HENRY DAVID THOREAU

Henry David Thoreau

WALDEN, THE MAINE WOODS, AND COLLECTED ESSAYS & POEMS

EDITIONS
The Library of America

Distributed to the trade
in the United States by Penguin Putnam Inc.
and in Canada by Penguin Books Canada Ltd.

Library of Congress Catalog Number: 2006053007
For cataloging information, see end of Index section.
ISBN 978-1-59853-010-0

———

Originally published in hardcover by
The Library of America in *A Week on the Concord
and Merrimack Rivers, Walden, The Maine Woods,
Cape Cod* (1985) and *Collected Essays and Poems* (2001)

First Library of America College Edition
Summer 2007

Manufactured in the United States of America

ROBERT F. SAYRE
AND
ELIZABETH HALL WITHERELL
SELECTED THE CONTENTS AND WROTE THE NOTES
FOR THIS VOLUME

Contents

WALDEN

or,
Life in the Woods

I do not propose to write an ode to dejection, but to brag as lustily as chanticleer in the morning, standing on his roost, if only to wake my neighbors up. —Page 69.

Contents

Economy

WHEN I wrote the following pages, or rather the bulk of them, I lived alone, in the woods, a mile from any neighbor, in a house which I had built myself, on the shore of Walden Pond, in Concord, Massachusetts, and earned my living by the labor of my hands only. I lived there two years and two months. At present I am a sojourner in civilized life again.

I should not obtrude my affairs so much on the notice of my readers if very particular inquiries had not been made by my townsmen concerning my mode of life, which some would call impertinent, though they do not appear to me at all impertinent, but, considering the circumstances, very natural and pertinent. Some have asked what I got to eat; if I did not feel lonesome; if I was not afraid; and the like. Others have been curious to learn what portion of my income I devoted to charitable purposes; and some, who have large families, how many poor children I maintained. I will therefore ask those of my readers who feel no particular interest in me to pardon me if I undertake to answer some of these questions in this book. In most books, the *I*, or first person, is omitted; in this it will be retained; that, in respect to egotism, is the main difference. We commonly do not remember that it is, after all, always the first person that is speaking. I should not talk so much about myself if there were any body else whom I knew as well. Unfortunately, I am confined to this theme by the narrowness of my experience. Moreover, I, on my side, require of every writer, first or last, a simple and sincere account of his own life, and not merely what he has heard of other men's lives; some such account as he would send to his kindred from a distant land; for if he has lived sincerely, it must have been in a distant land to me. Perhaps these pages are more particularly addressed to poor students. As for the rest of my readers, they will accept such portions as apply to them. I trust that none will stretch the seams in putting on the coat, for it may do good service to him whom it fits.

I would fain say something, not so much concerning the

Chinese and Sandwich Islanders as you who read these pages, who are said to live in New England; something about your condition, especially your outward condition or circumstances in this world, in this town, what it is, whether it is necessary that it be as bad as it is, whether it cannot be improved as well as not. I have travelled a good deal in Concord; and every where, in shops, and offices, and fields, the inhabitants have appeared to me to be doing penance in a thousand remarkable ways. What I have heard of Bramins sitting exposed to four fires and looking in the face of the sun; or hanging suspended, with their heads downward, over flames; or looking at the heavens over their shoulders "until it becomes impossible for them to resume their natural position, while from the twist of the neck nothing but liquids can pass into the stomach;" or dwelling, chained for life, at the foot of a tree; or measuring with their bodies, like caterpillars, the breadth of vast empires; or standing on one leg on the tops of pillars,—even these forms of conscious penance are hardly more incredible and astonishing than the scenes which I daily witness. The twelve labors of Hercules were trifling in comparison with those which my neighbors have undertaken; for they were only twelve, and had an end; but I could never see that these men slew or captured any monster or finished any labor. They have no friend Iolas to burn with a hot iron the root of the hydra's head, but as soon as one head is crushed, two spring up.

I see young men, my townsmen, whose misfortune it is to have inherited farms, houses, barns, cattle, and farming tools; for these are more easily acquired than got rid of. Better if they had been born in the open pasture and suckled by a wolf, that they might have seen with clearer eyes what field they were called to labor in. Who made them serfs of the soil? Why should they eat their sixty acres, when man is condemned to eat only his peck of dirt? Why should they begin digging their graves as soon as they are born? They have got to live a man's life, pushing all these things before them, and get on as well as they can. How many a poor immortal soul have I met well nigh crushed and smothered under its load, creeping down the road of life, pushing before it a barn seventy-five feet by forty, its Augean stables never cleansed, and one hundred acres of land, tillage, mowing, pasture, and wood-lot! The portionless, who struggle with no such unnecessary inherited encumbrances, find it labor enough to subdue and cultivate a few cubic feet of flesh.

But men labor under a mistake. The better part of the man is soon ploughed into the soil for compost. By a seeming fate, commonly called necessity, they are employed, as it says in an old book, laying up treasures which moth and rust will corrupt and thieves break through and steal. It is a fool's life, as they will find when they get to the end of it, if not before. It is said that Deucalion and Pyrrha created men by throwing stones over their heads behind them: —

> Inde genus durum sumus, experiensque laborum,
> Et documenta damus quâ simus origine nati.

Or, as Raleigh rhymes it in his sonorous way, —

> "From thence our kind hard-hearted is, enduring pain
>   and care,
> Approving that our bodies of a stony nature are."

So much for a blind obedience to a blundering oracle, throwing the stones over their heads behind them, and not seeing where they fell.

Most men, even in this comparatively free country, through mere ignorance and mistake, are so occupied with the factitious cares and superfluously coarse labors of life that its finer fruits cannot be plucked by them. Their fingers, from excessive toil, are too clumsy and tremble too much for that. Actually, the laboring man has not leisure for a true integrity day by day; he cannot afford to sustain the manliest relations to men; his labor would be depreciated in the market. He has no time to be any thing but a machine. How can he remember well his ignorance—which his growth requires—who has so often to use his knowledge? We should feed and clothe him gratuitously sometimes, and recruit him with our cordials, before we judge of him. The finest qualities of our nature, like the bloom on fruits, can be preserved only by the most delicate handling. Yet we do not treat ourselves nor one another thus tenderly.

Some of you, we all know, are poor, find it hard to live,

are sometimes, as it were, gasping for breath. I have no doubt that some of you who read this book are unable to pay for all the dinners which you have actually eaten, or for the coats and shoes which are fast wearing or are already worn out, and have come to this page to spend borrowed or stolen time, robbing your creditors of an hour. It is very evident what mean and sneaking lives many of you live, for my sight has been whetted by experience; always on the limits, trying to get into business and trying to get out of debt, a very ancient slough, called by the Latins *æs alienum*, another's brass, for some of their coins were made of brass; still living, and dying, and buried by this other's brass; always promising to pay, promising to pay, to-morrow, and dying to-day, insolvent; seeking to curry favor, to get custom, by how many modes, only not state-prison offences; lying, flattering, voting, contracting yourselves into a nutshell of civility, or dilating into an atmosphere of thin and vaporous generosity, that you may persuade your neighbor to let you make his shoes, or his hat, or his coat, or his carriage, or import his groceries for him; making yourselves sick, that you may lay up something against a sick day, something to be tucked away in an old chest, or in a stocking behind the plastering, or, more safely, in the brick bank; no matter where, no matter how much or how little.

I sometimes wonder that we can be so frivolous, I may almost say, as to attend to the gross but somewhat foreign form of servitude called Negro Slavery, there are so many keen and subtle masters that enslave both north and south. It is hard to have a southern overseer; it is worse to have a northern one; but worst of all when you are the slave-driver of yourself. Talk of a divinity in man! Look at the teamster on the highway, wending to market by day or night; does any divinity stir within him? His highest duty to fodder and water his horses! What is his destiny to him compared with the shipping interests? Does not he drive for Squire Make-a-stir? How godlike, how immortal, is he? See how he cowers and sneaks, how vaguely all the day he fears, not being immortal nor divine, but the slave and prisoner of his own opinion of himself, a fame won by his own deeds. Public opinion is a weak tyrant compared with our own private opinion.

What a man thinks of himself, that it is which determines, or rather indicates, his fate. Self-emancipation even in the West Indian provinces of the fancy and imagination,—what Wilberforce is there to bring that about? Think, also, of the ladies of the land weaving toilet cushions against the last day, not to betray too green an interest in their fates! As if you could kill time without injuring eternity.

The mass of men lead lives of quiet desperation. What is called resignation is confirmed desperation. From the desperate city you go into the desperate country, and have to console yourself with the bravery of minks and muskrats. A stereotyped but unconscious despair is concealed even under what are called the games and amusements of mankind. There is no play in them, for this comes after work. But it is a characteristic of wisdom not to do desperate things.

When we consider what, to use the words of the catechism, is the chief end of man, and what are the true necessaries and means of life, it appears as if men had deliberately chosen the common mode of living because they preferred it to any other. Yet they honestly think there is no choice left. But alert and healthy natures remember that the sun rose clear. It is never too late to give up our prejudices. No way of thinking or doing, however ancient, can be trusted without proof. What every body echoes or in silence passes by as true to-day may turn out to be falsehood to-morrow, mere smoke of opinion, which some had trusted for a cloud that would sprinkle fertilizing rain on their fields. What old people say you cannot do you try and find that you can. Old deeds for old people, and new deeds for new. Old people did not know enough once, perchance, to fetch fresh fuel to keep the fire a-going; new people put a little dry wood under a pot, and are whirled round the globe with the speed of birds, in a way to kill old people, as the phrase is. Age is no better, hardly so well, qualified for an instructor as youth, for it has not profited so much as it has lost. One may almost doubt if the wisest man has learned any thing of absolute value by living. Practically, the old have no very important advice to give the young, their own experience has been so partial, and their lives have been such miserable failures, for private reasons, as they must believe; and it may be that they have some faith left which belies that experience, and they are only less young than they were. I have lived some thirty years on this planet, and I have yet to hear the first syllable of valuable or even earnest advice from my seniors. They have told me nothing, and probably cannot tell me any thing, to the purpose. Here is life, an experiment to a great extent untried by me; but it does not avail me that they have tried it. If I have any experience which I think valuable, I am sure to reflect that this my Mentors said nothing about.

One farmer says to me, "You cannot live on vegetable food solely, for it furnishes nothing to make bones with;" and so he religiously devotes a part of his day to supplying his system with the raw material of bones; walking all the while he talks behind his oxen, which, with vegetable-made bones, jerk him and his lumbering plough along in spite of every obstacle. Some things are really necessaries of life in some circles, the most helpless and diseased, which in others are luxuries merely, and in others still are entirely unknown.

The whole ground of human life seems to some to have been gone over by their predecessors, both the heights and the valleys, and all things to have been cared for. According to Evelyn, "the wise Solomon prescribed ordinances for the very distances of trees; and the Roman prætors have decided how often you may go into your neighbor's land to gather the acorns which fall on it without trespass, and what share belongs to that neighbor." Hippocrates has even left directions how we should cut our nails; that is, even with the ends of the fingers, neither shorter nor longer. Undoubtedly the very tedium and ennui which presume to have exhausted the variety and the joys of life are as old as Adam. But man's capacities have never been measured; nor are we to judge of what he can do by any precedents, so little has been tried. Whatever have been thy failures hitherto, "be not afflicted, my child, for who shall assign to thee what thou hast left undone?"

We might try our lives by a thousand simple tests; as, for instance, that the same sun which ripens my beans illumines at once a system of earths like ours. If I had remembered this it would have prevented some mistakes. This was not the light in which I hoed them. The stars are the apexes of what wonderful triangles! What distant and different beings in the various mansions of the universe are contemplating the same one at the same moment! Nature and human life are as various as our several constitutions. Who shall say what prospect life offers to another? Could a greater miracle take place than for us to look through each other's eyes for an instant? We should live in all the ages of the world in an hour; ay, in all the worlds of the ages. History, Poetry, Mythology!—I know of no reading of another's experience so startling and informing as this would be.

The greater part of what my neighbors call good I believe in my soul to be bad, and if I repent of any thing, it is very likely to be my good behavior. What demon possessed me that I behaved so well? You may say the wisest thing you can old man,—you who have lived seventy years, not without honor of a kind,—I hear an irresistible voice which invites me away from all that. One generation abandons the enterprises of another like stranded vessels.

I think that we may safely trust a good deal more than we do. We may waive just so much care of ourselves as we honestly bestow elsewhere. Nature is as well adapted to our weakness as to our strength. The incessant anxiety and strain of some is a well nigh incurable form of disease. We are made to exaggerate the importance of what work we do; and yet how much is not done by us! or, what if we had been taken sick? How vigilant we are! determined not to live by faith if we can avoid it; all the day long on the alert, at night we unwillingly say our prayers and commit ourselves to uncertainties. So thoroughly and sincerely are we compelled to live, reverencing our life, and denying the possibility of change. This is the only way, we say; but there are as many ways as there can be drawn radii from one centre. All change is a miracle to contemplate; but it is a miracle which is taking place every instant. Confucius said, "To know that we know what we know, and that we do not know what we do not know, that is true knowledge." When one man has reduced a fact of the imagination to be a fact to his understanding, I foresee that all men will at length establish their lives on that basis.

*   *   *

Let us consider for a moment what most of the trouble and anxiety which I have referred to is about, and how much it is necessary that we be troubled, or, at least, careful. It would be some advantage to live a primitive and frontier life, though in the midst of an outward civilization, if only to learn what are the gross necessaries of life and what methods have been taken to obtain them; or even to look over the old day-books of the merchants, to see what it was that men most commonly bought at the stores, what they stored, that is, what are the grossest groceries. For the improvements of ages have had but little influence on the essential laws of man's existence; as our skeletons, probably, are not to be distinguished from those of our ancestors.

By the words, *necessary of life*, I mean whatever, of all that man obtains by his own exertions, has been from the first, or from long use has become, so important to human life that few, if any, whether from savageness, or poverty, or philosophy, ever attempt to do without it. To many creatures there is in this sense but one necessary of life, Food. To the bison of the prairie it is a few inches of palatable grass, with water to drink; unless he seeks the Shelter of the forest or the mountain's shadow. None of the brute creation requires more than Food and Shelter. The necessaries of life for man in this climate may, accurately enough, be distributed under the several heads of Food, Shelter, Clothing, and Fuel; for not till we have secured these are we prepared to entertain the true problems of life with freedom and a prospect of success. Man has invented, not only houses, but clothes and cooked food; and possibly from the accidental discovery of the warmth of fire, and the consequent use of it, at first a luxury, arose the present necessity to sit by it. We observe cats and dogs acquiring the same second nature. By proper Shelter and Clothing we legitimately retain our own internal heat; but with an excess of these, or of Fuel, that is, with an external heat greater than our own internal, may not cookery properly be said to begin? Darwin, the naturalist, says of the inhabitants of Tierra del Fuego, that while his own party, who were well clothed and sitting close to a fire, were far from too warm, these naked savages, who were farther off, were observed, to his great surprise, "to be streaming with perspiration at undergoing such a roasting." So, we are told, the New Hollander goes naked with impunity, while the European shivers in his clothes. Is it impossible to combine the hardiness of these savages with the intellectualness of the civilized man? According to Liebig, man's body is a stove, and food the fuel which keeps up the internal combustion in the lungs. In cold weather we eat more, in warm less. The animal heat is the result of a slow combustion, and disease and death take place when this is too rapid; or for want of fuel, or from some defect in the draught, the fire goes out. Of course the vital heat is not to be confounded with fire; but so much for analogy. It appears, therefore, from the above list, that the expression, *animal life*, is nearly synonymous with the expression, *animal heat*; for while Food may be regarded as the Fuel which keeps up the fire within us,—and Fuel serves only to prepare that Food or to increase the warmth of our bodies by addition from without,—Shelter and Clothing also serve only to retain the *heat* thus generated and absorbed.

The grand necessity, then, for our bodies, is to keep warm, to keep the vital heat in us. What pains we accordingly take, not only with our Food, and Clothing, and Shelter, but with our beds, which are our night-clothes, robbing the nests and breasts of birds to prepare this shelter within a shelter, as the mole has its bed of grass and leaves at the end of its burrow! The poor man is wont to complain that this is a cold world; and to cold, no less physical than social, we refer directly a great part of our ails. The summer, in some climates, makes possible to man a sort of Elysian life. Fuel, except to cook his Food, is then unnecessary; the sun is his fire, and many of the fruits are sufficiently cooked by its rays; while Food generally is more various, and more easily obtained, and Clothing and Shelter are wholly or half unnecessary. At the present day, and in this country, as I find by my own experience, a few implements, a knife, an axe, a spade, a wheelbarrow, &c., and for the studious, lamplight, stationery, and access to a few books, rank next to necessaries, and can all be obtained at a trifling cost. Yet some, not wise, go to the other side of the globe, to barbarous and unhealthy regions, and devote themselves to trade for ten or twenty years, in order that they may live,—that is, keep comfortably warm,—and die in New England at last. The luxuriously rich are not simply kept comfortably warm, but unnaturally hot; as I implied before, they are cooked, of course *à la mode*.

Most of the luxuries, and many of the so called comforts of life, are not only not indispensable, but positive hinderances to the elevation of mankind. With respect to luxuries and comforts, the wisest have ever lived a more simple and meagre life than the poor. The ancient philosophers, Chinese, Hindoo, Persian, and Greek, were a class than which none has been poorer in outward riches, none so rich in inward. We know not much about them. It is remarkable that *we* know so much of them as we do. The same is true of the more modern reformers and benefactors of their race. None can be an impartial or wise observer of human life but from the vantage ground of what *we* should call voluntary poverty. Of a life of luxury the fruit is luxury, whether in agriculture, or commerce, or literature, or art. There are nowadays professors of philosophy, but not philosophers. Yet it is admirable to profess because it was once admirable to live. To be a philosopher is not merely to have subtle thoughts, nor even to found a school, but so to love wisdom as to live according to its dictates, a life of simplicity, independence, magnanimity, and trust. It is to solve some of the problems of life, not only theoretically, but practically. The success of great scholars and thinkers is commonly a courtier-like success, not kingly, not manly. They make shift to live merely by conformity, practically as their fathers did, and are in no sense the progenitors of a nobler race of men. But why do men degenerate ever? What makes families run out? What is the nature of the luxury which enervates and destroys nations? Are we sure that there is none of it in our own lives? The philosopher is in advance of his age even in the outward form of his life. He is not fed, sheltered, clothed, warmed, like his contemporaries. How can a man be a philosopher and not maintain his vital heat by better methods than other men?

When a man is warmed by the several modes which I have described, what does he want next? Surely not more warmth of the same kind, as more and richer food, larger and more splendid houses, finer and more abundant clothing, more numerous incessant and hotter fires, and the like. When he has obtained those things which are necessary to life, there is another alternative than to obtain the superfluities; and that is, to adventure on life now, his vacation from humbler toil having commenced. The soil, it appears, is suited to the seed, for it has sent its radicle downward, and it may now send its shoot upward also with confidence. Why has man rooted himself thus firmly in the earth, but that he may rise in the same proportion into the heavens above?—for the nobler plants are valued for the fruit they bear at last in the air and light, far from the ground, and are not treated like the humbler esculents, which, though they may be biennials, are cultivated only till they have perfected their root, and often cut down at top for this purpose, so that most would not know them in their flowering season.

I do not mean to prescribe rules to strong and valiant natures, who will mind their own affairs whether in heaven or hell, and perchance build more magnificently and spend more lavishly than the richest, without ever impoverishing themselves, not knowing how they live,—if, indeed, there are any such, as has been dreamed; nor to those who find their encouragement and inspiration in precisely the present condition of things, and cherish it with the fondness and enthusiasm of lovers,—and, to some extent, I reckon myself in this number; I do not speak to those who are well employed, in whatever circumstances, and they know whether they are well employed or not;—but mainly to the mass of men who are discontented, and idly complaining of the hardness of their lot or of the times, when they might improve them. There are some who complain most energetically and inconsolably of any, because they are, as they say, doing their duty. I also have in my mind that seemingly wealthy, but most terribly impoverished class of all, who have accumulated dross, but know not how to use it, or get rid of it, and thus have forged their own golden or silver fetters.

If I should attempt to tell how I have desired to spend my life in years past, it would probably surprise those of my readers who are somewhat acquainted with its actual history;

it would certainly astonish those who know nothing about it. I will only hint at some of the enterprises which I have cherished.

In any weather, at any hour of the day or night, I have been anxious to improve the nick of time, and notch it on my stick too; to stand on the meeting of two eternities, the past and future, which is precisely the present moment; to toe that line. You will pardon some obscurities, for there are more secrets in my trade than in most men's, and yet not voluntarily kept, but inseparable from its very nature. I would gladly tell all that I know about it, and never paint "No Admittance" on my gate.

I long ago lost a hound, a bay horse, and a turtledove, and am still on their trail. Many are the travellers I have spoken concerning them, describing their tracks and what calls they answered to. I have met one or two who had heard the hound, and the tramp of the horse, and even seen the dove disappear behind a cloud, and they seemed as anxious to recover them as if they had lost them themselves.

To anticipate, not the sunrise and the dawn merely, but, if possible, Nature herself! How many mornings, summer and winter, before yet any neighbor was stirring about his business, have I been about mine! No doubt, many of my townsmen have met me returning from this enterprise, farmers starting for Boston in the twilight, or woodchoppers going to their work. It is true, I never assisted the sun materially in his rising, but, doubt not, it was of the last importance only to be present at it.

So many autumn, ay, and winter days, spent outside the town, trying to hear what was in the wind, to hear and carry it express! I well-nigh sunk all my capital in it, and lost my own breath into the bargain, running in the face of it. If it had concerned either of the political parties, depend upon it, it would have appeared in the Gazette with the earliest intelligence. At other times watching from the observatory of some cliff or tree, to telegraph any new arrival; or waiting at evening on the hill-tops for the sky to fall, that I might catch something, though I never caught much, and that, manna-wise, would dissolve again in the sun.

For a long time I was reporter to a journal, of no very wide circulation, whose editor has never yet seen fit to print the bulk of my contributions, and, as is too common with writers, I got only my labor for my pains. However, in this case my pains were their own reward.

For many years I was self-appointed inspector of snow storms and rain storms, and did my duty faithfully; surveyor, if not of highways, then of forest paths and all across-lot routes, keeping them open, and ravines bridged and passable at all seasons, where the public heel had testified to their utility.

I have looked after the wild stock of the town, which give a faithful herdsman a good deal of trouble by leaping fences; and I have had an eye to the unfrequented nooks and corners of the farm; though I did not always know whether Jonas or Solomon worked in a particular field to-day; that was none of my business. I have watered the red huckleberry, the sand cherry and the nettle tree, the red pine and the black ash, the white grape and the yellow violet, which might have withered else in dry seasons.

In short, I went on thus for a long time, I may say it without boasting, faithfully minding my business, till it became more and more evident that my townsmen would not after all admit me into the list of town officers, nor make my place a sinecure with a moderate allowance. My accounts, which I can swear to have kept faithfully, I have, indeed, never got audited, still less accepted, still less paid and settled. However, I have not set my heart on that.

Not long since, a strolling Indian went to sell baskets at the house of a well-known lawyer in my neighborhood. "Do you wish to buy any baskets?" he asked. "No, we do not want any," was the reply. "What!" exclaimed the Indian as he went out the gate, "do you mean to starve us?" Having seen his industrious white neighbors so well off,—that the lawyer had only to weave arguments, and by some magic wealth and standing followed, he had said to himself; I will go into business; I will weave baskets; it is a thing which I can do. Thinking that when he had made the baskets he would have done his part, and then it would be the white man's to buy them. He had not discovered that it was necessary for him to make it worth the other's while to buy them, or at least make him think that it was so, or to make something else which it would be worth his while to buy. I too had woven a kind of basket of a delicate texture, but I had not made it worth any one's while to buy them. Yet not the less, in my case, did I think it worth my while to weave them, and instead of studying how to make it worth men's while to buy my baskets, I studied rather how to avoid the necessity of selling them. The life which men praise and regard as successful is but one kind. Why should we exaggerate any one kind at the expense of the others?

Finding that my fellow-citizens were not likely to offer me any room in the court house, or any curacy or living any where else, but I must shift for myself, I turned my face more exclusively than ever to the woods, where I was better known. I determined to go into business at once, and not wait to acquire the usual capital, using such slender means as I had already got. My purpose in going to Walden Pond was not to live cheaply nor to live dearly there, but to transact some private business with the fewest obstacles; to be hindered from accomplishing which for want of a little common sense, a little enterprise and business talent, appeared not so sad as foolish.

I have always endeavored to acquire strict business habits; they are indispensable to every man. If your trade is with the Celestial Empire, then some small counting house on the coast, in some Salem harbor, will be fixture enough. You will export such articles as the country affords, purely native products, much ice and pine timber and a little granite, always in native bottoms. These will be good ventures. To oversee all the details yourself in person; to be at once pilot and captain, and owner and underwriter; to buy and sell and keep the accounts; to read every letter received, and write or read every letter sent; to superintend the discharge of imports night and day; to be upon many parts of the coast almost at the same time;—often the richest freight will be discharged upon a Jersey shore;—to be your own telegraph, unweariedly sweeping the horizon, speaking all passing vessels bound coastwise; to keep up a steady despatch of commodities, for the supply of such a distant and exorbitant market; to keep yourself informed of the state of the markets, prospects of war and peace every where, and anticipate the tendencies of trade and civilization,—taking advantage of the results of all exploring expeditions, using new passages and all improvements in navigation;—charts to be studied, the position of reefs and new lights and buoys to be ascertained, and ever, and ever, the logarithmic tables to be corrected, for by the error of some calculator the vessel often splits upon a rock that should have reached a friendly pier,—there is the untold fate of La Perouse;—universal science to be kept pace with, studying the lives of all great discoverers and navigators, great adventurers and merchants, from Hanno and the Phœnicians down to our day; in fine, account of stock to be taken from time to time, to know how you stand. It is a labor to task the faculties of a man,—such problems of profit and loss, of interest, of tare and tret, and gauging of all kinds in it, as demand a universal knowledge.

I have thought that Walden Pond would be a good place for business, not solely on account of the railroad and the ice trade; it offers advantages which it may not be good policy to divulge; it is a good port and a good foundation. No Neva marshes to be filled; though you must every where build on piles of your own driving. It is said that a flood-tide, with a westerly wind, and ice in the Neva, would sweep St. Petersburg from the face of the earth.

As this business was to be entered into without the usual capital, it may not be easy to conjecture where those means, that will still be indispensable to every such undertaking, were to be obtained. As for Clothing, to come at once to the practical part of the question, perhaps we are led oftener by the love of novelty, and a regard for the opinions of men, in procuring it, than by a true utility. Let him who has work to do recollect that the object of clothing is, first, to retain the vital heat, and secondly, in this state of society, to cover nakedness, and he may judge how much of any necessary or important work may be accomplished without adding to his wardrobe. Kings and queens who wear a suit but once, though made by some tailor or dress-maker to their majesties, cannot know the comfort of wearing a suit that fits. They are no better than wooden horses to hang the clean clothes on. Every day our garments become more assimilated to ourselves, receiving the impress of the wearer's character, until we hesitate to lay them aside, without such delay and medical appliances and some such solemnity even as our bodies. No man ever stood the lower in my estimation for having a patch in his clothes; yet I am sure that there is greater anxiety, commonly, to have fashionable, or at least clean and unpatched clothes, than to have a sound conscience. But even if the rent is not mended, perhaps the worst vice betrayed is improvidence. I sometimes try my acquaintances by such tests as this;—who could wear a patch, or two extra seams only, over the knee? Most behave as if they believed that their prospects for life would be ruined if they should do it. It would be easier for them to hobble to town with a broken leg than with a broken pantaloon. Often if an accident happens to a gentleman's legs, they can be mended; but if a similar accident happens to the legs of his pantaloons, there is no help for it; for he considers, not what is truly respectable, but what is respected. We know but few men, a great many coats and breeches. Dress a scarecrow in your last shift, you standing shiftless by, who would not soonest salute the scarecrow? Passing a cornfield the other day, close by a hat and coat on a stake, I recognized the owner of the farm. He was only a little more weather-beaten than when I saw him last. I have heard of a dog that barked at every stranger who approached his master's premises with clothes on, but was easily quieted by a naked thief. It is an interesting question how far men would retain their relative rank if they were divested of their clothes. Could you, in such a case, tell surely of any company of civilized men, which belonged to the most respected class? When Madam Pfeiffer, in her adventurous travels round the world, from east to west, had got so near home as Asiatic Russia, she says that she felt the necessity of wearing other than a travelling dress, when she went to meet the authorities, for she "was now in a civilized country, where —— — people are judged of by their clothes." Even in our democratic New England towns the accidental possession of wealth, and its manifestation in dress and equipage alone, obtain for the possessor almost universal respect. But they who yield such respect, numerous as they are, are so far heathen, and need to have a missionary sent to them. Beside, clothes introduced sewing, a kind of work which you may call endless; a woman's dress, at least, is never done.

A man who has at length found something to do will not need to get a new suit to do it in; for him the old will do, that has lain dusty in the garret for an indeterminate period. Old shoes will serve a hero longer than they have served his valet,—if a hero ever has a valet,—bare feet are older than shoes, and he can make them do. Only they who go to soirées and legislative halls must have new coats, coats to change as often as the man changes in them. But if my jacket and trousers, my hat and shoes, are fit to worship God in, they will do; will they not? Who ever saw his old clothes,—his old coat, actually worn out, resolved into its primitive elements, so that it was not a deed of charity to bestow it on some poor boy, by him perchance to be bestowed on some poorer still, or shall we say richer, who could do with less? I say, beware of all enterprises that require new clothes, and not rather a new wearer of clothes. If there is not a new man, how can the new clothes be made to fit? If you have any enterprise before you, try it in your old clothes. All men want, not something to *do with*, but something to *do*, or rather something to *be*. Perhaps we should never procure a new suit, however ragged or dirty the old, until we have so conducted, so enterprised or sailed in some way, that we feel like new men in the old, and that to retain it would be like keeping new wine in old bottles. Our moulting season, like that of the fowls, must be a crisis in our lives. The loon retires to solitary ponds to spend it. Thus also the snake casts its slough, and the caterpillar its wormy coat, by an internal industry and expansion; for clothes are but our outmost cuticle and mortal coil. Otherwise we shall be found sailing under false colors, and be inevitably cashiered at last by our own opinion, as well as that of mankind.

We don garment after garment, as if we grew like exogenous plants by addition without. Our outside and often thin and fanciful clothes are our epidermis or false skin, which partakes not of our life, and may be stripped off here and there without fatal injury; our thicker garments, constantly worn, are our cellular integument, or cortex; but our shirts are our

liber or true bark, which cannot be removed without girdling
and so destroying the man. I believe that all races at some
seasons wear something equivalent to the shirt. It is desirable
that a man be clad so simply that he can lay his hands on
himself in the dark, and that he live in all respects so compactly and preparedly, that, if an enemy take the town, he
can, like the old philosopher, walk out the gate empty-handed
without anxiety. While one thick garment is, for most purposes, as good as three thin ones, and cheap clothing can be
obtained at prices really to suit customers; while a thick coat
can be bought for five dollars, which will last as many years,
thick pantaloons for two dollars, cowhide boots for a dollar
and a half a pair, a summer hat for a quarter of a dollar, and
a winter cap for sixty-two and a half cents, or a better be
made at home at a nominal cost, where is he so poor that,
clad in such a suit, *of his own earning*, there will not be found
wise men to do him reverence?

When I ask for a garment of a particular form, my tailor-
ess tells me gravely, "They do not make them so now," not
emphasizing the "They" at all, as if she quoted an authority
as impersonal as the Fates, and I find it difficult to get made
what I want, simply because she cannot believe that I mean
what I say, that I am so rash. When I hear this oracular sentence, I am for a moment absorbed in thought, emphasizing
to myself each word separately that I may come at the meaning of it, that I may find out by what degree of consanguinity *They* are related to *me*, and what authority they may have
in an affair which affects me so nearly; and, finally, I am inclined to answer her with equal mystery, and without any
more emphasis of the "they,"—"It is true, they did not
make them so recently, but they do now." Of what use this
measuring of me if she does not measure my character, but
only the breadth of my shoulders, as it were a peg to hang
the coat on? We worship not the Graces, nor the Parcæ, but
Fashion. She spins and weaves and cuts with full authority.
The head monkey at Paris puts on a traveller's cap, and all
the monkeys in America do the same. I sometimes despair of
getting any thing quite simple and honest done in this world
by the help of men. They would have to be passed through
a powerful press first, to squeeze their old notions out of

them, so that they would not soon get upon their legs again, and then there would be some one in the company with a maggot in his head, hatched from an egg deposited there nobody knows when, for not even fire kills these things, and you would have lost your labor. Nevertheless, we will not forget that some Egyptian wheat was handed down to us by a mummy.

On the whole, I think that it cannot be maintained that dressing has in this or any country risen to the dignity of an art. At present men make shift to wear what they can get. Like shipwrecked sailors, they put on what they can find on the beach, and at a little distance, whether of space or time, laugh at each other's masquerade. Every generation laughs at the old fashions, but follows religiously the new. We are amused at beholding the costume of Henry VIII., or Queen Elizabeth, as much as if it was that of the King and Queen of the Cannibal Islands. All costume off a man is pitiful or grotesque. It is only the serious eye peering from and the sincere life passed within it, which restrain laughter and consecrate the costume of any people. Let Harlequin be taken with a fit of the colic and his trappings will have to serve that mood too. When the soldier is hit by a cannon ball rags are as becoming as purple.

The childish and savage taste of men and women for new patterns keeps how many shaking and squinting through kaleidoscopes that they may discover the particular figure which this generation requires to-day. The manufacturers have learned that this taste is merely whimsical. Of two patterns which differ only by a few threads more or less of a particular color, the one will be sold readily, the other lie on the shelf, though it frequently happens that after the lapse of a season the latter becomes the most fashionable. Comparatively, tattooing is not the hideous custom which it is called. It is not barbarous merely because the printing is skin-deep and unalterable.

I cannot believe that our factory system is the best mode by which men may get clothing. The condition of the operatives is becoming every day more like that of the English; and it cannot be wondered at, since, as far as I have heard or observed, the principal object is, not that mankind may be

well and honestly clad, but, unquestionably, that the corporations may be enriched. In the long run men hit only what
they aim at. Therefore, though they should fail immediately,
they had better aim at something high.

As for a Shelter, I will not deny that this is now a necessary of life, though there are instances of men having done
without it for long periods in colder countries than this.
Samuel Laing says that "The Laplander in his skin dress, and
in a skin bag which he puts over his head and shoulders, will
sleep night after night on the snow——in a degree of cold
which would extinguish the life of one exposed to it in any
woollen clothing." He had seen them asleep thus. Yet he
adds, "They are not hardier than other people." But, probably, man did not live long on the earth without discovering
the convenience which there is in a house, the domestic
comforts, which phrase may have originally signified the sat-
isfactions of the house more than of the family; though
these must be extremely partial and occasional in those climates where the house is associated in our thoughts with
winter or the rainy season chiefly, and two thirds of the
year, except for a parasol, is unnecessary. In our climate, in
the summer, it was formerly almost solely a covering at
night. In the Indian gazettes a wigwam was the symbol of a
day's march, and a row of them cut or painted on the bark
of a tree signified that so many times they had camped. Man
was not made so large limbed and robust but that he must
seek to narrow his world, and wall in a space such as fitted
him. He was at first bare and out of doors; but though this
was pleasant enough in serene and warm weather, by daylight, the rainy season and the winter, to say nothing of the
torrid sun, would perhaps have nipped his race in the bud if
he had not made haste to clothe himself with the shelter of a
house. Adam and Eve, according to the fable, wore the
bower before other clothes. Man wanted a home, a place of
warmth, or comfort, first of physical warmth, then the
warmth of the affections.

We may imagine a time when, in the infancy of the human race, some enterprising mortal crept into a hollow in a
rock for shelter. Every child begins the world again, to some

extent, and loves to stay out doors, even in wet and cold. It plays house, as well as horse, having an instinct for it. Who does not remember the interest with which when young he looked at shelving rocks, or any approach to a cave? It was the natural yearning of that portion of our most primitive ancestor which still survived in us. From the cave we have advanced to roofs of palm leaves, of bark and boughs, of linen woven and stretched, of grass and straw, of boards and shingles, of stones and tiles. At last, we know not what it is to live in the open air, and our lives are domestic in more senses than we think. From the hearth to the field is a great distance. It would be well perhaps if we were to spend more of our days and nights without any obstruction between us and the celestial bodies, if the poet did not speak so much from under a roof, or the saint dwell there so long. Birds do not sing in caves, nor do doves cherish their innocence in dovecots.

However, if one designs to construct a dwelling house, it behooves him to exercise a little Yankee shrewdness, lest after all he find himself in a workhouse, a labyrinth without a clew, a museum, an almshouse, a prison, or a splendid mausoleum instead. Consider first how slight a shelter is absolutely necessary. I have seen Penobscot Indians, in this town, living in tents of thin cotton cloth, while the snow was nearly a foot deep around them, and I thought that they would be glad to have it deeper to keep out the wind. Formerly, when how to get my living honestly, with freedom left for my proper pursuits, was a question which vexed me even more than it does now, for unfortunately I am become somewhat callous, I used to see a large box by the railroad, six feet long by three wide, in which the laborers locked up their tools at night, and it suggested to me that every man who was hard pushed might get such a one for a dollar, and, having bored a few auger holes in it, to admit the air at least, get into it when it rained and at night, and hook down the lid, and so have freedom in his love, and in his soul be free. This did not appear the worst, nor by any means a despicable alternative. You could sit up as late as you pleased, and, whenever you got up, go abroad without any landlord or house-lord dogging you for rent. Many a man is harassed to death to pay the rent of a larger and more luxurious box who would not have frozen to death in such a box as this. I am far from jesting. Economy is a subject which admits of being treated with levity, but it cannot so be disposed of. A comfortable house for a rude and hardy race, that lived mostly out of doors, was once made here almost entirely of such materials as Nature furnished ready to their hands. Gookin, who was superintendent of the Indians subject to the Massachusetts Colony, writing in 1674, says, "The best of their houses are covered very neatly, tight and warm, with barks of trees, slipped from their bodies at those seasons when the sap is up, and made into great flakes, with pressure of weighty timber, when they are green. . . . The meaner sort are covered with mats which they make of a kind of bulrush, and are also indifferently tight and warm, but not so good as the former. . . . Some I have seen, sixty or a hundred feet long and thirty feet broad. . . . I have often lodged in their wigwams, and found them as warm as the best English houses." He adds, that they were commonly carpeted and lined within with well-wrought embroidered mats, and were furnished with various utensils. The Indians had advanced so far as to regulate the effect of the wind by a mat suspended over the hole in the roof and moved by a string. Such a lodge was in the first instance constructed in a day or two at most, and taken down and put up in a few hours; and every family owned one, or its apartment in one.

In the savage state every family owns a shelter as good as the best, and sufficient for its coarser and simpler wants; but I think that I speak within bounds when I say that, though the birds of the air have their nests, and the foxes their holes, and the savages their wigwams, in modern civilized society not more than one half the families own a shelter. In the large towns and cities, where civilization especially prevails, the number of those who own a shelter is a very small fraction of the whole. The rest pay an annual tax for this outside garment of all, become indispensable summer and winter, which would buy a village of Indian wigwams, but now helps to keep them poor as long as they live. I do not mean to insist here on the disadvantage of hiring compared with owning, but it is evident that the savage owns his shelter because it costs so little, while the civilized man hires his commonly because he cannot afford to own it; nor can he, in the long run, any better afford to hire. But, answers one, by merely paying this tax the poor civilized man secures an abode which is a palace compared with the savage's. An annual rent of from twenty-five to a hundred dollars, these are the country rates, entitles him to the benefit of the improvements of centuries, spacious apartments, clean paint and paper, Rumford fireplace, back plastering, Venetian blinds, copper pump, spring lock, a commodious cellar, and many other things. But how happens it that he who is said to enjoy these things is so commonly a *poor* civilized man, while the savage, who has them not, is rich as a savage? If it is asserted that civilization is a real advance in the condition of man,—and I think that it is, though only the wise improve their advantages,—it must be shown that it has produced better dwellings without making them more costly; and the cost of a thing is the amount of what I will call life which is required to be exchanged for it, immediately or in the long run. An average house in this neighborhood costs perhaps eight hundred dollars, and to lay up this sum will take from ten to fifteen years of the laborer's life, even if he is not encumbered with a family;—estimating the pecuniary value of every man's labor at one dollar a day, for if some receive more, others receive less;—so that he must have spent more than half his life commonly before *his* wigwam will be earned. If we suppose him to pay a rent instead, this is but a doubtful choice of evils. Would the savage have been wise to exchange his wigwam for a palace on these terms?

It may be guessed that I reduce almost the whole advantage of holding this superfluous property as a fund in store against the future, so far as the individual is concerned, mainly to the defraying of funeral expenses. But perhaps a man is not required to bury himself. Nevertheless this points to an important distinction between the civilized man and the savage; and, no doubt, they have designs on us for our benefit, in making the life of a civilized people an *institution*, in which the life of the individual is to a great extent absorbed, in order to preserve and perfect that of the race. But I wish to show at what a sacrifice this advantage is at present obtained, and to suggest that we may possibly so live as to secure all the advantage without suffering any of the disadvantage. What mean ye by saying that the poor ye have always with you, or that the fathers have eaten sour grapes, and the children's teeth are set on edge?

"As I live, saith the Lord God, ye shall not have occasion any more to use this proverb in Israel."

"Behold all souls are mine; as the soul of the father, so also the soul of the son is mine: the soul that sinneth it shall die."

When I consider my neighbors, the farmers of Concord, who are at least as well off as the other classes, I find that for the most part they have been toiling twenty, thirty, or forty years, that they may become the real owners of their farms, which commonly they have inherited with encumbrances, or else bought with hired money,—and we may regard one third of that toil as the cost of their houses,—but commonly they have not paid for them yet. It is true, the encumbrances sometimes outweigh the value of the farm, so that the farm itself becomes one great encumbrance, and still a man is found to inherit it, being well acquainted with it, as he says. On applying to the assessors, I am surprised to learn that they cannot at once name a dozen in the town who own their farms free and clear. If you would know the history of these homesteads, inquire at the bank where they are mortgaged. The man who has actually paid for his farm with labor on it is so rare that every neighbor can point to him. I doubt if there are three such men in Concord. What has been said of the merchants, that a very large majority, even ninety-seven in a hundred, are sure to fail, is equally true of the farmers. With regard to the merchants, however, one of them says pertinently that a great part of their failures are not genuine pecuniary failures, but merely failures to fulfil their engagements, because it is inconvenient; that is, it is the moral character that breaks down. But this puts an infinitely worse face on the matter, and suggests, beside, that probably not even the other three succeed in saving their souls, but are perchance bankrupt in a worse sense than they who fail honestly. Bankruptcy and repudiation are the spring-boards from which much of our civilization vaults and turns its somersets, but the savage stands on the unelastic plank of famine. Yet the Middlesex Cattle Show goes off here with *éclat* annually, as if all the joints of the agricultural machine were suent.

The farmer is endeavoring to solve the problem of a livelihood by a formula more complicated than the problem itself. To get his shoestrings he speculates in herds of cattle. With consummate skill he has set his trap with a hair springe to catch comfort and independence, and then, as he turned away, got his own leg into it. This is the reason he is poor; and for a similar reason we are all poor in respect to a thousand savage comforts, though surrounded by luxuries. As Chapman sings,—

> "The false society of men—
> —for earthly greatness
> All heavenly comforts rarefies to air."

And when the farmer has got his house, he may not be the richer but the poorer for it, and it be the house that has got him. As I understand it, that was a valid objection urged by Momus against the house which Minerva made, that she "had not made it movable, by which means a bad neighborhood might be avoided;" and it may still be urged, for our houses are such unwieldy property that we are often imprisoned rather than housed in them; and the bad neighborhood to be avoided is our own scurvy selves. I know one or two families, at least, in this town, who, for nearly a generation, have been wishing to sell their houses in the outskirts and move into the village, but have not been able to accomplish it, and only death will set them free.

Granted that the *majority* are able at last either to own or hire the modern house with all its improvements. While civilization has been improving our houses, it has not equally improved the men who are to inhabit them. It has created palaces, but it was not so easy to create noblemen and kings. And *if the civilized man's pursuits are no worthier than the savage's, if he is employed the greater part of his life in obtaining gross necessaries and comforts merely, why should he have a better dwelling than the former?*

But how do the poor *minority* fare? Perhaps it will be found, that just in proportion as some have been placed in outward circumstances above the savage, others have been degraded below him. The luxury of one class is counterbalanced by the indigence of another. On the one side is the palace, on the other are the almshouse and "silent poor." The myriads who built the pyramids to be the tombs of the Pharaohs were fed on garlic, and it may be were not decently buried themselves. The mason who finishes the cornice of the palace returns at night perchance to a hut not so good as a wigwam. It is a mistake to suppose that, in a country where the usual evidences of civilization exist, the condition of a very large body of the inhabitants may not be as degraded as that of savages. I refer to the degraded poor, not now to the degraded rich. To know this I should not need to look farther than to the shanties which every where border our railroads, that last improvement in civilization; where I see in my daily walks human beings living in sties, and all winter with an open door, for the sake of light, without any visible, often imaginable, wood pile, and the forms of both old and young are permanently contracted by the long habit of shrinking from cold and misery, and the development of all their limbs and faculties is checked. It certainly is fair to look at that class by whose labor the works which distinguish this generation are accomplished. Such too, to a greater or less extent, is the condition of the operatives of every denomination in England, which is the great workhouse of the world. Or I could refer you to Ireland, which is marked as one of the white or enlightened spots on the map. Contrast the physical condition of the Irish with that of the North American Indian, or the South Sea Islander, or any other savage race before it was degraded by contact with the civilized man. Yet I have no doubt that that people's rulers are as wise as the average of civilized rulers. Their condition only proves what squalidness may consist with civilization. I hardly need refer now to the laborers in our Southern States who produce the staple exports of this country, and are themselves a staple production of the South. But to confine myself to those who are said to be in *moderate* circumstances.

Most men appear never to have considered what a house is, and are actually though needlessly poor all their lives because they think that they must have such a one as their neighbors have. As if one were to wear any sort of coat which the tailor might cut out for him, or, gradually leaving off palmleaf hat or cap of woodchuck skin, complain of hard times because he could not afford to buy him a crown! It is possible to invent a house still more convenient and luxurious than we have, which yet all would admit that man could not afford to pay for. Shall we always study to obtain more of these things, and not sometimes to be content with less? Shall the respectable citizen thus gravely teach, by precept and example, the necessity of the young man's providing a certain number of superfluous glow-shoes, and umbrellas, and empty guest chambers for empty guests, before he dies? Why should not our furniture be as simple as the Arab's or the Indian's? When I think of the benefactors of the race, whom we have apotheosized as messengers from heaven, bearers of divine gifts to man, I do not see in my mind any retinue at their heels, any car-load of fashionable furniture. Or what if I were to allow—would it not be a singular allowance?—that our furniture should be more complex than the Arab's, in proportion as we are morally and intellectually his superiors! At present our houses are cluttered and defiled with it, and a good housewife would sweep out the greater part into the dust hole, and not leave her morning's work undone. Morning work! By the blushes of Aurora and the music of Memnon, what should be man's *morning work* in this world? I had three pieces of limestone on my desk, but I was terrified to find that they required to be dusted daily, when the furniture of my mind was all undusted still, and I threw them out the window in disgust. How, then, could I have a furnished house? I would rather sit in the open air, for no dust gathers on the grass, unless where man has broken ground.

It is the luxurious and dissipated who set the fashions which the herd so diligently follow. The traveller who stops at the best houses, so called, soon discovers this, for the publicans presume him to be a Sardanapalus, and if he resigned himself to their tender mercies he would soon be completely emasculated. I think that in the railroad car we are inclined to spend more on luxury than on safety and convenience, and it threatens without attaining these to become no better than a modern drawing room, with its divans, and ottomans, and sunshades, and a hundred other oriental things, which we are taking west with us, invented for the ladies of the harem and the effeminate natives of the Celestial Empire, which Jonathan should be ashamed to know the names of. I would rather sit on a pumpkin and have it all to myself, than be crowded on a velvet cushion. I would rather ride on earth in an ox cart with a free circulation, than go to heaven in the fancy car of an excursion train and breathe a *malaria* all the way.

The very simplicity and nakedness of man's life in the primitive ages imply this advantage at least, that they left him still but a sojourner in nature. When he was refreshed with food and sleep he contemplated his journey again. He dwelt, as it were, in a tent in this world, and was either threading the valleys, or crossing the plains, or climbing the mountain tops. But lo! men have become the tools of their tools. The man who independently plucked the fruits when he was hungry is become a farmer; and he who stood under a tree for shelter, a housekeeper. We now no longer camp as for a night, but have settled down on earth and forgotten heaven. We have adopted Christianity merely as an improved method of *agri*-culture. We have built for this world a family mansion, and for the next a family tomb. The best works of art are the expression of man's struggle to free himself from this condition, but the effect of our art is merely to make this low state comfortable and that higher state to be forgotten. There is actually no place in this village for a work of *fine* art, if any had come down to us, to stand, for our lives, our houses and streets, furnish no proper pedestal for it. There is not a nail to hang a picture on, nor a shelf to receive the bust of a hero or a saint. When I consider how our houses are built and paid for, or not paid for, and their internal economy managed and sustained, I wonder that the floor does not give way under the visitor while he is admiring the gewgaws upon the mantel-piece, and let him through into the cellar, to some solid and honest though earthy foundation. I cannot but perceive that this so called rich and refined life is a thing jumped at, and I do not get on in the enjoyment of the *fine* arts which adorn it, my attention being wholly occupied with the jump; for I remember that the greatest genuine leap, due to human muscles alone, on record, is that of certain wandering Arabs, who are said to have cleared twenty-five feet on level ground. Without factitious support, man is sure to come to earth again beyond that distance. The first question which I am tempted to put to the proprietor of such great impropriety is, Who bolsters you? Are you one of the ninety-seven who fail? or of the three who succeed? Answer me these questions, and then perhaps I may look at your bawbles and find them ornamental. The cart before the horse is neither beautiful nor useful. Before we can adorn our houses with beautiful objects the walls must be stripped, and our lives must be stripped, and beautiful housekeeping and beautiful living be laid for a foundation: now, a taste for the beautiful is most cultivated out of doors, where there is no house and no housekeeper.

Old Johnson, in his "Wonder-Working Providence," speaking of the first settlers of this town, with whom he was contemporary, tells us that "they burrow themselves in the earth for their first shelter under some hillside, and, casting the soil aloft upon timber, they make a smoky fire against the earth, at the highest side." They did not "provide them houses," says he, "till the earth, by the Lord's blessing, brought forth bread to feed them," and the first year's crop was so light that "they were forced to cut their bread very thin for a long season." The secretary of the Province of New Netherland, writing in Dutch, in 1650, for the information of those who wished to take up land there, states more particularly, that "those in New Netherland, and especially in New England, who have no means to build farm houses at first according to their wishes, dig a square pit in the ground, cellar fashion, six or seven feet deep, as long and as broad as they think proper, case the earth inside with wood all round the wall, and line the wood with the bark of trees or something else to prevent the caving in of the earth; floor this cellar with plank, and wainscot it overhead for a ceiling, raise a roof of spars clear up, and cover the spars with bark or green sods, so that they can live dry and warm in these houses with their entire families for two, three, and four years, it being understood that partitions are run through those cellars which are adapted to the size of the family. The wealthy and principal men in New

England, in the beginning of the colonies, commenced their first dwelling houses in this fashion for two reasons; firstly, in order not to waste time in building, and not to want food the next season; secondly, in order not to discourage poor laboring people whom they brought over in numbers from Fatherland. In the course of three or four years, when the country became adapted to agriculture, they built themselves handsome houses, spending on them several thousands."

In this course which our ancestors took there was a show of prudence at least, as if their principle were to satisfy the more pressing wants first. But are the more pressing wants satisfied now? When I think of acquiring for myself one of our luxurious dwellings, I am deterred, for, so to speak, the country is not yet adapted to *human* culture, and we are still forced to cut our *spiritual* bread far thinner than our fore-fathers did their wheaten. Not that all architectural ornament is to be neglected even in the rudest periods; but let our houses first be lined with beauty, where they come in contact with our lives, like the tenement of the shellfish, and not overlaid with it. But, alas! I have been inside one or two of them, and know what they are lined with.

Though we are not so degenerate but that we might possibly live in a cave or a wigwam or wear skins to-day, it certainly is better to accept the advantages, though so dearly bought, which the invention and industry of mankind offer. In such a neighborhood as this, boards and shingles, lime and bricks, are cheaper and more easily obtained than suitable caves, or whole logs, or bark in sufficient quantities, or even well-tempered clay or flat stones. I speak understandingly on this subject, for I have made myself acquainted with it both theoretically and practically. With a little more wit we might use these materials so as to become richer than the richest now are, and make our civilization a blessing. The civilized man is a more experienced and wiser savage. But to make haste to my own experiment.

Near the end of March, 1845, I borrowed an axe and went down to the woods by Walden Pond, nearest to where I intended to build my house, and began to cut down some tall arrowy white pines, still in their youth, for timber. It is difficult to begin without borrowing, but perhaps it is the most generous course thus to permit your fellow-men to have an interest in your enterprise. The owner of the axe, as he released his hold on it, said that it was the apple of his eye; but I returned it sharper than I received it. It was a pleasant hillside where I worked, covered with pine woods, through which I looked out on the pond, and a small open field in the woods where pines and hickories were springing up. The ice in the pond was not yet dissolved, though there were some open spaces, and it was all dark colored and saturated with water. There were some slight flurries of snow during the days that I worked there; but for the most part when I came out on to the railroad, on my way home, its yellow sand heap stretched away gleaming in the hazy atmosphere, and the rails shone in the spring sun, and I heard the lark and pewee and other birds already come to commence another year with us. They were pleasant spring days, in which the winter of man's discontent was thawing as well as the earth, and the life that had lain torpid began to stretch itself. One day, when my axe had come off and I had cut a green hickory for a wedge, driving it with a stone, and had placed the whole to soak in a pond hole in order to swell the wood, I saw a striped snake run into the water, and he lay on the bottom, apparently without inconvenience, as long as I staid there, or more than a quarter of an hour; perhaps because he had not yet fairly come out of the torpid state. It appeared to me that for a like reason men remain in their present low and primitive condition; but if they should feel the influence of the spring of springs arousing them, they would of necessity rise to a higher and more ethereal life. I had previously seen the snakes in frosty mornings in my path with portions of their bodies still numb and inflexible, waiting for the sun to thaw them. On the 1st of April it rained and melted the ice, and in the early part of the day, which was very foggy, I heard a stray goose groping about over the pond and cackling as if lost, or like the spirit of the fog.

So I went on for some days cutting and hewing timber, and also studs and rafters, all with my narrow axe, not having many communicable or scholar-like thoughts, singing to myself,—

Men say they know many things;
But lo! they have taken wings,—
The arts and sciences,
And a thousand appliances;
The wind that blows
Is all that any body knows.

I hewed the main timbers six inches square, most of the studs on two sides only, and the rafters and floor timbers on one side, leaving the rest of the bark on, so that they were just as straight and much stronger than sawed ones. Each stick was carefully mortised or tenoned by its stump, for I had borrowed other tools by this time. My days in the woods were not very long ones; yet I usually carried my dinner of bread and butter, and read the newspaper in which it was wrapped, at noon, sitting amid the green pine boughs which I had cut off, and to my bread was imparted some of their fragrance, for my hands were covered with a thick coat of pitch. Before I had done I was more the friend than the foe of the pine tree, though I had cut down some of them, having become better acquainted with it. Sometimes a rambler in the wood was attracted by the sound of my axe, and we chatted pleasantly over the chips which I had made.

By the middle of April, for I made no haste in my work, but rather made the most of it, my house was framed and ready for the raising. I had already bought the shanty of James Collins, an Irishman who worked on the Fitchburg Railroad, for boards. James Collins' shanty was considered an uncommonly fine one. When I called to see it he was not at home. I walked about the outside, at first unobserved from within, the window was so deep and high. It was of small dimensions, with a peaked cottage roof, and not much else to be seen, the dirt being raised five feet all around as if it were a compost heap. The roof was the soundest part, though a good deal warped and made brittle by the sun. Door-sill there was none, but a perennial passage for the hens under the door board. Mrs. C. came to the door and asked me to view it from the inside. The hens were driven in by my approach. It was dark, and had a dirt floor for the most part, dank, clammy, and aguish, only here a board and there a board which would not bear removal. She lighted a lamp to show me the inside of the roof and the walls, and also that the board floor extended under the bed, warning me not to step into the cellar, a sort of dust hole two feet deep. In her own words, they were "good boards overhead, good boards all around, and a good window,"—of two whole squares originally, only the cat had passed out that way lately. There was a stove, a bed, and a place to sit, an infant in the house where it was born, a silk parasol, gilt-framed looking-glass, and a patent new coffee mill nailed to an oak sapling, all told. The bargain was soon concluded, for James had in the mean while returned. I to pay four dollars and twenty-five cents to-night, he to vacate at five to-morrow morning, selling to nobody else meanwhile: I to take possession at six. It were well, he said, to be there early, and anticipate certain indistinct but wholly unjust claims on the score of ground rent and fuel. This he assured me was the only encumbrance. At six I passed him and his family on the road. One large bundle held their all,—bed, coffee-mill, looking-glass, hens,—all but the cat, she took to the woods and became a wild cat, and, as I learned afterward, trod in a trap set for woodchucks, and so became a dead cat at last.

I took down this dwelling the same morning, drawing the nails, and removed it to the pond side by small cartloads, spreading the boards on the grass there to bleach and warp back again in the sun. One early thrush gave me a note or two as I drove along the woodland path. I was informed treacherously by a young Patrick that neighbor Seeley, an Irishman, in the intervals of the carting, transferred the still tolerable, straight, and drivable nails, staples, and spikes to his pocket, and then stood when I came back to pass the time of day, and look freshly up, unconcerned, with spring thoughts, at the devastation; there being a dearth of work, as he said. He was there to represent spectatordom, and help make this seemingly insignificant event one with the removal of the gods of Troy.

I dug my cellar in the side of a hill sloping to the south, where a woodchuck had formerly dug his burrow, down through sumach and blackberry roots, and the lowest stain of vegetation, six feet square by seven deep, to a fine sand where potatoes would not freeze in any winter. The sides were left shelving, and not stoned; but the sun having never shone on them, the sand still keeps its place. It was but two hours' work. I took particular pleasure in this breaking of ground, for in almost all latitudes men dig into the earth for an equable temperature. Under the most splendid house in the city is still to be found the cellar where they store their roots as of old, and long after the superstructure has disappeared posterity remark its dent in the earth. The house is still but a sort of porch at the entrance of a burrow.

At length, in the beginning of May, with the help of some of my acquaintances, rather to improve so good an occasion for neighborliness than from any necessity, I set up the frame of my house. No man was ever more honored in the character of his raisers than I. They are destined, I trust, to assist at the raising of loftier structures one day. I began to occupy my house on the 4th of July, as soon as it was boarded and roofed, for the boards were carefully feather-edged and lapped, so that it was perfectly impervious to rain; but before boarding I laid the foundation of a chimney at one end, bringing two cartloads of stones up the hill from the pond in my arms. I built the chimney after my hoeing in the fall, before a fire became necessary for warmth, doing my cooking in the mean while out of doors on the ground, early in the morning: which mode I still think is in some respects more convenient and agreeable than the usual one. When it stormed before my bread was baked, I fixed a few boards over the fire, and sat under them to watch my loaf, and passed some pleasant hours in that way. In those days, when my hands were much employed, I read but little, but the least scraps of paper which lay on the ground, my holder, or tablecloth, afforded me as much entertainment, in fact answered the same purpose as the Iliad.

It would be worth the while to build still more deliberately than I did, considering, for instance, what foundation a door, a window, a cellar, a garret, have in the nature of man, and perchance never raising any superstructure until we found a better reason for it than our temporal necessities even. There is some of the same fitness in a man's building his own house that there is in a bird's building its own nest. Who knows but if men constructed their dwellings with their own hands, and provided food for themselves and families simply and honestly enough, the poetic faculty would be universally developed, as birds universally sing when they are so engaged? But alas! we do like cowbirds and cuckoos, which lay their eggs in nests which other birds have built, and cheer no traveller with their chattering and unmusical notes. Shall we forever resign the pleasure of construction to the carpenter? What does architecture amount to in the experience of the mass of men? I never in all my walks came across a man engaged in so simple and natural an occupation as building his house. We belong to the community. It is not the tailor alone who is the ninth part of a man; it is as much the preacher, and the merchant, and the farmer. Where is this division of labor to end? and what object does it finally serve? No doubt another *may* also think for me; but it is not therefore desirable that he should do so to the exclusion of my thinking for myself.

True, there are architects so called in this country, and I have heard of one at least possessed with the idea of making architectural ornaments have a core of truth, a necessity, and hence a beauty, as if it were a revelation to him. All very well perhaps from his point of view, but only a little better than the common dilettantism. A sentimental reformer in architecture, he began at the cornice, not at the foundation. It was only how to put a core of truth within the ornaments, that every sugar plum in fact might have an almond or caraway seed in it,—though I hold that almonds are most wholesome without the sugar,—and not how the inhabitant, the in-dweller, might build truly within and without, and let the ornaments take care of themselves. What reasonable man ever supposed that ornaments were something outward and in the skin merely,—that the tortoise got his spotted shell, or the shellfish its mother-o'-pearl tints, by such a contract as the inhabitants of Broadway their Trinity Church? But a man has no more to do with the style of architecture of his house than a tortoise with that of its shell: nor need the soldier be so idle as to try to paint the precise *color* of his virtue on his standard. The enemy will find it out. He may turn pale when the trial comes. This man seemed to me to lean over the cornice

and timidly whisper his half truth to the rude occupants who
really knew it better than he. What of architectural beauty I
now see, I know has gradually grown from within outward,
out of the necessities and character of the indweller, who is
the only builder,—out of some unconscious truthfulness, and
nobleness, without ever a thought for the appearance; and
whatever additional beauty of this kind is destined to be produced will be preceded by a like unconscious beauty of life.
The most interesting dwellings in this country, as the painter
knows, are the most unpretending, humble log huts and cottages of the poor commonly; it is the life of the inhabitants
whose shells they are, and not any peculiarity in their surfaces
merely, which makes them *picturesque*; and equally interesting
will be the citizen's suburban box, when his life shall be as
simple and as agreeable to the imagination, and there is as
little straining after effect in the style of his dwelling. A great
proportion of architectural ornaments are literally hollow, and
a September gale would strip them off, like borrowed plumes,
without injury to the substantials. They can do without *architecture* who have no olives nor wines in the cellar. What if
an equal ado were made about the ornaments of style in literature, and the architects of our bibles spent as much time
about their cornices as the architects of our churches do? So
are made the *belles-lettres* and the *beaux-arts* and their professors. Much it concerns a man, forsooth, how a few sticks are
slanted over him or under him, and what colors are daubed
upon his box. It would signify somewhat, if, in any earnest
sense, *he* slanted them and daubed it; but the spirit having
departed out of the tenant, it is of a piece with constructing
his own coffin,—the architecture of the grave, and "carpenter," is but another name for "coffin-maker." One man says,
in his despair or indifference to life, take up a handful of the
earth at your feet, and paint your house that color. Is he
thinking of his last and narrow house? Toss up a copper for
it as well. What an abundance of leisure he must have! Why
do you take up a handful of dirt? Better paint your house
your own complexion; let it turn pale or blush for you. An
enterprise to improve the style of cottage architecture! When
you have got my ornaments ready I will wear them.

Before winter I built a chimney, and shingled the sides of

my house, which were already impervious to rain, with imperfect and sappy shingles made of the first slice of the log, whose edges I was obliged to straighten with a plane.

I have thus a tight shingled and plastered house, ten feet wide by fifteen long, and eight-feet posts, with a garret and a closet, a large window on each side, two trap doors, one door at the end, and a brick fireplace opposite. The exact cost of my house, paying the usual price for such materials as I used, but not counting the work, all of which was done by myself, was as follows; and I give the details because very few are able to tell exactly what their houses cost, and fewer still, if any, the separate cost of the various materials which compose them: —

Boards, ...	$8	03½,	mostly shanty boards.
Refuse shingles for roof and sides, . . .	4	00	
Laths, ...	1	25	
Two second-hand windows with glass, . .	2	43	
One thousand old brick, ...	4	00	
Two casks of lime, ...	2	40	That was high.
Hair, ...	0	31	More than I needed.
Mantle-tree iron, ...	0	15	
Nails, ...	3	90	
Hinges and screws, ...	0	14	
Latch, ...	0	10	
Chalk, ...	0	01	
Transportation, ...	1	40	I carried a good part on my back
In all, ...	$28	12½	

These are all the materials excepting the timber stones and sand, which I claimed by squatter's right. I have also a small wood-shed adjoining, made chiefly of the stuff which was left after building the house.

I intend to build me a house which will surpass any on the main street in Concord in grandeur and luxury, as soon as it pleases me as much and will cost me no more than my present one.

I thus found that the student who wishes for a shelter can obtain one for a lifetime at an expense not greater than the rent which he now pays annually. If I seem to boast more than is becoming, my excuse is that I brag for humanity rather than for myself; and my shortcomings and inconsistencies do not affect the truth of my statement. Notwithstanding much cant and hypocrisy,—chaff which I find it difficult to separate from my wheat, but for which I am as sorry as any man,—I will breathe freely and stretch myself in this respect, it is such a relief to both the moral and physical system; and I am resolved that I will not through humility become the devil's attorney. I will endeavor to speak a good word for the truth. At Cambridge College the mere rent of a student's room, which is only a little larger than my own, is thirty dollars each year, though the corporation had the advantage of building thirty-two side by side and under one roof, and the occupant suffers the inconvenience of many and noisy neighbors, and perhaps a residence in the fourth story. I cannot but think that if we had more true wisdom in these respects, not only less education would be needed, because, forsooth, more would already have been acquired, but the pecuniary expense of getting an education would in a great measure vanish. Those conveniences which the student requires at Cambridge or elsewhere cost him or somebody else ten times as great a sacrifice of life as they would with proper management on both sides. Those things for which the most money is demanded are never the things which the student most wants. Tuition, for instance, is an important item in the term bill, while for the far more valuable education which he gets by associating with the most cultivated of his contemporaries no charge is made. The mode of founding a college is, commonly, to get up a subscription of dollars and cents, and then following blindly the principles of a division of labor to its extreme, a principle which should never be followed but with circumspection,—to call in a contractor who makes this a subject of speculation, and he employs Irishmen or other operatives actually to lay the foundations, while the students that are to be are said to be fitting themselves for it; and for these oversights successive generations have to pay. I think that it would be *better than this*, for the students, or those who desire to be benefited by it, even to lay the foundation themselves. The student who secures his coveted leisure and retirement by systematically shirking any labor necessary to man obtains but an ignoble and unprofitable leisure, defrauding himself of the experience which alone can make leisure fruitful. "But," says one, "you do not mean that the students should go to work with their hands instead of their heads?" I do not mean that exactly, but I mean something which he might think a good deal like that; I mean that they should not *play* life, or *study* it merely, while the community supports them at this expensive game, but earnestly *live* it from beginning to end. How could youths better learn to live than by at once trying the experiment of living? Methinks this would exercise their minds as much as mathematics. If I wished a boy to know something about the arts and sciences, for instance, I would not pursue the common course, which is merely to send him into the neighborhood of some professor, where any thing is professed and practised but the art of life;—to survey the world through a telescope or a microscope, and never with his natural eye; to study chemistry, and not learn how his bread is made, or mechanics, and not learn how it is earned; to discover new satellites to Neptune, and not detect the motes in his eyes, or to what vagabond he is a satellite himself; or to be devoured by the monsters that swarm all around him, while contemplating the monsters in a drop of vinegar. Which would have advanced the most at the end of a month,—the boy who had made his own jackknife from the ore which he had dug and smelted, reading as much as would be necessary for this,—or the boy who had attended the lectures on metallurgy at the Institute in the mean while, and had received a Rogers' penknife from his father? Which would be most likely to cut his fingers?—To my astonishment I was informed on leaving college that I had studied navigation!—why, if I had taken one turn down the harbor I should have known more about it. Even the *poor* student studies and is taught only *political* economy, while that economy of living which is synonymous with philosophy is not even sincerely professed in our colleges. The consequence is, that while he is reading Adam Smith, Ricardo, and Say, he runs his father in debt irretrievably.

As with our colleges, so with a hundred "modern improvements;" there is an illusion about them; there is not always a positive advance. The devil goes on exacting compound interest to the last for his early share and numerous succeeding investments in them. Our inventions are wont to be pretty toys, which distract our attention from serious things. They

are but improved means to an unimproved end, an end which
it was already but too easy to arrive at; as railroads lead to
Boston or New York. We are in great haste to construct a
magnetic telegraph from Maine to Texas; but Maine and
Texas, it may be, have nothing important to communicate.
Either is in such a predicament as the man who was earnest
to be introduced to a distinguished deaf woman, but when
he was presented, and one end of her ear trumpet was put
into his hand, had nothing to say. As if the main object were
to talk fast and not to talk sensibly. We are eager to tunnel
under the Atlantic and bring the old world some weeks nearer
to the new; but perchance the first news that will leak
through into the broad, flapping American ear will be that
the Princess Adelaide has the whooping cough. After all, the
man whose horse trots a mile in a minute does not carry the
most important messages; he is not an evangelist, nor does he
come round eating locusts and wild honey. I doubt if Flying
Childers ever carried a peck of corn to mill.

One says to me, "I wonder that you do not lay up money;
you love to travel; you might take the cars and go to Fitchburg to-day and see the country." But I am wiser than that. I
have learned that the swiftest traveller is he that goes afoot. I
say to my friend, Suppose we try who will get there first. The
distance is thirty miles; the fare ninety cents. That is almost a
day's wages. I remember when wages were sixty cents a day
for laborers on this very road. Well, I start now on foot, and
get there before night; I have travelled at that rate by the
week together. You will in the mean while have earned your
fare, and arrive there some time to-morrow, or possibly this
evening, if you are lucky enough to get a job in season. Instead of going to Fitchburg, you will be working here the
greater part of the day. And so, if the railroad reached round
the world, I think that I should keep ahead of you; and as for
seeing the country and getting experience of that kind, I
should have to cut your acquaintance altogether.

Such is the universal law, which no man can ever outwit,
and with regard to the railroad even we may say it is as broad
as it is long. To make a railroad round the world available to
all mankind is equivalent to grading the whole surface of the
planet. Men have an indistinct notion that if they keep up this

activity of joint stocks and spades long enough all will at length ride somewhere, in next to no time, and for nothing; but though a crowd rushes to the depot, and the conductor shouts "All aboard!" when the smoke is blown away and the vapor condensed, it will be perceived that a few are riding, but the rest are run over,—and it will be called, and will be, "A melancholy accident." No doubt they can ride at last who shall have earned their fare, that is, if they survive so long, but they will probably have lost their elasticity and desire to travel by that time. This spending of the best part of one's life earning money in order to enjoy a questionable liberty during the least valuable part of it, reminds me of the Englishman who went to India to make a fortune first, in order that he might return to England and live the life of a poet. He should have gone up garret at once. "What!" exclaim a million Irishmen starting up from all the shanties in the land, "is not this railroad which we have built a good thing?" Yes, I answer, *comparatively* good, that is, you might have done worse; but I wish, as you are brothers of mine, that you could have spent your time better than digging in this dirt.

Before I finished my house, wishing to earn ten or twelve dollars by some honest and agreeable method, in order to meet my unusual expenses, I planted about two acres and a half of light and sandy soil near it chiefly with beans, but also a small part with potatoes, corn, peas, and turnips. The whole lot contains eleven acres, mostly growing up to pines and hickories, and was sold the preceding season for eight dollars and eight cents an acre. One farmer said that it was "good for nothing but to raise cheeping squirrels on." I put no manure on this land, not being the owner, but merely a squatter, and not expecting to cultivate so much again, and I did not quite hoe it all once. I got out several cords of stumps in ploughing, which supplied me with fuel for a long time, and left small circles of virgin mould, easily distinguishable through the summer by the greater luxuriance of the beans there. The dead and for the most part unmerchantable wood behind my house, and the driftwood from the pond, have supplied the remainder of my fuel. I was obliged to hire a team and a man for the ploughing, though I held the plough myself. My farm outgoes for the first season were, for implements, seed, work, &c., $14 72½. The seed corn was given me. This never costs any thing to speak of, unless you plant more than enough. I got twelve bushels of beans, and eighteen bushels of potatoes, beside some peas and sweet corn. The yellow corn and turnips were too late to come to any thing. My whole income from the farm was

	$23 44.
Deducting the outgoes, . . .	14 72½
there are left, ...	$8 71½,

beside produce consumed and on hand at the time this estimate was made of the value of $4 50,—the amount on hand much more than balancing a little grass which I did not raise. All things considered, that is, considering the importance of a man's soul and of to-day, notwithstanding the short time occupied by my experiment, nay, partly even because of its transient character, I believe that that was doing better than any farmer in Concord did that year.

The next year I did better still, for I spaded up all the land which I required, about a third of an acre, and I learned from the experience of both years, not being in the least awed by many celebrated works on husbandry, Arthur Young among the rest, that if one would live simply and eat only the crop which he raised, and raise no more than he ate, and not exchange it for an insufficient quantity of more luxurious and expensive things, he would need to cultivate only a few rods of ground, and that it would be cheaper to spade up that than to use oxen to plough it, and to select a fresh spot from time to time than to manure the old, and he could do all his necessary farm work as it were with his left hand at odd hours in the summer; and thus he would not be tied to an ox, or horse, or cow, or pig, as at present. I desire to speak impartially on this point, and as one not interested in the success or failure of the present economical and social arrangements. I was more independent than any farmer in Concord, for I was not anchored to a house or farm, but could follow the bent of my genius, which is a very crooked one, every moment. Beside being better off than they already, if my house had been burned or my crops had failed, I should have been nearly as well off as before.

I am wont to think that men are not so much the keepers of herds as herds are the keepers of men, the former are so much the freer. Men and oxen exchange work; but if we consider necessary work only, the oxen will be seen to have greatly the advantage, their farm is so much the larger. Man does some of his part of the exchange work in his six weeks of haying, and it is no boy's play. Certainly no nation that lived simply in all respects, that is, no nation of philosophers, would commit so great a blunder as to use the labor of animals. True, there never was and is not likely soon to be a nation of philosophers, nor am I certain it is desirable that there should be. However, *I* should never have broken a horse or bull and taken him to board for any work he might do for me, for fear I should become a horse-man or a herds-man merely; and if society seems to be the gainer by so doing, are we certain that what is one man's gain is not another's loss, and that the stable-boy has equal cause with his master to be satisfied? Granted that some public works would not have been constructed without this aid, and let man share the glory of such with the ox and horse; does it follow that he could not have accomplished works yet more worthy of himself in that case? When men begin to do, not merely unnecessary or artistic, but luxurious and idle work, with their assistance, it is inevitable that a few do all the exchange work with the oxen, or, in other words, become the slaves of the strongest. Man thus not only works for the animal within him, but, for a symbol of this, he works for the animal without him. Though we have many substantial houses of brick or stone, the prosperity of the farmer is still measured by the degree to which the barn overshadows the house. This town is said to have the largest houses for oxen cows and horses hereabouts, and it is not behindhand in its public buildings; but there are very few halls for free worship or free speech in this county. It should not be by their architecture, but why not even by their power of abstract thought, that nations should seek to commemorate themselves? How much more admirable the Bhagvat-Geeta than all the ruins of the East! Towers and temples are the luxury of princes. A simple and independent mind does not toil at the bidding of any prince. Genius is not a retainer to any emperor, nor is its material silver, or gold, or marble, except to a trifling extent. To what end, pray, is so much stone hammered? In Arcadia, when I was there, I did not see any hammering stone. Nations are possessed with an insane ambition to perpetuate the memory of themselves by the amount of hammered stone they leave. What if equal pains were taken to smooth and polish their manners? One piece of good sense would be more memorable than a monument as high as the moon. I love better to see stones in place. The grandeur of Thebes was a vulgar grandeur. More sensible is a rod of stone wall that bounds an honest man's field than a hundred-gated Thebes that has wandered farther from the true end of life. The religion and civilization which are barbaric and heathenish build splendid temples; but what you might call Christianity does not. Most of the stone a nation hammers goes toward its tomb only. It buries itself alive. As for the Pyramids, there is nothing to wonder at in them so much as the fact that so many men could be found degraded enough to spend their lives constructing a tomb for some ambitious booby, whom it would have been wiser and manlier to have drowned in the Nile, and then given his body to the dogs. I might possibly invent some excuse for them and him, but I have no time for it. As for the religion and love of art of the builders, it is much the same all the world over, whether the building be an Egyptian temple or the United States Bank. It costs more than it comes to. The mainspring is vanity, assisted by the love of garlic and bread and butter. Mr. Balcom, a promising young architect, designs it on the back of his Vitruvius, with hard pencil and ruler, and the job is let out to Dobson & Sons, stonecutters. When the thirty centuries begin to look down on it, mankind begin to look up at it. As for your high towers and monuments, there was a crazy fellow once in this town who undertook to dig through to China, and he got so far that, as he said, he heard the Chinese pots and kettles rattle; but I think that I shall not go out of my way to admire the hole which he made. Many are concerned about the monuments of the West and the East,—to know who built them. For my part,

I should like to know who in those days did not build them,—who were above such trifling. But to proceed with my statistics.

By surveying, carpentry, and day-labor of various other kinds in the village in the mean while, for I have as many trades as fingers, I had earned $13 34. The expense of food for eight months, namely, from July 4th to March 1st, the time when these estimates were made, though I lived there more than two years,—not counting potatoes, a little green corn, and some peas, which I had raised, nor considering the value of what was on hand at the last date, was

Rice,	$1	73½		
Molasses,	1	73	Cheapest form of the saccharine.	
Rye meal,	1	04¾		
Indian meal,	0	99¾	Cheaper than rye.	
Pork,	0	22		
Flour,	0	88	Costs more than Indian meal, both money and trouble.	
Sugar,	0	80		All experiments which failed.
Lard,	0	65		
Apples,	0	25		
Dried apple,	0	22		
Sweet potatoes,	0	10		
One pumpkin,	0	6		
One watermelon,	0	2		
Salt,	0	3		

Yes, I did eat $8 74, all told; but I should not thus unblushingly publish my guilt, if I did not know that most of my readers were equally guilty with myself, and that their deeds would look no better in print. The next year I sometimes caught a mess of fish for my dinner, and once I went so far as to slaughter a woodchuck which ravaged my bean-field,— effect his transmigration, as a Tartar would say,—and devour him, partly for experiment's sake; but though it afforded me a momentary enjoyment, notwithstanding a musky flavor, I saw that the longest use would not make that a good practice, however it might seem to have your woodchucks ready dressed by the village butcher.

Clothing and some incidental expenses within the same

dates, though little can be inferred from this item, amounted to

	$8	40¾
Oil and some household utensils, ...	2	00

So that all the pecuniary outgoes, excepting for washing and mending, which for the most part were done out of the house, and their bills have not yet been received,—and these are all and more than all the ways by which money necessarily goes out in this part of the world,—were

House, ...	$28	12½
Farm one year, ...	14	72½
Food eight months, ...	8	74
Clothing, &c., eight months, ...	8	40¾
Oil, &c., eight months, ...	2	00
In all, ...	$61	99¾

I address myself now to those of my readers who have a living to get. And to meet this I have for farm produce sold

	$23	44
Earned by day-labor, ...	13	34
In all, ...	$36	78,

which subtracted from the sum of the outgoes leaves a balance of $25 21¾ on the one side,—this being very nearly the means with which I started, and the measure of expenses to be incurred,—and on the other, beside the leisure and independence and health thus secured, a comfortable house for me as long as I choose to occupy it.

These statistics, however accidental and therefore uninstructive they may appear, as they have a certain completeness, have a certain value also. Nothing was given me of which I have not rendered some account. It appears from the above estimate, that my food alone cost me in money about twenty-seven cents a week. It was, for nearly two years after this, rye and Indian meal without yeast, potatoes, rice, a very little salt pork, molasses, and salt, and my drink water. It was fit that I should live on rice, mainly, who loved so well the philosophy of India. To meet the objections of some inveterate cavillers, I may as well state, that if I dined out occasionally, as I always had done, and I trust shall have opportunities to do again, it was frequently to the detriment of my domestic arrangements. But the dining out, being, as I have stated, a constant element, does not in the least affect a comparative statement like this.

I learned from my two years' experience that it would cost incredibly little trouble to obtain one's necessary food, even in this latitude; that a man may use as simple a diet as the animals, and yet retain health and strength. I have made a satisfactory dinner, satisfactory on several accounts, simply off a dish of purslane (*Portulaca oleracea*) which I gathered in my cornfield, boiled and salted. I give the Latin on account of the savoriness of the trivial name. And pray what more can a reasonable man desire, in peaceful times, in ordinary noons, than a sufficient number of ears of green sweet-corn boiled, with the addition of salt? Even the little variety which I used was a yielding to the demands of appetite, and not of health. Yet men have come to such a pass that they frequently starve, not for want of necessaries, but for want of luxuries; and I know a good woman who thinks that her son lost his life because he took to drinking water only.

The reader will perceive that I am treating the subject rather from an economic than a dietetic point of view, and he will not venture to put my abstemiousness to the test unless he has a well-stocked larder.

Bread I at first made of pure Indian meal and salt, genuine hoe-cakes, which I baked before my fire out of doors on a shingle or the end of a stick of timber sawed off in building my house; but it was wont to get smoked and to have a piny flavor. I tried flour also; but have at last found a mixture of rye and Indian meal most convenient and agreeable. In cold weather it was no little amusement to bake several small loaves of this in succession, tending and turning them as carefully as an Egyptian his hatching eggs. They were a real cereal fruit which I ripened, and they had to my senses a fragrance like that of other noble fruits, which I kept in as long as possible by wrapping them in cloths. I made a study of the ancient and indispensable art of bread-making, consulting such authorities as offered, going back to the primitive days and first invention of the unleavened kind, when from the wildness of nuts and meats men first reached the mildness and

refinement of this diet, and travelling gradually down in my
studies through that accidental souring of the dough which,
it is supposed, taught the leavening process, and through the
various fermentations thereafter, till I came to "good, sweet,
wholesome bread," the staff of life. Leaven, which some deem
the soul of bread, the *spiritus* which fills its cellular tissue,
which is religiously preserved like the vestal fire,—some precious bottle-full, I suppose, first brought over in the Mayflower, did the business for America, and its influence is still
rising, swelling, spreading, in cerealian billows over the
land,—this seed I regularly and faithfully procured from the
village, till at length one morning I forgot the rules, and
scalded my yeast; by which accident I discovered that even
this was not indispensable,—for my discoveries were not by
the synthetic but analytic process,—and I have gladly omitted
it since, though most housewives earnestly assured me that
safe and wholesome bread without yeast might not be, and
elderly people prophesied a speedy decay of the vital forces.
Yet I find it not to be an essential ingredient, and after going
without it for a year am still in the land of the living; and I
am glad to escape the trivialness of carrying a bottle-full in
my pocket, which would sometimes pop and discharge its
contents to my discomfiture. It is simpler and more respectable to omit it. Man is an animal who more than any other
can adapt himself to all climates and circumstances. Neither
did I put any sal soda, or other acid or alkali, into my bread.
It would seem that I made it according to the recipe which
Marcus Porcius Cato gave about two centuries before Christ.
"Panem depsticium sic facito. Manus mortariumque bene
lavato. Farinam in mortarium indito, aquæ paulatim addito,
subigitoque pulchre. Ubi bene subegeris, defingito, coqui-
toque sub testu." Which I take to mean—"Make kneaded
bread thus. Wash your hands and trough well. Put the meal
into the trough, add water gradually, and knead it thoroughly. When you have kneaded it well, mould it, and bake
it under a cover," that is, in a baking-kettle. Not a word about
leaven. But I did not always use this staff of life. At one time,
owing to the emptiness of my purse, I saw none of it for
more than a month.

Every New Englander might easily raise all his own breadstuffs in this land of rye and Indian corn, and not depend on distant and fluctuating markets for them. Yet so far are we from simplicity and independence that, in Concord, fresh and sweet meal is rarely sold in the shops, and hominy and corn in a still coarser form are hardly used by any. For the most part the farmer gives to his cattle and hogs the grain of his own producing, and buys flour, which is at least no more wholesome, at a greater cost, at the store. I saw that I could easily raise my bushel or two of rye and Indian corn, for the former will grow on the poorest land, and the latter does not require the best, and grind them in a hand-mill, and so do without rice and pork; and if I must have some concentrated sweet, I found by experiment that I could make a very good molasses either of pumpkins or beets, and I knew that I needed only to set out a few maples to obtain it more easily still, and while these were growing I could use various substitutes beside those which I have named, "For," as the Forefathers sang,—

> " we can make liquor to sweeten our lips
> Of pumpkins and parsnips and walnut-tree chips."

Finally, as for salt, that grossest of groceries, to obtain this might be a fit occasion for a visit to the seashore, or, if I did without it altogether, I should probably drink the less water. I do not learn that the Indians ever troubled themselves to go after it.

Thus I could avoid all trade and barter, so far as my food was concerned, and having a shelter already, it would only remain to get clothing and fuel. The pantaloons which I now wear were woven in a farmer's family,—thank Heaven there is so much virtue still in man; for I think the fall from the farmer to the operative as great and memorable as that from the man to the farmer;—and in a new country fuel is an encumbrance. As for a habitat, if I were not permitted still to squat, I might purchase one acre at the same price for which the land I cultivated was sold—namely, eight dollars and eight cents. But as it was, I considered that I enhanced the value of the land by squatting on it.

There is a certain class of unbelievers who sometimes ask me such questions as, if I think that I can live on vegetable

food alone; and to strike at the root of the matter at once,—
for the root is faith,—I am accustomed to answer such, that
I can live on board nails. If they cannot understand that, they
cannot understand much that I have to say. For my part, I
am glad to hear of experiments of this kind being tried; as
that a young man tried for a fortnight to live on hard, raw
corn on the ear, using his teeth for all mortar. The squirrel
tribe tried the same and succeeded. The human race is interested in these experiments, though a few old women who are
incapacitated for them, or who own their thirds in mills, may
be alarmed.

My furniture, part of which I made myself, and the rest
cost me nothing of which I have not rendered an account,
consisted of a bed, a table, a desk, three chairs, a looking-
glass three inches in diameter, a pair of tongs and andirons, a
kettle, a skillet, and a frying-pan, a dipper, a wash-bowl, two
knives and forks, three plates, one cup, one spoon, a jug for
oil, a jug for molasses, and a japanned lamp. None is so poor
that he need sit on a pumpkin. That is shiftlessness. There is
a plenty of such chairs as I like best in the village garrets to
be had for taking them away. Furniture! Thank God, I can
sit and I can stand without the aid of a furniture warehouse.
What man but a philosopher would not be ashamed to see
his furniture packed in a cart and going up country exposed
to the light of heaven and the eyes of men, a beggarly account
of empty boxes? That is Spaulding's furniture. I could never
tell from inspecting such a load whether it belonged to a so
called rich man or a poor one; the owner always seemed pov-
erty-stricken. Indeed, the more you have of such things the
poorer you are. Each load looks as if it contained the contents
of a dozen shanties; and if one shanty is poor, this is a dozen
times as poor. Pray, for what do we *move* ever but to get rid
of our furniture, our *exuviæ*; at last to go from this world to
another newly furnished, and leave this to be burned? It is the
same as if all these traps were buckled to a man's belt, and he
could not move over the rough country where our lines are
cast without dragging them,—dragging his trap. He was a
lucky fox that left his tail in the trap. The muskrat will gnaw
his third leg off to be free. No wonder man has lost his elas-

ticity. How often he is at a dead set! "Sir, if I may be so bold, what do you mean by a dead set?" If you are a seer, whenever you meet a man you will see all that he owns, ay, and much that he pretends to disown, behind him, even to his kitchen furniture and all the trumpery which he saves and will not burn, and he will appear to be harnessed to it and making what headway he can. I think that the man is at a dead set who has got through a knot hole or gateway where his sledge load of furniture cannot follow him. I cannot but feel compassion when I hear some trig, compact-looking man, seemingly free, all girded and ready, speak of his "furniture," as whether it is insured or not. "But what shall I do with my furniture?" My gay butterfly is entangled in a spider's web then. Even those who seem for a long while not to have any, if you inquire more narrowly you will find have some stored in somebody's barn. I look upon England to-day as an old gentleman who is travelling with a great deal of baggage, trumpery which has accumulated from long housekeeping, which he has not the courage to burn; great trunk, little trunk, bandbox and bundle. Throw away the first three at least. It would surpass the powers of a well man nowadays to take up his bed and walk, and I should certainly advise a sick one to lay down his bed and run. When I have met an immigrant tottering under a bundle which contained his all,— looking like an enormous wen which had grown out of the nape of his neck,—I have pitied him, not because that was his all, but because he had all *that* to carry. If I have got to drag my trap, I will take care that it be a light one and do not nip me in a vital part. But perchance it would be wisest never to put one's paw into it.

I would observe, by the way, that it costs me nothing for curtains, for I have no gazers to shut out but the sun and moon, and I am willing that they should look in. The moon will not sour milk nor taint meat of mine, nor will the sun injure my furniture or fade my carpet, and if he is sometimes too warm a friend, I find it still better economy to retreat behind some curtain which nature has provided, than to add a single item to the details of housekeeping. A lady once offered me a mat, but as I had no room to spare within the house, nor time to spare within or without to shake it, I declined it, preferring to wipe my feet on the sod before my door. It is best to avoid the beginnings of evil.

Not long since I was present at the auction of a deacon's effects, for his life had not been ineffectual: —

"The evil that men do lives after them."

As usual, a great proportion was trumpery which had begun to accumulate in his father's day. Among the rest was a dried tapeworm. And now, after lying half a century in his garret and other dust holes, these things were not burned; instead of a *bonfire*, or purifying destruction of them, there was an *auction*, or increasing of them. The neighbors eagerly collected to view them, bought them all, and carefully transported them to their garrets and dust holes, to lie there till their estates are settled, when they will start again. When a man dies he kicks the dust.

The customs of some savage nations might, perchance, be profitably imitated by us, for they at least go through the semblance of casting their slough annually; they have the idea of the thing, whether they have the reality or not. Would it not be well if we were to celebrate such a "busk," or "feast of first fruits," as Bartram describes to have been the custom of the Mucclasse Indians? "When a town celebrates the busk," says he, "having previously provided themselves with new clothes, new pots, pans, and other household utensils and furniture, they collect all their worn out clothes and other despicable things, sweep and cleanse their houses, squares, and the whole town, of their filth, which with all the remaining grain and other old provisions they cast together into one common heap, and consume it with fire. After having taken medicine, and fasted for three days, all the fire in the town is extinguished. During this fast they abstain from the gratification of every appetite and passion whatever. A general amnesty is proclaimed; all malefactors may return to their town. — "

"On the fourth morning, the high priest, by rubbing dry wood together, produces new fire in the public square, from whence every habitation in the town is supplied with the new and pure flame."

They then feast on the new corn and fruits and dance and

sing for three days, "and the four following days they receive visits and rejoice with their friends from neighboring towns who have in like manner purified and prepared themselves."

The Mexicans also practised a similar purification at the end of every fifty-two years, in the belief that it was time for the world to come to an end.

I have scarcely heard of a truer sacrament, that is, as the dictionary defines it, "outward and visible sign of an inward and spiritual grace," than this, and I have no doubt that they were originally inspired directly from Heaven to do thus, though they have no biblical record of the revelation.

For more than five years I maintained myself thus solely by the labor of my hands, and I found, that by working about six weeks in a year, I could meet all the expenses of living. The whole of my winters, as well as most of my summers, I had free and clear for study. I have thoroughly tried school-keeping, and found that my expenses were in proportion, or rather out of proportion, to my income, for I was obliged to dress and train, not to say think and believe, accordingly, and I lost my time into the bargain. As I did not teach for the good of my fellow-men, but simply for a livelihood, this was a failure. I have tried trade; but I found that it would take ten years to get under way in that, and that then I should probably be on my way to the devil. I was actually afraid that I might by that time be doing what is called a good business. When formerly I was looking about to see what I could do for a living, some sad experience in conforming to the wishes of friends being fresh in my mind to tax my ingenuity, I thought often and seriously of picking huckleberries; that surely I could do, and its small profits might suffice,—for my greatest skill has been to want but little,—so little capital it required, so little distraction from my wonted moods, I fool-ishly thought. While my acquaintances went unhesitatingly into trade or the professions, I contemplated this occupation as most like theirs; ranging the hills all summer to pick the berries which came in my way, and thereafter carelessly dispose of them; so, to keep the flocks of Admetus. I also dreamed that I might gather the wild herbs, or carry evergreens to such villagers as loved to be reminded of the woods, even to the city, by hay-cart loads. But I have since learned that trade curses every thing it handles; and though you trade in messages from heaven, the whole curse of trade attaches to the business.

As I preferred some things to others, and especially valued my freedom, as I could fare hard and yet succeed well, I did not wish to spend my time in earning rich carpets or other fine furniture, or delicate cookery, or a house in the Grecian or the Gothic style just yet. If there are any to whom it is no interruption to acquire these things, and who know how to use them when acquired, I relinquish to them the pursuit. Some are "industrious," and appear to love labor for its own sake, or perhaps because it keeps them out of worse mischief; to such I have at present nothing to say. Those who would not know what to do with more leisure than they now enjoy, I might advise to work twice as hard as they do,—work till they pay for themselves, and get their free papers. For myself I found that the occupation of a day-laborer was the most independent of any, especially as it required only thirty or forty days in a year to support one. The laborer's day ends with the going down of the sun, and he is then free to devote himself to his chosen pursuit, independent of his labor; but his employer, who speculates from month to month, has no respite from one end of the year to the other.

In short, I am convinced, both by faith and experience, that to maintain one's self on this earth is not a hardship but a pastime, if we will live simply and wisely; as the pursuits of the simpler nations are still the sports of the more artificial. It is not necessary that a man should earn his living by the sweat of his brow, unless he sweats easier than I do.

One young man of my acquaintance, who has inherited some acres, told me that he thought he should live as I did, *if he had the means.* I would not have any one adopt *my* mode of living on any account; for, beside that before he has fairly learned it I may have found out another for myself, I desire that there may be as many different persons in the world as possible; but I would have each one be very careful to find out and pursue *his own* way, and not his father's or his mother's or his neighbor's instead. The youth may build or plant or sail, only let him not be hindered from doing that which he tells me he would like to do. It is by a mathematical point only that we are wise, as the sailor or the fugitive slave keeps the polestar in his eye; but that is sufficient guidance for all our life. We may not arrive at our port within a calculable period, but we would preserve the true course.

Undoubtedly, in this case, what is true for one is truer still for a thousand, as a large house is not more expensive than a small one in proportion to its size, since one roof may cover, one cellar underlie, and one wall separate several apartments. But for my part, I preferred the solitary dwelling. Moreover, it will commonly be cheaper to build the whole yourself than to convince another of the advantage of the common wall; and when you have done this, the common partition, to be much cheaper, must be a thin one, and that other may prove a bad neighbor, and also not keep his side in repair. The only coöperation which is commonly possible is exceedingly partial and superficial; and what little true coöperation there is, is as if it were not, being a harmony inaudible to men. If a man has faith he will coöperate with equal faith every where; if he has not faith, he will continue to live like the rest of the world, whatever company he is joined to. To coöperate, in the highest as well as the lowest sense, means *to get our living together*. I heard it proposed lately that two young men should travel together over the world, the one without money, earning his means as he went, before the mast and behind the plough, the other carrying a bill of exchange in his pocket. It was easy to see that they could not long be companions or coöperate, since one would not *operate* at all. They would part at the first interesting crisis in their adventures. Above all, as I have implied, the man who goes alone can start to-day; but he who travels with another must wait till that other is ready, and it may be a long time before they get off.

But all this is very selfish, I have heard some of my townsmen say. I confess that I have hitherto indulged very little in philanthropic enterprises. I have made some sacrifices to a sense of duty, and among others have sacrificed this pleasure also. There are those who have used all their arts to persuade me to undertake the support of some poor family in the town; and if I had nothing to do,—for the devil finds employment for the idle,—I might try my hand at some such pastime as that. However, when I have thought to indulge myself in this respect, and lay their Heaven under an obligation by maintaining certain poor persons in all respects as comfortably as I maintain myself, and have even ventured so far as to make them the offer, they have one and all unhesitatingly preferred to remain poor. While my townsmen and women are devoted in so many ways to the good of their fellows, I trust that one at least may be spared to other and less humane pursuits. You must have a genius for charity as well as for any thing else. As for Doing-good, that is one of the professions which are full. Moreover, I have tried it fairly, and, strange as it may seem, am satisfied that it does not agree with my constitution. Probably I should not consciously and deliberately forsake my particular calling to do the good which society demands of me, to save the universe from annihilation; and I believe that a like but infinitely greater steadfastness elsewhere is all that now preserves it. But I would not stand between any man and his genius; and to him who does this work, which I decline, with his whole heart and soul and life, I would say, Persevere, even if the world call it doing evil, as it is most likely they will.

I am far from supposing that my case is a peculiar one; no doubt many of my readers would make a similar defence. At doing something,—I will not engage that my neighbors shall pronounce it good,—I do not hesitate to say that I should be a capital fellow to hire; but what that is, it is for my employer to find out. What *good* I do, in the common sense of that word, must be aside from my main path, and for the most part wholly unintended. Men say, practically, Begin where you are and such as you are, without aiming mainly to become of more worth, and with kindness aforethought go about doing good. If I were to preach at all in this strain, I should say rather, Set about being good. As if the sun should stop when he had kindled his fires up to the splendor of a moon or a star of the sixth magnitude, and go about like a Robin Goodfellow, peeping in at every cottage window, inspiring lunatics, and tainting meats, and making darkness visible, instead of steadily increasing his genial heat and beneficence till he is of such brightness that no mortal can look him in the face, and then, and in the mean while too, going about the world in his own orbit, doing it good, or rather, as a truer philosophy has discovered, the world going about him getting good. When Phaeton, wishing to prove his heavenly birth by his beneficence, had the sun's chariot but one day, and drove out of the beaten track, he burned several blocks of houses in the lower streets of heaven, and scorched the surface of the earth, and dried up every spring, and made the great desert of Sahara, till at length Jupiter hurled him headlong to the earth with a thunderbolt, and the sun, through grief at his death, did not shine for a year.

There is no odor so bad as that which arises from goodness tainted. It is human, it is divine, carrion. If I knew for a certainty that a man was coming to my house with the conscious design of doing me good, I should run for my life, as from that dry and parching wind of the African deserts called the simoom, which fills the mouth and nose and ears and eyes with dust till you are suffocated, for fear that I should get some of his good done to me,—some of its virus mingled with my blood. No,—in this case I would rather suffer evil the natural way. A man is not a good *man* to me because he will feed me if I should be starving, or warm me if I should be freezing, or pull me out of a ditch if I should ever fall into one. I can find you a Newfoundland dog that will do as much. Philanthropy is not love for one's fellow-man in the broadest sense. Howard was no doubt an exceedingly kind and worthy man in his way, and has his reward; but, comparatively speaking, what are a hundred Howards to *us*, if their philanthropy do not help *us* in our best estate, when we are most worthy to be helped? I never heard of a philanthropic meeting in which it was sincerely proposed to do any good to me, or the like of me.

The Jesuits were quite balked by those Indians who, being burned at the stake, suggested new modes of torture to their tormentors. Being superior to physical suffering, it sometimes chanced that they were superior to any consolation which the missionaries could offer; and the law to do as you would be done by fell with less persuasiveness on the ears of those, who, for their part, did not care how they were done by, who

loved their enemies after a new fashion, and came very near
freely forgiving them all they did.

Be sure that you give the poor the aid they most need,
though it be your example which leaves them far behind. If
you give money, spend yourself with it, and do not merely
abandon it to them. We make curious mistakes sometimes.
Often the poor man is not so cold and hungry as he is dirty
and ragged and gross. It is partly his taste, and not merely his
misfortune. If you give him money, he will perhaps buy more
rags with it. I was wont to pity the clumsy Irish laborers who
cut ice on the pond, in such mean and ragged clothes, while
I shivered in my more tidy and somewhat more fashionable
garments, till, one bitter cold day, one who had slipped into
the water came to my house to warm him, and I saw him
strip off three pairs of pants and two pairs of stockings ere he
got down to the skin, though they were dirty and ragged
enough, it is true, and that he could afford to refuse the *extra*
garments which I offered him, he had so many *intra* ones.
This ducking was the very thing he needed. Then I began to
pity myself, and I saw that it would be a greater charity to
bestow on me a flannel shirt than a whole slop-shop on him.
There are a thousand hacking at the branches of evil to one
who is striking at the root, and it may be that he who bestows the largest amount of time and money on the needy is
doing the most by his mode of life to produce that misery
which he strives in vain to relieve. It is the pious slave-breeder
devoting the proceeds of every tenth slave to buy a Sunday's
liberty for the rest. Some show their kindness to the poor by
employing them in their kitchens. Would they not be kinder
if they employed themselves there? You boast of spending a
tenth part of your income in charity; may be you should
spend the nine tenths so, and done with it. Society recovers
only a tenth part of the property then. Is this owing to the
generosity of him in whose possession it is found, or to the
remissness of the officers of justice?

Philanthropy is almost the only virtue which is sufficiently
appreciated by mankind. Nay, it is greatly overrated; and it is
our selfishness which overrates it. A robust poor man, one
sunny day here in Concord, praised a fellow-townsman to
me, because, as he said, he was kind to the poor; meaning

himself. The kind uncles and aunts of the race are more esteemed than its true spiritual fathers and mothers. I once
heard a reverend lecturer on England, a man of learning and
intelligence, after enumerating her scientific, literary, and political worthies, Shakspeare, Bacon, Cromwell, Milton, Newton, and others, speak next of her Christian heroes, whom, as
if his profession required it of him, he elevated to a place far
above all the rest, as the greatest of the great. They were
Penn, Howard, and Mrs. Fry. Every one must feel the falsehood and cant of this. The last were not England's best men
and women; only, perhaps, her best philanthropists.

I would not subtract any thing from the praise that is due
to philanthropy, but merely demand justice for all who by
their lives and works are a blessing to mankind. I do not value
chiefly a man's uprightness and benevolence, which are, as it
were, his stem and leaves. Those plants of whose greenness
withered we make herb tea for the sick, serve but a humble
use, and are most employed by quacks. I want the flower and
fruit of a man; that some fragrance be wafted over from him
to me, and some ripeness flavor our intercourse. His goodness must not be a partial and transitory act, but a constant
superfluity, which costs him nothing and of which he is unconscious. This is a charity that hides a multitude of sins. The
philanthropist too often surrounds mankind with the remembrance of his own cast-off griefs as an atmosphere, and calls
it sympathy. We should impart our courage, and not our despair, our health and ease, and not our disease, and take care
that this does not spread by contagion. From what southern
plains comes up the voice of wailing? Under what latitudes
reside the heathen to whom we would send light? Who is that
intemperate and brutal man whom we would redeem? If any
thing ail a man, so that he does not perform his functions, if
he have a pain in his bowels even,—for that is the seat of
sympathy,—he forthwith sets about reforming—the world.
Being a microcosm himself, he discovers, and it is a true discovery, and he is the man to make it,—that the world has
been eating green apples; to his eyes, in fact, the globe itself
is a great green apple, which there is danger awful to think of
that the children of men will nibble before it is ripe; and
straightway his drastic philanthropy seeks out the Esquimaux

and the Patagonian, and embraces the populous Indian and Chinese villages; and thus, by a few years of philanthropic activity, the powers in the mean while using him for their own ends, no doubt, he cures himself of his dyspepsia, the globe acquires a faint blush on one or both of its cheeks, as if it were beginning to be ripe, and life loses its crudity and is once more sweet and wholesome to live. I never dreamed of any enormity greater than I have committed. I never knew, and never shall know, a worse man than myself.

I believe that what so saddens the reformer is not his sympathy with his fellows in distress, but, though he be the holiest son of God, is his private ail. Let this be righted, let the spring come to him, the morning rise over his couch, and he will forsake his generous companions without apology. My excuse for not lecturing against the use of tobacco is, that I never chewed it; that is a penalty which reformed tobacco-chewers have to pay; though there are things enough I have chewed, which I could lecture against. If you should ever be betrayed into any of these philanthropies, do not let your left hand know what your right hand does, for it is not worth knowing. Rescue the drowning and tie your shoe-strings. Take your time, and set about some free labor.

Our manners have been corrupted by communication with the saints. Our hymn-books resound with a melodious cursing of God and enduring him forever. One would say that even the prophets and redeemers had rather consoled the fears than confirmed the hopes of man. There is nowhere recorded a simple and irrepressible satisfaction with the gift of life, any memorable praise of God. All health and success does me good, however far off and withdrawn it may appear; all disease and failure helps to make me sad and does me evil, however much sympathy it may have with me or I with it. If, then, we would indeed restore mankind by truly Indian, botanic, magnetic, or natural means, let us first be as simple and well as Nature ourselves, dispel the clouds which hang over our own brows, and take up a little life into our pores. Do not stay to be an overseer of the poor, but endeavor to become one of the worthies of the world.

I read in the Gulistan, or Flower Garden, of Sheik Sadi of Shiraz, that "They asked a wise man, saying; Of the many celebrated trees which the Most High God has created lofty and umbrageous, they call none azad, or free, excepting the cypress, which bears no fruit; what mystery is there in this? He replied; Each has its appropriate produce, and appointed season, during the continuance of which it is fresh and blooming, and during their absence dry and withered; to neither of which states is the cypress exposed, being always flourishing; and of this nature are the azads, or religious independents.—Fix not thy heart on that which is transitory; for the Dijlah, or Tigris, will continue to flow through Bagdad after the race of caliphs is extinct: if thy hand has plenty, be liberal as the date tree; but if it affords nothing to give away, be an azad, or free man, like the cypress."

COMPLEMENTAL VERSES.

THE PRETENSIONS OF POVERTY.

"Thou dost presume too much, poor needy wretch,
 To claim a station in the firmament,
 Because thy humble cottage, or thy tub,
 Nurses some lazy or pedantic virtue
 In the cheap sunshine or by shady springs,
 With roots and pot-herbs; where thy right hand,
 Tearing those humane passions from the mind,
 Upon whose stocks fair blooming virtues flourish,
 Degradeth nature, and benumbeth sense,
 And, Gorgon-like, turns active men to stone.
 We not require the dull society
 Of your necessitated temperance,
 Or that unnatural stupidity
 That knows nor joy nor sorrow; nor your forc'd
 Falsely exalted passive fortitude
 Above the active. This low abject brood,
 That fix their seats in mediocrity,
 Become your servile minds; but we advance
 Such virtues only as admit excess,
 Brave, bounteous acts, regal magnificence,
 All-seeing prudence, magnanimity
 That knows no bound, and that heroic virtue
 For which antiquity hath left no name,
 But patterns only, such as Hercules,
 Achilles, Theseus. Back to thy loath'd cell;
 And when thou seest the new enlightened sphere,
 Study to know but what those worthies were."

T. CAREW.

66

Where I Lived, and What I Lived For

A̲T A CERTAIN season of our life we are accustomed to consider every spot as the possible site of a house. I have
thus surveyed the country on every side within a dozen miles
of where I live. In imagination I have bought all the farms in
succession, for all were to be bought, and I knew their price.
I walked over each farmer's premises, tasted his wild apples,
discoursed on husbandry with him, took his farm at his price,
at any price, mortgaging it to him in my mind; even put a
higher price on it,—took every thing but a deed of it,—took
his word for his deed, for I dearly love to talk,—cultivated it,
and him too to some extent, I trust, and withdrew when I
had enjoyed it long enough, leaving him to carry it on. This
experience entitled me to be regarded as a sort of real-estate
broker by my friends. Wherever I sat, there I might live, and
the landscape radiated from me accordingly. What is a house
but a *sedes*, a seat?—better if a country seat. I discovered
many a site for a house not likely to be soon improved, which
some might have thought too far from the village, but to my
eyes the village was too far from it. Well, there I might live, I
said; and there I did live, for an hour, a summer and a winter
life; saw how I could let the years run off, buffet the winter
through, and see the spring come in. The future inhabitants
of this region, wherever they may place their houses, may be
sure that they have been anticipated. An afternoon sufficed to
lay out the land into orchard woodlot and pasture, and to
decide what fine oaks or pines should be left to stand before
the door, and whence each blasted tree could be seen to the
best advantage; and then I let it lie, fallow perchance, for a
man is rich in proportion to the number of things which he
can afford to let alone.

My imagination carried me so far that I even had the refusal of several farms,—the refusal was all I wanted,—but I
never got my fingers burned by actual possession. The nearest
that I came to actual possession was when I bought the Hollowell Place, and had begun to sort my seeds, and collected
materials with which to make a wheelbarrow to carry it on or
off with; but before the owner gave me a deed of it, his

wife—every man has such a wife—changed her mind and
wished to keep it, and he offered me ten dollars to release
him. Now, to speak the truth, I had but ten cents in the
world, and it surpassed my arithmetic to tell, if I was that
man who had ten cents, or who had a farm, or ten dollars, or
all together. However, I let him keep the ten dollars and the
farm too, for I had carried it far enough; or rather, to be
generous, I sold him the farm for just what I gave for it, and,
as he was not a rich man, made him a present of ten dollars,
and still had my ten cents, and seeds, and materials for a
wheelbarrow left. I found thus that I had been a rich man
without any damage to my poverty. But I retained the landscape, and I have since annually carried off what it yielded
without a wheelbarrow. With respect to landscapes,—

> "I am monarch of all I *survey*,
>   My right there is none to dispute."

I have frequently seen a poet withdraw, having enjoyed the
most valuable part of a farm, while the crusty farmer supposed that he had got a few wild apples only. Why, the owner
does not know it for many years when a poet has put his farm
in rhyme, the most admirable kind of invisible fence, has
fairly impounded it, milked it, skimmed it, and got all the
cream, and left the farmer only the skimmed milk.

The real attractions of the Hollowell farm, to me, were; its
complete retirement, being about two miles from the village,
half a mile from the nearest neighbor, and separated from the
highway by a broad field; its bounding on the river, which
the owner said protected it by its fogs from frosts in the
spring, though that was nothing to me; the gray color and
ruinous state of the house and barn, and the dilapidated
fences, which put such an interval between me and the last
occupant; the hollow and lichen-covered apple trees, gnawed
by rabbits, showing what kind of neighbors I should have;
but above all, the recollection I had of it from my earliest
voyages up the river, when the house was concealed behind a
dense grove of red maples, through which I heard the house-
dog bark. I was in haste to buy it, before the proprietor finished getting out some rocks, cutting down the hollow apple
trees, and grubbing up some young birches which had sprung

up in the pasture, or, in short, had made any more of his improvements. To enjoy these advantages I was ready to carry it on; like Atlas, to take the world on my shoulders,—I never heard what compensation he received for that,—and do all those things which had no other motive or excuse but that I might pay for it and be unmolested in my possession of it; for I knew all the while that it would yield the most abundant crop of the kind I wanted if I could only afford to let it alone. But it turned out as I have said.

All that I could say, then, with respect to farming on a large scale, (I have always cultivated a garden,) was, that I had had my seeds ready. Many think that seeds improve with age. I have no doubt that time discriminates between the good and the bad; and when at last I shall plant, I shall be less likely to be disappointed. But I would say to my fellows, once for all, As long as possible live free and uncommitted. It makes but little difference whether you are committed to a farm or the county jail.

Old Cato, whose "De Re Rusticâ" is my "Cultivator," says, and the only translation I have seen makes sheer nonsense of the passage, "When you think of getting a farm, turn it thus in your mind, not to buy greedily; nor spare your pains to look at it, and do not think it enough to go round it once. The oftener you go there the more it will please you, if it is good." I think I shall not buy greedily, but go round and round it as long as I live, and be buried in it first, that it may please me the more at last.

The present was my next experiment of this kind, which I purpose to describe more at length; for convenience, putting the experience of two years into one. As I have said, I do not propose to write an ode to dejection, but to brag as lustily as chanticleer in the morning, standing on his roost, if only to wake my neighbors up.

When first I took up my abode in the woods, that is, began to spend my nights as well as days there, which, by accident, was on Independence Day, or the fourth of July, 1845, my house was not finished for winter, but was merely a defence against the rain, without plastering or chimney, the walls being of rough weather-stained boards, with wide chinks,

which made it cool at night. The upright white hewn studs
and freshly planed door and window casings gave it a clean
and airy look, especially in the morning, when its timbers
were saturated with dew, so that I fancied that by noon some
sweet gum would exude from them. To my imagination it
retained throughout the day more or less of this auroral character, reminding me of a certain house on a mountain which
I had visited the year before. This was an airy and unplastered
cabin, fit to entertain a travelling god, and where a goddess
might trail her garments. The winds which passed over my
dwelling were such as sweep over the ridges of mountains,
bearing the broken strains, or celestial parts only, of terrestrial
music. The morning wind forever blows, the poem of creation is uninterrupted; but few are the ears that hear it.
Olympus is but the outside of the earth every where.

The only house I had been the owner of before, if I except a boat, was a tent, which I used occasionally when making excursions in the summer, and this is still rolled up in
my garret; but the boat, after passing from hand to hand,
has gone down the stream of time. With this more substantial shelter about me, I had made some progress toward settling in the world. This frame, so slightly clad, was a sort of
crystallization around me, and reacted on the builder. It was
suggestive somewhat as a picture in outlines. I did not need
to go out doors to take the air, for the atmosphere within
had lost none of its freshness. It was not so much within
doors as behind a door where I sat, even in the rainiest
weather. The Harivansa says, "An abode without birds is
like a meat without seasoning." Such was not my abode, for
I found myself suddenly neighbor to the birds; not by having imprisoned one, but having caged myself near them. I
was not only nearer to some of those which commonly frequent the garden and the orchard, but to those wilder and
more thrilling songsters of the forest which never, or rarely, serenade a villager,—the wood-thrush, the veery, the scarlet tanager, the field-sparrow, the whippoorwill, and many
others.

I was seated by the shore of a small pond, about a mile and
a half south of the village of Concord and somewhat higher
than it, in the midst of an extensive wood between that town

and Lincoln, and about two miles south of that our only field known to fame, Concord Battle Ground; but I was so low in the woods that the opposite shore, half a mile off, like the rest, covered with wood, was my most distant horizon. For the first week, whenever I looked out on the pond it impressed me like a tarn high up on the side of a mountain, its bottom far above the surface of other lakes, and, as the sun arose, I saw it throwing off its nightly clothing of mist, and here and there, by degrees, its soft ripples or its smooth reflecting surface was revealed, while the mists, like ghosts, were stealthily withdrawing in every direction into the woods, as at the breaking up of some nocturnal conventicle. The very dew seemed to hang upon the trees later into the day than usual, as on the sides of mountains.

This small lake was of most value as a neighbor in the intervals of a gentle rain storm in August, when, both air and water being perfectly still, but the sky overcast, mid-afternoon had all the serenity of evening, and the wood-thrush sang around, and was heard from shore to shore. A lake like this is never smoother than at such a time; and the clear portion of the air above it being shallow and darkened by clouds, the water, full of light and reflections, becomes a lower heaven itself so much the more important. From a hill top near by, where the wood had been recently cut off, there was a pleasing vista southward across the pond, through a wide indentation in the hills which form the shore there, where their opposite sides sloping toward each other suggested a stream flowing out in that direction through a wooded valley, but stream there was none. That way I looked between and over the near green hills to some distant and higher ones in the horizon, tinged with blue. Indeed, by standing on tiptoe I could catch a glimpse of some of the peaks of the still bluer and more distant mountain ranges in the north-west, those true-blue coins from heaven's own mint, and also of some portion of the village. But in other directions, even from this point, I could not see over or beyond the woods which surrounded me. It is well to have some water in your neighborhood, to give buoyancy to and float the earth. One value even of the smallest well is, that when you look into it you see that earth is not continent but insular. This is as important as that it keeps butter cool. When I looked across the pond from this peak toward the Sudbury meadows, which in time of flood I distinguished elevated perhaps by a mirage in their seething valley, like a coin in a basin, all the earth beyond the pond appeared like a thin crust insulated and floated even by this small sheet of intervening water, and I was reminded that this on which I dwelt was but *dry land*.

Though the view from my door was still more contracted, I did not feel crowded or confined in the least. There was pasture enough for my imagination. The low shrub-oak plateau to which the opposite shore arose, stretched away toward the prairies of the West and the steppes of Tartary, affording ample room for all the roving families of men. "There are none happy in the world but beings who enjoy freely a vast horizon,"—said Damodara, when his herds required new and larger pastures.

Both place and time were changed, and I dwelt nearer to those parts of the universe and to those eras in history which had most attracted me. Where I lived was as far off as many a region viewed nightly by astronomers. We are wont to imagine rare and delectable places in some remote and more celestial corner of the system, behind the constellation of Cassiopeia's Chair, far from noise and disturbance. I discovered that my house actually had its site in such a withdrawn, but forever new and unprofaned, part of the universe. If it were worth the while to settle in those parts near to the Pleiades or the Hyades, to Aldebaran or Altair, then I was really there, or at an equal remoteness from the life which I had left behind, dwindled and twinkling with as fine a ray to my nearest neighbor, and to be seen only in moonless nights by him. Such was that part of creation where I had squatted;—

> "There was a shepherd that did live,
>   And held his thoughts as high
>   As were the mounts whereon his flocks
>   Did hourly feed him by."

What should we think of the shepherd's life if his flocks always wandered to higher pastures than his thoughts?

Every morning was a cheerful invitation to make my life of equal simplicity, and I may say innocence, with Nature herself. I have been as sincere a worshipper of Aurora as the Greeks. I got up early and bathed in the pond; that was a religious exercise, and one of the best things which I did. They say that characters were engraven on the bathing tub of king Tching-thang to this effect: "Renew thyself completely each day; do it again, and again, and forever again." I can understand that. Morning brings back the heroic ages. I was as much affected by the faint hum of a mosquito making its invisible and unimaginable tour through my apartment at earliest dawn, when I was sitting with door and windows open, as I could be by any trumpet that ever sang of fame. It was Homer's requiem; itself an Iliad and Odyssey in the air, singing its own wrath and wanderings. There was something cosmical about it; a standing advertisement, till forbidden, of the everlasting vigor and fertility of the world. The morning, which is the most memorable season of the day, is the awakening hour. Then there is least somnolence in us; and for an hour, at least, some part of us awakes which slumbers all the rest of the day and night. Little is to be expected of that day, if it can be called a day, to which we are not awakened by our Genius, but by the mechanical nudgings of some servitor, are not awakened by our own newly-acquired force and aspirations from within, accompanied by the undulations of celestial music, instead of factory bells, and a fragrance filling the air—to a higher life than we fell asleep from; and thus the darkness bear its fruit, and prove itself to be good, no less than the light. That man who does not believe that each day contains an earlier, more sacred, and auroral hour than he has yet profaned, has despaired of life, and is pursuing a descending and darkening way. After a partial cessation of his sensuous life, the soul of man, or its organs rather, are reinvigorated each day, and his Genius tries again what noble life it can make. All memorable events, I should say, transpire in morning time and in a morning atmosphere. The Vedas say, "All intelligences awake with the morning." Poetry and art, and the fairest and most memorable of the actions of men, date from such an hour. All poets and heroes, like Memnon, are the children of Aurora, and emit their music at sunrise. To him whose elastic and vigorous thought keeps pace with the sun, the day is a perpetual morning. It matters not what the clocks say or the attitudes and labors of men. Morning is when I am awake and there is a dawn in me. Moral reform is the effort to throw off sleep. Why is it that men give so poor an account of their day if they have not been slumbering? They are not such poor calculators. If they had not been overcome with drowsiness they would have performed something. The millions are awake enough for physical labor; but only one in a million is awake enough for effective intellectual exertion, only one in a hundred millions to a poetic or divine life. To be awake is to be alive. I have never yet met a man who was quite awake. How could I have looked him in the face?

We must learn to reawaken and keep ourselves awake, not by mechanical aids, but by an infinite expectation of the dawn, which does not forsake us in our soundest sleep. I know of no more encouraging fact than the unquestionable ability of man to elevate his life by a conscious endeavor. It is something to be able to paint a particular picture, or to carve a statue, and so to make a few objects beautiful; but it is far more glorious to carve and paint the very atmosphere and medium through which we look, which morally we can do. To affect the quality of the day, that is the highest of arts. Every man is tasked to make his life, even in its details, worthy of the contemplation of his most elevated and critical hour. If we refused, or rather used up, such paltry information as we get, the oracles would distinctly inform us how this might be done.

I went to the woods because I wished to live deliberately, to front only the essential facts of life, and see if I could not learn what it had to teach, and not, when I came to die, discover that I had not lived. I did not wish to live what was not life, living is so dear; nor did I wish to practise resignation, unless it was quite necessary. I wanted to live deep and suck out all the marrow of life, to live so sturdily and Spartan-like as to put to rout all that was not life, to cut a broad swath and shave close, to drive life into a corner, and reduce it to its lowest terms, and, if it proved to be mean, why then to get the whole and genuine meanness of it, and publish its meanness to the world; or if it were sublime, to know it by experience, and be able to give a true account of it in my next excursion. For most men, it appears to me, are in a strange uncertainty about it, whether it is of the devil or of God, and have *somewhat hastily* concluded that it is the chief end of man here to "glorify God and enjoy him forever."

Still we live meanly, like ants; though the fable tells us that we were long ago changed into men; like pygmies we fight with cranes; it is error upon error, and clout upon clout, and our best virtue has for its occasion a superfluous and evitable wretchedness. Our life is frittered away by detail. An honest man has hardly need to count more than his ten fingers, or in extreme cases he may add his ten toes, and lump the rest. Simplicity, simplicity, simplicity! I say, let your affairs be as two or three, and not a hundred or a thousand; instead of a million count half a dozen, and keep your accounts on your thumb nail. In the midst of this chopping sea of civilized life, such are the clouds and storms and quick-sands and thousand-and-one items to be allowed for, that a man has to live, if he would not founder and go to the bottom and not make his port at all, by dead reckoning, and he must be a great calculator indeed who succeeds. Simplify, simplify. Instead of three meals a day, if it be necessary eat but one; instead of a hundred dishes, five; and reduce other things in proportion. Our life is like a German Confederacy, made up of petty states, with its boundary forever fluctuating, so that even a German cannot tell you how it is bounded at any moment. The nation itself, with all its so called internal improvements, which, by the way, are all external and superficial, is just such an unwieldy and overgrown establishment, cluttered with furniture and tripped up by its own traps, ruined by luxury and heedless expense, by want of calculation and a worthy aim, as the million households in the land; and the only cure for it as for them is in a rigid economy, a stern and more than Spartan simplicity of life and elevation of purpose. It lives too fast. Men think that it is essential that the *Nation* have commerce, and export ice, and talk through a telegraph, and ride thirty miles an hour, without a doubt, whether *they* do or not; but whether we should live like baboons or like men, is a little uncertain. If we do not get out sleepers, and forge rails, and devote days and nights to the work, but go to tinkering upon our *lives* to improve *them*, who will build railroads? And if railroads are not built, how shall we get to heaven in season? But if we stay at home and mind our business, who will want railroads? We do not ride on the railroad; it rides upon us. Did you ever think what those sleepers are that underlie the railroad? Each one is a man, an Irishman, or a Yankee man. The rails are laid on them, and they are covered with sand, and the cars run smoothly over them. They are sound sleepers, I assure you. And every few years a new lot is laid down and run over; so that, if some have the pleasure of riding on a rail, others have the misfortune to be ridden upon. And when they run over a man that is walking in his sleep, a supernumerary sleeper in the wrong position, and wake him up, they suddenly stop the cars, and make a hue and cry about it, as if this were an exception. I am glad to know that it takes a gang of men for every five miles to keep the sleepers down and level in their beds as it is, for this is a sign that they may sometime get up again.

Why should we live with such hurry and waste of life? We are determined to be starved before we are hungry. Men say that a stitch in time saves nine, and so they take a thousand stitches to-day to save nine to-morrow. As for *work*, we haven't any of any consequence. We have the Saint Vitus' dance, and cannot possibly keep our heads still. If I should only give a few pulls at the parish bell-rope, as for a fire, that is, without setting the bell, there is hardly a man on his farm in the outskirts of Concord, notwithstanding that press of engagements which was his excuse so many times this morning, nor a boy, nor a woman, I might almost say, but would forsake all and follow that sound, not mainly to save property from the flames, but, if we will confess the truth, much more to see it burn, since burn it must, and we, be it known, did not set it on fire,—or to see it put out, and have a hand in it, if that is done as handsomely; yes, even if it were the parish church itself. Hardly a man takes a half hour's nap after dinner, but when he wakes he holds up his head and asks, "What's the news?" as if the rest of mankind had stood his sentinels. Some give directions to be waked every half hour, doubtless for no other purpose; and then, to pay for it, they tell what they have dreamed. After a night's sleep the news is as indispensable as the breakfast. "Pray tell me any thing new that has happened to a man any where on this globe,"—and he reads it over his coffee and rolls, that a man has had his eyes gouged out this morning on the Wachito River; never dreaming the while that he lives in the dark unfathomed mammoth cave of this world, and has but the rudiment of an eye himself.

For my part, I could easily do without the post-office. I think that there are very few important communications made through it. To speak critically, I never received more than one or two letters in my life—I wrote this some years ago—that were worth the postage. The penny-post is, commonly, an institution through which you seriously offer a man that penny for his thoughts which is so often safely offered in jest. And I am sure that I never read any memorable news in a newspaper. If we read of one man robbed, or murdered, or killed by accident, or one house burned, or one vessel wrecked, or one steamboat blown up, or one cow run over on the Western Railroad, or one mad dog killed, or one lot of grasshoppers in the winter,—we never need read of another. One is enough. If you are acquainted with the principle, what do you care for a myriad instances and applications? To a philosopher all *news*, as it is called, is gossip, and they who edit and read it are old women over their tea. Yet not a few are greedy after this gossip. There was such a rush, as I hear, the other day at one of the offices to learn the foreign news by the last arrival, that several large squares of plate glass belonging to the establishment were broken by the pressure,—news which I seriously think a ready wit might write a twelvemonth or twelve years beforehand with sufficient accuracy. As for Spain, for instance, if you know how to throw in Don Carlos and the Infanta, and Don Pedro and Seville and Granada, from time to time in the right proportions,—they may have changed the names a little since I saw the papers,—and serve up a bull-fight when other entertainments fail, it will be true to the letter, and give us as good an idea of the exact state or ruin of things in Spain as the most succinct and lucid reports under this head in the newspapers: and as for England, almost the last significant scrap of news from that quarter was the revolution of 1649; and if you have learned the history of her crops for an average year, you never need attend to that thing again, unless your speculations are of a merely pecuniary character. If one may judge who rarely looks into the newspapers, nothing new does ever happen in foreign parts, a French revolution not excepted.

What news! how much more important to know what that is which was never old! "Kieou pe yu (great dignitary of the state of Wei) sent a man to Khoung-tseu to know his news. Khoung-tseu caused the messenger to be seated near him, and questioned him in these terms: What is your master doing? The messenger answered with respect: My master desires to diminish the number of his faults, but he cannot come to the end of them. The messenger being gone, the philosopher remarked: What a worthy messenger! What a worthy messenger!" The preacher, instead of vexing the ears of drowsy farmers on their day of rest at the end of the week,—for Sunday is the fit conclusion of an ill-spent week, and not the fresh and brave beginning of a new one,—with this one other draggle-tail of a sermon, should shout with thundering voice,—"Pause! Avast! Why so seeming fast, but deadly slow?"

Shams and delusions are esteemed for soundest truths, while reality is fabulous. If men would steadily observe realities only, and not allow themselves to be deluded, life, to compare it with such things as we know, would be like a fairy tale and the Arabian Nights' Entertainments. If we respected only what is inevitable and has a right to be, music and poetry would resound along the streets. When we are unhurried and wise, we perceive that only great and worthy things have any permanent and absolute existence,—that petty fears and petty pleasures are but the shadow of the reality. This is always exhilarating and sublime. By closing the eyes and slumbering, and consenting to be deceived by shows, men establish and confirm their daily life of routine and habit every where, which still is built on purely illusory foundations. Children, who play life, discern its true law and relations more clearly than men, who fail to live it worthily, but who think that they are wiser by experience, that is, by failure. I have read in a Hindoo book, that "there was a king's son, who, being expelled in infancy from his native city, was brought up by a forester, and, growing up to maturity in that state, imagined himself to belong to the barbarous race with which he lived. One of his father's ministers having discovered him, revealed to him what he was, and the misconception of his character was removed, and he knew himself to be a prince. So soul," continues the Hindoo philosopher, "from the circumstances in which it is placed, mistakes its own character, until the truth is revealed to it by some holy teacher, and then it knows itself to be *Brahme*." I perceive that we inhabitants of New England live this mean life that we do because our vision does not penetrate the surface of things. We think that that *is* which *appears* to be. If a man should walk through this town and see only the reality, where, think you, would the "Mill-dam" go to? If he should give us an account of the realities he beheld there, we should not recognize the place in his description. Look at a meeting-house, or a court-house, or a jail, or a shop, or a dwelling-house, and say what that thing really is before a true gaze, and they would all go to pieces in your account of them. Men esteem truth remote, in the outskirts of the system, behind the farthest star, before Adam and after the last man. In eternity there is indeed something true and sublime. But all these times and places and occasions are now and here. God himself culminates in the present moment, and will never be more divine in the lapse of all the ages. And we are enabled to apprehend at all what is sublime and noble only by the perpetual instilling and drenching of the reality which surrounds us. The universe constantly and obediently answers to our conceptions; whether we travel fast or slow, the track is laid for us. Let us spend our lives in conceiving then. The poet or the artist never yet had so fair and noble a design but some of his posterity at least could accomplish it.

Let us spend one day as deliberately as Nature, and not be thrown off the track by every nutshell and mosquito's wing that falls on the rails. Let us rise early and fast, or break fast, gently and without perturbation; let company come and let company go, let the bells ring and the children cry,—determined to make a day of it. Why should we knock under and go with the stream? Let us not be upset and overwhelmed in that terrible rapid and whirlpool called a dinner, situated in the meridian shallows. Weather this danger and you are safe, for the rest of the way is down hill. With unrelaxed nerves, with morning vigor, sail by it, looking another way, tied to the mast like Ulysses. If the engine whistles, let it whistle till it is hoarse for its pains. If the bell rings, why should we run? We will consider what kind of music they are like. Let us settle ourselves, and work and wedge our feet downward through the mud and slush of opinion, and prejudice, and tradition, and delusion, and appearance, that alluvion which covers the globe, through Paris and London, through New York and Boston and Concord, through church and state, through poetry and philosophy and religion, till we come to a hard bottom and rocks in place, which we can call *reality*, and say, This is, and no mistake; and then begin, having a *point d'appui*, below freshet and frost and fire, a place where you might found a wall or a state, or set a lamp-post safely, or perhaps a gauge, not a Nilometer, but a Realometer, that future ages might know how deep a freshet of shams and appearances had gathered from time to time. If you stand right fronting and face to face to a fact, you will see the sun glimmer on both its surfaces, as if it were a cimeter, and feel its sweet edge dividing you through the heart and marrow, and so you will happily conclude your mortal career. Be it life or death, we crave only reality. If we are really dying, let us hear the rattle in our throats and feel cold in the extremities; if we are alive, let us go about our business.

Time is but the stream I go a-fishing in. I drink at it; but while I drink I see the sandy bottom and detect how shallow it is. Its thin current slides away, but eternity remains. I would drink deeper; fish in the sky, whose bottom is pebbly with stars. I cannot count one. I know not the first letter of the alphabet. I have always been regretting that I was not as wise as the day I was born. The intellect is a cleaver; it discerns and rifts its way into the secret of things. I do not wish to be any more busy with my hands than is necessary. My head is hands and feet. I feel all my best faculties concentrated in it. My instinct tells me that my head is an organ for burrowing, as some creatures use their snout and fore-paws, and with it I would mine and burrow my way through these hills.

I think that the richest vein is somewhere hereabouts; so by the divining rod and thin rising vapors I judge; and here I will begin to mine.

Reading

WITH A LITTLE more deliberation in the choice of their pursuits, all men would perhaps become essentially students and observers, for certainly their nature and destiny are interesting to all alike. In accumulating property for ourselves or our posterity, in founding a family or a state, or acquiring fame even, we are mortal; but in dealing with truth we are immortal, and need fear no change nor accident. The oldest Egyptian or Hindoo philosopher raised a corner of the veil from the statue of the divinity; and still the trembling robe remains raised, and I gaze upon as fresh a glory as he did, since it was I in him that was then so bold, and it is he in me that now reviews the vision. No dust has settled on that robe; no time has elapsed since that divinity was revealed. That time which we really improve, or which is improvable, is neither past, present, nor future.

My residence was more favorable, not only to thought, but to serious reading, than a university; and though I was beyond the range of the ordinary circulating library, I had more than ever come within the influence of those books which circulate round the world, whose sentences were first written on bark, and are now merely copied from time to time on to linen paper. Says the poet Mîr Camar Uddîn Mast, "Being seated to run through the region of the spiritual world; I have had this advantage in books. To be intoxicated by a single glass of wine; I have experienced this pleasure when I have drunk the liquor of the esoteric doctrines." I kept Homer's Iliad on my table through the summer, though I looked at his page only now and then. Incessant labor with my hands, at first, for I had my house to finish and my beans to hoe at the same time, made more study impossible. Yet I sustained myself by the prospect of such reading in future. I read one or two shallow books of travel in the intervals of my work, till that employment made me ashamed of myself, and I asked where it was then that *I* lived.

The student may read Homer or Æschylus in the Greek without danger of dissipation or luxuriousness, for it implies that he in some measure emulate their heroes, and consecrate morning hours to their pages. The heroic books, even if printed in the character of our mother tongue, will always be in a language dead to degenerate times; and we must laboriously seek the meaning of each word and line, conjecturing a larger sense than common use permits out of what wisdom and valor and generosity we have. The modern cheap and fertile press, with all its translations, has done little to bring us nearer to the heroic writers of antiquity. They seem as solitary, and the letter in which they are printed as rare and curious, as ever. It is worth the expense of youthful days and costly hours, if you learn only some words of an ancient language, which are raised out of the trivialness of the street, to be perpetual suggestions and provocations. It is not in vain that the farmer remembers and repeats the few Latin words which he has heard. Men sometimes speak as if the study of the classics would at length make way for more modern and practical studies; but the adventurous student will always study classics, in whatever language they may be written and however ancient they may be. For what are the classics but the noblest recorded thoughts of man? They are the only oracles which are not decayed, and there are such answers to the most modern inquiry in them as Delphi and Dodona never gave. We might as well omit to study Nature because she is old. To read well, that is, to read true books in a true spirit, is a noble exercise, and one that will task the reader more than any exercise which the customs of the day esteem. It requires a training such as the athletes underwent, the steady intention almost of the whole life to this object. Books must be read as deliberately and reservedly as they were written. It is not enough even to be able to speak the language of that nation by which they are written, for there is a memorable interval between the spoken and the written language, the language heard and the language read. The one is commonly transitory, a sound, a tongue, a dialect merely, almost brutish, and we learn it unconsciously, like the brutes, of our mothers. The other is the maturity and experience of that; if that is our mother tongue, this is our father tongue, a reserved and select expression, too significant to be heard by the ear, which we must be born again in order to speak. The crowds of men who merely *spoke* the Greek and Latin tongues in the middle ages were not entitled by the accident of birth to *read* the works of genius written in those languages; for these were not written in that Greek or Latin which they knew, but in the select language of literature. They had not learned the nobler dialects of Greece and Rome, but the very materials on which they were written were waste paper to them, and they prized instead a cheap contemporary literature. But when the several nations of Europe had acquired distinct though rude written languages of their own, sufficient for the purposes of their rising literatures, then first learning revived, and scholars were enabled to discern from that remoteness the treasures of antiquity. What the Roman and Grecian multitude could not *hear*, after the lapse of ages a few scholars *read*, and a few scholars only are still reading it.

However much we may admire the orator's occasional bursts of eloquence, the noblest written words are commonly as far behind or above the fleeting spoken language as the firmament with its stars is behind the clouds. *There* are the stars, and they who can may read them. The astronomers forever comment on and observe them. They are not exhalations like our daily colloquies and vaporous breath. What is called eloquence in the forum is commonly found to be rhetoric in the study. The orator yields to the inspiration of a transient occasion, and speaks to the mob before him, to those who can *hear* him; but the writer, whose more equable life is his occasion, and who would be distracted by the event and the crowd which inspire the orator, speaks to the intellect and heart of mankind, to all in any age who can *understand* him.

No wonder that Alexander carried the Iliad with him on his expeditions in a precious casket. A written word is the choicest of relics. It is something at once more intimate with us and more universal than any other work of art. It is the work of art nearest to life itself. It may be translated into every language, and not only be read but actually breathed from all human lips;—not be represented on canvas or in marble only, but be carved out of the breath of life itself. The symbol of an ancient man's thought becomes a modern man's speech. Two thousand summers have imparted to the monuments of Grecian literature, as to her marbles, only a maturer golden and autumnal tint, for they have carried their own serene and celestial atmosphere into all lands to protect them against the corrosion of time. Books are the treasured wealth of the world and the fit inheritance of generations and nations. Books, the oldest and the best, stand naturally and rightfully on the shelves of every cottage. They have no cause of their own to plead, but while they enlighten and sustain the reader his common sense will not refuse them. Their authors are a natural and irresistible aristocracy in every society, and, more than kings or emperors, exert an influence on mankind. When the illiterate and perhaps scornful trader has earned by enterprise and industry his coveted leisure and independence, and is admitted to the circles of wealth and fashion, he turns inevitably at last to those still higher but yet inaccessible circles of intellect and genius, and is sensible only of the imperfection of his culture and the vanity and insufficiency of all his riches, and further proves his good sense by the pains which he takes to secure for his children that intellectual culture whose want he so keenly feels; and thus it is that he becomes the founder of a family.

Those who have not learned to read the ancient classics in the language in which they were written must have a very imperfect knowledge of the history of the human race; for it is remarkable that no transcript of them has ever been made into any modern tongue, unless our civilization itself may be regarded as such a transcript. Homer has never yet been printed in English, nor Æschylus, nor Virgil even,—works as refined, as solidly done, and as beautiful almost as the morning itself; for later writers, say what we will of their genius, have rarely, if ever, equalled the elaborate beauty and finish and the lifelong and heroic literary labors of the ancients. They only talk of forgetting them who never knew them. It will be soon enough to forget them when we have the learning and the genius which will enable us to attend to and appreciate them. That age will be rich indeed when those relics which we call Classics, and the still older and more than classic but even less known Scriptures of the nations, shall have still further accumulated, when the Vaticans shall be filled with Vedas and Zendavestas and Bibles, with Homers and Dantes and Shakspeares, and all the centuries to come shall

have successively deposited their trophies in the forum of the
world. By such a pile we may hope to scale heaven at last.

The works of the great poets have never yet been read by
mankind, for only great poets can read them. They have only
been read as the multitude read the stars, at most astrologi-
cally, not astronomically. Most men have learned to read to
serve a paltry convenience, as they have learned to cipher in
order to keep accounts and not be cheated in trade; but of
reading as a noble intellectual exercise they know little or
nothing; yet this only is reading, in a high sense, not that
which lulls us as a luxury and suffers the nobler faculties to
sleep the while, but what we have to stand on tiptoe to read
and devote our most alert and wakeful hours to.

I think that having learned our letters we should read the
best that is in literature, and not be forever repeating our a b
abs, and words of one syllable, in the fourth or fifth classes,
sitting on the lowest and foremost form all our lives. Most
men are satisfied if they read or hear read, and perchance have
been convicted by the wisdom of one good book, the Bible,
and for the rest of their lives vegetate and dissipate their faculties in what is called easy reading. There is a work in several
volumes in our Circulating Library entitled Little Reading,
which I thought referred to a town of that name which I had
not been to. There are those who, like cormorants and os-
triches, can digest all sorts of this, even after the fullest dinner
of meats and vegetables, for they suffer nothing to be wasted.
If others are the machines to provide this provender, they are
the machines to read it. They read the nine thousandth tale
about Zebulon and Sephronia, and how they loved as none
had ever loved before, and neither did the course of their true
love run smooth,—at any rate, how it did run and stumble,
and get up again and go on! how some poor unfortunate got
up onto a steeple, who had better never have gone up as far
as the belfry; and then, having needlessly got him up there,
the happy novelist rings the bell for all the world to come
together and hear, O dear! how he did get down again! For
my part, I think that they had better metamorphose all such
aspiring heroes of universal noveldom into man weather-
cocks, as they used to put heroes among the constellations,
and let them swing round there till they are rusty, and not

come down at all to bother honest men with their pranks. The next time the novelist rings the bell I will not stir though the meeting-house burn down. "The Skip of the Tip-Toe-Hop, a Romance of the Middle Ages, by the celebrated author of 'Tittle-Tol-Tan,' to appear in monthly parts; a great rush; don't all come together." All this they read with saucer eyes, and erect and primitive curiosity, and with unwearied gizzard, whose corrugations even yet need no sharpening, just as some little four-year-old bencher his two-cent gilt-covered edition of Cinderella, —without any improvement, that I can see, in the pronunciation, or accent, or emphasis, or any more skill in extracting or inserting the moral. The result is dulness of sight, a stagnation of the vital circulations, and a general deliquium and sloughing off of all the intellectual faculties. This sort of gingerbread is baked daily and more sedulously than pure wheat or rye-and-Indian in almost every oven, and finds a surer market.

The best books are not read even by those who are called good readers. What does our Concord culture amount to? There is in this town, with a very few exceptions, no taste for the best or for very good books even in English literature, whose words all can read and spell. Even the college-bred and so called liberally educated men here and elsewhere have really little or no acquaintance with the English classics; and as for the recorded wisdom of mankind, the ancient classics and Bibles, which are accessible to all who will know of them, there are the feeblest efforts any where made to become acquainted with them. I know a woodchopper, of middle age, who takes a French paper, not for news as he says, for he is above that, but to "keep himself in practice," he being a Canadian by birth; and when I ask him what he considers the best thing he can do in this world, he says, beside this, to keep up and add to his English. This is about as much as the college bred generally do or aspire to do, and they take an English paper for the purpose. One who has just come from reading perhaps one of the best English books will find how many with whom he can converse about it? Or suppose he comes from reading a Greek or Latin classic in the original, whose praises are familiar even to the so called illiterate; he will find nobody at all to speak to, but must keep silence about it. Indeed, there is hardly the professor in our colleges, who, if he has mastered the difficulties of the language, has proportionally mastered the difficulties of the wit and poetry of a Greek poet, and has any sympathy to impart to the alert and heroic reader; and as for the sacred Scriptures, or Bibles of mankind, who in this town can tell me even their titles? Most men do not know that any nation but the Hebrews have had a scripture. A man, any man, will go considerably out of his way to pick up a silver dollar; but here are golden words, which the wisest men of antiquity have uttered, and whose worth the wise of every succeeding age have assured us of;—and yet we learn to read only as far as Easy Reading, the primers and class-books, and when we leave school, the "Little Reading," and story books, which are for boys and beginners; and our reading, our conversation and thinking, are all on a very low level, worthy only of pygmies and manikins.

I aspire to be acquainted with wiser men than this our Concord soil has produced, whose names are hardly known here. Or shall I hear the name of Plato and never read his book? As if Plato were my townsman and I never saw him,— my next neighbor and I never heard him speak or attended to the wisdom of his words. But how actually is it? His Dialogues, which contain what was immortal in him, lie on the next shelf, and yet I never read them. We are under-bred and low-lived and illiterate; and in this respect I confess I do not make any very broad distinction between the illiterateness of my townsman who cannot read at all, and the illiterateness of him who has learned to read only what is for children and feeble intellects. We should be as good as the worthies of antiquity, but partly by first knowing how good they were. We are a race of tit-men, and soar but little higher in our intellectual flights than the columns of the daily paper.

It is not all books that are as dull as their readers. There are probably words addressed to our condition exactly, which, if we could really hear and understand, would be more salutary than the morning or the spring to our lives, and possibly put a new aspect on the face of things for us. How many a man has dated a new era in his life from the reading of a book. The book exists for us perchance which will explain our miracles and reveal new ones. The at present unutterable things we may find somewhere uttered. These same questions that disturb and puzzle and confound us have in their turn occurred to all the wise men; not one has been omitted; and each has answered them, according to his ability, by his words and his life. Moreover, with wisdom we shall learn liberality. The solitary hired man on a farm in the outskirts of Concord, who has had his second birth and peculiar religious experience, and is driven as he believes into silent gravity and exclusiveness by his faith, may think it is not true; but Zoroaster, thousands of years ago, travelled the same road and had the same experience; but he, being wise, knew it to be universal, and treated his neighbors accordingly, and is even said to have invented and established worship among men. Let him humbly commune with Zoroaster then, and, through the liberalizing influence of all the worthies, with Jesus Christ himself, and let "our church" go by the board.

We boast that we belong to the nineteenth century and are making the most rapid strides of any nation. But consider how little this village does for its own culture. I do not wish to flatter my townsmen, nor to be flattered by them, for that will not advance either of us. We need to be provoked,—goaded like oxen, as we are, into a trot. We have a comparatively decent system of common schools, schools for infants only; but excepting the half-starved Lyceum in the winter, and latterly the puny beginning of a library suggested by the state, no school for ourselves. We spend more on almost any article of bodily aliment or ailment than on our mental aliment. It is time that we had uncommon schools, that we did not leave off our education when we begin to be men and women. It is time that villages were universities, and their elder inhabitants the fellows of universities, with leisure—if they are indeed so well off—to pursue liberal studies the rest of their lives. Shall the world be confined to one Paris or one Oxford forever? Cannot students be boarded here and get a liberal education under the skies of Concord? Can we not hire some Abelard to lecture to us? Alas! what with foddering the cattle and tending the store, we are kept from school too long, and our education is sadly neglected. In this country, the village should in some respects take the place of the nobleman of Europe. It should be the patron of the fine arts. It is rich enough. It wants only the magnanimity and refinement. It can spend money enough on such things as farmers and traders value, but it is thought Utopian to propose spending money for things which more intelligent men know to be of far more worth This town has spent seventeen thousand dollars on a town-house, thank fortune or politics, but probably it will not spend so much on living wit, the true meat to put into that shell, in a hundred years. The one hundred and twenty-five dollars annually subscribed for a Lyceum in the winter is better spent than any other equal sum raised in the town. If we live in the nineteenth century, why should we not enjoy the advantages which the nineteenth century offers? Why should our life be in any respect provincial? If we will read newspapers, why not skip the gossip of Boston and take the best newspaper in the world at once?— not be sucking the pap of "neutral family" papers, or browsing "Olive-Branches" here in New England. Let the reports of all the learned societies come to us, and we will see if they know any thing. Why should we leave it to Harper & Brothers and Redding & Co. to select our reading? As the nobleman of cultivated taste surrounds himself with whatever conduces to his culture,—genius—learning—wit—books— paintings—statuary—music—philosophical instruments, and the like; so let the village do,—not stop short at a pedagogue, a parson, a sexton, a parish library, and three selectmen, because our pilgrim forefathers got through a cold winter once on a bleak rock with these. To act collectively is according to the spirit of our institutions; and I am confident that, as our circumstances are more flourishing, our means are greater than the nobleman's. New England can hire all the wise men in the world to come and teach her, and board them round the while, and not be provincial at all. That is the *uncommon* school we want. Instead of noblemen, let us have noble villages of men. If it is necessary, omit one bridge over the river, go round a little there, and throw one arch at least over the darker gulf of ignorance which surrounds us.

Sounds

B UT WHILE we are confined to books, though the most
select and classic, and read only particular written languages, which are themselves but dialects and provincial, we
are in danger of forgetting the language which all things and
events speak without metaphor, which alone is copious and
standard. Much is published, but little printed. The rays
which stream through the shutter will be no longer remembered when the shutter is wholly removed. No method nor
discipline can supersede the necessity of being forever on the
alert. What is a course of history, or philosophy, or poetry,
no matter how well selected, or the best society, or the most
admirable routine of life, compared with the discipline of
looking always at what is to be seen? Will you be a reader, a
student merely, or a seer? Read your fate, see what is before
you, and walk on into futurity.

I did not read books the first summer; I hoed beans. Nay,
I often did better than this. There were times when I could
not afford to sacrifice the bloom of the present moment to
any work, whether of the head or hands. I love a broad margin to my life. Sometimes, in a summer morning, having
taken my accustomed bath, I sat in my sunny doorway from
sunrise till noon, rapt in a revery, amidst the pines and hickories and sumachs, in undisturbed solitude and stillness, while
the birds sang around or flitted noiseless through the house,
until by the sun falling in at my west window, or the noise
of some traveller's wagon on the distant highway, I was reminded of the lapse of time. I grew in those seasons like corn
in the night, and they were far better than any work of the
hands would have been. They were not time subtracted from
my life, but so much over and above my usual allowance. I
realized what the Orientals mean by contemplation and the
forsaking of works. For the most part, I minded not how the
hours went. The day advanced as if to light some work of
mine; it was morning, and lo, now it is evening, and nothing
memorable is accomplished. Instead of singing like the birds,
I silently smiled at my incessant good fortune. As the sparrow
had its trill, sitting on the hickory before my door, so had I

my chuckle or suppressed warble which he might hear out of
my nest. My days were not days of the week, bearing the
stamp of any heathen deity, nor were they minced into hours
and fretted by the ticking of a clock; for I lived like the Puri
Indians, of whom it is said that "for yesterday, to-day, and
to-morrow they have only one word, and they express the
variety of meaning by pointing backward for yesterday, forward for to-morrow, and overhead for the passing day." This
was sheer idleness to my fellow-townsmen, no doubt; but if
the birds and flowers had tried me by their standard, I should
not have been found wanting. A man must find his occasions
in himself, it is true. The natural day is very calm, and will
hardly reprove his indolence.

I had this advantage, at least, in my mode of life, over those
who were obliged to look abroad for amusement, to society
and the theatre, that my life itself was become my amusement
and never ceased to be novel. It was a drama of many scenes
and without an end. If we were always indeed getting our
living, and regulating our lives according to the last and best
mode we had learned, we should never be troubled with ennui. Follow your genius closely enough, and it will not fail to
show you a fresh prospect every hour. Housework was a
pleasant pastime. When my floor was dirty, I rose early, and,
setting all my furniture out of doors on the grass, bed and
bedstead making but one budget, dashed water on the floor,
and sprinkled white sand from the pond on it, and then with
a broom scrubbed it clean and white; and by the time the
villagers had broken their fast the morning sun had dried my
house sufficiently to allow me to move in again, and my meditations were almost uninterrupted. It was pleasant to see my
whole household effects out on the grass, making a little pile
like a gypsy's pack, and my three-legged table, from which I
did not remove the books and pen and ink, standing amid the
pines and hickories. They seemed glad to get out themselves,
and as if unwilling to be brought in. I was sometimes
tempted to stretch an awning over them and take my seat
there. It was worth the while to see the sun shine on these
things, and hear the free wind blow on them; so much more
interesting most familiar objects look out of doors than in the
house. A bird sits on the next bough, life-everlasting grows

under the table, and blackberry vines run round its legs; pine cones, chestnut burs, and strawberry leaves are strewn about. It looked as if this was the way these forms came to be transferred to our furniture, to tables, chairs, and bedsteads,—because they once stood in their midst.

My house was on the side of a hill, immediately on the edge of the larger wood, in the midst of a young forest of pitch pines and hickories, and half a dozen rods from the pond, to which a narrow footpath led down the hill. In my front yard grew the strawberry, blackberry, and life-everlasting, johnswort and golden-rod, shrub-oaks and sand-cherry, blueberry and ground-nut. Near the end of May, the sand-cherry, (*Cerasus pumila,*) adorned the sides of the path with its delicate flowers arranged in umbels cylindrically about its short stems, which last, in the fall, weighed down with good sized and handsome cherries, fell over in wreaths like rays on every side. I tasted them out of compliment to Nature, though they were scarcely palatable. The sumach, (*Rhus glabra,*) grew luxuriantly about the house, pushing up through the embankment which I had made, and growing five or six feet the first season. Its broad pinnate tropical leaf was pleasant though strange to look on. The large buds, suddenly pushing out late in the spring from dry sticks which had seemed to be dead, developed themselves as by magic into graceful green and tender boughs, an inch in diameter; and sometimes, as I sat at my window, so heedlessly did they grow and tax their weak joints, I heard a fresh and tender bough suddenly fall like a fan to the ground, when there was not a breath of air stirring, broken off by its own weight. In August, the large masses of berries, which, when in flower, had attracted many wild bees, gradually assumed their bright velvety crimson hue, and by their weight again bent down and broke the tender limbs.

As I sit at my window this summer afternoon, hawks are circling about my clearing; the tantivy of wild pigeons, flying by twos and threes athwart my view, or perching restless on the white-pine boughs behind my house, gives a voice to the air; a fishhawk dimples the glassy surface of the pond and brings up a fish; a mink steals out of the marsh before my door and seizes a frog by the shore; the sedge is bending under the weight of the reed-birds flitting hither and thither; and for the last half hour I have heard the rattle of railroad cars, now dying away and then reviving like the beat of a partridge, conveying travellers from Boston to the country. For I did not live so out of the world as that boy, who, as I hear, was put out to a farmer in the east part of the town, but ere long ran away and came home again, quite down at the heel and homesick. He had never seen such a dull and out-of-the-way place; the folks were all gone off; why, you couldn't even hear the whistle! I doubt if there is such a place in Massachusetts now:—

> "In truth, our village has become a butt
> For one of those fleet railroad shafts, and o'er
> Our peaceful plain its soothing sound is—Concord."

The Fitchburg Railroad touches the pond about a hundred rods south of where I dwell. I usually go to the village along its causeway, and am, as it were, related to society by this link. The men on the freight trains, who go over the whole length of the road, bow to me as to an old acquaintance, they pass me so often, and apparently they take me for an employee; and so I am. I too would fain be a track-repairer somewhere in the orbit of the earth.

The whistle of the locomotive penetrates my woods summer and winter, sounding like the scream of a hawk sailing over some farmer's yard, informing me that many restless city merchants are arriving within the circle of the town, or adventurous country traders from the other side. As they come under one horizon, they shout their warning to get off the track to the other, heard sometimes through the circles of two towns. Here come your groceries, country; your rations, countrymen! Nor is there any man so independent on his farm that he can say them nay. And here's your pay for them! screams the countryman's whistle; timber like long battering rams going twenty miles an hour against the city's walls, and chairs enough to seat all the weary and heavy laden that dwell within them. With such huge and lumbering civility the country hands a chair to the city. All the Indian huckleberry hills are stripped, all the cranberry meadows are raked into the city. Up comes the cotton, down goes the woven cloth; up comes the silk, down goes the woollen; up come the books, but down goes the wit that writes them.

When I meet the engine with its train of cars moving off with planetary motion,—or, rather, like a comet, for the beholder knows not if with that velocity and with that direction it will ever revisit this system, since its orbit does not look like a returning curve,—with its steam cloud like a banner streaming behind in golden and silver wreaths, like many a downy cloud which I have seen, high in the heavens, unfolding its masses to the light,—as if this travelling demigod, this cloud-compeller, would ere long take the sunset sky for the livery of his train; when I hear the iron horse make the hills echo with his snort like thunder, shaking the earth with his feet, and breathing fire and smoke from his nostrils, (what kind of winged horse or fiery dragon they will put into the new Mythology I don't know,) it seems as if the earth had got a race now worthy to inhabit it. If all were as it seems, and men made the elements their servants for noble ends! If the cloud that hangs over the engine were the perspiration of heroic deeds, or as beneficent to men as that which floats over the farmer's fields, then the elements and Nature herself would cheerfully accompany men on their errands and be their escort.

I watch the passage of the morning cars with the same feeling that I do the rising of the sun, which is hardly more regular. Their train of clouds stretching far behind and rising higher and higher, going to heaven while the cars are going to Boston, conceals the sun for a minute and casts my distant field into the shade, a celestial train beside which the petty train of cars which hugs the earth is but the barb of the spear. The stabler of the iron horse was up early this winter morning by the light of the stars amid the mountains, to fodder and harness his steed. Fire, too, was awakened thus early to put the vital heat in him and get him off. If the enterprise were as innocent as it is early! If the snow lies deep, they strap on his snow-shoes, and with the giant plough, plough a furrow from the mountains to the seaboard, in which the cars, like a following drill-barrow, sprinkle all the restless men and floating merchandise in the country for seed. All day the fire-steed flies over the country, stopping only that his master may rest, and I am awakened by his tramp and defiant snort at midnight, when in some remote glen in the woods he fronts the elements incased in ice and snow; and he will reach his stall only with the morning star, to start once more on his travels without rest or slumber. Or perchance, at evening, I hear him in his stable blowing off the superfluous energy of the day, that he may calm his nerves and cool his liver and brain for a few hours of iron slumber. If the enterprise were as heroic and commanding as it is protracted and unwearied!

Far through unfrequented woods on the confines of towns, where once only the hunter penetrated by day, in the darkest night dart these bright saloons without the knowledge of their inhabitants; this moment stopping at some brilliant station-house in town or city, where a social crowd is gathered, the next in the Dismal Swamp, scaring the owl and fox. The startings and arrivals of the cars are now the epochs in the village day. They go and come with such regularity and precision, and their whistle can be heard so far, that the farmers set their clocks by them, and thus one well conducted institution regulates a whole country. Have not men improved somewhat in punctuality since the railroad was invented? Do they not talk and think faster in the depot than they did in the stage-office? There is something electrifying in the atmosphere of the former place. I have been astonished at the miracles it has wrought; that some of my neighbors, who, I should have prophesied, once for all, would never get to Boston by so prompt a conveyance, are on hand when the bell rings. To do things "railroad fashion" is now the by-word; and it is worth the while to be warned so often and so sincerely by any power to get off its track. There is no stopping to read the riot act, no firing over the heads of the mob, in this case. We have constructed a fate, an *Atropos*, that never turns aside. (Let that be the name of your engine.) Men are advertised that at a certain hour and minute these bolts will be shot toward particular points of the compass; yet it interferes with no man's business, and the children go to school on the other track. We live the steadier for it. We are all educated thus to be sons of Tell. The air is full of invisible bolts. Every path but your own is the path of fate. Keep on your own track, then.

What recommends commerce to me is its enterprise and bravery. It does not clasp its hands and pray to Jupiter. I see these men every day go about their business with more or less courage and content, doing more even than they suspect, and perchance better employed than they could have consciously devised. I am less affected by their heroism who stood up for half an hour in the front line at Buena Vista, than by the steady and cheerful valor of the men who inhabit the snow-plough for their winter quarters; who have not merely the three-o'-clock in the morning courage, which Bonaparte thought was the rarest, but whose courage does not go to rest so early, who go to sleep only when the storm sleeps or the sinews of their iron steed are frozen. On this morning of the Great Snow, perchance, which is still raging and chilling men's blood, I hear the muffled tone of their engine bell from out the fog bank of their chilled breath, which announces that the cars *are coming*, without long delay, notwithstanding the veto of a New England north-east snow storm, and I behold the ploughmen covered with snow and rime, their heads peering above the mould-board which is turning down other than daisies and the nests of field-mice, like bowlders of the Sierra Nevada, that occupy an outside place in the universe.

Commerce is unexpectedly confident and serene, alert, adventurous, and unwearied. It is very natural in its methods withal, far more so than many fantastic enterprises and sentimental experiments, and hence its singular success. I am refreshed and expanded when the freight train rattles past me, and I smell the stores which go dispensing their odors all the way from Long Wharf to Lake Champlain, reminding me of foreign parts, of coral reefs, and Indian oceans, and tropical climes, and the extent of the globe. I feel more like a citizen of the world at the sight of the palm-leaf which will cover so many flaxen New England heads the next summer, the Manilla hemp and cocoa-nut husks, the old junk, gunny bags, scrap iron, and rusty nails. This car-load of torn sails is more legible and interesting now than if they should be wrought into paper and printed books. Who can write so graphically the history of the storms they have weathered as these rents have done? They are proof-sheets which need no correction. Here goes lumber from the Maine woods, which did not go

out to sea in the last freshet, risen four dollars on the thousand because of what did go out or was split up; pine, spruce,
cedar,—first, second, third and fourth qualities, so lately all
of one quality, to wave over the bear, and moose, and caribou. Next rolls Thomaston lime, a prime lot, which will get
far among the hills before it gets slacked. These rags in bales,
of all hues and qualities, the lowest condition to which cotton
and linen descend, the final result of dress,—of patterns
which are now no longer cried up, unless it be in Milwaukie,
as those splendid articles, English, French, or American
prints, ginghams, muslins, &c., gathered from all quarters
both of fashion and poverty, going to become paper of one
color or a few shades only, on which forsooth will be written
tales of real life, high and low, and founded on fact! This
closed car smells of salt fish, the strong New England and
commercial scent, reminding me of the Grand Banks and the
fisheries. Who has not seen a salt fish, thoroughly cured for
this world, so that nothing can spoil it, and putting the perseverance of the saints to the blush? with which you may
sweep or pave the streets, and split your kindlings, and the
teamster shelter himself and his lading against sun wind and
rain behind it,—and the trader, as a Concord trader once did,
hang it up by his door for a sign when he commences business, until at last his oldest customer cannot tell surely
whether it be animal, vegetable, or mineral, and yet it shall be
as pure as a snowflake, and if it be put into a pot and boiled,
will come out an excellent dun fish for a Saturday's dinner.
Next Spanish hides, with the tails still preserving their twist
and the angle of elevation they had when the oxen that wore
them were careering over the pampas of the Spanish main,
a type of all obstinacy, and evincing how almost hopeless and
incurable are all constitutional vices. I confess, that practically
speaking, when I have learned a man's real disposition, I have
no hopes of changing it for the better or worse in this state
of existence. As the Orientals say, "A cur's tail may be
warmed, and pressed, and bound round with ligatures, and
after a twelve years' labor bestowed upon it, still it will retain
its natural form." The only effectual cure for such inveteracies
as these tails exhibit is to make glue of them, which I believe
is what is usually done with them, and then they will stay put

and stick. Here is a hogshead of molasses or of brandy directed to John Smith, Cuttingsville, Vermont, some trader among the Green Mountains, who imports for the farmers near his clearing, and now perchance stands over his bulkhead and thinks of the last arrivals on the coast, how they may affect the price for him, telling his customers this moment, as he has told them twenty times before this morning, that he expects some by the next train of prime quality. It is advertised in the Cuttingsville Times.

While these things go up other things come down. Warned by the whizzing sound, I look up from my book and see some tall pine, hewn on far northern hills, which has winged its way over the Green Mountains and the Connecticut, shot like an arrow through the township within ten minutes, and scarce another eye beholds it; going

> "to be the mast
> Of some great ammiral."

And hark! here comes the cattle-train bearing the cattle of a thousand hills, sheepcots, stables, and cow-yards in the air, drovers with their sticks, and shepherd boys in the midst of their flocks, all but the mountain pastures, whirled along like leaves blown from the mountains by the September gales. The air is filled with the bleating of calves and sheep, and the hustling of oxen, as if a pastoral valley were going by. When the old bell-weather at the head rattles his bell, the mountains do indeed skip like rams and the little hills like lambs. A carload of drovers, too, in the midst, on a level with their droves now, their vocation gone, but still clinging to their useless sticks as their badge of office. But their dogs, where are they? It is a stampede to them; they are quite thrown out; they have lost the scent. Methinks I hear them barking behind the Peterboro' Hills, or panting up the western slope of the Green Mountains. They will not be in at the death. Their vocation, too, is gone. Their fidelity and sagacity are below par now. They will slink back to their kennels in disgrace, or perchance run wild and strike a league with the wolf and the fox. So is your pastoral life whirled past and away. But the bell rings, and I must get off the track and let the cars go by; —

What's the railroad to me?
I never go to see
Where it ends.
It fills a few hollows,
And makes banks for the swallows,
It sets the sand a-blowing,
And the blackberries a growing,

but I cross it like a cart-path in the woods. I will not have my
eyes put out and my ears spoiled by its smoke and steam and
hissing.

Now that the cars are gone by, and all the restless world
with them, and the fishes in the pond no longer feel their
rumbling, I am more alone than ever. For the rest of the long
afternoon, perhaps, my meditations are interrupted only by
the faint rattle of a carriage or team along the distant highway.

Sometimes, on Sundays, I heard the bells, the Lincoln, Acton, Bedford, or Concord bell, when the wind was favorable,
a faint, sweet, and, as it were, natural melody, worth importing into the wilderness. At a sufficient distance over the
woods this sound acquires a certain vibratory hum, as if the
pine needles in the horizon were the strings of a harp which
it swept. All sound heard at the greatest possible distance produces one and the same effect, a vibration of the universal
lyre, just as the intervening atmosphere makes a distant ridge
of earth interesting to our eyes by the azure tint it imparts to
it. There came to me in this case a melody which the air had
strained, and which had conversed with every leaf and needle
of the wood, that portion of the sound which the elements
had taken up and modulated and echoed from vale to vale.
The echo is, to some extent, an original sound, and therein is
the magic and charm of it. It is not merely a repetition of
what was worth repeating in the bell, but partly the voice of
the wood; the same trivial words and notes sung by a wood-
nymph.

At evening, the distant lowing of some cow in the horizon
beyond the woods sounded sweet and melodious, and at first
I would mistake it for the voices of certain minstrels by whom

I was sometimes serenaded, who might be straying over hill and dale; but soon I was not unpleasantly disappointed when it was prolonged into the cheap and natural music of the cow. I do not mean to be satirical, but to express my appreciation of those youths' singing, when I state that I perceived clearly that it was akin to the music of the cow, and they were at length one articulation of Nature.

Regularly at half past seven, in one part of the summer, after the evening train had gone by, the whippoorwills chanted their vespers for half an hour, sitting on a stump by my door, or upon the ridge pole of the house. They would begin to sing almost with as much precision as a clock, within five minutes of a particular time, referred to the setting of the sun, every evening. I had a rare opportunity to become acquainted with their habits. Sometimes I heard four or five at once in different parts of the wood, by accident one a bar behind another, and so near me that I distinguished not only the cluck after each note, but often that singular buzzing sound like a fly in a spider's web, only proportionally louder. Sometimes one would circle round and round me in the woods a few feet distant as if tethered by a string, when probably I was near its eggs. They sang at intervals throughout the night, and were again as musical as ever just before and about dawn.

When other birds are still the screech owls take up the strain, like mourning women their ancient u-lu-lu. Their dismal scream is truly Ben Jonsonian. Wise midnight hags! It is no honest and blunt tu-whit tu-who of the poets, but, without jesting, a most solemn graveyard ditty, the mutual consolations of suicide lovers remembering the pangs and the delights of supernal love in the infernal groves. Yet I love to hear their wailing, their doleful responses, trilled along the wood-side, reminding me sometimes of music and singing birds; as if it were the dark and tearful side of music, the regrets and sighs that would fain be sung. They are the spirits, the low spirits and melancholy forebodings, of fallen souls that once in human shape night-walked the earth and did the deeds of darkness, now expiating their sins with their wailing hymns or threnodies in the scenery of their transgressions. They give me a new sense of the variety and capacity of that nature which is our common dwelling. *Oh-o-o-o-o that I never had been bor-r-r-r-n!* sighs one on this side of the pond, and circles with the restlessness of despair to some new perch on the gray oaks. Then— *that I never had been bor-r-r-r-n!* echoes another on the farther side with tremulous sincerity, and— *bor-r-r-r-n!* comes faintly from far in the Lincoln woods.

I was also serenaded by a hooting owl. Near at hand you could fancy it the most melancholy sound in Nature, as if she meant by this to stereotype and make permanent in her choir the dying moans of a human being,—some poor weak relic of mortality who has left hope behind, and howls like an animal, yet with human sobs, on entering the dark valley, made more awful by a certain gurgling melodiousness,—I find myself beginning with the letters gl when I try to imitate it,—expressive of a mind which has reached the gelatinous mildewy stage in the mortification of all healthy and courageous thought. It reminded me of ghouls and idiots and insane howlings. But now one answers from far woods in a strain made really melodious by distance,— *Hoo hoo hoo, hoorer hoo*; and indeed for the most part it suggested only pleasing associations, whether heard by day or night, summer or winter.

I rejoice that there are owls. Let them do the idiotic and maniacal hooting for men. It is a sound admirably suited to swamps and twilight woods which no day illustrates, suggesting a vast and undeveloped nature which men have not recognized. They represent the stark twilight and unsatisfied thoughts which all have. All day the sun has shone on the surface of some savage swamp, where the single spruce stands hung with usnea lichens, and small hawks circulate above, and the chicadee lisps amid the evergreens, and the partridge and rabbit skulk beneath; but now a more dismal and fitting day dawns, and a different race of creatures awakes to express the meaning of Nature there.

Late in the evening I heard the distant rumbling of wagons over bridges,—a sound heard farther than almost any other at night,—the baying of dogs, and sometimes again the lowing of some disconsolate cow in a distant barn-yard. In the mean while all the shore rang with the trump of bullfrogs, the sturdy spirits of ancient wine-bibbers and wassailers, still

unrepentant, trying to sing a catch in their Stygian lake,—if
the Walden nymphs will pardon the comparison, for though
there are almost no weeds, there are frogs there,—who
would fain keep up the hilarious rules of their old festal
tables, though their voices have waxed hoarse and solemnly
grave, mocking at mirth, and the wine has lost its flavor, and
become only liquor to distend their paunches, and sweet intoxication never comes to drown the memory of the past, but
mere saturation and waterloggedness and distention. The
most aldermanic, with his chin upon a heart-leaf, which serves
for a napkin to his drooling chaps, under this northern shore
quaffs a deep draught of the once scorned water, and passes
round the cup with the ejaculation *tr-r-r-oonk, tr-r-r-oonk,
tr-r-r-oonk!* and straightway comes over the water from some
distant cove the same password repeated, where the next in
seniority and girth has gulped down to his mark; and when
this observance has made the circuit of the shores, then ejac-
ulates the master of ceremonies, with satisfaction, *tr-r-r-oonk!*
and each in his turn repeats the same down to the least distended, leakiest, and flabbiest paunched, that there be no mistake; and then the bowl goes round again and again, until the
sun disperses the morning mist, and only the patriarch is not
under the pond, but vainly bellowing *troonk* from time to
time, and pausing for a reply.

I am not sure that I ever heard the sound of cock-crowing
from my clearing, and I thought that it might be worth the
while to keep a cockerel for his music merely, as a singing
bird. The note of this once wild Indian pheasant is certainly
the most remarkable of any bird's, and if they could be naturalized without being domesticated, it would soon become
the most famous sound in our woods, surpassing the clangor
of the goose and the hooting of the owl; and then imagine
the cackling of the hens to fill the pauses when their lords'
clarions rested! No wonder that man added this bird to his
tame stock,—to say nothing of the eggs and drum-sticks. To
walk in a winter morning in a wood where these birds
abounded, their native woods, and hear the wild cockerels
crow on the trees, clear and shrill for miles over the resounding earth, drowning the feebler notes of other birds,—think
of it! It would put nations on the alert. Who would not be

early to rise, and rise earlier and earlier every successive day of his life, till he became unspeakably healthy, wealthy, and wise? This foreign bird's note is celebrated by the poets of all countries along with the notes of their native songsters. All climates agree with brave Chanticleer. He is more indigenous even than the natives. His health is ever good, his lungs are sound, his spirits never flag. Even the sailor on the Atlantic and Pacific is awakened by his voice; but its shrill sound never roused me from my slumbers. I kept neither dog, cat, cow, pig, nor hens, so that you would have said there was a deficiency of domestic sounds; neither the churn, nor the spinning wheel, nor even the singing of the kettle, nor the hissing of the urn, nor children crying, to comfort one. An old-fashioned man would have lost his senses or died of ennui before this. Not even rats in the wall, for they were starved out, or rather were never baited in,—only squirrels on the roof and under the floor, a whippoorwill on the ridge pole, a blue-jay screaming beneath the window, a hare or woodchuck under the house, a screech-owl or a cat-owl behind it, a flock of wild geese or a laughing loon on the pond, and a fox to bark in the night. Not even a lark or an oriole, those mild plantation birds, ever visited my clearing. No cockerels to crow nor hens to cackle in the yard. No yard! but unfenced Nature reaching up to your very sills. A young forest growing up under your windows, and wild sumachs and blackberry vines breaking through into your cellar; sturdy pitch-pines rubbing and creaking against the shingles for want of room, their roots reaching quite under the house. Instead of a scuttle or a blind blown off in the gale,—a pine tree snapped off or torn up by the roots behind your house for fuel. Instead of no path to the front-yard gate in the Great Snow,—no gate,—no front-yard,—and no path to the civilized world!

Solitude

THIS IS a delicious evening, when the whole body is one sense, and imbibes delight through every pore. I go and come with a strange liberty in Nature, a part of herself. As I walk along the stony shore of the pond in my shirt sleeves, though it is cool as well as cloudy and windy, and I see nothing special to attract me, all the elements are unusually congenial to me. The bullfrogs trump to usher in the night, and the note of the whippoorwill is borne on the rippling wind from over the water. Sympathy with the fluttering alder and poplar leaves almost takes away my breath; yet, like the lake, my serenity is rippled but not ruffled. These small waves raised by the evening wind are as remote from storm as the smooth reflecting surface. Though it is now dark, the wind still blows and roars in the wood, the waves still dash, and some creatures lull the rest with their notes. The repose is never complete. The wildest animals do not repose, but seek their prey now; the fox, and skunk, and rabbit, now roam the fields and woods without fear. They are Nature's watchmen, —links which connect the days of animated life.

When I return to my house I find that visitors have been there and left their cards, either a bunch of flowers, or a wreath of evergreen, or a name in pencil on a yellow walnut leaf or a chip. They who come rarely to the woods take some little piece of the forest into their hands to play with by the way, which they leave, either intentionally or accidentally. One has peeled a willow wand, woven it into a ring, and dropped it on my table. I could always tell if visitors had called in my absence, either by the bended twigs or grass, or the print of their shoes, and generally of what sex or age or quality they were by some slight trace left, as a flower dropped, or a bunch of grass plucked and thrown away, even as far off as the railroad, half a mile distant, or by the lingering odor of a cigar or pipe. Nay, I was frequently notified of the passage of a traveller along the highway sixty rods off by the scent of his pipe.

There is commonly sufficient space about us. Our horizon is never quite at our elbows. The thick wood is not just at our door, nor the pond, but somewhat is always clearing, familiar and worn by us, appropriated and fenced in some way, and reclaimed from Nature. For what reason have I this vast range and circuit, some square miles of unfrequented forest, for my privacy, abandoned to me by men? My nearest neighbor is a mile distant, and no house is visible from any place but the hill-tops within half a mile of my own. I have my horizon bounded by woods all to myself; a distant view of the railroad where it touches the pond on the one hand, and of the fence which skirts the woodland road on the other. But for the most part it is as solitary where I live as on the prairies. It is as much Asia or Africa as New England. I have, as it were, my own sun and moon and stars, and a little world all to myself. At night there was never a traveller passed my house, or knocked at my door, more than if I were the first or last man; unless it were in the spring, when at long intervals some came from the village to fish for pouts,—they plainly fished much more in the Walden Pond of their own natures, and baited their hooks with darkness,—but they soon retreated, usually with light baskets, and left "the world to darkness and to me," and the black kernel of the night was never profaned by any human neighborhood. I believe that men are generally still a little afraid of the dark, though the witches are all hung, and Christianity and candles have been introduced.

Yet I experienced sometimes that the most sweet and tender, the most innocent and encouraging society may be found in any natural object, even for the poor misanthrope and most melancholy man. There can be no very black melancholy to him who lives in the midst of Nature and has his senses still. There was never yet such a storm but it was Æolian music to a healthy and innocent ear. Nothing can rightly compel a simple and brave man to a vulgar sadness. While I enjoy the friendship of the seasons I trust that nothing can make life a burden to me. The gentle rain which waters my beans and keeps me in the house to-day is not drear and melancholy, but good for me too. Though it prevents my hoeing them, it is of far more worth than my hoeing. If it should continue so long as to cause the seeds to rot in the ground and destroy the potatoes in the low lands, it would still be good for the

grass on the uplands, and, being good for the grass, it would
be good for me. Sometimes, when I compare myself with
other men, it seems as if I were more favored by the gods
than they, beyond any deserts that I am conscious of; as if I
had a warrant and surety at their hands which my fellows
have not, and were especially guided and guarded. I do not
flatter myself, but if it be possible they flatter me. I have never
felt lonesome, or in the least oppressed by a sense of solitude,
but once, and that was a few weeks after I came to the woods,
when, for an hour, I doubted if the near neighborhood of
man was not essential to a serene and healthy life. To be alone
was something unpleasant. But I was at the same time conscious of a slight insanity in my mood, and seemed to foresee
my recovery. In the midst of a gentle rain while these
thoughts prevailed, I was suddenly sensible of such sweet and
beneficent society in Nature, in the very pattering of the
drops, and in every sound and sight around my house, an
infinite and unaccountable friendliness all at once like an atmosphere sustaining me, as made the fancied advantages of
human neighborhood insignificant, and I have never thought
of them since. Every little pine needle expanded and swelled
with sympathy and befriended me. I was so distinctly made
aware of the presence of something kindred to me, even in
scenes which we are accustomed to call wild and dreary, and
also that the nearest of blood to me and humanest was not a
person nor a villager, that I thought no place could ever be
strange to me again.—

> "Mourning untimely consumes the sad;
>   Few are their days in the land of the living,
>   Beautiful daughter of Toscar."

Some of my pleasantest hours were during the long rain
storms in the spring or fall, which confined me to the house
for the afternoon as well as the forenoon, soothed by their
ceaseless roar and pelting; when an early twilight ushered in
a long evening in which many thoughts had time to take root
and unfold themselves. In those driving north-east rains
which tried the village houses so, when the maids stood ready
with mop and pail in front entries to keep the deluge out, I
sat behind my door in my little house, which was all entry,

and thoroughly enjoyed its protection. In one heavy thunder shower the lightning struck a large pitch-pine across the pond, making a very conspicuous and perfectly regular spiral groove from top to bottom, an inch or more deep, and four or five inches wide, as you would groove a walking-stick. I passed it again the other day, and was struck with awe on looking up and beholding that mark, now more distinct than ever, where a terrific and resistless bolt came down out of the harmless sky eight years ago. Men frequently say to me, "I should think you would feel lonesome down there, and want to be nearer to folks, rainy and snowy days and nights especially." I am tempted to reply to such,—This whole earth which we inhabit is but a point in space. How far apart, think you, dwell the two most distant inhabitants of yonder star, the breadth of whose disk cannot be appreciated by our instruments? Why should I feel lonely? is not our planet in the Milky Way? This which you put seems to me not to be the most important question. What sort of space is that which separates a man from his fellows and makes him solitary? I have found that no exertion of the legs can bring two minds much nearer to one another. What do we want most to dwell near to? Not to many men surely, the depot, the post-office, the bar-room, the meeting-house, the school-house, the grocery, Beacon Hill, or the Five Points, where men most congregate, but to the perennial source of our life, whence in all our experience we have found that to issue; as the willow stands near the water and sends out its roots in that direction. This will vary with different natures, but this is the place where a wise man will dig his cellar. . . . I one evening overtook one of my townsmen, who has accumulated what is called "a handsome property,"—though I never got a *fair* view of it,—on the Walden road, driving a pair of cattle to market, who inquired of me how I could bring my mind to give up so many of the comforts of life. I answered that I was very sure I liked it passably well; I was not joking. And so I went home to my bed, and left him to pick his way through the darkness and the mud to Brighton,—or Bright-town,—which place he would reach some time in the morning.

Any prospect of awakening or coming to life to a dead man makes indifferent all times and places. The place where that may occur is always the same, and indescribably pleasant to all our senses. For the most part we allow only outlying and transient circumstances to make our occasions. They are, in fact, the cause of our distraction. Nearest to all things is that power which fashions their being. *Next* to us the grandest laws are continually being executed. *Next* to us is not the workman whom we have hired, with whom we love so well to talk, but the workman whose work we are.

"How vast and profound is the influence of the subtile powers of Heaven and of Earth!"

"We seek to perceive them, and we do not see them; we seek to hear them, and we do not hear them; identified with the substance of things, they cannot be separated from them."

"They cause that in all the universe men purify and sanctify their hearts, and clothe themselves in their holiday garments to offer sacrifices and oblations to their ancestors. It is an ocean of subtile intelligences. They are every where, above us, on our left, on our right; they environ us on all sides."

We are the subjects of an experiment which is not a little interesting to me. Can we not do without the society of our gossips a little while under these circumstances,—have our own thoughts to cheer us? Confucius says truly, "Virtue does not remain as an abandoned orphan; it must of necessity have neighbors."

With thinking we may be beside ourselves in a sane sense. By a conscious effort of the mind we can stand aloof from actions and their consequences; and all things, good and bad, go by us like a torrent. We are not wholly involved in Nature. I may be either the driftwood in the stream, or Indra in the sky looking down on it. I *may* be affected by a theatrical exhibition; on the other hand, I *may not* be affected by an actual event which appears to concern me much more. I only know myself as a human entity; the scene, so to speak, of thoughts and affections; and am sensible of a certain doubleness by which I can stand as remote from myself as from another. However intense my experience, I am conscious of the presence and criticism of a part of me, which, as it were, is not a part of me, but spectator, sharing no experience, but taking note of it; and that is no more I than it is you. When the play, it may be the tragedy, of life is over, the spectator goes his way. It was a kind of fiction, a work of the imagination only, so far as he was concerned. This doubleness may easily make us poor neighbors and friends sometimes.

I find it wholesome to be alone the greater part of the time. To be in company, even with the best, is soon wearisome and dissipating. I love to be alone. I never found the companion that was so companionable as solitude. We are for the most part more lonely when we go abroad among men than when we stay in our chambers. A man thinking or working is always alone, let him be where he will. Solitude is not measured by the miles of space that intervene between a man and his fellows. The really diligent student in one of the crowded hives of Cambridge College is as solitary as a dervis in the desert. The farmer can work alone in the field or the woods all day, hoeing or chopping, and not feel lonesome, because he is employed; but when he comes home at night he cannot sit down in a room alone, at the mercy of his thoughts, but must be where he can "see the folks," and recreate, and as he thinks remunerate, himself for his day's solitude; and hence he wonders how the student can sit alone in the house all night and most of the day without ennui and "the blues;" but he does not realize that the student, though in the house, is still at work in *his* field, and chopping in *his* woods, as the farmer in his, and in turn seeks the same recreation and society that the latter does, though it may be a more condensed form of it.

Society is commonly too cheap. We meet at very short intervals, not having had time to acquire any new value for each other. We meet at meals three times a day, and give each other a new taste of that old musty cheese that we are. We have had to agree on a certain set of rules, called etiquette and politeness, to make this frequent meeting tolerable, and that we need not come to open war. We meet at the post-office, and at the sociable, and about the fireside every night; we live thick and are in each other's way, and stumble over one another, and I think that we thus lose some respect for one another. Certainly less frequency would suffice for all important and hearty communications. Consider the girls in a factory,—never alone, hardly in their dreams. It would be better if there were but one inhabitant to a square mile, as where I live. The value of a man is not in his skin, that we should touch him.

I have heard of a man lost in the woods and dying of famine and exhaustion at the foot of a tree, whose loneliness was relieved by the grotesque visions with which, owing to bodily weakness, his diseased imagination surrounded him, and which he believed to be real. So also, owing to bodily and mental health and strength, we may be continually cheered by a like but more normal and natural society, and come to know that we are never alone.

I have a great deal of company in my house; especially in the morning, when nobody calls. Let me suggest a few comparisons, that some one may convey an idea of my situation. I am no more lonely than the loon in the pond that laughs so loud, or than Walden Pond itself. What company has that lonely lake, I pray? And yet it has not the blue devils, but the blue angels in it, in the azure tint of its waters. The sun is alone, except in thick weather, when there sometimes appear to be two, but one is a mock sun. God is alone,—but the devil, he is far from being alone; he sees a great deal of company; he is legion. I am no more lonely than a single mullein or dandelion in a pasture, or a bean leaf, or sorrel, or a horse-fly, or a humble-bee. I am no more lonely than the Mill Brook, or a weathercock, or the northstar, or the south wind, or an April shower, or a January thaw, or the first spider in a new house.

I have occasional visits in the long winter evenings, when the snow falls fast and the wind howls in the wood, from an old settler and original proprietor, who is reported to have dug Walden Pond, and stoned it, and fringed it with pine woods; who tells me stories of old time and of new eternity; and between us we manage to pass a cheerful evening with social mirth and pleasant views of things, even without apples or cider,—a most wise and humorous friend, whom I love much, who keeps himself more secret than ever did Goffe or Whalley; and though he is thought to be dead, none can show where he is buried. An elderly dame, too, dwells in my neighborhood, invisible to most persons, in whose odorous herb garden I love to stroll sometimes, gathering simples and listening to her fables; for she has a genius of unequalled fertility, and her memory runs back farther than mythology, and she can tell me the original of every fable, and on what fact every one is founded, for the incidents occurred when she was young. A ruddy and lusty old dame, who delights in all weathers and seasons, and is likely to outlive all her children yet.

The indescribable innocence and beneficence of Nature, — of sun and wind and rain, of summer and winter, — such health, such cheer, they afford forever! and such sympathy have they ever with our race, that all Nature would be affected, and the sun's brightness fade, and the winds would sigh humanely, and the clouds rain tears, and the woods shed their leaves and put on mourning in midsummer, if any man should ever for a just cause grieve. Shall I not have intelligence with the earth? Am I not partly leaves and vegetable mould myself?

What is the pill which will keep us well, serene, contented? Not my or thy great-grandfather's, but our great-grandmother Nature's universal, vegetable, botanic medicines, by which she has kept herself young always, outlived so many old Parrs in her day, and fed her health with their decaying fatness. For my panacea, instead of one of those quack vials of a mixture dipped from Acheron and the Dead Sea, which come out of those long shallow black-schooner looking wagons which we sometimes see made to carry bottles, let me have a draught of undiluted morning air. Morning air! If men will not drink of this at the fountain-head of the day, why, then, we must even bottle up some and sell it in the shops, for the benefit of those who have lost their subscription ticket to morning time in this world. But remember, it will not keep quite till noon-day even in the coolest cellar, but drive out the stopples long ere that and follow westward the steps of Aurora. I am no worshipper of Hygeia, who was the daughter of that old herb-doctor Æsculapius, and who is represented on monuments holding a serpent in one hand, and in the other a cup out of which the serpent sometimes drinks; but rather of Hebe, cupbearer to Jupiter, who was the daughter of Juno and wild lettuce, and who had the power of restoring gods and men to the vigor of youth. She was probably the only thoroughly sound-conditioned, healthy, and robust young lady that ever walked the globe, and wherever she came it was spring.

Visitors

I THINK that I love society as much as most, and am ready enough to fasten myself like a bloodsucker for the time to any full-blooded man that comes in my way. I am naturally no hermit, but might possibly sit out the sturdiest frequenter of the bar-room, if my business called me thither.

I had three chairs in my house; one for solitude, two for friendship, three for society. When visitors came in larger and unexpected numbers there was but the third chair for them all, but they generally economized the room by standing up. It is surprising how many great men and women a small house will contain. I have had twenty-five or thirty souls, with their bodies, at once under my roof, and yet we often parted without being aware that we had come very near to one another. Many of our houses, both public and private, with their almost innumerable apartments, their huge halls and their cellars for the storage of wines and other munitions of peace, appear to me extravagantly large for their inhabitants. They are so vast and magnificent that the latter seem to be only vermin which infest them. I am surprised when the herald blows his summons before some Tremont or Astor or Middlesex House, to see come creeping out over the piazza for all inhabitants a ridiculous mouse, which soon again slinks into some hole in the pavement.

One inconvenience I sometimes experienced in so small a house, the difficulty of getting to a sufficient distance from my guest when we began to utter the big thoughts in big words. You want room for your thoughts to get into sailing trim and run a course or two before they make their port. The bullet of your thought must have overcome its lateral and ricochet motion and fallen into its last and steady course before it reaches the ear of the hearer, else it may plough out again through the side of his head. Also, our sentences wanted room to unfold and form their columns in the interval. Individuals, like nations, must have suitable broad and natural boundaries, even a considerable neutral ground, between them. I have found it a singular luxury to talk across the pond to a companion on the opposite side. In my house we were so near that we could not begin to hear,—we could not speak low enough to be heard; as when you throw two stones into calm water so near that they break each other's undulations. If we are merely loquacious and loud talkers, then we can afford to stand very near together, cheek by jowl, and feel each other's breath; but if we speak reservedly and thoughtfully, we want to be farther apart, that all animal heat and moisture may have a chance to evaporate. If we would enjoy the most intimate society with that in each of us which is without, or above, being spoken to, we must not only be silent, but commonly so far apart bodily that we cannot possibly hear each other's voice in any case. Referred to this standard, speech is for the convenience of those who are hard of hearing; but there are many fine things which we cannot say if we have to shout. As the conversation began to assume a loftier and grander tone, we gradually shoved our chairs farther apart till they touched the wall in opposite corners, and then commonly there was not room enough.

My "best" room, however, my withdrawing room, always ready for company, on whose carpet the sun rarely fell, was the pine wood behind my house. Thither in summer days, when distinguished guests came, I took them, and a priceless domestic swept the floor and dusted the furniture and kept the things in order.

If one guest came he sometimes partook of my frugal meal, and it was no interruption to conversation to be stirring a hasty-pudding, or watching the rising and maturing of a loaf of bread in the ashes, in the mean while. But if twenty came and sat in my house there was nothing said about dinner, though there might be bread enough for two, more than if eating were a forsaken habit; but we naturally practised abstinence; and this was never felt to be an offence against hospitality, but the most proper and considerate course. The waste and decay of physical life, which so often needs repair, seemed miraculously retarded in such a case, and the vital vigor stood its ground. I could entertain thus a thousand as well as twenty; and if any ever went away disappointed or hungry from my house when they found me at home, they may depend upon it that I sympathized with them at least. So easy is it, though many housekeepers doubt it, to establish new and better customs in the place of the old. You need not rest your reputation on the dinners you give. For my own part, I was never so effectually deterred from frequenting a man's house, by any kind of Cerberus whatever, as by the parade one made about dining me, which I took to be a very polite and roundabout hint never to trouble him so again. I think I shall never revisit those scenes. I should be proud to have for the motto of my cabin those lines of Spenser which one of my visitors inscribed on a yellow walnut leaf for a card: —

> "Arrivéd there, the little house they fill,
>   Ne looke for entertainment where none was;
>   Rest is their feast, and all things at their will:
>   The noblest mind the best contentment has."

When Winslow, afterward governor of the Plymouth Colony, went with a companion on a visit of ceremony to Massassoit on foot through the woods, and arrived tired and hungry at his lodge, they were well received by the king, but nothing was said about eating that day. When the night arrived, to quote their own words, — "He laid us on the bed with himself and his wife, they at the one end and we at the other, it being only plank, laid a foot from the ground, and a thin mat upon them. Two more of his chief men, for want of room, pressed by and upon us; so that we were worse weary of our lodging than of our journey." At one o'clock the next day Massassoit "brought two fishes that he had shot," about thrice as big as a bream; "these being boiled, there were at least forty looked for a share in them. The most ate of them. This meal only we had in two nights and a day; and had not one of us bought a partridge, we had taken our journey fasting." Fearing that they would be light-headed for want of food and also sleep, owing to "the savages' barbarous singing, (for they used to sing themselves asleep,)" and that they might get home while they had strength to travel, they departed. As for lodging, it is true they were but poorly entertained, though what they found an inconvenience was no doubt intended for an honor; but as far as eating was concerned, I do not see how the Indians could have done better. They had nothing to eat themselves, and they were wiser than to think that apologies could supply the place of food to their guests; so they drew their belts tighter and said nothing about it. Another time when Winslow visited them, it being a season of plenty with them, there was no deficiency in this respect.

As for men, they will hardly fail one any where. I had more visitors while I lived in the woods than at any other period of my life; I mean that I had some. I met several there under more favorable circumstances than I could any where else. But fewer came to see me upon trivial business. In this respect, my company was winnowed by my mere distance from town. I had withdrawn so far within the great ocean of solitude, into which the rivers of society empty, that for the most part, so far as my needs were concerned, only the finest sediment was deposited around me. Beside, there were wafted to me evidences of unexplored and uncultivated continents on the other side.

Who should come to my lodge this morning but a true Homeric or Paphlagonian man,—he had so suitable and poetic a name that I am sorry I cannot print it here,—a Canadian, a wood-chopper and post-maker, who can hole fifty posts in a day, who made his last supper on a woodchuck which his dog caught. He, too, has heard of Homer, and, "if it were not for books," would "not know what to do rainy days," though perhaps he has not read one wholly through for many rainy seasons. Some priest who could pronounce the Greek itself taught him to read his verse in the testament in his native parish far away; and now I must translate to him, while he holds the book, Achilles' reproof to Patroclus for his sad countenance.—"Why are you in tears, Patroclus, like a young girl?"—

"Or have you alone heard some news from Phthia?
They say that Menœtius lives yet, son of Actor,
And Peleus lives, son of Æacus, among the Myrmidons,
Either of whom having died, we should greatly grieve."

He says, "That's good." He has a great bundle of white-oak bark under his arm for a sick man, gathered this Sunday morning. "I suppose there's no harm in going after such a thing to-day," says he. To him Homer was a great writer, though what his writing was about he did not know. A more simple and natural man it would be hard to find. Vice and disease, which cast such a sombre moral hue over the world, seemed to have hardly any existence for him. He was about twenty-eight years old, and had left Canada and his father's house a dozen years before to work in the States, and earn money to buy a farm with at last, perhaps in his native country. He was cast in the coarsest mould; a stout but sluggish body, yet gracefully carried, with a thick sunburnt neck, dark bushy hair, and dull sleepy blue eyes, which were occasionally lit up with expression. He wore a flat gray cloth cap, a dingy wool-colored greatcoat, and cowhide boots. He was a great consumer of meat, usually carrying his dinner to his work a couple of miles past my house,—for he chopped all summer,—in a tin pail; cold meats, often cold woodchucks, and coffee in a stone bottle which dangled by a string from his belt; and sometimes he offered me a drink. He came along early, crossing my bean-field, though without anxiety or haste to get to his work, such as Yankees exhibit. He wasn't a-going to hurt himself. He didn't care if he only earned his board. Frequently he would leave his dinner in the bushes, when his dog had caught a woodchuck by the way, and go back a mile and a half to dress it and leave it in the cellar of the house where he boarded, after deliberating first for half an hour whether he could not sink it in the pond safely till nightfall,— loving to dwell long upon these themes. He would say, as he went by in the morning, "How thick the pigeons are! If working every day were not my trade, I could get all the meat I should want by hunting,—pigeons, woodchucks, rabbits, partridges,—by gosh! I could get all I should want for a week in one day."

He was a skilful chopper, and indulged in some flourishes and ornaments in his art. He cut his trees level and close to the ground, that the sprouts which came up afterward might be more vigorous and a sled might slide over the stumps; and instead of leaving a whole tree to support his corded wood, he would pare it away to a slender stake or splinter which you could break off with your hand at last.

He interested me because he was so quiet and solitary and so happy withal; a well of good humor and contentment which overflowed at his eyes. His mirth was without alloy. Sometimes I saw him at his work in the woods, felling trees, and he would greet me with a laugh of inexpressible satisfaction, and a salutation in Canadian French, though he spoke English as well. When I approached him he would suspend his work, and with half-suppressed mirth lie along the trunk of a pine which he had felled, and, peeling off the inner bark, roll it up into a ball and chew it while he laughed and talked. Such an exuberance of animal spirits had he that he sometimes tumbled down and rolled on the ground with laughter at any thing which made him think and tickled him. Looking round upon the trees he would exclaim,—"By George! I can enjoy myself well enough here chopping; I want no better sport." Sometimes, when at leisure, he amused himself all day in the woods with a pocket pistol, firing salutes to himself at regular intervals as he walked. In the winter he had a fire by which at noon he warmed his coffee in a kettle; and as he sat on a log to eat his dinner the chicadees would sometimes come round and alight on his arm and peck at the potato in his fingers; and he said that he "liked to have the little *fellers* about him."

In him the animal man chiefly was developed. In physical endurance and contentment he was cousin to the pine and the rock. I asked him once if he was not sometimes tired at night, after working all day; and he answered, with a sincere and serious look, "Gorrappit, I never was tired in my life." But the intellectual and what is called spiritual man in him were slumbering as in an infant. He had been instructed only in that innocent and ineffectual way in which the Catholic priests teach the aborigines, by which the pupil is never educated to the degree of consciousness, but only to the degree of trust and reverence, and a child is not made a man, but kept a child. When Nature made him, she gave him a strong body and contentment for his portion, and propped him on every side with reverence and reliance, that he might live out his threescore years and ten a child. He was so genuine and unsophisticated that no introduction would serve to introduce him, more than if you introduced a woodchuck to your neighbor. He had got to find him out as you did. He would not play any part. Men paid him wages for work, and so helped to feed and clothe him; but he never exchanged opinions with them. He was so simply and naturally humble—if he can be called humble who never aspires—that humility was no distinct quality in him, nor could he conceive of it. Wiser men were demigods to him. If you told him that such a one was coming, he did as if he thought that any thing so grand would expect nothing of himself, but take all the responsibility on itself, and let him be forgotten still. He never heard the sound of praise. He particularly reverenced the writer and the preacher. Their performances were miracles. When I told him that I wrote considerably, he thought for a long time that it was merely the handwriting which I meant, for he could write a remarkably good hand himself. I sometimes found the name of his native parish handsomely written in the snow by the highway, with the proper French accent, and knew that he had passed. I asked him if he ever wished to write his thoughts. He said that he had read and written letters for those who could not, but he never tried to write thoughts,—no, he could not, he could not tell what to put first, it would kill him, and then there was spelling to be attended to at the same time!

I heard that a distinguished wise man and reformer asked him if he did not want the world to be changed; but he answered with a chuckle of surprise in his Canadian accent, not knowing that the question had ever been entertained before, "No, I like it well enough." It would have suggested many things to a philosopher to have dealings with him. To a stranger he appeared to know nothing of things in general; yet I sometimes saw in him a man whom I had not seen before, and I did not know whether he was as wise as Shakspeare or as simply ignorant as a child, whether to suspect him of a fine poetic consciousness or of stupidity. A townsman told me that when he met him sauntering through the village in his small close-fitting cap, and whistling to himself, he reminded him of a prince in disguise.

His only books were an almanac and an arithmetic, in which last he was considerably expert. The former was a sort of cyclopædia to him, which he supposed to contain an abstract of human knowledge, as indeed it does to a considerable extent. I loved to sound him on the various reforms of the day, and he never failed to look at them in the most simple and practical light. He had never heard of such things before. Could he do without factories? I asked. He had worn the home-made Vermont gray, he said, and that was good. Could he dispense with tea and coffee? Did this country afford any beverage beside water? He had soaked hemlock leaves in water and drank it, and thought that was better than water in warm weather. When I asked him if he could do without money, he showed the convenience of money in such a way as to suggest and coincide with the most philosophical accounts of the origin of this institution, and the very derivation of the word *pecunia*. If an ox were his property, and he wished to get needles and thread at the store, he thought it would be inconvenient and impossible soon to go on mortgaging some portion of the creature each time to that amount. He could defend many institutions better than any philosopher, because, in describing them as they concerned him, he gave the true reason for their prevalence, and speculation had not suggested to him any other. At another time, hearing Plato's definition of a man,—a biped without feathers,—and that one exhibited a cock plucked and called it Plato's man, he thought it an important difference that the *knees* bent the wrong way. He would sometimes exclaim, "How I love to talk! By George, I could talk all day!" I asked him once, when I had not seen him for many months, if he had got a new idea this summer. "Good Lord," said he, "a man that has to work as I do, if he does not forget the ideas he has had, he will do well. May be the man you hoe with is inclined to race; then, by gorry, your mind must be there; you think of weeds." He would sometimes ask me first on such occasions, if I had made any improvement. One winter day I asked him if he was always satisfied with himself, wishing to suggest a substitute within him for the priest without, and some higher motive for living. "Satisfied!" said he; "some men are satisfied with one thing, and some with another. One man, perhaps, if he has got enough, will be satisfied to sit all day with his back to the fire and his belly to the table, by George!" Yet I never, by any manœuvring, could get him to take the spiritual view of things; the highest that he appeared to conceive of was a simple expediency, such as you might expect an animal to appreciate; and this, practically, is true of most men. If I suggested any improvement in his mode of life, he merely answered, without expressing any regret, that it was too late. Yet he thoroughly believed in honesty and the like virtues.

There was a certain positive originality, however slight, to be detected in him, and I occasionally observed that he was thinking for himself and expressing his own opinion, a phenomenon so rare that I would any day walk ten miles to observe it, and it amounted to the re-origination of many of the institutions of society. Though he hesitated, and perhaps failed to express himself distinctly, he always had a presentable thought behind. Yet his thinking was so primitive and immersed in his animal life, that, though more promising than a merely learned man's, it rarely ripened to any thing which can be reported. He suggested that there might be men of genius in the lowest grades of life, however permanently humble and illiterate, who take their own view always, or do not pretend to see at all; who are as bottomless even as Walden Pond was thought to be, though they may be dark and muddy.

Many a traveller came out of his way to see me and the inside of my house, and, as an excuse for calling, asked for a glass of water. I told them that I drank at the pond, and pointed thither, offering to lend them a dipper. Far off as I lived, I was not exempted from that annual visitation which occurs, methinks, about the first of April, when every body is on the move; and I had my share of good luck, though there were some curious specimens among my visitors. Half-witted men from the almshouse and elsewhere came to see me; but I endeavored to make them exercise all the wit they had, and make their confessions to me; in such cases making wit the theme of our conversation; and so was compensated. Indeed, I found some of them to be wiser than the so called *overseers* of the poor and selectmen of the town, and thought it was time that the tables were turned. With respect to wit, I learned that there was not much difference between the half and the whole. One day, in particular, an inoffensive, simple-minded pauper, whom with others I had often seen used as fencing stuff, standing or sitting on a bushel in the fields to keep cattle and himself from straying, visited me, and expressed a wish to live as I did. He told me, with the utmost simplicity and truth, quite superior, or rather *inferior*, to any thing that is called humility, that he was "deficient in intellect." These were his words. The Lord had made him so, yet he supposed the Lord cared as much for him as for another. "I have always been so," said he, "from my childhood; I never had much mind; I was not like other children; I am weak in the head. It was the Lord's will, I suppose." And there he was to prove the truth of his words. He was a metaphysical puzzle to me. I have rarely met a fellow-man on such promising ground,—it was so simple and sincere and so true all that he said. And, true enough, in proportion as he appeared to humble himself was he exalted. I did not know at first but it was the result of a wise policy. It seemed that from such a basis of truth and frankness as the poor weak-headed pauper had laid, our intercourse might go forward to something better than the intercourse of sages.

I had some guests from those not reckoned commonly among the town's poor, but who should be; who are among the world's poor, at any rate; guests who appeal, not to your hospitality, but to your *hospitalality*; who earnestly wish to be helped, and preface their appeal with the information that they are resolved, for one thing, never to help themselves. I require of a visitor that he be not actually starving, though he may have the very best appetite in the world, however he got it. Objects of charity are not guests. Men who did not know when their visit had terminated, though I went about my business again, answering them from greater and greater remoteness. Men of almost every degree of wit called on me in the migrating season. Some who had more wits than they knew what to do with; runaway slaves with plantation manners, who listened from time to time, like the fox in the fable, as if they heard the hounds a-baying on their track, and looked at me beseechingly, as much as to say,—

"O Christian, will you send me back?"

One real runaway slave, among the rest, whom I helped to forward toward the northstar. Men of one idea, like a hen with one chicken, and that a duckling; men of a thousand ideas, and unkempt heads, like those hens which are made to take charge of a hundred chickens, all in pursuit of one bug, a score of them lost in every morning's dew,—and become frizzled and mangy in consequence; men of ideas instead of legs, a sort of intellectual centipede that made you crawl all over. One man proposed a book in which visitors should write their names, as at the White Mountains; but, alas! I have too good a memory to make that necessary.

I could not but notice some of the peculiarities of my visitors. Girls and boys and young women generally seemed glad to be in the woods. They looked in the pond and at the flowers, and improved their time. Men of business, even farmers, thought only of solitude and employment, and of the great distance at which I dwelt from something or other; and though they said that they loved a ramble in the woods occasionally, it was obvious that they did not. Restless committed men, whose time was all taken up in getting a living or keeping it; ministers who spoke of God as if they enjoyed a monopoly of the subject, who could not bear all kinds of opinions; doctors, lawyers, uneasy housekeepers who pried into my cupboard and bed when I was out,—how came Mrs. —— to know that my sheets were not as clean as hers?—young men who had ceased to be young, and had concluded that it was safest to follow the beaten track of the professions,—all these generally said that it was not possible to do so much good in my position. Ay! there was the rub. The old and infirm and the timid, of whatever age or sex, thought most of sickness, and sudden accident and death; to them life seemed full of danger,—what danger is there if you don't think of any?—and they thought that a prudent man would carefully select the safest position, where Dr. B. might be on hand at a moment's warning. To them the village was literally a *com-munity*, a league for mutual defence, and you would suppose that they would not go a-huckleberrying without a medicine chest. The amount of it is, if a man is alive, there is always *danger* that he may die, though the danger must be allowed to be less in proportion as he is dead-and-alive to begin with. A man sits as many risks as he runs.

Finally, there were the self-styled reformers, the greatest bores of all, who thought that I was forever singing,—

> This is the house that I built;
> This is the man that lives in the house that I built;

but they did not know that the third line was,—

> These are the folks that worry the man
> That lives in the house that I built.

I did not fear the hen-harriers, for I kept no chickens; but I feared the men-harriers rather.

I had more cheering visitors than the last. Children come a-berrying, railroad men taking a Sunday morning walk in clean shirts, fishermen and hunters, poets and philosophers, in short, all honest pilgrims, who came out to the woods for freedom's sake, and really left the village behind, I was ready to greet with,—"Welcome, Englishmen! welcome, Englishmen!" for I had had communication with that race.

The Bean-Field

MEANWHILE my beans, the length of whose rows, added together, was seven miles already planted, were impatient to be hoed, for the earliest had grown considerably before the latest were in the ground; indeed they were not easily to be put off. What was the meaning of this so steady and self-respecting, this small Herculean labor, I knew not. I came to love my rows, my beans, though so many more than I wanted. They attached me to the earth, and so I got strength like Antæus. But why should I raise them? Only Heaven knows. This was my curious labor all summer,—to make this portion of the earth's surface, which had yielded only cinquefoil, blackberries, johnswort, and the like, before, sweet wild fruits and pleasant flowers, produce instead this pulse. What shall I learn of beans or beans of me? I cherish them, I hoe them, early and late I have an eye to them; and this is my day's work. It is a fine broad leaf to look on. My auxiliaries are the dews and rains which water this dry soil, and what fertility is in the soil itself, which for the most part is lean and effete. My enemies are worms, cool days, and most of all woodchucks. The last have nibbled for me a quarter of an acre clean. But what right had I to oust johnswort and the rest, and break up their ancient herb garden? Soon, however, the remaining beans will be too tough for them, and go forward to meet new foes.

When I was four years old, as I well remember, I was brought from Boston to this my native town, through these very woods and this field, to the pond. It is one of the oldest scenes stamped on my memory. And now to-night my flute has waked the echoes over that very water. The pines still stand here older than I; or, if some have fallen, I have cooked my supper with their stumps, and a new growth is rising all around, preparing another aspect for new infant eyes. Almost the same johnswort springs from the same perennial root in this pasture, and even I have at length helped to clothe that fabulous landscape of my infant dreams, and one of the results of my presence and influence is seen in these bean leaves, corn blades, and potato vines.

I planted about two acres and a half of upland; and as it was only about fifteen years since the land was cleared, and I myself had got out two or three cords of stumps, I did not give it any manure; but in the course of the summer it appeared by the arrow-heads which I turned up in hoeing, that an extinct nation had anciently dwelt here and planted corn and beans ere white men came to clear the land, and so, to some extent, had exhausted the soil for this very crop.

Before yet any woodchuck or squirrel had run across the road, or the sun had got above the shrub-oaks, while all the dew was on, though the farmers warned me against it,—I would advise you to do all your work if possible while the dew is on,—I began to level the ranks of haughty weeds in my bean-field and throw dust upon their heads. Early in the morning I worked barefooted, dabbling like a plastic artist in the dewy and crumbling sand, but later in the day the sun blistered my feet. There the sun lighted me to hoe beans, pacing slowly backward and forward over that yellow gravelly upland, between the long green rows, fifteen rods, the one end terminating in a shrub oak copse where I could rest in the shade, the other in a blackberry field where the green berries deepened their tints by the time I had made another bout. Removing the weeds, putting fresh soil about the bean stems, and encouraging this weed which I had sown, making the yellow soil express its summer thought in bean leaves and blossoms rather than in wormwood and piper and millet grass, making the earth say beans instead of grass,—this was my daily work. As I had little aid from horses or cattle, or hired men or boys, or improved implements of husbandry, I was much slower, and became much more intimate with my beans than usual. But labor of the hands, even when pursued to the verge of drudgery, is perhaps never the worst form of idleness. It has a constant and imperishable moral, and to the scholar it yields a classic result. A very *agricola laboriosus* was I to travellers bound westward through Lincoln and Wayland to nobody knows where; they sitting at their ease in gigs, with elbows on knees, and reins loosely hanging in festoons; I the home-staying, laborious native of the soil. But soon my homestead was out of their sight and thought. It was the only open and cultivated field for a great distance on either side of the road; so they made the most of it; and sometimes the man in the field heard more of travellers' gossip and comment than was meant for his ear: "Beans so late! peas so late!"—for I continued to plant when others had began to hoe,—the ministerial husbandman had not suspected it. "Corn, my boy, for fodder; corn for fodder." "Docs he *live* there?" asks the black bonnet of the gray coat; and the hard-featured farmer reins up his grateful dobbin to inquire what you are doing where he sees no manure in the furrow, and recommends a little chip dirt, or any little waste stuff, or it may be ashes or plaster. But here were two acres and a half of furrows, and only a hoe for cart and two hands to draw it,—there being an aversion to other carts and horses,—and chip dirt far away. Fellow-travellers as they rattled by compared it aloud with the fields which they had passed, so that I came to know how I stood in the agricultural world. This was one field not in Mr. Coleman's report. And, by the way, who estimates the value of the crop which Nature yields in the still wilder fields unimproved by man? The crop of *English* hay is carefully weighed, the moisture calculated, the silicates and the potash; but in all dells and pond holes in the woods and pastures and swamps grows a rich and various crop only unreaped by man. Mine was, as it were, the connecting link between wild and cultivated fields; as some states are civilized, and others half-civilized, and others savage or barbarous, so my field was, though not in a bad sense, a half-cultivated field. They were beans cheerfully returning to their wild and primitive state that I cultivated, and my hoe played the *Rans des Vaches* for them.

Near at hand, upon the topmost spray of a birch, sings the brown-thrasher—or red mavis, as some love to call him—all the morning, glad of your society, that would find out another farmer's field if yours were not here. While you are planting the seed, he cries,—"Drop it, drop it,—cover it up, cover it up,—pull it up, pull it up, pull it up." But this was not corn, and so it was safe from such enemies as he. You may wonder what his rigmarole, his amateur Paganini performances on one string or on twenty, have to do with your planting, and yet prefer it to leached ashes or plaster. It was a cheap sort of top dressing in which I had entire faith.

As I drew a still fresher soil about the rows with my hoe, I disturbed the ashes of unchronicled nations who in primeval years lived under these heavens, and their small implements of war and hunting were brought to the light of this modern day. They lay mingled with other natural stones, some of which bore the marks of having been burned by Indian fires, and some by the sun, and also bits of pottery and glass brought hither by the recent cultivators of the soil. When my hoe tinkled against the stones, that music echoed to the woods and the sky, and was an accompaniment to my labor which yielded an instant and immeasurable crop. It was no longer beans that I hoed, nor I that hoed beans; and I remembered with as much pity as pride, if I remembered at all, my acquaintances who had gone to the city to attend the oratorios. The night-hawk circled overhead in the sunny afternoons—for I sometimes made a day of it—like a mote in the eye, or in heaven's eye, falling from time to time with a swoop and a sound as if the heavens were rent, torn at last to very rags and tatters, and yet a seamless cope remained; small imps that fill the air and lay their eggs on the ground on bare sand or rocks on the tops of hills, where few have found them; graceful and slender like ripples caught up from the pond, as leaves are raised by the wind to float in the heavens; such kindredship is in Nature. The hawk is aerial brother of the wave which he sails over and surveys, those his perfect air-inflated wings answering to the elemental unfledged pinions of the sea. Or sometimes I watched a pair of hen-hawks circling high in the sky, alternately soaring and descending, approaching and leaving one another, as if they were the imbodiment of my own thoughts. Or I was attracted by the passage of wild pigeons from this wood to that, with a slight quivering winnowing sound and carrier haste; or from under a rotten stump my hoe turned up a sluggish portentous and outlandish spotted salamander, a trace of Egypt and the Nile, yet our contemporary. When I paused to lean on my hoe, these sounds and sights I heard and saw any where in the row, a part of the inexhaustible entertainment which the country offers.

On gala days the town fires its great guns, which echo like popguns to these woods, and some waifs of martial music occasionally penetrate thus far. To me, away there in my bean-field at the other end of the town, the big guns sounded as if a puff ball had burst; and when there was a military turnout of which I was ignorant, I have sometimes had a vague sense all the day of some sort of itching and disease in the horizon, as if some eruption would break out there soon, either scarlatina or canker-rash, until at length some more favorable puff of wind, making haste over the fields and up the Wayland road, brought me information of the "trainers." It seemed by the distant hum as if somebody's bees had swarmed, and that the neighbors, according to Virgil's advice, by a faint *tintinnabulum* upon the most sonorous of their domestic utensils, were endeavoring to call them down into the hive again. And when the sound died quite away, and the hum had ceased, and the most favorable breezes told no tale, I knew that they had got the last drone of them all safely into the Middlesex hive, and that now their minds were bent on the honey with which it was smeared.

I felt proud to know that the liberties of Massachusetts and of our fatherland were in such safe keeping; and as I turned to my hoeing again I was filled with an inexpressible confidence, and pursued my labor cheerfully with a calm trust in the future.

When there were several bands of musicians, it sounded as if all the village was a vast bellows, and all the buildings expanded and collapsed alternately with a din. But sometimes it was a really noble and inspiring strain that reached these woods, and the trumpet that sings of fame, and I felt as if I could spit a Mexican with a good relish,—for why should we always stand for trifles?—and looked round for a woodchuck or a skunk to exercise my chivalry upon. These martial strains seemed as far away as Palestine, and reminded me of a march of crusaders in the horizon, with a slight tantivy and tremulous motion of the elm-tree tops which overhang the village. This was one of the *great* days; though the sky had from my clearing only the same everlastingly great look that it wears daily, and I saw no difference in it.

It was a singular experience that long acquaintance which I cultivated with beans, what with planting, and hoeing, and harvesting, and threshing, and picking over, and selling them,—the last was the hardest of all,—I might add eating, for I did taste. I was determined to know beans. When they were growing, I used to hoe from five o'clock in the morning till noon, and commonly spent the rest of the day about other affairs. Consider the intimate and curious acquaintance one makes with various kinds of weeds,—it will bear some iteration in the account, for there was no little iteration in the labor,—disturbing their delicate organizations so ruthlessly, and making such invidious distinctions with his hoe, levelling whole ranks of one species, and sedulously cultivating another. That's Roman wormwood,—that's pigweed,—that's sorrel,—that's piper-grass,—have at him, chop him up, turn his roots upward to the sun, don't let him have a fibre in the shade, if you do he'll turn himself t'other side up and be as green as a leek in two days. A long war, not with cranes, but with weeds, those Trojans who had sun and rain and dews on their side. Daily the beans saw me come to their rescue armed with a hoe, and thin the ranks of their enemies, filling up the trenches with weedy dead. Many a lusty crest-waving Hector, that towered a whole foot above his crowding comrades, fell before my weapon and rolled in the dust.

Those summer days which some of my contemporaries devoted to the fine arts in Boston or Rome, and others to contemplation in India, and others to trade in London or New York, I thus, with the other farmers of New England, devoted to husbandry. Not that I wanted beans to eat, for I am by nature a Pythagorean, so far as beans are concerned, whether they mean porridge or voting, and exchanged them for rice; but, perchance, as some must work in fields if only for the sake of tropes and expression, to serve a parable-maker one day. It was on the whole a rare amusement, which, continued too long, might have become a dissipation. Though I gave them no manure, and did not hoe them all once, I hoed them unusually well as far as I went, and was paid for it in the end, "there being in truth," as Evelyn says, "no compost or lætation whatsoever comparable to this continual motion, repastination, and turning of the mould with the spade." "The earth," he adds elsewhere, "especially if fresh, has a certain magnetism in it, by which it attracts the salt, power, or virtue (call it either) which gives it life, and is the logic of all the labor and stir we keep about it, to sustain us; all dungings and other sordid temperings being but the vicars succedaneous to this improvement." Moreover, this being one of those "worn-out and exhausted lay fields which enjoy their sabbath," had perchance, as Sir Kenelm Digby thinks likely, attracted "vital spirits" from the air. I harvested twelve bushels of beans.

But to be more particular; for it is complained that Mr. Coleman has reported chiefly the expensive experiments of gentlemen farmers; my outgoes were, —

For a hoe, ...	$0 54
Ploughing, harrowing, and furrowing, ...	7 50, Too much.
Beans for seed, ...	3 12½
Potatoes "	1 33
Peas "	0 40
Turnip seed, ...	0 06
White line for crow fence, ...	0 02
Horse cultivator and boy three hours, ...	1 00
Horse and cart to get crop, ...	0 75
In all, ...	$14 72½

My income was, (patrem familias vendacem, non emacem esse oportet,) from

Nine bushels and twelve quarts of beans sold, ...	$16 94
Five " large potatoes, ...	2 50
Nine " small "	2 25
Grass, ...	1 00
Stalks, ...	0 75
In all, ...	$23 44
Leaving a pecuniary profit, as I have elsewhere said, of	$8 71½.

This is the result of my experience in raising beans. Plant the common small white bush bean about the first of June, in rows three feet by eighteen inches apart, being careful to select fresh round and unmixed seed. First look out for worms, and supply vacancies by planting anew. Then look out for woodchucks, if it is an exposed place, for they will nibble off the earliest tender leaves almost clean as they go; and again, when the young tendrils make their appearance, they have notice of it, and will shear them off with both buds and young pods, sitting erect like a squirrel. But above all harvest as early as possible, if you would escape frosts and have a fair and salable crop; you may save much loss by this means.

This further experience also I gained. I said to myself, I will not plant beans and corn with so much industry another summer, but such seeds, if the seed is not lost, as sincerity, truth, simplicity, faith, innocence, and the like, and see if they will not grow in this soil, even with less toil and manurance, and sustain me, for surely it has not been exhausted for these crops. Alas! I said this to myself; but now another summer is gone, and another, and another, and I am obliged to say to you, Reader, that the seeds which I planted, if indeed they *were* the seeds of those virtues, were wormeaten or had lost their vitality, and so did not come up. Commonly men will only be brave as their fathers were brave, or timid. This generation is very sure to plant corn and beans each new year precisely as the Indians did centuries ago and taught the first settlers to do, as if there were a fate in it. I saw an old man the other day, to my astonishment, making the holes with a hoe for the seventieth time at least, and not for himself to lie down in! But why should not the New Englander try new adventures, and not lay so much stress on his grain, his potato and grass crop, and his orchards?— raise other crops than these? Why concern ourselves so much about our beans for seed, and not be concerned at all about a new generation of men? We should really be fed and cheered if when we met a man we were sure to see that some of the qualities which I have named, which we all prize more than those other productions, but which are for the most part broadcast and floating in the air, had taken root and grown in him. Here comes such a subtile and ineffable quality, for instance, as truth or justice, though the slightest amount or new variety of it, along the road. Our ambassadors should be instructed to send home such seeds as these, and Congress help to distribute them over all the land. We should never stand upon ceremony with sincerity. We should never cheat and insult and banish one another by our meanness, if there were present the kernel of worth and friendliness. We should not meet thus in haste. Most men I do not meet at all, for they seem not to have time; they are busy about their beans. We would not deal with a man thus plodding ever, leaning on a hoe or a spade as a staff between his work, not as a mushroom, but partially risen out of the

earth, something more than erect, like swallows alighted and
walking on the ground. —

> "And as he spake, his wings would now and then
> Spread, as he meant to fly, then close again,"

so that we should suspect that we might be conversing with
an angel. Bread may not always nourish us; but it always does
us good, it even takes stiffness out of our joints, and makes
us supple and buoyant, when we knew not what ailed us, to
recognize any generosity in man or Nature, to share any unmixed and heroic joy.

Ancient poetry and mythology suggest, at least, that husbandry was once a sacred art; but it is pursued with irreverent
haste and heedlessness by us, our object being to have large
farms and large crops merely. We have no festival, nor procession, nor ceremony, not excepting our Cattle-shows and so
called Thanksgivings, by which the farmer expresses a sense
of the sacredness of his calling, or is reminded of its sacred
origin. It is the premium and the feast which tempt him. He
sacrifices not to Ceres and the Terrestrial Jove, but to the infernal Plutus rather. By avarice and selfishness, and a grovelling habit, from which none of us is free, of regarding the soil
as property, or the means of acquiring property chiefly, the
landscape is deformed, husbandry is degraded with us, and
the farmer leads the meanest of lives. He knows Nature but
as a robber. Cato says that the profits of agriculture are particularly pious or just, (*maximeque pius quæstus,*) and according to Varro the old Romans "called the same earth Mother
and Ceres, and thought that they who cultivated it led a pious
and useful life, and that they alone were left of the race of
King Saturn."

We are wont to forget that the sun looks on our cultivated
fields and on the prairies and forests without distinction.
They all reflect and absorb his rays alike, and the former make
but a small part of the glorious picture which he beholds in
his daily course. In his view the earth is all equally cultivated
like a garden. Therefore we should receive the benefit of his
light and heat with a corresponding trust and magnanimity.
What though I value the seed of these beans, and harvest that
in the fall of the year? This broad field which I have looked

at so long looks not to me as the principal cultivator, but away from me to influences more genial to it, which water and make it green. These beans have results which are not harvested by me. Do they not grow for woodchucks partly? The ear of wheat, (in Latin *spica*, obsoletely *speca*, from *spe*, hope,) should not be the only hope of the husbandman; its kernel or grain (*granum*, from *gerendo*, bearing,) is not all that it bears. How, then, can our harvest fail? Shall I not rejoice also at the abundance of the weeds whose seeds are the granary of the birds? It matters little comparatively whether the fields fill the farmer's barns. The true husbandman will cease from anxiety, as the squirrels manifest no concern whether the woods will bear chestnuts this year or not, and finish his labor with every day, relinquishing all claim to the produce of his fields, and sacrificing in his mind not only his first but his last fruits also.

The Village

AFTER HOEING, or perhaps reading and writing, in the forenoon, I usually bathed again in the pond, swimming across one of its coves for a stint, and washed the dust of labor from my person, or smoothed out the last wrinkle which study had made, and for the afternoon was absolutely free. Every day or two I strolled to the village to hear some of the gossip which is incessantly going on there, circulating either from mouth to mouth, or from newspaper to newspaper, and which, taken in homœopathic doses, was really as refreshing in its way as the rustle of leaves and the peeping of frogs. As I walked in the woods to see the birds and squirrels, so I walked in the village to see the men and boys; instead of the wind among the pines I heard the carts rattle. In one direction from my house there was a colony of muskrats in the river meadows; under the grove of elms and buttonwoods in the other horizon was a village of busy men, as curious to me as if they had been prairie dogs, each sitting at the mouth of its burrow, or running over to a neighbor's to gossip. I went there frequently to observe their habits. The village appeared to me a great news room; and on one side, to support it, as once at Redding & Company's on State Street, they kept nuts and raisins, or salt and meal and other groceries. Some have such a vast appetite for the former commodity, that is, the news, and such sound digestive organs, that they can sit forever in public avenues without stirring, and let it simmer and whisper through them like the Etesian winds, or as if inhaling ether, it only producing numbness and insensibility to pain,—otherwise it would often be painful to hear,—without affecting the consciousness. I hardly ever failed, when I rambled through the village, to see a row of such worthies, either sitting on a ladder sunning themselves, with their bodies inclined forward and their eyes glancing along the line this way and that, from time to time, with a voluptuous expression, or else leaning against a barn with their hands in their pockets, like caryatides, as if to prop it up. They, being commonly out of doors, heard whatever was in the wind. These are the coarsest mills, in which all gossip is first rudely digested or cracked up before it is emptied into finer and more delicate hoppers within doors. I observed that the vitals of the village were the grocery, the bar-room, the post-office, and the bank; and, as a necessary part of the machinery, they kept a bell, a big gun, and a fire-engine, at convenient places; and the houses were so arranged as to make the most of mankind, in lanes and fronting one another, so that every traveller had to run the gantlet, and every man, woman, and child might get a lick at him. Of course, those who were stationed nearest to the head of the line, where they could most see and be seen, and have the first blow at him, paid the highest prices for their places; and the few straggling inhabitants in the outskirts, where long gaps in the line began to occur, and the traveller could get over walls or turn aside into cow paths, and so escape, paid a very slight ground or window tax. Signs were hung out on all sides to allure him; some to catch him by the appetite, as the tavern and victualling cellar; some by the fancy, as the dry goods store and the jeweller's; and others by the hair or the feet or the skirts, as the barber, the shoemaker, or the tailor. Besides, there was a still more terrible standing invitation to call at every one of these houses, and company expected about these times. For the most part I escaped wonderfully from these dangers, either by proceeding at once boldly and without deliberation to the goal, as is recommended to those who run the gantlet, or by keeping my thoughts on high things, like Orpheus, who, "loudly singing the praises of the gods to his lyre, drowned the voices of the Sirens, and kept out of danger." Sometimes I bolted suddenly, and nobody could tell my whereabouts, for I did not stand much about gracefulness, and never hesitated at a gap in a fence. I was even accustomed to make an irruption into some houses, where I was well entertained, and after learning the kernels and very last sieve-ful of news, what had subsided, the prospects of war and peace, and whether the world was likely to hold together much longer, I was let out through the rear avenues, and so escaped to the woods again.

It was very pleasant, when I staid late in town, to launch myself into the night, especially if it was dark and tempestuous, and set sail from some bright village parlor or lecture room, with a bag of rye or Indian meal upon my shoulder, for my snug harbor in the woods, having made all tight without and withdrawn under hatches with a merry crew of thoughts, leaving only my outer man at the helm, or even tying up the helm when it was plain sailing. I had many a genial thought by the cabin fire "as I sailed." I was never cast away nor distressed in any weather, though I encountered some severe storms. It is darker in the woods, even in common nights, than most suppose. I frequently had to look up at the opening between the trees above the path in order to learn my route, and, where there was no cart-path, to feel with my feet the faint track which I had worn, or steer by the known relation of particular trees which I felt with my hands, passing between two pines for instance, not more than eighteen inches apart, in the midst of the woods, invariably in the darkest night. Sometimes, after coming home thus late in a dark and muggy night, when my feet felt the path which my eyes could not see, dreaming and absent-minded all the way, until I was aroused by having to raise my hand to lift the latch, I have not been able to recall a single step of my walk, and I have thought that perhaps my body would find its way home if its master should forsake it, as the hand finds its way to the mouth without assistance. Several times, when a visitor chanced to stay into evening, and it proved a dark night, I was obliged to conduct him to the cart-path in the rear of the house, and then point out to him the direction he was to pursue, and in keeping which he was to be guided rather by his feet than his eyes. One very dark night I directed thus on their way two young men who had been fishing in the pond. They lived about a mile off through the woods, and were quite used to the route. A day or two after one of them told me that they wandered about the greater part of the night, close by their own premises, and did not get home till toward morning, by which time, as there had been several heavy showers in the mean while, and the leaves were very wet, they were drenched to their skins. I have heard of many going astray even in the village streets, when the darkness was so thick that you could cut it with a knife, as the saying is. Some who live in the outskirts, having come to town a-shopping in their wagons, have been obliged to put up for the night; and

gentlemen and ladies making a call have gone half a mile out
of their way, feeling the sidewalk only with their feet, and not
knowing when they turned. It is a surprising and memorable,
as well as valuable experience, to be lost in the woods any
time. Often in a snow storm, even by day, one will come out
upon a well-known road, and yet find it impossible to tell
which way leads to the village. Though he knows that he has
travelled it a thousand times, he cannot recognize a feature in
it, but it is as strange to him as if it were a road in Siberia.
By night, of course, the perplexity is infinitely greater. In our
most trivial walks, we are constantly, though unconsciously,
steering like pilots by certain well-known beacons and headlands, and if we go beyond our usual course we still carry in
our minds the bearing of some neighboring cape; and not till
we are completely lost, or turned round,—for a man needs
only to be turned round once with his eyes shut in this world
to be lost,—do we appreciate the vastness and strangeness of
Nature. Every man has to learn the points of compass again
as often as he awakes, whether from sleep or any abstraction.
Not till we are lost, in other words, not till we have lost the
world, do we begin to find ourselves, and realize where we
are and the infinite extent of our relations.

One afternoon, near the end of the first summer, when I
went to the village to get a shoe from the cobbler's, I was
seized and put into jail, because, as I have elsewhere related,
I did not pay a tax to, or recognize the authority of, the state
which buys and sells men, women, and children, like cattle at
the door of its senate-house. I had gone down to the woods
for other purposes. But, wherever a man goes, men will pursue and paw him with their dirty institutions, and, if they can,
constrain him to belong to their desperate odd-fellow society.
It is true, I might have resisted forcibly with more or less
effect, might have run "amok" against society; but I preferred
that society should run "amok" against me, it being the desperate party. However, I was released the next day, obtained
my mended shoe, and returned to the woods in season to get
my dinner of huckleberries on Fair-Haven Hill. I was never
molested by any person but those who represented the state.
I had no lock nor bolt but for the desk which held my papers,
not even a nail to put over my latch or windows. I never

fastened my door night or day, though I was to be absent several days; not even when the next fall I spent a fortnight in the woods of Maine. And yet my house was more respected than if it had been surrounded by a file of soldiers. The tired rambler could rest and warm himself by my fire, the literary amuse himself with the few books on my table, or the curious, by opening my closet door, see what was left of my dinner, and what prospect I had of a supper. Yet, though many people of every class came this way to the pond, I suffered no serious inconvenience from these sources, and I never missed any thing but one small book, a volume of Homer, which perhaps was improperly gilded, and this I trust a soldier of our camp has found by this time. I am convinced, that if all men were to live as simply as I then did, thieving and robbery would be unknown. These take place only in communities where some have got more than is sufficient while others have not enough. The Pope's Homers would soon get properly distributed.—

> "Nec bella fuerunt,
> Faginus astabat dum scyphus ante dapes."
> "Nor wars did men molest,
> When only beechen bowls were in request."

"You who govern public affairs, what need have you to employ punishments? Love virtue, and the people will be virtuous. The virtues of a superior man are like the wind; the virtues of a common man are like the grass; the grass, when the wind passes over it, bends."

The Ponds

SOMETIMES, having had a surfeit of human society and gossip, and worn out all my village friends, I rambled still farther westward than I habitually dwell, into yet more unfrequented parts of the town, "to fresh woods and pastures new," or, while the sun was setting, made my supper of huckleberries and blueberries on Fair Haven Hill, and laid up a store for several days. The fruits do not yield their true flavor to the purchaser of them, nor to him who raises them for the market. There is but one way to obtain it, yet few take that way. If you would know the flavor of huckleberries, ask the cow-boy or the partridge. It is a vulgar error to suppose that you have tasted huckleberries who never plucked them. A huckleberry never reaches Boston; they have not been known there since they grew on her three hills. The ambrosial and essential part of the fruit is lost with the bloom which is rubbed off in the market cart, and they become mere provender. As long as Eternal Justice reigns, not one innocent huckleberry can be transported thither from the country's hills.

Occasionally, after my hoeing was done for the day, I joined some impatient companion who had been fishing on the pond since morning, as silent and motionless as a duck or a floating leaf, and, after practising various kinds of philosophy, had concluded commonly, by the time I arrived, that he belonged to the ancient sect of Cœnobites. There was one older man, an excellent fisher and skilled in all kinds of woodcraft, who was pleased to look upon my house as a building erected for the convenience of fishermen; and I was equally pleased when he sat in my doorway to arrange his lines. Once in a while we sat together on the pond, he at one end of the boat, and I at the other; but not many words passed between us, for he had grown deaf in his later years, but he occasionally hummed a psalm, which harmonized well enough with my philosophy. Our intercourse was thus altogether one of unbroken harmony, far more pleasing to remember than if it had been carried on by speech. When, as was commonly the case, I had none to commune with, I used to raise the echoes by striking with a paddle on the side of my boat, filling the surrounding woods with circling and dilating sound, stirring them up as the keeper of a menagerie his wild beasts, until I elicited a growl from every wooded vale and hill-side.

In warm evenings I frequently sat in the boat playing the flute, and saw the perch, which I seemed to have charmed, hovering around me, and the moon travelling over the ribbed bottom, which was strewed with the wrecks of the forest. Formerly I had come to this pond adventurously, from time to time, in dark summer nights, with a companion, and making a fire close to the water's edge, which we thought attracted the fishes, we caught pouts with a bunch of worms strung on a thread; and when we had done, far in the night, threw the burning brands high into the air like skyrockets, which, coming down into the pond, were quenched with a loud hissing, and we were suddenly groping in total darkness. Through this, whistling a tune, we took our way to the haunts of men again. But now I had made my home by the shore.

Sometimes, after staying in a village parlor till the family had all retired, I have returned to the woods, and, partly with a view to the next day's dinner, spent the hours of midnight fishing from a boat by moonlight, serenaded by owls and foxes, and hearing, from time to time, the creaking note of some unknown bird close at hand. These experiences were very memorable and valuable to me,—anchored in forty feet of water, and twenty or thirty rods from the shore, surrounded sometimes by thousands of small perch and shiners, dimpling the surface with their tails in the moonlight, and communicating by a long flaxen line with mysterious nocturnal fishes which had their dwelling forty feet below, or sometimes dragging sixty feet of line about the pond as I drifted in the gentle night breeze, now and then feeling a slight vibration along it, indicative of some life prowling about its extremity, of dull uncertain blundering purpose there, and slow to make up its mind. At length you slowly raise, pulling hand over hand, some horned pout squeaking and squirming to the upper air. It was very queer, especially in dark nights, when your thoughts had wandered to vast and cosmogonal themes in other spheres, to feel this faint jerk, which came to interrupt your dreams and link you to Nature again. It seemed as if I might next cast my line upward into the air, as well as downward into this element which was scarcely more dense. Thus I caught two fishes as it were with one hook.

The scenery of Walden is on a humble scale, and, though very beautiful, does not approach to grandeur, nor can it much concern one who has not long frequented it or lived by its shore; yet this pond is so remarkable for its depth and purity as to merit a particular description. It is a clear and deep green well, half a mile long and a mile and three quarters in circumference, and contains about sixty-one and a half acres; a perennial spring in the midst of pine and oak woods, without any visible inlet or outlet except by the clouds and evaporation. The surrounding hills rise abruptly from the water to the height of forty to eighty feet, though on the southeast and east they attain to about one hundred and one hundred and fifty feet respectively, within a quarter and a third of a mile. They are exclusively woodland. All our Concord waters have two colors at least, one when viewed at a distance, and another, more proper, close at hand. The first depends more on the light, and follows the sky. In clear weather, in summer, they appear blue at a little distance, especially if agitated, and at a great distance all appear alike. In stormy weather they are sometimes of a dark slate color. The sea, however, is said to be blue one day and green another without any perceptible change in the atmosphere. I have seen our river, when, the landscape being covered with snow, both water and ice were almost as green as grass. Some consider blue "to be the color of pure water, whether liquid or solid." But, looking directly down into our waters from a boat, they are seen to be of very different colors. Walden is blue at one time and green at another, even from the same point of view. Lying between the earth and the heavens, it partakes of the color of both. Viewed from a hill-top it reflects the color of the sky, but near at hand it is of a yellowish tint next the shore where you can see the sand, then a light green, which gradually deepens to a uniform dark green in the body of the pond. In some lights, viewed even from a hill-top, it is of a vivid green next the shore. Some have re-

ferred this to the reflection of the verdure; but it is equally
green there against the railroad sand-bank, and in the spring,
before the leaves are expanded, and it may be simply the result of the prevailing blue mixed with the yellow of the sand.
Such is the color of its iris. This is that portion, also, where
in the spring, the ice being warmed by the heat of the sun
reflected from the bottom, and also transmitted through the
earth, melts first and forms a narrow canal about the still frozen middle. Like the rest of our waters, when much agitated,
in clear weather, so that the surface of the waves may reflect
the sky at the right angle, or because there is more light
mixed with it, it appears at a little distance of a darker blue
than the sky itself; and at such a time, being on its surface,
and looking with divided vision, so as to see the reflection, I
have discerned a matchless and indescribable light blue, such
as watered or changeable silks and sword blades suggest,
more cerulean than the sky itself, alternating with the original
dark green on the opposite sides of the waves, which last appeared but muddy in comparison. It is a vitreous greenish
blue, as I remember it, like those patches of the winter sky
seen through cloud vistas in the west before sundown. Yet a
single glass of its water held up to the light is as colorless as
an equal quantity of air. It is well known that a large plate of
glass will have a green tint, owing, as the makers say, to its
"body," but a small piece of the same will be colorless. How
large a body of Walden water would be required to reflect a
green tint I have never proved. The water of our river is black
or a very dark brown to one looking directly down on it, and,
like that of most ponds, imparts to the body of one bathing
in it a yellowish tinge; but this water is of such crystalline
purity that the body of the bather appears of an alabaster
whiteness, still more unnatural, which, as the limbs are mag-
nified and distorted withal, produces a monstrous effect, making fit studies for a Michael Angelo.

The water is so transparent that the bottom can easily be
discerned at the depth of twenty-five or thirty feet. Paddling
over it, you may see many feet beneath the surface the schools
of perch and shiners, perhaps only an inch long, yet the former easily distinguished by their transverse bars, and you
think that they must be ascetic fish that find a subsistence

there. Once, in the winter, many years ago, when I had been cutting holes through the ice in order to catch pickerel, as I stepped ashore I tossed my axe back on to the ice, but, as if some evil genius had directed it, it slid four or five rods directly into one of the holes, where the water was twenty-five feet deep. Out of curiosity, I lay down on the ice and looked through the hole, until I saw the axe a little on one side, standing on its head, with its helve erect and gently swaying to and fro with the pulse of the pond; and there it might have stood erect and swaying till in the course of time the handle rotted off, if I had not disturbed it. Making another hole directly over it with an ice chisel which I had, and cutting down the longest birch which I could find in the neighborhood with my knife, I made a slip-noose, which I attached to its end, and, letting it down carefully, passed it over the knob of the handle, and drew it by a line along the birch, and so pulled the axe out again.

The shore is composed of a belt of smooth rounded white stones like paving stones, excepting one or two short sand beaches, and is so steep that in many places a single leap will carry you into water over your head; and were it not for its remarkable transparency, that would be the last to be seen of its bottom till it rose on the opposite side. Some think it is bottomless. It is nowhere muddy, and a casual observer would say that there were no weeds at all in it; and of noticeable plants, except in the little meadows recently overflowed, which do not properly belong to it, a closer scrutiny does not detect a flag nor a bulrush, nor even a lily, yellow or white, but only a few small heart-leaves and potamogetons, and perhaps a water-target or two; all which however a bather might not perceive; and these plants are clean and bright like the element they grow in. The stones extend a rod or two into the water, and then the bottom is pure sand, except in the deepest parts, where there is usually a little sediment, probably from the decay of the leaves which have been wafted on to it so many successive falls, and a bright green weed is brought up on anchors even in midwinter.

We have one other pond just like this, White Pond in Nine Acre Corner, about two and a half miles westerly; but, though I am acquainted with most of the ponds within a

dozen miles of this centre, I do not know a third of this pure
and well-like character. Successive nations perchance have
drank at, admired, and fathomed it, and passed away, and still
its water is green and pellucid as ever. Not an intermitting
spring! Perhaps on that spring morning when Adam and Eve
were driven out of Eden Walden Pond was already in existence, and even then breaking up in a gentle spring rain accompanied with mist and a southerly wind, and covered with
myriads of ducks and geese, which had not heard of the fall,
when still such pure lakes sufficed them. Even then it had
commenced to rise and fall, and had clarified its waters and
colored them of the hue they now wear, and obtained a patent of heaven to be the only Walden Pond in the world and
distiller of celestial dews. Who knows in how many un-
remembered nations' literatures this has been the Castalian
Fountain? or what nymphs presided over it in the Golden
Age? It is a gem of the first water which Concord wears in
her coronet.

Yet perchance the first who came to this well have left some
trace of their footsteps. I have been surprised to detect encircling the pond, even where a thick wood has just been cut
down on the shore, a narrow shelf-like path in the steep hill-
side, alternately rising and falling, approaching and receding
from the water's edge, as old probably as the race of man
here, worn by the feet of aboriginal hunters, and still from
time to time unwittingly trodden by the present occupants of
the land. This is particularly distinct to one standing on the
middle of the pond in winter, just after a light snow has
fallen, appearing as a clear undulating white line, unobscured
by weeds and twigs, and very obvious a quarter of a mile off
in many places where in summer it is hardly distinguishable
close at hand. The snow reprints it, as it were, in clear white
type alto-relievo. The ornamented grounds of villas which
will one day be built here may still preserve some trace of this.

The pond rises and falls, but whether regularly or not, and
within what period, nobody knows, though, as usual, many
pretend to know. It is commonly higher in the winter and
lower in the summer, though not corresponding to the general wet and dryness. I can remember when it was a foot or
two lower, and also when it was at least five feet higher, than

when I lived by it. There is a narrow sand-bar running into it, with very deep water on one side, on which I helped boil a kettle of chowder, some six rods from the main shore, about the year 1824, which it has not been possible to do for twenty-five years; and on the other hand, my friends used to listen with incredulity when I told them, that a few years later I was accustomed to fish from a boat in a secluded cove in the woods, fifteen rods from the only shore they knew, which place was long since converted into a meadow. But the pond has risen steadily for two years, and now, in the summer of '52, is just five feet higher than when I lived there, or as high as it was thirty years ago, and fishing goes on again in the meadow. This makes a difference of level, at the outside, of six or seven feet; and yet the water shed by the surrounding hills is insignificant in amount, and this overflow must be referred to causes which affect the deep springs. This same summer the pond has begun to fall again. It is remarkable that this fluctuation, whether periodical or not, appears thus to require many years for its accomplishment. I have observed one rise and a part of two falls, and I expect that a dozen or fifteen years hence the water will again be as low as I have ever known it. Flints' Pond, a mile eastward, allowing for the disturbance occasioned by its inlets and outlets, and the smaller intermediate ponds also, sympathize with Walden, and recently attained their greatest height at the same time with the latter. The same is true, as far as my observation goes, of White Pond.

This rise and fall of Walden at long intervals serves this use at least; the water standing at this great height for a year or more, though it makes it difficult to walk round it, kills the shrubs and trees which have sprung up about its edge since the last rise, pitch-pines, birches, alders, aspens, and others, and, falling again, leaves an unobstructed shore; for, unlike many ponds and all waters which are subject to a daily tide, its shore is cleanest when the water is lowest. On the side of the pond next my house, a row of pitch pines fifteen feet high has been killed and tipped over as if by a lever, and thus a stop put to their encroachments; and their size indicates how many years have elapsed since the last rise to this height. By this fluctuation the pond asserts its title to a shore, and thus the *shore* is *shorn*, and the trees cannot hold it by right of possession. These are the lips of the lake on which no beard grows. It licks its chaps from time to time. When the water is at its height, the alders, willows, and maples send forth a mass of fibrous red roots several feet long from all sides of their stems in the water, and to the height of three or four feet from the ground, in the effort to maintain themselves; and I have known the high-blueberry bushes about the shore, which commonly produce no fruit, bear an abundant crop under these circumstances.

Some have been puzzled to tell how the shore became so regularly paved. My townsmen have all heard the tradition, the oldest people tell me that they heard it in their youth, that anciently the Indians were holding a pow-wow upon a hill here, which rose as high into the heavens as the pond now sinks deep into the earth, and they used much profanity, as the story goes, though this vice is one of which the Indians were never guilty, and while they were thus engaged the hill shook and suddenly sank, and only one old squaw, named Walden, escaped, and from her the pond was named. It has been conjectured that when the hill shook these stones rolled down its side and became the present shore. It is very certain, at any rate, that once there was no pond here, and now there is one; and this Indian fable does not in any respect conflict with the account of that ancient settler whom I have mentioned, who remembers so well when he first came here with his divining rod, saw a thin vapor rising from the sward, and the hazel pointed steadily downward, and he concluded to dig a well here. As for the stones, many still think that they are hardly to be accounted for by the action of the waves on these hills; but I observe that the surrounding hills are remarkably full of the same kind of stones, so that they have been obliged to pile them up in walls on both sides of the railroad cut nearest the pond; and, moreover, there are most stones where the shore is most abrupt; so that, unfortunately, it is no longer a mystery to me. I detect the paver. If the name was not derived from that of some English locality,—Saffron Walden, for instance,—one might suppose that it was called, originally, *Walled-in* Pond.

The pond was my well ready dug. For four months in the

year its water is as cold as it is pure at all times; and I think that it is then as good as any, if not the best, in the town. In the winter, all water which is exposed to the air is colder than springs and wells which are protected from it. The temperature of the pond water which had stood in the room where I sat from five o'clock in the afternoon till noon the next day, the sixth of March, 1846, the thermometer having been up to 65° or 70° some of the time, owing partly to the sun on the roof, was 42°, or one degree colder than the water of one of the coldest wells in the village just drawn. The temperature of the Boiling Spring the same day was 45°, or the warmest of any water tried, though it is the coldest that I know of in summer, when, beside, shallow and stagnant surface water is not mingled with it. Moreover, in summer, Walden never becomes so warm as most water which is exposed to the sun, on account of its depth. In the warmest weather I usually placed a pailful in my cellar, where it became cool in the night, and remained so during the day; though I also resorted to a spring in the neighborhood. It was as good when a week old as the day it was dipped, and had no taste of the pump. Whoever camps for a week in summer by the shore of a pond, needs only bury a pail of water a few feet deep in the shade of his camp to be independent on the luxury of ice.

There have been caught in Walden, pickerel, one weighing seven pounds, to say nothing of another which carried off a reel with great velocity, which the fisherman safely set down at eight pounds because he did not see him, perch and pouts, some of each weighing over two pounds, shiners, chivins or roach, (*Leuciscus pulchellus*,) a very few breams, and a couple of eels, one weighing four pounds,—I am thus particular because the weight of a fish is commonly its only title to fame, and these are the only eels I have heard of here;—also, I have a faint recollection of a little fish some five inches long, with silvery sides and a greenish back, somewhat dace-like in its character, which I mention here chiefly to link my facts to fable. Nevertheless, this pond is not very fertile in fish. Its pickerel, though not abundant, are its chief boasts. I have seen at one time lying on the ice pickerel of at least three different kinds; a long and shallow one, steel-colored, most like those caught in the river; a bright golden kind, with greenish reflections and remarkably deep, which is the most common here; and another, golden-colored, and shaped like the last, but peppered on the sides with small dark brown or black spots, intermixed with a few faint blood-red ones, very much like a trout. The specific name *reticulatus* would not apply to this; it should be *guttatus* rather. These are all very firm fish, and weigh more than their size promises. The shiners, pouts, and perch also, and indeed all the fishes which inhabit this pond, are much cleaner, handsomer, and firmer fleshed than those in the river and most other ponds, as the water is purer, and they can easily be distinguished from them. Probably many ichthyologists would make new varieties of some of them. There are also a clean race of frogs and tortoises, and a few muscles in it; muskrats and minks leave their traces about it, and occasionally a travelling mud-turtle visits it. Sometimes, when I pushed off my boat in the morning, I disturbed a great mud-turtle which had secreted himself under the boat in the night. Ducks and geese frequent it in the spring and fall, the white-bellied swallows (*Hirundo bicolor*) skim over it, the kingfishers sound their alarm around it and the peetweets (*Totanus macularius*) "teter" along its stony shores all summer. I have sometimes disturbed a fishhawk sitting on a white-pine over the water; but I doubt if it is ever profaned by the wing of a gull, like Fair Haven. At most, it tolerates one annual loon. These are all the animals of consequence which frequent it now.

You may see from a boat, in calm weather, near the sandy eastern shore, where the water is eight or ten feet deep, and also in some other parts of the pond, some circular heaps half a dozen feet in diameter by a foot in height, consisting of small stones less than a hen's egg in size, where all around is bare sand. At first you wonder if the Indians could have formed them on the ice for any purpose, and when the ice melted, they sank to the bottom; but they are too regular and some of them plainly too fresh for that. They are similar to those found in rivers; but as there are no suckers nor lampreys here, I know not by what fish they could be made. Perhaps they are the nests of the chivin. These lend a pleasing mystery to the bottom.

The shore is irregular enough not to be monotonous. I

have in my mind's eye the western indented with deep bays, the bolder northern, and the beautifully scolloped southern shore, where successive capes overlap each other and suggest unexplored coves between. The forest has never so good a setting, nor is so distinctly beautiful, as when seen from the middle of a small lake amid hills which rise from the water's edge; for the water in which it is reflected not only makes the best foreground in such a case, but, with its winding shore, the most natural and agreeable boundary to it. There is no rawness nor imperfection in its edge there, as where the axe has cleared a part, or a cultivated field abuts on it. The trees have ample room to expand on the water side, and each sends forth its most vigorous branch in that direction. There Nature has woven a natural selvage, and the eye rises by just gradations from the low shrubs of the shore to the highest trees. There are few traces of man's hand to be seen. The water laves the shore as it did a thousand years ago.

A lake is the landscape's most beautiful and expressive feature. It is earth's eye; looking into which the beholder measures the depth of his own nature. The fluviatile trees next the shore are the slender eyelashes which fringe it, and the wooded hills and cliffs around are its overhanging brows.

Standing on the smooth sandy beach at the east end of the pond, in a calm September afternoon, when a slight haze makes the opposite shore line indistinct, I have seen whence came the expression, "the glassy surface of a lake." When you invert your head, it looks like a thread of finest gossamer stretched across the valley, and gleaming against the distant pine woods, separating one stratum of the atmosphere from another. You would think that you could walk dry under it to the opposite hills, and that the swallows which skim over might perch on it. Indeed, they sometimes dive below the line, as it were by mistake, and are undeceived. As you look over the pond westward you are obliged to employ both your hands to defend your eyes against the reflected as well as the true sun, for they are equally bright; and if, between the two, you survey its surface critically, it is literally as smooth as glass, except where the skater insects, at equal intervals scattered over its whole extent, by their motions in the sun produce the finest imaginable sparkle on it, or, perchance, a duck

plumes itself, or, as I have said, a swallow skims so low as to
touch it. It may be that in the distance a fish describes an arc
of three or four feet in the air, and there is one bright flash
where it emerges, and another where it strikes the water;
sometimes the whole silvery arc is revealed; or here and there,
perhaps, is a thistle-down floating on its surface, which the
fishes dart at and so dimple it again. It is like molten glass
cooled but not congealed, and the few motes in it are pure
and beautiful like the imperfections in glass. You may often
detect a yet smoother and darker water, separated from the
rest as if by an invisible cobweb, boom of the water nymphs,
resting on it. From a hill-top you can see a fish leap in almost
any part; for not a pickerel or shiner picks an insect from this
smooth surface but it manifestly disturbs the equilibrium of
the whole lake. It is wonderful with what elaborateness this
simple fact is advertised,—this piscine murder will out,—and
from my distant perch I distinguish the circling undulations
when they are half a dozen rods in diameter. You can even
detect a water-bug (*Gyrinus*) ceaselessly progressing over the
smooth surface a quarter of a mile off; for they furrow the
water slightly, making a conspicuous ripple bounded by two
diverging lines, but the skaters glide over it without rippling
it perceptibly. When the surface is considerably agitated there
are no skaters nor water-bugs on it, but apparently, in calm
days, they leave their havens and adventurously glide forth
from the shore by short impulses till they completely cover it.
It is a soothing employment, on one of those fine days in the
fall when all the warmth of the sun is fully appreciated, to sit
on a stump on such a height as this, overlooking the pond,
and study the dimpling circles which are incessantly inscribed
on its otherwise invisible surface amid the reflected skies and
trees. Over this great expanse there is no disturbance but it is
thus at once gently smoothed away and assuaged, as, when a
vase of water is jarred, the trembling circles seek the shore and
all is smooth again. Not a fish can leap or an insect fall on the
pond but it is thus reported in circling dimples, in lines of
beauty, as it were the constant welling up of its fountain, the
gentle pulsing of its life, the heaving of its breast. The thrills
of joy and thrills of pain are undistinguishable. How peaceful
the phenomena of the lake! Again the works of man shine as

in the spring. Ay, every leaf and twig and stone and cobweb sparkles now at mid-afternoon as when covered with dew in a spring morning. Every motion of an oar or an insect produces a flash of light; and if an oar falls, how sweet the echo!

In such a day, in September or October, Walden is a perfect forest mirror, set round with stones as precious to my eye as if fewer or rarer. Nothing so fair, so pure, and at the same time so large, as a lake, perchance, lies on the surface of the earth. Sky water. It needs no fence. Nations come and go without defiling it. It is a mirror which no stone can crack, whose quicksilver will never wear off, whose gilding Nature continually repairs; no storms, no dust, can dim its surface ever fresh;—a mirror in which all impurity presented to it sinks, swept and dusted by the sun's hazy brush,—this the light dust-cloth,—which retains no breath that is breathed on it, but sends its own to float as clouds high above its surface, and be reflected in its bosom still.

A field of water betrays the spirit that is in the air. It is continually receiving new life and motion from above. It is intermediate in its nature between land and sky. On land only the grass and trees wave, but the water itself is rippled by the wind. I see where the breeze dashes across it by the streaks or flakes of light. It is remarkable that we can look down on its surface. We shall, perhaps, look down thus on the surface of air at length, and mark where a still subtler spirit sweeps over it.

The skaters and water-bugs finally disappear in the latter part of October, when the severe frosts have come; and then and in November, usually, in a calm day, there is absolutely nothing to ripple the surface. One November afternoon, in the calm at the end of a rain storm of several days' duration, when the sky was still completely overcast and the air was full of mist, I observed that the pond was remarkably smooth, so that it was difficult to distinguish its surface; though it no longer reflected the bright tints of October, but the sombre November colors of the surrounding hills. Though I passed over it as gently as possible, the slight undulations produced by my boat extended almost as far as I could see, and gave a ribbed appearance to the reflections. But, as I was looking over the surface, I saw here and there at a distance a faint glimmer, as if some skater insects which had escaped the frosts might be collected there, or, perchance, the surface, being so smooth, betrayed where a spring welled up from the bottom. Paddling gently to one of these places, I was surprised to find myself surrounded by myriads of small perch, about five inches long, of a rich bronze color in the green water, sporting there and constantly rising to the surface and dimpling it, sometimes leaving bubbles on it. In such transparent and seemingly bottomless water, reflecting the clouds, I seemed to be floating through the air as in a balloon, and their swimming impressed me as a kind of flight or hovering, as if they were a compact flock of birds passing just beneath my level on the right or left, their fins, like sails, set all around them. There were many such schools in the pond, apparently improving the short season before winter would draw an icy shutter over their broad skylight, sometimes giving to the surface an appearance as if a slight breeze struck it, or a few raindrops fell there. When I approached carelessly and alarmed them, they made a sudden plash and rippling with their tails, as if one had struck the water with a brushy bough, and instantly took refuge in the depths. At length the wind rose, the mist increased, and the waves began to run, and the perch leaped much higher than before, half out of water, a hundred black points, three inches long, at once above the surface. Even as late as the fifth of December, one year, I saw some dimples on the surface, and thinking it was going to rain hard immediately, the air being full of mist, I made haste to take my place at the oars and row homeward; already the rain seemed rapidly increasing, though I felt none on my cheek, and I anticipated a thorough soaking. But suddenly the dimples ceased, for they were produced by the perch, which the noise of my oars had scared into the depths, and I saw their schools dimly disappearing; so I spent a dry afternoon after all.

An old man who used to frequent this pond nearly sixty years ago, when it was dark with surrounding forests, tells me that in those days he sometimes saw it all alive with ducks and other water fowl, and that there were many eagles about it. He came here a-fishing, and used an old log canoe which he found on the shore. It was made of two white-pine logs dug out and pinned together, and was cut off square at the ends. It was very clumsy, but lasted a great many years before it became water-logged and perhaps sank to the bottom. He did not know whose it was; it belonged to the pond. He used to make a cable for his anchor of strips of hickory bark tied together. An old man, a potter, who lived by the pond before the Revolution, told him once that there was an iron chest at the bottom, and that he had seen it. Sometimes it would come floating up to the shore; but when you went toward it, it would go back into deep water and disappear. I was pleased to hear of the old log canoe, which took the place of an Indian one of the same material but more graceful construction, which perchance had first been a tree on the bank, and then, as it were, fell into the water, to float there for a generation, the most proper vessel for the lake. I remember that when I first looked into these depths there were many large trunks to be seen indistinctly lying on the bottom, which had either been blown over formerly, or left on the ice at the last cutting, when wood was cheaper; but now they have mostly disappeared.

When I first paddled a boat on Walden, it was completely surrounded by thick and lofty pine and oak woods, and in some of its coves grape vines had run over the trees next the water and formed bowers under which a boat could pass. The hills which form its shores are so steep, and the woods on them were then so high, that, as you looked down from the west end, it had the appearance of an amphitheatre for some kind of sylvan spectacle. I have spent many an hour, when I was younger, floating over its surface as the zephyr willed, having paddled my boat to the middle, and lying on my back across the seats, in a summer forenoon, dreaming awake, until I was aroused by the boat touching the sand, and I arose to see what shore my fates had impelled me to; days when idleness was the most attractive and productive industry. Many a forenoon have I stolen away, preferring to spend thus the most valued part of the day; for I was rich, if not in money, in sunny hours and summer days, and spent them lavishly; nor do I regret that I did not waste more of them in the workshop or the teacher's desk. But since I left those shores the woodchoppers have still further laid them waste, and now for many a year there will be no more rambling through the aisles of the wood, with occasional vistas through which you see the water. My Muse may be excused if she is silent henceforth. How can you expect the birds to sing when their groves are cut down?

Now the trunks of trees on the bottom, and the old log canoe, and the dark surrounding woods, are gone, and the villagers, who scarcely know where it lies, instead of going to the pond to bathe or drink, are thinking to bring its water, which should be as sacred as the Ganges at least, to the village in a pipe, to wash their dishes with!—to earn their Walden by the turning of a cock or drawing of a plug! That devilish Iron Horse, whose ear-rending neigh is heard throughout the town, has muddied the Boiling Spring with his foot, and he it is that has browsed off all the woods on Walden shore; that Trojan horse, with a thousand men in his belly, introduced by mercenary Greeks! Where is the country's champion, the Moore of Moore Hall, to meet him at the Deep Cut and thrust an avenging lance between the ribs of the bloated pest?

Nevertheless, of all the characters I have known, perhaps Walden wears best, and best preserves its purity. Many men have been likened to it, but few deserve that honor. Though the woodchoppers have laid bare first this shore and then that, and the Irish have built their sties by it, and the railroad has infringed on its border, and the ice-men have skimmed it once, it is itself unchanged, the same water which my youthful eyes fell on; all the change is in me. It has not acquired one permanent wrinkle after all its ripples. It is perennially young, and I may stand and see a swallow dip apparently to pick an insect from its surface as of yore. It struck me again to-night, as if I had not seen it almost daily for more than twenty years,—Why, here is Walden, the same woodland lake that I discovered so many years ago; where a forest was cut down last winter another is springing up by its shore as lustily as ever; the same thought is welling up to its surface that was then; it is the same liquid joy and happiness to itself and its Maker, ay, and it *may* be to me. It is the work of a brave man surely, in whom there was no guile! He rounded this water with his hand, deepened and clarified it in his thought, and in his will bequeathed it to Concord. I see by its face that it is visited by the same reflection; and I can almost say, Walden, is it you?

> It is no dream of mine,
> To ornament a line;
> I cannot come nearer to God and Heaven
> Than I live to Walden even.
> I am its stony shore,
> And the breeze that passes o'er;
> In the hollow of my hand
> Are its water and its sand,
> And its deepest resort
> Lies high in my thought.

The cars never pause to look at it; yet I fancy that the engineers and firemen and brakemen, and those passengers who have a season ticket and see it often, are better men for the sight. The engineer does not forget at night, or his nature does not, that he has beheld this vision of serenity and purity once at least during the day. Though seen but once, it helps to wash out State-street and the engine's soot. One proposes that it be called "God's Drop."

I have said that Walden has no visible inlet nor outlet, but it is on the one hand distantly and indirectly related to Flints' Pond, which is more elevated, by a chain of small ponds coming from that quarter, and on the other directly and manifestly to Concord River, which is lower, by a similar chain of ponds through which in some other geological period it may have flowed, and by a little digging, which God forbid, it can be made to flow thither again. If by living thus reserved and austere, like a hermit in the woods, so long, it has acquired such wonderful purity, who would not regret that the comparatively impure waters of Flints' Pond should be mingled with it, or itself should ever go to waste its sweetness in the ocean wave?

Flints', or Sandy Pond, in Lincoln, our greatest lake and inland sea, lies about a mile east of Walden. It is much larger, being said to contain one hundred and ninety-seven acres, and is more fertile in fish; but it is comparatively shallow, and not remarkably pure. A walk through the woods thither was often my recreation. It was worth the while, if only to feel the wind blow on your cheek freely, and see the waves run, and remember the life of mariners. I went a-chestnutting there in the fall, on windy days, when the nuts were dropping into the water and were washed to my feet; and one day, as I crept along its sedgy shore, the fresh spray blowing in my face, I came upon the mouldering wreck of a boat, the sides gone, and hardly more than the impression of its flat bottom left amid the rushes; yet its model was sharply defined, as if it were a large decayed pad, with its veins. It was as impressive a wreck as one could imagine on the sea-shore, and had as good a moral. It is by this time mere vegetable mould and undistinguishable pond shore, through which rushes and flags have pushed up. I used to admire the ripple marks on the sandy bottom, at the north end of this pond, made firm and hard to the feet of the wader by the pressure of the water, and the rushes which grew in Indian file, in waving lines, corresponding to these marks, rank behind rank, as if the waves had planted them. There also I have found, in considerable quantities, curious balls, composed apparently of fine grass or roots, of pipewort perhaps, from half an inch to four inches in diameter, and perfectly spherical. These wash back and forth in shallow water on a sandy bottom, and are sometimes cast on the shore. They are either solid grass, or have a little sand in the middle. At first you would say that they were formed by the action of the waves, like a pebble; yet the smallest are made of equally coarse materials, half an inch long, and they are produced only at one season of the year. Moreover, the waves, I suspect, do not so much construct as wear down a material which has already acquired consistency. They preserve their form when dry for an indefinite period.

Flints' Pond! Such is the poverty of our nomenclature. What right had the unclean and stupid farmer, whose farm abutted on this sky water, whose shores he has ruthlessly laid bare, to give his name to it? Some skin-flint, who loved better the reflecting surface of a dollar, or a bright cent, in which he could see his own brazen face; who regarded even the wild ducks which settled in it as trespassers; his fingers grown into crooked and horny talons from the long habit of grasping harpy-like;—so it is not named for me. I go not there to see him nor to hear of him; who never *saw* it, who never bathed in it, who never loved it, who never protected it, who never spoke a good word for it, nor thanked God that he had made it. Rather let it be named from the fishes that swim in it, the wild fowl or quadrupeds which frequent it, the wild flowers which grow by its shores, or some wild man or child the thread of whose history is interwoven with its own; not from him who could show no title to it but the deed which a like-minded neighbor or legislature gave him,—him who thought only of its money value; whose presence perchance cursed all the shore; who exhausted the land around it, and would fain have exhausted the waters within it; who regretted only that it was not English hay or cranberry meadow,—there was nothing to redeem it, forsooth, in his eyes,—and would have drained and sold it for the mud at its bottom. It did not turn his mill, and it was no *privilege* to him to behold it. I respect not his labors, his farm where every thing has its price; who would carry the landscape, who would carry his God, to market, if he could get any thing for him; who goes to market *for* his god as it is; on whose farm nothing grows free, whose fields bear no crops, whose meadows no flowers, whose trees no fruits, but dollars; who loves not the beauty of his fruits, whose fruits are not ripe for him till they are turned to dollars. Give me the poverty that enjoys true wealth. Farmers are respectable and interesting to me in proportion as they are poor,—poor farmers. A model farm! where the house stands like a fungus in a muck-heap, chambers for men, horses, oxen, and swine, cleansed and uncleansed, all contiguous to one another! Stocked with men! A great grease-spot, redolent of manures and buttermilk! Under a high state of cultivation, being manured with the hearts and brains of men! As if you were to raise your potatoes in the church-yard! Such is a model farm.

No, no; if the fairest features of the landscape are to be named after men, let them be the noblest and worthiest men alone. Let our lakes receive as true names at least as the Icarian Sea, where "still the shore" a "brave attempt resounds."

Goose Pond, of small extent, is on my way to Flints'; Fair-

Haven, an expansion of Concord River, said to contain some
seventy acres, is a mile south-west; and White Pond, of about
forty acres, is a mile and a half beyond Fair-Haven. This is
my lake country. These, with Concord River, are my water
privileges; and night and day, year in year out, they grind
such grist as I carry to them.

Since the woodcutters, and the railroad, and I myself have
profaned Walden, perhaps the most attractive, if not the most
beautiful, of all our lakes, the gem of the woods, is White
Pond;—a poor name from its commonness, whether derived
from the remarkable purity of its waters or the color of its
sands. In these as in other respects, however, it is a lesser twin
of Walden. They are so much alike that you would say they
must be connected under ground. It has the same stony
shore, and its waters are of the same hue. As at Walden, in
sultry dog-day weather, looking down through the woods on
some of its bays which are not so deep but that the reflection
from the bottom tinges them, its waters are of a misty bluish-
green or glaucous color. Many years since I used to go there
to collect the sand by cart-loads, to make sand-paper with,
and I have continued to visit it ever since. One who frequents
it proposes to call it Virid Lake. Perhaps it might be called
Yellow-Pine Lake, from the following circumstance. About
fifteen years ago you could see the top of a pitch-pine, of the
kind called yellow-pine hereabouts, though it is not a distinct
species, projecting above the surface in deep water, many rods
from the shore. It was even supposed by some that the pond
had sunk, and this was one of the primitive forest that formerly stood there. I find that even so long ago as 1792, in a
"Topographical Description of the Town of Concord," by one
of its citizens, in the Collections of the Massachusetts Historical Society, the author, after speaking of Walden and White
Ponds, adds: "In the middle of the latter may be seen, when
the water is very low, a tree which appears as if it grew in the
place where it now stands, although the roots are fifty feet
below the surface of the water; the top of this tree is broken
off, and at that place measures fourteen inches in diameter."
In the spring of '49 I talked with the man who lives nearest
the pond in Sudbury, who told me that it was he who got
out this tree ten or fifteen years before. As near as he could

remember, it stood twelve or fifteen rods from the shore, where the water was thirty or forty feet deep. It was in the winter, and he had been getting out ice in the forenoon, and had resolved that in the afternoon, with the aid of his neighbors, he would take out the old yellow-pine. He sawed a channel in the ice toward the shore, and hauled it over and along and out on to the ice with oxen; but, before he had gone far in his work, he was surprised to find that it was wrong end upward, with the stumps of the branches pointing down, and the small end firmly fastened in the sandy bottom. It was about a foot in diameter at the big end, and he had expected to get a good saw-log, but it was so rotten as to be fit only for fuel, if for that. He had some of it in his shed then. There were marks of an axe and of woodpeckers on the but. He thought that it might have been a dead tree on the shore, but was finally blown over into the pond, and after the top had become water-logged, while the but-end was still dry and light, had drifted out and sunk wrong end up. His father, eighty years old, could not remember when it was not there. Several pretty large logs may still be seen lying on the bottom, where, owing to the undulation of the surface, they look like huge water snakes in motion.

This pond has rarely been profaned by a boat, for there is little in it to tempt a fisherman. Instead of the white lily, which requires mud, or the common sweet flag, the blue flag (*Iris versicolor*) grows thinly in the pure water, rising from the stony bottom all around the shore, where it is visited by humming birds in June, and the color both of its bluish blades and its flowers, and especially their reflections, are in singular harmony with the glaucous water.

White Pond and Walden are great crystals on the surface of the earth, Lakes of Light. If they were permanently congealed, and small enough to be clutched, they would, perchance, be carried off by slaves, like precious stones, to adorn the heads of emperors; but being liquid, and ample, and secured to us and our successors forever, we disregard them, and run after the diamond of Kohinoor. They are too pure to have a market value; they contain no muck. How much more beautiful than our lives, how much more transparent than our characters, are they! We never learned meanness of them.

How much fairer than the pool before the farmer's door, in which his ducks swim! Hither the clean wild ducks come. Nature has no human inhabitant who appreciates her. The birds with their plumage and their notes are in harmony with the flowers, but what youth or maiden conspires with the wild luxuriant beauty of Nature? She flourishes most alone, far from the towns where they reside. Talk of heaven! ye disgrace earth.

Baker Farm

SOMETIMES I rambled to pine groves, standing like temples, or like fleets at sea, full-rigged, with wavy boughs, and rippling with light, so soft and green and shady that the Druids would have forsaken their oaks to worship in them; or to the cedar wood beyond Flints' Pond, where the trees, covered with hoary blue berries, spiring higher and higher, are fit to stand before Valhalla, and the creeping juniper covers the ground with wreaths full of fruit; or to swamps where the usnea lichen hangs in festoons from the white-spruce trees, and toad-stools, round tables of the swamp gods, cover the ground, and more beautiful fungi adorn the stumps, like butterflies or shells, vegetable winkles; where the swamp-pink and dogwood grow, the red alder-berry glows like eyes of imps, the waxwork grooves and crushes the hardest woods in its folds, and the wild-holly berries make the beholder forget his home with their beauty, and he is dazzled and tempted by nameless other wild forbidden fruits, too fair for mortal taste. Instead of calling on some scholar, I paid many a visit to particular trees, of kinds which are rare in this neighborhood, standing far away in the middle of some pasture, or in the depths of a wood or swamp, or on a hill-top; such as the black-birch, of which we have some handsome specimens two feet in diameter; its cousin the yellow-birch, with its loose golden vest, perfumed like the first; the beech, which has so neat a bole and beautifully lichen-painted, perfect in all its details, of which, excepting scattered specimens, I know but one small grove of sizable trees left in the township, supposed by some to have been planted by the pigeons that were once baited with beech nuts near by; it is worth the while to see the silver grain sparkle when you split this wood; the bass; the hornbeam; the *Celtis occidentalis*, or false elm, of which we have but one well-grown; some taller mast of a pine, a shingle tree, or a more perfect hemlock than usual, standing like a pagoda in the midst of the woods; and many others I could mention. These were the shrines I visited both summer and winter.

Once it chanced that I stood in the very abutment of a

rainbow's arch, which filled the lower stratum of the atmosphere, tinging the grass and leaves around, and dazzling me as if I looked through colored crystal. It was a lake of rainbow light, in which, for a short while, I lived like a dolphin. If it had lasted longer it might have tinged my employments and life. As I walked on the railroad causeway, I used to wonder at the halo of light around my shadow, and would fain fancy myself one of the elect. One who visited me declared that the shadows of some Irishmen before him had no halo about them, that it was only natives that were so distinguished. Benvenuto Cellini tells us in his memoirs, that, after a certain terrible dream or vision which he had during his confinement in the castle of St. Angelo, a resplendent light appeared over the shadow of his head at morning and evening, whether he was in Italy or France, and it was particularly conspicuous when the grass was moist with dew. This was probably the same phenomenon to which I have referred, which is especially observed in the morning, but also at other times, and even by moonlight. Though a constant one, it is not commonly noticed, and, in the case of an excitable imagination like Cellini's, it would be basis enough for superstition. Beside, he tells us that he showed it to very few. But are they not indeed distinguished who are conscious that they are regarded at all?

I set out one afternoon to go a-fishing to Fair-Haven, through the woods, to eke out my scanty fare of vegetables. My way led through Pleasant Meadow, an adjunct of the Baker Farm, that retreat of which a poet has since sung, beginning,—

> "Thy entry is a pleasant field,
> Which some mossy fruit trees yield
> Partly to a ruddy brook,
> By gliding musquash undertook,
> And mercurial trout,
> Darting about."

I thought of living there before I went to Walden. I "hooked" the apples, leaped the brook, and scared the musquash and the trout. It was one of those afternoons which seem indefinitely long before one, in which many events may happen, a large portion of our natural life, though it was already half spent when I started. By the way there came up a shower, which compelled me to stand half an hour under a pine, piling boughs over my head, and wearing my handkerchief for a shed; and when at length I had made one cast over the pickerel-weed, standing up to my middle in water, I found myself suddenly in the shadow of a cloud, and the thunder began to rumble with such emphasis that I could do no more than listen to it. The gods must be proud, thought I, with such forked flashes to rout a poor unarmed fisherman. So I made haste for shelter to the nearest hut, which stood half a mile from any road, but so much the nearer to the pond, and had long been uninhabited: —

> "And here a poet builded,
>   In the completed years,
> For behold a trivial cabin
>   That to destruction steers."

So the Muse fables. But therein, as I found, dwelt now John Field, an Irishman, and his wife, and several children, from the broad-faced boy who assisted his father at his work, and now came running by his side from the bog to escape the rain, to the wrinkled, sibyl-like, cone-headed infant that sat upon its father's knee as in the palaces of nobles, and looked out from its home in the midst of wet and hunger inquisitively upon the stranger, with the privilege of infancy, not knowing but it was the last of a noble line, and the hope and cynosure of the world, instead of John Field's poor starveling brat. There we sat together under that part of the roof which leaked the least, while it showered and thundered without. I had sat there many times of old before the ship was built that floated this family to America. An honest, hard-working, but shiftless man plainly was John Field; and his wife, she too was brave to cook so many successive dinners in the recesses of that lofty stove; with round greasy face and bare breast, still thinking to improve her condition one day; with the never absent mop in one hand, and yet no effects of it visible any where. The chickens, which had also taken shelter here from the rain, stalked about the room like members of the family, too humanized methought to roast well. They stood and looked in my eye or pecked at my shoe significantly. Meanwhile my host told me his story, how hard he worked "bogging" for a neighboring farmer, turning up a meadow with a spade or bog hoe at the rate of ten dollars an acre and the use of the land with manure for one year, and his little broadfaced son worked cheerfully at his father's side the while, not knowing how poor a bargain the latter had made. I tried to help him with my experience, telling him that he was one of my nearest neighbors, and that I too, who came a-fishing here, and looked like a loafer, was getting my living like himself; that I lived in a tight light and clean house, which hardly cost more than the annual rent of such a ruin as his commonly amounts to; and how, if he chose, he might in a month or two build himself a palace of his own; that I did not use tea, nor coffee, nor butter, nor milk, nor fresh meat, and so did not have to work to get them; again, as I did not work hard, I did not have to eat hard, and it cost me but a trifle for my food; but as he began with tea, and coffee, and butter, and milk, and beef, he had to work hard to pay for them, and when he had worked hard he had to eat hard again to repair the waste of his system,—and so it was as broad as it was long, indeed it was broader than it was long, for he was discontented and wasted his life into the bargain; and yet he had rated it as a gain in coming to America, that here you could get tea, and coffee, and meat every day. But the only true America is that country where you are at liberty to pursue such a mode of life as may enable you to do without these, and where the state does not endeavor to compel you to sustain the slavery and war and other superfluous expenses which directly or indirectly result from the use of such things. For I purposely talked to him as if he were a philosopher, or desired to be one. I should be glad if all the meadows on the earth were left in a wild state, if that were the consequence of men's beginning to redeem themselves. A man will not need to study history to find out what is best for his own culture. But alas! the culture of an Irishman is an enterprise to be undertaken with a sort of moral bog hoe. I told him, that as he worked so hard at bogging, he required thick boots and stout clothing, which yet were soon soiled and worn out, but

I wore light shoes and thin clothing, which cost not half so much, though he might think that I was dressed like a gentleman, (which, however, was not the case,) and in an hour or two, without labor, but as a recreation, I could, if I wished, catch as many fish as I should want for two days, or earn enough money to support me a week. If he and his family would live simply, they might all go a-huckleberrying in the summer for their amusement. John heaved a sigh at this, and his wife stared with arms a-kimbo, and both appeared to be wondering if they had capital enough to begin such a course with, or arithmetic enough to carry it through. It was sailing by dead reckoning to them, and they saw not clearly how to make their port so; therefore I suppose they still take life bravely, after their fashion, face to face, giving it tooth and nail, not having skill to split its massive columns with any fine entering wedge, and rout it in detail;—thinking to deal with it roughly, as one should handle a thistle. But they fight at an overwhelming disadvantage,—living, John Field, alas! without arithmetic, and failing so.

"Do you ever fish?" I asked. "O yes, I catch a mess now and then when I am lying by; good perch I catch." "What's your bait?" "I catch shiners with fish-worms, and bait the perch with them." "You'd better go now, John," said his wife with glistening and hopeful face; but John demurred.

The shower was now over, and a rainbow above the eastern woods promised a fair evening; so I took my departure. When I had got without I asked for a dish, hoping to get a sight of the well bottom, to complete my survey of the premises; but there, alas! are shallows and quicksands, and rope broken withal, and bucket irrecoverable. Meanwhile the right culinary vessel was selected, water was seemingly distilled, and after consultation and long delay passed out to the thirsty one,—not yet suffered to cool, not yet to settle. Such gruel sustains life here, I thought; so, shutting my eyes, and excluding the motes by a skilfully directed under-current, I drank to genuine hospitality the heartiest draught I could. I am not squeamish in such cases when manners are concerned.

As I was leaving the Irishman's roof after the rain, bending my steps again to the pond, my haste to catch pickerel, wading in retired meadows, in sloughs and bog-holes, in forlorn

and savage places, appeared for an instant trivial to me who
had been sent to school and college; but as I ran down the
hill toward the reddening west, with the rainbow over my
shoulder, and some faint tinkling sounds borne to my ear
through the cleansed air, from I know not what quarter, my
Good Genius seemed to say,—Go fish and hunt far and wide
day by day,   farther and wider,—and rest thee by many
brooks and hearth-sides without misgiving. Remember thy
Creator in the days of thy youth. Rise free from care before
the dawn, and seek adventures. Let the noon find thee by
other lakes, and the night overtake thee every where at home.
There are no larger fields than these, no worthier games than
may here be played. Grow wild according to thy nature, like
these sedges and brakes, which will never become English
hay. Let the thunder rumble; what if it threaten ruin to farmers' crops? that is not its errand to thee. Take shelter under
the cloud, while they flee to carts and sheds. Let not to get a
living be thy trade, but thy sport. Enjoy the land, but own it
not. Through want of enterprise and faith men are where they
are, buying and selling, and spending their lives like serfs.

O Baker Farm!

> "Landscape where the richest element
> Is a little sunshine innocent." * *

> "No one runs to revel
> On thy rail-fenced lea." * *

> "Debate with no man hast thou,
>   With questions art never perplexed,
> As tame at the first sight as now,
>   In thy plain russet gabardine dressed." * *

> "Come ye who love,
>   And ye who hate,
> Children of the Holy Dove,
>   And Guy Faux of the state,
> And hang conspiracies
> From the tough rafters of the trees!"

Men come tamely home at night only from the next field

or street, where their household echoes haunt, and their life pines because it breathes its own breath over again; their shadows morning and evening reach farther than their daily steps. We should come home from far, from adventures, and perils, and discoveries every day, with new experience and character.

Before I had reached the pond some fresh impulse had brought out John Field, with altered mind, letting go "bogging" ere this sunset. But he, poor man, disturbed only a couple of fins while I was catching a fair string, and he said it was his luck; but when we changed seats in the boat luck changed seats too. Poor John Field!—I trust he does not read this, unless he will improve by it,—thinking to live by some derivative old country mode in this primitive new country,— to catch perch with shiners. It is good bait sometimes, I allow. With his horizon all his own, yet he a poor man, born to be poor, with his inherited Irish poverty or poor life, his Adam's grandmother and boggy ways, not to rise in this world, he nor his posterity, till their wading webbed bog-trotting feet get *talaria* to their heels.

Higher Laws

As I came home through the woods with my string of fish, trailing my pole, it being now quite dark, I caught a glimpse of a woodchuck stealing across my path, and felt a strange thrill of savage delight, and was strongly tempted to seize and devour him raw; not that I was hungry then, except for that wildness which he represented. Once or twice, however, while I lived at the pond, I found myself ranging the woods, like a half-starved hound, with a strange abandonment, seeking some kind of venison which I might devour, and no morsel could have been too savage for me. The wildest scenes had become unaccountably familiar. I found in myself, and still find, an instinct toward a higher, or, as it is named, spiritual life, as do most men, and another toward a primitive rank and savage one, and I reverence them both. I love the wild not less than the good. The wildness and adventure that are in fishing still recommended it to me. I like sometimes to take rank hold on life and spend my day more as the animals do. Perhaps I have owed to this employment and to hunting, when quite young, my closest acquaintance with Nature. They early introduce us to and detain us in scenery with which otherwise, at that age, we should have little acquaintance. Fishermen, hunters, woodchoppers, and others, spending their lives in the fields and woods, in a peculiar sense a part of Nature themselves, are often in a more favorable mood for observing her, in the intervals of their pursuits, than philosophers or poets even, who approach her with expectation. She is not afraid to exhibit herself to them. The traveller on the prairie is naturally a hunter, on the head waters of the Missouri and Columbia a trapper, and at the Falls of St. Mary a fisherman. He who is only a traveller learns things at second-hand and by the halves, and is poor authority. We are most interested when science reports what those men already know practically or instinctively, for that alone is a true *humanity*, or account of human experience.

They mistake who assert that the Yankee has few amusements, because he has not so many public holidays, and men and boys do not play so many games as they do in England, for here the more primitive but solitary amusements of hunting fishing and the like have not yet given place to the former. Almost every New England boy among my contemporaries shouldered a fowling piece between the ages of ten and fourteen; and his hunting and fishing grounds were not limited like the preserves of an English nobleman, but were more boundless even than those of a savage. No wonder, then, that he did not oftener stay to play on the common. But already a change is taking place, owing, not to an increased humanity, but to an increased scarcity of game, for perhaps the hunter is the greatest friend of the animals hunted, not excepting the Humane Society.

Moreover, when at the pond, I wished sometimes to add fish to my fare for variety. I have actually fished from the same kind of necessity that the first fishers did. Whatever humanity I might conjure up against it was all factitious, and concerned my philosophy more than my feelings. I speak of fishing only now, for I had long felt differently about fowling, and sold my gun before I went to the woods. Not that I am less humane than others, but I did not perceive that my feelings were much affected. I did not pity the fishes nor the worms. This was habit. As for fowling, during the last years that I carried a gun my excuse was that I was studying ornithology, and sought only new or rare birds. But I confess that I am now inclined to think that there is a finer way of studying ornithology than this. It requires so much closer attention to the habits of the birds, that, if for that reason only, I have been willing to omit the gun. Yet notwithstanding the objection on the score of humanity, I am compelled to doubt if equally valuable sports are ever substituted for these; and when some of my friends have asked me anxiously about their boys, whether they should let them hunt, I have answered, yes,—remembering that it was one of the best parts of my education,—*make* them hunters, though sportsmen only at first, if possible, mighty hunters at last, so that they shall not find game large enough for them in this or any vegetable wilderness,—hunters as well as fishers of men. Thus far I am of the opinion of Chaucer's nun, who

> "yave not of the text a pulled hen
> That saith that hunters ben not holy men."

There is a period in the history of the individual, as of the race, when the hunters are the "best men," as the Algonquins called them. We cannot but pity the boy who has never fired a gun, he is no more humane, while his education has been sadly neglected. This was my answer with respect to those youths who were bent on this pursuit, trusting that they would soon outgrow it. No humane being, past the thoughtless age of boyhood, will wantonly murder any creature, which holds its life by the same tenure that he does. The hare in its extremity cries like a child. I warn you, mothers, that my sympathies do not always make the usual phil-*anthropic* distinctions.

Such is oftenest the young man's introduction to the forest, and the most original part of himself. He goes thither at first as a hunter and fisher, until at last, if he has the seeds of a better life in him, he distinguishes his proper objects, as a poet or naturalist it may be, and leaves the gun and fish-pole behind. The mass of men are still and always young in this respect. In some countries a hunting person is no uncommon sight. Such a one might make a good shepherd's dog, but is far from being the Good Shepherd. I have been surprised to consider that the only obvious employment, except wood-chopping, ice-cutting, or the like business, which ever to my knowledge detained at Walden Pond for a whole half day any of my fellow-citizens, whether fathers or children of the town, with just one exception, was fishing. Commonly they did not think that they were lucky, or well paid for their time, unless they got a long string of fish, though they had the opportunity of seeing the pond all the while. They might go there a thousand times before the sediment of fishing would sink to the bottom and leave their purpose pure; but no doubt such a clarifying process would be going on all the while. The governor and his council faintly remember the pond, for they went a-fishing there when they were boys; but now they are too old and dignified to go a-fishing, and so they know it no more forever. Yet even they expect to go to heaven at last. If the legislature regards it, it is chiefly to regulate the number of hooks to be used there; but they know nothing about the hook of hooks with which to angle for the pond itself, impaling the legislature for a bait. Thus, even in civilized communities, the embryo man passes through the hunter stage of development.

I have found repeatedly, of late years, that I cannot fish without falling a little in self-respect. I have tried it again and again. I have skill at it, and, like many of my fellows, a certain instinct for it, which revives from time to time, but always when I have done I feel that it would have been better if I had not fished. I think that I do not mistake. It is a faint intimation, yet so are the first streaks of morning. There is unquestionably this instinct in me which belongs to the lower orders of creation; yet with every year I am less a fisherman, though without more humanity or even wisdom; at present I am no fisherman at all. But I see that if I were to live in a wilderness I should again be tempted to become a fisher and hunter in earnest. Beside, there is something essentially unclean about this diet and all flesh, and I began to see where housework commences, and whence the endeavor, which costs so much, to wear a tidy and respectable appearance each day, to keep the house sweet and free from all ill odors and sights. Having been my own butcher and scullion and cook, as well as the gentleman for whom the dishes were served up, I can speak from an unusually complete experience. The practical objection to animal food in my case was its uncleanness; and, besides, when I had caught and cleaned and cooked and eaten my fish, they seemed not to have fed me essentially. It was insignificant and unnecessary, and cost more than it came to. A little bread or a few potatoes would have done as well, with less trouble and filth. Like many of my contemporaries, I had rarely for many years used animal food, or tea, or coffee, &c.; not so much because of any ill effects which I had traced to them, as because they were not agreeable to my imagination. The repugnance to animal food is not the effect of experience, but is an instinct. It appeared more beautiful to live low and fare hard in many respects; and though I never did so, I went far enough to please my imagination. I believe that every man who has ever been earnest to preserve his higher or poetic faculties in the best condition has been particularly inclined to abstain from animal food, and from much food of any kind. It is a significant fact, stated by entomologists, I find it in Kirby and Spence, that "some insects in their perfect state, though furnished with organs of feeding, make no use of them;" and they lay it down as "a general rule, that almost all insects in this state eat much less than in that of larvæ. The voracious caterpillar when transformed into a butterfly," . . "and the gluttonous maggot when become a fly," content themselves with a drop or two of honey or some other sweet liquid. The abdomen under the wings of the butterfly still represents the larva. This is the tid-bit which tempts his insectivorous fate. The gross feeder is a man in the larva state; and there are whole nations in that condition, nations without fancy or imagination, whose vast abdomens betray them.

It is hard to provide and cook so simple and clean a diet as will not offend the imagination; but this, I think, is to be fed when we feed the body; they should both sit down at the same table. Yet perhaps this may be done. The fruits eaten temperately need not make us ashamed of our appetites, nor interrupt the worthiest pursuits. But put an extra condiment into your dish, and it will poison you. It is not worth the while to live by rich cookery. Most men would feel shame if caught preparing with their own hands precisely such a dinner, whether of animal or vegetable food, as is every day prepared for them by others. Yet till this is otherwise we are not civilized, and, if gentlemen and ladies, are not true men and women. This certainly suggests what change is to be made. It may be vain to ask why the imagination will not be reconciled to flesh and fat. I am satisfied that it is not. Is it not a reproach that man is a carnivorous animal? True, he can and does live, in a great measure, by preying on other animals; but this is a miserable way,—as any one who will go to snaring rabbits, or slaughtering lambs, may learn,—and he will be regarded as a benefactor of his race who shall teach man to confine himself to a more innocent and wholesome diet. Whatever my own practice may be, I have no doubt that it is a part of the destiny of the human race, in its gradual improvement, to leave off eating animals, as surely as the savage tribes have left off eating each other when they came in contact with the more civilized.

If one listens to the faintest but constant suggestions of his genius, which are certainly true, he sees not to what extremes, or even insanity, it may lead him; and yet that way, as he grows more resolute and faithful, his road lies. The faintest assured objection which one healthy man feels will at length prevail over the arguments and customs of mankind. No man ever followed his genius till it misled him. Though the result were bodily weakness, yet perhaps no one can say that the consequences were to be regretted, for these were a life in conformity to higher principles. If the day and the night are such that you greet them with joy, and life emits a fragrance like flowers and sweet-scented herbs, is more elastic, more starry, more immortal,—that is your success. All nature is your congratulation, and you have cause momentarily to bless yourself. The greatest gains and values are farthest from being appreciated. We easily come to doubt if they exist. We soon forget them. They are the highest reality. Perhaps the facts most astounding and most real are never communicated by man to man. The true harvest of my daily life is somewhat as intangible and indescribable as the tints of morning or evening. It is a little star-dust caught, a segment of the rainbow which I have clutched.

Yet, for my part, I was never unusually squeamish; I could sometimes eat a fried rat with a good relish, if it were necessary. I am glad to have drunk water so long, for the same reason that I prefer the natural sky to an opium-eater's heaven. I would fain keep sober always; and there are infinite degrees of drunkenness. I believe that water is the only drink for a wise man; wine is not so noble a liquor; and think of dashing the hopes of a morning with a cup of warm coffee, or of an evening with a dish of tea! Ah, how low I fall when I am tempted by them! Even music may be intoxicating. Such apparently slight causes destroyed Greece and Rome, and will destroy England and America. Of all ebriosity, who does not prefer to be intoxicated by the air he breathes? I have found it to be the most serious objection to coarse labors long continued, that they compelled me to eat and drink coarsely also.

But to tell the truth, I find myself at present somewhat less particular in these respects. I carry less religion to the table, ask no blessing; not because I am wiser than I was, but, I am obliged to confess, because, however much it is to be regretted, with years I have grown more coarse and indifferent. Perhaps these questions are entertained only in youth, as most believe of poetry. My practice is "nowhere," my opinion is here. Nevertheless I am far from regarding myself as one of those privileged ones to whom the Ved refers when it says, that "he who has true faith in the Omnipresent Supreme Being may eat all that exists," that is, is not bound to inquire what is his food, or who prepares it; and even in their case it is to be observed, as a Hindoo commentator has remarked, that the Vedant limits this privilege to "the time of distress."

Who has not sometimes derived an inexpressible satisfaction from his food in which appetite had no share? I have been thrilled to think that I owed a mental perception to the commonly gross sense of taste, that I have been inspired through the palate, that some berries which I had eaten on a hill-side had fed my genius. "The soul not being mistress of herself," says Thseng-tseu, "one looks, and one does not see; one listens, and one does not hear; one eats, and one does not know the savor of food." He who distinguishes the true savor of his food can never be a glutton; he who does not cannot be otherwise. A puritan may go to his brown-bread crust with as gross an appetite as ever an alderman to his turtle. Not that food which entereth into the mouth defileth a man, but the appetite with which it is eaten. It is neither the quality nor the quantity, but the devotion to sensual savors; when that which is eaten is not a viand to sustain our animal, or inspire our spiritual life, but food for the worms that possess us. If the hunter has a taste for mud-turtles, muskrats, and other such savage tid-bits, the fine lady indulges a taste for jelly made of a calf's foot, or for sardines from over the sea, and they are even. He goes to the mill-pond, she to her preserve-pot. The wonder is how they, how you and I, can live this slimy beastly life, eating and drinking.

Our whole life is startlingly moral. There is never an instant's truce between virtue and vice. Goodness is the only investment that never fails. In the music of the harp which trembles round the world it is the insisting on this which thrills us. The harp is the travelling patterer for the Universe's Insurance Company, recommending its laws, and our little goodness is all the assessment that we pay. Though the youth at last grows indifferent, the laws of the universe are not indifferent, but are forever on the side of the most sensitive. Listen to every zephyr for some reproof, for it is surely there, and he is unfortunate who does not hear it. We cannot touch a string or move a stop but the charming moral transfixes us. Many an irksome noise, go a long way off, is heard as music, a proud sweet satire on the meanness of our lives.

We are conscious of an animal in us, which awakens in proportion as our higher nature slumbers. It is reptile and sensual, and perhaps cannot be wholly expelled; like the worms which, even in life and health, occupy our bodies. Possibly we may withdraw from it, but never change its nature. I fear that it may enjoy a certain health of its own; that we may be well, yet not pure. The other day I picked up the lower jaw of a hog, with white and sound teeth and tusks, which suggested that there was an animal health and vigor distinct from the spiritual. This creature succeeded by other means than temperance and purity. "That in which men differ from brute beasts," says Mencius, "is a thing very inconsiderable; the common herd lose it very soon; superior men preserve it carefully." Who knows what sort of life would result if we had attained to purity? If I knew so wise a man as could teach me purity I would go to seek him forthwith. "A command over our passions, and over the external senses of the body, and good acts, are declared by the Ved to be indispensable in the mind's approximation to God." Yet the spirit can for the time pervade and control every member and function of the body, and transmute what in form is the grossest sensuality into purity and devotion. The generative energy, which, when we are loose, dissipates and makes us unclean, when we are continent invigorates and inspires us. Chastity is the flowering of man; and what are called Genius, Heroism, Holiness, and the like, are but various fruits which succeed it. Man flows at once to God when the channel of purity is open. By turns our purity inspires and our impurity casts us down. He is blessed who is assured that the animal is dying out in him day

by day, and the divine being established. Perhaps there is
none but has cause for shame on account of the inferior and
brutish nature to which he is allied. I fear that we are such
gods or demigods only as fauns and satyrs, the divine allied
to beasts, the creatures of appetite, and that, to some extent,
our very life is our disgrace. —

"How happy's he who hath due place assigned
    To his beasts and disaforested his mind!

> *   *   *   *   *

Can use his horse, goat, wolf, and ev'ry beast,
And is not ass himself to all the rest!
Else man not only is the herd of swine,
But he's those devils too which did incline
Them to a headlong rage, and made them worse."

All sensuality is one, though it takes many forms; all purity
is one. It is the same whether a man eat, or drink, or cohabit,
or sleep sensually. They are but one appetite, and we only
need to see a person do any one of these things to know how
great a sensualist he is. The impure can neither stand nor sit
with purity. When the reptile is attacked at one mouth of his
burrow, he shows himself at another. If you would be chaste,
you must be temperate. What is chastity? How shall a man
know if he is chaste? He shall not know it. We have heard of
this virtue, but we know not what it is. We speak conform-
ably to the rumor which we have heard. From exertion come
wisdom and purity; from sloth ignorance and sensuality. In
the student sensuality is a sluggish habit of mind. An unclean
person is universally a slothful one, one who sits by a stove,
whom the sun shines on prostrate, who reposes without
being fatigued. If you would avoid uncleanness, and all the
sins, work earnestly, though it be at cleaning a stable. Nature
is hard to be overcome, but she must be overcome. What
avails it that you are Christian, if you are not purer than the
heathen, if you deny yourself no more, if you are not more
religious? I know of many systems of religion esteemed
heathenish whose precepts fill the reader with shame, and

provoke him to new endeavors, though it be to the performance of rites merely.

I hesitate to say these things, but it is not because of the subject,—I care not how obscene my *words* are,—but because I cannot speak of them without betraying my impurity. We discourse freely without shame of one form of sensuality, and are silent about another. We are so degraded that we cannot speak simply of the necessary functions of human nature. In earlier ages, in some countries, every function was reverently spoken of and regulated by law. Nothing was too trivial for the Hindoo lawgiver, however offensive it may be to modern taste. He teaches how to eat, drink, cohabit, void excrement and urine, and the like, elevating what is mean, and does not falsely excuse himself by calling these things trifles.

Every man is the builder of a temple, called his body, to the god he worships, after a style purely his own, nor can he get off by hammering marble instead. We are all sculptors and painters, and our material is our own flesh and blood and bones. Any nobleness begins at once to refine a man's features, any meanness or sensuality to imbrute them.

John Farmer sat at his door one September evening, after a hard day's work, his mind still running on his labor more or less. Having bathed he sat down to recreate his intellectual man. It was a rather cool evening, and some of his neighbors were apprehending a frost. He had not attended to the train of his thoughts long when he heard some one playing on a flute, and that sound harmonized with his mood. Still he thought of his work; but the burden of his thought was, that though this kept running in his head, and he found himself planning and contriving it against his will, yet it concerned him very little. It was no more than the scurf of his skin, which was constantly shuffled off. But the notes of the flute came home to his ears out of a different sphere from that he worked in, and suggested work for certain faculties which slumbered in him. They gently did away with the street, and the village, and the state in which he lived. A voice said to him,—Why do you stay here and live this mean moiling life, when a glorious existence is possible for you? Those same stars twinkle over other fields than these.—But how to come out of this condition and actually migrate thither? All that he could think of was to practise some new austerity, to let his mind descend into his body and redeem it, and treat himself with ever increasing respect.

Brute Neighbors

SOMETIMES I had a companion in my fishing, who came through the village to my house from the other side of the town, and the catching of the dinner was as much a social exercise as the eating of it.

Hermit. I wonder what the world is doing now. I have not heard so much as a locust over the sweet-fern these three hours. The pigeons are all asleep upon their roosts,—no flutter from them. Was that a farmer's noon horn which sounded from beyond the woods just now? The hands are coming in to boiled salt beef and cider and Indian bread. Why will men worry themselves so? He that does not eat need not work. I wonder how much they have reaped. Who would live there where a body can never think for the barking of Bose? And O, the housekeeping! to keep bright the devil's door-knobs, and scour his tubs this bright day! Better not keep a house. Say, some hollow tree; and then for morning calls and dinner-parties! Only a woodpecker tapping. O, they swarm; the sun is too warm there; they are born too far into life for me. I have water from the spring, and a loaf of brown bread on the shelf.—Hark! I hear a rustling of the leaves. Is it some ill-fed village hound yielding to the instinct of the chase? or the lost pig which is said to be in these woods, whose tracks I saw after the rain? It comes on apace; my sumachs and sweet-briers tremble.—Eh, Mr. Poet, is it you? How do you like the world to-day?

Poet. See those clouds; how they hang! That's the greatest thing I have seen to-day. There's nothing like it in old paintings, nothing like it in foreign lands,—unless when we were off the coast of Spain. That's a true Mediterranean sky. I thought, as I have my living to get, and have not eaten to-day, that I might go a-fishing. That's the true industry for poets. It is the only trade I have learned. Come, let's along.

Hermit. I cannot resist. My brown bread will soon be gone. I will go with you gladly soon, but I am just concluding a serious meditation. I think that I am near the end of it. Leave me alone, then, for a while. But that we may not be delayed, you shall be digging the bait meanwhile. Angleworms are rarely to be met with in these parts, where the soil was never fattened with manure; the race is nearly extinct. The sport of digging the bait is nearly equal to that of catching the fish, when one's appetite is not too keen; and this you may have all to yourself to-day. I would advise you to set in the spade down yonder among the ground-nuts, where you see the johnswort waving. I think that I may warrant you one worm to every three sods you turn up, if you look well in among the roots of the grass, as if you were weeding. Or, if you choose to go farther, it will not be unwise, for I have found the increase of fair bait to be very nearly as the squares of the distances.

Hermit alone. Let me see; where was I? Methinks I was nearly in this frame of mind; the world lay about at this angle. Shall I go to heaven or a-fishing? If I should soon bring this meditation to an end, would another so sweet occasion be likely to offer? I was as near being resolved into the essence of things as ever I was in my life. I fear my thoughts will not come back to me. If it would do any good, I would whistle for them. When they make us an offer, is it wise to say, We will think of it? My thoughts have left no track, and I cannot find the path again. What was it that I was thinking of? It was a very hazy day. I will just try these three sentences of Con-fut-see; they may fetch that state about again. I know not whether it was the dumps or a budding ecstasy. Mem. There never is but one opportunity of a kind.

Poet. How now, Hermit, is it too soon? I have got just thirteen whole ones, beside several which are imperfect or undersized; but they will do for the smaller fry; they do not cover up the hook so much. Those village worms are quite too large; a shiner may make a meal off one without finding the skewer.

Hermit. Well, then, let's be off. Shall we to the Concord? There's good sport there if the water be not too high.

Why do precisely these objects which we behold make a world? Why has man just these species of animals for his neighbors; as if nothing but a mouse could have filled this crevice? I suspect that Pilpay & Co. have put animals to their best use, for they are all beasts of burden, in a sense, made to carry some portion of our thoughts.

The mice which haunted my house were not the common ones, which are said to have been introduced into the country, but a wild native kind not found in the village. I sent one to a distinguished naturalist, and it interested him much. When I was building, one of these had its nest underneath the house, and before I had laid the second floor, and swept out the shavings, would come out regularly at lunch time and pick up the crums at my feet. It probably had never seen a man before; and it soon became quite familiar, and would run over my shoes and up my clothes. It could readily ascend the sides of the room by short impulses, like a squirrel, which it resembled in its motions. At length, as I leaned with my elbow on the bench one day, it ran up my clothes, and along my sleeve, and round and round the paper which held my dinner, while I kept the latter close, and dodged and played at bo-peep with it; and when at last I held still a piece of cheese between my thumb and finger, it came and nibbled it, sitting in my hand, and afterward cleaned its face and paws, like a fly, and walked away.

A phœbe soon built in my shed, and a robin for protection in a pine which grew against the house. In June the partridge, (*Tetrao umbellus,*) which is so shy a bird, led her brood past my windows, from the woods in the rear to the front of my house, clucking and calling to them like a hen, and in all her behavior proving herself the hen of the woods. The young suddenly disperse on your approach, at a signal from the mother, as if a whirlwind had swept them away, and they so exactly resemble the dried leaves and twigs that many a traveller has placed his foot in the midst of a brood, and heard the whir of the old bird as she flew off, and her anxious calls and mewing, or seen her trail her wings to attract his attention, without suspecting their neighborhood. The parent will sometimes roll and spin round before you in such a dishabille, that you cannot, for a few moments, detect what kind of creature it is. The young squat still and flat, often running their heads under a leaf, and mind only their mother's directions given from a distance, nor will your approach make them run again and betray themselves. You may even tread on them, or have your eyes on them for a minute, without discovering them. I have held them in my open hand at such a time, and still their only care, obedient to their mother and their instinct, was to squat there without fear or trembling. So perfect is this instinct, that once, when I had laid them on the leaves again, and one accidentally fell on its side, it was found with the rest in exactly the same position ten minutes afterward. They are not callow like the young of most birds, but more perfectly developed and precocious even than chickens. The remarkably adult yet innocent expression of their open and serene eyes is very memorable. All intelligence seems reflected in them. They suggest not merely the purity of infancy, but a wisdom clarified by experience. Such an eye was not born when the bird was, but is coeval with the sky it reflects. The woods do not yield another such a gem. The traveller does not often look into such a limpid well. The ignorant or reckless sportsman often shoots the parent at such a time, and leaves these innocents to fall a prey to some prowling beast or bird, or gradually mingle with the decaying leaves which they so much resemble. It is said that when hatched by a hen they will directly disperse on some alarm, and so are lost, for they never hear the mother's call which gathers them again. These were my hens and chickens.

It is remarkable how many creatures live wild and free though secret in the woods, and still sustain themselves in the neighborhood of towns, suspected by hunters only. How retired the otter manages to live here! He grows to be four feet long, as big as a small boy, perhaps without any human being getting a glimpse of him. I formerly saw the raccoon in the woods behind where my house is built, and probably still heard their whinnering at night. Commonly I rested an hour or two in the shade at noon, after planting, and ate my lunch, and read a little by a spring which was the source of a swamp and of a brook, oozing from under Brister's Hill, half a mile from my field. The approach to this was through a succession of descending grassy hollows, full of young pitch-pines, into a larger wood about the swamp. There, in a very secluded and shaded spot, under a spreading white-pine, there was yet a clean firm sward to sit on. I had dug out the spring and made a well of clear gray water, where I could dip up a pailful

without roiling it, and thither I went for this purpose almost
every day in midsummer, when the pond was warmest.
Thither too the wood-cock led her brood, to probe the mud
for worms, flying but a foot above them down the bank,
while they ran in a troop beneath; but at last, spying me, she
would leave her young and circle round and round me, nearer
and nearer, till within four or five feet, pretending broken
wings and legs, to attract my attention and get off her young,
who would already have taken up their march, with faint wiry
peep, single file through the swamp, as she directed. Or I
heard the peep of the young when I could not see the parent
bird. There too the turtle-doves sat over the spring, or fluttered from bough to bough of the soft white-pines over my
head; or the red squirrel, coursing down the nearest bough,
was particularly familiar and inquisitive. You only need sit still
long enough in some attractive spot in the woods that all its
inhabitants may exhibit themselves to you by turns.

I was witness to events of a less peaceful character. One day
when I went out to my wood-pile, or rather my pile of
stumps, I observed two large ants, the one red, the other
much larger, nearly half an inch long, and black, fiercely contending with one another. Having once got hold they never
let go, but struggled and wrestled and rolled on the chips
incessantly. Looking farther, I was surprised to find that the
chips were covered with such combatants, that it was not a
duellum, but a *bellum*, a war between two races of ants, the
red always pitted against the black, and frequently two red
ones to one black. The legions of these Myrmidons covered
all the hills and vales in my wood-yard, and the ground was
already strewn with the dead and dying, both red and black.
It was the only battle which I have ever witnessed, the only
battle-field I ever trod while the battle was raging; internecine
war; the red republicans on the one hand, and the black im-
perialists on the other. On every side they were engaged in
deadly combat, yet without any noise that I could hear, and
human soldiers never fought so resolutely. I watched a couple
that were fast locked in each other's embraces, in a little
sunny valley amid the chips, now at noon-day prepared to
fight till the sun went down, or life went out. The smaller red
champion had fastened himself like a vice to his adversary's

front, and through all the tumblings on that field never for an instant ceased to gnaw at one of his feelers near the root, having already caused the other to go by the board; while the stronger black one dashed him from side to side, and, as I saw on looking nearer, had already divested him of several of his members. They fought with more pertinacity than bull-dogs. Neither manifested the least disposition to retreat. It was evident that their battle-cry was Conquer or die. In the mean while there came along a single red ant on the hill-side of this valley, evidently full of excitement, who either had des-patched his foe, or had not yet taken part in the battle; prob-ably the latter, for he had lost none of his limbs; whose mother had charged him to return with his shield or upon it. Or perchance he was some Achilles, who had nourished his wrath apart, and had now come to avenge or rescue his Patro-clus. He saw this unequal combat from afar,—for the blacks were nearly twice the size of the red,—he drew near with rapid pace till he stood on his guard within half an inch of the combatants; then, watching his opportunity, he sprang upon the black warrior, and commenced his operations near the root of his right fore-leg, leaving the foe to select among his own members; and so there were three united for life, as if a new kind of attraction had been invented which put all other locks and cements to shame. I should not have won-dered by this time to find that they had their respective mu-sical bands stationed on some eminent chip, and playing their national airs the while, to excite the slow and cheer the dying combatants. I was myself excited somewhat even as if they had been men. The more you think of it, the less the differ-ence. And certainly there is not the fight recorded in Concord history, at least, if in the history of America, that will bear a moment's comparison with this, whether for the numbers en-gaged in it, or for the patriotism and heroism displayed. For numbers and for carnage it was an Austerlitz or Dresden, Concord Fight! Two killed on the patriots' side, and Luther Blanchard wounded! Why here every ant was a Buttrick,— "Fire! for God's sake fire!"—and thousands shared the fate of Davis and Hosmer. There was not one hireling there. I have no doubt that it was a principle they fought for, as much as our ancestors, and not to avoid a three-penny tax on their tea;

and the results of this battle will be as important and memorable to those whom it concerns as those of the battle of
Bunker Hill, at least.

I took up the chip on which the three I have particularly
described were struggling, carried it into my house, and
placed it under a tumbler on my window-sill, in order to see
the issue. Holding a microscope to the first-mentioned red
ant, I saw that, though he was assiduously gnawing at the
near fore-leg of his enemy, having severed his remaining
feeler, his own breast was all torn away, exposing what vitals
he had there to the jaws of the black warrior, whose breast-
plate was apparently too thick for him to pierce; and the dark
carbuncles of the sufferer's eyes shone with ferocity such as
war only could excite. They struggled half an hour longer under the tumbler, and when I looked again the black soldier
had severed the heads of his foes from their bodies, and the
still living heads were hanging on either side of him like
ghastly trophies at his saddle-bow, still apparently as firmly
fastened as ever, and he was endeavoring with feeble struggles, being without feelers and with only the remnant of a
leg, and I know not how many other wounds, to divest himself of them; which at length, after half an hour more, he
accomplished. I raised the glass, and he went off over the
window-sill in that crippled state. Whether he finally survived
that combat, and spent the remainder of his days in some
Hotel des Invalides, I do not know; but I thought that his
industry would not be worth much thereafter. I never learned
which party was victorious, nor the cause of the war; but I
felt for the rest of that day as if I had had my feelings excited
and harrowed by witnessing the struggle, the ferocity and carnage, of a human battle before my door.

Kirby and Spence tell us that the battles of ants have long
been celebrated and the date of them recorded, though they
say that Huber is the only modern author who appears to
have witnessed them. "Æneas Sylvius," say they, "after giving
a very circumstantial account of one contested with great obstinacy by a great and small species on the trunk of a pear
tree," adds that " 'This action was fought in the pontificate of
Eugenius the Fourth, in the presence of Nicholas Pistoriensis,
an eminent lawyer, who related the whole history of the

battle with the greatest fidelity.' A similar engagement between great and small ants is recorded by Olaus Magnus, in
which the small ones, being victorious, are said to have buried
the bodies of their own soldiers, but left those of their giant
enemies a prey to the birds. This event happened previous to
the expulsion of the tyrant Christiern the Second from Sweden." The battle which I witnessed took place in the Presi
dency of Polk, five years before the passage of Webster's
Fugitive-Slave Bill.

Many a village Bose, fit only to course a mud-turtle in a
victualling cellar, sported his heavy quarters in the woods,
without the knowledge of his master, and ineffectually
smelled at old fox burrows and woodchucks' holes; led perchance by some slight cur which nimbly threaded the wood,
and might still inspire a natural terror in its denizens;—now
far behind his guide, barking like a canine bull toward some
small squirrel which had treed itself for scrutiny, then, cantering off, bending the bushes with his weight, imagining that
he is on the track of some stray member of the jerbilla family.
Once I was surprised to see a cat walking along the stony
shore of the pond, for they rarely wander so far from home.
The surprise was mutual. Nevertheless the most domestic cat,
which has lain on a rug all her days, appears quite at home in
the woods, and, by her sly and stealthy behavior, proves herself more native there than the regular inhabitants. Once,
when berrying, I met with a cat with young kittens in the
woods, quite wild, and they all, like their mother, had their
backs up and were fiercely spitting at me. A few years before
I lived in the woods there was what was called a "winged
cat" in one of the farm-houses in Lincoln nearest the pond,
Mr. Gilian Baker's. When I called to see her in June, 1842,
she was gone a-hunting in the woods, as was her wont, (I am
not sure whether it was a male or female, and so use the more
common pronoun,) but her mistress told me that she came
into the neighborhood a little more than a year before, in
April, and was finally taken into their house; that she was of
a dark brownish-gray color, with a white spot on her throat,
and white feet, and had a large bushy tail like a fox; that in
the winter the fur grew thick and flatted out along her sides,
forming strips ten or twelve inches long by two and a half

wide, and under her chin like a muff, the upper side loose, the under matted like felt, and in the spring these appendages dropped off. They gave me a pair of her "wings," which I keep still. There is no appearance of a membrane about them. Some thought it was part flying-squirrel or some other wild animal, which is not impossible, for, according to naturalists, prolific hybrids have been produced by the union of the marten and domestic cat. This would have been the right kind of cat for me to keep, if I had kept any; for why should not a poet's cat be winged as well as his horse?

In the fall the loon (*Colymbus glacialis*) came, as usual, to moult and bathe in the pond, making the woods ring with his wild laughter before I had risen. At rumor of his arrival all the Mill-dam sportsmen are on the alert, in gigs and on foot, two by two and three by three, with patent rifles and conical balls and spy-glasses. They come rustling through the woods like autumn leaves, at least ten men to one loon. Some station themselves on this side of the pond, some on that, for the poor bird cannot be omnipresent; if he dive here he must come up there. But now the kind October wind rises, rustling the leaves and rippling the surface of the water, so that no loon can be heard or seen, though his foes sweep the pond with spy-glasses, and make the woods resound with their discharges. The waves generously rise and dash angrily, taking sides with all waterfowl, and our sportsmen must beat a retreat to town and shop and unfinished jobs. But they were too often successful. When I went to get a pail of water early in the morning I frequently saw this stately bird sailing out of my cove within a few rods. If I endeavored to overtake him in a boat, in order to see how he would manœuvre, he would dive and be completely lost, so that I did not discover him again, sometimes, till the latter part of the day. But I was more than a match for him on the surface. He commonly went off in a rain.

As I was paddling along the north shore one very calm October afternoon, for such days especially they settle on to the lakes, like the milkweed down, having looked in vain over the pond for a loon, suddenly one, sailing out from the shore toward the middle a few rods in front of me, set up his wild laugh and betrayed himself. I pursued with a paddle and he dived, but when he came up I was nearer than before. He dived again, but I miscalculated the direction he would take, and we were fifty rods apart when he came to the surface this time, for I had helped to widen the interval; and again he laughed long and loud, and with more reason than before. He manœuvred so cunningly that I could not get within half a dozen rods of him. Each time, when he came to the surface, turning his head this way and that, he coolly surveyed the water and the land, and apparently chose his course so that he might come up where there was the widest expanse of water and at the greatest distance from the boat. It was surprising how quickly he made up his mind and put his resolve into execution. He led me at once to the widest part of the pond, and could not be driven from it. While he was thinking one thing in his brain, I was endeavoring to divine his thought in mine. It was a pretty game, played on the smooth surface of the pond, a man against a loon. Suddenly your adversary's checker disappears beneath the board, and the problem is to place yours nearest to where his will appear again. Sometimes he would come up unexpectedly on the opposite side of me, having apparently passed directly under the boat. So long-winded was he and so unweariable, that when he had swum farthest he would immediately plunge again, nevertheless; and then no wit could divine where in the deep pond, beneath the smooth surface, he might be speeding his way like a fish, for he had time and ability to visit the bottom of the pond in its deepest part. It is said that loons have been caught in the New York lakes eighty feet beneath the surface, with hooks set for trout,—though Walden is deeper than that. How surprised must the fishes be to see this ungainly visitor from another sphere speeding his way amid their schools! Yet he appeared to know his course as surely under water as on the surface, and swam much faster there. Once or twice I saw a ripple where he approached the surface, just put his head out to reconnoitre, and instantly dived again. I found that it was as well for me to rest on my oars and wait his reappearing as to endeavor to calculate where he would rise; for again and again, when I was straining my eyes over the surface one way, I would suddenly be startled by his unearthly laugh behind me. But why, after displaying so

much cunning, did he invariably betray himself the moment
he came up by that loud laugh? Did not his white breast
enough betray him? He was indeed a silly loon, I thought. I
could commonly hear the plash of the water when he came
up, and so also detected him. But after an hour he seemed as
fresh as ever, dived as willingly and swam yet farther than at
first. It was surprising to see how serenely he sailed off with
unruffled breast when he came to the surface, doing all the
work with his webbed feet beneath. His usual note was this
demoniac laughter, yet somewhat like that of a water-fowl;
but occasionally, when he had balked me most successfully
and come up a long way off, he uttered a long-drawn
unearthly howl, probably more like that of a wolf than any
bird; as when a beast puts his muzzle to the ground and deliberately howls. This was his looning,—perhaps the wildest
sound that is ever heard here, making the woods ring far and
wide. I concluded that he laughed in derision of my efforts,
confident of his own resources. Though the sky was by this
time overcast, the pond was so smooth that I could see where
he broke the surface when I did not hear him. His white
breast, the stillness of the air, and the smoothness of the water
were all against him. At length, having come up fifty rods off,
he uttered one of those prolonged howls, as if calling on the
god of loons to aid him, and immediately there came a wind
from the east and rippled the surface, and filled the whole air
with misty rain, and I was impressed as if it were the prayer
of the loon answered, and his god was angry with me; and so
I left him disappearing far away on the tumultuous surface.

For hours, in fall days, I watched the ducks cunningly tack
and veer and hold the middle of the pond, far from the
sportsman; tricks which they will have less need to practise in
Louisiana bayous. When compelled to rise they would sometimes circle round and round and over the pond at a considerable height, from which they could easily see to other ponds
and the river, like black motes in the sky; and, when I
thought they had gone off thither long since, they would settle down by a slanting flight of a quarter of a mile on to a
distant part which was left free; but what beside safety they
got by sailing in the middle of Walden I do not know, unless
they love its water for the same reason that I do.

House-Warming

IN OCTOBER I went a-graping to the river meadows, and loaded myself with clusters more precious for their beauty and fragrance than for food. There too I admired, though I did not gather, the cranberries, small waxen gems, pendants of the meadow grass, pearly and red, which the farmer plucks with an ugly rake, leaving the smooth meadow in a snarl, heedlessly measuring them by the bushel and the dollar only, and sells the spoils of the meads to Boston and New York; destined to be *jammed*, to satisfy the tastes of lovers of Nature there. So butchers rake the tongues of bison out of the prairie grass, regardless of the torn and drooping plant. The barberry's brilliant fruit was likewise food for my eyes merely; but I collected a small store of wild apples for coddling, which the proprietor and travellers had overlooked. When chestnuts were ripe I laid up half a bushel for winter. It was very exciting at that season to roam the then boundless chestnut woods of Lincoln,—they now sleep their long sleep under the railroad,—with a bag on my shoulder, and a stick to open burrs with in my hand, for I did not always wait for the frost, amid the rustling of leaves and the loud reproofs of the red-squirrels and the jays, whose half-consumed nuts I sometimes stole, for the burrs which they had selected were sure to contain sound ones. Occasionally I climbed and shook the trees. They grew also behind my house, and one large tree which almost overshadowed it, was, when in flower, a bouquet which scented the whole neighborhood, but the squirrels and the jays got most of its fruit; the last coming in flocks early in the morning and picking the nuts out of the burrs before they fell. I relinquished these trees to them and visited the more distant woods composed wholly of chestnut. These nuts, as far as they went, were a good substitute for bread. Many other substitutes might, perhaps, be found. Digging one day for fish-worms I discovered the ground-nut (*Apios tuberosa*) on its string, the potato of the aborigines, a sort of fabulous fruit, which I had begun to doubt if I had ever dug and eaten in childhood, as I had told, and had not dreamed it. I had often since seen its crimpled red velvety blossom supported by the stems of other plants without knowing it to be the same. Cultivation has well nigh exterminated it. It has a sweetish taste, much like that of a frostbitten potato, and I found it better boiled than roasted. This tuber seemed like a faint promise of Nature to rear her own children and feed them simply here at some future period. In these days of fatted cattle and waving grain-fields, this humble root, which was once the *totem* of an Indian tribe, is quite forgotten, or known only by its flowering vine; but let wild Nature reign here once more, and the tender and luxurious English grains will probably disappear before a myriad of foes, and without the care of man the crow may carry back even the last seed of corn to the great corn-field of the Indian's God in the southwest, whence he is said to have brought it; but the now almost exterminated ground-nut will perhaps revive and flourish in spite of frosts and wildness, prove itself indigenous, and resume its ancient importance and dignity as the diet of the hunter tribe. Some Indian Ceres or Minerva must have been the inventor and bestower of it; and when the reign of poetry commences here, its leaves and string of nuts may be represented on our works of art.

Already, by the first of September, I had seen two or three small maples turned scarlet across the pond, beneath where the white stems of three aspens diverged, at the point of a promontory, next the water. Ah, many a tale their color told! And gradually from week to week the character of each tree came out, and it admired itself reflected in the smooth mirror of the lake. Each morning the manager of this gallery substituted some new picture, distinguished by more brilliant or harmonious coloring, for the old upon the walls.

The wasps came by thousands to my lodge in October, as to winter quarters, and settled on my windows within and on the walls over-head, sometimes deterring visitors from entering. Each morning, when they were numbed with cold, I swept some of them out, but I did not trouble myself much to get rid of them; I even felt complimented by their regarding my house as a desirable shelter. They never molested me seriously, though they bedded with me; and they gradually disappeared, into what crevices I do not know, avoiding winter and unspeakable cold.

Like the wasps, before I finally went into winter quarters
in November, I used to resort to the north-east side of Walden, which the sun, reflected from the pitch-pine woods and
the stony shore, made the fire-side of the pond; it is so much
pleasanter and wholesomer to be warmed by the sun while
you can be, than by an artificial fire. I thus warmed myself by
the still glowing embers which the summer, like a departed
hunter, had left.

When I came to build my chimney I studied masonry. My
bricks being second-hand ones required to be cleaned with a
trowel, so that I learned more than usual of the qualities of
bricks and trowels. The mortar on them was fifty years old,
and was said to be still growing harder; but this is one of
those sayings which men love to repeat whether they are true
or not. Such sayings themselves grow harder and adhere more
firmly with age, and it would take many blows with a trowel
to clean an old wiseacre of them. Many of the villages of Mes-
opotamia are built of second-hand bricks of a very good quality, obtained from the ruins of Babylon, and the cement on
them is older and probably harder still. However that may be,
I was struck by the peculiar toughness of the steel which bore
so many violent blows without being worn out. As my bricks
had been in a chimney before, though I did not read the
name of Nebuchadnezzar on them, I picked out as many fire-
place bricks as I could find, to save work and waste, and I
filled the spaces between the bricks about the fire-place with
stones from the pond shore, and also made my mortar with
the white sand from the same place. I lingered most about
the fireplace, as the most vital part of the house. Indeed, I
worked so deliberately, that though I commenced at the
ground in the morning, a course of bricks raised a few inches
above the floor served for my pillow at night; yet I did not
get a stiff neck for it that I remember; my stiff neck is of older
date. I took a poet to board for a fortnight about those times,
which caused me to be put to it for room. He brought his
own knife, though I had two, and we used to scour them by
thrusting them into the earth. He shared with me the labors
of cooking. I was pleased to see my work rising so square and
solid by degrees, and reflected, that, if it proceeded slowly, it

was calculated to endure a long time. The chimney is to some extent an independent structure, standing on the ground and rising through the house to the heavens; even after the house is burned it still stands sometimes, and its importance and independence are apparent. This was toward the end of summer. It was now November.

The north wind had already begun to cool the pond, though it took many weeks of steady blowing to accomplish it, it is so deep. When I began to have a fire at evening, before I plastered my house, the chimney carried smoke particularly well, because of the numerous chinks between the boards. Yet I passed some cheerful evenings in that cool and airy apartment, surrounded by the rough brown boards full of knots, and rafters with the bark on high over-head. My house never pleased my eye so much after it was plastered, though I was obliged to confess that it was more comfortable. Should not every apartment in which man dwells be lofty enough to create some obscurity over-head, where flickering shadows may play at evening about the rafters? These forms are more agreeable to the fancy and imagination than fresco paintings or other the most expensive furniture. I now first began to inhabit my house, I may say, when I began to use it for warmth as well as shelter. I had got a couple of old fire-dogs to keep the wood from the hearth, and it did me good to see the soot form on the back of the chimney which I had built, and I poked the fire with more right and more satisfaction than usual. My dwelling was small, and I could hardly entertain an echo in it; but it seemed larger for being a single apartment and remote from neighbors. All the attractions of a house were concentrated in one room; it was kitchen, chamber, parlor, and keeping-room; and whatever satisfaction parent or child, master or servant, derive from living in a house, I enjoyed it all. Cato says, the master of a family (*patremfamilias*) must have in his rustic villa "cellam oleariam, vinariam, dolia multa, uti lubeat caritatem expectare, et rei, et virtuti, et gloriæ erit," that is, "an oil and wine cellar, many casks, so that it may be pleasant to expect hard times; it will be for his advantage, and virtue, and glory." I had in my cellar a firkin of potatoes, about two quarts of peas with the weevil in them, and on my shelf a little rice, a jug of molasses, and of rye and Indian meal a peck each.

I sometimes dream of a larger and more populous house, standing in a golden age, of enduring materials, and without ginger-bread work, which shall still consist of only one room, a vast, rude, substantial, primitive hall, without ceiling or plastering, with bare rafters and purlins supporting a sort of lower heaven over one's head,—useful to keep off rain and snow; where the king and queen posts stand but to receive your homage, when you have done reverence to the prostrate Saturn of an older dynasty on stepping over the sill; a cavernous house, wherein you must reach up a torch upon a pole to see the roof; where some may live in the fire-place, some in the recess of a window, and some on settles, some at one end of the hall, some at another, and some aloft on rafters with the spiders, if they choose; a house which you have got into when you have opened the outside door, and the ceremony is over; where the weary traveller may wash, and eat, and converse, and sleep, without further journey; such a shelter as you would be glad to reach in a tempestuous night, containing all the essentials of a house, and nothing for house-keeping; where you can see all the treasures of the house at one view, and every thing hangs upon its peg that a man should use; at once kitchen, pantry, parlor, chamber, store-house, and garret; where you can see so necessary a thing as a barrel or a ladder, so convenient a thing as a cupboard, and hear the pot boil, and pay your respects to the fire that cooks your dinner and the oven that bakes your bread, and the necessary furniture and utensils are the chief ornaments; where the washing is not put out, nor the fire, nor the mistress, and perhaps you are sometimes requested to move from off the trap-door, when the cook would descend into the cellar, and so learn whether the ground is solid or hollow beneath you without stamping. A house whose inside is as open and manifest as a bird's nest, and you cannot go in at the front door and out at the back without seeing some of its inhabitants; where to be a guest is to be presented with the freedom of the house, and not to be carefully excluded from seven eighths of it, shut up in a particular cell, and told to make yourself at home there,—in solitary confinement. Nowadays the host does not admit you to *his* hearth, but has got the mason to build one for yourself somewhere in his alley, and hospitality is the art of *keeping* you at the greatest distance. There is as much secrecy about the cooking as if he had a design to poison you. I am aware that I have been on many a man's premises, and might have been legally ordered off, but I am not aware that I have been in many men's houses. I might visit in my old clothes a king and queen who lived simply in such a house as I have described, if I were going their way; but backing out of a modern palace will be all that I shall desire to learn, if ever I am caught in one.

It would seem as if the very language of our parlors would lose all its nerve and degenerate into *parlaver* wholly, our lives pass at such remoteness from its symbols, and its metaphors and tropes are necessarily so far fetched, through slides and dumb-waiters, as it were; in other words, the parlor is so far from the kitchen and workshop. The dinner even is only the parable of a dinner, commonly. As if only the savage dwelt near enough to Nature and Truth to borrow a trope from them. How can the scholar, who dwells away in the North West Territory or the Isle of Man, tell what is parliamentary in the kitchen?

However, only one or two of my guests were ever bold enough to stay and eat a hasty-pudding with me; but when they saw that crisis approaching they beat a hasty retreat rather, as if it would shake the house to its foundations. Nevertheless, it stood through a great many hasty-puddings.

I did not plaster till it was freezing weather. I brought over some whiter and cleaner sand for this purpose from the opposite shore of the pond in a boat, a sort of conveyance which would have tempted me to go much farther if necessary. My house had in the mean while been shingled down to the ground on every side. In lathing I was pleased to be able to send home each nail with a single blow of the hammer, and it was my ambition to transfer the plaster from the board to the wall neatly and rapidly. I remembered the story of a conceited fellow, who, in fine clothes, was wont to lounge about the village once, giving advice to workmen. Venturing one day to substitute deeds for words, he turned up his cuffs, seized a plasterer's board, and having loaded his trowel with-

out mishap, with a complacent look toward the lathing overhead, made a bold gesture thitherward; and straightway, to
his complete discomfiture, received the whole contents in his
ruffled bosom. I admired anew the economy and convenience
of plastering, which so effectually shuts out the cold and takes
a handsome finish, and I learned the various casualties to
which the plasterer is liable. I was surprised to see how thirsty
the bricks were which drank up all the moisture in my plaster
before I had smoothed it, and how many pailfuls of water it
takes to christen a new hearth. I had the previous winter
made a small quantity of lime by burning the shells of the
Unio fluviatilis, which our river affords, for the sake of the
experiment; so that I knew where my materials came from. I
might have got good limestone within a mile or two and
burned it myself, if I had cared to do so.

The pond had in the mean while skimmed over in the shad-
iest and shallowest coves, some days or even weeks before the
general freezing. The first ice is especially interesting and perfect, being hard, dark, and transparent, and affords the best
opportunity that ever offers for examining the bottom where
it is shallow; for you can lie at your length on ice only an
inch thick, like a skater insect on the surface of the water, and
study the bottom at your leisure, only two or three inches
distant, like a picture behind a glass, and the water is necessarily always smooth then. There are many furrows in the
sand where some creature has travelled about and doubled on
its tracks; and, for wrecks, it is strewn with the cases of cadis
worms made of minute grains of white quartz. Perhaps these
have creased it, for you find some of their cases in the furrows, though they are deep and broad for them to make. But
the ice itself is the object of most interest, though you must
improve the earliest opportunity to study it. If you examine
it closely the morning after it freezes, you find that the greater
part of the bubbles, which at first appeared to be within it,
are against its under surface, and that more are continually
rising from the bottom; while the ice is as yet comparatively
solid and dark, that is, you see the water through it. These
bubbles are from an eightieth to an eighth of an inch in
diameter, very clear and beautiful, and you see your face

reflected in them through the ice. There may be thirty or forty of them to a square inch. There are also already within the ice narrow oblong perpendicular bubbles about half an inch long, sharp cones with the apex upward; or oftener, if the ice is quite fresh, minute spherical bubbles one directly above another, like a string of beads. But these within the ice are not so numerous nor obvious as those beneath. I sometimes used to cast on stones to try the strength of the ice, and those which broke through carried in air with them, which formed very large and conspicuous white bubbles beneath. One day when I came to the same place forty-eight hours afterward, I found that those large bubbles were still perfect, though an inch more of ice had formed, as I could see distinctly by the seam in the edge of a cake. But as the last two days had been very warm, like an Indian summer, the ice was not now transparent, showing the dark green color of the water, and the bottom, but opaque and whitish or gray, and though twice as thick was hardly stronger than before, for the air bubbles had greatly expanded under this heat and run together, and lost their regularity; they were no longer one directly over another, but often like silvery coins poured from a bag, one overlapping another, or in thin flakes, as if occupying slight cleavages. The beauty of the ice was gone, and it was too late to study the bottom. Being curious to know what position my great bubbles occupied with regard to the new ice, I broke out a cake containing a middling sized one, and turned it bottom upward. The new ice had formed around and under the bubble, so that it was included between the two ices. It was wholly in the lower ice, but close against the upper, and was flattish, or perhaps slightly lenticular, with a rounded edge, a quarter of an inch deep by four inches in diameter; and I was surprised to find that directly under the bubble the ice was melted with great regularity in the form of a saucer reversed, to the height of five eighths of an inch in the middle, leaving a thin partition there between the water and the bubble, hardly an eighth of an inch thick; and in many places the small bubbles in this partition had burst out downward, and probably there was no ice at all under the largest bubbles, which were a foot in diameter. I inferred that the infinite number of minute bubbles which I had first seen against the under surface of the ice were now frozen in likewise, and that each, in its degree, had operated like a burning glass on the ice beneath to melt and rot it. These are the little air-guns which contribute to make the ice crack and whoop.

At length the winter set in in good earnest, just as I had finished plastering, and the wind began to howl around the house as if it had not had permission to do so till then. Night after night the geese came lumbering in in the dark with a clangor and a whistling of wings, even after the ground was covered with snow, some to alight in Walden, and some flying low over the woods toward Fair Haven, bound for Mexico. Several times, when returning from the village at ten or eleven o'clock at night, I heard the tread of a flock of geese, or else ducks, on the dry leaves in the woods by a pond-hole behind my dwelling, where they had come up to feed, and the faint honk or quack of their leader as they hurried off. In 1845 Walden froze entirely over for the first time on the night of the 22d of December, Flints' and other shallower ponds and the river having been frozen ten days or more; in '46, the 16th; in '49, about the 31st; and in '50, about the 27th of December; in '52, the 5th of January; in '53, the 31st of December. The snow had already covered the ground since the 25th of November, and surrounded me suddenly with the scenery of winter. I withdrew yet farther into my shell, and endeavored to keep a bright fire both within my house and within my breast. My employment out of doors now was to collect the dead wood in the forest, bringing it in my hands or on my shoulders, or sometimes trailing a dead pine tree under each arm to my shed. An old forest fence which had seen its best days was a great haul for me. I sacrificed it to Vulcan, for it was past serving the god Terminus. How much more interesting an event is that man's supper who has just been forth in the snow to hunt, nay, you might say, steal, the fuel to cook it with! His bread and meat are sweet. There are enough fagots and waste wood of all kinds in the forests of most of our towns to support many fires, but which at present warm none, and, some think, hinder the growth of the young wood. There was also the drift-wood of the pond. In the course of the summer I had discovered a raft of pitch-pine logs with the bark on, pinned together by the Irish when the railroad was built. This I hauled up partly on the shore. After soaking two years and then lying high six months it was perfectly sound, though waterlogged past drying. I amused myself one winter day with sliding this piece-meal across the pond, nearly half a mile, skating behind with one end of a log fifteen feet long on my shoulder, and the other on the ice; or I tied several logs together with a birch withe, and then, with a longer birch or alder which had a hook at the end, dragged them across. Though completely waterlogged and almost as heavy as lead, they not only burned long, but made a very hot fire; nay, I thought that they burned better for the soaking, as if the pitch, being confined by the water, burned longer as in a lamp.

Gilpin, in his account of the forest borderers of England, says that "the encroachments of trespassers, and the houses and fences thus raised on the borders of the forest," were "considered as great nuisances by the old forest law, and were severely punished under the name of *purprestures*, as tending *ad terrorem ferarum — ad nocumentum forestæ*, &c.," to the frightening of the game and the detriment of the forest. But I was interested in the preservation of the venison and the vert more than the hunters or wood-choppers, and as much as though I had been the Lord Warden himself; and if any part was burned, though I burned it myself by accident, I grieved with a grief that lasted longer and was more inconsolable than that of the proprietors; nay, I grieved when it was cut down by the proprietors themselves. I would that our farmers when they cut down a forest felt some of that awe which the old Romans did when they came to thin, or let in the light to, a consecrated grove, (*lucum conlucare,*) that is, would believe that it is sacred to some god. The Roman made an expiatory offering, and prayed, Whatever god or goddess thou art to whom this grove is sacred, be propitious to me, my family, and children, &c.

It is remarkable what a value is still put upon wood even in this age and in this new country, a value more permanent and universal than that of gold. After all our discoveries and inventions no man will go by a pile of wood. It is as precious to us as it was to our Saxon and Norman ancestors. If they made their bows of it, we make our gun-stocks of it. Michaux, more than thirty years ago, says that the price of wood for fuel in New York and Philadelphia "nearly equals, and sometimes exceeds, that of the best wood in Paris, though this immense capital annually requires more than three hundred thousand cords, and is surrounded to the distance of three hundred miles by cultivated plains." In this town the price of wood rises almost steadily, and the only question is, how much higher it is to be this year than it was the last. Mechanics and tradesmen who come in person to the forest on no other errand, are sure to attend the wood auction, and even pay a high price for the privilege of gleaning after the wood-chopper. It is now many years that men have resorted to the forest for fuel and the materials of the arts; the New Englander and the New Hollander, the Parisian and the Celt, the farmer and Robinhood, Goody Blake and Harry Gill, in most parts of the world the prince and the peasant, the scholar and the savage, equally require still a few sticks from the forest to warm them and cook their food. Neither could I do without them.

Every man looks at his wood-pile with a kind of affection. I loved to have mine before my window, and the more chips the better to remind me of my pleasing work. I had an old axe which nobody claimed, with which by spells in winter days, on the sunny side of the house, I played about the stumps which I had got out of my bean-field. As my driver prophesied when I was ploughing, they warmed me twice, once while I was splitting them, and again when they were on the fire, so that no fuel could give out more heat. As for the axe, I was advised to get the village blacksmith to "jump" it; but I jumped him, and, putting a hickory helve from the woods into it, made it do. If it was dull, it was at least hung true.

A few pieces of fat pine were a great treasure. It is interesting to remember how much of this food for fire is still concealed in the bowels of the earth. In previous years I had often gone "prospecting" over some bare hill-side, where a pitch-pine wood had formerly stood, and got out the fat pine roots. They are almost indestructible. Stumps thirty or forty years old, at least, will still be sound at the core, though the sapwood has all become vegetable mould, as appears by the scales of the thick bark forming a ring level with the earth four or five inches distant from the heart. With axe and shovel you explore this mine, and follow the marrowy store, yellow as beef tallow, or as if you had struck on a vein of gold, deep into the earth. But commonly I kindled my fire with the dry leaves of the forest, which I had stored up in my shed before the snow came. Green hickory finely split makes the woodchopper's kindlings, when he has a camp in the woods. Once in a while I got a little of this. When the villagers were lighting their fires beyond the horizon, I too gave notice to the various wild inhabitants of Walden vale, by a smoky streamer from my chimney, that I was awake. —

> Light-winged Smoke, Icarian bird,
> Melting thy pinions in thy upward flight,
> Lark without song, and messenger of dawn,
> Circling above the hamlets as thy nest;
> Or else, departing dream, and shadowy form
> Of midnight vision, gathering up thy skirts;
> By night star-veiling, and by day
> Darkening the light and blotting out the sun;
> Go thou my incense upward from this hearth,
> And ask the gods to pardon this clear flame.

Hard green wood just cut, though I used but little of that, answered my purpose better than any other. I sometimes left a good fire when I went to take a walk in a winter afternoon; and when I returned, three or four hours afterward, it would be still alive and glowing. My house was not empty though I was gone. It was as if I had left a cheerful housekeeper behind. It was I and Fire that lived there; and commonly my housekeeper proved trustworthy. One day, however, as I was splitting wood, I thought that I would just look in at the window and see if the house was not on fire; it was the only time I remember to have been particularly anxious on this score; so I looked and saw that a spark had caught my bed, and I went in and extinguished it when it had burned a place as big as my hand. But my house occupied so sunny and sheltered a position, and its roof was so low, that I could afford to let the fire go out in the middle of almost any winter day.

The moles nested in my cellar, nibbling every third potato, and making a snug bed even there of some hair left after plastering and of brown paper; for even the wildest animals love comfort and warmth as well as man, and they survive the winter only because they are so careful to secure them. Some of my friends spoke as if I was coming to the woods on purpose to freeze myself. The animal merely makes a bed, which he warms with his body in a sheltered place; but man, having discovered fire, boxes up some air in a spacious apartment, and warms that, instead of robbing himself, makes that his bed, in which he can move about divested of more cumbrous clothing, maintain a kind of summer in the midst of winter, and by means of windows even admit the light, and with a lamp lengthen out the day. Thus he goes a step or two beyond instinct, and saves a little time for the fine arts. Though, when I had been exposed to the rudest blasts a long time, my whole body began to grow torpid, when I reached the genial atmosphere of my house I soon recovered my faculties and prolonged my life. But the most luxuriously housed has little to boast of in this respect, nor need we trouble ourselves to speculate how the human race may be at last destroyed. It would be easy to cut their threads any time with a little sharper blast from the north. We go on dating from Cold Fridays and Great Snows; but a little colder Friday, or greater snow, would put a period to man's existence on the globe.

The next winter I used a small cooking-stove for economy, since I did not own the forest; but it did not keep fire so well as the open fire-place. Cooking was then, for the most part, no longer a poetic, but merely a chemic process. It will soon be forgotten, in these days of stoves, that we used to roast potatoes in the ashes, after the Indian fashion. The stove not only took up room and scented the house, but it concealed the fire, and I felt as if I had lost a companion. You can always see a face in the fire. The laborer, looking into it at evening, purifies his thoughts of the dross and earthiness which they have accumulated during the day. But I could no longer sit and look into the fire, and the pertinent words of a poet recurred to me with new force. —

"Never, bright flame, may be denied to me
Thy dear, life imaging, close sympathy.
What but my hopes shot upward e'er so bright?
What but my fortunes sunk so low in night?

Why art thou banished from our hearth and hall,
Thou who art welcomed and beloved by all?
Was thy existence then too fanciful
For our life's common light, who are so dull?
Did thy bright gleam mysterious converse hold
With our congenial souls? secrets too bold?
Well, we are safe and strong, for now we sit
Beside a hearth where no dim shadows flit,
Where nothing cheers nor saddens, but a fire
Warms feet and hands—nor does to more aspire;
By whose compact utilitarian heap
The present may sit down and go to sleep,
Nor fear the ghosts who from the dim past walked,
And with us by the unequal light of the old wood fire
    talked."

Former Inhabitants; and Winter Visitors

I WEATHERED some merry snow storms, and spent some cheerful winter evenings by my fire-side, while the snow whirled wildly without, and even the hooting of the owl was hushed. For many weeks I met no one in my walks but those who came occasionally to cut wood and sled it to the village. The elements, however, abetted me in making a path through the deepest snow in the woods, for when I had once gone through the wind blew the oak leaves into my tracks, where they lodged, and by absorbing the rays of the sun melted the snow, and so not only made a dry bed for my feet, but in the night their dark line was my guide. For human society I was obliged to conjure up the former occupants of these woods. Within the memory of many of my townsmen the road near which my house stands resounded with the laugh and gossip of inhabitants, and the woods which border it were notched and dotted here and there with their little gardens and dwellings, though it was then much more shut in by the forest than now. In some places, within my own remembrance, the pines would scrape both sides of a chaise at once, and women and children who were compelled to go this way to Lincoln alone and on foot did it with fear, and often ran a good part of the distance. Though mainly but a humble route to neighboring villages, or for the woodman's team, it once amused the traveller more than now by its variety, and lingered longer in his memory. Where now firm open fields stretch from the village to the woods, it then ran through a maple swamp on a foundation of logs, the remnants of which, doubtless, still underlie the present dusty highway, from the Stratten, now the Alms House, Farm, to Brister's Hill.

East of my bean-field, across the road, lived Cato Ingraham, slave of Duncan Ingraham, Esquire, gentleman of Concord village; who built his slave a house, and gave him permission to live in Walden Woods;—Cato, not Uticensis, but Concordiensis. Some say that he was a Guinea Negro. There are a few who remember his little patch among the walnuts, which he let grow up till he should be old and need them; but a younger and whiter speculator got them at last.

He too, however, occupies an equally narrow house at present. Cato's half-obliterated cellar hole still remains, though known to few, being concealed from the traveller by a fringe of pines. It is now filled with the smooth sumach, (*Rhus glabra*,) and one of the earliest species of golden-rod (*Solidago stricta*) grows there luxuriantly.

Here, by the very corner of my field, still nearer to town, Zilpha, a colored woman, had her little house, where she spun linen for the townsfolk, making the Walden Woods ring with her shrill singing, for she had a loud and notable voice. At length, in the war of 1812, her dwelling was set on fire by English soldiers, prisoners on parole, when she was away, and her cat and dog and hens were all burned up together. She led a hard life, and somewhat inhumane. One old frequenter of these woods remembers, that as he passed her house one noon he heard her muttering to herself over her gurgling pot,—"Ye are all bones, bones!" I have seen bricks amid the oak copse there.

Down the road, on the right hand, on Brister's Hill, lived Brister Freeman, "a handy Negro," slave of Squire Cummings once,—there where grow still the apple-trees which Brister planted and tended; large old trees now, but their fruit still wild and ciderish to my taste. Not long since I read his epitaph in the old Lincoln burying-ground, a little on one side, near the unmarked graves of some British grenadiers who fell in the retreat from Concord,—where he is styled "Sippio Brister,"—Scipio Africanus he had some title to be called,—"a man of color," as if he were discolored. It also told me, with staring emphasis, when he died; which was but an indirect way of informing me that he ever lived. With him dwelt Fenda, his hospitable wife, who told fortunes, yet pleasantly,—large, round, and black, blacker than any of the children of night, such a dusky orb as never rose on Concord before or since.

Farther down the hill, on the left, on the old road in the woods, are marks of some homestead of the Stratten family; whose orchard once covered all the slope of Brister's Hill, but was long since killed out by pitch-pines, excepting a few stumps, whose old roots furnish still the wild stocks of many a thrifty village tree.

Nearer yet to town, you come to Breed's location, on the other side of the way, just on the edge of the wood; ground famous for the pranks of a demon not distinctly named in old mythology, who has acted a prominent and astounding part in our New England life, and deserves, as much as any mythological character, to have his biography written one day; who first comes in the guise of a friend or hired man, and then robs and murders the whole family,—New-England Rum. But history must not yet tell the tragedies enacted here; let time intervene in some measure to assuage and lend an azure tint to them. Here the most indistinct and dubious tradition says that once a tavern stood; the well the same, which tempered the traveller's beverage and refreshed his steed. Here then men saluted one another, and heard and told the news, and went their ways again.

Breed's hut was standing only a dozen years ago, though it had long been unoccupied. It was about the size of mine. It was set on fire by mischievous boys, one Election night, if I do not mistake. I lived on the edge of the village then, and had just lost myself over Davenant's Gondibert, that winter that I labored with a lethargy,—which, by the way, I never knew whether to regard as a family complaint, having an uncle who goes to sleep shaving himself, and is obliged to sprout potatoes in a cellar Sundays, in order to keep awake and keep the Sabbath, or as the consequence of my attempt to read Chalmers' collection of English poetry without skipping. It fairly overcame my Nervii. I had just sunk my head on this when the bells rung fire, and in hot haste the engines rolled that way, led by a straggling troop of men and boys, and I among the foremost, for I had leaped the brook. We thought it was far south over the woods,—we who had run to fires before,—barn, shop, or dwelling-house, or all together. "It's Baker's barn," cried one. "It is the Codman Place," affirmed another. And then fresh sparks went up above the wood, as if the roof fell in, and we all shouted "Concord to the rescue!" Wagons shot past with furious speed and crushing loads, bearing, perchance, among the rest, the agent of the Insurance Company, who was bound to go however far; and ever and anon the engine bell tinkled behind, more slow and sure, and rearmost of all, as it was afterward whispered, came they who set the fire and gave the alarm. Thus we kept on like true idealists, rejecting the evidence of our senses, until at a turn in the road we heard the crackling and actually felt the heat of the fire from over the wall, and realized, alas! that we were there. The very nearness of the fire but cooled our ardor. At first we thought to throw a frog-pond on to it; but concluded to let it burn, it was so far gone and so worthless. So we stood round our engine, jostled one another, expressed our sentiments through speaking trumpets, or in lower tone referred to the great conflagrations which the world has witnessed, including Bascom's shop, and, between ourselves, we thought that, were we there in season with our "tub," and a full frog-pond by, we could turn that threatened last and universal one into another flood. We finally retreated without doing any mischief,—returned to sleep and Gondibert. But as for Gondibert, I would except that passage in the preface about wit being the soul's powder,—"but most of mankind are strangers to wit, as Indians are to powder."

It chanced that I walked that way across the fields the following night, about the same hour, and hearing a low moaning at this spot, I drew near in the dark, and discovered the only survivor of the family that I know, the heir of both its virtues and its vices, who alone was interested in this burning, lying on his stomach and looking over the cellar wall at the still smouldering cinders beneath, muttering to himself, as is his wont. He had been working far off in the river meadows all day, and had improved the first moments that he could call his own to visit the home of his fathers and his youth. He gazed into the cellar from all sides and points of view by turns, always lying down to it, as if there was some treasure, which he remembered, concealed between the stones, where there was absolutely nothing but a heap of bricks and ashes. The house being gone, he looked at what there was left. He was soothed by the sympathy which my mere presence implied, and showed me, as well as the darkness permitted, where the well was covered up; which, thank Heaven, could never be burned; and he groped long about the wall to find the well-sweep which his father had cut and mounted, feeling for the iron hook or staple by which a burden had been

fastened to the heavy end,—all that he could now cling to,—
to convince me that it was no common "rider." I felt it, and
still remark it almost daily in my walks, for by it hangs the
history of a family.

Once more, on the left, where are seen the well and lilac
bushes by the wall, in the now open field, lived Nutting and
Le Grosse. But to return toward Lincoln.

Farther in the woods than any of these, where the road
approaches nearest to the pond, Wyman the potter squatted,
and furnished his townsmen with earthen ware, and left descendants to succeed him. Neither were they rich in worldly
goods, holding the land by sufferance while they lived; and
there often the sheriff came in vain to collect the taxes, and
"attached a chip," for form's sake, as I have read in his accounts, there being nothing else that he could lay his hands
on. One day in midsummer, when I was hoeing, a man who
was carrying a load of pottery to market stopped his horse
against my field and inquired concerning Wyman the younger. He had long ago bought a potter's wheel of him, and
wished to know what had become of him. I had read of the
potter's clay and wheel in Scripture, but it had never occurred
to me that the pots we use were not such as had come down
unbroken from those days, or grown on trees like gourds
somewhere, and I was pleased to hear that so fictile an art
was ever practised in my neighborhood.

The last inhabitant of these woods before me was an Irishman, Hugh Quoil, (if I have spelt his name with coil
enough,) who occupied Wyman's tenement,—Col. Quoil, he
was called. Rumor said that he had been a soldier at Waterloo. If he had lived I should have made him fight his battles
over again. His trade here was that of a ditcher. Napoleon
went to St. Helena; Quoil came to Walden Woods. All I
know of him is tragic. He was a man of manners, like one
who had seen the world, and was capable of more civil speech
than you could well attend to. He wore a great coat in midsummer, being affected with the trembling delirium, and his
face was the color of carmine. He died in the road at the foot
of Brister's Hill shortly after I came to the woods, so that I
have not remembered him as a neighbor. Before his house
was pulled down, when his comrades avoided it as "an un-

lucky castle," I visited it. There lay his old clothes curled up by use, as if they were himself, upon his raised plank bed. His pipe lay broken on the hearth, instead of a bowl broken at the fountain. The last could never have been the symbol of his death, for he confessed to me that, though he had heard of Brister's Spring, he had never seen it; and soiled cards, kings of diamonds spades and hearts, were scattered over the floor. One black chicken which the administrator could not catch, black as night and as silent, not even croaking, awaiting Reynard, still went to roost in the next apartment. In the rear there was the dim outline of a garden, which had been planted but had never received its first hoeing, owing to those terrible shaking fits, though it was now harvest time. It was over-run with Roman wormwood and beggar-ticks, which last stuck to my clothes for all fruit. The skin of a woodchuck was freshly stretched upon the back of the house, a trophy of his last Waterloo; but no warm cap or mittens would he want more.

Now only a dent in the earth marks the site of these dwellings, with buried cellar stones, and strawberries, raspberries, thimble-berries, hazel-bushes, and sumachs growing in the sunny sward there; some pitch-pine or gnarled oak occupies what was the chimney nook, and a sweet-scented black-birch, perhaps, waves where the door-stone was. Sometimes the well dent is visible, where once a spring oozed; now dry and tearless grass; or it was covered deep,—not to be discovered till some late day,—with a flat stone under the sod, when the last of the race departed. What a sorrowful act must that be,—the covering up of wells! coincident with the opening of wells of tears. These cellar dents, like deserted fox burrows, old holes, are all that is left where once were the stir and bustle of human life, and "fate, free-will, foreknowledge absolute," in some form and dialect or other were by turns discussed. But all I can learn of their conclusions amounts to just this, that "Cato and Brister pulled wool;" which is about as edifying as the history of more famous schools of philosophy.

Still grows the vivacious lilac a generation after the door and lintel and the sill are gone, unfolding its sweet-scented flowers each spring, to be plucked by the musing traveller; planted and tended once by children's hands, in front-yard

plots,—now standing by wall-sides in retired pastures, and
giving place to new-rising forests;—the last of that stirp, sole
survivor of that family. Little did the dusky children think
that the puny slip with its two eyes only, which they stuck in
the ground in the shadow of the house and daily watered,
would root itself so, and outlive them and house itself in the
rear that shaded it, and grown man's garden and orchard, and
tell their story faintly to the lone wanderer a half century after
they had grown up and died,—blossoming as fair, and smell-
ing as sweet, as in that first spring. I mark its still tender, civil,
cheerful, lilac colors.

But this small village, germ of something more, why did it
fail while Concord keeps its ground? Were there no natural
advantages,—no water privileges, forsooth? Ay, the deep
Walden Pond and cool Brister's Spring,—privilege to drink
long and healthy draughts at these, all unimproved by these
men but to dilute their glass. They were universally a thirsty
race. Might not the basket, stable-broom, mat-making, corn-
parching, linen-spinning, and pottery business have thrived
here, making the wilderness to blossom like the rose, and a
numerous posterity have inherited the land of their fathers?
The sterile soil would at least have been proof against a lowland degeneracy. Alas! how little does the memory of these
human inhabitants enhance the beauty of the landscape!
Again, perhaps, Nature will try, with me for a first settler, and
my house raised last spring to be the oldest in the hamlet.

I am not aware that any man has ever built on the spot
which I occupy. Deliver me from a city built on the site of a
more ancient city, whose materials are ruins, whose gardens
cemeteries. The soil is blanched and accursed there, and before that becomes necessary the earth itself will be destroyed.
With such reminiscences I repeopled the woods and lulled
myself asleep.

At this season I seldom had a visitor. When the snow lay
deepest no wanderer ventured near my house for a week or
fortnight at a time, but there I lived as snug as a meadow
mouse, or as cattle and poultry which are said to have survived for a long time buried in drifts, even without food; or
like that early settler's family in the town of Sutton, in this

state, whose cottage was completely covered by the great snow of 1717 when he was absent, and an Indian found it only by the hole which the chimney's breath made in the drift, and so relieved the family. But no friendly Indian concerned himself about me; nor needed he, for the master of the house was at home. The Great Snow! How cheerful it is to hear of! When the farmers could not get to the woods and swamps with their teams, and were obliged to cut down the shade trees before their houses, and when the crust was harder cut off the trees in the swamps ten feet from the ground, as it appeared the next spring.

In the deepest snows, the path which I used from the highway to my house, about half a mile long, might have been represented by a meandering dotted line, with wide intervals between the dots. For a week of even weather I took exactly the same number of steps, and of the same length, coming and going, stepping deliberately and with the precision of a pair of dividers in my own deep tracks,—to such routine the winter reduces us,—yet often they were filled with heaven's own blue. But no weather interfered fatally with my walks, or rather my going abroad, for I frequently tramped eight or ten miles through the deepest snow to keep an appointment with a beech-tree, or a yellow-birch, or an old acquaintance among the pines; when the ice and snow causing their limbs to droop, and so sharpening their tops, had changed the pines into fir-trees; wading to the tops of the highest hills when the snow was nearly two feet deep on a level, and shaking down another snow-storm on my head at every step; or sometimes creeping and floundering thither on my hands and knees, when the hunters had gone into winter quarters. One afternoon I amused myself by watching a barred owl (*Strix nebulosa*) sitting on one of the lower dead limbs of a white-pine, close to the trunk, in broad daylight, I standing within a rod of him. He could hear me when I moved and cronched the snow with my feet, but could not plainly see me. When I made most noise he would stretch out his neck, and erect his neck feathers, and open his eyes wide; but their lids soon fell again, and he began to nod. I too felt a slumberous influence after watching him half an hour, as he sat thus with his eyes half open, like a cat, winged brother of the cat. There was

only a narrow slit left between their lids, by which he preserved a peninsular relation to me; thus, with half-shut eyes,
looking out from the land of dreams, and endeavoring to realize me, vague object or mote that interrupted his visions. At
length, on some louder noise or my nearer approach, he
would grow uneasy and sluggishly turn about on his perch,
as if impatient at having his dreams disturbed; and when he
launched himself off and flapped through the pines, spreading
his wings to unexpected breadth, I could not hear the slightest sound from them. Thus, guided amid the pine boughs
rather by a delicate sense of their neighborhood than by sight,
feeling his twilight way as it were with his sensitive pinions,
he found a new perch, where he might in peace await the
dawning of his day.

As I walked over the long causeway made for the railroad
through the meadows, I encountered many a blustering and
nipping wind, for nowhere has it freer play; and when the
frost had smitten me on one cheek, heathen as I was, I turned
to it the other also. Nor was it much better by the carriage
road from Brister's Hill. For I came to town still, like a
friendly Indian, when the contents of the broad open fields
were all piled up between the walls of the Walden road, and
half an hour sufficed to obliterate the tracks of the last traveller. And when I returned new drifts would have formed,
through which I floundered, where the busy north-west wind
had been depositing the powdery snow round a sharp angle
in the road, and not a rabbit's track, nor even the fine print,
the small type, of a meadow mouse was to be seen. Yet I
rarely failed to find, even in mid-winter, some warm and
springy swamp where the grass and the skunk-cabbage still
put forth with perennial verdure, and some hardier bird occasionally awaited the return of spring.

Sometimes, notwithstanding the snow, when I returned
from my walk at evening I crossed the deep tracks of a wood-
chopper leading from my door, and found his pile of whittlings on the hearth, and my house filled with the odor of his
pipe. Or on a Sunday afternoon, if I chanced to be at home,
I heard the cronching of the snow made by the step of a long-
headed farmer, who from far through the woods sought my
house, to have a social "crack;" one of the few of his vocation

who are "men on their farms;" who donned a frock instead of a professor's gown, and is as ready to extract the moral out of church or state as to haul a load of manure from his barn-yard. We talked of rude and simple times, when men sat about large fires in cold bracing weather, with clear heads; and when other dessert failed, we tried our teeth on many a nut which wise squirrels have long since abandoned, for those which have the thickest shells are commonly empty.

The one who came from farthest to my lodge, through deepest snows and most dismal tempests, was a poet. A farmer, a hunter, a soldier, a reporter, even a philosopher, may be daunted; but nothing can deter a poet, for he is actuated by pure love. Who can predict his comings and goings? His business calls him out at all hours, even when doctors sleep. We made that small house ring with boisterous mirth and resound with the murmur of much sober talk, making amends then to Walden vale for the long silences. Broadway was still and deserted in comparison. At suitable intervals there were regular salutes of laughter, which might have been referred indifferently to the last uttered or the forth-coming jest. We made many a "bran new" theory of life over a thin dish of gruel, which combined the advantages of conviviality with the clear-headedness which philosophy requires.

I should not forget that during my last winter at the pond there was another welcome visitor, who at one time came through the village, through snow and rain and darkness, till he saw my lamp through the trees, and shared with me some long winter evenings. One of the last of the philosophers,— Connecticut gave him to the world,—he peddled first her wares, afterwards, as he declares, his brains. These he peddles still, prompting God and disgracing man, bearing for fruit his brain only, like the nut its kernel. I think that he must be the man of the most faith of any alive. His words and attitude always suppose a better state of things than other men are acquainted with, and he will be the last man to be disappointed as the ages revolve. He has no venture in the present. But though comparatively disregarded now, when his day comes, laws unsuspected by most will take effect, and masters of families and rulers will come to him for advice.—

"How blind that cannot see serenity!"

A true friend of man; almost the only friend of human prog-ress. An Old Mortality, say rather an Immortality, with un-wearied patience and faith making plain the image engraven in men's bodies, the God of whom they are but defaced and leaning monuments. With his hospitable intellect he embraces children, beggars, insane, and scholars, and entertains the thought of all, adding to it commonly some breadth and ele-gance. I think that he should keep a caravansary on the world's highway, where philosophers of all nations might put up, and on his sign should be printed, "Entertainment for man, but not for his beast. Enter ye that have leisure and a quiet mind, who earnestly seek the right road." He is perhaps the sanest man and has the fewest crotchets of any I chance to know; the same yesterday and to-morrow. Of yore we had sauntered and talked, and effectually put the world behind us; for he was pledged to no institution in it, freeborn, *ingenuus*. Whichever way we turned, it seemed that the heavens and the earth had met together, since he enhanced the beauty of the landscape. A blue-robed man, whose fittest roof is the over-arching sky which reflects his serenity. I do not see how he can ever die; Nature cannot spare him.

Having each some shingles of thought well dried, we sat and whittled them, trying our knives, and admiring the clear yellowish grain of the pumpkin pine. We waded so gently and reverently, or we pulled together so smoothly, that the fishes of thought were not scared from the stream, nor feared any angler on the bank, but came and went grandly, like the clouds which float through the western sky, and the mother-o'-pearl flocks which sometimes form and dissolve there. There we worked, revising mythology, rounding a fable here and there, and building castles in the air for which earth of-fered no worthy foundation. Great Looker! Great Expecter! to converse with whom was a New England Night's Enter-tainment. Ah! such discourse we had, hermit and philoso-pher, and the old settler I have spoken of,—we three,—it expanded and racked my little house; I should not dare to say how many pounds' weight there was above the atmospheric pressure on every circular inch; it opened its seams so that

they had to be calked with much dulness thereafter to stop
the consequent leak;—but I had enough of that kind of
oakum already picked.

There was one other with whom I had "solid seasons,"
long to be remembered, at his house in the village, and who
looked in upon me from time to time; but I had no more for
society there.

There too, as every where, I sometimes expected the Visitor who never comes. The Vishnu Purana says, "The house-
holder is to remain at eventide in his court-yard as long as it
takes to milk a cow, or longer if he pleases, to await the arrival of a guest." I often performed this duty of hospitality,
waited long enough to milk a whole herd of cows, but did
not see the man approaching from the town.

Winter Animals

WHEN THE PONDS were firmly frozen, they afforded not only new and shorter routes to many points, but new views from their surfaces of the familiar landscape around them. When I crossed Flints' Pond, after it was covered with snow, though I had often paddled about and skated over it, it was so unexpectedly wide and so strange that I could think of nothing but Baffin's Bay. The Lincoln hills rose up around me at the extremity of a snowy plain, in which I did not remember to have stood before; and the fishermen, at an indeterminable distance over the ice, moving slowly about with their wolfish dogs, passed for sealers or Esquimaux, or in misty weather loomed like fabulous creatures, and I did not know whether they were giants or pygmies. I took this course when I went to lecture in Lincoln in the evening, travelling in no road and passing no house between my own hut and the lecture room. In Goose Pond, which lay in my way, a colony of muskrats dwelt, and raised their cabins high above the ice, though none could be seen abroad when I crossed it. Walden, being like the rest usually bare of snow, or with only shallow and interrupted drifts on it, was my yard, where I could walk freely when the snow was nearly two feet deep on a level elsewhere and the villagers were confined to their streets. There, far from the village street, and except at very long intervals, from the jingle of sleigh-bells, I slid and skated, as in a vast moose-yard well trodden, overhung by oak woods and solemn pines bent down with snow or bristling with icicles.

For sounds in winter nights, and often in winter days, I heard the forlorn but melodious note of a hooting owl indefinitely far; such a sound as the frozen earth would yield if struck with a suitable plectrum, the very *lingua vernacula* of Walden Wood, and quite familiar to me at last, though I never saw the bird while it was making it. I seldom opened my door in a winter evening without hearing it; *Hoo hoo hoo, hoorer hoo,* sounded sonorously, and the first three syllables accented somewhat like *how der do*; or sometimes *hoo hoo* only. One night in the beginning of winter, before the pond froze over, about nine o'clock, I was startled by the loud honking of a goose, and, stepping to the door, heard the sound of their wings like a tempest in the woods as they flew low over my house. They passed over the pond toward Fair Haven, seemingly deterred from settling by my light, their commodore honking all the while with a regular beat. Suddenly an unmistakable cat-owl from very near me, with the most harsh and tremendous voice I ever heard from any inhabitant of the woods, responded at regular intervals to the goose, as if determined to expose and disgrace this intruder from Hudson's Bay by exhibiting a greater compass and volume of voice in a native, and *boo-hoo* him out of Concord horizon. What do you mean by alarming the citadel at this time of night consecrated to me? Do you think I am ever caught napping at such an hour, and that I have not got lungs and a larynx as well as yourself? *Boo-hoo, boo-hoo, boo-hoo!* It was one of the most thrilling discords I ever heard. And yet, if you had a discriminating ear, there were in it the elements of a concord such as these plains never saw nor heard.

I also heard the whooping of the ice in the pond, my great bed-fellow in that part of Concord, as if it were restless in its bed and would fain turn over, were troubled with flatulency and bad dreams; or I was waked by the cracking of the ground by the frost, as if some one had driven a team against my door, and in the morning would find a crack in the earth a quarter of a mile long and a third of an inch wide.

Sometimes I heard the foxes as they ranged over the snow crust, in moonlight nights, in search of a partridge or other game, barking raggedly and demoniacally like forest dogs, as if laboring with some anxiety, or seeking expression, struggling for light and to be dogs outright and run freely in the streets; for if we take the ages into our account, may there not be a civilization going on among brutes as well as men? They seemed to me to be rudimental, burrowing men, still standing on their defence, awaiting their transformation. Sometimes one came near to my window, attracted by my light, barked a vulpine curse at me, and then retreated.

Usually the red squirrel (*Sciurus Hudsonius*) waked me in the dawn, coursing over the roof and up and down the sides of the house, as if sent out of the woods for this purpose. In the course of the winter I threw out half a bushel of ears of sweet-corn, which had not got ripe, on to the snow crust by my door, and was amused by watching the motions of the various animals which were baited by it. In the twilight and the night the rabbits came regularly and made a hearty meal. All day long the red squirrels came and went, and afforded me much entertainment by their manœuvres. One would approach at first warily through the shrub-oaks, running over the snow crust by fits and starts like a leaf blown by the wind, now a few paces this way, with wonderful speed and waste of energy, making inconceivable haste with his "trotters," as if it were for a wager, and now as many paces that way, but never getting on more than half a rod at a time; and then suddenly pausing with a ludicrous expression and a gratuitous somerset, as if all the eyes in the universe were fixed on him, — for all the motions of a squirrel, even in the most solitary recesses of the forest, imply spectators as much as those of a dancing girl, — wasting more time in delay and circumspection than would have sufficed to walk the whole distance, — I never saw one walk, — and then suddenly, before you could say Jack Robinson, he would be in the top of a young pitch-pine, winding up his clock and chiding all imaginary spectators, soliloquizing and talking to all the universe at the same time, — for no reason that I could ever detect, or he himself was aware of, I suspect. At length he would reach the corn, and selecting a suitable ear, frisk about in the same uncertain trigonometrical way to the topmost stick of my wood-pile, before my window, where he looked me in the face, and there sit for hours, supplying himself with a new ear from time to time, nibbling at first voraciously and throwing the half-naked cobs about; till at length he grew more dainty still and played with his food, tasting only the inside of the kernel, and the ear, which was held balanced over the stick by one paw, slipped from his careless grasp and fell to the ground, when he would look over at it with a ludicrous expression of uncertainty, as if suspecting that it had life, with a mind not made up whether to get it again, or a new one, or be off; now thinking of corn, then listening to hear what was in the wind. So the

little impudent fellow would waste many an ear in a forenoon; till at last, seizing some longer and plumper one, considerably bigger than himself, and skilfully balancing it, he
would set out with it to the woods, like a tiger with a buffalo, by the same zig-zag course and frequent pauses,
scratching along with it as if it were too heavy for him and
falling all the while, making its fall a diagonal between a perpendicular and horizontal, being determined to put it
through at any rate;—a singularly frivolous and whimsical
fellow;—and so he would get off with it to where he lived,
perhaps carry it to the top of a pine tree forty or fifty rods
distant, and I would afterwards find the cobs strewn about
the woods in various directions.

At length the jays arrive, whose discordant screams were
heard long before, as they were warily making their approach an eighth of a mile off, and in a stealthy and sneaking manner they flit from tree to tree, nearer and nearer, and
pick up the kernels which the squirrels have dropped. Then,
sitting on a pitch-pine bough, they attempt to swallow in
their haste a kernel which is too big for their throats and
chokes them; and after great labor they disgorge it, and
spend an hour in the endeavor to crack it by repeated blows
with their bills. They were manifestly thieves, and I had not
much respect for them; but the squirrels, though at first shy,
went to work as if they were taking what was their own.

Meanwhile also came the chicadees in flocks, which picking up the crums the squirrels had dropped, flew to the
nearest twig, and placing them under their claws, hammered
away at them with their little bills, as if it were an insect in
the bark, till they were sufficiently reduced for their slender
throats. A little flock of these tit-mice came daily to pick a
dinner out of my wood-pile, or the crums at my door, with
faint flitting lisping notes, like the tinkling of icicles in the
grass, or else with sprightly *day day day*, or more rarely, in
spring-like days, a wiry summery *phe-be* from the wood-side.
They were so familiar that at length one alighted on an armful of wood which I was carrying in, and pecked at the
sticks without fear. I once had a sparrow alight upon my
shoulder for a moment while I was hoeing in a village garden, and I felt that I was more distinguished by that circum-

stance than I should have been by any epaulet I could have worn. The squirrels also grew at last to be quite familiar, and occasionally stepped upon my shoe, when that was the nearest way.

When the ground was not yet quite covered, and again near the end of winter, when the snow was melted on my south hill-side and about my wood-pile, the partridges came out of the woods morning and evening to feed there. Whichever side you walk in the woods the partridge bursts away on whirring wings, jarring the snow from the dry leaves and twigs on high, which comes sifting down in the sun-beams like golden dust; for this brave bird is not to be scared by winter. It is frequently covered up by drifts, and, it is said, "sometimes plunges from on wing into the soft snow, where it remains concealed for a day or two." I used to start them in the open land also, where they had come out of the woods at sunset to "bud" the wild apple-trees. They will come regularly every evening to particular trees, where the cunning sportsman lies in wait for them, and the distant orchards next the woods suffer thus not a little. I am glad that the partridge gets fed, at any rate. It is Nature's own bird which lives on buds and diet-drink.

In dark winter mornings, or in short winter afternoons, I sometimes heard a pack of hounds threading all the woods with hounding cry and yelp, unable to resist the instinct of the chase, and the note of the hunting horn at intervals, proving that man was in the rear. The woods ring again, and yet no fox bursts forth on to the open level of the pond, nor following pack pursuing their Actæon. And perhaps at evening I see the hunters returning with a single brush trailing from their sleigh for a trophy, seeking their inn. They tell me that if the fox would remain in the bosom of the frozen earth he would be safe, or if he would run in a straight line away no fox-hound could overtake him; but, having left his pursuers far behind, he stops to rest and listen till they come up, and when he runs he circles round to his old haunts, where the hunters await him. Sometimes, however, he will run upon a wall many rods, and then leap off far to one side, and he appears to know that water will not retain his scent. A hunter told me that he once saw a fox pursued by hounds burst out on to Walden when the ice was covered with shallow puddles, run part way across, and then return to the same shore. Ere long the hounds arrived, but here they lost the scent. Sometimes a pack hunting by themselves would pass my door, and circle round my house, and yelp and hound without regarding me, as if afflicted by a species of madness, so that nothing could divert them from the pursuit. Thus they circle until they fall upon the recent trail of a fox, for a wise hound will forsake every thing else for this. One day a man came to my hut from Lexington to inquire after his hound that made a large track, and had been hunting for a week by himself. But I fear that he was not the wiser for all I told him, for every time I attempted to answer his questions he interrupted me by asking, "What do you do here?" He had lost a dog, but found a man.

One old hunter who has a dry tongue, who used to come to bathe in Walden once every year when the water was warmest, and at such times looked in upon me, told me, that many years ago he took his gun one afternoon and went out for a cruise in Walden Wood; and as he walked the Wayland road he heard the cry of hounds approaching, and ere long a fox leaped the wall into the road, and as quick as thought leaped the other wall out of the road, and his swift bullet had not touched him. Some way behind came an old hound and her three pups in full pursuit, hunting on their own account, and disappeared again in the woods. Late in the afternoon, as he was resting in the thick woods south of Walden, he heard the voice of the hounds far over toward Fair Haven still pursuing the fox; and on they came, their hounding cry which made all the woods ring sounding nearer and nearer, now from Well-Meadow, now from the Baker Farm. For a long time he stood still and listened to their music, so sweet to a hunter's ear, when suddenly the fox appeared, threading the solemn aisles with an easy coursing pace, whose sound was concealed by a sympathetic rustle of the leaves, swift and still, keeping the ground, leaving his pursuers far behind; and, leaping upon a rock amid the woods, he sat erect and listening, with his back to the hunter. For a moment compassion restrained the latter's arm; but that was a short-lived mood, and as quick as

thought can follow thought his piece was levelled, and
whang!—the fox rolling over the rock lay dead on the
ground. The hunter still kept his place and listened to the
hounds. Still on they came, and now the near woods resounded through all their aisles with their demoniac cry. At
length the old hound burst into view with muzzle to the
ground, and snapping the air as if possessed, and ran directly
to the rock; but spying the dead fox she suddenly ceased her
hounding, as if struck dumb with amazement, and walked
round and round him in silence; and one by one her pups
arrived, and, like their mother, were sobered into silence by
the mystery. Then the hunter came forward and stood in
their midst, and the mystery was solved. They waited in silence while he skinned the fox, then followed the brush a
while, and at length turned off into the woods again. That
evening a Weston Squire came to the Concord hunter's cottage to inquire for his hounds, and told how for a week they
had been hunting on their own account from Weston
woods. The Concord hunter told him what he knew and offered him the skin; but the other declined it and departed.
He did not find his hounds that night, but the next day
learned that they had crossed the river and put up at a farm-
house for the night, whence, having been well fed, they took
their departure early in the morning.

The hunter who told me this could remember one Sam
Nutting, who used to hunt bears on Fair Haven Ledges, and
exchange their skins for rum in Concord village; who told
him, even, that he had seen a moose there. Nutting had a
famous fox-hound named Burgoyne,—he pronounced it
Bugine,—which my informant used to borrow. In the
"Wast Book" of an old trader of this town, who was also a captain, town-clerk, and representative, I find the following
entry. Jan. 18th, 1742–3, "John Melven Cr. by 1 Grey Fox
0—2—3;" they are not now found here; and in his leger,
Feb. 7th, 1743, Hezekiah Stratton has credit "by ½ a Catt skin
0—1—4½;" of course, a wild-cat, for Stratton was a ser-
geant in the old French war, and would not have got credit
for hunting less noble game. Credit is given for deer skins
also, and they were daily sold. One man still preserves the
horns of the last deer that was killed in this vicinity, and an-

other has told me the particulars of the hunt in which his uncle was engaged. The hunters were formerly a numerous and merry crew here. I remember well one gaunt Nimrod who would catch up a leaf by the road-side and play a strain on it wilder and more melodious, if my memory serves me, than any hunting horn.

At midnight, when there was a moon, I sometimes met with hounds in my path prowling about the woods, which would skulk out of my way, as if afraid, and stand silent amid the bushes till I had passed.

Squirrels and wild mice disputed for my store of nuts. There were scores of pitch-pines around my house, from one to four inches in diameter, which had been gnawed by mice the previous winter,—a Norwegian winter for them, for the snow lay long and deep, and they were obliged to mix a large proportion of pine bark with their other diet. These trees were alive and apparently flourishing at mid-summer, and many of them had grown a foot, though completely girdled; but after another winter such were without exception dead. It is remarkable that a single mouse should thus be allowed a whole pine tree for its dinner, gnawing round instead of up and down it; but perhaps it is necessary in order to thin these trees, which are wont to grow up densely.

The hares (*Lepus Americanus*) were very familiar. One had her form under my house all winter, separated from me only by the flooring, and she startled me each morning by her hasty departure when I began to stir,—thump, thump, thump, striking her head against the floor timbers in her hurry. They used to come round my door at dusk to nibble the potato parings which I had thrown out, and were so nearly the color of the ground that they could hardly be distinguished when still. Sometimes in the twilight I alternately lost and recovered sight of one sitting motionless under my window. When I opened my door in the evening, off they would go with a squeak and a bounce. Near at hand they only excited my pity. One evening one sat by my door two paces from me, at first trembling with fear, yet unwilling to move; a poor wee thing, lean and bony, with ragged ears and sharp nose, scant tail and slender paws. It looked as if Nature no longer contained the breed of nobler bloods, but

stood on her last toes. Its large eyes appeared young and unhealthy, almost dropsical. I took a step, and lo, away it scud
with an elastic spring over the snow crust, straightening its
body and its limbs into graceful length, and soon put the
forest between me and itself,—the wild free venison, asserting its vigor and the dignity of Nature. Not without reason
was its slenderness. Such then was its nature. (*Lepus*, *levipes*,
light-foot, some think.)

What is a country without rabbits and partridges? They
are among the most simple and indigenous animal products;
ancient and venerable families known to antiquity as to
modern times; of the very hue and substance of Nature,
nearest allied to leaves and to the ground,—and to one another; it is either winged or it is legged. It is hardly as if you
had seen a wild creature when a rabbit or a partridge bursts
away, only a natural one, as much to be expected as rustling
leaves. The partridge and the rabbit are still sure to thrive,
like true natives of the soil, whatever revolutions occur. If
the forest is cut off, the sprouts and bushes which spring up
afford them concealment, and they become more numerous
than ever. That must be a poor country indeed that does not
support a hare. Our woods teem with them both, and
around every swamp may be seen the partridge or rabbit
walk, beset with twiggy fences and horse-hair snares, which
some cow-boy tends.

The Pond in Winter

AFTER A STILL winter night I awoke with the impression that some question had been put to me, which I had been endeavoring in vain to answer in my sleep, as what—how—when—where? But there was dawning Nature, in whom all creatures live, looking in at my broad windows with serene and satisfied face, and no question on *her* lips. I awoke to an answered question, to Nature and daylight. The snow lying deep on the earth dotted with young pines, and the very slope of the hill on which my house is placed, seemed to say, Forward! Nature puts no question and answers none which we mortals ask. She has long ago taken her resolution. "O Prince, our eyes contemplate with admiration and transmit to the soul the wonderful and varied spectacle of this universe. The night veils without doubt a part of this glorious creation; but day comes to reveal to us this great work, which extends from earth even into the plains of the ether."

Then to my morning work. First I take an axe and pail and go in search of water, if that be not a dream. After a cold and snowy night it needed a divining rod to find it. Every winter the liquid and trembling surface of the pond, which was so sensitive to every breath, and reflected every light and shadow, becomes solid to the depth of a foot or a foot and a half, so that it will support the heaviest teams, and perchance the snow covers it to an equal depth, and it is not to be distinguished from any level field. Like the marmots in the surrounding hills, it closes its eye-lids and becomes dormant for three months or more. Standing on the snow-covered plain, as if in a pasture amid the hills, I cut my way first through a foot of snow, and then a foot of ice, and open a window under my feet, where, kneeling to drink, I look down into the quiet parlor of the fishes, pervaded by a softened light as through a window of ground glass, with its bright sanded floor the same as in summer; there a perennial waveless serenity reigns as in the amber twilight sky, corresponding to the cool and even temperament of the inhabitants. Heaven is under our feet as well as over our heads.

Early in the morning, while all things are crisp with frost,

men come with fishing reels and slender lunch, and let down
their fine lines through the snowy field to take pickerel and
perch; wild men, who instinctively follow other fashions and
trust other authorities than their townsmen, and by their
goings and comings stitch towns together in parts where else
they would be ripped. They sit and eat their luncheon in stout
fear-naughts on the dry oak leaves on the shore, as wise in
natural lore as the citizen is in artificial. They never consulted
with books, and know and can tell much less than they have
done. The things which they practise are said not yet to be
known. Here is one fishing for pickerel with grown perch for
bait. You look into his pail with wonder as into a summer
pond, as if he kept summer locked up at home, or knew
where she had retreated. How, pray, did he get these in mid-
winter? O, he got worms out of rotten logs since the ground
froze, and so he caught them. His life itself passes deeper in
Nature than the studies of the naturalist penetrate; himself a
subject for the naturalist. The latter raises the moss and bark
gently with his knife in search of insects; the former lays open
logs to their core with his axe, and moss and bark fly far and
wide. He gets his living by barking trees. Such a man has
some right to fish, and I love to see Nature carried out in
him. The perch swallows the grub-worm, the pickerel swallows the perch, and the fisherman swallows the pickerel; and
so all the chinks in the scale of being are filled.

When I strolled around the pond in misty weather I was
sometimes amused by the primitive mode which some ruder
fisherman had adopted. He would perhaps have placed alder
branches over the narrow holes in the ice, which were four or
five rods apart and an equal distance from the shore, and having fastened the end of the line to a stick to prevent its being
pulled through, have passed the slack line over a twig of the
alder, a foot or more above the ice, and tied a dry oak leaf to
it, which, being pulled down, would show when he had a
bite. These alders loomed through the mist at regular intervals as you walked half way round the pond.

Ah, the pickerel of Walden! when I see them lying on the
ice, or in the well which the fisherman cuts in the ice, making
a little hole to admit the water, I am always surprised by their
rare beauty, as if they were fabulous fishes, they are so foreign

to the streets, even to the woods, foreign as Arabia to our
Concord life. They possess a quite dazzling and transcendent
beauty which separates them by a wide interval from the cadaverous cod and haddock whose fame is trumpeted in our
streets. They are not green like the pines, nor gray like the
stones, nor blue like the sky; but they have, to my eyes, if
possible, yet rarer colors, like flowers and precious stones, as
if they were the pearls, the animalized *nuclei* or crystals of the
Walden water. They, of course, are Walden all over and all
through; are themselves small Waldens in the animal kingdom, Waldenses. It is surprising that they are caught here,—
that in this deep and capacious spring, far beneath the rattling
teams and chaises and tinkling sleighs that travel the Walden
road, this great gold and emerald fish swims. I never chanced
to see its kind in any market; it would be the cynosure of all
eyes there. Easily, with a few convulsive quirks, they give up
their watery ghosts, like a mortal translated before his time to
the thin air of heaven.

As I was desirous to recover the long lost bottom of Walden Pond, I surveyed it carefully, before the ice broke up,
early in '46, with compass and chain and sounding line. There
have been many stories told about the bottom, or rather no
bottom, of this pond, which certainly had no foundation for
themselves. It is remarkable how long men will believe in the
bottomlessness of a pond without taking the trouble to sound
it. I have visited two such Bottomless Ponds in one walk in
this neighborhood. Many have believed that Walden reached
quite through to the other side of the globe. Some who have
lain flat on the ice for a long time, looking down through the
illusive medium, perchance with watery eyes into the bargain,
and driven to hasty conclusions by the fear of catching cold
in their breasts, have seen vast holes "into which a load of hay
might be driven," if there were any body to drive it, the un-
doubted source of the Styx and entrance to the Infernal Regions from these parts. Others have gone down from the
village with a "fifty-six" and a wagon load of inch rope, but
yet have failed to find any bottom; for while the "fifty-six"
was resting by the way, they were paying out the rope in the
vain attempt to fathom their truly immeasurable capacity for

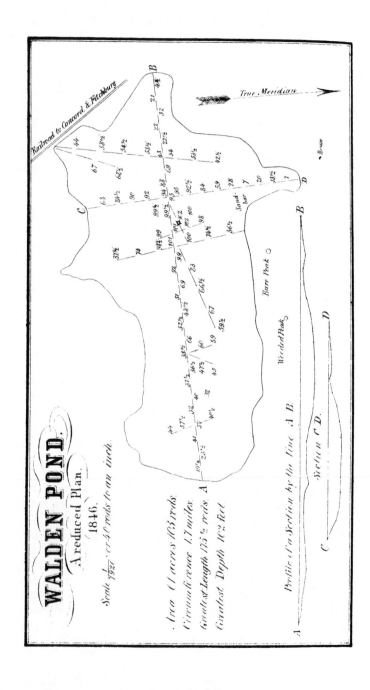

WALDEN POND.
A reduced Plan.
1846.

Scale 7 9/10 rods or 40 rods to an inch.

Area 61 acres 103 rods.
Circumference 1.7 miles.
Greatest Length 175 1/2 rods. A
Greatest Depth 102 feet

Railroad to Concord & Fitchburg

True Meridian

Burr Peak

Wooded Peak

Brush

Sand bar

Profile of a Section by the line A.B.

Section C.D.

marvellousness. But I can assure my readers that Walden has a reasonably tight bottom at a not unreasonable, though at an unusual, depth. I fathomed it easily with a cod-line and a stone weighing about a pound and a half, and could tell accurately when the stone left the bottom, by having to pull so much harder before the water got underneath to help me. The greatest depth was exactly one hundred and two feet; to which may be added the five feet which it has risen since, making one hundred and seven. This is a remarkable depth for so small an area; yet not an inch of it can be spared by the imagination. What if all ponds were shallow? Would it not react on the minds of men? I am thankful that this pond was made deep and pure for a symbol. While men believe in the infinite some ponds will be thought to be bottomless.

A factory owner, hearing what depth I had found, thought that it could not be true, for, judging from his acquaintance with dams, sand would not lie at so steep an angle. But the deepest ponds are not so deep in proportion to their area as most suppose, and, if drained, would not leave very remarkable valleys. They are not like cups between the hills; for this one, which is so unusually deep for its area, appears in a vertical section through its centre not deeper than a shallow plate. Most ponds, emptied, would leave a meadow no more hollow than we frequently see. William Gilpin, who is so admirable in all that relates to landscapes, and usually so correct, standing at the head of Loch Fyne, in Scotland, which he describes as "a bay of salt water, sixty or seventy fathoms deep, four miles in breadth," and about fifty miles long, surrounded by mountains, observes, "If we could have seen it immediately after the diluvian crash, or whatever convulsion of Nature occasioned it, before the waters gushed in, what a horrid chasm it must have appeared!

> So high as heaved the tumid hills, so low
> Down sunk a hollow bottom, broad, and deep,
> Capacious bed of waters——."

But if, using the shortest diameter of Loch Fyne, we apply these proportions to Walden, which, as we have seen, appears already in a vertical section only like a shallow plate, it will appear four times as shallow. So much for the *increased* horrors of the chasm of Loch Fyne when emptied. No doubt many a smiling valley with its stretching cornfields occupies exactly such a "horrid chasm," from which the waters have receded, though it requires the insight and the far sight of the geologist to convince the unsuspecting inhabitants of this fact. Often an inquisitive eye may detect the shores of a primitive lake in the low horizon hills, and no subsequent elevation of the plain has been necessary to conceal their history. But it is easiest, as they who work on the highways know, to find the hollows by the puddles after a shower. The amount of it is, the imagination, give it the least license, dives deeper and soars higher than Nature goes. So, probably, the depth of the ocean will be found to be very inconsiderable compared with its breadth.

As I sounded through the ice I could determine the shape of the bottom with greater accuracy than is possible in surveying harbors which do not freeze over, and I was surprised at its general regularity. In the deepest part there are several acres more level than almost any field which is exposed to the sun wind and plough. In one instance, on a line arbitrarily chosen, the depth did not vary more than one foot in thirty rods; and generally, near the middle, I could calculate the variation for each one hundred feet in any direction beforehand within three or four inches. Some are accustomed to speak of deep and dangerous holes even in quiet sandy ponds like this, but the effect of water under these circumstances is to level all inequalities. The regularity of the bottom and its conformity to the shores and the range of the neighboring hills were so perfect that a distant promontory betrayed itself in the soundings quite across the pond, and its direction could be determined by observing the opposite shore. Cape becomes bar, and plain shoal, and valley and gorge deep water and channel.

When I had mapped the pond by the scale of ten rods to an inch, and put down the soundings, more than a hundred in all, I observed this remarkable coincidence. Having noticed that the number indicating the greatest depth was apparently in the centre of the map, I laid a rule on the map lengthwise, and then breadthwise, and found, to my surprise, that the line of greatest length intersected the line of greatest breadth *exactly* at the point of greatest depth, notwithstanding that the middle is so nearly level, the outline of the pond far from regular, and the extreme length and breadth were got by measuring into the coves; and I said to myself, Who knows but this hint would conduct to the deepest part of the ocean as well as of a pond or puddle? Is not this the rule also for the height of mountains, regarded as the opposite of valleys? We know that a hill is not highest at its narrowest part.

Of five coves, three, or all which had been sounded, were observed to have a bar quite across their mouths and deeper water within, so that the bay tended to be an expansion of water within the land not only horizontally but vertically, and to form a basin or independent pond, the direction of the two capes showing the course of the bar. Every harbor on the seacoast, also, has its bar at its entrance. In proportion as the mouth of the cove was wider compared with its length, the water over the bar was deeper compared with that in the basin. Given, then, the length and breadth of the cove, and the character of the surrounding shore, and you have almost elements enough to make out a formula for all cases.

In order to see how nearly I could guess, with this experience, at the deepest point in a pond, by observing the outlines of its surface and the character of its shores alone, I made a plan of White Pond, which contains about forty-one acres, and, like this, has no island in it, nor any visible inlet or outlet; and as the line of greatest breadth fell very near the line of least breadth, where two opposite capes approached each other and two opposite bays receded, I ventured to mark a point a short distance from the latter line, but still on the line of greatest length, as the deepest. The deepest part was found to be within one hundred feet of this, still farther in the direction to which I had inclined, and was only one foot deeper, namely, sixty feet. Of course, a stream running through, or an island in the pond, would make the problem much more complicated.

If we knew all the laws of Nature, we should need only one fact, or the description of one actual phenomenon, to infer all the particular results at that point. Now we know only a few laws, and our result is vitiated, not, of course, by any confusion or irregularity in Nature, but by our ignorance of essential elements in the calculation. Our notions of law and harmony are commonly confined to those instances which we detect; but the harmony which results from a far greater number of seemingly conflicting, but really concurring, laws, which we have not detected, is still more wonderful. The particular laws are as our points of view, as, to the traveller, a mountain outline varies with every step, and it has an infinite number of profiles, though absolutely but one form. Even when cleft or bored through it is not comprehended in its entireness.

What I have observed of the pond is no less true in ethics. It is the law of average. Such a rule of the two diameters not only guides us toward the sun in the system and the heart in man, but draw lines through the length and breadth of the aggregate of a man's particular daily behaviors and waves of life into his coves and inlets, and where they intersect will be the height or depth of his character. Perhaps we need only to know how his shores trend and his adjacent country or circumstances, to infer his depth and concealed bottom. If he is surrounded by mountainous circumstances, an Achillean shore, whose peaks overshadow and are reflected in his bosom, they suggest a corresponding depth in him. But a low and smooth shore proves him shallow on that side. In our bodies, a bold projecting brow falls off to and indicates a corresponding depth of thought. Also there is a bar across the entrance of our every cove, or particular inclination; each is our harbor for a season, in which we are detained and partially land-locked. These inclinations are not whimsical usually, but their form, size, and direction are determined by the promontories of the shore, the ancient axes of elevation. When this bar is gradually increased by storms, tides, or currents, or there is a subsidence of the waters, so that it reaches to the surface, that which was at first but an inclination in the shore in which a thought was harbored becomes an individual lake, cut off from the ocean, wherein the thought secures its own conditions, changes, perhaps, from salt to fresh, becomes a sweet sea, dead sea, or a marsh. At the advent of each individual into this life, may we not suppose that such a bar has risen to the surface somewhere? It is true, we are such poor navigators that our thoughts, for the most part, stand off and on upon a harborless coast, are conversant only with the bights of the bays of poesy, or steer for the public ports of entry, and go into the dry docks of science, where they merely refit for this world, and no natural currents concur to individualize them.

As for the inlet or outlet of Walden, I have not discovered any but rain and snow and evaporation, though perhaps, with a thermometer and a line, such places may be found, for where the water flows into the pond it will probably be coldest in summer and warmest in winter. When the ice-men were at work here in '46–7, the cakes sent to the shore were one day rejected by those who were stacking them up there, not being thick enough to lie side by side with the rest; and the cutters thus discovered that the ice over a small space was two or three inches thinner than elsewhere, which made them think that there was an inlet there. They also showed me in another place what they thought was a "leach hole," through which the pond leaked out under a hill into a neighboring meadow, pushing me out on a cake of ice to see it. It was a small cavity under ten feet of water; but I think that I can warrant the pond not to need soldering till they find a worse leak than that. One has suggested, that if such a "leach hole" should be found, its connection with the meadow, if any existed, might be proved by conveying some colored powder or sawdust to the mouth of the hole, and then putting a strainer over the spring in the meadow, which would catch some of the particles carried through by the current.

While I was surveying, the ice, which was sixteen inches thick, undulated under a slight wind like water. It is well known that a level cannot be used on ice. At one rod from the shore its greatest fluctuation, when observed by means of a level on land directed toward a graduated staff on the ice, was three quarters of an inch, though the ice appeared firmly attached to the shore. It was probably greater in the middle. Who knows but if our instruments were delicate enough we might detect an undulation in the crust of the earth? When two legs of my level were on the shore and the third on the ice, and the sights were directed over the latter, a rise or fall of the ice of an almost infinitesimal amount made a difference of several feet on a tree across the pond. When I began to cut holes for sounding, there were three or four inches of water on the ice under a deep snow which had sunk it thus far; but the water began immediately to run into these holes, and continued to run for two days in deep streams, which wore away the ice on every side, and contributed essentially, if not mainly, to dry the surface of the pond; for, as the water ran in, it raised and floated the ice. This was somewhat like cutting a hole in the bottom of a ship to let the water out. When such holes freeze, and a rain succeeds, and finally a new freezing forms a fresh smooth ice over all, it is beautifully mottled internally by dark figures, shaped somewhat like a spider's web, what you may call ice rosettes, produced by the channels worn by the water flowing from all sides to a centre. Sometimes, also, when the ice was covered with shallow puddles, I saw a double shadow of myself, one standing on the head of the other, one on the ice, the other on the trees or hill-side.

While yet it is cold January, and snow and ice are thick and solid, the prudent landlord comes from the village to get ice to cool his summer drink; impressively, even pathetically wise, to foresee the heat and thirst of July now in January,— wearing a thick coat and mittens! when so many things are not provided for. It may be that he lays up no treasures in this world which will cool his summer drink in the next. He cuts and saws the solid pond, unroofs the house of fishes, and carts off their very element and air, held fast by chains and stakes like corded wood, through the favoring winter air, to wintry cellars, to underlie the summer there. It looks like solidified azure, as, far off, it is drawn through the streets. These ice-cutters are a merry race, full of jest and sport, and when I went among them they were wont to invite me to saw pit-fashion with them, I standing underneath.

In the winter of '46–7 there came a hundred men of Hyperborean extraction swoop down on to our pond one morning, with many car-loads of ungainly-looking farming tools, sleds, ploughs, drill-barrows, turf-knives, spades, saws, rakes, and each man was armed with a double-pointed pike-staff, such as is not described in the New-England Farmer or the Cultivator. I did not know whether they had come to sow a crop of winter rye, or some other kind of grain recently introduced from Iceland. As I saw no manure, I judged that they meant to skim the land, as I had done, thinking the soil was deep and had lain fallow long enough. They said that a gentleman farmer, who was behind the scenes, wanted to double his money, which, as I understood, amounted to half a million already; but in order to cover each one of his dollars with another, he took off the only coat, ay, the skin itself, of Walden Pond in the midst of a hard winter. They went to work at once, ploughing, harrowing, rolling, furrowing, in admirable order, as if they were bent on making this a model farm; but when I was looking sharp to see what kind of seed they dropped into the furrow, a gang of fellows by my side suddenly began to hook up the virgin mould itself, with a peculiar jerk, clean down to the sand, or rather the water,—for it was a very springy soil,—indeed all the *terra firma* there was, and haul it away on sleds, and then I guessed that they must be cutting peat in a bog. So they came and went every day, with a peculiar shriek from the locomotive, from and to some point of the polar regions, as it seemed to me, like a flock of arctic snow-birds. But sometimes Squaw Walden had her revenge, and a hired man, walking behind his team, slipped through a crack in the ground down toward Tartarus, and he who was so brave before suddenly became but the ninth part of a man, almost gave up his animal heat, and was glad to take refuge in my house, and acknowledged that there was some virtue in a stove; or sometimes the frozen soil took a piece of steel out of a ploughshare, or a plough got set in the furrow and had to be cut out.

To speak literally, a hundred Irishmen, with Yankee overseers, came from Cambridge every day to get out the ice. They divided it into cakes by methods too well known to require description, and these, being sledded to the shore, were rapidly hauled off on to an ice platform, and raised by grappling irons and block and tackle, worked by horses, on to a stack, as surely as so many barrels of flour, and there placed evenly side by side, and row upon row, as if they formed the solid base of an obelisk designed to pierce the clouds. They told me that in a good day they could get out a thousand tons, which was the yield of about one acre. Deep ruts and "cradle holes" were worn in the ice, as on *terra*

firma, by the passage of the sleds over the same track, and the
horses invariably ate their oats out of cakes of ice hollowed
out like buckets. They stacked up the cakes thus in the open
air in a pile thirty-five feet high on one side and six or seven
rods square, putting hay between the outside layers to exclude
the air; for when the wind, though never so cold, finds a
passage through, it will wear large cavities, leaving slight supports or studs only here and there, and finally topple it down.
At first it looked like a vast blue fort or Valhalla; but when
they began to tuck the coarse meadow hay into the crevices,
and this became covered with rime and icicles, it looked like
a venerable moss-grown and hoary ruin, built of azure-tinted
marble, the abode of Winter, that old man we see in the almanac,—his shanty, as if he had a design to estivate with us.
They calculated that not twenty-five per cent. of this would
reach its destination, and that two or three per cent. would be
wasted in the cars. However, a still greater part of this heap
had a different destiny from what was intended; for, either
because the ice was found not to keep so well as was expected, containing more air than usual, or for some other reason, it never got to market. This heap, made in the winter of
'46–7 and estimated to contain ten thousand tons, was finally
covered with hay and boards; and though it was unroofed the
following July, and a part of it carried off, the rest remaining
exposed to the sun, it stood over that summer and the next
winter, and was not quite melted till September 1848. Thus
the pond recovered the greater part.

Like the water, the Walden ice, seen near at hand, has a
green tint, but at a distance is beautifully blue, and you can
easily tell it from the white ice of the river, or the merely
greenish ice of some ponds, a quarter of a mile off. Sometimes one of those great cakes slips from the ice-man's sled
into the village street, and lies there for a week like a great
emerald, an object of interest to all passers. I have noticed
that a portion of Walden which in the state of water was
green will often, when frozen, appear from the same point of
view blue. So the hollows about this pond will, sometimes,
in the winter, be filled with a greenish water somewhat like
its own, but the next day will have frozen blue. Perhaps the
blue color of water and ice is due to the light and air they

contain, and the most transparent is the bluest. Ice is an interesting subject for contemplation. They told me that they had some in the ice-houses at Fresh Pond five years old which was as good as ever. Why is it that a bucket of water soon becomes putrid, but frozen remains sweet forever? It is commonly said that this is the difference between the affections and the intellect.

Thus for sixteen days I saw from my window a hundred men at work like busy husbandmen, with teams and horses and apparently all the implements of farming, such a picture as we see on the first page of the almanac; and as often as I looked out I was reminded of the fable of the lark and the reapers, or the parable of the sower, and the like; and now they are all gone, and in thirty days more, probably, I shall look from the same window on the pure sea-green Walden water there, reflecting the clouds and the trees, and sending up its evaporations in solitude, and no traces will appear that a man has ever stood there. Perhaps I shall hear a solitary loon laugh as he dives and plumes himself, or shall see a lonely fisher in his boat, like a floating leaf, beholding his form reflected in the waves, where lately a hundred men securely labored.

Thus it appears that the sweltering inhabitants of Charleston and New Orleans, of Madras and Bombay and Calcutta, drink at my well. In the morning I bathe my intellect in the stupendous and cosmogonal philosophy of the Bhagvat Geeta, since whose composition years of the gods have elapsed, and in comparison with which our modern world and its literature seem puny and trivial; and I doubt if that philosophy is not to be referred to a previous state of existence, so remote is its sublimity from our conceptions. I lay down the book and go to my well for water, and lo! there I meet the servant of the Bramin, priest of Brahma and Vishnu and Indra, who still sits in his temple on the Ganges reading the Vedas, or dwells at the root of a tree with his crust and water jug. I meet his servant come to draw water for his master, and our buckets as it were grate together in the same well. The pure Walden water is mingled with the sacred water of the Ganges. With favoring winds it is wafted past the site of the fabulous islands of Atlantis and the Hesperides, makes the periplus of Hanno, and, floating by Ternate and Tidore and the mouth of the Persian Gulf, melts in the tropic gales of the Indian seas, and is landed in ports of which Alexander only heard the names.

Spring

THE OPENING of large tracts by the ice-cutters commonly causes a pond to break up earlier; for the water, agitated by the wind, even in cold weather, wears away the surrounding ice. But such was not the effect on Walden that year, for she had soon got a thick new garment to take the place of the old. This pond never breaks up so soon as the others in this neighborhood, on account both of its greater depth and its having no stream passing through it to melt or wear away the ice. I never knew it to open in the course of a winter, not excepting that of '52—3, which gave the ponds so severe a trial. It commonly opens about the first of April, a week or ten days later than Flints' Pond and Fair-Haven, beginning to melt on the north side and in the shallower parts where it began to freeze. It indicates better than any water hereabouts the absolute progress of the season, being least affected by transient changes of temperature. A severe cold of a few days' duration in March may very much retard the opening of the former ponds, while the temperature of Walden increases almost uninterruptedly. A thermometer thrust into the middle of Walden on the 6th of March, 1847, stood at 32°, or freezing point; near the shore at 33°; in the middle of Flints' Pond, the same day, at 32½°; at a dozen rods from the shore, in shallow water, under ice a foot thick, at 36°. This difference of three and a half degrees between the temperature of the deep water and the shallow in the latter pond, and the fact that a great proportion of it is comparatively shallow, show why it should break up so much sooner than Walden. The ice in the shallowest part was at this time several inches thinner than in the middle. In mid-winter the middle had been the warmest and the ice thinnest there. So, also, every one who has waded about the shores of a pond in summer must have perceived how much warmer the water is close to the shore, where only three or four inches deep, than a little distance out, and on the surface where it is deep, than near the bottom. In spring the sun not only exerts an influence through the increased temperature of the air and earth, but its heat passes through ice a foot or more thick, and is reflected from the bottom in shallow water, and so also warms the water and melts the under side of the ice, at the same time that it is melting it more directly above, making it uneven, and causing the air bubbles which it contains to extend themselves upward and downward until it is completely honey-combed, and at last disappears suddenly in a single spring rain. Ice has its grain as well as wood, and when a cake begins to rot or "comb," that is, assume the appearance of honey-comb, whatever may be its position, the air cells are at right angles with what was the water surface. Where there is a rock or a log rising near to the surface the ice over it is much thinner, and is frequently quite dissolved by this reflected heat; and I have been told that in the experiment at Cambridge to freeze water in a shallow wooden pond, though the cold air circulated underneath, and so had access to both sides, the reflection of the sun from the bottom more than counterbalanced this advantage. When a warm rain in the middle of the winter melts off the snow-ice from Walden, and leaves a hard dark or transparent ice on the middle, there will be a strip of rotten though thicker white ice, a rod or more wide, about the shores, created by this reflected heat. Also, as I have said, the bubbles themselves within the ice operate as burning glasses to melt the ice beneath.

The phenomena of the year take place every day in a pond on a small scale. Every morning, generally speaking, the shallow water is being warmed more rapidly than the deep, though it may not be made so warm after all, and every evening it is being cooled more rapidly until the morning. The day is an epitome of the year. The night is the winter, the morning and evening are the spring and fall, and the noon is the summer. The cracking and booming of the ice indicate a change of temperature. One pleasant morning after a cold night, February 24th, 1850, having gone to Flints' Pond to spend the day, I noticed with surprise, that when I struck the ice with the head of my axe, it resounded like a gong for many rods around, or as if I had struck on a tight drum-head. The pond began to boom about an hour after sunrise, when it felt the influence of the sun's rays slanted upon it from over the hills; it stretched itself and yawned like a waking man with a gradually increasing tumult, which was kept up three or four hours. It took a short siesta at noon, and boomed once more toward night, as the sun was withdrawing his influence. In the right stage of the weather a pond fires its evening gun with great regularity. But in the middle of the day, being full of cracks, and the air also being less elastic, it had completely lost its resonance, and probably fishes and muskrats could not then have been stunned by a blow on it. The fishermen say that the "thundering of the pond" scares the fishes and prevents their biting. The pond does not thunder every evening, and I cannot tell surely when to expect its thundering; but though I may perceive no difference in the weather, it does. Who would have suspected so large and cold and thick-skinned a thing to be so sensitive? Yet it has its law to which it thunders obedience when it should as surely as the buds expand in the spring. The earth is all alive and covered with papillæ. The largest pond is as sensitive to atmospheric changes as the globule of mercury in its tube.

One attraction in coming to the woods to live was that I should have leisure and opportunity to see the spring come in. The ice in the pond at length begins to be honey-combed, and I can set my heel in it as I walk. Fogs and rains and warmer suns are gradually melting the snow; the days have grown sensibly longer; and I see how I shall get through the winter without adding to my wood-pile, for large fires are no longer necessary. I am on the alert for the first signs of spring, to hear the chance note of some arriving bird, or the striped squirrel's chirp, for his stores must be now nearly exhausted, or see the woodchuck venture out of his winter quarters. On the 13th of March, after I had heard the bluebird, song-sparrow, and red-wing, the ice was still nearly a foot thick. As the weather grew warmer, it was not sensibly worn away by the water, nor broken up and floated off as in rivers, but, though it was completely melted for half a rod in width about the shore, the middle was merely honey-combed and saturated with water, so that you could put your foot through it when six inches thick; but by the next day evening, perhaps, after a warm rain followed by fog, it would have wholly disappeared, all gone off with the fog, spirited away. One year I went across the middle only five days before it disappeared entirely.

In 1845 Walden was first completely open on the 1st of April; in '46, the 25th of March; in '47, the 8th of April; in '51, the 28th of March; in '52, the 18th of April; in '53, the 23d of March; in '54, about the 7th of April.

Every incident connected with the breaking up of the rivers and ponds and the settling of the weather is particularly interesting to us who live in a climate of so great extremes. When the warmer days come, they who dwell near the river hear the ice crack at night with a startling whoop as loud as artillery, as if its icy fetters were rent from end to end, and within a few days see it rapidly going out. So the alligator comes out of the mud with quakings of the earth. One old man, who has been a close observer of Nature, and seems as thoroughly wise in regard to all her operations as if she had been put upon the stocks when he was a boy, and he had helped to lay her keel,—who has come to his growth, and can hardly acquire more of natural lore if he should live to the age of Methuselah,—told me, and I was surprised to hear him express wonder at any of Nature's operations, for I thought that there were no secrets between them, that one spring day he took his gun and boat, and thought that he would have a little sport with the ducks. There was ice still on the meadows, but it was all gone out of the river, and he dropped down without obstruction from Sudbury, where he lived, to Fair-Haven Pond, which he found, unexpectedly, covered for the most part with a firm field of ice. It was a warm day, and he was surprised to see so great a body of ice remaining. Not seeing any ducks, he hid his boat on the north or back side of an island in the pond, and then concealed himself in the bushes on the south side, to await them. The ice was melted for three or four rods from the shore, and there was a smooth and warm sheet of water, with a muddy bottom, such as the ducks love, within, and he thought it likely that some would be along pretty soon. After he had lain still there about an hour he heard a low and seemingly very distant sound, but singularly grand and impressive, unlike any thing he had ever heard, gradually swelling and increasing as if it would have a universal and memorable ending, a sullen rush and roar, which seemed to him all at once like the sound of a vast body of fowl coming in to settle there, and, seizing his gun, he started up in haste and excited; but he found, to his surprise, that the whole body of the ice had started while he lay there, and drifted in to the shore, and the sound he had heard was made by its edge grating on the shore,—at first gently nibbled and crumbled off, but at length heaving up and scattering its wrecks along the island to a considerable height before it came to a stand still.

At length the sun's rays have attained the right angle, and warm winds blow up mist and rain and melt the snow banks, and the sun dispersing the mist smiles on a checkered landscape of russet and white smoking with incense, through which the traveller picks his way from islet to islet, cheered by the music of a thousand tinkling rills and rivulets whose veins are filled with the blood of winter which they are bearing off.

Few phenomena gave me more delight than to observe the forms which thawing sand and clay assume in flowing down the sides of a deep cut on the railroad through which I passed on my way to the village, a phenomenon not very common on so large a scale, though the number of freshly exposed banks of the right material must have been greatly multiplied since railroads were invented. The material was sand of every degree of fineness and of various rich colors, commonly mixed with a little clay. When the frost comes out in the spring, and even in a thawing day in the winter, the sand begins to flow down the slopes like lava, sometimes bursting out through the snow and overflowing it where no sand was to be seen before. Innumerable little streams overlap and interlace one with another, exhibiting a sort of hybrid product, which obeys half way the law of currents, and half way that of vegetation. As it flows it takes the forms of sappy leaves or vines, making heaps of pulpy sprays a foot or more in depth, and resembling, as you look down on them, the laciniated lobed and imbricated thalluses of some lichens; or you are reminded of coral, of leopards' paws or birds' feet, of brains or lungs or bowels, and excrements of all kinds. It is a truly *grotesque* vegetation, whose forms and color we see imitated in bronze, a sort of architectural foliage more ancient and typical than acanthus, chiccory, ivy, vine, or any vegetable leaves; destined perhaps, under some circumstances, to become a puzzle to future geologists. The whole cut impressed me as if it were a cave with its stalactites laid open to the light. The various shades of the sand are singularly rich and agreeable, embracing the different iron colors, brown, gray, yellowish, and reddish. When the flowing mass reaches the drain at the foot of the bank it spreads out flatter into *strands*, the separate streams losing their semi-cylindrical form and gradually becoming more flat and broad, running together as they are more moist, till they form an almost flat *sand*, still variously and beautifully shaded, but in which you can trace the original forms of vegetation; till at length, in the water itself, they are converted into *banks*, like those formed off the mouths of rivers, and the forms of vegetation are lost in the ripple marks on the bottom.

The whole bank, which is from twenty to forty feet high, is sometimes overlaid with a mass of this kind of foliage, or sandy rupture, for a quarter of a mile on one or both sides, the produce of one spring day. What makes this sand foliage remarkable is its springing into existence thus suddenly. When I see on the one side the inert bank,—for the sun acts on one side first,—and on the other this luxuriant foliage, the creation of an hour, I am affected as if in a peculiar sense I stood in the laboratory of the Artist who made the world and me,—had come to where he was still at work, sporting on this bank, and with excess of energy strewing his fresh designs about. I feel as if I were nearer to the vitals of the globe, for this sandy overflow is something such a foliaceous mass as the vitals of the animal body. You find thus in the very sands an anticipation of the vegetable leaf. No wonder that the earth expresses itself outwardly in leaves, it so labors with the idea inwardly. The atoms have already learned this law, and are pregnant by it. The overhanging leaf sees here its prototype. *Internally*, whether in the globe or animal body, it is a moist thick *lobe*, a word especially applicable to the liver and lungs and the *leaves* of fat, (λείβω, *labor*, *lapsus*, to flow or slip downward, a lapsing; λοβος, *globus*, lobe, globe; also lap, flap, and many other words,) *externally* a dry thin *leaf*, even as the *f* and *v* are a pressed and dried *b*. The radicals of lobe are *lb*, the soft mass of the *b* (single lobed, or B, double lobed,) with a liquid *l* behind it pressing it forward. In globe, *glb*, the guttural *g* adds to the meaning the capacity of the throat. The feathers and wings of birds are still drier and thinner leaves. Thus, also, you pass from the lumpish grub in the earth to the airy and fluttering butterfly. The very globe continually transcends and translates itself, and becomes winged in its orbit. Even ice begins with delicate crystal leaves, as if it had flowed into moulds which the fronds of water plants have impressed on the watery mirror. The whole tree itself is but one leaf, and rivers are still vaster leaves whose pulp is intervening earth, and towns and cities are the ova of insects in their axils.

When the sun withdraws the sand ceases to flow, but in the morning the streams will start once more and branch and branch again into a myriad of others. You here see perchance how blood vessels are formed. If you look closely you observe that first there pushes forward from the thawing mass a stream of softened sand with a drop-like point, like the ball of the finger, feeling its way slowly and blindly downward, until at last with more heat and moisture, as the sun gets higher, the most fluid portion, in its effort to obey the law to which the most inert also yields, separates from the latter and forms for itself a meandering channel or artery within that, in which is seen a little silvery stream glancing like lightning from one stage of pulpy leaves or branches to another, and ever and anon swallowed up in the sand. It is wonderful how rapidly yet perfectly the sand organizes itself as it flows, using the best material its mass affords to form the sharp edges of its channel. Such are the sources of rivers. In the silicious matter which the water deposits is perhaps the bony system, and in the still finer soil and organic matter the fleshy fibre or cellular tissue. What is man but a mass of thawing clay? The ball of the human finger is but a drop congealed. The fingers and toes flow to their extent from the thawing mass of the body. Who knows what the human body would expand and flow out to under a more genial heaven? Is not the hand a spreading *palm* leaf with its lobes and veins? The ear may be regarded, fancifully, as a lichen, *umbilicaria*, on the side of the head, with its lobe or drop. The lip (*labium*, from *labor* (?)) laps or lapses from the sides of the cavernous mouth. The nose is a manifest congealed drop or stalactite.

The chin is a still larger drop, the confluent dripping of the face. The cheeks are a slide from the brows into the valley of the face, opposed and diffused by the cheek bones. Each rounded lobe of the vegetable leaf, too, is a thick and now loitering drop, larger or smaller; the lobes are the fingers of the leaf; and as many lobes as it has, in so many directions it tends to flow, and more heat or other genial influences would have caused it to flow yet farther.

Thus it seemed that this one hillside illustrated the principle of all the operations of Nature. The Maker of this earth but patented a leaf. What Champollion will decipher this hiero-glyphic for us, that we may turn over a new leaf at last? This phenomenon is more exhilarating to me than the luxuriance and fertility of vineyards. True, it is somewhat excrementi-tious in its character, and there is no end to the heaps of liver lights and bowels, as if the globe were turned wrong side outward; but this suggests at least that Nature has some bow-els, and there again is mother of humanity. This is the frost coming out of the ground; this is Spring. It precedes the green and flowery spring, as mythology precedes regular po-etry. I know of nothing more purgative of winter fumes and indigestions. It convinces me that Earth is still in her swad-dling clothes, and stretches forth baby fingers on every side. Fresh curls spring from the baldest brow. There is nothing inorganic. These foliaceous heaps lie along the bank like the slag of a furnace, showing that Nature is "in full blast" within. The earth is not a mere fragment of dead history, stratum upon stratum like the leaves of a book, to be studied by geologists and antiquaries chiefly, but living poetry like the leaves of a tree, which precede flowers and fruit,—not a fossil earth, but a living earth; compared with whose great central life all animal and vegetable life is merely parasitic. Its throes will heave our exuviæ from their graves. You may melt your metals and cast them into the most beautiful moulds you can; they will never excite me like the forms which this molten earth flows out into. And not only it, but the institutions upon it, are plastic like clay in the hands of the potter.

Ere long, not only on these banks, but on every hill and plain and in every hollow, the frost comes out of the ground like a dormant quadruped from its burrow, and seeks the sea with music, or migrates to other climes in clouds. Thaw with his gentle persuasion is more powerful than Thor with his hammer. The one melts, the other but breaks in pieces.

When the ground was partially bare of snow, and a few warm days had dried its surface somewhat, it was pleasant to compare the first tender signs of the infant year just peeping forth with the stately beauty of the withered vegetation which had withstood the winter,—life-everlasting, golden-rods, pinweeds, and graceful wild grasses, more obvious and interesting frequently than in summer even, as if their beauty was not ripe till then; even cotton-grass, cat-tails, mulleins, johnswort, hard-hack, meadow-sweet, and other strong stemmed plants, those unexhausted granaries which entertain the earliest birds,—decent weeds, at least, which widowed Nature wears. I am particularly attracted by the arching and sheaf-like top of the wool-grass; it brings back the summer to our winter memories, and is among the forms which art loves to copy, and which, in the vegetable kingdom, have the same relation to types already in the mind of man that astronomy has. It is an antique style older than Greek or Egyptian. Many of the phenomena of Winter are suggestive of an inexpressible tenderness and fragile delicacy. We are accustomed to hear this king described as a rude and boisterous tyrant; but with the gentleness of a lover he adorns the tresses of Summer.

At the approach of spring the red-squirrels got under my house, two at a time, directly under my feet as I sat reading or writing, and kept up the queerest chuckling and chirruping and vocal pirouetting and gurgling sounds that ever were heard; and when I stamped they only chirruped the louder, as if past all fear and respect in their mad pranks, defying humanity to stop them. No you don't—chickaree—chickaree. They were wholly deaf to my arguments, or failed to perceive their force, and fell into a strain of invective that was irresistible.

The first sparrow of spring! The year beginning with younger hope than ever! The faint silvery warblings heard over the partially bare and moist fields from the blue-bird, the song-sparrow, and the red-wing, as if the last flakes of winter tinkled as they fell! What at such a time are histories, chronologies, traditions, and all written revelations? The brooks sing carols and glees to the spring. The marsh-hawk sailing low over the meadow is already seeking the first slimy life that awakes. The sinking sound of melting snow is heard in all dells, and the ice dissolves apace in the ponds. The grass flames up on the hillsides like a spring fire,—"et primitus oritur herba imbribus primoribus evocata,"—as if the earth sent forth an inward heat to greet the returning sun; not yellow but green is the color of its flame;—the symbol of perpetual youth, the grass-blade, like a long green ribbon, streams from the sod into the summer, checked indeed by the frost, but anon pushing on again, lifting its spear of last year's hay with the fresh life below. It grows as steadily as the rill oozes out of the ground. It is almost identical with that, for in the growing days of June, when the rills are dry, the grass blades are their channels, and from year to year the herds drink at this perennial green stream, and the mower draws from it betimes their winter supply. So our human life but dies down to its root, and still puts forth its green blade to eternity.

Walden is melting apace. There is a canal two rods wide along the northerly and westerly sides, and wider still at the east end. A great field of ice has cracked off from the main body. I hear a song-sparrow singing from the bushes on the shore,— *olit, olit, olit,* — *chip, chip, chip, che char,* — *che wiss, wiss, wiss.* He too is helping to crack it. How handsome the great sweeping curves in the edge of the ice, answering somewhat to those of the shore, but more regular! It is unusually hard, owing to the recent severe but transient cold, and all watered or waved like a palace floor. But the wind slides eastward over its opaque surface in vain, till it reaches the living surface beyond. It is glorious to behold this ribbon of water sparkling in the sun, the bare face of the pond full of glee and youth, as if it spoke the joy of the fishes within it, and of the sands on its shore,—a silvery sheen as from the scales of a *leuciscus,* as it were all one active fish. Such is the contrast between winter and spring. Walden was dead and is alive again. But this spring it broke up more steadily, as I have said.

The change from storm and winter to serene and mild

weather, from dark and sluggish hours to bright and elastic ones, is a memorable crisis which all things proclaim. It is seemingly instantaneous at last. Suddenly an influx of light filled my house, though the evening was at hand, and the clouds of winter still overhung it, and the eaves were dripping with sleety rain. I looked out the window, and lo! where yesterday was cold gray ice there lay the transparent pond already calm and full of hope as on a summer evening, reflecting a summer evening sky in its bosom, though none was visible overhead, as if it had intelligence with some remote horizon. I heard a robin in the distance, the first I had heard for many a thousand years, methought, whose note I shall not forget for many a thousand more,—the same sweet and powerful song as of yore. O the evening robin, at the end of a New England summer day! If I could ever find the twig he sits upon! I mean *he*; I mean *the twig*. This at least is not the *Turdus migratorius*. The pitch-pines and shrub-oaks about my house, which had so long drooped, suddenly resumed their several characters, looked brighter, greener, and more erect and alive, as if effectually cleansed and restored by the rain. I knew that it would not rain any more. You may tell by looking at any twig of the forest, ay, at your very wood-pile, whether its winter is past or not. As it grew darker, I was startled by the *honking* of geese flying low over the woods, like weary travellers getting in late from southern lakes, and indulging at last in unrestrained complaint and mutual consolation. Standing at my door, I could hear the rush of their wings; when, driving toward my house, they suddenly spied my light, and with hushed clamor wheeled and settled in the pond. So I came in, and shut the door, and passed my first spring night in the woods.

In the morning I watched the geese from the door through the mist, sailing in the middle of the pond, fifty rods off, so large and tumultuous that Walden appeared like an artificial pond for their amusement. But when I stood on the shore they at once rose up with a great flapping of wings at the signal of their commander, and when they had got into rank circled about over my head, twenty-nine of them, and then steered straight to Canada, with a regular *honk* from the leader at intervals, trusting to break their fast in muddier pools. A "plump" of ducks rose at the same time and took the route to the north in the wake of their noisier cousins.

For a week I heard the circling groping clangor of some solitary goose in the foggy mornings, seeking its companion, and still peopling the woods with the sound of a larger life than they could sustain. In April the pigeons were seen again flying express in small flocks, and in due time I heard the martins twittering over my clearing, though it had not seemed that the township contained so many that it could afford me any, and I fancied that they were peculiarly of the ancient race that dwelt in hollow trees ere white men came. In almost all climes the tortoise and the frog are among the precursors and heralds of this season, and birds fly with song and glancing plumage, and plants spring and bloom, and winds blow, to correct this slight oscillation of the poles and preserve the equilibrium of Nature.

As every season seems best to us in its turn, so the coming in of spring is like the creation of Cosmos out of Chaos and the realization of the Golden Age.—

> "Eurus ad Auroram, Nabathæaque regna recessit,
> Persidaque, et radiis juga subdita matutinis."

> "The East-Wind withdrew to Aurora and the Nabathæan
>   kingdom,
> And the Persian, and the ridges placed under the morning
>   rays.
>
>   *   *   *   *
>
> Man was born. Whether that Artificer of things,
> The origin of a better world, made him from the divine
>   seed;
> Or the earth being recent and lately sundered from the
>   high
> Ether, retained some seeds of cognate heaven."

A single gentle rain makes the grass many shades greener. So our prospects brighten on the influx of better thoughts. We should be blessed if we lived in the present always, and took advantage of every accident that befell us, like the grass which confesses the influence of the slightest dew that falls on it; and did not spend our time in atoning for the neglect of past opportunities, which we call doing our duty. We loiter in winter while it is already spring. In a pleasant spring morning all men's sins are forgiven. Such a day is a truce to vice. While such a sun holds out to burn, the vilest sinner may return. Through our own recovered innocence we discern the innocence of our neighbors. You may have known your neighbor yesterday for a thief, a drunkard, or a sensualist, and merely pitied or despised him, and despaired of the world; but the sun shines bright and warm this first spring morning, recreating the world, and you meet him at some serene work, and see how his exhausted and debauched veins expand with still joy and bless the new day, feel the spring influence with the innocence of infancy, and all his faults are forgotten. There is not only an atmosphere of good will about him, but even a savor of holiness groping for expression, blindly and ineffectually perhaps, like a new-born instinct, and for a short hour the south hill-side echoes to no vulgar jest. You see some innocent fair shoots preparing to burst from his gnarled rind and try another year's life, tender and fresh as the youngest plant. Even he has entered into the joy of his Lord. Why the jailer does not leave open his prison doors,—why the judge does not dismiss his case,—why the preacher does not dismiss his congregation! It is because they do not obey the hint which God gives them, nor accept the pardon which he freely offers to all.

"A return to goodness produced each day in the tranquil and beneficent breath of the morning, causes that in respect to the love of virtue and the hatred of vice, one approaches a little the primitive nature of man, as the sprouts of the forest which has been felled. In like manner the evil which one does in the interval of a day prevents the germs of virtues which began to spring up again from developing themselves and destroys them.

"After the germs of virtue have thus been prevented many times from developing themselves, then the beneficent breath of evening does not suffice to preserve them. As soon as the breath of evening does not suffice longer to preserve them, then the nature of man does not differ much from that of the brute. Men seeing the nature of this man like that of the brute, think that he has never possessed the innate faculty of reason. Are those the true and natural sentiments of man?"

"The Golden Age was first created, which without any
   avenger
Spontaneously without law cherished fidelity and rectitude.
Punishment and fear were not; nor were threatening words
   read
On suspended brass; nor did the suppliant crowd fear
The words of their judge; but were safe without an
   avenger.
Not yet the pine felled on its mountains had descended
To the liquid waves that it might see a foreign world,
And mortals knew no shores but their own.
         *   *   *   *
There was eternal spring, and placid zephyrs with warm
Blasts soothed the flowers born without seed."

On the 29th of April, as I was fishing from the bank of the river near the Nine-Acre-Corner bridge, standing on the quaking grass and willow roots, where the muskrats lurk, I heard a singular rattling sound, somewhat like that of the sticks which boys play with their fingers, when, looking up, I observed a very slight and graceful hawk, like a night-hawk, alternately soaring like a ripple and tumbling a rod or two over and over, showing the underside of its wings, which gleamed like a satin ribbon in the sun, or like the pearly inside of a shell. This sight reminded me of falconry and what no-bleness and poetry are associated with that sport. The Merlin it seemed to me it might be called: but I care not for its name. It was the most ethereal flight I had ever witnessed. It did not simply flutter like a butterfly, nor soar like the larger hawks, but it sported with proud reliance in the fields of air; mount-ing again and again with its strange chuckle, it repeated its free and beautiful fall, turning over and over like a kite, and then recovering from its lofty tumbling, as if it had never set its foot on *terra firma*. It appeared to have no companion in the universe,—sporting there alone,—and to need none but the morning and the ether with which it played. It was not lonely, but made all the earth lonely beneath it. Where was the parent which hatched it, its kindred, and its father in the heavens? The tenant of the air, it seemed related to the earth but by an egg hatched some time in the crevice of a crag;— or was its native nest made in the angle of a cloud, woven of the rainbow's trimmings and the sunset sky, and lined with some soft midsummer haze caught up from earth? Its eyry now some cliffy cloud.

Beside this I got a rare mess of golden and silver and bright cupreous fishes, which looked like a string of jewels. Ah! I have penetrated to those meadows on the morning of many a first spring day, jumping from hummock to hummock, from willow root to willow root, when the wild river valley and the woods were bathed in so pure and bright a light as would have waked the dead, if they had been slumbering in their graves, as some suppose. There needs no stronger proof of immortality. All things must live in such a light. O Death, where was thy sting? O Grave, where was thy victory, then?

Our village life would stagnate if it were not for the unexplored forests and meadows which surround it. We need the tonic of wildness,—to wade sometimes in marshes where the bittern and the meadow-hen lurk, and hear the booming of the snipe; to smell the whispering sedge where only some wilder and more solitary fowl builds her nest, and the mink crawls with its belly close to the ground. At the same time that we are earnest to explore and learn all things, we require that all things be mysterious and unexplorable, that land and sea be infinitely wild, unsurveyed and unfathomed by us because unfathomable. We can never have enough of Nature. We must be refreshed by the sight of inexhaustible vigor, vast and Titanic features, the sea-coast with its wrecks, the wilderness with its living and its decaying trees, the thunder cloud, and the rain which lasts three weeks and produces freshets. We need to witness our own limits transgressed, and some life pasturing freely where we never wander. We are cheered when we observe the vulture feeding on the carrion which disgusts and disheartens us and deriving health and strength from the repast. There was a dead horse in the hollow by the path to my house, which compelled me sometimes to go out of my way, especially in the night when the air was heavy, but the assurance it gave me of the strong appetite and inviolable health of Nature was my compensation for this. I love to see that Nature is so rife with life that myriads can be afforded to be sacrificed and suffered to prey on one another; that tender organizations can be so serenely squashed out of existence like pulp,—tadpoles which herons gobble up, and tortoises and toads run over in the road; and that sometimes it has rained flesh and blood! With the liability to accident, we must see how little account is to be made of it. The impression made on a wise man is that of universal innocence. Poison is not poisonous after all, nor are any wounds fatal. Compassion is a very untenable ground. It must be expeditious. Its pleadings will not bear to be stereotyped.

Early in May, the oaks, hickories, maples, and other trees, just putting out amidst the pine woods around the pond, imparted a brightness like sunshine to the landscape, especially in cloudy days, as if the sun were breaking through mists and shining faintly on the hill-sides here and there. On the third or fourth of May I saw a loon in the pond, and during the first week of the month I heard the whippoorwill, the brown-thrasher, the veery, the wood-pewee, the chewink, and other birds. I had heard the wood-thrush long before. The phœbe had already come once more and looked in at my door and window, to see if my house was cavern-like enough for her, sustaining herself on humming wings with clinched talons, as if she held by the air, while she surveyed the premises. The sulphur-like pollen of the pitch-pine soon covered the pond and the stones and rotten wood along the shore, so that you could have collected a barrel-ful. This is the "sulphur showers" we hear of. Even in Calidas' drama of Sacontala, we read of "rills dyed yellow with the golden dust of the lotus." And so the seasons went rolling on into summer, as one rambles into higher and higher grass.

Thus was my first year's life in the woods completed; and the second year was similar to it. I finally left Walden September 6th, 1847.

Conclusion

To the sick the doctors wisely recommend a change of air and scenery. Thank Heaven, here is not all the world. The buck-eye does not grow in New England, and the mocking-bird is rarely heard here. The wild-goose is more of a cosmopolite than we; he breaks his fast in Canada, takes a luncheon in the Ohio, and plumes himself for the night in a southern bayou. Even the bison, to some extent, keeps pace with the seasons, cropping the pastures of the Colorado only till a greener and sweeter grass awaits him by the Yellowstone. Yet we think that if rail-fences are pulled down, and stone-walls piled up on our farms, bounds are henceforth set to our lives and our fates decided. If you are chosen town-clerk, for-sooth, you cannot go to Tierra del Fuego this summer: but you may go to the land of infernal fire nevertheless. The universe is wider than our views of it.

Yet we should oftener look over the tafferel of our craft, like curious passengers, and not make the voyage like stupid sailors picking oakum. The other side of the globe is but the home of our correspondent. Our voyaging is only great-circle sailing, and the doctors prescribe for diseases of the skin merely. One hastens to Southern Africa to chase the giraffe; but surely that is not the game he would be after. How long, pray, would a man hunt giraffes if he could? Snipes and woodcocks also may afford rare sport; but I trust it would be nobler game to shoot one's self.—

> "Direct your eye sight inward, and you'll find
> A thousand regions in your mind
> Yet undiscovered. Travel them, and be
> Expert in home-cosmography."

What does Africa,—what does the West stand for? Is not our own interior white on the chart? black though it may prove, like the coast, when discovered. Is it the source of the Nile, or the Niger, or the Mississippi, or a North-West Passage around this continent, that we would find? Are these the problems which most concern mankind? Is Franklin the only man who is lost, that his wife should be so earnest to find

him? Does Mr. Grinnell know where he himself is? Be rather
the Mungo Park, the Lewis and Clarke and Frobisher, of your
own streams and oceans; explore your own higher latitudes,—with shiploads of preserved meats to support you, if
they be necessary; and pile the empty cans sky-high for a sign.
Were preserved meats invented to preserve meat merely? Nay,
be a Columbus to whole new continents and worlds within
you, opening new channels, not of trade, but of thought.
Every man is the lord of a realm beside which the earthly
empire of the Czar is but a petty state, a hummock left by the
ice. Yet some can be patriotic who have no *self*-respect, and
sacrifice the greater to the less. They love the soil which
makes their graves, but have no sympathy with the spirit
which may still animate their clay. Patriotism is a maggot in
their heads. What was the meaning of that South-Sea Exploring Expedition, with all its parade and expense, but an indirect recognition of the fact, that there are continents and seas
in the moral world, to which every man is an isthmus or an
inlet, yet unexplored by him, but that it is easier to sail many
thousand miles through cold and storm and cannibals, in a
government ship, with five hundred men and boys to assist
one, than it is to explore the private sea, the Atlantic and
Pacific Ocean of one's being alone.—

> "Erret, et extremos alter scrutetur Iberos.
> Plus habet hic vitæ, plus habet ille viæ."

Let them wander and scrutinize the outlandish Australians.
I have more of God, they more of the road.

It is not worth the while to go round the world to count the
cats in Zanzibar. Yet do this even till you can do better, and
you may perhaps find some "Symmes' Hole" by which to get
at the inside at last. England and France, Spain and Portugal,
Gold Coast and Slave Coast, all front on this private sea; but
no bark from them has ventured out of sight of land, though
it is without doubt the direct way to India. If you would learn
to speak all tongues and conform to the customs of all nations, if you would travel farther than all travellers, be naturalized in all climes, and cause the Sphinx to dash her head
against a stone, even obey the precept of the old philosopher,

and Explore thyself. Herein are demanded the eye and the nerve. Only the defeated and deserters go to the wars, cowards that run away and enlist. Start now on that farthest western way, which does not pause at the Mississippi or the Pacific, nor conduct toward a worn-out China or Japan, but leads on direct a tangent to this sphere, summer and winter, day and night, sun down, moon down, and at last earth down too.

It is said that Mirabeau took to highway robbery "to ascertain what degree of resolution was necessary in order to place one's self in formal opposition to the most sacred laws of society." He declared that "a soldier who fights in the ranks does not require half so much courage as a foot-pad,"—"that honor and religion have never stood in the way of a well-considered and a firm resolve." This was manly, as the world goes; and yet it was idle, if not desperate. A saner man would have found himself often enough "in formal opposition" to what are deemed "the most sacred laws of society," through obedience to yet more sacred laws, and so have tested his resolution without going out of his way. It is not for a man to put himself in such an attitude to society, but to maintain himself in whatever attitude he find himself through obedience to the laws of his being, which will never be one of opposition to a just government, if he should chance to meet with such.

I left the woods for as good a reason as I went there. Perhaps it seemed to me that I had several more lives to live, and could not spare any more time for that one. It is remarkable how easily and insensibly we fall into a particular route, and make a beaten track for ourselves. I had not lived there a week before my feet wore a path from my door to the pond-side; and though it is five or six years since I trod it, it is still quite distinct. It is true, I fear that others may have fallen into it, and so helped to keep it open. The surface of the earth is soft and impressible by the feet of men; and so with the paths which the mind travels. How worn and dusty, then, must be the highways of the world, how deep the ruts of tradition and conformity! I did not wish to take a cabin passage, but rather to go before the mast and on the deck of the world, for there I could best see the moonlight amid the mountains. I do not wish to go below now.

I learned this, at least, by my experiment; that if one advances confidently in the direction of his dreams, and endeavors to live the life which he has imagined, he will meet with a success unexpected in common hours. He will put some things behind, will pass an invisible boundary; new, universal, and more liberal laws will begin to establish themselves around and within him; or the old laws be expanded, and interpreted in his favor in a more liberal sense, and he will live with the license of a higher order of beings. In proportion as he simplifies his life, the laws of the universe will appear less complex, and solitude will not be solitude, nor poverty poverty, nor weakness weakness. If you have built castles in the air, your work need not be lost; that is where they should be. Now put the foundations under them.

It is a ridiculous demand which England and America make, that you shall speak so that they can understand you. Neither men nor toad-stools grow so. As if that were important, and there were not enough to understand you without them. As if Nature could support but one order of understandings, could not sustain birds as well as quadrupeds, flying as well as creeping things, and *hush* and *who*, which Bright can understand, were the best English. As if there were safety in stupidity alone. I fear chiefly lest my expression may not be *extra- vagant* enough, may not wander far enough beyond the narrow limits of my daily experience, so as to be adequate to the truth of which I have been convinced. *Extra vagance!* it depends on how you are yarded. The migrating buffalo, which seeks new pastures in another latitude, is not extravagant like the cow which kicks over the pail, leaps the cow-yard fence, and runs after her calf, in milking time. I desire to speak somewhere *without* bounds; like a man in a waking moment, to men in their waking moments; for I am convinced that I cannot exaggerate enough even to lay the foundation of a true expression. Who that has heard a strain of music feared then lest he should speak extravagantly any more forever? In view of the future or possible, we should live quite laxly and undefined in front, our outlines dim and misty on that side; as our shadows reveal an insensible perspiration toward the sun. The volatile truth of our words should continually betray the inadequacy of the residual statement. Their truth is instantly *translated*; its literal monument alone remains. The words which express our faith and piety are not definite; yet they are significant and fragrant like frankincense to superior natures.

Why level downward to our dullest perception always, and praise that as common sense? The commonest sense is the sense of men asleep, which they express by snoring. Sometimes we are inclined to class those who are once-and-a-half witted with the half-witted, because we appreciate only a third part of their wit. Some would find fault with the morning-red, if they ever got up early enough. "They pretend," as I hear, "that the verses of Kabir have four different senses; illusion, spirit, intellect, and the exoteric doctrine of the Vedas;" but in this part of the world it is considered a ground for complaint if a man's writings admit of more than one interpretation. While England endeavors to cure the potato-rot, will not any endeavor to cure the brain-rot, which prevails so much more widely and fatally?

I do not suppose that I have attained to obscurity, but I should be proud if no more fatal fault were found with my pages on this score than was found with the Walden ice. Southern customers objected to its blue color, which is the evidence of its purity, as if it were muddy, and preferred the Cambridge ice, which is white, but tastes of weeds. The purity men love is like the mists which envelop the earth, and not like the azure ether beyond.

Some are dinning in our ears that we Americans, and moderns generally, are intellectual dwarfs compared with the ancients, or even the Elizabethan men. But what is that to the purpose? A living dog is better than a dead lion. Shall a man go and hang himself because he belongs to the race of pygmies, and not be the biggest pygmy that he can? Let every one mind his own business, and endeavor to be what he was made.

Why should we be in such desperate haste to succeed, and in such desperate enterprises? If a man does not keep pace with his companions, perhaps it is because he hears a different drummer. Let him step to the music which he hears, however measured or far away. It is not important that he should mature as soon as an apple-tree or an oak. Shall he turn his spring into summer? If the condition of things which we were made for is not yet, what were any reality which we can substitute? We will not be shipwrecked on a vain reality. Shall we with pains erect a heaven of blue glass over ourselves, though when it is done we shall be sure to gaze still at the true ethereal heaven far above, as if the former were not?

There was an artist in the city of Kouroo who was disposed to strive after perfection. One day it came into his mind to make a staff. Having considered that in an imperfect work time is an ingredient, but into a perfect work time does not enter, he said to himself, It shall be perfect in all respects, though I should do nothing else in my life. He proceeded instantly to the forest for wood, being resolved that it should not be made of unsuitable material; and as he searched for and rejected stick after stick, his friends gradually deserted him, for they grew old in their works and died, but he grew not older by a moment. His singleness of purpose and resolution, and his elevated piety, endowed him, without his knowledge, with perennial youth. As he made no compromise with Time, Time kept out of his way, and only sighed at a distance because he could not overcome him. Before he had found a stock in all respects suitable the city of Kouroo was a hoary ruin, and he sat on one of its mounds to peel the stick. Before he had given it the proper shape the dynasty of the Candahars was at an end, and with the point of the stick he wrote the name of the last of that race in the sand, and then resumed his work. By the time he had smoothed and polished the staff Kalpa was no longer the pole-star; and ere he had put on the ferule and the head adorned with precious stones, Brahma had awoke and slumbered many times. But why do I stay to mention these things? When the finishing stroke was put to his work, it suddenly expanded before the eyes of the astonished artist into the fairest of all the creations of Brahma. He had made a new system in making a staff, a world with full and fair proportions; in which, though the old cities and dynasties had passed away, fairer and more glorious ones had taken their places. And now he saw by the heap of shavings still fresh at his feet, that, for him and his work, the former lapse of time had been an illusion, and that no more time had elapsed than is required for a single scintil-

lation from the brain of Brahma to fall on and inflame the
tinder of a mortal brain. The material was pure, and his art
was pure; how could the result be other than wonderful?

No face which we can give to a matter will stead us so well
at last as the truth. This alone wears well. For the most part,
we are not where we are, but in a false position. Through an
infirmity of our natures, we suppose a case, and put ourselves
into it, and hence are in two cases at the same time, and it is
doubly difficult to get out. In sane moments we regard only
the facts, the case that is. Say what you have to say, not what
you ought. Any truth is better than make-believe. Tom Hyde,
the tinker, standing on the gallows, was asked if he had any
thing to say. "Tell the tailors," said he, "to remember to make
a knot in their thread before they take the first stitch." His
companion's prayer is forgotten.

However mean your life is, meet it and live it; do not shun
it and call it hard names. It is not so bad as you are. It looks
poorest when you are richest. The fault-finder will find faults
even in paradise. Love your life, poor as it is. You may perhaps have some pleasant, thrilling, glorious hours, even in a
poor-house. The setting sun is reflected from the windows of
the alms-house as brightly as from the rich man's abode; the
snow melts before its door as early in the spring. I do not see
but a quiet mind may live as contentedly there, and have as
cheering thoughts, as in a palace. The town's poor seem to
me often to live the most independent lives of any. May be
they are simply great enough to receive without misgiving.
Most think that they are above being supported by the town;
but it oftener happens that they are not above supporting
themselves by dishonest means, which should be more disrep-
utable. Cultivate poverty like a garden herb, like sage. Do not
trouble yourself much to get new things, whether clothes or
friends. Turn the old; return to them. Things do not change;
we change. Sell your clothes and keep your thoughts. God
will see that you do not want society. If I were confined to a
corner of a garret all my days, like a spider, the world would
be just as large to me while I had my thoughts about me. The
philosopher said: "From an army of three divisions one can
take away its general, and put it in disorder; from the man
the most abject and vulgar one cannot take away his

thought." Do not seek so anxiously to be developed, to subject yourself to many influences to be played on; it is all dissipation. Humility like darkness reveals the heavenly lights. The shadows of poverty and meanness gather around us, "and lo! creation widens to our view." We are often reminded that if there were bestowed on us the wealth of Crœsus, our aims must still be the same, and our means essentially the same. Moreover, if you are restricted in your range by poverty, if you cannot buy books and newspapers, for instance, you are but confined to the most significant and vital experiences; you are compelled to deal with the material which yields the most sugar and the most starch. It is life near the bone where it is sweetest. You are defended from being a trifler. No man loses ever on a lower level by magnanimity on a higher. Superfluous wealth can buy superfluities only. Money is not required to buy one necessary of the soul.

I live in the angle of a leaden wall, into whose composition was poured a little alloy of bell metal. Often, in the repose of my mid-day, there reaches my ears a confused *tintinnabulum* from without. It is the noise of my contemporaries. My neighbors tell me of their adventures with famous gentlemen and ladies, what notabilities they met at the dinner-table; but I am no more interested in such things than in the contents of the Daily Times. The interest and the conversation are about costume and manners chiefly; but a goose is a goose still, dress it as you will. They tell me of California and Texas, of England and the Indies, of the Hon. Mr. —— of Georgia or of Massachusetts, all transient and fleeting phenomena, till I am ready to leap from their court-yard like the Mameluke bey. I delight to come to my bearings,—not walk in procession with pomp and parade, in a conspicuous place, but to walk even with the Builder of the universe, if I may,—not to live in this restless, nervous, bustling, trivial Nineteenth Century, but stand or sit thoughtfully while it goes by. What are men celebrating? They are all on a committee of arrangements, and hourly expect a speech from somebody. God is only the president of the day, and Webster is his orator. I love to weigh, to settle, to gravitate toward that which most strongly and rightfully attracts me;—not hang by the beam of the scale and try to weigh less,—not suppose a case, but take the case that is; to travel the only path I can, and that on which no power can resist me. It affords me no satisfaction to commence to spring an arch before I have got a solid foundation. Let us not play at kittlybenders. There is a solid bottom every where. We read that the traveller asked the boy if the swamp before him had a hard bottom. The boy replied that it had. But presently the traveller's horse sank in up to the girths, and he observed to the boy, "I thought you said that this bog had a hard bottom." "So it has," answered the latter, "but you have not got half way to it yet." So it is with the bogs and quicksands of society; but he is an old boy that knows it. Only what is thought said or done at a certain rare coincidence is good. I would not be one of those who will foolishly drive a nail into mere lath and plastering; such a deed would keep me awake nights. Give me a hammer, and let me feel for the furrowing. Do not depend on the putty. Drive a nail home and clinch it so faithfully that you can wake up in the night and think of your work with satisfaction,—a work at which you would not be ashamed to invoke the Muse. So will help you God, and so only. Every nail driven should be as another rivet in the machine of the universe, you carrying on the work.

Rather than love, than money, than fame, give me truth. I sat at a table where were rich food and wine in abundance, and obsequious attendance, but sincerity and truth were not; and I went away hungry from the inhospitable board. The hospitality was as cold as the ices. I thought that there was no need of ice to freeze them. They talked to me of the age of the wine and the fame of the vintage; but I thought of an older, a newer, and purer wine, of a more glorious vintage, which they had not got, and could not buy. The style, the house and grounds and "entertainment" pass for nothing with me. I called on the king, but he made me wait in his hall, and conducted like a man incapacitated for hospitality. There was a man in my neighborhood who lived in a hollow tree. His manners were truly regal. I should have done better had I called on him.

How long shall we sit in our porticoes practising idle and musty virtues, which any work would make impertinent? As if one were to begin the day with long-suffering, and hire a

man to hoe his potatoes; and in the afternoon go forth to
practise Christian meekness and charity with goodness aforethought! Consider the China pride and stagnant self-com-
placency of mankind. This generation reclines a little to
congratulate itself on being the last of an illustrious line; and
in Boston and London and Paris and Rome, thinking of its
long descent, it speaks of its progress in art and science and
literature with satisfaction. There are the Records of the
Philosophical Societies, and the public Eulogies of *Great
Men!* It is the good Adam contemplating his own virtue.
"Yes, we have done great deeds, and sung divine songs, which
shall never die,"—that is, as long as *we* can remember them.
The learned societies and great men of Assyria,—where are
they? What youthful philosophers and experimentalists we
are! There is not one of my readers who has yet lived a whole
human life. These may be but the spring months in the life
of the race. If we have had the seven-years' itch, we have not
seen the seventeen-year locust yet in Concord. We are acquainted with a mere pellicle of the globe on which we live.
Most have not delved six feet beneath the surface, nor leaped
as many above it. We know not where we are. Beside, we are
sound asleep nearly half our time. Yet we esteem ourselves
wise, and have an established order on the surface. Truly, we
are deep thinkers, we are ambitious spirits! As I stand over
the insect crawling amid the pine needles on the forest floor,
and endeavoring to conceal itself from my sight, and ask myself why it will cherish those humble thoughts, and hide its
head from me who might perhaps be its benefactor, and impart to its race some cheering information, I am reminded of
the greater Benefactor and Intelligence that stands over me
the human insect.

There is an incessant influx of novelty into the world, and
yet we tolerate incredible dulness. I need only suggest what
kind of sermons are still listened to in the most enlightened
countries. There are such words as joy and sorrow, but they
are only the burden of a psalm, sung with a nasal twang,
while we believe in the ordinary and mean. We think that we
can change our clothes only. It is said that the British Empire
is very large and respectable, and that the United States are a
first-rate power. We do not believe that a tide rises and falls

behind every man which can float the British Empire like a chip, if he should ever harbor it in his mind. Who knows what sort of seventeen-year locust will next come out of the ground? The government of the world I live in was not framed, like that of Britain, in after-dinner conversations over the wine.

The life in us is like the water in the river. It may rise this year higher than man has ever known it, and flood the parched uplands; even this may be the eventful year, which will drown out all our muskrats. It was not always dry land where we dwell. I see far inland the banks which the stream anciently washed, before science began to record its freshets. Every one has heard the story which has gone the rounds of New England, of a strong and beautiful bug which came out of the dry leaf of an old table of apple-tree wood, which had stood in a farmer's kitchen for sixty years, first in Connecticut, and afterward in Massachusetts,—from an egg deposited in the living tree many years earlier still, as appeared by counting the annual layers beyond it; which was heard gnawing out for several weeks, hatched perchance by the heat of an urn. Who does not feel his faith in a resurrection and immortality strengthened by hearing of this? Who knows what beautiful and winged life, whose egg has been buried for ages under many concentric layers of woodenness in the dead dry life of society, deposited at first in the alburnum of the green and living tree, which has been gradually converted into the semblance of its well-seasoned tomb,—heard perchance gnawing out now for years by the astonished family of man, as they sat round the festive board,—may unexpectedly come forth from amidst society's most trivial and handselled furniture, to enjoy its perfect summer life at last!

I do not say that John or Jonathan will realize all this; but such is the character of that morrow which mere lapse of time can never make to dawn. The light which puts out our eyes is darkness to us. Only that day dawns to which we are awake. There is more day to dawn. The sun is but a morning star.

THE END.

THE MAINE WOODS

Contents

Ktaadn

O N THE 31st of August, 1846, I left Concord in Massachusetts for Bangor and the backwoods of Maine, by way of the railroad and steamboat, intending to accompany a relative of mine engaged in the lumber-trade in Bangor, as far as a dam on the west branch of the Penobscot, in which property he was interested. From this place, which is about one hundred miles by the river above Bangor, thirty miles from the Houlton military road, and five miles beyond the last log-hut, I proposed to make excursions to Mount Ktaadn, the second highest mountain in New England, about thirty miles distant, and to some of the lakes of the Penobscot, either alone or with such company as I might pick up there. It is unusual to find a camp so far in the woods at that season, when lumbering operations have ceased, and I was glad to avail myself of the circumstance of a gang of men being employed there at that time in repairing the injuries caused by the great freshet in the spring. The mountain may be approached more easily and directly on horseback and on foot from the northeast side, by the Aroostook road, and the Wassataquoik River; but in that case you see much less of the wilderness, none of the glorious river and lake scenery, and have no experience of the batteau and the boatman's life. I was fortunate also in the season of the year, for in the summer myriads of black flies, mosquitoes, and midges, or, as the Indians call them, "no-see-ems," make travelling in the woods almost impossible; but now their reign was nearly over.

Ktaadn, whose name is an Indian word signifying highest land, was first ascended by white men in 1804. It was visited by Professor J. W. Bailey of West Point in 1836; by Dr. Charles T. Jackson, the State Geologist, in 1837; and by two young men from Boston in 1845. All these have given accounts of their expeditions. Since I was there, two or three other parties have made the excursion, and told their stories. Besides these, very few, even among backwoodsmen and hunters, have ever climbed it, and it will be a long time before the tide of fashionable travel sets that way. The mountainous region of the State of Maine stretches from near the White

Mountains, northeasterly one hundred and sixty miles, to the head of the Aroostook River, and is about sixty miles wide. The wild or unsettled portion is far more extensive. So that some hours only of travel in this direction will carry the curious to the verge of a primitive forest, more interesting, perhaps, on all accounts, than they would reach by going a thousand miles westward.

The next forenoon, Tuesday, September 1st, I started with my companion in a buggy from Bangor for "up river," expecting to be overtaken the next day night at Mattawamkeag Point, some sixty miles off, by two more Bangoreans, who had decided to join us in a trip to the mountain. We had each a knapsack or bag filled with such clothing and articles as were indispensable, and my companion carried his gun.

Within a dozen miles of Bangor we passed through the villages of Stillwater and Oldtown, built at the falls of the Penobscot; which furnish the principal power by which the Maine woods are converted into lumber. The mills are built directly over and across the river. Here is a close jam, a hard rub, at all seasons; and then the once green tree, long since white, I need not say as the driven snow, but as a driven log, becomes lumber merely. Here your inch, your two and your three inch stuff begin to be, and Mr. Sawyer marks off those spaces which decide the destiny of so many prostrate forests. Through this steel riddle, more or less coarse, is the arrowy Maine forest, from Ktaadn and Chesuncook, and the head-waters of the St. John, relentlessly sifted, till it comes out boards, clapboards, laths, and shingles such as the wind can take, still perchance to be slit and slit again, till men get a size that will suit. Think how stood the white-pine tree on the shore of Chesuncook, its branches soughing with the four winds, and every individual needle trembling in the sunlight,—think how it stands with it now,—sold, perchance, to the New England Friction-Match Company! There were in 1837, as I read, two hundred and fifty saw-mills on the Penobscot and its tributaries above Bangor, the greater part of them in this immediate neighborhood, and they sawed two hundred millions of feet of boards annually. To this is to be added the lumber of the Kennebec, Androscoggin, Saco, Passamaquoddy, and other streams. No wonder that we hear so

often of vessels which are becalmed off our coast, being surrounded a week at a time by floating lumber from the Maine
woods. The mission of men there seems to be, like so many
busy demons, to drive the forest all out of the country, from
every solitary beaver-swamp and mountain-side, as soon as
possible.

At Oldtown we walked into a batteau-manufactory. The
making of batteaux is quite a business here for the supply of
the Penobscot River. We examined some on the stocks. They
are light and shapely vessels, calculated for rapid and rocky
streams, and to be carried over long portages on men's shoulders, from twenty to thirty feet long, and only four or four
and a half wide, sharp at both ends like a canoe, though
broadest forward on the bottom, and reaching seven or eight
feet over the water, in order that they may slip over rocks as
gently as possible. They are made very slight, only two boards
to a side, commonly secured to a few light maple or other
hard-wood knees, but inward are of the clearest and widest
white-pine stuff, of which there is a great waste on account
of their form, for the bottom is left perfectly flat, not only
from side to side, but from end to end. Sometimes they become "hogging" even, after long use, and the boatmen then
turn them over and straighten them by a weight at each end.
They told us that one wore out in two years, or often in a
single trip, on the rocks, and sold for from fourteen to sixteen
dollars. There was something refreshing and wildly musical to
my ears in the very name of the white man's canoe, reminding
me of Charlevoix and Canadian Voyageurs. The batteau is
a sort of mongrel between the canoe and the boat, a fur-
trader's boat.

The ferry here took us past the Indian island. As we left
the shore, I observed a short, shabby, washerwoman-looking
Indian—they commonly have the woe-begone look of the
girl that cried for spilt milk—just from "up river"—land on
the Oldtown side near a grocery, and, drawing up his canoe,
take out a bundle of skins in one hand, and an empty keg or
half-barrel in the other, and scramble up the bank with them.
This picture will do to put before the Indian's history, that is,
the history of his extinction. In 1837 there were three hundred
and sixty-two souls left of this tribe. The island seemed

deserted to-day, yet I observed some new houses among the weather-stained ones, as if the tribe had still a design upon life; but generally they have a very shabby, forlorn, and cheerless look, being all back side and woodshed, not homesteads, even Indian homesteads, but instead of home or abroadsteads, for their life is *domi aut militiæ*, at home or at war, or now rather *venatus*, that is, a hunting, and most of the latter. The church is the only trim-looking building, but that is not Abenaki, that was Rome's doings. Good Canadian it may be, but it is poor Indian. These were once a powerful tribe. Politics are all the rage with them now. I even thought that a row of wigwams, with a dance of powwows, and a prisoner tortured at the stake, would be more respectable than this.

We landed in Milford, and rode along on the east side of the Penobscot, having a more or less constant view of the river, and the Indian islands in it, for they retain all the islands as far up as Nickatow, at the mouth of the East Branch. They are generally well-timbered, and are said to be better soil than the neighboring shores. The river seemed shallow and rocky, and interrupted by rapids, rippling and gleaming in the sun. We paused a moment to see a fish-hawk dive for a fish down straight as an arrow, from a great height, but he missed his prey this time. It was the Houlton road on which we were now travelling, over which some troops were marched once towards Mars' Hill, though not to Mars' *field*, as it proved. It is the main, almost the only, road in these parts, as straight and well made, and kept in as good repair, as almost any you will find anywhere. Everywhere we saw signs of the great freshet,—this house standing awry, and that where it was not founded, but where it was found, at any rate, the next day; and that other with a water-logged look, as if it were still airing and drying its basement, and logs with everybody's marks upon them, and sometimes the marks of their having served as bridges, strewn along the road. We crossed the Sunkhaze, a summery Indian name, the Olemmon, Passadumkeag, and other streams, which make a greater show on the map than they now did on the road. At Passadumkeag we found anything but what the name implies,—earnest politicians, to wit,—white ones, I mean,—on the alert, to know how the election was likely to go; men who talked rapidly, with subdued voice, and a sort of factitious earnestness, you could not help believing, hardly waiting for an introduction, one on each side of your buggy, endeavoring to say much in little, for they see you hold the whip impatiently, but always saying little in much. Caucuses they have had, it seems, and caucuses they are to have again,—victory and defeat. Somebody may be elected, somebody may not. One man, a total stranger, who stood by our carriage in the dusk, actually frightened the horse with his asseverations, growing more solemnly positive as there was less in him to be positive about. So Passadumkeag did not look on the map. At sundown, leaving the river-road awhile for shortness, we went by way of Enfield, where we stopped for the night. This, like most of the localities bearing names on this road, was a place to name, which, in the midst of the unnamed and unincorporated wilderness, was to make a distinction without a difference, it seemed to me. Here, however, I noticed quite an orchard of healthy and well-grown apple-trees, in a bearing state, it being the oldest settler's house in this region, but all natural fruit, and comparatively worthless for want of a grafter. And so it is generally, lower down the river. It would be a good speculation, as well as a favor conferred on the settlers, for a Massachusetts boy to go down there with a trunk full of choice scions, and his grafting apparatus, in the spring.

The next morning we drove along through a high and hilly country, in view of Cold-Stream Pond, a beautiful lake four or five miles long, and came into the Houlton road again, here called the military road, at Lincoln, forty-five miles from Bangor, where there is quite a village for this country,—the principal one above Oldtown. Learning that there were several wigwams here, on one of the Indian islands, we left our horse and wagon, and walked through the forest half a mile to the river, to procure a guide to the mountain. It was not till after considerable search that we discovered their habitations,—small huts, in a retired place, where the scenery was unusually soft and beautiful, and the shore skirted with pleasant meadows and graceful elms. We paddled ourselves across to the island-side in a canoe, which we found on the shore. Near where we landed sat an Indian girl ten or twelve years old, on a rock in the water, in the sun, washing, and humming or moaning a song meanwhile. It was an aboriginal strain. A salmon-spear, made wholly of wood, lay on the shore, such as they might have used before white men came. It had an elastic piece of wood fastened to one side of its point, which slipped over and closed upon the fish, somewhat like the contrivance for holding a bucket at the end of a well-pole. As we walked up to the nearest house, we were met by a sally of a dozen wolfish-looking dogs, which may have been lineal descendants from the ancient Indian dogs, which the first voyageurs describe as "their wolves." I suppose they were. The occupant soon appeared, with a long pole in his hand, with which he beat off the dogs, while he parleyed with us. A stalwart, but dull and greasy-looking fellow, who told us, in his sluggish way, in answer to our questions, as if it were the first serious business he had to do that day, that there *were* Indians going "up river"—he and one other—to-day, before noon. And who was the other? Louis Neptune, who lives in the next house. Well, let us go over and see Louis together. The same doggish reception, and Louis Neptune makes his appearance,—a small, wiry man, with puckered and wrinkled face, yet he seemed the chief man of the two; the same, as I remembered, who had accompanied Jackson to the mountain in '37. The same questions were put to Louis, and the same information obtained, while the other Indian stood by. It appeared that they were going to start by noon, with two canoes, to go up to Chesuncook to hunt moose,— to be gone a month. "Well, Louis, suppose you get to the Point [to the Five Islands, just below Mattawamkeag], to camp, we walk on up the West Branch to-morrow,—four of us,—and wait for you at the dam, or this side. You overtake us to-morrow or next day, and take us into your canoes. We stop for you, you stop for us. We pay you for your trouble." "Ye!" replied Louis, "may be you carry some provision for all,—some pork,—some bread,—and so pay." He said, "Me sure get some moose"; and when I asked if he thought Po-mola would let us go up, he answered that we must plant one bottle of rum on the top; he had planted good many; and when he looked again, the rum was all gone. He had been up two or three times: he had planted letter,—English, German, French, &c. These men were slightly clad in shirt and pantaloons, like laborers with us in warm weather. They did not invite us into their houses, but met us outside. So we left the Indians, thinking ourselves lucky to have secured such guides and companions.

There were very few houses along the road, yet they did not altogether fail, as if the law by which men are dispersed over the globe were a very stringent one, and not to be resisted with impunity or for slight reasons. There were even the germs of one or two villages just beginning to expand. The beauty of the road itself was remarkable. The various evergreens, many of which are rare with us,—delicate and beautiful specimens of the larch, arbor-vitæ, ball-spruce, and fir-balsam, from a few inches to many feet in height,—lined its sides, in some places like a long, front yard, springing up from the smooth grass-plots which uninterruptedly border it, and are made fertile by its wash; while it was but a step on either hand to the grim, untrodden wilderness, whose tangled labyrinth of living, fallen, and decaying trees only the deer and moose, the bear and wolf, can easily penetrate. More perfect specimens than any front-yard plot can show, grew there to grace the passage of the Houlton teams.

About noon we reached the Mattawamkeag, fifty-six miles from Bangor by the way we had come, and put up at a frequented house still on the Houlton road, where the Houlton stage stops. Here was a substantial covered bridge over the Mattawamkeag, built, I think they said, some seventeen years before. We had dinner,—where, by the way, and even at breakfast, as well as supper, at the public-houses on this road, the front rank is composed of various kinds of "sweet cakes," in a continuous line from one end of the table to the other. I think I may safely say that there was a row of ten or a dozen plates of this kind set before us two here. To account for which, they say that, when the lumberers come out of the woods, they have a craving for cakes and pies, and such sweet things, which there are almost unknown, and this is the *supply* to satisfy that *demand*. The supply is always equal to the demand, and these hungry men think a good deal of getting their money's worth. No doubt the balance of victuals is restored by the time they reach Bangor,—Mattawamkeag takes off the raw edge. Well, over this front rank, I say, you, coming from the "sweet cake" side, with a cheap philosophic indifference though it may be, have to assault what there is behind, which I do not by any means mean to insinuate is insufficient in quantity or quality to supply that other demand, of men, not from the woods, but from the towns, for venison and strong country fare. After dinner we strolled down to the "Point," formed by the junction of the two rivers, which is said to be the scene of an ancient battle between the Eastern Indians and the Mohawks, and searched there carefully for relics, though the men at the bar-room had never heard of such things; but we found only some flakes of arrow-head stone, some points of arrow-heads, one small leaden bullet, and some colored beads, the last to be referred, perhaps, to early fur-trader days. The Mattawamkeag, though wide, was a mere river's bed, full of rocks and shallows at this time, so that you could cross it almost dry-shod in boots; and I could hardly believe my companion, when he told me that he had been fifty or sixty miles up it in a batteau, through distant and still uncut forests. A batteau could hardly find a harbor now at its mouth. Deer and carribou, or reindeer, are taken here in the winter, in sight of the house.

Before our companions arrived, we rode on up the Houlton road seven miles, to Molunkus, where the Aroostook road comes into it, and where there is a spacious public house in the woods, called the "Molunkus House," kept by one Libbey, which looked as if it had its hall for dancing and for military drills. There was no other evidence of man but this huge shingle palace in this part of the world; but sometimes even this is filled with travellers. I looked off the piazza round the corner of the house up the Aroostook road, on which there was no clearing in sight. There was a man just adventuring upon it this evening in a rude, original, what you may call Aroostook wagon,—a mere seat, with a wagon swung under it, a few bags on it, and a dog asleep to watch them. He offered to carry a message for us to anybody in that country, cheerfully. I suspect that, if you should go to the end of the world, you would find somebody there going farther, as if just starting for home at sundown, and having a last word before he drove off. Here, too, *was* a small trader, whom I did not see at first, who kept a store—but no great store, certainly—in a small box over the way, behind the Molunkus sign-post. It looked like the balance-box of a patent hay-scales. As for his house, we could only conjecture where that was; he may have been a boarder in the Molunkus House. I saw him standing in his shop-door,—his shop was so small, that, if a traveller should make demonstrations of entering in, *he* would have to go out by the back way, and confer with his customer through a window, about his goods in the cellar, or, more probably, bespoken, and yet on the way. I should have gone in, for I felt a real impulse to trade, if I had not stopped to consider what would become of him. The day before, we had walked into a shop, over against an inn where we stopped, the puny beginning of trade, which would grow at last into a firm copartnership in the future town or city,— indeed, it was already "Somebody & Co.," I forget who. The woman came forward from the penetralia of the attached house, for "Somebody & Co." was in the burning, and she sold us percussion-caps, canalés and smooth, and knew their prices and qualities, and which the hunters preferred. Here was a little of everything in a small compass to satisfy the wants and the ambition of the woods,—a stock selected with what pains and care, and brought home in the wagon-box, or a corner of the Houlton team; but there seemed to me, as usual, a preponderance of children's toys,—dogs to bark, and cats to mew, and trumpets to blow, where natives there hardly are yet. As if a child, born into the Maine woods, among the pine-cones and cedar-berries, could not do with-out such a sugar-man, or skipping-jack, as the young Roth-schild has.

I think that there was not more than one house on the road to Molunkus, or for seven miles. At that place we got over the fence into a new field, planted with potatoes, where the logs were still burning between the hills; and, pulling up the vines, found good-sized potatoes, nearly ripe, growing like weeds, and turnips mixed with them. The mode of clearing and planting is, to fell the trees, and burn once what will burn, then cut them up into suitable lengths, roll into heaps, and burn again; then, with a hoe, plant potatoes where you can come at the ground between the stumps and charred logs; for a first crop the ashes sufficing for manure, and no hoeing being necessary the first year. In the fall, cut, roll, and burn again, and so on, till the land is cleared; and soon it is ready for grain, and to be laid down. Let those talk of poverty and hard times who will in the towns and cities; cannot the emigrant who can pay his fare to New York or Boston pay five dollars more to get here,—I paid three, all told, for my passage from Boston to Bangor, two hundred and fifty miles,—and be as rich as he pleases, where land virtually costs nothing, and houses only the labor of building, and he may begin life as Adam did? If he will still remember the distinction of poor and rich, let him bespeak him a narrower house forthwith.

When we returned to the Mattawamkeag, the Houlton stage had already put up there; and a Province man was betraying his greenness to the Yankees by his questions. Why Province money won't pass here at par, when States' money is good at Frederickton,—though this, perhaps, was sensible enough. From what I saw then, it appears that the Province man was now the only real Jonathan, or raw country bumpkin, left so far behind by his enterprising neighbors that he did n't know enough to put a question to them. No people can long continue provincial in character who have the propensity for politics and whittling, and rapid travelling, which the Yankees have, and who are leaving the mother country behind in the variety of their notions and inventions. The possession and exercise of practical talent merely are a sure and rapid means of intellectual culture and independence.

The last edition of Greenleaf's Map of Maine hung on the wall here, and, as we had no pocket-map, we resolved to trace a map of the lake country. So, dipping a wad of tow into the lamp, we oiled a sheet of paper on the oiled table-cloth, and, in good faith, traced what we afterwards ascertained to be a labyrinth of errors, carefully following the outlines of the imaginary lakes which the map contains. The Map of the Public Lands of Maine and Massachusetts is the only one I have seen that at all deserves the name. It was while we were engaged in this operation that our companions arrived. They had seen the Indians' fire on the Five Islands, and so we concluded that all was right.

Early the next morning we had mounted our packs, and

prepared for a tramp up the West Branch, my companion having turned his horse out to pasture for a week or ten days, thinking that a bite of fresh grass, and a taste of running water, would do him as much good as backwoods fare and new country influences his master. Leaping over a fence, we began to follow an obscure trail up the northern bank of the Penobscot. There was now no road further, the river being the only highway, and but half a dozen log-huts confined to its banks, to be met with for thirty miles. On either hand, and beyond, was a wholly uninhabited wilderness, stretching to Canada. Neither horse nor cow, nor vehicle of any kind, had ever passed over this ground; the cattle, and the few bulky articles which the loggers use, being got up in the winter on the ice, and down again before it breaks up. The evergreen woods had a decidedly sweet and bracing fragrance; the air was a sort of diet-drink, and we walked on buoyantly in Indian file, stretching our legs. Occasionally there was a small opening on the bank, made for the purpose of log-rolling, where we got a sight of the river,—always a rocky and rippling stream. The roar of the rapids, the note of a whistler-duck on the river, of the jay and chickadee around us, and of the pigeon-woodpecker in the openings, were the sounds that we heard. This was what you might call a bran-new country; the only roads were of Nature's making, and the few houses were camps. Here, then, one could no longer accuse institutions and society, but must front the true source of evil.

There are three classes of inhabitants who either frequent or inhabit the country which we had now entered;—first, the loggers, who, for a part of the year, the winter and spring, are far the most numerous, but in the summer, except a few explorers for timber, completely desert it; second, the few settlers I have named, the only permanent inhabitants, who live on the verge of it, and help raise supplies for the former; third, the hunters, mostly Indians, who range over it in their season.

At the end of three miles, we came to the Mattaseunk stream and mill, where there was even a rude wooden railroad running down to the Penobscot, the last railroad we were to see. We crossed one tract, on the bank of the river, of more than a hundred acres of heavy timber, which had just been felled and burnt over, and was still smoking. Our trail lay through the midst of it, and was wellnigh blotted out. The trees lay at full length, four or five feet deep, and crossing each other in all directions, all black as charcoal, but perfectly sound within, still good for fuel or for timber; soon they would be cut into lengths and burnt again. Here were thousands of cords, enough to keep the poor of Boston and New York amply warm for a winter, which only cumbered the ground and were in the settler's way. And the whole of that solid and interminable forest is doomed to be gradually devoured thus by fire, like shavings, and no man be warmed by it. At Crocker's log-hut, at the mouth of Salmon River, seven miles from the Point, one of the party commenced distributing a store of small cent picture-books among the children, to teach them to read, and also newspapers, more or less recent, among the parents, than which nothing can be more acceptable to a backwoods people. It was really an important item in our outfit, and, at times, the only currency that would circulate. I walked through Salmon River with my shoes on, it being low water, but not without wetting my feet. A few miles farther we came to "Marm Howard's," at the end of an extensive clearing, where there were two or three log-huts in sight at once, one on the opposite side of the river, and a few graves, even surrounded by a wooden paling, where already the rude forefathers of *a* hamlet lie, and a thousand years hence, perchance, some poet will write his "Elegy in a Country Churchyard." The "Village Hampdens," the "mute, inglorious Miltons," and Cromwells, "guiltless of" their "country's blood," were yet unborn.

> "Perchance in this *wild* spot *there will be* laid
>   Some heart once pregnant with celestial fire;
> Hands that the rod of empire might have swayed,
>   Or waked to ecstasy the living lyre."

The next house was Fisk's, ten miles from the Point, at the mouth of the East Branch, opposite to the island Nickatow, or the Forks, the last of the Indian islands. I am particular to give the names of the settlers and the distances, since every log-hut in these woods is a public house, and such information is of no little consequence to those who may have occasion to travel this way. Our course here crossed the Penobscot, and followed the southern bank. One of the party, who entered the house in search of some one to set us over, reported a very neat dwelling, with plenty of books, and a new wife, just imported from Boston, wholly new to the woods. We found the East Branch a large and rapid stream at its mouth, and much deeper than it appeared. Having with some difficulty discovered the trail again, we kept up the south side of the West Branch, or main river, passing by some rapids called Rock-Ebeeme, the roar of which we heard through the woods, and, shortly after, in the thickest of the wood, some empty loggers' camps, still new, which were occupied the previous winter. Though we saw a few more afterwards, I will make one account serve for all. These were such houses as the lumberers of Maine spend the winter in, in the wilderness. There were the camps and the hovels for the cattle, hardly distinguishable, except that the latter had no chimney. These camps were about twenty feet long by fifteen wide, built of logs,—hemlock, cedar, spruce, or yellow birch,—one kind alone, or all together, with the bark on; two or three large ones first, one directly above another, and notched together at the ends, to the height of three or four feet, then of smaller logs resting upon transverse ones at the ends, each of the last successively shorter than the other, to form the roof. The chimney was an oblong square hole in the middle, three or four feet in diameter, with a fence of logs as high as the ridge. The interstices were filled with moss, and the roof was shingled with long and handsome splints of cedar, or spruce, or pine, rifted with a sledge and cleaver. The fire-place, the most important place of all, was in shape and size like the chimney, and directly under it, defined by a log fence or fender on the ground, and a heap of ashes, a foot or two deep, within, with solid benches of split logs running round it. Here the fire usually melts the snow, and dries the rain before it can descend to quench it. The faded beds of arbor-vitæ leaves extended under the eaves on either hand. There was the place for the water-pail, pork-barrel, and wash-basin, and generally a dingy pack of cards left on a log. Usually a good deal of whittling was expended on the latch, which was made of wood, in the form of an iron one. These houses are made comfortable by the huge fires, which can be afforded night and day. Usually the scenery about them is drear and savage enough; and the loggers' camp is as completely in the woods as a fungus at the foot of a pine in a swamp; no outlook but to the sky overhead; no more clearing than is made by cutting down the trees of which it is built, and those which are necessary for fuel. It only it be well sheltered and convenient to his work, and near a spring, he wastes no thought on the prospect. They are very proper forest houses, the stems of the trees collected together and piled up around a man to keep out wind and rain,—made of living green logs, hanging with moss and lichen, and with the curls and fringes of the yellow-birch bark, and dripping with resin, fresh and moist, and redolent of swampy odors, with that sort of vigor and perennialness even about them that toadstools suggest.* The logger's fare consists of tea, molasses, flour, pork (sometimes beef), and beans. A great proportion of the beans raised in Massachusetts find their market here. On expeditions it is only hard bread and pork, often raw, slice upon slice, with tea or water, as the case may be.

The primitive wood is always and everywhere damp and mossy, so that I travelled constantly with the impression that I was in a swamp; and only when it was remarked that this or that tract, judging from the quality of the timber on it, would make a profitable clearing, was I reminded, that if the sun were let in it would make a dry field, like the few I had seen, at once. The best shod for the most part travel with wet feet. If the ground was so wet and spongy at this, the dryest part of a dry season, what must it be in the spring? The woods hereabouts abounded in beech and yellow birch, of

*Springer, in his "Forest Life" (1851), says that they first remove the leaves and turf from the spot where they intend to build a camp, for fear of fire; also, that "the spruce-tree is generally selected for camp-building, it being light, straight, and quite free from sap"; that "the roof is finally covered with the boughs of the fir, spruce, and hemlock, so that when the snow falls upon the whole, the warmth of the camp is preserved in the coldest weather"; and that they make the log seat before the fire, called the "Deacon's Seat," of a spruce or fir split in halves, with three or four stout limbs left on one side for legs, which are not likely to get loose.

which last there were some very large specimens; also spruce, cedar, fir, and hemlock; but we saw only the stumps of the white pine here, some of them of great size, these having been already culled out, being the only tree much sought after, even as low down as this. Only a little spruce and hemlock beside had been logged here. The Eastern wood which is sold for fuel in Massachusetts all comes from below Bangor. It was the pine alone, chiefly the white pine, that had tempted any but the hunter to precede us on this route.

Waite's farm, thirteen miles from the Point, is an extensive and elevated clearing, from which we got a fine view of the river, rippling and gleaming far beneath us. My companions had formerly had a good view of Ktaadn and the other mountains here, but to-day it was so smoky that we could see nothing of them. We could overlook an immense country of uninterrupted forest, stretching away up the East Branch toward Canada, on the north and northwest, and toward the Aroostook valley on the northeast; and imagine what wild life was stirring in its midst. Here was quite a field of corn for this region, whose peculiar dry scent we perceived a third of a mile off, before we saw it.

Eighteen miles from the Point brought us in sight of McCauslin's, or "Uncle George's," as he was familiarly called by my companions, to whom he was well known, where we intended to break our long fast. His house was in the midst of an extensive clearing of intervale, at the mouth of the Little Schoodic River, on the opposite or north bank of the Penobscot. So we collected on a point of the shore, that we might be seen, and fired our gun as a signal, which brought out his dogs forthwith, and thereafter their master, who in due time took us across in his batteau. This clearing was bounded abruptly, on all sides but the river, by the naked stems of the forest, as if you were to cut only a few feet square in the midst of a thousand acres of mowing, and set down a thimble therein. He had a whole heaven and horizon to himself, and the sun seemed to be journeying over his clearing only the livelong day. Here we concluded to spend the night, and wait for the Indians, as there was no stopping-place so convenient above. He had seen no Indians pass, and this did not often happen without his knowledge. He thought that his dogs sometimes gave notice of the approach of Indians half an hour before they arrived.

McCauslin was a Kennebec man, of Scotch descent, who had been a waterman twenty-two years, and had driven on the lakes and head-waters of the Penobscot five or six springs in succession, but was now settled here to raise supplies for the lumberers and for himself. He entertained us a day or two with true Scotch hospitality, and would accept no recompense for it. A man of a dry wit and shrewdness, and a general intelligence which I had not looked for in the backwoods. In fact, the deeper you penetrate into the woods, the more intelligent, and, in one sense, less countrified do you find the inhabitants; for always the pioneer has been a traveller, and, to some extent, a man of the world; and, as the distances with which he is familiar are greater, so is his information more general and far reaching than the villager's. If I were to look for a narrow, uninformed, and countrified mind, as opposed to the intelligence and refinement which are thought to emanate from cities, it would be among the rusty inhabitants of an old-settled country, on farms all run out and gone to seed with life-everlasting, in the towns about Boston, even on the high-road in Concord, and not in the backwoods of Maine.

Supper was got before our eyes in the ample kitchen, by a fire which would have roasted an ox; many whole logs, four feet long, were consumed to boil our tea-kettle,—birch, or beech, or maple, the same summer and winter; and the dishes were soon smoking on the table, late the arm-chair, against the wall, from which one of the party was expelled. The arms of the chair formed the frame on which the table rested; and, when the round top was turned up against the wall, it formed the back of the chair, and was no more in the way than the wall itself. This, we noticed, was the prevailing fashion in these log-houses, in order to economize in room. There were piping-hot wheaten cakes, the flour having been brought up the river in batteaux,—no Indian bread, for the upper part of Maine, it will be remembered, is a wheat country,—and ham, eggs, and potatoes, and milk and cheese, the produce of the farm; and also shad and salmon, tea sweetened with molasses, and sweet cakes, in contradistinction to the hot cakes not sweetened, the one white, the other yellow, to wind up with.

Such we found was the prevailing fare, ordinary and extraordinary, along this river. Mountain cranberries (*Vaccinium Vitis-Idæa*), stewed and sweetened, were the common dessert. Everything here was in profusion, and the best of its kind. Butter was in such plenty that it was commonly used, before it was salted, to grease boots with.

In the night we were entertained by the sound of raindrops on the cedar-splints which covered the roof, and awaked the next morning with a drop or two in our eyes. It had set in for a storm, and we made up our minds not to forsake such comfortable quarters with this prospect, but wait for Indians and fair weather. It rained and drizzled and gleamed by turns, the livelong day. What we did there, how we killed the time, would perhaps be idle to tell; how many times we buttered our boots, and how often a drowsy one was seen to sidle off to the bedroom. When it held up, I strolled up and down the bank, and gathered the harebell and cedar-berries, which grew there; or else we tried by turns the long-handled axe on the logs before the door. The axe-helves here were made to chop standing on the log,—a primitive log of course,—and were, therefore, nearly a foot longer than with us. One while we walked over the farm and visited his well-filled barns with McCauslin. There were one other man and two women only here. He kept horses, cows, oxen, and sheep. I think he said that he was the first to bring a plough and a cow so far; and he might have added the last, with only two exceptions. The potato-rot had found him out here, too, the previous year, and got half or two thirds of his crop, though the seed was of his own raising. Oats, grass, and potatoes were his staples; but he raised, also, a few carrots and turnips, and "a little corn for the hens," for this was all that he dared risk, for fear that it would not ripen. Melons, squashes, sweet-corn, beans, tomatoes, and many other vegetables, could not be ripened there.

The very few settlers along this stream were obviously tempted by the cheapness of the land mainly. When I asked McCauslin why more settlers did not come in, he answered, that one reason was, they could not buy the land, it belonged to individuals or companies who were afraid that their wild lands would be settled, and so incorporated into towns, and they be taxed for them; but to settling on the States' land there was no such hinderance. For his own part, he wanted no neighbors,—he did n't wish to see any road by his house. Neighbors, even the best, were a trouble and expense, especially on the score of cattle and fences. They might live across the river, perhaps, but not on the same side.

The chickens here were protected by the dogs. As Mc-Causlin said, "The old one took it up first, and she taught the pup, and now they had got it into their heads that it would n't do to have anything of the bird kind on the premises." A hawk hovering over was not allowed to alight, but barked off by the dogs circling underneath; and a pigeon, or a "yellow-hammer," as they called the pigeon-woodpecker, on a dead limb or stump, was instantly expelled. It was the main business of their day, and kept them constantly coming and going. One would rush out of the house on the least alarm given by the other.

When it rained hardest, we returned to the house, and took down a tract from the shelf. There was the Wandering Jew, cheap edition, and fine print, the Criminal Calendar, and Parish's Geography, and flash novels two or three. Under the pressure of circumstances, we read a little in these. With such aid, the press is not so feeble an engine, after all. This house, which was a fair specimen of those on this river, was built of huge logs, which peeped out everywhere, and were chinked with clay and moss. It contained four or five rooms. There were no sawed boards, or shingles, or clapboards, about it; and scarcely any tool but the axe had been used in its construction. The partitions were made of long clapboard-like splints, of spruce or cedar, turned to a delicate salmon color by the smoke. The roof and sides were covered with the same, instead of shingles and clapboards, and some of a much thicker and larger size were used for the floor. These were all so straight and smooth, that they answered the purpose admirably; and a careless observer would not have suspected that they were not sawed and planed. The chimney and hearth were of vast size, and made of stone. The broom was a few twigs of arbor-vitæ tied to a stick; and a pole was suspended over the hearth, close to the ceiling, to dry stockings and clothes on. I noticed that the floor was full of small, dingy holes, as if made with a gimlet, but which were, in fact, made by the spikes, nearly an inch long, which the lumberers wear in their boots to prevent their slipping on wet logs. Just above McCauslin's, there is a rocky rapid, where logs jam in the spring; and many "drivers" are there collected, who frequent his house for supplies; these were their tracks which I saw.

At sundown McCauslin pointed away over the forest, across the river, to signs of fair weather amid the clouds,— some evening redness there. For even there the points of compass held; and there was a quarter of the heavens appropriated to sunrise and another to sunset.

The next morning, the weather proving fair enough for our purpose, we prepared to start, and, the Indians having failed us, persuaded McCauslin, who was not unwilling to revisit the scenes of his driving, to accompany us in their stead, intending to engage one other boatman on the way. A strip of cotton cloth for a tent, a couple of blankets, which would suffice for the whole party, fifteen pounds of hard bread, ten pounds of "clear" pork, and a little tea, made up "Uncle George's" pack. The last three articles were calculated to be provision enough for six men for a week, with what we might pick up. A tea-kettle, a frying-pan, and an axe, to be obtained at the last house, would complete our outfit.

We were soon out of McCauslin's clearing, and in the ever green woods again. The obscure trail made by the two settlers above, which even the woodman is sometimes puzzled to discern, erelong crossed a narrow, open strip in the woods overrun with weeds, called the Burnt Land, where a fire had raged formerly, stretching northward nine or ten miles, to Millinocket Lake. At the end of three miles, we reached Shad Pond, or Noliseemack, an expansion of the river. Hodge, the Assistant State Geologist, who passed through this on the 25th of June, 1837, says, "We pushed our boat through an acre or more of buck-beans, which had taken root at the bottom, and bloomed above the surface in the greatest profusion and beauty." Thomas Fowler's house is four miles from McCauslin's, on the shore of the pond, at the mouth of the Millinocket River, and eight miles from the lake of the same name, on the latter stream. This lake affords a more direct course to Ktaadn, but we preferred to follow the Penobscot and the Pamadumcook lakes. Fowler was just completing a new log-hut, and was sawing out a window through the logs, nearly two feet thick, when we arrived. He had begun to paper his house with spruce-bark, turned inside out, which had a good effect, and was in keeping with the circumstances. Instead of water we got here a draught of beer, which, it was allowed, would be better; clear and thin, but strong and stringent as the cedar-sap. It was as if we sucked at the very teats of Nature's pine-clad bosom in these parts,—the sap of all Millinocket botany commingled,—the topmost, most fantastic, and spiciest sprays of the primitive wood, and whatever invigorating and stringent gum or essence it afforded steeped and dissolved in it,—a lumberer's drink, which would acclimate and naturalize a man at once,—which would make him see green, and, if he slept, dream that he heard the wind sough among the pines. Here was a fife, praying to be played on, through which we breathed a few tuneful strains,— brought hither to tame wild beasts. As we stood upon the pile of chips by the door, fish-hawks were sailing overhead; and here, over Shad Pond, might daily be witnessed the tyranny of the bald-eagle over that bird. Tom pointed away over the lake to a bald-eagle's nest, which was plainly visible more than a mile off, on a pine, high above the surrounding forest, and was frequented from year to year by the same pair, and held sacred by him. There were these two houses only there, his low hut and the eagles' airy cart-load of fagots. Thomas Fowler, too, was persuaded to join us, for two men were necessary to manage the batteau, which was soon to be our carriage, and these men needed to be cool and skilful for the navigation of the Penobscot. Tom's pack was soon made, for he had not far to look for his waterman's boots, and a red-flannel shirt. This is the favorite color with lumbermen; and red flannel is reputed to possess some mysterious virtues, to be most healthful and convenient in respect to perspiration. In every gang there will be a large proportion of red birds. We took here a poor and leaky batteau, and began to pole up the Millinocket two miles, to the elder Fowler's, in order to avoid the Grand Falls of the Penobscot, intending to exchange our batteau there for a better. The Millinocket is a small, shallow, and sandy stream, full of what I took to be lamprey-eels' or suckers' nests, and lined with musquash cabins, but free from rapids, according to Fowler, excepting at its outlet from the lake. He was at this time engaged in cutting the native grass,—rush-grass and meadow-clover, as he called it,—on the meadows and small, low islands of this stream. We noticed flattened places in the grass on either side, where, he said, a moose had laid down the night before, adding, that there were thousands in these meadows.

Old Fowler's, on the Millinocket, six miles from Mc-Causlin's, and twenty-four from the Point, is the last house. Gibson's, on the Sowadnehunk, is the only clearing above, but that had proved a failure, and was long since deserted. Fowler is the oldest inhabitant of these woods. He formerly lived a few miles from here, on the south side of the West Branch, where he built his house sixteen years ago, the first house built above the Five Islands. Here our new batteau was to be carried over the first portage of two miles, round the Grand Falls of the Penobscot, on a horse-sled made of saplings, to jump the numerous rocks in the way; but we had to wait a couple of hours for them to catch the horses, which were pastured at a distance, amid the stumps, and had wandered still farther off. The last of the salmon for this season had just been caught, and were still fresh in pickle, from which enough was extracted to fill our empty kettle, and so graduate our introduction to simpler forest fare. The week before they had lost nine sheep here out of their first flock, by the wolves. The surviving sheep came round the house, and seemed frightened, which induced them to go and look for the rest, when they found seven dead and lacerated, and two still alive. These last they carried to the house, and, as Mrs. Fowler said, they were merely scratched in the throat, and had no more visible wound than would be produced by the prick of a pin. She sheared off the wool from their throats, and washed them, and put on some salve, and turned them out, but in a few moments they were missing, and had not been found since. In fact, they were all poisoned, and those that were found swelled up at once, so that they saved neither skin nor wool. This realized the old fables of the wolves and the sheep, and convinced me that that ancient hostility still existed. Verily, the shepherd-boy did not need to sound a false alarm this time. There were steel traps by the door, of various sizes, for wolves, otter, and bears, with large claws instead of teeth, to catch in their sinews. Wolves are frequently killed with poisoned bait.

At length, after we had dined here on the usual backwoods fare, the horses arrived, and we hauled our batteau out of the water, and lashed it to its wicker carriage, and, throwing in our packs, walked on before, leaving the boatmen and driver, who was Tom's brother, to manage the concern. The route, which led through the wild pasture where the sheep were killed, was in some places the roughest ever travelled by horses, over rocky hills, where the sled bounced and slid along, like a vessel pitching in a storm; and one man was as necessary to stand at the stern, to prevent the boat from being wrecked, as a helmsman in the roughest sea. The philosophy of our progress was something like this: when the runners struck a rock three or four feet high, the sled bounced back and upwards at the same time; but, as the horses never ceased pulling, it came down on the top of the rock, and so we got over. This portage probably followed the trail of an ancient Indian carry round these falls. By two o'clock we, who had walked on before, reached the river above the falls, not far from the outlet of Quakish Lake, and waited for the batteau to come up. We had been here but a short time, when a thunder-shower was seen coming up from the west, over the still invisible lakes, and that pleasant wilderness which we were so eager to become acquainted with; and soon the heavy drops began to patter on the leaves around us. I had just selected the prostrate trunk of a huge pine, five or six feet in diameter, and was crawling under it, when, luckily, the boat arrived. It would have amused a sheltered man to witness the manner in which it was unlashed, and whirled over, while the first water-spout burst upon us. It was no sooner in the hands of the eager company than it was abandoned to the first revolutionary impulse, and to gravity, to adjust it; and they might have been seen all stooping to its shelter, and wriggling under like so many eels, before it was fairly deposited on the ground. When all were under, we propped up the lee side, and busied ourselves there whittling thole-pins for rowing, when we should reach the lakes; and made the woods ring, between the claps of thunder, with such boat-songs as we could remember. The horses stood sleek and shining with the rain, all drooping and crestfallen, while deluge after deluge washed over us; but the bottom of a boat may be relied on for a tight roof. At length, after two hours' delay at this place, a streak of fair weather appeared in the northwest, whither our course now lay, promising a serene evening for our voyage; and the driver returned with his horses, while we made haste to launch our boat, and commence our voyage in good earnest.

There were six of us, including the two boatmen. With our packs heaped up near the bows, and ourselves disposed as baggage to trim the boat, with instructions not to move in case we should strike a rock, more than so many barrels of pork, we pushed out into the first rapid, a slight specimen of the stream we had to navigate. With Uncle George in the stern, and Tom in the bows, each using a spruce pole about twelve feet long, pointed with iron,* and poling on the same side, we shot up the rapids like a salmon, the water rushing and roaring around, so that only a practised eye could distinguish a safe course, or tell what was deep water and what rocks, frequently grazing the latter on one or both sides, with a hundred as narrow escapes as ever the Argo had in passing through the Symplegades. I, who had had some experience in boating, had never experienced any half so exhilarating before. We were lucky to have exchanged our Indians, whom we did not know, for these men, who, together with Tom's brother, were reputed the best boatmen on the river, and were at once indispensable pilots and pleasant companions. The canoe is smaller, more easily upset, and sooner worn out; and the Indian is said not to be so skilful in the management of the batteau. He is, for the most part, less to be relied on, and more disposed to sulks and whims. The utmost familiarity with dead streams, or with the ocean, would not prepare a man for this peculiar navigation; and the most skilful boatman anywhere else would here be obliged to take out his boat and carry round a hundred times, still with great risk, as well as delay, where the practised batteau-man poles up with

*The Canadians call it *picquer de fond*.

comparative ease and safety. The hardy "voyageur" pushes with incredible perseverance and success quite up to the foot of the falls, and then only carries round some perpendicular ledge, and launches again in

"The torrent's smoothness, ere it dash below,"

to struggle with the boiling rapids above. The Indians say that the river once ran both ways, one half up and the other down, but that, since the white man came, it all runs down, and now they must laboriously pole their canoes against the stream, and carry them over numerous portages. In the summer, all stores—the grindstone and the plough of the pioneer, flour, pork, and utensils for the explorer—must be conveyed up the river in batteaux; and many a cargo and many a boatman is lost in these waters. In the winter, however, which is very equable and long, the ice is the great highway, and the loggers' team penetrates to Chesuncook Lake, and still higher up, even two hundred miles above Bangor. Imagine the solitary sled-track running far up into the snowy and evergreen wilderness, hemmed in closely for a hundred miles by the forest, and again stretching straight across the broad surfaces of concealed lakes!

We were soon in the smooth water of the Quakish Lake, and took our turns at rowing and paddling across it. It is a small, irregular, but handsome lake, shut in on all sides by the forest, and showing no traces of man but some low boom in a distant cove, reserved for spring use. The spruce and cedar on its shores, hung with gray lichens, looked at a distance like the ghosts of trees. Ducks were sailing here and there on its surface, and a solitary loon, like a more living wave,—a vital spot on the lake's surface,—laughed and frolicked, and showed its straight leg, for our amusement. Joe Merry Mountain appeared in the northwest, as if it were looking down on this lake especially; and we had our first, but a partial view of Ktaadn, its summit veiled in clouds, like a dark isthmus in that quarter, connecting the heavens with the earth. After two miles of smooth rowing across this lake, we found ourselves in the river again, which was a continuous rapid for one mile, to the dam, requiring all the strength and skill of our boatmen to pole up it.

This dam is a quite important and expensive work for this country, whither cattle and horses cannot penetrate in the summer, raising the whole river ten feet, and flooding, as they said, some sixty square miles by means of the innumerable lakes with which the river connects. It is a lofty and solid structure, with sloping piers some distance above, made of frames of logs filled with stones, to break the ice.* Here every log pays toll as it passes through the sluices.

We filed into the rude logger's camp at this place, such as I have described, without ceremony, and the cook, at that moment the sole occupant, at once set about preparing tea for his visitors. His fireplace, which the rain had converted into a mud-puddle, was soon blazing again, and we sat down on the log benches around it to dry us. On the well-flattened and somewhat faded beds of arbor-vitæ leaves, which stretched on either hand under the eaves behind us, lay an odd leaf of the Bible, some genealogical chapter out of the Old Testament; and, half buried by the leaves, we found Emerson's Address on West India Emancipation, which had been left here formerly by one of our company, and *had made two converts to the Liberty party here*, as I was told; also, an odd number of the Westminster Review, for 1834, and a pamphlet entitled History of the Erection of the Monument on the grave of Myron Holly. This was the readable, or reading matter, in a lumberer's camp in the Maine woods, thirty miles from a road, which would be given up to the bears in a fortnight. These things were well thumbed and soiled. This gang was headed by one John Morrison, a good specimen of a Yankee; and was necessarily composed of men not bred to the business of dam-building, but who were Jacks-at-all-trades, handy with the axe, and other simple implements, and well skilled in wood and water craft. We had hot cakes for our supper even here, white as snow-balls, but without butter, and the never-failing sweet cakes, with which we filled our pockets, foreseeing that we should not soon meet with the like again. Such delicate puff-balls seemed a singular diet for back-

---

*Even the Jesuit missionaries, accustomed to the St. Lawrence and other rivers of Canada, in their first expeditions to the Abenaquinois, speak of rivers *ferrées de rochers*, shod with rocks. See also No. 10 Relations, for 1647, p. 185.

woodsmen. There was also tea without milk, sweetened with molasses. And so, exchanging a word with John Morrison and his gang when we had returned to the shore, and also exchanging our batteau for a better still, we made haste to improve the little daylight that remained. This camp, exactly twenty-nine miles from Mattawamkeag Point, by the way we had come, and about one hundred from Bangor by the river, was the last human habitation of any kind in this direction. Beyond, there was no trail; and the river and lakes, by batteaux and canoes, was considered the only practicable route. We were about thirty miles by the river from the summit of Ktaadn, which was in sight, though not more than twenty, perhaps, in a straight line.

It being about the full of the moon, and a warm and pleasant evening, we decided to row five miles by moonlight to the head of the North Twin Lake, lest the wind should rise on the morrow. After one mile of river, or what the boatmen call "thoroughfare,"—for the river becomes at length only the connecting link between the lakes,—and some slight rapid which had been mostly made smooth water by the dam, we entered the North Twin Lake just after sundown, and steered across for the river "thoroughfare," four miles distant. This is a noble sheet of water, where one may get the impression which a new country and a "lake of the woods" are fitted to create. There was the smoke of no log-hut nor camp of any kind to greet us, still less was any lover of nature or musing traveller watching our batteau from the distant hills; not even the Indian hunter was there, for he rarely climbs them, but hugs the river like ourselves. No face welcomed us but the fine fantastic sprays of free and happy evergreen trees, waving one above another in their ancient home. At first the red clouds hung over the western shore as gorgeously as if over a city, and the lake lay open to the light with even a civilized aspect, as if expecting trade and commerce, and towns and villas. We could distinguish the inlet to the South Twin, which is said to be the larger, where the shore was misty and blue, and it was worth the while to look thus through a narrow opening across the entire expanse of a concealed lake to its own yet more dim and distant shore. The shores rose gently to ranges of low hills covered with forests; and though, in fact, the most valuable white pine timber, even about this lake, had been culled out, this would never have been suspected by the voyager. The impression, which indeed corresponded with the fact, was, as if we were upon a high table-land between the States and Canada, the northern side of which is drained by the St. John and Chaudiere, the southern by the Penobscot and Kennebec. There was no bold mountainous shore, as we might have expected, but only isolated hills and mountains rising here and there from the plateau. The country is an archipelago of lakes,—the lake-country of New England. Their levels vary but a few feet, and the boatmen, by short portages, or by none at all, pass easily from one to another. They say that at very high water the Penobscot and the Kennebec flow into each other, or at any rate, that you may lie with your face in the one and your toes in the other. Even the Penobscot and St. John have been connected by a canal, so that the lumber of the Allegash, instead of going down the St. John, comes down the Penobscot; and the Indian's tradition, that the Penobscot once ran both ways for his convenience, is, in one sense, partially realized to-day.

None of our party but McCauslin had been above this lake, so we trusted to him to pilot us, and we could not but confess the importance of a pilot on these waters. While it is river, you will not easily forget which way is up stream; but when you enter a lake, the river is completely lost, and you scan the distant shores in vain to find where it comes in. A stranger is, for the time at least, lost, and must set about a voyage of discovery first of all to find the river. To follow the windings of the shore when the lake is ten miles, or even more, in length, and of an irregularity which will not soon be mapped, is a wearisome voyage, and will spend his time and his provisions. They tell a story of a gang of experienced woodmen sent to a location on this stream, who were thus lost in the wilderness of lakes. They cut their way through thickets, and carried their baggage and their boats over from lake to lake, sometimes several miles. They carried into Millinocket Lake, which is on another stream, and is ten miles square, and contains a hundred islands. They explored its shores thoroughly, and then carried into another, and another, and it was a week of toil and anxiety before they found the Penobscot River again, and then their provisions were exhausted, and they were obliged to return.

While Uncle George steered for a small island near the head of the lake, now just visible, like a speck on the water, we rowed by turns swiftly over its surface, singing such boat-songs as we could remember. The shores seemed at an indefinite distance in the moonlight. Occasionally we paused in our singing and rested on our oars, while we listened to hear if the wolves howled, for this is a common serenade, and my companions affirmed that it was the most dismal and unearthly of sounds; but we heard none this time. If we did not *hear*, however, we did *listen*, not without a reasonable expectation; that at least I have to tell,—only some utterly uncivilized, big-throated owl hooted loud and dismally in the drear and boughy wilderness, plainly not nervous about his solitary life, nor afraid to hear the echoes of his voice there. We remembered also that possibly moose were silently watching us from the distant coves, or some surly bear or timid caribou had been startled by our singing. It was with new emphasis that we sang there the Canadian boat-song,—

> "Row, brothers, row, the stream runs fast,
> The Rapids are near and the daylight's past!"—

which describes precisely our own adventure, and was inspired by the experience of a similar kind of life,—for the rapids were ever near, and the daylight long past; the woods on shore looked dim, and many an Utawas' tide here emptied into the lake.

> "Why should we yet our sail unfurl?
> There is not a breath the blue wave to curl!
> But, when the wind blows off the shore,
> O sweetly we'll rest our weary oar."

> "Utawas' tide! this trembling moon,
> Shall see us float o'er thy surges soon."

At last we glided past the "green isle" which had been our landmark, all joining in the chorus; as if by the watery links of rivers and of lakes we were about to float over unmeasured zones of earth, bound on unimaginable adventures,—

"Saint of this green isle! hear our prayers,
O grant us cool heavens and favoring airs!"

About nine o'clock we reached the river, and ran our boat into a natural haven between some rocks, and drew her out on the sand. This camping-ground McCauslin had been familiar with in his lumbering days, and he now struck it unerringly in the moonlight, and we heard the sound of the rill which would supply us with cool water emptying into the lake. The first business was to make a fire, an operation which was a little delayed by the wetness of the fuel and the ground, owing to the heavy showers of the afternoon. The fire is the main comfort of the camp, whether in summer or winter, and is about as ample at one season as at another. It is as well for cheerfulness as for warmth and dryness. It forms one side of the camp; one bright side at any rate. Some were dispersed to fetch in dead trees and boughs, while Uncle George felled the birches and beeches which stood convenient, and soon we had a fire some ten feet long by three or four high, which rapidly dried the sand before it. This was calculated to burn all night. We next proceeded to pitch our tent; which operation was performed by sticking our two spike-poles into the ground in a slanting direction, about ten feet apart, for rafters, and then drawing our cotton cloth over them, and tying it down at the ends, leaving it open in front, shed-fashion. But this evening the wind carried the sparks on to the tent and burned it. So we hastily drew up the batteau just within the edge of the woods before the fire, and propping up one side three or four feet high, spread the tent on the ground to lie on; and with the corner of a blanket, or what more or less we could get to put over us, lay down with our heads and bodies under the boat, and our feet and legs on the sand toward the fire. At first we lay awake, talking of our course, and finding ourselves in so convenient a posture for studying the heavens, with the moon and stars shining in our faces, our conversation naturally turned upon astronomy, and we recounted by turns the most interesting discoveries in that science. But at length we composed ourselves seriously to sleep. It was interesting, when awakened at midnight, to watch the grotesque and fiend-like forms and motions of some one of

the party, who, not being able to sleep, had got up silently to
arouse the fire, and add fresh fuel, for a change; now stealthily
lugging a dead tree from out the dark, and heaving it on, now
stirring up the embers with his fork, or tiptoeing about to
observe the stars, watched, perchance, by half the prostrate
party in breathless silence; so much the more intense because
they were awake, while each supposed his neighbor sound
asleep. Thus aroused, I too brought fresh fuel to the fire, and
then rambled along the sandy shore in the moonlight, hoping
to meet a moose, come down to drink, or else a wolf. The
little rill tinkled the louder, and peopled all the wilderness for
me; and the glassy smoothness of the sleeping lake, laving the
shores of a new world, with the dark, fantastic rocks rising
here and there from its surface, made a scene not easily described. It has left such an impression of stern, yet gentle,
wildness on my memory as will not soon be effaced. Not far
from midnight we were one after another awakened by rain
falling on our extremities; and as each was made aware of the
fact by cold or wet, he drew a long sigh and then drew up
his legs, until gradually we had all sidled round from lying at
right angles with the boat, till our bodies formed an acute
angle with it, and were wholly protected. When next we
awoke, the moon and stars were shining again, and there
were signs of dawn in the east. I have been thus particular in
order to convey some idea of a night in the woods.

We had soon launched and loaded our boat, and, leaving
our fire blazing, were off again before breakfast. The lumberers rarely trouble themselves to put out their fires, such is the
dampness of the primitive forest; and this is one cause, no
doubt, of the frequent fires in Maine, of which we hear so
much on smoky days in Massachusetts. The forests are held
cheap after the white pine has been culled out; and the explorers and hunters pray for rain only to clear the atmosphere
of smoke. The woods were so wet to-day, however, that there
was no danger of our fire spreading. After poling up half a
mile of river, or thoroughfare, we rowed a mile across the
foot of Pamadumcook Lake, which is the name given on the
map to this whole chain of lakes, as if there was but one,
though they are, in each instance, distinctly separated by a
reach of the river, with its narrow and rocky channel and its

rapids. This lake, which is one of the largest, stretched north-west ten miles, to hills and mountains in the distance. Mc-Causlin pointed to some distant, and as yet inaccessible, forests of white pine, on the sides of a mountain in that direction. The Joe Merry Lakes, which lay between us and Moosehead, on the west, were recently, if they are not still, "surrounded by some of the best timbered land in the State." By another thoroughfare we passed into Deep Cove, a part of the same lake, which makes up two miles, toward the northeast, and rowing two miles across this, by another short thoroughfare, entered Ambejijis Lake.

At the entrance to a lake we sometimes observed what is technically called "fencing stuff," or the unhewn timbers of which booms are formed, either secured together in the water, or laid up on the rocks and lashed to trees, for spring use. But it was always startling to discover so plain a trail of civilized man there. I remember that I was strangely affected, when we were returning, by the sight of a ring-bolt well drilled into a rock, and fastened with lead, at the head of this solitary Ambejijis Lake.

It was easy to see that driving logs must be an exciting as well as arduous and dangerous business. All winter long the logger goes on piling up the trees which he has trimmed and hauled in some dry ravine at the head of a stream, and then in the spring he stands on the bank and whistles for Rain and Thaw, ready to wring the perspiration out of his shirt to swell the tide, till suddenly, with a whoop and halloo from him, shutting his eyes, as if to bid farewell to the existing state of things, a fair proportion of his winter's work goes scrambling down the country, followed by his faithful dogs, Thaw and Rain and Freshet and Wind, the whole pack in full cry, toward the Orono Mills. Every log is marked with the owner's name, cut in the sapwood with an axe or bored with an auger, so deep as not to be worn off in the driving, and yet not so as to injure the timber; and it requires considerable ingenuity to invent new and simple marks where there are so many owners. They have quite an alphabet of their own, which only the practised can read. One of my companions read off from his memorandum-book some marks of his own logs, among which there were crosses, belts, crow's feet, girdles, &c., as, "Y—girdle—crow-foot," and various other devices. When the logs have run the gauntlet of innumerable rapids and falls, each on its own account, with more or less jamming and bruising, those bearing various owners' marks being mixed up together,—since all must take advantage of the same freshet,—they are collected together at the heads of the lakes, and surrounded by a boom fence of floating logs, to prevent their being dispersed by the wind, and are thus towed altogether, like a flock of sheep, across the lake, where there is no current, by a windlass, or boom-head, such as we sometimes saw standing on an island or head-land, and, if circumstances permit, with the aid of sails and oars. Sometimes, notwithstanding, the logs are dispersed over many miles of lake surface in a few hours by winds and freshets, and thrown up on distant shores, where the driver can pick up only one or two at a time, and return with them to the thoroughfare; and before he gets his flock well through Ambejijis or Pamadumcook, he makes many a wet and uncomfortable camp on the shore. He must be able to navigate a log as if it were a canoe, and be as indifferent to cold and wet as a muskrat. He uses a few efficient tools,—a lever commonly of rock-maple, six or seven feet long, with a stout spike in it, strongly feruled on, and a long spike-pole, with a screw at the end of the spike to make it hold. The boys along shore learn to walk on floating logs as city boys on sidewalks. Sometimes the logs are thrown up on rocks in such positions as to be irrecoverable but by another freshet as high, or they jam together at rapids and falls, and accumulate in vast piles, which the driver must start at the risk of his life. Such is the lumber business, which depends on many accidents, as the early freezing of the rivers, that the teams may get up in season, a sufficient freshet in the spring, to fetch the logs down, and many others.* I quote Michaux on Lumbering on the Kennebec, then the source of the best white-pine lumber car-

*"A steady current or pitch of water is preferable to one either rising or diminishing; as, when rising rapidly, the water at the middle of the river is considerably higher than at the shores,—so much so as to be distinctly perceived by the eye of a spectator on the banks, presenting an appearance like a turnpike road. The lumber, therefore, is always sure to incline from the centre of the channel toward either shore."—Springer.

ried to England. "The persons engaged in this branch of industry are generally emigrants from New Hampshire. . . . .
In the summer they unite in small companies, and traverse
these vast solitudes in every direction, to ascertain the places
in which the pines abound. After cutting the grass and converting it into hay for the nourishment of the cattle to be
employed in their labor, they return home. In the beginning
of the winter they enter the forests again, establish themselves
in huts covered with the bark of the canoe-birch, or the
arbor-vitæ; and, though the cold is so intense that the mercury
sometimes remains for several weeks from 40° to 50° [Fahr.]
below the point of congelation, they persevere, with unabated
courage, in their work." According to Springer, the company
consists of choppers, swampers,—who make roads,—barker
and loader, teamster, and cook. "When the trees are felled,
they cut them into logs from fourteen to eighteen feet long,
and, by means of their cattle, which they employ with great
dexterity, drag them to the river, and after stamping on them
a mark of property, roll them on its frozen bosom. At the
breaking of the ice, in the spring, they float down with the
current. . . . . The logs that are not drawn the first year,"
adds Michaux, "are attacked by large worms, which form
holes about two lines in diameter, in every direction; but, if
stripped of their bark, they will remain uninjured for thirty
years."

Ambejijis, this quiet Sunday morning, struck me as the
most beautiful lake we had seen. It is said to be one of the
deepest. We had the fairest view of Joe Merry, Double Top,
and Ktaadn, from its surface. The summit of the latter had a
singularly flat, table-land appearance, like a short highway,
where a demigod might be let down to take a turn or two in
an afternoon, to settle his dinner. We rowed a mile and a half
to near the head of the lake, and, pushing through a field of
lily-pads, landed, to cook our breakfast, by the side of a large
rock, known to McCauslin. Our breakfast consisted of tea,
with hard bread and pork, and fried salmon, which we ate
with forks neatly whittled from alder-twigs, which grew
there, off strips of birch-bark for plates. The tea was black tea,
without milk to color or sugar to sweeten it, and two tin
dippers were our tea-cups. This beverage is as indispensable

to the loggers as to any gossiping old women in the land, and they, no doubt, derive great comfort from it. Here was the site of an old logger's camp, remembered by McCauslin, now overgrown with weeds and bushes. In the midst of a dense underwood we noticed a whole brick, on a rock, in a small run, clean and red and square as in a brick-yard, which had been brought thus far formerly for tamping. Some of us afterward regretted that we had not carried this on with us to the top of the mountain, to be left there for our mark. It would certainly have been a simple evidence of civilized man. McCauslin said, that large wooden crosses, made of oak, still sound, were sometimes found standing in this wilderness, which were set up by the first Catholic missionaries who came through to the Kennebec.

In the next nine miles, which were the extent of our voyage, and which it took us the rest of the day to get over, we rowed across several small lakes, poled up numerous rapids and thoroughfares, and carried over four portages. I will give the names and distances, for the benefit of future tourists. First, after leaving Ambejijis Lake, we had a quarter of a mile of rapids to the portage, or carry of ninety rods around Ambejijis Falls; then a mile and a half through Passamagamet Lake, which is narrow and river-like, to the falls of the same name,—Ambejijis stream coming in on the right; then two miles through Katepskonegan Lake to the portage of ninety rods around Katepskonegan Falls, which name signifies "carrying-place,"—Passamagamet stream coming in on the left; then three miles through Pockwockomus Lake, a slight expansion of the river, to the portage of forty rods around the falls of the same name,—Katepskonegan stream coming in on the left; then three quarters of a mile through Abolja-carmegus Lake, similar to the last, to the portage of forty rods around the falls of the same name; then half a mile of rapid water to the Sowadnehunk dead-water, and the Aboljackna-gesic stream.

This is generally the order of names as you ascend the river: First, the lake, or, if there is no expansion, the dead-water; then the falls; then the stream emptying into the lake, or river above, all of the same name. First we came to Passamagamet Lake, then to Passamagamet Falls, then to Passamagamet stream, emptying in. This order and identity of names, it will be perceived, is quite philosophical, since the dead-water or lake is always at least partially produced by the stream emptying in above; and the first fall below, which is the outlet of that lake, and where that tributary water makes its first plunge, also naturally bears the same name.

At the portage around Ambejijis Falls I observed a pork-barrel on the shore, with a hole eight or nine inches square cut in one side, which was set against an upright rock; but the bears, without turning or upsetting the barrel, had gnawed a hole in the opposite side, which looked exactly like an enormous rat hole, big enough to put their heads in; and at the bottom of the barrel were still left a few mangled and slabbered slices of pork. It is usual for the lumberers to leave such supplies as they cannot conveniently carry along with them at carries or camps, to which the next comers do not scruple to help themselves, they being the property, commonly, not of an individual, but a company, who can afford to deal liberally.

I will describe particularly how we got over some of these portages and rapids, in order that the reader may get an idea of the boatman's life. At Ambejijis Falls, for instance, there was the roughest path imaginable cut through the woods; at first up hill, at an angle of nearly forty-five degrees, over rocks and logs without end. This was the manner of the portage. We first carried over our baggage, and deposited it on the shore at the other end; then returning to the batteau, we dragged it up the hill by the painter, and onward, with frequent pauses, over half the portage. But this was a bungling way, and would soon have worn out the boat. Commonly, three men walk over with a batteau weighing from three to five or six hundred pounds on their heads and shoulders, the tallest standing under the middle of the boat, which is turned over, and one at each end, or else there are two at the bows. More cannot well take hold at once. But this requires some practice, as well as strength, and is in any case extremely laborious, and wearing to the constitution, to follow. We were, on the whole, rather an invalid party, and could render our boatmen but little assistance. Our two men at length took the batteau upon their shoulders, and, while two of us steadied it, to prevent it from rocking and wearing into their shoulders, on which they placed their hats folded, walked bravely over the remaining distance, with two or three pauses. In the same manner they accomplished the other portages. With this crushing weight they must climb and stumble along over fallen trees and slippery rocks of all sizes, where those who walked by the sides were continually brushed off, such was the narrowness of the path. But we were fortunate not to have to cut our path in the first place. Before we launched our boat, we scraped the bottom smooth again, with our knives, where it had rubbed on the rocks, to save friction.

To avoid the difficulties of the portage, our men determined to " warp up" the Passamagamet Falls; so while the rest walked over the portage with the baggage, I remained in the batteau, to assist in warping up. We were soon in the midst of the rapids, which were more swift and tumultuous than any we had poled up, and had turned to the side of the stream for the purpose of warping, when the boatmen, who felt some pride in their skill, and were ambitious to do something more than usual, for my benefit, as I surmised, took one more view of the rapids, or rather the falls; and, in answer to one's question, whether we could n't get up there, the other answered that he guessed he 'd try it. So we pushed again into the midst of the stream, and began to struggle with the current. I sat in the middle of the boat to trim it, moving slightly to the right or left as it grazed a rock. With an uncertain and wavering motion we wound and bolted our way up, until the bow was actually raised two feet above the stern at the steepest pitch; and then, when everything depended upon his exertions, the bowman's pole snapped in two; but before he had time to take the spare one, which I reached him, he had saved himself with the fragment upon a rock; and so we got up by a hair's breadth; and Uncle George exclaimed that that was never done before, and he had not tried it if he had not known whom he had got in the bow, nor he in the bow, if he had not known him in the stern. At this place there was a regular portage cut through the woods, and our boatmen had never known a batteau to ascend the falls. As near as I can remember, there was a perpendicular fall here, at the worst place of the whole Penobscot River, two or three feet at least.

I could not sufficiently admire the skill and coolness with which they performed this feat, never speaking to each other. The bowman, not looking behind, but knowing exactly what the other is about, works as if he worked alone. Now sounding in vain for a bottom in fifteen feet of water, while the boat falls back several rods, held straight only with the greatest skill and exertion; or, while the sternman obstinately holds his ground, like a turtle, the bowman springs from side to side with wonderful suppleness and dexterity, scanning the rapids and the rocks with a thousand eyes; and now, having got a bite at last, with a lusty shove, which makes his pole bend and quiver, and the whole boat tremble, he gains a few feet upon the river. To add to the danger, the poles are liable at any time to be caught between the rocks, and wrenched out of their hands, leaving them at the mercy of the rapids,— the rocks, as it were, lying in wait, like so many alligators, to catch them in their teeth, and jerk them from your hands, before you have stolen an effectual shove against their palates. The pole is set close to the boat, and the prow is made to overshoot, and just turn the corners of the rocks, in the very teeth of the rapids. Nothing but the length and lightness, and the slight draught of the batteau, enables them to make any headway. The bowman must quickly choose his course; there is no time to deliberate. Frequently the boat is shoved between rocks where both sides touch, and the waters on either hand are a perfect maelstrom.

Half a mile above this, two of us tried our hands at poling up a slight rapid; and we were just surmounting the last difficulty when an unlucky rock confounded our calculations; and while the batteau was sweeping round irrecoverably amid the whirlpool, we were obliged to resign the poles to more skilful hands.

Katepskonegan is one of the shallowest and weediest of the lakes, and looked as if it might abound in pickerel. The falls of the same name, where we stopped to dine, are considerable and quite picturesque. Here Uncle George had seen trout caught by the barrelful; but they would not rise to our bait at this hour. Half-way over this carry, thus far in the Maine wilderness on its way to the Provinces, we noticed a large, flaming, Oak Hall hand-bill, about two feet long, wrapped round the trunk of a pine, from which the bark had been stript, and to which it was fast glued by the pitch. This should be recorded among the advantages of this mode of advertising, that so, possibly, even the bears and wolves, moose, deer, otter, and beaver, not to mention the Indian, may learn where they can fit themselves according to the latest fashion, or, at least, recover some of their own lost garments. We christened this, the Oak Hall carry.

The forenoon was as serene and placid on this wild stream in the woods, as we are apt to imagine that Sunday in summer usually is in Massachusetts. We were occasionally startled by the scream of a bald-eagle, sailing over the stream in front of our batteau; or of the fish-hawks, on whom he levies his contributions. There were, at intervals, small meadows of a few acres on the sides of the stream, waving with uncut grass, which attracted the attention of our boatmen, who regretted that they were not nearer to their clearings, and calculated how many stacks they might cut. Two or three men sometimes spend the summer by themselves, cutting the grass in these meadows, to sell to the loggers in the winter, since it will fetch a higher price on the spot than in any market in the State. On a small isle, covered with this kind of rush, or cut grass, on which we landed, to consult about our further course, we noticed the recent track of a moose, a large, roundish hole, in the soft wet ground, evincing the great size and weight of the animal that made it. They are fond of the water, and visit all these island-meadows, swimming as easily from island to island as they make their way through the thickets on land. Now and then we passed what McCauslin called a pokelogan, an Indian term for what the drivers might have reason to call a poke-logs-in, an inlet that leads nowhere. If you get in, you have got to get out again the same way. These, and the frequent "run-rounds" which come into the river again, would embarrass an inexperienced voyager not a little.

The carry around Pockwockomus Falls was exceedingly rough and rocky, the batteau having to be lifted directly from the water up four or five feet on to a rock, and launched again down a similar bank. The rocks on this portage were covered with the *dents* made by the spikes in the lumberers' boots while staggering over under the weight of their batteaux; and you could see where the surface of some large rocks on which they had rested their batteaux was worn quite smooth with use. As it was, we had carried over but half the usual portage at this place for this stage of the water, and launched our boat in the smooth wave just curving to the fall, prepared to struggle with the most violent rapid we had to encounter. The rest of the party walked over the remainder of the portage, while I remained with the boatmen to assist in warping up. One had to hold the boat while the others got in to prevent it from going over the falls. When we had pushed up the rapids as far as possible, keeping close to the shore, Tom seized the painter and leaped out upon a rock just visible in the water, but he lost his footing, notwithstanding his spiked boots, and was instantly amid the rapids; but recovering himself by good luck, and reaching another rock, he passed the painter to me, who had followed him, and took his place again in the bows. Leaping from rock to rock in the shoal water, close to the shore, and now and then getting a bite with the rope round an upright one, I held the boat while one reset his pole, and then all three forced it upward against any rapid. This was " warping up." When a part of us walked round at such a place, we generally took the precaution to take out the most valuable part of the baggage, for fear of being swamped.

As we poled up a swift rapid for half a mile above Abolja-carmegus Falls, some of the party read their own marks on the huge logs which lay piled up high and dry on the rocks on either hand, the relics probably of a jam which had taken place here in the Great Freshet in the spring. Many of these would have to wait for another great freshet, perchance, if they lasted so long, before they could be got off. It was singular enough to meet with property of theirs which they had never seen, and where they had never been before, thus detained by freshets and rocks when on its way to them. Methinks that must be where all my property lies, cast up on the rocks on some distant and unexplored stream, and waiting for an unheard-of freshet to fetch it down. O make haste, ye gods, with your winds and rains, and start the jam before it rots!

The last half-mile carried us to the Sowadnehunk dead-water, so called from the stream of the same name, signifying "running between mountains," an important tributary which comes in a mile above. Here we decided to camp, about twenty miles from the Dam, at the mouth of Murch Brook and the Aboljacknagesic, mountain streams, broad off from Ktaadn, and about a dozen miles from its summit; having made fifteen miles this day.

We had been told by McCauslin that we should here find trout enough: so, while some prepared the camp, the rest fell to fishing. Seizing the birch-poles which some party of Indians, or white hunters, had left on the shore, and baiting our hooks with pork, and with trout, as soon as they were caught, we cast our lines into the mouth of the Aboljacknagesic, a clear, swift, shallow stream, which came in from Ktaadn. Instantly a shoal of white chivin (*Leucisci pulchelli*), silvery roaches, cousin-trout, or what not, large and small, prowling thereabouts, fell upon our bait, and one after another were landed amidst the bushes. Anon their cousins, the true trout, took their turn, and alternately the speckled trout, and the silvery roaches, swallowed the bait as fast as we could throw in; and the finest specimens of both that I have ever seen, the largest one weighing three pounds, were heaved upon the shore, though at first in vain, to wriggle down into the water again, for we stood in the boat; but soon we learned to remedy this evil: for one, who had lost his hook, stood on shore to catch them as they fell in a perfect shower around him,— sometimes, wet and slippery, full in his face and bosom, as his arms were outstretched to receive them. While yet alive, before their tints had faded, they glistened like the fairest flowers, the product of primitive rivers; and he could hardly trust his senses, as he stood over them, that these jewels should have swam away in that Aboljacknagesic water for so long, so many dark ages;—these bright fluviatile flowers, seen of Indians only, made beautiful, the Lord only knows why, to swim there! I could understand better, for this, the truth of mythology, the fables of Proteus, and all those beautiful sea-monsters,—how all history, indeed, put to a terrestrial use, is mere history; but put to a celestial, is mythology always.

But there is the rough voice of Uncle George, who com-

mands at the frying-pan, to send over what you've got, and
then you may stay till morning. The pork sizzles, and cries for
fish. Luckily for the foolish race, and this particularly foolish
generation of trout, the night shut down at last, not a little
deepened by the dark side of Ktaadn, which, like a permanent
shadow, reared itself from the eastern bank. Lescarbot, writing in 1609, tells us that the Sieur Champdoré, who, with one
of the people of the Sieur de Monts, ascended some fifty
leagues up the St. John in 1608, found the fish so plenty,
"qu'en mettant la chaudière sur le feu ils en avoient pris suf-
fisamment pour eux dîsner avant que l'eau fust chaude." Their
descendants here are no less numerous. So we accompanied
Tom into the woods to cut cedar-twigs for our bed. While he
went ahead with the axe, and lopt off the smallest twigs of
the flat-leaved cedar, the arbor-vitæ of the gardens, we gathered them up, and returned with them to the boat, until it
was loaded. Our bed was made with as much care and skill as
a roof is shingled; beginning at the foot, and laying the twig
end of the cedar upward, we advanced to the head, a course
at a time, thus successively covering the stub-ends, and producing a soft and level bed. For us six it was about ten feet
long by six in breadth. This time we lay under our tent, having pitched it more prudently with reference to the wind and
the flame, and the usual huge fire blazed in front. Supper was
eaten off a large log, which some freshet had thrown up. This
night we had a dish of arbor-vitæ, or cedar-tea, which the
lumberer sometimes uses when other herbs fail, —

> "A quart of arbor-vitæ,
> To make him strong and mighty,"

but I had no wish to repeat the experiment. It had too medicinal a taste for my palate. There was the skeleton of a
moose here, whose bones some Indian hunters had picked on
this very spot.

In the night I dreamed of trout-fishing; and, when at
length I awoke, it seemed a fable that this painted fish swam
there so near my couch, and rose to our hooks the last evening, and I doubted if I had not dreamed it all. So I arose
before dawn to test its truth, while my companions were still
sleeping. There stood Ktaadn with distinct and cloudless out-

line in the moonlight; and the rippling of the rapids was the only sound to break the stillness. Standing on the shore, I once more cast my line into the stream, and found the dream to be real and the fable true. The speckled trout and silvery roach, like flying-fish, sped swiftly through the moonlight air, describing bright arcs on the dark side of Ktaadn, until moonlight, now fading into daylight, brought satiety to my mind, and the minds of my companions, who had joined me.

By six o'clock, having mounted our packs and a good blanketful of trout, ready dressed, and swung up such baggage and provision as we wished to leave behind, upon the tops of saplings, to be out of the reach of bears, we started for the summit of the mountain, distant, as Uncle George said the boatmen called it, about four miles, but as I judged, and as it proved, nearer fourteen. He had never been any nearer the mountain than this, and there was not the slightest trace of man to guide us farther in this direction. At first, pushing a few rods up the Aboljacknagesic, or "open-land stream," we fastened our batteau to a tree, and travelled up the north side, through burnt lands, now partially overgrown with young aspens, and other shrubbery; but soon, recrossing this stream, where it was about fifty or sixty feet wide, upon a jam of logs and rocks,—and you could cross it by this means almost anywhere,—we struck at once for the highest peak, over a mile or more of comparatively open land still, very gradually ascending the while. Here it fell to my lot, as the oldest mountain-climber, to take the lead. So, scanning the woody side of the mountain, which lay still at an indefinite distance, stretched out some seven or eight miles in length before us, we determined to steer directly for the base of the highest peak, leaving a large slide, by which, as I have since learned, some of our predecessors ascended, on our left. This course would lead us parallel to a dark seam in the forest, which marked the bed of a torrent, and over a slight spur, which extended southward from the main mountain, from whose bare summit we could get an outlook over the country, and climb directly up the peak, which would then be close at hand. Seen from this point, a bare ridge at the extremity of the open land, Ktaadn presented a different aspect from any mountain I have seen, there being a greater proportion of naked rock rising abruptly from the forest; and we looked up at this blue barrier as if it were some fragment of a wall which anciently bounded the earth in that direction. Setting the compass for a northeast course, which was the bearing of the southern base of the highest peak, we were soon buried in the woods.

We soon began to meet with traces of bears and moose, and those of rabbits were everywhere visible. The tracks of moose, more or less recent, to speak literally, covered every square rod on the sides of the mountain; and these animals are probably more numerous there now than ever before, being driven into this wilderness, from all sides, by the settlements. The track of a full-grown moose is like that of a cow, or larger, and of the young, like that of a calf. Sometimes we found ourselves travelling in faint paths, which they had made, like cow-paths in the woods, only far more indistinct, being rather openings, affording imperfect vistas through the dense underwood, than trodden paths; and everywhere the twigs had been browsed by them, clipt as smoothly as if by a knife. The bark of trees was stript up by them to the height of eight or nine feet, in long, narrow strips, an inch wide, still showing the distinct marks of their teeth. We expected nothing less than to meet a herd of them every moment, and our Nimrod held his shooting-iron in readiness; but we did not go out of our way to look for them, and, though numerous, they are so wary that the unskilful hunter might range the forest a long time before he could get sight of one. They are sometimes dangerous to encounter, and will not turn out for the hunter, but furiously rush upon him and trample him to death, unless he is lucky enough to avoid them by dodging round a tree. The largest are nearly as large as a horse, and weigh sometimes one thousand pounds; and it is said that they can step over a five-feet gate in their ordinary walk. They are described as exceedingly awkward-looking animals, with their long legs and short bodies, making a ludicrous figure when in full run, but making great headway nevertheless. It seemed a mystery to us how they could thread these woods, which it required all our suppleness to accomplish,—climbing, stooping, and winding, alternately. They are said to drop their long and branching horns, which usually spread five or six feet, on their backs, and make their way easily by the weight of their bodies. Our boatmen said, but I know not with how much truth, that their horns are apt to be gnawed away by vermin while they sleep. Their flesh, which is more like beef than venison, is common in Bangor market.

We had proceeded on thus seven or eight miles, till about noon, with frequent pauses to refresh the weary ones, crossing a considerable mountain stream, which we conjectured to be Murch Brook, at whose mouth we had camped, all the time in woods, without having once seen the summit, and rising very gradually, when the boatmen, beginning to despair a little, and fearing that we were leaving the mountain on one side of us, for they had not entire faith in the compass, McCauslin climbed a tree, from the top of which he could see the peak, when it appeared that we had not swerved from a right line, the compass down below still ranging with his arm, which pointed to the summit. By the side of a cool mountain rill, amid the woods, where the water began to partake of the purity and transparency of the air, we stopped to cook some of our fishes, which we had brought thus far in order to save our hard bread and pork, in the use of which we had put ourselves on short allowance. We soon had a fire blazing, and stood around it, under the damp and sombre forest of firs and birches, each with a sharpened stick, three or four feet in length, upon which he had spitted his trout, or roach, previously well gashed and salted, our sticks radiating like the spokes of a wheel from one centre, and each crowding his particular fish into the most desirable exposure, not with the truest regard always to his neighbor's rights. Thus we regaled ourselves, drinking meanwhile at the spring, till one man's pack, at least, was considerably lightened, when we again took up our line of march.

At length we reached an elevation sufficiently bare to afford a view of the summit, still distant and blue, almost as if retreating from us. A torrent, which proved to be the same we had crossed, was seen tumbling down in front, literally from out of the clouds. But this glimpse at our whereabouts was soon lost, and we were buried in the woods again. The wood was chiefly yellow birch, spruce, fir, mountain-ash, or round-wood, as the Maine people call it, and moose-wood. It was the worst kind of travelling; sometimes like the densest scrub-oak patches with us. The cornel, or bunch-berries, were very abundant, as well as Solomon's seal and moose-berries. Blue-berries were distributed along our whole route; and in one place the bushes were drooping with the weight of the fruit, still as fresh as ever. It was the 7th of September. Such patches afforded a grateful repast, and served to bait the tired party forward. When any lagged behind, the cry of "blue-berries" was most effectual to bring them up. Even at this ele-vation we passed through a moose-yard, formed by a large flat rock, four or five rods square, where they tread down the snow in winter. At length, fearing that if we held the direct course to the summit, we should not find any water near our camping-ground, we gradually swerved to the west, till, at four o'clock, we struck again the torrent which I have men-tioned, and here, in view of the summit, the weary party de-cided to camp that night.

While my companions were seeking a suitable spot for this purpose, I improved the little daylight that was left, in climb-ing the mountain alone. We were in a deep and narrow ra-vine, sloping up to the clouds, at an angle of nearly forty-five degrees, and hemmed in by walls of rock, which were at first covered with low trees, then with impenetrable thickets of scraggy birches and spruce-trees, and with moss, but at last bare of all vegetation but lichens, and almost continually draped in clouds. Following up the course of the torrent which occupied this,—and I mean to lay some emphasis on this word *up*,—pulling myself up by the side of perpendicu-lar falls of twenty or thirty feet, by the roots of firs and birches, and then, perhaps, walking a level rod or two in the thin stream, for it took up the whole road, ascending by huge steps, as it were, a giant's stairway, down which a river flowed, I had soon cleared the trees, and paused on the suc-cessive shelves, to look back over the country. The torrent was from fifteen to thirty feet wide, without a tributary, and seemingly not diminishing in breadth as I advanced; but still it came rushing and roaring down, with a copious tide, over and amidst masses of bare rock, from the very clouds, as though a waterspout had just burst over the mountain. Leav-ing this at last, I began to work my way, scarcely less arduous than Satan's anciently through Chaos, up the nearest, though not the highest peak. At first scrambling on all fours over the tops of ancient black spruce-trees (*Abies nigra*), old as the flood, from two to ten or twelve feet in height, their tops flat and spreading, and their foliage blue, and nipt with cold, as if for centuries they had ceased growing upward against the bleak sky, the solid cold. I walked some good rods erect upon the tops of these trees, which were overgrown with moss and mountain-cranberries. It seemed that in the course of time they had filled up the intervals between the huge rocks, and the cold wind had uniformly levelled all over. Here the principle of vegetation was hard put to it. There was apparently a belt of this kind running quite round the mountain, though, perhaps, nowhere so remarkable as here. Once, slumping through, I looked down ten feet, into a dark and cavernous region, and saw the stem of a spruce, on whose top I stood, as on a mass of coarse basket-work, fully nine inches in diameter at the ground. These holes were bears' dens, and the bears were even then at home. This was the sort of garden I made my way *over*, for an eighth of a mile, at the risk, it is true, of treading on some of the plants, not seeing any path *through* it,—certainly the most treacherous and porous country I ever travelled.

> "Nigh foundered on he fares,
> Treading the crude consistence, half on foot,
> Half flying."

But nothing could exceed the toughness of the twigs,—not one snapped under my weight, for they had slowly grown. Having slumped, scrambled, rolled, bounced, and walked, by turns, over this scraggy country, I arrived upon a side-hill, or rather side-mountain, where rocks, gray, silent rocks, were the flocks and herds that pastured, chewing a rocky cud at sunset. They looked at me with hard gray eyes, without a bleat or a low. This brought me to the skirt of a cloud, and bounded my walk that night. But I had already seen that Maine country when I turned about, waving, flowing, rippling, down below.

When I returned to my companions, they had selected a camping-ground on the torrent's edge, and were resting on the ground; one was on the sick list, rolled in a blanket, on a damp shelf of rock. It was a savage and dreary scenery enough; so wildly rough, that they looked long to find a level and open space for the tent. We could not well camp higher, for want of fuel; and the trees here seemed so evergreen and sappy, that we almost doubted if they would acknowledge the influence of fire; but fire prevailed at last, and blazed here, too, like a good citizen of the world. Even at this height we met with frequent traces of moose, as well as of bears. As here was no cedar, we made our bed of coarser feathered spruce; but at any rate the feathers were plucked from the live tree. It was, perhaps, even a more grand and desolate place for a night's lodging than the summit would have been, being in the neighborhood of those wild trees, and of the torrent. Some more aerial and finer-spirited winds rushed and roared through the ravine all night, from time to time arousing our fire, and dispersing the embers about. It was as if we lay in the very nest of a young whirlwind. At midnight, one of my bedfellows, being startled in his dreams by the sudden blazing up to its top of a fir-tree, whose green boughs were dried by the heat, sprang up, with a cry, from his bed, thinking the world on fire, and drew the whole camp after him.

In the morning, after whetting our appetite on some raw pork, a wafer of hard bread, and a dipper of condensed cloud or waterspout, we all together began to make our way up the falls, which I have described; this time choosing the right hand, or highest peak, which was not the one I had approached before. But soon my companions were lost to my sight behind the mountain ridge in my rear, which still seemed ever retreating before me, and I climbed alone over huge rocks, loosely poised, a mile or more, still edging toward the clouds; for though the day was clear elsewhere, the summit was concealed by mist. The mountain seemed a vast aggregation of loose rocks, as if some time it had rained rocks, and they lay as they fell on the mountain sides, nowhere fairly at rest, but leaning on each other, all rocking-stones, with cavities between, but scarcely any soil or smoother shelf. They were the raw materials of a planet dropped from an unseen quarry, which the vast chemistry of nature would anon work up, or work down, into the smiling and verdant plains and valleys of earth. This was an undone extremity of the globe; as in lignite, we see coal in the process of formation.

At length I entered within the skirts of the cloud which seemed forever drifting over the summit, and yet would never be gone, but was generated out of that pure air as fast as it flowed away; and when, a quarter of a mile farther, I reached the summit of the ridge, which those who have seen in clearer weather say is about five miles long, and contains a thousand acres of table-land, I was deep within the hostile ranks of clouds, and all objects were obscured by them. Now the wind would blow me out a yard of clear sunlight, wherein I stood; then a gray, dawning light was all it could accomplish, the cloud-line ever rising and falling with the wind's intensity. Sometimes it seemed as if the summit would be cleared in a few moments, and smile in sunshine: but what was gained on one side was lost on another. It was like sitting in a chimney and waiting for the smoke to blow away. It was, in fact, a cloud-factory,—these were the cloud-works, and the wind turned them off done from the cool, bare rocks. Occasionally, when the windy columns broke in to me, I caught sight of a dark, damp crag to the right or left; the mist driving cease-lessly between it and me. It reminded me of the creations of the old epic and dramatic poets, of Atlas, Vulcan, the Cy-clops, and Prometheus. Such was Caucasus and the rock where Prometheus was bound. Æschylus had no doubt vis-ited such scenery as this. It was vast, Titanic, and such as man never inhabits. Some part of the beholder, even some vital part, seems to escape through the loose grating of his ribs as he ascends. He is more lone than you can imagine. There is less of substantial thought and fair understanding in him, than in the plains where men inhabit. His reason is dispersed and shadowy, more thin and subtile, like the air. Vast, Titanic, inhuman Nature has got him at disadvantage, caught him alone, and pilfers him of some of his divine faculty. She does not smile on him as in the plains. She seems to say sternly, why came ye here before your time? This ground is not pre-pared for you. Is it not enough that I smile in the valleys? I have never made this soil for thy feet, this air for thy breath-ing, these rocks for thy neighbors. I cannot pity nor fondle thee here, but forever relentlessly drive thee hence to where I *am* kind. Why seek me where I have not called thee, and then complain because you find me but a stepmother? Shouldst thou freeze or starve, or shudder thy life away, here is no shrine, nor altar, nor any access to my ear.

> "Chaos and ancient Night, I come no spy
> With purpose to explore or to disturb
> The secrets of your realm, but . . .
> .   .   .   .   .   as my way
> Lies through your spacious empire up to light."

The tops of mountains are among the unfinished parts of the globe, whither it is a slight insult to the gods to climb and pry into their secrets, and try their effect on our humanity. Only daring and insolent men, perchance, go there. Simple races, as savages, do not climb mountains,—their tops are sacred and mysterious tracts never visited by them. Pomola is always angry with those who climb to the summit of Ktaadn.

According to Jackson, who, in his capacity of geological surveyor of the State, has accurately measured it,—the altitude of Ktaadn is 5,300 feet, or a little more than one mile above the level of the sea,—and he adds, "It is then evidently the highest point in the State of Maine, and is the most abrupt granite mountain in New England." The peculiarities of that spacious table-land on which I was standing, as well as the remarkable semi-circular precipice or basin on the eastern side, were all concealed by the mist. I had brought my whole pack to the top, not knowing but I should have to make my descent to the river, and possibly to the settled portion of the State alone, and by some other route, and wishing to have a complete outfit with me. But at length, fearing that my companions would be anxious to reach the river before night, and knowing that the clouds might rest on the mountain for days, I was compelled to descend. Occasionally, as I came down, the wind would blow me a vista open, through which I could see the country eastward, boundless forests, and lakes, and streams, gleaming in the sun, some of them emptying into the East Branch. There were also new mountains in sight in that direction. Now and then some small bird of the sparrow family would flit away before me, unable to command its course, like a fragment of the gray rock blown off by the wind.

I found my companions where I had left them, on the side of the peak, gathering the mountain cranberries, which filled every crevice between the rocks, together with blueberries, which had a spicier flavor the higher up they grew, but were not the less agreeable to our palates. When the country is settled, and roads are made, these cranberries will perhaps become an article of commerce. From this elevation, just on the skirts of the clouds, we could overlook the country, west and south, for a hundred miles. There it was, the State of Maine, which we had seen on the map, but not much like that,—immeasurable forest for the sun to shine on, that eastern *stuff* we hear of in Massachusetts. No clearing, no house. It did not look as if a solitary traveller had cut so much as a walking-stick there. Countless lakes,—Moosehead in the southwest, forty miles long by ten wide, like a gleaming silver platter at the end of the table; Chesuncook, eighteen long by three wide, without an island; Millinocket, on the south, with its hundred islands; and a hundred others without a name; and mountains also, whose names, for the most part, are known only to the Indians. The forest looked like a firm grass sward, and the effect of these lakes in its midst has been well compared, by one who has since visited this same spot, to that of a "mirror broken into a thousand fragments, and wildly scattered over the grass, reflecting the full blaze of the sun." It was a large farm for somebody, when cleared. According to the Gazetteer, which was printed before the boundary question was settled, this single Penobscot county, in which we were, was larger than the whole State of Vermont, with its fourteen counties; and this was only a part of the wild lands of Maine. We are concerned now, however, about natural, not political limits. We were about eighty miles, as the bird flies, from Bangor, or one hundred and fifteen, as we had rode, and walked, and paddled. We had to console ourselves with the reflection that this view was probably as good as that from the peak, as far as it went; and what were a mountain without its attendant clouds and mists? Like ourselves, neither Bailey nor Jackson had obtained a clear view from the summit.

Setting out on our return to the river, still at an early hour in the day, we decided to follow the course of the torrent, which we supposed to be Murch Brook, as long as it would not lead us too far out of our way. We thus travelled about four miles in the very torrent itself, continually crossing and recrossing it, leaping from rock to rock, and jumping with the stream down falls of seven or eight feet, or sometimes sliding down on our backs in a thin sheet of water. This ravine had been the scene of an extraordinary freshet in the spring, apparently accompanied by a slide from the mountain. It must have been filled with a stream of stones and water, at least twenty feet above the present level of the torrent. For a rod or two, on either side of its channel, the trees were barked and splintered up to their tops, the birches bent over, twisted, and sometimes finely split, like a stable-broom; some, a foot in diameter, snapped off, and whole clumps of trees bent over with the weight of rocks piled on them. In one place we noticed a rock, two or three feet in diameter, lodged nearly twenty feet high in the crotch of a tree. For the whole four miles, we saw but one rill emptying in, and the volume of water did not seem to be increased from the first. We travelled thus very rapidly with a downward impetus, and grew remarkably expert at leaping from rock to rock, for leap we must, and leap we did, whether there was any rock at the right distance or not. It was a pleasant picture when the foremost turned about and looked up the winding ravine, walled in with rocks and the green forest, to see, at intervals of a rod or two, a red-shirted or green-jacketed mountaineer against the white torrent, leaping down the channel with his pack on his back, or pausing upon a convenient rock in the midst of the torrent to mend a rent in his clothes, or unstrap the dipper at his belt to take a draught of the water. At one place we were startled by seeing, on a little sandy shelf by the side of the stream, the fresh print of a man's foot, and for a moment realized how Robinson Crusoe felt in a similar case; but at last we remembered that we had struck this stream on our way up, though we could not have told where, and one had descended into the ravine for a drink. The cool air above, and the continual bathing of our bodies in mountain water, alternate foot, sitz, douche, and plunge baths, made this walk exceedingly refreshing, and we had travelled only a mile or two, after leaving the torrent, before every thread of our clothes was as dry as usual, owing perhaps to a peculiar quality in the atmosphere.

After leaving the torrent, being in doubt about our course, Tom threw down his pack at the foot of the loftiest spruce tree at hand, and shinned up the bare trunk, some twenty feet, and then climbed through the green tower, lost to our sight, until he held the topmost spray in his hand.* Mc-Causlin, in his younger days, had marched through the wilderness with a body of troops, under General Somebody, and with one other man did all the scouting and spying service. The General's word was, "Throw down the top of that tree," and there was no tree in the Maine woods so high that it did not lose its top in such a case. I have heard a story of two men being lost once in these woods, nearer to the settlements than this, who climbed the loftiest pine they could find, some six feet in diameter at the ground, from whose top they discovered a solitary clearing and its smoke. When at this height, some two hundred feet from the ground, one of them became dizzy, and fainted in his companion's arms, and the latter had to accomplish the descent with him, alternately fainting and reviving, as best he could. To Tom we cried, Where away does the summit bear? where the burnt lands? The last he could only conjecture; he descried, however, a little meadow and pond, lying probably in our course, which we concluded to steer for. On reaching this secluded meadow, we found fresh tracks of moose on the shore of the pond, and the water was still unsettled as if they had fled before us. A little farther, in a dense thicket, we seemed to be still on their trail. It was a small meadow, of a few acres, on the mountain side, concealed by the forest, and perhaps never seen by a white man

---

*"The spruce-tree," says Springer in '51, "is generally selected, principally for the superior facilities which its numerous limbs afford the climber. To gain the first limbs of this tree, which are from twenty to forty feet from the ground, a smaller tree is undercut and lodged against it, clambering up which the top of the spruce is reached. In some cases, when a very elevated position is desired, the spruce-tree is lodged against the trunk of some lofty pine, up which we ascend to a height twice that of the surrounding forest."

To indicate the direction of pines, he throws down a branch, and a man at the ground takes the bearing.

before, where one would think that the moose might browse
and bathe, and rest in peace. Pursuing this course, we soon
reached the open land, which went sloping down some miles
toward the Penobscot.

Perhaps I most fully realized that this was primeval, untamed, and forever untameable *Nature*, or whatever else men
call it, while coming down this part of the mountain. We
were passing over "Burnt Lands," burnt by lightning, perchance, though they showed no recent marks of fire, hardly
so much as a charred stump, but looked rather like a natural
pasture for the moose and deer, exceedingly wild and desolate, with occasional strips of timber crossing them, and low
poplars springing up, and patches of blueberries here and
there. I found myself traversing them familiarly, like some
pasture run to waste, or partially reclaimed by man; but when
I reflected what man, what brother or sister or kinsman of
our race made it and claimed it, I expected the proprietor to
rise up and dispute my passage. It is difficult to conceive of a
region uninhabited by man. We habitually presume his presence and influence everywhere. And yet we have not seen
pure Nature, unless we have seen her thus vast and drear and
inhuman, though in the midst of cities. Nature was here
something savage and awful, though beautiful. I looked with
awe at the ground I trod on, to see what the Powers had
made there, the form and fashion and material of their work.
This was that Earth of which we have heard, made out of
Chaos and Old Night. Here was no man's garden, but the
unhandselled globe. It was not lawn, nor pasture, nor mead,
nor woodland, nor lea, nor arable, nor waste-land. It was the
fresh and natural surface of the planet Earth, as it was made
for ever and ever,—to be the dwelling of man, we say,—so
Nature made it, and man may use it if he can. Man was not
to be associated with it. It was Matter, vast, terrific,—not his
Mother Earth that we have heard of, not for him to tread on,
or be buried in,—no, it were being too familiar even to let
his bones lie there,—the home, this, of Necessity and Fate.
There was there felt the presence of a force not bound to be
kind to man. It was a place for heathenism and superstitious
rites,—to be inhabited by men nearer of kin to the rocks and
to wild animals than we. We walked over it with a certain

awe, stopping, from time to time, to pick the blueberries which grew there, and had a smart and spicy taste. Perchance where *our* wild pines stand, and leaves lie on their forest floor, in Concord, there were once reapers, and husbandmen planted grain; but here not even the surface had been scarred by man, but it was a specimen of what God saw fit to make this world What is it to be admitted to a museum, to see a myriad of particular things, compared with being shown some star's surface, some hard matter in its home! I stand in awe of my body, this matter to which I am bound has become so strange to me. I fear not spirits, ghosts, of which I am one, — *that* my body might, — but I fear bodies, I tremble to meet them. What is this Titan that has possession of me? Talk of mysteries! — Think of our life in nature, — daily to be shown matter, to come in contact with it, — rocks, trees, wind on our cheeks! the *solid* earth! the *actual* world! the *common sense! Contact! Contact! Who* are we? *where* are we?

Erelong we recognized some rocks and other features in the landscape which we had purposely impressed on our memories, and, quickening our pace, by two o'clock we reached the batteau.* Here we had expected to dine on trout, but in this glaring sunlight they were slow to take the bait, so we were compelled to make the most of the crumbs of our hard bread and our pork, which were both nearly exhausted. Meanwhile we deliberated whether we should go up the river a mile farther, to Gibson's clearing, on the Sowadnehunk, where there was a deserted log-hut, in order to get a half-inch auger, to mend one of our spike-poles with. There were young spruce-trees enough around us, and we had a spare spike, but nothing to make a hole with. But as it was uncertain whether we should find any tools left there, we patched up the broken pole, as well as we could, for the downward voyage, in which there would be but little use for it. Moreover, we were unwilling to lose any time in this expedition, lest the wind should rise before we reached the larger lakes, and detain us; for a moderate wind produces quite a sea on these waters, in which a batteau will not live for a moment; and on one

*The bears had not touched things on our possessions. They sometimes tear a batteau to pieces for the sake of the tar with which it is besmeared.

occasion McCauslin had been delayed a week at the head of
the North Twin, which is only four miles across. We were
nearly out of provisions, and ill prepared in this respect for
what might possibly prove a week's journey round by the
shore, fording innumerable streams, and threading a trackless
forest, should any accident happen to our boat.

It was with regret that we turned our backs on Chesuncook, which McCauslin had formerly logged on, and the Allegash lakes. There were still longer rapids and portages
above; among the last the Rippogenus Portage, which he described as the most difficult on the river, and three miles long.
The whole length of the Penobscot is two hundred and seventy-five miles, and we are still nearly one hundred miles from
its source. Hodge, the assistant State Geologist, passed up
this river in 1837, and by a portage of only one mile and three-
quarters crossed over into the Allegash, and so went down
that into the St. John, and up the Madawaska to the Grand
Portage across to the St. Lawrence. His is the only account
that I know, of an expedition through to Canada in this direction. He thus describes his first sight of the latter river,
which, to compare small things with great, is like Balboa's
first sight of the Pacific from the mountains of the Isthmus of
Darien. "When we first came in sight of the St. Lawrence,"
he says, "from the top of a high hill, the view was most striking, and much more interesting to me from having been shut
up in the woods for the two previous months. Directly before
us lay the broad river, extending across nine or ten miles, its
surface broken by a few islands and reefs, and two ships riding at anchor near the shore. Beyond, extended ranges of uncultivated hills, parallel with the river. The sun was just going
down behind them, and gilding the whole scene with its parting rays."

About four o'clock, the same afternoon, we commenced
our return voyage, which would require but little if any poling. In shooting rapids the boatmen use large and broad paddles, instead of poles, to guide the boat with. Though we
glided so swiftly, and often smoothly, down, where it had
cost us no slight effort to get up, our present voyage was
attended with far more danger: for if we once fairly struck
one of the thousand rocks by which we were surrounded the

boat would be swamped in an instant. When a boat is swamped under these circumstances, the boatmen commonly find no difficulty in keeping afloat at first, for the current keeps both them and their cargo up for a long way down the stream; and if they can swim, they have only to work their way gradually to the shore. The greatest danger is of being caught in an eddy behind some larger rock, where the water rushes up stream faster than elsewhere it does down, and being carried round and round under the surface till they are drowned. McCauslin pointed out some rocks which had been the scene of a fatal accident of this kind. Sometimes the body is not thrown out for several hours. He himself had performed such a circuit once, only his legs being visible to his companions; but he was fortunately thrown out in season to recover his breath.* In shooting the rapids, the boatman has this problem to solve: to choose a circuitous and safe course amid a thousand sunken rocks, scattered over a quarter or half a mile, at the same time that he is moving steadily on at the rate of fifteen miles an hour. Stop he cannot; the only question is, where will he go? The bow-man chooses the course with all his eyes about him, striking broad off with his paddle, and drawing the boat by main force into her course. The stern-man faithfully follows the bow.

We were soon at the Aboljacarmegus Falls. Anxious to avoid the delay, as well as the labor, of the portage here, our boatmen went forward first to reconnoitre, and concluded to let the batteau down the falls, carrying the baggage only over the portage. Jumping from rock to rock until nearly in the middle of the stream, we were ready to receive the boat and let her down over the first fall, some six or seven feet perpendicular. The boatmen stand upon the edge of a shelf of rock, where the fall is perhaps nine or ten feet perpendicular, in from one to two feet of rapid water, one on each side of the boat, and let it slide gently over, till the bow is run out ten or twelve feet in the air; then, letting it drop squarely, while

---

*I cut this from a newspaper. "On the 11th (instant?) [May, '49], on Rappogenes Falls, Mr. John Delantee, of Orono, Me., was drowned while running logs. He was a citizen of Orono, and was twenty-six years of age. His companions found his body, enclosed it in bark, and buried it in the solemn woods."

one holds the painter, the other leaps in, and his companion following, they are whirled down the rapids to a new fall, or to smooth water. In a very few minutes they had accomplished a passage in safety, which would be as foolhardy for the unskilful to attempt as the descent of Niagara itself. It seemed as if it needed only a little familiarity, and a little more skill, to navigate down such falls as Niagara itself with safety. At any rate, I should not despair of such men in the rapids above table-rock, until I saw them actually go over the falls, so cool, so collected, so fertile in resources are they. One might have thought that these were falls, and that falls were not to be waded through with impunity, like a mud-puddle. There was really danger of their losing their sublimity in losing their power to harm us. Familiarity breeds contempt. The boatman pauses, perchance, on some shelf beneath a table-rock under the fall, standing in some cove of back-water two feet deep, and you hear his rough voice come up through the spray, coolly giving directions how to launch the boat this time.

Having carried round Pockwockomus Falls, our oars soon brought us to the Katepskonegan, or Oak Hall carry, where we decided to camp half way over, leaving our batteau to be carried over in the morning on fresh shoulders. One shoulder of each of the boatmen showed a red spot as large as one's hand, worn by the batteau on this expedition; and this shoulder, as it did all the work, was perceptibly lower than its fellow, from long service. Such toil soon wears out the strongest constitution. The drivers are accustomed to work in the cold water in the spring, rarely ever dry; and if one falls in all over he rarely changes his clothes till night, if then, even. One who takes this precaution is called by a particular nickname, or is turned off. None can lead this life who are not almost amphibious. McCauslin said soberly, what is at any rate a good story to tell, that he had seen where six men were wholly under water at once, at a jam, with their shoulders to handspikes. If the log did not start, then they had to put out their heads to breathe. The driver works as long as he can see, from dark to dark, and at night has not time to eat his supper and dry his clothes fairly, before he is asleep on his cedar bed. We lay that night on the very bed made by such a party, stretching our tent over the poles which were still standing, but reshingling the damp and faded bed with fresh leaves.

In the morning we carried our boat over and launched it, making haste lest the wind should rise. The boatmen ran down Passamagamet, and, soon after, Ambejijis Falls, while we walked round with the baggage. We made a hasty breakfast at the head of Ambejijis Lake, on the remainder of our pork, and were soon rowing across its smooth surface again, under a pleasant sky, the mountain being now clear of clouds, in the northeast. Taking turns at the oars, we shot rapidly across Deep Cove, the foot of Pamadumcook, and the North Twin, at the rate of six miles an hour, the wind not being high enough to disturb us, and reached the Dam at noon. The boatmen went through one of the log sluices in the batteau, where the fall was ten feet at the bottom, and took us in below. Here was the longest rapid in our voyage, and perhaps the running this was as dangerous and arduous a task as any. Shooting down sometimes at the rate, as we judged, of fifteen miles an hour, if we struck a rock we were split from end to end in an instant. Now, like a bait bobbing for some river monster, amid the eddies, now darting to this side of the stream, now to that, gliding swift and smooth near to our destruction, or striking broad off with the paddle and drawing the boat to right or left with all our might, in order to avoid a rock. I suppose that it was like running the rapids of the Saute de St. Marie, at the outlet of Lake Superior, and our boatmen probably displayed no less dexterity than the Indians there do. We soon ran through this mile, and floated in Quakish Lake.

After such a voyage, the troubled and angry waters, which once had seemed terrible and not to be trifled with, appeared tamed and subdued; they had been bearded and worried in their channels, pricked and whipped into submission with the spike-pole and paddle, gone through and through with impunity, and all their spirit and their danger taken out of them, and the most swollen and impetuous rivers seemed but playthings henceforth. I began, at length, to understand the boatman's familiarity with, and contempt for, the rapids. "Those Fowler boys," said Mrs. McCauslin, "are perfect ducks for the water." They had run down to Lincoln, according to her, thirty or forty miles, in a batteau, in the night, for a doctor, when it was so dark that they could not see a rod before them, and the river was swollen so as to be almost a continuous rapid, so that the doctor *cried*, when they brought him up by daylight, "Why, Tom, how did you see to steer?" "We did n't steer much,—only kept her straight." And yet they met with no accident. It is true, the more difficult rapids are higher up than this.

When we reached the Millinocket opposite to Tom's house, and were waiting for his folks to set us over, for we had left our batteau above the Grand Falls, we discovered two canoes, with two men in each, turning up this stream from Shad Pond, one keeping the opposite side of a small island before us, while the other approached the side where we were standing, examining the banks carefully for muskrats as they came along. The last proved to be Louis Neptune and his companion, now, at last, on their way up to Chesuncook after moose; but they were so disguised that we hardly knew them. At a little distance they might have been taken for Quakers, with their broad-brimmed hats, and overcoats with broad capes, the spoils of Bangor, seeking a settlement in this Sylvania,—or, nearer at hand, for fashionable gentlemen the morning after a spree. Met face to face, these Indians in their native woods looked like the sinister and slouching fellows whom you meet picking up strings and paper in the streets of a city. There is, in fact, a remarkable and unexpected resemblance between the degraded savage and the lowest classes in a great city. The one is no more a child of nature than the other. In the progress of degradation the distinction of races is soon lost. Neptune at first was only anxious to know what we "kill," seeing some partridges in the hands of one of the party, but we had assumed too much anger to permit of a reply. We thought Indians had some honor before. But—"Me been sick. O, me unwell now. You make bargain, then me go." They had in fact been delayed so long by a drunken frolic at the Five Islands, and they had not yet recovered from its effects. They had some young musquash in their canoes, which they dug out of the banks with a hoe, for food, not for their skins, for musquash are their principal food on these expeditions. So they went on up the Millinocket, and we kept down the bank of the Penobscot, after recruiting ourselves with a draught of Tom's beer, leaving Tom at his home.

Thus a man shall lead his life away here on the edge of the wilderness, on Indian Millinocket stream, in a new world, far in the dark of a continent, and have a flute to play at evening here, while his strains echo to the stars, amid the howling of wolves; shall live, as it were, in the primitive age of the world, a primitive man. Yet he shall spend a sunny day, and in this century be my contemporary; perchance shall read some scattered leaves of literature, and sometimes talk with me. Why read history, then, if the ages and the generations are now? He lives three thousand years deep into time, an age not yet described by poets. Can you well go further back in history than this? Ay! ay!—for there turns up but now into the mouth of Millinocket stream a still more ancient and primitive man, whose history is not brought down even to the former. In a bark vessel sewn with the roots of the spruce, with hornbeam paddles, he dips his way along. He is but dim and misty to me, obscured by the æons that lie between the bark-canoe and the batteau. He builds no house of logs, but a wigwam of skins. He eats no hot bread and sweet cake, but musquash and moose-meat and the fat of bears. He glides up the Millinocket and is lost to my sight, as a more distant and misty cloud is seen flitting by behind a nearer, and is lost in space. So he goes about his destiny, the red face of man.

After having passed the night, and buttered our boots for the last time, at Uncle George's, whose dogs almost devoured him for joy at his return, we kept on down the river the next day, about eight miles on foot, and then took a batteau, with a man to pole it, to Mattawamkeag, ten more. At the middle of that very night, to make a swift conclusion to a long story, we dropped our buggy over the half-finished bridge at Oldtown, where we heard the confused din and clink of a hundred saws, which never rest, and at six o'clock the next morning one of the party was steaming his way to Massachusetts.

What is most striking in the Maine wilderness is the continuousness of the forest, with fewer open intervals or glades than you had imagined. Except the few burnt-lands, the narrow intervals on the rivers, the bare tops of the high mountains, and the lakes and streams, the forest is uninterrupted. It is even more grim and wild than you had anticipated, a damp and intricate wilderness, in the spring everywhere wet and miry. The aspect of the country, indeed, is universally stern and savage, excepting the distant views of the forest from hills, and the lake prospects, which are mild and civilizing in a degree. The lakes are something which you are unprepared for; they lie up so high, exposed to the light, and the forest is diminished to a fine fringe on their edges, with here and there a blue mountain, like amethyst jewels set around some jewel of the first water,—so anterior, so superior, to all the changes that are to take place on their shores, even now civil and refined, and fair as they can ever be. These are not the artificial forests of an English king,—a royal preserve merely. Here prevail no forest laws but those of nature. The aborigines have never been dispossessed, nor nature disforested.

It is a country full of evergreen trees, of mossy silver birches and watery maples, the ground dotted with insipid, small, red berries, and strewn with damp and moss-grown rocks,—a country diversified with innumerable lakes and rapid streams, peopled with trout and various species of *leucisci*, with salmon, shad, and pickerel, and other fishes; the forest resounding at rare intervals with the note of the chicadee, the blue-jay, and the woodpecker, the scream of the fish-hawk and the eagle, the laugh of the loon, and the whistle of ducks along the solitary streams; at night, with the hooting of owls and howling of wolves; in summer, swarming with myriads of black flies and mosquitoes, more formidable than wolves to the white man. Such is the home of the moose, the bear, the caribou, the wolf, the beaver, and the Indian. Who shall describe the inexpressible tenderness and immortal life of the grim forest, where Nature, though it be mid-winter, is ever in her spring, where the moss-grown and decaying trees are not old, but seem to enjoy a perpetual youth; and blissful, innocent Nature, like a serene infant, is too happy to make a noise, except by a few tinkling, lisping birds and trickling rills?

What a place to live, what a place to die and be buried in!

There certainly men would live forever, and laugh at death and the grave. There they could have no such thoughts as are associated with the village graveyard,—that make a grave out of one of those moist evergreen hummocks!

> Die and be buried who will,
>   I mean to live here still;
> My nature grows ever more young
>   The primitive pines among.

I am reminded by my journey how exceedingly new this country still is. You have only to travel for a few days into the interior and back parts even of many of the old States, to come to that very America which the Northmen, and Cabot, and Gosnold, and Smith, and Raleigh visited. If Columbus was the first to discover the islands, Americus Vespucius and Cabot, and the Puritans, and we their descendants, have discovered only the shores of America. While the republic has already acquired a history world-wide, America is still unsettled and unexplored. Like the English in New Holland, we live only on the shores of a continent even yet, and hardly know where the rivers come from which float our navy. The very timber and boards and shingles of which our houses are made, grew but yesterday in a wilderness where the Indian still hunts and the moose runs wild. New York has her wilderness within her own borders; and though the sailors of Europe are familiar with the soundings of her Hudson, and Fulton long since invented the steamboat on its waters, an Indian is still necessary to guide her scientific men to its headwaters in the Adirondac country.

Have we even so much as discovered and settled the shores? Let a man travel on foot along the coast, from the Passamaquoddy to the Sabine, or to the Rio Bravo, or to wherever the end is now, if he is swift enough to overtake it, faithfully following the windings of every inlet and of every cape, and stepping to the music of the surf,—with a desolate fishing-town once a week, and a city's port once a month to cheer him, and putting up at the light-houses, when there are any,—and tell me if it looks like a discovered and settled country, and not rather, for the most part, like a desolate island, and No-man's Land.

We have advanced by leaps to the Pacific, and left many a
lesser Oregon and California unexplored behind us. Though
the railroad and the telegraph have been established on the
shores of Maine, the Indian still looks out from her interior
mountains over all these to the sea. There stands the city of
Bangor, fifty miles up the Penobscot, at the head of navigation for vessels of the largest class, the principal lumber depot
on this continent, with a population of twelve thousand, like
a star on the edge of night, still hewing at the forests of which
it is built, already overflowing with the luxuries and refinement of Europe, and sending its vessels to Spain, to England,
and to the West Indies for its groceries,—and yet only a few
axe-men have gone "up river," into the howling wilderness
which feeds it. The bear and deer are still found within its
limits; and the moose, as he swims the Penobscot, is entangled amid its shipping, and taken by foreign sailors in its harbor. Twelve miles in the rear, twelve miles of railroad, are
Orono and the Indian Island, the home of the Penobscot
tribe, and then commence the batteau and the canoe, and the
military road; and sixty miles above, the country is virtually
unmapped and unexplored, and there still waves the virgin
forest of the New World.

Chesuncook

At 5 P. M., September 13th, 1853, I left Boston, in the steamer, for Bangor, by the outside course. It was a warm and still night,—warmer, probably, on the water than on the land, and the sea was as smooth as a small lake in summer, merely rippled. The passengers went singing on the deck, as in a parlor, till ten o'clock. We passed a vessel on her beam-ends on a rock just outside the islands, and some of us thought that she was the "rapt ship" which ran

> "on her side so low
> That she drank water, and her keel ploughed air,"

not considering that there was no wind, and that she was under bare poles. Now we have left the islands behind and are off Nahant. We behold those features which the discoverers saw, apparently unchanged. Now we see the Cape Ann lights, and now pass near a small village-like fleet of mackerel-fishers at anchor, probably off Gloucester. They salute us with a shout from their low decks; but I understand their "Good evening" to mean, "Don't run against me, Sir." From the wonders of the deep we go below to yet deeper sleep. And then the absurdity of being waked up in the night by a man who wants the job of blacking your boots! It is more inevitable than sea-sickness, and may have something to do with it. It is like the ducking you get on crossing the line the first time. I trusted that these old customs were abolished. They might with the same propriety insist on blacking your face. I heard of one man who complained that somebody had stolen his boots in the night; and when he found them, he wanted to know what they had done to them,—they had spoiled them,—he never put that stuff on them; and the boot-black narrowly escaped paying damages.

Anxious to get out of the whale's belly, I rose early, and joined some old salts, who were smoking by a dim light on a sheltered part of the deck. We were just getting into the river. They knew all about it, of course. I was proud to find that I had stood the voyage so well, and was not in the least digested. We brushed up and watched the first signs of dawn through an open port; but the day seemed to hang fire. We inquired the time; none of my companions had a chronometer. At length an African prince rushed by, observing, "Twelve o'clock, gentlemen!" and blew out the light. It was moon-rise. So I slunk down into the monster's bowels again.

The first land we make is Monhegan Island, before dawn, and next St. George's Islands, seeing two or three lights. Whitehead, with its bare rocks and funereal bell, is interesting. Next I remember that the Camden Hills attracted my eyes, and afterward the hills about Frankfort. We reached Bangor about noon.

When I arrived, my companion that was to be had gone up river, and engaged an Indian, Joe Aitteon, a son of the Governor, to go with us to Chesuncook Lake. Joe had conducted two white men a-moose-hunting in the same direction the year before. He arrived by cars at Bangor that evening, with his canoe and a companion, Sabattis Solomon, who was going to leave Bangor the following Monday with Joe's father, by way of the Penobscot, and join Joe in moose-hunting at Chesuncook, when we had done with him. They took supper at my friend's house and lodged in his barn, saying that they should fare worse than that in the woods. They only made Watch bark a little, when they came to the door in the night for water, for he does not like Indians.

The next morning Joe and his canoe were put on board the stage for Moosehead Lake, sixty and odd miles distant, an hour before we started in an open wagon. We carried hard bread, pork, smoked beef, tea, sugar, etc., seemingly enough for a regiment; the sight of which brought together reminded me by what ignoble means we had maintained our ground hitherto. We went by the Avenue Road, which is quite straight and very good, north-westward toward Moosehead Lake, through more than a dozen flourishing towns, with almost every one its academy,—not one of which, however, is on my General Atlas, published, alas! in 1824; so much are they before the age, or I behind it! The earth must have been considerably lighter to the shoulders of General Atlas then.

It rained all this day and till the middle of the next forenoon, concealing the landscape almost entirely; but we had hardly got out of the streets of Bangor before I began to be exhilarated by the sight of the wild fir and spruce-tops, and those of other primitive evergreens, peering through the mist in the horizon. It was like the sight and odor of cake to a schoolboy. He who rides and keeps the beaten track studies the fences chiefly. Near Bangor, the fence-posts, on account of the frost's heaving them in the clayey soil, were not planted in the ground, but were mortised into a transverse horizontal beam lying on the surface. Afterwards, the prevailing fences were log ones, with sometimes a Virginia fence, or else rails slanted over crossed stakes,—and these zigzagged or played leap-frog all the way to the lake, keeping just ahead of us. After getting out of the Penobscot Valley, the country was unexpectedly level, or consisted of very even and equal swells, for twenty or thirty miles, never rising above the general level, but affording, it is said, a very good prospect in clear weather, with frequent views of Ktaadn,—straight roads and long hills. The houses were far apart, commonly small and of one story, but framed. There was very little land under cultivation, yet the forest did not often border the road. The stumps were frequently as high as one's head, showing the depth of the snows. The white hay-caps, drawn over small stacks of beans or corn in the fields, on account of the rain, were a novel sight to me. We saw large flocks of pigeons, and several times came within a rod or two of partridges in the road. My companion said, that, in one journey out of Bangor, he and his son had shot sixty partridges from his buggy. The mountain-ash was now very handsome, as also the wayfarer's-tree or hobble-bush, with its ripe purple berries mixed with red. The Canada thistle, an introduced plant, was the prevailing weed all the way to the lake,—the road-side in many places, and fields not long cleared, being densely filled with it as with a crop, to the exclusion of everything else. There were also whole fields full of ferns, now rusty and withering, which in older countries are commonly confined to wet ground. There were very few flowers, even allowing for the lateness of the season. It chanced that I saw no asters in bloom along the road for fifty miles, though they were so abundant then in Massachusetts,—except in one place one or two of the Aster acuminatus,—and no golden-rods till within twenty miles of Monson, where I saw a three-ribbed one. There were many late buttercups, however, and the two fire-weeds, Erechthites and Epilobium, commonly where there had been a burning, and at last the pearly everlasting. I noticed occasionally very long troughs which supplied the road with water, and my companion said that three dollars annually were granted by the State to one man in each school-district, who provided and maintained a suitable water-trough by the road-side, for the use of travellers,—a piece of intelligence as refreshing to me as the water itself. That legislature did not sit in vain. It was an Oriental act, which made me wish that I was still farther down East,—another Maine law, which I hope we may get in Massachusetts. That State is banishing bar-rooms from its highways, and conducting the mountain-springs thither.

The country was first decidedly mountainous in Garland, Sangerville, and onwards, twenty-five or thirty miles from Bangor. At Sangerville, where we stopped at mid-afternoon to warm and dry ourselves, the landlord told us that he had found a wilderness where we found him. At a fork in the road between Abbot and Monson, about twenty miles from Moosehead Lake, I saw a guide-post surmounted by a pair of moose-horns, spreading four or five feet, with the word "Monson" painted on one blade, and the name of some other town on the other. They are sometimes used for ornamental hat-trees, together with deers' horns, in front entries; but, after the experience which I shall relate, I trust that I shall have a better excuse for killing a moose than that I may hang my hat on his horns. We reached Monson, fifty miles from Bangor, and thirteen from the lake, after dark.

At four o'clock the next morning, in the dark, and still in the rain, we pursued our journey. Close to the academy in this town they have erected a sort of gallows for the pupils to practice on. I thought that they might as well hang at once all who need to go through such exercises in so new a country, where there is nothing to hinder their living an out-door life. Better omit Blair, and take the air. The country about the south end of the lake is quite mountainous, and the road began to feel the effects of it. There is one hill which, it is calculated, it takes twenty-five minutes to ascend. In many places the road was in that condition called *repaired*, having just been whittled into the required semi-cylindrical form with the shovel and scraper, with all the softest inequalities in the middle, like a hog's back with the bristles up, and Jehu was expected to keep astride of the spine. As you looked off each side of the bare sphere into the horizon, the ditches were awful to behold,—a vast hollowness, like that between Saturn and his ring. At a tavern hereabouts the hostler greeted our horse as an old acquaintance, though he did not remember the driver. He said that he had taken care of that little mare for a short time, a year or two before, at the Mount Kineo House, and thought she was not in as good condition as then. Every man to his trade. I am not acquainted with a single horse in the world, not even the one that kicked me.

Already we had thought that we saw Moosehead Lake from a hill-top, where an extensive fog filled the distant lowlands, but we were mistaken. It was not till we were within a mile or two of its south end that we got our first view of it,—a suitably wild-looking sheet of water, sprinkled with small, low islands, which were covered with shaggy spruce and other wild wood,—seen over the infant port of Greenville, with mountains on each side and far in the north, and a steamer's smoke-pipe rising above a roof. A pair of moose-horns ornamented a corner of the public-house where we left our horse, and a few rods distant lay the small steamer Moosehead, Captain King. There was no village, and no summer road any farther in this direction,—but a winter road, that is, one passable only when deep snow covers its inequalities, from Greenville up the east side of the lake to Lily Bay, about twelve miles.

I was here first introduced to Joe. He had ridden all the way on the outside of the stage, the day before, in the rain, giving way to ladies, and was well wetted. As it still rained, he asked if we were going to "put it through." He was a good-looking Indian, twenty-four years old, apparently of unmixed blood, short and stout, with a broad face and reddish complexion, and eyes, methinks, narrower and more turned-up at the outer corners than ours, answering to the description of his race. Beside his under-clothing, he wore a red-flannel shirt, woollen pants, and a black Kossuth hat, the ordinary dress of the lumberman, and, to a considerable extent, of the Penobscot Indian. When, afterward, he had occasion to take off his shoes and stockings, I was struck with the smallness of his feet. He had worked a good deal as a lumberman, and appeared to identify himself with that class. He was the only one of the party who possessed an India-rubber jacket. The top strip or edge of his canoe was worn nearly through by friction on the stage.

At eight o'clock the steamer, with her bell and whistle, scaring the moose, summoned us on board. She was a well-appointed little boat, commanded by a gentlemanly captain, with patent life-seats and metallic life-boat, and dinner on board, if you wish. She is chiefly used by lumberers for the transportation of themselves, their boats, and supplies, but also by hunters and tourists. There was another steamer, named Amphitrite, laid up close by; but, apparently, her name was not more trite than her hull. There were also two or three large sail-boats in port. These beginnings of commerce on a lake in the wilderness are very interesting, — these larger white birds that come to keep company with the gulls. There were but few passengers, and not one female among them: a St. Francis Indian, with his canoe and moose-hides, two explorers for lumber, three men who landed at Sandbar Island, and a gentleman who lives on Deer Island, eleven miles up the lake, and owns also Sugar Island, between which and the former the steamer runs; these, I think, were all beside ourselves. In the saloon was some kind of musical instrument, cherubim, or seraphim, to soothe the angry waves; and there, very properly, was tacked up the map of the public lands of Maine and Massachusetts, a copy of which I had in my pocket.

The heavy rain confining us to the saloon awhile, I discoursed with the proprietor of Sugar Island on the condition of the world in Old Testament times. But at length, leaving this subject as fresh as we found it, he told me that he had lived about this lake twenty or thirty years, and yet had not been to the head of it for twenty-one years. He faces the other way. The explorers had a fine new birch on board, larger than ours, in which they had come up the Piscataquis from Howland, and they had had several messes of trout already. They were going to the neighborhood of Eagle and Chamberlain Lakes, or the head-waters of the St. John, and offered to keep us company as far as we went. The lake to-day was rougher than I found the ocean, either going or returning, and Joe remarked that it would swamp his birch. Off Lily Bay it is a dozen miles wide, but it is much broken by islands. The scenery is not merely wild, but varied and interesting; mountains were seen, farther or nearer, on all sides but the northwest, their summits now lost in the clouds; but Mount Kineo is the principal feature of the lake, and more exclusively belongs to it. After leaving Greenville, at the foot, which is the nucleus of a town some eight or ten years old, you see but three or four houses for the whole length of the lake, or about forty miles, three of them the public houses at which the steamer is advertised to stop, and the shore is an unbroken wilderness. The prevailing wood seemed to be spruce, fir, birch, and rock-maple. You could easily distinguish the hard wood from the soft, or "black growth," as it is called, at a great distance,—the former being smooth, round-topped, and light green, with a bowery and cultivated look.

Mount Kineo, at which the boat touched, is a peninsula with a narrow neck, about midway the lake on the east side. The celebrated precipice is on the east or land side of this, and is so high and perpendicular that you can jump from the top, many hundred feet, into the water, which makes up behind the point. A man on board told us that an anchor had been sunk ninety fathoms at its base before reaching bottom! Probably it will be discovered erelong that some Indian maiden jumped off it for love once, for true love never could have found a path more to its mind. We passed quite close to the rock here, since it is a very bold shore, and I observed marks of a rise of four or five feet on it. The St. Francis Indian expected to take in his boy here, but he was not at the landing. The father's sharp eyes, however, detected a canoe with his boy in it far away under the mountain, though no one else could see it. "Where is the canoe?" asked the captain, "I don't see it"; but he held on, nevertheless, and by and by it hove in sight.

We reached the head of the lake about noon. The weather had, in the meanwhile, cleared up, though the mountains were still capped with clouds. Seen from this point, Mount Kineo, and two other allied mountains ranging with it northeasterly, presented a very strong family likeness, as if all cast in one mould. The steamer here approached a long pier projecting from the northern wilderness, and built of some of its logs,—and whistled, where not a cabin nor a mortal was to be seen. The shore was quite low, with flat rocks on it, overhung with black ash, arbor-vitæ, etc., which at first looked as if they did not care a whistle for us. There was not a single cabman to cry "Coach!" or inveigle us to the United States Hotel. At length a Mr. Hinckley, who has a camp at the other end of the "carry," appeared with a truck drawn by an ox and a horse over a rude log-railway through the woods. The next thing was to get our canoe and effects over the carry from this lake, one of the heads of the Kennebec, into the Penobscot River. This railway from the lake to the river occupied the middle of a clearing two or three rods wide and perfectly straight through the forest. We walked across while our baggage was drawn behind. My companion went ahead to be ready for partridges, while I followed, looking at the plants.

This was an interesting botanical locality for one coming from the South to commence with; for many plants which are rather rare, and one or two which are not found at all, in the eastern part of Massachusetts, grew abundantly between the rails,—as Labrador tea, Kalmia glauca, Canada blueberry (which was still in fruit, and a second time in bloom), Clintonia and Linnæa borealis, which last a lumberer called *moxon*, creeping snowberry, painted trillium, large-flowered bellwort, etc. I fancied that the Aster radula, Diplopappus umbellatus, Solidago lanceolatus, red trumpet-weed, and many others which were conspicuously in bloom on the shore of the lake and on the carry, had a peculiarly wild and primitive look there. The spruce and fir trees crowded to the track on each side to welcome us, the arbor-vitæ, with its changing leaves, prompted us to make haste, and the sight of the canoe-birch gave us spirits to do so. Sometimes an evergreen just fallen lay across the track with its rich burden of cones, looking, still, fuller of life than our trees in the most favorable positions. You did not expect to find such *spruce* trees in the wild woods, but they evidently attend to their toilets each morning even there. Through such a front-yard did we enter that wilderness.

There was a very slight rise above the lake,—the country appearing like, and perhaps being, partly a swamp,—and at length a gradual descent to the Penobscot, which I was surprised to find here a large stream, from twelve to fifteen rods wide, flowing from west to east, or at right angles with the lake, and not more than two and a half miles from it. The distance is nearly twice too great on the Map of the Public Lands, and on Colton's Map of Maine, and Russell Stream is placed too far down. Jackson makes Moosehead Lake to be nine hundred and sixty feet above high water in Portland harbor. It is higher than Chesuncook, for the lumberers consider the Penobscot, where we struck it, twenty-five feet lower than Moosehead,—though eight miles above it is said to be the highest, so that the water can be made to flow either way, and the river falls a good deal between here and Chesuncook. The carryman called this about one hundred and forty miles above Bangor by the river, or two hundred from the ocean, and fifty-five miles below Hilton's, on the Canada road, the first clearing above, which is four and a half miles from the source of the Penobscot.

At the north end of the carry, in the midst of a clearing of sixty acres or more, there was a log camp of the usual construction, with something more like a house adjoining, for the accommodation of the carryman's family and passing lumberers. The bed of withered fir-twigs smelled very sweet, though really very dirty. There was also a store-house on the bank of the river, containing pork, flour, iron, batteaux, and birches, locked up.

We now proceeded to get our dinner, which always turned out to be tea, and to pitch canoes, for which purpose a large iron pot lay permanently on the bank. This we did in company with the explorers. Both Indians and whites use a mixture of rosin and grease for this purpose,—that is, for the pitching, not the dinner. Joe took a small brand from the fire and blew the heat and flame against the pitch on his birch, and so melted and spread it. Sometimes he put his mouth over the suspected spot and sucked, to see if it admitted air; and at one place, where we stopped, he set his canoe high on crossed stakes, and poured water into it. I narrowly watched his motions, and listened attentively to his observations, for

we had employed an Indian mainly that I might have an opportunity to study his ways. I heard him swear once, mildly,
during this operation, about his knife being as dull as a
hoe,—an accomplishment which he owed to his intercourse
with the whites; and he remarked, "We ought to have some
tea before we start; we shall be hungry before we kill that
moose."

At mid-afternoon we embarked on the Penobscot. Our
birch was nineteen and a half feet long by two and a half at
the widest part, and fourteen inches deep within, both ends
alike, and painted green, which Joe thought affected the pitch
and made it leak. This, I think, was a middling-sized one.
That of the explorers was much larger, though probably not
much longer. This carried us three with our baggage, weighing in all between five hundred and fifty and six hundred
pounds. We had two heavy, though slender, rock-maple paddles, one of them of bird's-eye maple. Joe placed birch-bark
on the bottom for us to sit on, and slanted cedar splints
against the cross-bars to protect our backs, while he himself
sat upon a cross-bar in the stern. The baggage occupied the
middle or widest part of the canoe. We also paddled by turns
in the bows, now sitting with our legs extended, now sitting
upon our legs, and now rising upon our knees; but I found
none of these positions endurable, and was reminded of the
complaints of the old Jesuit missionaries of the torture they
endured from long confinement in constrained positions in
canoes, in their long voyages from Quebec to the Huron
country; but afterwards I sat on the cross-bars, or stood up,
and experienced no inconvenience.

It was dead water for a couple of miles. The river had been
raised about two feet by the rain, and lumberers were hoping
for a flood sufficient to bring down the logs that were left in
the spring. Its banks were seven or eight feet high, and
densely covered with white and black spruce,—which, I
think, must be the commonest trees thereabouts,—fir, arbor-
vitæ, canoe, yellow, and black birch, rock, mountain, and a
few red maples, beech, black and mountain ash, the large-
toothed aspen, many civil looking elms, now imbrowned,
along the stream, and at first a few hemlocks also. We had not
gone far before I was startled by seeing what I thought was

an Indian encampment, covered with a red flag, on the bank, and exclaimed, "Camp!" to my comrades. I was slow to discover that it was a red maple changed by the frost. The immediate shores were also densely covered with the speckled alder, red osier, shrubby-willows or sallows, and the like. There were a few yellow-lily-pads still left, half-drowned, along the sides, and sometimes a white one. Many fresh tracks of moose were visible where the water was shallow, and on the shore, and the lily-stems were freshly bitten off by them.

After paddling about two miles, we parted company with the explorers, and turned up Lobster Stream, which comes in on the right, from the southeast. This was six or eight rods wide, and appeared to run nearly parallel with the Penobscot. Joe said that it was so called from small fresh-water lobsters found in it. It is the Matahumkeag of the maps. My companion wished to look for moose signs, and intended, if it proved worth the while, to camp up that way, since the Indian advised it. On account of the rise of the Penobscot the water ran up this stream quite to the pond of the same name, or two miles. The Spencer Mountains, east of the north end of Moosehead Lake, were now in plain sight in front of us. The kingfisher flew before us, the pigeon woodpecker was seen and heard, and nuthatches and chicadees close at hand. Joe said that they called the chicadee *kecunnilessu* in his language. I will not vouch for the spelling of what possibly was never spelt before, but I pronounced after him till he said it would do. We passed close to a woodcock, which stood perfectly still on the shore, with feathers puffed up, as if sick. This Joe said they called *nipsquecohossus*. The kingfisher was *skuscumonsuck*; bear was *wassus*; Indian Devil, *lunxus*; the mountain-ash, *upahsis*. This was very abundant and beautiful. Moose-tracks were not so fresh along this stream, except in a small creek about a mile up it, where a large log had lodged in the spring, marked "W-cross-girdle-crow-foot." We saw a pair of moose-horns on the shore, and I asked Joe if a moose had shed them; but he said there was a head attached to them, and I knew that they did not shed their heads more than once in their lives.

After ascending about a mile and a half, to within a short distance of Lobster Lake, we returned to the Penobscot. Just below the mouth of the Lobster we found quick water, and the river expanded to twenty or thirty rods in width. The moose-tracks were quite numerous and fresh here. We noticed in a great many places narrow and well-trodden paths by which they had come down to the river, and where they had slid on the steep and clayey bank. Their tracks were either close to the edge of the stream, those of the calves distinguishable from the others, or in shallow water; the holes made by their feet in the soft bottom being visible for a long time. They were particularly numerous where there was a small bay, or *pokelogan*, as it is called, bordered by a strip of meadow, or separated from the river by a low peninsula covered with coarse grass, wool-grass, etc., wherein they had waded back and forth and eaten the pads. We detected the remains of one in such a spot. At one place, where we landed to pick up a summer duck, which my companion had shot, Joe peeled a canoe-birch for bark for his hunting-horn. He then asked if we were not going to get the other duck, for his sharp eyes had seen another fall in the bushes a little farther along, and my companion obtained it. I now began to notice the bright red berries of the tree-cranberry, which grows eight or ten feet high, mingled with the alders and cornel along the shore. There was less hard wood than at first.

After proceeding a mile and three quarters below the mouth of the Lobster, we reached, about sundown, a small island at the head of what Joe called the Moosehorn Deadwater, (the Moosehorn, in which he was going to hunt that night, coming in about three miles below,) and on the upper end of this we decided to camp. On a point at the lower end lay the carcass of a moose killed a month or more before. We concluded merely to prepare our camp, and leave our baggage here, that all might be ready when we returned from moosehunting. Though I had not come a-hunting, and felt some compunctions about accompanying the hunters, I wished to see a moose near at hand, and was not sorry to learn how the Indian managed to kill one. I went as reporter or chaplain to the hunters,—and the chaplain has been known to carry a gun himself. After clearing a small space amid the dense spruce and fir trees, we covered the damp ground with a shingling of fir-twigs, and, while Joe was preparing his birch-horn and pitching his canoe,—for this had to be done whenever we stopped long enough to build a fire, and was the principal labor which he took upon himself at such times,—we collected fuel for the night, large wet and rotting logs, which had lodged at the head of the island, for our hatchet was too small for effective chopping; but we did not kindle a fire, lest the moose should smell it. Joe set up a couple of forked stakes, and prepared half a dozen poles, ready to cast one of our blankets over in case it rained in the night, which precaution, however, was omitted the next night. We also plucked the ducks which had been killed for breakfast.

While we were thus engaged in the twilight, we heard faintly, from far down the stream, what sounded like two strokes of a woodchopper's axe, echoing dully through the grim solitude. We are wont to liken many sounds, heard at a distance in the forest, to the stroke of an axe, because they resemble each other under those circumstances, and that is the one we commonly hear there. When we told Joe of this, he exclaimed, "By George, I'll bet that was a moose! They make a noise like that." These sounds affected us strangely, and by their very resemblance to a familiar one, where they probably had so different an origin, enhanced the impression of solitude and wildness.

At starlight we dropped down the stream, which was a dead-water for three miles, or as far as the Moosehorn; Joe telling us that we must be very silent, and he himself making no noise with his paddle, while he urged the canoe along with effective impulses. It was a still night, and suitable for this purpose,—for if there is wind, the moose will smell you,—and Joe was very confident that he should get some. The harvest moon had just risen, and its level rays began to light up the forest on our right, while we glided downward in the shade on the same side, against the little breeze that was stirring. The lofty, spiring tops of the spruce and fir were very black against the sky, and more distinct than by day, close bordering this broad avenue on each side; and the beauty of the scene, as the moon rose above the forest, it would not be easy to describe. A bat flew over our heads, and we heard a few faint notes of birds from time to time, perhaps the myrtle-bird for one, or the sudden plunge of a musquash, or saw one crossing the stream before us, or heard the sound of a rill emptying in, swollen by the recent rain. About a mile below the island, when the solitude seemed to be growing more complete every moment, we suddenly saw the light and heard the crackling of a fire on the bank, and discovered the camp of the two explorers; they standing before it in their red shirts, and talking aloud of the adventures and profits of the day. They were just then speaking of a bargain, in which, as I understood, somebody had cleared twenty-five dollars. We glided by without speaking, close under the bank, within a couple of rods of them; and Joe, taking his horn, imitated the call of the moose, till we suggested that they might fire on us. This was the last we saw of them, and we never knew whether they detected or suspected us.

I have often wished since that I was with them. They search for timber over a given section, climbing hills and often high trees to look off,—explore the streams by which it is to be driven, and the like,—spend five or six weeks in the woods, they two alone, a hundred miles or more from any town,— roaming about, and sleeping on the ground where night overtakes them,—depending chiefly on the provisions they carry with them, though they do not decline what game they come across,—and then in the fall they return and make report to their employers, determining the number of teams that will be required the following winter. Experienced men get three or four dollars a day for this work. It is a solitary and adventurous life, and comes nearest to that of the trapper of the West, perhaps. They work ever with a gun as well as an axe, let their beards grow, and live without neighbors, not on an open plain, but far within a wilderness.

This discovery accounted for the sounds which we had heard, and destroyed the prospect of seeing moose yet awhile. At length, when we had left the explorers far behind, Joe laid down his paddle, drew forth his birch horn,—a straight one, about fifteen inches long and three or four wide at the mouth, tied round with strips of the same bark,—and standing up, imitated the call of the moose,— *ugh-ugh-ugh*, or *oo-oo-oo-oo*, and then a prolonged *oo-o-o-o-o-o-o*, and listened attentively for several minutes. We asked him what kind of noise he expected to hear. He said, that, if a moose heard it, he guessed we should find out; we should hear him coming half a mile off; he would come close to, perhaps into, the water, and my companion must wait till he got fair sight, and then aim just behind the shoulder.

The moose venture out to the river-side to feed and drink at night. Earlier in the season the hunters do not use a horn to call them out, but steal upon them as they are feeding along the sides of the stream, and often the first notice they have of one is the sound of the water dropping from its muzzle. An Indian whom I heard imitate the voice of the moose, and also that of the caribou and the deer, using a much longer horn than Joe's, told me that the first could be heard eight or ten miles, sometimes; it was a loud sort of bellowing sound, clearer and more sonorous than the lowing of cattle,—the caribou's a sort of snort,—and the small deer's like that of a lamb.

At length we turned up the Moosehorn, where the Indians at the carry had told us that they killed a moose the night before. This is a very meandering stream, only a rod or two in width, but comparatively deep, coming in on the right, fitly enough named Moosehorn, whether from its windings or its inhabitants. It was bordered here and there by narrow meadows between the stream and the endless forest, affording favorable places for the moose to feed, and to call them out on. We proceeded half a mile up this, as through a narrow, winding canal, where the tall, dark spruce and firs and arborvitæ towered on both sides in the moonlight, forming a perpendicular forest-edge of great height, like the spires of a Venice in the forest. In two places stood a small stack of hay on the bank, ready for the lumberer's use in the winter, looking strange enough there. We thought of the day when this might be a brook winding through smooth-shaven meadows on some gentleman's grounds; and seen by moonlight then, excepting the forest that now hems it in, how little changed it would appear!

Again and again Joe called the moose, placing the canoe close by some favorable point of meadow for them to come out on, but listened in vain to hear one come rushing through the woods, and concluded that they had been hunted too much thereabouts. We saw, many times, what to our imaginations looked like a gigantic moose, with his horns peering from out the forest-edge; but we saw the forest only, and not its inhabitants, that night. So at last we turned about. There was now a little fog on the water, though it was a fine, clear night above. There were very few sounds to break the stillness of the forest. Several times we heard the hooting of a great horned-owl, as at home, and told Joe that he would call out the moose for him, for he made a sound considerably like the horn,—but Joe answered, that the moose had heard that sound a thousand times, and knew better; and oftener still we were startled by the plunge of a musquash. Once, when Joe had called again, and we were listening for moose, we heard, come faintly echoing, or creeping from far, through the moss-clad aisles, a dull, dry, rushing sound, with a solid core to it, yet as if half smothered under the grasp of the luxuriant and fungus-like forest, like the shutting of a door in some distant entry of the damp and shaggy wilderness. If we had not been there, no mortal had heard it. When we asked Joe in a whisper what it was, he answered,—"Tree fall." There is something singularly grand and impressive in the sound of a tree falling in a perfectly calm night like this, as if the agencies which overthrow it did not need to be excited, but worked with a subtle, deliberate, and conscious force, like a boa-constrictor, and more effectively then than even in a windy day. If there is any such difference, perhaps it is because trees with the dews of the night on them are heavier than by day.

Having reached the camp, about ten o'clock, we kindled our fire and went to bed. Each of us had a blanket, in which he lay on the fir-twigs, with his extremities toward the fire, but nothing over his head. It was worth the while to lie down in a country where you could afford such great fires; that was one whole side, and the bright side, of our world. We had first rolled up a large log some eighteen inches through and ten feet long, for a back-log, to last all night, and then piled on the trees to the height of three or four feet, no matter how green or damp. In fact, we burned as much wood that night as would, with economy and an air-tight stove, last a poor family in one of our cities all winter. It was very agreeable, as well as independent, this lying in the open air, and the fire kept our uncovered extremities warm enough. The Jesuit missionaries used to say, that, in their journeys with the Indians in Canada, they lay on a bed which had never been shaken up since the creation, unless by earthquakes. It is surprising with what impunity and comfort one who has always lain in a warm bed in a close apartment, and studiously avoided drafts of air, can lie down on the ground without a shelter, roll himself in a blanket, and sleep before a fire, in a frosty, autumn night, just after a long rain-storm, and even come soon to enjoy and value the fresh air.

I lay awake awhile, watching the ascent of the sparks through the firs, and sometimes their descent in half-extinguished cinders on my blanket. They were as interesting as fireworks, going up in endless, successive crowds, each after an explosion, in an eager, serpentine course, some to five or six rods above the tree-tops before they went out. We do not suspect how much our chimneys have concealed; and now air-tight stoves have come to conceal all the rest. In the course of the night, I got up once or twice and put fresh logs on the fire, making my companions curl up their legs.

When we awoke in the morning, (Saturday, September 17,) there was considerable frost whitening the leaves. We heard the sound of the chickaree, and a few faintly lisping birds, and also of ducks in the water about the island. I took a botanical account of stock of our domains before the dew was off, and found that the ground-hemlock, or American yew, was the prevailing under-shrub. We breakfasted on tea, hard bread, and ducks.

Before the fog had fairly cleared away, we paddled down the stream again, and were soon past the mouth of the Moosehorn. These twenty miles of the Penobscot, between Moosehead and Chesuncook Lakes, are comparatively smooth, and a great part dead-water; but from time to time it is shallow and rapid, with rocks or gravel-beds, where you can wade across. There is no expanse of water, and no break in the forest, and the meadow is a mere edging here and there. There are no hills near the river nor within sight, except one or two distant mountains seen in a few places. The banks are from six to ten feet high, but once or twice rise gently to higher ground. In many places the forest on the bank was but a thin strip, letting the light through from some alder-swamp or meadow behind. The conspicuous berry-bearing bushes and trees along the shore were the red osier, with its whitish fruit, hobble-bush, mountain-ash, tree-cranberry, choke-cherry, now ripe, alternate cornel, and naked viburnum. Following Joe's example, I ate the fruit of the last, and also of the hobble-bush, but found them rather insipid and seedy. I looked very narrowly at the vegetation, as we glided along close to the shore, and frequently made Joe turn aside for me to pluck a plant, that I might see by comparison what was primitive about my native river. Horehound, horsemint, and the sensitive fern grew close to the edge, under the willows and alders, and wool-grass on the islands, as along the Assabet River in Concord. It was too late for flowers, except a few asters, golden-rods, etc. In several places we noticed the slight frame of a camp, such as we had prepared to set up, amid the forest by the river-side, where some lumberers or hunters had passed a night,—and sometimes steps cut in the muddy or clayey bank in front of it.

We stopped to fish for trout at the mouth of a small stream called Ragmuff, which came in from the west, about two miles below the Moosehorn. Here were the ruins of an old lumbering-camp, and a small space, which had formerly been cleared and burned over, was now densely overgrown with the red cherry and raspberries. While we were trying for trout, Joe, Indian-like, wandered off up the Ragmuff on his own errands, and when we were ready to start was far beyond call. So we were compelled to make a fire and get our dinner here, not to lose time. Some dark reddish birds, with grayer females, (perhaps purple finches,) and myrtle-birds in their summer dress, hopped within six or eight feet of us and our smoke. Perhaps they smelled the frying pork. The latter bird, or both, made the lisping notes which I had heard in the forest. They suggested that the few small birds found in the wilderness are on more familiar terms with the lumberman and hunter than those of the orchard and clearing with the farmer. I have since found the Canada jay, and partridges, both the black and the common, equally tame there, as if they had not yet learned to mistrust man entirely. The chicadee, which is at home alike in the primitive woods and in our wood-lots, still retains its confidence in the towns to a re-markable degree.

Joe at length returned, after an hour and a half, and said that he had been two miles up the stream exploring, and had seen a moose, but, not having the gun, he did not get him. We made no complaint, but concluded to look out for Joe the next time. However, this may have been a mere mistake, for we had no reason to complain of him afterwards. As we con-tinued down the stream, I was surprised to hear him whis-tling "O Susanna," and several other such airs, while his paddle urged us along. Once he said, "Yes, Sir-ee." His com-mon word was "Sartain." He paddled, as usual, on one side only, giving the birch an impulse by using the side as a ful-crum. I asked him how the ribs were fastened to the side rails. He answered, "I don't know, I never noticed." Talking with him about subsisting wholly on what the woods yielded, game, fish, berries, etc., I suggested that his ancestors did so; but he answered, that he had been brought up in such a way that he could not do it. "Yes," said he, "that's the way they got a living, like wild fellows, wild as bears. By George! I shan't go into the woods without provision,—hard bread, pork, etc." He had brought on a barrel of hard bread and stored it at the carry for his hunting. However, though he was a Governor's son, he had not learned to read.

At one place below this, on the east side, where the bank was higher and drier than usual, rising gently from the shore to a slight elevation, some one had felled the trees over twenty or thirty acres, and left them drying in order to burn. This was the only preparation for a house between the Moosehead carry and Chesuncook, but there was no hut nor inhabitants there yet. The pioneer thus selects a site for his house, which will, perhaps, prove the germ of a town.

My eyes were all the while on the trees, distinguishing be-tween the black and white spruce and the fir. You paddle along in a narrow canal through an endless forest, and the vision I have in my mind's eye, still, is of the small, dark, and sharp tops of tall fir and spruce trees, and pagoda-like arbor-vitæs, crowded together on each side, with various hard woods, intermixed. Some of the arbor-vitæs were at least sixty feet high. The hard woods, occasionally occurring exclusively, were less wild to my eye. I fancied them ornamental grounds, with farm-houses in the rear. The canoe and yellow birch, beech, maple, and elm are Saxon and Norman; but the spruce and fir, and pines generally, are Indian. The soft engravings which adorn the annuals give no idea of a stream in such a wilderness as this. The rough sketches in Jackson's Reports on the Geology of Maine answer much better. At one place we saw a small grove of slender sapling white-pines, the only collection of pines that I saw on this voyage. Here and there, however, was a full-grown, tall, and slender, but defective one, what lumbermen call a *konchus* tree, which they ascertain with their axes, or by the knots. I did not learn whether this word was Indian or English. It reminded me of the Greek κόγχη, a conch or shell, and I amused myself with fancying that it might signify the dead sound which the trees yield when struck. All the rest of the pines had been driven off.

How far men go for the material of their houses! The inhabitants of the most civilized cities, in all ages, send into far, primitive forests, beyond the bounds of their civilization, where the moose and bear and savage dwell, for their pine-boards for ordinary use. And, on the other hand, the savage soon receives from cities, iron arrow-points, hatchets, and guns, to point his savageness with.

The solid and well-defined fir-tops, like sharp and regular spear-heads, black against the sky, gave a peculiar, dark, and sombre look to the forest. The spruce-tops have a similar, but more ragged outline,—their shafts also merely feathered below. The firs were somewhat oftener regular and dense pyramids. I was struck by this universal spiring upward of the forest evergreens. The tendency is to slender, spiring tops, while they are narrower below. Not only the spruce and fir, but even the arbor-vitæ and white-pine, unlike the soft, spreading second-growth, of which I saw none, all spire upwards, lifting a dense spear-head of cones to the light and air, at any rate, while their branches straggle after as they may; as Indians lift the ball over the heads of the crowd in their desperate game. In this they resemble grasses, as also palms somewhat. The hemlock is commonly a tent-like pyramid from the ground to its summit.

After passing through some long rips, and by a large island, we reached an interesting part of the river called the Pine-Stream Dead-Water, about six miles below Ragmuff, where the river expanded to thirty rods in width and had many islands in it, with elms and canoe-birches, now yellowing, along the shore, and we got our first sight of Ktaadn.

Here, about two o'clock, we turned up a small branch three or four rods wide, which comes in on the right from the south, called Pine-Stream, to look for moose signs. We had gone but a few rods before we saw very recent signs along the water's edge, the mud lifted up by their feet being quite fresh, and Joe declared that they had gone along there but a short time before. We soon reached a small meadow on the east side, at an angle in the stream, which was, for the most part, densely covered with alders. As we were advancing along the edge of this, rather more quietly than usual, perhaps, on account of the freshness of the signs,—the design being to camp up this stream, if it promised well,—I heard a slight crackling of twigs deep in the alders, and turned Joe's attention to it; whereupon he began to push the canoe back rapidly; and we had receded thus half a dozen rods, when we suddenly spied two moose standing just on the edge of the open part of the meadow which we had passed, not more than six or seven rods distant, looking round the alders at us. They made me think of great frightened rabbits, with their long ears and half-inquisitive, half-frightened looks; the true denizens of the forest, (I saw at once,) filling a vacuum which now first I discovered had not been filled for me,— *moose-men*, *wood-eaters*, the word is said to mean,—clad in a sort of Vermont gray, or homespun. Our Nimrod, owing to the retrograde movement, was now the farthest from the game; but being warned of its neighborhood, he hastily stood up, and, while we ducked, fired over our heads one barrel at the foremost, which alone he saw, though he did not know what kind of creature it was; whereupon this one dashed across the meadow and up a high bank on the northeast, so rapidly as to leave but an indistinct impression of its outlines on my mind. At the same instant, the other, a young one, but as tall as a horse, leaped out into the stream, in full sight, and there stood cowering for a moment, or rather its disproportionate lowness behind gave it that appearance, and uttering two or three trumpeting squeaks. I have an indistinct recollection of seeing the old one pause an instant on the top of the bank in the woods, look toward its shivering young, and then dash away again. The second barrel was levelled at the calf, and when we expected to see it drop in the water, after a little hesitation, it, too, got out of the water, and dashed up the hill, though in a somewhat different direction. All this was the work of a few seconds, and our hunter, having never seen a moose before, did not know but they were deer, for they stood partly in the water, nor whether he had fired at the same one twice or not. From the style in which they went off, and the fact that he was not used to standing up and firing from a canoe, I judged that we should not see anything more of them. The Indian said that they were a cow and her calf,— a yearling, or perhaps two years old, for they accompany their dams so long; but, for my part, I had not noticed much difference in their size. It was but two or three rods across the meadow to the foot of the bank, which, like all the world thereabouts, was densely wooded; but I was surprised to notice, that, as soon as the moose had passed behind the veil of the woods, there was no sound of footsteps to be heard from the soft, damp moss which carpets that forest, and long before we landed, perfect silence reigned. Joe said, "If you wound 'em moose, me sure get 'em."

We all landed at once. My companion reloaded; the Indian fastened his birch, threw off his hat, adjusted his waistband, seized the hatchet, and set out. He told me afterward, casually, that before we landed he had seen a drop of blood on the bank, when it was two or three rods off. He proceeded rapidly up the bank and through the woods, with a peculiar, elastic, noiseless, and stealthy tread, looking to right and left on the ground, and stepping in the faint tracks of the wounded moose, now and then pointing in silence to a single drop of blood on the handsome, shining leaves of the Clintonia Borealis, which, on every side, covered the ground, or to a dry fern-stem freshly broken, all the while chewing some leaf or else the spruce gum. I followed, watching his motions more than the trail of the moose. After following the trail about forty rods in a pretty direct course, stepping over fallen trees and winding between standing ones, he at length lost it, for there were many other moose-tracks there, and, returning once more to the last blood-stain, traced it a little way and lost it again, and, too soon, I thought, for a good hunter, gave it up entirely. He traced a few steps, also, the tracks of the calf; but, seeing no blood, soon relinquished the search.

I observed, while he was tracking the moose, a certain reticence or moderation in him. He did not communicate several observations of interest which he made, as a white man would have done, though they may have leaked out afterward. At another time, when we heard a slight crackling of twigs and he landed to reconnoitre, he stepped lightly and gracefully, stealing through the bushes with the least possible noise, in a way in which no white man does,—as it were, finding a place for his foot each time.

About half an hour after seeing the moose, we pursued our voyage up Pine-Stream, and soon, coming to a part which was very shoal and also rapid, we took out the baggage, and proceeded to carry it round, while Joe got up with the canoe alone. We were just completing our portage and I was absorbed in the plants, admiring the leaves of the aster macrophyllus, ten inches wide, and plucking the seeds of the great round-leaved orchis, when Joe exclaimed from the stream that he had killed a moose. He had found the cow-moose lying dead, but quite warm, in the middle of the stream, which was so shallow that it rested on the bottom, with hardly a third of its body above water. It was about an hour after it was shot, and it was swollen with water. It had run about a hundred rods and sought the stream again, cutting off a slight bend. No doubt, a better hunter would have tracked it to this spot at once. I was surprised at its great size, horse-like, but Joe said it was not a large cow-moose. My companion went in search of the calf again. I took hold of the ears of the moose, while Joe pushed his canoe down stream toward a favorable shore, and so we made out, though with some difficulty, its long nose frequently sticking in the bottom, to drag it into still shallower water. It was a brownish black, or perhaps a dark iron-gray, on the back and sides, but lighter beneath and in front. I took the cord which served for the canoe's painter, and with Joe's assistance measured it carefully, the greatest distances first, making a knot each time.

The painter being wanted, I reduced these measures that night with equal care to lengths and fractions of my umbrella, beginning with the smallest measures, and untying the knots as I proceeded; and when we arrived at Chesuncook the next day, finding a two-foot rule there, I reduced the last to feet and inches; and, moreover, I made myself a two-foot rule of a thin and narrow strip of black ash which would fold up conveniently to six inches. All this pains I took because I did not wish to be obliged to say merely that the moose was very large. Of the various dimensions which I obtained I will mention only two. The distance from the tips of the hoofs of the fore-feet, stretched out, to the top of the back between the shoulders, was seven feet and five inches. I can hardly believe my own measure, for this is about two feet greater than the height of a tall horse. [Indeed, I am now satisfied that this measurement was incorrect, but the other measures given here I can warrant to be correct, having proved them in a more recent visit to those woods.] The extreme length was eight feet and two inches. Another cow-moose, which I have since measured in those woods with a tape, was just six feet from the tip of the hoof to the shoulders, and eight feet long as she lay.

When afterward I asked an Indian at the carry how much taller the male was, he answered, "Eighteen inches," and made me observe the height of a cross-stake over the fire, more than four feet from the ground, to give me some idea of the depth of his chest. Another Indian, at Oldtown, told me that they were nine feet high to the top of the back, and that one which he tried weighed eight hundred pounds. The length of the spinal projections between the shoulders is very great. A white hunter, who was the best authority among hunters that I could have, told me that the male was *not* eighteen inches taller than the female; yet he agreed that he was sometimes nine feet high to the top of the back, and weighed a thousand pounds. Only the male has horns, and they rise two feet or more above the shoulders,—spreading three or four, and sometimes six feet,—which would make him in all, sometimes, eleven feet high! According to this calculation, the moose is as tall, though it may not be as large, as the great Irish elk, Megaceros Hibernicus, of a former period, of which

Mantell says that it "very far exceeded in magnitude any living species, the skeleton" being "upward of ten feet high from the ground to the highest point of the antlers." Joe said, that, though the moose shed the whole horn annually, each new horn has an additional prong; but I have noticed that they sometimes have more prongs on one side than on the other. I was struck with the delicacy and tenderness of the hoofs, which divide very far up, and the one half could be pressed very much behind the other, thus probably making the animal surer-footed on the uneven ground and slippery moss-covered logs of the primitive forest. They were very unlike the stiff and battered feet of our horses and oxen. The bare, horny part of the fore-foot was just six inches long, and the two portions could be separated four inches at the extremities.

The moose is singularly grotesque and awkward to look at. Why should it stand so high at the shoulders? Why have so long a head? Why have no tail to speak of? for in my examination I overlooked it entirely. Naturalists say it is an inch and a half long. It reminded me at once of the camelopard, high before and low behind,—and no wonder, for, like it, it is fitted to browse on trees. The upper lip projected two inches beyond the lower for this purpose. This was the kind of man that was at home there; for, as near as I can learn, that has never been the residence, but rather the hunting-ground of the Indian. The moose will perhaps one day become extinct; but how naturally then, when it exists only as a fossil relic, and unseen as that, may the poet or sculptor invent a fabulous animal with similar branching and leafy horns,—a sort of fucus or lichen in bone,—to be the inhabitant of such a forest as this!

Here, just at the head of the murmuring rapids, Joe now proceeded to skin the moose with a pocket-knife, while I looked on; and a tragical business it was,—to see that still warm and palpitating body pierced with a knife, to see the warm milk stream from the rent udder, and the ghastly naked red carcass appearing from within its seemly robe, which was made to hide it. The ball had passed through the shoulder-blade diagonally and lodged under the skin on the opposite side, and was partially flattened. My companion keeps it to show to his grandchildren. He has the shanks of another moose which he has since shot, skinned and stuffed, ready to be made into boots by putting in a thick leather sole. Joe said, if a moose stood fronting you, you must not fire, but advance toward him, for he will turn slowly and give you a fair shot. In the bed of this narrow, wild, and rocky stream, between two lofty walls of spruce and firs, a mere cleft in the forest which the stream had made, this work went on. At length Joe had stripped off the hide and dragged it trailing to the shore, declaring that it weighed a hundred pounds, though probably fifty would have been nearer the truth. He cut off a large mass of the meat to carry along, and another, together with the tongue and nose, he put with the hide on the shore to lie there all night, or till we returned. I was surprised that he thought of leaving this meat thus exposed by the side of the carcass, as the simplest course, not fearing that any creature would touch it; but nothing did. This could hardly have happened on the bank of one of our rivers in the eastern part of Massachusetts; but I suspect that fewer small wild animals are prowling there than with us. Twice, however, in this excursion I had a glimpse of a species of large mouse.

This stream was so withdrawn, and the moose-tracks were so fresh, that my companions, still bent on hunting, concluded to go farther up it and camp, and then hunt up or down at night. Half a mile above this, at a place where I saw the aster puniceus and the beaked hazel, as we paddled along, Joe, hearing a slight rustling amid the alders, and seeing something black about two rods off, jumped up and whispered, "Bear!" but before the hunter had discharged his piece, he corrected himself to "Beaver!"—"Hedgehog!" The bullet killed a large hedgehog more than two feet and eight inches long. The quills were rayed out and flattened on the hinder part of its back, even as if it had lain on that part, but were erect and long between this and the tail. Their points, closely examined, were seen to be finely bearded or barbed, and shaped like an awl, that is, a little concave, to give the barbs effect. After about a mile of still water, we prepared our camp on the right side, just at the foot of a considerable fall. Little chopping was done that night, for fear of scaring the moose. We had moose-meat fried for supper. It tasted like tender beef, with perhaps more flavor,—sometimes like veal.

After supper, the moon having risen, we proceeded to hunt a mile up this stream, first "carrying" about the falls. We made a picturesque sight, wending single-file along the shore, climbing over rocks and logs,—Joe, who brought up the rear, twirling his canoe in his hands as if it were a feather, in places where it was difficult to get along without a burden. We launched the canoe again from the ledge over which the stream fell, but after half a mile of still water, suitable for hunting, it became rapid again, and we were compelled to make our way along the shore, while Joe endeavored to get up in the birch alone, though it was still very difficult for him to pick his way amid the rocks in the night. We on the shore found the worst of walking, a perfect chaos of fallen and drifted trees, and of bushes projecting far over the water, and now and then we made our way across the mouth of a small tributary on a kind of net-work of alders. So we went tumbling on in the dark, being on the shady side, effectually scaring all the moose and bears that might be thereabouts. At length we came to a standstill, and Joe went forward to reconnoitre; but he reported that it was still a continuous rapid as far as he went, or half a mile, with no prospect of improvement, as if it were coming down from a mountain. So we turned about, hunting back to the camp through the still water. It was a splendid moonlight night, and I, getting sleepy as it grew late,—for I had nothing to do,—found it difficult to realize where I was. This stream was much more unfrequented than the main one, lumbering operations being no longer carried on in this quarter. It was only three or four rods wide, but the firs and spruce through which it trickled seemed yet taller by contrast. Being in this dreamy state, which the moonlight enhanced, I did not clearly discern the shore, but seemed, most of the time, to be floating through ornamental grounds,—for I associated the fir-tops with such scenes;—very high up some Broadway, and beneath or between their tops, I thought I saw an endless succession of porticos and columns, cornices and façades, verandas and churches. I did not merely fancy this, but in my drowsy state such was the illusion. I fairly lost myself in sleep several times, still dreaming of that architecture and the nobility that dwelt behind and might issue from it; but all at once I would be aroused and brought back to a sense of my actual position by the sound of Joe's birch horn in the midst of all this silence calling the moose, *ugh, ugh, oo-oo-oo-oo-oo-oo*, and I prepared to hear a furious moose come rushing and crashing through the forest, and see him burst out on to the little strip of meadow by our side.

But, on more accounts than one, I had had enough of moose-hunting. I had not come to the woods for this purpose, nor had I foreseen it, though I had been willing to learn how the Indian manœuvred; but one moose killed was as good, if not as bad, as a dozen. The afternoon's tragedy, and my share in it, as it affected the innocence, destroyed the pleasure of my adventure. It is true, I came as near as is possible to come to being a hunter and miss it, myself; and as it is, I think that I could spend a year in the woods, fishing and hunting, just enough to sustain myself, with satisfaction. This would be next to living like a philosopher on the fruits of the earth which you had raised, which also attracts me. But this hunting of the moose merely for the satisfaction of killing him,—not even for the sake of his hide,—without making any extraordinary exertion or running any risk yourself, is too much like going out by night to some wood-side pasture and shooting your neighbor's horses. These are God's own horses, poor, timid creatures, that will run fast enough as soon as they smell you, though they *are* nine feet high. Joe told us of some hunters who a year or two before had shot down several oxen by night, somewhere in the Maine woods, mistaking them for moose. And so might any of the hunters; and what is the difference in the sport, but the name? In the former case, having killed one of God's and *your own* oxen, you strip off its hide,—because that is the common trophy, and, moreover, you have heard that it may be sold for moccasins,—cut a steak from its haunches, and leave the huge carcass to smell to heaven for you. It is no better, at least, than to assist at a slaughter-house.

This afternoon's experience suggested to me how base or coarse are the motives which commonly carry men into the wilderness. The explorers and lumberers generally are all hirelings, paid so much a day for their labor, and as such they have no more love for wild nature than wood-sawyers have for forests. Other white men and Indians who come here are for the most part hunters, whose object is to slay as many moose and other wild animals as possible. But, pray, could not one spend some weeks or years in the solitude of this vast wilderness with other employments than these,—employments perfectly sweet and innocent and ennobling? For one that comes with a pencil to sketch or sing, a thousand come with an axe or rifle. What a coarse and imperfect use Indians and hunters make of Nature! No wonder that their race is so soon exterminated. I already, and for weeks afterward, felt my nature the coarser for this part of my woodland experience, and was reminded that our life should be lived as tenderly and daintily as one would pluck a flower.

With these thoughts, when we reached our camping-ground, I decided to leave my companions to continue moose-hunting down the stream, while I prepared the camp, though they requested me not to chop much nor make a large fire, for fear I should scare their game. In the midst of the damp fir-wood, high on the mossy bank, about nine o'clock of this bright moonlight night, I kindled a fire, when they were gone, and, sitting on the fir-twigs, within sound of the falls, examined by its light the botanical specimens which I had collected that afternoon, and wrote down some of the reflections which I have here expanded; or I walked along the shore and gazed up the stream, where the whole space above the falls was filled with mellow light. As I sat before the fire on my fir-twig seat, without walls above or around me, I remembered how far on every hand that wilderness stretched, before you came to cleared or cultivated fields, and wondered if any bear or moose was watching the light of my fire; for Nature looked sternly upon me on account of the murder of the moose.

Strange that so few ever come to the woods to see how the pine lives and grows and spires, lifting its evergreen arms to the light,—to see its perfect success; but most are content to behold it in the shape of many broad boards brought to market, and deem *that* its true success! But the pine is no more lumber than man is, and to be made into boards and houses is no more its true and highest use than the truest use of a man is to be cut down and made into manure. There is a higher law affecting our relation to pines as well as to men. A pine cut down, a dead pine, is no more a pine than a dead human carcass is a man. Can he who has discovered only some of the values of whalebone and whale oil be said to have discovered the true use of the whale? Can he who slays the elephant for his ivory be said to have "seen the elephant"? These are petty and accidental uses; just as if a stronger race were to kill us in order to make buttons and flageolets of our bones; for everything may serve a lower as well as a higher use. Every creature is better alive than dead, men and moose and pine-trees, and he who understands it aright will rather preserve its life than destroy it.

Is it the lumberman, then, who is the friend and lover of the pine, stands nearest to it, and understands its nature best? Is it the tanner who has barked it, or he who has boxed it for turpentine, whom posterity will fable to have been changed into a pine at last? No! no! it is the poet; he it is who makes the truest use of the pine,—who does not fondle it with an axe, nor tickle it with a saw, nor stroke it with a plane,—who knows whether its heart is false without cutting into it,—who has not bought the stumpage of the township on which it stands. All the pines shudder and heave a sigh when *that* man steps on the forest floor. No, it is the poet, who loves them as his own shadow in the air, and lets them stand. I have been into the lumber-yard, and the carpenter's shop, and the tannery, and the lampblack-factory, and the turpentine clearing; but when at length I saw the tops of the pines waving and reflecting the light at a distance high over all the rest of the forest, I realized that the former were not the highest use of the pine. It is not their bones or hide or tallow that I love most. It is the living spirit of the tree, not its spirit of turpentine, with which I sympathize, and which heals my cuts. It is as immortal as I am, and perchance will go to as high a heaven, there to tower above me still.

Erelong, the hunters returned, not having seen a moose, but, in consequence of my suggestions, bringing a quarter of the dead one, which, with ourselves, made quite a load for the canoe.

After breakfasting on moose-meat, we returned down Pine Stream on our way to Chesuncook Lake, which was about five miles distant. We could see the red carcass of the moose lying in Pine Stream when nearly half a mile off. Just below the mouth of this stream were the most considerable rapids between the two lakes, called Pine-Stream Falls, where were large flat rocks washed smooth, and at this time you could easily wade across above them. Joe ran down alone while we walked over the portage, my companion collecting spruce gum for his friends at home, and I looking for flowers. Near the lake, which we were approaching with as much expectation as if it had been a university,—for it is not often that the stream of our life opens into such expansions,—were islands, and a low and meadowy shore with scattered trees, birches, white and yellow, slanted over the water, and maples,—many of the white birches killed, apparently by inundations. There was considerable native grass; and even a few cattle—whose movements we heard, though we did not see them, mistaking them at first for moose—were pastured there.

On entering the lake, where the stream runs southeasterly, and for some time before, we had a view of the mountains about Ktaadn, (*Katahdinauguoh* one says they are called,) like a cluster of blue fungi of rank growth, apparently twenty-five or thirty miles distant, in a southeast direction, their summits concealed by clouds. Joe called some of them the *Souadneunk* mountains. This is the name of a stream there, which another Indian told us meant "Running between mountains." Though some lower summits were afterward uncovered, we got no more complete view of Ktaadn while we were in the woods. The clearing to which we were bound was on the right of the mouth of the river, and was reached by going round a low point, where the water was shallow to a great distance from the shore. Chesuncook Lake extends northwest and southeast, and is called eighteen miles long and three wide, without an island. We had entered the northwest corner of it, and when near the shore could see only part way down it. The principal mountains visible from the land here were those already mentioned, between southeast and east, and a few summits a little west of north, but generally the north and northwest horizon about the St. John and the British boundary was compara-tively level.

Ansell Smith's, the oldest and principal clearing about this lake, appeared to be quite a harbor for *bateaux* and canoes; seven or eight of the former were lying about, and there was a small scow for hay, and a capstan on a platform, now high and dry, ready to be floated and anchored to tow rafts with. It was a very primitive kind of harbor, where boats were drawn up amid the stumps,—such a one, methought, as the Argo might have been launched in. There were five other huts with small clearings on the opposite side of the lake, all at this end and visible from this point. One of the Smiths told me that it was so far cleared that they came here to live and built the present house four years before, though the family had been here but a few months.

I was interested to see how a pioneer lived on this side of the country. His life is in some respects more adventurous than that of his brother in the West; for he contends with winter as well as the wilderness, and there is a greater interval of time at least between him and the army which is to follow. Here immigration is a tide which may ebb when it has swept away the pines; there it is not a tide, but an inundation, and roads and other improvements come steadily rushing after.

As we approached the log-house, a dozen rods from the lake, and considerably elevated above it, the projecting ends of the logs lapping over each other irregularly several feet at the corners gave it a very rich and picturesque look, far removed from the meanness of weather-boards. It was a very spacious, low building, about eighty feet long, with many large apartments. The walls were well clayed between the logs, which were large and round, except on the upper and under sides, and as visible inside as out, successive bulging cheeks gradually lessening upwards and tuned to each other with the axe, like Pandean pipes. Probably the musical forest-gods had not yet cast them aside; they never do till they are split or the bark is gone. It was a style of architecture not described by Vitruvius, I suspect, though possibly hinted at in the biography of Orpheus; none of your frilled or fluted columns, which have cut such a false swell, and support nothing but a gable end and their builder's pretensions,— that is, with the multitude; and as for "ornamentation," one of those words with a dead tail which architects very properly use to describe their flourishes, there were the lichens and mosses and fringes of bark, which nobody troubled himself about. We certainly leave the handsomest paint and clapboards behind in the woods, when we strip off the bark and poison ourselves with white-lead in the towns. We get but half the spoils of the forest. For beauty, give me trees with the fur on. This house was designed and constructed with the freedom of stroke of a forester's axe, without other compass and square than Nature uses. Wherever the logs were cut off by a window or door, that is, were not kept in place by alternate overlapping, they were held one upon another by very large pins, driven in diagonally on each side, where branches might have been, and then cut off so close up and down as not to project beyond the bulge of the log, as if the logs clasped each other in their arms. These logs were posts, studs, boards, clapboards, laths, plaster, and nails, all in one. Where the citizen uses a mere sliver or board, the pioneer uses the whole trunk of a tree. The house had large stone chimneys, and was roofed with spruce-bark. The windows were imported, all but the casings. One end was a regular logger's camp, for the boarders, with the usual fir floor and log benches. Thus this house was but a slight departure from the hollow tree, which the bear still inhabits,—being a hollow made with trees piled up, with a coating of bark like its original.

The cellar was a separate building, like an ice-house, and it answered for a refrigerator at this season, our moose-meat being kept there. It was a potato-hole with a permanent roof. Each structure and institution here was so primitive that you could at once refer it to its source; but our buildings commonly suggest neither their origin nor their purpose. There was a large, and what farmers would call handsome, barn, part of whose boards had been sawed by a whip-saw; and the saw-pit, with its great pile of dust, remained before the house. The long split shingles on a portion of the barn were laid a foot to the weather, suggesting what kind of weather they have there. Grant's barn at Caribou Lake was said to be still larger, the biggest ox-nest in the woods, fifty feet by a hundred. Think of a monster barn in that primitive forest lifting its gray back above the tree-tops! Man makes very much such a nest for his domestic animals, of withered grass and fodder, as the squirrels and many other wild creatures do for themselves.

There was also a blacksmith's shop, where plainly a good deal of work was done. The oxen and horses used in lumbering operations were shod, and all the iron-work of sleds, etc., was repaired or made here. I saw them load a *bateau* at the Moosehead carry, the next Tuesday, with about thirteen hundred weight of bar iron for this shop. This reminded me how primitive and honorable a trade was Vulcan's. I do not hear that there was any carpenter or tailor among the gods. The smith seems to have preceded these and every other mechanic at Chesuncook as well as on Olympus, and his family is the most widely dispersed, whether he be christened John or Ansell.

Smith owned two miles down the lake by half a mile in width. There were about one hundred acres cleared here. He cut seventy tons of English hay this year on this ground, and twenty more on another clearing, and he uses it all himself in lumbering operations. The barn was crowded with pressed hay and a machine to press it. There was a large garden full of roots, turnips, beets, carrots, potatoes, etc., all of great size. They said that they were worth as much here as in New York. I suggested some currants for sauce, especially as they had no apple-trees set out, and showed how easily they could be obtained.

There was the usual long-handled axe of the primitive woods by the door, three and a half feet long,—for my new black-ash rule was in constant use,—and a large, shaggy dog, whose nose, report said, was full of porcupine quills. I can testify that he looked very sober. This is the usual fortune of pioneer dogs, for they have to face the brunt of the battle for their race, and act the part of Arnold Winkelried without intending it. If he should invite one of his town friends up this way, suggesting moose-meat and unlimited freedom, the latter might pertinently inquire, "What is that sticking in your nose?" When a generation or two have used up all the enemies' darts, their successors lead a comparatively easy life. We owe to our fathers analogous blessings. Many old people receive pensions for no other reason, it seems to me, but as a compensation for having lived a long

time ago. No doubt our town dogs still talk, in a snuffling
way, about the days that tried dogs' noses. How they got a
cat up there I do not know, for they are as shy as my aunt
about entering a canoe. I wondered that she did not run up
a tree on the way; but perhaps she was bewildered by the
very crowd of opportunities.

Twenty or thirty lumberers, Yankee and Canadian, were
coming and going,—Aleck among the rest,—and from time
to time an Indian touched here. In the winter there are sometimes a hundred men lodged here at once. The most interesting piece of news that circulated among them appeared to be,
that four horses belonging to Smith, worth seven hundred
dollars, had passed by farther into the woods a week before.

The white-pine-tree was at the bottom or farther end of all
this. It is a war against the pines, the only real Aroostook or
Penobscot war. I have no doubt that they lived pretty much
the same sort of life in the Homeric age, for men have always
thought more of eating than of fighting; then, as now, their
minds ran chiefly on the "hot bread and sweet cakes"; and the
fur and lumber trade is an old story to Asia and Europe. I
doubt if men ever made a trade of heroism. In the days of
Achilles, even, they delighted in big barns, and perchance in
pressed hay, and he who possessed the most valuable team
was the best fellow.

We had designed to go on at evening up the Caucomgomoc, whose mouth was a mile or two distant, to the lake of
the same name, about ten miles off; but some Indians of
Joe's acquaintance, who were making canoes on the Caucomgomoc, came over from that side, and gave so poor an
account of the moose-hunting, so many had been killed
there lately, that my companions concluded not to go there.
Joe spent this Sunday and the night with his acquaintances.
The lumberers told me that there were many moose hereabouts, but no caribou or deer. A man from Oldtown had
killed ten or twelve moose, within a year, so near the house
that they heard all his guns. His name may have been Hercules, for aught I know, though I should rather have expected to hear the rattling of his club; but, no doubt, he
keeps pace with the improvements of the age, and uses a
Sharpe's rifle now; probably he gets all his armor made and

repaired at Smith's shop. One moose had been killed and another shot at within sight of the house within two years. I do not know whether Smith has yet got a poet to look after the cattle, which, on account of the early breaking up of the ice, are compelled to summer in the woods, but I would suggest this office to such of my acquaintances as love to write verses and go a-gunning.

After a dinner, at which apple-sauce was the greatest luxury to me, but our moose-meat was oftenest called for by the lumberers, I walked across the clearing into the forest, southward, returning along the shore. For my dessert, I helped myself to a large slice of the Chesuncook woods, and took a hearty draught of its waters with all my senses. The woods were as fresh and full of vegetable life as lichen in wet weather, and contained many interesting plants; but unless they are of white pine, they are treated with as little respect here as a mildew, and in the other case they are only the more quickly cut down. The shore was of coarse, flat, slate rocks, often in slabs, with the surf beating on it. The rocks and bleached drift-logs, extending some way into the shaggy woods, showed a rise and fall of six or eight feet, caused partly by the dam at the outlet. They said that in winter the snow was three feet deep on a level here, and sometimes four or five,—that the ice on the lake was two feet thick, clear, and four feet including the snow-ice. Ice had already formed in vessels.

We lodged here this Sunday night in a comfortable bed-room, apparently the best one; and all that I noticed unusual in the night—for I still kept taking notes, like a spy in the camp—was the creaking of the thin split boards, when any of our neighbors stirred.

Such were the first rude beginnings of a town. They spoke of the practicability of a winter-road to the Moosehead carry, which would not cost much, and would connect them with steam and staging and all the busy world. I almost doubted if the lake would be then the self-same lake,—preserve its form and identity, when the shores should be cleared and settled; as if these lakes and streams which explorers report never awaited the advent of the citizen.

The sight of one of these frontier-houses, built of these

great logs, whose inhabitants have unflinchingly maintained their ground many summers and winters in the wilderness, reminds me of famous forts, like Ticonderoga or Crown Point, which have sustained memorable sieges. They are especially winter-quarters, and at this season this one had a partially deserted look, as if the siege were raised a little, the snow-banks being melted from before it, and its garrison accordingly reduced. I think of their daily food as rations,—it is called "supplies"; a Bible and a great-coat are munitions of war, and a single man seen about the premises is a sentinel on duty. You expect that he will require the countersign, and will perchance take you for Ethan Allen, come to demand the surrender of his fort in the name of the Continental Congress. It is a sort of ranger service. Arnold's expedition is a daily experience with these settlers. They can prove that they were out at almost any time; and I think that all the first generation of them deserve a pension more than any that went to the Mexican war.

Early the next morning we started on our return up the Penobscot, my companion wishing to go about twenty-five miles above the Moosehead carry to a camp near the junction of the two forks, and look for moose there. Our host allowed us something for the quarter of the moose which we had brought, and which he was glad to get. Two explorers from Chamberlain Lake started at the same time that we did. Red-flannel shirts should be worn in the woods, if only for the fine contrast which this color makes with the evergreens and the water. Thus I thought when I saw the forms of the explorers in their birch, poling up the rapids before us, far off against the forest. It is the surveyor's color also, most distinctly seen under all circumstances. We stopped to dine at Ragmuff, as before. My companion it was who wandered up the stream to look for moose this time, while Joe went to sleep on the bank, so that we felt sure of him; and I improved the opportunity to botanize and bathe. Soon after starting again, while Joe was gone back in the canoe for the frying-pan, which had been left, we picked a couple of quarts of tree-cranberries for a sauce.

I was surprised by Joe's asking me how far it was to the Moosehorn. He was pretty well acquainted with this stream, but he had noticed that I was curious about distances, and had several maps. He, and Indians generally, with whom I have talked, are not able to describe dimensions or distances in our measures with any accuracy. He could tell perhaps, at what time we should arrive, but not how far it was. We saw a few wood-ducks, sheldrakes, and black ducks, but they were not so numerous there at that season as on our river at home. We scared the same family of wood-ducks before us, going and returning. We also heard the note of one fish-hawk, somewhat like that of a pigeon-woodpecker, and soon after saw him perched near the top of a dead white-pine against the island where we had first camped, while a company of peetweets were twittering and teetering about over the carcass of a moose on a low sandy spit just beneath. We drove the fish-hawk from perch to perch, each time eliciting a scream or whistle, for many miles before us. Our course being up-stream, we were obliged to work much harder than before, and had frequent use for a pole. Sometimes all three of us paddled together, standing up, small and heavily laden as the canoe was. About six miles from Moosehead, we began to see the mountains east of the north end of the lake, and at four o'clock we reached the carry.

The Indians were still encamped here. There were three, including the St. Francis Indian who had come in the steamer with us. One of the others was called Sabattis. Joe and the St. Francis Indian were plainly clear Indian, the other two apparently mixed Indian and white; but the difference was confined to their features and complexions, for all that I could see. We here cooked the tongue of the moose for supper,—having left the nose, which is esteemed the choicest part, at Chesuncook, boiling, it being a good deal of trouble to prepare it. We also stewed our tree-cranberries, (*Viburnum opulus,*) sweetening them with sugar. The lumberers sometimes cook them with molasses. They were used in Arnold's expedition. This sauce was very grateful to us who had been confined to hard bread, pork, and moose-meat, and, notwithstanding their seeds, we all three pronounced them equal to the common cranberry; but perhaps some allowance is to be made for our forest appetites. It would be worth the while to cultivate them, both for beauty and for food. I afterward saw them in a garden in Bangor. Joe said that they were called *ebeemenar*.

While we were getting supper, Joe commenced curing the moose-hide, on which I had sat a good part of the voyage, he having already cut most of the hair off with his knife at the Caucomgomoc. He set up two stout forked poles on the bank, seven or eight feet high, and as much asunder east and west, and having cut slits eight or ten inches long, and the same distance apart, close to the edge, on the sides of the hide, he threaded poles through them, and then, placing one of the poles on the forked stakes, tied the other down tightly at the bottom. The two ends also were tied with cedar-bark, their usual string, to the upright poles, through small holes at short intervals. The hide, thus stretched, and slanted a little to the north, to expose its flesh side to the sun, measured, in the extreme, eight feet long by six high. Where any flesh still adhered, Joe boldly scored it with his knife to lay it open to the sun. It now appeared somewhat spotted and injured by the duck shot. You may see the old frames on which hides have been stretched at many camping-places in these woods.

For some reason or other, the going to the forks of the Penobscot was given up, and we decided to stop here, my companion intending to hunt down the stream at night. The Indians invited us to lodge with them, but my companion inclined to go to the log-camp on the carry. This camp was close and dirty, and had an ill smell, and I preferred to accept the Indians' offer, if we did not make a camp for ourselves; for, though they were dirty, too, they were more in the open air, and were much more agreeable, and even refined company, than the lumberers. The most interesting question entertained at the lumberers' camp was, which man could "handle" any other on the carry; and, for the most part, they possessed no qualities which you could not lay hands on. So we went to the Indians' camp or wigwam.

It was rather windy, and therefore Joe concluded to hunt after midnight, if the wind went down, which the other Indians thought it would not do, because it was from the south. The two mixed-bloods, however, went off up the river for moose at dark, before we arrived at their camp. This Indian camp was a slight, patched-up affair, which had stood there

several weeks, built shed-fashion, open to the fire on the west.
If the wind changed, they could turn it round. It was formed
by two forked stakes and a cross-bar, with rafters slanted from
this to the ground. The covering was partly an old sail, partly
birch-bark, quite imperfect, but securely tied on, and coming
down to the ground on the sides. A large log was rolled up
at the back side for a head-board, and two or three moose-
hides were spread on the ground with the hair up. Various
articles of their wardrobe were tucked around the sides and
corners, or under the roof. They were smoking moose-meat
on just such a crate as is represented by With, in De Bry's
"Collectio Peregrinationum," published in 1588, and which the
natives of Brazil called *boucan*, (whence buccaneer,) on
which were frequently shown pieces of human flesh drying
along with the rest. It was erected in front of the camp over
the usual large fire, in the form of an oblong square. Two
stout forked stakes, four or five feet apart and five feet high,
were driven into the ground at each end, and then two poles
ten feet long were stretched across over the fire, and smaller
ones laid transversely on these a foot apart. On the last hung
large, thin slices of moose-meat smoking and drying, a space
being left open over the centre of the fire. There was the
whole heart, black as a thirty-two pound ball, hanging at one
corner. They said, that it took three or four days to cure this
meat, and it would keep a year or more. Refuse pieces lay
about on the ground in different stages of decay, and some
pieces also in the fire, half buried and sizzling in the ashes, as
black and dirty as an old shoe. These last I at first thought
were thrown away, but afterwards found that they were being
cooked. Also a tremendous rib-piece was roasting before the
fire, being impaled on an upright stake forced in and out between the ribs. There was a moose-hide stretched and curing
on poles like ours, and quite a pile of cured skins close by.
They had killed twenty-two moose within two months, but,
as they could use but very little of the meat, they left the
carcasses on the ground. Altogether it was about as savage a
sight as was ever witnessed, and I was carried back at once
three hundred years. There were many torches of birch-bark,
shaped like straight tin horns, lying ready for use on a stump
outside.

For fear of dirt, we spread our blankets over their hides, so as not to touch them anywhere. The St. Francis Indian and Joe alone were there at first, and we lay on our backs talking with them till midnight. They were very sociable, and, when they did not talk with us, kept up a steady chatting in their own language. We heard a small bird just after dark, which, Joe said, sang at a certain hour in the night,—at ten o'clock, he believed. We also heard the hylodes and tree-toads, and the lumberers singing in their camp a quarter of a mile off. I told them that I had seen pictured in old books pieces of human flesh drying on these crates; whereupon they repeated some tradition about the Mohawks eating human flesh, what parts they preferred, etc., and also of a battle with the Mohawks near Moosehead, in which many of the latter were killed; but I found that they knew but little of the history of their race, and could be entertained by stories about their ancestors as readily as any way. At first I was nearly roasted out, for I lay against one side of the camp, and felt the heat reflected not only from the birch-bark above, but from the side; and again I remembered the sufferings of the Jesuit missionaries, and what extremes of heat and cold the Indians were said to endure. I struggled long between my desire to remain and talk with them, and my impulse to rush out and stretch myself on the cool grass; and when I was about to take the last step, Joe, hearing my murmurs, or else being uncomfortable himself, got up and partially dispersed the fire. I suppose that that is Indian manners,—to defend yourself.

While lying there listening to the Indians, I amused myself with trying to guess at their subject by their gestures, or some proper name introduced. There can be no more startling evidence of their being a distinct and comparatively aboriginal race, than to hear this unaltered Indian language, which the white man cannot speak nor understand. We may suspect change and deterioration in almost every other particular, but the language which is so wholly unintelligible to us. It took me by surprise, though I had found so many arrow-heads, and convinced me that the Indian was not the invention of historians and poets. It was a purely wild and primitive American sound, as much as the barking of a *chickaree*, and I could not understand a syllable of it; but Paugus, had he been there, would have understood it. These Abenakis gossiped, laughed, and jested, in the language in which Eliot's Indian Bible is written, the language which has been spoken in New England who shall say how long? These were the sounds that issued from the wigwams of this country before Columbus was born; they have not yet died away; and, with remarkably few exceptions, the language of their forefathers is still copious enough for them. I felt that I stood, or rather lay, as near to the primitive man of America, that night, as any of its discoverers ever did.

In the midst of their conversation, Joe suddenly appealed to me to know how long Moosehead Lake was.

Meanwhile, as we lay there, Joe was making and trying his horn, to be ready for hunting after midnight. The St. Francis Indian also amused himself with sounding it, or rather calling through it; for the sound is made with the voice, and not by blowing through the horn. The latter appeared to be a speculator in moose-hides. He bought my companion's for two dollars and a quarter, green. Joe said that it was worth two and a half at Oldtown. Its chief use is for moccasins. One or two of these Indians wore them. I was told, that, by a recent law of Maine, foreigners are not allowed to kill moose there at any season; white Americans can kill them only at a particular season, but the Indians of Maine at all seasons. The St. Francis Indian accordingly asked my companion for a *wighiggin*, or bill, to show, since he was a foreigner. He lived near Sorel. I found that he could write his name very well, *Tahmunt Swasen*. One Ellis, an old white man of Guilford, a town through which we passed, not far from the south end of Moosehead, was the most celebrated moose-hunter of those parts. Indians and whites spoke with equal respect of him. Tahmunt said, that there were more moose here than in the Adirondack country in New York, where he had hunted; that three years before there were a great many about, and there were a great many now in the woods, but they did not come out to the water. It was of no use to hunt them at midnight,—they would not come out then. I asked Sabattis, after he came home, if the moose never attacked him. He answered, that you must not fire many times so as to mad him. "I fire once and hit him in the right place, and in the morning

I find him. He won't go far. But if you keep firing, you mad him. I fired once five bullets, every one through the heart, and he did not mind 'em at all; it only made him more mad." I asked him if they did not hunt them with dogs. He said, that they did so in winter, but never in the summer, for then it was of no use; they would run right off straight and swiftly a hundred miles.

Another Indian said, that the moose, once scared, would run all day. A dog will hang to their lips, and be carried along till he is swung against a tree and drops off. They cannot run on a "glaze," though they can run in snow four feet deep; but the caribou can run on ice. They commonly find two or three moose together. They cover themselves with water, all but their noses, to escape flies. He had the horns of what he called "the black moose that goes in low lands." These spread three or four feet. The "red moose" was another kind, "running on mountains," and had horns which spread six feet. Such were his distinctions. Both can move their horns. The broad flat blades are covered with hair, and are so soft, when the animal is alive, that you can run a knife through them. They regard it as a good or bad sign, if the horns turn this way or that. His caribou horns had been gnawed by mice in his wigwam, but he thought that the horns neither of the moose nor of the caribou were ever gnawed while the creature was alive, as some have asserted. An Indian, whom I met after this at Old-town, who had carried about a bear and other animals of Maine to exhibit, told me that thirty years ago there were not so many moose in Maine as now; also, that the moose were very easily tamed, and would come back when once fed, and so would deer, but not caribou. The Indians of this neighborhood are about as familiar with the moose as we are with the ox, having associated with them for so many generations. Father Rasles, in his Dictionary of the Abenaki Language, gives not only a word for the male moose, (*aianbé,*) and another for the female, (*hèrar,*) but for the bone which is in the middle of the heart of the moose (!), and for his left hind-leg.

There were none of the small deer up there; they are more common about the settlements. One ran into the city of Bangor two years before, and jumped through a window of costly plate glass, and then into a mirror, where it thought it recognized one of its kind, and out again, and so on, leaping over the heads of the crowd, until it was captured. This the inhabitants speak of as the deer that went a-shopping. The last-mentioned Indian spoke of the *lunxus* or Indian devil, (which I take to be the cougar, and not the *Gulo luscus*,) as the only animal in Maine which man need fear; it would follow a man, and did not mind a fire. He also said, that beavers were getting to be pretty numerous again, where we went, but their skins brought so little now that it was not profitable to hunt them.

I had put the ears of our moose, which were ten inches long, to dry along with the moose-meat over the fire, wishing to preserve them; but Sabattis told me that I must skin and cure them, else the hair would all come off. He observed, that they made tobacco-pouches of the skins of their ears, putting the two together inside to inside. I asked him how he got fire; and he produced a little cylindrical box of friction-matches. He also had flints and steel, and some punk, which was not dry; I think it was from the yellow birch. "But suppose you upset, and all these and your powder get wet." "Then," said he, " we wait till we get to where there is some fire." I produced from my pocket a little vial, containing matches, stoppled water-tight, and told him, that, though we were upset, we should still have some dry matches; at which he stared without saying a word.

We lay awake thus a long while talking, and they gave us the meaning of many Indian names of lakes and streams in the vicinity,—especially Tahmunt. I asked the Indian name of Moosehead Lake. Joe answered, *Sebamook*; Tahmunt pronounced it *Sebemook*. When I asked what it meant, they answered, Moosehead Lake. At length, getting my meaning, they alternately repeated the word over to themselves, as a philologist might,—*Sebamook*,—*Sebamook*,—now and then comparing notes in Indian; for there was a slight difference in their dialects; and finally Tahmunt said, "Ugh! I know,"— and he rose up partly on the moose-hide,—"like as here is a place, and there is a place," pointing to different parts of the hide, "and you take water from there and fill this, and it stays here; that is *Sebamook*." I understood him to mean that it was a reservoir of water which did not run away, the river coming in on one side and passing out again near the same place, leaving a permanent bay. Another Indian said, that it meant Large-Bay Lake, and that *Sebago* and *Sebec*, the names of other lakes, were kindred words, meaning large open water. Joe said that *Seboois* meant Little River. I observed their inability, often described, to convey an abstract idea. Having got the idea, though indistinctly, they groped about in vain for words with which to express it. Tahmunt thought that the whites called it Moosehead Lake, because Mount Kineo, which commands it, is shaped like a moose's head, and that Moose River was so called "because the mountain points right across the lake to its mouth." John Josselyn, writing about 1673, says, "Twelve miles from Casco Bay, and passable for men and horses, is a lake, called by the Indians Sebug. On the brink thereof, at one end, is the famous rock, shaped like a moose deer or helk, diaphanous, and called the Moose Rock." He appears to have confounded Sebamook with Sebago, which is nearer, but has no "diaphanous" rock on its shore.

I give more of their definitions, for what they are worth,— partly *because* they differ sometimes from the commonly received ones. They never analyzed these words before. After long deliberation and repeating of the word, for it gave much trouble, Tahmunt said that *Chesuncook* meant a place where many streams emptied in (?), and he enumerated them,— Penobscot, Umbazookskus, Cusabesex, Red Brook, etc.— "*Caucomgomoc*,—what does that mean?" "What are those large white birds?" he asked. "Gulls," said I. "Ugh! Gull Lake."— *Pammadumcook*, Joe thought, meant the Lake with Gravelly Bottom or Bed.— *Kenduskeag*, Tahmunt concluded at last, after asking if birches went up it, for he said that he was not much acquainted with it, meant something like this: "You go up Penobscot till you come to *Kenduskeag*, and you go by, you don't turn up there. That is *Kenduskeag*." (?) Another Indian, however, who knew the river better, told us afterward that it meant Little Eel River.— *Mattawamkeag* was a place where two rivers meet. (?)— *Penobscot* was Rocky River. One writer says, that this was "originally the name of only a section of the main channel, from the head of the tidewater to a short distance above Oldtown."

A very intelligent Indian, whom we afterward met, son-in-law of Neptune, gave us also these other definitions: — *Umbazookskus*, Meadow Stream; *Millinoket*, Place of Islands; *Aboljacarmegus*, Smooth-Ledge Falls (and Dead-Water); *Aboljacarmeguscook*, the stream emptying in; (the last was the word he gave when I asked about *Aboljacknagesic*, which he did not recognize;) *Mattahumkeag*, Sand-Creek Pond; *Piscataquis*, Branch of a River.

I asked our hosts what *Musketaquid*, the Indian name of Concord, Massachusetts, meant; but they changed it to *Musketicook*, and repeated that, and Tahmunt said that it meant Dead Stream, which is probably true. *Cook* appears to mean stream, and perhaps *quid* signifies the place or ground. When I asked the meaning of the names of two of our hills, they answered that they were another language. As Tahmunt said that he traded at Quebec, my companion inquired the meaning of the word *Quebec*, about which there has been so much question. He did not know, but began to conjecture. He asked what those great ships were called that carried soldiers. "Men-of-war," we answered. "Well," he said, " when the English ships came up the river, they could not go any farther, it was so narrow there; they must go back, — go-back, — that 's Que-bec." I mention this to show the value of his authority in the other cases.

Late at night the other two Indians came home from moose-hunting, not having been successful, aroused the fire again, lighted their pipes, smoked awhile, took something strong to drink, and ate some moose-meat, and, finding what room they could, lay down on the moose-hides; and thus we passed the night, two white men and four Indians, side by side.

When I awoke in the morning the weather was drizzling. One of the Indians was lying outside, rolled in his blanket, on the opposite side of the fire, for want of room. Joe had neglected to awake my companion, and he had done no hunting that night. Tahmunt was making a cross-bar for his canoe with a singularly shaped knife, such as I have since seen other Indians using. The blade was thin, about three quarters of an inch wide, and eight or nine inches long, but curved out of its plane into a hook, which he said made it more convenient to shave with. As the Indians very far north and northwest use the same kind of knife, I suspect that it was made according to an aboriginal pattern, though some white artisans may use a similar one. The Indians baked a loaf of flour bread in a spider on its edge before the fire for their breakfast; and while my companion was making tea, I caught a dozen sizable fishes in the Penobscot, two kinds of sucker and one trout. After we had breakfasted by ourselves, one of our bedfellows, who had also breakfasted, came along, and, being invited, took a cup of tea, and finally, taking up the common platter, licked it clean. But he was nothing to a white fellow, a lumberer, who was continually stuffing himself with the Indians' moose-meat, and was the butt of his companions accordingly. He seems to have thought that it was a feast "to eat all." It is commonly said that the white man finally surpasses the Indian on his own ground, and it was proved true in this case. I cannot swear to his employment during the hours of darkness, but I saw him at it again as soon as it was light, though he came a quarter of a mile to his work.

The rain prevented our continuing any longer in the woods; so giving some of our provisions and utensils to the Indians, we took leave of them. This being the steamer's day, I set out for the lake at once.

I walked over the carry alone and waited at the head of the lake. An eagle, or some other large bird, flew screaming away from its perch by the shore at my approach. For an hour after I reached the shore there was not a human being to be seen, and I had all that wide prospect to myself. I thought that I heard the sound of the steamer before she came in sight on the open lake. I noticed at the landing, when the steamer came in, one of our bedfellows, who had been a-moose-hunting the night before, now very sprucely dressed in a clean white shirt and fine black pants, a true Indian dandy, who had evidently come over the carry to show himself to any arrivers on the north shore of Moosehead Lake, just as New York dandies take a turn up Broadway and stand on the steps of a hotel.

Midway the lake we took on board two manly-looking middle-aged men, with their *bateau*, who had been exploring for six weeks as far as the Canada line, and had let their beards grow. They had the skin of a beaver, which they had recently caught, stretched on an oval hoop, though the fur was not good at that season. I talked with one of them, telling him that I had come all this distance partly to see where the white-pine, the Eastern stuff of which our houses are built, grew, but that on this and a previous excursion into another part of Maine I had found it a scarce tree; and I asked him where I must look for it. With a smile, he answered, that he could hardly tell me. However, he said that he had found enough to employ two teams the next winter in a place where there was thought to be none left. What was considered a "top-top" tree now was not looked at twenty years ago, when he first went into the business; but they succeeded very well now with what was considered quite inferior timber then. The explorer used to cut into a tree higher and higher up, to see if it was false-hearted, and if there was a rotten heart as big as his arm, he let it alone; but now they cut such a tree, and sawed it all around the rot, and it made the very best of boards, for in such a case they were never shaky.

One connected with lumbering operations at Bangor told me that the largest pine belonging to his firm, cut the previous winter, "scaled" in the woods four thousand five hundred feet, and was worth ninety dollars in the log at the Bangor boom in Oldtown. They cut a road three and a half miles long for this tree alone. He thought that the principal locality for the white-pine that came down the Penobscot now was at the head of the East Branch and the Allegash, about Webster Stream and Eagle and Chamberlain Lakes. Much timber has been stolen from the public lands. (Pray, what kind of forest-warden is the Public itself?) I heard of one man who, having discovered some particularly fine trees just within the boundaries of the public lands, and not daring to employ an accomplice, cut them down, and by means of block and tackle, without cattle, tumbled them into a stream, and so succeeded in getting off with them without the least assistance. Surely, stealing pine-trees in this way is not so mean as robbing hen-roosts.

We reached Monson that night, and the next day rode to Bangor, all the way in the rain again, varying our route a little. Some of the taverns on this road, which were particularly dirty, were plainly in a transition state from the camp to the house.

The next forenoon we went to Oldtown. One slender old Indian on the Oldtown shore, who recognized my companion, was full of mirth and gestures, like a Frenchman. A Catholic priest crossed to the island in the same *bateau* with us. The Indian houses are framed, mostly of one story, and in rows one behind another, at the south end of the island, with a few scattered ones. I counted about forty, not including the church and what my companion called the council-house. The last, which I suppose is their town-house, was regularly framed and shingled like the rest. There were several of two stories, quite neat, with front-yards enclosed, and one at least had green blinds. Here and there were moose-hides stretched and drying about them. There were no cart-paths, nor tracks of horses, but foot-paths; very little land cultivated, but an abundance of weeds, indigenous and naturalized; more introduced weeds than useful vegetables, as the Indian is said to cultivate the vices rather than the virtues of the white man. Yet this village was cleaner than I expected, far cleaner than such Irish villages as I have seen. The children were not particularly ragged nor dirty. The little boys met us with bow in hand and arrow on string, and cried, "Put up a cent." Verily, the Indian has but a feeble hold on his bow now; but the curiosity of the white man is insatiable, and from the first he has been eager to witness this forest accomplishment. That elastic piece of wood with its feathered dart, so sure to be unstrung by contact with civilization, will serve for the type, the coat-of-arms of the savage. Alas for the Hunter Race! the white man has driven off their game, and substituted a cent in its place. I saw an Indian woman washing at the water's edge. She stood on a rock, and, after dipping the clothes in the stream, laid them on the rock, and beat them with a short club. In the graveyard, which was crowded with graves, and overrun with weeds, I noticed an inscription in Indian, painted on a wooden grave-board. There was a large wooden cross on the island.

Since my companion knew him, we called on Governor Neptune, who lived in a little "ten-footer," one of the humblest of them all. Personalities are allowable in speaking of public men, therefore I will give the particulars of our visit. He was a-bed. When we entered the room, which was one half of the house, he was sitting on the side of the bed. There was a clock hanging in one corner. He had on a black frock-coat, and black pants, much worn, white cotton shirt, socks, a red silk handkerchief about his neck, and a straw hat. His black hair was only slightly grayed. He had very broad cheeks, and his features were decidedly and refreshingly different from those of any of the upstart Native American party whom I have seen. He was no darker than many old white men. He told me that he was eighty-nine; but he was going a-moose-hunting that fall, as he had been the previous one. Probably his companions did the hunting. We saw various squaws dodging about. One sat on the bed by his side and helped him out with his stories. They were remarkably cor-pulent, with smooth, round faces, apparently full of good-humor. Certainly our much-abused climate had not dried up their adipose substance. While we were there,—for we stayed a good while,—one went over to Oldtown, returned and cut out a dress, which she had bought, on another bed in the room. The Governor said, that "he could remember when the moose were much larger; that they did not use to be in the woods, but came out of the water, as all deer did. Moose was whale once. Away down Merrimack way, a whale came ashore in a shallow bay. Sea went out and left him, and he came up on land a moose. What made them know he was a whale was, that at first, before he began to run in bushes, he had no bow-els inside, but"——and then the squaw who sat on the bed by his side, as the Governor's aid, and had been putting in a word now and then and confirming the story, asked me what we called that soft thing we find along the sea-shore. "Jelly-fish," I suggested. "Yes," said he, "no bowels, but jelly-fish."

There may be some truth in what he said about the moose growing larger formerly; for the quaint John Josselyn, a phy-sician who spent many years in this very district of Maine in the seventeenth century, says, that the tips of their horns "are sometimes found to be two fathoms asunder,"—and he is particular to tell us that a fathom is six feet,—"and [they are] in height, from the toe of the fore foot to the pitch of the shoulder, twelve foot, both which hath been taken by some of my sceptique readers to be monstrous lies"; and he adds, "There are certain transcendentia in every creature, which are the indelible characters of God, and which discover God." This is a greater dilemma to be caught in than is presented by the cranium of the young Bechuana ox, apparently another of the *transcendentia*, in the collection of Thomas Steel, Upper Brook Street, London, whose "entire length of horn, from tip to tip, along the curve, is 13 ft. 5 in.; distance (straight) between the tips of the horns, 8 ft. 8½ in." However, the size both of the moose and the cougar, as I have found, is generally rather underrated than overrated, and I should be inclined to add to the popular estimate a part of what I subtracted from Josselyn's.

But we talked mostly with the Governor's son-in-law, a very sensible Indian; and the Governor, being so old and deaf, permitted himself to be ignored, while we asked questions about him. The former said, that there were two political parties among them,—one in favor of schools, and the other opposed to them, or rather they did not wish to resist the priest, who was opposed to them. The first had just prevailed at the election and sent their man to the legislature. Neptune and Aitteon and he himself were in favor of schools. He said, "If Indians got learning, they would keep their money." When we asked where Joe's father, Aitteon, was, he knew that he must be at Lincoln, though he was about going a-moose-hunting, for a messenger had just gone to him there to get his signature to some papers. I asked Neptune if they had any of the old breed of dogs yet. He answered, "Yes." "But that," said I, pointing to one that had just come in, "is a Yankee dog." He assented. I said that he did not look like a good one. "O yes!" he said, and he told, with much gusto, how, the year before, he had caught and held by the throat a wolf. A very small black puppy rushed into the room and made at the Governor's feet, as he sat in his stockings with his legs dangling from the bedside. The Governor rubbed his hands and dared him to come on, entering into the sport with spirit. Nothing more that was significant transpired, to my knowledge, during this interview. This was the first time that

I ever called on a governor, but, as I did not ask for an office, I can speak of it with the more freedom.

An Indian who was making canoes behind a house, looking up pleasantly from his work,—for he knew my companion,—said that his name was Old John Pennyweight. I had heard of him long before, and I inquired after one of his contemporaries, Joe Four-pence-ha'penny; but, alas! he no longer circulates. I made a faithful study of canoe-building, and I thought that I should like to serve an apprenticeship at that trade for one season, going into the woods for bark with my "boss," making the canoe there, and returning in it at last.

While the *bateau* was coming over to take us off, I picked up some fragments of arrow-heads on the shore, and one broken stone chisel, which were greater novelties to the Indians than to me. After this, on Old Fort Hill, at the bend of the Penobscot, three miles above Bangor, looking for the site of an Indian town which some think stood thereabouts, I found more arrow-heads, and two little dark and crumbling fragments of Indian earthenware, in the ashes of their fires. The Indians on the Island appeared to live quite happily and to be well treated by the inhabitants of Oldtown.

We visited Veazie's mills, just below the Island, where were sixteen sets of saws,—some gang saws, sixteen in a gang, not to mention circular saws. On one side, they were hauling the logs up an inclined plane by water-power; on the other, passing out the boards, planks, and sawed timber, and forming them into rafts. The trees were literally drawn and quartered there. In forming the rafts, they use the lower three feet of hard-wood saplings, which have a crooked and knobbed but-end, for bolts, passing them up through holes bored in the corners and sides of the rafts, and keying them. In another apartment they were making fence-slats, such as stand all over New England, out of odds and ends,—and it may be that I saw where the picket-fence behind which I dwell at home came from. I was surprised to find a boy collecting the long edgings of boards as fast as cut off, and thrusting them down a hopper, where they were *ground up* beneath the mill, that they might be out of the way; otherwise they accumulate in vast piles by the side of the building, increasing the danger from fire, or, floating off, they obstruct the river. This was not only a saw-mill, but a grist-mill, then. The inhabitants of Oldtown, Stillwater, and Bangor cannot suffer for want of kindling stuff, surely. Some get their living exclusively by picking up the drift-wood and selling it by the cord in the winter. In one place I saw where an Irishman, who keeps a team and a man for the purpose, had covered the shore for a long distance with regular piles, and I was told that he had sold twelve hundred dollars' worth in a year. Another, who lived by the shore, told me that he got all the material of his out-buildings and fences from the river; and in that neighborhood I perceived that this refuse wood was frequently used instead of sand to fill hollows with, being apparently cheaper than dirt.

I got my first clear view of Ktaadn, on this excursion, from a hill about two miles northwest of Bangor, whither I went for this purpose. After this I was ready to return to Massachusetts.

Humboldt has written an interesting chapter on the primitive forest, but no one has yet described for me the difference between that wild forest which once occupied our oldest townships, and the tame one which I find there to-day. It is a difference which would be worth attending to. The civilized man not only clears the land permanently to a great extent, and cultivates open fields, but he tames and cultivates to a certain extent the forest itself. By his mere presence, almost, he changes the nature of the trees as no other creature does. The sun and air, and perhaps fire, have been introduced, and grain raised where it stands. It has lost its wild, damp, and shaggy look, the countless fallen and decaying trees are gone, and consequently that thick coat of moss which lived on them is gone too. The earth is comparatively bare and smooth and dry. The most primitive places left with us are the swamps, where the spruce still grows shaggy with usnea. The surface of the ground in the Maine woods is everywhere spongy and saturated with moisture. I noticed that the plants which cover the forest floor there are such as are commonly confined to swamps with us,—the *Clintonia borealis*, orchises, creeping snowberry, and others; and the prevailing aster there is the

Aster acuminatus, which with us grows in damp and shady woods. The asters *cordifolius* and *macrophyllus* also are common, asters of little or no color, and sometimes without petals. I saw no soft, spreading, second-growth white-pines, with smooth bark, acknowledging the presence of the wood-chopper, but even the young white-pines were all tall and slender rough-barked trees.

Those Maine woods differ essentially from ours. There you are never reminded that the wilderness which you are threading is, after all, some villager's familiar wood-lot, some widow's thirds, from which her ancestors have sledded fuel for generations, minutely described in some old deed which is recorded, of which the owner has got a plan too, and old bound-marks may be found every forty rods, if you will search. 'T is true, the map may inform you that you stand on land granted by the State to some academy, or on Bingham's purchase; but these names do not impose on you, for you see nothing to remind you of the academy or of Bingham. What were the "forests" of England to these? One writer relates of the Isle of Wight, that in Charles the Second's time "there were woods in the island so complete and extensive, that it is said a squirrel might have travelled in several parts many leagues together on the top of the trees." If it were not for the rivers, (and he might go round their heads,) a squirrel could here travel thus the whole breadth of the country.

We have as yet had no adequate account of a primitive pine-forest. I have noticed that in a physical atlas lately published in Massachusetts, and used in our schools, the " wood land" of North America is limited almost solely to the valleys of the Ohio and some of the Great Lakes, and the great pine-forests of the globe are not represented. In our vicinity, for instance, New Brunswick and Maine are exhibited as bare as Greenland. It may be that the children of Greenville, at the foot of Moosehead Lake, who surely are not likely to be scared by an owl, are referred to the valley of the Ohio to get an idea of a forest; but they would not know what to do with their moose, bear, caribou, beaver, etc., there. Shall we leave it to an Englishman to inform us, that "in North America, both in the United States and Canada, are the most extensive pine-forests in the world"? The greater part of New Brunswick, the northern half of Maine, and adjacent parts of Canada, not to mention the northeastern part of New York and other tracts farther off, are still covered with an almost unbroken pine-forest.

But Maine, perhaps, will soon be where Massachusetts is. A good part of her territory is already as bare and commonplace as much of our neighborhood, and her villages generally are not so well shaded as ours. We seem to think that the earth must go through the ordeal of sheep-pasturage before it is habitable by man. Consider Nahant, the resort of all the fashion of Boston,—which peninsula I saw but indistinctly in the twilight, when I steamed by it, and thought that it was unchanged since the discovery. John Smith described it in 1614 as "the Mattahunts, two pleasant isles of groves, gardens, and cornfields"; and others tell us that it was once well wooded, and even furnished timber to build the wharves of Boston. Now it is difficult to make a tree grow there, and the visitor comes away with a vision of Mr. Tudor's ugly fences, a rod high, designed to protect a few pear-shrubs. And what are we coming to in our Middlesex towns?—a bald, staring town-house, or meeting-house, and a bare liberty-pole, as leafless as it is fruitless, for all I can see. We shall be obliged to import the timber for the last, hereafter, or splice such sticks as we have;—and our ideas of liberty are equally mean with these. The very willow-rows lopped every three years for fuel or powder,—and every sizable pine and oak, or other forest tree, cut down within the memory of man! As if individual speculators were to be allowed to export the clouds out of the sky, or the stars out of the firmament, one by one. We shall be reduced to gnaw the very crust of the earth for nutriment.

They have even descended to smaller game. They have lately, as I hear, invented a machine for chopping up huckleberry-bushes fine, and so converting them into fuel!—bushes which, for fruit alone, are worth all the pear-trees in the country many times over. (I can give you a list of the three best kinds, if you want it.) At this rate, we shall all be obliged to let our beards grow at least, if only to hide the nakedness of the land and make a sylvan appearance. The farmer sometimes talks of "brushing up," simply as if bare ground looked better than clothed ground, than that which wears its natural vesture,—as if the wild hedges, which, perhaps, are more to his children than his whole farm beside, were *dirt*. I know of one who deserves to be called the Tree-hater, and, perhaps, to leave this for a new patronymic to his children. You would think that he had been warned by an oracle that he would be killed by the fall of a tree, and so was resolved to anticipate them. The journalists think that they cannot say too much in favor of such "improvements" in husbandry; it is a safe theme, like piety; but as for the beauty of one of these "model farms," I would as lief see a patent churn and a man turning it. They are, commonly, places merely where somebody is making money, it may be counterfeiting. The virtue of making two blades of grass grow where only one grew before does not begin to be superhuman.

Nevertheless, it was a relief to get back to our smooth, but still varied landscape. For a permanent residence, it seemed to me that there could be no comparison between this and the wilderness, necessary as the latter is for a resource and a background, the raw material of all our civilization. The wilderness is simple, almost to barrenness. The partially cultivated country it is which chiefly has inspired, and will continue to inspire, the strains of poets, such as compose the mass of any literature. Our woods are sylvan, and their inhabitants woodmen and rustics,—that is, *selvaggia*, and the inhabitants are *salvages*. A civilized man, using the word in the ordinary sense, with his ideas and associations, must at length pine there, like a cultivated plant, which clasps its fibres about a crude and undissolved mass of peat. At the extreme North, the voyagers are obliged to dance and act plays for employment. Perhaps our own woods and fields,—in the best wooded towns, where we need not quarrel about the huckleberries,—with the primitive swamps scattered here and there in their midst, but not prevailing over them, are the perfection of parks and groves, gardens, arbors, paths, vistas, and landscapes. They are the natural consequence of what art and refinement we as a people have,—the common which each village possesses, its true paradise, in comparison with which all elaborately and wilfully wealth-constructed parks and gardens are paltry imitations. Or, I would rather say, such *were* our groves twenty years ago. The poet's, commonly, is not a logger's path, but a woodman's. The logger and pioneer have preceded him, like John the Baptist; eaten the wild honey, it may be, but the locusts also; banished decaying wood and the spongy mosses which feed on it, and built hearths and humanized Nature for him.

But there are spirits of a yet more liberal culture, to whom no simplicity is barren. There are not only stately pines, but fragile flowers, like the orchises, commonly described as too delicate for cultivation, which derive their nutriment from the crudest mass of peat. These remind us, that, not only for strength, but for beauty, the poet must, from time to time, travel the logger's path and the Indian's trail, to drink at some new and more bracing fountain of the Muses, far in the recesses of the wilderness.

The kings of England formerly had their forests "to hold the king's game," for sport or food, sometimes destroying villages to create or extend them; and I think that they were impelled by a true instinct. Why should not we, who have renounced the king's authority, have our national preserves, where no villages need be destroyed, in which the bear and panther, and some even of the hunter race, may still exist, and not be "civilized off the face of the earth,"—our forests, not to hold the king's game merely, but to hold and preserve the king himself also, the lord of creation,—not for idle sport or food, but for inspiration and our own true re-creation? or shall we, like villains, grub them all up, poaching on our own national domains?

The Allegash and East Branch

I STARTED on my third excursion to the Maine woods Monday, July 20th, 1857, with one companion, arriving at Bangor the next day at noon. We had hardly left the steamer, when we passed Molly Molasses in the street. As long as she lives the Penobscots may be considered extant as a tribe. The succeeding morning, a relative of mine, who is well acquainted with the Penobscot Indians, and who had been my companion in my two previous excursions into the Maine woods, took me in his wagon to Oldtown, to assist me in obtaining an Indian for this expedition. We were ferried across to the Indian Island in a batteau. The ferryman's boy had got the key to it, but the father who was a blacksmith, after a little hesitation, cut the chain with a cold-chisel on a rock. He told us that the Indians were nearly all gone to the seaboard and to Massachusetts, partly on account of the small-pox, of which they are very much afraid, having broken out in Oldtown, and it was doubtful whether we should find a suitable one at home. The old chief Neptune, however, was there still. The first man we saw on the island was an Indian named Joseph Polis, whom my relative had known from a boy, and now addressed familiarly as "Joe." He was dressing a deerskin in his yard. The skin was spread over a slanting log, and he was scraping it with a stick, held by both hands. He was stoutly built, perhaps a little above the middle height, with a broad face, and, as others said, perfect Indian features and complexion. His house was a two-story white one with blinds, the best looking that I noticed there, and as good as an average one on a New England village street. It was surrounded by a garden and fruit-trees, single cornstalks standing thinly amid the beans. We asked him if he knew any good Indian who would like to go into the woods with us, that is, to the Allegash Lakes, by way of Moosehead, and return by the East Branch of the Penobscot, or vary from this as we pleased. To which he answered, out of that strange remoteness in which the Indian ever dwells to the white man, "Me like to go myself; me want to get some moose"; and kept on scraping the skin. His brother had

been into the woods with my relative only a year or two before, and the Indian now inquired what the latter had done
to him, that he did not come back, for he had not seen nor
heard from him since.

At length we got round to the more interesting topic again.
The ferryman had told us that all the best Indians were gone
except Polis, who was one of the aristocracy. He to be sure
would be the best man we could have, but if he went at all
would want a great price; so we did not expect to get him.
Polis asked at first two dollars a day, but agreed to go for a
dollar and a half, and fifty cents a week for his canoe. He
would come to Bangor with his canoe by the seven o'clock
train that evening,—we might depend on him. We thought
ourselves lucky to secure the services of this man, who was
known to be particularly steady and trustworthy.

I spent the afternoon with my companion, who had remained in Bangor, in preparing for our expedition, purchasing provisions, hard bread, pork, coffee, sugar, &c., and some
India-rubber clothing.

We had at first thought of exploring the St. John from its
source to its mouth, or else to go up the Penobscot by its
East Branch to the lakes of the St. John, and return by way
of Chesuncook and Moosehead. We had finally inclined to the
last route, only reversing the order of it, going by way of
Moosehead, and returning by the Penobscot, otherwise it
would have been all the way up stream and taken twice as
long.

At evening the Indian arrived in the cars, and I led the way
while he followed me three quarters of a mile to my friend's
house, with the canoe on his head. I did not know the exact
route myself, but steered by the lay of the land, as I do in
Boston, and I tried to enter into conversation with him, but
as he was puffing under the weight of his canoe, not having
the usual apparatus for carrying it, but, above all, was an Indian, I might as well have been thumping on the bottom of
his birch the while. In answer to the various observations
which I made by way of breaking the ice, he only grunted
vaguely from beneath his canoe once or twice, so that I knew
he was there.

Early the next morning (July 23d) the stage called for us,

the Indian having breakfasted with us, and already placed the baggage in the canoe to see how it would go. My companion and I had each a large knapsack as full as it would hold, and we had two large India-rubber bags which held our provision and utensils. As for the Indian, all the baggage he had, beside his axe and gun, was a blanket, which he brought loose in his hand. However, he had laid in a store of tobacco and a new pipe for the excursion. The canoe was securely lashed diagonally across the top of the stage, with bits of carpet tucked under the edge to prevent its chafing. The very accommodating driver appeared as much accustomed to carrying canoes in this way as bandboxes.

At the Bangor House we took in four men bound on a hunting excursion, one of the men going as cook. They had a dog, a middling-sized brindled cur, which ran by the side of the stage, his master showing his head and whistling from time to time; but after we had gone about three miles the dog was suddenly missing, and two of the party went back for him, while the stage, which was full of passengers, waited. I suggested that he had taken the back track for the Bangor House. At length one man came back, while the other kept on. This whole party of hunters declared their intention to stop till the dog was found; but the very obliging driver was ready to wait a spell longer. He was evidently unwilling to lose so many passengers, who would have taken a private conveyance, or perhaps the other line of stages, the next day. Such progress did we make with a journey of over sixty miles, to be accomplished that day, and a rain-storm just setting in. We discussed the subject of dogs and their instincts till it was threadbare, while we waited there, and the scenery of the suburbs of Bangor is still distinctly impressed on my memory. After full half an hour the man returned, leading the dog by a rope. He had overtaken him just as he was entering the Bangor House. He was then tied on the top of the stage, but being wet and cold, several times in the course of the journey he jumped off, and I saw him dangling by his neck. This dog was depended on to stop bears with. He had already stopped one somewhere in New Hampshire, and I can testify that he stopped a stage in Maine. This party of four probably paid nothing for the dog's ride, nor for his run, while our party of three paid two dollars, and were charged four for the light canoe which lay still on the top.

It soon began to rain, and grew more and more stormy as the day advanced. This was the third time that I had passed over this route, and it rained steadily each time all day. We accordingly saw but little of the country. The stage was crowded all the way, and I attended the more to my fellow-travellers. If you had looked inside this coach you would have thought that we were prepared to run the gauntlet of a band of robbers, for there were four or five guns on the front seat, the Indian's included, and one or two on the back one, each man holding his darling in his arms. One had a gun which carried twelve to a pound. It appeared that this party of hunters was going our way, but much farther down the Allegash and St. John, and thence up some other stream, and across to the Ristigouche and the Bay of Chaleur, to be gone six weeks. They had canoes, axes, and supplies deposited some distance along the route. They carried flour, and were to have new bread made every day. Their leader was a handsome man about thirty years old, of good height, but not apparently robust, of gentlemanly address and faultless toilet; such a one as you might expect to meet on Broadway. In fact, in the popular sense of the word, he was the most "gentlemanly" appearing man in the stage, or that we saw on the road. He had a fair white complexion, as if he had always lived in the shade, and an intellectual face, and with his quiet manners might have passed for a divinity student who had seen something of the world. I was surprised to find, on talking with him in the course of the day's journey, that he was a hunter at all,—for his gun was not much exposed,—and yet more to find that he was probably the chief white hunter of Maine, and was known all along the road. He had also hunted in some of the States farther south and west. I afterwards heard him spoken of as one who could endure a great deal of exposure and fatigue without showing the effect of it; and he could not only use guns, but make them, being himself a gunsmith. In the spring, he had saved a stage-driver and two passengers from drowning in the backwater of the Piscataquis in Foxcroft on this road, having swum ashore in the freezing water and made a raft and got them off,—though the horses were drowned,—at great risk to himself, while the only other man who could swim withdrew to the nearest house to prevent freezing. He could now ride over this road for nothing. He knew our man, and remarked that we had a good Indian there, a good hunter; adding that he was said to be worth $6,000. The Indian also knew him, and said to me, "the great hunter."

The former told me that he practised a kind of still hunting, new or uncommon in those parts, that the caribou, for instance, fed round and round the same meadow, returning on the same path, and he lay in wait for them.

The Indian sat on the front seat, saying nothing to anybody, with a stolid expression of face, as if barely awake to what was going on. Again I was struck by the peculiar vagueness of his replies when addressed in the stage, or at the taverns. He really never said anything on such occasions. He was merely stirred up, like a wild beast, and passively muttered some insignificant response. His answer, in such cases, was never the consequence of a positive mental energy, but vague as a puff of smoke, suggesting no *responsibility*, and if you considered it, you would find that you had got nothing out of him. This was instead of the conventional palaver and smartness of the white man, and equally profitable. Most get no more than this out of the Indian, and pronounce him stolid accordingly. I was surprised to see what a foolish and impertinent style a Maine man, a passenger, used in addressing him, as if he were a child, which only made his eyes glisten a little. A tipsy Canadian asked him at a tavern, in a drawling tone, if he smoked, to which he answered with an indefinite "yes." "Won't you lend me your pipe a little while?" asked the other. He replied, looking straight by the man's head, with a face singularly vacant to all neighboring interests, "Me got no pipe"; yet I had seen him put a new one, with a supply of tobacco, into his pocket that morning.

Our little canoe, so neat and strong, drew a favorable criticism from all the wiseacres among the tavern loungers along the road. By the roadside, close to the wheels, I noticed a splendid great purple-fringed orchis with a spike as big as an epilobium, which I would fain have stopped the stage to pluck, but as this had never been known to stop a bear, like the cur on the stage, the driver would probably have thought it a waste of time.

When we reached the lake, about half past eight in the evening, it was still steadily raining, and harder than before; and, in that fresh, cool atmosphere, the hylodes were peeping and the toads ringing about the lake universally, as in the spring with us. It was as if the seasons had revolved backward two or three months, or I had arrived at the abode of perpetual spring.

We had expected to go upon the lake at once, and after paddling up two or three miles, to camp on one of its islands; but on account of the steady and increasing rain, we decided to go to one of the taverns for the night, though, for my own part, I should have preferred to camp out.

About four o'clock the next morning, (July 24th,) though it was quite cloudy, accompanied by the landlord to the water's edge, in the twilight, we launched our canoe from a rock on the Moosehead Lake. When I was there four years before we had a rather small canoe for three persons, and I had thought that this time I would get a larger one, but the present one was even smaller than that. It was 18¼ feet long by 2 feet 6½ inches wide in the middle, and one foot deep within, as I found by measurement, and I judged that it would weigh not far from eighty pounds. The Indian had recently made it himself, and its smallness was partly compensated for by its newness, as well as stanchness and solidity, it being made of very thick bark and ribs. Our baggage weighed about 166 pounds, so that the canoe carried about 600 pounds in all, or the weight of four men. The principal part of the baggage was, as usual, placed in the middle of the broadest part, while we stowed ourselves in the chinks and crannies that were left before and behind it, where there was no room to extend our legs, the loose articles being tucked into the ends. The canoe was thus as closely packed as a market-basket, and might possibly have been upset without spilling any of its contents. The Indian sat on a cross-bar in the stern, but we flat on the bottom, with a splint or chip behind our backs, to protect them from the cross-bar, and one of us commonly paddled with the Indian. He foresaw that we should not want a pole till we reached the Umbazookskus River, it being either dead water or down stream so far, and he was prepared to make a sail of his blanket in the bows, if the wind should be fair; but we never used it.

It had rained more or less the four previous days, so that we thought we might count on some fair weather. The wind was at first southwesterly.

Paddling along the eastern side of the lake in the still of the morning, we soon saw a few sheldrakes, which the Indian called *Shecorways*, and some peetweets *Naramekechus*, on the rocky shore; we also saw and heard loons, *medawisla*, which he said was a sign of wind. It was inspiriting to hear the regular dip of the paddles, as if they were our fins or flippers, and to realize that we were at length fairly embarked. We who had felt strangely as stage-passengers and tavern-lodgers were suddenly naturalized there and presented with the freedom of the lakes and the woods. Having passed the small rocky isles within two or three miles of the foot of the lake, we had a short consultation respecting our course, and inclined to the western shore for the sake of its lee; for otherwise, if the wind should rise, it would be impossible for us to reach Mount Kineo, which is about midway up the lake on the east side, but at its narrowest part, where probably we could recross if we took the western side. The wind is the chief obstacle to crossing the lakes, especially in so small a canoe. The Indian remarked several times that he did not like to cross the lakes "in littlum canoe," but nevertheless, "just as we say, it made no odds to him." He sometimes took a straight course up the middle of the lake between Sugar and Deer Islands, when there was no wind.

Measured on the map, Moosehead Lake is twelve miles wide at the widest place, and thirty miles long in a direct line, but longer as it lies. The captain of the steamer called it thirty-eight miles as he steered. We should probably go about forty. The Indian said that it was called "*Mspame*, because large water." Squaw Mountain rose darkly on our left, near the outlet of the Kennebec, and what the Indian called Spencer Bay Mountain, on the east, and already we saw Mount Kineo before us in the north.

Paddling near the shore, we frequently heard the *pe-pe* of the olive-sided fly-catcher, also the wood-pewee, and the kingfisher, thus early in the morning. The Indian reminding us that he could not work without eating, we stopped to breakfast on the main shore, southwest of Deer Island, at a spot where the *Mimulus ringens* grew abundantly. We took out our bags, and the Indian made a fire under a very large bleached log, using white-pine bark from a stump, though he said that hemlock was better, and kindling with canoe-birch bark. Our table was a large piece of freshly peeled birch-bark, laid wrong-side-up, and our breakfast consisted of hard bread, fried pork, and strong coffee, well sweetened, in which we did not miss the milk.

While we were getting breakfast a brood of twelve black dippers, half grown, came paddling by within three or four rods, not at all alarmed; and they loitered about as long as we stayed, now huddled close together, within a circle of eighteen inches in diameter, now moving off in a long line, very cunningly. Yet they bore a certain proportion to the great Moosehead Lake on whose bosom they floated, and I felt as if they were under its protection.

Looking northward from this place it appeared as if we were entering a large bay, and we did not know whether we should be obliged to diverge from our course and keep outside a point which we saw, or should find a passage between this and the mainland. I consulted my map and used my glass, and the Indian did the same, but we could not find our place exactly on the map, nor could we detect any break in the shore. When I asked the Indian the way, he answered "I don't know," which I thought remarkable, since he had said that he was familiar with the lake; but it appeared that he had never been up this side. It was misty dog-day weather, and we had already penetrated a smaller bay of the same kind, and knocked the bottom out of it, though we had been obliged to pass over a small bar, between an island and the shore, where there was but just breadth and depth enough to float the canoe, and the Indian had observed, "Very easy makum bridge here," but now it seemed that, if we held on, we should be fairly embayed. Presently, however, though we had not stirred, the mist lifted somewhat, and revealed a break in the shore northward, showing that the point was a portion of Deer Island, and that our course lay westward of it. Where it had seemed a continuous shore even through a glass, one portion was now seen by the naked eye to be much more distant than the other which overlapped it, merely by the greater thickness of the mist which still rested on it, while the nearer or island portion was comparatively bare and green. The line of separation was very distinct, and the Indian immediately remarked, "I guess you and I go there,—I guess there's room for my canoe there." This was his common expression instead of saying we. He never addressed us by our names, though curious to know how they were spelled and what they meant, while we called him Polis. He had already guessed very accurately at our ages, and said that he was forty-eight.

After breakfast I emptied the melted pork that was left into the lake, making what sailors call a "slick," and watching to see how much it spread over and smoothed the agitated surface. The Indian looked at it a moment and said, "That make hard paddlum thro'; hold 'em canoe. So say old times."

We hastily reloaded, putting the dishes loose in the bows, that they might be at hand when wanted, and set out again. The western shore, near which we paddled along, rose gently to a considerable height, and was everywhere densely covered with the forest, in which was a large proportion of hard wood to enliven and relieve the fir and spruce.

The Indian said that the usnea lichen which we saw hanging from the trees was called *chorchorque*. We asked him the names of several small birds which we heard this morning. The wood-thrush, which was quite common, and whose note he imitated, he said was called *Adelungquamooktum*; but sometimes he could not tell the name of some small bird which I heard and knew, but he said, "I tell all the birds about here,—this country; can't tell littlum noise, but I see 'em, then I can tell."

I observed that I should like to go to school to him to learn his language, living on the Indian island the while; could not that be done? "O, yer," he replied, "good many do so." I asked how long he thought it would take. He said one week. I told him that in this voyage I would tell him all I knew, and he should tell me all he knew, to which he readily agreed.

The birds sang quite as in our woods,—the red-eye, redstart, veery, wood-pewee, etc., but we saw no bluebirds in all our journey, and several told me in Bangor that they had not the bluebird there. Mt. Kineo, which was generally visible, though occasionally concealed by islands or the mainland in front, had a level bar of cloud concealing its summit, and all the mountain-tops about the lake were cut off at the same height. Ducks of various kinds—sheldrake, summer ducks, etc.—were quite common, and ran over the water before us as fast as a horse trots. Thus they were soon out of sight.

The Indian asked the meaning of *reality*, as near as I could make out the word, which he said one of us had used; also of "*interrent*," that is intelligent. I observed that he could rarely sound the letter r, but used l, as also r for l sometimes; as *load* for road, *pickelel* for pickerel, *Soogle* Island for Sugar Island, *lock* for rock, etc. Yet he trilled the r pretty well after me.

He generally added the syllable *um* to his words when he could,—as padl*um*, etc. I have once heard a Chippewa lecture, who made his audience laugh unintentionally by putting *m* after the word *too*, which word he brought in continually and unnecessarily, accenting and prolonging this sound into *m ar* sonorously as if it were necessary to bring in so much of his vernacular as a relief to his organs, a compensation for twisting his jaws about, and putting his tongue into every corner of his mouth, as he complained that he was obliged to do when he spoke English. There was so much of the Indian accent resounding through his English, so much of the "bow-arrow tang" as my neighbor calls it, and I have no doubt that word seemed to him the best pronounced. It was a wild and refreshing sound, like that of the wind among the pines, or the booming of the surf on the shore.

I asked him the meaning of the word *Musketicook*, the Indian name of Concord River. He pronounced it *Muskéeticook*, emphasizing the second syllable with a peculiar guttural sound, and said that it meant "Dead-water," which it is, and in this definition he agreed exactly with the St. Francis Indian with whom I talked in 1853.

On a point on the mainland some miles southwest of Sandbar Island, where we landed to stretch our legs and look at the vegetation, going inland a few steps, I discovered a fire still glowing beneath its ashes, where somebody had breakfasted, and a bed of twigs prepared for the following night. So I knew not only that they had just left, but that they designed to return, and by the breadth of the bed that there was more than one in the party. You might have gone within six feet of these signs without seeing them. There grew the beaked hazel, the only hazel which I saw on this journey, the *Diervilla*, rue seven feet high, which was very abundant on all the lake and river shores, and *Cornus stolonifera*, or red osier, whose bark, the Indian said, was good to smoke, and was called *maquoxigill*, "tobacco before white people came to this country, Indian tobacco."

The Indian was always very careful in approaching the shore, lest he should injure his canoe on the rocks, letting it swing round slowly sidewise, and was still more particular that we should not step into it on shore, nor till it floated free, and then should step gently lest we should open its seams, or make a hole in the bottom. He said that he would tell us when to jump.

Soon after leaving this point we passed the mouth of the Kennebec, and heard and saw the falls at the dam there, for even Moosehead Lake is dammed. After passing Deer Island, we saw the little steamer from Greenville, far east in the middle of the lake, and she appeared nearly stationary. Sometimes we could hardly tell her from an island which had a few trees on it. Here we were exposed to the wind from over the whole breadth of the lake, and ran a little risk of being swamped. While I had my eye fixed on the spot where a large fish had leaped, we took in a gallon or two of water, which filled my lap; but we soon reached the shore and took the canoe over the bar, at Sand-bar Island, a few feet wide only, and so saved a considerable distance. One landed first at a more sheltered place, and walking round caught the canoe by the prow, to prevent it being injured against the shore.

Again we crossed a broad bay opposite the mouth of Moose River, before reaching the narrow strait at Mount Kineo, made what the voyageurs call a *traverse*, and found the water quite rough. A very little wind on these broad lakes raises a sea which will swamp a canoe. Looking off from a lee shore, the surface may appear to be very little agitated, almost smooth, a mile distant, or if you see a few white crests they appear nearly level with the rest of the lake; but when you get out so far, you may find quite a sea running, and erelong, before you think of it, a wave will gently creep up the side of the canoe and fill your lap, like a monster deliberately covering you with its slime before it swallows you, or it will strike the canoe violently and break into it. The same thing may happen when the wind rises suddenly, though it were perfectly calm and smooth there a few minutes before; so that nothing can save you, unless you can swim ashore, for it is impossible to get into a canoe again when it is upset. Since you sit flat on the bottom, though the danger should not be imminent, a little water is a great inconvenience, not to mention the wetting of your provisions. We rarely crossed even a bay directly, from point to point, when there was wind, but made a slight curve corresponding somewhat to the shore, that we might the sooner reach it if the wind increased.

When the wind is aft, and not too strong, the Indian makes a spritsail of his blanket. He thus easily skims over the whole length of this lake in a day.

The Indian paddled on one side, and one of us on the other, to keep the canoe steady, and when he wanted to change hands he would say "t'other side." He asserted, in answer to our questions, that he had never upset a canoe himself, though he may have been upset by others.

Think of our little egg-shell of a canoe tossing across that great lake, a mere black speck to the eagle soaring above it.

My companion trailed for trout as we paddled along, but the Indian warning him that a big fish might upset us, for there are some very large ones there, he agreed to pass the line quickly to him in the stern if he had a bite. Beside trout, I heard of cusk, white-fish, &c., as found in this lake.

While we were crossing this bay, where Mount Kineo rose dark before us, within two or three miles, the Indian repeated the tradition respecting this mountain's having anciently been a cow moose,—how a mighty Indian hunter, whose name I forget, succeeding in killing this queen of the moose tribe with great difficulty, while her calf was killed somewhere among the islands in Penobscot Bay, and, to his eyes, this mountain had still the form of the moose in a reclining posture, its precipitous side presenting the outline of her head.

He told this at some length, though it did not amount to much, and with apparent good faith, and asked us how we supposed the hunter could have killed such a mighty moose as that,—how we could do it. Whereupon a man-of-war to fire broadsides into her was suggested, etc. An Indian tells such a story as if he thought it deserved to have a good deal said about it, only he has not got it to say, and so he makes up for the deficiency by a drawling tone, long-windedness, and a dumb wonder which he hopes will be contagious.

We approached the land again through pretty rough water, and then steered directly across the lake, at its narrowest part, to the eastern side, and were soon partly under the lee of the mountain, about a mile north of the Kineo House, having paddled about twenty miles. It was now about noon.

We designed to stop there that afternoon and night, and spent half an hour looking along the shore northward for a suitable place to camp. We took out all our baggage at one place in vain, it being too rocky and uneven, and while engaged in this search we made our first acquaintance with the moose-fly. At length, half a mile farther north, by going half a dozen rods into the dense spruce and fir wood on the side of the mountain, almost as dark as a cellar, we found a place sufficiently clear and level to lie down on, after cutting away a few bushes. We required a space only seven feet by six for our bed, the fire being four or five feet in front, though it made no odds how rough the hearth was; but it was not always easy to find this in those woods. The Indian first cleared a path to it from the shore with his axe, and we then carried up all our baggage, pitched our tent, and made our bed, in order to be ready for foul weather, which then threatened us, and for the night. He gathered a large armful of fir twigs, breaking them off, which he said were the best for our bed, partly, I thought, because they were the largest and could be most rapidly collected. It had been raining more or less for four or five days, and the wood was even damper than usual, but he got dry bark for the fire from the under-side of a dead leaning hemlock, which, he said, he could always do.

This noon his mind was occupied with a law question, and I referred him to my companion, who was a lawyer. It appeared that he had been buying land lately, (I think it was a hundred acres,) but there was probably an incumbrance to it, somebody else claiming to have bought some grass on it for this year. He wished to know to whom the grass belonged, and was told that if the other man could prove that he bought the grass before he, Polis, bought the land, the former could take it, whether the latter knew it or not. To which he only answered, "Strange!" He went over this several times, fairly sat down to it, with his back to a tree, as if he meant to confine us to this topic henceforth; but as he made no headway, only reached the jumping-off place of his wonder at white men's institutions after each explanation, we let the subject die.

He said that he had fifty acres of grass, potatoes, &c., somewhere above Oldtown, beside some about his house; that he hired a good deal of his work, hoeing, &c., and preferred white men to Indians, because "they keep steady, and know how."

After dinner we returned southward along the shore, in the canoe, on account of the difficulty of climbing over the rocks and fallen trees, and began to ascend the mountain along the edge of the precipice. But a smart shower coming up just then, the Indian crept under his canoe, while we, being protected by our rubber coats, proceeded to botanize. So we sent him back to the camp for shelter, agreeing that he should come there for us with his canoe toward night. It had rained a little in the forenoon, and we trusted that this would be the clearing-up shower, which it proved; but our feet and legs were thoroughly wet by the bushes. The clouds breaking away a little, we had a glorious wild view, as we ascended, of the broad lake with its fluctuating surface and numerous forest-clad islands, extending beyond our sight both north and south, and the boundless forest undulating away from its shores on every side, as densely packed as a rye-field, and enveloping nameless mountains in succession; but above all, looking westward over a large island was visible a very distant part of the lake, though we did not then suspect it to be Moosehead,—at first a mere broken white line seen through the tops of the island trees, like hay-caps, but spreading to a lake when we got higher. Beyond this we saw what appears to be called Bald Mountain on the map, some twenty-five miles distant, near the sources of the Penobscot. It was a perfect lake of the woods. But this was only a transient gleam, for the rain was not quite over.

Looking southward, the heavens were completely overcast, the mountains capped with clouds, and the lake generally wore a dark and stormy appearance, but from its surface just north of Sugar Island, six or eight miles distant, there was reflected upward to us through the misty air a bright blue tinge from the distant unseen sky of another latitude beyond. They probably had a clear sky then at Greenville, the south end of the lake. Standing on a mountain in the midst of a lake, where would you look for the first sign of approaching fair weather? Not into the heavens, it seems, but into the lake.

Again we mistook a little rocky islet seen through the "drisk," with some taller bare trunks or stumps on it, for the steamer with its smoke-pipes, but as it had not changed its position after half an hour, we were undeceived. So much do the works of man resemble the works of nature. A moose might mistake a steamer for a floating isle, and not be scared till he heard its puffing or its whistle.

If I wished to see a mountain or other scenery under the most favorable auspices, I would go to it in foul weather, so as to be there when it cleared up; we are then in the most suitable mood, and nature is most fresh and inspiring. There is no serenity so fair as that which is just established in a tearful eye.

Jackson, in his Report on the Geology of Maine, in 1838, says of this mountain: "Hornstone, which will answer for flints, occurs in various parts of the State, where trap-rocks have acted upon silicious slate. The largest mass of this stone known in the world is Mount Kineo, upon Moosehead Lake, which appears to be entirely composed of it, and rises seven hundred feet above the lake level. This variety of hornstone I have seen in every part of New England in the form of Indian arrow-heads, hatchets, chisels, etc., which were probably obtained from this mountain by the aboriginal inhabitants of the country." I have myself found hundreds of arrow-heads made of the same material. It is generally slate-colored, with white specks, becoming a uniform white where exposed to the light and air, and it breaks with a conchoidal fracture, producing a ragged cutting edge. I noticed some conchoidal hollows more than a foot in diameter. I picked up a small thin piece which had so sharp an edge that I used it as a dull knife, and to see what I could do, fairly cut off an aspen one inch thick with it, by bending it and making many cuts; though I cut my fingers badly with the back of it in the meanwhile.

From the summit of the precipice which forms the southern and eastern sides of this mountain peninsula, and is its most remarkable feature, being described as five or six hundred feet high, we looked, and probably might have jumped down to the water, or to the seemingly dwarfish trees on the narrow neck of land which connects it with the main. It is a dangerous place to try the steadiness of your nerves. Hodge says that these cliffs descend "perpendicularly ninety feet" below the surface of the water.

The plants which chiefly attracted our attention on this mountain were the mountain cinquefoil (*Potentilla tridentata*), abundant and in bloom still at the very base, by the water-side, though it is usually confined to the summits of mountains in our latitude; very beautiful harebells overhanging the precipice; bear-berry; the Canada blueberry (*Vaccinium Canadense*), similar to the *V. Pennsylvanicum* our earliest one, but entire leaved and with a downy stem and leaf; I have not seen it in Massachusetts; *Diervilla trifida*; *Microstylis ophioglossoides*, an orchidaceous plant new to us; wild holly (*Nemopanthes Canadensis*); the great round-leaved orchis (*Platanthera orbiculata*), not long in bloom; *Spiranthes cernua*, at the top; bunch-berry, reddening as we ascended, green at the base of the mountain, red at the top; and the small fern, *Woodsia ilvensis*, growing in tufts, now in fruit. I have also received *Liparis liliifolia*, or twayblade, from this spot. Having explored the wonders of the mountain, and the weather being now entirely cleared up, we commenced the descent. We met the Indian, puffing and panting, about one third of the way up, but thinking that he must be near the top, and saying that it took his breath away. I thought that superstition had something to do with his fatigue. Perhaps he believed that he was climbing over the back of a tremendous moose. He said that he had never ascended Kineo. On reaching the canoe we found that he had caught a lake trout weighing about three pounds, at the depth of twenty-five or thirty feet, while we were on the mountain.

When we got to the camp, the canoe was taken out and turned over, and a log laid across it to prevent its being blown away. The Indian cut some large logs of damp and rotten hard wood to smoulder and keep fire through the night. The trout was fried for supper. Our tent was of thin cotton cloth and quite small, forming with the ground a triangular prism closed at the rear end, six feet long, seven wide, and four high, so that we could barely sit up in the middle. It required two forked stakes, a smooth ridge-pole, and a dozen or more pins to pitch it. It kept off dew and wind, and an ordinary rain, and answered our purpose well enough. We reclined within it till bedtime, each with his baggage at his head, or else sat about the fire, having hung our wet clothes on a pole before the fire for the night.

As we sat there, just before night, looking out through the dusky wood, the Indian heard a noise which he said was made by a snake. He imitated it at my request, making a low whistling note,—*pheet—pheet*,—two or three times repeated, somewhat like the peep of the hylodes, but not so loud. In answer to my inquiries, he said that he had never seen them while making it, but going to the spot he finds the snake. This, he said on another occasion, was a sign of rain. When I had selected this place for our camp, he had remarked that there were snakes there,—he saw them. But they won't do any hurt, I said. "O no," he answered, "just as you say, it makes no difference to me."

He lay on the right side of the tent, because, as he said, he was partly deaf in one ear, and he wanted to lie with his good ear up. As we lay there, he inquired if I ever heard "Indian sing." I replied that I had not often, and asked him if he would not favor us with a song. He readily assented, and lying on his back, with his blanket wrapped around him, he commenced a slow, somewhat nasal, yet musical chant, in his own language, which probably was taught his tribe long ago by the Catholic missionaries. He translated it to us, sentence by sentence, afterward, wishing to see if we could remember it. It proved to be a very simple religious exercise or hymn, the burden of which was, that there was only one God who ruled all the world. This was hammered (or sung) out very thin, so that some stanzas wellnigh meant nothing at all, merely keeping up the idea. He then said that he would sing us a Latin song; but we did not detect any Latin, only one or two Greek words in it,—the rest may have been Latin with the Indian pronunciation.

His singing carried me back to the period of the discovery of America, to San Salvador and the Incas, when Europeans first encountered the simple faith of the Indian. There was, indeed, a beautiful simplicity about it; nothing of the dark and savage, only the mild and infantile. The sentiments of humility and reverence chiefly were expressed.

It was a dense and damp spruce and fir wood in which we lay, and, except for our fire, perfectly dark; and when I awoke in the night, I either heard an owl from deeper in the forest behind us, or a loon from a distance over the lake. Getting up some time after midnight to collect the scattered brands together, while my companions were sound asleep, I observed, partly in the fire, which had ceased to blaze, a perfectly regular elliptical ring of light, about five inches in its shortest diameter, six or seven in its longer, and from one eighth to one quarter of an inch wide. It was fully as bright as the fire, but not reddish or scarlet like a coal, but a white and slumbering light, like the glowworm's. I could tell it from the fire only by its whiteness. I saw at once that it must be phosphorescent wood, which I had so often heard of, but never chanced to see. Putting my finger on it, with a little hesitation, I found that it was a piece of dead moose-wood (*Acer striatum*) which the Indian had cut off in a slanting direction the evening before. Using my knife, I discovered that the light proceeded from that portion of the sap-wood immediately under the bark, and thus presented a regular ring at the end, which, indeed, appeared raised above the level of the wood, and when I pared off the bark and cut into the sap, it was all aglow along the log. I was surprised to find the wood quite hard and apparently sound, though probably decay had commenced in the sap, and I cut out some little triangular chips, and placing them in the hollow of my hand, carried them into the camp, waked my companion, and showed them to him. They lit up the inside of my hand, revealing the lines and wrinkles, and appearing exactly like coals of fire raised to a white heat, and I saw at once how, probably, the Indian jugglers had imposed on their people and on travellers, pretending to hold coals of fire in their mouths.

I also noticed that part of a decayed stump within four or five feet of the fire, an inch wide and six inches long, soft and shaking wood, shone with equal brightness.

I neglected to ascertain whether our fire had anything to do with this, but the previous day's rain and long-continued wet weather undoubtedly had.

I was exceedingly interested by this phenomenon, and already felt paid for my journey. It could hardly have thrilled me more if it had taken the form of letters, or of the human face. If I had met with this ring of light while groping in this forest alone, away from any fire, I should have been still more surprised. I little thought that there was such a light shining in the darkness of the wilderness for me.

The next day the Indian told me their name for this light,—*Artoosoqu'*,—and on my inquiring concerning the will-o'-the-wisp, and the like phenomena, he said that his "folks" sometimes saw fires passing along at various heights, even as high as the trees, and making a noise. I was prepared after this to hear of the most startling and unimagined phenomena witnessed by "his folks," they are abroad at all hours and seasons in scenes so unfrequented by white men. Nature must have made a thousand revelations to them which are still secrets to us.

I did not regret my not having seen this before, since I now saw it under circumstances so favorable. I was in just the frame of mind to see something wonderful, and this was a phenomenon adequate to my circumstances and expectation, and it put me on the alert to see more like it. I exulted like "a pagan suckled in a creed" that had never been worn at all, but was bran new, and adequate to the occasion. I let science slide, and rejoiced in that light as if it had been a fellow-creature. I saw that it was excellent, and was very glad to know that it was so cheap. A scientific *explanation*, as it is called, would have been altogether out of place there. That is for pale daylight. Science with its retorts would have put me to sleep; it was the opportunity to be ignorant that I improved. It suggested to me that there was something to be seen if one had eyes. It made a believer of me more than before. I believed that the woods were not tenantless, but choke-full of honest spirits as good as myself any day,—not an empty chamber, in which chemistry was left to work alone, but an inhabited house,—and for a few moments I enjoyed fellowship with them. Your so-called wise man goes trying to persuade himself that there is no entity there but himself and his traps, but it is a great deal easier to believe the truth. It suggested, too, that the same experience always gives birth to the same sort of belief or religion. One revelation has been made to the Indian, another to the white man. I have much to learn of the Indian, nothing of the missionary. I am not sure but all that would tempt me to teach the Indian my religion would be his promise to teach me *his*. Long enough I had heard of irrelevant things; now at length I was glad to make acquaintance with the light that dwells in rotten wood. Where is all your knowledge gone to? It evaporates completely, for it has no depth.

I kept those little chips and wet them again the next night, but they emitted no light.

SATURDAY, July 25.

At breakfast this Saturday morning, the Indian, evidently curious to know what would be expected of him the next day, whether we should go along or not, asked me how I spent the Sunday when at home. I told him that I commonly sat in my chamber reading, etc., in the forenoon, and went to walk in the afternoon. At which he shook his head and said, "Er, that is ver bad." "How do you spend it?" I asked. He said that he did no work, that he went to church at Oldtown when he was at home; in short, he did as he had been taught by the whites. This led to a discussion in which I found myself in the minority. He stated that he was a Protestant, and asked me if I was. I did not at first know what to say, but I thought that I could answer with truth that I was.

When we were washing the dishes in the lake, many fishes,

apparently chivin, came close up to us to get the particles of grease.

The weather seemed to be more settled this morning, and we set out early in order to finish our voyage up the lake before the wind arose. Soon after starting the Indian directed our attention to the Northeast Carry, which we could plainly see, about thirteen miles distant in that direction as measured on the map, though it is called much farther. This carry is a rude wooden railroad, running north and south about two miles, perfectly straight, from the lake to the Penobscot, through a low tract, with a clearing three or four rods wide; but low as it is, it passes over the height of land there. This opening appeared as a clear bright, or light point in the horizon, resting on the edge of the lake, whose breadth a hair could have covered at a considerable distance from the eye, and of no appreciable height. We should not have suspected it to be visible if the Indian had not drawn our attention to it. It was a remarkable kind of light to steer for,—daylight seen through a vista in the forest,—but visible as far as an ordinary beacon by night.

We crossed a deep and wide bay which makes eastward north of Kineo, leaving an island on our left, and keeping up the eastern side of the lake. This way or that led to some Tomhegan or *Socatarian* stream, up which the Indian had hunted, and whither I longed to go. The last name, however, had a bogus sound, too much like sectarian for me, as if a missionary had tampered with it; but I know that the Indians were very liberal. I think I should have inclined to the Tomhegan first.

We then crossed another broad bay, which, as we could no longer observe the shore particularly, afforded ample time for conversation. The Indian said that he had got his money by hunting, mostly high up the west branch of the Penobscot, and toward the head of the St. John; he had hunted there from a boy, and knew all about that region. His game had been, beaver, otter, black cat (or fisher), sable, moose, &c. Loup cervier (or Canada lynx) were plenty yet in burnt grounds. For food in the woods, he uses partridges, ducks, dried moose-meat, hedge-hog, &c. Loons, too, were good, only "bile 'em good." He told us at some length how he had

suffered from starvation when a mere lad, being overtaken by
winter when hunting with two grown Indians in the northern
part of Maine, and obliged to leave their canoe on account of
ice.

Pointing into the bay, he said that it was the way to various
lakes which he knew. Only solemn bear-haunted mountains,
with their great wooded slopes, were visible; where, as man
is not, we suppose some other power to be. My imagination
personified the slopes themselves, as if by their very length
they would waylay you, and compel you to camp again on
them before night. Some invisible glutton would seem to
drop from the trees and gnaw at the heart of the solitary
hunter who threaded those woods; and yet I was tempted to
walk there. The Indian said that he had been along there several times.

I asked him how he guided himself in the woods. "O," said
he, "I can tell good many ways." When I pressed him further,
he answered, "Sometimes I lookum side-hill," and he glanced
toward a high hill or mountain on the eastern shore, "great
difference between the north and south, see where the sun
has shone most. So trees,—the large limbs bend toward
south. Sometimes I lookum locks" (rocks). I asked what he
saw on the rocks, but he did not describe anything in particular, answering vaguely, in a mysterious or drawling tone,
"Bare locks on lake shore,—great difference between N. S. E.
W. side,—can tell what the sun has shone on." "Suppose,"
said I, "that I should take you in a dark night, right up here
into the middle of the woods a hundred miles, set you down,
and turn you round quickly twenty times, could you steer
straight to Oldtown?" "O yer," said he, "have done pretty
much same thing. I will tell you. Some years ago I met an old
white hunter at Millinocket; very good hunter. He said he
could go anywhere in the woods. He wanted to hunt with
me that day, so we start. We chase a moose all the forenoon,
round and round, till middle of afternoon, when we kill him.
Then I said to him, now you go straight to camp. Don't go
round and round where we 've been, but go straight. He said,
I can't do that, I don't know where I am. Where you think
camp? I asked. He pointed so. Then I laugh at him. I take
the lead and go right off the other way, cross our tracks many

times, straight camp." "How do you do that?" asked I. "O, I can't tell *you*," he replied. "Great difference between me and white man."

It appeared as if the sources of information were so various that he did not give a distinct, conscious attention to any one, and so could not readily refer to any when questioned about it, but he found his way very much as an animal does. Perhaps what is commonly called instinct in the animal, in this case is merely a sharpened and educated sense. Often, when an Indian says, "I don't know," in regard to the route he is to take, he does not mean what a white man would by those words, for his Indian instinct may tell him still as much as the most confident white man knows. He does not carry things in his head, nor remember the route exactly, like a white man, but relies on himself at the moment. Not having experienced the need of the other sort of knowledge, all labelled and arranged, he has not acquired it.

The white hunter with whom I talked in the stage knew some of the resources of the Indian. He said that he steered by the wind, or by the limbs of the hemlocks, which were largest on the south side; also sometimes, when he knew that there was a lake near, by firing his gun and listening to hear the direction and distance of the echo from over it.

The course we took over this lake, and others afterward, was rarely direct, but a succession of curves from point to point, digressing considerably into each of the bays; and this was not merely on account of the wind, for the Indian, looking toward the middle of the lake, said it was hard to go there, easier to keep near the shore, because he thus got over it by successive reaches and saw by the shore how he got along.

The following will suffice for a common experience in crossing lakes in a canoe. As the forenoon advanced the wind increased. The last bay which we crossed before reaching the desolate pier at the northeast carry, was two or three miles over, and the wind was southwesterly. After going a third of the way, the waves had increased so as occasionally to wash into the canoe, and we saw that it was worse and worse ahead. At first we might have turned about, but were not willing to. It would have been of no use to follow the course of the shore, for not only the distance would have been much greater, but the waves ran still higher there on account of the greater sweep the wind had. At any rate it would have been dangerous now to alter our course, because the waves would have struck us at an advantage. It will not do to meet them at right angles, for then they will wash in both sides, but you must take them quartering. So the Indian stood up in the canoe, and exerted all his skill and strength for a mile or two, while I paddled right along in order to give him more steerage-way. For more than a mile he did not allow a single wave to strike the canoe as it would, but turned it quickly from this side to that, so that it would always be on or near the crest of a wave when it broke, where all its force was spent, and we merely settled down with it. At length I jumped out on to the end of the pier, against which the waves were dashing violently, in order to lighten the canoe, and catch it at the landing, which was not much sheltered; but just as I jumped we took in two or three gallons of water. I remarked to the Indian, "You managed that well," to which he replied: "Ver few men do that. Great many waves; when I look out for one, another come quick."

While the Indian went to get cedar-bark, &c., to carry his canoe with, we cooked the dinner on the shore, at this end of the carry, in the midst of a sprinkling rain.

He prepared his canoe for carrying in this wise. He took a cedar shingle or splint eighteen inches long and four or five wide, rounded at one end, that the corners might not be in the way, and tied it with cedar-bark by two holes made midway, near the edge on each side, to the middle crossbar of the canoe. When the canoe was lifted upon his head bottom up, this shingle, with its rounded end uppermost, distributed the weight over his shoulders and head, while a band of cedar-bark, tied to the cross-bar on each side of the shingle, passed round his breast, and another longer one, outside of the last, round his forehead; also a hand on each side rail served to steer the canoe and keep it from rocking. He thus carried it with his shoulders, head, breast, forehead, and both hands, as if the upper part of his body were all one hand to clasp and hold it. If you know of a better way, I should like to hear of it. A cedar-tree furnished all the gear in this case, as it had the woodwork of the canoe. One of the paddles rested on the crossbars in the bows. I took the canoe upon my head and found that I could carry it with ease, though the straps were not fitted to my shoulders; but I let him carry it, not caring to establish a different precedent, though he said that if I would carry the canoe, he would take all the rest of the baggage, except my companion's. This shingle remained tied to the crossbar throughout the voyage, was always ready for the carries, and also served to protect the back of one passenger.

We were obliged to go over this carry twice, our load was so great. But the carries were an agreeable variety, and we improved the opportunity to gather the rare plants which we had seen, when we returned empty-handed.

We reached the Penobscot about four o'clock, and found there some St. Francis Indians encamped on the bank, in the same place where I camped with four Indians four years before. They were making a canoe, and, as then, drying moose-meat. The meat looked very suitable to make a *black* broth at least. Our Indian said it was not good. Their camp was covered with spruce-bark. They had got a young moose, taken in the river a fortnight before, confined in a sort of cage of logs piled up cob-fashion, seven or eight feet high. It was quite tame, about four feet high, and covered with moose-flies. There was a large quantity of cornel (*C. stolonifera*), red maple, and also willow and aspen boughs, stuck through between the logs on all sides, but-ends out, and on their leaves it was browsing. It looked at first as if it were in a bower rather than a pen.

Our Indian said that *he* used *black* spruce-roots to sew canoes with, obtaining it from high lands or mountains. The St. Francis Indian thought that *white* spruce-roots might be best. But the former said, "No good, break, can't split 'em"; also that they were hard to get, deep in ground, but the black were near the surface, on higher land, as well as tougher. He said that the white spruce was *subekoondark*, black, *skusk*. I told him I thought that I could make a canoe, but he expressed great doubt of it; at any rate, he thought that my work would not be "neat" the first time. An Indian at Greenville had told me that the winter bark, that is, bark taken off before the sap flows in May, was harder and much better than summer bark.

Having reloaded, we paddled down the Penobscot, which, as the Indian remarked, and even I detected, remembering how it looked before, was uncommonly full. We soon after saw a splended yellow lily (*Lilium Canadense*) by the shore, which I plucked. It was six feet high, and had twelve flowers, in two whorls, forming a pyramid, such as I have seen in Concord. We afterward saw many more thus tall along this stream, and also still more numerous on the East Branch, and, on the latter, one which I thought approached yet nearer to the *Lilium superbum*. The Indian asked what we called it, and said that the "loots" (roots) were good for soup, that is, to cook with meat, to thicken it, taking the place of flour. They get them in the fall. I dug some, and found a mass of bulbs pretty deep in the earth, two inches in diameter, looking, and even tasting, somewhat like raw green corn on the ear.

When we had gone about three miles down the Penobscot, we saw through the tree-tops a thunder-shower coming up in the west, and we looked out a camping-place in good season, about five o'clock, on the west side, not far below the mouth of what Joe Aitteon, in '53, called Lobster Stream, coming from Lobster Pond. Our present Indian, however, did not admit this name, nor even that of *Matahumkeag*, which is on the map, but called the lake *Beskabekuk*.

I will describe, once for all, the routine of camping at this season. We generally told the Indian that we would stop at the first suitable place, so that he might be on the lookout for it. Having observed a clear, hard, and flat beach to land on, free from mud, and from stones which would injure the canoe, one would run up the bank to see if there were open and level space enough for the camp between the trees, or if it could be easily cleared, preferring at the same time a cool place, on account of insects. Sometimes we paddled a mile or more before finding one to our minds, for where the shore was suitable, the bank would often be too steep, or else too low and grassy, and therefore mosquitoey. We then took out the baggage and drew up the canoe, sometimes turning it over on shore for safety. The Indian cut a path to the spot we had selected, which was usually within two or three rods of the water, and we carried up our baggage. One, perhaps, takes canoe-birch bark, always at hand, and dead dry wood or bark, and kindles a fire five or six feet in front of where we intend to lie. It matters not, commonly, on which side this is, because there is little or no wind in so dense a wood at that season; and then he gets a kettle of water from the river, and takes out the pork, bread, coffee, &c., from their several packages.

Another, meanwhile, having the axe, cuts down the nearest dead rock-maple or other dry hard wood, collecting several large logs to last through the night, also a green stake, with a notch or fork to it, which is slanted over the fire, perhaps resting on a rock or forked stake, to hang the kettle on, and two forked stakes and a pole for the tent.

The third man pitches the tent, cuts a dozen or more pins with his knife, usually of moose-wood, the common under-wood, to fasten it down with, and then collects an armful or two of fir-twigs,* arbor-vitæ, spruce, or hemlock, whichever is at hand, and makes the bed, beginning at either end, and laying the twigs wrong-side up, in regular rows, covering the stub-ends of the last row; first, however, filling the hollows, if there are any, with coarser material. Wrangel says that his guides in Siberia first strewed a quantity of dry brushwood on the ground, and then cedar twigs on that.

Commonly, by the time the bed is made, or within fifteen or twenty minutes, the water boils, the pork is fried, and supper is ready. We eat this sitting on the ground, or a stump, if there is any, around a large piece of birch-bark for a table, each holding a dipper in one hand and a piece of ship-bread or fried pork in the other, frequently making a pass with his hand, or thrusting his head into the smoke, to avoid the mosquitoes.

Next, pipes are lit by those who smoke, and veils are donned by those who have them, and we hastily examine and dry our plants, anoint our faces and hands, and go to bed,— and—the mosquitoes.

Though you have nothing to do but see the country, there's rarely any time to spare, hardly enough to examine a

*These twigs are called in Rasle's Dictionary, *Sediak*.

plant, before the night or drowsiness is upon you.

Such was the ordinary experience, but this evening we had camped earlier on account of the rain, and had more time.

We found that our camp to-night was on an old, and now more than usually indistinct, supply-road, running along the river. What is called a road there shows no ruts or trace of wheels, for they are not used; nor, indeed, of runners, since they are used only in the winter, when the snow is several feet deep. It is only an indistinct vista through the wood, which it takes an experienced eye to detect.

We had no sooner pitched our tent than the thunder-shower burst on us, and we hastily crept under it, drawing our bags after us, curious to see how much of a shelter our thin cotton roof was going to be in this excursion. Though the violence of the rain forced a fine shower through the cloth before it was fairly wetted and shrunk, with which we were well bedewed, we managed to keep pretty dry, only a box of matches having been left out and spoiled, and before we were aware of it the shower was over, and only the dripping trees imprisoned us.

Wishing to see what fishes there were in the river there, we cast our lines over the wet bushes on the shore, but they were repeatedly swept down the swift stream in vain. So, leaving the Indian, we took the canoe just before dark, and dropped down the river a few rods to fish at the mouth of a sluggish brook on the opposite side. We pushed up this a rod or two, where, perhaps, only a canoe had been before. But though there were a few small fishes, mostly *chivin*, there, we were soon driven off by the mosquitoes. While there we heard the Indian fire his gun twice in such rapid succession that we thought it must be double-barrelled, though we observed afterward that it was single. His object was to clean out and dry it after the rain, and he then loaded it with ball, being now on ground where he expected to meet with large game. This sudden, loud, crashing noise in the still aisles of the forest, affected me like an insult to nature, or ill manners at any rate, as if you were to fire a gun in a hall or temple. It was not heard far, however, except along the river, the sound being rapidly hushed up or absorbed by the damp trees and mossy ground.

The Indian made a little smothered fire of damp leaves close to the back of the camp, that the smoke might drive through and keep out the mosquitoes; but just before we fell asleep this suddenly blazed up, and came near setting fire to the tent. We were considerably molested by mosquitoes at this camp.

Sunday, July 26.

The note of the white-throated sparrow, a very inspiriting but almost wiry sound, was the first heard in the morning, and with this all the woods rang. This was the prevailing bird in the northern part of Maine. The forest generally was all alive with them at this season, and they were proportionally numerous and musical about Bangor. They evidently breed in that State. Wilson did not know where they bred, and says, "Their only note is a kind of chip." Though commonly unseen, their simple *ah, te-te-te, te-te-te, te-te-te*, so sharp and piercing, was as distinct to the ear as the passage of a spark of fire shot into the darkest of the forest would be to the eye. I thought that they commonly uttered it as they flew. I hear this note for a few days only in the spring, as they go through Concord, and in the fall see them again going southward, but then they are mute. We were commonly aroused by their lively strain very early. What a glorious time they must have in that wilderness, far from mankind and election day!

I told the Indian that we would go to church to Chesuncook this (Sunday) morning, some fifteen miles. It was settled weather at last. A few swallows flitted over the water, we heard the white throats along the shore, the phebe notes of the chicadee, and, I believe, red-starts, and moose-flies of large size pursued us in mid-stream.

The Indian thought that we should lie by on Sunday. Said he, "We come here lookum things, look all round; but come Sunday, lock up all that, and then Monday look again." He spoke of an Indian of his acquaintance who had been with some ministers to Ktaadn, and had told him how they conducted. This he described in a low and solemn voice. "They make a long prayer every morning and night, and at every meal. Come Sunday," said he, "they stop 'em, no go at all that day,—keep still,—preach all day,—first one then another, just like church. O, ver good men." "One day," said he, "going along a river, they came to the body of a man in the water, drowned good while, all ready fall to pieces. They go right ashore,—stop there, go no farther that day,—they have meeting there, preach and pray just like Sunday. Then they get poles and lift up the body, and they go back and carry the body with them. O, they ver good men."

I judged from this account that their every camp was a camp-meeting, and they had mistaken their route,—they should have gone to Eastham; that they wanted an opportunity to preach somewhere more than to see Ktaadn. I read of another similar party that seem to have spent their time there singing the songs of Zion. I was glad that I did not go to that mountain with such slow coaches.

However, the Indian added, plying the paddle all the while, that if we would go along, he must go with us, he our man, and he suppose that if he no takum pay for what he do Sunday, then ther 's no harm, but if he takum pay, then wrong. I told him that he was stricter than white men. Nevertheless, I noticed that he did not forget to reckon in the Sundays at last.

He appeared to be a very religious man, and said his prayers in a loud voice, in Indian, kneeling before the camp, morning and evening,—sometimes scrambling up again in haste when he had forgotten this, and saying them with great rapidity. In the course of the day, he remarked, not very originally, "Poor man rememberum God more than rich."

We soon passed the island where I had camped four years before, and I recognized the very spot. The dead water, a mile or two below it, the Indian called, *Beska bekukskishtuk*, from the lake *Beskabekuk*, which empties in above. This dead water, he said, was "a great place for moose always." We saw the grass bent where a moose came out the night before, and the Indian said that he could smell one as far as he could see him; but, he added, that if he should see five or six to-day close by canoe, he no shoot 'em. Accordingly, as he was the only one of the party who had a gun, or had come a-hunting, the moose were safe.

Just below this, a cat-owl flew heavily over the stream, and he, asking if I knew what it was, imitated very well the common *hoo, hoo, hoo, hoorer, hoo*, of our woods; making a hard, guttural sound, "Ugh, ugh, ugh,—ugh, ugh." When we passed the Moose-horn, he said that it had no name. What Joe Aitteon had called Ragmuff, he called *Pay tay te quick*, and said that it meant Burnt Ground Stream. We stopped there, where I had stopped before, and I bathed in this tributary. It was shallow but cold, apparently too cold for the Indian, who stood looking on. As we were pushing away again, a white-headed eagle sailed over our heads. A reach some miles above Pine Stream, where there were several islands, the Indian said was *Nonglangyis*, dead-water. Pine Stream he called Black River, and said that its Indian name was *Karsaootuk*. He could go to Caribou Lake that way.

We carried a part of the baggage about Pine Stream Falls, while the Indian went down in the canoe. A Bangor merchant had told us that two men in his employ were drowned some time ago while passing these falls in a bateau, and a third clung to a rock all night, and was taken off in the morning. There were magnificent great purple-fringed orchises on this carry and the neighboring shores. I measured the largest canoe-birch which I saw in this journey near the end of the carry. It was 14½ feet in circumference at two feet from the ground, but at five feet divided into three parts. The canoe-birches thereabouts were commonly marked by conspicuous dark spiral ridges, with a groove between, so that I thought at first that they had been struck by lightning, but, as the Indian said, it was evidently caused by the grain of the tree. He cut a small, woody knob, as big as a filbert, from the trunk of a fir, apparently an old balsam vesicle filled with wood, which he said was good medicine.

After we had embarked and gone half a mile, my companion remembered that he had left his knife, and we paddled back to get it, against the strong and swift current. This taught us the difference between going up and down the stream, for while we were working our way back a quarter of a mile, we should have gone down a mile and a half at least. So we landed, and while he and the Indian were gone back for it, I watched the motions of the foam, a kind of white water-fowl near the shore, forty or fifty rods below. It alternately appeared and disappeared behind the rock, being carried round by an eddy. Even this semblance of life was interesting on that lonely river.

Immediately below these falls was the Chesuncook deadwater, caused by the flowing back of the lake. As we paddled slowly over this, the Indian told us a story of his hunting thereabouts, and something more interesting about himself. It appeared that he had represented his tribe at Augusta, and also once at Washington, where he had met some Western chiefs. He had been consulted at Augusta, and gave advice, which he said was followed, respecting the eastern boundary of Maine, as determined by highlands and streams, at the time of the difficulties on that side. He was employed with the surveyors on the line. Also he had called on Daniel Webster in Boston, at the time of his Bunker Hill oration.

I was surprised to hear him say that he liked to go to Boston, New York, Philadelphia, &c., &c.; that he would like to live there. But then, as if relenting a little, when he thought what a poor figure he would make there, he added, "I suppose, I live in New York, I be poorest hunter, I expect." He understood very well both his superiority and his inferiority to the whites. He criticised the people of the United States as compared with other nations, but the only distinct idea with which he labored was, that they were "very strong," but, like some individuals, "too fast." He must have the credit of saying this just before the general breaking down of railroads and banks. He had a great idea of education, and would occasionally break out into such expressions as this, "Kademy—a-cad-e-my—good thing—I suppose they usum Fifth Reader there. . . . . You been college?"

From this dead-water the outlines of the mountains about Ktaadn were visible. The top of Ktaadn was concealed by a cloud, but the Souneunk Mountains were nearer, and quite visible. We steered across the northwest end of the lake, from which we looked down south-southeast, the whole length to Joe Merry Mountain, seen over its extremity. It is an agreeable change to cross a lake, after you have been shut up in the woods, not only on account of the greater expanse of water, but also of sky. It is one of the surprises which Nature has in store for the traveller in the forest. To look down, in this case, over eighteen miles of water, was liberating and civilizing even. No doubt, the short distance to which you can see in the woods, and the general twilight, would at length react on the inhabitants, and make them *salvages*. The lakes also reveal the mountains, and give ample scope and range to our thought. The very gulls which we saw sitting on the rocks, like white specks, or circling about, reminded me of custom-house officers. Already there were half a dozen log-huts about this end of the lake, though so far from a road. I perceive that in these woods the earliest settlements are, for various reasons, clustering about the lakes, but partly, I think, for the sake of the neighborhood as the oldest clearings. They are forest schools already established,—great centres of light. Water is a pioneer which the settler follows, taking advantage of its improvements.

Thus far only I had been before. About noon we turned northward, up a broad kind of estuary, and at its northeast corner found the Caucomgomoc River, and after going about a mile from the lake, reached the Umbazookskus, which comes in on the right at a point where the former river, coming from the west, turns short to the south. Our course was up the Umbazookskus, but as the Indian knew of a good camping-place, that is, a cool place where there were few mosquitoes, about half a mile farther up the Caucomgomoc, we went thither. The latter river, judging from the map, is the longer and principal stream, and, therefore, its name must prevail below the junction. So quickly we changed the civilizing sky of Chesuncook for the dark wood of the Caucomgomoc. On reaching the Indian's camping-ground, on the south side, where the bank was about a dozen feet high, I read on the trunk of a fir-tree blazed by an axe an inscription in charcoal which had been left by him. It was surmounted by a drawing of a bear paddling a canoe, which he said was the sign which had been used by his family always. The drawing, though rude, could not be mistaken for anything but a bear, and he doubted my ability to copy it. The inscription ran thus, *verbatim et literatim*. I interline the English of his Indian as he gave it to me.

July 26,
1853.

Niasoseh
We alone Joseph
 Polis   *elioi*
 Polis   start
 sia   *olta*
 for   Oldtown
 onke   *ni*
 right   away.
 quambi

July 15,
1855.
Niasoseb.

He added now below:—

1857,
July 26.
Io.   Polis.

This was one of his homes. I saw where he had sometimes stretched his moose-hides on the opposite or sunny north side of the river, where there was a narrow meadow.

After we had selected a place for our camp, and kindled our fire, almost exactly on the site of the Indian's last camp here, he, looking up, observed, "That tree danger." It was a dead part, more than a foot in diameter, of a large canoe-birch, which branched at the ground. This branch, rising thirty feet or more, slanted directly over the spot which we had chosen for our bed. I told him to try it with his axe; but he could not shake it perceptibly, and, therefore, seemed inclined to disregard it, and my companion expressed his willingness to run the risk. But it seemed to me that we should be fools to lie under it, for though the lower part was firm, the top, for aught we knew, might be just ready to fall, and we should at any rate be very uneasy if the wind arose in the night. It is a common accident for men camping in the woods to be killed by a falling tree. So the camp was moved to the other side of the fire.

It was, as usual, a damp and shaggy forest, that Caucomgomoc one, and the most you knew about it was, that on this side it stretched toward the settlements, and on that to still more unfrequented regions. You carried so much topography in your mind always,—and sometimes it seemed to make a considerable difference whether you sat or lay nearer the settlements, or farther off, than your companions,—were the rear or frontier man of the camp. But there is really the same difference between our positions wherever we may be camped, and some are nearer the frontiers on feather-beds in the towns than others on fir-twigs in the backwoods.

The Indian said that the Umbazookskus, being a dead stream with broad meadows, was a good place for moose, and he frequently came a-hunting here, being out alone three weeks or more from Oldtown. He sometimes, also, went a-hunting to the Seboois Lakes, taking the stage, with his gun and ammunition, axe and blankets, hard bread and pork, perhaps for a hundred miles of the way, and jumped off at the wildest place on the road, where he was at once at home, and every rod was a tavern-site for him. Then, after a short journey through the woods, he would build a spruce-bark canoe in one day, putting but few ribs into it, that it might be light, and after doing his hunting with it on the lakes, would return with his furs the same way he had come. Thus you have an Indian availing himself cunningly of the advantages of civilization, without losing any of his woodcraft, but proving himself the more successful hunter for it.

This man was very clever and quick to learn anything in his line. Our tent was of a kind new to him; but when he had once seen it pitched it was surprising how quickly he would find and prepare the pole and forked stakes to pitch it with, cutting and placing them right the first time, though I am sure that the majority of white men would have blundered several times.

This river came from Caucomgomoc Lake, about ten miles farther up. Though it was sluggish here, there were falls not far above us, and we saw the foam from them go by from time to time. The Indian said that *Caucomgomoc* meant Big-gull Lake, (i. e. Herring-gull, I suppose,) *gomoc* meaning lake. Hence this was *Caucomgomoctook*, or the river from that lake. This was the Penobscot *Caucomgomoc-took*. There was another St. John one not far north. He finds the eggs of this gull, sometimes twenty together, as big as hen's eggs, on rocky ledges on the west side of Millinocket River, for instance, and eats them.

Now I thought I would observe how he spent his Sunday. While I and my companion were looking about at the trees and river, he went to sleep. Indeed, he improved every opportunity to get a nap, whatever the day.

Rambling about the woods at this camp, I noticed that they consisted chiefly of firs, black spruce, and some white, red maple, canoe-birch, and, along the river, the hoary alder, *Alnus incana*. I name them in the order of their abundance. The *Viburnum nudum* was a common shrub, and of smaller plants, there were the dwarf-cornel, great round-leaved orchis, abundant and in bloom (a greenish-white flower growing in little communities), *Uvularia grandiflora*, whose stem tasted like a cucumber, *Pyrola secunda*, apparently the commonest Pyrola in those woods, now out of bloom, *Pyrola elliptica*, and *Chiogenes hispidula*. The *Clintonia borealis*, with ripe berries, was very abundant, and perfectly at home there. Its leaves, disposed commonly in triangles about its stem, were just as handsomely formed and green, and its berries as blue and glossy, as if it grew by some botanist's favorite path.

I could trace the outlines of large birches that had fallen long ago, collapsed and rotted and turned to soil, by faint yellowish-green lines of feather-like moss, eighteen inches wide and twenty or thirty feet long, crossed by other similar lines.

I heard a Maryland yellow-throat's midnight strain, wood-thrush, kingfisher (tweezer bird), or parti-colored warbler, and a night-hawk. I also heard and saw red squirrels, and heard a bull-frog. The Indian said that he heard a snake.

Wild as it was, it was hard for me to get rid of the associations of the settlements. Any steady and monotonous sound, to which I did not distinctly attend, passed for a sound of human industry. The waterfalls which I heard were not without their dams and mills to my imagination,—and several times I found that I had been regarding the steady rushing sound of the wind from over the woods beyond the rivers as that of a train of cars,—the cars at Quebec. Our minds anywhere, when left to themselves, are always thus busily drawing conclusions from false premises.

I asked the Indian to make us a sugar-bowl of birch-bark, which he did, using the great knife which dangled in a sheath from his belt; but the bark broke at the corners when he bent it up, and he said it was not good; that there was a great difference in this respect between the bark of one canoe-birch and that of another, i. e. one cracked more easily than another. I used some thin and delicate sheets of this bark which he split and cut, in my flower-book; thinking it would be good to separate the dried specimens from the green.

My companion, wishing to distinguish between the black and white spruce, asked Polis to show him a twig of the latter, which he did at once, together with the black; indeed, he could distinguish them about as far as he could see them; but as the two twigs appeared very much alike, my companion asked the Indian to point out the difference; whereupon the latter, taking the twigs, instantly remarked, as he passed his hand over them successively in a stroking manner, that the white was rough (i. e. the needles stood up nearly perpendicular), but the black smooth (i. e. as if bent or combed down). This was an obvious difference, both to sight and touch. However, if I remember rightly, this would not serve to distinguish the white spruce from the light-colored variety of the black.

I asked him to let me see him get some black spruce root, and make some thread. Whereupon, without looking up at the trees overhead, he began to grub in the ground, instantly distinguishing the black spruce roots, and cutting off a slender one, three or four feet long, and as big as a pipe-stem, he split the end with his knife, and taking a half between the thumb and forefinger of each hand, rapidly separated its whole length into two equal semi-cylindrical halves; then giving me another root, he said, "You try." But in my hands it immediately ran off one side, and I got only a very short piece. In short, though it looked very easy, I found that there was a great art in splitting these roots. The split is skilfully humored by bending short with this hand or that, and so kept in the middle. He then took off the bark from each half, pressing a short piece of cedar bark against the convex side with both hands, while he drew the root upward with his teeth. An Indian's teeth are strong, and I noticed that he used his often where we should have used a hand. They amounted to a third hand. He thus obtained, in a moment, a very neat, tough, and flexible string, which he could tie into a knot, or make into a fish-line even. It is said that in Norway and Sweden the roots of the Norway spruce (*Abies excelsa*) are used in the same way for the same purpose. He said that you would be obliged to give half a dollar for spruce root enough for a canoe, thus prepared. He had hired the sewing of his own canoe, though he made all the rest. The root in his canoe was of a pale slate color, probably acquired by exposure to the weather, or perhaps from being boiled in water first.

He had discovered the day before that his canoe leaked a little, and said that it was owing to stepping into it violently, which forced the water under the edge of the horizontal seams on the side. I asked him where he would get pitch to mend it with, for they commonly use hard-pitch, obtained of the whites at Oldtown. He said that he could make something very similar, and equally good, not of spruce gum, or the like, but of material which we had with us; and he wished me to guess what. But I could not, and he would not tell me, though he showed me a ball of it when made, as big as a pea, and like black pitch, saying, at last, that there were some things which a man did not tell even his wife. It may have been his own discovery. In Arnold's expedition the pioneers used for their canoe "the turpentine of the pine, and the scrapings of the pork-bag."

Being curious to see what kind of fishes there were in this dark, deep, sluggish river, I cast in my line just before night, and caught several small somewhat yellowish sucker-like fishes, which the Indian at once rejected, saying that they were *Michigan* fish (i. e. *soft* and *stinking* fish) and good for nothing. Also, he would not touch a pout, which I caught, and said that neither Indians nor whites thereabouts ever ate them, which I thought was singular, since they are esteemed in Massachusetts, and he had told me that he ate hedgehogs, loons, &c. But he said that some small silvery fishes, which I called white chivin, which were similar in size and form to the first, were the best fish in the Penobscot waters, and if I would toss them up the bank to him, he would cook them for me. After cleaning them, not very carefully, leaving the heads on, he laid them on the coals and so broiled them.

Returning from a short walk, he brought a vine in his hand, and asked me if I knew what it was, saying that it made the best tea of anything in the woods. It was the Creeping Snowberry (*Chiogenes hispidula*), which was quite common there, its berries just grown. He called it *cowosnebagosar*, which name implies that it grows where old prostrate trunks have collapsed and rotted. So we determined to have some tea made of this to-night. It had a slight checkerberry flavor, and we both agreed that it was really better than the black tea which we had brought. We thought it quite a discovery, and that it might well be dried, and sold in the shops. I, for one, however, am not an old tea-drinker, and cannot speak with authority to others. It would have been particularly good to carry along for a cold drink during the day, the water thereabouts being invariably warm. The Indian said that they also used for tea a certain herb which grew in low ground, which he did not find there, and *Ledum*, or Labrador tea, which I have since found and tried in Concord; also hemlock leaves, the last especially in the winter, when the other plants were covered with snow; and various other things; but he did not approve of *arbor vitæ*, which I said I had drunk in those woods. We could have had a new kind of tea every night.

Just before night we saw a *musquash*, (he did not say musk-rat,) the only one we saw in this voyage, swimming downward on the opposite side of the stream. The Indian, wishing to get one to eat, hushed us, saying, "Stop, me call 'em"; and sitting flat on the bank, he began to make a curious squeaking, wiry sound with his lips, exerting himself considerably. I was greatly surprised,—thought that I had at last got into the wilderness, and that he was a wild man indeed, to be talking to a musquash! I did not know which of the two was the strangest to me. He seemed suddenly to have quite forsaken humanity, and gone over to the musquash side. The musquash, however, as near as I could see, did not turn aside, though he may have hesitated a little, and the Indian said that he saw our fire; but it was evident that he was in the habit of calling the musquash to him, as he said. An acquaintance of mine who was hunting moose in the woods a month after this, tells me that his Indian in this way repeatedly called the musquash within reach of his paddle in the moonlight, and struck at them.

The Indian said a particularly long prayer this Sunday evening, as if to atone for working in the morning.

MONDAY, July 27.

Having rapidly loaded the canoe, which the Indian always carefully attended to, that it might be well trimmed, and each having taken a look, as usual, to see that nothing was left, we set out again, descending the Caucomgomoc, and turning northeasterly up the *Umbazookskus*. This name, the Indian said, meant *Much Meadow River*. We found it a very meadowy stream, and dead water, and now very wide on account of the rains, though, he said, it was sometimes quite narrow. The space between the woods, chiefly bare meadow, was from fifty to two hundred rods in breadth, and is a rare place for moose. It reminded me of the Concord; and what increased the resemblance, was one old musquash house almost afloat.

In the water on the meadows grew sedges, wool-grass, the common blue-flag abundantly, its flower just showing itself above the high water, as if it were a blue water-lily, and higher in the meadows a great many clumps of a peculiar narrow-leaved willow (*Salix petiolaris*), which is common in our river meadows. It was the prevailing one here, and the Indian said that the musquash ate much of it; and here also grew the red osier (*Cornus stolonifera*), its large fruit now whitish.

Though it was still early in the morning, we saw night-hawks circling over the meadow, and as usualy heard the *Pepe* (*Muscicapa Cooperi*), which is one of the prevailing birds in these woods, and the robin.

It was unusual for the woods to be so distant from the shore, and there was quite an echo from them, but when I was shouting in order to awake it, the Indian reminded me that I should scare the moose, which he was looking out for, and which we all wanted to see. The word for echo was *Pocka-dunkquaywayle*.

A broad belt of dead larch-trees along the distant edge of the meadow, against the forest on each side, increased the usual wildness of the scenery. The Indian called these juniper, and said that they had been killed by the back water caused by the dam at the outlet of Chesuncook Lake, some twenty miles distant. I plucked at the water's edge the *Asclepias incarnata*, with quite handsome flowers, a brighter red than our variety (the *pulchra*). It was the only form of it which I saw there.

Having paddled several miles up the Umbazookskus, it suddenly contracted to a mere brook, narrow and swift, the larches and other trees approaching the bank and leaving no open meadow, and we landed to get a black-spruce pole for pushing against the stream. This was the first occasion for one. The one selected was quite slender, cut about ten feet long, merely whittled to a point, and the bark shaved off. The stream, though narrow and swift, was still deep, with a muddy bottom, as I proved by diving to it. Beside the plants which I have mentioned, I observed on the bank here the *Salix cordata* and *rostrata*, *Ranunculus recurvatus*, and *Rubus triflorus* with ripe fruit.

While we were thus employed, two Indians in a canoe hove in sight round the bushes, coming down stream. Our Indian knew one of them, an old man, and fell into conversation with him in Indian. He belonged at the foot of Moosehead. The other was of another tribe. They were returning from hunting. I asked the younger if they had seen any moose, to which he said no; but I, seeing the moose-hides sticking out from a great bundle made with their blankets in the middle of the canoe, added, "Only their hides." As he was a foreigner, he may have wished to deceive me, for it is against the law for white men and foreigners to kill moose in Maine at this season. But, perhaps, he need not have been alarmed, for the moose-wardens are not very particular. I heard quite directly of one, who being asked by a white man going into the woods what he would say if he killed a moose, answered, "If you bring me a quarter of it, I guess you won't be troubled." His duty being, as he said, only to prevent the "indiscriminate" slaughter of them for their hides. I suppose that he would consider it an *indiscriminate* slaughter when a quarter was not reserved for himself. Such are the perquisites of this office.

We continued along through the most extensive larch wood which I had seen,—tall and slender trees with fantastic branches. But though this was the prevailing tree here, I do not remember that we saw any afterward. You do not find straggling trees of this species here and there throughout the wood, but rather a little forest of them. The same is the case with the white and red pines, and some other trees, greatly to the convenience of the lumberer. They are of a social habit, growing in "veins," "clumps," "groups," or "communities," as the explorers call them, distinguishing them far away, from the top of a hill or a tree, the white pines towering above the surrounding forest, or else they form extensive forests by themselves. I would have liked to come across a large community of pines, which had never been invaded by the lumbering army.

We saw some fresh moose tracks along the shore, but the Indian said that the moose were not driven out of the woods by the flies, as usual at this season, on account of the abundance of water everywhere. The stream was only from one and one half to three rods wide, quite winding, with occasional small islands, meadows, and some very swift and shallow places. When we came to an island, the Indian never hesitated which side to take, as if the current told him which was the shortest and deepest. It was lucky for us that the water was so high. We had to walk but once on this stream, carrying a part of the load, at a swift and shallow reach, while he got up with the canoe, not being obliged to take out, though he said it was very strong water. Once or twice we passed the red wreck of a bateau which had been stove some spring.

While making this portage I saw many splendid specimens of the great purple-fringed orchis, three feet high. It is remarkable that such delicate flowers should here adorn these wilderness paths.

Having resumed our seats in the canoe, I felt the Indian wiping my back, which he had acccidentally spat upon. He said it was a sign that I was going to be married.

The Umbazookskus River is called ten miles long. Having polled up the narrowest part some three or four miles, the next opening in the sky was over Umbazookskus Lake, which we suddenly entered about eleven o'clock in the forenoon. It stretches northwesterly four or five miles, with what the Indian called the Caucomgomoc Mountain seen far beyond it. It was an agreeable change.

This lake was very shallow a long distance from the shore, and I saw stone heaps on the bottom, like those in the Assabet at home. The canoe ran into one. The Indian thought that they were made by an eel. Joe Aitteon in 1853 thought that they were made by chub. We crossed the southeast end of the lake to the carry into Mud Pond.

Umbazookskus Lake is the head of the Penobscot in this direction, and Mud Pond is the nearest head of the Allegash, one of the chief sources of the St. John. Hodge, who went through this way to the St. Lawrence in the service of the State, calls the portage here a mile and three quarters long, and states that Mud Pond has been found to be fourteen feet higher than Umbazookskus Lake. As the west branch of the Penobscot at the Moosehead carry is considered about twenty-five feet lower than Moosehead Lake, it appears that the Penobscot in the upper part of its course runs in a broad and shallow valley, between the Kennebec and St. Johns, and lower than either of them, though, judging from the map, you might expect it to be the highest.

Mud Pond is about half-way from Umbazookskus to Chamberlain Lake, into which it empties, and to which we were bound. The Indian said that this was the wettest carry in the State, and as the season was a very wet one, we anticipated an unpleasant walk. As usual he made one large bundle of the pork-keg, cooking utensils, and other loose traps, by tying them up in his blanket. We should be obliged to go over the carry twice, and our method was to carry one half part way, and then go back for the rest.

Our path ran close by the door of a log-hut in a clearing at this end of the carry, which the Indian, who alone entered it, found to be occupied by a Canadian and his family, and that the man had been blind for a year. He seemed peculiarly unfortunate to be taken blind there, where there were so few eyes to see for him. He could not even be led out of that country by a dog, but must be taken down the rapids as passively as a barrel of flour. This was the first house above Chesuncook, and the last on the Penobscot waters, and was built here, no doubt, because it was the route of the lumberers in the winter and spring.

After a slight ascent from the lake through the springy soil of the Canadian's clearing, we entered on a level and very wet and rocky path through the universal dense evergreen forest, a loosely paved gutter merely, where we went leaping from rock to rock and from side to side, in the vain attempt to keep out of the water and mud. We concluded that it was yet Penobscot water, though there was no flow to it. It was on this carry that the white hunter whom I met in the stage, as he told me, had shot two bears a few months before. They stood directly in the path, and did not turn out for him. They might be excused for not turning out there, or only taking the right as the law directs. He said that at this season bears were found on the mountains and hillsides, in search of berries, and were apt to be saucy,—that we might come across them up Trout Stream; and he added, what I hardly credited, that many Indians slept in their canoes, not daring to sleep on land, on account of them.

Here commences what was called, twenty years ago, the best timber land in the State. This very spot was described as "covered with the greatest abundance of pine," but now this appeared to me, comparatively, an uncommon tree there,— and yet you did not see where any more could have stood, amid the dense growth of cedar, fir, &c. It was then proposed to cut a canal from lake to lake here, but the outlet was finally made farther east, at Telos Lake, as we shall see.

The Indian with his canoe soon disappeared before us; but erelong he came back and told us to take a path which turned off westward, it being better walking, and, at my suggestion, he agreed to leave a bough in the regular carry at that place, that we might not pass it by mistake. Thereafter, he said, we were to keep the main path, and he added, "You see 'em my tracks." But I had not much faith that we could distinguish his tracks, since others had passed over the carry within a few days.

We turned off at the right place, but were soon confused by numerous logging-paths, coming into the one we were on, by which lumberers had been to pick out those pines which I have mentioned. However, we kept what we considered the main path, though it was a winding one, and in this, at long intervals, we distinguished a faint trace of a footstep. This, though comparatively unworn, was at first a better, or, at least, a drier road, than the regular carry which we had left. It led through an arbor-vitæ wilderness of the grimmest character. The great fallen and rotting trees had been cut through and rolled aside, and their huge trunks abutted on the path on each side, while others still lay across it two or three feet high. It was impossible for us to discern the Indian's trail in the elastic moss, which, like a thick carpet, covered every rock and fallen tree, as well as the earth. Nevertheless, I did occasionally detect the track of a man, and I gave myself some credit for it. I carried my whole load at once, a heavy knapsack, and a large India-rubber bag, containing our bread and a blanket, swung on a paddle; in all, about sixty pounds; but my companion preferred to make two journeys, by short stages, while I waited for him. We could not be sure that we were not depositing our loads each time farther off from the true path.

As I sat waiting for my companion, he would seem to be gone a long time, and I had ample opportunity to make observations on the forest. I now first began to be seriously molested by the black-fly, a very small but perfectly formed fly of that color, about one tenth of an inch long, which I first felt, and then saw, in swarms about me, as I sat by a wider and more than usually doubtful fork in this dark forest-path. The hunters tell bloody stories about them, — how they settle in a ring about your neck, before you know it, and are wiped off in great numbers with your blood. But remembering that I had a wash in my knapsack, prepared by a thoughtful hand in Bangor, I made haste to apply it to my face and hands, and was glad to find it effectual, as long as it was fresh, or for twenty minutes, not only against black-flies, but all the insects that molested us. They would not alight on the part thus defended. It was composed of sweet-oil and oil of turpentine, with a little oil of spearmint, and camphor. However, I finally concluded that the remedy was worse than the disease. It was so disagreeable and inconvenient to have your face and hands covered with such a mixture.

Three large slate-colored birds of the jay genus (*Garrulus Canadensis*), the Canada-jay, moose-bird, meat-bird, or what not, came flitting silently and by degrees toward me, and hopped down the limbs inquisitively to within seven or eight feet. They were more clumsy and not nearly so handsome as the blue-jay. Fish-hawks, from the lake, uttered their sharp whistling notes low over the top of the forest near me, as if they were anxious about a nest there.

After I had sat there some time, I noticed at this fork in the path a tree which had been blazed, and the letters "Chamb. L." written on it with red chalk. This I knew to mean Chamberlain Lake. So I concluded that on the whole we were on the right course, though as we had come nearly two miles, and saw no signs of Mud Pond, I did harbor the suspicion that we might be on a direct course to Chamberlain Lake, leaving out Mud Pond. This I found by my map would be about five miles northeasterly, and I then took the bearing by my compass.

My companion having returned with his bag, and also defended his face and hands with the insect-wash, we set forward again. The walking rapidly grew worse, and the path more indistinct, and at length, after passing through a patch of *calla palustris*, still abundantly in bloom, we found ourselves in a more open and regular swamp, made less passable than ordinary by the unusual wetness of the season. We sank a foot deep in water and mud at every step, and sometimes up to our knees, and the trail was almost obliterated, being no more than that a musquash leaves in similar places, when he parts the floating sedge. In fact, it probably was a musquash trail in some places. We concluded that if Mud Pond was as muddy as the approach to it was wet, it certainly deserved its name. It would have been amusing to behold the dogged and deliberate pace at which we entered that swamp, without interchanging a word, as if determined to go through it, though it should come up to our necks. Having penetrated a considerable distance into this, and found a tussuck on which we could deposit our loads, though there was no place to sit, my companion went back for the rest of his pack. I had thought to observe on this carry when we crossed the dividing line between the Penobscot and St. John, but as my feet had hardly been out of water the whole distance, and it was all level and stagnant, I began to despair of finding it. I remembered hearing a good deal about the "highlands" dividing the waters of the Penobscot from those of the St. John, as well as the St. Lawrence, at the time of the northeast boundary dispute, and I observed by my map, that the line claimed by Great Britain as the boundary prior to 1842 passed between Umbazookskus Lake and Mud Pond, so that we had either crossed or were then on it. These, then, according to *her* interpretation of the treaty of '83, were the "highlands which divide those rivers that empty themselves into the St. Lawrence from those which fall into the Atlantic Ocean." Truly an interesting spot to stand on,— if that were it,—though you could not sit down there. I thought that if the commissioners themselves, and the king of Holland with them, had spent a few days here, with their packs upon their backs, looking for that "highland," they would have had an interesting time, and perhaps it would have modified their views of the question somewhat. The king of Holland would have been in his element. Such were my meditations while my companion was gone back for his bag.

It was a cedar swamp, through which the peculiar note of the white-throated sparrow rang loud and clear. There grew the side-saddle flower, Labrador tea, *Kalmia glauca*, and, what was new to me, the Low Birch (*Betula pumila*), a little round-leafed shrub, two or three feet high only. We thought to name this swamp after the latter.

After a long while my companion came back, and the Indian with him. We had taken the wrong road, and the Indian had lost us. He had very wisely gone back to the Canadian's camp, and asked him which way we had probably gone, since he could better understand the ways of white men, and he told him correctly that we had undoubtedly taken the supply road to Chamberlain Lake (slender supplies they would get over such a road at this season). The Indian was greatly surprised that we should have taken what he called a "tow"

(i. e. tote or toting or supply) road, instead of a carry path,—
that we had not followed his tracks,—said it was "strange,"
and evidently thought little of our woodcraft.

Having held a consultation, and eaten a mouthful of
bread, we concluded that it would, perhaps, be nearer for us
two now to keep on to Chamberlain Lake, omitting Mud
Pond, than to go back and start anew for the last place,
though the Indian had never been through this way, and
knew nothing about it. In the meanwhile he would go back
and finish carrying over his canoe and bundle to Mud Pond,
cross that, and go down its outlet and up Chamberlain Lake,
and trust to meet us there before night. It was now a little
after noon. He supposed that the water in which we stood
had flowed back from Mud Pond, which could not be far off
eastward, but was unapproachable through the dense cedar
swamp.

Keeping on, we were erelong agreeably disappointed by
reaching firmer ground, and we crossed a ridge where the
path was more distinct, but there was never any outlook
over the forest. While descending the last, I saw many specimens of the great round-leaved orchis, of large size; one
which I measured had leaves, as usual, flat on the ground,
nine and a half inches long, and nine wide, and was two feet
high. The dark, damp wilderness is favorable to some of
these orchidaceous plants, though they are too delicate for
cultivation. I also saw the swamp gooseberry (*Ribes lacustre*),
with green fruit, and in all the low ground, where it was not
too wet, the *Rubus triflorus* in fruit. At one place I heard a
very clear and piercing note from a small hawk, like a single
note from a white-throated sparrow, only very much louder,
as he dashed through the tree-tops over my head. I wondered that he allowed himself to be disturbed by our presence, since it seemed as if he could not easily find his nest
again himself in that wilderness. We also saw and heard several times the red squirrel, and often, as before observed, the
bluish scales of the fir cones which it had left on a rock or
fallen tree. This, according to the Indian, is the only squirrel
found in those woods, except a very few striped ones. It
must have a solitary time in that dark evergreen forest,

where there is so little life, seventy-five miles from a road as we had come. I wondered how he could call any particular tree there his home; and yet he would run up the stem of one out of the myriads, as if it were an old road to him. How can a hawk ever find him there? I fancied that he must be glad to see us, though he did seem to chide us. One of those sombre fir and spruce woods is not complete unless you hear from out its cavernous mossy and twiggy recesses his fine alarum,—his spruce voice, like the working of the sap through some crack in a tree,—the working of the spruce-beer. Such an impertinent fellow would occasionally try to alarm the wood about me. "O," said I, "I am well acquainted with your family, I know your cousins in Concord very well. Guess the mail 's irregular in these parts, and you 'd like to hear from 'em." But my overtures were vain, for he would withdraw by his aerial turnpikes into a more distant cedar-top, and spring his rattle again.

We then entered another swamp, at a necessarily slow pace, where the walking was worse than ever, not only on account of the water, but the fallen timber, which often obliterated the indistinct trail entirely. The fallen trees were so numerous, that for long distances the route was through a succession of small yards, where we climbed over fences as high as our heads, down into water often up to our knees, and then over another fence into a second yard, and so on; and going back for his bag my companion once lost his way and came back without it. In many places the canoe would have run if it had not been for the fallen timber. Again it would be more open, but equally wet, too wet for trees to grow, and no place to sit down. It was a mossy swamp, which it required the long legs of a moose to traverse, and it is very likely that we scared some of them in our transit, though we saw none. It was ready to echo the growl of a bear, the howl of a wolf, or the scream of a panther; but when you get fairly into the middle of one of these grim forests, you are surprised to find that the larger inhabitants are not at home commonly, but have left only a puny red squirrel to bark at you. Generally speaking, a howling wilderness does not howl: it is the imagination of the traveller that does the howling. I did, however, see one dead porcupine; perhaps he had succumbed to the difficulties of the way. These bristly fellows are a very suitable small fruit of such unkempt wildernesses.

Making a logging-road in the Maine woods is called "swamping it," and they who do the work are called "swampers." I now perceived the fitness of the term. This was the most perfectly swamped of all the roads I ever saw. Nature must have co-operated with art here. However, I suppose they would tell you that this name took its origin from the fact that the chief work of road-makers in those woods is to make the swamps passable. We came to a stream where the bridge, which had been made of logs tied together with cedar bark, had been broken up, and we got over as we could. This probably emptied into Mud Pond, and perhaps the Indian might have come up it and taken us in there if he had known it. Such as it was, this ruined bridge was the chief evidence that we were on a path of any kind.

We then crossed another low rising ground, and I, who wore shoes, had an opportunity to wring out my stockings, but my companion, who used boots, had found that this was not a safe experiment for him, for he might not be able to get his wet boots on again. He went over the whole ground, or water, three times, for which reason our progress was very slow; beside that the water softened our feet, and to some extent unfitted them for walking. As I sat waiting for him, it would naturally seem an unaccountable time that he was gone. Therefore, as I could see through the woods that the sun was getting low, and it was uncertain how far the lake might be, even if we were on the right course, and in what part of the world we should find ourselves at nightfall, I proposed that I should push through with what speed I could, leaving boughs to mark my path, and find the lake and the Indian, if possible, before night, and send the latter back to carry my companion's bag.

Having gone about a mile, and got into low ground again, I heard a noise like the note of an owl, which I soon discovered to be made by the Indian, and answering him, we soon came together. He had reached the lake, after crossing Mud Pond, and running some rapids below it, and had come up about a mile and a half on our path. If he had not come back to meet us, we probably should not have found him that night, for the path branched once or twice before reaching this particular part of the lake. So he went back for my companion and his bag, while I kept on. Having waded through another stream where the bridge of logs had been broken up and half floated away,—and this was not altogether worse than our ordinary walking, since it was less muddy,—we continued on, through alternate mud and water, to the shore of Apmoojenegamook Lake, which we reached in season for a late supper, instead of dining there, as we had expected, having gone without our dinner. It was at least five miles by the way we had come, and as my companion had gone over most of it three times, he had walked full a dozen miles, bad as it was. In the winter, when the water is frozen, and the snow is four feet deep, it is no doubt a tolerable path to a footman. As it was, I would not have missed that walk for a good deal. If you want an exact recipe for making such a road, take one part Mud Pond, and dilute it with equal parts of Umbazookskus and Apmoojenegamook; then send a family of musquash through to locate it, look after the grades and culverts, and finish it to their minds, and let a hurricane follow to do the fencing.

We had come out on a point extending into Apmoojenegamook, or Chamberlain Lake, west of the outlet of Mud Pond, where there was a broad, gravelly, and rocky shore, encumbered with bleached logs and trees. We were rejoiced to see such dry things in that part of the world. But at first we did not attend to dryness so much as to mud and wetness. We all three walked into the lake up to our middle to wash our clothes.

This was another noble lake, called twelve miles long, east and west; if you add Telos Lake, which, since the dam was built, has been connected with it by dead water, it will be twenty; and it is apparently from a mile and a half to two miles wide. We were about midway its length, on the south side. We could see the only clearing in these parts, called the "Chamberlain Farm," with two or three log buildings close together, on the opposite shore, some two and a half miles distant. The smoke of our fire on the shore brought over two men in a canoe from the farm, that being a common signal agreed on when one wishes to cross. It took them about half an hour to come over, and they had their labor for their pains this time. Even the English name of the lake had a wild, woodland sound, reminding me of that Chamberlain who killed Paugus at Lovewell's fight.

After putting on such dry clothes as we had, and hanging the others to dry on the pole which the Indian arranged over the fire, we ate our supper, and lay down on the pebbly shore with our feet to the fire, without pitching our tent, making a thin bed of grass to cover the stones.

Here first I was molested by the little midge called the No-see-em (*Simulium nocivum*, the latter word is not the Latin for no-see-em), especially over the sand at the water's edge, for it is a kind of sand-fly. You would not observe them but for their light-colored wings. They are said to get under your clothes, and produce a feverish heat, which I suppose was what I felt that night.

Our insect foes in this excursion, to sum them up, were, first, mosquitoes, the chief ones, but only troublesome at night, or when we sat still on shore by day; second, black flies (*Simulium molestum*), which molested us more or less on the carries by day, as I have before described, and sometimes in narrower parts of the stream. Harris mistakes when he says that they are not seen after June. Third, moose-flies. The big ones, Polis said, were called *Bososquasis*. It is a stout brown fly, much like a horse-fly, about eleven sixteenths of an inch long, commonly rusty colored beneath, with unspotted wings. They can bite smartly, according to Polis, but are easily avoided or killed. Fourth, the No-see-ems above mentioned. Of all these, the mosquitoes are the only ones that troubled me seriously; but, as I was provided with a wash and a veil, they have not made any deep impression.

The Indian would not use our wash to protect his face and hands, for fear that it would hurt his skin, nor had he any veil; he, therefore, suffered from insects now, and throughout this journey, more than either of us. I think that he suffered more than I did, when neither of us was protected. He regularly tied up his face in his handkerchief, and buried it in his blanket, and he now finally lay down on the sand between us and the fire for the sake of the smoke, which he tried to make enter his blanket about his face, and for the same purpose he lit his pipe and breathed the smoke into his blanket.

As we lay thus on the shore, with nothing between us and the stars, I inquired what stars he was acquainted with, or had names for. They were the Great Bear, which he called by this name, the Seven Stars, which he had no English name for, "the morning star," and "the north star."

In the middle of the night, as indeed each time that we lay on the shore of a lake, we heard the voice of the loon, loud and distinct, from far over the lake. It is a very wild sound, quite in keeping with the place and the circumstances of the traveller, and very unlike the voice of a bird. I could lie awake for hours listening to it, it is so thrilling. When camping in such a wilderness as this, you are prepared to hear sounds from some of its inhabitants which will give voice to its wildness. Some idea of bears, wolves, or panthers runs in your head naturally, and when this note is first heard very far off at midnight, as you lie with your ear to the ground, — the forest being perfectly still about you, you take it for granted that it is the voice of a wolf or some other wild beast, for only the last part is heard when at a distance, — you conclude that it is a pack of wolves baying the moon, or, perchance, cantering after a moose. Strange as it may seem, the "mooing" of a cow on a mountain-side comes nearest to my idea of the voice of a bear; and this bird's note resembled that. It was the unfailing and characteristic sound of those lakes. We were not so lucky as to hear wolves howl, though that is an occasional serenade. Some friends of mine, who two years ago went up the Caucomgomoc River, were serenaded by wolves while moose-hunting by moonlight. It was a sudden burst, as if a hundred demons had broke loose, — a startling sound enough, which, if any, would make your hair stand on end, and all was still again. It lasted but a moment, and you 'd have thought there were twenty of them, when probably there were only two or three. They heard it twice only, and they said that it gave expression to the wilderness which it lacked before. I heard of some men who, while skinning a moose lately in those woods, were driven off from the carcass by a pack of wolves, which ate it up.

This of the loon — I do not mean its laugh, but its

looning—is a long-drawn call, as it were, sometimes singularly human to my ear,— *hoo-hoo-ooooo*, like the hallooing of a man on a very high key, having thrown his voice into his head. I have heard a sound exactly like it when breathing heavily through my own nostrils, half awake at ten at night, suggesting my affinity to the loon; as if its language were but a dialect of my own, after all. Formerly, when lying awake at midnight in those woods, I had listened to hear some words or syllables of their language, but it chanced that I listened in vain until I heard the cry of the loon. I have heard it occasionally on the ponds of my native town, but there its wildness is not enhanced by the surrounding scenery.

I was awakened at midnight by some heavy, low-flying bird, probably a loon, flapping by close over my head, along the shore. So, turning the other side of my half-clad body to the fire, I sought slumber again.

TUESDAY, July 28.

When we awoke we found a heavy dew on our blankets. I lay awake very early, and listened to the clear, shrill *ah-tette-tette-te*, of the white-throated sparrow, repeated at short intervals, without the least variation, for half an hour, as if it could not enough express its happiness. Whether my companions heard it or not, I know not, but it was a kind of matins to me, and the event of that forenoon.

It was a pleasant sunrise, and we had a view of the mountains in the southeast. Ktaadn appeared about southeast by south. A double-topped mountain, about southeast by east, and another portion of the same, east-southeast. The last the Indian called Nerlumskeechticook, and said that it was at the head of the East Branch, and we should pass near it on our return that way.

We did some more washing in the lake this morning, and with our clothes hung about on the dead trees and rocks, the shore looked like washing-day at home. The Indian, taking the hint, borrowed the soap, and walking into the lake, washed his only cotton shirt on his person, then put on his pants and let it dry on him.

I observed that he wore a cotton shirt, originally white, a greenish flannel one over it, but no waistcoat, flannel drawers, and strong linen or duck pants, which also had been white, blue woollen stockings, cowhide boots, and a Kossuth hat. He carried no change of clothing, but putting on a stout, thick jacket, which he laid aside in the canoe, and seizing a full-sized axe, his gun and ammunition, and a blanket, which would do for a sail or knapsack, if wanted, and strapping on his belt, which contained a large sheath-knife, he walked off at once, ready to be gone all summer. This looked very independent; a few simple and effective tools, and no India-rubber clothing. He was always the first ready to start in the morning, and if it had not held some of our property would not have been obliged to roll up his blanket. Instead of carrying a large bundle of his own extra clothing, &c., he brought back the great-coats of moose tied up in his blanket. I found that his outfit was the result of a long experience, and in the main was hardly to be improved on, unless by washing or an extra shirt. Wanting a button here, he walked off to a place where some Indians had recently encamped, and searched for one, but I believe in vain.

Having softened our stiffened boots and shoes with the pork fat, the usual disposition of what was left at breakfast, we crossed the lake early, steering in a diagonal direction northwesterly about four miles, to the outlet, which was not to be discovered till we were close to it. The Indian name, Apmoojenegamook, means lake that is crossed, because the usual course lies across, and not along it. This is the largest of the Allegash lakes, and was the first St. John's water that we floated on. It is shaped in the main like Chesuncook. There are no mountains or high hills very near it. At Bangor we had been told of a township many miles farther northwest; it was indicated to us as containing the highest land thereabouts, where, by climbing a particular tree in the forest, we could get a general idea of the country. I have no doubt that the last was good advice, but we did not go there. We did not now intend to go far down the Allegash, but merely to get a view of the great lakes which are its source, and then return this way to the East Branch of the Penobscot. The water now, by good rights, flowed northward, if it could be said to flow at all.

After reaching the middle of the lake, we found the waves

as usual pretty high, and the Indian warned my companion, who was nodding, that he must not allow himself to fall asleep in the canoe lest he should upset us; adding, that when Indians want to sleep in a canoe, they lie down straight on the bottom. But in this crowded one that was impossible. However, he said that he would nudge him if he saw him nodding.

A belt of dead trees stood all around the lake, some far out in the water, with others prostrate behind them, and they made the shore, for the most part, almost inaccessible. This is the effect of the dam at the outlet. Thus the natural sandy or rocky shore, with its green fringe, was concealed and destroyed. We coasted westward along the north side, searching for the outlet, about one quarter of a mile distant from this savage-looking shore, on which the waves were breaking violently, knowing that it might easily be concealed amid this rubbish, or by the over-lapping of the shore. It is remarkable how little these important gates to a lake are blazoned. There is no triumphal arch over the modest inlet or outlet, but at some undistinguished point it trickles in or out through the uninterrupted forest, almost as through a sponge.

We reached the outlet in about an hour, and carried over the dam there, which is quite a solid structure, and about one quarter of a mile farther there was a second dam. The reader will perceive that the result of this particular damming about Chamberlain Lake is, that the head-waters of the St. John are made to flow by Bangor. They have thus dammed all the larger lakes, raising their broad surfaces many feet; Moosehead, for instance, some forty miles long, with its steamer on it; thus turning the forces of nature against herself, that they might float their spoils out of the country. They rapidly run out of these immense forests all the finer, and more accessible pine timber, and then leave the bears to watch the decaying dams, not clearing nor cultivating the land, nor making roads, nor building houses, but leaving it a wilderness, as they found it. In many parts, only these dams remain, like deserted beaver-dams. Think how much land they have flowed, without asking Nature's leave! When the State wishes to endow an academy or university, it grants it a tract of forest land: one saw represents an academy; a gang, a university.

The wilderness experiences a sudden rise of all her streams and lakes, she feels ten thousand vermin gnawing at the base of her noblest trees, many combining, drag them off, jarring over the roots of the survivors, and tumble them into the nearest stream, till the fairest having fallen, they scamper off to ransack some new wilderness, and all is still again. It is as when a migrating army of mice girdles a forest of pines. The chopper fells trees from the same motive that the mouse gnaws them,—to get his living. You tell me that he has a more interesting family than the mouse. That is as it happens. He speaks of a "berth" of timber, a good place for him to get into, just as a worm might. When the chopper would praise a pine, he will commonly tell you that the one he cut was so big that a yoke of oxen stood on its stump; as if that were what the pine had grown for, to become the footstool of oxen. In my mind's eye, I can see these unwieldy tame deer, with a yoke binding them together, and brazen-tipped horns betraying their servitude, taking their stand on the stump of each giant pine in succession throughout this whole forest, and chewing their cud there, until it is nothing but an ox-pasture, and run out at that. As if it were good for the oxen, and some terebinthine or other medicinal quality ascended into their nostrils. Or is their elevated position intended merely as a symbol of the fact that the pastoral comes next in order to the sylvan or hunter life?

The character of the logger's admiration is betrayed by his very mode of expressing it. If he told all that was in his mind, he would say, it was so big that I cut it down and then a yoke of oxen could stand on its stump. He admires the log, the carcass or corpse, more than the tree. Why, my dear sir, the tree might have stood on its own stump, and a great deal more comfortably and firmly than a yoke of oxen can, if you had not cut it down. What right have you to celebrate the virtues of the man you murdered?

The Anglo-American can indeed cut down, and grub up all this waving forest, and make a stump speech, and vote for Buchanan on its ruins, but he cannot converse with the spirit of the tree he fells, he cannot read the poetry and mythology which retire as he advances. He ignorantly erases mythologi-cal tablets in order to print his handbills and town-meeting warrants on them. Before he has learned his a b c in the beautiful but mystic lore of the wilderness which Spenser and Dante had just begun to read, he cuts it down, coins a *pine-tree* shilling, (as if to signify the pine's value to him,) puts up a *dee*strict school-house, and introduces Webster's spelling-book.

Below the last dam, the river being swift and shallow, though broad enough, we two walked about half a mile to lighten the canoe. I made it a rule to carry my knapsack when I walked, and also to keep it tied to a cross-bar when in the canoe, that it might be found with the canoe if we should upset.

I heard the dog-day locust here, and afterward on the carries, a sound which I had associated only with more open, if not settled countries. The area for locusts must be small in the Maine woods.

We were now fairly on the Allegash River, which name our Indian said meant hemlock bark. These waters flow northward about 100 miles, at first very feebly, then southeasterly 250 more to the Bay of Fundy. After perhaps two miles of river, we entered Heron Lake, called on the map *Pongokwa-hem*, scaring up forty or fifty young *shecorways*, sheldrakes, at the entrance, which ran over the water with great rapidity, as usual in a long line.

This was the fourth great lake, lying northwest and southeast, like Chesuncook, and most of the long lakes in that neighborhood, and, judging from the map, it is about ten miles long. We had entered it on the southwest side, and saw a dark mountain northeast over the lake, not very far off nor high, which the Indian said was called *Peaked Mountain*, and used by explorers to look for timber from. There was also some other high land more easterly. The shores were in the same ragged and unsightly condition, encumbered with dead timber, both fallen and standing, as in the last lake, owing to the dam on the Allegash below. Some low points or islands were almost drowned.

I saw something white a mile off on the water, which turned out to be a great gull on a rock in the middle, which the Indian would have been glad to kill and eat, but it flew away long before we were near; and also a flock of summer ducks that were about the rock with it. I asking him about herons, since this was Heron Lake, he said that he found the blue heron's nests in the hard-wood trees. I thought that I saw a light-colored object move along the opposite or northern shore, four or five miles distant. He did not know what it could be, unless it were a moose, though he had never seen a white one; but he said that he could distinguish a moose "anywhere on shore, clear across the lake."

Rounding a point, we stood across a bay for a mile and a half or two miles, toward a large island, three or four miles down the lake. We met with ephemeræ (shad-fly) midway, about a mile from the shore, and they evidently fly over the whole lake. On Moosehead I had seen a large devil's-needle half a mile from the shore, coming from the middle of the lake, where it was three or four miles wide at least. It had probably crossed. But at last, of course, you come to lakes so large that an insect cannot fly across them; and this, perhaps, will serve to distinguish a large lake from a small one.

We landed on the southeast side of the island, which was rather elevated, and densely wooded, with a rocky shore, in season for an early dinner. Somebody had camped there not long before, and left the frame on which they stretched a moose-hide, which our Indian criticised severely, thinking it showed but little woodcraft. Here were plenty of the shells of crayfish, or fresh-water lobsters, which had been washed ashore, such as have given a name to some ponds and streams. They are commonly four or five inches long. The Indian proceeded at once to cut a canoe-birch, slanted it up against another tree on the shore, tying it with a withe, and lay down to sleep in its shade.

When we were on the Caucomgomoc, he recommended to us a new way home, the very one which we had first thought of, by the St. John. He even said that it was easier, and would take but little more time than the other, by the east branch of the Penobscot, though very much farther round; and taking the map, he showed where we should be each night, for he was familiar with the route. According to his calculation, we should reach the French settlements the next night after this, by keeping northward down the Allegash, and when we got into the main St. John the banks would be more or less settled all the way; as if that were a recommendation. There would be but one or two falls, with short carrying-places, and we should go down the stream very fast, even a hundred miles a day, if the wind allowed; and he indicated where we should carry over into Eel River to save a bend below Woodstock in New Brunswick, and so into the Schoodic Lake, and thence to the Mattawamkeag. It would be about three hundred and sixty miles to Bangor this way, though only about one hundred and sixty by the other; but in the former case we should explore the St. John from its source through two thirds of its course, as well as the Schoodic Lake and Mattawamkeag,—and we were again tempted to go that way. I feared, however, that the banks of the St. John were too much settled. When I asked him which course would take us through the wildest country, he said the route by the East Branch. Partly from this consideration, as also from its shortness, we resolved to adhere to the latter route, and perhaps ascend Ktaadn on the way. We made this island the limit of our excursion in this direction.

We had now seen the largest of the Allegash Lakes. The next dam " was about fifteen miles" farther north, down the Allegash, and it was dead water so far. We had been told in Bangor of a man who lived alone, a sort of hermit, at that dam, to take care of it, who spent his time tossing a bullet from one hand to the other, for want of employment,—as if we might want to call on him. This sort of tit-for-tat intercourse between his two hands, bandying to and fro a leaden subject, seems to have been his symbol for society.

This island, according to the map, was about a hundred and ten miles in a straight line north-northwest from Bangor, and about ninety-nine miles east-southeast from Quebec. There was another island visible toward the north end of the lake, with an elevated clearing on it; but we learned afterward that it was not inhabited, had only been used as a pasture for cattle which summered in these woods, though our informant said that there was a hut on the mainland near the outlet of the lake. This unnaturally smooth-shaven, squarish spot, in the midst of the otherwise uninterrupted forest, only reminded us how uninhabited the country was. You would sooner expect to meet with a bear than an ox in such a clearing. At any rate, it must have been a surprise to the bears when they came across it. Such, seen far or near, you know at once to be man's work, for Nature never does it. In order to let in the light to the earth as on a lake, he clears off the forest on the hillsides and plains, and sprinkles fine grass-seed, like an enchanter, and so carpets the earth with a firm sward.

Polis had evidently more curiosity respecting the few settlers in those woods than we. If nothing was said, he took it for granted that we wanted to go straight to the next log-hut. Having observed that we came by the log-huts at Chesuncook, and the blind Canadian's at the Mud Pond carry, without stopping to communicate with the inhabitants, he took occasion now to suggest that the usual way was, when you came near a house, to go to it, and tell the inhabitants what you had seen or heard, and then they tell you what they had seen; but we laughed, and said that we had had enough of houses for the present, and had come here partly to avoid them.

In the mean while, the wind, increasing, blew down the Indian's birch and created such a sea that we found ourselves prisoners on the island, the nearest shore, which was the western, being perhaps a mile distant, and we took the canoe out to prevent its drifting away. We did not know but we should be compelled to spend the rest of the day and the night there. At any rate, the Indian went to sleep again in the shade of his birch, my companion busied himself drying his plants, and I rambled along the shore westward, which was quite stony, and obstructed with fallen bleached or drifted trees for four or five rods in width. I found growing on this broad rocky and gravelly shore the *Salix rostrata, discolor*, and *lucida, Ranunculus recurvatus, Potentilla Norvegica, Scutellaria lateriflora, Eupatorium purpureum, Aster Tradescanti, Mentha Canadensis, Epilobium angustifolium*, abundant, *Lycopus sinuatus, Solidago lanceolata, Spiræa salicifolia, Antennaria margaritacea, Prunella, Rumex acetosella*, Raspberries, Wool-grass, *Onoclea*, &c. The nearest trees were *Betula papyracea* and *excelsa*, and *Populus tremuloides*. I give these names because it was my farthest northern point.

Our Indian said that he was a doctor, and could tell me some medicinal use for every plant I could show him. I immediately tried him. He said that the inner bark of the aspen (*Populus tremuloides*) was good for sore eyes; and so with various other plants, proving himself as good as his word. According to his account, he had acquired such knowledge in his youth from a wise old Indian with whom he associated, and he lamented that the present generation of Indians "had lost a great deal."

He said that the caribou was a "very great runner," that there was none about this lake now, though there used to be many, and pointing to the belt of dead trees caused by the dams, he added, "No likum stump,—when he sees that he scared."

Pointing southeasterly over the lake and distant forest, he observed, "Me go Oldtown in three days." I asked how he would get over the swamps and fallen trees. "O," said he, "in winter all covered, go anywhere on snow-shoes, right across lakes." When I asked how he went, he said, "First I go Ktaadn, west side, then I go Millinocket, then Pamadumcook, then Nickatou, then Lincoln, then Oldtown," or else he went a shorter way by the Piscataquis. What a wilderness walk for a man to take alone! None of your half-mile swamps, none of your mile-wide woods merely, as on the skirts of our towns, without hotels, only a dark mountain or a lake for guide-board and station, over ground much of it impassable in summer!

It reminded me of Prometheus Bound. Here was travelling of the old heroic kind over the unaltered face of nature. From the Allegash, or Hemlock River, and Pongoquahem Lake, across great Apmoojenegamook, and leaving the Nerlum-skeechticook Mountain on his left, he takes his way under the bear-haunted slopes of Souneunk and Ktaadn Mountains to Pamadumcook and Millinocket's inland seas, (where often gulls'-eggs may increase his store,) and so on to the forks of the Nickatou, (*nia soseb* "we alone Joseph" seeing what our folks see,) ever pushing the boughs of the fir and spruce aside, with his load of furs, contending day and night, night and day, with the shaggy demon vegetation, travelling through the mossy graveyard of trees. Or he could go by "that rough tooth of the sea," Kineo, great source of arrows and of spears to the ancients, when weapons of stone were used. Seeing and hearing moose, caribou, bears, porcupines, lynxes, wolves, and panthers. Places where he might live and die and never hear of the United States, which make such a noise in the world,—never hear of America, so called from the name of a European gentleman.

There is a lumberer's road called the Eagle Lake road, from the Seboois to the east side of this lake. It may seem strange that any road through such a wilderness should be passable, even in winter, when the snow is three or four feet deep, but at that season, wherever lumbering operations are actively carried on, teams are continually passing on the single track, and it becomes as smooth almost as a railway. I am told that in the Aroostook country the sleds are required by law to be of one width, (four feet,) and sleighs must be altered to fit the track, so that one runner may go in one rut and the other follow the horse. Yet it is very bad turning out.

We had for some time seen a thunder-shower coming up from the west over the woods of the island, and heard the muttering of the thunder, though we were in doubt whether it would reach us; but now the darkness rapidly increasing, and a fresh breeze rustling the forest, we hastily put up the plants which we had been drying, and with one consent made a rush for the tent material and set about pitching it. A place was selected and stakes and pins cut in the shortest possible time, and we were pinning it down lest it should be blown away, when the storm suddenly burst over us.

As we lay huddled together under the tent, which leaked considerably about the sides, with our baggage at our feet, we listened to some of the grandest thunder which I ever heard,—rapid peals, round and plump, bang, bang, bang, in succession, like artillery from some fortress in the sky; and the lightning was proportionally brilliant. The Indian said, "It must be good powder." All for the benefit of the moose and us, echoing far over the concealed lakes. I thought it must be a place which the thunder loved, where the lightning practised to keep its hand in, and it would do no harm to shatter a few pines. What had become of the ephemeræ and devil's-needles then? Were they prudent enough to seek harbor before the storm? Perhaps their motions might guide the voyageur.

Looking out I perceived that the violent shower falling on the lake had almost instantaneously flattened the waves,—the commander of that fortress had smoothed it for us so,—and it clearing off, we resolved to start immediately, before the wind raised them again.

Going outside, I said that I saw clouds still in the south-west, and heard thunder there. The Indian asked if the thunder went "lound" (round), saying that if it did we should have more rain. I thought that it did. We embarked, nevertheless, and paddled rapidly back toward the dams. The white-throated sparrows on the shore were about, singing, *Ah te, e, e, te, e, e, te,* or else *ah te, e, e, te, e, e, te, e, e, te, e, e.*

At the outlet of Chamberlain Lake we were overtaken by another gusty rain-storm, which compelled us to take shelter, the Indian under his canoe on the bank, and we ran under the edge of the dam. However, we were more scared than wet. From my covert I could see the Indian peeping out from beneath his canoe to see what had become of the rain. When we had taken our respective places thus once or twice, the rain not coming down in earnest, we commenced rambling about the neighborhood, for the wind had by this time raised such waves on the lake that we could not stir, and we feared that we should be obliged to camp there. We got an early supper on the dam and tried for fish there, while waiting for the tumult to subside. The fishes were not only few, but small and worthless, and the Indian declared that there were no good fishes in the St. John's waters; that we must wait till we got to the Penobscot waters.

At length, just before sunset, we set out again. It was a wild evening when we coasted up the north side of this Apmoo-jenegamook Lake. One thunder-storm was just over, and the waves which it had raised still running with violence, and another storm was now seen coming up in the southwest, far over the lake; but it might be worse in the morning, and we wished to get as far as possible on our way up the lake while we might. It blowed hard against the northern shore about an eighth of a mile distant on our left, and there was just as much sea as our shallow canoe would bear, without our taking unusual care. That which we kept off, and toward which the waves were driving, was as dreary and harborless a shore as you can conceive. For half a dozen rods in width it was a perfect maze of submerged trees, all dead and bare and bleaching, some standing half their original height, others prostrate, and criss-across, above or beneath the surface, and mingled with them were loose trees and limbs and stumps, beating about. Imagine the wharves of the largest city in the world, decayed, and the earth and planking washed away, leaving the spiles standing in loose order, but often of twice the ordinary height, and mingled with and beating against them the wreck of ten thousand navies, all their spars and timbers, while there rises from the water's edge the densest and grimmest wilderness, ready to supply more material when the former fails, and you may get a faint idea of that coast. We could not have landed if we would, without the greatest danger of being swamped; so blow as it might, we must depend on coasting by it. It was twilight, too, and that stormy cloud was advancing rapidly in our rear. It was a pleasant excitement, yet we were glad to reach, at length, in the dusk, the cleared shore of the Chamberlain Farm.

We landed on a low and thinly wooded point there, and while my companions were pitching the tent, I ran up to the house to get some sugar, our six pounds being gone; — it was no wonder they were, for Polis had a sweet tooth. He would first fill his dipper nearly a third full of sugar, and then add the coffee to it. Here was a clearing extending back from the lake to a hill-top, with some dark-colored log buildings and a storehouse in it, and half a dozen men standing in front of the principal hut, greedy for news. Among them was the man who tended the dam on the Allegash and tossed the bullet. He having charge of the dams, and learning that we were going to Webster Stream the next day, told me that some of their men, who were haying at Telos Lake, had shut the dam at the canal there in order to catch trout, and if we wanted more water to take us through the canal we might raise the gate, for he would like to have it raised. The Chamberlain Farm is no doubt a cheerful opening in the woods, but such was the lateness of the hour that it has left but a dusky impression on my mind. As I have said, the influx of light merely is civilizing, yet I fancied that they walked about on Sundays in their clearing somewhat as in a prison-yard.

They were unwilling to spare more than four pounds of brown sugar,—unlocking the storehouse to get it,—since they only kept a little for such cases as this, and they charged twenty cents a pound for it, which certainly it was worth to get it up there.

When I returned to the shore it was quite dark, but we had a rousing fire to warm and dry us by, and a snug apartment behind it. The Indian went up to the house to inquire after a brother who had been absent hunting a year or two, and while another shower was beginning, I groped about cutting spruce and arbor-vitæ twigs for a bed. I preferred the arbor-vitæ on account of its fragrance, and spread it particularly thick about the shoulders. It is remarkable with what pure satisfaction the traveller in these woods will reach his camping-ground on the eve of a tempestuous night like this, as if he had got to his inn, and, rolling himself in his blanket, stretch himself on his six feet by two bed of dripping fir-twigs, with a thin sheet of cotton for roof, snug as a meadow-mouse in its nest. Invariably our best nights were those when it rained, for then we were not troubled with mosquitoes.

You soon come to disregard rain on such excursions, at least in the summer, it is so easy to dry yourself, supposing a dry change of clothing is not to be had. You can much sooner dry you by such a fire as you can make in the woods than in anybody's kitchen, the fireplace is so much larger, and wood so much more abundant. A shed-shaped tent will catch and reflect the heat like a Yankee-baker, and you may be drying while you are sleeping.

Some who have leaky roofs in the towns may have been kept awake, but we were soon lulled asleep by a steady, soaking rain, which lasted all night. To-night, the rain not coming at once with violence, the twigs were soon dried by the reflected heat.

WEDNESDAY, July 29.

When we awoke it had done raining, though it was still cloudy. The fire was put out, and the Indian's boots, which stood under the eaves of the tent, were half full of water. He was much more improvident in such respects than either of us, and he had to thank us for keeping his powder dry. We decided to cross the lake at once, before breakfast, or while we could; and before starting I took the bearing of the shore which we wished to strike, S. S. E. about three miles distant, lest a sudden misty rain should conceal it when we were midway. Though the bay in which we were was perfectly quiet and smooth, we found the lake already wide awake outside, but not dangerously or unpleasantly so; nevertheless, when you get out on one of those lakes in a canoe like this, you do not forget that you are completely at the mercy of the wind, and a fickle power it is. The playful waves may at any time become too rude for you in their sport, and play right on over you. We saw a few *she-cor-ways* and a *fish-hawk* thus early, and after much steady paddling and dancing over the dark waves of Apmoojenegamook, we found ourselves in the neighborhood of the southern land, heard the waves breaking on it, and turned our thoughts wholly to that side. After coasting eastward along this shore a mile or two, we breakfasted on a rocky point, the first convenient place that offered.

It was well enough that we crossed thus early, for the waves now ran quite high, and we should have been obliged to go round somewhat, but beyond this point we had comparatively smooth water. You can commonly go along one side or the other of a lake, when you cannot cross it.

The Indian was looking at the hard-wood ridges from time to time, and said that he would like to buy a few hundred acres somewhere about this lake, asking our advice. It was to buy as near the crossing place as possible.

My companion and I having a minute's discussion on some point of ancient history, were amused by the attitude which the Indian, who could not tell what we were talking about, assumed. He constituted himself umpire, and, judging by our air and gesture, he very seriously remarked from time to time, "you beat," or "he beat."

Leaving a spacious bay, a northeasterly prolongation of Chamberlain Lake, on our left, we entered through a short strait into a small lake a couple of miles over, called on the map *Telasinis*, but the Indian had no distinct name for it, and thence into *Telos* Lake, which he called *Paytaywecomgomoc*, or Burnt-Ground Lake. This curved round toward the northeast, and may have been three or four miles long as we paddled.

He had not been here since 1825. He did not know what Telos
meant; thought it was not Indian. He used the word "*Spoke-
logan*" (for an inlet in the shore which led nowhere), and
when I asked its meaning said that there was "no Indian in
'em." There was a clearing, with a house and barn, on the
southwest shore, temporarily occupied by some men who
were getting the hay, as we had been told; also a clearing for
a pasture on a hill on the west side of the lake.

We landed on a rocky point on the northeast side, to look
at some Red Pines (*Pinus resinosa*), the first we had noticed,
and get some cones, for our few which grow in Concord do
not bear any.

The outlet from the lake into the East Branch of the Penobscot is an artificial one, and it was not very apparent where
it was exactly, but the lake ran curving far up northeasterly
into two narrow valleys or ravines, as if it had for a long time
been groping its way toward the Penobscot waters, or remembered when it anciently flowed there; by observing
where the horizon was lowest, and following the longest of
these, we at length reached the dam, having come about a
dozen miles from the last camp. Somebody had left a line set
for trout, and the jackknife with which the bait had been cut
on the dam beside it, an evidence that man was near, and on
a deserted log close by a loaf of bread baked in a Yankee-
baker. These proved the property of a solitary hunter, whom
we soon met, and canoe and gun and traps were not far off.
He told us that it was twenty miles farther on our route to
the foot of Grand Lake, where you could catch as many trout
as you wanted, and that the first house below the foot of the
lake, on the East Branch, was Hunt's, about forty-five miles
farther; though there was one about a mile and a half up
Trout stream, some fifteen miles ahead, but it was rather a
blind route to it. It turned out that, though the stream was
in our favor, we did not reach the next house till the morning
of the third day after this. The nearest permanently inhabited
house behind us was now a dozen miles distant, so that the
interval between the two nearest houses on our route was
about sixty miles.

This hunter, who was a quite small, sunburnt man, having
already carried his canoe over, and baked his loaf, had

nothing so interesting and pressing to do as to observe our transit. He had been out a month or more alone. How much more wild and adventurous his life than that of the hunter in Concord woods, who gets back to his house and the mill-dam every night! Yet they in the towns who have wild oats to sow commonly sow them on cultivated and comparatively exhausted ground. And as for the rowdy world in the large cities, so little enterprise has it that it never adventures in this direction, but like vermin clubs together in alleys and drinking-saloons, its highest accomplishment, perchance, to run beside a fire-engine and throw brickbats. But the former is comparatively an independent and successful man, getting his living in a way that he likes, without disturbing his human neighbors. How much more respectable also is the life of the solitary pioneer or settler in these, or any woods,—having real difficulties, not of his own creation, drawing his subsistence directly from nature,—than that of the helpless multitudes in the towns who depend on gratifying the extremely artificial wants of society and are thrown out of employment by hard times!

Here for the first time we found the raspberries really plenty,—that is, on passing the height of land between the Allegash and the East Branch of the Penobscot; the same was true of the blueberries.

Telos Lake, the head of the St. John on this side, and Webster Pond, the head of the East Branch of the Penobscot, are only about a mile apart, and they are connected by a ravine, in which but little digging was required to make the water of the former, which is the highest, flow into the latter. This canal, which is something less than a mile long and about four rods wide, was made a few years before my first visit to Maine. Since then the lumber of the upper Allegash and its lakes has been run down the Penobscot, that is, up the Allegash, which here consists principally of a chain of large and stagnant lakes, whose thoroughfares, or river-links, have been made nearly equally stagnant by damming, and then down the Penobscot. The rush of the water has produced such changes in the canal that it has now the appearance of a very rapid mountain stream flowing through a ravine, and you would not suspect that any digging had been required to persuade the waters of the St. John to flow into the Penobscot here. It was so winding that one could see but little way down.

It is stated by Springer, in his "Forest Life," that the cause of this canal being dug was this. According to the treaty of 1842 with Great Britain, it was agreed that all the timber run down the St. John, which rises in Maine, " when within the Province of New Brunswick . . . . shall be dealt with as if it were the produce of the said Province," which was thought by our side to mean that it should be free from taxation. Immediately, the Province, wishing to get something out of the Yankees, levied a duty on all the timber that passed down the St. John; but to satisfy its own subjects "made a corresponding discount on the stumpage charged those hauling timber from the crown lands." The result was that the Yankees made the St. John run the other way, or down the Penobscot, so that the Province lost both its duty and its water, while the Yankees, being greatly enriched, had reason to thank it for the suggestion.

It is wonderful how well watered this country is. As you paddle across a lake, bays will be pointed out to you, by following up which, and perhaps the tributary stream which empties in, you may, after a short portage, or possibly, at some seasons, none at all, get into another river, which empties far away from the one you are on. Generally, you may go in any direction in a canoe, by making frequent but not very long portages. You are only realizing once more what all nature distinctly remembers here, for no doubt the waters flowed thus in a former geological period, and instead of being a lake country, it was an archipelago. It seems as if the more youthful and impressible streams can hardly resist the numerous invitations and temptations to leave their native beds and run down their neighbors' channels. Your carries are often over half-submerged ground, on the dry channels of a former period. In carrying from one river to another, I did not go over such high and rocky ground as in going about the falls of the same river. For in the former case I was once lost in a swamp, as I have related, and, again, found an artificial canal which appeared to be natural.

I remember once dreaming of pushing a canoe up the rivers

of Maine, and that, when I had got so high that the channels were dry, I kept on through the ravines and gorges, nearly as well as before, by pushing a little harder, and now it seemed to me that my dream was partially realized.

Wherever there is a channel for water, there is a road for the canoe. The pilot of the steamer which ran from Oldtown up the Penobscot in 1854 told me that she drew only fourteen inches, and would run easily in two feet of water, though they did not like to. It is said that some Western steamers can run on a heavy dew, whence we can imagine what a canoe may do. Montresor, who was sent from Quebec by the English about 1760 to explore the route to the Kennebec, over which Arnold afterward passed, supplied the Penobscot near its source with water by opening the beaver-dams, and he says, "This is often done." He afterward states that the Governor of Canada had forbidden to molest the beaver about the outlet of the Kennebec from Moosehead Lake, on account of the service which their dams did by raising the water for navigation.

This canal, so called, was a considerable and extremely rapid and rocky river. The Indian decided that there was water enough in it without raising the dam, which would only make it more violent, and that he would run down it alone, while we carried the greater part of the baggage. Our provision being about half consumed, there was the less left in the canoe. We had thrown away the pork-keg, and wrapt its contents in birch bark, which is the unequalled wrapping-paper of the woods.

Following a moist trail through the forest, we reached the head of Webster Pond about the same time with the Indian, notwithstanding the velocity with which he moved, our route being the most direct. The Indian name of Webster Stream, of which this pond is the source, is, according to him, *Madunkehunk*, i. e. Height of Land, and of the pond, *Madunke-hunk-gamooc*, or Height of Land Pond. The latter was two or three miles long. We passed near a pine on its shore which had been splintered by lightning, perhaps the day before. This was the first proper East Branch Penobscot water that we came to.

At the outlet of Webster Lake was another dam, at which

we stopped and picked raspberries, while the Indian went down the stream a half-mile through the forest, to see what he had got to contend with. There was a deserted log camp here, apparently used the previous winter, with its "hovel" or barn for cattle. In the hut was a large fir-twig bed, raised two feet from the floor, occupying a large part of the single apartment, a long narrow table against the wall, with a stout log bench before it, and above the table a small window, the only one there was, which admitted a feeble light. It was a simple and strong fort erected against the cold, and suggested what valiant trencher work had been done there. I discovered one or two curious wooden traps, which had not been used for a long time, in the woods near by. The principal part consisted of a long and slender pole.

We got our dinner on the shore, on the upper side of the dam. As we were sitting by our fire, concealed by the earth bank of the dam, a long line of sheldrake, half grown, came waddling over it from the water below, passing within about a rod of us, so that we could almost have caught them in our hands. They were very abundant on all the streams and lakes which we visited, and every two or three hours they would rush away in a long string over the water before us, twenty to fifty of them at once, rarely ever flying, but running with great rapidity up or down the stream, even in the midst of the most violent rapids, and apparently as fast up as down, or else crossing diagonally, the old, as it appeared, behind, and driving them, and flying to the front from time to time, as if to direct them. We also saw many small black dippers, which behaved in a similar manner, and, once or twice, a few black ducks.

An Indian at Oldtown had told us that we should be obliged to carry ten miles between Telos Lake on the St. John's and Second Lake on the East Branch of the Penobscot; but the lumberers whom we met assured us that there would not be more than a mile of carry. It turned out that the Indian, who had lately been over this route, was nearest right, as far as we were concerned. However, if one of us could have assisted the Indian in managing the canoe in the rapids, we might have run the greater part of the way; but as he was alone in the management of the canoe in such places, we were obliged to walk the greater part. I did not feel quite ready to try such an experiment on Webster Stream, which has so bad a reputation. According to my observation, a bateau, properly manned, shoots rapids as a matter of course, which a single Indian with a canoe carries round.

My companion and I carried a good part of the baggage on our shoulders, while the Indian took that which would be least injured by wet in the canoe. We did not know when we should see him again, for he had not been this way since the canal was cut, nor for more than thirty years. He agreed to stop when he got to smooth water, come up and find our path if he could, and halloo for us, and after waiting a reasonable time go on and try again,—and we were to look out in like manner for him.

He commenced by running through the sluice-way and over the dam, as usual, standing up in his tossing canoe, and was soon out of sight behind a point in a wild gorge. This Webster Stream is well known to lumbermen as a difficult one. It is exceedingly rapid and rocky, and also shallow, and can hardly be considered navigable, unless that may mean that what is launched in it is sure to be carried swiftly down it, though it may be dashed to pieces by the way. It is somewhat like navigating a thunder-spout. With commonly an irresistible force urging you on, you have got to choose your own course each moment, between the rocks and shallows, and to get into it, moving forward always with the utmost possible moderation, and often holding on, if you can, that you may inspect the rapids before you.

By the Indian's direction we took an old path on the south side, which appeared to keep down the stream, though at a considerable distance from it, cutting off bends, perhaps to Second Lake, having first taken the course from the map with a compass, which was northeasterly, for safety. It was a wild wood-path, with a few tracks of oxen which had been driven over it, probably to some old camp clearing, for pasturage, mingled with the tracks of moose which had lately used it. We kept on steadily for about an hour without putting down our packs, occasionally winding around or climbing over a fallen tree, for the most part far out of sight and hearing of the river; till, after walking about three miles, we were glad to find that the path came to the river again at an old camp ground, where there was a small opening in the forest, at which we paused. Swiftly as the shallow and rocky river ran here, a continuous rapid with dancing waves, I saw, as I sat on the shore, a long string of sheldrakes, which something scared, run up the opposite side of the stream by me, with the same ease that they commonly did down it, just touching the surface of the waves, and getting an impulse from them as they flowed from under them; but they soon came back, driven by the Indian, who had fallen a little behind us, on account of the windings. He shot round a point just above, and came to land by us with considerable water in his canoe. He had found it, as he said, "very strong water," and had been obliged to land once before to empty out what he had taken in. He complained that it strained him to paddle so hard in order to keep his canoe straight in its course, having no one in the bows to aid him, and, shallow as it was, said that it would be no joke to upset there, for the force of the water was such that he had as lief I would strike him over the head with a paddle as have that water strike him. Seeing him come out of that gap was as if you should pour water down an inclined and zigzag trough, then drop a nutshell into it, and taking a short cut to the bottom, get there in time to see it come out, notwithstanding the rush and tumult, right side up, and only partly full of water.

After a moment's breathing space, while I held his canoe, he was soon out of sight again around another bend, and we, shouldering our packs, resumed our course.

We did not at once fall into our path again, but made our way with difficulty along the edge of the river, till at length, striking inland through the forest, we recovered it. Before going a mile we heard the Indian calling to us. He had come up through the woods and along the path to find us, having reached sufficiently smooth water to warrant his taking us in. The shore was about one fourth of a mile distant, through a dense, dark forest, and as he led us back to it, winding rapidly about to the right and left, I had the curiosity to look down carefully, and found that he was following his steps backward. I could only occasionally perceive his trail in the moss, and yet he did not appear to look down nor hesitate an instant, but led us out exactly to his canoe. This surprised me, for without a compass, or the sight or noise of the river to guide us, we could not have kept our course many minutes, and could have retraced our steps but a short distance, with a great deal of pains and very slowly, using a laborious circumspection. But it was evident that he could go back through the forest wherever he had been during the day.

After this rough walking in the dark woods it was an agreeable change to glide down the rapid river in the canoe once more. This river, which was about the size of our Assabet (in Concord), though still very swift, was almost perfectly smooth here, and showed a very visible declivity, a regularly inclined plane, for several miles, like a mirror set a little aslant, on which we coasted down. This very obvious regular descent, particularly plain when I regarded the water-line against the shores, made a singular impression on me, which the swiftness of our motion probably enhanced, so that we seemed to be gliding down a much steeper declivity than we were, and that we could not save ourselves from rapids and falls if we should suddenly come to them. My companion did not perceive this slope, but I have a surveyor's eyes, and I satisfied myself that it was no ocular illusion. You could tell at a glance on approaching such a river, which way the water flowed, though you might perceive no motion. I observed the angle at which a level line would strike the surface, and calculated the amount of fall in a rod, which did not need to be remarkably great to produce this effect.

It was very exhilarating, and the perfection of travelling, quite unlike floating on our dead Concord River, the coasting down this inclined mirror, which was now and then gently winding, down a mountain, indeed, between two evergreen forests, edged with lofty dead white pines, sometimes slanted half-way over the stream, and destined soon to bridge it. I saw some monsters there, nearly destitute of branches, and scarcely diminishing in diameter for eighty or ninety feet.

As we thus swept along, our Indian repeated in a deliberate and drawling tone the words "Daniel Webster, great lawyer," apparently reminded of him by the name of the stream, and he described his calling on him once in Boston, at what he supposed was his boarding-house. He had no business with him, but merely went to pay his respects, as we should say. In answer to our questions, he described his person well enough. It was on the day after Webster delivered his Bunker Hill oration, which I believe Polis heard. The first time he called he waited till he was tired without seeing him, and then went away. The next time, he saw him go by the door of the room in which he was waiting several times, in his shirt-sleeves, without noticing him. He thought that if he had come to see Indians, they would not have treated him so. At length, after very long delay, he came in, walked toward him, and asked in a loud voice, gruffly, "What do you want?" and he, thinking at first, by the motion of his hand, that he was going to strike him, said to himself, "You'd better take care, if you try that I shall know what to do." He did not like him, and declared that all he said "was not worth talk about a musquash." We suggested that probably Mr. Webster was very busy, and had a great many visitors just then.

Coming to falls and rapids, our easy progress was suddenly terminated. The Indian went along shore to inspect the water, while we climbed over the rocks, picking berries. The peculiar growth of blueberries on the tops of large rocks here made the impression of high land, and indeed this was the Height-of-land stream. When the Indian came back, he remarked, "You got to walk; ver strong water." So, taking out his canoe, he launched it again below the falls, and was soon out of sight. At such times, he would step into the canoe, take up his paddle, and, with an air of mystery, start off, looking far down stream, and keeping his own counsel, as if absorbing all the intelligence of forest and stream into himself; but I sometimes detected a little fun in his face, which could yield to my sympathetic smile, for he was thoroughly good-humored. We meanwhile scrambled along the shore with our packs, without any path. This was the last of *our* boating for the day.

The prevailing rock here was a kind of slate, standing on its edges, and my companion, who was recently from California, thought it exactly like that in which the gold is found, and said that if he had had a pan he would have liked to wash a little of the sand here.

The Indian now got along much faster than we, and waited

for us from time to time. I found here the only cool spring that I drank at anywhere on this excursion, a little water filling a hollow in the sandy bank. It was a quite memorable event, and due to the elevation of the country, for wherever else we had been the water in the rivers and the streams emptying in was dead and warm, compared with that of a mountainous region. It was very bad walking along the shore over fallen and drifted trees and bushes, and rocks, from time to time swinging ourselves round over the water, or else taking to a gravel bar or going inland. At one place, the Indian being ahead, I was obliged to take off all my clothes in order to ford a small but deep stream emptying in, while my companion, who was inland, found a rude bridge, high up in the woods, and I saw no more of him for some time. I saw there very fresh moose tracks, found a new golden-rod to me (perhaps *Solidago thyrsoidea*), and I passed one white-pine log, which had lodged, in the forest near the edge of the stream, which was quite five feet in diameter at the but. Probably its size detained it.

Shortly after this, I overtook the Indian at the edge of some burnt land, which extended three or four miles at least, beginning about three miles above Second Lake, which we were expecting to reach that night, and which is about ten miles from Telos Lake. This burnt region was still more rocky than before, but, though comparatively open, we could not yet see the lake. Not having seen my companion for some time, I climbed, with the Indian, a singular high rock on the edge of the river, forming a narrow ridge only a foot or two wide at top, in order to look for him; and after calling many times, I at length heard him answer from a considerable distance inland, he having taken a trail which led off from the river, perhaps directly to the lake, and was now in search of the river again. Seeing a much higher rock, of the same character, about one third of a mile farther east, or down stream, I proceeded toward it, through the burnt land, in order to look for the lake from its summit, supposing that the Indian would keep down the stream in his canoe, and hallooing all the while that my companion might join me on the way. Before we came together, I noticed where a moose, which possibly I had scared by my shouting, had apparently just run along a

large rotten trunk of a pine, which made a bridge, thirty or
forty feet long, over a hollow, as convenient for him as for
me. The tracks were as large as those of an ox, but an ox
could not have crossed there. This burnt land was an exceedingly wild and desolate region. Judging by the weeds and
sprouts, it appeared to have been burnt about two years before. It was covered with charred trunks, either prostrate or
standing, which crocked our clothes and hands, and we could
not easily have distinguished a bear there by his color. Great
shells of trees, sometimes unburnt without, or burnt on one
side only, but black within, stood twenty or forty feet high.
The fire had run up inside, as in a chimney, leaving the sap-
wood. Sometimes we crossed a rocky ravine fifty feet wide,
on a fallen trunk; and there were great fields of fire-weed
(*Epilobium angustifolium*) on all sides, the most extensive that
I ever saw, which presented great masses of pink. Intermixed
with these were blueberry and raspberry bushes.

Having crossed a second rocky ridge, like the first, when I
was beginning to ascend the third, the Indian, whom I had
left on the shore some fifty rods behind, beckoned to me to
come to him, but I made sign that I would first ascend the
highest rock before me, whence I expected to see the lake.
My companion accompanied me to the top. This was formed
just like the others. Being struck with the perfect parallelism
of these singular rock-hills, however much one might be in
advance of another, I took out my compass and found that
they lay northwest and southeast, the rock being on its edge,
and sharp edges they were. This one, to speak from memory,
was perhaps a third of a mile in length, but quite narrow,
rising gradually from the northwest to the height of about
eighty feet, but steep on the southeast end. The southwest
side was as steep as an ordinary roof, or as we could safely
climb; the northeast was an abrupt precipice from which you
could jump clean to the bottom, near which the river flowed;
while the level top of the ridge, on which you walked along,
was only from one to three or four feet in width. For a rude
illustration, take the half of a pear cut in two lengthwise, lay
it on its flat side, the stem to the northwest, and then halve it
vertically in the direction of its length, keeping the southwest
half. Such was the general form.

There was a remarkable series of these great rock-waves revealed by the burning; breakers, as it were. No wonder that the river that found its way through them was rapid and obstructed by falls. No doubt the absence of soil on these rocks, or its dryness where there was any, caused this to be a very thorough burning. We could see the lake over the woods, two or three miles ahead, and that the river made an abrupt turn southward around the northwest end of the cliff on which we stood, or a little above us, so that we had cut off a bend, and that there was an important fall in it a short distance below us. I could see the canoe a hundred rods behind, but now on the opposite shore, and supposed that the Indian had concluded to take out and carry round some bad rapids on that side, and that that might be what he had beckoned to me for; but after waiting a while I could still see nothing of him, and I observed to my companion that I wondered where he was, though I began to suspect that he had gone inland to look for the lake from some hill-top on that side, as we had done. This proved to be the case; for after I had started to return to the canoe, I heard a faint halloo, and descried him on the top of a distant rocky hill on that side. But as, after a long time had elapsed, I still saw his canoe in the same place, and he had not returned to it, and appeared in no hurry to do so, and, moreover, as I remembered that he had previously beckoned to me, I thought that there might be something more to delay him than I knew, and began to return northwest, along the ridge, toward the angle in the river. My companion, who had just been separated from us, and had even contemplated the necessity of camping alone, wishing to husband his steps, and yet to keep with us, inquired where I was going; to which I answered, that I was going far enough back to communicate with the Indian, and that then I thought we had better go along the shore together, and keep him in sight.

When we reached the shore, the Indian appeared from out the woods on the opposite side, but on account of the roar of the water it was difficult to communicate with him. He kept along the shore westward to his canoe, while we stopped at the angle where the stream turned southward around the precipice. I again said to my companion, that we would keep along the shore and keep the Indian in sight. We started to do so, being close together, the Indian behind us having launched his canoe again, but just then I saw the latter, who had crossed to our side, forty or fifty rods behind, beckoning to me, and I called to my companion, who had just disappeared behind large rocks at the point of the precipice, three or four rods before me, on his way down the stream, that I was going to help the Indian a moment. I did so,—helped get the canoe over a fall, lying with my breast over a rock, and holding one end while he received it below,—and within ten or fifteen minutes at most I was back again at the point where the river turned southward, in order to catch up with my companion, while Polis glided down the river alone, parallel with me. But to my surprise, when I rounded the precipice, though the shore was bare of trees, not of rocks, for a quarter of a mile at least, my companion was not to be seen. It was as if he had sunk into the earth. This was the more unaccountable to me, because I knew that his feet were since our swamp walk very sore, and that he wished to keep with the party; and besides this was very bad walking, climbing over or about the rocks. I hastened along, hallooing and searching for him, thinking he might be concealed behind a rock, yet doubting if he had not taken the other side of the precipice, but the Indian had got along still faster in his canoe, till he was arrested by the falls, about a quarter of a mile below. He then landed, and said that we could go no farther that night. The sun was setting, and on account of falls and rapids we should be obliged to leave this river and carry a good way into another farther east. The first thing then was to find my companion, for I was now very much alarmed about him, and I sent the Indian along the shore down stream, which began to be covered with unburnt wood again just below the falls, while I searched backward about the precipice which we had passed. The Indian showed some unwillingness to exert himself, complaining that he was very tired, in consequence of his day's work, that it had strained him very much getting down so many rapids alone; but he went off calling somewhat like an owl. I remembered that my companion was near-sighted, and I feared that he had either fallen from the precipice, or fainted and sunk down amid the rocks beneath it. I shouted and searched above and below this

precipice in the twilight till I could not see, expecting nothing
less than to find his body beneath it. For half an hour I anticipated and believed only the worst. I thought what I should
do the next day, if I did not find him, what I *could* do in such
a wilderness, and how his relatives would feel, if I should
return without him. I felt that if he were really lost away from
the river there, it would be a desperate undertaking to find
him; and where were they who could help you? What would
it be to raise the country, where there were only two or three
camps, twenty or thirty miles apart, and no road, and perhaps
nobody at home? Yet we must try the harder, the less the
prospect of success.

I rushed down from this precipice to the canoe in order to
fire the Indian's gun, but found that my companion had the
caps. I was still thinking of getting it off when the Indian
returned. He had not found him, but he said that he had seen
his tracks once or twice along the shore. This encouraged me
very much. He objected to firing the gun, saying that if my
companion heard it, which was not likely, on account of the
roar of the stream, it would tempt him to come toward us,
and he might break his neck in the dark. For the same reason
we refrained from lighting a fire on the highest rock. I proposed that we should both keep down the stream to the lake,
or that I should go at any rate, but the Indian said, "No use,
can't do anything in the dark; come morning, then we find
'em. No harm,—he make 'em camp. No bad animals here, no
gristly bears, such as in California, where he 's been,—warm
night,—he well off as you and I." I considered that if he was
well he could do without us. He had just lived eight years in
California, and had plenty of experience with wild beasts and
wilder men, was peculiarly accustomed to make journeys of
great length, but if he were sick or dead, he was near where
we were. The darkness in the woods was by this so thick that
it alone decided the question. We must camp where we were.
I knew that he had his knapsack, with blankets and matches,
and, if well, would fare no worse than we, except that he
would have no supper nor society.

This side of the river being so encumbered with rocks, we
crossed to the eastern or smoother shore, and proceeded to
camp there, within two or three rods of the Falls. We pitched

no tent, but lay on the sand, putting a few handfuls of grass and twigs under us, there being no evergreen at hand. For fuel we had some of the charred stumps. Our various bags of provisions had got quite wet in the rapids, and I arranged them about the fire to dry. The fall close by was the principal one on this stream, and it shook the earth under us. It was a cool, because dewy, night; the more so, probably, owing to the nearness of the falls. The Indian complained a good deal, and thought afterward that he got a cold there which occasioned a more serious illness. We were not much troubled by mosquitoes at any rate. I lay awake a good deal from anxiety, but, unaccountably to myself, was at length comparatively at ease respecting him. At first I had apprehended the worst, but now I had little doubt but that I should find him in the morning. From time to time I fancied that I heard his voice calling through the roar of the falls from the opposite side of the river; but it is doubtful if we could have heard him across the stream there. Sometimes I doubted whether the Indian had really seen his tracks, since he manifested an unwillingness to make much of a search, and then my anxiety returned.

It was the most wild and desolate region we had camped in, where, if anywhere, one might expect to meet with befitting inhabitants, but I heard only the squeak of a night-hawk flitting over. The moon in her first quarter, in the fore part of the night, setting over the bare rocky hills, garnished with tall, charred, and hollow stumps or shells of trees, served to reveal the desolation.

THURSDAY, July 30.

I aroused the Indian early this morning to go in search of our companion, expecting to find him within a mile or two, farther down the stream. The Indian wanted his breakfast first, but I reminded him that my companion had had neither breakfast nor supper. We were obliged first to carry our canoe and baggage over into another stream, the main East Branch, about three fourths of a mile distant, for Webster Stream was no farther navigable. We went twice over this carry, and the dewy bushes wet us through like water up to the middle; I hallooed in a high key from time to time, though I had little expectation that I could be heard over the roar of the rapids, and moreover we were necessarily on the opposite side of the stream to him. In going over this portage the last time, the Indian, who was before me with the canoe on his head, stumbled and fell heavily once, and lay for a moment silent, as if in pain. I hastily stepped forward to help him, asking if he was much hurt, but after a moment's pause, without replying, he sprang up and went forward. He was all the way subject to taciturn fits, but they were harmless ones.

We had launched our canoe and gone but little way down the East Branch, when I heard an answering shout from my companion, and soon after saw him standing on a point where there was a clearing a quarter of a mile below, and the smoke of his fire was rising near by. Before I saw him I naturally shouted again and again, but the Indian curtly remarked, "He hears you," as if once was enough. It was just below the mouth of Webster Stream. When we arrived, he was smoking his pipe, and said that he had passed a pretty comfortable night, though it was rather cold, on account of the dew.

It appeared that when we stood together the previous evening, and I was shouting to the Indian across the river, he, being near-sighted, had not seen the Indian nor his canoe, and when I went back to the Indian's assistance, did not see which way I went, and supposed that we were below and not above him, and so, making haste to catch up, he ran away from us. Having reached this clearing, a mile or more below our camp, the night overtook him, and he made a fire in a little hollow, and lay down by it in his blanket, still thinking that we were ahead of him. He thought it likely that he had heard the Indian call once the evening before, but mistook it for an owl. He had seen one botanical rarity before it was dark,—pure white *Epilobium angustifolium* amidst the fields of pink ones, in the burnt lands. He had already stuck up the remnant of a lumberer's shirt, found on the point, on a pole by the water-side, for a signal, and attached a note to it, to inform us that he had gone on to the lake, and that if he did not find us there, he would be back in a couple of hours. If he had not found us soon, he had some thoughts of going back in search of the solitary hunter whom we had met at Telos Lake, ten miles behind, and, if successful, hire him to take him to Bangor. But if this hunter had moved as fast as we, he would have been twenty miles off by this time, and who could guess in what direction? It would have been like looking for a needle in a hay-mow, to search for him in these woods. He had been considering how long he could live on berries alone.

We substituted for his note a card containing our names and destination, and the date of our visit, which Polis neatly enclosed in a piece of birch-bark to keep it dry. This has probably been read by some hunter or explorer ere this.

We all had good appetites for the breakfast which we made haste to cook here, and then, having partially dried our clothes, we glided swiftly down the winding stream toward Second Lake.

As the shores became flatter with frequent gravel and sand bars, and the stream more winding in the lower land near the lake, elms and ash trees made their appearance; also the wild yellow lily (*Lilium Canadense*), some of whose bulbs I collected for a soup. On some ridges the burnt land extended as far as the lake. This was a very beautiful lake, two or three miles long, with high mountains on the southwest side, the (as our Indian said) *Nerlumskeechticook*, i. e. Dead-Water Mountain. It appears to be the same called Carbuncle Mountain on the map. According to Polis, it extends in separate elevations all along this and the next lake, which is much larger. The lake, too, I think, is called by the same name, or perhaps with the addition of *gamoc* or *mooc*. The morning was a bright one, and perfectly still and serene, the lake as smooth as glass, we making the only ripples as we paddled into it. The dark mountains about it were seen through a glaucous mist, and the brilliant white stems of canoe-birches mingled with the other woods around it. The wood-thrush sang on the distant shore, and the laugh of some loons, sporting in a concealed western bay, as if inspired by the morning, came distinct over the lake to us, and, what was remarkable, the echo which ran round the lake was much louder than the original note; probably because, the loons being in a regularly curving bay under the mountain, we were exactly in the focus of many echoes, the sound being reflected like light from a concave mirror. The beauty of the scene may have been enhanced to our eyes by the fact that we had just come together again after a night of some anxiety. This reminded me of the Ambejijis Lake on the West Branch, which I crossed in my first coming to Maine. Having paddled down three quarters of the lake, we came to a stand still, while my companion let down for fish. A white (or whitish) gull sat on a rock which rose above the surface in mid-lake not far off, quite in harmony with the scene; and as we rested there in the warm sun, we heard one loud crashing or crackling sound from the forest, forty or fifty rods distant, as of a stick broken by the foot of some large animal. Even this was an interesting incident there. In the midst of our dreams of giant lake-trout, even then supposed to be nibbling, our fisherman drew up a diminutive red perch, and we took up our paddles again in haste.

It was not apparent where the outlet of this lake was, and while the Indian thought it was in one direction, I thought it was in another. He said, "I bet you fourpence it is there," but he still held on in my direction, which proved to be the right one. As we were approaching the outlet, it being still early in the forenoon, he suddenly exclaimed, "Moose! moose!" and told us to be still. He put a cap on his gun, and standing up in the stern, rapidly pushed the canoe straight toward the shore and the moose. It was a cow-moose, about thirty rods off, standing in the water by the side of the outlet, partly behind some fallen timber and bushes, and at that distance she did not look very large. She was flapping her large ears, and from time to time poking off the flies with her nose from some part of her body. She did not appear much alarmed by our neighborhood, only occasionally turned her head and looked straight at us, and then gave her attention to the flies again. As we approached nearer, she got out of the water, stood higher and regarded us more suspiciously. Polis pushed the canoe steadily forward in the shallow water, and I for a moment forgot the moose in attending to some pretty rose-colored Polygonums just rising above the surface, but the canoe soon grounded in the mud eight or ten rods distant from the moose, and the Indian seized his gun and prepared to fire. After standing still a moment, she turned slowly, as usual, so as to expose her side, and he improved this moment to fire, over our heads. She thereupon moved off eight or ten rods at a moderate pace, across a shallow bay, to an old standing-place of hers, behind some fallen red maples, on the opposite shore, and there she stood still again a dozen or fourteen rods from us, while the Indian hastily loaded and fired twice at her, without her moving. My companion, who passed him his caps and bullets, said that Polis was as excited as a boy of fifteen, that his hand trembled, and he once put his ramrod back up-side down. This was remarkable for so experienced a hunter. Perhaps he was anxious to make a good shot before us. The white hunter had told me that the Indians were not good shots, because they were excited, though he said that we had got a good hunter with us.

The Indian now pushed quickly and quietly back, and a long distance round, in order to get into the outlet,—for he had fired over the neck of a peninsula between it and the lake,—till we approached the place where the moose had stood, when he exclaimed, "She is a goner," and was surprised that we did not see her as soon as he did. There, to be sure, she lay perfectly dead, with her tongue hanging out, just where she had stood to receive the last shots, looking unexpectedly large and horse-like, and we saw where the bullets had scored the trees.

Using a tape, I found that the moose measured just six feet from the shoulder to the tip of the hoof, and was eight feet long as she lay. Some portions of the body, for a foot in diameter, were almost covered with flies, apparently the common fly of our woods, with a dark spot on the wing, and not the very large ones which occasionally pursued us in mid-stream, though both are called moose-flies.

Polis, preparing to skin the moose, asked me to help him find a stone on which to sharpen his large knife. It being all a flat alluvial ground where the moose had fallen, covered with red maples, &c., this was no easy matter; we searched far and wide, a long time, till at length I found a flat kind of slate-stone, and soon after he returned with a similar one, on which he soon made his knife very sharp.

While he was skinning the moose, I proceeded to ascertain what kind of fishes were to be found in the sluggish and muddy outlet. The greatest difficulty was to find a pole. It was almost impossible to find a slender, straight pole ten or twelve feet long in those woods. You might search half an hour in vain. They are commonly spruce, arbor-vitæ, fir, &c., short, stout, and branchy, and do not make good fish-poles, even after you have patiently cut off all their tough and scraggy branches. The fishes were red perch and chivin.

The Indian having cut off a large piece of sirloin, the upper lip and the tongue, wrapped them in the hide, and placed them in the bottom of the canoe, observing that there was "one man," meaning the weight of one. Our load had previously been reduced some thirty pounds, but a hundred pounds were now added, a serious addition, which made our quarters still more narrow, and considerably increased the danger on the lakes and rapids, as well as the labor of the carries. The skin was ours according to custom, since the Indian was in our employ, but we did not think of claiming it. He being a skilful dresser of moose-hides, would make it worth seven or eight dollars to him, as I was told. He said that he sometimes earned fifty or sixty dollars in a day at them; he had killed ten moose in one day, though the skinning and all took two days. This was the way he had got his property. There were the tracks of a calf thereabouts, which he said would come "by, by," and he could get it if we cared to wait, but I cast cold water on the project.

We continued along the outlet toward Grand Lake, through a swampy region, by a long, winding, and narrow dead water, very much choked up by wood, where we were obliged to land sometimes in order to get the canoe over a log. It was hard to find any channel, and we did not know but we should be lost in the swamp. It abounded in ducks, as usual. At length we reached Grand Lake, which the Indian called *Matungamook*.

At the head of this we saw, coming in from the southwest, with a sweep apparently from a gorge in the mountains, Trout Stream, or *Uncardnerheese*, which name, the Indian said, had something to do with mountains.

We stopped to dine on an interesting high rocky island, soon after entering Matungamook Lake, securing our canoe to the cliffy shore. It is always pleasant to step from a boat on to a large rock or cliff. Here was a good opportunity to dry our dewy blankets on the open sunny rock. Indians had recently camped here, and accidentally burned over the western end of the island, and Polis picked up a gun-case of blue broadcloth, and said that he knew the Indian it belonged to, and would carry it to him. His tribe is not so large but he may know all its effects. We proceeded to make a fire and cook our dinner amid some pines, where our predecessors had done the same, while the Indian busied himself about his moose-hide on the shore, for he said that he thought it a good plan for one to do all the cooking, i. e. I suppose if that one were not himself. A peculiar evergreen overhung our fire, which at first glance looked like a pitch pine (*P. rigida*), with leaves little more than an inch long, spruce-like, but we found it to be the *Pinus Banksiana*,—"Banks's, or the Labrador Pine," also called Scrub Pine, Gray Pine, &c., a new tree to us. These must have been good specimens, for several were thirty or thirty-five feet high, which is 2 or 3 times the height commonly assigned them. Michaux says that it grows further north than any of our pines, but he did not find it any where more than 10 feet high. Richardson found it forty feet high and upward, and states that the porcupine feeds on its bark. Here also grew the Red Pine (*Pinus resinosa*).

I saw where the Indians had made canoes in a little secluded hollow in the woods, on the top of the rock, where they were out of the wind, and large piles of whittlings remained. This must have been a favorite resort for their ancestors, and, indeed, we found here the point of an arrow-head, such as they have not used for two centuries and now know not how to make. The Indian, picking up a stone, remarked to me, "That very strange lock (rock)." It was a piece of hornstone, which I told him his tribe had probably brought here centuries before to make arrow-heads of. He also picked up a yellowish curved bone by the side of our fireplace and asked me to guess what it was. It was one of the upper incisors of a beaver, on which some party had feasted within a year or two. I found also most of the teeth, and the skull, &c. We here dined on fried moose-meat.

One who was my companion in my two previous excursions to these woods, tells me that when hunting up the Caucomgomoc, about two years ago, he found himself dining one day on moose-meat, mud-turtle, trout, and beaver, and he thought that there were few places in the world where these dishes could easily be brought together on one table.

After the almost incessant rapids and falls of the Madunke-hunk (Height-of-Land, or Webster Stream), we had just passed through the dead-water of Second Lake, and were now in the much larger dead-water of Grand Lake, and I thought the Indian was entitled to take an extra nap here. Ktaadn, near which we were to pass the next day, is said to mean "Highest Land." So much geography is there in their names. The Indian navigator naturally distinguishes by a name those parts of a stream where he has encountered quick water and falls, and again, the lakes and smooth water where he can rest his weary arms, since those are the most interesting and memorable parts to him. The very sight of the *Nerlumskeechticook*, or Dead-Water Mountains, a day's journey off over the forest, as we first saw them, must awaken in him pleasing memories. And not less interesting is it to the white traveller, when he is crossing a placid lake in these out-of-the-way woods, perhaps thinking that he is in some sense one of the earlier discoverers of it, to be reminded that it was thus well known and suitably named by Indian hunters perhaps a thousand years ago.

Ascending the precipitous rock which formed this long narrow island, I was surprised to find that its summit was a narrow ridge, with a precipice on one side, and that its axis of elevation extended from northwest to southeast, exactly like that of the great rocky ridges at the commencement of the Burnt Ground, ten miles northwesterly. The same arrangement prevailed here, and we could plainly see that the mountain ridges on the west of the lake trended the same way. Splendid large harebells nodded over the edge and in the clefts of the cliff, and the blueberries (*Vaccinium Canadense*) were for the first time really abundant in the thin soil on its top. There was no lack of them henceforward on the East Branch. There was a fine view hence over the sparkling lake, which looked pure and deep, and had two or three, in all, rocky islands in it. Our blankets being dry, we set out again, the Indian as usual having left his gazette on a tree. This time it was we three in a canoe, my companion smoking. We paddled southward down this handsome lake, which appeared to extend nearly as far east as south, keeping near the western shore, just outside a small island, under the dark *Nerlumskeechticook* mountain. For I had observed on my map that this was the course. It was three or four miles across it. It struck me that the outline of this mountain on the southwest of the lake, and of another beyond it, was not only like that of the huge rock waves of Webster Stream, but in the main like Kineo, on Moosehead Lake, having a similar but less abrupt precipice at the southeast end; in short, that all the prominent hills and ridges hereabouts were larger or smaller Kineos, and that possibly there was such a relation between Kineo and the rocks of Webster Stream.

The Indian did not know exactly where the outlet was, whether at the extreme southwest angle or more easterly, and had asked to see my plan at the last stopping-place, but I had forgotten to show it to him. As usual, he went feeling his way by a middle course between two probable points, from which he could diverge either way at last without losing much distance. In approaching the south shore, as the clouds looked gusty, and the waves ran pretty high, we so steered as to get partly under the lee of an island, though at a great distance from it.

I could not distinguish the outlet till we were almost in it, and heard the water falling over the dam there.

Here was a considerable fall, and a very substantial dam, but no sign of a cabin or camp. The hunter whom we met at Telos Lake had told us that there were plenty of trout here, but at this hour they did not rise to the bait, only cousin trout, from the very midst of the rushing waters. There are not so many fishes in these rivers as in the Concord.

While we loitered here, Polis took occasion to cut with his big knife some of the hair from his moose-hide, and so lightened and prepared it for drying. I noticed at several old Indian camps in the woods the pile of hair which they had cut from their hides.

Having carried over the dam, he darted down the rapids, leaving us to walk for a mile or more, where for the most part there was no path, but very thick and difficult travelling near the stream. At length he would call to let us know where he was waiting for us with his canoe, when, on account of the windings of the stream, we did not know where the shore was, but he did not call often enough, forgetting that we were not Indians. He seemed to be very saving of his breath,—yet he would be surprised if we went by, or did not strike the right spot. This was not because he was unaccommodating, but a proof of superior manners. Indians like to get along with the least possible communication and ado. He was really paying us a great compliment all the while, thinking that we preferred a hint to a kick.

At length, climbing over the willows and fallen trees, when this was easier than to go round or under them, we overtook the canoe, and glided down the stream in smooth but swift water for several miles. I here observed again, as at Webster Stream, and on a still larger scale the next day, that the river was a smooth and regularly inclined plane down which we coasted. As we thus glided along we started the first black ducks which we had distinguished.

We decided to camp early to-night, that we might have ample time before dark; so we stopped at the first favorable shore, where there was a narrow gravelly beach on the western side, some five miles below the outlet of the lake. It was an interesting spot, where the river began to make a great bend to the east, and the last of the peculiar moose-faced *Nerlumskeechticook* mountains not far southwest of Grand Lake rose dark in the northwest a short distance behind, displaying its gray precipitous southeast side, but we could not see this without coming out upon the shore.

Two steps from the water on either side, and you come to the abrupt bushy and rooty if not turfy edge of the bank, four or five feet high, where the interminable forest begins, as if the stream had but just cut its way through it.

It is surprising on stepping ashore anywhere into this unbroken wilderness to see so often, at least within a few rods of the river, the marks of the axe, made by lumberers who have either camped here, or driven logs past in previous springs. You will see perchance where, going on the same errand that you do, they have cut large chips from a tall white-pine stump for their fire. While we were pitching the camp

and getting supper, the Indian cut the rest of the hair from
his moose-hide, and proceeded to extend it vertically on a
temporary frame between two small trees, half a dozen feet
from the opposite side of the fire, lashing and stretching it
with arbor-vitæ bark, which was always at hand, and in this
case was stripped from one of the trees it was tied to. Asking
for a new kind of tea, he made us some, pretty good, of
the checkerberry (*Gaultheria procumbens*), which covered the
ground, dropping a little bunch of it tied up with cedar bark
into the kettle; but it was not quite equal to the *Chiogenes*.
We called this therefore Checkerberry-tea Camp.

I was struck with the abundance of the *Linnæa borealis*,
checkerberry, and *Chiogenes hispidula*, almost everywhere in
the Maine woods. The wintergreen (*Chimaphila umbellata*)
was still in bloom here, and *Clintonia* berries were abundant
and ripe. This handsome plant is one of the most common in
that forest. We here first noticed the moose-wood in fruit on
the banks. The prevailing trees were spruce (commonly
black), arbor-vitæ, canoe-birch, (black ash and elms beginning
to appear,) yellow birch, red maple, and a little hemlock
skulking in the forest. The Indian said that the white-maple
punk was the best for tinder, that yellow-birch punk was
pretty good, but hard. After supper he put on the moose
tongue and lips to boil, cutting out the *septum*. He showed
me how to write on the under side of birch bark, with a black
spruce twig, which is hard and tough and can be brought to
a point.

The Indian wandered off into the woods a short distance
just before night, and, coming back, said, "Me found great
treasure—fifty, sixty dollars worth." "What's that?" we
asked. "Steel traps, under a log, thirty or forty, I did n't count
'em. I guess Indian work—worth three dollars apiece." It was
a singular coincidence that he should have chanced to walk to
and look under that particular log, in that trackless forest.

I saw chivin and chub in the stream when washing my
hands, but my companion tried in vain to catch them. I also
heard the sound of bull-frogs from a swamp on the opposite
side, thinking at first that they were moose; a duck paddled
swiftly by; and sitting in that dusky wilderness, under that
dark mountain, by the bright river which was full of reflected

light, still I heard the wood-thrush sing, as if no higher civilization could be attained. By this time the night was upon us.

You commonly make your camp just at sundown, and are collecting wood, getting your supper, or pitching your tent while the shades of night are gathering around and adding to the already dense gloom of the forest. You have no time to explore or look around you before it is dark. You may penetrate half a dozen rods farther into that twilight wilderness, after some dry bark to kindle your fire with, and wonder what mysteries lie hidden still deeper in it, say at the end of a long day's walk; or you may run down to the shore for a dipper of water, and get a clearer view for a short distance up or down the stream, and while you stand there, see a fish leap, or duck alight in the river, or hear a wood-thrush or robin sing in the woods. That is as if you had been to town or civilized parts. But there is no sauntering off to see the country, and ten or fifteen rods seems a great way from your companions, and you come back with the air of a much travelled man, as from a long journey, with adventures to relate, though you may have heard the crackling of the fire all the while,—and at a hundred rods you might be lost past recovery, and have to camp out. It is all mossy and *moosey*. In some of those dense fir and spruce woods there is hardly room for the smoke to go up. The trees are a *standing* night, and every fir and spruce which you fell is a plume plucked from night's raven wing. Then at night the general stillness is more impressive than any sound, but occasionally you hear the note of an owl farther or nearer in the woods, and if near a lake, the semi-human cry of the loons at their unearthly revels.

To-night the Indian lay between the fire and his stretched moose-hide, to avoid the mosquitoes. Indeed, he also made a small smoky fire of damp leaves at his head and his feet, and then as usual rolled up his head in his blanket. We with our veils and our wash were tolerably comfortable, but it would be difficult to pursue any sedentary occupation in the woods at this season: you cannot see to read much by the light of a fire through a veil in the evening, nor handle pencil and paper well with gloves or anointed fingers.

The Indian said, "You and I kill moose last night, therefore use 'em best wood. Always use hard wood to cook moose-meat." His "best wood" was rock-maple. He cast the moose's lip into the fire, to burn the hair off, and then rolled it up with the meat to carry along. Observing that we were sitting down to breakfast without any pork, he said, with a very grave look, "Me want some fat," so he was told that he might have as much as he would fry.

We had smooth but swift water for a considerable distance, where we glided rapidly along, scaring up ducks and kingfishers. But as usual, our smooth progress erelong came to an end, and we were obliged to carry canoe and all about half a mile down the right bank, around some rapids or falls. It required sharp eyes sometimes to tell which side was the carry, before you went over the falls, but Polis never failed to land us rightly. The raspberries were particularly abundant and large here, and all hands went to eating them, the Indian remarking on their size.

Often on bare rocky carries the trail was so indistinct that I repeatedly lost it, but when I walked behind him I observed that he could keep it almost like a hound, and rarely hesitated, or, if he paused a moment on a bare rock, his eye immediately detected some sign which would have escaped me. Frequently *we* found no path at all at these places, and were to him unaccountably delayed. He would only say it was "ver strange."

We had heard of a Grand Fall on this stream, and thought that each fall we came to must be it, but after christening several in succession with this name, we gave up the search. There were more Grand or Petty Falls than I can remember.

I cannot tell how many times we had to walk on account of falls or rapids. We were expecting all the while that the river would take a final leap and get to smooth water, but there was no improvement this forenoon. However, the carries were an agreeable variety. So surely as we stepped out of the canoe and stretched our legs we found ourselves in a blueberry and raspberry garden, each side of our rocky trail around the falls being lined with one or both. There was not a carry on the main East Branch where we did not find an abundance of both these berries, for these were the rockiest places, and partially cleared, such as these plants prefer, and there had been none to gather the finest before us.

In our three journeys over the carries, for we were obliged to go over the ground three times whenever the canoe was taken out, we did full justice to the berries, and they were just what we wanted to correct the effect of our hard bread and pork diet. Another name for making a portage would have been going a berrying. We also found a few *Amelanchier*, or *service* berries, though most were abortive, but they held on rather more generally than they do in Concord. The Indian called them *Pemoymenuk*, and said that they bore much fruit in some places. He sometimes also ate the northern wild red cherries, saying that they were good medicine, but they were scarcely edible.

We bathed and dined at the foot of one of these carries. It was the Indian who commonly reminded us that it was dinner-time, sometimes even by turning the prow to the shore. He once made an indirect, but lengthy apology, by saying that we might think it strange, but that one who worked hard all day was very particular to have his dinner in good season. At the most considerable fall on this stream, when I was walking over the carry, close behind the Indian, he observed a track on the rock, which was but slightly covered with soil, and, stooping, muttered "caribou." When we returned, he observed a much larger track near the same place, where some animal's foot had sunk into a small hollow in the rock, partly filled with grass and earth, and he exclaimed with surprise, "What that?" "Well, what is it?" I asked. Stooping and laying his hand in it, he answered with a mysterious air, and in a half whisper, "Devil [that is, Indian Devil, or cougar] ledges about here—very bad animal—pull 'em *locks* all to pieces." "How long since it was made?" I asked. "To-day or yesterday," said he. But when I asked him afterward if he was sure it was the devil's track, he said he did not know. I had been told that the scream of a cougar was heard about Ktaadn recently, and we were not far from that mountain.

We spent at least half the time in walking to-day, and the walking was as bad as usual, for the Indian being alone, commonly ran down far below the foot of the carries before he waited for us. The carry-paths themselves were more than usually indistinct, often the route being revealed only by the countless small holes in the fallen timber made by the tacks in the drivers' boots, or where there *was* a slight trail we did not find it. It was a tangled and perplexing thicket, through which we stumbled and threaded our way, and when we had finished a mile of it, our starting-point seemed far away. We were glad that we had not got to walk to Bangor along the banks of this river, which would be a journey of more than a hundred miles. Think of the denseness of the forest, the fallen trees and rocks, the windings of the river, the streams emptying in and the frequent swamps to be crossed. It made you shudder. Yet the Indian from time to time pointed out to us where he had thus crept along day after day when he was a boy of ten, and in a starving condition. He had been hunting far north of this with two grown Indians. The winter came on unexpectedly early, and the ice compelled them to leave their canoe at Grand Lake, and walk down the bank. They shouldered their furs and started for Oldtown. The snow was not deep enough for snow-shoes, or to cover the inequalities of the ground. Polis was soon too weak to carry any burden; but he managed to catch one otter. This was the most they all had to eat on this journey, and he remembered how good the yellow-lily roots were, made into a soup with the otter oil. He shared this food equally with the other two, but being so small he suffered much more than they. He waded through the Mattawamkeag at its mouth, when it was freezing cold and came up to his chin, and he, being very weak and emaciated, expected to be swept away. The first house which they reached was at Lincoln, and thereabouts they met a white teamster with supplies, who seeing their condition gave them as much of his load as they could eat. For six months after getting home he was very low, and did not expect to live, and was perhaps always the worse for it.

We could not find much more than half of this day's journey on our maps (the "Map of the Public Lands of Maine and Massachusetts," and "Colton's Railroad and Township Map of Maine," which copies the former). By the maps there was not more than fifteen miles between camps, at the outside, and yet we had been busily progressing all day, and much of the time very rapidly.

For seven or eight miles below that succession of "Grand" falls, the aspect of the banks as well as the character of the stream was changed. After passing a tributary from the northeast, perhaps Bowlin Stream, we had good swift smooth water, with a regular slope, such as I have described. Low, grassy banks and muddy shores began. Many elms, as well as maples, and more ash trees overhung the stream, and supplanted the spruce.

My lily-roots having been lost when the canoe was taken out at a carry, I landed late in the afternoon, at a low and grassy place amid maples, to gather more. It was slow work grubbing them up amid the sand, and the mosquitoes were all the while feasting on me. Mosquitoes, black flies, &c., pursued us in mid-channel, and we were glad sometimes to get into violent rapids, for then we escaped them.

A red-headed woodpecker flew across the river, and the Indian remarked that it was good to eat. As we glided swiftly down the inclined plane of the river, a great cat-owl launched itself away from a stump on the bank, and flew heavily across the stream, and the Indian, as usual, imitated its note. Soon the same bird flew back in front of us, and we afterwards passed it perched on a tree. Soon afterward a white-headed eagle sailed down the stream before us. We drove him several miles, while we were looking for a good place to camp, for we expected to be overtaken by a shower,—and still we could distinguish him by his white tail, sailing away from time to time from some tree by the shore still farther down the stream. Some shecorways, being surprised by us, a part of them dived, and we passed directly over them, and could trace their course here and there by a bubble on the surface, but we did not see them come up. Polis detected once or twice what he called a "tow" road, an indistinct path leading into the forest. In the mean while we passed the mouth of the Seboois on our left. This did not look so large as our stream, which was indeed the main one. It was some time before we found a camping-place, for the shore was either too grassy and muddy, where mosquitoes abounded, or too steep a hillside. The Indian said that there were but few mosquitoes on a steep hillside. We examined a good place, where somebody had camped a long time; but it seemed pitiful to occupy an old site, where there was so much room to choose, so we continued on. We at length found a place to our minds, on the west bank, about a mile below the mouth of the Seboois, where, in a very dense spruce wood above a gravelly shore, there seemed to be but few insects. The trees were so thick that we were obliged to clear a space to build our fire and lie down in, and the young spruce trees that were left were like the wall of an apartment rising around us. We were obliged to pull ourselves up a steep bank to get there. But the place which you have selected for your camp, though never so rough and grim, begins at once to have its attractions, and becomes a very centre of civilization to you: "Home is home, be it never so homely."

It turned out that the mosquitoes were more numerous here than we had found them before, and the Indian complained a good deal, though he lay, as the night before, between three fires and his stretched hide. As I sat on a stump by the fire, with a veil and gloves on trying to read, he observed, "I make you candle," and in a minute he took a piece of birch bark about two inches wide and rolled it hard, like an allumette fifteen inches long, lit it, and fixed it by the other end horizontally in a split stick three feet high, stuck it in the ground, turning the blazing end to the wind, and telling me to snuff it from time to time. It answered the purpose of a candle pretty well.

I noticed, as I had done before, that there was a lull among the mosquitoes about midnight, and that they began again in the morning. Nature is thus merciful. But apparently they need rest as well as we. Few if any creatures are equally active all night. As soon as it was light I saw, through my veil, that the inside of the tent about our heads was quite blackened with myriads, each one of their wings when flying, as has been calculated, vibrating some three thousand times in a minute, and their combined hum was almost as bad to endure as their stings. I had an uncomfortable night on this account, though I am not sure that one succeeded in his attempt to sting me. We did not suffer so much from insects on this excursion as the statements of some who have explored these woods in midsummer led us to anticipate. Yet I have no doubt that at some seasons and in some places they are a much more serious pest. The Jesuit Hierome Lalemant, of Quebec, reporting the death of Father Reni Menard, who was abandoned, lost his way, and died in the woods, among the Ontarios near Lake Superior, in 1661, dwells chiefly on his probable sufferings from the attacks of mosquitoes when too weak to defend himself, adding that there was a frightful number of them in those parts, "and so insupportable," says he, "that the three Frenchmen who have made that voyage, affirm that there was no other means of defending one's self but to run always without stopping, and it was even necessary for two of them to be employed in driving off these creatures while the third wanted to drink, otherwise he could not have done it." I have no doubt that this was said in good faith.

August 1.

I caught two or three large red chivin (*Leuciscus pulchellus*) early this morning, within twenty feet of the camp, which, added to the moose-tongue, that had been left in the kettle boiling over night, and to our other stores, made a sumptuous breakfast. The Indian made us some hemlock tea instead of coffee, and we were not obliged to go as far as China for it; indeed, not quite so far as for the fish. This was tolerable, though he said it was not strong enough. It was interesting to see so simple a dish as a kettle of water with a handful of green hemlock sprigs in it, boiling over the huge fire in the open air, the leaves fast losing their lively green color, and know that it was for our breakfast.

We were glad to embark once more, and leave some of the mosquitoes behind. We had passed the *Wassataquoik* without perceiving it. This, according to the Indian, is the name of the main East Branch itself, and not properly applied to this small tributary alone, as on the maps.

We found that we had camped about a mile above Hunt's, which is on the east bank, and is the last house for those who ascend Ktaadn on this side.

We also had expected to ascend it from this point, but omitted it on account of the chafed feet of one of my companions. The Indian, however, suggested that perhaps he might get a pair of moccasins at this place, and that he could walk very easily in them without hurting his feet, wearing several pairs of stockings, and he said beside that they were so porous that when you had taken in water it all drained out again in a little while. We stopped to get some sugar, but found that the family had moved away, and the house was unoccupied, except temporarily by some men who were getting the hay. They told us that the road to Ktaadn left the river eight miles above; also that perhaps we could get some sugar at Fisk's, fourteen miles below. I do not remember that we saw the mountain at all from the river. I noticed a seine here stretched on the bank, which probably had been used to catch salmon. Just below this, on the west bank, we saw a moose-hide stretched, and with it a bearskin, which was comparatively very small. I was the more interested in this sight, because it was near here that a townsman of ours, then quite a lad, and alone, killed a large bear some years ago. The Indian said that they belonged to Joe Aitteon, my last guide, but how he told I do not know. He was probably hunting near, and had left them for the day. Finding that we were going directly to Oldtown, he regretted that he had not taken more of the moose-meat to his family, saying that in a short time, by drying it, he could have made it so light as to have brought away the greater part, leaving the bones. We once or twice inquired after the lip, which is a famous tit-bit, but he said, "That go Oldtown for my old woman; don't get it every day."

Maples grew more and more numerous. It was lowering, and rained a little during the forenoon, and, as we expected a wetting, we stopped early and dined on the east side of a small expansion of the river, just above what are probably called Whetstone Falls, about a dozen miles below Hunt's. There were pretty fresh moose-tracks by the water-side. There were singular long ridges hereabouts, called "horsebacks," covered with ferns. My companion having lost his pipe asked the Indian if he could not make him one. "O yer," said he, and in a minute rolled up one of birch-bark, telling him to wet the bowl from time to time. Here also he left his gazette on a tree.

We carried round the falls just below, on the west side. The rocks were on their edges, and very sharp. The distance was about three fourths of a mile. When we had carried over one load, the Indian returned by the shore, and I by the path; and though I made no particular haste, I was nevertheless surprised to find him at the other end as soon as I. It was remarkable how easily he got along over the worst ground. He said to me, "I take canoe and you take the rest, suppose you can keep along with me?" I thought that he meant, that while he ran down the rapids I should keep along the shore, and be ready to assist him from time to time, as I had done before; but as the walking would be very bad, I answered, "I suppose you will go too fast for me, but I will try." But I was to go by the path, he said. This I thought would not help the matter, I should have so far to go to get to the river-side when he wanted me. But neither was this what he meant. He was proposing a race over the carry, and asked me if I thought I could keep along with him by the same path, adding that I must be pretty smart to do it. As his load, the canoe, would be much the heaviest and bulkiest, though the simplest, I thought that I ought to be able to do it, and said that I would try. So I proceeded to gather up the gun, axe, paddle, kettle, frying-pan, plates, dippers, carpets, &c., &c., and while I was thus engaged he threw me his cow-hide boots. "What, are these in the bargain?" I asked. "O yer," said he; but before I could make a bundle of my load I saw him disappearing over a hill with the canoe on his head; so, hastily scraping the various articles together, I started on the run, and immediately went by him in the bushes, but I had no sooner left him out of sight in a rocky hollow, than the greasy plates, dippers, &c., took to themselves wings, and while I was employed in gathering them up again, he went by me; but hastily pressing the sooty kettle to my side, I started once more, and soon passing him again, I saw him no more on the carry. I do not mention this as anything of a feat, for it was but poor running on my part, and he was obliged to move with great caution for fear of breaking his canoe as well as his neck. When he made his appearance, puffing and panting like myself, in answer to my inquiries where he had been, he said, "Locks (rocks) cut 'em feet," and laughing added, "O, me love to play sometimes." He said that he and his companions when they came to carries several miles long used to try who would get over first; each perhaps with a canoe on his head.

I bore the sign of the kettle on my brown linen sack for the rest of the voyage.

We made a second carry on the west side, around some falls about a mile below this. On the mainland were Norway pines, indicating a new geological formation, and it was such a dry and sandy soil as we had not noticed before.

As we approached the mouth of the East Branch, we passed two or three huts, the first sign of civilization after Hunt's, though we saw no road as yet; we heard a cow-bell, and even saw an infant held up to a small square window to see us pass, but apparently the infant and the mother that held it were the only inhabitants then at home for several miles. This took the wind out of our sails, reminding us that we were travellers surely, while it was a native of the soil, and had the advantage of us. Conversation flagged. I would only hear the Indian, perhaps, ask my companion, "You load my pipe?" He said that he smoked alder bark, for medicine. On entering the West Branch at Nickertow it appeared much larger than the East. Polis remarked that the former was all gone and lost now, that it was all smooth water hence to Oldtown, and he threw away his pole which was cut on the Umbazookskus. Thinking of the rapids, he said once or twice, that you would n't catch him to go East Branch again; but he did not by any means mean all that he said.

Things are quite changed since I was here eleven years ago. Where there were but one or two houses, I now found quite a village, with saw-mills and a store (the latter was locked, but its contents were so much the more safely stored), and there was a stage-road to Mattawamkeag, and the rumor of a stage. Indeed, a steamer had ascended thus far once, when the water was very high. But we were not able to get any sugar, only a better shingle to lean our backs against.

We camped about two miles below Nickertow, on the south side of the West Branch, covering with fresh twigs the withered bed of a former traveller, and feeling that we were now in a settled country, especially when in the evening we heard an ox sneeze in its wild pasture across the river. Wherever you land along the frequented part of the river, you have not far to go to find these sites of temporary inns, the withered bed of flattened twigs, the charred sticks, and perhaps the tent-poles. And not long since, similar beds were spread along the Connecticut, the Hudson, and the Delaware, and longer still ago, by the Thames and Seine, and they now help to make the soil where private and public gardens, mansions and palaces are. We could not get fir twigs for our bed here, and the spruce was harsh in comparison, having more twig in proportion to its leaf, but we improved it somewhat with hemlock. The Indian remarked as before, "Must have hard wood to cook moose-meat," as if that were a maxim, and proceeded to get it. My companion cooked some in California fashion, winding a long string of the meat round a stick and slowly turning it in his hand before the fire. It was very good. But the Indian not approving of the mode, or because he was not allowed to cook it his own way, would not taste it. After the regular supper we attempted to make a lily soup of the bulbs which I had brought along, for I wished to learn all I could before I got out of the woods. Following the Indian's directions, for he began to be sick, I washed the bulbs carefully, minced some moose-meat and some pork, salted and boiled all together, but we had not patience to try the experiment fairly, for he said it must be boiled till the roots were completely softened so as to thicken the soup like flour; but though we left it on all night, we found it dried to the kettle in the morning, and not yet boiled to a flour. Perhaps the roots were not ripe enough, for they commonly gather them in the fall. As it was, it was palatable enough, but it reminded me of the Irishman's limestone broth. The other ingredients were enough alone. The Indian's name for these bulbs was *Sheepnoc*. I stirred the soup by accident with a striped maple or moose-wood stick, which I had peeled, and he remarked that its bark was an emetic.

He prepared to camp as usual between his moose-hide and the fire, but it beginning to rain suddenly, he took refuge under the tent with us, and gave us a song before falling asleep. It rained hard in the night and spoiled another box of matches for us, which the Indian had left out, for he was very careless; but, as usual, we had so much the better night for the rain, since it kept the mosquitoes down.

SUNDAY, August 2,—

Was a cloudy and unpromising morning. One of us observed to the Indian, "You did not stretch your moose-hide
last night, did you, Mr. Polis?" Whereat he replied, in a tone
of surprise, though perhaps not of ill humor: "What you ask
me that question for? Suppose I stretch 'em, you see 'em. May
be your way talking, may be all right, no Indian way." I had
observed that he did not wish to answer the same question
more than once, and was often silent when it was put again
for the sake of certainty, as if he were moody. Not that he
was incommunicative, for he frequently commenced a long-
winded narrative of his own accord,—repeated at length the
tradition of some old battle, or some passage in the recent
history of his tribe in which he had acted a prominent part,
from time to time drawing a long breath, and resuming the
thread of his tale, with the true story-teller's leisureliness, perhaps after shooting a rapid,—prefacing with " we-ll-by-by,"
&c., as he paddled along. Especially after the day's work was
over, and he had put himself in posture for the night, he
would be unexpectedly sociable, exhibit even the *bonhommie*
of a Frenchman, and we would fall asleep before he got
through his periods.

Nickertow is called eleven miles from Mattawamkeag by
the river. Our camp was, therefore, about nine miles from the
latter place.

The Indian was quite sick this morning with the colic. I
thought that he was the worse for the moose-meat he had
eaten.

We reached the Mattawamkeag at half past eight in the
morning, in the midst of a drizzling rain, and after buying
some sugar set out again.

The Indian growing much worse, we stopped in the north
part of Lincoln to get some brandy for him, but failing in
this, an apothecary recommended Brandreth's pills, which he
refused to take, because he was not acquainted with them. He
said to me, "Me doctor—first study my case, find out what
ail 'em—then I know what to take." We dropped down a
little farther, and stopped at mid-forenoon on an island and
made him a dipper of tea. Here too we dined and did some

washing and botanizing, while he lay on the bank. In the afternoon we went on a little farther, though the Indian was no better. *"Burntibus,"* as he called it, was a long smooth lake-like reach below the Five Islands. He said that he owned a hundred acres somewhere up this way. As a thunder-shower appeared to be coming up, we stopped opposite a barn on the west bank, in Chester, about a mile above Lincoln. Here at last we were obliged to spend the rest of the day and night, on account of our patient, whose sickness did not abate. He lay groaning under his canoe on the bank, looking very woe-begone, yet it was only a common case of colic. You would not have thought, if you had seen him lying about thus, that he was the proprietor of so many acres in that neighborhood, was worth $6,000, and had been to Washington. It seemed to me that, like the Irish, he made a greater ado about his sickness than a Yankee does, and was more alarmed about himself. We talked somewhat of leaving him with his people in Lincoln,—for that is one of their homes,—and taking the stage the next day, but he objected on account of the expense, saying, "Suppose me well in morning, you and I go Oldtown by noon."

As we were taking our tea at twilight, while he lay groaning still under his canoe, having at length found out "what ail him," he asked me to get him a dipper of water. Taking the dipper in one hand, he seized his powder-horn with the other, and pouring into it a charge or two of powder, stirred it up with his finger, and drank it off. This was all he took to-day after breakfast beside his tea.

To save the trouble of pitching our tent, when we had secured our stores from wandering dogs, we camped in the solitary half-open barn near the bank, with the permission of the owner, lying on new-mown hay four feet deep. The fragrance of the hay, in which many ferns, &c. were mingled, was agreeable, though it was quite alive with grasshoppers which you could hear crawling through it. This served to graduate our approach to houses and feather-beds. In the night some large bird, probably an owl, flitted through over our heads, and very early in the morning we were awakened by the twittering of swallows which had their nests there.

We started early before breakfast, the Indian being considerably better, and soon glided by Lincoln, and after another long and handsome lake-like reach, we stopped to breakfast on the west shore, two or three miles below this town.

We frequently passed Indian Islands with their small houses on them. The Governor, Aitteon, lives in one of them, in Lincoln.

The Penobscot Indians seem to be more social, even, than the whites. Ever and anon in the deepest wilderness of Maine you come to the log-hut of a Yankee or Canada settler, but a Penobscot never takes up his residence in such a solitude. They are not even scattered about on their islands in the Penobscot, which are all within the settlements, but gathered together on two or three,—though not always on the best soil,—evidently for the sake of society. I saw one or two houses not now used by them, because, as our Indian Polis said, they were too solitary.

The small river emptying in at Lincoln is the Matanawcook, which also, we noticed, was the name of a steamer moored there. So we paddled and floated along, looking into the mouths of rivers. When passing the Mohawk Rips, or, as the Indian called them, "Mohog lips," four or five miles below Lincoln, he told us at length the story of a fight between his tribe and the Mohawks there, anciently,—how the latter were overcome by stratagem, the Penobscots using concealed knives,—but they could not for a long time kill the Mohawk chief, who was a very large and strong man, though he was attacked by several canoes at once, when swimming alone in the river.

From time to time we met Indians in their canoes, going up river. Our man did not commonly approach them, but exchanged a few words with them at a distance in his tongue. These were the first Indians we had met since leaving the *Umbazookskus*.

At Piscataquis Falls, just above the river of that name, we walked over the wooden railroad on the eastern shore, about one and a half miles long, while the Indian glided down the rapids. The steamer from Oldtown stops here, and passengers take a new boat above. Piscataquis, whose mouth we here passed, means "branch." It is obstructed by falls at its mouth, but can be navigated with bateaux or canoes above through a settled country, even to the neighborhood of Moosehead Lake, and we had thought at first of going that way. We were not obliged to get out of the canoe after this on account of falls or rapids, nor, indeed, was it quite necessary here. We took less notice of the scenery to-day, because we were in quite a settled country. The river became broad and sluggish, and we saw a blue heron winging its way slowly down the stream before us.

We passed the Passadumkeag River on our left and saw the blue *Olamon* mountains at a distance in the southeast. Hereabouts our Indian told us at length the story of their contention with the priest respecting schools. He thought a great deal of education and had recommended it to his tribe. His argument in its favor was, that if you had been to college and learnt to calculate, you could "keep 'em property,—no other way." He said that his boy was the best scholar in the school at Oldtown, to which he went with whites. He himself is a Protestant, and goes to church regularly in Oldtown. According to his account, a good many of his tribe are Protestants, and many of the Catholics also are in favor of schools. Some years ago they had a schoolmaster, a Protestant, whom they liked very well. The priest came and said that they must send him away, and finally he had such influence, telling them that they would go to the bad place at last if they retained him, that they sent him away. The school party, though numerous, were about giving up. Bishop Fenwick came from Boston and used his influence against them. But our Indian told his side that they must not give up, must hold on, they were the strongest. If they gave up, then they would have no party. But they answered that it was "no use, priest too strong, we 'd better give up." At length he persuaded them to make a stand.

The priest was going for a sign to cut down the liberty-pole. So Polis and his party had a secret meeting about it; he got ready fifteen or twenty stout young men, "stript 'em naked, and painted 'em like old times," and told them that when the priest and his party went to cut down the liberty-pole, they were to rush up, take hold of it and prevent them, and he assured them that there would be no war, only a noise, "no war where priest is." He kept his men concealed in a house near by, and when the priest's party were about to cut down the liberty-pole, the fall of which would have been a death-blow to the school party, he gave a signal, and his young men rushed out and seized the pole. There was a great uproar, and they were about coming to blows, but the priest interfered, saying, "No war, no war," and so the pole stands, and the school goes on still.

We thought that it showed a good deal of tact in him, to seize this occasion and take his stand on it; proving how well he understood those with whom he had to deal.

The Olamon River comes in from the east in Greenbush a few miles below the Passadumkeag. When we asked the meaning of this name, the Indian said that there was an island opposite its mouth which was called *Olarmon*. That in old times, when visitors were coming to Oldtown, they used to stop there to dress and fix up or paint themselves. "What is that which ladies used?" he asked. Rouge? Red vermilion? "Yer," he said, "that is *larmon*, a kind of clay or red paint, which they used to get here."

We decided that we too would stop at this island, and fix up our inner man, at least, by dining.

It was a large island with an abundance of hemp-nettle, but I did not notice any kind of red paint there. The Olarmon River, at its mouth at least, is a dead stream. There was another large island in that neighborhood, which the Indian called *"Soogle"* (i. e. Sugar) Island.

About a dozen miles before reaching Oldtown he inquired, "How you like 'em your pilot?" But we postponed an answer till we had got quite back again.

The *Sunkhaze*, another short dead stream, comes in from the east two miles above Oldtown. There is said to be some of the best deer ground in Maine on this stream. Asking the meaning of this name, the Indian said, "Suppose you are going down Penobscot, just like we, and you see a canoe come out of bank and go along before you, but you no see 'em stream. That is *Sunkhaze*."

He had previously complimented me on my paddling, saying that I paddled "just like anybody," giving me an Indian name which meant "great paddler." When off this stream he said to me, who sat in the bows, "Me teach you paddle." So turning toward the shore he got out, came forward and placed my hands as he wished. He placed one of them quite outside the boat, and the other parallel with the first, grasping the paddle near the end, not over the flat extremity, and told me to slide it back and forth on the side of the canoe. This, I found, was a great improvement which I had not thought of, saving me the labor of lifting the paddle each time, and I wondered that he had not suggested it before. It is true, before our baggage was reduced we had been obliged to sit with our legs drawn up, and our knees above the side of the canoe, which would have prevented our paddling thus, or perhaps he was afraid of wearing out his canoe, by constant friction on the side.

I told him that I had been accustomed to sit in the stern, and lifting my paddle at each stroke, getting a pry on the side each time, and I still paddled partly as if in the stern. He then wanted to see me paddle in the stern. So, changing paddles, for he had the longer and better one, and turning end for end, he sitting flat on the bottom and I on the crossbar, he began to paddle very hard, trying to turn the canoe, looking over his shoulder and laughing, but finding it in vain he relaxed his efforts, though we still sped along a mile or two very swiftly. He said that he had no fault to find with my paddling in the stern, but I complained that he did not paddle according to his own directions in the bows.

Opposite the Sunkhaze is the main boom of the Penobscot, where the logs from far up the river are collected and assorted.

As we drew near to Oldtown I asked Polis if he was not glad to get home again; but there was no relenting to his wildness, and he said, "It makes no difference to me where I am." Such is the Indian's pretence always.

We approached the Indian Island through the narrow strait called "Cook." He said, "I 'xpect we take in some water there, river so high,—never see it so high at this season. Very rough water there, but short; swamp steamboat once. Don't you paddle till I tell you, then you paddle right along." It was a very short rapid. When we were in the midst of it he shouted "paddle," and we shot through without taking in a drop.

Soon after the Indian houses came in sight, but I could not at first tell my companion which of two or three large white ones was our guide's. He said it was the one with blinds.

We landed opposite his door at about four in the afternoon, having come some forty miles this day. From the Piscataquis we had come remarkably and unaccountably quick, probably as fast as the stage on the bank, though the last dozen miles was dead water.

Polis wanted to sell us his canoe, said it would last seven or eight years, or with care, perhaps ten; but we were not ready to buy it.

We stopped for an hour at his house, where my companion shaved with his razor, which he pronounced in very good condition. Mrs. P. wore a hat and had a silver brooch on her breast, but she was not introduced to us. The house was roomy and neat. A large new map of Oldtown and the Indian Island hung on the wall, and a clock opposite to it. Wishing to know when the cars left Oldtown, Polis's son brought one of the last Bangor papers, which I saw was directed to "Joseph Polis," from the office.

This was the last that I saw of Joe Polis. We took the last train, and reached Bangor that night.

Appendix

I. TREES.

THE prevailing trees (I speak only of what I saw) on the east and west branches of the Penobscot and on the upper part of the Allegash were the fir, spruce (both black and white), and arbor-vitæ, or "cedar." The fir has the darkest foliage, and, together with the spruce, makes a very dense "black growth," especially on the upper parts of the rivers. A dealer in lumber with whom I talked called the former a weed, and it is commonly regarded as fit neither for timber nor fuel. But it is more sought after as an ornamental tree than any other evergreen of these woods except the arbor-vitæ. The black spruce is much more common than the white. Both are tall and slender trees. The arbor-vitæ, which is of a more cheerful hue, with its light-green fans, is also tall and slender, though sometimes two feet in diameter. It often fills the swamps.

Mingled with the former, and also here and there forming extensive and more open woods by themselves, indicating, it is said, a better soil, were canoe and yellow birches (the former was always at hand for kindling a fire,—we saw no small white-birches in that wilderness), and sugar and red maples.

The Aspen (*Populus tremuloides*) was very common on burnt grounds. We saw many straggling white pines, commonly unsound trees, which had therefore been skipped by the choppers; these were the largest trees we saw; and we occasionally passed a small wood in which this was the prevailing tree; but I did not notice nearly so many of these trees as I can see in a single walk in Concord. The speckled or hoary alder (*Alnus incana*) abounds everywhere along the muddy banks of rivers and lakes, and in swamps. Hemlock could commonly be found for tea, but was nowhere abundant. Yet F. A. Michaux states that in Maine, Vermont, and the upper part of New Hampshire, &c., the hemlock forms three fourths of the evergreen woods, the rest being black spruce. It belongs to cold hillsides.

The elm and black ash were very common along the lower and stiller parts of the streams, where the shores were flat and grassy or there were low gravelly islands. They made a pleasing variety in the scenery, and we felt as if nearer home while gliding past them.

The above fourteen trees made the bulk of the woods which we saw.

The larch (Juniper), beech, and Norway pine (*Pinus resinosa*, red pine), were only occasionally seen in particular places. The *Pinus Banksiana* (gray or Northern scrub-pine), and a single small red oak (*Quercus rubra*) only, are on islands in Grand Lake, on the East Branch.

The above are almost all peculiarly Northern trees, and found chiefly, if not solely, on mountains southward.

II. FLOWERS AND SHRUBS.

IT appears that in a forest like this the great majority of flowers, shrubs, and grasses are confined to the banks of the rivers and lakes, and to the meadows, more open swamps, burnt lands, and mountain-tops; comparatively very few indeed penetrate the woods. There is no such dispersion even of wild-flowers as is commonly supposed, or as exists in a cleared and settled country. Most of our wild-flowers, so called, may be considered as naturalized in the localities where they grow. Rivers and lakes are the great protectors of such plants against the aggressions of the forest, by their annual rise and fall keeping open a narrow strip where these more delicate plants have light and space in which to grow. They are the *protégés* of the rivers. These narrow and straggling bands and isolated groups are, in a sense, the pioneers of civilization. Birds, quadrupeds, insects, and man also, in the main, follow the flowers, and the latter in his turn makes more room for them and for berry-bearing shrubs, birds, and small quadrupeds. One settler told me that not only blackberries and raspberries, but mountain-maples came in, in the clearing and burning.

Though plants are often referred to primitive woods as

their locality, it cannot be true of very many, unless the woods are supposed to include such localities as I have mentioned. Only those which require but little light, and can bear the drip of the trees, penetrate the woods, and these have commonly more beauty in their leaves than in their pale and almost colorless blossoms.

The prevailing flowers and conspicuous small plants of the *woods*, which I noticed, were: *Clintonia borealis*, *Linnæa*, checkerberry (*Gaultheria procumbens*), *Aralia nudicaulis* (wild sarsaparilla), great round-leaved orchis, *Dalibarda repens*, *Chiogenes hispidula* (creeping snowberry), *Oxalis acetosella* (common wood-sorrel), *Aster acuminatus*, *Pyrola secunda* (one-sided pyrola), *Medeola Virginica* (Indian cucumber-root), small *Circæa* (enchanter's nightshade), and perhaps *Cornus Canadensis* (dwarf cornel).

Of these, the last of July, 1857, only the *Aster acuminatus* and great round-leaved *orchis* were conspicuously in bloom.

The most common flowers of the *river* and *lake shores* were: *Thalictrum cornuti* (meadow-rue), *Hypericum ellipticum*, *mutilum*, and *Canadense* (St. John's-wort), horsemint, horehound, *Lycopus Virginicus* and *Europæus*, var. *sinuatus* (bugle-weed), *Scutellaria galericulata* (skull-cap), *Solidago lanceolata* and *squarrosa* East Branch (golden-rod), *Diplopappus umbellatus* (double-bristled aster), *Aster radula*, *Cicuta maculata* and *bulbifera* (water-hemlock), meadow-sweet, *Lysimachia stricta* and *ciliata* (loose-strife), *Galium trifidum* (small bed-straw), *Lilium Canadense* (wild yellow-lily), *Platanthera peramœna* and *psycodes* (great purple orchis and small purple-fringed orchis), *Mimulus ringens* (monkey-flower), dock (water), blue flag, *Hydrocotyle Americana* (marsh pennywort), *Sanicula Canadensis?* (black snake-root), *Clematis Virginiana?* (common virgin's-bower), *Nasturtium palustre* (marsh cress), *Ranunculus recurvatus* (hooked crowfoot), *Asclepias incarnata* (swamp milkweed), *Aster Tradescanti* (Tradescant's aster), *Aster miser*, also *longifolius*, *Eupatorium purpureum* apparently, lake shores (Joe-Pye-weed), *Apocynum Cannabinum* East Branch (Indian hemp), *Polygonum cilinode* (bind-weed), and others. Not to mention among inferior orders wool-grass and the sensitive fern.

In the water, *Nuphar advena* (yellow pond-lily), some *potamogetons* (pond-weed), *Sagittaria variabilis* (arrow-head), *Sium lineare?* (water-parsnip).

Of these, those conspicuously in flower the last of July, 1857, were: rue, *Solidago lanceolata* and *squarrosa*, *Diplopappus umbellatus*, *Aster radula*, *Lilium Canadense*, great and small purple orchis, *Mimulus ringens*, blue flag, virgin's-bower, &c.

The characteristic flowers in *swamps* were: *Rubus triflorus* (dwarf raspberry), *Calla palustris* (water-arum), and *Sarracenia purpurea* (pitcher-plant). On *burnt grounds*: *Epilobium angustifolium*, in full bloom (great willow-herb), and *Erechthites hieracifolia* (fire-weed). On *cliffs*: *Campanula rotundifolia* (harebell), *Cornus Canadensis* (dwarf cornel), *Arctostaphylos uva-ursi* (bearberry), *Potentilla tridentata* (mountain cinquefoil), *Pteris aquilina* (common brake). At *old camps, carries, and logging-paths*: *Cirsium arvense* (Canada thistle), *Prunella vulgaris* (common self-heal), clover, herds-grass, *Achillea millefolium* (common yarrow), *Leucanthemum vulgare* (whiteweed), *Aster macrophyllus*, *Halenia deflexa* East Branch (spurred gentian), *Antennaria margaritacea* (pearly everlasting), *Actæa rubra* and *alba*, wet carries (red and white cohosh), *Desmodium Canadense* (tick-trefoil), sorrel.

The handsomest and most interesting flowers were the great purple orchises, rising ever and anon, with their great purple spikes perfectly erect, amid the shrubs and grasses of the shore. It seemed strange that they should be made to grow there in such profusion, seen of moose and moose-hunters only, while they are so rare in Concord. I have never seen this species flowering nearly so late with us, or with the small one.

The prevailing underwoods were: *Dirca palustris* (moose-wood), *Acer spicatum* (mountain maple), *Viburnum lantanoides* (hobble-bush), and frequently *Taxus baccata*, var. *Canadensis* (American yew).

The prevailing shrubs and small trees along the shore were: *osier rouge* and alders (before mentioned); sallows, or small willows, of two or three kinds, as *Salix humilis*, *rostrata*, and *discolor?*, *Sambucus Canadensis* (black elder), rose, *Viburnum opulus* and *nudum* (cranberry-tree and withe-rod), *Pyrus*

Americana (American mountain-ash), *Corylus rostrata* (beaked hazel-nut), *Diervilla trifida* (bush-honeysuckle), *Prunus Virginiana* (choke-cherry), *Myrica gale* (sweet-gale), *Nemopanthes Canadensis* (mountain holly), *Cephalanthus occidentalis* (button-bush), *Ribes prostratum*, in some places (fetid currant).

More particularly of shrubs and small trees in *swamps*: some willows, *Kalmia glauca* (pale laurel), *Ledum latifolium* and *palustre* (Labrador tea), *Ribes lacustre* (swamp gooseberry), and in one place *Betula pumila* (low birch). At *camps and carries*: raspberry, *Vaccinium Canadense* (Canada blueberry), *Prunus Pennsylvanica* also along shore (wild red cherry), *Amelanchier Canadensis* (shad-bush), *Sambucus pubens* (red-berried elder). Among those peculiar to the *mountains* would be the *Vaccinium vitis-idæa* (cow-berry).

Of plants commonly regarded as *introduced* from Europe, I observed at Ansel Smith's clearing, Chesuncook, abundant in 1857: *Ranunculus acris* (buttercups), *Plantago major* (common plantain), *Chenopodium album* (lamb's-quarters), *Capsella bursa-pastoris*, 1853 (shepherd's-purse), *Spergula arvensis*, also, north shore of Moosehead, in 1853, and elsewhere, 1857 (corn-spurrey), *Taraxacum dens-leonis*—regarded as indigenous by Gray, but evidently introduced there—(common dandelion), *Polygonum Persicaria* and *hydropiper*, by a logging-path in woods at Smith's (lady's-thumb and smart-weed), *Rumex acetosella*, common at carries (sheep-sorrel), *Trifolium pratense*, 1853, and carries frequent (red clover), *Leucanthemum vulgare*, carries (white weed), *Phleum pratense*, carries, 1853–7 (herd's-grass), *Verbena hastata* (blue vervain), *Cirsium arvense*, abundant at camps 1857 (Canada thistle), *Rumex crispus?*, West Branch, 1853? (curled dock), *Verbascum thapsus*, between Bangor and lake, 1853 (common mullein).

It appears that I saw about a dozen plants which had accompanied man as far into the woods as Chesuncook, and had naturalized themselves there, in 1853. Plants begin thus early to spring by the side of a logging-path,—a mere vista through the woods, which can only be used in the winter, on account of the stumps and fallen trees,—which at length are the roadside plants in old settlements. The pioneers of such are planted in part by the first cattle, which cannot be summered in the woods.

III. LIST OF PLANTS.

THE following is a list of the plants which I noticed in the Maine woods, in the years 1853 and 1857. (Those marked * not in woods.)

1. THOSE WHICH ATTAINED THE HEIGHT OF TREES.

Alnus incana (speckled or hoary alder), abundant along streams, &c.

Thuja occidentalis (American arbor-vitæ), one of the prevailing.

Fraxinus sambucifolia (black ash), very common, especially near dead water. The Indian spoke of "yellow ash" as also found there.

Populus tremuloides (American aspen), very common, especially on burnt lands, almost as white as birches.

Populus grandidentata (large-toothed aspen), perhaps two or three.

Fagus ferruginea (American beech), not uncommon, at least on the West Branch (saw more in 1846).

Betula papyracea (canoe-birch), prevailing everywhere and about Bangor.

Betula excelsa (yellow birch), very common.

Betula lenta (black birch), on the West Branch, in 1853.

Betula alba (American white birch), about Bangor only.

Ulmus Americana (American or white elm), West Branch and low down the East Branch, i. e. on the lower and alluvial part of the river, very common.

Larix Americana (American or black larch), very common on the Umbazookskus, some elsewhere.

Abies Canadensis (hemlock-spruce), not abundant, some on the West Branch, and a little everywhere.

Acer saccharinum (sugar maple), very common.

Acer rubrum (red or swamp maple), very common.

Acer dasycarpum (white or silver maple), a little low on East Branch and in Chesuncook woods.

Quercus rubra (red oak), one on an island in Grand Lake, East Branch, and, according to a settler, a few on the east side of Chesuncook Lake; a few also about Bangor in 1853.

Pinus strobus (white pine), scattered along, most abundant at Heron Lake.

Pinus resinosa (red pine), Telos and Grand Lake, a little afterwards here and there.

Abies balsamea (balsam fir), perhaps the most common tree, especially in the upper parts of rivers.

Abies nigra (black or double spruce), next to the last the most common, if not equally common, and on mountains.

Abies alba (white or single spruce), common with the last along the rivers.

Pinus Banksiana (gray or Northern scrub-pine), a few on an island in Grand Lake.

Twenty-three in all (23).

2. SMALL TREES AND SHRUBS.

Prunus depressa (dwarf-cherry), on gravel bars, East Branch, near Hunt's, with green fruit, obviously distinct from the *pumila* of river and meadows.

Vaccinium corymbosum (common swamp blueberry), Bucksport.

Vaccinium Canadense (Canada blueberry), carries and rocky hills everywhere as far south as Bucksport.

Vaccinium Pennsylvanicum (dwarf-blueberry?), Whetstone Falls.

Betula pumila (low birch), Mud Pond Swamp.

Prinos verticillata (black alder, '57), now placed with *Ilex* by Gray, 2d ed.

Cephalanthus occidentalis (button-bush).

Prunus Pennsylvanica (wild red cherry), very common at camps, carries, &c., along rivers; fruit ripe August 1, 1857.

Prunus Virginiana (choke-cherry), river-side, common.

Cornus alternifolia (alternate-leaved cornel), West Branch, 1853.

Ribes prostratum (fetid currant), common along streams, on Webster Stream.

Sambucus Canadensis (common elder), common along river-sides.

Sambucus pubens (red-berried elder), not quite so common, roadsides toward Moosehead, and on carries afterward, fruit beautiful.

Ribes lacustre (swamp-gooseberry), swamps, common, Mud Pond Swamp and Webster Stream; not ripe July 29, 1857.

Corylus rostrata (beaked hazel-nut), common.

Taxus baccata, var. *Canadensis* (American yew), a common under-shrub at an island in West Branch and Chesuncook woods.

Viburnum lantanoides (hobble-bush), common, especially in Chesuncook woods; fruit ripe in September, 1853, not in July, 1857.

Viburnum opulus (cranberry-tree), on West Branch; one in flower still, July 25, 1857.

Viburnum nudum (withe-rod), common along rivers.

Kalmia glauca (pale laurel), swamps, common, as at Moosehead carry and Chamberlain swamp.

Kalmia angustifolia (lamb-kill), with *Kalmia glauca*.

Acer spicatum (mountain maple), a prevailing underwood.

Acer striatum (striped maple), in fruit July 30, 1857; green the first year; green, striped with white, the second; darker, the third, with dark blotches.

Cornus stolonifera (red-osier dogwood), prevailing shrub on shore of West Branch; fruit still white in August, 1857.

Pyrus Americana (American mountain ash), common along shores.

Amelanchier Canadensis (shad-bush), rocky carries, &c.; considerable fruit in 1857.

Rubus strigosus (wild red raspberry), very abundant, burnt grounds, camps, and carries, but not ripe till we got to Chamberlain dam and on East Branch.

Rosa Carolina (swamp-rose), common on the shores of lakes, &c.

*Rhus typhina** (stag-horn sumac).

Myrica gale (sweet-gale), common.

Nemopanthes Canadensis (mountain holly), common in low ground, Moosehead carry, and on Mount Kineo.

Cratægus (*coccinea*? scarlet-fruited thorn), not uncommon; with hard fruit in September, 1853.

Salix (near to *petiolaris*, petioled willow), very common in Umbazookskus meadows.

Salix rostrata (long-beaked willow), common.

Salix humilis (low bush-willow), common.

Salix discolor (glaucous willow?).

Salix lucida (shining willow), at island in Heron lake.

Dirca palustris (moose-wood), common.

In all, 38.

3. SMALL SHRUBS AND HERBACEOUS PLANTS.

Agrimonia Eupatoria (common agrimony), not uncommon.

Circæa Alpina (enchanter's nightshade), very common· in woods.

Nasturtium palustre (marsh cress), var. *hispidum*, common as at A. Smith's.

Aralia hispida (bristly sarsaparilla), on West Branch, both years.

Aralia nudicaulis (wild sarsaparilla), Chesuncook woods.

Sagittaria variabilis (arrow-head), common at Moosehead and afterward.

Arum triphyllum (Indian turnip), now *arisæma*, Moosehead carry in 1853.

Asclepias incarnata (swamp milk-weed), Umbazookskus River and after, redder than ours, and a different variety from our var. *pulchra*.

Aster acuminatus (pointed-leaved aster), the prevailing aster in woods, not long open on South Branch July 31st; two or more feet high.

Aster macrophyllus (large-leaved aster), common, and the whole plant surprisingly fragrant, like a medicinal herb, just out at Telos Dam July 29, 1857, and after to Bangor and Bucksport; bluish flower (in woods on Pine Stream and at Chesuncook in 1853).

Aster radula (rough-leaved aster), common, Moosehead carry and after.

Aster miser (petty aster), in 1853 on West Branch, and common on Chesuncook shore.

Aster longifolius (willow-leaved blue aster), 1853, Moosehead and Chesuncook shores.

Aster cordifolius (heart-leaved aster), 1853, West Branch.

Aster Tradescanti (Tradescant's aster), 1857. A narrow-leaved one Chesuncook shore, 1853.

Aster, *longifolius* like, with small flowers, West Branch, 1853.

Aster puniceus (rough-stemmed aster), Pine Stream.

Diplopappus umbellatus (large *diplopappus* aster), common along river.

Arctostaphylos uva-ursi (bear-berry), Kineo, &c., 1857.

Polygonum cilinode (fringe-jointed false buckwheat), common.

Bidens cernua (bur-marigold), 1853, West Branch.

Ranunculus acris (buttercups), abundant at Smith's dam, Chesuncook, 1853.

Rubus triflorus (dwarf-raspberry), low grounds and swamps, common.

Utricularia vulgaris* (greater bladder-wort), Pushaw.

Iris versicolor (larger blue-flag), common Moosehead, West Branch, Umbazookskus, &c.

Sparganium (bur-reed).

Calla palustris (water-arum), in bloom July 27, 1857, Mud Pond Swamp.

Lobelia cardinalis (cardinal-flower), apparently common, but out of bloom August, 1857.

Cerastium nutans (clammy wild chickweed?).

Gaultheria procumbens (checkerberry), prevailing everywhere in woods along banks of rivers.

Stellaria media* (common chickweed), Bangor.

Chiogenes hispidula (creeping snowberry), very common in woods.

Cicuta maculata (water-hemlock).

Cicuta bulbifera (bulb-bearing water-hemlock), Penobscot and Chesuncook shore, 1853.

Galium trifidum (small bed-straw), common.

Galium Aparine (cleavers?), Chesuncook, 1853.

Galium, one kind on Pine Stream, 1853.

Trifolium pratense (red-clover), on carries, &c.

Actæa spicata, var. *alba* (white cohosh), Chesuncook woods 1853, and East Branch 1857.

Actæa var. *rubra* (red cohosh), East Branch 1857.

Vaccinium vitis-idæa (cow-berry), Ktaadn, very abundant.

Cornus Canadensis (dwarf-cornel), in woods Chesuncook 1853; just ripe at Kineo July 24, 1857, common; still in bloom, Moosehead carry September 16, 1853.

Medeola Virginica (Indian cucumber-root), West Branch and Chesuncook woods.

Dalibarda repens (Dalibarda), Moosehead carry and after, common. In flower still, August 1, 1857.

Taraxacum dens-leonis (common dandelion), Smith's 1853, only there. Is it not foreign?

Diervilla trifida (bush honeysuckle), very common.

Rumex hydrolapathum? (great water-dock), in 1857; noticed it was large seeded in 1853, common.

Rumex crispus? (curled-dock), West Branch 1853.

Apocynum cannabinum (Indian hemp), Kineo, *Bradford*, and East Branch 1857, at Whetstone Falls.

Apocynum androsæmifolium (spreading dogbane), Kineo, *Bradford*.

Clintonia borealis (Clintonia), all over woods; fruit just ripening July 25, 1857.

A lemna (duckweed), Pushaw 1857.

Elodea Virginica (marsh St. John's-wort), Moosehead 1853.

Epilobium angustifolium (great willow-herb), great fields on burnt lands; some white at Webster Stream.

Epilobium coloratum (purple-veined willow-herb), once in 1857.

Eupatorium purpureum (Joe-Pye-weed), Heron, Moosehead, and Chesuncook lake-shores, common.

Allium (onion), a new kind to me in bloom, without bulbs above, on rocks near Whetstone Falls? East Branch.

Halenia deflexa (spurred gentian), carries on East Branch, common.

Geranium Robertianum (Herb Robert).

Solidago lanceolata (bushy golden-rod), very common.

Solidago, one of the three-ribbed, in both years.

Solidago thyrsoidea (large mountain golden-rod), one on Webster Stream.

Solidago squarrosa (large-spiked golden-rod), the most common on East Branch.

Solidago altissima (rough hairy golden-rod), not uncommon both years.

Coptis trifolia (three-leaved gold-thread).

Smilax herbacea (carrion-flower), not uncommon both years.

*Spiræa tomentosa** (hardhack), Bangor.

Campanula rotundifolia (harebell), cliffs Kineo, Grand Lake, &c.

Hieracium (hawk-weed), not uncommon.

Veratrum viride (American white hellebore).

Lycopus Virginicus (bugle-weed), 1857.

Lycopus Europæus (water-horehound), var. *sinuatus*, Heron Lake shore.

Chenopodium album (lamb's-quarters), Smith's.

Mentha Canadensis (wild mint), very common.

Galeopsis tetrahit (common hemp-nettle), Olarmon Isle, abundant, and below, in prime August 3, 1857.

Houstonia cærulea (bluets), now *Oldenlandia* (Gray, 2d ed.), 1857.

Hydrocotyle Americana (marsh pennywort), common.

Hypericum ellipticum (elliptical-leaved St. John's-wort), common.

Hypericum mutilum (small St. John's-wort), both years, common.

Hypericum Canadense (Canadian St. John's-wort), Moosehead Lake and Chesuncook shores, 1853.

Trientalis Americana (star-flower), Pine Stream, 1853.

Lobelia inflata (Indian tobacco).

Spiranthes cernuus (ladies' tresses), Kineo and after.

Nabalus (rattlesnake root), 1857; *altissimus* (tall white lettuce), Chesuncook woods, 1853.

Antennaria margaritacea (pearly everlasting), common, Moosehead, Smith's, &c.

Lilium Canadense (wild yellow lily), very common and large, West and East Branch; one on East Branch, 1857, with strongly revolute petals, and leaves perfectly smooth beneath, but not larger than the last, and apparently only a variety.

Linnæa borealis (Linnæa), almost everywhere in woods.

Lobelia Dortmanna (water-lobelia), pond in Bucksport.

Lysimachia ciliata (hairy-stalked loosestrife), very common, Chesuncook shore and East Branch.

Lysimachia stricta (upright loosestrife), very common.

Microstylis ophioglossoides (adder's-mouth), Kineo.

Spiræa salicifolia (common meadow-sweet), common.

Mimulus ringens (monkey-flower), common, lake-shores, &c.

Scutellaria galericulata (skullcap), very common.

Scutellaria lateriflora (mad-dog skullcap), Heron Lake, 1857, Chesuncook, 1853.

Platanthera psycodes (small purple-fringed orchis), very common, East Branch and Chesuncook, 1853.

Platanthera fimbriata (large purple-fringed orchis), very common, West Branch and Umbazookskus, 1857.

Platanthera orbiculata (large round-leaved orchis), very common in woods, Moosehead and Chamberlain carries, Caucomgomoc, &c.

Amphicarpæa monoica (hog peanut).

Aralia racemosa (spikenard), common, Moosehead carry, Telos Lake, &c., and after; out about August 1, 1857.

Plantago major (common plantain), common in open land at Smith's in 1853.

Pontederia cordata* (pickerel-weed), only near Oldtown, 1857.

Potamogeton (pond-weed), not common.

Potentilla tridentata (mountain cinquefoil), Kineo.

Potentilla Norvegica (cinquefoil), Heron Lake shore and Smith's.

Polygonum amphibium (water-persicaria), var. *aquaticum*, Second Lake.

Polygonum Persicaria (lady's-thumb), log-path Chesuncook, 1853.

Nuphar advena (yellow pond-lily), not abundant.

Nymphæa odorata (sweet water-lily), a few in West Branch, 1853.

Polygonum hydropiper (smart-weed), log-path, Chesuncook.

Pyrola secunda (one-sided pyrola), very common, Caucomgomoc.

Pyrola elliptica (shin-leaf), Caucomgomoc River.

Ranunculus Flammula (spearwort, var. *reptans*).

Ranunculus recurvatus (hooked crowfoot), Umbazookskus landing, &c.

Typha latifolia* (common cat-tail or reed-mace), extremely abundant between Bangor and Portland.

Sanicula Marylandica (black snake-root), Moosehead carry and after.

Aralia nudicaulis (wild sarsaparilla).

Capsella bursa-pastoris (shepherd's-purse), Smith's, 1853.

Prunella vulgaris (self-heal), very common everywhere.

Erechthites hieracifolia (fireweed), 1857, and Smith's open land, 1853.

Sarracenia purpurea (pitcher-plant), Mud Pond swamp.

Smilacina bifolia (false Solomon's-seal), 1857, and Chesuncook woods, 1853.

Smilacina racemosa (false spikenard?), Umbazookskus carry (July 27, 1853).

Veronica scutellata (marsh speedwell).

Spergula arvensis (corn spurrey), 1857, not uncommon, 1853, Moosehead and Smith's.

Fragaria (strawberry), 1853 Smith's, 1857 Bucksport.

Thalictrum Cornuti (meadow-rue), very common, especially along rivers, tall, and conspicuously in bloom in July, 1857.

Cirsium arvense (Canada thistle), abundant at camps and highway sides in the north of Maine.

Cirsium muticum (swamp-thistle), well in bloom Webster Stream, August 31.

Rumex acetosella (sheep-sorrel), common by river and log-paths, as Chesuncook log-path.

Impatiens fulva (spotted touch-me-not).

Trillium erythrocarpum (painted trillium), common West Branch and Moosehead carry.

Verbena hastata (blue vervain).

Clematis Virginiana (common virgin's-bower), common on river banks, feathered in September, 1853, in bloom July, 1857.

Leucanthemum vulgare (white-weed).

Sium lineare (water-parsnip), 1857, and Chesuncook shore, 1853.

Achillea millefolium (common yarrow), by river and log-paths, and Smith's.

Desmodium Canadense (Canadian tick-trefoil), not uncommon.

Oxalis acetosella (common wood-sorrel), still out July 25, 1853, at Moosehead carry and after.

Oxalis stricta (yellow wood-sorrel), 1853, at Smith's and his wood-path.

Liparis liliifolia (tway-blade), Kineo, *Bradford.*

Uvularia grandiflora (large-flowered bellwort), woods, common.

Uvularia sessilifolia (sessile-leaved bellwort), Chesuncook woods, 1853.

In all, 145.

4. OF LOWER ORDER.

Scirpus Eriophorum (wool-grass), very common, especially on low islands. A coarse grass, four or five feet high, along the river.

Phleum pratense (herd's-grass), on carries, at camps and clearings.

Equisetum sylvaticum (sylvatic horse-tail).

Pteris aquilina (brake), Kineo and after.

Onoclea sensibilis (sensitive-fern), very common along the river sides; some on the gravelly shore of Heron Lake Island.

Polypodium Dryopteris (brittle polypody).

Woodsia Ilvensis (rusty Woodsia), Kineo.

Lycopodium lucidulum (toothed club-moss).

Usnea (a parmeliaceous lichen), common on various trees.

IV. LIST OF BIRDS

WHICH I SAW IN MAINE BETWEEN JULY 24 AND AUGUST 3, 1857.

A very small hawk at Great Falls, on Webster Stream.

Haliætus leucocephalus (white-headed or bald-eagle), at Ragmuff, and above and below Hunt's, and on pond below Mattawamkeag.

Pandion haliætus (fish-hawk or osprey), heard, also seen on East Branch.

Bubo Virginianus (cat-owl), near Camp Island, also above mouth of Seboois, from a stump back and forth, also near Hunt's on a tree.

Icterus phœniceus (red-winged blackbird), Umbazookskus River.

Corvus Americanus (American crow), a few, as at outlet of Grand Lake; a peculiar cawing.

Fringilla Canadensis (tree-sparrow), think I saw one on Mount Kineo July 24, which behaved as if it had a nest there.

Garrulus cristatus (blue-jay).

Parus atricapillus (chicadee), a few.

Muscicapa tyrannus (king-bird).

Muscicapa Cooperii (olive-sided fly-catcher), everywhere a prevailing bird.

Muscicapa virens (wood pewee), Moosehead, and I think beyond.

Muscicapa ruticilla (American redstart), Moosehead.

Vireo olivaceus (red-eyed vireo), everywhere common.

Turdus migratorius (red-breasted robin), some everywhere.

Turdus melodus (wood-thrush), common in all the woods.

Turdus Wilsonii (Wilson's thrush), Moosehead and beyond.

Turdus aurocapillus (golden-crowned thrush or oven-bird), Moosehead.

Fringilla albicollis (white-throated sparrow), Kineo and after, apparently nesting; the prevailing bird early and late.

Fringilla melodia (song-sparrow), at Moosehead or beyond.

Sylvia pinus (pine warbler), one part of voyage.

Muscicapa acadica (small pewee), common.

Trichas Marylandica (Maryland yellow-throat), everywhere.

Coccyzus Americanus? (yellow-billed cuckoo), common.

Picus erythrocephalus (red-headed woodpecker), heard and saw; and good to eat.

Sitta Carolinensis? (white-breasted American nuthatch), heard.

Alcedo alcyon (belted kingfisher), very common.

Caprimulgus Americanus (night-hawk).

Tetrao umbellus (partridge), Moosehead carry, &c.

Tetrao cupido? (pinnated grouse), Webster Stream.

Ardea cærulea (blue heron), lower part of Penobscot.

Totanus macularius (spotted sandpiper or peetweet), everywhere.

Larus argentatus? (herring-gull), Heron Lake on rocks, and Chamberlain. Smaller gull on Second Lake.

Anas obscura (dusky or black duck), once in East Branch.

Anas sponsa (summer or wood duck), everywhere.

Fuligula albeola (spirit duck or dipper), common.

Colymbus glacialis (great Northern diver or loon), in all the lakes. A swallow; the night-warbler? once or twice.

Mergus Merganser (buff-breasted merganser or sheldrake), common on lakes and rivers.

V. QUADRUPEDS.

A bat on West Branch; beaver skull at Grand Lake; Mr. Thatcher ate beaver with moose on the Caucomgomoc. A muskrat on the last stream; the red squirrel is common in the depths of the woods; a dead porcupine on Chamberlain road; a cow moose and tracks of calf; skin of a bear, just killed.

VI. OUTFIT FOR AN EXCURSION.

The following will be a good outfit for one who wishes to make an excursion of *twelve* days into the Maine woods in July, with a companion, and one Indian for the same purposes that I did.

Wear,— a check shirt, stout old shoes, thick socks, a neck ribbon, thick waistcoat, thick pants, old Kossuth hat, a linen sack.

Carry,— in an India-rubber knapsack, with a large flap, two shirts (check), one pair thick socks, one pair drawers, one flannel shirt, two pocket-handkerchiefs, a light India-rubber coat or a thick woollen one, two bosoms and collars to go and come with, one napkin, pins, needles, thread, one blanket, best gray, seven feet long.

Tent,— six by seven feet, and four feet high in middle, will do; veil and gloves and insect-wash, or, better, mosquito-bars to cover all at night; best pocket-map, and perhaps description of the route; compass; plant-book and red blotting-paper; paper and stamps, botany, small pocket spy-glass for birds, pocket microscope, tape-measure, insect-boxes.

Axe, full size if possible, jackknife, fish-lines, two only apiece, with a few hooks and corks ready, and with pork for bait in a packet, rigged; matches (some also in a small vial in the waist-coat pocket); soap, two pieces; large knife and iron spoon (for all); three or four old newspapers, much twine, and several rags for dishcloths; twenty feet of strong cord, four-quart tin pail for kettle, two tin dippers, three tin plates, a fry-pan.

Provisions.—Soft hardbread, twenty-eight pounds; pork, sixteen pounds; sugar, twelve pounds; one pound black tea or three pounds coffee, one box or a pint of salt, one quart Indian meal, to fry fish in; six lemons, good to correct the pork and warm water; perhaps two or three pounds of rice, for variety. You will probably get some berries, fish, &c., beside.

A gun is not worth the carriage, unless you go as hunters. The pork should be in an open keg, sawed to fit; the sugar, tea or coffee, meal, salt, &c., should be put in separate water-tight India-rubber bags, tied with a leather string; and all the provisions, and part of the rest of the baggage, put into two large India-rubber bags, which have been proved to be water-tight and durable. Expense of preceding outfit is twenty-four dollars.

An Indian may be hired for about one dollar and fifty cents per day, and perhaps fifty cents a week for his canoe (this depends on the demand). The canoe should be a strong and tight one. This expense will be nineteen dollars.

Such an excursion need not cost more than twenty-five dollars apiece, starting at the foot of Moosehead, if you already possess or can borrow a reasonable part of the outfit. If you take an Indian and canoe at Oldtown, it will cost seven or eight dollars more to transport them to the lake.

VII. A LIST OF INDIAN WORDS.

1. *Katadn*, said to mean *Highest Land*, Rale puts for mt. *Pemadene*; for *Grai, pierre à aiguiser, Kitadañgan*. (v. Potter.)

Mattawamkeag, place where two rivers meet. (Indian of carry.) (v. Williamson's History of Maine, and Willis.)

Molunkus.

Ebeeme, rock.

Noliseemack; other name, Shad Pond.

Kecunnilessu, chicadee.

Nipsquecohossus, woodcock.

Skuscumonsuk, kingfisher. Has it not the pl. termination *uk* here, or *suk*?

Wassus, bear, *aouessous*. Rale.

Lunxus, Indian-devil.

Upahsis, mountain-ash.

} Joe.

Moose, (is it called, or does it mean, wood-eater?) *mous*, Rale.

Katahdinauguoh, said to mean mountains about Ktaadn.

Ebemena, tree-cranberry. *Ibimin*, *nar*, red, bad fruit. Rale.

} Joe.

Wighiggin, a bill or writing, *aouixigan*, "*Livre, lettre, peinture, ecriture.*" Rale.

} Ind'n of carry.

Sebamook, Large-bay Lake, *Peqouasebem*; add *ar* for plural, *lac* or *étang*. Rale. *Ouaürinaügamek*, *anse dans un lac*. Rale. *Mspame*, large water. Polis.

} Nicholai.

Sebago and *Sebec*, large open water.

Chesuncook, place where many streams empty in. (v. Willis and Potter.)

Caucomgomoc, Gull Lake. (*Caucomgomoc*, the lake; *caucomgomoc-took*, the river, Polis.)

} Tahmunt, &c.

Pammadumcook.

Kenduskieg, Little Eel River. (v. Willis.)

Nicholai.

Penobscot, Rocky River. *Puapeskou*, stone. (Rale v. Springer.)

} Ind'n of carry.

Umbazookskus, meadow stream. (Much-meadow river, Polis.)

Millinocket, place of Islands.

Souneunk, that runs between Mountains.

Aboljacarmegus, Smooth-ledge Falls and Deadwater.

} Nicholai.

Aboljacarmeguscook, the river there.

Muskiticook, Dead Stream. (Indian of carry.) *Meskikou*, or *Meskikouikou*, a place where there is grass. (Rale.) *Muskéeticook*, Dead water. (Polis.)

Mattahumkeag, Sand-creek Pond.
Piscataquis, branch of a river. } Nicholai.

Shecorways, sheldrakes.
Naramekechus, peetweet. } Polis.
Medawisla, loon.

Orignal, Moosehead Lake. (Montresor.)
Chor-chor-que, usnea.
Adelungquamooktum, wood-thrush.
Bematinichtik, high land generally. (Mt. *Pema-*
dené, Rale.) } Polis
Maquoxigil, bark of red osier, Indian tobacco.

Kineo, flint (Williamson; old Indian hunter).
(Hodge.)

Artoosoqu', phosphorescence.
Subekoondark, white spruce.
Skusk, black spruce.
Beskabekuk, the "Lobster Lake" of maps.
Beskabekuk shishtook, the dead water below the
island.
Paytaytequick, Burnt-Ground Stream, what Joe
called *Ragmuff*.
Nonlangyis, the name of a dead-water between
the last and Pine Stream.
Karsaootuk, Black River (or Pine Stream). *Mka-*
zéouighen, black. Rale. } Polis.

Michigan, fimus. Polis applied it to a sucker,
or a poor, good-for-nothing fish. *Fiante* (?)
mitsegan, Rale. (Pickering puts the ? after the
first word.)
Cowosnebagosar, Chiogenes hispidula, means,
grows where trees have rotted.
Pockadunkquaywayle, echo. *Pagadañkoueouérré*.
Rale. } Polis.

Bososquasis, moose-fly.
Nerlumskeechtcook (or *quoik*?), (or *skeetcook*),
Dead water, and applied to the mountains near.
Apmoojenegamook, lake that is crossed.
Allegash, hemlock-bark. (v. Willis.)
Paytaywecongomec, Burnt-Ground Lake, *Telos*.

Madunkehunk, Height-of-land Stream (Webster Stream).

Madunkehunk-gamooc, Height-of-land Lake.

Matungamooc, Grand Lake.

Uncardnerheese, Trout Stream.

Wassataquoik (or -*cook*), Salmon River, East Branch. (v. Willis.)

Pemoymenuk, Amelanchier berries, "*Pemoua-imin*, *nak*, a black fruit. Rale." Has it not here the plural ending?

Polis.

Sheepnoc, *Lilium Canadense* bulbs. "*Sipen*, *nak*, white, larger than *penak*." Rale.

Paytgumkiss, Petticoat (where a small river comes into the Penobscot below Nickatow).

Burntibus, a lake-like reach in the Penobscot.

Passadumkeag, "where the water falls into the Penobscot above the falls." (Williamson.) *Païsidaňkioui* is, *au dessus de la montagne*. Rale.

Olarmon, or *larmon*, (Polis) red paint. "Vermilion, paint, *Ouramaň*." Rale.

Sunkhaze, "See canoe come out; no see 'em stream." (Polis.) The mouth of a river, according to Rale, is *Saňghe-détegoue*. The place where one stream empties into another, thus ♂, is *saňktaïoui*. (v. Willis.)

Tomhegan Br. (at Moosehead). "*Hatchet, temahigan*." Rale.

Nickatow, "*Nicketaoutegué*, or *Niketoutegoue*, *rivière qui fourche*." Rale.

2. From WILLIAM WILLIS, on the Language of the Abnaquies. Maine Hist. Coll., Vol. IV.

Abalajako-megus (river near Ktaadn).

Aitteon (name of a pond and sachem).

Apmogenegamook (name of a lake).

Allagash (a bark camp). Sockbasin, a Penobscot, told him, "The Indians gave this name to the lake from the fact of their keeping a hunting-camp there."

Bamonewengamock, head of Allagash, Cross Lake. (Sock-basin.)

Chesuncook, Big Lake. (Sockbasin.)

Caucongamock (a lake).

Ebeeme, mountains that have plums on them. (Sockbasin.)

Ktaadn. Sockbasin pronounces this Ka-tah-din, and said it meant "large mountain or large thing."

Kenduskeag (the place of Eels).

Kineo (flint), mountain on the border, &c.

Metawamkeag, a river with a smooth gravelly bottom. (Sockbasin.)

Metanawcook.

Millinoket, a lake with many islands in it. (Sockbasin.)

Matakeunk (river).

Molunkus (river).

Nicketow, Neccotoh, where two streams meet ("Forks of the Penobscot").

Negas (Indian village on the Kenduskeag).

Orignal (Montresor's name for Moosehead Lake).

Ponguongamook, Allagash, name of a Mohawk Indian killed there. (Sockbasin.)

Penobscot, *Penobskeag*, French *Pentagoet*, &c.

Pougohwaken (Heron Lake).

Pemadumcook (lake).

Passadumkeag, where water goes into the river above falls. (Williamson.)

Ripogenus (river).

Sunkhaze (river), Dead water.

Souneunk.

Seboomook. Sockbasin says this word means "the shape of a Moose's head, and was given to the lake," &c. *Howard* says differently.

Seboois, a brook, a small river. (Sockbasin.)

Sebec (river).

Sebago (great water).

Telos (lake).

Telasinis (lake).

Umbagog (lake), doubled up; so called from its form. (Sockbasin.)

Umbazookskus (lake).

Wassatiquoik, a mountain river. (Sockbasin.)

Judge C. E. Potter of Manchester, New Hampshire, adds in November, 1855:—

"*Chesuncook*. This is formed from *Chesunk*, or *Sehunk* (a goose), and *Auke* (a place), and means 'The Goose Place.' Chesunk, or Sehunk, is the sound made by the wild geese when flying."

Ktaadn. This is doubtless a corruption of *Kees* (high), and *Auke* (a place).

Penobscot, *Penapse* (stone, rock-place), and *Auke* (place).

Suncook, Goose-place, *Sehunk-auke*.

The Judge says that *schoot* means to rush, and hence *schoodic* from this and *auke* (a place where water rushes), and that *schoon* means the same; and that the Marblehead people and others have derived the words *scoon* and *scoot* from the Indians, and hence schooner; refers to a Mr. Chute.

THE END.

ESSAYS

Aulus Persius Flaccus

I F YOU have imagined what a divine work is spread out for the poet, and approach this author too, in the hope of finding the field at length fairly entered on, you will hardly dissent from the words of the prologue,

> "Ipse semipaganus
> Ad sacra Vatum carmen affero nostrum."

Here is none of the interior dignity of Virgil, nor the elegance and fire of Horace, nor will any Sibyl be needed to remind you, that from those older Greek poets, there is a sad descent to Persius. Scarcely can you distinguish one harmonious sound, amid this unmusical bickering with the follies of men.

One sees how music has its place in thought, but hardly as yet in language. When the Muse arrives, we wait for her to remould language, and impart to it her own rhythm. Hitherto the verse groans and labors with its load, but goes not forward blithely, singing by the way. The best ode may be parodied, indeed is itself a parody, and has a poor and trivial sound, like a man stepping on the rounds of a ladder. Homer, and Shakspeare, and Milton, and Marvell, and Wordsworth, are but the rustling of leaves and crackling of twigs in the forest, and not yet the sound of any bird. The Muse has never lifted up her voice to sing. Most of all satire will not be sung. A Juvenal or Persius do not marry music to their verse, but are measured fault-finders at best; stand but just outside the faults they condemn, and so are concerned rather about the monster they have escaped, than the fair prospect before them. Let them live on an age, not a secular one, and they will have travelled out of his shadow and harm's way, and found other objects to ponder.

As long as there is satire, the poet is, as it were, *particeps criminis.* One sees not but he had best let bad take care of itself, and have to do only with what is beyond suspicion. If you light on the least vestige of truth, and it is the weight of the whole body still which stamps the faintest trace, an eternity will not suffice to extol it, while no evil is so huge, but you grudge to bestow on it a moment of hate. Truth never turns to rebuke falsehood; her own straightforwardness is the severest correction. Horace would not have written satire so well, if he had not been inspired by it, as by a passion, and fondly cherished his vein. In his odes, the love always exceeds the hate, so that the severest satire still sings itself, and the poet is satisfied, though the folly be not corrected.

A sort of necessary order in the development of Genius is, first, Complaint; second, Plaint; third, Love. Complaint, which is the condition of Persius, lies not in the province of poetry. Ere long the enjoyment of a superior good would have changed his disgust into regret. We can never have much sympathy with the complainer; for after searching nature through, we conclude he must be both plaintiff and defendant too, and so had best come to a settlement without a hearing.

I know not but it would be truer to say, that the highest strain of the muse is essentially plaintive. The saint's are still *tears* of joy.

But the divinest poem, or the life of a great man, is the severest satire; as impersonal as nature herself, and like the sighs of her winds in the woods, which convey ever a slight reproof to the hearer. The greater the genius, the keener the edge of the satire.

Hence have we to do only with the rare and fragmentary traits, which least belong to Persius, or, rather, are the properest utterance of his muse; since that which he says best at any time is what he can best say at all times. The Spectators and Ramblers have not failed to cull some quotable sentences from this garden too, so pleasant is it to meet even the most familiar truth in a new dress, when, if our neighbor had said it, we should have passed it by as hackneyed. Out of these six satires, you may perhaps select some twenty lines, which fit so well as many thoughts, that they will recur to the scholar almost as readily as a natural image; though when translated into familiar language, they lose that insular emphasis, which fitted them for quotation. Such lines as the following no translation can render commonplace. Contrasting the man of true religion with those, that, with jealous privacy, would fain carry on a secret commerce with the gods, he says,—

"Haud cuivis promptum est, murmurque humilesque
   susurros
Tollere de templis; et aperto vivere voto."

To the virtuous man, the universe is the only sanctum sanctorum, and the penetralia of the temple are the broad noon
of his existence. Why should he betake himself to a subterranean crypt, as if it were the only holy ground in all the
world he had left unprofaned? The obedient soul would only
the more discover and familiarize things, and escape more and
more into light and air, as having henceforth done with secrecy, so that the universe shall not seem open enough for it.
At length, it is neglectful even of that silence which is consistent with true modesty, but by its independence of all confidence in its disclosures, makes that which it imparts so private
to the hearer, that it becomes the care of the whole world that
modesty be not infringed.

To the man who cherishes a secret in his breast, there is a
still greater secret unexplored. Our most indifferent acts may
be matter for secrecy, but whatever we do with the utmost
truthfulness and integrity, by virtue of its pureness, must be
transparent as light.

In the third satire he asks,

"Est aliquid quò tendis, et in quod dirigis arcum?
An passim sequeris corvos, testâve, lutove,
Securus quò pes ferat, atque ex tempore vivis?"

Language seems not to have justice done it, but is obviously
cramped and narrowed in its significance, when any meanness
is described. The truest construction is not put upon it. What
may readily be fashioned into a rule of wisdom, is here thrown
in the teeth of the sluggard, and constitutes the front of his
offence. Universally, the innocent man will come forth from
the sharpest inquisition and lecturings, the combined din of
reproof and commendation, with a faint sound of eulogy in
his ears. Our vices lie ever in the direction of our virtues, and
in their best estate are but plausible imitations of the latter.
Falsehood never attains to the dignity of entire falseness, but
is only an inferior sort of truth; if it were more thoroughly
false, it would incur danger of becoming true.

"Securus quò pes ferat, atque ex tempore *vivit*,"

is then the motto of a wise man. For first, as the subtle discernment of the language would have taught us, with all his negligence he is still secure; but the sluggard, notwithstanding his heedlessness, is insecure.

The life of a wise man is most of all extemporaneous, for he lives out of an eternity that includes all time. He is a child each moment, and reflects wisdom. The far darting thought of the child's mind tarries not for the development of manhood; it lightens itself, and needs not draw down lightning from the clouds. When we bask in a single ray from the mind of Zoroaster, we see how all subsequent time has been an idler, and has no apology for itself. But the cunning mind travels farther back than Zoroaster each instant, and comes quite down to the present with its revelation. All the thrift and industry of thinking give no man any stock in life; his credit with the inner world is no better, his capital no larger. He must try his fortune again to-day as yesterday. All questions rely on the present for their solution. Time measures nothing but itself. The word that is written may be postponed, but not that on the lip. If this is what the occasion says, let the occasion say it. From a real sympathy, all the world is forward to prompt him who gets up to live without his creed in his pocket.

In the fifth satire, which is the best, I find,

"Stat contrà ratio, et secretam garrit in aurem.
Ne liceat facere id, quod quis vitiabit agendo."

Only they who do not see how anything might be better done are forward to try their hand on it. Even the master workman must be encouraged by the reflection, that his awkwardness will be incompetent to do that harm, to which his skill may fail to do justice. Here is no apology for neglecting to do many things from a sense of our incapacity,—for what deed does not fall maimed and imperfect from our hands?— but only a warning to bungle less.

The satires of Persius are the farthest possible from inspired; evidently a chosen, not imposed subject. Perhaps I have given him credit for more earnestness than is apparent;

but certain it is, that that which alone we can call Persius, which is forever independent and consistent, was in earnest, and so sanctions the sober consideration of all. The artist and his work are not to be separated. The most wilfully foolish man cannot stand aloof from his folly, but the deed and the doer together make ever one sober fact. The buffoon may not bribe you to laugh always at his grimaces; they shall sculpture themselves in Egyptian granite, to stand heavy as the pyramids on the ground of his character.

The Service

Spes sibi quisque. Virgil
Each one his own hope.

THE brave man is the elder son of creation, who has stept boyantly into his inheritance, while the coward, who is the younger, waiteth patiently till he decease. He rides as wide of this earth's gravity as a star, and by yielding incessantly to all the impulses of the soul, is constantly drawn upward and becomes a fixed star. His bravery deals not so much in resolute action, as healthy and assured rest; its palmy state is a staying at home and compelling alliance in all directions. So stands his life to heaven, as some fair sunlit tree against the western horizon, and by sunrise is planted on some eastern hill, to glisten in the first rays of the dawn. The brave man braves nothing, nor knows he of his bravery. He is that sixth champion against Thebes, whom, when the proud devices of the rest have been recorded, the poet describes as "bearing a full orbed shield of solid brass,"

> "But there was no device upon its circle,
> For not to seem just but to be is his wish."

He does not present a gleaming edge to ward off harm, for that will oftenest attract the lightning, but rather is the all pervading ether, which the lightning does not strike but purify. So is the profanity of his companion as a flash across the face of his sky, which lights up and reveals its serene depths. Earth cannot shock the heavens, but its dull vapor and foul smoke make a bright cloud spot in the ether, and anon the sun, like a cunning artificer, will cut and paint it, and set it for a jewel in the breast of the sky.

His greatness is not measurable. His is not such a greatness as when we would erect a stupendous piece of art, and send far and near for materials, intending to lay the foundations deeper, and rear the structure higher, than ever, for hence results only a remarkable bulkiness without grandeur, lacking those true and simple proportions which are independent of size. He was not builded by that unwise generation, that would fain have reached the heavens by piling one brick upon another, but by a far wiser, that builded inward and not outward, having found out a shorter way, through the observance of a higher art. The pyramids some artisan may measure with his line; but if he give you the dimensions of the Parthenon in feet and inches, the figures will not embrace it like a cord, but dangle from its entablature like an elastic drapery.

His eye is the focus in which all the rays, from whatever side, are collected; for, itself being within and central, the entire circumference is revealed to it. Just as we scan the whole concave of the heavens at a glance, but can compass only one side of the pebble at our feet. So does his discretion give prevalence to his valor. "Discretion is the wise man's soul," saith the poet. His prudence may safely go many strides beyond the utmost rashness of the coward; for, while he observes strictly the golden mean, he seems to run through all extremes with impunity. Like the sun, which, to the poor worldling, now appears in the zenith, now in the horizon, and again is faintly reflected from the moon's disk, and has the credit of describing an entire great circle, crossing the equinoctial and solstitial colures, without detriment to his steadfastness or mediocrity. The golden mean, in ethics as in physics, is the center of the system, and that about which all revolve; and, though to a distant and plodding planet it be the uttermost extreme, yet one day, when that planet's year is complete, it will be found to be central. They who are alarmed lest Virtue should so far demean herself, as to be extremely good, have not yet wholly embraced her, but described only a slight arc of a few seconds about her, and from so small and ill defined a curvature, you can calculate no center whatever, but their mean is no better than meanness, nor their medium than mediocrity.

The coward wants resolution, which the brave man can do without. He recognizes no faith but a creed, thinking this straw, by which he is moored, does him good service, because his sheet anchor does not drag. "The house roof fights with the rain; he who is under shelter does not know it." In his religion, the ligature, which should be muscle and sinew, is rather like that thread which the accomplices of Cylon held in their hands, when they went abroad from the temple of Minerva, the other end being attached to the statue of the goddess. But frequently, as in their case, the thread breaks, being stretched, and he is left without an asylum.

The divinity in man is the true vestal fire of the temple, which is never permitted to go out, but burns as steadily, and with as pure a flame, on the obscure provincial altar, as in Numa's temple at Rome. In the meanest are all the materials of manhood, only they are not rightly disposed. We say justly that the weak person is flat, for like all flat substances, he does not stand in the direction of his strength, that is, on his edge, but affords a convenient surface to put upon. He slides all the way through life. Most things are strong in one direction; a straw longitudinally; a board in the direction of its edge; a knee transversely to its grain; but the brave man is a perfect sphere, which cannot fall on its flat side, and is equally strong every way. The coward is wretchedly spheroidal at best, too much educated or drawn out on one side, and depressed on the other; or may be likened to a hollow sphere, whose disposition of matter is best when the greatest bulk is intended.

We shall not attain to be spherical by lying on one or the other side for an eternity, but only by resigning ourselves implicitly to the law of gravity in us, shall we find our axis coincident with the celestial axis, and by revolving incessantly through all circles, acquire a perfect sphericity. Mankind, like the earth, revolve mainly from west to east, and so are flattened at the poles. But does not philosophy give hint of a movement commencing to be rotary at the poles too, which in a millennium will have acquired increased rapidity, and help restore an equilibrium? And when at length every star in the nebulae and milky way, has looked down with mild radiance for a season, exerting its whole influence as the pole star, the demands of science will in some degree be satisfied.

The grand and majestic have always somewhat of the undulatoriness of the sphere. It is the secret of majesty in the rolling gait of the elephant, and of all grace in action and in art. Always the line of beauty is a curve. When with pomp a huge sphere is drawn along the streets, by the efforts of a hundred men, I seem to discover each striving to imitate its gait, and keep step with it,—if possible to swell to its own diameter. But onward it moves, and conquers the multitude with its majesty. What shame then, that our lives, which might so well be the source of planetary motion, and sanction the order of the spheres, should be full of abruptness and angulosity, so as not to roll nor move majestically.

The Romans "made Fortune sirname to Fortitude," for fortitude is that alchemy that turns all things to good fortune. The man of fortitude, whom the Latins called *fortis*, is no other than that lucky person whom *fors* favors, or *vir summae fortis*. If we will, every bark may "carry Caesar and Caesar's fortune." For an impenetrable shield, stand inside yourself; he was no artist, but an artisan, who first made shields of brass. For armor of proof, *meâ virtute me involvo*, I wrap myself in my virtue;

> "Tumble me down; and I will sit
> Upon my ruins, smiling yet."

If you let a single ray of light through the shutter, it will go on diffusing itself without limit till it enlighten the world, but the shadow that was never so wide at first, as rapidly contracts till it comes to naught. The shadow of the moon, when it passes nearest the sun, is lost in space ere it can reach our earth to eclipse it. Always the system shines with uninterrupted light, for as the sun is so much larger than any planet, no shadow can travel far into space. We may bask always in the light of the system, always may step back out of the shade. No man's shadow is as large as his body, if the rays make a right angle with the reflecting surface. Let our lives be passed under the equator, with the sun in the meridian.

There is no ill which may not be dissipated like the dark, if you let in a stronger light upon it. Overcome evil with good. Practise no such narrow economy as they, whose bravery amounts to no more light than a farthing candle, before which most objects cast a shadow wider than themselves.

Nature refuses to sympathize with our sorrow, she has not provided for, but by a thousand contrivances against it; she has bevelled the margins of the eyelids, that the tears may not overflow on the cheeks. It was a conceit of Plutarch, accounting for the preference given to signs observed on the left hand, that men may have thought "things terrestrial and mortal directly over against heavenly and divine things, and do conjecture that the things which to us are on the left hand, the gods send down from their right hand." If we are not blind, we shall see how a right hand is stretched over all, as well the unlucky as lucky, and that the ordering soul is only right handed, distributing with one palm all our fates.

What first suggested that necessity was grim, and made fate to be so fatal? The strongest is always the least violent. Necessity is my eastern cushion on which I recline. My eye revels in its prospect as in the summer haze. I ask no more but to be left alone with it. It is the bosom of time and the lap of eternity. To be necessary is to be needful, and necessity is only another name for inflexibility of good. How I welcome my grim fellow, and walk arm in arm with him. Let me too be such a Necessity as he. I love him, he is so flexile, and yields to me as the air to my body. I leap and dance in his midst, and play with his beard till he smiles. I greet thee my elder brother, who with thy touch ennoblest all things. Then is holiday when naught intervenes betwixt me and thee. Must it be so,—then is it good. The stars are thy interpreters to me.

Over Greece hangs the divine necessity ever a mellower heaven of itself, whose light gilds the Acropolis and a thousand fanes and groves.

WHAT MUSIC SHALL WE HAVE?

> Each more medodious note I hear
> Brings this reproach to me,
> That I alone afford the ear,
> Who would the music be.

THE brave man is the sole patron of music; he recognizes it for his mother tongue; a more mellifluous and articulate language than words, in comparison with which, speech is recent and temporary. It is his voice. His language must have the same majestic movement and cadence, that philosophy assigns to the heavenly bodies. The steady flux of his thought constitutes time in music. The universe falls in and keeps pace

with it, which before proceeded singly and discordant. Hence
are poetry and song. When Bravery first grew afraid and went
to war, it took music along with it. The soul delighted still to
hear the echo of her own voice. Especially the soldier insists
on agreement and harmony always. To secure these he falls
out. Indeed, it is that friendship there is in war that makes it
chivalrous and heroic. It was the dim sentiment of a noble
friendship for the purest soul the world has seen, that gave to
Europe a crusading era. War is but the compelling of peace. If
the soldier marches to the sack of a town, he must be preceded by drum and trumpet, which shall identify his cause
with the accordant universe. All things thus echo back his own
spirit, and thus the hostile territory is preoccupied for him.
He is no longer insulated, but infinitely related and familiar.
The roll call musters for him all the forces of nature.

There is as much music in the world as virtue. In a world
of peace and love music would be the universal language, and
men greet each other in the fields in such accents, as a
Beethoven now utters at rare intervals from a distance. All
things obey music as they obey virtue. It is the herald of
virtue. It is God's voice. In it are the centripetal and centrifugal forces. The universe needed only to hear a divine melody,
that every star might fall into its proper place, and assume its
true sphericity. It entails a surpassing affluence on the meanest thing; riding sublime over the heads of sages, and soothing the din of philosophy. When we listen to it we are so wise
that we need not to know. All sounds, and more than all, silence, do fife and drum for us. The least creaking doth whet
all our senses, and emit a tremulous light, like the aurora borealis, over things. As polishing expresses the vein in marble,
and the grain in wood, so music brings out what of heroic
lurks anywhere. It is either a sedative or a tonic to the soul. I
read that "Plato thinks the gods never gave men music, the
science of melody and harmony, for mere delectation or to
tickle the ear; but that the discordant parts of the circulations,
and beauteous fabric of the soul, and that of it that roves
about the body, and many times for want of tune and air,
breaks forth into many extravagances and excesses, might be
sweetly recalled and artfully wound up to their former consent and agreement."

A sudden burst from a horn startles us, as if one had rashly provoked a wild beast. We admire his boldness, he dares wake the echoes which he cannot put to rest. The sound of a bugle in the stillness of the night, sends forth its voice to the farthest stars, and marshals them in new order and harmony. Instantly it finds a fit sounding board in the heavens. The notes flash out on the horizon like heat lightning, quickening the pulse of creation. The heavens say, Now is this my own earth.

To the sensitive soul the Universe has her own fixed measure and rhythm, which is its measure also and constitutes the regularity and health of its pulse. When the body marches to the measure of the soul then is true courage and invincible strength.

The coward would reduce this thrilling sphere music to a universal wail,—this melodious chant to a nasal cant. He thinks to conciliate all hostile influences by compelling his neighborhood into a partial concord with himself, but his music is no better than a jingle, which is akin to a jar,—jars regularly recurring. He blows a feeble blast of slender melody, because nature can have no more sympathy with such a soul, than it has of cheerful melody in itself. Hence hears he no accordant note in the universe, and is a coward, or consciously outcast and deserted man. But the brave man, without drum or trumpet, compels concord everywhere by the universality and tunefulness of his soul.

Let not the faithful sorrow that he has no ear for the more fickle and subtle harmonies of creation, if he be awake to the slower measure of virtue and truth. If his pulse does not beat in unison with the musician's quips and turns, it accords with the pulse beat of the ages.

A man's life should be a stately march to an unheard music, and when to his fellows it seems irregular and inharmonious, he will be stepping to a livelier measure, which only his nicer ear can detect. There will be no halt ever, but at most a marching on his post, or such a pause as is richer than any sound—when the deepened melody is no longer heard, but implicitly consented to with the whole life and being. He will take a false step never, even in the most arduous circumstances, for then the music will not fail to swell into corresponding volume and distinctness and rule the movement it accompanies.

NOT HOW MANY BUT WHERE THE ENEMY ARE

"What's brave, what's noble,
Let's do it after the high Roman fashion."
Shakspeare

WHEN my eye falls on the stupendous masses of the clouds, tossed into such irregular greatness across the cope of my sky, I feel that their grandeur is thrown away on the meanness of my employment. In vain the sun through morning and noon rolls defiance to man, and, as he sinks behind his cloudy fortress in the west, challenges him to equal greatness in his career; but from his humbleness he looks up to the domes, and minarets, and gilded battlements of the eternal city, and is content to be a suburban dweller outside the walls. We look in vain over earth for a Roman greatness, to take up the gauntlet which the heavens throw down. Idomeneus would not have demurred at the freshness of the last morning that rose to us, as unfit occasion to display his valor in; and of some such evening as this, methinks, that Greek fleet came to anchor in the bay of Aulis. Would that it were to us the eve of a more than ten years' war, a tithe of whose exploits, and Achillean withdrawals, and godly interferences, would stock a library of Iliads. Better that we have some of that testy spirit of knight errantry, and if we are so blind as to think the world is not rich enough nowadays to afford a real foe to combat, with our trusty swords and double handed maces, hew and mangle some unreal phantom of the brain. In the pale and shivering fogs of the morning, gathering them up betimes, and withdrawing sluggishly to their daylight haunts, I see Falsehood sneaking from the full blaze of truth, and with good relish could do execution on their rearward ranks with the first brand that came to hand. We too are such puny creatures as to be put to flight by the sun, and suffer our ardor to grow cool in proportion as his increases; our own short lived chivalry sounds a retreat with the fumes and vapors of the night, and we turn to meet mankind with its meek face preaching peace, and such nonresistance as the chaff that rides before the whirlwind. Let not our Peace be proclaimed by the rust on our swords, or our inability to draw them from their scabbards, but let her at least have so much work on her hands, as to keep those swords bright and sharp. The very dogs that bay the moon from farmyards o' these nights, do evince more heroism than is tamely barked forth in all the civil exhortations and war sermons of the age. And that day and night, which should be set down indelibly in men's hearts, must be learned from the pages of an almanack. One cannot wonder at the owlish habits of the race, which does not distinguish when its day ends and night begins, for as night is the season of rest, it would be hard to say when its toil ended and its rest began. Not to it

> —returns
> Day, or the sweet approach of even or morn,
> Or sight of vernal bloom, or summer's rose,
> Or flocks, or herds, or human face divine;
> But cloud instead, and ever-during dark
> Surrounds—

And so the time lapses without epoch or era, and we know some half score of mornings and evenings by tradition only. Almost the night is grieved and leaves her tears on the forelock of day, that men will not rush to her embrace, and fulfil, at length, the pledge so forwardly given in the youth of time. Men are a circumstance to themselves, instead of causing the universe to stand around the mute witness of their manhood, and the stars to forget their sphere music and chant an elegiac strain, that heroism should have departed out of their ranks and gone over to humanity.

It is not enough that our life is an easy one; we must live on the stretch, retiring to our rest like soldiers on the eve of a battle, looking forward with ardor to the strenuous sortie of the morrow. "Sit not down in the popular seats and common level of virtues, but endeavor to make them heroical. Offer not only peace offerings but holocausts unto God." To the brave soldier the rust and leisure of peace are harder than the fatigues of war. As our bodies court physical encounters, and languish in the mild and even climate of the tropics, so our souls thrive best on unrest and discontent. The soul is a sterner master than any King Frederick, for a true bravery would subject our bodies to rougher usage than even a grenadier could withstand. We too are dwellers within the purlieus of the camp. When the sun breaks through the morning mist, I seem to hear the din of war louder than when his chariot thundered on the plains of Troy. The thin fields of vapor spread like gauze over the woods, form extended lawns whereon high tournament is held

> before each van
> Prick forth the aery knights, and couch their spears,
> Till thickest legions close.

It behoves us to make life a steady progression, and not be defeated by its opportunities. The stream which first fell a drop from heaven, should be filtered by events till it burst out into springs of greater purity, and extract a diviner flavor from the accidents through which it passes. Shall man wear out sooner than the sun, and not rather dawn as freshly, and with such native dignity stalk down the hills of the east into the bustling vale of life, with as lofty and serene a countenance to roll onward through midday, to a yet fairer and more promising setting? In the crimson colors of the west I discern the budding hues of dawn. To my western brother it is rising pure and bright as it did to me, but only the evening exhibits in the still rear of day, the beauty which through morning and noon escaped me. Is not that which we call the gross atmosphere of evening the accumulated deed of the day, which absorbs the rays of beauty, and shows more richly than the naked promise of the dawn? Let us look to it, that by earnest toil in the heat of the noon, we get ready a rich western blaze against the evening.

Nor need we fear that the time will hang heavy when our toil is done, for our task is not such a piece of day labor, that a man must be thinking what he shall do next for a livelihood, but such, that as it began in endeavor, so will it end only when no more in heaven or on earth remains to be endeavored. Effort is the prerogative of virtue. Let not death be the sole task of life, the moment when we are rescued from death to life. And set to work,—if indeed that can be called a task which all things do but alleviate. Nor will we suffer our hands to lose one jot of their handiness by looking behind to a mean recompense, knowing that our endeavor cannot be thwarted, nor we be cheated of our earnings unless by not earning them.

It concerns us rather to be somewhat here present than to leave something behind us; for, if that were to be considered, it is never the deed men praise, but some marble or canvass which are only a staging to the real work. The hugest and most effective deed may have no sensible result at all on earth, but may paint itself in the heavens with new stars and constellations. When in rare moments our whole being strives with one consent, which we name a yearning, we may not hope that our work will stand in any artist's gallery on earth. The bravest deed, which for the most part is left quite out of history, which alone wants the staleness of a deed done, and the uncertainty of a deed doing, is the life of a great man. To perform exploits is to be temporarily bold, as becomes a courage that ebbs and flows, the soul quite vanquished by its own deed subsiding into indifference and cowardice, but the exploit of a brave life consists in its momentary completeness.

Every stroke of the chisel must enter our own flesh and bone, he is a mere idolater and apprentice to art who suffers it to grate dully on marble; for the true art is not merely a sublime consolation, and holiday labor, which the gods have given to sickly mortals, but such a masterpiece, as you may imagine a dweller on the table lands of central Asia might produce, with threescore and ten years for canvass, and the faculties of a man for tools,—a human life,—wherein you might hope to discover more than the freshness of Guido's Aurora, or the mild light of Titian's landscapes;—no bald imitation nor even rival of nature, but rather the restored original of which she is the reflection. For such a masterpiece as this, whole galleries of Greece and Italy are a mere mixing of colors and preparatory quarrying of marble.

Of such sort, then, be our crusade, which, while it inclines chiefly to the hearty good will and activity of war, rather than the insincerity and sloth of peace, will set an example to both of calmness and energy;—as unconcerned for victory as careless of defeat, not seeking to lengthen our term of service, nor

to cut it short by a reprieve, but earnestly applying ourselves to the campaign before us. Nor let our warfare be a
boorish and uncourteous one, but a higher courtesy attend
its higher chivalry, though not to the slackening of its
tougher duties and severer discipline; that so our camp may
be a palaestra, wherein the dormant energies and affections
of men may tug and wrestle, not to their discomfiture, but
to their mutual exercise and development.

What were Godfrey and Gonzalo unless we breathed a life
into them, and enacted their exploits as a prelude to our own?
The past is the canvass on which our idea is painted,—the dim
prospectus of our future field. We are dreaming of what we
are to do. Methinks I hear the clarion sound, and clang of
corselet and buckler, from many a silent hamlet of the soul.
The signal gun has long since sounded and we are not yet on
our posts. Let us make such haste as the morning, and such
delay as the evening.

Natural History of Massachusetts

Reports—on the Fishes, Reptiles, and Birds; the Herbaceous Plants and Quadrupeds; the Insects Injurious to Vegetation; and the Invertebrate Animals—of Massachusetts. Published agreeably to an Order of the Legislature, by the Commissioners on the Zoological and Botanical Survey of the State.

PRELIMINARY NOTE.

We were thinking how we might best celebrate the good deed which the State of Massachusetts has done, in procuring the Scientific Survey of the Commonwealth, whose result is recorded in these volumes, when we found a near neighbor and friend of ours, dear also to the Muses, a native and an inhabitant of the town of Concord, who readily undertook to give us such comments as he had made on these books, and, better still, notes of his own conversation with nature in the woods and waters of this town. With all thankfulness we begged our friend to lay down the oar and fishing line, which none can handle better, and assume the pen, that Isaak Walton and White of Selborne might not want a successor, nor the fair meadows, to which we also have owed a home and the happiness of many years, their poet.

EDITOR OF THE DIAL.

Concord, Mass.

Books of natural history make the most cheerful winter reading. I read in Audubon with a thrill of delight, when the snow covers the ground, of the magnolia, and the Florida keys, and their warm sea breezes; of the fence-rail, and the cotton-tree, and the migrations of the rice-bird; of the breaking up of winter in Labrador, and the melting of the snow on the forks of the Missouri; and owe an accession of health to these reminiscences of luxuriant nature.

> Within the circuit of this plodding life
> There enter moments of an azure hue,
> Untarnished fair as is the violet
> Or anemone, when the spring strews them

By some meandering rivulet, which make
The best philosophy untrue that aims
But to console man for his grievances.
I have remembered when the winter came,
High in my chamber in the frosty nights,
When in the still light of the cheerful moon,
On every twig and rail and jutting spout,
The icy spears were adding to their length
Against the arrows of the coming sun,
How in the shimmering noon of summer past
Some unrecorded beam slanted across
The upland pastures where the Johnswort grew;
Or heard, amid the verdure of my mind,
The bee's long smothered hum, on the blue flag
Loitering amidst the mead; or busy rill,
Which now through all its course stands still and dumb
Its own memorial,—purling at its play
Along the slopes, and through the meadows next,
Until its youthful sound was hushed at last
In the staid current of the lowland stream;
Or seen the furrows shine but late upturned,
And where the fieldfare followed in the rear,
When all the fields around lay bound and hoar
Beneath a thick integument of snow.
So by God's cheap economy made rich
To go upon my winter's task again.

I am singularly refreshed in winter when I hear of service berries, poke-weed, juniper. Is not heaven made up of these cheap summer glories? There is a singular health in those words Labrador and East Main, which no desponding creed recognises. How much more than federal are these states. If there were no other vicissitudes than the seasons, our interest would never tire. Much more is adoing than Congress wots of. What journal do the persimmon and the buckeye keep, and the sharp-shinned hawk? What is transpiring from summer to winter in the Carolinas, and the Great Pine Forest, and the Valley of the Mohawk? The merely political aspect of the land is never very cheering; men are degraded when considered as the members of a political organization. On this

side all lands present only the symptoms of decay. I see but
Bunker Hill and Sing-Sing, the District of Columbia and
Sullivan's Island, with a few avenues connecting them. But
paltry are they all beside one blast of the east or the south
wind which blows over them.

In society you will not find health, but in nature. Unless
our feet at least stood in the midst of nature, all our faces
would be pale and livid. Society is always diseased, and the
best is the most so. There is no scent in it so wholesome as
that of the pines, nor any fragrance so penetrating and
restorative as the life-everlasting in high pastures. I would
keep some book of natural history always by me as a sort of
elixir, the reading of which should restore the tone of the system. To the sick, indeed, nature is sick, but to the well, a
fountain of health. To him who contemplates a trait of natural
beauty no harm nor disappointment can come. The doctrines
of despair, of spiritual or political tyranny or servitude, were
never taught by such as shared the serenity of nature. Surely
good courage will not flag here on the Atlantic border, as
long as we are flanked by the Fur Countries. There is enough
in that sound to cheer one under any circumstances. The
spruce, the hemlock, and the pine will not countenance despair. Methinks some creeds in vestries and churches do forget the hunter wrapped in furs by the Great Slave Lake, and
that the Esquimaux sledges are drawn by dogs, and in the
twilight of the northern night, the hunter does not give over
to follow the seal and walrus on the ice. They are of sick and
diseased imaginations who would toll the world's knell so
soon. Cannot these sedentary sects do better than prepare the
shrouds and write the epitaphs of those other busy living
men? The practical faith of all men belies the preacher's consolation. What is any man's discourse to me, if I am not sensible of something in it as steady and cheery as the creak of
crickets? In it the woods must be relieved against the sky.
Men tire me when I am not constantly greeted and refreshed
as by the flux of sparkling streams. Surely joy is the condition
of life. Think of the young fry that leap in ponds, the myriads
of insects ushered into being on a summer evening, the incessant note of the hyla with which the woods ring in the
spring, the nonchalance of the butterfly carrying accident and

change painted in a thousand hues upon its wings, or the brook minnow stoutly stemming the current, the lustre of whose scales worn bright by the attrition is reflected upon the bank.

We fancy that this din of religion, literature, and philosophy, which is heard in pulpits, lyceums, and parlors, vibrates through the universe, and is as catholic a sound as the creaking of the earth's axle; but if a man sleep soundly, he will forget it all between sunset and dawn. It is the three-inch swing of a pendulum in a cupboard, which the great pulse of nature vibrates by and through each instant. When we lift our eyelids and open our ears, it disappears with smoke and rattle like the cars on a railroad. When I detect a beauty in any of the recesses of nature, I am reminded, by the serene and retired spirit in which it requires to be contemplated, of the inexpressible privacy of a life,—how silent and unambitious it is. The beauty there is in mosses must be considered from the holiest, quietest nook. What an admirable training is science for the more active warfare of life. Indeed, the unchallenged bravery, which these studies imply, is far more impressive than the trumpeted valor of the warrior. I am pleased to learn that Thales was up and stirring by night not unfrequently, as his astronomical discoveries prove. Linnæus, setting out for Lapland, surveys his "comb" and "spare shirt," "leathern breeches" and "gauze cap to keep off gnats," with as much complacency as Bonaparte a park of artillery for the Russian campaign. The quiet bravery of the man is admirable. His eye is to take in fish, flower, and bird, quadruped and biped. Science is always brave, for to know, is to know good; doubt and danger quail before her eye. What the coward overlooks in his hurry, she calmly scrutinizes, breaking ground like a pioneer for the array of arts that follow in her train. But cowardice is unscientific; for there cannot be a science of ignorance. There may be a science of bravery, for that advances; but a retreat is rarely well conducted; if it is, then is it an orderly advance in the face of circumstances.

But to draw a little nearer to our promised topics. Entomology extends the limits of being in a new direction, so that I walk in nature with a sense of greater space and freedom. It suggests besides, that the universe is not rough-hewn, but perfect in its details. Nature will bear the closest inspection; she invites us to lay our eye level with the smallest leaf, and take an insect view of its plain. She has no interstices; every part is full of life. I explore, too, with pleasure, the sources of the myriad sounds which crowd the summer noon, and which seem the very grain and stuff of which eternity is made. Who does not remember the shrill roll-call of the harvest fly? There were ears for these sounds in Greece long ago, as Anacreon's ode will show.

> "We pronounce thee happy, Cicada,
> For on the tops of the trees,
> Drinking a little dew,
> Like any king thou singest.
> For thine are they all,
> Whatever thou seest in the fields,
> And whatever the woods bear.
> Thou art the friend of the husbandmen,
> In no respect injuring any one;
> And thou art honored among men,
> Sweet prophet of summer.
> The Muses love thee,
> And Phœbus himself loves thee,
> And has given thee a shrill song;
> Age does not wrack thee,
> Thou skilful, earthborn, song-loving,
> Unsuffering, bloodless one;
> Almost thou art like the gods."

In the autumn days, the creaking of crickets is heard at noon over all the land, and as in summer they are heard chiefly at night-fall, so then by their incessant chirp they usher in the evening of the year. Nor can all the vanities that vex the world alter one whit the measure that night has chosen. Every pulse-beat is in exact time with the cricket's chant and the tickings of the deathwatch in the wall. Alternate with these if you can.

About two hundred and eighty birds either reside permanently in the State, or spend the summer only, or make us a passing visit. Those which spend the winter with us have obtained our warmest sympathy. The nut-hatch and chicadee flitting in company through the dells of the wood, the one harshly scolding at the intruder, the other with a faint lisping note enticing him on, the jay screaming in the orchard, the crow cawing in unison with the storm, the partridge, like a russet link extended over from autumn to spring, preserving unbroken the chain of summers, the hawk with warrior-like firmness abiding the blasts of winter, the robin* and lark lurking by warm springs in the woods, the familiar snow-bird culling a few seeds in the garden, or a few crumbs in the yard, and occasionally the shrike, with heedless and unfrozen melody bringing back summer again;—

> His steady sails he never furls
> At any time o' year,
> And perching now on Winter's curls,
> He whistles in his ear.

As the spring advances and the ice is melting in the river, our earliest and straggling visitors make their appearance. Again does the old Teian poet sing as well for New England as for Greece, in the

RETURN OF SPRING.

> "Behold, how spring appearing,
> The Graces send forth roses;
> Behold, how the wave of the sea
> Is made smooth by the calm;
> Behold, how the duck dives;
> Behold, how the crane travels;
> And Titan shines constantly bright.
> The shadows of the clouds are moving;
> The works of man shine;
> The earth puts forth fruits;
> The fruit of the olive puts forth.

---

*A white robin and a white quail have occasionally been seen. It is mentioned in Audubon as remarkable that the nest of a robin should be found on the ground; but this bird seems to be less particular than most in the choice of a building spot. I have seen its nest placed under the thatched roof of a deserted barn, and in one instance, where the adjacent country was nearly destitute of trees, together with two of the phœbe, upon the end of a board in the loft of a sawmill, but a few feet from the saw, which vibrated several inches with the motion of the machinery.

> The cup of Bacchus is crowned,
> Along the leaves, along the branches,
> The fruit, bending them down, flourishes."

The ducks alight at this season in the still water, in company with the gulls, which do not fail to improve an east wind to visit our meadows, and swim about by twos and threes, pluming themselves, and diving to peck at the root of the lily, and the cranberries which the frost has not loosened. The first flock of geese is seen beating to north, in long harrows and waving lines, the gingle of the song-sparrow salutes us from the shrubs and fences, the plaintive note of the lark comes clear and sweet from the meadow, and the bluebird, like an azure ray, glances past us in our walk. The fish-hawk, too, is occasionally seen at this season sailing majestically over the water, and he who has once observed it will not soon forget the majesty of its flight. It sails the air like a ship of the line, worthy to struggle with the elements, falling back from time to time like a ship on its beam ends, and holding its talons up as if ready for the arrows, in the attitude of the national bird. It is a great presence, as of the master of river and forest. Its eye would not quail before the owner of the soil, but make him feel like an intruder on its domains. And then its retreat, sailing so steadily away, is a kind of advance. I have by me one of a pair of ospreys, which have for some years fished in this vicinity, shot by a neighboring pond, measuring more than two feet in length, and six in the stretch of its wings. Nuttall mentions that "The ancients, particularly Aristotle, pretended that the ospreys taught their young to gaze at the sun, and those who were unable to do so were destroyed. Linnæus even believed, on ancient authority, that one of the feet of this bird had all the toes divided, while the other was partly webbed, so that it could swim with one foot, and grasp a fish with the other." But that educated eye is now dim, and those talons are nerveless. Its shrill scream seems yet to linger in its throat, and the roar of the sea in its wings. There is the tyranny of Jove in its claws, and his wrath in the erectile feathers of the head and neck. It reminds me of the Argonautic expedition, and would inspire the dullest to take flight over Parnassus.

The booming of the bittern, described by Goldsmith and Nuttall, is frequently heard in our fens, in the morning and evening, sounding like a pump, or the chopping of wood in a frosty morning in some distant farm-yard. The manner in which this sound is produced I have not seen anywhere described. On one occasion, the bird has been seen by one of my neighbors to thrust its bill into the water, and suck up as much as it could hold, then raising its head, it pumped it out again with four or five heaves of the neck, throwing it two or three feet, and making the sound each time.

At length the summer's eternity is ushered in by the cackle of the flicker among the oaks on the hill-side, and a new dynasty begins with calm security.

In May and June the woodland quire is in full tune, and given the immense spaces of hollow air, and this curious human ear, one does not see how the void could be better filled.

> Each summer sound
> Is a summer round.

As the season advances, and those birds which make us but a passing visit depart, the woods become silent again, and but few feathers ruffle the drowsy air. But the solitary rambler may still find a response and expression for every mood in the depths of the wood.

> Sometimes I hear the veery's* clarion,
> Or brazen trump of the impatient jay,
> And in secluded woods the chicadee
> Doles out her scanty notes, which sing the praise
> Of heroes, and set forth the loveliness
> Of virtue evermore.

The phœbe still sings in harmony with the sultry weather by the brink of the pond, nor are the desultory hours of noon in the midst of the village without their minstrel.

---

*This bird, which is so well described by Nuttall, but is apparently unknown by the author of the Report, is one of the most common in the woods in this vicinity, and in Cambridge I have heard the college yard ring with its trill. The boys call it "*yorrick*," from the sound of its querulous and chiding note, as it flits near the traveller through the underwood. The cowbird's egg is occasionally found in its nest, as mentioned by Audubon.

> Upon the lofty elm tree sprays
> The vireo rings the changes sweet,
> During the trivial summer days,
> Striving to lift our thoughts above the street.

With the autumn begins in some measure a new spring. The plover is heard whistling high in the air over the dry pastures, the finches flit from tree to tree, the bobolinks and flickers fly in flocks, and the goldfinch rides on the earliest blast, like a winged hyla peeping amid the rustle of the leaves. The crows, too, begin now to congregate; you may stand and count them as they fly low and straggling over the landscape, singly or by twos and threes, at intervals of half a mile, until a hundred have passed.

I have seen it suggested somewhere that the crow was brought to this country by the white man; but I shall as soon believe that the white man planted these pines and hemlocks. He is no spaniel to follow our steps; but rather flits about the clearings like the dusky spirit of the Indian, reminding me oftener of Philip and Powhatan, than of Winthrop and Smith. He is a relic of the dark ages. By just so slight, by just so lasting a tenure does superstition hold the world ever; there is the rook in England, and the crow in New England.

> Thou dusky spirit of the wood,
> Bird of an ancient brood,
> Flitting thy lonely way,
> A meteor in the summer's day,
> From wood to wood, from hill to hill,
> Low over forest, field, and rill,
> What wouldst thou say?
> Why shouldst thou haunt the day?
> What makes thy melancholy float?
> What bravery inspires thy throat,
> And bears thee up above the clouds,
> Over desponding human crowds,
> Which far below
> Lay thy haunts low?

The late walker or sailer, in the October evenings, may hear the murmuring of the snipe, circling over the meadows, the most spirit-like sound in nature; and still later in the autumn, when the frosts have tinged the leaves, a solitary loon pays a visit to our retired ponds, where he may lurk undisturbed till the season of moulting is passed, making the woods ring with his wild laughter. This bird, the Great Northern Diver, well deserves its name; for when pursued with a boat, it will dive, and swim like a fish under water, for sixty rods or more, as fast as a boat can be paddled, and its pursuer, if he would discover his game again, must put his ear to the surface to hear where it comes up. When it comes to the surface, it throws the water off with one shake of its wings, and calmly swims about until again disturbed.

These are the sights and sounds which reach our senses oftenest during the year. But sometimes one hears a quite new note, which has for back ground other Carolinas and Mexicos than the books describe, and learns that his ornithology has done him no service.

It appears from the Report that there are about forty quadrupeds belonging to the State, and among these one is glad to hear of a few bears, wolves, lynxes, and wildcats.

When our river overflows its banks in the spring, the wind from the meadows is laden with a strong scent of musk, and by its freshness advertises me of an unexplored wildness. Those backwoods are not far off then. I am affected by the sight of the cabins of the musk-rat, made of mud and grass, and raised three or four feet along the river, as when I read of the barrows of Asia. The musk-rat is the beaver of the settled States. Their number has even increased within a few years in this vicinity. Among the rivers which empty into the Merrimack, the Concord is known to the boatmen as a dead stream. The Indians are said to have called it Musketaquid, or Prairie river. Its current being much more sluggish, and its water more muddy than the rest, it abounds more in fish and game of every kind. According to the History of the town, "The fur trade here was once very important. As early as 1641, a company was formed in the colony, of which Major Willard of Concord was superintendent, and had the exclusive right to trade with the Indians in furs and other articles; and for this right they were obliged to pay into the public treasury one twentieth of all the furs they obtained." There are trappers in our midst still, as well as on the streams of the far west, who night and morning go the round of their traps, without fear of the Indian. One of these takes from one hundred and fifty to two hundred musk-rats in a year, and even thirty-six have been shot by one man in a day. Their fur, which is not nearly as valuable as formerly, is in good condition in the winter and spring only; and upon the breaking up of the ice, when they are driven out of their holes by the water, the greatest number is shot from boats, either swimming or resting on their stools, or slight supports of grass and reeds, by the side of the stream. Though they exhibit considerable cunning at other times, they are easily taken in a trap, which has only to be placed in their holes, or wherever they frequent, without any bait being used, though it is sometimes rubbed with their musk. In the winter the hunter cuts holes in the ice, and shoots them when they come to the surface. Their burrows are usually in the high banks of the river, with the entrance under water, and rising within to above the level of high water. Sometimes their nests, composed of dried meadow grass and flags, may be discovered where the bank is low and spongy, by the yielding of the ground under the feet. They have from three to seven or eight young in the spring.

Frequently, in the morning or evening, a long ripple is seen in the still water, where a musk-rat is crossing the stream, with only its nose above the surface, and sometimes a green bough in its mouth to build its house with. When it finds itself observed, it will dive and swim five or six rods under water, and at length conceal itself in its hole, or the weeds. It will remain under water for ten minutes at a time, and on one occasion has been seen, when undisturbed, to form an air bubble under the ice, which contracted and expanded as it breathed at leisure. When it suspects danger on shore, it will stand erect like a squirrel, and survey its neighborhood for several minutes, without moving.

In the fall, if a meadow intervene between their burrows and the stream, they erect cabins of mud and grass, three or four feet high, near its edge. These are not their breeding places, though young are sometimes found in them in late freshets, but rather their hunting lodges, to which they resort in the winter with their food, and for shelter. Their food consists chiefly of flags and fresh water muscles, the shells of the latter being left in large quantities around their lodges in the spring.

The Penobscot Indian wears the entire skin of a musk-rat, with the legs and tail dangling, and the head caught under his girdle, for a pouch, into which he puts his fishing tackle, and essences to scent his traps with.

The bear, wolf, lynx, wildcat, deer, beaver, and marten, have disappeared; the otter is rarely if ever seen at present; and the mink is less common than formerly.

Perhaps of all our untamed quadrupeds, the fox has obtained the widest and most familiar reputation, from the time of Pilpay and Æsop to the present day. His recent tracks still give variety to a winter's walk. I tread in the steps of the fox that has gone before me by some hours, or which perhaps I have started, with such a tiptoe of expectation, as if I were on the trail of the Spirit itself which resides in the wood, and expected soon to catch it in its lair. I am curious to know what has determined its graceful curvatures, and how surely they were coincident with the fluctuations of some mind. I know which way a mind wended, what horizon it faced, by the setting of these tracks, and whether it moved slowly or rapidly, by their greater or less intervals and distinctness; for the swiftest step leaves yet a lasting trace. Sometimes you will see the trails of many together, and where they have gambolled and gone through a hundred evolutions, which testify to a singular listlessness and leisure in nature.

When I see a fox run across the pond on the snow, with the carelessness of freedom, or at intervals trace his course in the sunshine along the ridge of a hill, I give up to him sun and earth as to their true proprietor. He does not go in the sun, but it seems to follow him, and there is a visible sympathy between him and it. Sometimes, when the snow lies light, and but five or six inches deep, you may give chase and come up with one on foot. In such a case he will show a remarkable presence of mind, choosing only the safest direction, though he may lose ground by it. Notwithstanding his fright, he will take no step which is not beautiful. His pace is a sort of leopard canter, as if he were in no wise impeded by the snow, but were husbanding his strength all the while. When the ground is uneven, the course is a series of graceful curves, conforming to the shape of the surface. He runs as though there were not a bone in his back, occasionally dropping his muzzle to the ground for a rod or two, and then tossing his head aloft, when satisfied of his course. When he comes to a declivity, he will put his fore feet together, and slide swiftly down it, shoving the snow before him. He treads so softly that you would hardly hear it from any nearness, and yet with such expression, that it would not be quite inaudible at any distance.

Of fishes, seventy-five genera and one hundred and seven species are described in the Report. The fisherman will be startled to learn that there are but about a dozen kinds in the ponds and streams of any inland town; and almost nothing is known of their habits. Only their names and residence make one love fishes. I would know even the number of their fin rays, and how many scales compose the lateral line. I am the wiser in respect to all knowledges, and the better qualified for all fortunes, for knowing that there is a minnow in the brook. Methinks I have need even of his sympathy and to be his fellow in a degree.

I have experienced such simple delight in the trivial matters of fishing and sporting, formerly, as might have inspired the muse of Homer or Shakspeare; and now when I turn the pages and ponder the plates of the Angler's Souvenir, I am fain to exclaim,—

> "Can these things be,
> And overcome us like a summer's cloud?"

Next to nature it seems as if man's actions were the most natural, they so gently accord with her. The small seines of flax stretched across the shallow and transparent parts of our river, are no more intrusion than the cobweb in the sun. I stay my boat in mid current, and look down in the sunny water to see the civil meshes of his nets, and wonder how the blustering people of the town could have done this elvish work. The twine looks like a new river weed, and is to the river as a beautiful memento of man's presence in nature, discovered as silently and delicately as a foot-print in the sand.

When the ice is covered with snow, I do not suspect the wealth under my feet; that there is as good as a mine under me wherever I go. How many pickerel are poised on easy fin fathoms below the loaded wain. The revolution of the seasons must be a curious phenomenon to them. At length the sun and wind brush aside their curtain, and they see the heavens again.

Early in the spring, after the ice has melted, is the time for spearing fish. Suddenly the wind shifts from north-east and east to west and south, and every icicle, which has tinkled on the meadow grass so long, trickles down its stem, and seeks its level unerringly with a million comrades. The steam curls up from every roof and fence.

> I see the civil sun drying earth's tears,
> Her tears of joy, which only faster flow.

In the brooks is heard the slight grating sound of small cakes of ice, floating with various speed, full of content and promise, and where the water gurgles under a natural bridge, you may hear these hasty rafts hold conversation in an under tone. Every rill is a channel for the juices of the meadow. In the ponds the ice cracks with a merry and inspiriting din, and down the larger streams is whirled grating hoarsely, and crashing its way along, which was so lately a highway for the woodman's team and the fox, sometimes with the tracks of the skaters still fresh upon it, and the holes cut for pickerel. Town committees anxiously inspect the bridges and causeways, as if by mere eye-force to intercede with the ice, and save the treasury.

> The river swelleth more and more,
> Like some sweet influence stealing o'er
> The passive town; and for a while
> Each tussuck makes a tiny isle,
> Where, on some friendly Ararat,
> Resteth the weary water-rat.
>
> No ripple shows Musketaquid,
> Her very current e'en is hid,
> As deepest souls do calmest rest,

When thoughts are swelling in the breast,
And she that in the summer's drought
Doth make a rippling and a rout,
Sleeps from Nahshawtuck to the Cliff,
Unruffled by a single skiff.
But by a thousand distant hills
The louder roar a thousand rills,
And many a spring which now is dumb,
And many a stream with smothered hum,
Doth swifter well and faster glide,
Though buried deep beneath the tide.

Our village shows a rural Venice,
Its broad lagoons where yonder fen is;
As lovely as the Bay of Naples
Yon placid cove amid the maples;
And in my neighbor's field of corn
I recognise the Golden Horn.

Here Nature taught from year to year,
When only red men came to hear,
Methinks 't was in this school of art
Venice and Naples learned their part,
But still their mistress, to my mind,
Her young disciples leaves behind.

The fisherman now repairs and launches his boat. The best time for spearing is at this season, before the weeds have begun to grow, and while the fishes lie in the shallow water, for in summer they prefer the cool depths, and in the autumn they are still more or less concealed by the grass. The first requisite is fuel for your crate; and for this purpose the roots of the pitch pine are commonly used, found under decayed stumps, where the trees have been felled eight or ten years.

With a crate, or jack, made of iron hoops, to contain your fire, and attached to the bow of your boat about three feet from the water, a fish-spear with seven tines, and fourteen feet long, a large basket, or barrow, to carry your fuel and bring back your fish, and a thick outer garment, you are equipped for a cruise. It should be a warm and still evening; and then with a fire crackling merrily at the prow, you may launch forth like a cucullo into the night. The dullest soul cannot go upon such an expedition without some of the spirit of adventure; as if he had stolen the boat of Charon and gone down the Styx on a midnight expedition into the realms of Pluto. And much speculation does this wandering star afford to the musing night-walker, leading him on and on, jack-o'lantern-like, over the meadows; or if he is wiser, he amuses himself with imagining what of human life, far in the silent night, is flitting moth-like round its candle. The silent navigator shoves his craft gently over the water, with a smothered pride and sense of benefaction, as if he were the phosphor, or light-bringer, to these dusky realms, or some sister moon, blessing the spaces with her light. The waters, for a rod or two on either hand and several feet in depth, are lit up with more than noon-day distinctness, and he enjoys the opportunity which so many have desired, for the roofs of a city are indeed raised, and he surveys the midnight economy of the fishes. There they lie in every variety of posture, some on their backs, with their white bellies uppermost, some suspended in mid water, some sculling gently along with a dreamy motion of the fins, and others quite active and wide awake,—a scene not unlike what the human city would present. Occasionally he will encounter a turtle selecting the choicest morsels, or a musk-rat resting on a tussuck. He may exercise his dexterity, if he sees fit, on the more distant and active fish, or fork the nearer into his boat, as potatoes out of a pot, or even take the sound sleepers with his hands. But these last accomplishments he will soon learn to dispense with, distinguishing the real object of his pursuit, and find compensation in the beauty and never ending novelty of his position. The pines growing down to the water's edge will show newly as in the glare of a conflagration, and as he floats under the willows with his light, the song-sparrow will often wake on her perch, and sing that strain at midnight, which she had meditated for the morning. And when he has done, he may have to steer his way home through the dark by the north star, and he will feel himself some degrees nearer to it for having lost his way on the earth.

The fishes commonly taken in this way are pickerel, suckers, perch, eels, pouts, breams, and shiners,—from thirty to sixty weight in a night. Some are hard to be recognised in the unnatural light, especially the perch, which, his dark bands being exaggerated, acquires a ferocious aspect. The number of these transverse bands, which the Report states to be seven, is, however, very variable, for in some of our ponds they have nine and ten even.

It appears that we have eight kinds of tortoises, twelve snakes,—but one of which is venomous,—nine frogs and toads, nine salamanders, and one lizard, for our neighbors.

I am particularly attracted by the motions of the serpent tribe. They make our hands and feet, the wings of the bird, and the fins of the fish seem very superfluous, as if nature had only indulged her fancy in making them. The black snake will dart into a bush when pursued, and circle round and round with an easy and graceful motion, amid the thin and bare twigs, five or six feet from the ground, as a bird flits from bough to bough, or hang in festoons between the forks. Elasticity and flexibleness in the simpler forms of animal life are equivalent to a complex system of limbs in the higher; and we have only to be as wise and wily as the serpent, to perform as difficult feats without the vulgar assistance of hands and feet.

In April, the snapping turtle, *Emysaurus serpentina*, is frequently taken on the meadows and in the river. The fisherman, taking sight over the calm surface, discovers its snout projecting above the water, at the distance of many rods, and easily secures his prey through its unwillingness to disturb the water by swimming hastily away, for, gradually drawing its head under, it remains resting on some limb or clump of grass. Its eggs, which are buried at a distance from the water, in some soft place, as a pigeon bed, are frequently devoured by the skunk. It will catch fish by day-light, as a toad catches flies, and is said to emit a transparent fluid from its mouth to attract them.

Nature has taken more care than the fondest parent for the education and refinement of her children. Consider the silent influence which flowers exert, no less upon the ditcher in the meadow than the lady in the bower. When I walk in the woods, I am reminded that a wise purveyor has been there before me; my most delicate experience is typified there. I am struck with the pleasing friendships and unanimities of nature, as when the moss on the trees takes the form of their leaves. In the most stupendous scenes you will see delicate and fragile features, as slight wreathes of vapor, dew-lines, feathery sprays, which suggest a high refinement, a noble blood and breeding, as it were. It is not hard to account for elves and fairies; they represent this light grace, this ethereal gentility. Bring a spray from the wood, or a crystal from the brook, and place it on your mantel, and your household ornaments will seem plebeian beside its nobler fashion and bearing. It will wave superior there, as if used to a more refined and polished circle. It has a salute and a response to all your enthusiasm and heroism.

In the winter, I stop short in the path to admire how the trees grow up without forethought, regardless of the time and circumstances. They do not wait as man does, but now is the golden age of the sapling. Earth, air, sun, and rain, are occasion enough; they were no better in primeval centuries. The "winter of *their* discontent" never comes. Witness the buds of the native poplar standing gaily out to the frost on the sides of its bare switches. They express a naked confidence. With cheerful heart one could be a sojourner in the wilderness, if he were sure to find there the catkins of the willow or the alder. When I read of them in the accounts of northern adventurers, by Baffin's Bay or Mackenzie's river, I see how even there too I could dwell. They are our little vegetable redeemers. Methinks our virtue will hold out till they come again. They are worthy to have had a greater than Minerva or Ceres for their inventor. Who was the benignant goddess that bestowed them on mankind?

Nature is mythical and mystical always, and works with the license and extravagance of genius. She has her luxurious and florid style as well as art. Having a pilgrim's cup to make, she gives to the whole, stem, bowl, handle, and nose, some fantastic shape, as if it were to be the car of some fabulous marine deity, a Nereus or Triton.

In the winter, the botanist needs not confine himself to his books and herbarium, and give over his out-door pursuits, but study a new department of vegetable physiology, what may be called crystalline botany, then. The winter of 1837 was unusually favorable for this. In December of that year the

Genius of vegetation seemed to hover by night over its summer haunts with unusual persistency. Such a hoar-frost, as is
very uncommon here or anywhere, and whose full effects can
never be witnessed after sunrise, occurred several times. As I
went forth early on a still frosty morning, the trees looked like
airy creatures of darkness caught napping, on this side huddled together with their grey hairs streaming in a secluded
valley, which the sun had not penetrated, on that hurrying off
in Indian file along some water-course, while the shrubs and
grasses, like elves and fairies of the night, sought to hide their
diminished heads in the snow. The river, viewed from the
high bank, appeared of a yellowish green color, though all
the landscape was white. Every tree, shrub, and spire of
grass, that could raise its head above the snow, was covered
with a dense ice-foliage, answering, as it were, leaf for leaf to
its summer dress. Even the fences had put forth leaves in the
night. The centre, diverging, and more minute fibres were
perfectly distinct, and the edges regularly indented. These
leaves were on the side of the twig or stubble opposite to the
sun, meeting it for the most part at right angles, and there
were others standing out at all possible angles upon these and
upon one another, with no twig or stubble supporting them.
When the first rays of the sun slanted over the scene, the
grasses seemed hung with innumerable jewels, which jingled
merrily as they were brushed by the foot of the traveller, and
reflected all the hues of the rainbow as he moved from side to
side. It struck me that these ghost leaves and the green ones
whose forms they assume, were the creatures of but one law;
that in obedience to the same law the vegetable juices swell
gradually into the perfect leaf, on the one hand, and the crystalline particles troop to their standard in the same order, on
the other. As if the material were indifferent, but the law one
and invariable, and every plant in the spring but pushed up
into and filled a permanent and eternal mould, which, summer and winter, forever is waiting to be filled.

This foliate structure is common to the coral and the
plumage of birds, and to how large a part of animate and
inanimate nature. The same independence of law on matter is
observable in many other instances, as in the natural rhymes,
when some animal form, color, or odor, has its counterpart in

some vegetable. As, indeed, all rhymes imply an eternal melody, independent of any particular sense.

As confirmation of the fact, that vegetation is but a kind of crystallization, every one may observe how, upon the edge of the melting frost on the window, the needle-shaped particles are bundled together so as to resemble fields waving with grain, or shocks rising here and there from the stubble; on one side the vegetation of the torrid zone, high towering palms and wide-spread bannians, such as are seen in pictures of oriental scenery; on the other, arctic pines stiff frozen, with downcast branches.

Vegetation has been made the type of all growth; but as in crystals the law is more obvious, their material being more simple, and for the most part more transient and fleeting, would it not be as philosophical as convenient, to consider all growth, all filling up within the limits of nature, but a crystallization more or less rapid?

On this occasion, in the side of the high bank of the river, wherever the water or other cause had formed a cavity, its throat and outer edge, like the entrance to a citadel, bristled with a glistening ice-armor. In one place you might see minute ostrich feathers, which seemed the waving plumes of the warriors filing into the fortress; in another, the glancing, fan-shaped banners of the Lilliputian host; and in another, the needle-shaped particles collected into bundles, resembling the plumes of the pine, might pass for a phalanx of spears. From the under side of the ice in the brooks, where there was a thicker ice below, depended a mass of crystallization, four or five inches deep, in the form of prisms, with their lower ends open, which, when the ice was laid on its smooth side, resembled the roofs and steeples of a Gothic city, or the vessels of a crowded haven under a press of canvass. The very mud in the road, where the ice had melted, was crystallized with deep rectilinear fissures, and the crystalline masses in the sides of the ruts resembled exactly asbestos in the disposition of their needles. Around the roots of the stubble and flower-stalks, the frost was gathered into the form of irregular conical shells, or fairy rings. In some places the ice-crystals were lying upon granite rocks, directly over crystals of quartz, the frost-work of a longer night, crystals of a longer period, but to some eye unprejudiced by the short term of human life, melting as fast as the former.

In the Report on the Invertebrate Animals, this singular fact is recorded, which teaches us to put a new value on time and space. "The distribution of the marine shells is well worthy of notice as a geological fact. Cape Cod, the right arm of the Commonwealth, reaches out into the ocean, some fifty or sixty miles. It is nowhere many miles wide; but this narrow point of land has hitherto proved a barrier to the migrations of many species of Mollusca. Several genera and numerous species, which are separated by the intervention of only a few miles of land, are effectually prevented from mingling by the Cape, and do not pass from one side to the other. * * * * Of the one hundred and ninety-seven marine species, eighty-three do not pass to the south shore, and fifty are not found on the north shore of the Cape."

That common muscle, the *Unio complanatus*, or more properly *fluviatilis*, left in the spring by the musk-rat upon rocks and stumps, appears to have been an important article of food with the Indians. In one place, where they are said to have feasted, they are found in large quantities, at an elevation of thirty feet above the river, filling the soil to the depth of a foot, and mingled with ashes and Indian remains.

The works we have placed at the head of our chapter, with as much license as the preacher selects his text, are such as imply more labor than enthusiasm. The State wanted complete catalogues of its natural riches, with such additional facts merely as would be directly useful.

The Reports on Fishes, Reptiles, Insects, and Invertebrate Animals, however, indicate labor and research, and have a value independent of the object of the legislature.

Those on Herbaceous Plants and Birds cannot be of much value, as long as Bigelow and Nuttall are accessible. They serve but to indicate, with more or less exactness, what species are found in the State. We detect several errors ourselves, and a more practised eye would no doubt expand the list.

The Quadrupeds deserved a more final and instructive report than they have obtained.

These volumes deal much in measurements and minute descriptions, not interesting to the general reader, with only here and there a colored sentence to allure him, like those plants growing in dark forests, which bear only leaves without blossoms. But the ground was comparatively unbroken, and we will not complain of the pioneer, if he raises no flowers with his first crop. Let us not underrate the value of a fact; it will one day flower in a truth. It is astonishing how few facts of importance are added in a century to the natural history of any animal. The natural history of man himself is still being gradually written. Men are knowing enough after their fashion. Every countryman and dairymaid knows that the coats of the fourth stomach of the calf will curdle milk, and what particular mushroom is a safe and nutritious diet. You cannot go into any field or wood, but it will seem as if every stone had been turned, and the bark on every tree ripped up. But after all, it is much easier to discover than to see when the cover is off. It has been well said that "the attitude of inspection is prone." Wisdom does not inspect, but behold. We must look a long time before we can see. Slow are the beginnings of philosophy. He has something demoniacal in him, who can discern a law, or couple two facts. We can imagine a time when,—"Water runs down hill,"—may have been taught in the schools. The true man of science will know nature better by his finer organization; he will smell, taste, see, hear, feel, better than other men. His will be a deeper and finer experience. We do not learn by inference and deduction, and the application of mathematics to philosophy, but by direct intercourse and sympathy. It is with science as with ethics, we cannot know truth by contrivance and method; the Baconian is as false as any other, and with all the helps of machinery and the arts, the most scientific will still be the healthiest and friendliest man, and possess a more perfect Indian wisdom.

A Walk to Wachusett

The needles of the pine,
All to the west incline.

Concord, July, 19, 1842.

SUMMER and winter our eyes had rested on the dim outline of the mountains, to which distance and indistinctness lent a grandeur not their own, so that they served equally to interpret all the allusions of poets and travellers; whether with Homer, on a spring morning, we sat down on the many-peaked Olympus, or, with Virgil, and his compeers, roamed the Etrurian and Thessalian hills, or with Humboldt measured the more modern Andes and Teneriffe.

With frontier strength ye stand your ground,
With grand content ye circle round,
Tumultuous silence for all sound,
Ye distant nursery of rills,
Monadnock, and the Peterboro' hills;
Like some vast fleet,
Sailing through rain and sleet,
Through winter's cold and summer's heat;
Still holding on, upon your high emprise,
Until ye find a shore amid the skies;
Not skulking close to land,
With cargo contraband,
For they who sent a venture out by ye
Have set the sun to see
Their honesty.
Ships of the line, each one,
Ye to the westward run,
Always before the gale,
Under a press of sail,
With weight of metal all untold.
I seem to feel ye, in my firm seat here,
Immeasurable depth of hold,
And breadth of beam, and length of running gear.

Methinks ye take luxurious pleasure
In your novel western leisure;
So cool your brows, and freshly blue,
As Time had nought for ye to do;
For ye lie at your length,
An unappropriated strength,
Unhewn primeval timber,
For knees so stiff, for masts so limber;
The stock of which new earths are made,
One day to be our western trade,
Fit for the stanchions of a world
Which through the seas of space is hurled.

While we enjoy a lingering ray,
Ye still o'ertop the western day,
Reposing yonder, on God's croft,
Like solid stacks of hay.
Edged with silver, and with gold,
The clouds hang o'er in damask fold,
And with such depth of amber light
The west is dight,
Where still a few rays slant,
That even heaven seems extravagant.
On the earth's edge mountains and trees
Stand as they were on air graven,
Or as the vessels in a haven
Await the morning breeze.
I fancy even
Through your defiles windeth the way to heaven;
And yonder still, in spite of history's page,
Linger the golden and the silver age;
Upon the laboring gale
The news of future centuries is brought,
And of new dynasties of thought,
From your remotest vale.

But special I remember thee,
Wachusett, who like me
Standest alone without society.
Thy far blue eye,
A remnant of the sky,

Seen through the clearing or the gorge,
Or from the windows of the forge,
Doth leaven all it passes by.
Nothing is true,
But stands 'tween me and you,
Thou western pioneer,
Who knowst not shame nor fear,
By venturous spirit driven,
Under the eaves of heaven,
And can'st expand thee there,
And breathe enough of air?
Upholding heaven, holding down earth,
Thy pastime from they birth,
Not steadied by the one, nor leaning on the other;
May I approve myself thy worthy brother!

At length, like Rasselas, and other inhabitants of happy valleys, we resolved to scale the blue wall which bounds the western horizon, though not without misgivings, that thereafter no visible fairy land would exist for us. But we will not leap at once to our journey's end, though near, but imitate Homer, who conducts his reader over the plain, and along the resounding sea, though it be but to the tent of Achilles. In the spaces of thought are the reaches of land and water, where men go and come. The landscape lies far and fair within, and the deepest thinker is the farthest travelled. Taking advantage of the early hour, on a pleasant morning in July, my companion and I passed rapidly through Acton and Stow, stopping to rest and refresh us on the bank of a small stream, a tributary of the Assabet, in the latter town. As we traversed the cool woods of Acton, with stout staves in our hands, we were cheered by the song of the red-eye, the thrushes, the phœbe, and the cuckoo; and as we passed through the open country, we inhaled the fresh scent of every field, and all nature lay passive, to be viewed and travelled. Every rail, every farm-house, seen dimly in the twilight, every tinkling sound told of peace and purity, and we moved happily along the dark roads, enjoying not such privacy as the day leaves when it withdraws, but such as it has not profaned. It was solitude with light, which is better than darkness. But anon, the sound of the mower's rifle was heard in the fields, and this, too, mingled with the herd of days.

This part of our route lay through the country of hops. Perhaps there is no plant which so well supplies the want of the vine in American scenery, and reminds the traveller so often of Italy, and the South of France, as this, whether he traverses the country when the hop-fields, as now, present solid and regular masses of verdure, hanging in graceful festoons from pole to pole, the cool coverts where fresh gales are born to refresh the way-farer, or in September, when the women and children, and the neighbors from far and near, are gathered to pick the hops into long troughs, or later still, when the poles stand piled in immense pyramids in the yards, or lie in heaps by the roadside.

The culture of the hop, with the processes of picking, drying in the kiln, and packing for the market, as well as the uses to which it is applied, so analogous to the culture and uses of the grape, may afford a theme for future poets.

The mower in the adjacent meadow could not tell us the name of the brook on whose banks we had rested, or whether it had any, but his younger companion, perhaps his brother, knew that it was Great Brook. Though they stood very near together in the field, the things they knew were very far apart; nor did they suspect each other's reserved knowledge, till the stranger came by. In Bolton, while we rested on the rails of a cottage fence, the strains of music which issued from within, perhaps in compliment to us sojourners, reminded us that thus far men were fed by the accustomed pleasures. So soon did we begin to learn that man's life is rounded with the same few facts, the same simple relations everywhere, and it is vain to travel to find it new. The flowers grow more various ways than he. But coming soon to higher land, which afforded a prospect of the mountains, we thought we had not travelled in vain, if it were only to hear a truer and wilder pronunciation of their names, from the lips of a farmer by the roadside; not *Way*-tatic, *Way*-chusett, but *Wor*-tatic, *Wor*-chusett. It made us ashamed of our tame and civil pronunciation, and we looked upon him as born and bred farther west than we. His tongue had a more generous accent than ours, as if breath was cheaper when it wagged. A countryman, who

speaks but seldom, talks copiously, as it were, as his wife sets
cream and cheese before you without stint. Before noon we
had reached the highlands in the western part of Bolton,
overlooking the valley of Lancaster, and affording the first fair
and open prospect into the west, and here, on the top of a
hill, in the shade of some oaks, near to where a spring bub-
bled out from a leaden pipe, we rested during the heat of the
day, reading Virgil, and enjoying the scenery. It was such a
place as one feels to be on the outside of the earth, for from
it we could, in some measure, see the form and structure of
the globe. There lay the object of our journey, coming upon
us with unchanged proportions, though with a less ethereal
aspect than had greeted our morning gaze, while further
north, in successive order, slumbered the sister mountains
along the horizon.

We could get no further into the Æneid than

> —atque altæ mœnia Romæ,
> —and the wall of high Rome,

before we were constrained to reflect by what myriad tests a
work of genius has to be tried; that Virgil, away in Rome, two
thousand years off, should have to unfold his meaning, the inspiration of Italian vales, to the pilgrim on the New England
hills. This life so raw and modern, that so civil and ancient,
and yet we read Virgil, mainly to be reminded of the identity
of human nature in all ages, and by the poet's own account,
we are both the children of a late age, and live equally under
the reign of Jupiter.

> "He shook honey from the leaves, and removed fire,
> And stayed the wine, everywhere flowing in rivers,
> That experience, by meditating, might invent various arts
> By degrees, and seek the blade of corn in furrows,
> And strike out hidden fire from the veins of the flint."

The old world stands severely behind the new, as one mountain yonder towers behind another, more dim and distant.
Rome imposes her story still upon this late generation. The
very children in the school we have this morning passed, have
gone through her wars, and recited her alarms, ere they
have heard of the wars of the neighboring Lancaster. The

roving eye still rests inevitably on her hills. She still holds up
the skirts of the sky, and makes the past remote.

The lay of the land hereabouts is well worthy the attention
of the traveller. The hill on which we were resting makes
part of an extensive range, running from south-west to northeast, across the country, and separating the waters of the
Nashua from those of the Concord, whose banks we had left
in the morning, and by bearing in mind this fact, we could
easily determine whither each brook was bound that crossed
our path. Parallel to this, and fifteen miles further west, beyond the deep and broad valley in which lie Groton, Shirley,
Lancaster, and Boylston, runs the Wachusett range, in the
same general direction. The descent into the valley on the
Nashua side is, by far, the most sudden; and a couple of miles
brought us to the southern branch of that river, a shallow but
rapid stream, flowing between high and gravelly banks. But
we soon learned that there were no *gelidæ valles* into which we
had descended, and missing the coolness of the morning air,
feared it had become the sun's turn to try his power upon us.

> "The sultry sun had gained the middle sky,
> And not a tree, and not an herb was nigh,"

and with melancholy pleasure we echoed the melodious plaint
of our fellow-traveller Hassan, in the desert,

> "Sad was the hour, and luckless was the day,
> When first from Schiraz's walls I bent my way."

The air lay lifeless between the hills, as in a seething caldron, with no leaf stirring, and instead of the fresh odor of
grass and clover, with which we had before been regaled, the
dry scent of every herb seemed merely medicinal. Yielding,
therefore, to the heat, we strolled into the woods, and along
the course of a rivulet, on whose banks we loitered, observing
at our leisure the products of these new fields. He who traverses the woodland paths, at this season, will have occasion
to remember the small drooping bell-like flowers and slender
red stem of the dogs-bane, and the coarser stem and berry of
the poke, which are both common in remoter and wilder
scenes; and if "the sun casts such a reflecting heat from the
sweet fern," as makes him faint, when he is climbing the bare

hills, as they complained who first penetrated into these parts, the cool fragrance of the swamp pink restores him again, when traversing the valleys between.

On we went, and late in the afternoon refreshed ourselves by bathing our feet in every rill that crossed the road, and anon, as we were able to walk in the shadows of the hills, recovered our morning elasticity. Passing through Sterling, we reached the banks of the Stillwater, in the western part of the town, at evening, where is a small village collected. We fancied that there was already a certain western look about this place, a smell of pines and roar of water, recently confined by dams, belying its name, which were exceedingly grateful. When the first inroad has been made, a few acres levelled, and a few houses erected, the forest looks wilder than ever. Left to herself, nature is always more or less civilized, and delights in a certain refinement; but where the axe has encroached upon the edge of the forest, the dead and unsightly limbs of the pine, which she had concealed with green banks of verdure, are exposed to sight. This village had, as yet, no post-office, nor any settled name. As we entered upon its street, the villagers gazed after us, with a complacent, almost compassionate look, as if we were just making our debut in the world, at a late hour. "Nevertheless," did they seem to say, "come and study us, and learn men and manners." So is each one's world but a clearing in the forest, so much open and inclosed ground. The landlord had not yet returned from the field with his men, and the cows had yet to be milked. But though we met with no very hospitable reception here at first, we remembered the inscription on the wall of the Swedish inn, and were comforted, "You will find at Trolhate excellent bread, meat, and wine, provided you bring them with you." But I must confess it did somewhat disturb our pleasure, in this withdrawn spot, to have our own village newspaper handed us by our host, as if the greatest charm the country offered to the traveller was the facility of communication with the town. Let it recline on its own everlasting hills, and not be looking out from their summits for some petty Boston or New York in the horizon.

At intervals we heard the murmuring of water, and the slumberous breathing of crickets throughout the night, and

left the inn the next morning in the grey twilight, after it had
been hallowed by the night air, and when only the innocent
cows were stirring, with a kind of regret. It was only four
miles to the base of the mountain, and the scenery was already more picturesque. Our road lay along the course of the
Stillwater, which was breaking at the bottom of a deep ravine,
filled with pines and rocks, tumbling fresh from the mountains, so soon, alas! to commence its career of usefulness. At
first a cloud hung between us and the summit, but it was
soon blown away. As we gathered the raspberries, which grew
abundantly by the roadside, that action seemed consistent
with a lofty prudence, as well as agreeable to the palate, as if
the traveller who ascends into a mountainous region should
fortify himself by eating of such light ambrosial fruits as grow
there, and drinking of the springs which gush out from the
mountain sides, as he gradually inhales the subtler and purer
atmosphere of those elevated places, thus propitiating the
mountain gods, by a sacrifice of their own fruits. The gross
products of the plains and valleys are for such as dwell therein;
but surely the juices of this berry have relation to the thin air
of the mountain tops.

In due time we began to ascend the mountain, passing,
first, through a maple wood, then a denser forest, which gradually became dwarfed, till there were no trees whatever. We at
length pitched our tent on the summit. It is but nineteen
hundred feet above the village of Princeton, and three thousand above the level of the sea; but by this slight elevation, it
is infinitely removed from the plain, and when we have
reached it, we feel a sense of remoteness, as if we had travelled
into distant regions, to Arabia Petrea, or the farthest east, so
withdrawn and solitary it seems. A robin upon a staff, was the
highest object in sight, thus easily triumphing over the height
of nature. Swallows were flying about us, and the chewink
and cuckoos were heard near at hand. The summit consists of
a few acres, destitute of trees, covered with bare rocks, interspersed with blueberry bushes, raspberries, gooseberries,
strawberries, moss, and a fine wiry grass. The common yellow
lily, and dwarf cornel, grow abundantly in the crevices of the
rocks. This clear space, which is gently rounded, is bounded a
few feet lower by a thick shrubbery of oaks, with maples, as-

pens, beeches, cherries, and occasionally a mountain-ash intermingled, among which we found the bright blueberries of the Solomon's Seal, and the fruit of the pyrola. From the foundation of a wooden observatory, which was formerly erected on the highest point, forming a rude hollow structure of stone, a dozen feet in diameter, and five or six in height, we could dimly see Monadnock, rising in simple grandeur, in the north-west, nearly a thousand feet higher, still the "far blue mountain," though with an altered profile. But the first day the weather was so hazy that it was in vain we endeavored to unravel the obscurity. It was like looking into the sky again, and the patches of forest here and there seemed to flit like clouds over a lower heaven. As to voyagers of an aerial Polynesia, the earth seemed like an island in the ether; on every side, even as low as we, the sky shutting down, like an unfathomable deep, around it. A blue Pacific island, where who knows what islanders inhabit? and as we sail near its shores we see the waving of trees, and hear the lowing of kine.

We read Virgil and Wordsworth in our tent, with new pleasure there, while waiting for a clearer atmosphere, nor did the weather prevent our appreciating the simple truth and beauty of Peter Bell:

> "And he had lain beside his asses,
>   On lofty Cheviot hills."

> "And he had trudged through Yorkshire dales,
>   Among the rocks and winding *scars*,
>   Where deep and low the hamlets lie
>   Beneath their little patch of sky,
>   And little lot of stars."

Who knows but this hill may one day be a Helvellyn, or even a Parnassus, and the Muses haunt here, and other Homers frequent the neighboring plains,

> Not unconcerned Wachusett rears his head
>   Above the field, so late from nature won,
> With patient brow reserved, as one who read
>   New annals in the history of man.

The blueberries which the mountain afforded, added to the milk we had brought, made our frugal supper, while for entertainment, the even-song of the wood-thrush rung along the ridge. Our eyes rested on no painted ceiling, nor carpeted hall, but on skies of nature's painting, and hills and forests of her embroidery. Before sunset, we rambled along the ridge to the north, while a hawk soared still above us. It was a place where gods might wander, so solemn and solitary, and removed from all contagion with the plain. As the evening came on, the haze was condensed in vapor, and the landscape became more distinctly visible, and numerous sheets of water were brought to light,

> Et jam summa procul villarum culmina fumant,
> Majoresque cadunt altis de montibus umbræ.

> And now the tops of the villas smoke afar off,
> And the shadows fall longer from the high mountains.

As we stood on the stone tower while the sun was setting, we saw the shades of night creep gradually over the valleys of the east, and the inhabitants withdrew to their houses, and shut their doors, while the moon silently rose up, and took possession of that part. And then the same scene was repeated on the west side, as far as the Connecticut and the Green Mountains, and the sun's rays fell on us two alone, of all New England men.

It was the night but one before the full of the moon, so that we enjoyed uninterrupted light, so bright that we could see to read Wordsworth distinctly, and when in the evening we strolled on the summit, there was a fire blazing on Monadnock, which lighted up the whole western horizon, and by making us aware of a community of mountains, made our position seem less solitary. But at length the wind drove us to the shelter of our tent, and we closed its door for the night, and fell asleep.

It was a rich treat to hear the wind roar over the rocks, at intervals, when we waked, for it had grown quite cold and windy. The night was, in its elements, simple even to majesty in that bleak place—a bright moonlight and a piercing wind. It was at no time darker than twilight within the tent, and we could easily see the moon through its transparent roof as we lay; for there was the moon still above us, with Jupiter and Saturn on either hand, looking down on Wachusett, and it was a satisfaction to know that they were our fellow-travellers still, as high and out of our reach, as our own destiny. Truly the stars were given for a consolation to man. We should not know but our life were fated to be always grovelling, but it is permitted to behold them, and surely they are deserving of a fair destiny. We see laws which never fail, of whose failure we never conceived; and their lamps burn all the night, too, as well as all day, so rich and lavish is that nature, which can afford this superfluity of light.

The morning twilight began as soon as the moon had set, and we arose and kindled our fire, whose blaze might have been seen for thirty miles around. As the day-light increased, it was remarkable how rapidly the wind went down. There was no dew on the summit, but coldness supplied its place. When the dawn had reached its prime, we enjoyed the view of a distinct horizon line, and could fancy ourselves at sea, and the distant hills the waves in the horizon, as seen from the deck of a vessel. The cherry-birds flitted around us, the nesthatch and flicker were heard among the bushes, the titmouse perched within a few feet, and the song of the woodthrush again rung along the ridge. At length we saw the sun rise up out of the sea, and shine on Massachusetts, and from this moment the atmosphere grew more and more transparent till the time of our departure, and we began to realize the extent of the view, and how the earth, in some degree, answered to the heavens in breadth, the white villages to the constellations in the sky. There was little of the sublimity and grandeur which belong to mountain scenery, but an immense landscape to ponder on a summer's day. We could see how ample and roomy is nature. As far as the eye could reach, there was little life in the landscape; the few birds that flitted past did not crowd. The travellers on the remote highways, which intersect the country on every side, had no fellow-travellers for miles, before or behind. On every side, the eye ranged over successive circles of towns, rising one above another, like the terraces of a vineyard, till they were lost in the horizon. Wachusett is, in fact, the observatory of the state.

There lay Massachusetts, spread out before us in its length and breadth, like a map. There was the level horizon, which told of the sea on the east and south, the well-known hills of New Hampshire on the north, and the misty summit of the Hoosac and Green Mountains, first made visible to us the evening before, blue and unsubstantial, like some bank of clouds which the morning wind would dissipate, on the north-west and west. These last distant ranges, on which the eye rests unwearied, commence with an abrupt boulder in the north, beyond the Connecticut, and travel southward, with three or four peaks dimly seen. But Monadnock, rearing its masculine front in the north-west, is the grandest feature. As we beheld it we knew that it was the height of land between the two rivers, on this side the valley of the Merrimack, or that of the Connecticut, fluctuating with their blue seas of air. These rival vales, gradually extending their population and commerce along their respective streams, to what destiny who shall tell? Watatic, and the neighboring hills in this state and in New Hampshire, are a continuation of the same elevated range on which we were standing. But that New Hampshire bluff—that promontory of a state—causing day and night on this our state of Massachussets, will longest haunt our dreams.

We could, at length, realize the place mountains occupy on the land, and how they come into the general scheme of the universe. When first we climb their summits, and observe their lesser irregularities, we do not give credit to the comprehensive intelligence which shaped them; but when afterward we behold their outlines in the horizon, we confess that the hand which moulded their opposite slopes, making one to balance the other, worked round a deep centre, and was privy to the plan of the universe. So is the least part of nature in its bearings, referred to all space. These lesser mountain ranges, as well as the Alleghanies, run from north-east to south-west, and parallel with these mountain streams are the more fluent rivers, answering to the general direction of the coast, the bank of the great ocean stream itself. Even the clouds, with their thin bars, fall into the same direction by preference, and such is the course of the prevailing winds, and the migration of men and birds. A mountain chain determines many things for the statesman and philosopher. The improvements of civilization rather creep along its sides than cross its summit. How often is it a barrier to prejudice and fanaticism? In passing over these heights of land, through their thin atmosphere, the follies of the plain are refined and purified. As many species of plants do not scale their summits, so many species of folly do not cross the Alleghanies; it is only the hardy mountain plant that creeps quite over the ridge, and descends into the valley beyond.

It adds not a little grandeur to our conception of the flight of birds, especially of the duck tribe, and such as fly high in the air, to have ascended a mountain. We can now see what landmarks they are to their migrations; how the Catskills and Highlands have hardly sunk to them, when Wachusett and Monadnock open a passage to the north-east—how they are guided, too, in their course by the rivers and valleys, and who knows but by the stars, as well as the mountain ranges, and not by the petty landmarks which we use? The bird whose eye takes in the Green Mountains on the one side, and the ocean on the other, need not be at a loss to find its way.

At noon we descended the mountain, and having returned to the abodes of men, turned our faces to the east again; measuring our progress, from time to time, by the more ethereal hues, which the mountain assumed. Passing swiftly through Stillwater and Sterling, as with a downward impetus, (the reader will excuse the abruptness of the descent,) we found ourselves almost at home again in the green meadows of Lancaster, so like our own Concord, for both are watered by two streams which unite near their centres, and have many other features in common. There is an unexpected refinement about this scenery; level prairies of great extent, interspersed with elms, and hop-fields, and groves of trees, give it almost a classic appearance. This, it will be remembered, was the scene of Mrs. Rowlandson's capture, and of other events in the Indian wars, but from this July afternoon, and under that mild exterior, those times seemed as remote as the irruption of the Goths. They were the dark age of New England. On beholding a picture of a New England village as it then appeared, with a fair open prospect, and a light on trees and rivers, as if it were broad noon, we find we had not thought the sun shone in those days, or that men lived in broad day-

light then. We do not imagine the sun shining on hill and valley during Philip's war, nor on the war-path of Paugus, or
Standish, or Church, or Lovell, with serene summer weather,
but a dim twilight or night did those events transpire in. They
must have fought in the shade of their own dusky deeds.

At length, as we plodded along the dusty roads, our
thoughts became as dusty as they; all thought indeed stopped,
thinking broke down, or proceeded only passively in a sort of
rhythmical cadence of the confused material of thought, and
we found ourselves mechanically repeating some familiar measure which timed with our tread; some verse of the Robin
Hood ballads, for instance, which one can recommend to
travel by.

> "Swearers are swift, sayd lyttle John,
>   As the wind blows over the hill;
> For if it be never so loud this night,
>   To-morrow it may be still."

And so it went up hill and down till a stone interrupted the
line, when a new verse was chosen.

> "His shoote it was but loosely shot,
>   Yet flewe not the arrowe in vaine,
> For it met one of the sheriffe's men,
>   And William-a-Trent was slaine."

There is, however, this consolation to the most way-worn
traveller, upon the dustiest road, that the path his feet describe is so perfectly symbolical of human life—now climbing
the hills, now descending into the vales. From the summits he
beholds the heavens and the horizon, from the vales he looks
up to the heights again. He is treading his old lessons still,
and though he may be very weary and travel-worn, it is yet
sincere experience.

Leaving the Nashua, we changed our route a little, and arrived at Stillriver village, in the western part of Harvard, just
as the sun was setting. From this place, which lies to the
northward, upon the western slope of the same range of hills,
on which we had spent the noon before, in the adjacent town,
the prospect is beautiful, and the grandeur of the mountain
outlines unsurpassed. There was such a repose and quiet here

at this hour, as if the very hill-sides were enjoying the scene, and as we passed slowly along, looking back over the country we had traversed, and listening to the evening song of the robin, we could not help contrasting the equanimity of nature with the bustle and impatience of man. His words and actions presume always a crisis near at hand, but she is forever silent and unpretending.

We rested that night at Harvard, and the next morning, while one bent his steps to the nearer village of Groton, the other took his separate and solitary way to the peaceful meadows of Concord; but let him not forget to record the brave hospitality of a farmer and his wife, who generously entertained him at their board, though the poor wayfarer could only congratulate the one on the continuance of hayweather, and silently accept the kindness of the other. Refreshed by this instance of generosity, no less than by the substantial viands set before him, he pushed forward with new vigor, and reached the banks of the Concord before the sun had climbed many degrees into the heavens.

And now that we have returned to the desert life of the plain, let us endeavor to impart a little of that mountain grandeur into it. We will remember within what walls we lie, and understand that this level life too has its summit, and why from the mountain top the deepest valleys have a tinge of blue; that there is elevation in every hour, as no part of the earth is so low that the heavens may not be seen from, and we have only to stand on the summit of our hour to command an uninterrupted horizon.

Sir Walter Raleigh

PERHAPS no one in English history better represents the heroic character than Sir Walter Raleigh; for Sidney has got to be almost as shadowy as Arthur himself. Raleigh's somewhat antique & Roman virtues appear in his numerous military and naval adventures, in his knightly conduct toward the Queen, in his poems and his employments in the tower, and not least in his death, but more than all in his constant soldier-like bearing and promise. He was the Bayard of peaceful as well as warlike enterprise, & few lives which are the subject of recent & trustworthy history are so agreeable to the imagination. Notwithstanding his temporary unpopularity, he especially possessed those prevalent and popular qualities which command the admiration of men. If an English Plutarch were to be written, Raleigh would be the best Greek or Roman among them all. He was one whose virtues if they were not distinctly great yet gave to virtue a current stamp and value as it were by the very grace and loftiness with which he carried them—one of nature's noblemen, who possessed the requisites to true nobility, without which no heraldry nor blood can avail. Among savages he would still have been the chief. He seems to have had, not a profounder or grander, but, so to speak, more, nature, than other men. The enthusiastic and often extravagant, but always hearty & emphatic tone in which he is spoken of by his contemporaries is not the least remarkable fact about him, and it does not matter much whether the current stories are true or not, since they at least prove his reputation.

It is not his praise to have been a saint and a seer in his generation, but "one of the gallantest worthies that ever England bred". The stories about him testify to a character rather than a virtue. As, for instance, that "he was damnably proud. Old Sir Robert Harley, of Brampton-Brian Castle, (who knew him), would say, 'twas a great question, who was the proudest, Sir Walter or Sir Thomas Overbury, but the difference that was, was judged on Sir Thomas' side;" that "In his youth his companions were boisterous blades, but generally those that had wit." A young contemporary says, "I have heard his enemies confess, that he was one of the weightiest and wisest men that this island ever bred". And another gives this character of him—"Who hath not known or read of this prodigy of wit and fortune, Sir Walter Raleigh, a man unfortunate in nothing else but in the greatness of his wit and advancement, whose eminent worth was such, both in domestic policy, foreign expeditions, and discoveries, in arts and literature, both practic and contemplative, that it might seem at once, to conquer example and imitation".

And what we are told of his personal appearance is accordant with the rest; that "he had in the outward man a good presence, in a handsome and well-compacted person", that "he was a tall, handsome, and bold man," and his "was thought a very good face", though "his countenance was somewhat spoiled by the unusual height of his forehead." "He was such a person (every way), that (as King Charles I. says of the Lord Strafford) a prince would rather be afraid of, than ashamed of—" and had an "awfulness and ascendency in his aspect over other mortals". And we are not disappointed to learn that he indulged in a splendid dress, and "notwithstanding his so great mastership in style, and his conversation with the learnedest and politest persons, yet he spake broad Devonshire to his dying day."

Such a character as this was well suited to the times in which he lived. His age was an unusually stirring one. The discovery of America and the successful progress of the Reformation opened a field for both the intellectual and physical energies of his generation. Its fathers were Calvin, and Knox, and Cranmer, and Pizarro, and Garcilaso; and its immediate forefathers Luther, and Raphael, and Bayard, and Angelo, and Ariosto, and Copernicus, and Machiavel, and Erasmus, and Cabot, and Ximenes, and Columbus. Its device might have been an anchor, a sword, and a quill. The Pizarro laid by his sword at intervals and took to his letters. The Columbus set sail for newer worlds still, by voyages which needed not the patronage of princes. The Bayard alighted from his steed to seek adventures no less arduous than heretofore, upon the ocean, and in the western world; and the Luther who had reformed religion, began now to reform politics and science.

In his youth, however it may have concerned him, Camoens was writing a heroic poem in Portugal, and the arts still had their representative in Paul Veronese of Italy. He may have been one to welcome the works of Tasso and Montaigne to England, and when he looked about him, have found such men as Cervantes & Sidney, men of like pursuits & not altogether dissimilar genius from himself, for his contemporaries, a Drake to rival him on the sea, and a Hudson in western adventure, a Halley, a Galileo, and a Kepler, for his astronomers, a Bacon, a Behmen, and a Burton, for his philosophers, and a Jonson—a Spenser, and a Shakspeare, his poets for refreshment and inspiration.

But that we may know how worthy he himself was to make one of this illustrious company, and appreciate this great activity and versatility of his genius, we will glance hastily at the various aspects of his life.

He was a proper knight, a born cavalier, and in the intervals of war betook himself still to the most vigorous arts of peace, though as if diverted from his proper aim. He makes us doubt if there is not some worthier apology for war than has been discovered, for its modes and manners were an instinct with him, and though in his writings he takes frequent occasion sincerely to condemn its folly, and show the better policy and advantage of peace, yet he speaks with the uncertain authority of a warrior still, to whom those juster wars are not simply the dire necessity implied. In whatever he is engaged we seem to see a plume waving over his head, and a sword dangling at his side. Born in 1552, the last year of the reign of Edward VI, we find that not long after, by such instinct as the young crab seeks the sea shore, he has already marched into France, as one of "a troop of a hundred gentlemen volunteers", who are described as "a gallant company, nobly mounted and accoutred, having on their colors the motto, *Finem det mihi virtus*"—Let valor be my end. And so in fact he marched on through life with this motto in his heart always.

All the peace of those days seems to have been but a truce, or casual interruption of the order of war. War with Spain especially was so much the rule rather than the exception, that the navigators and commanders of these two nations when abroad, acted on the presumption that their countries were at war at home, though they had left them at peace, and their respective colonies in America carried on war at their convenience with no infraction of the treaties between the mother countries. Raleigh especially seems to have regarded the Spaniards as his natural enemies, and he was not backward to develop this part of his nature.

When England was threatened with foreign invasion, the Queen looked to him especially for advice and assistance, and none was better able to give them than he. We cannot but admire the tone in which he speaks of his island, and how it is to be best defended, and the navy its chief strength maintained and improved. He speaks from England as his castle and his, as no other man's, is the voice of the state, for he does not assert the interests of an individual but of a commonwealth, and we see in him revived a Roman patriotism. His actions as they were public and for the public, were fit to be publicly rewarded, and we accordingly read with equanimity of gold chains and monopolies and other emoluments conferred on him from time to time for his various services—his military successes in Ireland "that commonwealth of common woe", as he even then described it,—his enterprise in the harbor of Cadiz,—his capture of Fayal from the Spaniards, and other exploits which perhaps more than anything else got him fame and a name during his life time.

If war was his earnest work, it was his pastime too, for in the peaceful intervals we hear of his participating heartily and bearing off the palm in the birth-day tournaments and tilting matches of the Queen, where the combatants vied with each other mainly who should come on to the ground in the most splendid dress and equipments—those tilts where it is said that his political rival Essex, whose wealth enabled him to lead the costliest train, but who ran very ill, and was thought the poorest knight of all, was wont to change his suit from orange to green, that it might be said that there was one in green who ran worse than one in orange.

None of the worthies of that age can be duly appreciated if we neglect to consider them in their relation to the new world. The stirring spirits stood with but one foot on the land. There were Drake, Hawkins, Hudson, Frobisher, and many others, and their worthy companion was Raleigh. As a navigator and naval commander he had few equals, and if the reader who has attended to his other actions inquires how he filled up the odd years, he will find that they were spent in numerous voyages to America, for the purposes of discovery and colonization, so that he would be more famous for these enterprises if they were not overshadowed by the number and variety of his pursuits.

His persevering care and oversight as the patron of Virginia, discovered and planted under his auspices in 1584 present him in an interesting light to the American reader. The work of colonization was well suited to his genius, and if the security of England herself had not required his attention and presence at this time he would possibly have realized some of his dreams in plantations and cities on our coast.

England has since felt the benefit of his experience in naval affairs. He was one of the first to assert their importance to her and exerted himself especially for the improvement of naval architecture on which he has left a treatise. And he also composed a discourse on the art of war at sea, a subject which at that time had never been treated.

We can least bear to consider Raleigh as a courtier, though the court of England at that time was a field not altogether unworthy of such a courtier. His competitors for fame and favor there, were Burleigh, Leicester, Sussex, Buckingham, and, be it remembered, Sir Philip Sidney, whose Arcadia was just finished when Raleigh came to court—his natural companion and other self, as it were, as if nature, in her anxiety to confer one specimen of a true knight and courtier on that age, had cast two in the same mould, lest one should miscarry. These two kindred spirits are said to have been mutually attracted toward each other. And there too was Queen Elizabeth herself, the centre of the court and of the kingdom, to whose service he consecrates himself, not so much as a subject to his sovereign, but as a knight to the service of his mistress. His intercourse with the Queen may well have begun with the incident of the cloak, for such continued to be its character afterwards. It has in the description an air of romance and might fitly have made a part of his friend Sidney's Arcadia. We are inclined to consider him as some knight, and a knight errant too, who had strayed into the precincts of the court, and practised there the arts which he had learned in bower and hall and in the lists.—Not that he knew not how to govern states as well as queens, but he brought to the task the gallantry and graces of chivalry as well as the judgment and experience of a practical modern Englishman. "The Queen", says one, "began to be taken with his elocution, and loved to hear his reasons to her demands, and the truth is she took him for a kind of oracle which nettled them all." He rose rapidly in her favor and became her indispensable counsellor in all matters which concerned the state, for he was minutely acquainted with the affairs of England, and none better understood her commercial interests. But though he made a good use of his influence for the most part when obtained, he could descend to the grossest flattery to obtain it, and we could wish him forever banished from the court, whose favors he so earnestly sought. But that he who was one while "the Queen of England's poor captive," could sometimes assume a manly and independent tone with her appears from his answer when she once exclaimed, on his asking a favor for a friend, "When, Sir Walter, will you cease to be a beggar?" "When your gracious majesty ceases to be a benefactor."

His court life exhibits him in mean and frivolous relations which make him lose that respect in our eyes which he had acquired elsewhere. The base use he made of his recovered influence, (after having been banished from the court and even suffered imprisonment in consequence of the Queen's displeasure,) to procure the disgrace and finally the execution of his rival Essex, who had been charged with treason, is the foulest stain upon his escutcheon, the one which it is hardest to reconcile with the nobleness and generosity which we are inclined to attribute to such a character. Revenge is most unheroic. Also his acceptance of bribes afterwards for using his influence in behalf of the Earl's adherents is not to be excused by the usage of the times. The times may change, but the laws of integrity and magnanimity are immutable. Nor are the terms on which he was the friend of Cecil, from motives of policy merely, more tolerable to consider. Yet we cannot but think that he frequently travelled a higher, though a parallel course with the mob, and though he had their suffrage, to some extent deserves the praise which Jonson applies to another—

"That to the vulgar canst thyself apply,
Treading a better path not contrary."

We gladly make haste to consider him in what the world calls his misfortune, after the death of Elizabeth and the accession of James 1st, when his essentially nobler nature was separated from the base company of the court, and the contaminations which his loyalty could not resist, though by imprisonment and the scaffold.

His enemies had already prejudiced the king against him before his accession to the throne, and when at length the English nobility were presented to his majesty, who, it will be remembered, was a Scotchman, and Raleigh's name was told, "Raleigh", exclaimed the king, "O my soule, mon, I have heard rawly of thee." His efforts to limit the king's power of introducing Scots into England, contributed to increase his jealousy and dislike, and he was shortly after accused by Lord Cobham of participating in a conspiracy to place the Lady Arabella Stuart on the throne, and owing mainly, it is thought, to the King's resentment, was tried and falsely convicted of high treason—though his accuser retracted in writing his whole accusation before the conclusion of the trial.

In connexion with his behavior to Essex, it should be remembered that by his conduct on his own trial he in a great measure removed the ill-will which existed against him on that account. At his trial, which is said to have been most unjustly and insolently conducted by Sir Edward Coke on the part of the Crown, "He answered" says one, "with that temper, wit, learning, courage, and judgment, that save that it went with the hazzard of his life, it was the happiest day that ever he spent. The two first that brought the news [of his condemnation] to the king were Roger Ashton, and a Scotsman, whereof one affirmed that never any man spake so well in times past, nor would do in the world to come: and the other said, that whereas when he saw him first, he was so led with the common hatred, that he would have gone a hundred miles to have seen him hanged, he would, ere he parted, have gone a thousand to have saved his life." Another says he "behaved himself so worthily, so wisely, and so temperately, that in half a day the mind of all the company was changed from the extremest hate to the extremest pity." And another "to the lords humble, but not prostrate; to the jury affable, but not fawning; to the king's counsel patient, but not yielding to the imputations laid upon him, or neglecting to repel them with the spirit which became an injured and honorable man." And finally he followed the sheriff out of court in the expressive words of Sir Thomas Overbury, "with admirable erection, but yet in such sort as became a man condemned."

Raleigh prepared himself for immediate execution, but after his pretended accomplices had gone through the ceremony of a mock execution and been pardoned by the King, it satisfied the policy of his enemies to retain him a prisoner in the tower for 13 years, with the sentence of death still unrevoked. In the meanwhile he solaced himself in his imprisonment with writing a history of the world and cultivating poetry and philosophy as the noblest deeds compatible with his confinement.

It is satisfactory to contrast with his mean personal relations while at court his connexion in the tower with the young prince Henry whose tastes and aspirations were of a stirring kind, as his friend and instructor. He addresses some of his shorter pieces to him, and in some instances they seem to have been written expressly for his use. He preaches to him as he was well able, from experience, a wiser philosophy than he had himself practised, and was particularly anxious to correct in him a love of popularity—which he had discovered, and gave him useful maxims for his conduct when he should take his father's place.

He lost neither health nor spirits by 13 years of captivity, but after having spent this the literary era of his life as in the retirement of his study, and having written the history of the old world, he began to dream of actions which would supply materials to the future historian of the new. It is interesting to consider him, a close prisoner as he was, preparing for voyages and adventures, which would require to roam more broadly than was consistent with the comfort or ambition of his freest contemporaries.

Already in 1595 8 years before his imprisonment, it will be remembered he had undertaken his first voyage to Guiana in person—mainly it is said to recover favor with the Queen—but doubtless it was much more to recover favor with himself and exercise his genius in fields more worthy of him than a corrupt court.

He continued to cherish this his favorite project, though a prisoner, and at length in the 13th year of his imprisonment, though the influence of his friends, and his confident assertions respecting the utility of the expedition to his country, he obtained his release and set sail for Guiana with twelve ships. But unfortunately he neglected to procure a formal pardon from the king, trusting to the opinion of Lord Bacon that this was unnecessary, since the sentence of death against him was virtually annulled, by the lives of others being committed to his hands. Acting on this presumption, and with the best intentions toward his country, and only his usual jealousy of Spain, he undertook to make good his engagements to himself and this world.

It is not easy for us at this day to realize what extravagant expectations Europe had formed respecting the wealth of the new world. We might suppose two whole continents with their adjacent seas & oceans, equal to the present known globe—stretching from pole to pole, and possessing every variety of soil, climate and productions, lying unexplored today—what would be the speculations of Broadway & State street?

The few travellers who had penetrated into the country of Guiana, whither Raleigh was bound, brought back accounts of noble streams flowing through majestic forests and a depth and luxuriance of soil which made England seem a barren waste in comparison. Its mineral wealth was reported to be as inexhaustible as the cupidity of its discoverers was unbounded. The very surface of the ground was said to be resplendent with gold, and men went covered with gold-dust, as Hottentots with grease. Raleigh was informed while at Trinidad by the Spanish governor who was his prisoner, that one John Martinez had at length penetrated into this country and the stories told by him of the wealth and extent of its cities, surpass the narratives of Marco Polo himself. He is said, in particular, to have reached the city of Manoa, to which he first gave the name of El Dorado, or The Gilded, the Indians conducting him blindfolded, "not removing the veil from his eyes till he was ready to enter the city. It was at noon that he passed the gates, and it took him all that day and the next, walking from sunrise to sunset, before he arrived at the Palace of Inga, where he resided for seven months, till he had made himself master of the language of the country". These, and even more fanciful accounts had Raleigh heard and pondered, both before and after his first visit to the country. No one was more familiar with the stories, both true and fabulous, respecting the discovery and resources of the new world, and none had a better right to know what great commanders and navigators had done there or anywhere than he. Such information would naturally flow to him of its own accord. That his ardor and faith were hardly cooled by actual observation may be gathered from the tone of his own description. He was the first Englishman who ascended the Orinoco, and he thus describes the adjacent country.

"On the banks were divers sorts of fruits good to eat, besides flowers and trees, of that variety as would be sufficient to make ten volumes of herbals. We relieved ourselves many times with the fruits of the country, and sometimes with fowl and fish; we saw also birds of all colors,—some carnation, some crimson, some tawny, purple, green, watched, and of all other sorts, both simple and mixed; as it was unto us a great good passing of the time to behold them."

The following is his description of the waterfalls and the province of Canuri, through which last the river runs.

"When we ascended to the tops of the first hills of the plains adjoining to the river, we beheld that wonderful breach of waters which was precipitated down Caroli, and might from that mountain see the river how it ran in three parts above twenty miles off; there appeared ten or twelve falls in sight, every one as high over the other as a church-tower, the water descending with that fury that the rebound made it seem as if it had been all covered over with a great shower of rain, and in some places we took it for a smoke that had risen over some great town. For mine own part I was well persuaded from thence to have returned, being a very ill footman; but the rest were all so desirous to go near the said strange thunder of waters, as they drew me on by little and little into the next valley. . . . . I never saw a more beautiful country nor more lively prospects: hills so raised here and there over the valleys; the river winding into divers branches; the plains adjoining, without bush or stubble, all fair green grass; the ground of hard sand, easy to march on either for horse or foot; the deer crossing in every path; the birds towards the evening singing on every tree with a thousand several tunes; cranes and herons, of white, crimson and carnation, perching on the river's side; the air fresh, with a gentle easterly wind; and every stone that we stopped to take up promising either gold or silver by his complexion."

In another place he says "To conclude, it is a country as yet untouched by the natives of the old world: never sacked, turned, or wrought; the face of the earth hath not been torn, nor the virtue and salt of the soil spent by manurance."

To the fabulous accounts of preceding adventurers Raleigh added many others equally absurd and poetical, as for instance, of a tribe "with eyes in their shoulders, and mouths in their breasts,"—but, it seems to us, with entire good faith, and no such flagrant intent to deceive as he has been accused of. "Weak policy it would be in me", says he, "to betray myself or my country with imaginations; neither am I so far in love with that watching, care, peril, disease, hard fare, and other mischiefs that accompany such voyages, as to woo myself again into any of them, were I not assured that the sun covereth not so much riches in any other part of the earth." It is easy to see that he was tempted not so much by the lustre of the gold, as by the splendor of the enterprise itself. It was the best move that peace allowed. The expeditions to Guiana and the ensuing golden dreams were not wholly unworthy of him, though he accomplished little more in the first voyage than to take formal possession of the country in the name of the Queen, and in the second, of the Spanish town of St. Thomas, as his enemies would say, in the name of himself. Perceiving that the Spaniards, who had been secretly informed of his designs through their ambassador in England, were prepared to thwart his endeavors, and resist his progress in the country, he procured the capture of this their principal town, which was also burnt against his orders.

But it seems to us that no *particular* exception is to be taken against these high-handed measures, though his enemies have made the greatest handle of them. His behavior on this occasion was part and parcel of his constant character. It would not be easy to say when he ceased to be an honorable soldier and became a freebooter, nor indeed is it of so much importance to inquire of a man what actions he performed at one and what at another period, as what manner of man he was at all periods. It was after all the same Raleigh who had won so much renown by land & sea, at home and abroad. It was his forte to deal vigorously with men, whether as a statesman, a courtier, a navigator, a planter of colonies, an accused person, a prisoner, an explorer of continents, or a military or naval commander, and it was a right hero's maxim of his that "good success admits of no examination", which in a liberal sense is true enough, for good success can only spring from good conduct; and that there was no cant in him on the subject of war, appears from his saying which indeed is very true, that "The necessity of war, which among human actions is most lawless, hath some kind of affinity and near resemblance with the necessity of law." It is to be remembered too that if the Spaniards found him a restless and uncompromising enemy—the Indians experienced in him a humane and gentle defender, and on his second visit to Guiana remembered his name and welcomed him with enthusiasm.

We are told that the Spanish Ambassador, on receiving intelligence of his doings in this country, rushed in to the presence of King James, exclaiming "Piratas—piratas"—pirates—pirates. And the king, to gratify his resentment, without bringing him to trial for this alledged new offence—with characteristic meanness and pusillanimity caused him to be executed upon the old sentence soon after his return to England.

The circumstances of his execution and how he bore himself on that memorable occasion when the sentence of death passed 15 years before was revived against him, after as a historian in his confinement he had visited the old world in his free imagination, and as an unrestrained adventurer the New, with his fleets and in person—are perhaps too well known to be repeated.—The reader will excuse our hasty rehearsal of the final scene.

We can pardon though not without hesitation his supposed attempt at suicide in the prospect of defeat and disgrace. No one can read his letter to his wife written while he was contemplating this act, without being reminded of the Roman Cato, and admiring while he condemns him. "I know", says he "that it is forbidden to destroy ourselves; but I trust it is forbidden in this sort—that we destroy not ourselves despairing of God's mercy."

Though his greatness seems to have forsaken him in his feigning himself sick and the base methods he took to avoid being brought to trial, yet he recovered himself at last, and happily withstood the trials which awaited him.

The night before his execution, besides writing letters of farewell to his wife, containing the most practical advice for the conduct of her life, he appears to have spent the time in writing verses on his condition, and among others this couplet "On the Snuff of a Candle".

> "Cowards fear to die; but courage stout,
>   Rather than live in snuff, will be put out."

And perhaps the following verses for an epitaph on himself,

> "Even such is time, that takes on trust
>   Our youth, our joys, our all we have,
>   And pays us but with age and dust;
>   Who in the dark and silent grave,
>   When we have wandered all our ways,
>   Shuts up the story of our days!
>   But from this earth, this grave, this dust,
>   The Lord shall raise me up, I trust."

His execution was appointed on Lord Mayor's day, that the pageants and shows might divert the attention of the people, but those pageants have long since been forgotten, while this tragedy is still remembered. He took a pipe of tobacco before he went to the scaffold, and appeared there with a serene countenance so that a stranger could not have told which was the condemned person. After exculpating himself in a speech to the people, and without ostentation having felt the edge of the axe, and disposed himself once as he wished to lie, he made a solemn prayer, and being directed to place himself so that his face should look to the east, his characteristic answer was "It mattered little how the head lay provided the heart was right."

The executioner being over-awed by his behavior was unable at first to perform his office—when Raleigh slowly raising his head exclaimed, "Strike away man, don't be afraid." "He was the most fearless of death," says the Bishop who attended him, "that ever was known, and the most resolute and confident, yet with reverence and conscience."

But we would not exaggerate the importance of these things—the death scenes of great men are agreeable to consider only when they make another and harmonious chapter of their lives, and we have accompanied our hero thus far, because he lived, so to speak, unto the end.

In his history of the world occurs this sentence:

"O eloquent, just, and mighty Death! Whom none could advise, thou hast persuaded, what none hath dared, thou hast done; and whom all the world hath flattered, thou only hast cast out of the world & despised; thou hast drawn together all the far-stretched greatness, all the pride, cruelty, and ambition of man, and covered it all over with these two narrow words,—Hic Iacet!"

Perhaps Raleigh was the man of the most general information and universal accomplishment of any in England. Though he excelled greatly in but few departments, yet he reached a more valuable mediocrity in many. "He seemed", said Fuller, "to be like Cato Uticensis, born to that only which he was about." He said he had been "a soldier, a sea-captain, and a courtier," but he had been much more than this. He embraced in his studies music, ornamental gardening, painting, history, antiquities, chemistry, and many arts beside. Especially he is said to have been "a great chemist," and "studied most in his sea-voyages, where he carried always a trunk of books along with him, and had nothing to divert him," and where also he carried his favorite pictures. In the tower, too, says one, "he doth spend all the day in distillations," and that this was more than a temporary recreation appears from the testimony of one who says he was operator to him for twelve years. Here also he conversed on poetry, philosophy, and literature with Hoskins, his fellow prisoner, whom Ben Jonson mentions as "the person who had polished him." He was a political economist far in advance of his age, and a sagacious and influential speaker in the House of

Commons. Science is indebted to him in more ways than one. In the midst of pressing public cares he interested himself to establish some means of universal communication between men of Science, for their mutual benefit, and actually set up what he termed, "an office of address", for this purpose. As a Mathematician he was the friend of Harriot, Dee, and the Earl of Northumberland. As an Antiquarian, he was a member of the first antiquarian society established in England, along with Spelman, Selden, Cotton, Camden, Savile, & Stow. He is said to have been the founder of the Mermaid Club, which met in Fleet Street, to which Shakspeare, Ben Jonson, Fletcher, Beaumont, Carew, Donne, &c., belonged. He has the fame of having first introduced the potato from Virginia, and the cherry from the Canaries into Ireland, where his garden was, and his manor of Sherborne "he beautified with gardens, and orchards, and groves of much variety and delight." And this fact evincing his attention to horticulture is related, that once, on occasion of the Queen's visiting him, he artificially retarded the ripening of some cherries, by stretching a wet canvass over the tree and removed it on a sunny day, so as to present the fruit ripe to the Queen a month later than usual. Not to omit a more doubtful, but not less celebrated benefit, it is said, that on the return of his first colonists from Virginia in 1586, tobacco was first effectually introduced into England, and its use encouraged by his influence and example.—And finally not to be outdone by the quacks, he invented a cordial which became very celebrated and bore his name, and was even administered to the Queen, and to the Prince in his last illness. One Febure writes that "Sir Walter, being a worthy successor of Mithridates, Matheolus, B. Valentine, Paracelsus, and others, has he affirms, selected all that is choicest in the animal, vegetable, and mineral world, and moreover manifested so much art and experience in the preparation of this great and admirable cordial as will of itself render him immortal."

We come at last to consider him as a literary man and a writer, concerning which aspect of his life we are least indebted to the historian for our facts.

As he was heroic with the sword, so was he with the pen. The History of the World, the task which he selected for his prison hours, was heroic in the undertaking and heroic in the achievement. The easy and cheerful heart with which he endured his confinement, turning his prison into a study, a parlor, and a laboratory, and his prison-yard into a garden, so that men did not so much pity as admire him—the steady purpose with which he set about fighting his battles, prosecuting his discoveries, and gathering his laurels, with the pen, if he might no longer do so with regiments & fleets—is itself an exploit. In writing the history of the world he was indeed at liberty; for he who contemplates truth and universal laws is free, whatever walls immure his body;—though to our brave prisoner thus employed mankind may have seemed but his poor fellow prisoners still.

Though this remarkable work interests us more, on the whole, as a part of the history of Raleigh, than as the history of the world, yet it was done like himself, and with no small success. The historian of Greece and Rome is usually unmanned by his subject as a peasant crouches before lords, but Raleigh, though he succumbs to the imposing fame of tradition and antediluvian story, and exhibits unnecessary reverence for a prophet or patriarch, from his habit of innate religious courtesy to the church, has done better than this whenever a hero offered. He stalks down through the aisles of the past, as through the avenues of a camp, with poets and historians for his heralds and guides, and from whatever side the faintest trump reaches his ear that way does he promptly turn, though to the neglect of many a gaudy pavilion.

From a work so little read in these days we will venture to quote as specimens the following criticisms on Alexander and the character of Epaminondas. They will at any rate teach our lips no bad habits. There is a natural emphasis in his style, like a man's tread, and a breathing space between the sentences, which the best of more modern writing does not furnish. His chapters are like English parks or rather like a Western forest, where the larger growth keeps down the underwood, and one may ride on horse back through the openings.

"Certainly the things that this king did, were marvellous, and would hardly have been undertaken by any man else; and though his father had determined to have invaded the lesser Asia, it is like enough that he would have contented himself with some part thereof, and not have discovered the river of Indus, as this man did. The swift course of victory, wherewith he ran over so large a portion of the world, in so short a space, may justly be imputed unto this, that he was never encountered by an equal spirit, concurring with equal power against him. Hereby it came to pass that his actions being limited by no greater opposition, than desart places, and the mere length of tedious journies could make, were like the Colossus of Rhodes, and not so much to be admired for the workmanship, though therein also praiseworthy, as for the huge bulk. For certainly the things performed by Xenophon, discover as brave a spirit as Alexander's, and working no less exquisitely, though the effects were less material, as were also the forces and power of command, by which it wrought. But he that would find the exact pattern of a noble commander, must look upon such as Epaminondas, that encountering worthy captains, and those better followed than themselves, have by their singular virtue overtopped their valiant enemies, and still prevailed over those, that would not have yielded one foot to any other. Such as these are, do seldom live to obtain great empires. For it is a work of more labor and longer time, to master the equal force of one hardy and well-ordered state, than to tread down and utterly subdue a multitude of servile nations, compounding the body of a gross unwieldly empire. Wherefore these *Parvo Potentes*, men that with little have done much upon enemies of like ability, are to be regarded as choice examples of worth; but great conquerors, to be rather admired for the substance of their actions, than the exquisite managing: exactness and greatness concurring so seldom, that I can find no instance of both in one, save only that brave Roman, Caesar."

Of Epaminondas he says, "So died Epaminondas, the worthiest man that ever was bred in that nation of Greece, and hardly to be matched in any age or country; for he equalled all others in the several virtues which in each of them were singular. His justice and sincerity, his temperance, wisdom, and high magnanimity, were no way inferior to his military virtues; in every part whereof he so excelled, that he could not but properly be called a wary, a valiant, a politic, a bountiful, and a provident captain. Neither was his private conversation unanswerable to those high parts which gave him praise abroad; for he was grave, and yet very affable and courteous; resolute in public business, but in his own particular, easy and of much mildness; a lover of his people, bearing with men's infirmities; witty and pleasant in speech—far from insolence; master of his own affections, and furnished with all qualities that might win and keep love. To these graces were added great ability of body, and much eloquence, and very deep knowledge in all parts of philosophy and learning; wherewith his mind being enlightened, rested not in the sweetness of contemplation, but broke forth into such effects as gave unto Thebes, which had ever been an underling, a dreadful reputation among all people adjoining, and the highest command in Greece".

For the most part an author only *writes* history, treating it as a dead subject, but Raleigh *tells* it, like a fresh story. A man of action himself, he knew when there was an action coming worthy to be related, and does not disappoint the reader, as is too commonly the case, by recording merely the traditionary admiration or wonder. In commenting upon the military actions of the ancients he easily and naturally digresses to some perhaps equal action of his own, or within his experience, and tells how they should have drawn up their fleets or men, with the authority of an admiral or general. The alacrity with which he adverts to some action within his experience, and slides down from the dignified impersonality of the historian into the familiarity and interest of a party and eye-witness, is as attractive as rare. He is often without reproach the Caesar of his own story. He treats Scipio—Pompey—Hannibal, and the rest, quite like equals, and he speaks like an eye-witness, and gives life and reality to the narrative by his very lively understanding and relating of it, especially in those parts in which the mere scholar is most likely to fail. Every reader has observed what a dust the historian commonly raises about the field of battle, to serve as an apology for not making clear the disposition and manoeuvring of the parties, so that the clearest idea one gets is of a very vague counteraction, or standing over against one another of two forces. In this history we, at least, have faith that these things are right. Our author describes an ancient battle with the vivacity and truth of an eye-witness, and perhaps in criticising the disposition of the forces, saying they should have stood thus or so, sometimes enforces his assertions in some such style, as "I remember being in the harbor of Cadiz &c.," so that, as in Herodotus and Thucydides, we associate the historian with the exploits he describes, but in this case not on account of his fame as a writer—but for the conspicuous part he acted on the world's stage—and his name is of equal mark to us with those of his heroes, so in the present instance, not only for his valor as a writer, but the part he acted in his generation, the life of the author seems fit to make the last chapter in the history he is writing. We expect that when his history is brought to a close it will include his own exploits. However, this is hardly a work to be consulted as authority now-a-days, but on the subject of its author's character. The natural breadth and grasp of the man is seen in the preface itself, which is a sermon with human life for its text. In the first books he discusses with childlike earnestness and an ingenuity which they little deserved the absurd and frivolous questions which engaged the theology and philosophy of his day. But even these are recommended by his sincerity and fine imagination, while the subsequent parts, or story itself, have the merit of being far more credible and lifelike than is common. He shows occasionally a poet's imagination and the innocence and purity of a child as it were under a knight's dress, such as were worthy of the friend of Spenser. The nobleness of his nature is everywhere apparent. The gentle and steady heart with which he cultivates philosophy and poetry in his prison, dissolving in the reader's imagination, the very walls and bars by his childlike confidence in truth and his own destiny, are affecting. Even Astrology, or, as he has elsewhere called it, "Star learning", comes recommended from his pen, and science will not refuse it.

"And certainly it cannot be doubted", says he, "but the stars are instruments of far greater use, than to give an obscure light, and for men to gaze on after sunset: it being manifest, that the diversity of seasons, the winters, & summers, more hot and cold, are not so uncertained by the sun and moon alone, who alway keep one and the same course; but that the stars have also their working therein.

And if we cannot deny but that God hath given virtues to springs & fountains, to cold earth, to plants and stones, minerals, and to the excremental parts of the basest living creatures, why should we rob the beautiful stars of their working powers? for seeing they are many in number, and of eminent beauty and magnitude, we may not think, that in the treasury of his wisdom, who is infinite, there can be wanting (even for every star) a peculiar virtue and operation; as every herb, plant, fruit, and flower adorning the face of the earth, hath the like. For as these were not created to beautifie the earth alone, and to cover and shadow her dusty face, but otherwise for the use of man and beast, to feed them and cure them; so were not those uncountable glorious bodies set in the firmament, to no other end, than to adorn it; but for instruments and organs of his divine Providence, so far as it hath pleased his just will to determine. Origen upon this place of *Genesis, Let there be light in the firmament, &c.*, affirmeth that the stars are not causes (meaning perchance binding causes;) but are as open books, wherein are contained and set down all things whatsoever to come; but not to be read by the eyes of human wisdom: which latter part I believe well, and this saying of Syracides withal; *That there are hid yet greater things than these be, and we have seen but a few of his works.* And though, for the capacity of men, we know somewhat, yet in the true and uttermost virtues of herbs and plants, which our selves sow and set, and which grow under our feet, we are in effect ignorant; much more in the powers and working of celestial bodies. . . . But in this question of fate, the middle course is to be followed, that as with the heathen we do not bind God to his creatures; so on the contrary, we do not rob those beautiful creatures of their powers and offices. . . . And that they wholly direct the reasonless mind, I am resolved; For all those which were created mortal, as birds beasts and the like, are left to their natural appetites; over all which, celestial bodies (as instruments and executioners of God's providence) have absolute dominion. . . . And S. Augustine: *Deus regit inferiora corpora per superiora, God ruleth the bodies below by those above;* . . . . It was therefore truly affirmed, *Sapiens adjuvabit opus astrorum, quemadmodum agricola terrae naturam; A wise man assisteth the work of the stars, as the husbandman helpeth the nature of the soil.* . . . . Lastly, we ought all to know, that God created the stars as he did the rest of the universal; whose influences may be called his reserved and unwritten laws. . . . But it was well said of *Plotinus* that the stars were significant, but not efficient, giving them yet something less than their due: and therefore as I do not consent with them who would make those glorious creatures of God virtueless: so I think that we derogate from his eternal and absolute power and providence, to ascribe to them the same dominion over our immortal souls, which they have over all bodily substances, and perishable natures: for the souls of men loving and fearing God, receive influence from that divine light it self, whereof the sun's clarity, and that of the stars, is by *Plato* called but a shadow. *Lumen est umbra Dei, Deus est lumen luminis;* Light is the shadow of God's brightness, who is the light of light."

We are reminded by this of Dubartas' poem on the "Probability of the Celestial Orbs being inhabited," translated by Sylvester.

> "I not believe that the great architect
>   With all these fires the heavenly arches deck'd
>   Only for shew, and with these glistering shields
>   T'amaze poor shepherds, watching in the fields;
>   I not believe that the least flow'r which pranks
>   Our garden borders, or our common banks,
>   And the least stone, that in her warming lap
>   Our mother earth doth covetously wrap,
>   Hath some peculiar virtue of its own,
>   And that the glorious stars of heav'n have none."

Nor is the following brief review and exaltation of the subject of all history unworthy of a place in this History of the World.

"Man, thus compounded and formed by God, was an abstract or model, or brief story in the universal: . . . . for out of the earth and dust was formed the flesh of man, and therefore heavy and lumpish: the bones of his body we may compare to the hard rocks and stones, and therefore strong and durable; of which Ovid;

Inde genus durum sumus, experiensque laborum,
Et documenta damus qua simus origine nati:

From thence our kind hard-hearted is, enduring pain and
care,
Approving, that our bodies of a stony nature are.

His bloud, which disperseth itself by the branches of veins
through all the body, may be resembled to those waters,
which are carried by brooks and rivers over all the earth; his
breath to the air, his natural heat to the inclosed warmth
which the earth hath in it self, which, stirred up by the heat
of the sun, assisteth nature in the speedier procreation of
those varieties, which the earth bringeth forth; our radical
moisture, oil or balsamum (whereon the natural heat feedeth
and is maintained) is resembled to the fat and fertility of the
earth; the hair of man's body, which adorns or overshadows
it, to the grass, which covereth the upper face and skin of the
earth; our generative power, to nature, which produceth all
things; our determinations to the light, wandering, and unstable clouds, carried everywhere with uncertain winds; our
eyes to the light of the sun and moon; and the beauty of our
youth, to the flowers of the spring, which either, in a very
short time, or with the sun's heat, dry up and wither away, or
the fierce puffs of wind blow them from the stalks; the
thoughts of our mind, to the motion of angels; and our pure
understanding (formerly called *mens* and that which always
looketh upwards) to those intellectual natures, which are always present with God; and lastly, our immortal souls (while
they are righteous) are by God himself beautified with the
title of his own image and similitude." But man is not in all
things like nature. "For this tide of man's life, after it once
turneth and declineth, ever runneth with a perpetual ebb and
falling stream, but never floweth again: our leaf once fallen,
springeth no more; neither doth the sun or the summer adorn
us again, with the garments of new leaves and flowers."

There is a flowing rhythm in some of these sentences like
the rippling of rivers—hardly to be matched in any prose or
verse. The following is his poem on the decay of oracles and
of pantheism.

"The fire which the Chaldeans worshipped for a god, is

crept into every man's chimney, which the lack of fuel starveth, water quencheth, and want of air suffocateth: Jupiter is no more vexed with Juno's jealousies; Death hath persuaded him to chastity, and her to patience; and that time which hath devoured it self, hath also eaten up both the bodies and images of him and his: yea their stately temples of stone and dureful marble. The houses and sumptuous buildings erected to Baal, can no where be found upon the earth, nor any monument of that glorious temple consecrated to Diana. There are none now in Phoenicia that lament the death of Adonis; nor any in Lybia, Creta, Thessalia, or elsewhere, that can ask counsel or help from Jupiter. The great god Pan hath broken his pipes, Apollo's priests are become speechless; and the trade of riddles in Oracles, with the Devil's telling men's fortunes therein, is taken up by counterfeit Egyptians and cozening Astrologers."

In his "Discourse of War in General" commencing with almost a heroic verse, "The ordinary theme and argument of history is war," are many things well thought and many more well said. He thus expands the maxim that corporations have no soul. "But no senate nor civil assembly can be under such natural impulses to honor and justice as single persons. For a majority is no-body when that majority is separated, and a collective body can have no synteresis, or divine ray, which is in the mind of every man, never assenting to evil, but upbraiding and tormenting him when he does it: but the honor and conscience that lies in the majority is too thin and diffusive to be efficacious; for a number can do a great wrong, and call it right, and not one of that majority blush for it." If his philosophy is for the most part poor, yet the conception and expression are rich and generous. His maxims are not true or impartial, but are conceived with a certain magnanimity which was natural to him, as if a selfish policy could easily afford to give place in him to a more universal and true.

As a fact evincing Raleigh's poetic culture and taste, it is said that in a visit to the poet Spenser, on the banks of the Mulla, which is described in "Colin Clout's come home again," he anticipated the judgment of posterity with respect to the Fairy Queen, and by his sympathy and advice encouraged the poet to go on with his work, which, by the advice of other friends, among whom was Sidney, he had laid aside. His own poems, though insignificant in respect to number and length, and not collected into a separate volume, or surely accredited to Raleigh, deserve the distinct attention of the lover of English poetry, and leave such an impression on the mind that this leaf of his laurels, for the time, well nigh overshadows all the rest. In these few rhymes, as in that country he describes, his life naturally culminates, and his secret aspirations appear. They are in some respects more trustworthy testimonials to his character than state papers or tradition; for poetry is a piece of very private history which unostentatiously lets us into the secret of a man's life, and is to the reader, what the eye is to the beholder, the characteristic feature, which cannot be distorted or made to deceive.

The pleasing poem entitled "A Description of the Country's Recreations", also printed among the poems of Sir Henry Wotton, is well known. The following, which bears evident marks of his pen, we will quote for its secure and continent rhythm.

"False Love and True Love."

"As you came from the holy land
        Of Walsingham,
    Met you not with my true love
        By the way as you came?
    How shall I know your true love,
        That have met many one
    As I went to the holy land,
        That have come, that have gone.
    She is neither white nor brown,
        But as the heavens fair;
    There is none hath so divine a form
        In the earth or the air.
    Such a one did I meet, good sir,
        Such an angelic face;
    Who like a queen, like a nymph did appear,
        By her gait, by her grace:
    She hath left me here all alone,
        All alone as unknown,

Who sometimes did me lead with herself,
    And me loved as her own:
What's the cause that she leaves you alone
    And a new way doth take:
Who loved you once as her own
    And her joy did you make?
I have loved her all my youth,
    But now, old as you see,
Love likes not the falling fruit
    From the withered tree:
Know that love is a careless child
    And forgets promise past,
He is blind, he is deaf, when he list,
    And in faith never fast:
His desire is a dureless content,
    And a trustless joy;
He is won with a world of despair,
    And is lost with a toy:
Of women-kind such indeed is the love,
    Or the word love abused;
Under which many childish desires
    And conceits are excused:
But true love is a durable fire
    In the mind ever burning;
Never sick, never old, never dead,
    From itself never turning."

The following will be new to many of our readers.

"The Shepherd's Praise of his sacred Diana"

"Prais'd be Diana's fair and harmless light;
    Prais'd be the dews wherewith she moists the ground;
  Prais'd be her beams, the glory of the night;
    Prais'd be her power, by which all powers abound!

Prais'd be her nymphs, with whom she decks the woods;
    Prais'd be her knights, in whom true honor lives;
Prais'd be that force by which she moves the floods!
    Let that Diana shine, which all these gives!

In heaven, queen she is among the spheres;
>   She mistress-like, makes all things to be pure;
Eternity in her oft-change she bears;
>   She, Beauty is; by her, the fair endure.

Time wears her not; she doth his chariot guide;
>   Mortality below her orb is placed;
By her the virtues of the stars down slide;
>   In her is Virtue's perfect image cast!

A knowledge pure it is her worth to know:
With Circes let them dwell that think not so!"

Though we discover in his verses the vices of the courtier, and they are not equally sustained, as if his genius were warped by the frivolous society of the Court, he was capable of rising to unusual heights. His genius seems to have been fitted for short flights of unmatched sweetness and vigor, but by no means for the sustained loftiness of the epic poet. One who read his verses would say that he had not grown to be the man he promised. They have occasionally a strength of character and heroic tone rarely expressed or appreciated, and possess an excellence so peculiar, as to be almost unique specimens of their kind in the language. Those which have reference to his death have been oftenest quoted, and are the best. "The Soul's Errand" deserves to be remembered till her mission is accomplished in the world. We quote the following, not so well known—with some omissions, from the commencement of

"His Pilgrimage".

"Give me my scallop-shell of quiet,
>   My staff of faith to walk upon;
My scrip of joy, immortal diet;
>   My bottle of salvation;
My gown of glory, hope's true gage,
And thus I'll take my pilgrimage.

Blood must be my body's balmer,
>   No other balm will here be given,
Whilst my soul like a quiet palmer,
>   Travels to the land of heaven,
Over the silver mountains,

Where spring the nectar fountains;
    There will I kiss
    The bowl of bliss,
And drink mine everlasting fill
Upon every milken hill.
My soul will be adry before,
But after, it will thirst no more.

In that serene and blissful day,
    More peaceful pilgrims I shall see,
That have cast off their rags of clay,
    And walk apparell'd fresh like me."

But he wrote his poems, after all, rather with ships and fleets, and regiments of men and horse. At his bidding navies took their place in the channel, and even from prison he fitted out fleets with which to realize his golden dreams, and invited his companions to fresh adventures.

Raleigh might well be studied if only for the excellence of his style, for he is remarkable even in the midst of so many masters. All the distinguished writers of that period possess a greater vigor and naturalness than the more modern, and when we read a quotation from one of them in the midst of a modern author, we seem to have come suddenly upon a greener ground and greater depth and strength of soil. It is as if a green bough were laid across the page, and we are refreshed as by the sight of fresh grass in mid winter or early spring. You have constantly the warrant of life & experience in what you read. The little that is said is supplied by implication of the much that was done. The sentences are verdurous and blooming as evergreen and flowers, because they are rooted in fact and experience, but our false and florid sentences have only the tints of flowers without their sap or roots. Indeed where shall we look for standard English but to the words of a standard man? The word which is best said came very near not being spoken at all, for it is cousin to a deed which would have been better done. It must have taken the place of a deed by some urgent necessity, even by some misfortune, so that the truest writer will be some captive knight after all. And perhaps the fates had such a design, when having stored Raleigh so richly with the substance of life and experience, they made him a fast prisoner, and compelled him to make his words his deeds, and transfer to his expression the emphasis and sincerity of his action.

The necessity of labor, and conversation with many men and things, to the scholar, is rarely well remembered. Steady labor with the hands which engrosses the attention also, is the best method of removing palaver out of one's style both of talking and writing. If he has worked hard from morning till night, though he may have grieved that he could not be watching the train of his thoughts during that time, yet the few hasty lines which at evening record his day's experience will be more musical and true, than his freest but idle fancy could have furnished. He will not idly dance at his work who has wood to cut and cord before night-fall in the short days of winter, but every stroke will be husbanded and ring soberly through the wood; and so will the strokes of that scholar's pen, which at evening record the story of the day, ring soberly on the ear of the reader long after echoes of his axe have died away. The scholar may be sure he writes the tougher truth for the calluses on his palms. They give firmness to the sentence. We are often astonished by the force and precision of style to which hard working men, unpractised in writing, easily attain, when required to make the effort. As if sincerity and plainness, those ornaments of style, were better taught on the farm or in the workshop, than in the schools. The sentences written by such rude hands are nervous and tough, like hardened thongs, the sinews of the deer, or the roots of the pine. The scholar might frequently emulate the propriety and emphasis of the farmer's call to his team, and confess that if that were written it would surpass his labored sentences. Whose are the truly *labored* sentences? From the weak and flimsy periods of the politician and literary man we are glad to turn even to the description of work, the simple record of the month's labor in the farmer's almanack, to restore our tone and spirits. We like that a sentence should read as if its author, had he held a plough instead of a pen, could have drawn a furrow deep and straight to the end. The scholar requires hard labor to give an impetus to his thought; he will learn to grasp the pen firmly so, and wield it gracefully and effectually as an axe or sword. When we consider the weak and nerveless periods of some literary men, who perchance in feet and inches come up to the standard of their race, and are not deficient in girth also, we are amazed at the immense sacrifice of thews and sinews. What! these proportions, these bones, and this their work! Hands which could have felled an ox have hewed this fragile matter which would not have tasked a lady's fingers. Can this be a stalwart man's work, who has a marrow in his back, and a tendon Achilles in his heel? They who set up Stonehenge did somewhat, if they only laid out their strength for once, and stretched themselves.

Yet after all the truly efficient laborer will be found not to crowd his day with work, but saunter to his task surrounded by a wide halo of ease and leisure, and then do but what he likes best. He is anxious only about the kernels of time. Though the hen should set all day she could lay only one egg, and besides would not have picked up materials for another.

A perfectly healthy sentence is extremely rare. Sometimes we read one which was written while the world went round, while grass grew and water ran. But for the most part we miss the hue and fragrance of the thought. As if we could be satisfied with the dews of the morning or evening without their colors, or the heavens without their azure. The most attractive sentences are perhaps not the wisest but the surest and roundest. They are spoken firmly and conclusively as if the author had a right to know what he says; and if not wise, they have at least been well learned. At least he does not stand on a rolling stone, but is well assured of his footing—and if you dispute their doctrine you will yet allow that there is truth in their assurance. Raleigh's are of this sort, spoken with entire satisfaction and heartiness. They are not so much philosophy as poetry. With him it was always well done and nobly said. His learning was in his hand and he carried it by him and used it as adroitly as his sword. Aubrey says "He was no slug". He wields his pen as one who sits at his ease in his chair, and has a healthy and able body to back his wits, and not a torpid and diseased one to fetter them. In whichever hand is the pen we are sure there is a sword in the other. He sits with his armor on, and with one ear open to hear if the trumpet sound, as one who has stolen a little leisure from the duties of a camp; and we are confident that the whole man sat down to the writing of his books, as real and palpable as an Englishman can be; and not some curious brain only. Such a man's mere daily exercise in literature might well attract us, and Cecil has said, "He can toil terribly."

Raleigh seems to have been too genial and loyal a soul to resist the temptations of a court; but if to his genius and culture could have been added the temperament of Geo. Fox or Oliver Cromwell, perhaps the world would have had reason longer to remember him. He was however the most generous nature that could be drawn into the precincts of a court, and carried the courtier's life almost to the highest pitch of magnanimity and grace it was capable of. He was liberal and generous, as a prince,—that is, within bounds; heroic, as a knight in armor,—but not as a defenceless man. His was not the heroism of a Luther but of a Bayard, and had more of grace than of honest truth in it. He had more taste than appetite. There may be something petty in a refined taste,—it easily degenerates into effeminacy. It does not consider the broadest use, and is not content with simple good and bad, but is often fastidious, and curious, or nice only.

His faults, as we have hinted before, were those of a courtier and a soldier. In his counsels and aphorisms we see not unfrequently the haste and rashness of the soldier strangely mingled with the wisdom of the philosopher. Though his philosophy was not wide nor profound, it was continually giving way to the generosity of his nature, and he was not hard to be won to the right.

What he touches he adorns by a greater humanity and native nobleness, but he touches not the truest nor deepest. He does not in any sense unfold the new but embellishes the old, and with all his inclination to originality, he never was quite original, or steered his own course. He was of so fair and susceptible a nature rather than broad or deep that he delayed to slake his thirst at the nearest and most turbid wells of truth and beauty, and his homage to the least fair and noble, left no room for homage to the all fair. The misfortune and incongruity of the man appear in the fact that he was at once the author of the "Maxims of State", and "The Soul's Errand."

When we reconsider what we have said in the foregoing pages, we hesitate to apply any of their eulogy to the actual and historical Raleigh, or any of their condemnation to that ideal Raleigh which he suggests, for we must know the man of history as we know our contemporaries, not so much by his deeds, which often belie his real character, as by the expectation he begets in us—and there is a bloom and halo about the character of Raleigh which defies a close and literal scrutiny, and robs us of our critical acumen. With all his heroism, he was not heroic enough; with all his manliness, he was servile and dependent; with all his aspirations, he was ambitious. He was not upright nor constant, yet we would have trusted him; he could flatter and cringe, yet we should have respected him; and he could accept a bribe, yet we should confidently have appealed to his generosity.

Such a life is useful for us to contemplate as suggesting that a man is not to be measured by the virtue of his described actions or the wisdom of his expressed thoughts merely, but by that free character he is, and is felt to be, under all circumstances. Even talent is respectable only when it indicates a depth of character unfathomed. Surely, it is better that our wisdom appear in the constant success of our spirits, than in our business or the maxims which fall from our lips merely. We want not only a revelation but a nature behind to sustain it. Many silent, as well as famous, lives have been the result of no mean thought though it was never adequately expressed nor conceived; and perhaps the most illiterate and unphilosophical mind may yet be accustomed to think to the extent of the noblest action. We all know those in our own circle who do injustice to their entire character in their conversation and in writing, but who, if actually set over against us would not fail to make a wiser impression than many a wise thinker and speaker.

We are not a little profited by any life which teaches us not to despair of the race, and such effect has the steady and cheerful bravery of Raleigh. To march sturdily through life patiently and resolutely looking defiance at one's foes, that is one way, but we cannot help being more attracted by that kind of heroism which relaxes its brows in the presence of danger, and does not need to maintain itself strictly, but by a kind of sympathy with the universe, generously adorns the scene and the occasion, and loves valor so well that itself would be the defeated party only to behold it. When we consider the vast Xerxean army of reformers in these days, we cannot doubt that many a grim soul goes silent, the hero of some small intestine war; and it is somewhat to begin to live on corn bread solely for one who has before lived on bolted wheat;—but of this sort are not the deeds to be sung. These are not the Arthurs that inflame the imaginations of men. All fair action is the product of enthusiasm, and nature herself does nothing in the prose mood. We would fain witness a heroism which is literally illustrious, whose daily life is of the stuff of which our dreams are made—so that the world shall regard less what it does than how it does it, and its actions unsettle the common standards, and have a right to be done, however wrong they may be to the moralist.

Mere gross health and cheerfulness are no slight attraction, and some biographies have this charm mainly. For the most part the best man's spirit makes a fearful sprite to haunt his grave, and it adds not a little therefore to the credit of Little John, the celebrated follower of Robin Hood, reflecting favorably on the character of his life, that his grave was "long celebrous for the yielding of excellent whetstones".

A great cheerfulness indeed have all great wits and heroes possessed, almost a prophane levity to such as understood them not, but their religion had the broader basis of health and permanence. For the hero too has his religion, though it is the very opposite to that of the ascetic. It demands not a narrower cell but a wider world. He is perhaps the very best man of the world; the poet active, the saint enterprising; not the most godlike, but the most manlike. There have been souls of a heroic stamp, for whom this world seemed expressly made; as if creation had at last succeeded, for it seems to be thrown away on the saint; and their presence enhances the beauty and ampleness of nature herself, and where they walk, as Virgil says of the abodes of the blessed,

"Largior hic campos aether et lumine vestit
Purpureo: Solemque suum, sua sidera norunt."

Here a more copious air invests the fields, and clothes
With purple light: And they know their own sun and their
own stars.

Dark Ages

W E should read history as little critically as we consider the landscape, and be more interested by the atmospheric tints, and various lights and shades which the intervening spaces create, than by its groundwork and composition. It is the morning now turned evening and seen in the west,—the same sun, but a new light and atmosphere. Its beauty is like the sunset; not a fresco painting on a wall, flat and bounded, but atmospheric and roving or free. In reality history fluctuates as the face of the landscape from morning to evening. What is of moment is its hue and color. Time hides no treasures; we want not its *then* but its *now*. We do not complain that the mountains in the horizon are blue and indistinct; they are the more like the heavens.

Of what moment are facts that can be lost,—which need to be commemorated? The monument of death will outlast the memory of the dead. The pyramids do not tell the tale that was confided to them; the living fact commemorates itself. Why look in the dark for light? Strictly speaking, the historical societies have not recovered one fact from oblivion, but are themselves instead of the fact that is lost. The researcher is more memorable than the researched. The crowd stood admiring the mist, and the dim outlines of the trees seen through it, when one of their number advanced to explore the phenomenon, and with fresh admiration, all eyes were turned on his dimly retreating figure. It is astonishing with how little coöperation of the societies, the past is remembered. Its story has indeed had a different muse than has been assigned it. There is a good instance of the manner in which all history began, in Alwákidi's Arabian Chronicle. "I was informed by *Ahmed Almatîn Aljorhami*, who had it from *Rephâa Ebn Kais Alámiri*, who had it from *Saiph Ebn Jabalah Alchátgami*, who had it from *Thabet Ebn Alkamah*, who said he was present at the action." These fathers of history were not anxious to preserve, but to learn the fact; and hence it was not forgotten. Critical acumen is exerted in vain to uncover the past; the *past* cannot be *presented*; we cannot know what we are not. But one veil hangs over past, present, and future, and it is the province of the historian to find out not what was, but what is. Where a battle has been fought, you will find nothing but the bones of men and beasts; where a battle is being fought there are hearts beating. We will sit on a mound and muse, and not try to make these skeletons stand on their legs again. Does nature remember, think you, that they *were* men, or not rather that they *are* bones?

Ancient history has an air of antiquity; it should be more modern. It is written as if the spectator should be thinking of the backside of the picture on the wall, or as if the author expected the dead would be his readers, and wished to detail to them their own experience. Men seem anxious to accomplish an orderly retreat through the centuries, earnestly rebuilding the works behind, as they are battered down by the encroachments of time; but while they loiter, they and their works both fall a prey to the arch enemy. It has neither the venerableness of antiquity, nor the freshness of the modern. It does as if it would go to the beginning of things, which natural history might with reason assume to do; but consider the Universal History, and then tell us—when did burdock and plantain sprout first? It has been so written for the most part, that the times it describes are with remarkable propriety called *dark ages*. They are dark, as one has observed, because we are so in the dark about them. The sun rarely shines in history, what with the dust and confusion; and when we meet with any cheering fact which implies the presence of this luminary, we excerpt and modernize it. As when we read in the history of the Saxons, that Edwin of Northumbria "caused stakes to be fixed in the highways where he had seen a clear spring," and "brazen dishes were chained to them, to refresh the weary sojourner, whose fatigues Edwin had himself experienced." This is worth all Arthur's twelve battles.

But it is fit the past should be dark; though the darkness is not so much a quality of the past, as of tradition. It is not a distance of time but a distance of relation, which makes thus dusky its memorials. What is near to the heart of this generation is fair and bright still. Greece lies outspread fair and sunshiny in floods of light, for there is the sun and day-light in her literature and art. Homer does not allow us to forget that the sun shone—nor Phidias, nor the Parthenon. Yet no era has been wholly dark, nor will we too hastily submit to the historian, and congratulate ourselves on a blaze of light. If we could pierce the obscurity of those remote years we should find it light enough; only there is not our day.—Some creatures are made to see in the dark.—There has always been the same amount of light in the world. The new and missing stars, the comets and eclipses do not affect the general illumination, for only our glasses appreciate them. The eyes of the oldest fossil remains, they tell us, indicate that the same laws of light prevailed then as now. Always the laws of light are the same, but the modes and degrees of seeing vary. The gods are partial to no era, but steadily shines their light in the heavens, while the eye of the beholder is turned to stone. There was but the eye and the sun from the first. The ages have not added a new ray to the one, nor altered a fibre of the other.

A Winter Walk

THE wind has gently murmured through the blinds, or puffed with feathery softness against the windows, and occasionally sighed like a summer zephyr lifting the leaves along, the livelong night. The meadow mouse has slept in his snug gallery in the sod, the owl has sat in a hollow tree in the depth of the swamp, the rabbit, the squirrel, and the fox have all been housed. The watch-dog has lain quiet on the hearth, and the cattle have stood silent in their stalls. The earth itself has slept, as it were its first, not its last sleep, save when some street-sign or wood-house door, has faintly creaked upon its hinge, cheering forlorn nature at her midnight work.—The only sound awake twixt Venus and Mars,—advertising us of a remote inward warmth, a divine cheer and fellowship, where gods are met together, but where it is very bleak for men to stand. But while the earth has slumbered, all the air has been alive with feathery flakes, descending, as if some northern Ceres reigned, showering her silvery grain over all the fields.

We sleep and at length awake to the still reality of a winter morning. The snow lies warm as cotton or down upon the window-sill; the broadened sash and frosted panes admit a dim and private light, which enhances the snug cheer within. The stillness of the morning is impressive. The floor creaks under our feet as we move toward the window to look abroad through some clear space over the fields. We see the roofs stand under their snow burden. From the eaves and fences hang stalactites of snow, and in the yard stand stalagmites covering some concealed core. The trees and shrubs rear white arms to the sky on every side, and where were walls and fences, we see fantastic forms stretching in frolic gambols across the dusky landscape, as if nature had strewn her fresh designs over the fields by night as models for man's art.

Silently we unlatch the door, letting the drift fall in, and step abroad to face the cutting air. Already the stars have lost some of their sparkle, and a dull leaden mist skirts the horizon. A lurid brazen light in the east proclaims the approach of day, while the western landscape is dim and spectral still, and clothed in a sombre Tartarean light, like the shadowy realms. They are Infernal sounds only that you hear,—the crowing of cocks, the barking of dogs, the chopping of wood, the lowing of kine, all seem to come from Pluto's barn-yard and beyond the Styx;—not for any melancholy they suggest, but their twilight bustle is too solemn and mysterious for earth. The recent tracks of the fox or otter, in the yard, remind us that each hour of the night is crowded with events, and the primeval nature is still working and making tracks in the snow. Opening the gate, we tread briskly along the lone country road, crunching the dry and crisped snow under our feet, or aroused by the sharp clear creak of the wood-sled, just starting for the distant market, from the early farmer's door, where it has lain the summer long, dreaming amid the chips and stubble. For through the drifts and powdered windows we see the farmer's early candle, like a paled star, emitting a lonely beam, as if some severe virtue were at its matins there. And one by one the smokes begin to ascend from the chimneys amidst the trees and snows.

> The sluggish smoke curls up from some deep dell,
> The stiffened air exploring in the dawn,
> And making slow acquaintance with the day;
> Delaying now upon its heavenward course,
> In wreathed loiterings dallying with itself,
> With as uncertain purpose and slow deed,
> As its half-wakened master by the hearth,
> Whose mind still slumbering and sluggish thoughts
> Have not yet swept into the onward current
> Of the new day;—and now it streams afar,
> The while the chopper goes with step direct,
> And mind intent to swing the early axe.
> First in the dusky dawn he sends abroad
> His early scout, his emissary, smoke,
> The earliest, latest pilgrim from the roof,
> To feel the frosty air, inform the day;
> And while he crouches still beside the hearth,
> Nor musters courage to unbar the door,
> It has gone down the glen with the light wind,
> And o'er the plain unfurled its venturous wreath,

Draped the tree tops, loitered upon the hill,
And warmed the pinions of the early bird;
And now, perchance, high in the crispy air,
Has caught sight of the day o'er the earth's edge,
And greets its master's eye at his low door,
As some refulgent cloud in the upper sky.

We hear the sound of wood-chopping at the farmers' doors, far over the frozen earth, the baying of the house dog, and the distant clarion of the cock. The thin and frosty air conveys only the finer particles of sound to our ears, with short and sweet vibrations, as the waves subside soonest on the purest and lightest liquids, in which gross substances sink to the bottom. They come clear and bell-like, and from a greater distance in the horizon, as if there were fewer impediments than in summer to make them faint and ragged. The ground is sonorous, like seasoned wood, and even the ordinary rural sounds are melodious, and the jingling of the ice on the trees is sweet and liquid. There is the least possible moisture in the atmosphere, all being dried up, or congealed, and it is of such extreme tenuity and elasticity, that it becomes a source of delight. The withdrawn and tense sky seems groined like the aisles of a cathedral, and the polished air sparkles as if there were crystals of ice floating in it. Those who have resided in Greenland, tell us, that, when it freezes, "the sea smokes like burning turf land, and a fog or mist arises, called frost smoke," which "cutting smoke frequently raises blisters on the face and hands, and is very pernicious to the health." But this pure stinging cold is an elixir to the lungs, and not so much a frozen mist, as a crystallized mid-summer haze, refined and purified by cold.

The sun at length rises through the distant woods, as if with the faint clashing swinging sound of cymbals, melting the air with his beams, and with such rapid steps the morning travels, that already his rays are gilding the distant western mountains. We step hastily along through the powdery snow, warmed by an inward heat, enjoying an Indian summer still, in the increased glow of thought and feeling. Probably if our lives were more conformed to nature, we should not need to defend ourselves against her heats and colds, but find her our constant nurse and friend, as do plants and quadrupeds. If our bodies were fed with pure and simple elements, and not with a stimulating and heating diet, they would afford no more pasture for cold than a leafless twig, but thrive like the trees, which find even winter genial to their expansion.

The wonderful purity of nature at this season is a most pleasing fact. Every decayed stump and moss-grown stone and rail, and the dead leaves of autumn, are concealed by a clean napkin of snow. In the bare fields and tinkling woods, see what virtue survives. In the coldest and bleakest places, the warmest charities still maintain a foot-hold. A cold and searching wind drives away all contagion, and nothing can withstand it but what has a virtue in it; and accordingly, whatever we meet with in cold and bleak places, as the tops of mountains, we respect for a sort of sturdy innocence, a Puritan toughness. All things beside seem to be called in for shelter, and what stays out must be part of the original frame of the universe, and of such valor as God himself. It is invigorating to breathe the cleansed air. Its greater fineness and purity are visible to the eye, and we would fain stay out long and late, that the gales may sigh through us too, as through the leafless trees, and fit us for the winter:—as if we hoped so to borrow some pure and steadfast virtue, which will stead us in all seasons.

At length we have reached the edge of the woods, and shut out the gadding town. We enter within their covert as we go under the roof of a cottage, and cross its threshold, all ceiled and banked up with snow. They are glad and warm still, and as genial and cheery in winter as in summer. As we stand in the midst of the pines, in the flickering and checkered light which straggles but little way into their maze, we wonder if the towns have ever heard their simple story. It seems to us that no traveller has ever explored them, and notwithstanding the wonders which science is elsewhere revealing every day, who would not like to hear their annals? Our humble villages in the plain, are their contribution. We borrow from the forest the boards which shelter, and the sticks which warm us. How important is their evergreen to the winter, that portion of the summer which does not fade, the permanent year, the unwithered grass. Thus simply, and with little expense of altitude, is the surface of the earth diversified. What would human life be without forests, those natural cities? From the tops of mountains they appear like smooth shaven lanes, yet whither shall we walk but in this taller grass?

There is a slumbering subterranean fire in nature which never goes out, and which no cold can chill. It finally melts the great snow, and in January or July is only buried under a thicker or thinner covering. In the coldest day it flows somewhere, and the snow melts around every tree. This field of winter rye, which sprouted late in the fall, and now speedily dissolves the snow, is where the fire is very thinly covered. We feel warmed by it. In the winter, warmth stands for all virtue, and we resort in thought to a trickling rill, with its bare stones shining in the sun, and to warm springs in the woods, with as much eagerness as rabbits and robins. The steam which rises from swamps and pools, is as dear and domestic as that of our own kettle. What fire could ever equal the sunshine of a winter's-day, when the meadow mice come out by the wallsides, and the chicadee lisps in the defiles of the wood? The warmth comes directly from the sun, and is not radiated from the earth, as in summer; and when we feel his beams on our back as we are treading some snowy dell, we are grateful as for a special kindness, and bless the sun which has followed us into that by-place.

This subterranean fire has its altar in each man's breast, for in the coldest day, and on the bleakest hill, the traveler cherishes a warmer fire within the folds of his cloak than is kindled on any hearth. A healthy man, indeed, is the complement of the seasons, and in winter, summer is in his heart. There is the south. Thither have all birds and insects migrated, and around the warm springs in his breast are gathered the robin and the lark.

In this glade covered with bushes of a year's growth, see how the silvery dust lies on every seared leaf and twig, deposited in such infinite and luxurious forms as by their very variety atone for the absence of color. Observe the tiny tracks of mice around every stem, and the triangular tracks of the rabbit. A pure elastic heaven hangs over all, as if the impurities of the summer sky, refined and shrunk by the chaste winter's cold, had been winnowed from the heavens upon the earth.

Nature confounds her summer distinction at this season. The heavens seem to be nearer the earth. The elements are less reserved and distinct. Water turns to ice, rain to snow. The day is but a Scandinavian night. The winter is an arctic summer.

How much more living is the life that is in nature, the furred life which still survives the stinging nights, and, from amidst fields and woods covered with frost and snow, sees the sun rise.

> "The foodless wilds
> Pour forth their brown inhabitants."

The grey-squirrel and rabbit are brisk and playful in the remote glens, even on the morning of the cold Friday. Here is our Lapland and Labrador, and for our Esquimaux and Knistenaux, Dog-ribbed Indians, Novazemblaites, and Spitzbergeners, are there not the ice-cutter and wood-chopper, the fox, muskrat, and mink?

Still, in the midst of the arctic day, we may trace the summer to its retreats, and sympathize with some contemporary life. Stretched over the brooks, in the midst of the frost-bound meadows, we may observe the submarine cottages of the caddice worms, the larvæ of the Plicipennes. Their small cylindrical caves built around themselves, composed of flags, sticks, grass, and withered leaves, shells and pebbles, in form and color like the wrecks which strew the bottom—now drifting along over the pebbly bottom, now whirling in tiny eddies and dashing down steep falls, or sweeping rapidly along with the current, or else swaying to and fro at the end of some grass blade or root. Anon they will leave their sunken habitations, and crawling up the stems of plants, or floating on the surface like gnats, or perfect insects, henceforth flutter over the surface of the water, or sacrifice their short lives in the flame of our candles at evening. Down yonder little glen the shrubs are drooping under their burden, and the red alder-berries contrast with the white ground. Here are the marks of a myriad feet which have already been abroad. The sun rises as proudly over such a glen, as over the valley of the Seine or the Tiber, and it seems the residence of a pure and self-subsistent valor, such as they never witnessed; which never knew defeat nor fear. Here reign the simplicity and purity of a primitive age, and a health and hope far remote from towns and cities. Standing quite alone, far in the forest, while the wind is shaking down snow from the trees, and leaving the only human tracks behind us, we find our reflections of a richer variety than the life of cities. The chicadee and nut-hatch are more inspiring society than the statesmen and philosophers, and we shall return to these last, as to more vulgar companions. In this lonely glen, with its brook draining the slopes, its creased ice and crystals of all hues, where the spruces and hemlocks stand up on either side, and the rush and sere wild oats in the rivulet itself, our lives are more serene and worthy to contemplate.

As the day advances, the heat of the sun is reflected by the hillsides, and we hear a faint but sweet music, where flows the rill released from its fetters, and the icicles are melting on the trees; and the nut-hatch and partridge are heard and seen. The south wind melts the snow at noon, and the bare ground appears with its withered grass and leaves, and we are invigorated by the perfume which expands from it, as by the scent of strong meats.

Let us go into this deserted woodman's hut, and see how he has passed the long winter nights and the short and stormy days. For here man has lived under this south hill-side, and it seems a civilized and public spot. We have such associations as when the traveller stands by the ruins of Palmyra or Hecatompolis. Singing birds and flowers perchance have begun to appear here, for flowers as well as weeds follow in the footsteps of man. These hemlocks whispered over his head, these hickory logs were his fuel, and these pitch-pine roots kindled his fire; yonder foaming rill in the hollow, whose thin and airy vapor still ascends as busily as ever, though he is far off now, was his well. These hemlock boughs, and the straw upon this raised platform, were his bed, and this broken dish held his drink. But he has not been here this season, for the phœbes built their nest upon this shelf last summer. I find some embers left, as if he had but just gone out, where he baked his pot of beans, and while at evening he smoked his pipe, whose stemless bowl lies in the ashes, chatted with his only companion, if perchance he had any, about the depth of the snow on the morrow, already falling fast and thick without, or disputed whether the last sound was the screech of an owl, or the creak of a bough, or imagination only; and through this broad chimney-throat, in the late winter evening, ere he stretched himself upon the straw, he looked up to learn the progress of the storm, and seeing the bright stars of Cassiopeia's chair shining brightly down upon him, fell contentedly asleep.

See how many traces from which we may learn the chopper's history. From this stump we may guess the sharpness of his axe, and from the slope of the stroke, on which side he stood, and whether he cut down the tree without going round it or changing hands; and from the flexure of the splinters we may know which way it fell. This one chip contains inscribed on it the whole history of the wood-chopper and of the world. On this scrap of paper, which held his sugar or salt, perchance, or was the wadding of his gun, sitting on a log in the forest, with what interest we read the tattle of cities, of those larger huts, empty and to let, like this, in High-streets, and Broad-ways. The eaves are dripping on the south side of this simple roof, while the titmouse lisps in the pine, and the genial warmth of the sun around the door is somewhat kind and human.

After two seasons, this rude dwelling does not deform the scene. Already the birds resort to it, to build their nests, and you may track to its door the feet of many quadrupeds. Thus, for a long time, nature overlooks the encroachment and profanity of man. The wood still cheerfully and unsuspiciously echoes the strokes of the axe that fells it, and while they are few and seldom, they enhance its wildness, and all the elements strive to naturalize the sound.

Now our path begins to ascend gradually to the top of this high hill, from whose precipitous south side, we can look over the broad country, of forest, and field, and river, to the distant snowy mountains. See yonder thin column of smoke curling up through the woods from some invisible farmhouse; the standard raised over some rural homestead. There must be a warmer and more genial spot there below, as where we detect the vapor from a spring forming a cloud above the trees. What fine relations are established between the traveller who discovers this airy column from some eminence in the forest, and him who sits below. Up goes the smoke as silently and naturally as the vapor exhales from the leaves, and as busy disposing itself in wreathes as the housewife on the hearth below. It is a hieroglyphic of man's life, and suggests more intimate and important things than the boiling of a pot. Where its fine column rises above the forest, like an ensign, some human life has planted itself,—and such is the beginning of Rome, the establishment of the arts, and the foundation of empires, whether on the prairies of America, or the steppes of Asia.

And now we descend again to the brink of this woodland lake, which lies in a hollow of the hills, as if it were their expressed juice, and that of the leaves, which are annually steeped in it. Without outlet or inlet to the eye, it has still its history, in the lapse of its waves, in the rounded pebbles on its shore, and on the pines which grow down to its brink. It has not been idle, though sedentary, but, like Abu Musa, teaches that "sitting still at home is the heavenly way; the going out is the way of the world." Yet in its evaporation it travels as far as any. In summer it is the earth's liquid eye; a mirror in the breast of nature. The sins of the wood are washed out in it. See how the woods form an amphitheatre about it, and it is an arena for all the genialness of nature. All trees direct the traveller to its brink, all paths seek it out, birds fly to it, quadrupeds flee to it, and the very ground inclines toward it. It is nature's saloon, where she has sat down to her toilet. Consider her silent economy and tidiness; how the sun comes with his evaporation to sweep the dust from its surface each morning, and a fresh surface is constantly welling up; and annually, after whatever impurities have accumulated herein, its liquid transparency appears again in the spring. In summer a hushed music seems to sweep across its surface. But now a plain sheet of snow conceals it from our eyes, except when the wind has swept the ice bare, and the sere leaves are gliding from side to side, tacking and veering on their tiny voyages. Here is one just keeled up against a pebble on shore, a dry beach leaf, rocking still, as if it would soon start again. A skilful engineer, methinks, might project its course since it fell from the parent stem. Here are all the elements for such a calculation. Its present position, the direction of the wind, the level of the pond, and how much more is given. In its scarred edges and veins is its log rolled up.

We fancy ourselves in the interior of a larger house. The surface of the pond is our deal table or sanded floor, and the woods rise abruptly from its edge, like the walls of a cottage. The lines set to catch pickerel through the ice look like a larger culinary preparation, and the men stand about on the white ground like pieces of forest furniture. The actions of these men, at the distance of half a mile over the ice and snow, impress us as when we read the exploits of Alexander in history. They seem not unworthy of the scenery, and as momentous as the conquest of kingdoms.

Again we have wandered through the arches of the wood, until from its skirts we hear the distant booming of ice from yonder bay of the river, as if it were moved by some other and subtler tide than oceans know. To me it has a strange sound of home, thrilling as the voice of one's distant and noble kindred. A mild summer sun shines over forest and lake, and though there is but one green leaf for many rods, yet nature enjoys a serene health. Every sound is fraught with the same mysterious assurance of health, as well now the creaking of the boughs in January, as the soft sough of the wind in July.

> When Winter fringes every bough
>   With his fantastic wreath,
> And puts the seal of silence now
>   Upon the leaves beneath;
>
> When every stream in its pent-house
>   Goes gurgling on its way,
> And in his gallery the mouse
>   Nibbleth the meadow hay;
>
> Methinks the summer still is nigh,
>   And lurketh underneath,
> As that same meadow mouse doth lie
>   Snug in the last year's heath.

And if perchance the chicadee
   Lisp a faint note anon,
The snow is summer's canopy,
   Which she herself put on.

Fair blossoms deck the cheerful trees,
   And dazzling fruits depend,
The north wind sighs a summer breeze,
   The nipping frosts to fend,

Bringing glad tidings unto me,
   The while I stand all ear,
Of a serene eternity,
   Which need not winter fear.

Out on the silent pond straightway
   The restless ice doth crack,
And pond sprites merry gambols play
   Amid the deafening rack.

Eager I hasten to the vale,
   As if I heard brave news,
How nature held high festival,
   Which it were hard to lose.

I gambol with my neighbor ice,
   And sympathizing quake,
As each new crack darts in a trice
   Across the gladsome lake.

One with the cricket in the ground,
   And faggot on the hearth,
Resounds the rare domestic sound
   Along the forest path.

Before night we will take a journey on skates along the course of this meandering river, as full of novelty to one who sits by the cottage fire all the winter's day, as if it were over the polar ice, with captain Parry or Franklin; following the winding of the stream, now flowing amid hills, now spreading out into fair meadows, and forming a myriad coves and bays where the pine and hemlock overarch. The river flows in the rear of the towns, and we see all things from a new and wilder side. The fields and gardens come down to it with a frankness, and freedom from pretension, which they do not wear on the highway. It is the outside and edge of the earth. Our eyes are not offended by violent contrasts. The last rail of the farmer's fence is some swaying willow bough, which still preserves its freshness, and here at length all fences stop, and we no longer cross any road. We may go far up within the country now by the most retired and level road, never climbing a hill, but by broad levels ascending to the upland meadows. It is a beautiful illustration of the law of obedience, the flow of a river; the path for a sick man, a highway down which an acorn cup may float secure with its freight. Its slight occasional falls, whose precipices would not diversify the landscape, are celebrated by mist and spray, and attract the traveller from far and near. From the remote interior, its current conducts him by broad and easy steps, or by one gentle inclined plain, to the sea. Thus by an early and constant yielding to the inequalities of the ground, it secures itself the easiest passage.

No dominion of nature is quite closed to man at all times, and now we draw near to the empire of the fishes. Our feet glide swiftly over unfathomed depths, where in summer our line tempted the pout and perch, and where the stately pickerel lurked in the long corridors, formed by the bulrushes. The deep, impenetrable marsh, where the heron waded, and bittern squatted, is made pervious to our swift shoes, as if a thousand railroads had been made into it. With one impulse we are carried to the cabin of the muskrat, that earliest settler, and see him dart away under the transparent ice, like a furred fish, to his hole in the bank; and we glide rapidly over meadows where lately "the mower whet his scythe," through beds of frozen cranberries mixed with meadow grass. We skate near to where the blackbird, the pewee, and the kingbird hung their nests over the water, and the hornets builded from the maple on the swamp. How many gay warblers now following the sun, have radiated from this nest of silver birch and thistle down. On the swamp's outer edge was hung the supermarine village, where no foot penetrated. In this hollow tree the wood-duck reared her brood, and slid away each day to forage in yonder fen.

In winter, nature is a cabinet of curiosities, full of dried specimens, in their natural order and position. The meadows and forests are a *hortus siccus*. The leaves and grasses stand perfectly pressed by the air without screw or gum, and the bird's nests are not hung on an artificial twig, but where they builded them. We go about dry-shod to inspect the summer's work in the rank swamp, and see what a growth have got the alders, the willows, and the maples; testifying to how many warm suns, and fertilizing dews and showers. See what strides their boughs took in the luxuriant summer,—and anon these dormant buds will carry them onward and upward another span into the heavens.

Occasionally we wade through fields of snow, under whose depths the river is lost for many rods, to appear again to the right or left, where we least expected; still holding on its way underneath, with a faint, stertorous, rumbling sound, as if, like the bear and marmot, it too had hibernated, and we had followed its faint summer trail to where it earthed itself in snow and ice. At first we should have thought that rivers would be empty and dry in mid winter, or else frozen solid till the spring thawed them; but their volume is not diminished even, for only a superficial cold bridges their surface. The thousand springs which feed the lakes and streams are flowing still. The issues of a few surface springs only are closed, and they go to swell the deep reservoirs. Nature's wells are below the frost. The summer brooks are not filled with snow-water, nor does the mower quench his thirst with that alone. The streams are swollen when the snow melts in the spring, because nature's work has been delayed, the water being turned into ice and snow, whose particles are less smooth and round, and do not find their level so soon.

Far over the ice, between the hemlock woods and snow-clad hills, stands the pickerel fisher, his lines set in some retired cove, like a Finlander, with his arms thrust into the pouches of his dreadnought; with dull, snowy, fishy thoughts, himself a finless fish, separated a few inches from his race; dumb, erect, and made to be enveloped in clouds and snows, like the pines on shore. In these wild scenes, men stand about in the scenery, or move deliberately and heavily, having sacrificed the sprightliness and vivacity of towns to the dumb sobriety of nature. He does not make the scenery less wild, more than the jays and muskrats, but stands there as a part of it, as the natives are represented in the voyages of early navigators, at Nootka sound, and on the North-west coast, with their furs about them, before they were tempted to loquacity by a scrap of iron. He belongs to the natural family of man, and is planted deeper in nature and has more root than the inhabitants of towns. Go to him, ask what luck, and you will learn that he too is a worshipper of the unseen. Hear with what sincere deference and waving gesture in his tone, he speaks of the lake pickerel, which he has never seen, his primitive and ideal race of pickerel. He is connected with the shore still, as by a fish-line, and yet remembers the season when he took fish through the ice on the pond, while the peas were up in his garden at home.

But now, while we have loitered, the clouds have gathered again, and a few straggling snow-flakes are beginning to descend. Faster and faster they fall, shutting out the distant objects from sight. The snow falls on every wood and field, and no crevice is forgotten; by the river and the pond, on the hill and in the valley. Quadrupeds are confined to their coverts, and the birds sit upon their perches this peaceful hour. There is not so much sound as in fair weather, but silently and gradually every slope, and the grey walls and fences, and the polished ice, and the sere leaves, which were not buried before, are concealed, and the tracks of men and beasts are lost. With so little effort does nature reassert her rule, and blot out the traces of men. Hear how Homer has described the same. "The snow flakes fall thick and fast on a winter's day. The winds are lulled, and the snow falls incessant, covering the top of the mountains, and the hills, and the plains where the lotus tree grows, and the cultivated fields, and they are falling by the inlets and shores of the foaming sea, but are silently dissolved by the waves." The snow levels all things, and infolds them deeper on the bosom of nature, as, in the slow summer, vegetation creeps up to the entablature of the temple, and the turrets of the castle, and helps her to prevail over art.

The surly night-wind rustles through the wood, and warns

us to retrace our steps, while the sun goes down behind the thickening storm, and birds seek their roosts, and cattle their stalls.

> "Drooping the lab'rer ox
> Stands covered o'er with snow, and *now* demands
> The fruit of all his toil."

Though winter is represented in the almanac as an old man, facing the wind and sleet, and drawing his cloak about him, we rather think of him as a merry wood-chopper, and warm-blooded youth, as blithe as summer. The unexplored grandeur of the storm keeps up the spirits of the traveller. It does not trifle with us, but has a sweet earnestness. In winter we lead a more inward life. Our hearts are warm and merry, like cottages under drifts, whose windows and doors are half concealed, but from whose chimneys the smoke cheerfully ascends. The imprisoning drifts increase the sense of comfort which the house affords, and in the coldest days we are content to sit over the hearth and see the sky through the chimney top, enjoying the quiet and serene life that may be had in a warm corner by the chimney side, or feeling our pulse by listening to the low of cattle in the street, or the sound of the flail in distant barns all the long afternoon. No doubt a skilful physician could determine our health by observing how these simple and natural sounds affected us. We enjoy now, not an oriental, but a boreal leisure, around warm stoves and fire-places, and watch the shadow of motes in the sunbeams.

Sometimes our fate grows too homely and familiarly serious ever to be cured. Consider how for three months the human destiny is wrapped in furs. The good Hebrew revelation takes no cognizance of all this cheerful snow. Is there no religion for the temperate and frigid zones? We know of no scripture which records the pure benignity of the gods on a New England winter night. Their praises have never been sung, only their wrath deprecated. The best scripture, after all, records but a meagre faith. Its saints live reserved and austere. Let a brave devout man spend the year in the woods of Maine or Labrador, and see if the Hebrew scriptures speak adequately of his condition and experience, from the setting in of winter to the breaking up of the ice.

Now commences, the long winter evening around the farmer's hearth, when the thoughts of the indwellers travel far abroad, and men are by nature and necessity charitable and liberal to all creatures. Now is the happy resistance to cold, when the farmer reaps his reward, and thinks of his preparedness for winter, and through the glittering panes, sees with equanimity "the mansion of the northern bear," for now the storm is over,

> "The full ethereal round,
> Infinite worlds disclosing to the view,
> Shines out intensely keen; and all one cope
> Of starry glitter glows from pole to pole."

The Landlord

U NDER the one word, house, are included the school house, the alms house, the jail, the tavern, the dwelling house; and the meanest shed or cave in which men live, contains the elements of all these. But no where on the earth stands the entire and perfect house. The Parthenon, St. Peter's, the Gothic minster, the palace, the hovel, are but imperfect executions of an imperfect idea. Who would dwell in them? Perhaps to the eye of the gods, the cottage is more holy than the Parthenon, for they look down with no especial favor upon the shrines formally dedicated to them, and that should be the most sacred roof which shelters most of humanity. Surely, then, the gods who are most interested in the human race preside over the Tavern, where especially men congregate. Methinks I see the thousand shrines erected to Hospitality shining afar in all countries, as well Mahometan and Jewish, as Christian, khans, and caravansaries, and inns, whither all pilgrims without distinction resort.

Likewise we look in vain east or west over the earth to find the perfect man; but each represents only some particular excellence. The Landlord is a man of more open and general sympathies, who possesses a spirit of hospitality which is its own reward, and feeds and shelters men from pure love of the creatures. To be sure, this profession is as often filled by imperfect characters, and such as have sought it from unworthy motives, as any other, but so much the more should we prize the true and honest Landlord when we meet with him.

Who has not imagined to himself a country inn, where the traveller shall really feel *in*, and at home, and at his public house, who was before at his private house; whose host is indeed a *host*, and a *lord* of the *land*, a self-appointed brother of his race; called to his place, beside, by all the winds of heaven and his good genius, as truly as the preacher is called to preach; a man of such universal sympathies, and so broad and genial a human nature, that he would fain sacrifice the tender but narrow ties of private friendship, to a broad, sunshiny, fair-weather-and-foul friendship for his race; who loves men, not as a philosopher, with philanthropy, nor as an overseer of the poor, with charity, but by a necessity of his nature, as he loves dogs and horses; and standing at his open door from morning till night, would fain see more and more of them come along the highway, and is never satiated. To him the sun and moon are but travellers, the one by day and the other by night; and they too patronise his house. To his imagination all things travel save his sign-post and himself; and though you may be his neighbor for years, he will show you only the civilities of the road. But on the other hand, while nations and individuals are alike selfish and exclusive, he loves all men equally; and if he treats his nearest neighbor as a stranger, since he has invited all nations to share his hospitality, the farthest travelled is in some measure kindred to him who takes him into the bosom of his family.

He keeps a house of entertainment at the sign of the Black Horse or the Spread Eagle, and is known far and wide, and his fame travels with increasing radius every year. All the neighborhood is in his interest, and if the traveller ask how far to a tavern, he receives some such answer as this: "Well, sir, there's a house about three miles from here, where they haven't taken down their sign yet; but it's only ten miles to Slocum's, and that's a capital house, both for man and beast." At three miles he passes a cheerless barrack, standing desolate behind its sign-post, neither public nor private, and has glimpses of a discontented couple who have mistaken their calling. At ten miles see where the Tavern stands,—really an *entertaining* prospect,—so public and inviting that only the rain and snow do not enter. It is no gay pavilion, made of bright stuffs, and furnished with nuts and gingerbread, but as plain and sincere as a caravansary; located in no Tarrytown, where you receive only the civilities of commerce, but far in the fields it exercises a primitive hospitality, amid the fresh scent of new hay and raspberries, if it be summer time, and the tinkling of cow-bells from invisible pastures; for it is a land flowing with milk and honey, and the newest milk courses in a broad deep stream across the premises.

In these retired places the tavern is first of all a house—elsewhere, last of all, or never—and warms and shelters its inhabitants. It is as simple and sincere in its essentials as the caves in which the first men dwelt, but it is also as open and public. The traveller steps across the threshold, and lo! he too is master, for he only can be called proprietor of the house here who behaves with most propriety in it. The Landlord stands clear back in nature, to my imagination, with his axe and spade felling trees and raising potatoes with the vigor of a pioneer; with Promethean energy making nature yield her increase to supply the wants of so many; and he is not so exhausted, nor of so short a stride, but that he comes forward even to the highway to this wide hospitality and publicity. Surely, he has solved some of the problems of life. He comes in at his back door, holding a log fresh cut for the hearth upon his shoulder with one hand, while he greets the newly arrived traveller with the other.

Here at length we have free range, as not in palaces, nor cottages, nor temples, and intrude no where. All the secrets of housekeeping are exhibited to the eyes of men, above and below, before and behind. This is the necessary way to live, men have confessed, in these days, and shall he skulk and hide? And why should we have any serious disgust at kitchens? Perhaps they are the holiest recess of the house. There is the hearth, after all,—and the settle, and the faggots, and the kettle, and the crickets. We have pleasant reminiscences of these. They are the heart, the left ventricle, the very vital part of the house. Here the real and sincere life which we meet in the streets was actually fed and sheltered. Here burns the taper that cheers the lonely traveller by night, and from this hearth ascend the smokes that populate the valley to his eyes by day. On the whole, a man may not be so little ashamed of any other part of his house, for here is his sincerity and earnest, at least. It may not be here that the besoms are plied most—it is not here that they need to be, for dust will not settle on the kitchen floor more than in nature.

Hence it will not do for the Landlord to possess too fine a nature. He must have health above the common accidents of life, subject to no modern fashionable diseases; but no taste, rather a vast relish or appetite. His sentiments on all subjects will be delivered as freely as the wind blows; there is nothing private or individual in them, though still original, but they are public, and of the hue of the heavens over his house,—a certain out-of-door obviousness and transparency not to be disputed. What he does, his manners are not to be complained of, though abstractly offensive, for it is what man does, and in him the race is exhibited. When he eats, he is liver and bowels, and the whole digestive apparatus to the company, and so all admit the thing is done. He must have no idiosyncracies, no particular bents or tendencies to this or that, but a general, uniform, and healthy development, such as his portly person indicates, offering himself equally on all sides to men. He is not one of your peaked and inhospitable men of genius, with particular tastes, but, as we said before, has one uniform relish, and taste which never aspires higher than a tavern sign, or the cut of a weather-cock. The man of genius, like a dog with a bone, or the slave who has swallowed a diamond, or a patient with the gravel, sits afar and retired, off the road, hangs out no sign of refreshment for man and beast, but says, by all possible hints and signs, I wish to be alone—good-bye— farewell. But the landlord can afford to live without privacy. He entertains no private thought, he cherishes no solitary hour, no sabbath day, but thinks—enough to assert the dignity of reason—and talks, and reads the newspaper. What he does not tell to one traveller, he tells to another. He never wants to be alone, but sleeps, wakes, eats, drinks, sociably, still remembering his race. He walks abroad through the thoughts of men, and the Iliad and Shakspeare are tame to him, who hears the rude but homely incidents of the road from every traveller. The mail might drive through his brain in the midst of his most lonely soliloquy, without disturbing his equanimity, provided it brought plenty of news and passengers. There can be no *pro*-fanity where there is no fane behind, and the whole world may see quite round him. Perchance his lines have fallen to him in dustier places, and he has heroically sat down where two roads meet, or at the Four Corners, or the Five Points, and his life is sublimely trivial for the good of men. The dust of travel blows ever in his eyes, and they preserve their clear, complacent look. The hourlies and half-hourlies, the dailies and weeklies, whirl on well worn tracks, round and round his house, as if it were the goal in the stadium, and still he sits within in unruffled serenity, with no show of retreat. His neighbor dwells timidly behind a screen of poplars and willows, and a fence with sheafs of spears at regular intervals, or defended against the tender palms of visitors by sharp spikes,—but the traveller's wheels rattle over the door-step of the tavern, and he cracks his whip in the entry. He is truly glad to see you, and sincere as the bull's-eye over his door. The traveller seeks to find, wherever he goes, some one who will stand in this broad and catholic relation to him, who will be an inhabitant of the land to him a stranger, and represent its human nature, as the rock stands for its inanimate nature; and this is he. As his crib furnishes provender for the traveller's horse, and his larder provisions for his appetite, so his conversation furnishes the necessary aliment to his spirits. He knows very well what a man wants, for he is a man himself, and as it were the farthest travelled, though he has never stirred from his door. He understands his needs and destiny. He would be well fed and lodged, there can be no doubt, and have the transient sympathy of a cheerful companion, and of a heart which always prophesies fair weather. And after all the greatest men, even, want much more the sympathy which every one can give, than that which the great only can impart. If he is not the most upright, let us allow him this praise, that he is the most downright of men. He has a hand to shake and to be shaken, and takes a sturdy and unquestionable interest in you, as if he had assumed the care of you, but if you will break his neck, he will even give you the best advice as to the method.

The great poets have not been ungrateful to their landlords. Mine host of the Tabard inn, in the Prologue to the Canterbury Tales, was an honor to his profession:

> "A semely man our Hoste was, with alle,
> For to han been an marshal in an halle.
> A large man he was, with eyen stepe;
> A fairer burgeis is ther non in Chepe:
> Bold of his speche, and wise, and well ytaught,
> And of manhood him lacked righte naught.
> Eke thereto, was he right a mery man,
> And after souper plaien he began,
> And spake of mirthe amonges other thinges,
> Whan that we hadden made our reckoninges."

He is the true house-band, and centre of the company—of greater fellowship and practical social talent than any. He it is, that proposes that each shall tell a tale to while away the time to Canterbury, and leads them himself, and concludes with his own tale:

> "Now, by my fader's soule that is ded,
> But ye be mery, smiteth of my hed:
> Hold up your hondes withouten more speche."

If we do not look up to the Landlord, we look round for him on all emergencies, for he is a man of infinite experience, who unites hands with wit. He is a more public character than a statesman—a publican, and not consequently a sinner; and surely, he, if any, should be exempted from taxation and military duty.

Talking with our host is next best and instructive to talking with one's self. It is a more conscious soliloquy; as it were, to speak generally, and try what we would say provided we had an audience. He has indulgent and open ears, and does not require petty and particular statements. "Heigho!" exclaims the traveller. Them's my sentiments, thinks mine host, and stands ready for what may come next, expressing the purest sympathy by his demeanor. "Hot as blazes!" says the other,—— "Hard weather, sir,—not much stirring now-a-days," says he. He is wiser than to contradict his guest in any case; he lets him go on, he lets him travel.

The latest sitter leaves him standing far in the night, prepared to live right on, while suns rise and set, and his "goodnight" has as brisk a sound as his "good-morning," and the earliest riser finds him tasting his liquors in the bar ere flies begin to buzz, with a countenance fresh as the morning star over the sanded floor,—and not as one who had watched all night for travellers. And yet, if beds be the subject of conversation, it will appear that no man has been a sounder sleeper in his time.

Finally, as for his moral character, we do not hesitate to say, that he has no grain of vice or meanness in him, but represents just that degree of virtue which all men relish without being obliged to respect. He is a good man, as his bitters are good—an unquestionable goodness. Not what is called a good man,—good to be considered, as a work of art in galleries and museums,—but a good fellow, that is, good to be associated with. Who ever thought of the religion of an innkeeper—whether he was joined to the Church, partook of the sacrament, said his prayers, feared God, or the like? No doubt he has had his experiences, has felt a change, and is a firm believer in the perseverance of the saints. In this last, we suspect, does the peculiarity of his religion consist. But he keeps an inn, and not a conscience. How many fragrant charities, and sincere social virtues are implied in this daily offering of himself to the public. He cherishes good will to all, and gives the wayfarer as good and honest advice to direct him on his road, as the priest.

To conclude, the tavern will compare favorably with the church. The church is the place where prayers and sermons are delivered, but the tavern is where they are to take effect, and if the former are good, the latter cannot be bad.

Paradise (To Be) Regained*

W E LEARN that Mr. Etzler is a native of Germany, and originally published his book in Pennsylvania, ten or twelve years ago; and now a second English edition, from the original American one, is demanded by his readers across the water, owing, we suppose, to the recent spread of Fourier's doctrines. It is one of the signs of the times. We confess that we have risen from reading this book with enlarged ideas, and grander conceptions of our duties in this world. It did expand us a little. It is worth attending to, if only that it entertains large questions. Consider what Mr. Etzler proposes:

"Fellow Men! I promise to show the means of creating a paradise within ten years, where everything desirable for human life may be had by every man in superabundance, without labor, and without pay; where the whole face of nature shall be changed into the most beautiful forms, and man may live in the most magnificent palaces, in all imaginable refinements of luxury, and in the most delightful gardens; where he may accomplish, without labor, in one year, more than hitherto could be done in thousands of years; may level mountains, sink valleys, create lakes, drain lakes and swamps, and intersect the land everywhere with beautiful canals, and roads for transporting heavy loads of many thousand tons, and for travelling one thousand miles in twenty-four hours; may cover the ocean with floating islands movable in any desired direction with immense power and celerity, in perfect security, and with all comforts and luxuries, bearing gardens and palaces, with thousands of families, and provided with rivulets of sweet water; may explore the interior of the globe, and travel from pole to pole in a fortnight; provide himself with means, unheard of yet, for increasing his knowledge of the world, and so his intelligence; lead a life of continual happiness, of enjoyments yet unknown; free himself from almost all the evils that afflict mankind, except death, and even put death far beyond the common period of human life, and finally render it less afflicting. Mankind may thus live in and enjoy a new world, far superior to the present, and raise themselves far higher in the scale of being."

*The Paradise within the Reach of all Men, without Labor, by Powers of Nature and Machinery. An Address to all intelligent Men. In two parts. By J. A. Etzler. Part First. Second English Edition. pp. 55. London, 1842.

It would seem from this and various indications beside, that there is a transcendentalism in mechanics as well as in ethics. While the whole field of the one reformer lies beyond the boundaries of space, the other is pushing his schemes for the elevation of the race to its utmost limits. While one scours the heavens, the other sweeps the earth. One says he will reform himself, and then nature and circumstances will be right. Let us not obstruct ourselves, for that is the greatest friction. It is of little importance though a cloud obstruct the view of the astronomer compared with his own blindness. The other will reform nature and circumstances, and then man will be right. Talk no more vaguely, says he, of reforming the world—I will reform the globe itself. What matters it whether I remove this humor out of my flesh, or the pestilent humor from the fleshy part of the globe? Nay, is not the latter the more generous course? At present the globe goes with a shattered constitution in its orbit. Has it not asthma, and ague, and fever, and dropsy, and flatulence, and pleurisy, and is it not afflicted with vermin? Has it not its healthful laws counteracted, and its vital energy which will yet redeem it? No doubt the simple powers of nature properly directed by man would make it healthy and paradise; as the laws of man's own constitution but wait to be obeyed, to restore him to health and happiness. Our panaceas cure but few ails, our general hospitals are private and exclusive. We must set up another Hygeian than is now worshipped. Do not the quacks even direct small doses for children, larger for adults, and larger still for oxen and horses? Let us remember that we are to prescribe for the globe itself.

This fair homestead has fallen to us, and how little have we done to improve it, how little have we cleared and hedged and ditched! We are too inclined to go hence to a "better land," without lifting a finger, as our farmers are moving to the Ohio soil; but would it not be more heroic and faithful to till and redeem this New-England soil of the world? The still youthful energies of the globe have only to be directed in their proper channel. Every gazette brings accounts of the untutored freaks of the wind—shipwrecks and hurricanes which the mariner and planter accept as special or general providences; but they touch our consciences, they remind us of our sins. Another deluge would disgrace mankind. We confess we never had much respect for that antediluvian race. A thorough-bred business man cannot enter heartily upon the business of life without first looking into his accounts. How many things are now at loose ends. Who knows which way the wind will blow to-morrow? Let us not succumb to nature. We will marshal the clouds and restrain the tempests; we will bottle up pestilent exhalations, we will probe for earthquakes, grub them up; and give vent to the dangerous gases; we will disembowel the volcano, and extract its poison, take its seed out. We will wash water, and warm fire, and cool ice, and underprop the earth. We will teach birds to fly, and fishes to swim, and ruminants to chew the cud. It is time we had looked into these things.

And it becomes the moralist, too, to inquire what man might do to improve and beautify the system; what to make the stars shine more brightly, the sun more cheery and joyous, the moon more placid and content. Could he not heighten the tints of flowers and the melody of birds? Does he perform his duty to the inferior races? Should he not be a god to them? What is the part of magnanimity to the whale and the beaver? Should we not fear to exchange places with them for a day, lest by their behavior they should shame us? Might we not treat with magnanimity the shark and the tiger, not descend to meet them on their own level, with spears of sharks' teeth and bucklers of tiger's skin? We slander the hyena; man is the fiercest and cruelest animal. Ah! he is of little faith; even the erring comets and meteors would thank him, and return his kindness in their kind.

How meanly and grossly do we deal with nature! Could we not have a less gross labor? What else do these fine inventions suggest,—magnetism, the daguerreotype, electricity? Can we not do more than cut and trim the forest,—can we not assist in its interior economy, in the circulation of the sap? Now we work superficially and violently. We do not suspect how much might be done to improve our relation with animated nature; what kindness and refined courtesy there might be.

There are certain pursuits which, if not wholly poetic and true, do at least suggest a nobler and finer relation to nature than we know. The keeping of bees, for instance, is a very slight interference. It is like directing the sunbeams. All nations, from the remotest antiquity, have thus fingered nature. There are Hymettus and Hybla, and how many bee-renowned spots beside? There is nothing gross in the idea of these little herds,—their hum like the faintest low of kine in the meads. A pleasant reviewer has lately reminded us that in some places they are led out to pasture where the flowers are most abundant. "Columella tells us," says he, "that the inhabitants of Arabia sent their hives into Attica to benefit by the later-blowing flowers." Annually are the hives, in immense pyramids, carried up the Nile in boats, and suffered to float slowly down the stream by night, resting by day, as the flowers put forth along the banks; and they determine the richness of any locality, and so the profitableness of delay, by the sinking of the boat in the water. We are told, by the same reviewer, of a man in Germany, whose bees yielded more honey than those of his neighbors, with no apparent advantage; but at length he informed them that he had turned his hives one degree more to the east, and so his bees, having two hours the start in the morning, got the first sip of honey. True, there is treachery and selfishness behind all this; but these things suggest to the poetic mind what might be done.

Many examples there are of a grosser interference, yet not without their apology. We saw last summer, on the side of a mountain, a dog employed to churn for a farmer's family, travelling upon a horizontal wheel, and though he had sore eyes, an alarming cough, and withal a demure aspect, yet their bread did get buttered for all that. Undoubtedly, in the most brilliant successes, the first rank is always sacrificed. Much useless travelling of horses, *in extenso*, has of late years been improved for man's behoof, only two forces being taken advantage of,—the gravity of the horse, which is the centripetal, and his centrifugal inclination to go a-head. Only these two elements in the calculation. And is not the creature's whole economy better economized thus? Are not all finite beings better pleased with motions relative than absolute? And what is the great globe itself but such a wheel,—a larger tread-mill,—so that our horse's freest steps over prairies are oftentimes balked and rendered of no avail by the earth's motion on its axis? But here he is the central agent and motive power; and, for variety of scenery, being provided with a window in front, do not the ever-varying activity and fluctuating energy of the creature himself work the effect of the most varied scenery on a country road? It must be confessed that horses at present work too exclusively for men, rarely men for horses; and the brute degenerates in man's society.

It will be seen that we contemplate a time when man's will shall be law to the physical world, and he shall no longer be deterred by such abstractions as time and space, height and depth, weight and hardness, but shall indeed be the lord of creation. "Well," says the faithless reader, " 'life is short, but art is long;' where is the power that will effect all these changes?" This it is the very object of Mr. Etzler's volume to show. At present, he would merely remind us that there are innumerable and immeasurable powers already existing in nature, unimproved on a large scale, or for generous and universal ends, amply sufficient for these purposes. He would only indicate their existence, as a surveyor makes known the existence of a water-power on any stream; but for their application he refers us to a sequel to this book, called the "Mechanical System." A few of the most obvious and familiar of these powers are, the Wind, the Tide, the Waves, the Sunshine. Let us consider their value.

First, there is the power of the Wind, constantly exerted over the globe. It appears from observation of a sailing-vessel, and from scientific tables, that the average power of the wind is equal to that of one horse for every one hundred square feet. "We know," says our author—

"that ships of the first class carry sails two hundred feet high; we may, therefore, equally, on land, oppose to the wind surfaces of the same height. Imagine a line of such surfaces one mile, or about 5,000 feet, long; they would then contain 1,000,000 square feet. Let these surfaces intersect the direction of the wind at right angles, by some contrivance, and receive, consequently, its full power at all times. Its average power being equal to one horse for every 100 square feet, the total power would be equal to 1,000,000 divided by 100, or 10,000 horses' power. Allowing the power of one horse to equal that of ten men, the power of 10,000 horses is equal to 100,000 men. But as men cannot work uninterruptedly, but want about half the time for sleep and repose, the same power would be equal to 200,000 men. . . . We are not limited to the height of 200 feet; we might extend, if required, the application of this power to the height of the clouds, by means of kites."

But we will have one such fence for every square mile of the globe's surface, for, as the wind usually strikes the earth at an angle of more than two degrees, which is evident from observing its effect on the high sea, it admits of even a closer approach. As the surface of the globe contains about 200,000,000 square miles, the whole power of the wind on these surfaces would equal 40,000,000,000,000 men's power, and "would perform 80,000 times as much work as all the men on earth could effect with their nerves."

If it should be objected that this computation includes the surface of the ocean and uninhabitable regions of the earth, where this power could not be applied for our purposes, Mr. Etzler is quick with his reply—"But, you will recollect," says he, "that I have promised to show the means for rendering the ocean as inhabitable as the most fruitful dry land; and I do not exclude even the polar regions."

The reader will observe that our author uses the fence only as a convenient formula for expressing the power of the wind, and does not consider it a necessary method of its application. We do not attach much value to this statement of the comparative power of the wind and horse, for no common ground is mentioned on which they can be compared. Undoubtedly, each is incomparably excellent in its way, and every general comparison made for such practical purposes as are contemplated, which gives a preference to the one, must be made with some unfairness to the other. The scientific tables are, for the most part, true only in a tabular sense. We suspect that a loaded wagon, with a light sail, ten feet square, would not have been blown so far by the end of the year, under equal circumstances, as a common racer or dray horse would have drawn it. And how many crazy structures on our globe's surface, of the same dimensions, would wait for dry-rot if the traces of one horse were hitched to them, even to their windward side? Plainly, this is not the principle of comparison. But even the steady and constant force of the horse may be rated as equal to his weight at least. Yet we should prefer to let the zephyrs and gales bear, with all their weight, upon our fences, than that Dobbin, with feet braced, should lean ominously against them for a season.

Nevertheless, here is an almost incalculable power at our disposal, yet how trifling the use we make of it. It only serves to turn a few mills, blow a few vessels across the ocean, and a few trivial ends besides. What a poor compliment do we pay to our indefatigable and energetic servant!

"If you ask, perhaps, why this power is not used, if the statement be true, I have to ask in return, why is the power of steam so lately come to application? so many millions of men boiled water every day for many thousand years; they must have frequently seen that boiling water, in tightly closed pots or kettles, would lift the cover or burst the vessel with great violence. The power of steam was, therefore, as commonly known down to the least kitchen or wash-woman, as the power of wind; but close observation and reflection were bestowed neither on the one nor the other."

Men having discovered the power of falling water, which after all is comparatively slight, how eagerly do they seek out and improve these *privileges*? Let a difference of but a few feet in level be discovered on some stream near a populous town, some slight occasion for gravity to act, and the whole economy of the neighborhood is changed at once. Men do indeed speculate about and with this power as if it were the only privilege. But meanwhile this aerial stream is falling from far greater heights with more constant flow, never shrunk by drought, offering mill-sites wherever the wind blows; a Niagara in the air, with no Canada side;—only the application is hard.

There are the powers too of the Tide and Waves, constantly ebbing and flowing, lapsing and relapsing, but they serve man in but few ways. They turn a few tide mills, and perform a few other insignificant and accidental services only. We all perceive the effect of the tide; how imperceptibly it creeps up into our harbors and rivers, and raises the heaviest navies as easily as the lightest ship. Everything that floats must yield to it. But man, slow to take nature's constant hint of assistance, makes slight and irregular use of this power, in careening ships and getting them afloat when aground.

The following is Mr. Etzler's calculation on this head: To form a conception of the power which the tide affords, let us imagine a surface of 100 miles square, or 10,000 square miles, where the tide rises and sinks, on an average, 10 feet; how many men would it require to empty a basin of 10,000 square miles area, and 10 feet deep, filled with sea-water, in 6¼ hours and fill it again in the same time? As one man can raise 8 cubic feet of sea-water per minute, and in 6¼ hours 3,000, it would take 1,200,000,000 men, or as they could work only half the time, 2,400,000,000, to raise 3,000,000,000,000 cubic feet, or the whole quantity required in the given time.

This power may be applied in various ways. A large body, of the heaviest materials that will float, may first be raised by it, and being attached to the end of a balance reaching from the land, or from a stationary support, fastened to the bottom, when the tide falls, the whole weight will be brought to bear upon the end of the balance. Also when the tide rises it may be made to exert a nearly equal force in the opposite direction. It can be employed whenever a *point d'appui* can be obtained.

"However, the application of the tide being by establishments fixed on the ground, it is natural to begin with them near the shores in shallow water, and upon sands, which may be extended gradually further into the sea. The shores of the continent, islands, and sands, being generally surrounded by shallow water, not exceeding from 50 to 100 fathoms in depth, for 20, 50, or 100 miles and upward. The coasts of North America, with their extensive sand-banks, islands, and rocks, may easily afford, for this purpose, a ground about 3,000 miles long, and, on an average, 100 miles broad, or 300,000 square miles, which, with a power of 240,000 men per square mile, as stated, at 10 feet tide, will be equal to 72,000 millions of men, or for every mile of coast, a power of 24,000,000 men."

"Rafts, of any extent, fastened on the ground of the sea, along the shore, and stretching far into the sea, may be covered with fertile soil, bearing vegetables and trees, of every description, the finest gardens, equal to those the firm land may admit of, and buildings and machineries, which may operate, not only on the sea, where they are, but which also, by means of mechanical connections, may extend their operations for many miles into the continent. (Etzler's Mechanical System, page 24.) Thus this power may cultivate the artificial soil for many miles upon the surface of the sea, near the shores, and, for several miles, the dry land, along the shore, in the most superior manner imaginable; it may build cities along the shore, consisting of the most magnificent palaces, every one surrounded by gardens and the most delightful sceneries; it may level the hills and unevennesses, or raise eminences for enjoying open prospect into the country and upon the sea; it may cover the barren shore with fertile soil, and beautify the same in various ways; it may clear the sea of shallows, and make easy the approach to the land, not merely of vessels, but of large floating islands, which may come from, and go to distant parts of the world, islands that have every commodity and security for their inhabitants which the firm land affords."

"Thus may a power, derived from the gravity of the moon and the ocean, hitherto but the objects of idle curiosity to the studious man, be made eminently subservient for creating the most delightful abodes along the coasts, where men may enjoy at the same time all the advantages of sea and dry land; the coasts may hereafter be continuous paradisiacal skirts between land and sea, everywhere crowded with the densest population. The shores and the sea along them will be no more as raw nature presents them now, but everywhere of easy and charming access, not even molested by the roar of waves, shaped as it may suit the purposes of their inhabitants; the sea will be cleared of every obstruction to free passage every-where, and its productions in fishes, etc., will be gathered in large, appropriate receptacles, to present them to the inhabitants of the shores and of the sea."

Verily, the land would wear a busy aspect at the spring and neap tide, and these island ships—these *terræ infirmæ*—which realise the fables of antiquity, affect our imagination. We have often thought that the fittest locality for a human dwelling was on the edge of the land, that there the constant lesson and impression of the sea might sink deep into the life and character of the landsman, and perhaps impart a marine tint to his imagination. It is a noble word, that *mariner*—one who is conversant with the sea. There should be more of what it signifies in each of us. It is a worthy country to belong to—we look to see him not disgrace it. Perhaps we should be equally mariners and terreners, and even our Green Mountains need some of that sea-green to be mixed with them.

The computation of the power of the waves is less satisfactory. While only the average power of the wind, and the average height of the tide, were taken before now, the extreme height of the waves is used, for they are made to rise ten feet above the level of the sea, to which, adding ten more for depression, we have twenty feet, or the extreme height of a wave. Indeed, the power of the waves, which is produced by the wind blowing obliquely and at disadvantage upon the water, is made to be, not only three thousand times greater than that of the tide, but one hundred times greater than that of the wind itself, meeting its object at right angles. Moreover, this power is measured by the area of the vessel, and not by its length mainly, and it seems to be forgotten that the motion of the waves is chiefly undulatory, and exerts a power only within the limits of a vibration, else the very continents, with their extensive coasts, would soon be set adrift.

Finally, there is the power to be derived from sunshine, by the principle on which Archimedes contrived his burning mirrors, a multiplication of mirrors reflecting the rays of the sun upon the same spot, till the requisite degree of heat is obtained. The principal application of this power will be to the boiling of water and production of steam.

"How to create rivulets of sweet and wholesome water, on floating islands, in the midst of the ocean, will be no riddle now. Seawater changed into steam, will distil into sweet water, leaving the salt on the bottom. Thus the steam engines on floating islands, for their propulsion and other mechanical purposes, will serve, at the same time, for the distillery of sweet water, which, collected in basins, may be led through channels over the island, while, where required, it may be refrigerated by artificial means, and changed into cool water, surpassing, in salubrity, the best spring water, because nature hardly ever distils water so purely, and without admixture of less wholesome matter."

So much for these few and more obvious powers, already used to a trifling extent. But there are innumerable others in nature, not described nor discovered. These, however, will do for the present. This would be to make the sun and the moon equally our satellites. For, as the moon is the cause of the tides, and the sun the cause of the wind, which, in turn, is the cause of the waves, all the work of this planet would be performed by these far influences.

"But as these powers are very irregular and subject to interruptions; the next object is to show how they may be converted into powers that operate continually and uniformly for ever, until the machinery be worn out, or, in other words, into perpetual motions." . . . "Hitherto the power of the wind has been applied immediately upon the machinery for use, and we have had to wait the chances of the wind's blowing; while the operation was stopped as soon as the wind ceased to blow. But the manner, which I shall state hereafter, of applying this power, is to make it operate only for collecting or storing up power, and then to take out of this store, at any time, as much as may be wanted for final operation upon the machines. The power stored up is to react as required, and may do so long after the original power of the wind has ceased. And though the wind should cease for intervals of many months, we may have by the same power a uniform perpetual motion in a very simple way."

"The weight of a clock being wound up gives us an image of reaction. The sinking of this weight is the reaction of winding it up. It is not necessary to wait till it has run down before we wind up the weight, but it may be wound up at any time, partly or totally; and if done always before the weight reaches the bottom, the clock will be going perpetually. In a similar, though not in the same way, we may cause a reaction on a larger scale. We may raise, for instance, water by the immediate application of wind or steam to a pond upon some eminence, out of which, through an outlet, it may fall upon some wheel or other contrivance for setting machinery a going. Thus we may store up water in some eminent pond, and take out of this store, at any time, as much water through the outlet as we want to employ, by which means the original power may react for many days after it has ceased." . . . "Such reservoirs of moderate elevation or size need not be made artificially, but will be found made by nature very frequently, requiring but little aid for their completion. They require no regularity of form. Any valley with lower grounds in its vicinity, would answer the purpose. Small crevices may be filled up. Such places may be eligible for the beginning of enterprises of this kind."

The greater the height, of course the less water required. But suppose a level and dry country; then hill and valley, and "eminent pond," are to be constructed by main force; or if the springs are unusually low, then dirt and stones may be used, and the disadvantage arising from friction will be counterbalanced by their greater gravity. Nor shall a single rood of dry land be sunk in such artificial ponds as may be wasted, but their surfaces "may be covered with rafts decked with fertile earth, and all kinds of vegetables which may grow there as well as anywhere else."

And finally, by the use of thick envelopes retaining the heat, and other contrivances, "the power of steam caused by sunshine may react at will, and thus be rendered perpetual, no matter how often or how long the sunshine may be interrupted. (Etzler's Mechanical System)."

Here is power enough, one would think, to accomplish somewhat. These are the powers below. Oh ye millwrights, ye engineers, ye operatives and speculators of every class, never again complain of a want of power; it is the grossest form of infidelity. The question is not how we shall execute, but what. Let us not use in a niggardly manner what is thus generously offered.

Consider what revolutions are to be effected in agriculture. First, in the new country, a machine is to move along taking out trees and stones to any required depth, and piling them up in convenient heaps; then the same machine, "with a little alteration," is to plane the ground perfectly, till there shall be no hills nor valleys, making the requisite canals, ditches and roads, as it goes along. The same machine, "with some other little alterations," is then to sift the ground thoroughly, supply fertile soil from other places if wanted, and plant it; and finally, the same machine "with a little addition," is to reap and gather in the crop, thresh and grind it, or press it to oil, or prepare it any way for final use. For the description of these machines we are referred to "Etzler's Mechanical System, pages 11 to 27." We should be pleased to see that "Mechanical System," though we have not been able to ascertain whether it has been published, or only exists as yet in the design of the author. We have great faith in it. But we cannot stop for applications now.

"Any wilderness, even the most hideous and sterile, may be converted into the most fertile and delightful gardens. The most dismal swamps may be cleared of all their spontaneous growth, filled up and levelled, and intersected by canals, ditches and aqueducts, for draining them entirely. The soil, if required, may be meliorated, by covering or mixing it with rich soil taken from distant places, and the same be mouldered to fine dust, levelled, sifted from all roots, weeds and stones, and sowed and planted in the most beautiful order and symmetry, with fruit trees and vegetables of every kind that may stand the climate."

New facilities for transportation and locomotion are to be adopted:

"Large and commodious vehicles, for carrying many thousand tons, running over peculiarly adapted level roads, at the rate of forty miles per hour, or one thousand miles per day, may transport men and things, small houses, and whatever may serve for comfort and ease, by land. Floating islands, constructed of logs, or of wooden-stuff prepared in a similar manner, as is to be done with stone, and of live trees, which may be reared so as to interlace one another, and strengthen the whole, may be covered with gardens and palaces, and propelled by powerful engines, so as to run at an equal rate through seas and oceans. Thus, man may move, with the celerity of a bird's flight, in terrestrial paradises, from one climate to another, and see the world in all its variety, exchanging, with distant nations, the surplus of productions. The journey from one pole to another may be performed in a fortnight; the visit to a transmarine country in a week or two; or a journey round the world in one or two months by land and water. And why pass a dreary winter every year while there is yet room enough on the globe where nature is blessed with a perpetual summer, and with a far greater variety and luxuriance of vegetation? More than one-half the surface of the globe has no winter. Men will have it in their power to remove and prevent all bad influences of climate, and to enjoy, perpetually, only that temperature which suits their constitution and feeling best."

Who knows but by accumulating the power until the end of the present century, using meanwhile only the smallest allowance, reserving all that blows, all that shines, all that ebbs and flows, all that dashes, we may have got such a reserved accumulated power as to run the earth off its track into a new orbit, some summer, and so change the tedious vicissitude of the seasons? Or, perchance, coming generations will not abide the dissolution of the globe, but, availing themselves of future inventions in aerial locomotion, and the navigation of space, the entire race may migrate from the earth, to settle some vacant and more western planet, it may be still healthy, perchance unearthy, not composed of dirt and stones, whose primary strata only are strewn, and where no weeds are sown.

It took but little art, a simple application of natural laws, a canoe, a paddle, and a sail of matting, to people the isles of the Pacific, and a little more will people the shining isles of space. Do we not see in the firmament the lights carried along the shore by night, as Columbus did? Let us not despair nor mutiny.

"The dwellings also ought to be very different from what is known, if the full benefit of our means is to be enjoyed. They are to be of a structure for which we have no name yet. They are to be neither palaces, nor temples, nor cities, but a combination of all, superior to whatever is known. Earth may be baked into bricks, or even vitrified stone by heat,—we may bake large masses of any size and form into stone and vitrified substance of the greatest durability, lasting even thousands of years, out of clayey earth, or of stones ground to dust, by the application of burning mirrors. This is to be done in the open air, without other preparation than gathering the substance, grinding and mixing it with water and cement, moulding or casting it, and bringing the focus of the burning mirrors of proper size upon the same. The character of the architecture is to be quite different from what it ever has been hitherto; large solid masses are to be baked or cast in one piece, ready shaped in any form that may be desired. The building may, therefore, consist of columns two hundred feet high and upwards, of proportionate thickness, and of one entire piece of vitrified substance; huge pieces are to be moulded so as to join and hook on to each other firmly, by proper joints and folds, and not to yield in any way without breaking."

"Foundries, of any description, are to be heated by burning mirrors, and will require no labor, except the making of the first moulds and the superintendence for gathering the metal and taking the finished articles away."

Alas, in the present state of science, we must take the finished articles away; but think not that man will always be a victim of circumstances.

The countryman who visited the city and found the streets cluttered with bricks and lumber, reported that it was not yet finished, and one who considers the endless repairs and reforming of our houses, might well wonder when they will be done. But why may not the dwellings of men on this earth be built once for all of some durable material, some Roman or Etruscan masonry which will stand, so that time shall only adorn and beautify them? Why may we not finish the outward world for posterity, and leave them leisure to attend to the inner? Surely, all the gross necessities and economies might be cared for in a few years. All might be built and baked and stored up, during this, the term-time of the world, against the vacant eternity, and the globe go provisioned and furnished like our public vessels, for its voyage through space, as through some Pacific ocean, while we would "tie up the rudder and sleep before the wind," as those who sail from Lima to Manilla.

But, to go back a few years in imagination, think not that life in these crystal palaces is to bear any analogy to life in our present humble cottages. Far from it. Clothed, once for all, in some "flexible stuff," more durable than George Fox's suit of leather, composed of "fibres of vegetables," "glutinated" together by some "cohesive substances," and made into sheets, like paper, of any size or form, man will put far from him corroding care and the whole host of ills.

"The twenty-five halls in the inside of the square are to be each two hundred feet square and high; the forty corridors, each one hundred feet long and twenty wide; the eighty galleries, each from 1,000 to 1,250 feet long; about 7,000 private rooms, the whole surrounded and intersected by the grandest and most splendid colonnades imaginable; floors, ceilings, columns with their various beautiful and fanciful intervals, all shining, and reflecting to infinity all objects and persons, with splendid lustre of all beautiful colors, and fanciful shapes and pictures. All galleries, outside and within the halls, are to be provided with many thousand commodious and most elegant vehicles, in which persons may move up and down, like birds, in perfect security, and without exertion. Any member may procure himself all the common articles of his daily wants, by a short turn of some crank, without leaving his apartment; he may, at any time, bathe himself in cold or warm water, or in steam, or in some artificially prepared liquor for invigorating health. He may, at any time, give to the air in his apartment that temperature that suits his feeling best. He may cause, at any time, an agreeable scent of various kinds. He may, at any time, meliorate his breathing air,—that main vehicle of vital power. Thus, by a proper application of the physical knowledge of our days, man may be kept in a perpetual serenity of mind, and if there is no incurable disease or defect in his organism, in constant vigor of health, and his life be prolonged beyond any parallel which present times afford."

"One or two persons are sufficient to direct the kitchen business. They have nothing else to do but to superintend the cookery, and to watch the time of the victuals being done, and then to remove them, with the table and vessels, into the dining-hall, or to the respective private apartments, by a slight motion of the hand at some crank. Any extraordinary desire of any person may be satisfied by going to the place where the thing is to be had; and anything that requires a particular preparation in cooking or baking, may be done by the person who desires it."

This is one of those instances in which the individual genius is found to consent, as indeed it always does, at last, with the universal. These last sentences have a certain sad and sober truth, which reminds us of the scripture of all nations. All expression of truth does at length take the deep ethical form. Here is hint of a place the most eligible of any in space, and of a servitor, in comparison with whom, all other helps dwindle into insignificance. We hope to hear more of him anon, for even a crystal palace would be deficient without his invaluable services.

And as for the environs of the establishment,

"There will be afforded the most enrapturing views to be fancied, cut of the private apartments, from the galleries, from the roof, from its turrets and cupolas,—gardens as far as the eye can see, full of fruits and flowers, arranged in the most beautiful order, with walks, colonnades, aqueducts, canals, ponds, plains, amphitheatres, terraces, fountains, sculptural works, pavilions, gondolas, places for public amusement, etc., to delight the eye and fancy, the taste and smell." . . . "The walks and roads are to be paved with hard vitrified, large plates, so as to be always clean from all dirt in any weather or season. . . . The channels being of vitrified substance, and the water perfectly clear, and filtrated or distilled if required, may afford the most beautiful scenes imaginable, while a variety of fishes is seen clear down to the bottom playing about, and the canals may afford at the same time, the means of gliding smoothly along between various sceneries of art and nature, in beautiful gondolas, while their surface and borders may be covered with fine land and aquatic birds. The walks may be covered with porticos adorned with magnificent columns, statues and sculptural works; all of vitrified substance, and lasting for ever, while the beauties of nature around heighten the magnificence and deliciousness."

"The night affords no less delight to fancy and feelings. An infinite variety of grand, beautiful and fanciful objects and sceneries, radiating with crystalline brilliancy, by the illumination of gas-light; the human figures themselves, arrayed in the most beautiful pomp fancy may suggest, or the eye desire, shining even with brilliancy of stuffs and diamonds, like stones of various colors, elegantly shaped and arranged around the body; all reflected a thousand-fold in huge mirrors and reflectors of various forms; theatrical scenes of a grandeur and magnificence, and enrapturing illusions, unknown yet, in which any person may be either a spectator or actor; the speech and the songs reverberating with increased sound, rendered more sonorous and harmonious than by nature, by vaultings that are moveable into any shape at any time; the sweetest and most impressive harmony of music, produced by song and instruments partly not known yet, may thrill through the nerves and vary with other amusements and delights."

"At night the roof, and the inside and outside of the whole square, are illuminated by gas-light, which in the mazes of many-colored crystal-like colonnades and vaultings, is reflected with a brilliancy that gives to the whole a lustre of precious stones, as far as the eye can see,—such are the future abodes of men." . . . "Such is the life reserved to true intelligence, but withheld from ignorance, prejudice, and stupid adherence to custom." . . . "Such is the domestic life to be enjoyed by every human individual that will partake of it. Love and affection may there be fostered and enjoyed without any of the obstructions that oppose, diminish, and destroy them in the present state of men." . . . "It would be as ridiculous, then, to dispute and quarrel about the means of life, as it would be now about water to drink along mighty rivers, or about the permission to breathe air in the atmosphere, or about sticks in our extensive woods."

Thus is Paradise to be Regained, and that old and stern decree at length reversed. Man shall no more earn his living by the sweat of his brow. All labor shall be reduced to "a short turn of some crank," and "taking the finished article away." But there is a crank,—oh, how hard to be turned! Could there not be a crank upon a crank,—an infinitely small crank?—we would fain inquire. No,—alas! not. But there is a certain divine energy in every man, but sparingly employed as yet, which may be called the crank within,—the crank after all,—the prime mover in all machinery,—quite indispensable to all work. Would that we might get our hands on its handle! In fact no work can be shirked. It may be postponed indefinitely, but not infinitely. Nor can any really important work be made easier by co-operation or machinery. Not one particle of labor now threatening any man can be routed without being performed. It cannot be hunted out of the vicinity like jackals and hyenas. It will not run. You may begin by sawing the little sticks, or you may saw the great sticks first, but sooner or later you must saw them both.

We will not be imposed upon by this vast application of forces. We believe that most things will have to be accomplished still by the application called Industry. We are rather pleased after all to consider the small private, but both constant and accumulated force, which stands behind every spade in the field. This it is that makes the valleys shine, and the deserts really bloom. Sometimes, we confess, we are so degenerate as to reflect with pleasure on the days when men were yoked like cattle, and drew a crooked stick for a plough. After all, the great interests and methods were the same.

It is a rather serious objection to Mr. Etzler's schemes, that they require time, men, and money, three very superfluous and inconvenient things for an honest and well-disposed man to deal with. "The whole world," he tells us, "might therefore be really changed into a paradise, within less than ten years, commencing from the first year of an association for the purpose of constructing and applying the machinery." We are sensible of a startling incongruity when time and money are mentioned in this connection. The ten years which are proposed would be a tedious while to wait, if every man were at his post and did his duty, but quite too short a period, if we are to take time for it. But this fault is by no means peculiar to Mr. Etzler's schemes. There is far too much hurry and bustle, and too little patience and privacy, in all our methods, as if something were to be accomplished in centuries. The true reformer does not want time, nor money, nor co-operation, nor advice. What is time but the stuff delay is made of? And depend upon it, our virtue will not live on the interest of our money. He expects no income but our outgoes; so soon as we begin to count the cost the cost begins. And as for advice, the information floating in the atmosphere of society is as evanescent and unserviceable to him as gossamer for clubs of Hercules. There is absolutely no common sense; it is common nonsense. If we are to risk a cent or a drop of our blood, who then shall advise us? For ourselves, we are too young for experience. Who is old enough? We are older by faith than by experience. In the unbending of the arm to do the deed there is experience worth all the maxims in the world.

"It will now be plainly seen that the execution of the proposals is not proper for individuals. Whether it be proper for government at this time, before the subject has become popular, is a question to be decided; all that is to be done, is to step forth, after mature reflection, to confess loudly one's conviction, and to constitute societies. Man is powerful but in union with many. Nothing great, for the improvement of his own condition, or that of his fellow men, can ever be effected by individual enterprise."

Alas! this is the crying sin of the age, this want of faith in the prevalence of a man. Nothing can be effected but by one man. He who wants help wants everything. True, this is the condition of our weakness, but it can never be the means of our recovery. We must first succeed alone, that we may enjoy our success together. We trust that the social movements which we witness indicate an aspiration not to be thus cheaply satisfied. In this matter of reforming the world, we have little faith in corporations; not thus was it first formed.

But our author is wise enough to say, that the raw materials for the accomplishment of his purposes, are "iron, copper, wood, earth chiefly, and a union of men whose eyes and understanding are not shut up by preconceptions." Aye, this last may be what we want mainly,—a company of "odd fellows" indeed.

"Small shares of twenty dollars will be sufficient,"—in all, from "200,000 to 300,000,"—"to create the first establishment for a whole community of from 3000 to 4000 individuals"—at the end of five years we shall have a principal of 200 millions of dollars, and so paradise will be wholly regained at the end of the tenth year. But, alas, the ten years have already elapsed, and there are no signs of Eden yet, for want of the requisite funds to begin the enterprise in a hopeful manner. Yet it seems a safe investment. Perchance they could be hired at a low rate, the property being mortgaged for security, and, if necessary, it could be given up in any stage of the enterprise, without loss, with the fixtures.

Mr. Etzler considers this "Address as a touchstone, to try whether our nation is in any way accessible to these great truths, for raising the human creature to a superior state of existence, in accordance with the knowledge and the spirit of the most cultivated minds of the present time." He has prepared a constitution, short and concise, consisting of twenty-one articles, so that wherever an association may spring up, it may go into operation without delay; and the editor informs us that "Communications on the subject of this book may be addressed to C. F. Stollmeyer, No. 6, Upper Charles street, Northampton square, London."

But we see two main difficulties in the way. First, the successful application of the powers by machinery, (we have not yet seen the "Mechanical System,") and, secondly, which is infinitely harder, the application of man to the work by faith. This it is, we fear, which will prolong the ten years to ten thousand at least. It will take a power more than "80,000 times greater than all the men on earth could effect with their nerves," to persuade men to use that which is already offered them. Even a greater than this physical power must be brought to bear upon that moral power. Faith, indeed, is all the reform that is needed; it is itself a reform. Doubtless, we are as slow to conceive of Paradise as of Heaven, of a perfect natural as of a perfect spiritual world. We see how past ages have loitered and erred; "Is perhaps our generation free from irrationality and error? Have we perhaps reached now the summit of human wisdom, and need no more to look out for mental or physical improvement?" Undoubtedly, we are never so visionary as to be prepared for what the next hour may bring forth.

Μέλλει· τὸ θεῖον δ'ἐστι τοιοῦτον φύσει.

The Divine is about to be, and such is its nature. In our wisest moments we are secreting a matter, which, like the lime of the shell fish, incrusts us quite over, and well for us, if, like it, we cast our shells from time to time, though they be pearl and of fairest tint. Let us consider under what disadvantages science has hitherto labored before we pronounce thus confidently on her progress.

"There was never any system in the productions of human labor; but they came into existence and fashion as chance directed men." "Only a few professional men of learning occupy themselves with teaching natural philosophy, chemistry, and the other branches of the sciences of nature, to a very limited extent, for very limited purposes, with very limited means." "The science of mechanics is but in a state of infancy. It is true, improvements are made upon improvements, instigated by patents of government; but they are made accidentally or at hap-hazard. There is no general system of this science, mathematical as it is, which developes its principles in their full extent, and the outlines of the application to which they lead. There is no idea of comparison between what is explored and what is yet to be explored in this science. The ancient Greeks placed mathematics at the head of their education. But we are glad to have filled our memory with notions, without troubling ourselves much with reasoning about them."

Mr. Etzler is not one of the enlightened practical men, the pioneers of the actual, who move with the slow deliberate tread of science, conserving the world; who execute the dreams of the last century, though they have no dreams of their own; yet he deals in the very raw but still solid material of all inventions. He has more of the practical than usually belongs to so bold a schemer, so resolute a dreamer. Yet his success is in theory, and not in practice, and he feeds our faith rather than contents our understanding. His book wants order, serenity, dignity, everything,—but it does not fail to impart what only man can impart to man of much importance, his own faith. It is true his dreams are not thrilling nor bright enough, and he leaves off to dream where he who dreams just before the dawn begins. His castles in the air fall to the ground, because they are not built lofty enough; they should be secured to heaven's roof. After all, the theories and speculations of men concern us more than their puny execution. It is with a certain coldness and languor that we loiter about the actual and so called practical. How little do the most wonderful inventions of modern times detain us. They insult nature. Every machine, or particular application, seems a slight outrage against universal laws. How many fine inventions are there which do not clutter the ground? We think that those only succeed which minister to our sensible and animal wants, which bake or brew, wash or warm, or the like. But are those of no account which are patented by fancy and imagination, and succeed so admirably in our dreams that they give the tone still to our waking thoughts? Already nature is serving all those uses which science slowly derives on a much higher and grander scale to him that will be served by her. When the sunshine falls on the path of the poet, he enjoys all those pure benefits and pleasures which the arts slowly and partially realize from age to age. The winds which fan his cheek waft him the sum of that profit and happiness which their lagging inventions supply.

The chief fault of this book is, that it aims to secure the greatest degree of gross comfort and pleasure merely. It paints a Mahometan's heaven, and stops short with singular abruptness when we think it is drawing near to the precincts of the Christian's,—and we trust we have not made here a distinction without a difference. Undoubtedly if we were to reform this outward life truly and thoroughly, we should find no duty of the inner omitted. It would be employment for our whole nature; and what we should do thereafter would be as vain a question as to ask the bird what it will do when its nest is built and its brood reared. But a moral reform must take place first, and then the necessity of the other will be superseded, and we shall sail and plough by its force alone. There is a speedier way than the Mechanical System can show to fill up marshes, to drown the roar of the waves, to tame hyenas, secure agreeable environs, diversify the land, and refresh it with "rivulets of sweet water," and that is by the power of rectitude and true behavior. It is only for a little while, only occasionally, methinks, that we want a garden. Surely a good man need not be at the labor to level a hill for the sake of a prospect, or raise fruits and flowers, and construct floating islands, for the sake of a paradise. He enjoys better prospects than lie behind any hill. Where an angel travels it will be paradise all the way, but where Satan travels it will be burning marl and cinders. What says Veeshnoo Sarma? "He whose mind is at ease is possessed of all riches. Is it not the same to one whose foot is enclosed in a shoe, as if the whole surface of the earth were covered with leather?"

He who is conversant with the supernal powers will not worship these inferior deities of the wind, the waves, tide, and sunshine. But we would not disparage the importance of such calculations as we have described. They are truths in physics, because they are true in ethics. The moral powers no one would presume to calculate. Suppose we could compare the moral with the physical, and say how many horse-power the force of love, for instance, blowing on every square foot of a man's soul, would equal. No doubt we are well aware of this force; figures would not increase our respect for it; the sunshine is equal to but one ray of its heat. The light of the sun is but the shadow of love. "The souls of men loving and fearing God," says Raleigh, "receive influence from that divine light itself, whereof the sun's clarity, and that of the stars, is by Plato called but a shadow. *Lumen est umbra Dei, Deus est Lumen Luminis.* Light is the shadow of God's brightness, who is the light of light," and, we may add, the heat of heat. Love is the wind, the tide, the waves, the sunshine. Its power is incalculable; it is many horse power. It never ceases, it never slacks; it can move the globe without a resting-place; it can warm without fire; it can feed without meat; it can clothe without garments; it can shelter without roof; it can make a paradise within which will dispense with a paradise without. But though the wisest men in all ages have labored to publish this force, and every human heart is, sooner or later, more or less, made to feel it, yet how little is actually applied to social ends. True, it is the motive power of all successful social machinery; but, as in physics, we have made the elements do only a little drudgery for us, steam to take the place of a few horses, wind of a few oars, water of a few cranks and hand-mills; as the mechanical forces have not yet been generously and largely applied to make the physical world answer to the ideal, so the power of love has been but meanly and sparingly applied, as yet. It has patented only such machines as the almshouses, the hospital, and the Bible Society, while its infinite wind is still blowing, and blowing down these very structures, too, from time to time. Still less are we accumulating its power, and preparing to act with greater energy at a future time. Shall we not contribute our shares to this enterprise, then?

Homer. Ossian. Chaucer.

EXTRACTS FROM A LECTURE ON POETRY,
READ BEFORE THE CONCORD LYCEUM,
NOVEMBER 29, 1843, BY HENRY D. THOREAU.

HOMER.

THE wisest definition of poetry the poet will instantly prove false by setting aside its requisitions. We can therefore publish only our advertisement of it.

There is no doubt that the loftiest written wisdom is rhymed or measured, is in form as well as substance poetry; and a volume, which should contain the condensed wisdom of mankind, need not have one rhythmless line. Yet poetry, though the last and finest result, is a natural fruit. As naturally as the oak bears an acorn, and the vine a gourd, man bears a poem, either spoken or done. It is the chief and most memorable success, for history is but a prose narrative of poetic deeds. What else have the Hindoos, the Persians, the Babylonians, the Egyptians, done, that can be told? It is the simplest relation of phenomena, and describes the commonest sensations with more truth than science does, and the latter at a distance slowly mimics its style and methods. The poet sings how the blood flows in his veins. He performs his functions, and is so well that he needs such stimulus to sing only as plants to put forth leaves and blossoms. He would strive in vain to modulate the remote and transient music which he sometimes hears, since his song is a vital function like breathing, and an integral result like weight. It is not the overflowing of life but its subsidence rather, and is drawn from under the feet of the poet. It is enough if Homer but say the sun sets. He is as serene as nature, and we can hardly detect the enthusiasm of the bard. It is as if nature spoke. He presents to us the simplest pictures of human life, so that childhood itself can understand them, and the man must not think twice to appreciate his naturalness. Each reader discovers for himself, that succeeding poets have done little else

than copy his similes. His more memorable passages are as
naturally bright, as gleams of sunlight in misty weather.
Nature furnishes him not only with words, but with stereotyped lines and sentences from her mint.

"As from the clouds appears the full moon,
  All shining, and then again it goes behind the shadowy
      clouds,
  So Hector, at one time appeared among the foremost,
  And at another in the rear, commanding; and all with brass
  He shone, like to the lightning of ægis-bearing Zeus."

He conveys the least information, even the hour of the day,
with such magnificence, and vast expense of natural imagery,
as if it were a message from the gods.

"While it was dawn, and sacred day was advancing,
  For that space the weapons of both flew fast, and the people
      fell;
  But when now the woodcutter was preparing his morning
      meal
  In the recesses of the mountain, and had wearied his hands
  With cutting lofty trees, and satiety came to his mind,
  And the desire of sweet food took possession of his
      thoughts;
  Then the Danaans by their valor broke the phalanxes,
  Shouting to their companions from rank to rank."

When the army of the Trojans passed the night under arms,
keeping watch lest the enemy should re-embark under cover
of the dark,

"They, thinking great things, upon the neutral ground of war,
  Sat all the night; and many fires burned for them.
  As when in the heavens the stars round the bright moon
  Appear beautiful, and the air is without wind;
  And all the heights, and the extreme summits,
  And the shady valleys appear; and the shepherd rejoices in
      his heart;

So between the ships and the streams of Xanthus
Appeared the fires of the Trojans before Ilium."

The "white-armed goddess Juno," sent by the Father of
gods and men for Iris and Apollo,

"Went down the Idæan mountains to far Olympus,
As when the mind of a man, who has come over much earth,
Sallies forth, and he reflects with rapid thoughts,
There was I, and there, and remembers many things;
So swiftly the august Juno hastening flew through the air,
And came to high Olympus."

There are few books which are fit to be remembered in our
wisest hours, but the Iliad is brightest in the serenest days,
and imbodies still all the sunlight that fell on Asia Minor. No
modern joy or ecstasy of ours can lower its height or dim its
lustre; but there it lies in the east of literature, as it were the
earliest, latest production of the mind. The ruins of Egypt oppress and stifle us with their dust, foulness preserved in cassia
and pitch, and swathed in linen; the death of that which never
lived. But the rays of Greek poetry struggle down to us, and
mingle with the sunbeams of the recent day. The statue of
Memnon is cast down, but the shaft of the Iliad still meets the
sun in his rising.

So too, no doubt, Homer had his Homer, and Orpheus his
Orpheus, in the dim antiquity which preceded them. The
mythological system of the ancients, and it is still the only
mythology of the moderns, the poem of mankind, interwoven
so wonderfully with their astronomy, and matching in
grandeur and harmony with the architecture of the Heavens
themselves, seems to point to a time when a mightier genius
inhabited the earth. But man is the great poet, and not
Homer nor Shakspeare; and our language itself, and the common arts of life are his work. Poetry is so universally true and
independent of experience, that it does not need any particular biography to illustrate it, but we refer it sooner or later to
some Orpheus or Linus, and after ages to the genius of humanity, and the gods themselves.

OSSIAN.*

The genuine remains of Ossian, though of less fame and extent, are in many respects of the same stamp with the Iliad itself. He asserts the dignity of the bard no less than Homer, and in his era we hear of no other priest than he. It will not avail to call him a heathen because he personifies the sun and addresses it; and what if his heroes did "worship the ghosts of their fathers," their thin, airy, and unsubstantial forms? we but worship the ghosts of our fathers in more substantial forms. We cannot but respect the vigorous faith of those heathen, who sternly believed somewhat, and are inclined to say to the critics, who are offended by their superstitious rites, don't interrupt these men's prayers. As if we knew more about human life and a God, than the heathen and ancients. Does English theology contain the recent discoveries?

Ossian reminds us of the most refined and rudest eras, of Homer, Pindar, Isaiah, and the American Indian. In his poetry, as in Homer's, only the simplest and most enduring features of humanity are seen, such essential parts of a man as Stonehenge exhibits of a temple; we see the circles of stone, and the upright shaft alone. The phenomena of life acquire almost an unreal and gigantic size seen through his mists. Like all older and grander poetry, it is distinguished by the few elements in the lives of its heroes. They stand on the heath, between the stars and the earth, shrunk to the bones and sinews. The earth is a boundless plain for their deeds. They lead such a simple, dry, and everlasting life, as hardly needs depart with the flesh, but is transmitted entire from age to age. There are but few objects to distract their sight, and their life is as unencumbered as the course of the stars they gaze at.

---

* "The Genuine Remains of Ossian, Literally Translated, with a Preliminary Dissertation, by Patrick Macgregor. Published under the Patronage of the Highland Society of London. 1 vol. 12mo. London, 1841." We take pleasure in recommending this, the first literal English translation of the Gaelic originals of Ossian, which were left by Macpherson, and published agreeably to his intention, in 1807.

"The wrathful kings, on cairns apart,
  Look forward from behind their shields,
  And mark the wandering stars,
  That brilliant westward move."

It does not cost much for these heroes to live. They want not
much furniture. They are such forms of men only as can be
seen afar through the mist, and have no costume nor dialect,
but for language there is the tongue itself, and for costume
there are always the skins of beasts and the bark of trees to be
had. They live out their years by the vigor of their constitutions. They survive storms and the spears of their foes, and
perform a few heroic deeds, and then,

"Mounds will answer questions of them,
  For many future years."

Blind and infirm, they spend the remnant of their days listening to the lays of the bards, and feeling the weapons which
laid their enemies low, and when at length they die, by a convulsion of nature, the bard allows us a short misty glance into
futurity, yet as clear, perchance, as their lives had been. When
Mac-Roine was slain,

"His soul departed to his warlike sires,
  To follow misty forms of boars,
  In tempestuous islands bleak."

The hero's cairn is erected, and the bard sings a brief significant strain, which will suffice for epitaph and biography.

"The weak will find his bow in the dwelling,
  The feeble will attempt to bend it."

Compared with this simple, fibrous life, our civilized history appears the chronicle of debility, of fashion, and the arts
of luxury. But the civilized man misses no real refinement in
the poetry of the rudest era. It reminds him that civilization
does but dress men. It makes shoes, but it does not toughen
the soles of the feet. It makes cloth of finer texture, but it
does not touch the skin. Inside the civilized man stands the
savage still in the place of honor. We are those blue-eyed,
yellow-haired Saxons, those slender, dark-haired Normans.

The profession of the bard attracted more respect in those days from the importance attached to fame. It was his province to record the deeds of heroes. When Ossian hears the traditions of inferior bards, he exclaims,

> "I straightway seize the unfutile tales,
> And send them down in faithful verse."

His philosophy of life is expressed in the opening of the third Duan of Ca-Lodin.

> "Whence have sprung the things that are?
> And whither roll the passing years?
> Where does time conceal its two heads,
> In dense impenetrable gloom,
> Its surface marked with heroes' deeds alone?
> I view the generations gone;
> The past appears but dim;
> As objects by the moon's faint beams,
> Reflected from a distant lake.
> I see, indeed, the thunder-bolts of war,
> But there the unmighty joyless dwell,
> All those who send not down their deeds
> To far, succeeding times."

The ignoble warriors die and are forgotten;

> "Strangers come to build a tower,
> And throw their ashes overhand;
> Some rusted swords appear in dust;
> One, bending forward, says,
> 'The arms belonged to heroes gone;
> We never heard their praise in song.'"

The grandeur of the similes is another feature which characterizes great poetry. Ossian seems to speak a gigantic and universal language. The images and pictures occupy even much space in the landscape, as if they could be seen only from the sides of mountains, and plains with a wide horizon, or across arms of the sea. The machinery is so massive that it cannot be less than natural. Oivana says to the spirit of her father, "Grey-haired Torkil of Torne," seen in the skies,

"Thou glidest away like receding ships."

So when the hosts of Fingal and Starne approach to battle,

"With murmurs loud, like rivers far,
The race of Torne hither moved."

And when compelled to retire,

"dragging his spear behind,
Cudulin sank in the distant wood,
Like a fire unblazing ere it dies."

Nor did Fingal want a proper audience when he spoke;

"A thousand orators inclined
To hear the lay of Fingal."

The threats too would have deterred a man. Vengeance and terror were real. Trenmore threatens the young warrior, whom he meets on a foreign strand,

"Thy mother shall find thee pale on the shore,
While lessening on the waves she spies
The sails of him who slew her son."

If Ossian's heroes weep, it is from excess of strength, and not from weakness, a sacrifice or libation of fertile natures, like the perspiration of stone in summer's heat. We hardly know that tears have been shed, and it seems as if weeping were proper only for babes and heroes. Their joy and their sorrow are made of one stuff, like rain and snow, the rainbow and the mist. When Fillan was worsted in fight, and ashamed in the presence of Fingal,

"He strode away forthwith,
And bent in grief above a stream,
His cheeks bedewed with tears.
From time to time the thistles gray
He lopped with his inverted lance."

Crodar, blind and old, receives Ossian, son of Fingal, who comes to aid him in war,

" 'My eyes have failed,' says he, 'Crodar is blind,
   Is thy strength like that of thy fathers?
   Stretch, Ossian, thine arm to the hoary-haired.'
     I gave my arm to the king.
   The aged hero seized my hand;
   He heaved a heavy sigh;
   Tears flowed incessant down his cheek.
   'Strong art thou, son of the mighty,
   Though not so dreadful as Morven's prince. * * *
   Let my feast be spread in the hall,
   Let every sweet-voiced minstrel sing;
   Great is he who is within my wall,
   Sons of wave-echoing Croma.' "

Even Ossian himself, the hero-bard, pays tribute to the superior strength of his father Fingal.

"How beauteous, mighty man, was thy mind,
   Why succeeded Ossian without its strength?"

CHAUCER.

What a contrast between the stern and desolate poetry of Ossian, and that of Chaucer, and even of Shakspeare and Milton, much more of Dryden, and Pope, and Gray. Our summer of English poetry, like the Greek and Latin before it, seems well advanced toward its fall, and laden with the fruit and foliage of the season, with bright autumnal tints, but soon the winter will scatter its myriad clustering and shading leaves, and leave only a few desolate and fibrous boughs to sustain the snow and rime, and creak in the blasts of ages. We cannot escape the impression, that the Muse has stooped a little in her flight, when we come to the literature of civilized eras. Now first we hear of various ages and styles of poetry, but the poetry of runic monuments is for every age. The bard has lost the dignity and sacredness of his office. He has no more the bardic rage, and only conceives the deed, which he formerly stood ready to perform. Hosts of warriors, earnest for battle, could not mistake nor dispense with the ancient bard. His lays were heard in the pauses of the fight. There was no danger of his being overlooked by his contemporaries. But now the hero and the bard are of different professions. When we come to the pleasant English verse, it seems as if the storms had all cleared away, and it would never thunder and lighten more. The poet has come within doors, and exchanged the forest and crag for the fireside, the hut of the Gael, and Stonehenge with its circles of stones, for the house of the Englishman. No hero stands at the door prepared to break forth into song or heroic action, but we have instead a homely Englishman, who cultivates the art of poetry. We see the pleasant fireside, and hear the crackling fagots in all the verse. The towering and misty imagination of the bard has descended into the plain, and become a lowlander, and keeps flocks and herds. Poetry is one man's trade, and not all men's religion, and is split into many styles. It is pastoral, and lyric, and narrative, and didactic.

Notwithstanding the broad humanity of Chaucer, and the many social and domestic comforts which we meet with in his verse, we have to narrow our vision somewhat to consider him, as if he occupied less space in the landscape, and did not stretch over hill and valley as Ossian does. Yet, seen from the side of posterity, as the father of English poetry, preceded by a long silence or confusion in history, unenlivened by any strain of pure melody, we easily come to reverence him. Passing over the earlier continental poets, since we are bound to the pleasant archipelago of English poetry, Chaucer's is the first name after that misty weather in which Ossian lived, which can detain us long. Indeed, though he represents so different a culture and society, he may be regarded as in many respects the Homer of the English poets. Perhaps he is the youthfullest of them all. We return to him as to the purest well, the fountain furthest removed from the highway of desultory life. He is so natural and cheerful, compared with later poets, that we might almost regard him as a personification of spring. To the faithful reader his muse has even given an aspect to his times, and when he is fresh from perusing him, they seem related to the golden age. It is still the poetry of youth and life, rather than of thought; and though the moral vein is obvious and constant, it has not yet banished the sun and daylight from his verse. The loftiest strains of the muse are, for the most part, sublimely plaintive, and not a carol as free as nature's. The content which the sun shines to celebrate from morning to evening is unsung. The muse solaces herself, and is not ravished but consoled. There is a catastrophe implied, and a tragic element in all our verse, and less of the lark and morning dews, than of the nightingale and evening shades. But in Homer and Chaucer there is more of the innocence and serenity of youth, than in the more modern and moral poets. The Iliad is not sabbath but morning reading, and men cling to this old song, because they have still moments of unbaptized and uncommitted life, which give them an appetite for more. It represents no creed nor opinion, and we read it with a rare sense of freedom and irresponsibility, as if we trod on native ground, and were autochthones of the soil.

Chaucer had eminently the habits of a literary man and a scholar. We do not enough allow for the prevalence of this class. There were never any times so stirring, that there were not to be found some sedentary still. Through all those outwardly active ages, there were still monks in cloisters writing or copying folios. He was surrounded by the din of arms. The battles of Hallidon Hill and Neville's Cross, and the still more memorable battles of Crecy and Poictiers, were fought in his youth, but these did not concern our poet much, Wicliffe much more. He seems to have regarded himself always as one privileged to sit and converse with books. He helped to establish the literary class. His character, as one of the fathers of the English language, would alone make his works important, even those which have little poetical merit. A great philosophical and moral poet gives permanence to the language he uses, by making the best sound convey the best sense. He was as simple as Wordsworth in preferring his homely but vigorous Saxon tongue, when it was neglected by the court, and had not yet attained to the dignity of a literature, and rendered a similar service to his country to that which Dante rendered to Italy. If Greek sufficeth for Greek, and Arabic for Arabian, and Hebrew for Jew, and Latin for Latin, then English shall suffice for him, for any of these will serve to teach truth "right as divers pathes leaden divers folke the right waye to Rome." In the Testament of Love he writes, "Let then clerkes enditen in Latin, for they have the propertie

of science, and the knowinge in that facultie, and lette Frenchmen in their Frenche also enditen their queinte termes, for it
is kyndely to their mouthes, and let us shewe our fantasies
in soche wordes as we lerneden of our dames tonge."

He will know how to appreciate Chaucer best, who has
come down to him the natural way, through the meagre pastures of Saxon and ante-Chaucerian poetry; and yet so human
and wise he seems after such diet, that he is liable to misjudge
him still. In the Saxon poetry extant, in the earliest English,
and the contemporary Scottish poetry, there is less to remind
the reader of the rudeness and vigor of youth, than of the feebleness of a declining age. It is for the most part translation
or imitation merely, with only an occasional and slight tinge
of poetry, and oftentimes the falsehood and exaggeration of
fable, without its imagination to redeem it. It is astonishing to
how few thoughts so many sincere efforts give utterance. But
as they never sprang out of nature, so they will never root
themselves in nature. There are few traces of original genius,
and we look in vain to find antiquity restored, humanized,
and made blithe again, by the discovery of some natural sympathy between it and the present. But when we come to
Chaucer we are relieved of many a load. He is fresh and modern still, and no dust settles on his true passages. It lightens
along the line, and we are reminded that flowers have
bloomed, and birds sung, and hearts beaten, in England.
Before the earnest gaze of the reader the rust and moss of
time gradually drop off, and the original green life is revealed.
He was a homely and domestic man, and did breathe quite as
modern men do. Only one trait, one little incident of human
biography needs to be truly recorded, that all the world may
think the author fit to wear the laurel crown. In the dearth we
have described, and at this distance of time, the bare processes
of living read like poetry, for all of human good or ill, heroic
or vulgar, lies very near to them. All that is truly great and interesting to men, runs thus as level a course, and is as unaspir-
ing, as the plough in the furrow.

There is no wisdom which can take place of humanity, and
we find *that* in Chaucer. We can expand in his breadth
and think we could be that man's acquaintance. He was worthy to be a citizen of England, while Petrarch and Boccaccio

lived in Italy, and Tell and Tamerlane in Switzerland and in Asia, and Bruce in Scotland, and Wickliffe, and Gower, and Edward the Third, and John of Gaunt, and the Black Prince, were his own countrymen; all stout and stirring names. The fame of Roger Bacon came down from the preceding century, and the name of Dante still exerted the influence of a living presence. On the whole, Chaucer impresses us, as greater than his reputation, and not a little like Homer and Shakspeare, for he would have held up his head in their company. Among early English poets he is the landlord and host, and has the authority of such. The affectionate mention, which succeeding early poets make of him, coupling him with Homer and Virgil, is to be taken into the account in estimating his character and influence. King James and Dunbar of Scotland speak with more love and reverence of him, than any modern author of his predecessors of the last century. The same childlike relation is without parallel now. We read him without criticism for the most part, for he pleads not his own cause, but speaks for his readers, and has that greatness of trust and reliance which compels popularity. He confides in the reader, and speaks privily with him, keeping nothing back. And in return his reader has great confidence in him, that he tells no lies, and reads his story with indulgence, as if it were the circumlocution of a child, but discovers afterwards that he has spoken with more directness and economy of words than a sage. He is never heartless,

> "For first the thing is thought within the hart,
>   Er any word out from the mouth astart."

And so new as all his theme in those days, that he had not to invent, but only to tell.

We admire Chaucer for his sturdy English wit. The easy height he speaks from in his Prologue to the Canterbury Tales, as if he were equal to any of the company there assembled, is as good as any particular excellence in it. But though it is full of good sense and humanity, it is not transcendent poetry. For picturesque description of persons it is, perhaps, without a parallel in English poetry; yet it is essentially humorous, as the loftiest genius never is. Humor, however broad and genial, takes a narrower view than enthusiasm. The whole story of Chanticlere and Dame Partlett, in the Nonne's Preeste's tale, is genuine humanity. I know of nothing better in its kind, no more successful fabling of birds and beasts. If it is said of Shakspeare, that he is now Hamlet, and then Falstaff, it may be said of Chaucer that he sympathizes with brutes as well as men, and assumes their nature that he may speak from it. In this tale he puts on the very feathers and stature of the cock. To his own finer vein he added all the common wit and wisdom of his time, and every where in his works his remarkable knowledge of the world, and nice perception of character, his rare common sense and proverbial wisdom, are apparent. His genius does not soar like Milton's, but is genial and familiar. It shows great tenderness and delicacy, but not the heroic sentiment. It is only a greater portion of humanity with all its weakness. It is not heroic, as Raleigh's, nor pious, as Herbert's, nor philosophical, as Shakspeare's, but it is the child of the English muse, that child which is the father of the man. It is for the most part only an exceeding naturalness, perfect sincerity, with the behavior of a child rather than of a man.

Gentleness and delicacy of character are every where apparent in his verse. The simplest and humblest words come readily to his lips. No one can read the Prioress' tale, understanding the spirit in which it was written, and in which the child sings, *O alma redemptoris mater*, or the account of the departure of Custance with her child upon the sea, in the Man of Lawe's tale, without feeling the native innocence and refinement of the author. Nor can we be mistaken respecting the essential purity of his character, disregarding the apology of the manners of the age. His sincere sorrow in his later days for the grossness of his earlier works, and that he "cannot recall and annull" much that he had written, "but, alas, they are now continued from man to man, and I cannot do what I desire," is not to be forgotten. A simple pathos and feminine gentleness, which Wordsworth occasionally approaches, but does not equal, are peculiar to him. We are tempted to say, that his genius was feminine, not masculine. It was such a feminineness, however, as is rarest to find in woman, though not the appreciation of it. Perhaps it is not to be found at all in woman, but is only the feminine in man.

Such pure, childlike love of nature is not easily to be matched. Nor is it strange, that the poetry of so rude an age should contain such sweet and polished praise of nature, for her charms are not enhanced by civilization, as society's are, but by her own original and permanent refinement she at last subdues and educates man.

Chaucer's remarkably trustful and affectionate character appears in his familiar, yet innocent and reverent, manner of speaking of his God. He comes into his thought without any false reverence, and with no more parade than the zephyr to his ear. If nature is our mother, then God is our father. There is less love and simple practical trust in Shakspeare and Milton. How rarely in our English tongue do we find expressed any affection for God. There is no sentiment so rare as the love of God. Herbert almost alone expresses it, "Ah, my dear God!" Our poet uses similar words, and whenever he sees a beautiful person, or other object, prides himself on the "maistry" of his God. He reverently recommends Dido to be his bride,

> "if that God that heaven and yearth made,
> Would have a love for beauty and goodnesse,
> And womanhede, trouth, and semeliness."

He supplies the place to his imagination of the saints of the Catholic calendar, and has none of the attributes of a Scandinavian deity.

But, in justification of our praise, we must refer the hearer to his works themselves; to the Prologue to the Canterbury Tales, the account of Gentilesse, the Flower and the Leaf, the stories of Griselda, Virginia, Ariadne, and Blanche the Dutchesse, and much more of less distinguished merit. There are many poets of more taste and better manners, who knew how to leave out their dulness, but such negative genius cannot detain us long; we shall return to Chaucer still with love. Even the clown has taste, whose dictates, though he disregards them, are higher and purer than those which the artist obeys; and some natures, which are rude and ill developed, have yet a higher standard of perfection, than others which are refined and well balanced. Though the peasant's cot is dark, it has the evening star for taper, while the nobleman's saloon is meanly lighted. If we have to wander through many dull and prosaic passages in Chaucer, we have at least the satisfaction of knowing that it is not an artificial dulness, but too easily matched by many passages in life, and it is, perhaps, more pleasing, after all, to meet with a fine thought in its natural setting. We confess we feel a disposition commonly to concentrate sweets, and accumulate pleasures, but the poet may be presumed always to speak as a traveller, who leads us through a varied scenery, from one eminence to another, and, from time to time, a single casual thought rises naturally and inevitably, with such majesty and escort only as the first stars at evening. And surely fate has enshrined it in these circumstances for some end. Nature strews her nuts and flowers broadcast, and never collects them into heaps. This was the soil it grew in, and this the hour it bloomed in; if sun, wind, and rain, came here to cherish and expand the flower, shall not we come here to pluck it?

A true poem is distinguished, not so much by a felicitous expression, or any thought it suggests, as by the atmosphere which surrounds it. Most have beauty of outline merely, and are striking as the form and bearing of a stranger, but true verses come toward us indistinctly, as the very kernel of all friendliness, and envelope us in their spirit and fragrance. Much of our poetry has the very best manners, but no character. It is only an unusual precision and elasticity of speech, as if its author had taken, not an intoxicating draught, but an electuary. It has the distinct outline of sculpture, and chronicles an early hour. Under the influence of passion all men speak thus distinctly, but wrath is not always divine.

There are two classes of men called poets. The one cultivates life, the other art; one seeks food for nutriment, the other for flavor; one satisfies hunger, the other gratifies the palate. There are two kinds of writing, both great and rare; one that of genius, or the inspired, the other of intellect and taste, in the intervals of inspiration. The former is above criticism, always correct, giving the law to criticism. It vibrates and pulsates with life forever. It is sacred, and to be read with reverence, as the works of nature are studied. There are few instances of a sustained style of this kind; perhaps every man has spoken words, but the speaker is then careless of the record. Such a style removes us out of personal relations with its author, we do not take his words on our lips, but his sense into our hearts. It is the stream of inspiration, which bubbles out, now here, now there, now in this man, now in that. It matters not through what ice-crystals it is seen, now a fountain, now the ocean stream running under ground. It is in Shakspeare, Alpheus, in Burns, Arethuse; but ever the same. The other is self-possessed and wise. It is reverent of genius, and greedy of inspiration. It is conscious in the highest and the least degree. It consists with the most perfect command of the faculties. It dwells in a repose as of the desert, and objects are as distinct in it as oases or palms in the horizon of sand. The train of thought moves with subdued and measured step, like a caravan. But the pen is only an instrument in its hand, and not instinct with life, like a longer arm. It leaves a thin varnish or glaze over all its work. The works of Goethe furnish remarkable instances of the latter.

There is no just and serene criticism as yet. Our taste is too delicate and particular. It says nay to the poet's work, but never yea to his hope. It invites him to adorn his deformities, and not to cast them off by expansion, as the tree its bark. We are a people who live in a bright light, in houses of pearl and porcelain, and drink only light wines, whose teeth are easily set on edge by the least natural sour. If we had been consulted, the back bone of the earth would have been made, not of granite, but of Bristol spar. A modern author would have died in infancy in a ruder age. But the poet is something more than a scald, "a smoother and polisher of language"; he is a Cincinnatus in literature, and occupies no west end of the world, but, like the sun, indifferently selects his rhymes, and with a liberal taste weaves into his verse the planet and the stubble.

In these old books the stucco has long since crumbled away, and we read what was sculptured in the granite. They are rude and massive in their proportions, rather than smooth and delicate in their finish. The workers in stone polish only their chimney ornaments, but their pyramids are roughly done. There is a soberness in a rough aspect, as of unhewn granite, which addresses a depth in us, but a polished surface hits only the ball of the eye. The true finish is the work of time and the use to which a thing is put. The elements are still polishing the pyramids. Art may varnish and gild, but it can do no more. A work of genius is rough-hewn from the first, because it anticipates the lapse of time, and has an in-grained polish, which still appears when fragments are broken off, an essential quality of its substance. Its beauty is at the same time its strength, and it breaks with a lustre. The great poem must have the stamp of greatness as well as its essence. The reader easily goes within the shallowest contemporary poetry, and informs it with all the life and promise of the day, as the pilgrim goes within the temple, and hears the faintest strains of the worshippers; but it will have to speak to posterity, traversing these deserts, through the ruins of its outmost walls, by the grandeur and beauty of its proportions.

Herald of Freedom

W̲E̲ H̲A̲V̲E̲ occasionally, for several years, met with a number of this spirited journal, edited, as abolitionists need
not be informed, by Nathaniel P. Rogers, once a counsellor at
law in Plymouth, still further up the Merrimack, but now, in
his riper years, come down the hills thus far, to be the Herald
of Freedom to those parts. We have been refreshed not a little by the cheap cordial of his editorials, flowing like his own
mountain-torrents, now clear and sparkling, now foaming and
gritty, and always spiced with the essence of the fir and the
Norway pine; but never dark nor muddy, nor threatening
with smothered murmurs, like the rivers of the plain. The effect of one of his effusions reminds us of what the hy-
dropathists say about the electricity in fresh spring-water,
compared with that which has stood over night to suit weak
nerves. We do not know of another notable and public instance of such pure, youthful, and hearty indignation at all
wrong. The church itself must love it, if it have any heart,
though he is said to have dealt rudely with its sanctity. His
clean attachment to the right, however, sanctions the severest
rebuke we have read.

We have neither room, nor inclination, to criticise this paper, or its cause, at length, but would speak of it in the free
and uncalculating spirit of its author. Mr. Rogers seems to us
to occupy an honorable and manly position in these days, and
in this country, making the press a living and breathing organ
to reach the hearts of men, and not merely "fine paper, and
good type," with its civil pilot sitting aft, and magnanimously
waiting for the news to arrive,—the vehicle of the earliest
news, but the *latest intelligence*,—recording the indubitable
and last results, the marriages and deaths, alone. The present
editor is wide awake, and standing on the beak of his ship;
not as a scientific explorer under government, but a yankee
sealer, rather, who makes those unexplored continents his
harbors in which to refit for more adventurous cruises. He is
a fund of news and freshness in himself,—has the gift of
speech, and the knack of writing, and if anything important

takes place in the Granite State, we may be sure that we shall hear of it in good season. No other paper that we know keeps pace so well with one forward wave of the restless public thought and sentiment of New England, and asserts so faithfully and ingenuously the largest liberty in all things. There is, beside, more unpledged poetry in his prose, than in the verses of many an accepted rhymer; and we are occasionally advertised by a mellow hunter's note from his trumpet, that, unlike most reformers, his feet are still where they should be, on the turf, and that he looks out from a serener natural life into the turbid arena of politics. Nor is slavery always a sombre theme with him, but invested with the colors of his wit and fancy, and an evil to be abolished by other means than sorrow and bitterness of complaint. He will fight this fight with what cheer may be. But to speak of his composition. It is a genuine yankee style, without fiction,—real guessing and calculating to some purpose, and reminds us occasionally, as does all free, brave, and original writing, of its great master in these days, Thomas Carlyle. It has a life above grammar, and a meaning which need not be parsed to be understood. But like those same mountain-torrents, there is rather too much slope to his channel, and the rainbow sprays and evaporations go double-quick-time to heaven, while the body of his water falls headlong to the plain. We would have more pause and deliberation, occasionally, if only to bring his tide to a head,—more frequent expansions of the stream, still, bottomless mountain tarns, perchance island seas, and at length the deep ocean itself.

We cannot do better than enrich our pages with a few extracts from such articles as we have at hand. Who can help sympathizing with his righteous impatience, when invited to hold his peace or endeavor to convince the understandings of the people by well ordered arguments?

"Bandy *compliments* and *arguments* with the somnambulist, on 'table rock,' when all the waters of Lake Superior are thundering in the great horse-shoe, and deafening the very war of the elements! Would you not shout to him with a clap of thunder through a speaking-trumpet, if you could command it,—if possible to reach his senses in his appaling extremity! Did Jonah *argufy* with the city of Nineveh,—'yet forty days,' cried the vagabond prophet, 'and

Nineveh shall be overthrown!' That was his salutation. And did the 'Property and Standing' turn up their noses at him, and set the mob on to him? Did the clergy *discountenance* him, and call him extravagant, misguided, a divider of churches, a disturber of parishes? What would have become of that city, if they had done this? Did they 'approve his *principles*' but dislike his '*measures*' and his '*spirit*'!!

"Slavery must be cried down, denounced down, ridiculed down, and pro-slavery with it, or rather before it. Slavery will go when pro-slavery starts. The sheep will follow when the bell-wether leads. Down, then, with the bloody system, out of the land with it, and out of the world with it,—into the Red Sea with it. Men *sha'nt* be enslaved in this country any longer. Women and children *sha'nt* be flogged here any longer. If you undertake to hinder us, the worst is your own." . . . "But this is all fanaticism. *Wait and see.*"

He thus raises the anti-slavery 'war-whoop' in New Hampshire, when an important convention is to be held, sending the summons

"To none but the whole-hearted, fully-committed, cross-the-Rubicon spirits." . . . "From rich 'old Cheshire,' from Rockingham, with her horizon setting down away to the salt sea." . . . "From where the sun sets behind Kearsarge, even to where he rises gloriously over *Moses Norris's* own town of *Pittsfield*; and from Amoskeag to Ragged Mountains,—Coos—Upper Coos, home of the everlasting hills, send out your bold advocates of human rights,—wherever they lay, scattered by lonely lake, or Indian stream, or 'Grant,' or 'Location,'—from the trout-haunted brooks of the Amoriscoggin, and where the adventurous streamlet takes up its mountain march for the St. Lawrence.

"Scattered and insulated men, wherever the light of philanthropy and liberty has beamed in upon your solitary spirits, come down to us like your streams and clouds;—and our own Grafton, all about among your dear hills, and your mountain-flanked valleys—whether you *home* along the swift Ammonoosuck, the cold Pemigewassett, or the ox-bowed Connecticut." . . .

"We are slow, brethren, dishonorably slow, in a cause like ours. Our feet should be as 'hinds' feet.' 'Liberty lies bleeding.' The leaden-colored wing of slavery obscures the land with its baleful shadow. Let us come together, and inquire at the hand of the Lord, what is to be done."

And again; on occasion of the New England Convention, in the Second-Advent Tabernacle, in Boston, he desires to try one more blast, as it were, 'on Fabyan's White Mountain horn.'

"Ho, then, people of the Bay State,—men, women, and children; children, women, and men, scattered friends of the *friendless*, wheresoever ye inhabit,—if habitations ye have, as such friends have not *always*,—along the sea-beat border of Old Essex and the Puritan Landing, and up beyond sight of the sea-cloud, among the inland hills, where the sun rises and sets upon the dry land, in that vale of the Connecticut, too fair for human content, and too fertile for virtuous industry,—where deepens that haughtiest of earth's streams, on its seaward way, proud with the pride of old Massachusetts. Are there any friends of the friendless negro haunting such a valley as this? In God's name, I fear there are none, or few, for the very scene looks apathy and oblivion to the genius of humanity. I blow you the summons though. Come, if any of you are there.

"And gallant little Rhode Island; *transcendent* abolitionists of the tiny commonwealth. I need not call you. You are *called* the year round, and, instead of sleeping in your tents, stand harnessed, and with trumpets in your hands,—every one!

"Connecticut! yonder, the home of the Burleighs, the Monroes, and the Hudsons, and the native land of old George Benson! are you ready? 'All ready!'

"Maine here, off east, looking from my mountain post, like an everglade. Where is your Sam. Fessenden, who stood storm-proof 'gainst New Organization in '38? Has he too much name as a jurist and an orator, to be found at a New England Convention in '43? God forbid. Come one and all of you from 'Down East,' to Boston, on the 30th, and let the sails of your coasters whiten all the sea-road. Alas! there are scarce enough of you to man a fishing boat. Come up, mighty in your fewness.

"And green Vermont, what has become of your anti-slavery host,— thick as your mountain maples,—mastering your very politics,—not by balance of power, but by sturdy majority. Where are you now? Will you be at the *Advent* Meeting on the 30th of May? Has anti-slavery waxed too trying for your off-hand, how-are-ye, humanity? Have you heard the voice of Freedom of late? Next week will answer.

"Poor, cold, winter-ridden New-Hampshire,—winter-killed, I like to have said,—she will be there, bare-foot, and bare-legged, making tracks like her old bloody-footed volunteers at Trenton. She will be there, if she can work her passage. I guess her minstrelsy* will,—for birds can go independently of car, or tardy stage-coach." . . .

"Let them come as Macaulay says they did to the siege of Rome, when they did not leave old men and women enough to *begin* the harvests. Oh how few we should be, if every soul of us were there.

*The Hutchinsons.

How few, and yet it is the entire muster-roll of Freedom for all the land. We should have to beat up for recruits to complete the army of Gideon, or the *platoon* at the Spartan straits. The foe are like the grasshoppers for *multitude*, as for *moral power*. Thick grass mows the easier, as the Goth said of the enervated millions of falling Rome. They can't stand too thick, nor too tall for the anti-slavery scythe. Only be there at the mowing."

In noticing the doings of another Convention, he thus congratulates himself on the liberty of speech which anti-slavery concedes to all,—even to the Folsoms and Lamsons:—

"Denied a chance to speak elsewhere, because they are not mad after the fashion, they all flock to the anti-slavery boards as a kind of Asylum. And so the poor old enterprise has to father all the oddity of the times. It is a glory to anti-slavery, that she can allow the poor friends the right of speech. I hope she will always keep herself able to afford it. Let the constables wait on the State House, and Jail, and the *Meeting Houses*. Let the door-keeper at the Anti-Slavery Hall be that tall, celestial-faced Woman, that carries the flag on the National Standard, and says, 'without *concealment*,' as well as 'without compromise.' Let every body in, who has sanity enough to see the beauty of brotherly kindness, and let them say their fantasies, and magnanimously bear with them, seeing unkind pro-slavery drives them in upon *us*. We shall have *saner* and *sensibler* meetings then, than all others in the land put together."

More recently, speaking of the use which some of the clergy have made of Webster's plea in the Girard case, as a seasonable aid to the church, he proceeds:

"Webster is a great man, and the clergy run under his wing. They had better employ him as counsel against the Comeouters. He would'nt trust the defence on the Girard will plea though, if they did. He would not risk his fame on it, as a religious argument. He would go and consult William Bassett, of Lynn, on the principles of the 'Comeouters,' to learn their strength; and he would get him a testament, and go into it as he does into the Constitution, and after a year's study of it he would hardly come off in the argument as he did from the conflict with Carolina Hayne. On looking into the case, he would advise the clergy not to go to trial,—to settle,—or, if they could'nt to 'leave it out' to a reference of 'orthodox deacons.' "

We will quote from the same sheet his indignant and touching satire on the funeral of those public officers who were killed by the explosion on board the Princeton, together with the President's slave; an accident which reminds us how closely slavery is linked with the government of this nation. The President coming to preside over a nation of *free* men, and the man who stands *next to him a slave*!

"I saw account," says he, "of the burial of those slaughtered politicians. The hearses passed along, of Upshur, Gilmer, Kennon, Maxcy, and Gardner,—but the dead slave, who fell in company with them on the deck of the Princeton, was not there. He was held their equal by the impartial gun-burst, but not allowed by the *bereaved* nation a share in the funeral." . . . "Out upon their funeral, and upon the paltry procession that went in its train. Why did'nt they enquire for the body of the *other man* who fell on that deck! And why has'nt the nation inquired, and its press? I saw account of the scene in a barbarian print, called the Boston Atlas, and it was dumb on the absence of that body, as if no such man had fallen. Why, I demand in the name of human nature, was that sixth man of the game brought down by that great shot, left unburied and above ground,— for there is no account yet that his body has been allowed the rites of sepulture." . . . "They did'nt bury him even as a slave. They did'nt assign him a jim-crow place in that solemn procession, that he might follow to wait upon his enslavers in the land of spirits. They have gone there without slaves or waiters." . . . "The poor black man,—they enslaved and imbruted him all his life, and now he is dead, they have, for aught appears, left him to decay and waste above ground. Let the civilized world take note of the circumstance."

Such timely, pure, and unpremeditated expressions of a public sentiment, such publicity of genuine indignation and humanity, as abound every where in this journal, are the most generous gifts which a man can make.

But since our voyage Rogers has died, and now there is no one in New England to express the indignation or contempt which may still be felt at any cant or inhumanity.

When, on a certain occasion, one said to him, "Why do you go about as you do, agitating the community on the subject of abolition? Jesus Christ never preached abolitionism:" he replied, "Sir, I have two answers to your appeal to Jesus Christ. First, I deny your proposition, that he never preached abolition. That single precept of his—'Whatsoever ye would that men should do to you, do ye even so to them'—reduced to *practice*, would abolish slavery over the whole earth in twenty-four hours. That is my first answer. I deny your proposition. Secondly, granting your proposition to be true— and admitting what I deny—that Jesus Christ did not preach the abolition of slavery, then I say, *he did'nt do his duty.*"

His was not the wisdom of the head, but of the heart. If perhaps he had all the faults, he had more than the usual virtues of the radical. He loved his native soil, her hills and streams, like a Burns or Scott. As he rode to an antislavery convention, he viewed the country with a poet's eye, and some of his letters written back to his editorial substitute contain as true and pleasing pictures of New England life and scenery as are anywhere to be found.

Whoever heard of Swamscot before? "Swamscot is all fishermen. Their business is all on the deep. Their village is ranged along the ocean margin, where their brave little fleets lay drawn up, and which are out at day-break on the mighty blue—where you may see them brooding at anchor—still and intent at their *profound* trade, as so many flies on the back of a wincing horse, and for whose wincings they care as little as the Swamscot Fishers heed the restless heavings of the sea around their barks. Every thing about savors of fish. Nets hang out on every enclosure. Flakes, for curing the fish are attached to almost every dwelling. Every body has a boat—and you'll see a huge pair of sea boots lying before almost every door. The air too savors strongly of the common finny vocation. Beautiful little beaches slope out from the dwellings into the Bay, all along the village—where the fishing boats lie keeled up, at low water, with their useless anchors hooked deep into the sand. A stranded bark is a sad sight—especially if it is above high water mark, where the next tide can't relieve it and set it afloat again. The Swamscot boats though, all look cheery, and as if sure of the next sea-flow. The people are said to be the freest in the region—owing perhaps to their bold and adventurous life. The Priests can't ride them *out into the deep*, as they can the shore folks."

His style and vein though often exaggerated and affected were more native to New England than those of any of her sons, and unfinished as his pieces were, yet their literary merit has been overlooked.

Wendell Phillips Before Concord Lyceum

CONCORD, MASS. MARCH 12TH, 1845.

Mr. Editor:

We have now, for the third winter, had our spirits refreshed, and our faith in the destiny of the commonwealth strengthened, by the presence and the eloquence of Wendell Phillips; and we wish to tender to him our thanks and our sympathy. The admission of this gentleman into the Lyceum has been strenuously opposed by a respectable portion of our fellow citizens, who themselves, we trust, whose descendants, at least, we know, will be as faithful conservers of the true order, whenever that shall be the order of the day,—and in each instance, the people have voted that they *would hear him*, by coming themselves and bringing their friends to the lecture room, and being very silent that they *might* hear. We saw some men and women, who had long ago *come out, going in* once more through the free and hospitable portals of the Lyceum; and many of our neighbors confessed, that they had had a 'sound season' this once.

It was the speaker's aim to show what the state, and above all the church, had to do, and now, alas! have done, with Texas and slavery, and how much, on the other hand, the individual should have to do with church and state. These were fair themes, and not mistimed; and his words were addressed to 'fit audience, *and not* few.'

We must give Mr. Phillips the credit of being a clean, erect, and what was once called a consistent man. He at least is not responsible for slavery, nor for American Independence; for the hypocrisy and superstition of the church, nor the timidity and selfishness of the state; nor for the indifference and willing ignorance of any. He stands so distinctly, so firmly, and so effectively, alone, and one honest man is so much more than a host, that we cannot but feel that he does himself injustice when he reminds us of 'the American Society, which he represents.' It is rare that we have the pleasure of listening to so clear and orthodox a speaker, who obviously has so few cracks or flaws in his moral nature—who, having words at his command in a remarkable degree, has much more than words, if these should fail, in his unquestionable earnestness and integrity—and, aside from their admiration at his rhetoric, secures the genuine respect of his audience. He unconsciously tells his biography as he proceeds, and we see him early and earnestly deliberating on these subjects, and wisely and bravely, without counsel or consent of any, occupying a ground at first, from which the varying tides of public opinion cannot drive him.

No one could mistake the genuine modesty and truth with which he affirmed, when speaking of the framers of the Constitution,—'I am wiser than they,' which with him has improved these sixty years' experience of its working; or the uncompromising consistency and frankness of the prayer which concluded, not like the Thanksgiving proclamations, with—'God save the Commonwealth of Massachusetts,' but God dash it into a thousand pieces, till there shall not remain a fragment on which a man can stand, and dare not tell his name—referring to the case of Frederick _____. To our disgrace we know not what to call him, unless Scotland will lend us the spoils of one of her Douglasses, out of history or fiction, for a season, till we be hospitable and brave enough to hear his proper name,—a fugitive slave in one more sense than we; who has proved himself the possessor of a *fair* intellect, and has won a colorless reputation in these parts; and who, we trust, will be as superior to degradation from the sympathies of Freedom, as from the antipathies of slavery. When, said Mr. Phillips, he communicated to a New-Bedford audience, the other day, his purpose of writing his life, and telling his name, and the name of his master, and the place he ran from, the murmur ran round the room, and was anxiously whispered by the sons of the Pilgrims, 'He had better not!' and it was echoed under the shadow of Concord monument, 'He had better not!'

We would fain express our appreciation of the freedom and steady wisdom, so rare in the reformer, with which he declared that he was not born to abolish slavery, but to do right. We have heard a few, a very few, good political speakers, who afforded us the pleasure of great intellectual power and acuteness, of soldier-like steadiness, and of a graceful and natural oratory; but in this man the audience might detect a sort of moral principle and integrity, which was more stable than their firmness, more discriminating than his own intellect, and more graceful than his rhetoric, which was not working for temporary or trivial ends. It is so rare and encouraging to listen to an orator, who is content with another alliance than with the popular party, or even with the sympathising school of the martyrs, who can afford sometimes to be his own auditor if the mob stay away, and hears himself without reproof, that we feel ourselves in danger of slandering all mankind by affirming, that here is one, who is at the same time an eloquent speaker and a righteous man.

Perhaps, on the whole, the most interesting fact elicited by these addresses, is the readiness of the people at large, of whatever sect or party, to entertain, with good will and hospitality, the most revolutionary and heretical opinions, when frankly and adequately, and in some sort cheerfully, expressed. Such clear and candid declaration of opinion served like an electuary to whet and clarify the intellect of all parties, and furnished each one with an additional argument for that right he asserted.

We consider Mr. Phillips one of the most conspicuous and efficient champions of a true church and state now in the field, and would say to him, and such as are like him—'God speed you.' If you know of any champion in the ranks of his opponents, who has the valor and courtesy even of Paynim chivalry, if not the Christian graces and refinement of this knight, you will do us a service by directing him to these fields forthwith, where the lists are now open, and he shall be hospitably entertained. For as yet the Red-cross knight has shown us only the gallant device upon his shield, and his admirable command of his steed, prancing and curvetting in the empty lists; but we wait to see who, in the actual breaking of lances, will come tumbling upon the plain.

Thomas Carlyle and His Works

THOMAS CARLYLE is a Scotchman, born about fifty years ago, "at Ecclefechan, Annandale," according to one authority. "His parents 'good farmer people,' his father an elder in the Secession church there, and a man of strong native sense, whose words were said to 'nail a subject to the wall.'" We also hear of his "excellent mother," still alive, and of "her fine old covenanting accents, concerting with his transcendental tones." He seems to have gone to school at Annan, on the shore of the Solway Frith, and there, as he himself writes, "heard of famed professors, of high matters classical, mathematical, a whole Wonderland of Knowledge," from Edward Irving, then a young man "fresh from Edinburgh, with college prizes &c."—"come to see our schoolmaster, who had also been his." From this place, they say, you can look over into Wordsworth's country. Here first he may have become acquainted with Nature, with woods, such as are there, and rivers and brooks, some of whose names we have heard, and the last lapses of Atlantic billows. He got some of his education, too, more or less liberal, out of the University of Edinburgh, where, according to the same authority, he had to "support himself," partly by "private tuition, translations for the booksellers, &c.," and afterward, as we are glad to hear, "taught an academy in Dysart, at the same time that Irving was teaching in Kirkaldy," the usual middle passage of a literary life. He was destined for the church, but not by the powers that rule man's life; made his literary début in Fraser's Magazine, long ago; read here and there in English and French, with more or less profit, we may suppose, such of us at least as are not particularly informed, and at length found some words which spoke to his condition in the German language, and set himself earnestly to unravel that mystery—with what success many readers know.

After his marriage he "resided partly at Comely Bank, Edinburgh; and for a year or two at Craigenputtock, a wild and solitary farm-house in the upper part of Dumfriesshire," at which last place, amid barren heather hills, he was visited by our countryman Emerson. With Emerson he still corresponds. He was early intimate with Edward Irving, and continued to be his friend until the latter's death. Concerning this "freest, brotherliest, bravest human soul," and Carlyle's relation to him, those whom it concerns will do well to consult a notice of his death in Fraser's Magazine for 1835, reprinted in the Miscellanies. He also corresponded with Goethe. Laterly, we hear, the poet Sterling was his only intimate acquaintance in England.

He has spent the last quarter of his life in London, writing books; has the fame, as all readers know, of having made England acquainted with Germany, in late years, and done much else that is novel and remarkable in literature. He especially is the literary man of those parts. You may imagine him living in altogether a retired and simple way, with small family, in a quiet part of London, called Chelsea, a little out of the din of commerce, in "Cheyne Row," there, not far from the "Chelsea Hospital." "A little past this, and an old ivy-clad church, with its buried generations lying around it," writes one traveller, "you come to an antique street running at right angles with the Thames, and, a few steps from the river, you find Carlyle's name on the door."

"A Scotch lass ushers you into the second story front chamber, which is the spacious workshop of the world maker." Here he sits a long time together, with many books and papers about him; many new books, we have been told, on the upper shelves, uncut, with the "author's respects" in them; in late months, with many manuscripts in an old English hand, and innumerable pamphlets, from the public libraries, relating to the Cromwellian period; now, perhaps, looking out into the street on brick and pavement, for a change, and now upon some rod of grass ground in the rear; or, perchance, he steps over to the British Museum, and makes that his studio for the time. This is the fore part of the day; that is the way with literary men commonly; and then in the afternoon, we presume, he takes a short run of a mile or so through the suburbs out into the country; we think he would run that way, though so short a trip might not take him to very sylvan or rustic places. In the meanwhile, people are calling to *see* him, from various quarters, very few worthy of being *seen* by him, "distinguished travellers from America," not a few, to all and sundry of whom he gives freely of his yet unwritten rich and flashing soliloquy, in exchange for whatever they may have to offer; speaking his English, as they say, with a "broad Scotch accent," talking, to their astonishment and to ours, very much as he writes, a sort of Carlylese, his discourse "coming to its climaxes, ever and anon, in long, deep, chest-shaking bursts of laughter."

He goes to Scotland sometimes to visit his native heath-clad hills, having some interest still in the earth there; such names as Craigenputtock and Ecclefechan, which we have already quoted, stand for habitable places there to him; or he rides to the seacoast of England in his vacations, upon his horse Yankee, bought by the sale of his books here, as we have been told.

How, after all, he gets his living; what proportion of his daily bread he earns by day-labor or job-work with his pen, what he inherits, what steals—questions whose answers are so significant, and not to be omitted in his biography—we, alas! are unable to answer here. It may be worth the while to state that he is not a Reformer, in our sense of the term, eats, drinks, and sleeps, thinks and believes, professes and practices, not according to the New England standard, nor to the Old English wholly. Nevertheless, we are told that he is a sort of lion in certain quarters there, "an amicable centre for men of the most opposite opinions," and "listened to as an oracle," "smoking his perpetual pipe."

A rather tall, gaunt figure, with intent face, dark hair and complexion, and the air of a student; not altogether well in body, from sitting too long in his workhouse, he, born in the border country and descended from moss-troopers, it may be. We have seen several pictures of him here; one, a full length portrait, with hat and overall, if it did not tell us much, told the fewest lies; another, we remember, was well said to have "too combed a look;" one other also we have seen in which we discern some features of the man we are thinking of; but the only ones worth remembering, after all, are those which he has unconsciously drawn of himself.

When we remember how these volumes came over to us, with their encouragement and provocation from month to month, and what commotion they created in many private breasts, we wonder that the country did not ring, from shore to shore, from the Atlantic to the Pacific, with its greeting; and the Boones and Crocketts of the West make haste to hail him, whose wide humanity embraces them too. Of all that the packets have brought over to us, has there been any richer cargo than this? What else has been English news for so long a season? What else, of late years, has been England to us—to us who read books, we mean? Unless we remembered it as the scene where the age of Wordsworth was spending itself, and a few younger muses were trying their wings, and from time to time, as the residence of Landor; Carlyle alone, since the death of Coleridge, has kept the promise of England. It is the best apology for all the bustle and the sin of commerce, that it has made us acquainted with the thoughts of this man. Commerce would not concern us much if it were not for such results as this. New England owes him a debt which she will be slow to recognize. His earlier essays reached us at a time when Coleridge's were the only recent words which had made any notable impression so far, and they found a field unoccupied by him, before yet any words of moment had been uttered in our midst. He had this advantage, too, in a teacher, that he stood near to his pupils; and he has no doubt afforded reasonable encouragement and sympathy to many an independent but solitary thinker. Through him, as usher, we have been latterly, in a great measure, made acquainted with what philosophy and criticism the nineteenth century had to offer—admitted, so to speak, to the privileges of the century; and what he may yet have to say, is still expected here with more interest than any thing else from that quarter.

It is remarkable, but on the whole, perhaps, not to be lamented, that the world is so unkind to a new book. Any distinguished traveller who comes to our shores, is likely to get more dinners and speeches of welcome than he can well dispose of, but the best books, if noticed at all, meet with coldness and suspicion, or, what is worse, gratuitous, off-hand criticism. It is plain that the reviewers, both here and abroad, do not know how to dispose of this man. They approach him too easily, as if he were one of the men of letters about town, who grace Mr. Somebody's administration, merely; but he already belongs to literature, and depends neither on the favor of reviewers, nor the honesty of booksellers, nor the pleasure of readers for his success. He has more to impart than to receive from his generation. He is another such a strong and finished workman in his craft as Samuel Johnson was, and like him, makes the literary class respectable. As few are yet out of their apprenticeship, or even if they learn to be able writers, are at the same time able and valuable thinkers. The aged and critical eye, especially, is incapacitated to appreciate the works of this author. To such their meaning is impalpable and evanescent, and they seem to abound only in obstinate mannerisms, Germanisms, and whimsical ravings of all kinds, with now and then an unaccountably true and sensible remark. On the strength of this last, Carlyle is admitted to have what is called genius. We hardly know an old man to whom these volumes are not hopelessly sealed. The language, they say, is foolishness and a stumbling-block to them; but to many a clear-headed boy, they are plainest English, and despatched with such hasty relish as his bread and milk. The fathers wonder how it is that the children take to this diet so readily, and digest it with so little difficulty. They shake their heads with mistrust at their free and easy delight, and remark that "Mr. Carlyle is a very learned man;" for they, too, not to be out of fashion, have got grammar and dictionary, if the truth were known, and with the best faith cudgelled their brains to get a little way into the jungle, and they could not but confess, as often as they found the clue, that it was as intricate as Blackstone to follow, if you read it honestly. But merely reading, even with the best intentions, is not enough, you must almost have written these books yourself. Only he who has had the good fortune to read them in the nick of time, in the most perceptive and recipient season of life, can give any adequate account of them.

Many have tasted of this well with an odd suspicion, as if it were some fountain Arethuse which had flowed under the sea from Germany, as if the materials of his books had lain in some garret there, in danger of being appropriated for waste paper. Over what German ocean, from what Hercynian forest, he has been imported, piece-meal, into England, or whether he has now all arrived, we are not informed. This article is not invoiced in Hamburg, nor in London. Perhaps it was contraband. However, we suspect that this sort of goods cannot be imported in this way. No matter how skillful the stevedore, all things being got into sailing trim, wait for a Sunday, and aft wind, and then weigh anchor, and run up the main-sheet—straightway what of transcendent and permanent value is there resists the aft wind, and will doggedly stay behind that Sunday—it does not travel Sundays; while biscuit and pork make headway, and sailors cry heave-yo! it must part company, if it open a seam. It is not quite safe to send out a venture in this kind, unless yourself go supercargo. Where a man goes, there he is; but the slightest virtue is immovable—it is real estate, not personal; who would keep it, must consent to be bought and sold with it.

However, we need not dwell on this charge of a German extraction, it being generally admitted, by this time, that Carlyle is English, and an inhabitant of London. He has the English for his mother tongue, though with a Scotch accent, or never so many accents, and thoughts also, which are the legitimate growth of native soil, to utter therewith. His style is eminently colloquial—and no wonder it is strange to meet with in a book. It is not literary or classical; it has not the music of poetry, nor the pomp of philosophy, but the rhythms and cadences of conversation endlessly repeated. It resounds with emphatic, natural, lively, stirring tones, muttering, rattling, exploding, like shells and shot, and with like execution. So far as it is a merit in composition, that the written answer to the spoken word, and the spoken word to a fresh and pertinent thought in the mind, as well as to the half thoughts, the tumultuary misgivings and expectancies, this author is, perhaps, not to be matched in literature. In the streets men laugh and cry, but in books, never; they "whine, put finger i' the eye, and sob" only. One would think that all books of late, had adopted the falling inflexion. "A mother, if she wishes to sing her child to sleep," say the musical men, "will always adopt the falling inflexion." Would they but choose the rising inflexion, and wake the child up for once.

He is no mystic either, more than Newton or Arkwright, or Davy—and tolerates none. Not one obscure line, or half line, did he ever write. His meaning lies plain as the daylight, and he who runs may read; indeed, only he who runs *can* read, and keep up with the meaning. It has the distinctness of picture to his mind, and he tells us only what he sees printed in largest English type upon the face of things. He utters substantial English thoughts in plainest English dialects; for it must be confessed, he speaks more than one of these. All the shires of England, and all the shires of Europe, are laid under contribution to his genius; for to be English does not mean to be exclusive and narrow, and adapt one's self to the apprehension of his nearest neighbor only. And yet no writer is more thoroughly Saxon. In the translation of those fragments of Saxon poetry, we have met with the same rhythm that occurs so often in his poem on the French Revolution. And if you would know where many of those obnoxious Carlyleisms and Germanisms came from, read the best of Milton's prose, read those speeches of Cromwell which he has brought to light, or go and listen once more to your mother's tongue. So much for his German extraction.

Indeed, for fluency and skill in the use of the English tongue, he is a master unrivaled. His felicity and power of expression surpass even any of his special merits as a historian and critic. Therein his experience has not failed him, but furnished him with such a store of winged, aye, and legged words, as only a London life, perchance, could give account of; we had not understood the wealth of the language before. Nature is ransacked, and all the resorts and purlieus of humanity are taxed, to furnish the fittest symbol for his thought. He does not go to the dictionary, the word-book, but to the word-manufactory itself, and has made endless work for the lexicographers—yes, he has that same English for his mother-tongue, that you have, but with him it is no dumb, muttering, mumbling faculty, concealing the thoughts, but a keen, unwearied, resistless weapon. He has such command of it as neither you nor I have; and it would be well for any who have a lost horse to advertise, or a town-meeting warrant, or a sermon, or a letter to write, to study this universal letter-writer, for he knows more than the grammar or the dictionary.

The style is worth attending to, as one of the most important features of the man which we at this distance can discern. It is for once quite equal to the matter. It can carry all its load, and never breaks down nor staggers. His books are solid and workmanlike, as all that England does; and they are graceful and readable also. They tell of huge labor done, well done, and all the rubbish swept away, like the bright cutlery which glitters in shop-windows, while the coke and ashes, the turnings, filings, dust, and borings, lie far away at Birmingham, unheard of. He is a masterly clerk, scribe, reporter, and writer. He can reduce to writing most things—gestures, winks, nods, significant looks, patois, brogue, accent, pantomime, and how much that had passed for silence before, does he represent by written words. The countryman who puzzled the city lawyer, requiring him to write, among other things, his call to his horses, would hardly have puzzled him; he would have found a word for it, all right and classical, that would have started his team for him. Consider the ceaseless tide of speech forever flowing in countless cellars, garrets, *parlors*; that of the French, says Carlyle, "only ebbs toward the short hours of night," and what a drop in the bucket is the printed word. Feeling, thought, speech, writing, and we might add, poetry, inspiration—for so the circle is completed; how they gradually dwindle at length, passing through successive colanders, into your history and classics, from the roar of the ocean, the murmur of the forest, to the squeak of a mouse; so much only parsed and spelt out, and punctuated, at last. The few who can talk like a book, they only get reported commonly. But this writer reports a new "Lieferung."

One wonders how so much, after all, was expressed in the old way, so much here depends upon the emphasis, tone, pronunciation, style, and spirit of the reading. No writer uses so profusely all the aids to intelligibility which the printer's art affords. You wonder how others had contrived to write so many pages without emphatic or italicised words, they are so expressive, so natural, so indispensable here, as if none had ever used the demonstrative pronouns demonstratively before. In another's sentences the thought, though it may be immortal, is, as it were, embalmed, and does not *strike* you, but here it is so freshly living, even the body of it, not having passed through the ordeal of death, that it stirs in the very extremities, and the smallest particles and pronouns are all alive with it. It is not simple dictionary *it*, yours or mine, but IT. The words did not come at the command of grammar, but of a tyrannous, inexorable meaning; not like standing soldiers, by vote of parliament, but any able-bodied countryman pressed into the service, for "sire, it is not a revolt, it is a revolution."

We have never heard him speak, but we should say that Carlyle was a rare talker. He has broken the ice, and streams freely forth like a spring torrent. He does not trace back the stream of his thought, silently adventurous, up to its fountain-head, but is borne away with it, as it rushes through his brain like a torrent to overwhelm and fertilize. He holds a talk with you. His audience is such a tumultuous mob of thirty thousand, as assembled at the University of Paris, before printing was invented. Philosophy, on the other hand, does not talk, but write, or, when it comes personally before an audience, lecture or read; and therefore it must be read tomorrow, or a thousand years hence. But the talker must naturally be attended to at once; he does not talk on without an audience; the winds do not long bear the sound of his voice. Think of Carlyle reading his French Revolution to any audience. One might say it was never written, but spoken; and thereafter reported and printed, that those not within sound of his voice might know something about it. Some men read to you something which they have written, in a dead *language*, of course, but it may be in a living *letter*, in a Syriac, or Roman, or Runic character. Men must *speak* English who can *write* Sanscrit; and they must speak a modern language who write, perchance, an ancient and universal one. We do not live in those days when the learned used a learned language. There is no writing of Latin with Carlyle, but as Chaucer, with all reverence to Homer, and Virgil, and Messieurs the Normans, sung his poetry in the homely Saxon tongue,—and Locke has at least the merit of having done philosophy into English—so Carlyle has done a different philosophy still further into English, and thrown open the doors of literature and criticism to the populace.

Such a style—so diversified and variegated! It is like the face of a country; it is like a New England landscape, with farm-houses and villages, and cultivated spots, and belts of forests and blueberry-swamps round about it, with the fragrance of shad-blossoms and violets on certain winds. And as for the reading of it, it is novel enough to the reader who has used only the diligence, and old-line mail-coach. It is like travelling, sometimes on foot, sometimes in a gig tandem; sometimes in a full coach, over highways, mended and unmended, for which you will prosecute the town; on level roads, through French departments, by Simplon roads over the Alps, and now and then he hauls up for a relay, and yokes in an unbroken colt of a Pegasus for a leader, driving off by cart-paths, and across lots, by corduroy roads and gridiron bridges; and where the bridges are gone, not even a string-piece left, and the reader has to set his breast and swim. You have got an expert driver this time, who has driven ten thousand miles, and was never known to upset; can drive six in hand on the edge of a precipice, and touch the leaders anywhere with his snapper.

With wonderful art he grinds into paint for his picture all his moods and experiences, so that all his forces may be brought to the encounter. Apparently writing without a particular design or responsibility, setting down his soliloquies from time to time, taking advantage of all his humors, when at length the hour comes to declare himself, he puts down in plain English, without quotation marks, what he, Thomas Carlyle, is ready to defend in the face of the world, and fathers the rest, often quite as defensible, only more modest, or plain spoken, or insinuating, upon "Sauerteig," or some other gentleman long employed on the subject. Rolling his subject how many ways in his mind, he meets it now face to face, wrestling with it at arm's length, and striving to get it down, or throws it over his head; and if that will not do, or whether it will do or not, tries the back-stitch and side-hug with it, and downs it again—scalps it, draws and quarters it, hangs it in chains, and leaves it to the winds and dogs. With his brows knit, his mind made up, his will resolved and resistless, he advances, crashing his way through the host of weak, half-formed, *dilettante* opinions, honest and dishonest ways of thinking, with their standards raised, sentimentalities and conjectures, and tramples them all into dust. See how he prevails; you don't even hear the groans of the wounded and dying. Certainly it is not so well worth the while to look through any man's eyes at history, for the time, as through his; and his way of looking at things is fastest getting adopted by his generation.

It is not in man to determine what his style shall be. He might as well determine what his thoughts shall be. We would not have had him write always as in the chapter on Burns, and the Life of Schiller, and elsewhere. No; his thoughts were ever irregular and impetuous. Perhaps as he grows older and writes more he acquires a truer expression; it is in some respects manlier, freer, struggling up to a level with its fountain-head. We think it is the richest prose style we know of.

Who cares what a man's style is, so it is intelligible—as intelligible as his thought. Literally and really, the style is no more than the *stylus*, the pen he writes with—and it is not worth scraping and polishing, and gilding, unless it will write his thoughts the better for it. It is something for use, and not to look at. The question for us is not whether Pope had a fine style, wrote with a peacock's feather, but whether he uttered useful thoughts. Translate a book a dozen times from one language to another, and what becomes of its style? Most books would be worn out and disappear in this ordeal. The pen which wrote it is soon destroyed, but the poem survives. We believe that Carlyle has, after all, more readers, and is better known to-day for this very originality of style, and that posterity will have reason to thank him for emancipating the language, in some measure, from the fetters which a merely conservative, aimless, and pedantic literary class had imposed upon it, and setting an example of greater freedom and naturalness. No man's thoughts are new, but the style of their expression is the never failing novelty which cheers and refreshes men. If we were to answer the question, whether the mass of men, as we know them, talk as the standard authors and reviewers write, or rather as this man writes, we should say that he alone begins to write their language at all, and that the former is, for the most part, the mere effigies of a language, not the best method of concealing one's thoughts even, but frequently a method of doing without thoughts at all.

In his graphic description of Richter's style, Carlyle describes his own pretty nearly; and no doubt he first got his own tongue loosened at that fountain, and was inspired by it to equal freedom and originality. "The language," as he says of Richter, "groans with indescribable metaphors and allusions to all things, human and divine, flowing onward, not like a river, but like an inundation; circling in complex eddies, chafing and gurgling, now this way, now that;" but in Carlyle, "the proper current" never "sinks out of sight amid the boundless uproar." Again: "His very language is Titanian—deep, strong, tumultuous, shining with a thousand hues, fused from a thousand elements, and winding in labyrinthic mazes."

In short, if it is desirable that a man be eloquent, that he talk much, and address himself to his own age mainly, then this is not a bad style of doing it. But if it is desired rather that he pioneer into unexplored regions of thought, and speak to silent centuries to come, then, indeed, we could wish that he had cultivated the style of Goethe more, that of Richter less; not that Goethe's is the kind of utterance most to be prized by mankind, but it will serve for a model of the best that can be successfully cultivated.

But for style, and fine writing, and Augustan ages—that is but a poor style, and vulgar writing, and a degenerate age, which allows us to remember these things. This man has something to communicate. Carlyle's are not, in the common sense, works of art in their origin and aim; and yet, perhaps, no living English writer evinces an equal literary talent. They are such works of art only as the plough, and corn-mill, and steam-engine—not as pictures and statues. Others speak with greater emphasis to scholars, as such, but none so earnestly and effectually to all who can read. Others give their advice, he gives his sympathy also. It is no small praise that he does not take upon himself the airs, has none of the whims, none of the pride, the nice vulgarities, the starched, impoverished isolation, and cold glitter of the spoiled children of genius. He does not need to husband his pearl, but excels by a greater humanity and sincerity.

He is singularly serious and untrivial. We are every where impressed by the rugged, unwearied, and rich sincerity of the man. We are sure that he never sacrificed one jot of his honest thought to art or whim, but to utter himself in the most direct and effectual way, that is the endeavor. These are merits which will wear well. When time has worn deeper into the substance of these books, this grain will appear. No such sermons have come to us here out of England, in late years, as those of this preacher; sermons to kings, and sermons to peasants, and sermons to all intermediate classes. It is in vain that John Bull, or any of his cousins, turns a deaf ear, and pretends not to hear them, nature will not soon be weary of repeating them. There are words less obviously true, more for the ages to hear, perhaps, but none so impossible for this age not to hear. What a cutting cimiter was that "Past and Present," going through heaps of silken stuffs, and glibly through the necks of men, too, without their knowing it, leaving no trace. He has the earnestness of a prophet. In an age of pedantry and dilettantism, he has no grain of these in his composition. There is no where else, surely, in recent readable English, or other books, such direct and effectual teaching, reproving, encouraging, stimulating, earnestly, vehemently, almost like Mahomet, like Luther; not looking behind him to see how his *Opera Omnia* will look, but forward to other work to be done. His writings are a gospel to the young of this generation; they will hear his manly, brotherly speech with responsive joy, and press forward to older or newer gospels.

We should omit a main attraction in these books, if we said nothing of their humor. Of this indispensable pledge of sanity, without some leaven of which the abstruse thinker may justly be suspected of mysticism, fanaticism, or insanity, there is a superabundance in Carlyle. Especially the transcendental philosophy needs the leaven of humor to render it light and digestible. In his later and longer works it is an unfailing accompaniment, reverberating through pages and chapters, long sustained without effort. The very punctuation, the italics, the quotation marks, the blank spaces and dashes, and the capitals, each and all are pressed into its service.

Every man, of course, has his fane, from which even the most innocent conscious humor is excluded; but in proportion as the writer's position is high above his fellows, the range of his humor is extended. To the thinker, all the institutions of men, as all imperfection, viewed from the point of equanimity, are legitimate subjects of humor. Whatever is not necessary, no matter how sad or personal, or universal a grievance, is, indeed, a jest more or less sublime.

Carlyle's humor is vigorous and Titanic, and has more sense in it than the sober philosophy of many another. It is not to be disposed of by laughter and smiles merely; it gets to be too serious for that—only they may laugh who are not hit by it. For those who love a merry jest, this is a strange kind of fun—rather too practical joking, if they understand it. The pleasant humor which the public loves, is but the innocent pranks of the ball-room, harmless flow of animal spirits, the light plushy pressure of dandy pumps, in comparison. But when an elephant takes to treading on your corns, why then you are lucky if you sit high, or wear cowhide. His humor is always subordinate to a serious purpose, though often the real charm for the reader, is not so much in the essential progress and final upshot of the chapter, as in this indirect side-light illustration of every hue. He sketches first with strong, practical English pencil, the essential features in outline, black on white, more faithfully than Dryasdust would have done, telling us wisely whom and what to mark, to save time, and then with brush of camel's hair, or sometimes with more expeditious swab, he lays on the bright and fast colors of his humor everywhere. One piece of solid work, be it known, we have determined to do, about which let there be no jesting, but all things else under the heavens, to the right and left of that, are for the time fair game. To us this humor is not wearisome, as almost every other is. Rabelais, for instance, is intolerable; one chapter is better than a volume—it may be sport to him, but it is death to us. A mere humorist, indeed, is a most unhappy man; and his readers are most unhappy also.

Humor is not so distinct a quality as for the purposes of criticism, it is commonly regarded, but allied to every, even the divinest faculty. The familiar and cheerful conversation about every hearth-side, if it be analyzed, will be found to be sweetened by this principle. There is not only a never-failing, pleasant, and earnest humor kept up there, embracing the domestic affairs, the dinner, and the scolding, but there is also a constant run upon the neighbors, and upon church and state, and to cherish and maintain this, in a great measure, the fire is kept burning, and the dinner provided. There will be neighbors, parties to a very genuine, even romantic friendship, whose whole audible salutation and intercourse, abstaining from the usual cordial expressions, grasping of hands, or affectionate farewells, consists in the mutual play and interchange of a genial and healthy humor, which excepts nothing, not even themselves, in its lawless range. The child plays continually, if you will let it, and all its life is a sort of practical humor of a very pure kind, often of so fine and ethereal a nature, that its parents, its uncles and cousins, can in no wise participate in it, but must stand aloof in silent admiration, and reverence even. The more quiet the more profound it is. Even nature is observed to have her playful moods or aspects, of which man seems sometimes to be the sport.

But, after all, we could sometimes dispense with the humor, though unquestionably incorporated in the blood, if it were replaced by this author's gravity. We should not apply to himself, without qualification, his remarks on the humor of Richter. With more repose in his inmost being, his humor would become more thoroughly genial and placid. Humor is apt to imply but a half satisfaction at best. In his pleasantest and most genial hour, man smiles but as the globe smiles, and the works of nature. The fruits *dry* ripe, and much as we relish some of them in their green and pulpy state, we lay up for our winter store, not out of these, but the rustling autumnal harvests. Though we never weary of this vivacious wit, while we are perusing its work, yet when we remember it from afar, we sometimes feel balked and disappointed, missing the security, the simplicity, and frankness, even the occasional magnanimity of acknowledged dullness and bungling. This never-failing success and brilliant talent become a reproach. To the most practical reader the humor is certainly too obvious and constant a quality. When we are to have dealings with a man, we prize the good faith and valor of soberness and gravity. There is always a more impressive statement than consists with these victorious comparisons. Besides, humor does not wear well. It is commonly enough said, that a joke will not bear repeating. The deepest humor will not keep.

Humors do not circulate but stagnate, or circulate partially. In the oldest literature, in the Hebrew, the Hindoo, the Persian, the Chinese, it is rarely humor, even the most divine, which still survives, but the most sober and private, painful or joyous thoughts, maxims of duty, to which the life of all men may be referred. After time has sifted the literature of a people, there is left only their Scripture, for that is writing, *par excellence.* This is as true of the poets, as of the philosophers and moralists by profession; for what subsides in any of these is the moral only, to re-appear as dry land at some remote epoch.

We confess that Carlyle's humor is rich, deep, and variegated, in direct communication with the back bone and risible muscles of the globe—and there is nothing like it; but much as we relish this jovial, this rapid and delugeous way of conveying one's views and impressions, when we would not converse but meditate, we pray for a man's diamond edition of his thought, without the colored illuminations in the margin—the fishes and dragons, and unicorns, the red or the blue ink, but its initial letter in distinct skeleton type, and the whole so clipped and condensed down to the very essence of it, that time will have little to do. We know not but we shall immigrate soon, and would fain take with us all the treasures of the east, and all kinds of *dry*, portable soups, in small tin canisters, which contain whole herds of English beeves, boiled down, will be acceptable.

The difference between this flashing, fitful writing and pure philosophy, is the difference between flame and light. The flame, indeed, yields light, but when we are so near as to observe the flame, we are apt to be incommoded by the heat and smoke. But the sun, that old Platonist, is set so far off in the heavens, that only a genial summer-heat and ineffable day-light can reach us. But many a time, we confess, in wintery weather, we have been glad to forsake the sun-light, and warm us by these Promethean flames.

Carlyle must undoubtedly plead guilty to the charge of mannerism. He not only has his vein, but his peculiar manner of working it. He has a style which can be imitated, and sometimes is an imitator of himself. Every man, though born and bred in the metropolis of the world, will still have some provincialism adhering to him; but in proportion as his aim is simple and earnest, he approaches at once the most ancient and the most modern men. There is no mannerism in the Scriptures. The style of proverbs, and indeed of all *maxims*, whether measured by sentences or by chapters, if they may be said to have any style, is one, and as the expression of one voice, merely an account of the matter by the latest witness. It is one advantage enjoyed by men of science, that they use only formulas which are universal. The common language and the common sense of mankind, it is most uncommon to meet with in the individual. Yet liberty of thought and speech is only liberty to think the universal thought, and speak the universal language of men, instead of being enslaved to a particular mode. Of this universal speech there is very little. It is equable and sure; from a depth within man which is beyond education and prejudice.

Certainly, no critic has anywhere said what is more to the purpose, than this which Carlyle's own writings furnish, which we quote, as well for its intrinsic merit as for its pertinence here. "It is true," says he, thinking of Richter, "the beaten paths of literature lead the safeliest to the goal; and the talent pleases us most, which submits to shine with new gracefulness through old forms. Nor is the noblest and most peculiar mind too noble or peculiar for working by prescribed laws; Sophocles, Shakspeare, Cervantes, and in Richter's own age, Goethe, how little did they innovate on the given forms of composition, how much in the spirit they breathed into them! All this is true; and Richter must lose of our esteem in proportion." And again, in the chapter on Goethe, "We read Goethe for years before we come to see wherein the distinguishing peculiarity of his understanding, of his disposition, even of his way of writing, consists! It seems quite a simple style, [that of his?] remarkable chiefly for its calmness, its perspicuity, in short, its commonness; and yet it is the most uncommon of all styles." And this, too, translated for us by the same pen from Schiller, which we will apply not merely to the outward form of his works, but to their inner form and substance. He is speaking of the artist. "Let some beneficent divinity snatch him, when a suckling, from the breast of his mother, and nurse him with the milk of a better time, that he may ripen to his full stature beneath a distant Grecian sky. And having grown to manhood, let him return, a foreign shape, into his century; not, however, to delight it by his presence, but, dreadful, like the son of Agamemnon, to purify it. The matter of his works he will take from the present, but their form he will derive from a nobler time; nay, from beyond all time, from the absolute unchanging unity of his own nature."

But enough of this. Our complaint is already out of all proportion to our discontent.

Carlyle's works, it is true, have not the stereotyped success which we call classic. They are a rich but inexpensive entertainment, at which we are not concerned lest the host has strained or impoverished himself to feed his guests. It is not the most lasting word, nor the loftiest wisdom, but rather the word which comes last. For his genius it was reserved to give expression to the thoughts which were throbbing in a million breasts. He has plucked the ripest fruit in the public garden; but this fruit already least concerned the tree that bore it, which was rather perfecting the bud at the foot of the leaf stalk. His works are not to be studied, but read with a swift satisfaction. Their flavor and gust is like what poets tell of the froth of wine, which can only be tasted once and hastily. On a review we can never find the pages we had read. The first impression is the truest and the deepest, and there is no reprint, no *double entendre*, so to speak, for the alert reader. Yet they are in some degree true natural products in this respect. All things are but once, and never repeated. The first faint blushes of the morning, gilding the mountain tops, the pale phosphor and saffron-colored clouds do verily transport us to the morning of creation; but what avails it to travel eastward, or look again there an hour hence? We should be as far in the day ourselves, mounting toward our meridian. These works were designed for such complete success that they serve but for a single occasion. It is the luxury of art, when its own instrument is manufactured for each particular and present use. The knife which slices the bread of Jove ceases to be a knife when this service is rendered.

But he is wilfully and pertinaciously unjust, even scurrilous, impolite, ungentlemanly; calls us "Imbeciles," "Dilettantes,"

"Philistines," implying sometimes what would not sound well expressed. If he would adopt the newspaper style, and take back these hard names—but where is the reader who does not derive some benefit from these epithets, applying them to himself? Think not that with each repetition of them there is a fresh overflowing of bile; oh no! Perhaps none at all after the first time, only a faithfulness, the right name being found, to apply it—"They are the same ones we meant before"—and ofttimes with a genuine sympathy and encouragement expressed. Indeed, there appears in all his writings a hearty and manly sympathy with all misfortune and wretchedness, and not a weak and sniveling one. They who suspect a Mephistophiles, or sneering, satirical devil, under all, have not learned the secret of true humor, which sympathizes with the gods themselves, in view of their grotesque, half-finished creatures.

He is, in fact, the best tempered, and not the least impartial of reviewers. He goes out of his way to do justice to profligates and quacks. There is somewhat even Christian, in the rarest and most peculiar sense, in his universal brotherliness, his simple, child-like endurance, and earnest, honest endeavor, with sympathy for the like. And this fact is not insignificant, that he is almost the only writer of biography, of the lives of men, in modern times. So kind and generous a tribute to the genius of Burns cannot be expected again, and is not needed. We honor him for his noble reverence for Luther, and his patient, almost reverent study of Goethe's genius, anxious that no shadow of his author's meaning escape him for want of trustful attention. There is nowhere else, surely, such determined and generous love of whatever is manly in history. His just appreciation of any, even inferior talent, especially of all sincerity, under whatever guise, and all true men of endeavor, must have impressed every reader. Witness the chapters on Werner, Heyne, even Cagliostro, and others. He is not likely to underrate his man. We are surprised to meet with such a discriminator of kingly qualities in these republican and democratic days, such genuine loyalty all thrown away upon the world.

Carlyle, to adopt his own classification, is himself the hero, as literary man. There is no more notable working-man in

England, in Manchester or Birmingham, or the mines round about. We know not how many hours a-day he toils, nor for what wages, exactly, we only know the results for us. We hear through the London fog and smoke the steady systole, diastole, and vibratory hum, from "Somebody's Works" there; the "Print Works," say some; the "Chemicals," say others; where something, at any rate, is manufactured which we remember to have seen in the market. This is the place, then. Literature has come to mean, to the ears of laboring men, something idle, something cunning and pretty merely, because the nine hundred and ninety-nine really write for fame or for amusement. But as the laborer works, and soberly by the sweat of his brow earns bread for his body, so this man *works* anxiously and *sadly*, to get bread of life, and dispense it. We cannot do better than quote his own estimate of labor from Sartor Resartus.

"Two men I honor, and no third. First; the toil-worn craftsman that with earth-made implement laboriously conquers the earth, and makes her man's. Venerable to me is the hard hand; crooked, coarse, wherein, notwithstanding, lies a cunning virtue, indefeasibly royal, as of the sceptre of this planet. Venerable, too, is the rugged face, all weather-tanned, besoiled, with its rude intelligence; for it is the face of a man living manlike. Oh, but the more venerable for thy rudeness, and even because we must pity as well as love thee. Hardly-entreated brother! For us was thy back so bent, for us were thy straight limbs and fingers so deformed; thou wert our conscript, on whom the lot fell, and fighting our battles wert so marred. For in thee, too, lay a god-created form, but it was not to be unfolded; encrusted must it stand with the thick adhesions and defacements of labor; and thy body, like thy soul, was not to know freedom. Yet toil on, toil on; *thou* art in thy duty, be out of it who may; thou toilest for the altogether indispensable, for daily bread."

"A second man I honor, and still more highly; him who is seen toiling for the spiritually indispensable; not daily bread, but the bread of life. Is not he, too, in his duty, endeavoring toward inward harmony, revealing this, by act or by word, through all his outward endeavors, be they high or low? Highest of all, when his outward and his inward endeavor are one; when we can name him Artist; not earthly craftsman only, but inspired thinker, that with heaven-made implement conquers heaven for us. If the poor and humble toil that we have food, must not the high and glorious toil for him in return, that he have light, have guidance, freedom, immortality? These two in all their degrees, I honor; all else is chaff and dust, which let the wind blow whither it listeth."

"Unspeakably touching is it, however, when I find both dignities united; and he that must toil outwardly for the lowest of man's wants, is also toiling inwardly for the highest. Sublimer in this world know I nothing than a peasant saint, could such now anywhere be met with. Such a one will take thee back to Nazareth itself; thou wilt see the splendor of heaven spring forth from the humblest depths of earth, like a light shining in great darkness."

Notwithstanding the very genuine, admirable, and loyal tributes to Burns, Schiller, Goethe, and others, Carlyle is not a critic of poetry. In the book of heroes, Shakspeare, the hero, as poet, comes off rather slimly. His sympathy, as we said, is with the men of endeavor; not using the life got, but still bravely getting their life. "In fact," as he says of Cromwell, "every where we have to notice the decisive, practical *eye* of this man; how he drives toward the practical and practicable; has a genuine insight into what *is* fact." You must have very stout legs to get noticed at all by him. He is thoroughly English in his love of practical men, and dislike for cant, and ardent enthusiastic heads that are not supported by any legs. He would kindly knock them down that they may regain some vigor by touching their mother earth. We have often wondered how he ever found out Burns, and must still refer a good share of his delight in him to neighborhood and early association. The Lycidas and Comus appearing in Blackwood's Magazine, would probably go unread by him, nor lead him to expect a Paradise Lost. The condition of England question is a practical one. The condition of England demands a hero, not a poet. Other things demand a poet; the poet answers other demands. Carlyle in London, with this question pressing on him so urgently, sees no occasion for minstrels and rhapsodists there. Kings may have their bards when there are any kings. Homer would *certainly* go a begging there. He lives in Chelsea, not on the plains of Hindostan, nor on the prairies of the West, where settlers are scarce, and a man must at least go *whistling* to himself.

What he says of poetry is rapidly uttered, and suggestive of a thought, rather than the deliberate development of any. He answers your question, What is poetry? by writing a special poem, as that Norse one, for instance, in the Book of Heroes, altogether wild and original;—answers your question, What is light? by kindling a blaze which dazzles you, and pales sun and moon, and not as a peasant might, by opening a shutter. And, certainly, you would say that this question never could be answered but by the grandest of poems; yet he has not dull breath and stupidity enough, perhaps, to give the most deliberate and universal answer, such as the fates wring from illiterate and unthinking men. He answers like Thor, with a stroke of his hammer, whose dint makes a valley in the earth's surface.

Carlyle is not a *seer*, but a brave looker-on and *reviewer*, not the most free and catholic observer of men and events, for they are likely to find him preoccupied, but unexpectedly free and catholic when they fall within the focus of his lens. He does not live in the present hour, and read men and books as they occur for his theme, but having chosen this, he directs his studies to this end.

But if he supplies us with arguments and illustrations against himself, we will remember that we may perhaps be convicted of error from the same source—stalking on these lofty reviewer's stilts so far from the green pasturage around. If we look again at his page, we are apt to retract somewhat that we have said. Often a genuine poetic feeling dawns through it, like the texture of the earth seen through the dead grass and leaves in the spring. There is indeed more poetry in this author than criticism on poetry. He often reminds us of the ancient Scald, inspired by the grimmer features of life, dwelling longer on Dante than on Shakspeare. We have not recently met with a more solid and unquestionable piece of poetic work than that episode of "The Ancient Monk," in Past and Present, at once idyllic, narrative, heroic; a beautiful restoration of a past age. There is nothing like it elsewhere that we know of. The History of the French Revolution is a poem, at length got translated into prose; an Iliad, indeed, as he himself has it—"The destructive wrath of Sansculottism: this is what we speak, having unhappily no voice for singing."

One improvement we could suggest in this last, as indeed in most epics, that he should let in the sun oftener upon his picture. It does not often enough appear, but it is all revolution, the old way of human life turned simply bottom upward, so that when at length we are inadvertently reminded of the "Brest Shipping," a St. Domingo colony, and that anybody thinks of owning plantations, and simply turning up the soil there, and that now at length, after some years of this revolution, there is a falling off in the importation of sugar, we feel a queer surprise. Had they not sweetened their water with Revolution then? It would be well if there were several chapters headed "Work for the Month"—Revolution-work inclusive, of course—"Altitude of the Sun," "State of the Crops and Markets," "Meteorological Observations," "Attractive Industry," "Day Labor," &c., just to remind the reader that the French peasantry did something beside go without breeches, burn châteaus, get ready knotted cords, and embrace and throttle one another by turns. These things are sometimes hinted at, but they deserve a notice more in proportion to their importance. We want not only a background to the picture, but a ground under the feet also. We remark, too, occasionally, an unphilosophical habit, common enough elsewhere, in Alison's History of Modern Europe, for instance, of saying, undoubtedly with effect, that if a straw had not fallen this way or that, why then—but, of course, it is as easy in philosophy to make kingdoms rise and fall as straws. The old adage is as true for our purpose, which says that a miss is as good as a mile. Who shall say how near the man came to being killed who was not killed? If an apple had not fallen then we had never heard of Newton and the law of gravitation; as if they could not have contrived to let fall a pear as well.

The poet is blithe and cheery ever, and as well as nature. Carlyle has not the simple Homeric health of Wordsworth, nor the deliberate philosophic turn of Coleridge, nor the scholastic taste of Landor, but, though sick and under re-

straint, the constitutional vigor of one of his old Norse heroes, struggling in a lurid light, with Jötuns still, striving to
throw the old woman, and "she was Time"—striving to lift
the big cat—and that was "The Great World-Serpent, which,
tail in mouth, girds and keeps up the whole created world."
The smith, though so brawny and tough, I should not call the
healthiest man. There is too much shop-work, too great extremes of heat and cold, and incessant ten-pound-ten and
thrashing of the anvil, in his life. But the haymaker's is a true
sunny perspiration, produced by the extreme of summer heat
only, and conversant with the blast of the zephyr, not of the
forge-bellows. We know very well the nature of this man's
sadness, but we do not know the nature of his gladness.
There sits Bull in the court all the year round, with his hoarse
bark and discontented growl—not a cross dog, only a canine
habit, verging to madness some think—now separated from
the shuddering travellers only by the paling, now heard afar in
the horizon, even melodious there; baying the moon o'
nights, *baying the sun by day*, with his mastiff mouth. He
never goes after the cows, nor stretches in the sun, nor plays
with the children. Pray give him a longer rope, ye gods, or let
him go at large, and never taste raw meat more.

The poet will maintain serenity in spite of all disappoint-
ments. He is expected to preserve an unconcerned and
healthy outlook over the world while he lives. *Philosophia
practica est eruditionis meta*, philosophy practiced is the goal
of learning; and for that other, *Oratoris est celare artem*, we
might read, *Herois est celare pugnam*, the hero will conceal his
struggles. Poetry is the only life got, the only work done, the
only pure product and free labor of man, performed only
when he has put all the world under his feet, and conquered
the last of his foes.

Carlyle speaks of Nature with a certain unconscious pathos
for the most part. She is to him a receded but ever memorable splendor, casting still a reflected light over all his
scenery. As we read his books here in New England, where
there are potatoes enough, and every man can get his living
peacefully and sportively as the birds and bees, and need think
no more of that, it seems to us as if by the world he often
meant London, at the head of the tide upon the Thames, the

sorest place on the face of the earth, the very citadel of con-
servatism. Possibly a South African village might have furnished a more hopeful, and more exacting audience, or in the
silence of the wilderness and the desert, he might have addressed himself more entirely to his true audience posterity.

In his writings, we should say that he, as conspicuously as
any, though with little enough expressed or even conscious
sympathy, represents the Reformer class, and all the better for
not being the acknowledged leader of any. In him the universal plaint is most settled, unappeasable and serious. Until a
thousand named and nameless grievances are righted, there
will be no repose for him in the lap of nature, or the seclusion
of science and literature. By foreseeing it he hastens the crisis
in the affairs of England, and is as good as many years added
to her history.

As we said, we have no adequate word from him concerning poets—Homer, Shakspeare; nor more, we might add, of
Saints—Jesus; nor philosophers—Socrates, Plato; nor mys-
tics—Swedenborg. He has no articulate sympathy at least
with such as these as yet. Odin, Mahomet, Cromwell, will
have justice at his hands, and we would leave him to write the
eulogies of all the giants of the will, but the kings of men,
whose kingdoms are wholly in the hearts of their subjects,
strictly transcendent and moral greatness, what is highest and
worthiest in character, he is not inclined to dwell upon or
point to. To do himself justice, and set some of his readers
right, he should give us some transcendent hero at length, to
rule his demigods and Titans; develop, perhaps, his reserved
and dumb reverence for Christ, not speaking to a London or
Church of England audience merely. Let *not* "sacred silence
meditate that sacred matter" forever, but let us have sacred
speech and sacred scripture thereon. True reverence is not
necessarily dumb, but ofttimes prattling and hilarious as children in the spring.

Every man will include in his list of worthies those whom
he himself best represents. Carlyle, and our countryman
Emerson, whose place and influence must ere long obtain a
more distinct recognition, are, to a certain extent, the complement of each other. The age could not do with one of
them, it cannot do with both. To make a broad and rude dis-

tinction, to suit our present purpose, the former, as critic, deals with the men of action—Mahomet, Luther, Cromwell; the latter with the thinkers—Plato, Shakspeare, Goethe, for though both have written upon Goethe, they do not meet in him. The one has more sympathy with the heroes, or practical reformers, the other with the observers, or philosophers Put these worthies together, and you will have a pretty fair representation of mankind; yet with one or more memorable exceptions. To say nothing of Christ, who yet awaits a just appreciation from literature, the peacefully practical hero, whom Columbus may represent, is obviously slighted; but above and after all, the Man of the Age, come to be called working-man, it is obvious that none yet speaks to his condition, for the speaker is not yet in his condition. There is poetry and prophecy to cheer him, and advice of the head and heart to the hands; but no very memorable coöperation, it must be confessed, since the Christian era, or rather since Prometheus tried it. It is even a note-worthy fact, that a man addresses effectually in another only himself still, and what he himself does and is, alone can he prompt the other to do and to become. Like speaks to like only; labor to labor, philosophy to philosophy, criticism to criticism, poetry to poetry, &c. Literature speaks how much still to the past, how little to the future, how much to the east, how little to the west—

> In the East fames are won,
> In the West deeds are done.

One more merit in Carlyle, let the subject be what it may, is the freedom of prospect he allows, the entire absence of cant and dogma. He removes many cart-loads of rubbish, and leaves open a broad highway. His writings are all unfenced on the side of the future and the possible. He does not place himself across the passage out of his books, so that none may go freely out, but rather by the entrance, inviting all to come in and go through. No gins, no net-work, no pickets here, to restrain the free thinking reader. In many books called philosophical, we find ourselves running hither and thither, under and through, and sometimes quite unconsciously straddling some imaginary fence-work, which in our clairvoyance we had not noticed, but fortunately, not with such fatal consequences as happen to those birds which fly against a white-washed wall, mistaking it for fluid air. As we proceed the wreck of this dogmatic tissue collects about the organs of our perception, like cobwebs about the muzzles of hunting dogs in dewy mornings. If we look up with such eyes as these authors furnish, we see no heavens, but a low pent-roof of straw or tiles, as if we stood under a shed, with no sky-light through which to glimpse the blue.

Carlyle, though he does but inadvertently direct our eyes to the open heavens, nevertheless, lets us wander broadly underneath, and shows them to us reflected in innumerable pools and lakes. We have from him, occasionally, some hints of a possible science of astronomy even, and revelation of heavenly arcana, but nothing definite hitherto.

These volumes contain not the highest, but a very practicable wisdom, which startles and provokes, rather than informs us. Carlyle does not oblige us to think; we have thought enough for him already, but he compels us to act. We accompany him rapidly through an endless gallery of pictures, and glorious reminiscences of experiences unimproved. "Have you not had Moses and the prophets? Neither will ye be persuaded if one should rise from the dead." There is no calm philosophy of life here, such as you might put at the end of the Almanac, to hang over the farmer's hearth, how men shall live in these winter, in these summer days. No philosophy, properly speaking, of love, or friendship, or religion, or politics, or education, or nature, or spirit; perhaps a nearer approach to a philosophy of kingship, and of the place of the literary man, than of any thing else. A rare preacher, with prayer, and psalm, and sermon, and benediction, but no contemplation of man's life from serene oriental ground, nor yet from the stirring occidental. No thanksgiving sermon for the holydays, or the Easter vacations, when all men submit to float on the full currents of life. When we see with what spirits, though with little heroism enough, wood-choppers, drovers, and apprentices, take and spend life, playing all day long, sunning themselves, shading themselves, eating, drinking, sleeping, we think that the philosophy of their life written would be such a level natural history as the Gardener's

Calendar, and the works of the early botanists, inconceivably slow to come to practical conclusions; its premises away off before the first morning light, ere the heather was introduced into the British isles, and no inferences to be drawn during this noon of the day, not till after the remote evening shadows have begun to fall around.

There is no philosophy here for philosophers, only as every man is said to have his philosophy. No system but such as is the man himself; and, indeed, he stands compactly enough. No progress beyond the first assertion and challenge, as it were, with trumpet blast. One thing is certain, that we had best be doing something in good earnest, henceforth forever; that's an indispensable philosophy. The before impossible precept, *"know thyself,"* he translates into the partially possible one, *"know what thou canst work at."* Sartor Resartus is, perhaps, the sunniest and most philosophical, as it is the most autobiographical of his works, in which he drew most largely on the experience of his youth. But we miss everywhere a calm depth, like a lake, even stagnant, and must submit to rapidity and whirl, as on skates, with all kinds of skillful and antic motions, sculling, sliding, cutting punch-bowls and rings, forward and backward. The talent is very nearly equal to the genius. Sometimes it would be preferable to wade slowly through a Serbonian bog, and feel the juices of the meadow. We should say that he had not speculated far, but faithfully, living up to it. He lays all the stress still on the most elementary and initiatory maxims, introductory to philosophy. It is the experience of the religionist. He pauses at such a quotation as, "It is only with renunciation that life, properly speaking, can be said to begin;" or, "Doubt of any sort cannot be removed except by action;" or, "Do the duty which lies nearest thee." The chapters entitled, "The Everlasting No," and "The Everlasting Yea," contain what you might call the religious experience of his hero. In the latter, he assigns to him these words, brief, but as significant as any we remember in this author:—"One BIBLE I know, of whose plenary inspiration doubt is not so much as possible; nay, with my own eyes I saw the God's-hand writing it: thereof all other Bibles are but leaves." This belongs to "The Everlasting Yea;" yet he lingers unaccountably in "The Everlasting No," under the negative pole. "Truth!" he still cries with Teufelsdröckh, "though the heavens crush me for following her: no falsehood! though a whole celestial Lubberland were the price of apostacy." Again, "Living without God in the world, of God's light I was not utterly bereft; if my as yet sealed eyes, with their unspeakable longing, could nowhere see Him, nevertheless, in my heart He was present, and His heaven-written law still stood legible and sacred there." Again, "Ever from that time, [*the era of his Protest,*] the temper of my misery was changed: not fear or whining sorrow was it, but indignation and grim, fire-eyed defiance." And in the "Centre of Indifference," as editor, he observes, that "it was no longer a quite hopeless unrest," and then proceeds, not in his best style, "For the fire-baptized soul, long so scathed and thunder-riven, here feels its own freedom, which feeling is its Baphometic Baptism: the citadel of its whole kingdom it has thus gained by assault, and will keep inexpugnable; outward from which the remaining dominions, not, indeed, without hard battling, will doubtless by degrees be conquered and pacificated."

Beside some philosophers of larger vision, Carlyle stands like an honest, half-despairing boy, grasping at some details only of their world systems. Philosophy, certainly, is some account of truths, the fragments and very insignificant parts of which man will practice in this work-shop; truths infinite and in harmony with infinity; in respect to which the very objects and ends of the so-called practical philosopher, will be mere propositions, like the rest. It would be no reproach to a philosopher, that he knew the future better than the past, or even than the present. It is better worth knowing. He will prophesy, tell what is to be, or in other words, what alone is, under appearances, laying little stress on the boiling of the pot, or the Condition of England question. He has no more to do with the condition of England than with her national debt, which a vigorous generation would not inherit. The philosopher's conception of things will, above all, be truer than other men's, and his philosophy will subordinate all the circumstances of life. To live like a philosopher, is to live, not foolishly, like other men, but wisely, and according to universal laws. In this, which was the ancient sense, we think there has been no philosopher in modern times. The wisest and most practical men of recent history, to whom this epithet has been hastily applied, have lived comparatively meagre lives, of conformity and tradition, such as their fathers transmitted to them. But a man may live in what style he can. Between earth and heaven, there is room for all kinds. If he take counsel of fear and prudence, he has already failed. One who believed, by his very constitution, some truth which a few words express, would make a revolution never to be forgotten in this world; for it needs but a fraction of truth to found houses and empires on.

However, such distinctions as poet and philosopher, do not much assist our final estimate of a man; we do not lay much stress on them. "A man's a man for a' that." If Carlyle does not take two steps in philosophy, are there any who take three? Philosophy having crept clinging to the rocks, so far, puts out its feelers many ways in vain. It would be hard to surprise him by the relation of any important human experience, but in some nook or corner of his works, you will find that this, too, was sometimes dreamed of in his philosophy.

To sum up our most serious objections, in a few words, we should say that Carlyle indicates a depth,—and we mean not impliedly, but distinctly,—which he neglects to fathom. We want to know more about that which he wants to know as well. If any luminous star, or undissolvable nebula, is visible from his station, which is not visible from ours, the interests of science require that the fact be communicated to us. The universe expects every man to do his duty in his parallel of latitude. We want to hear more of his inmost life; his hymn and prayer, more; his elegy and eulogy, less; that he should speak more from his character, and less from his talent; communicate centrally with his readers, and not by a side; that he should say what he believes, without suspecting that men disbelieve it, out of his never-misunderstood nature. Homer and Shakspeare speak directly and confidently to us. The confidence implied in the unsuspicious tone of the world's worthies, is a great and encouraging fact. Dig up some of the earth you stand on, and show that. If he gave us religiously the meagre results of his experience, his style would be less picturesque and diversified, but more attractive and impressive. His genius can cover all the land with gorgeous palaces, but the reader does not abide in them, but pitches his tent rather in the desert and on the mountain peak.

When we look about for something to quote, as the fairest specimen of the man, we confess that we labor under an unusual difficulty; for his philosophy is so little of the proverbial or sentential kind, and opens so gradually, rising insensibly from the reviewer's level, and developing its thought completely and in detail, that we look in vain for the brilliant passages, for point and antithesis, and must end by quoting his works entire. What in a writer of less breadth would have been the proposition which would have bounded his discourse, his column of victory, his Pillar of Hercules, and *ne plus ultra*, is in Carlyle frequently the same thought unfolded; no Pillar of Hercules, but a considerable prospect, north and south, along the Atlantic coast. There are other pillars of Hercules, like beacons and light-houses, still further in the horizon, toward Atlantis, set up by a few ancient and modern travellers; but, so far as this traveller goes, he clears and colonizes, and all the surplus population of London is bound thither at once. What we would quote is, in fact, his vivacity, and not any particular wisdom or sense, which last is ever synonymous with sentence, [*sententia*,] as in his contemporaries, Coleridge, Landor and Wordsworth.

We have not attempted to discriminate between his works, but have rather regarded them all as one work, as is the man himself. We have not examined so much as remembered them. To do otherwise, would have required a more indifferent, and perhaps even less just review, than the present. The several chapters were thankfully received, as they came out, and now we find it impossible to say which was best; perhaps each was best in its turn. They do not require to be remembered by chapters—that is a merit—but are rather remembered as a well-known strain, reviving from time to time, when it had nearly died away, and always inspiring us to worthier and more persistent endeavors.

In his last work, "The Letters and Speeches of Oliver Cromwell," Carlyle has added a chapter to the history of England; has actually written a chapter of her history, and, in comparison with this, there seems to be no other,—this, and the thirty thousand or three hundred thousand pamphlets in the British Museum, and that is all. This book is a practical comment on Universal History. What if there were a British Museum in Athens and Babylon, and nameless cities! It throws light on the history of the Iliad and the labors of Pisistratus. History is, then, an account of memorable events that have sometime transpired, and not an incredible and confused fable, quarters for scholars merely, or a gymnasium for poets and orators. We may say that he has dug up a hero, who was buried alive in his battle-field, hauled him out of his cairn, on which every passer had cast a pamphlet. We had heard of their digging up Arthurs before to be sure they were there; and, to be sure they were there, their bones, seven feet of them; but they had to bury them again. Others have helped to make known Shakspeare, Milton, Herbert, to give a name to such treasures as we all possessed; but, in this instance, not only a lost character has been restored to our imaginations, but palpably a living body, as it were, to our senses, to wear and sustain the former. His Cromwell's restoration, if England will read it faithfully, and addressed to New England too. Every reader will make his own application.

To speak deliberately, we think that in this instance, vague rumor and a vague history have for the first time been subjected to a rigid scrutiny, and the wheat, with at least novel fidelity, sifted from the chaff; so that there remain for result,—First, Letters and Speeches of Oliver Cromwell, now for the first time read or readable, and well nigh as complete as the fates will permit; secondly, Deeds, making an imperfect and fragmentary life, which may, with probability, be fathered upon him; thirdly, this wreck of an ancient picture, the present editor has, to the best of his ability, restored, sedulously scraping away the daubings of successive bunglers, and endeavoring to catch the spirit of the artist himself. Not the worst, nor a barely possible, but for once the most favorable construction has been put upon this evidence of the life of a man, and the result is a picture of the ideal Cromwell, the perfection of the painter's art. Possibly this was the actual man. At any rate, this only can contain the actual hero. We confess that when we read these Letters and Speeches, unquestionably Cromwell's, with open and confident mind, we get glimpses occasionally of a grandeur and heroism, which even this editor has not proclaimed. His "Speeches" make us forget modern orators, and might go right into the next edition of the Old Testament, without alteration. Cromwell *was* another sort of man than *we* had taken him to be. These Letters and Speeches have supplied the lost key to his character. Verily another soldier than Bonaparte; rejoicing in the triumph of a psalm; to whom psalms were for Magna Charta and Heralds' Book, and whose victories were "crowning mercies." For stern, antique, and practical religion, a man unparalleled, since the Jewish dispensation, in the line of kings. An old Hebrew warrior, indeed, and last right-hand man of the Lord of Hosts, that has blown his ram's horn about Jericho. Yet, with a remarkable common sense and unexpected liberality, there was joined in him, too, such a divine madness, though with large and sublime features, as that of those dibblers of beans on St. George's Hill, whom Carlyle tells of. He still listened to ancient and decaying oracles. If his actions were not always what Christianity or the truest philosophy teaches, still they never fail to impress us as noble, and however violent, will always be pardoned to the great purpose and sincerity of the man. His unquestionable hardness, not to say willfulness, not prevailing by absolute truth and greatness of character, but honestly striving to bend things to his will, is yet grateful to consider in this or any age. As John Maidstone said, "He was a strong man in the dark perils of war; in the high places of the field, hope shone in him like a pillar of fire, when it had gone out in the others." And as Milton sang, whose least testimony cannot be spared—

"Our chief of men,
Guided by faith and matchless fortitude."

None ever spake to Cromwell before, sending a word of cheer across the centuries—not the "hear!" "hear!" of modern parliaments, but the congratulation and sympathy of a brother soul. The Letters and Speeches owe not a little to the "Intercalations" and "Annotations" of the "latest of the Commentators." The reader will not soon forget how like a happy merchant in the crowd, listening to his favorite speaker, he is all on the alert, and sympathetic, nudging his neighbors

from time to time, and throwing in his responsive or inter-
rogatory word. All is good, both that which he didn't hear,
and that which he did. He not only makes him speak audibly,
but he makes all parties listen to him, all England sitting
round, and give in their comments, "groans," or "blushes,"
or "assent;" indulging sometimes in triumphant malicious
applications to the present day, when there is a palpable hit;
supplying the look and attitude of the speaker, and the tone
of his voice, and even rescuing his unutterable, wrecked and
submerged thought,—for this orator begins speaking anywhere within sight of the beginning, and leaves off when the
conclusion is visible. Our merchant listens, restless, meanwhile, encouraging his fellow-auditors, when the speech
grows dim and involved, and pleasantly congratulating them,
when it runs smoothly; or, in touching soliloquy, he exclaims,
"Poor Oliver, noble Oliver"—"Courage, my brave one!"

And all along, between the Letters and Speeches, as readers
well remember, he has ready such a fresh top-of-the-morning
salutation as conjures up the spirits of those days, and men go
marching over English sward, not wired skeletons, but with
firm, elastic muscles, and clang of armor on their thighs, if
they wore swords, or the twang of psalms and canticles on
their lips. His blunt, "Who are you?" put to the shadowy
ghosts of history, they vanish into deeper obscurity than ever.
Vivid phantasmagorian pictures of what is transpiring in
England in the meanwhile, there are, not a few, better than if
you had been there to see.

All of Carlyle's works might well enough be embraced
under the title of one of them, a good specimen brick,
"On Heroes, Hero-worship, and the Heroic in History." Of
this department, he is the Chief Professor in the World's
University, and even leaves Plutarch behind. Such intimate
and living, such loyal and generous sympathy with the heroes
of history, not one in one age only, but forty in forty ages,
such an unparalleled reviewing and greeting of all past worth,
with exceptions, to be sure,—but exceptions were the rule,
before,—it was, indeed, to make this the age of review writing, as if now one period of the human story were completing itself, and getting its accounts settled. This soldier has
told the stories with new emphasis, and will be a memorable

hander-down of fame to posterity. And with what wise discrimination he has selected his men, with reference both to
his own genius and to theirs: Mahomet,—Dante,—Cromwell,—Voltaire,—Johnson,—Burns,—Goethe,—Richter,—Schiller,
—Mirabeau; could any of these have been spared? These we
wanted to hear about. We have not as commonly the cold
and refined judgment of the scholar and critic merely, but
something more human and affecting. These eulogies have
the glow and warmth of friendship. There is sympathy not
with mere fames, and formless, incredible things, but with
kindred men,—not transiently, but life-long he has walked
with them.

The attitude of some, in relation to Carlyle's love of heroes,
and men of the sword, reminds us of the procedure at the
anti-slavery meetings, when some member, being warmed,
begins to speak with more latitude than usual of the Bible or
the Church, for a few prudent and devout ones to spring a
prayer upon him, as the saying is; that is, propose suddenly to
unite in prayer, and so solemnize the minds of the audience,
or dismiss them at once; which may oftener be to interrupt a
true prayer by most gratuitous profanity. But the spring of
this trap, we are glad to learn, has grown somewhat rusty, and
is not so sure of late.

No doubt, some of Carlyle's worthies, should they ever return to earth, would find themselves unpleasantly put upon
their good behavior, to sustain their characters; but if he can
return a man's life more perfect to our hands, than it was left
at his death, following out the design of its author, we shall
have no great cause to complain. We do not want a Daguerreotype likeness. All biography is the life of Adam,—a
much-experienced man,—and time withdraws something partial from the story of every individual, that the historian may
supply something general. If these virtues were not in this
man, perhaps they are in his biographer,—no fatal mistake.
Really, in any other sense, we never do, nor desire to, come at
the historical man,—unless we rob his grave, that is the nearest
approach. Why did he die, then? *He* is with his bones, surely.

No doubt, Carlyle has a propensity to *exaggerate* the heroic
in history, that is, he creates you an ideal hero rather than another thing, he has most of that material. This we allow in all

its senses, and in one narrower sense it is not so convenient.
Yet what were history if he did not exaggerate it? How comes
it that history never has to wait for facts, but for a man to
write it? The ages may go on forgetting the facts never so
long, he can remember two for every one forgotten. The
musty records of history, like the catacombs, contain the perishable remains, but only in the breast of genius are embalmed the souls of heroes. There is very little of what is
called criticism here; it is love and reverence, rather, which
deal with qualities not relatively, but absolutely great; for
whatever is admirable in a man is something infinite, to which
we cannot set bounds. These sentiments allow the mortal to
die, the immortal and divine to survive. There is something
antique, even in his style of treating his subject, reminding us
that Heroes and Demi-gods, Fates and Furies, still exist, the
common man is nothing to him, but after death the hero is
apotheosized and has a place in heaven, as in the religion of
the Greeks.

Exaggeration! was ever any virtue attributed to a man without exaggeration? was ever any vice, without infinite exaggeration? Do we not exaggerate ourselves to ourselves, or do we
recognize ourselves for the actual men we are? Are we not all
great men? Yet what are we actually to speak of? We live by
exaggeration, what else is it to anticipate more than we enjoy?
The lightning is an exaggeration of the light. Exaggerated history is poetry, and truth referred to a new standard. To a
small man every greater is an exaggeration. He who cannot
exaggerate is not qualified to utter truth. No truth we think
was ever expressed but with this sort of emphasis, so that for
the time there seemed to be no other. Moreover, you must
speak loud to those who are hard of hearing, and so you acquire a habit of shouting to those who are not. By an immense exaggeration we appreciate our Greek poetry and
philosophy, and Egyptian ruins; our Shakspeares and Miltons,
our Liberty and Christianity. We give importance to this hour
over all other hours. We do not live by justice, but by grace.
As the sort of justice which concerns us in our daily intercourse is not that administered by the judge, so the historical
justice which we prize is not arrived at by nicely balancing the
evidence. In order to appreciate any, even the humblest man,

you must first, by some good fortune, have acquired a sentiment of admiration, even of reverence, for him, and there never were such exaggerators as these. Simple admiration for a hero renders a juster verdict than the wisest criticism, which necessarily degrades what is high to its own level. There is no danger in short of saying too much in praise of one man, provided you can say more in praise of a better man. If by exaggeration a man can create for us a hero, where there was nothing but dry bones before, we will thank him, and let Dryasdust administer historical justice. This is where a true history properly begins, when some genius arises, who can turn the dry and musty records into poetry. As we say, looking to the future, that what is best is truest, so, in one sense, we may say looking into the past, for the only past that we are to look at, must also be future to us. The great danger is not of excessive partiality or sympathy with one, but of a shallow justice to many, in which, after all, none gets his deserts. Who has not experienced that praise is truer than naked justice? As if man were to be the judge of his fellows, and should repress his rising sympathy with the prisoner at the bar, considering the many honest men abroad, whom he had never countenanced.

To try him by the German rule of referring an author to his own standard, we will quote the following from Carlyle's remarks on history, and leave the reader to consider how far his practice has been consistent with his theory. "Truly, if History is Philosophy teaching by experience, the writer fitted to compose history, is hitherto an unknown man. The experience itself would require all knowledge to record it, were the All-wisdom needful for such Philosophy as would interpret it, to be had for asking. Better were it that mere earthly historians should lower such pretensions, more suitable for omniscience than for human science; and aiming only at some picture of the things acted, which picture itself, will at best be a poor approximation, leave the inscrutable purport of them an acknowledged secret; or, at most, in reverent Faith, far different from that teaching of Philosophy, pause over the mysterious vestiges of Him, whose path is in the great deep of Time, whom history indeed reveals, but only all History and in Eternity, will clearly reveal."

•

Who lives in London to tell this generation who have been the great men of our race? We have read that on some exposed place in the city of Geneva, they have fixed a brazen indicater for the use of travellers, with the names of the mountain summits in the horizon marked upon it, "so that by taking sight across the index you can distinguish them at once. You will not mistake Mont Blanc, if you see him, but until you get accustomed to the panorama, you may easily mistake one of his court for the king." It stands there a piece of mute brass, that seems nevertheless to know in what vicinity it is: and there perchance it will stand, when the nation that placed it there has passed away, still in sympathy with the mountains, forever discriminating in the desert.

So, we may say, stands this man, pointing as long as he lives, in obedience to some spiritual magnetism, to the summits in the historical horizon, for the guidance of his fellows.

Truly, our greatest blessings are very cheap. To have our sunlight without paying for it, without any duty levied,—to have our poet there in England, to furnish us entertainment, and what is better, provocation, from year to year, all our lives long, to make the world seem richer for us, the age more respectable, and life better worth the living,—all without expense of acknowledgment even, but silently accepted out of the east, like morning light as a matter of course.

Civil Disobedience

I HEARTILY accept the motto,—"That government is best which governs least"; and I should like to see it acted up to more rapidly and systematically. Carried out, it finally amounts to this, which also I believe,—"That government is best which governs not at all"; and when men are prepared for it, that will be the kind of government which they will have. Government is at best but an expedient; but most governments are usually, and all governments are sometimes, inexpedient. The objections which have been brought against a standing army, and they are many and weighty, and deserve to prevail, may also at last be brought against a standing government. The standing army is only an arm of the standing government. The government itself, which is only the mode which the people have chosen to execute their will, is equally liable to be abused and perverted before the people can act through it. Witness the present Mexican war, the work of comparatively a few individuals using the standing government as their tool; for, in the outset, the people would not have consented to this measure.

This American government,—what is it but a tradition, though a recent one, endeavoring to transmit itself unimpaired to posterity, but each instant losing some of its integrity? It has not the vitality and force of a single living man; for a single man can bend it to his will. It is a sort of wooden gun to the people themselves. But it is not the less necessary for this; for the people must have some complicated machinery or other, and hear its din, to satisfy that idea of government which they have. Governments show thus how successfully men can be imposed on, even impose on themselves, for their own advantage. It is excellent, we must all allow. Yet this government never of itself furthered any enterprise, but by the alacrity with which it got out of its way. *It* does not keep the country free. *It* does not settle the West. *It* does not educate. The character inherent in the American people has done all that has been accomplished; and it would have done somewhat more, if the government had not sometimes got in its way. For government is an expedient by which men would fain succeed in letting one another alone; and, as has been said, when it is most expedient, the governed are most let alone by it. Trade and commerce, if they were not made of India-rubber, would never manage to bounce over the obstacles which legislators are continually putting in their way; and, if one were to judge these men wholly by the effects of their actions and not partly by their intentions, they would deserve to be classed and punished with those mischievous persons who put obstructions on the railroads.

But, to speak practically and as a citizen, unlike those who call themselves no-government men, I ask for, not at once no government, but *at once* a better government. Let every man make known what kind of government would command his respect, and that will be one step toward obtaining it.

After all, the practical reason why, when the power is once in the hands of the people, a majority are permitted, and for a long period continue, to rule, is not because they are most likely to be in the right, nor because this seems fairest to the minority, but because they are physically the strongest. But a government in which the majority rule in all cases cannot be based on justice, even as far as men understand it. Can there not be a government in which majorities do not virtually decide right and wrong, but conscience?—in which majorities decide only those questions to which the rule of expediency is applicable? Must the citizen ever for a moment, or in the least degree, resign his conscience to the legislator? Why has every man a conscience, then? I think that we should be men first, and subjects afterward. It is not desirable to cultivate a respect for the law, so much as for the right. The only obligation which I have a right to assume, is to do at any time what I think right. It is truly enough said, that a corporation has no conscience; but a corporation of conscientious men is a corporation *with* a conscience. Law never made men a whit more just; and, by means of their respect for it, even the well-disposed are daily made the agents of injustice. A common and natural result of an undue respect for law is, that you may see a file of soldiers, colonel, captain, corporal, privates, powder-monkeys, and all, marching in admirable order over hill and dale to the wars, against their wills, ay, against their common sense and consciences, which makes it very steep marching indeed, and produces a palpitation of the heart. They have no doubt that it is a damnable business in which they are concerned; they are all peaceably inclined. Now, what are they? Men at all? or small movable forts and magazines, at the service of some unscrupulous man in power? Visit the Navy-Yard, and behold a marine, such a man as an American government can make, or such as it can make a man with its black arts,—a mere shadow and reminiscence of humanity, a man laid out alive and standing, and already, as one may say, buried under arms with funeral accompaniments, though it may be,—

> "Not a drum was heard, not a funeral note,
>   As his corse to the rampart we hurried;
> Not a soldier discharged his farewell shot
>   O'er the grave where our hero we buried."

The mass of men serve the state thus, not as men mainly, but as machines, with their bodies. They are the standing army, and the militia, jailers, constables, posse comitatus, &c. In most cases there is no free exercise whatever of the judgment or of the moral sense; but they put themselves on a level with wood and earth and stones; and wooden men can perhaps be manufactured that will serve the purpose as well. Such command no more respect than men of straw or a lump of dirt. They have the same sort of worth only as horses and dogs. Yet such as these even are commonly esteemed good citizens. Others,—as most legislators, politicians, lawyers, ministers, and office-holders,—serve the state chiefly with their heads; and, as they rarely make any moral distinctions, they are as likely to serve the Devil, without *intending* it, as God. A very few, as heroes, patriots, martyrs, reformers in the great sense, and *men*, serve the state with their consciences also, and so necessarily resist it for the most part; and they are commonly treated as enemies by it. A wise man will only be useful as a man, and will not submit to be "clay," and "stop a hole to keep the wind away," but leave that office to his dust at least:—

> "I am too high-born to be propertied
> To be a secondary at control,
> Or useful serving-man and instrument
> To any sovereign state throughout the world."

He who gives himself entirely to his fellow-men appears to them useless and selfish; but he who gives himself partially to them is pronounced a benefactor and philanthropist.

How does it become a man to behave toward this American government to-day? I answer, that he cannot without disgrace be associated with it. I cannot for an instant recognize that political organization as *my* government which is the *slave's* government also.

All men recognize the right of revolution; that is, the right to refuse allegiance to, and to resist, the government, when its tyranny or its inefficiency are great and unendurable. But almost all say that such is not the case now. But such was the case, they think, in the Revolution of '75. If one were to tell me that this was a bad government because it taxed certain foreign commodities brought to its ports, it is most probable that I should not make an ado about it, for I can do without them. All machines have their friction; and possibly this does enough good to counterbalance the evil. At any rate, it is a great evil to make a stir about it. But when the friction comes to have its machine, and oppression and robbery are organized, I say, let us not have such a machine any longer. In other words, when a sixth of the population of a nation which has undertaken to be the refuge of liberty are slaves, and a whole country is unjustly overrun and conquered by a foreign army, and subjected to military law, I think that it is not too soon for honest men to rebel and revolutionize. What makes this duty the more urgent is the fact, that the country so overrun is not our own, but ours is the invading army.

Paley, a common authority with many on moral questions, in his chapter on the "Duty of Submission to Civil Government," resolves all civil obligation into expediency; and he proceeds to say, "that so long as the interest of the whole society requires it, that is, so long as the established government cannot be resisted or changed without public inconveniency, it is the will of God that the established government be obeyed, and no longer. . . . . This principle being admitted, the justice of every particular case of resistance is reduced to a computation of the quantity of the danger and grievance on the one side, and of the probability and expense of redressing it on the other." Of this, he says, every man shall judge for himself. But Paley appears never to have contemplated those cases to which the rule of expediency does not apply, in which a people, as well as an individual, must do justice, cost what it may. If I have unjustly wrested a plank from a drowning man, I must restore it to him though I drown myself. This, according to Paley, would be inconvenient. But he that would save his life, in such a case, shall lose it. This people must cease to hold slaves, and to make war on Mexico, though it cost them their existence as a people.

In their practice, nations agree with Paley; but does any one think that Massachusetts does exactly what is right at the present crisis?

> "A drab of state, a cloth-o'-silver slut,
>   To have her train borne up, and her soul trail in
>   the dirt."

Practically speaking, the opponents to a reform in Massachusetts are not a hundred thousand politicians at the South, but a hundred thousand merchants and farmers here, who are more interested in commerce and agriculture than they are in humanity, and are not prepared to do justice to the slave and to Mexico, *cost what it may*. I quarrel not with far-off foes, but with those who, near at home, co-operate with, and do the bidding of, those far away, and without whom the latter would be harmless. We are accustomed to say, that the mass of men are unprepared; but improvement is slow, because the few are not materially wiser or better than the many. It is not so important that many should be as good as you, as that there be some absolute goodness somewhere; for that will leaven the whole lump. There are thousands who are *in opinion* opposed to slavery and to the war, who yet in effect do nothing to put an end to them; who, esteeming themselves children of Washington and Franklin, sit down with their hands in their pockets, and say that they know not what to do, and do nothing; who even postpone the question of freedom to the question of free-trade, and quietly read the prices-current along with the latest advices from Mexico, after dinner, and, it may be, fall asleep over them both. What is the price-current of an honest man and patriot to-day? They hesitate, and they regret, and sometimes they petition; but they do nothing in earnest and with effect. They will wait, well disposed, for others to remedy the evil, that they may no longer have it to regret. At most, they give only a cheap vote, and a feeble countenance and God-speed, to the right, as it goes by them. There are nine hundred and ninety-nine patrons of virtue to one virtuous man. But it is easier to deal with the real possessor of a thing than with the temporary guardian of it.

All voting is a sort of gaming, like checkers or backgammon, with a slight moral tinge to it, a playing with right and wrong, with moral questions; and betting naturally accompanies it. The character of the voters is not staked. I cast my vote, perchance, as I think right; but I am not vitally concerned that that right should prevail. I am willing to leave it to the majority. Its obligation, therefore, never exceeds that of expediency. Even voting *for the right* is *doing* nothing for it. It is only expressing to men feebly your desire that it should prevail. A wise man will not leave the right to the mercy of chance, nor wish it to prevail through the power of the majority. There is but little virtue in the action of masses of men. When the majority shall at length vote for the abolition of slavery, it will be because they are indifferent to slavery, or because there is but little slavery left to be abolished by their vote. *They* will then be the only slaves. Only *his* vote can hasten the abolition of slavery who asserts his own freedom by his vote.

I hear of a convention to be held at Baltimore, or elsewhere, for the selection of a candidate for the Presidency, made up chiefly of editors, and men who are politicians by profession; but I think, what is it to any independent, intelligent, and respectable man what decision they may come to? Shall we not have the advantage of his wisdom and honesty, nevertheless? Can we not count upon some independent votes? Are there not many individuals in the country who do not attend conventions? But no: I find that the respectable man, so called, has immediately drifted from his position, and despairs of his country, when his country has more reason to despair of him. He forthwith adopts one of the candidates thus selected as the only *available* one, thus proving that he is himself *available* for any purposes of the demagogue. His vote is of no more worth than that of any unprincipled foreigner or hireling native, who may have been bought. O for a man who is a *man*, and, as my neighbor says, has a bone in his back which you cannot pass your hand through! Our statistics are at fault: the population has been returned too large. How many *men* are there to a square thousand miles in this country? Hardly one. Does not America offer any inducement for men to settle here? The American has dwindled into an Odd Fellow,—one who may be known by the development of his organ of gregariousness, and a manifest lack of intellect and cheerful self-reliance; whose first and chief concern, on coming into the world, is to see that the Almshouses are in good repair; and, before yet he has lawfully donned the virile garb, to collect a fund for the support of the widows and orphans that may be; who, in short, ventures to live only by the aid of the Mutual Insurance company, which has promised to bury him decently.

It is not a man's duty, as a matter of course, to devote himself to the eradication of any, even the most enormous wrong; he may still properly have other concerns to engage him; but it is his duty, at least, to wash his hands of it, and, if he gives it no thought longer, not to give it practically his support. If I devote myself to other pursuits and contemplations, I must first see, at least, that I do not pursue them sitting upon another man's shoulders. I must get off him first, that he may pursue his contemplations too. See what gross inconsistency is tolerated. I have heard some of my townsmen say, "I should like to have them order me out to help put down an insurrection of the slaves, or to march to Mexico;—see if I would go"; and yet these very men have each, directly by their allegiance, and so indirectly, at least, by their money, furnished a substitute. The soldier is applauded who refuses to serve in an unjust war by those who do not refuse to sustain the unjust government which makes the war; is applauded by those whose own act and authority he disregards and sets at naught;

as if the State were penitent to that degree that it hired one to scourge it while it sinned, but not to that degree that it left off sinning for a moment. Thus, under the name of Order and Civil Government, we are all made at last to pay homage to and support our own meanness. After the first blush of sin comes its indifference; and from immoral it becomes, as it were, *un*moral, and not quite unnecessary to that life which we have made.

The broadest and most prevalent error requires the most disinterested virtue to sustain it. The slight reproach to which the virtue of patriotism is commonly liable, the noble are most likely to incur. Those who, while they disapprove of the character and measures of a government, yield to it their allegiance and support, are undoubtedly its most conscientious supporters, and so frequently the most serious obstacles to reform. Some are petitioning the State to dissolve the Union, to disregard the requisitions of the President. Why do they not dissolve it themselves,—the union between themselves and the State,—and refuse to pay their quota into its treasury? Do not they stand in the same relation to the State, that the State does to the Union? And have not the same reasons prevented the State from resisting the Union, which have prevented them from resisting the State?

How can a man be satisfied to entertain an opinion merely, and enjoy *it*? Is there any enjoyment in it, if his opinion is that he is aggrieved? If you are cheated out of a single dollar by your neighbor, you do not rest satisfied with knowing that you are cheated, or with saying that you are cheated, or even with petitioning him to pay you your due; but you take effectual steps at once to obtain the full amount, and see that you are never cheated again. Action from principle, the perception and the performance of right, changes things and relations; it is essentially revolutionary, and does not consist wholly with anything which was. It not only divides states and churches, it divides families; ay, it divides the *individual*, separating the diabolical in him from the divine.

Unjust laws exist: shall we be content to obey them, or shall we endeavor to amend them, and obey them until we have succeeded, or shall we transgress them at once? Men generally, under such a government as this, think that they ought to wait until they have persuaded the majority to alter them. They think that, if they should resist, the remedy would be worse than the evil. But it is the fault of the government itself that the remedy *is* worse than the evil. *It* makes it worse. Why is it not more apt to anticipate and provide for reform? Why does it not cherish its wise minority? Why does it cry and resist before it is hurt? Why does it not encourage its citizens to be on the alert to point out its faults, and *do* better than it would have them? Why does it always crucify Christ, and excommunicate Copernicus and Luther, and pronounce Washington and Franklin rebels?

One would think, that a deliberate and practical denial of its authority was the only offence never contemplated by government; else, why has it not assigned its definite, its suitable and proportionate penalty? If a man who has no property refuses but once to earn nine shillings for the State, he is put in prison for a period unlimited by any law that I know, and determined only by the discretion of those who placed him there; but if he should steal ninety times nine shillings from the State, he is soon permitted to go at large again.

If the injustice is part of the necessary friction of the machine of government, let it go, let it go: perchance it will wear smooth,—certainly the machine will wear out. If the injustice has a spring, or a pulley, or a rope, or a crank, exclusively for itself, then perhaps you may consider whether the remedy will not be worse than the evil; but if it is of such a nature that it requires you to be the agent of injustice to another, then, I say, break the law. Let your life be a counter friction to stop the machine. What I have to do is to see, at any rate, that I do not lend myself to the wrong which I condemn.

As for adopting the ways which the State has provided for remedying the evil, I know not of such ways. They take too much time, and a man's life will be gone. I have other affairs to attend to. I came into this world, not chiefly to make this a good place to live in, but to live in it, be it good or bad. A man has not everything to do, but something; and because he cannot do *everything*, it is not necessary that he should do *something* wrong. It is not my business to be petitioning the Governor or the Legislature any more than it is theirs to petition me; and, if they should not hear my petition, what should I do then? But in this case the State has provided no way: its very Constitution is the evil. This may seem to be harsh and stubborn and unconciliatory; but it is to treat with the utmost kindness and consideration the only spirit that can appreciate or deserves it. So is all change for the better, like birth and death, which convulse the body.

I do not hesitate to say, that those who call themselves Abolitionists should at once effectually withdraw their support, both in person and property, from the government of Massachusetts, and not wait till they constitute a majority of one, before they suffer the right to prevail through them. I think that it is enough if they have God on their side, without waiting for that other one. Moreover, any man more right than his neighbors constitutes a majority of one already.

I meet this American government, or its representative, the State government, directly, and face to face, once a year—no more—in the person of its tax-gatherer; this is the only mode in which a man situated as I am necessarily meets it; and it then says distinctly, Recognize me; and the simplest, the most effectual, and, in the present posture of affairs, the indispensablest mode of treating with it on this head, of expressing your little satisfaction with and love for it, is to deny it then. My civil neighbor, the tax-gatherer, is the very man I have to deal with,—for it is, after all, with men and not with parchment that I quarrel,—and he has voluntarily chosen to be an agent of the government. How shall he ever know well what he is and does as an officer of the government, or as a man, until he is obliged to consider whether he shall treat me, his neighbor, for whom he has respect, as a neighbor and well-disposed man, or as a maniac and disturber of the peace, and see if he can get over this obstruction to his neighborliness without a ruder and more impetuous thought or speech corresponding with his action. I know this well, that if one thousand, if one hundred, if ten men whom I could name,—if ten *honest* men only,—ay, if *one* HONEST man, in this State of Massachusetts, *ceasing to hold slaves*, were actually to withdraw from this copartnership, and be locked up in the county jail therefor, it would be the abolition of slavery in America. For it matters not how small the beginning may seem to be: what is once well done is done forever. But we love better to talk about it: that we say is our mission. Reform keeps many scores of newspapers in its service, but not one man. If my esteemed neighbor, the State's ambassador, who will devote his days to the settlement of the question of human rights in the Council Chamber, instead of being threatened with the prisons of Carolina, were to sit down the prisoner of Massachusetts, that State which is so anxious to foist the sin of slavery upon her sister,—though at present she can discover only an act of inhospitality to be the ground of a quarrel with her,—the Legislature would not wholly waive the subject the following winter.

Under a government which imprisons any unjustly, the true place for a just man is also a prison. The proper place to-day, the only place which Massachusetts has provided for her freer and less desponding spirits, is in her prisons, to be put out and locked out of the State by her own act, as they have already put themselves out by their principles. It is there that the fugitive slave, and the Mexican prisoner on parole, and the Indian come to plead the wrongs of his race, should find them; on that separate, but more free and honorable ground, where the State places those who are not *with* her, but *against* her,—the only house in a slave State in which a free man can abide with honor. If any think that their influence would be lost there, and their voices no longer afflict the ear of the State, that they would not be as an enemy within its walls, they do not know by how much truth is stronger than error, nor how much more eloquently and effectively he can combat injustice who has experienced a little in his own person. Cast your whole vote, not a strip of paper merely, but your whole influence. A minority is powerless while it conforms to the majority; it is not even a minority then; but it is irresistible when it clogs by its whole weight. If the alternative is to keep all just men in prison, or give up war and slavery, the State will not hesitate which to choose. If a thousand men were not to pay their tax-bills this year, that would not be a violent and bloody measure, as it would be to pay them, and enable the State to commit violence and shed innocent blood. This is, in fact, the definition of a peaceable revolution, if any such is possible. If the tax-gatherer, or any other public officer, asks me, as one has done, "But what shall I do?" my answer is, "If you really wish to do anything, resign your office." When the subject has refused allegiance, and the officer has resigned his office, then the revolution is accomplished. But even suppose blood should flow. Is there not a sort of blood shed when the conscience is wounded? Through this wound a man's real manhood and immortality flow out, and he bleeds to an everlasting death. I see this blood flowing now.

I have contemplated the imprisonment of the offender, rather than the seizure of his goods,—though both will serve the same purpose,—because they who assert the purest right, and consequently are most dangerous to a corrupt State, commonly have not spent much time in accumulating property. To such the State renders comparatively small service, and a slight tax is wont to appear exorbitant, particularly if they are obliged to earn it by special labor with their hands. If there were one who lived wholly without the use of money, the State itself would hesitate to demand it of him. But the rich man,—not to make any invidious comparison,—is always sold to the institution which makes him rich. Absolutely speaking, the more money, the less virtue; for money comes between a man and his objects, and obtains them for him; and it was certainly no great virtue to obtain it. It puts to rest many questions which he would otherwise be taxed to answer; while the only new question which it puts is the hard but superfluous one, how to spend it. Thus his moral ground is taken from under his feet. The opportunities of living are diminished in proportion as what are called the "means" are increased. The best thing a man can do for his culture when he is rich is to endeavor to carry out those schemes which he entertained when he was poor. Christ answered the Herodians according to their condition. "Show me the tribute-money," said he;—and one took a penny out of his pocket;—if you use money which has the image of Cæsar on it, and which he has made current and valuable, that is, *if you are men of the State*, and gladly enjoy the advantages of Cæsar's government, then pay him back some of his own when he demands it; "Render therefore to Cæsar that which is Cæsar's, and to God those things which are God's,"—leaving them no wiser than before as to which was which; for they did not wish to know.

When I converse with the freest of my neighbors, I perceive that, whatever they may say about the magnitude and seriousness of the question, and their regard for the public tranquillity, the long and the short of the matter is, that they cannot spare the protection of the existing government, and they dread the consequences to their property and families of disobedience to it. For my own part, I should not like to think that I ever rely on the protection of the State. But, if I deny the authority of the State when it presents its tax-bill, it will soon take and waste all my property, and so harass me and my children without end. This is hard. This makes it impossible for a man to live honestly, and at the same time comfortably, in outward respects. It will not be worth the while to accumulate property; that would be sure to go again. You must hire or squat somewhere, and raise but a small crop, and eat that soon. You must live within yourself, and depend upon yourself always tucked up and ready for a start, and not have many affairs. A man may grow rich in Turkey even, if he will be in all respects a good subject of the Turkish government. Confucius said: "If a state is governed by the principles of reason, poverty and misery are subjects of shame; if a state is not governed by the principles of reason, riches and honors are the subjects of shame." No: until I want the protection of Massachusetts to be extended to me in some distant Southern port, where my liberty is endangered, or until I am bent solely on building up an estate at home by peaceful enterprise, I can afford to refuse allegiance to Massachusetts, and her right to my property and life. It costs me less in every sense to incur the penalty of disobedience to the State, than it would to obey. I should feel as if I were worth less in that case.

Some years ago, the State met me in behalf of the Church, and commanded me to pay a certain sum toward the support of a clergyman whose preaching my father attended, but never I myself. "Pay," it said, "or be locked up in the jail." I declined to pay. But, unfortunately, another man saw fit to pay it. I did not see why the schoolmaster should be taxed to support the priest, and not the priest the schoolmaster; for I was not the State's schoolmaster, but I supported myself by voluntary subscription. I did not see why the lyceum should not present its tax-bill, and have the State to back its demand,

as well as the Church. However, at the request of the selectmen, I condescended to make some such statement as this in
writing:—"Know all men by these presents, that I, Henry
Thoreau, do not wish to be regarded as a member of any incorporated society which I have not joined." This I gave to
the town clerk; and he has it. The State, having thus learned
that I did not wish to be regarded as a member of that
church, has never made a like demand on me since; though it
said that it must adhere to its original presumption that time.
If I had known how to name them, I should then have signed
off in detail from all the societies which I never signed on to;
but I did not know where to find a complete list.

I have paid no poll-tax for six years. I was put into a jail
once on this account, for one night; and, as I stood considering the walls of solid stone, two or three feet thick, the door
of wood and iron, a foot thick, and the iron grating which
strained the light, I could not help being struck with the foolishness of that institution which treated me as if I were mere
flesh and blood and bones, to be locked up. I wondered that
it should have concluded at length that this was the best use
it could put me to, and had never thought to avail itself of my
services in some way. I saw that, if there was a wall of stone
between me and my townsmen, there was a still more difficult
one to climb or break through, before they could get to be as
free as I was. I did not for a moment feel confined, and the
walls seemed a great waste of stone and mortar. I felt as if I
alone of all my townsmen had paid my tax. They plainly did
not know how to treat me, but behaved like persons who are
underbred. In every threat and in every compliment there was
a blunder; for they thought that my chief desire was to stand
the other side of that stone wall. I could not but smile to see
how industriously they locked the door on my meditations,
which followed them out again without let or hindrance, and
they were really all that was dangerous. As they could not
reach me, they had resolved to punish my body; just as boys,
if they cannot come at some person against whom they have
a spite, will abuse his dog. I saw that the State was half-witted, that it was timid as a lone woman with her silver spoons,
and that it did not know its friends from its foes, and I lost all
my remaining respect for it, and pitied it.

Thus the State never intentionally confronts a man's sense, intellectual or moral, but only his body, his senses. It is not armed with superior wit or honesty, but with superior physical strength. I was not born to be forced. I will breathe after my own fashion. Let us see who is the strongest. What force has a multitude? They only can force me who obey a higher law than I. They force me to become like themselves. I do not hear of *men* being *forced* to live this way or that by masses of men. What sort of life were that to live? When I meet a government which says to me, "Your money or your life," why should I be in haste to give it my money? It may be in a great strait, and not know what to do: I cannot help that. It must help itself; do as I do. It is not worth the while to snivel about it. I am not responsible for the successful working of the machinery of society. I am not the son of the engineer. I perceive that, when an acorn and a chestnut fall side by side, the one does not remain inert to make way for the other, but both obey their own laws, and spring and grow and flourish as best they can, till one, perchance, overshadows and destroys the other. If a plant cannot live according to its nature, it dies; and so a man.

The night in prison was novel and interesting enough. The prisoners in their shirt-sleeves were enjoying a chat and the evening air in the doorway, when I entered. But the jailer said, "Come, boys, it is time to lock up"; and so they dispersed, and I heard the sound of their steps returning into the hollow apartments. My room-mate was introduced to me by the jailer, as "a first-rate fellow and a clever man." When the door was locked, he showed me where to hang my hat, and how he managed matters there. The rooms were white-washed once a month; and this one, at least, was the whitest, most simply furnished, and probably the neatest apartment in the town. He naturally wanted to know where I came from, and what brought me there; and, when I had told him, I asked him in my turn how he came there, presuming him to be an honest man, of course; and, as the world goes, I believe he was. "Why," said he, "they accuse me of burning a barn; but I never did it." As near as I could discover, he had probably gone to bed in a barn when drunk, and smoked his pipe there; and so a barn was burnt. He had the reputation of being a clever man, had been there some three months waiting for his trial to come on, and would have to wait as much longer; but he was quite domesticated and contented, since he got his board for nothing, and thought that he was well treated.

He occupied one window, and I the other; and I saw, that, if one stayed there long, his principal business would be to look out the window. I had soon read all the tracts that were left there, and examined where former prisoners had broken out, and where a grate had been sawed off, and heard the history of the various occupants of that room; for I found that even here there was a history and a gossip which never circulated beyond the walls of the jail. Probably this is the only house in the town where verses are composed, which are afterward printed in a circular form, but not published. I was shown quite a long list of verses which were composed by some young men who had been detected in an attempt to escape, who avenged themselves by singing them.

I pumped my fellow-prisoner as dry as I could, for fear I should never see him again; but at length he showed me which was my bed, and left me to blow out the lamp.

It was like travelling into a far country, such as I had never expected to behold, to lie there for one night. It seemed to me that I never had heard the town-clock strike before, nor the evening sounds of the village; for we slept with the windows open, which were inside the grating. It was to see my native village in the light of the Middle Ages, and our Concord was turned into a Rhine stream, and visions of knights and castles passed before me. They were the voices of old burghers that I heard in the streets. I was an involuntary spectator and auditor of whatever was done and said in the kitchen of the adjacent village-inn,—a wholly new and rare experience to me. It was a closer view of my native town. I was fairly inside of it. I never had seen its institutions before. This is one of its peculiar institutions; for it is a shire town. I began to comprehend what its inhabitants were about.

In the morning, our breakfasts were put through the hole in the door, in small oblong-square tin pans, made to fit, and holding a pint of chocolate, with brown bread, and an iron spoon. When they called for the vessels again, I was green enough to return what bread I had left; but my comrade seized it, and said that I should lay that up for lunch or dinner. Soon after he was let out to work at haying in a neighboring field, whither he went every day, and would not be back till noon; so he bade me good-day, saying that he doubted if he should see me again.

When I came out of prison,—for some one interfered, and paid that tax,—I did not perceive that great changes had taken place on the common, such as he observed who went in a youth, and emerged a tottering and gray-headed man; and yet a change had to my eyes come over the scene,—the town, and State, and country,—greater than any that mere time could effect. I saw yet more distinctly the State in which I lived. I saw to what extent the people among whom I lived could be trusted as good neighbors and friends; that their friendship was for summer weather only; that they did not greatly propose to do right; that they were a distinct race from me by their prejudices and superstitions, as the Chinamen and Malays are; that, in their sacrifices to humanity, they ran no risks, not even to their property; that, after all, they were not so noble but they treated the thief as he had treated them, and hoped, by a certain outward observance and a few prayers, and by walking in a particular straight though useless path from time to time, to save their souls. This may be to judge my neighbors harshly; for I believe that many of them are not aware that they have such an institution as the jail in their village.

It was formerly the custom in our village, when a poor debtor came out of jail, for his acquaintances to salute him, looking through their fingers, which were crossed to represent the grating of a jail window, "How do ye do?" My neighbors did not thus salute me, but first looked at me, and then at one another, as if I had returned from a long journey. I was put into jail as I was going to the shoemaker's to get a shoe which was mended. When I was let out the next morning, I proceeded to finish my errand, and having put on my mended shoe, joined a huckleberry party, who were impatient to put themselves under my conduct; and in half an hour,—for the horse was soon tackled,—was in the midst of a huckleberry field, on one of our highest hills, two miles off, and then the State was nowhere to be seen.

This is the whole history of "My Prisons."

I have never declined paying the highway tax, because I am as desirous of being a good neighbor as I am of being a bad subject; and, as for supporting schools, I am doing my part to educate my fellow-countrymen now. It is for no particular item in the tax-bill that I refuse to pay it. I simply wish to refuse allegiance to the State, to withdraw and stand aloof from it effectually. I do not care to trace the course of my dollar, if I could, till it buys a man or a musket to shoot one with,—the dollar is innocent,—but I am concerned to trace the effects of my allegiance. In fact, I quietly declare war with the State, after my fashion, though I will still make what use and get what advantage of her I can, as is usual in such cases.

If others pay the tax which is demanded of me, from a sympathy with the State, they do but what they have already done in their own case, or rather they abet injustice to a greater extent than the State requires. If they pay the tax from a mistaken interest in the individual taxed, to save his property, or prevent his going to jail, it is because they have not considered wisely how far they let their private feelings interfere with the public good.

This, then, is my position at present. But one cannot be too much on his guard in such a case, lest his action be biassed by obstinacy, or an undue regard for the opinions of men. Let him see that he does only what belongs to himself and to the hour.

I think sometimes, Why, this people mean well; they are only ignorant; they would do better if they knew how: why give your neighbors this pain to treat you as they are not inclined to? But I think again, this is no reason why I should do as they do, or permit others to suffer much greater pain of a different kind. Again, I sometimes say to myself, When many millions of men, without heat, without ill will, without personal feeling of any kind, demand of you a few shillings only, without the possibility, such is their constitution, of retracting or altering their present demand, and without the possibility, on your side, of appeal to any other millions, why expose yourself to this overwhelming brute force? You do not resist cold and hunger, the winds and the waves, thus obstinately; you quietly submit to a thousand similar necessities. You do not put your head into the fire. But just in proportion as I regard this as not wholly a brute force, but partly a human force, and consider that I have relations to those millions as to so many millions of men, and not of mere brute or inanimate things, I see that appeal is possible, first and instantaneously, from them to the Maker of them, and, secondly, from them to themselves. But, if I put my head deliberately into the fire, there is no appeal to fire or to the Maker of fire, and I have only myself to blame. If I could convince myself that I have any right to be satisfied with men as they are, and to treat them accordingly, and not according, in some respects, to my requisitions and expectations of what they and I ought to be, then, like a good Mussulman and fatalist, I should endeavor to be satisfied with things as they are, and say it is the will of God. And, above all, there is this difference between resisting this and a purely brute or natural force, that I can resist this with some effect; but I cannot expect, like Orpheus, to change the nature of the rocks and trees and beasts.

I do not wish to quarrel with any man or nation. I do not wish to split hairs, to make fine distinctions, or set myself up as better than my neighbors. I seek rather, I may say, even an excuse for conforming to the laws of the land. I am but too ready to conform to them. Indeed, I have reason to suspect myself on this head; and each year, as the tax-gatherer comes round, I find myself disposed to review the acts and position of the general and State governments, and the spirit of the people, to discover a pretext for conformity.

> "We must affect our country as our parents;
> And if at any time we alienate
> Our love or industry from doing it honor,
> We must respect effects and teach the soul
> Matter of conscience and religion,
> And not desire of rule or benefit."

I believe that the State will soon be able to take all my work of this sort out of my hands, and then I shall be no better a patriot than my fellow-countrymen. Seen from a lower point of view, the Constitution, with all its faults, is very good; the law and the courts are very respectable; even this State and this American government are, in many respects, very admirable and rare things, to be thankful for, such as a great many have described them; but seen from a point of view a little higher, they are what I have described them; seen from a higher still, and the highest, who shall say what they are, or that they are worth looking at or thinking of at all?

However, the government does not concern me much, and I shall bestow the fewest possible thoughts on it. It is not many moments that I live under a government, even in this world. If a man is thought-free, fancy-free, imagination-free, that which *is not* never for a long time appearing *to be* to him, unwise rulers or reformers cannot fatally interrupt him.

I know that most men think differently from myself; but those whose lives are by profession devoted to the study of these or kindred subjects, content me as little as any. States-men and legislators, standing so completely within the insti-tution, never distinctly and nakedly behold it. They speak of moving society, but have no resting-place without it. They may be men of a certain experience and discrimination, and have no doubt invented ingenious and even useful systems, for which we sincerely thank them; but all their wit and use-fulness lie within certain not very wide limits. They are wont to forget that the world is not governed by policy and expe-diency. Webster never goes behind government, and so can-not speak with authority about it. His words are wisdom to those legislators who contemplate no essential reform in the existing government; but for thinkers, and those who legislate for all time, he never once glances at the subject. I know of those whose serene and wise speculations on this theme would soon reveal the limits of his mind's range and hospital-ity. Yet, compared with the cheap professions of most reform-ers, and the still cheaper wisdom and eloquence of politicians in general, his are almost the only sensible and valuable words, and we thank Heaven for him. Comparatively, he is al-ways strong, original, and, above all, practical. Still his quality is not wisdom, but prudence. The lawyer's truth is not Truth, but consistency, or a consistent expediency. Truth is always in harmony with herself, and is not concerned chiefly to reveal the justice that may consist with wrong-doing. He well de-serves to be called, as he has been called, the Defender of the Constitution. There are really no blows to be given by him but defensive ones. He is not a leader, but a follower. His leaders are the men of '87. "I have never made an ef-fort," he says, "and never propose to make an effort; I have never countenanced an effort, and never mean to counte-nance an effort, to disturb the arrangement as originally made, by which the various States came into the Union." Still thinking of the sanction which the Constitution gives to slavery, he says, "Because it was a part of the original compact,—let it stand." Notwithstanding his special acute-ness and ability, he is unable to take a fact out of its merely political relations, and behold it as it lies absolutely to be dis-posed of by the intellect,—what, for instance, it behooves a man to do here in America to-day with regard to slavery,—

but ventures, or is driven, to make some such desperate answer as the following, while professing to speak absolutely,
and as a private man,—from which what new and singular
code of social duties might be inferred? "The manner," says
he, "in which the governments of those States where slavery
exists are to regulate it, is for their own consideration, under
their responsibility to their constituents, to the general laws of
propriety, humanity, and justice, and to God. Associations
formed elsewhere, springing from a feeling of humanity, or
any other cause, have nothing whatever to do with it. They
have never received any encouragement from me, and they
never will."*

They who know of no purer sources of truth, who have
traced up its stream no higher, stand, and wisely stand, by the
Bible and the Constitution, and drink at it there with reverence and humility; but they who behold where it comes trickling into this lake or that pool, gird up their loins once more,
and continue their pilgrimage toward its fountain-head.

No man with a genius for legislation has appeared in
America. They are rare in the history of the world. There are
orators, politicians, and eloquent men, by the thousand; but
the speaker has not yet opened his mouth to speak, who is capable of settling the much-vexed questions of the day. We
love eloquence for its own sake, and not for any truth which
it may utter, or any heroism it may inspire. Our legislators
have not yet learned the comparative value of free-trade and
of freedom, of union, and of rectitude, to a nation. They have
no genius or talent for comparatively humble questions of
taxation and finance, commerce and manufactures and agriculture. If we were left solely to the wordy wit of legislators
in Congress for our guidance, uncorrected by the seasonable
experience and the effectual complaints of the people,
America would not long retain her rank among the nations.
For eighteen hundred years, though perchance I have no
right to say it, the New Testament has been written; yet
where is the legislator who has wisdom and practical talent
enough to avail himself of the light which it sheds on the science of legislation?

*These extracts have been inserted since the Lecture was read.

The authority of government, even such as I am willing to submit to,—for I will cheerfully obey those who know and can do better than I, and in many things even those who neither know nor can do so well,—is still an impure one: to be strictly just, it must have the sanction and consent of the governed. It can have no pure right over my person and property but what I concede to it. The progress from an absolute to a limited monarchy, from a limited monarchy to a democracy, is a progress toward a true respect for the individual. Even the Chinese philosopher was wise enough to regard the individual as the basis of the empire. Is a democracy, such as we know it, the last improvement possible in government? Is it not possible to take a step further towards recognizing and organizing the rights of man? There will never be a really free and enlightened State, until the State comes to recognize the individual as a higher and independent power, from which all its own power and authority are derived, and treats him accordingly. I please myself with imagining a State at last which can afford to be just to all men, and to treat the individual with respect as a neighbor; which even would not think it inconsistent with its own repose, if a few were to live aloof from it, not meddling with it, nor embraced by it, who fulfilled all the duties of neighbors and fellow-men. A State which bore this kind of fruit, and suffered it to drop off as fast as it ripened, would prepare the way for a still more perfect and glorious State, which also I have imagined, but not yet anywhere seen.

Walking

I WISH to speak a word for Nature, for absolute freedom and wildness, as contrasted with a freedom and culture merely civil,—to regard man as an inhabitant, or a part and parcel of Nature, rather than a member of society. I wish to make an extreme statement, if so I may make an emphatic one, for there are enough champions of civilization: the minister, and the school-committee, and every one of you will take care of that.

I have met with but one or two persons in the course of my life who understood the art of Walking, that is, of taking walks,—who had a genius, so to speak, for *sauntering*: which word is beautifully derived "from idle people who roved about the country, in the Middle Ages, and asked charity, under pretence of going *à la Sainte Terre*," to the Holy Land, till the children exclaimed, "There goes a *Sainte-Terrer*," a Saunterer,—a Holy-Lander. They who never go to the Holy Land in their walks, as they pretend, are indeed mere idlers and vagabonds; but they who do go there are saunterers in the good sense, such as I mean. Some, however, would derive the word from *sans terre*, without land or a home, which, therefore, in the good sense, will mean, having no particular home, but equally at home everywhere. For this is the secret of successful sauntering. He who sits still in a house all the time may be the greatest vagrant of all; but the saunterer, in the good sense, is no more vagrant than the meandering river, which is all the while sedulously seeking the shortest course to the sea. But I prefer the first, which, indeed, is the most probable derivation. For every walk is a sort of crusade, preached by some Peter the Hermit in us, to go forth and reconquer this Holy Land from the hands of the Infidels.

It is true, we are but faint-hearted crusaders, even the walkers, nowadays, who undertake no persevering, never-ending enterprises. Our expeditions are but tours, and come round again at evening to the old hearth-side from which we set

out. Half the walk is but retracing our steps. We should go
forth on the shortest walk, perchance, in the spirit of undying
adventure, never to return,—prepared to send back our embalmed hearts only as relics to our desolate kingdoms. If you
are ready to leave father and mother, and brother and sister,
and wife and child and friends, and never see them again,—if
you have paid your debts, and made your will, and settled
all your affairs, and are a free man, then you are ready for a
walk.

To come down to my own experience, my companion and
I, for I sometimes have a companion, take pleasure in fancying ourselves knights of a new, or rather an old, order,—not
Equestrians or Chevaliers, not Ritters or Riders, but Walkers,
a still more ancient and honorable class, I trust. The chivalric
and heroic spirit which once belonged to the Rider seems
now to reside in, or perchance to have subsided into, the
Walker,—not the Knight, but Walker Errant. He is a sort of
fourth estate, outside of Church and State and People.

We have felt that we almost alone hereabouts practised this
noble art; though, to tell the truth, at least, if their own assertions are to be received, most of my townsmen would fain
walk sometimes, as I do, but they cannot. No wealth can buy
the requisite leisure, freedom, and independence, which are
the capital in this profession. It comes only by the grace of
God. It requires a direct dispensation from Heaven to become a walker. You must be born into the family of the
Walkers. *Ambulator nascitur, non fit.* Some of my townsmen,
it is true, can remember and have described to me some walks
which they took ten years ago, in which they were so blessed
as to lose themselves for half an hour in the woods; but I
know very well that they have confined themselves to the
highway ever since, whatever pretensions they may make to
belong to this select class. No doubt they were elevated for a
moment as by the reminiscence of a previous state of existence, when even they were foresters and outlaws.

> "When he came to grene wode,
> 　　In a mery mornynge,
> There he herde the notes small
> 　　Of byrdes mery syngynge.

> "It is ferre gone, sayd Robyn,
> That I was last here;
> Me lyste a lytell for to shote
> At the donne dere."

I think that I cannot preserve my health and spirits, unless I spend four hours a day at least—and it is commonly more than that—sauntering through the woods and over the hills and fields, absolutely free from all worldly engagements. You may safely say, A penny for your thoughts, or a thousand pounds. When sometimes I am reminded that the mechanics and shopkeepers stay in their shops not only all the forenoon, but all the afternoon too, sitting with crossed legs, so many of them,—as if the legs were made to sit upon, and not to stand or walk upon,—I think that they deserve some credit for not having all committed suicide long ago.

I, who cannot stay in my chamber for a single day without acquiring some rust, and when sometimes I have stolen forth for a walk at the eleventh hour of four o'clock in the afternoon, too late to redeem the day, when the shades of night were already beginning to be mingled with the daylight, have felt as if I had committed some sin to be atoned for,—I confess that I am astonished at the power of endurance, to say nothing of the moral insensibility, of my neighbors who confine themselves to shops and offices the whole day for weeks and months, ay, and years almost together. I know not what manner of stuff they are of,—sitting there now at three o'clock in the afternoon, as if it were three o'clock in the morning. Bonaparte may talk of the three-o'clock-in-the-morning courage, but it is nothing to the courage which can sit down cheerfully at this hour in the afternoon over against one's self whom you have known all the morning, to starve out a garrison to whom you are bound by such strong ties of sympathy. I wonder that about this time, or say between four and five o'clock in the afternoon, too late for the morning papers and too early for the evening ones, there is not a general explosion heard up and down the street, scattering a legion of antiquated and house-bred notions and whims to the four winds for an airing,—and so the evil cure itself.

How womankind, who are confined to the house still more than men, stand it I do not know; but I have ground to suspect that most of them do not *stand* it at all. When, early in a summer afternoon, we have been shaking the dust of the village from the skirts of our garments, making haste past those houses with purely Doric or Gothic fronts, which have such an air of repose about them, my companion whispers that probably about these times their occupants are all gone to bed. Then it is that I appreciate the beauty and the glory of architecture, which itself never turns in, but forever stands out and erect, keeping watch over the slumberers.

No doubt temperament, and, above all, age, have a good deal to do with it. As a man grows older, his ability to sit still and follow in-door occupations increases. He grows vespertinal in his habits as the evening of life approaches, till at last he comes forth only just before sundown, and gets all the walk that he requires in half an hour.

But the walking of which I speak has nothing in it akin to taking exercise, as it is called, as the sick take medicine at stated hours,—as the swinging of dumb-bells or chairs; but is itself the enterprise and adventure of the day. If you would get exercise, go in search of the springs of life. Think of a man's swinging dumb-bells for his health, when those springs are bubbling up in far-off pastures unsought by him!

Moreover, you must walk like a camel, which is said to be the only beast which ruminates when walking. When a traveller asked Wordsworth's servant to show him her master's study, she answered, "Here is his library, but his study is out of doors."

Living much out of doors, in the sun and wind, will no doubt produce a certain roughness of character,—will cause a thicker cuticle to grow over some of the finer qualities of our nature, as on the face and hands, or as severe manual labor robs the hands of some of their delicacy of touch. So staying in the house, on the other hand, may produce a softness and smoothness, not to say thinness of skin, accompanied by an increased sensibility to certain impressions. Perhaps we should be more susceptible to some influences important to our intellectual and moral growth, if the sun had shone and the wind blown on us a little less; and no doubt it is a nice matter to proportion rightly the thick and thin skin. But methinks that is a scurf that will fall off fast enough,—that the natural remedy is to be found in the proportion which the night bears to the day, the winter to the summer, thought to experience. There will be so much the more air and sunshine in our thoughts. The callous palms of the laborer are conversant with finer tissues of self-respect and heroism, whose touch thrills the heart, than the languid fingers of idleness. That is mere sentimentality that lies abed by day and thinks itself white, far from the tan and callus of experience.

When we walk, we naturally go to the fields and woods: what would become of us, if we walked only in a garden or a mall? Even some sects of philosophers have felt the necessity of importing the woods to themselves, since they did not go to the woods. "They planted groves and walks of Platanes," where they took *subdiales ambulationes* in porticos open to the air. Of course it is of no use to direct our steps to the woods, if they do not carry us thither. I am alarmed when it happens that I have walked a mile into the woods bodily, without getting there in spirit. In my afternoon walk I would fain forget all my morning occupations and my obligations to society. But it sometimes happens that I cannot easily shake off the village. The thought of some work will run in my head, and I am not where my body is,—I am out of my senses. In my walks I would fain return to my senses. What business have I in the woods, if I am thinking of something out of the woods? I suspect myself, and cannot help a shudder, when I find myself so implicated even in what are called good works,—for this may sometimes happen.

My vicinity affords many good walks; and though for so many years I have walked almost every day, and sometimes for several days together, I have not yet exhausted them. An absolutely new prospect is a great happiness, and I can still get this any afternoon. Two or three hours' walking will carry me to as strange a country as I expect ever to see. A single farmhouse which I had not seen before is sometimes as good as the dominions of the King of Dahomey. There is in fact a sort of harmony discoverable between the capabilities of the land-

scape within a circle of ten miles' radius, or the limits of an afternoon walk, and the threescore years and ten of human life.
It will never become quite familiar to you.

Nowadays almost all man's improvements, so called, as the
building of houses, and the cutting down of the forest and of
all large trees, simply deform the landscape, and make it more
and more tame and cheap. A people who would begin by
burning the fences and let the forest stand! I saw the fences
half consumed, their ends lost in the middle of the prairie, and
some worldly miser with a surveyor looking after his bounds,
while heaven had taken place around him, and he did not see
the angels going to and fro, but was looking for an old post-
hole in the midst of paradise. I looked again, and saw him
standing in the middle of a boggy, stygian fen, surrounded by
devils, and he had found his bounds without a doubt, three little stones, where a stake had been driven, and looking nearer,
I saw that the Prince of Darkness was his surveyor.

I can easily walk ten, fifteen, twenty, any number of miles,
commencing at my own door, without going by any house,
without crossing a road except where the fox and the mink
do: first along by the river, and then the brook, and then the
meadow and the wood-side. There are square miles in my
vicinity which have no inhabitant. From many a hill I can see
civilization and the abodes of man afar. The farmers and their
works are scarcely more obvious than woodchucks and their
burrows. Man and his affairs, church and state and school,
trade and commerce, and manufactures and agriculture, even
politics, the most alarming of them all,—I am pleased to see
how little space they occupy in the landscape. Politics is but a
narrow field, and that still narrower highway yonder leads to
it. I sometimes direct the traveller thither. If you would go
to the political world, follow the great road,—follow that
market-man, keep his dust in your eyes, and it will lead you
straight to it; for it, too, has its place merely, and does not
occupy all space. I pass from it as from a bean-field into the
forest, and it is forgotten. In one half-hour I can walk off to
some portion of the earth's surface where a man does not
stand from one year's end to another, and there, consequently, politics are not, for they are but as the cigar-smoke of
a man.

The village is the place to which the roads tend, a sort of expansion of the highway, as a lake of a river. It is the body of which roads are the arms and legs,—a trivial or quadrivial place, the thoroughfare and ordinary of travellers. The word is from the Latin *villa*, which, together with *via*, a way, or more anciently *ved* and *vella*, Varro derives from *veho*, to carry, because the villa is the place to and from which things are carried. They who got their living by teaming were said *vellaturam facere*. Hence, too, apparently, the Latin word *vilis* and our vile; also *villain*. This suggests what kind of degeneracy villagers are liable to. They are wayworn by the travel that goes by and over them, without travelling themselves.

Some do not walk at all; others walk in the highways; a few walk across lots. Roads are made for horses and men of business. I do not travel in them much, comparatively, because I am not in a hurry to get to any tavern or grocery or livery-stable or depot to which they lead. I am a good horse to travel, but not from choice a roadster. The landscape-painter uses the figures of men to mark a road. He would not make that use of my figure. I walk out into a Nature such as the old prophets and poets, Menu, Moses, Homer, Chaucer, walked in. You may name it America, but it is not America: neither Americus Vespucius, nor Columbus, nor the rest were the discoverers of it. There is a truer account of it in mythology than in any history of America, so called, that I have seen.

However, there are a few old roads that may be trodden with profit, as if they led somewhere now that they are nearly discontinued. There is the Old Marlborough Road, which does not go to Marlborough now, methinks, unless that is Marlborough where it carries me. I am the bolder to speak of it here, because I presume that there are one or two such roads in every town.

THE OLD MARLBOROUGH ROAD.

> Where they once dug for money,
> But never found any;
> Where sometimes Martial Miles
> Singly files,
> And Elijah Wood,

I fear for no good:
No other man,
Save Elisha Dugan,—
O man of wild habits,
Partridges and rabbits,
Who hast no cares
Only to set snares,
Who liv'st all alone,
Close to the bone,
And where life is sweetest
Constantly eatest.
When the spring stirs my blood
   With the instinct to travel,
   I can get enough gravel
On the Old Marlborough Road.
      Nobody repairs it,
      For nobody wears it;
      It is a living way,
      As the Christians say.
Not many there be
   Who enter therein,
Only the guests of the
   Irishman Quin.
What is it, what is it,
   But a direction out there,
And the bare possibility
   Of going somewhere?
      Great guide-boards of stone,
      But travellers none;
      Cenotaphs of the towns
      Named on their crowns.
      It is worth going to see
      Where you *might* be.
      What king
      Did the thing,
      I am still wondering;
      Set up how or when,
      By what selectmen,
      Gourgas or Lee,
      Clark or Darby?

They 're a great endeavor
To be something forever;
Blank tablets of stone,
Where a traveller might groan,
And in one sentence
Grave all that is known;
Which another might read,
In his extreme need.
I know one or two
Lines that would do,
Literature that might stand
All over the land,
Which a man could remember
Till next December,
And read again in the spring,
After the thawing.
If with fancy unfurled
You leave your abode,
You may go round the world
By the Old Marlborough Road.

At present, in this vicinity, the best part of the land is not private property; the landscape is not owned, and the walker enjoys comparative freedom. But possibly the day will come when it will be partitioned off into so-called pleasure-grounds, in which a few will take a narrow and exclusive pleasure only,—when fences shall be multiplied, and man-traps and other engines invented to confine men to the *public* road, and walking over the surface of God's earth shall be construed to mean trespassing on some gentleman's grounds. To enjoy a thing exclusively is commonly to exclude yourself from the true enjoyment of it. Let us improve our opportunities, then, before the evil days come.

What is it that makes it so hard sometimes to determine whither we will walk? I believe that there is a subtle magnetism in Nature, which, if we unconsciously yield to it, will direct us aright. It is not indifferent to us which way we walk. There is a right way; but we are very liable from heedlessness and stupidity to take the wrong one. We would fain take that walk, never yet taken by us through this actual world, which is perfectly symbolical of the path which we love to travel in the interior and ideal world; and sometimes, no doubt, we find it difficult to choose our direction, because it does not yet exist distinctly in our idea.

When I go out of the house for a walk, uncertain as yet whither I will bend my steps, and submit myself to my instinct to decide for me, I find, strange and whimsical as it may seem, that I finally and inevitably settle southwest, toward some particular wood or meadow or deserted pasture or hill in that direction. My needle is slow to settle,—varies a few degrees, and does not always point due southwest, it is true, and it has good authority for this variation, but it always settles between west and south-southwest. The future lies that way to me, and the earth seems more unexhausted and richer on that side. The outline which would bound my walks would be, not a circle, but a parabola, or rather like one of those cometary orbits which have been thought to be non-returning curves, in this case opening westward, in which my house occupies the place of the sun. I turn round and round irresolute sometimes for a quarter of an hour, until I decide, for the thousandth time, that I will walk into the southwest or west. Eastward I go only by force; but westward I go free. Thither no business leads me. It is hard for me to believe that I shall find fair landscapes or sufficient wildness and freedom behind the eastern horizon. I am not excited by the prospect of a walk thither; but I believe that the forest which I see in the western horizon stretches uninterruptedly towards the setting sun, and that there are no towns nor cities in it of enough consequence to disturb me. Let me live where I will, on this side is the city, on that the wilderness, and ever I am leaving the city more and more, and withdrawing into the wilderness. I should not lay so much stress on this fact, if I did not believe that something like this is the prevailing tendency of my countrymen. I must walk toward Oregon, and not toward Europe. And that way the nation is moving, and I may say that mankind progress from east to west. Within a few years we have witnessed the phenomenon of a southeastward migration, in the settlement of Australia; but this affects us as a retrograde movement, and, judging from the moral and physical character of the first generation of Australians, has not yet proved a successful experiment. The eastern Tartars think that there is nothing west beyond Thibet. "The world ends there," say they; "beyond there is nothing but a shoreless sea." It is unmitigated East where they live.

We go eastward to realize history and study the works of art and literature, retracing the steps of the race; we go westward as into the future, with a spirit of enterprise and adventure. The Atlantic is a Lethean stream, in our passage over which we have had an opportunity to forget the Old World and its institutions. If we do not succeed this time, there is perhaps one more chance for the race left before it arrives on the banks of the Styx; and that is in the Lethe of the Pacific, which is three times as wide.

I know not how significant it is, or how far it is an evidence of singularity, that an individual should thus consent in his pettiest walk with the general movement of the race; but I know that something akin to the migratory instinct in birds and quadrupeds,—which, in some instances, is known to have affected the squirrel tribe, impelling them to a general and mysterious movement, in which they were seen, say some, crossing the broadest rivers, each on its particular chip, with its tail raised for a sail, and bridging narrower streams with their dead,—that something like the *furor* which affects the domestic cattle in the spring, and which is referred to a worm in their tails,—affects both nations and individuals, either perennially or from time to time. Not a flock of wild geese cackles over our town, but it to some extent unsettles the value of real estate here, and, if I were a broker, I should probably take that disturbance into account.

> "Than longen folk to gon on pilgrimages,
> And palmeres for to seken strange strondes."

Every sunset which I witness inspires me with the desire to go to a West as distant and as fair as that into which the sun goes down. He appears to migrate westward daily, and tempt us to follow him. He is the Great Western Pioneer whom the nations follow. We dream all night of those mountain-ridges in the horizon, though they may be of vapor only, which were last gilded by his rays. The island of Atlantis, and the islands and gardens of the Hesperides, a sort of terrestrial paradise, appear to have been the Great West of the ancients, enveloped in mystery and poetry. Who has not seen in imagination, when looking into the sunset sky, the gardens of the Hesperides, and the foundation of all those fables?

Columbus felt the westward tendency more strongly than any before. He obeyed it, and found a New World for Castile and Leon. The herd of men in those days scented fresh pastures from afar.

> "And now the sun had stretched out all the hills,
> And now was dropped into the western bay;
> At last *he* rose, and twitched his mantle blue;
> To-morrow to fresh woods and pastures new."

Where on the globe can there be found an area of equal extent with that occupied by the bulk of our States, so fertile and so rich and varied in its productions, and at the same time so habitable by the European, as this is? Michaux, who knew but part of them, says that "the species of large trees are much more numerous in North America than in Europe; in the United States there are more than one hundred and forty species that exceed thirty feet in height; in France there are but thirty that attain this size." Later botanists more than confirm his observations. Humboldt came to America to realize his youthful dreams of a tropical vegetation, and he beheld it in its greatest perfection in the primitive forests of the Amazon, the most gigantic wilderness on the earth, which he has so eloquently described. The geographer Guyot, himself a European, goes farther,—farther than I am ready to follow him; yet not when he says,—"As the plant is made for the animal, as the vegetable world is made for the animal world, America is made for the man of the Old World. . . . . The man of the Old World sets out upon his way. Leaving the highlands of Asia, he descends from station to station towards Europe. Each of his steps is marked by a new civilization superior to the preceding, by a greater power of development. Arrived at the Atlantic, he pauses on the shore of this unknown ocean, the bounds of which he knows not, and turns upon his footprints for an instant." When he has exhausted the rich soil of Europe, and reinvigorated himself, "then recommences his adventurous career westward as in the earliest ages." So far Guyot.

From this western impulse coming in contact with the barrier of the Atlantic sprang the commerce and enterprise of modern times. The younger Michaux, in his "Travels West of the Alleghanies in 1802," says that the common inquiry in the newly settled West was, " 'From what part of the world have you come?' As if these vast and fertile regions would naturally be the place of meeting and common country of all the inhabitants of the globe."

To use an obsolete Latin word, I might say, *Ex Oriente lux; ex Occidente* FRUX. From the East light; from the West fruit.

Sir Francis Head, an English traveller and a Governor-General of Canada, tells us that "in both the northern and southern hemispheres of the New World, Nature has not only outlined her works on a larger scale, but has painted the whole picture with brighter and more costly colors than she used in delineating and in beautifying the Old World. . . . . The heavens of America appear infinitely higher, the sky is bluer, the air is fresher, the cold is intenser, the moon looks larger, the stars are brighter, the thunder is louder, the lightning is vivider, the wind is stronger, the rain is heavier, the mountains are higher, the rivers longer, the forests bigger, the plains broader." This statement will do at least to set against Buffon's account of this part of the world and its productions.

Linnæus said long ago, "Nescio quæ facies *læta, glabra* plantis Americanis: I know not what there is of joyous and smooth in the aspect of American plants"; and I think that in this country there are no, or at most very few, *Africanæ bestiæ*, African beasts, as the Romans called them, and that in this respect also it is peculiarly fitted for the habitation of man. We are told that within three miles of the centre of the East-Indian city of Singapore, some of the inhabitants are annually carried off by tigers; but the traveller can lie down in the woods at night almost anywhere in North America without fear of wild beasts.

These are encouraging testimonies. If the moon looks larger here than in Europe, probably the sun looks larger also. If the heavens of America appear infinitely higher, and the stars brighter, I trust that these facts are symbolical of the height to which the philosophy and poetry and religion of her inhabitants may one day soar. At length, perchance, the immaterial heaven will appear as much higher to the American mind, and the intimations that star it as much brighter. For I believe that climate does thus react on man,—as there is something in the mountain-air that feeds the spirit and inspires. Will not man grow to greater perfection intellectually as well as physically under these influences? Or is it unimportant how many foggy days there are in his life? I trust that we shall be more imaginative, that our thoughts will be clearer, fresher, and more ethereal, as our sky,—our understanding more comprehensive and broader, like our plains,—our intellect generally on a grander scale, like our thunder and lightning, our rivers and mountains and forests,—and our hearts shall even correspond in breadth and depth and grandeur to our inland seas. Perchance there will appear to the traveller something, he knows not what, of *læta* and *glabra*, of joyous and serene, in our very faces. Else to what end does the world go on, and why was America discovered?

To Americans I hardly need to say,—

"Westward the star of empire takes its way."

As a true patriot, I should be ashamed to think that Adam in paradise was more favorably situated on the whole than the backwoodsman in this country.

Our sympathies in Massachusetts are not confined to New England; though we may be estranged from the South, we sympathize with the West. There is the home of the younger sons, as among the Scandinavians they took to the sea for their inheritance. It is too late to be studying Hebrew; it is more important to understand even the slang of to-day.

Some months ago I went to see a panorama of the Rhine. It was like a dream of the Middle Ages. I floated down its historic stream in something more than imagination, under bridges built by the Romans, and repaired by later heroes, past cities and castles whose very names were music to my ears, and each of which was the subject of a legend. There were Ehrenbreitstein and Rolandseck and Coblentz, which I knew only in history. They were ruins that interested me chiefly. There seemed to come up from its waters and its vine-

clad hills and valleys a hushed music as of Crusaders departing for the Holy Land. I floated along under the spell of en-
chantment, as if I had been transported to an heroic age, and
breathed an atmosphere of chivalry.

Soon after, I went to see a panorama of the Mississippi, and
as I worked my way up the river in the light of to-day, and
saw the steamboats wooding up, counted the rising cities,
gazed on the fresh ruins of Nauvoo, beheld the Indians moving west across the stream, and, as before I had looked up the
Moselle, now looked up the Ohio and the Missouri, and
heard the legends of Dubuque and of Wenona's Cliff,—still
thinking more of the future than of the past or present,—I
saw that this was a Rhine stream of a different kind; that the
foundations of castles were yet to be laid, and the famous
bridges were yet to be thrown over the river; and I felt that
this was the heroic age itself, though we know it not, for the
hero is commonly the simplest and obscurest of men.

The West of which I speak is but another name for the
Wild; and what I have been preparing to say is, that in
Wildness is the preservation of the world. Every tree sends its
fibres forth in search of the Wild. The cities import it at any
price. Men plough and sail for it. From the forest and wilderness come the tonics and barks which brace mankind. Our ancestors were savages. The story of Romulus and Remus being
suckled by a wolf is not a meaningless fable. The founders of
every State which has risen to eminence have drawn their
nourishment and vigor from a similar wild source. It was because the children of the Empire were not suckled by the wolf
that they were conquered and displaced by the children of the
Northern forests who were.

I believe in the forest, and in the meadow, and in the night
in which the corn grows. We require an infusion of hemlock-
spruce or arbor-vitæ in our tea. There is a difference between
eating and drinking for strength and from mere gluttony. The
Hottentots eagerly devour the marrow of the koodoo and
other antelopes raw, as a matter of course. Some of our
Northern Indians eat raw the marrow of the Arctic reindeer,
as well as various other parts, including the summits of the
antlers, as long as they are soft. And herein, perchance, they

have stolen a march on the cooks of Paris. They get what usually goes to feed the fire. This is probably better than stall-fed beef and slaughter-house pork to make a man of. Give me a wildness whose glance no civilization can endure,—as if we lived on the marrow of koodoos devoured raw.

There are some intervals which border the strain of the wood-thrush, to which I would migrate,—wild lands where no settler has squatted it; to which, methinks, I am already acclimated.

The African hunter Cummings tells us that the skin of the eland, as well as that of most other antelopes just killed, emits the most delicious perfume of trees and grass. I would have every man so much like a wild antelope, so much a part and parcel of Nature, that his very person should thus sweetly advertise our senses of his presence, and remind us of those parts of Nature which he most haunts. I feel no disposition to be satirical, when the trapper's coat emits the odor of musquash even; it is a sweeter scent to me than that which commonly exhales from the merchant's or the scholar's garments. When I go into their wardrobes and handle their vestments, I am reminded of no grassy plains and flowery meads which they have frequented, but of dusty merchants' exchanges and libraries rather.

A tanned skin is something more than respectable, and perhaps olive is a fitter color than white for a man,—a denizen of the woods. "The pale white man!" I do not wonder that the African pitied him. Darwin the naturalist says, "A white man bathing by the side of a Tahitian was like a plant bleached by the gardener's art, compared with a fine, dark green one, growing vigorously in the open fields."

Ben Jonson exclaims,–

> "How near to good is what is fair!"

So I would say,—

> How near to good is what is *wild*!

Life consists with wildness. The most alive is the wildest. Not yet subdued to man, its presence refreshes him. One who pressed forward incessantly and never rested from his labors, who grew fast and made infinite demands on life, would al-

ways find himself in a new country or wilderness, and surrounded by the raw material of life. He would be climbing
over the prostrate stems of primitive forest-trees.

Hope and the future for me are not in lawns and cultivated
fields, not in towns and cities, but in the impervious and
quaking swamps. When, formerly, I have analyzed my partiality for some farm which I had contemplated purchasing, I
have frequently found that I was attracted solely by a few
square rods of impermeable and unfathomable bog,—a natural sink in one corner of it. That was the jewel which dazzled
me. I derive more of my subsistence from the swamps which
surround my native town than from the cultivated gardens in
the village. There are no richer parterres to my eyes than the
dense beds of dwarf andromeda (*Cassandra calyculata*) which
cover these tender places on the earth's surface. Botany cannot go farther than tell me the names of the shrubs which
grow there,—the high-blueberry, panicled andromeda, lamb-
kill, azalea, and rhodora,—all standing in the quaking sphag-
num. I often think that I should like to have my house front
on this mass of dull red bushes, omitting other flower plots
and borders, transplanted spruce and trim box, even gravelled
walks,—to have this fertile spot under my windows, not a few
imported barrow-fulls of soil only to cover the sand which
was thrown out in digging the cellar. Why not put my house,
my parlor, behind this plot, instead of behind that meagre as-
semblage of curiosities, that poor apology for a Nature and
Art, which I call my front-yard? It is an effort to clear up and
make a decent appearance when the carpenter and mason
have departed, though done as much for the passer-by as the
dweller within. The most tasteful front-yard fence was never
an agreeable object of study to me; the most elaborate ornaments, acorn-tops, or what not, soon wearied and disgusted
me. Bring your sills up to the very edge of the swamp, then,
(though it may not be the best place for a dry cellar,) so that
there be no access on that side to citizens. Front-yards are not
made to walk in, but, at most, through, and you could go in
the back way.

Yes, though you may think me perverse, if it were proposed
to me to dwell in the neighborhood of the most beautiful
garden that ever human art contrived, or else of a dismal

swamp, I should certainly decide for the swamp. How vain, then, have been all your labors, citizens, for me!

My spirits infallibly rise in proportion to the outward dreariness. Give me the ocean, the desert, or the wilderness! In the desert, pure air and solitude compensate for want of moisture and fertility. The traveller Burton says of it,—"Your *morale* improves; you become frank and cordial, hospitable and single-minded. . . . . In the desert, spirituous liquors excite only disgust. There is a keen enjoyment in a mere animal existence." They who have been travelling long on the steppes of Tartary say,—"On reëntering cultivated lands, the agitation, perplexity, and turmoil of civilization oppressed and suffocated us; the air seemed to fail us, and we felt every moment as if about to die of asphyxia." When I would recreate myself, I seek the darkest wood, the thickest and most interminable, and, to the citizen, most dismal swamp. I enter a swamp as a sacred place,—a *sanctum sanctorum*. There is the strength, the marrow of Nature. The wild-wood covers the virgin mould,—and the same soil is good for men and for trees. A man's health requires as many acres of meadow to his prospect as his farm does loads of muck. There are the strong meats on which he feeds. A town is saved, not more by the righteous men in it than by the woods and swamps that surround it. A township where one primitive forest waves above, while another primitive forest rots below,— such a town is fitted to raise not only corn and potatoes, but poets and philosophers for the coming ages. In such a soil grew Homer and Confucius and the rest, and out of such a wilderness comes the Reformer eating locusts and wild honey.

To preserve wild animals implies generally the creation of a forest for them to dwell in or resort to. So is it with man. A hundred years ago they sold bark in our streets peeled from our own woods. In the very aspect of those primitive and rugged trees, there was, methinks, a tanning principle which hardened and consolidated the fibres of men's thoughts. Ah! already I shudder for these comparatively degenerate days of my native village, when you cannot collect a load of bark of good thickness,—and we no longer produce tar and turpentine.

The civilized nations—Greece, Rome, England—have been sustained by the primitive forests which anciently rotted where they stand. They survive as long as the soil is not exhausted. Alas for human culture! little is to be expected of a nation, when the vegetable mould is exhausted, and it is compelled to make manure of the bones of its fathers. There the poet sustains himself merely by his own superfluous fat, and the philosopher comes down on his marrow-bones.

It is said to be the task of the American "to work the virgin soil," and that "agriculture here already assumes proportions unknown everywhere else." I think that the farmer displaces the Indian even because he redeems the meadow, and so makes himself stronger and in some respects more natural. I was surveying for a man the other day a single straight line one hundred and thirty-two rods long, through a swamp, at whose entrance might have been written the words which Dante read over the entrance to the infernal regions,—"Leave all hope, ye that enter,"—that is, of ever getting out again; where at one time I saw my employer actually up to his neck and swimming for his life in his property, though it was still winter. He had another similar swamp which I could not survey at all, because it was completely under water, and nevertheless, with regard to a third swamp, which I did *survey* from a distance, he remarked to me, true to his instincts, that he would not part with it for any consideration, on account of the mud which it contained. And that man intends to put a girdling ditch round the whole in the course of forty months, and so redeem it by the magic of his spade. I refer to him only as the type of a class.

The weapons with which we have gained our most important victories, which should be handed down as heirlooms from father to son, are not the sword and the lance, but the bush-whack, the turf-cutter, the spade, and the bog-hoe, rusted with the blood of many a meadow, and begrimed with the dust of many a hard-fought field. The very winds blew the Indian's cornfield into the meadow, and pointed out the way which he had not the skill to follow. He had no better implement with which to intrench himself in the land than a clam-shell. But the farmer is armed with plough and spade.

In Literature it is only the wild that attracts us. Dulness is but another name for tameness. It is the uncivilized free and wild thinking in "Hamlet" and the "Iliad," in all the Scriptures and Mythologies, not learned in the schools, that delights us. As the wild duck is more swift and beautiful than the tame, so is the wild—the mallard—thought, which 'mid falling dews wings its way above the fens. A truly good book is something as natural, and as unexpectedly and unaccountably fair and perfect, as a wild flower discovered on the prairies of the West or in the jungles of the East. Genius is a light which makes the darkness visible, like the lightning's flash, which perchance shatters the temple of knowledge itself,—and not a taper lighted at the hearth-stone of the race, which pales before the light of common day.

English literature, from the days of the minstrels to the Lake Poets,—Chaucer and Spenser and Milton, and even Shakspeare, included,—breathes no quite fresh and in this sense wild strain. It is an essentially tame and civilized literature, reflecting Greece and Rome. Her wilderness is a greenwood,—her wild man a Robin Hood. There is plenty of genial love of Nature, but not so much of Nature herself. Her chronicles inform us when her wild animals, but not when the wild man in her, became extinct.

The science of Humboldt is one thing, poetry is another thing. The poet to-day, notwithstanding all the discoveries of science, and the accumulated learning of mankind, enjoys no advantage over Homer.

Where is the literature which gives expression to Nature? He would be a poet who could impress the winds and streams into his service, to speak for him; who nailed words to their primitive senses, as farmers drive down stakes in the spring, which the frost has heaved; who derived his words as often as he used them,—transplanted them to his page with earth adhering to their roots; whose words were so true and fresh and natural that they would appear to expand like the buds at the approach of spring, though they lay half-smothered between two musty leaves in a library,—ay, to bloom and bear fruit there, after their kind, annually; for the faithful reader, in sympathy with surrounding Nature.

I do not know of any poetry to quote which adequately expresses this yearning for the Wild. Approached from this side, the best poetry is tame. I do not know where to find in any literature, ancient or modern, any account which contents me of that Nature with which even I am acquainted. You will perceive that I demand something which no Augustan nor Elizabethan age, which no *culture*, in short, can give. Mythology comes nearer to it than anything. How much more fertile a Nature, at least, has Grecian mythology its root in than English literature! Mythology is the crop which the Old World bore before its soil was exhausted, before the fancy and imagination were affected with blight; and which it still bears, wherever its pristine vigor is unabated. All other literatures endure only as the elms which overshadow our houses; but this is like the great dragon-tree of the Western Isles, as old as mankind, and, whether that does or not, will endure as long; for the decay of other literatures makes the soil in which it thrives.

The West is preparing to add its fables to those of the East. The valleys of the Ganges, the Nile, and the Rhine, having yielded their crop, it remains to be seen what the valleys of the Amazon, the Plate, the Orinoco, the St. Lawrence, and the Mississippi will produce. Perchance, when, in the course of ages, American liberty has become a fiction of the past,— as it is to some extent a fiction of the present,—the poets of the world will be inspired by American mythology.

The wildest dreams of wild men, even, are not the less true, though they may not recommend themselves to the sense which is most common among Englishmen and Americans to-day. It is not every truth that recommends itself to the common sense. Nature has a place for the wild clematis as well as for the cabbage. Some expressions of truth are reminiscent,—others merely *sensible*, as the phrase is,— others prophetic. Some forms of disease, even, may prophesy forms of health. The geologist has discovered that the figures of serpents, griffins, flying dragons, and other fanciful embellishments of heraldry, have their prototypes in the forms of fossil species which were extinct before man was created, and hence "indicate a faint and shadowy knowledge of a previous state of organic existence." The Hindoos dreamed that the earth rested on an elephant, and the elephant on a tortoise, and the tortoise on a serpent; and though it may be an unimportant coincidence, it will not be out of place here to state, that a fossil tortoise has lately been discovered in Asia large enough to support an elephant. I confess that I am partial to these wild fancies, which transcend the order of time and development. They are the sublimest recreation of the intellect. The partridge loves peas, but not those that go with her into the pot.

In short, all good things are wild and free. There is something in a strain of music, whether produced by an instrument or by the human voice,—take the sound of a bugle in a summer night, for instance,—which by its wildness, to speak without satire, reminds me of the cries emitted by wild beasts in their native forests. It is so much of their wildness as I can understand. Give me for my friends and neighbors wild men, not tame ones. The wildness of the savage is but a faint symbol of the awful ferity with which good men and lovers meet.

I love even to see the domestic animals reassert their native rights,—any evidence that they have not wholly lost their original wild habits and vigor; as when my neighbor's cow breaks out of her pasture early in the spring and boldly swims the river, a cold, gray tide, twenty-five or thirty rods wide, swollen by the melted snow. It is the buffalo crossing the Mississippi. This exploit confers some dignity on the herd in my eyes,—already dignified. The seeds of instinct are preserved under the thick hides of cattle and horses, like seeds in the bowels of the earth, an indefinite period.

Any sportiveness in cattle is unexpected. I saw one day a herd of a dozen bullocks and cows running about and frisking in unwieldy sport, like huge rats, even like kittens. They shook their heads, raised their tails, and rushed up and down a hill, and I perceived by their horns, as well as by their activity, their relation to the deer tribe. But, alas! a sudden loud *Whoa!* would have damped their ardor at once, reduced them from venison to beef, and stiffened their sides and sinews like the locomotive. Who but the Evil One has cried, "Whoa!" to mankind? Indeed, the life of cattle, like that of many men, is but a sort of locomotiveness; they move a side at a time, and man, by his machinery, is meeting the horse and ox half-way.

Whatever part the whip has touched is thenceforth palsied. Who would ever think of a *side* of any of the supple cat tribe, as we speak of a *side* of beef?

I rejoice that horses and steers have to be broken before they can be made the slaves of men, and that men themselves have some wild oats still left to sow before they become submissive members of society. Undoubtedly, all men are not equally fit subjects for civilization; and because the majority, like dogs and sheep, are tame by inherited disposition, this is no reason why the others should have their natures broken that they may be reduced to the same level. Men are in the main alike, but they were made several in order that they might be various. If a low use is to be served, one man will do nearly or quite as well as another; if a high one, individual excellence is to be regarded. Any man can stop a hole to keep the wind away, but no other man could serve so rare a use as the author of this illustration did. Confucius says,—"The skins of the tiger and the leopard, when they are tanned, are as the skins of the dog and the sheep tanned." But it is not the part of a true culture to tame tigers, any more than it is to make sheep ferocious; and tanning their skins for shoes is not the best use to which they can be put.

When looking over a list of men's names in a foreign language, as of military officers, or of authors who have written on a particular subject, I am reminded once more that there is nothing in a name. The name Menschikoff, for instance, has nothing in it to my ears more human than a whisker, and it may belong to a rat. As the names of the Poles and Russians are to us, so are ours to them. It is as if they had been named by the child's rigmarole,—*Iery wiery ichery van, tittle-tol-tan.* I see in my mind a herd of wild creatures swarming over the earth, and to each the herdsman has affixed some barbarous sound in his own dialect. The names of men are of course as cheap and meaningless as *Bose* and *Tray*, the names of dogs.

Methinks it would be some advantage to philosophy, if men were named merely in the gross, as they are known. It would be necessary only to know the genus, and perhaps the race or variety, to know the individual. We are not prepared to believe that every private soldier in a Roman army had a name of his own,—because we have not supposed that he had a character of his own. At present our only true names are nick-names. I knew a boy who, from his peculiar energy, was called "Buster" by his playmates, and this rightly supplanted his Christian name. Some travellers tell us that an Indian had no name given him at first, but earned it, and his name was his fame; and among some tribes he acquired a new name with every new exploit. It is pitiful when a man bears a name for convenience merely, who has earned neither name nor fame.

I will not allow mere names to make distinctions for me, but still see men in herds for all them. A familiar name can-not make a man less strange to me. It may be given to a sav-age who retains in secret his own wild title earned in the woods. We have a wild savage in us, and a savage name is per-chance somewhere recorded as ours. I see that my neighbor, who bears the familiar epithet William, or Edwin, takes it off with his jacket. It does not adhere to him when asleep or in anger, or aroused by any passion or inspiration. I seem to hear pronounced by some of his kin at such a time his original wild name in some jaw-breaking or else melodious tongue.

Here is this vast, savage, howling mother of ours, Nature, lying all around, with such beauty, and such affection for her children, as the leopard; and yet we are so early weaned from her breast to society, to that culture which is exclusively an in-teraction of man on man,—a sort of breeding in and in, which produces at most a merely English nobility, a civiliza-tion destined to have a speedy limit.

In society, in the best institutions of men, it is easy to de-tect a certain precocity. When we should still be growing chil-dren, we are already little men. Give me a culture which imports much muck from the meadows, and deepens the soil,—not that which trusts to heating manures, and im-proved implements and modes of culture only!

Many a poor sore-eyed student that I have heard of would grow faster, both intellectually and physically, if, instead of sit-ting up so very late, he honestly slumbered a fool's allowance.

There may be an excess even of informing light. Niépce, a Frenchman, discovered "actinism," that power in the sun's rays which produces a chemical effect,—that granite rocks, and stone structures, and statues of metal, "are all alike destructively acted upon during the hours of sunshine, and, but for provisions of Nature no less wonderful, would soon perish under the delicate touch of the most subtile of the agencies of the universe." But he observed that "those bodies which underwent this change during the daylight possessed the power of restoring themselves to their original conditions during the hours of night, when this excitement was no longer influencing them." Hence it has been inferred that "the hours of darkness are as necessary to the inorganic creation as we know night and sleep are to the organic kingdom." Not even does the moon shine every night, but gives place to darkness.

I would not have every man nor every part of a man cultivated, any more than I would have every acre of earth cultivated: part will be tillage, but the greater part will be meadow and forest, not only serving an immediate use, but preparing a mould against a distant future, by the annual decay of the vegetation which it supports.

There are other letters for the child to learn than those which Cadmus invented. The Spaniards have a good term to express this wild and dusky knowledge,—*Gramática parda*, tawny grammar,—a kind of mother-wit derived from that same leopard to which I have referred.

We have heard of a Society for the Diffusion of Useful Knowledge. It is said that knowledge is power; and the like. Methinks there is equal need of a Society for the Diffusion of Useful Ignorance, what we will call Beautiful Knowledge, a knowledge useful in a higher sense: for what is most of our boasted so-called knowledge but a conceit that we know something, which robs us of the advantage of our actual ignorance? What we call knowledge is often our positive ignorance; ignorance our negative knowledge. By long years of patient industry and reading of the newspapers—for what are the libraries of science but files of newspapers?—a man accumulates a myriad facts, lays them up in his memory, and then when in some spring of his life he saunters abroad into the Great Fields of thought, he, as it were, goes to grass like a horse, and leaves all his harness behind in the stable. I would say to the Society for the Diffusion of Useful Knowledge, sometimes,—Go to grass. You have eaten hay long enough. The spring has come with its green crop. The very cows are driven to their country pastures before the end of May; though I have heard of one unnatural farmer who kept his cow in the barn and fed her on hay all the year round. So, frequently, the Society for the Diffusion of Useful Knowledge treats its cattle.

A man's ignorance sometimes is not only useful, but beautiful,—while his knowledge, so called, is oftentimes worse than useless, besides being ugly. Which is the best man to deal with,—he who knows nothing about a subject, and, what is extremely rare, knows that he knows nothing, or he who really knows something about it, but thinks that he knows all?

My desire for knowledge is intermittent; but my desire to bathe my head in atmospheres unknown to my feet is perennial and constant. The highest that we can attain to is not Knowledge, but Sympathy with Intelligence. I do not know that this higher knowledge amounts to anything more definite than a novel and grand surprise on a sudden revelation of the insufficiency of all that we called Knowledge before,—a discovery that there are more things in heaven and earth than are dreamed of in our philosophy. It is the lighting up of the mist by the sun. Man cannot *know* in any higher sense than this, any more than he can look serenely and with impunity in the face of the sun: ‘Ὡς τὶ νοῶν, οὐ κεῖνον νοήσεις,—"You will not perceive that, as perceiving a particular thing," say the Chaldean Oracles.

There is something servile in the habit of seeking after a law which we may obey. We may study the laws of matter at and for our convenience, but a successful life knows no law. It is an unfortunate discovery certainly, that of a law which binds us where we did not know before that we were bound. Live free, child of the mist,—and with respect to knowledge we are all children of the mist. The man who takes the liberty to live is superior to all the laws, by virtue of his relation to the law-maker. "That is active duty," says the Vishnu Purana, "which is not for our bondage; that is knowledge which is for our liberation: all other duty is good only unto weariness; all other knowledge is only the cleverness of an artist."

It is remarkable how few events or crises there are in our histories; how little exercised we have been in our minds; how few experiences we have had. I would fain be assured that I am growing apace and rankly, though my very growth disturb this dull equanimity,—though it be with struggle through long, dark, muggy nights or seasons of gloom. It would be well, if all our lives were a divine tragedy even, instead of this trivial comedy or farce. Dante, Bunyan, and others, appear to have been exercised in their minds more than we: they were subjected to a kind of culture such as our district schools and colleges do not contemplate. Even Mahomet, though many may scream at his name, had a good deal more to live for, ay, and to die for, than they have commonly.

When, at rare intervals, some thought visits one, as perchance he is walking on a railroad, then indeed the cars go by without his hearing them. But soon, by some inexorable law, our life goes by and the cars return.

> "Gentle breeze, that wanderest unseen,
> And bendest the thistles round Loira of storms,
> Traveller of the windy glens,
> Why hast thou left my ear so soon?"

While almost all men feel an attraction drawing them to society, few are attracted strongly to Nature. In their relation to Nature men appear to me for the most part, notwithstanding their arts, lower than the animals. It is not often a beautiful relation, as in the case of the animals. How little appreciation of the beauty of the landscape there is among us! We have to be told that the Greeks called the world Κόσμος, Beauty, or Order, but we do not see clearly why they did so, and we esteem it at best only a curious philological fact.

For my part, I feel that with regard to Nature I live a sort of border life, on the confines of a world into which I make occasional and transient forays only, and my patriotism and allegiance to the State into whose territories I seem to retreat are those of a moss-trooper. Unto a life which I call natural I would gladly follow even a will-o'-the-wisp through bogs and sloughs unimaginable, but no moon nor fire-fly has shown me the causeway to it. Nature is a personality so vast and universal that we have never seen one of her features. The walker in the familiar fields which stretch around my native town sometimes finds himself in another land than is described in their owners' deeds, as it were in some far-away field on the confines of the actual Concord, where her jurisdiction ceases, and the idea which the word Concord suggests ceases to be suggested. These farms which I have myself surveyed, these bounds which I have set up appear dimly still as through a mist; but they have no chemistry to fix them; they fade from the surface of the glass; and the picture which the painter painted stands out dimly from beneath. The world with which we are commonly acquainted leaves no trace, and it will have no anniversary.

I took a walk on Spaulding's Farm the other afternoon. I saw the setting sun lighting up the opposite side of a stately pine wood. Its golden rays straggled into the aisles of the wood as into some noble hall. I was impressed as if some ancient and altogether admirable and shining family had settled there in that part of the land called Concord, unknown to me,—to whom the sun was servant,—who had not gone into society in the village,—who had not been called on. I saw their park, their pleasure-ground, beyond through the wood, in Spaulding's cranberry-meadow. The pines furnished them with gables as they grew. Their house was not obvious to vision; the trees grew through it. I do not know whether I heard the sounds of a suppressed hilarity or not. They seemed to recline on the sunbeams. They have sons and daughters. They are quite well. The farmer's cart-path, which leads directly through their hall, does not in the least put them out,—as the muddy bottom of a pool is sometimes seen through the reflected skies. They never heard of Spaulding, and do not know that he is their neighbor,—notwithstanding I heard him whistle as he drove his team through the house. Nothing can equal the serenity of their lives. Their coat of arms is simply a lichen. I saw it painted on the pines and oaks. Their attics were in the tops of the trees. They are of no politics. There was no noise of labor. I did not perceive that they were weaving or spinning. Yet I did detect, when the wind lulled and hearing was done away, the finest imaginable sweet musical hum,—as of a distant hive in May, which perchance was the sound of their thinking. They had no idle thoughts, and no one without could see their work, for their industry was not as in knots and excrescences embayed.

But I find it difficult to remember them. They fade irrevocably out of my mind even now while I speak and endeavor to recall them, and recollect myself. It is only after a long and serious effort to recollect my best thoughts that I become again aware of their cohabitancy. If it were not for such families as this, I think I should move out of Concord.

We are accustomed to say in New England that few and fewer pigeons visit us every year. Our forests furnish no mast for them. So, it would seem, few and fewer thoughts visit each growing man from year to year, for the grove in our minds is laid waste,—sold to feed unnecessary fires of ambition, or sent to mill, and there is scarcely a twig left for them to perch on. They no longer build nor breed with us. In some more genial season, perchance, a faint shadow flits across the landscape of the mind, cast by the *wings* of some thought in its vernal or autumnal migration, but, looking up, we are unable to detect the substance of the thought itself. Our winged thoughts are turned to poultry. They no longer soar, and they attain only to a Shanghai and Cochin-China grandeur. Those *gra-a-ate thoughts*, those *gra-a-ate men* you hear of!

We hug the earth,—how rarely we mount! Methinks we might elevate ourselves a little more. We might climb a tree, at least. I found my account in climbing a tree once. It was a tall white pine, on the top of a hill; and though I got well pitched, I was well paid for it, for I discovered new mountains in the horizon which I had never seen before,—so much more of the earth and the heavens. I might have walked about the foot of the tree for threescore years and ten, and yet I certainly should never have seen them. But, above all, I discovered around me,—it was near the end of June,—on the ends of the topmost branches only, a few minute and delicate red cone-like blossoms, the fertile flower of the white pine looking heavenward. I carried straightway to the village the topmost spire, and showed it to stranger jurymen who walked the streets,—for it was court-week,—and to farmers and lumber-dealers and wood-choppers and hunters, and not one had ever seen the like before, but they wondered as at a star dropped down. Tell of ancient architects finishing their works on the tops of columns as perfectly as on the lower and more visible parts! Nature has from the first expanded the minute blossoms of the forest only toward the heavens, above men's heads and unobserved by them. We see only the flowers that are under our feet in the meadows. The pines have developed their delicate blossoms on the highest twigs of the wood every summer for ages, as well over the heads of Nature's red children as of her white ones; yet scarcely a farmer or hunter in the land has ever seen them.

Above all, we cannot afford not to live in the present. He is blessed over all mortals who loses no moment of the passing life in remembering the past. Unless our philosophy hears the cock crow in every barn-yard within our horizon, it is belated. That sound commonly reminds us that we are growing rusty and antique in our employments and habits of thought. His philosophy comes down to a more recent time than ours. There is something suggested by it that is a newer testament,—the gospel according to this moment. He has not fallen astern; he has got up early, and kept up early, and to be where he is is to be in season, in the foremost rank of time. It is an expression of the health and soundness of Nature, a brag for all the world,—healthiness as of a spring burst forth, a new fountain of the Muses, to celebrate this last instant of time. Where he lives no fugitive slave laws are passed. Who has not betrayed his master many times since last he heard that note?

The merit of this bird's strain is in its freedom from all plaintiveness. The singer can easily move us to tears or to laughter, but where is he who can excite in us a pure morning joy? When, in doleful dumps, breaking the awful stillness of our wooden sidewalk on a Sunday, or, perchance, a watcher in the house of mourning, I hear a cockerel crow far or near, I think to myself, "There is one of us well, at any rate,"—and with a sudden gush return to my senses.

We had a remarkable sunset one day last November. I was walking in a meadow, the source of a small brook, when the sun at last, just before setting, after a cold gray day, reached a clear stratum in the horizon, and the softest, brightest morning sunlight fell on the dry grass and on the stems of the trees in the opposite horizon, and on the leaves of the shrub-oaks on the hill-side, while our shadows stretched long over the meadow eastward, as if we were the only motes in its beams. It was such a light as we could not have imagined a moment before, and the air also was so warm and serene that nothing was wanting to make a paradise of that meadow. When we reflected that this was not a solitary phenomenon, never to happen again, but that it would happen forever and ever an infinite number of evenings, and cheer and reassure the latest child that walked there, it was more glorious still.

The sun sets on some retired meadow, where no house is visible, with all the glory and splendor that it lavishes on cities, and, perchance, as it has never set before,—where there is but a solitary marsh-hawk to have his wings gilded by it, or only a musquash looks out from his cabin, and there is some little black-veined brook in the midst of the marsh, just beginning to meander, winding slowly round a decaying stump. We walked in so pure and bright a light, gilding the withered grass and leaves, so softly and serenely bright, I thought I had never bathed in such a golden flood, without a ripple or a murmur to it. The west side of every wood and rising ground gleamed like the boundary of Elysium, and the sun on our backs seemed like a gentle herdsman driving us home at evening.

So we saunter toward the Holy Land, till one day the sun shall shine more brightly than ever he has done, shall perchance shine into our minds and hearts, and light up our whole lives with a great awakening light, as warm and serene and golden as on a bank-side in autumn.

A Yankee in Canada

CHAPTER I.
CONCORD TO MONTREAL.

I FEAR that I have not got much to say about Canada, not having seen much; what I got by going to Canada was a cold. I left Concord, Massachusetts, Wednesday morning, September 25th, 1850, for Quebec. Fare, seven dollars there and back; distance from Boston, five hundred and ten miles; being obliged to leave Montreal on the return as soon as Friday, October 4th, or within ten days. I will not stop to tell the reader the names of my fellow-travellers; there were said to be fifteen hundred of them. I wished only to be set down in Canada, and take one honest walk there as I might in Concord woods of an afternoon.

The country was new to me beyond Fitchburg. In Ashburnham and afterward, as we were whirled rapidly along, I noticed the woodbine (*Ampelopsis quinquefolia*), its leaves now changed, for the most part on dead trees, draping them like a red scarf. It was a little exciting, suggesting bloodshed, or at least a military life, like an epaulet or sash, as if it were dyed with the blood of the trees whose wounds it was inadequate to stanch. For now the bloody autumn was come, and an Indian warfare was waged through the forest. These military trees appeared very numerous, for our rapid progress connected those that were even some miles apart. Does the woodbine prefer the elm? The first view of Monadnoc was obtained five or six miles this side of

Fitzwilliam, but nearest and best at Troy and beyond. Then there were the Troy cuts and embankments. Keene Street strikes the traveller favorably, it is so wide, level, straight, and long. I have heard one of my relatives, who was born and bred there, say that you could see a chicken run across it a mile off. I have also been told that when this town was settled they laid out a street four rods wide, but at a subsequent meeting of the proprietors one rose and remarked, "We have plenty of land, why not make the street eight rods wide?" and so they voted that it should be eight rods wide, and the town is known far and near for its handsome street. It was a cheap way of securing comfort, as well as fame, and I wish that all new towns would take pattern from this. It is best to lay our plans widely in youth, for then land is cheap, and it is but too easy to contract our views afterward. Youths so laid out, with broad avenues and parks, that they may make handsome and liberal old men! Show me a youth whose mind is like some Washington city of magnificent distances, prepared for the most remotely successful and glorious life after all, when those spaces shall be built over and the idea of the founder be realized. I trust that every New England boy will begin by laying out a Keene Street through his head, eight rods wide. I know one such Washington city of a man, whose lots as yet are only surveyed and staked out, and except a cluster of shanties here and there, only the Capitol stands there for all structures, and any day you may see from afar his princely idea borne coachwise along the spacious but yet empty avenues. Keene is built on a remarkably large and level interval, like the bed of a lake, and the surrounding hills, which are remote from its street, must afford some good walks. The scenery of mountain towns is commonly too much crowded. A town which is built on a plain of some extent, with an open horizon, and surrounded by hills at a distance, affords the best walks and views.

As we travel northwest up the country, sugar-maples, beeches, birches, hemlocks, spruce, butternuts, and ash trees prevail more and more. To the rapid traveller the number of elms in a town is the measure of its civility. One man in the cars has a bottle full of some liquor. The whole company smile whenever it is exhibited. I find no difficulty in con-

taining myself. The Westmoreland country looked attractive.
I heard a passenger giving the very obvious derivation of this
name, West-more-land, as if it were purely American, and he
had made a discovery; but I thought of "my cousin Westmoreland" in England. Every one will remember the approach to Bellows Falls, under a high cliff which rises from
the Connecticut. I was disappointed in the size of the river
here; it appeared shrunk to a mere mountain stream. The water was evidently very low. The rivers which we had crossed
this forenoon possessed more of the character of mountain
streams than those in the vicinity of Concord, and I was surprised to see everywhere traces of recent freshets, which had
carried away bridges and injured the railroad, though I had
heard nothing of it. In Ludlow, Mount Holly, and beyond,
there is interesting mountain scenery, not rugged and stupendous, but such as you could easily ramble over,—long narrow
mountain vales through which to see the horizon. You are in
the midst of the Green Mountains. A few more elevated blue
peaks are seen from the neighborhood of Mount Holly, perhaps Killington Peak is one. Sometimes, as on the Western
Railroad, you are whirled over mountainous embankments,
from which the scared horses in the valleys appear diminished
to hounds. All the hills blush; I think that autumn must be
the best season to journey over even the *Green* Mountains.
You frequently exclaim to yourself, what *red* maples! The
sugar-maple is not so red. You see some of the latter with rosy
spots or cheeks only, blushing on one side like fruit, while all
the rest of the tree is green, proving either some partiality in
the light or frosts, or some prematurity in particular branches.
Tall and slender ash-trees, whose foliage is turned to a dark
mulberry color, are frequent. The butternut, which is a remarkably spreading tree, is turned completely yellow, thus
proving its relation to the hickories. I was also struck by the
bright yellow tints of the yellow-birch. The sugar-maple is remarkable for its clean ankle. The groves of these trees looked
like vast forest sheds, their branches stopping short at a uniform height, four or five feet from the ground, like eaves, as
if they had been trimmed by art, so that you could look
under and through the whole grove with its leafy canopy, as
under a tent whose curtain is raised.

As you approach Lake Champlain you begin to see the New York mountains. The first view of the Lake at Vergennes is impressive, but rather from association than from any peculiarity in the scenery. It lies there so small (not appearing in that proportion to the width of the State that it does on the map), but beautifully quiet, like a picture of the Lake of Lucerne on a music-box, where you trace the name of Lucerne among the foliage; far more ideal than ever it looked on the map. It does not say, "Here I am, Lake Champlain," as the conductor might for it, but having studied the geography thirty years, you crossed over a hill one afternoon and beheld it. But it is only a glimpse that you get here. At Burlington you rush to a wharf and go on board a steamboat, two hundred and thirty-two miles from Boston. We left Concord at twenty minutes before eight in the morning, and were in Burlington about six at night, but too late to see the lake. We got our first fair view of the lake at dawn, just before reaching Plattsburg, and saw blue ranges of mountains on either hand, in New York and in Vermont, the former especially grand. A few white schooners, like gulls, were seen in the distance, for it is not waste and solitary like a lake in Tartary; but it was such a view as leaves not much to be said; indeed, I have postponed Lake Champlain to another day.

The oldest reference to these waters that I have yet seen is in the account of Cartier's discovery and exploration of the St. Lawrence in 1535. Samuel Champlain actually discovered and paddled up the Lake in July, 1609, eleven years before the settlement of Plymouth, accompanying a war-party of the Canadian Indians against the Iroquois. He describes the islands in it as not inhabited, although they are pleasant,—on account of the continual wars of the Indians, in consequence of which they withdraw from the rivers and lakes into the depths of the land, that they may not be surprised. "Continuing our course," says he, "in this lake, on the western side, viewing the country, I saw on the eastern side very high mountains, where there was snow on the summit. I inquired of the savages if those places were inhabited. They replied that they were, and that they were Iroquois, and that in those places there were beautiful valleys and plains fertile in corn, such as I have eaten in this country, with an infinity of other fruits." This is the earliest account of what is now Vermont.

The number of French Canadian gentlemen and ladies among the passengers, and the sound of the French language, advertised us by this time that we were being whirled towards some foreign vortex. And now we have left Rouse's Point, and entered the Sorel River, and passed the invisible barrier between the States and Canada. The shores of the Sorel, Richelieu, or St. John's River, are flat and reedy, where I had expected something more rough and mountainous for a natural boundary between two nations. Yet I saw a difference at once, in the few huts, in the pirogues on the shore, and as it were, in the shore itself. This was an interesting scenery to me, and the very reeds or rushes in the shallow water, and the tree-tops in the swamps, have left a pleasing impression. We had still a distant view behind us of two or three blue mountains in Vermont and New York. About nine o'clock in the forenoon we reached St. John's, an old frontier post three hundred and six miles from Boston and twenty-four from Montreal. We now discovered that we were in a foreign country, in a station-house of another nation. This building was a barn-like structure, looking as if it were the work of the villagers combined, like a log-house in a new settlement. My attention was caught by the double advertisements in French and English fastened to its posts, by the formality of the English, and the covert or open reference to their queen and the British lion. No gentlemanly conductor appeared, none whom you would know to be the conductor by his dress and demeanor; but erelong we began to see here and there a solid, red-faced, burly-looking Englishman, a little pursy perhaps, who made us ashamed of ourselves and our thin and nervous countrymen,—a grandfatherly personage, at home in his great-coat, who looked as if he might be a stage proprietor, certainly a railroad director, and knew, or had a right to know, when the cars did start. Then there were two or three pale-faced, black-eyed, loquacious Canadian French gentlemen there, shrugging their shoulders; pitted as if they had all had the small-pox. In the mean while some soldiers, red-coats, belonging to the barracks near by, were turned out to be drilled. At every important point in our route the soldiers showed themselves ready for us; though they were evidently rather raw recruits here, they manœuvred far better than our soldiers; yet, as usual, I heard some Yankees talk as if they were no great shakes, and they had seen the Acton Blues manœuvre as well. The officers spoke sharply to them, and appeared to be doing their part thoroughly. I heard one suddenly coming to the rear, exclaim, "Michael Donouy, take his name!" though I could not see what the latter did or omitted to do. It was whispered that Michael Donouy would have to suffer for that. I heard some of our party discussing the possibility of their driving these troops off the field with their umbrellas. I thought that the Yankee, though undisciplined, had this advantage at least, that he especially is a man who, everywhere and under all circumstances, is fully resolved to better his condition essentially, and therefore he could afford to be beaten at first; while the virtue of the Irishman, and to a great extent the Englishman, consists in merely maintaining his ground or condition. The Canadians here, a rather poor-looking race, clad in gray homespun, which gave them the appearance of being covered with dust, were riding about in caleches and small one-horse carts called charettes. The Yankees assumed that all the riders were racing, or at least exhibiting the paces of their horses, and saluted them accordingly. We saw but little of the village here, for nobody could tell us when the cars would start; that was kept a profound secret, perhaps for political reasons; and therefore we were tied to our seats. The inhabitants of St. John's and vicinity are described by an English traveller as "singularly unprepossessing," and before completing his period he adds, "besides, they are generally very much disaffected to the British crown." I suspect that that "besides" should have been a because.

At length, about noon, the cars began to roll towards La Prairie. The whole distance of fifteen miles was over a remarkably level country, resembling a Western prairie, with the mountains about Chambly visible in the northeast. This novel, but monotonous scenery, was exciting. At La Prairie we first took notice of the tinned roofs, but above all of the St. Lawrence, which looked like a lake; in fact it is considerably expanded here; it was nine miles across diagonally to

Montreal. Mount Royal in the rear of the city, and the island
of St. Helen's opposite to it, were now conspicuous. We
could also see the Sault St. Louis about five miles up the river,
and the Sault Norman still farther eastward. The former are
described as the most considerable rapids in the St. Lawrence;
but we could see merely a gleam of light there as from a cobweb in the sun. Soon the city of Montreal was discovered
with its tin roofs shining afar. Their reflections fell on the eye
like a clash of cymbals on the ear. Above all the church of
Notre Dame was conspicuous, and anon the Bonsecours mar-
ket-house, occupying a commanding position on the quay, in
the rear of the shipping. This city makes the more favorable
impression from being approached by water, and also being
built of stone, a gray limestone found on the island. Here,
after travelling directly inland the whole breadth of New
England, we had struck upon a city's harbor,—it made on me
the impression of a seaport,—to which ships of six hundred
tons can ascend, and where vessels drawing fifteen feet lie
close to the wharf, five hundred and forty miles from the
Gulf; the St. Lawrence being here two miles wide. There was
a great crowd assembled on the ferry-boat wharf and on the
quay to receive the Yankees, and flags of all colors were
streaming from the vessels to celebrate their arrival. When the
gun was fired, the gentry hurrahed again and again, and then
the Canadian caleche-drivers, who were most interested in the
matter, and who, I perceived, were separated from the former
by a fence, hurrahed their welcome; first the broadcloth, then
the homespun.

It was early in the afternoon when we stepped ashore. With
a single companion, I soon found my way to the church of
Notre Dame. I saw that it was of great size and signified
something. It is said to be the largest ecclesiastical structure in
North America, and can seat ten thousand. It is two hundred
and fifty-five and a half feet long, and the groined ceiling is
eighty feet above your head. The Catholic are the only
churches which I have seen worth remembering, which are
not almost wholly profane. I do not speak only of the rich and
splendid like this, but of the humblest of them as well.
Coming from the hurrahing mob and the rattling carriages,
we pushed aside the listed door of this church, and found

ourselves instantly in an atmosphere which might be sacred to thought and religion, if one had any. There sat one or two women who had stolen a moment from the concerns of the day, as they were passing; but, if there had been fifty people there, it would still have been the most solitary place imaginable. They did not look up at us, nor did one regard another. We walked softly down the broad-aisle with our hats in our hands. Presently came in a troop of Canadians, in their homespun, who had come to the city in the boat with us, and one and all kneeled down in the aisle before the high altar to their devotions, somewhat awkwardly, as cattle prepare to lie down, and there we left them. As if you were to catch some farmer's sons from Marlboro, come to cattle-show, silently kneeling in Concord meeting-house some Wednesday! Would there not soon be a mob peeping in at the windows? It is true, these Roman Catholics, priests and all, impress me as a people who have fallen far behind the significance of their symbols. It is as if an ox had strayed into a church and were trying to bethink himself. Nevertheless, they are capable of reverence; but we Yankees are a people in whom this sentiment has nearly died out, and in this respect we cannot bethink ourselves even as oxen. I did not mind the pictures nor the candles, whether tallow or tin. Those of the former which I looked at appeared tawdry. It matters little to me whether the pictures are by a neophyte of the Algonquin or the Italian tribe. But I was impressed by the quiet religious atmosphere of the place. It was a great cave in the midst of a city; and what were the altars and the tinsel but the sparkling stalactics, into which you entered in a moment, and where the still atmosphere and the sombre light disposed to serious and profitable thought? Such a cave at hand, which you can enter any day, is worth a thousand of our churches which are open only Sundays,—hardly long enough for an airing,—and then filled with a bustling congregation,—a church where the priest is the least part, where you do your own preaching, where the universe preaches to you and can be heard. I am not sure but this Catholic religion would be an admirable one if the priest were quite omitted. I think that I might go to church myself sometimes some Monday, if I lived in a city where there was such a one to go to. In Concord, to be sure, we do not need such.

Our forests are such a church, far grander and more sacred. We dare not leave *our* meeting-houses open for fear they would be profaned. Such a cave, such a shrine, in one of our groves, for instance, how long would it be respected? for what purposes would it be entered, by such baboons as we are? I think of its value not only to religion, but to philosophy and to poetry; besides a reading-room, to have a thinking-room in every city! Perchance the time will come when every house even will have not only its sleeping-rooms, and dining-room, and talking-room or parlor, but its thinking-room also, and the architects will put it into their plans. Let it be furnished and ornamented with whatever conduces to serious and creative thought. I should not object to the holy water, or any other simple symbol, if it were consecrated by the imagination of the worshippers.

I heard that some Yankees bet that the candles were not wax, but tin. A European assured them that they were wax; but, inquiring of the sexton, he was surprised to learn that they were tin filled with oil. The church was too poor to afford wax. As for the Protestant churches, here or elsewhere, they did not interest me, for it is only as caves that churches interest me at all, and in that respect they were inferior.

Montreal makes the impression of a larger city than you had expected to find, though you may have heard that it contains nearly sixty thousand inhabitants. In the newer parts it appeared to be growing fast like a small New York, and to be considerably Americanized. The names of the squares reminded you of Paris,—the Champ de Mars, the Place d'Armes, and others, and you felt as if a French revolution might break out any moment. Glimpses of Mount Royal rising behind the town, and the names of some streets in that direction, make one think of Edinburgh. That hill sets off this city wonderfully. I inquired at a principal bookstore for books published in Montreal. They said that there were none but school-books and the like; they got their books from the States. From time to time we met a priest in the streets, for they are distinguished by their dress, like the *civil* police. Like clergymen generally, with or without the gown, they made on us the impression of effeminacy. We also met some Sisters of Charity, dressed in black, with Shaker-shaped black bonnets and crosses, and cadaverous faces, who looked as if they had almost cried their eyes out, their complexions parboiled with scalding tears; insulting the daylight by their presence, having taken an oath not to smile. By cadaverous I mean that their faces were like the faces of those who have been dead and buried for a year, and then untombed, with the life's grief upon them, and yet, for some unaccountable reason, the process of decay arrested.

> "Truth never fails her servant, sir, nor leaves him
> With the day's shame upon him."

They waited demurely on the sidewalk while a truck laden with raisins was driven in at the seminary of St. Sulpice, never once lifting their eyes from the ground.

The soldier here, as everywhere in Canada, appeared to be put forward, and by his best foot. They were in the proportion of the soldiers to the laborers in an African ant-hill. The inhabitants evidently rely on them in a great measure for music and entertainment. You would meet with them pacing back and forth before some guard-house or passage-way, guarding, regarding, and disregarding all kinds of law by turns, apparently for the sake of the discipline to themselves, and not because it was important to exclude anybody from entering that way. They reminded me of the men who are paid for piling up bricks and then throwing them down again. On every prominent ledge you could see England's hands holding the Canadas, and I judged by the redness of her knuckles that she would soon have to let go. In the rear of such a guard-house, in a large gravelled square or parade-ground, called the Champ de Mars, we saw a large body of soldiers being drilled, we being as yet the only spectators. But they did not appear to notice us any more than the devotees in the church, but were seemingly as indifferent to fewness of spectators as the phenomena of nature are, whatever they might have been thinking under their helmets of the Yankees that were to come. Each man wore white kid gloves. It was one of the most interesting sights which I saw in Canada. The problem appeared to be how to smooth down all individual protuberances or idiosyncrasies, and make a thousand men move as one man, animated by one central will; and there was some approach to success. They obeyed the signals of a commander who stood at a great distance, wand in hand; and the precision, and promptness, and harmony of their movements could not easily have been matched. The harmony was far more remarkable than that of any choir or band, and obtained, no doubt, at a greater cost. They made on me the impression, not of many individuals, but of one vast centipede of a man, good for all sorts of pulling down; and why not then for some kinds of building up? If men could combine thus earnestly, and patiently, and harmoniously to some really worthy end, what might they not accomplish? They now put their hands, and partially perchance their heads, together, and the result is that they are the imperfect tools of an imperfect and tyrannical government. But if they could put their hands and heads and hearts and all together, such a co-operation and harmony would be the very end and success for which government now exists in vain,—a government, as it were, not only with tools, but stock to trade with.

I was obliged to frame some sentences that sounded like French in order to deal with the market-women, who, for the most part, cannot speak English. According to the guidebook the relative population of this city stands nearly thus: two fifths are French Canadian; nearly one fifth British Canadian; one and a half fifth English, Irish, and Scotch; somewhat less than one half fifth Germans, United States people, and others. I saw nothing like pie for sale, and no good cake to put in my bundle, such as you can easily find in our towns, but plenty of fair-looking apples, for which Montreal Island is celebrated, and also pears, cheaper, and I thought better than ours, and peaches, which, though they were probably brought from the South, were as cheap as they commonly are with us. So imperative is the law of demand and supply that, as I have been told, the market of Montreal is sometimes supplied with green apples from the State of New York some weeks even before they are ripe in the latter place. I saw here the spruce wax which the Canadians chew, done up in little silvered papers, a penny a roll; also a small and shrivelled fruit which they called *cerises* mixed with many little stems somewhat like raisins, but I soon returned what I had bought, finding them rather insipid, only putting a sample in my pocket. Since my return, I find on comparison that it is the fruit of the sweet viburnum (*Viburnum Lentago*), which with us rarely holds on till it is ripe.

I stood on the deck of the steamer John Munn, late in the afternoon, when the second and third ferry-boats arrived from La Prairie, bringing the remainder of the Yankees. I never saw so many caleches, cabs, charettes, and similar vehicles collected before, and doubt if New York could easily furnish more. The handsome and substantial stone quay, which stretches a mile along the river-side, and protects the street from the ice, was thronged with the citizens who had turned out on foot and in carriages to welcome or to behold the Yankees. It was interesting to see the caleche drivers dash up and down the slope of the quay with their active little horses. They drive much faster than in our cities. I have been told that some of them come nine miles into the city every morning and return every night, without changing their horses during the day. In the midst of the crowd of carts, I observed one deep one loaded with sheep with their legs tied together, and their bodies piled one upon another, as if the driver had forgotten that they were sheep and not yet mutton. A sight, I trust, peculiar to Canada, though I fear that it is not.

CHAPTER II.
QUEBEC AND MONTMORENCI.

About six o'clock we started for Quebec, one hundred and eighty miles distant by the river; gliding past Longueil and Boucherville on the right, and *Pointe aux Trembles*, "so called from having been originally covered with aspens," and *Bout de l'Isle*, or the end of the island, on the left. I repeat these names not merely for want of more substantial facts to record, but because they sounded singularly poetic to my ears. There certainly was no lie in them. They suggested that some simple, and, perchance, heroic human life might have transpired there. There is all the poetry in the world in a name. It is a poem which the mass of men hear and read. What is poetry in the common sense, but a string of such jingling names? I want nothing better than a good word. The name of a thing may easily be more than the thing itself to me. Inexpressibly beautiful appears the recognition by man of the least natural fact, and the allying his life to it. All the world reiterating this slender truth, that aspens once grew there; and the swift inference is, that men were there to see them. And so it would be with the names of our native and neighboring villages, if we had not profaned them.

The daylight now failed us, and we went below; but I endeavored to console myself for being obliged to make this voyage by night, by thinking that I did not lose a great deal, the shores being low and rather unattractive, and that the river itself was much the more interesting object. I heard something in the night about the boat being at William Henry, Three Rivers, and in the Richelieu Rapids, but I was still where I had been when I lost sight of *Pointe aux Trembles.* To hear a man who has been waked up at midnight in the cabin of a steamboat, inquiring, "Waiter, where are we now?" is, as if at any moment of the earth's revolution round the sun, or of the system round its centre, one were to raise himself up and inquire of one of the deck hands, "Where are we now?"

I went on deck at daybreak, when we were thirty or forty miles above Quebec. The banks were now higher and more interesting. There was an "uninterrupted succession of whitewashed cottages" on each side of the river. This is what every traveller tells. But it is not to be taken as an evidence of the populousness of the country in general, hardly even of the river banks. They have presented a similar appearance for a hundred years. The Swedish traveller and naturalist, Kalm, who descended this river in 1749, says: "It could really be called a village, beginning at Montreal and ending at Quebec, which is a distance of more than one hundred and eighty miles; for the farm-houses are never above five arpens, and sometimes but three asunder, a few places excepted." Even in 1684 Hontan said that the houses were not more than a gunshot apart at most. Erelong we passed Cape Rouge, eight miles above Quebec, the mouth of the Chaudière on the opposite or south side, New Liverpool Cove with its lumber rafts and some shipping; then Sillery and Wolfe's Cove and the Heights of Abraham on the north, with now a view of Cape Diamond, and the citadel in front. The approach to

Quebec was very imposing. It was about six o'clock in the morning when we arrived. There is but a single street under the cliff on the south side of the cape, which was made by blasting the rocks and filling up the river. Three-story houses did not rise more than one fifth or one sixth the way up the nearly perpendicular rock, whose summit is three hundred and forty-five feet above the water. We saw, as we glided past, the sign on the side of the precipice, part way up, pointing to the spot where Montgomery was killed in 1775. Formerly it was the custom for those who went to Quebec for the first time to be ducked, or else pay a fine. Not even the Governor General escaped. But we were too many to be ducked, even if the custom had not been abolished.*

Here we were, in the harbor of Quebec, still three hundred and sixty miles from the mouth of the St. Lawrence, in a basin two miles across, where the greatest depth is twenty-eight fathoms, and though the water is fresh, the tide rises seventeen to twenty-four feet,—a harbor "large and deep enough," says a British traveller, "to hold the English navy." I may as well state that, in 1844, the county of Quebec contained about forty-five thousand inhabitants (the city and suburbs having about forty-three thousand); about twenty-eight thousand being Canadians of French origin; eight thousand British; over seven thousand natives of Ireland; one thousand five hundred natives of England; the rest Scotch and others. Thirty-six thousand belong to the Church of Rome.

Separating ourselves from the crowd, we walked up a narrow street, thence ascended by some wooden steps, called the Break-neck Stairs, into another steep, narrow, and zigzag street, blasted through the rock, which last led through a low massive stone portal, called Prescott Gate, the principal thoroughfare into the Upper Town. This passage was defended by cannon, with a guard-house over it, a sentinel at his post, and other soldiers at hand ready to relieve him. I rubbed my eyes

---

*Hierosme Lalemant says in 1648, in his relation, he being Superior: "All those who come to New France know well enough the mountain of Notre Dame, because the pilots and sailors, being arrived at that part of the Great River which is opposite to those high mountains, baptize ordinarily for sport the new passengers, if they do not turn aside by some present the inundation of this baptism which one makes flow plentifully on their heads."

to be sure that I was in the nineteenth century, and was not entering one of those portals which sometimes adorn the frontispieces of new editions of old black-letter volumes. I thought it would be a good place to read Froissart's Chronicles. It was such a reminiscence of the Middle Ages as Scott's novels. Men apparently dwelt there for security. Peace be unto them! As if the inhabitants of New York were to go over to Castle William to live! What a place it must be to bring up children! Being safe through the gate we naturally took the street which was steepest, and after a few turns found ourselves on the Durham Terrace, a wooden platform on the site of the old castle of St. Louis, still one hundred and fifteen feet below the summit of the citadel, overlooking the Lower Town, the wharf where we had landed, the harbor, the Isle of Orleans, and the river and surrounding country to a great distance. It was literally a *splendid* view. We could see six or seven miles distant, in the northeast, an indentation in the lofty shore of the northern channel, apparently on one side of the harbor, which marked the mouth of the Montmorenci, whose celebrated fall was only a few rods in the rear.

At a shoe-shop, whither we were directed for this purpose, we got some of our American money changed into English. I found that American hard money would have answered as well, excepting cents, which fell very fast before their pennies, it taking two of the former to make one of the latter, and often the penny, which had cost us two cents, did us the service of one cent only. Moreover, our robust cents were compelled to meet on even terms a crew of vile half-penny tokens, and bungtown coppers, which had more brass in their composition, and so perchance made their way in the world. Wishing to get into the citadel, we were directed to the Jesuits' Barracks,—a good part of the public buildings here are barracks,—to get a pass of the Town Major. We did not heed the sentries at the gate, nor did they us, and what under the sun they were placed there for, unless to hinder a free circulation of the air, was not apparent. There we saw soldiers eating their breakfasts in their mess-room, from bare wooden tables in camp fashion. We were continually meeting with soldiers in the streets, carrying funny little tin pails of all shapes, even semicircular, as if made to pack conveniently. I supposed that they contained their dinners,—so many slices of bread and butter to each, perchance. Sometimes they were carrying some kind of military chest on a sort of bier or hand-barrow, with a springy, undulating, military step, all passengers giving way to them, even the charette-drivers stopping for them to pass,—as if the battle were being lost from an inadequate supply of powder. There was a regiment of Highlanders, and, as I understood, of Royal Irish, in the city; and by this time there was a regiment of Yankees also. I had already observed, looking up even from the water, the head and shoulders of some General Poniatowsky, with an enormous cocked hat and gun, peering over the roof of a house, away up where the chimney caps commonly are with us, as it were a caricature of war and military awfulness; but I had not gone far up St. Louis Street before my riddle was solved, by the apparition of a real live Highlander under a cocked hat, and with his knees out, standing and marching sentinel on the ramparts, between St. Louis and St. John's Gate. (It must be a holy war that is waged there.) We stood close by without fear and looked at him. His legs were somewhat tanned, and the hair had begun to grow on them, as some of our wise men predict that it will in such cases, but I did not think they were remarkable in any respect. Notwithstanding all his warlike gear, when I inquired of him the way to the Plains of Abraham, he could not answer me without betraying some bashfulness through his broad Scotch. Soon after, we passed another of these creatures standing sentry at the St. Louis Gate, who let us go by without shooting us, or even demanding the countersign. We then began to go through the gate, which was so thick and tunnel-like, as to remind me of those lines in Claudian's Old Man of Verona, about the getting out of the gate being the greater part of a journey;—as you might imagine yourself crawling through an architectural vignette *at the end* of a black-letter volume. We were then reminded that we had been in a fortress, from which we emerged by numerous zigzags in a ditch-like road, going a considerable distance to advance a few rods, where they could have shot us two or three times over, if their minds had been disposed as their guns were. The greatest, or rather the most prominent, part of this city was constructed with the design to offer the dead-est resistance to leaden and iron missiles that might be cast against it. But it is a remarkable meteorological and psycho-logical fact, that it is rarely known to rain lead with much vi-olence, except on places so constructed. Keeping on about a mile we came to the Plains of Abraham,—for having got through with the Saints, we come next to the Patriarchs. Here the Highland regiment was being reviewed, while the band stood on one side and played,—methinks it was *La Claire Fontaine*, the national air of the Canadian French. This is the site where a real battle once took place, to commemo-rate which they have had a sham fight here almost every day since. The Highlanders manœuvred very well, and if the pre-cision of their movements was less remarkable, they did not appear so stiffly erect as the English or Royal Irish, but had a more elastic and graceful gait, like a herd of their own red deer, or as if accustomed to stepping down the sides of moun-tains. But they made a sad impression on the whole, for it was obvious that all true manhood was in the process of being drilled out of them. I have no doubt that soldiers well drilled are, as a class, peculiarly destitute of originality and indepen-dence. The officers appeared like men dressed above their condition. It is impossible to give the soldier a good educa-tion, without making him a deserter. His natural foe is the government that drills him. What would any philanthropist, who felt an interest in these men's welfare, naturally do, but first of all teach them so to respect themselves, that they could not be hired for this work, whatever might be the conse-quences to this government or that;—not drill a few, but ed-ucate all. I observed one older man among them, gray as a wharf-rat, and supple as the Devil, marching lock-step with the rest who would have to pay for that elastic gait.

We returned to the citadel along the heights, plucking such flowers as grew there. There was an abundance of succory still in blossom, broad-leaved golden-rod, buttercups, thorn-bushes, Canada thistles, and ivy, on the very summit of Cape Diamond. I also found the bladder-campion in the neighbor-hood. We there enjoyed an extensive view, which I will de-scribe in another place. Our pass, which stated that all the rules were "to be strictly enforced," as if they were determined to keep up the semblance of reality to the last gasp, opened to us the Dalhousie Gate, and we were conducted over the citadel by a bare-legged Highlander in cocked hat and full regimentals. He told us that he had been here about three years, and had formerly been stationed at Gibraltar. As if his regiment, having perchance been nestled amid the rocks of Edinburgh Castle, must flit from rock to rock thenceforth over the earth's surface, like a bald eagle, or other bird of prey, from eyrie to eyrie. As we were going out, we met the Yankees coming in, in a body, headed by a red-coated officer called the commandant, and escorted by many citizens, both English and French Canadian. I therefore immediately fell into the procession, and went round the citadel again with more intelligent guides, carrying, as before, all my effects with me. Seeing that nobody walked with the red-coated commandant, I attached myself to him, and though I was not what is called well-dressed, he did not know whether to repel me or not, for I talked like one who was not aware of any deficiency in that respect. Probably there was not one among all the Yankees who went to Canada this time, who was not more splendidly dressed than I was. It would have been a poor story if I had not enjoyed some distinction. I had on my "bad-weather clothes," like Olaf Trygesson the Northman, when he went to the Thing in England, where, by the way, he won his bride. As we stood by the thirty-two-pounder on the summit of Cape Diamond, which is fired three times a day, the commandant told me that it would carry to the Isle of Orleans, four miles distant, and that no hostile vessel could come round the island. I now saw the subterranean or, rather, "casemated barracks" of the soldiers, which I had not noticed before, though I might have walked over them. They had very narrow windows, serving as loop-holes for musketry, and small iron chimneys rising above the ground. There we saw the soldiers at home and in an undress, splitting wood,—I looked to see whether with swords or axes,—and in various ways endeavoring to realize that their nation was now at peace with this part of the world. A part of each regiment, chiefly officers, are allowed to marry. A grandfatherly, would-be witty Englishman could give a Yankee whom he was patronizing no reason for the bare knees of the Highlanders,

other than oddity. The rock within the citadel is a little convex, so that shells falling on it would roll toward the circumference, where the barracks of the soldiers and officers are; it
has been proposed, therefore, to make it slightly concave, so
that they may roll into the centre, where they would be comparatively harmless; and it is estimated that to do this would
cost twenty thousand pounds sterling. It may be well to remember this when I build my next house, and have the roof
"all correct" for bombshells.

At mid-afternoon we made haste down *Sault-au-Matelot*
street, towards the Falls of Montmorenci, about eight miles
down the St. Lawrence, on the north side, leaving the further
examination of Quebec till our return. On our way, we saw
men in the streets sawing logs pit-fashion, and afterward,
with a common wood-saw and horse, cutting the planks into
squares for paving the streets. This looked very shiftless, especially in a country abounding in water-power, and reminded me that I was no longer in Yankee land. I found, on
inquiry, that the excuse for this was, that labor was so cheap;
and I thought, with some pain, how cheap men are here! I
have since learned that the English traveller, Warburton, remarked, soon after landing at Quebec, that everything was
cheap there but men. That must be the difference between
going thither from New and from Old England. I had already
observed the dogs harnessed to their little milk-carts, which
contain a single large can, lying asleep in the gutters regardless of the horses, while they rested from their labors, at different stages of the ascent in the Upper Town. I was surprised
at the regular and extensive use made of these animals for
drawing, not only milk, but groceries, wood, &c. It reminded
me that the dog commonly is not put to any use. Cats catch
mice; but dogs only worry the cats. Kalm, a hundred years
ago, saw sledges here for ladies to ride in, drawn by a pair of
dogs. He says, "A middle-sized dog is sufficient to draw a single person, when the roads are good"; and he was told by old
people, that horses were very scarce in their youth, and almost all the land-carriage was then effected by dogs. They
made me think of the Esquimaux, who, in fact, are the next
people on the north. Charlevoix says, that the first horses
were introduced in 1665.

We crossed Dorchester Bridge, over the St. Charles, the little river in which Cartier, the discoverer of the St. Lawrence, put his ships, and spent the winter of 1535, and found ourselves on an excellent macadamized road, called *Le Chemin de Beauport*. We had left Concord Wednesday morning, and we endeavored to realize that now, Friday morning, we were taking a walk in Canada, in the Seigniory of Beauport, a foreign country, which a few days before had seemed almost as far off as England and France. Instead of rambling to Flint's Pond or the Sudbury Meadows, we found ourselves, after being a little detained in cars and steamboats,—after spending half a night at Burlington, and half a day at Montreal,—taking a walk down the bank of the St. Lawrence to the Falls of Montmorenci and elsewhere. Well, I thought to myself, here I am in a foreign country; let me have my eyes about me, and take it all in. It already looked and felt a good deal colder than it had in New England, as we might have expected it would. I realized fully that I was four degrees nearer the pole, and shuddered at the thought; and I wondered if it were possible that the peaches might not be all gone when I returned. It was an atmosphere that made me think of the fur-trade, which is so interesting a department in Canada, for I had for all head-covering a thin palm-leaf hat without lining, that cost twenty-five cents, and over my coat one of those unspeakably cheap, as well as thin, brown linen sacks of the Oak Hall pattern, which every summer appear all over New England, thick as the leaves upon the trees. It was a thoroughly Yankee costume, which some of my fellow-travellers wore in the cars to save their coats a dusting. I wore mine, at first, because it looked better than the coat it covered, and last, because two coats were warmer than one, though one was thin and dirty. I never wear my best coat on a journey, though perchance I could show a certificate to prove that I have a more costly one, at least, at home, if that were all that a gentleman required. It is not wise for a traveller to go dressed. I should no more think of it than of putting on a clean dicky and blacking my shoes to go a-fishing; as if you were going out to dine, when, in fact, the genuine traveller is going out to work hard, and fare harder,—to eat a crust by the wayside whenever he can get it. Honest travelling is about as dirty work as you can do, and a man needs a pair of overalls for it. As for blacking my shoes in such a case, I should as soon think of blacking my face. I carry a piece of tallow to preserve the leather, and keep out the water; that's all; and many an officious shoe-black, who carried off my shoes when I was slumbering, mistaking me for a gentleman, has had occasion to repent it before he produced a gloss on them.

My pack, in fact, was soon made, for I keep a short list of those articles which, from frequent experience, I have found indispensable to the foot-traveller; and, when I am about to start, I have only to consult that, to be sure that nothing is omitted, and, what is more important, nothing superfluous inserted. Most of my fellow-travellers carried carpet-bags, or valises. Sometimes one had two or three ponderous yellow valises in his clutch, at each hitch of the cars, as if we were going to have another rush for seats; and when there was a rush in earnest, and there were not a few, I would see my man in the crowd, with two or three affectionate lusty fellows along each side of his arm, between his shoulder and his valises, which last held them tight to his back, like the nut on the end of a screw. I could not help asking in my mind, What so great cause for showing Canada to those valises, when perhaps your very nieces had to stay at home for want of an escort? I should have liked to be present when the custom-house officer came aboard of him, and asked him to declare upon his honor if he had anything but wearing apparel in them. Even the elephant carries but a small trunk on his journeys. The perfection of travelling is to travel without baggage. After considerable reflection and experience, I have concluded that the best bag for the foot-traveller is made with a handkerchief, or, if he study appearances, a piece of stiff brown paper, well tied up, with a fresh piece within to put outside when the first is torn. That is good for both town and country, and none will know but you are carrying home the silk for a new gown for your wife, when it may be a dirty shirt. A bundle which you can carry literally under your arm, and which will shrink and swell with its contents. I never found the carpet-bag of equal capacity, which was not a bundle of itself. We styled ourselves the Knights of the Umbrella and the Bundle; for wherever we went, whether to Notre Dame or Mount

Royal, or the Champ-de-Mars, to the Town Major's or the Bishop's Palace, to the Citadel, with a bare-legged Highlander for our escort, or to the Plains of Abraham, to dinner or to bed, the umbrella and the bundle went with us; for we wished to be ready to digress at any moment. We made it our home nowhere in particular, but everywhere where our umbrella and bundle were. It would have been an amusing circumstance, if the Mayor of one of those cities had politely asked us where we were staying. We could only have answered, that we were staying with his Honor for the time being. I was amused when, after our return, some green ones inquired if we found it easy to get accommodated; as if we went abroad to get accommodated, when we can get that at home.

We met with many charettes, bringing wood and stone to the city. The most ordinary looking horses travelled faster than ours, or, perhaps they were ordinary looking, because, as I am told, the Canadians do not use the curry-comb. Moreover, it is said, that on the approach of winter their horses acquire an increased quantity of hair, to protect them from the cold. If this be true, some of our horses would make you think winter were approaching, even in midsummer. We soon began to see women and girls at work in the fields, digging potatoes alone, or bundling up the grain which the men cut. They appeared in rude health, with a great deal of color in their cheeks, and, if their occupation had made them coarse, it impressed me as better in its effects than making shirts at fourpence apiece, or doing nothing at all; unless it be chewing slate pencils, with still smaller results. They were much more agreeable objects, with their great broad-brimmed hats and flowing dresses, than the men and boys. We afterwards saw them doing various other kinds of work; indeed, I thought that we saw more women at work out of doors than men. On our return, we observed in this town a girl with Indian boots, nearly two feet high, taking the harness off a dog. The purity and transparency of the atmosphere were wonderful. When we had been walking an hour, we were surprised, on turning round, to see how near the city, with its glittering tin roofs, still looked. A village ten miles off did not appear to be more than three or four. I was convinced that you could see objects distinctly there much farther than here. It is true the villages are of a dazzling white, but the dazzle is to be referred, perhaps, to the transparency of the atmosphere as much as to the whitewash.

We were now fairly in the village of Beauport, though there was still but one road. The houses stood close upon this, without any front-yards, and at any angle with it, as if they had dropped down, being set with more reference to the road which the sun travels. It being about sundown, and the Falls not far off, we began to look round for a lodging, for we preferred to put up at a private house, that we might see more of the inhabitants. We inquired first at the most promising looking houses, if, indeed, any were promising. When we knocked, they shouted some French word for come in, perhaps *entrez*, and we asked for a lodging in English; but we found, unexpectedly, that they spoke French only. Then we went along and tried another house, being generally saluted by a rush of two or three little curs, which readily distinguished a foreigner, and which we were prepared now to hear bark in French. Our first question would be, *Parlez-vous Anglais?* but the invariable answer was, *Non, monsieur;* and we soon found that the inhabitants were exclusively French Canadians, and nobody spoke English at all, any more than in France; that, in fact, we were in a foreign country, where the inhabitants uttered not one familiar sound to us. Then we tried by turns to talk French with them, in which we succeeded sometimes pretty well, but for the most part, pretty ill. *Pouvez-vous nous donner un lit cette nuit?* we would ask, and then they would answer with French volubility, so that we could catch only a word here and there. We could understand the women and children generally better than the men, and they us; and thus, after a while, we would learn that they had no more beds than they used.

So we were compelled to inquire: *Y a-t-il une maison publique ici?* (*auberge* we should have said, perhaps, for they seemed never to have heard of the other), and they answered at length that there was no tavern, unless we could get lodgings at the mill, *le moulin*, which we had passed; or they would direct us to a grocery, and almost every house had a small grocery at one end of it. We called on the public notary or village lawyer, but he had no more beds nor English than the rest. At one house there was so good a misunderstanding at once established through the politeness of all parties, that we were encouraged to walk in and sit down, and ask for a glass of water; and having drank their water, we thought it was as good as to have tasted their salt. When our host and his wife spoke of their poor accommodations, meaning for themselves, we assured them that they were good enough, for we thought that they were only apologizing for the poorness of the accommodations they were about to offer us, and we did not discover our mistake till they took us up a ladder into a loft, and showed to our eyes what they had been laboring in vain to communicate to our brains through our ears, that they had but that one apartment with its few beds for the whole family. We made our *a-dieus* forthwith, and with gravity, perceiving the literal signification of that word. We were finally taken in at a sort of public-house, whose master worked for Patterson, the proprietor of the extensive sawmills driven by a portion of the Montmorenci stolen from the fall, whose roar we now heard. We here talked, or murdered French all the evening, with the master of the house and his family, and probably had a more amusing time than if we had completely understood one another. At length they showed us to a bed in their best chamber, very high to get into, with a low wooden rail to it. It had no cotton sheets, but coarse, home-made, dark colored, linen ones. Afterward, we had to do with sheets still coarser than these, and nearly the color of our blankets. There was a large open buffet loaded with crockery, in one corner of the room, as if to display their wealth to travellers, and pictures of Scripture scenes, French, Italian, and Spanish, hung around. Our hostess came back directly to inquire if we would have brandy for breakfast. The next morning, when I asked their names, she took down the temperance pledges of herself and husband, and children, which were hanging against the wall. They were Jean Baptiste Binet, and his wife, Geneviève Binet. Jean Baptiste is the sobriquet of the French Canadians.

After breakfast we proceeded to the fall, which was within half a mile, and at this distance its rustling sound, like the wind among the leaves, filled all the air. We were disappointed to find that we were in some measure shut out from the west side of the fall by the private grounds and fences of Patterson, who appropriates not only a part of the water for his mill, but a still larger part of the prospect, so that we were obliged to trespass. This gentleman's mansion-house and grounds were formerly occupied by the Duke of Kent, father to Queen Victoria. It appeared to me in bad taste for an individual, though he were the father of Queen Victoria, to obtrude himself with his land titles, or at least his fences, on so remarkable a natural phenomenon, which should, in every sense, belong to mankind. Some falls should even be kept sacred from the intrusion of mills and factories, as water privileges in another than the millwright's sense. This small river falls perpendicularly nearly two hundred and fifty feet at one pitch. The St. Lawrence falls only one hundred and sixty-four feet at Niagara. It is a very simple and noble fall, and leaves nothing to be desired; but the most that I could say of it would only have the force of one other testimony to assure the reader that it is there. We looked directly down on it from the point of a projecting rock, and saw far below us, on a low promontory, the grass kept fresh and green by the perpetual drizzle, looking like moss. The rock is a kind of slate, in the crevices of which grew ferns and golden-rods. The prevailing trees on the shores were spruce and arbor-vitæ,—the latter very large and now full of fruit,—also aspens, alders, and the mountain-ash with its berries. Every emigrant who arrives in this country by way of the St. Lawrence, as he opens a point of the Isle of Orleans, sees the Montmorenci tumbling into the Great River thus magnificently in a vast white sheet, making its contribution with emphasis. Roberval's pilot, Jean Alphonse, saw this fall thus, and described it, in 1542. It is a splendid introduction to the scenery of Quebec. Instead of an artificial fountain in its square, Quebec has this magnificent natural waterfall to adorn one side of its harbor. Within the mouth of the chasm below, which can be entered only at ebb tide, we had a grand view at once of Quebec and of the fall. Kalm says that the noise of the fall is sometimes heard at Quebec, about eight miles distant, and is a sign of a northeast wind. The side of this chasm, of soft and crumbling slate too steep to climb, was among the memorable features of the

scene. In the winter of 1829 the frozen spray of the fall, descending on the ice of the St. Lawrence, made a hill one hundred and twenty-six feet high. It is an annual phenomenon
which some think may help explain the formation of glaciers.

In the vicinity of the fall we began to notice what looked
like our red-fruited thorn bushes, grown to the size of ordinary apple-trees, very common, and full of large red or yellow
fruit, which the inhabitants called *pommettes*, but I did not
learn that they were put to any use.

CHAPTER III.

ST. ANNE.

By the middle of the forenoon, though it was a rainy day,
we were once more on our way down the north bank of the
St. Lawrence, in a northeasterly direction, toward the Falls of
St. Anne, which are about thirty miles from Quebec. The settled, more level, and fertile portion of Canada East may be
described rudely as a triangle, with its apex slanting toward
the northeast, about one hundred miles wide at its base, and
from two to three, or even four hundred miles long, if you
reckon its narrow northeastern extremity; it being the immediate valley of the St. Lawrence and its tributaries, rising by
a single or by successive terraces toward the mountains on
either hand. Though the words Canada East on the map
stretch over many rivers and lakes and unexplored wildernesses, the actual Canada, which might be the colored portion of the map, is but a little clearing on the banks of the
river, which one of those syllables would more than cover.
The banks of the St. Lawrence are rather low from Montreal
to the Richelieu Rapids, about forty miles above Quebec.
Thence they rise gradually to Cape Diamond, or Quebec.
Where we now were, eight miles northeast of Quebec, the
mountains which form the northern side of this triangle were
only five or six miles distant from the river, gradually departing farther and farther from it, on the west, till they reach the
Ottawa, and making haste to meet it on the east, at Cape
Tourmente, now in plain sight about twenty miles distant. So
that we were travelling in a very narrow and sharp triangle
between the mountains and the river, tilted up toward

the mountains on the north, never losing sight of our great fellow-traveller on our right. According to Bouchette's Topographical Description of the Canadas, we were in the Seigniory of the Côte de Beaupré, in the county of Mont-morenci, and the district of Quebec; in that part of Canada which was the first to be settled, and where the face of the country and the population have undergone the least change from the beginning, where the influence of the States and of Europe is least felt, and the inhabitants see little or nothing of the world over the walls of Quebec. This Seigniory was granted in 1636, and is now the property of the Seminary of Quebec. It is the most mountainous one in the province. There are some half a dozen parishes in it, each containing a church, parsonage-house, grist-mill, and several saw-mills. We were now in the most westerly parish called Ange Gardien, or the Guardian Angel, which is bounded on the west by the Montmorenci. The north bank of the St. Lawrence here is formed on a grand scale. It slopes gently, either directly from the shore, or from the edge of an interval, till, at the distance of about a mile, it attains the height of four or five hundred feet. The single road runs along the side of the slope two or three hundred feet above the river at first, and from a quarter of a mile to a mile distant from it, and affords fine views of the north channel, which is about a mile wide, and of the beautiful Isle of Orleans, about twenty miles long by five wide, where grow the best apples and plums in the Quebec District.

Though there was but this single road, it was a continuous village for as far as we walked this day and the next, or about thirty miles down the river, the houses being as near together all the way as in the middle of one of our smallest straggling country villages, and we could never tell by their number when we were on the skirts of a parish, for the road never ran through the fields or woods. We were told that it was just six miles from one parish church to another. I thought that we saw every house in Ange Gardien. Therefore, as it was a muddy day, we never got out of the mud, nor out of the vil-lage, unless we got over the fence; then indeed, if it was on the north side, we were out of the civilized world. There were sometimes a few more houses near the church, it is true, but we had only to go a quarter of a mile from the road to the top of the bank to find ourselves on the verge of the uninhabited, and, for the most part, unexplored wilderness stretching toward Hudson's Bay. The farms accordingly were extremely long and narrow, each having a frontage on the river. Bouchette accounts for this peculiar manner of laying out a village by referring to "the social character of the Canadian peasant, who is singularly fond of neighborhood," also to the advantage arising from a concentration of strength in Indian times. Each farm, called *terre*, he says, is, in nine cases out of ten, three arpents wide by thirty deep, that is, very nearly thirty-five by three hundred and forty-nine of our rods; sometimes one half arpent by thirty, or one to sixty; sometimes, in fact, a few yards by half a mile. Of course it costs more for fences. A remarkable difference between the Canadian and the New England character appears from the fact that in 1745, the French government were obliged to pass a law forbidding the farmers or *censitaires* building on land less than one and a half arpents front by thirty or forty deep, under a certain penalty, in order to compel emigration, and bring the seigneur's estates all under cultivation; and it is thought that they have now less reluctance to leave the paternal roof than formerly, "removing beyond the sight of the parish spire, or the sound of the parish bell." But I find that in the previous or seventeenth century, the complaint, often renewed, was of a totally opposite character, namely, that the inhabitants dispersed and exposed themselves to the Iroquois. Accordingly, about 1664, the king was obliged to order that "they should make no more clearings except one next to another, and that they should reduce their parishes to the form of the parishes in France as much as possible." The Canadians of those days, at least, possessed a roving spirit of adventure which carried them further, in exposure to hardship and danger, than ever the New England colonist went, and led them, though not to clear and colonize the wilderness, yet to range over it as *coureurs de bois*, or runners of the woods, or as Hontan prefers to call them *coureurs de risques*, runners of risks; to say nothing of their enterprising priesthood; and Charlevoix thinks that if the authorities had taken the right steps to prevent the youth from ranging the woods (*de courir les bois*) they would have had an excellent militia to fight the Indians and English.

The road, in this clayey looking soil, was exceedingly muddy in consequence of the night's rain. We met an old woman directing her dog, which was harnessed to a little cart, to the least muddy part of it. It was a beggarly sight. But harnessed to the cart as he was, we heard him barking after we had passed, though we looked anywhere but to the cart to see where the dog was that barked. The houses commonly fronted the south, whatever angle they might make with the road; and frequently they had no door nor cheerful window on the roadside. Half the time they stood fifteen to forty rods from the road, and there was no very obvious passage to them, so that you would suppose that there must be another road running by them. They were of stone, rather coarsely mortared, but neatly whitewashed, almost invariably one story high and long in proportion to their height, with a shingled roof, the shingles being pointed, for ornament, at the eaves, like the pickets of a fence, and also one row half-way up the roof. The gables sometimes projected a foot or two at the ridge-pole only. Yet they were very humble and unpretending dwellings. They commonly had the date of their erection on them. The windows opened in the middle, like blinds, and were frequently provided with solid shutters. Sometimes, when we walked along the back side of a house which stood near the road, we observed stout stakes leaning against it, by which the shutters, now pushed half open, were fastened at night; within, the houses were neatly ceiled with wood not painted. The oven was commonly out of doors, built of stone and mortar, frequently on a raised platform of planks. The cellar was often on the opposite side of the road, in front of or behind the houses, looking like an ice-house with us with a lattice door for summer. The very few mechanics whom we met had an old-Bettyish look, in their aprons and *bonnets rouges*, like fools' caps. The men wore commonly the same *bonnet rouge*, or red woollen or worsted cap, or sometimes blue or gray, looking to us as if they had got up with their night-caps on, and, in fact, I afterwards found that they had. Their clothes were of the cloth of the country, *étoffe du pays*, gray or some other plain color. The women looked stout, with gowns that stood out stiffly, also, for the most part, apparently of some home-made stuff. We also saw some specimens of the more characteristic winter dress of the Canadian, and I have since frequently detected him in New England by his coarse gray homespun capote and picturesque red sash, and his well-furred cap, made to protect his ears against the severity of his climate.

It drizzled all day, so that the roads did not improve. We began now to meet with wooden crosses frequently, by the roadside, about a dozen feet high, often old and toppling down, sometimes standing in a square wooden platform, sometimes in a pile of stones, with a little niche containing a picture of the Virgin and Child, or of Christ alone, sometimes with a string of beads, and covered with a piece of glass to keep out the rain, with the words, *pour la vierge*, or *Iniri*, on them. Frequently, on the cross-bar, there would be quite a collection of symbolical knickknacks, looking like an Italian's board; the representation in wood of a hand, a hammer, spikes, pincers, a flask of vinegar, a ladder, &c., the whole, perchance, surmounted by a weathercock; but I could not look at an honest weathercock in this walk without mistrusting that there was some covert reference in it to St. Peter. From time to time we passed a little one-story chapel-like building, with a tin-roofed spire, a shrine, perhaps it would be called, close to the pathside, with a lattice door, through which we could see an altar, and pictures about the walls; equally open, through rain and shine, though there was no getting into it. At these places the inhabitants kneeled and perhaps breathed a short prayer. We saw one school-house in our walk, and listened to the sounds which issued from it; but it appeared like a place where the process, not of enlightening, but of obfuscating the mind was going on, and the pupils received only so much light as could penetrate the shadow of the Catholic Church. The churches were very picturesque, and their interior much more showy than the dwelling-houses promised. They were of stone, for it was ordered, in 1699, that that should be their material. They had tinned spires, and quaint ornaments. That of l'Ange Gardien had a dial on it, with the Middle Age Roman numerals on its face, and some images in niches on the outside. Probably its counterpart has

existed in Normandy for a thousand years. At the church of
Chateau Richer, which is the next parish to l'Ange Gardien,
we read, looking over the wall, the inscriptions in the adjacent
churchyard, which began with, "*Ici gît*" or "*Repose*," and one
over a boy contained, "*Priez pour lui.*" This answered as well
as Père la Chaise. We knocked at the door of the curé's house
here, when a sleek friar-like personage, in his sacerdotal robe,
appeared. To our *Parlez-vous Anglais?* even he answered,
"*Non, monsieur*"; but at last we made him understand what
we wanted. It was to find the ruins of the old *chateau*. "*Ah!
oui! oui!*" he exclaimed, and, donning his coat, hastened
forth, and conducted us to a small heap of rubbish which we
had already examined. He said that fifteen years before, it was
plus considérable. Seeing at that moment three little red birds
fly out of a crevice in the ruins, up into an arbor-vitæ tree,
which grew out of them, I asked him their names, in such
French as I could muster, but he neither understood me nor
ornithology; he only inquired where we had *appris à parler
Français*; we told him, *dans les États-Unis*; and so we bowed
him into his house again. I was surprised to find a man wearing a black coat, and with apparently no work to do, even in
that part of the world.

The universal salutation from the inhabitants whom we met
was *bon jour*, at the same time touching the hat; with *bon
jour*, and touching your hat, you may go smoothly through
all Canada East. A little boy, meeting us, would remark, "*Bon
jour, Monsieur; le chemin est mauvais*," Good morning, sir; it
is bad walking. Sir Francis Head says that the immigrant is
forward to "appreciate the happiness of living in a land in
which the old country's servile custom of touching the hat
does not exist," but he was thinking of Canada West, of
course. It would, indeed, be a serious bore to be obliged to
touch your hat several times a day. A Yankee has not leisure
for it.

We saw peas, and even beans, collected into heaps in the
fields. The former are an important crop here, and, I suppose,
are not so much infested by the weevil as with us. There were
plenty of apples, very fair and sound, by the roadside, but
they were so small as to suggest the origin of the apple in the
crab. There was also a small red fruit which they called *snells*,

and another, also red and very acid, whose name a little boy wrote for me "*pinbéna*." It is probably the same with, or similar to, the *pembina* of the voyageurs, a species of viburnum, which, according to Richardson, has given its name to many of the rivers of Rupert's Land. The forest trees were spruce, arbor-vitæ, firs, birches, beeches, two or three kinds of maple, bass-wood, wild-cherry, aspens, &c., but no pitch pines (*Pinus rigida*). I saw very few, if any, trees which had been set out for shade or ornament. The water was commonly running streams or springs in the bank by the roadside, and was excellent. The parishes are commonly separated by a stream, and frequently the farms. I noticed that the fields were furrowed or thrown into beds seven or eight feet wide to dry the soil.

At the *Rivière du Sault à la Puce*, which, I suppose, means the River of the Fall of the Flea, was advertised in English, as the sportsmen are English, "The best Snipe-shooting grounds," over the door of a small public-house. These words being English affected me as if I had been absent now ten years from my country, and for so long had not heard the sound of my native language, and every one of them was as interesting to me as if I had been a snipe-shooter, and they had been snipes. The prunella or self-heal, in the grass here, was an old acquaintance. We frequently saw the inhabitants washing, or cooking for their pigs, and in one place hackling flax by the roadside. It was pleasant to see these usually domestic operations carried on out of doors, even in that cold country.

At twilight we reached a bridge over a little river, the boundary between Chateau Richer and St. Anne, *le premier pont de St. Anne*, and at dark the church of *La Bonne St. Anne*. Formerly vessels from France, when they came in sight of this church, gave "a general discharge of their artillery," as a sign of joy that they had escaped all the dangers of the river. Though all the while we had grand views of the adjacent country far up and down the river, and, for the most part, when we turned about, of Quebec in the horizon behind us, and we never beheld it without new surprise and admiration; yet, throughout our walk, the Great River of Canada on our right hand was the main feature in the landscape, and this expands so rapidly below the Isle of Orleans, and creates such a breadth of level horizon above its waters in that direction, that, looking down the river as we approached the extremity of that island, the St. Lawrence seemed to be opening into the ocean, though we were still about three hundred and twenty-five miles from what can be called its mouth.*

When we inquired here for a *maison publique* we were directed apparently to that private house where we were most likely to find entertainment. There were no guideboards where we walked, because there was but one road; there were no shops nor signs, because there were no artisans to speak of, and the people raised their own provisions; and there were no taverns, because there were no travellers. We here bespoke lodging and breakfast. They had, as usual, a large old-fashioned, two-storied box-stove in the middle of the room, out of which, in due time, there was sure to be forthcoming a supper, breakfast, or dinner. The lower half held the fire, the upper the hot air, and as it was a cool Canadian evening, this was a comforting sight to us. Being four or five feet high it warmed the whole person as you stood by it. The stove was plainly a very important article of furniture in Canada, and was not set aside during the summer. Its size, and the respect which was paid to it, told of the severe winters which it had seen and prevailed over. The master of the house, in his long-pointed, red woollen cap, had a thoroughly antique physiognomy of the old Norman stamp. He might have come over with Jacques Cartier. His was the hardest French to understand of any we had heard yet, for there was a great difference between one speaker and another, and this man talked with a pipe in his mouth beside, a kind of tobacco French. I asked him what he called his dog. He shouted *Brock!* (the name of the breed). We like to hear the cat called *min*,—min! min! min! I inquired if we could cross the river here to the Isle of Orleans, thinking to return that way when we had been to the

*From McCulloch's Geographical Dictionary we learn that "immediately beyond the Island of Orleans it is a mile broad; where the Saguenay joins it, eighteen miles; at Point Peter, upwards of thirty; at the Bay of Seven Islands, seventy miles; and at the Island of Anticosti (about three hundred and fifty miles from Quebec) it rolls a flood into the ocean nearly one hundred miles across."

Falls. He answered, "*S'il ne fait pas un trop grand vent,*" If there is not too much wind. They use small boats, or pirogues, and the waves are often too high for them. He wore, as usual, something between a moccasin and a boot, which he called *bottes Indiennes,* Indian boots, and had made himself. The tops were of calf or sheep-skin, and the soles of cowhide turned up like a mocassin. They were yellow or reddish, the leather never having been tanned nor colored. The women wore the same. He told us that he had travelled ten leagues due north into the bush. He had been to the Falls of St. Anne, and said that they were more beautiful, but not greater, than Montmorenci, *plus beau, mais non plus grand que Montmorenci.* As soon as we had retired, the family commenced their devotions. A little boy officiated, and for a long time we heard him muttering over his prayers.

In the morning, after a breakfast of tea, maple-sugar, bread and butter, and what I suppose is called *potage* (potatoes and meat boiled with flour), the universal dish as we found, perhaps the national one, I ran over to the Church of La Bonne St. Anne, whose matin bell we had heard, it being Sunday morning. Our book said that this church had "long been an object of interest, from the miraculous cures said to have been wrought on visitors to the shrine." There was a profusion of gilding, and I counted more than twenty-five crutches suspended on the walls, some for grown persons, some for children, which it was to be inferred so many sick had been able to dispense with; but they looked as if they had been made to order by the carpenter who made the church. There were one or two villagers at their devotions at that early hour, who did not look up, but when they had sat a long time with their little book before the picture of one saint, went to another. Our whole walk was through a thoroughly Catholic country, and there was no trace of any other religion. I doubt if there are any more simple and unsophisticated Catholics anywhere. Emery de Caen, Champlain's contemporary, told the Huguenot sailors that "Monseigneur, the Duke de Ventadour (Viceroy), did not wish that they should sing psalms in the Great River."

On our way to the Falls, we met the habitans coming to the Church of La Bonne St. Anne, walking or riding in charettes by families. I remarked that they were universally of small stature. The toll-man at the bridge over the St. Anne was the first man we had chanced to meet, since we left Quebec, who could speak a word of English. How good French the inhabitants of this part of Canada speak, I am not competent to say; I only know that it is not made impure by being mixed with English. I do not know why it should not be as good as is spoken in Normandy. Charlevoix, who was here a hundred years ago, observes, "The French language is nowhere spoken with greater purity, there being no accent perceptible"; and Potherie said "they had no dialect, which, indeed, is generally lost in a colony."

The falls, which we were in search of, are three miles up the St. Anne. We followed for a short distance a foot-path up the east bank of this river, through handsome sugar-maple and arbor-vitæ groves. Having lost the path which led to a house where we were to get further directions, we dashed at once into the woods, steering by guess and by compass, climbing directly through woods, a steep hill, or mountain, five or six hundred feet high, which was, in fact, only the bank of the St. Lawrence. Beyond this we by good luck fell into another path, and following this or a branch of it, at our discretion, through a forest consisting of large white pines,—the first we had seen in our walk,—we at length heard the roar of falling water, and came out at the head of the Falls of St. Anne. We had descended into a ravine or cleft in the mountain, whose walls rose still a hundred feet above us, though we were near its top, and we now stood on a very rocky shore, where the water had lately flowed a dozen feet higher, as appeared by the stones and drift-wood, and large birches twisted and splintered as a farmer twists a withe. Here the river, one or two hundred feet wide, came flowing rapidly over a rocky bed out of that interesting wilderness which stretches toward Hudson's Bay and Davis's Straits. Ha-ha Bay, on the Saguenay, was about one hundred miles north of where we stood. Looking on the map, I find that the first country on the north which bears a name is that part of Rupert's Land called East Main. This river, called after the holy Anne, flowing from such a direction, here tumbled over a precipice, at present by three channels, how far down I do not know, but far enough for all our purposes, and to as good a distance as if twice as far. It matters little whether you call it one, or two, or three hundred feet; at any rate, it was a sufficient Water-privilege for us. I crossed the principal channel directly over the verge of the fall, where it was contracted to about fifteen feet in width by a dead tree, which had been dropped across and secured in a cleft of the opposite rock, and a smaller one a few feet higher, which served for a hand-rail. This bridge was rotten as well as small and slippery, being stripped of bark, and I was obliged to seize a moment to pass when the falling water did not surge over it, and mid-way, though at the expense of wet feet, I looked down probably more than a hundred feet, into the mist and foam below. This gave me the freedom of an island of precipitous rock, by which I descended as by giant steps, the rock being composed of large cubical masses, clothed with delicate close-hugging lichens of various colors, kept fresh and bright by the moisture, till I viewed the first fall from the front, and looked down still deeper to where the second and third channels fell into a remarkably large circular basin worn in the stone. The falling water seemed to jar the very rocks, and the noise to be ever increasing. The vista down stream was through a narrow and deep cleft in the mountain, all white suds at the bottom; but a sudden angle in this gorge prevented my seeing through to the bottom of the fall. Returning to the shore, I made my way down stream through the forest to see how far the fall extended, and how the river came out of that adventure. It was to clamber along the side of a precipitous mountain of loose mossy rocks, covered with a damp primitive forest, and terminating at the bottom in an abrupt precipice over the stream. This was the east side of the fall. At length, after a quarter of a mile, I got down to still water, and, on looking up through the winding gorge, I could just see to the foot of the fall which I had before examined; while from the opposite side of the stream, here much contracted, rose a perpendicular wall, I will not venture to say how many hundred feet, but only that it was the highest perpendicular wall of bare rock that I ever saw. In front of me tumbled in from the summit of the cliff a tributary stream, making a beautiful cascade, which was a remarkable fall in itself, and there was a cleft in this precipice, apparently four or five feet wide, perfectly straight up and down from top to bottom, which, from its cavernous depth and darkness, appeared merely as *a black streak*. This precipice is not sloped, nor is the material soft and crumbling slate as at Montmorenci, but it rises perfectly perpendicular, like the side of a mountain fortress, and is cracked into vast cubical masses of gray and black rock shining with moisture, as if it were the ruin of an ancient wall built by Titans. Birches, spruces, mountain-ashes with their bright red berries, arbor-vitæs, white pines, alders, &c., overhung this chasm on the very verge of the cliff and in the crevices, and here and there were buttresses of rock supporting trees part way down, yet so as to enhance, not injure, the effect of the bare rock. Take it altogether, it was a most wild and rugged and stupendous chasm, so deep and narrow where a river had worn itself a passage through a mountain of rock, and all around was the comparatively untrodden wilderness.

This was the limit of our walk down the St. Lawrence. Early in the afternoon we began to retrace our steps, not being able to cross the north channel and return by the Isle of Orleans, on account of the *trop grand vent*, or too great wind. Though the waves did run pretty high, it was evident that the inhabitants of Montmorenci County were no sailors, and made but little use of the river. When we reached the bridge, between St. Anne and Chateau Richer, I ran back a little way to ask a man in the field the name of the river which we were crossing, but for a long time I could not make out what he said, for he was one of the more unintelligible Jacques Cartier men. At last it flashed upon me that it was *La Rivière au Chien*, or the Dog River, which my eyes beheld, which brought to my mind the life of the Canadian voyageur and *coureur de bois*, a more western and wilder Arcadia, methinks, than the world has ever seen; for the Greeks, with all their wood and river gods, were not so qualified to name the natural features of a country, as the ancestors of these French Canadians; and if any people had a right to substitute their own for the Indian names, it was they. They have preceded the pioneer on our own frontiers, and named the *prairie* for us. *La Rivière au Chien* cannot, by any license of language, be translated into Dog River, for that is not such a giving it to the dogs, and recognizing their place in creation as the French implies. One of the tributaries of the St. Anne is named *La Rivière de la Rose*; and farther east are, *La Rivière de la Blondelle*, and *La Rivière de la Friponne*. Their very *rivière* meanders more than our *river*.

Yet the impression which this country made on me was commonly different from this. To a traveller from the Old World, Canada East may appear like a new country, and its inhabitants like colonists, but to me, coming from New England, and being a very green traveller withal,—notwithstanding what I have said about Hudson's Bay,—it appeared as old as Normandy itself, and realized much that I had heard of Europe and the Middle Ages. Even the names of humble Canadian villages affected me as if they had been those of the renowned cities of antiquity. To be told by a habitan, when I asked the name of a village in sight, that it is *St. Fereole* or *St. Anne*, the *Guardian Angel* or the *Holy Joseph's*; or of a mountain, that it was *Bélange* or *St. Hyacinthe*! As soon as you leave the States, these saintly names begin. *St. John* is the first town you stop at (fortunately we did not see it), and thenceforward, the names of the mountains, and streams, and villages reel, if I may so speak, with the intoxication of poetry;— *Chambly, Longueil, Pointe aux Trembles, Bartholomy*, &c., &c.; as if it needed only a little foreign accent, a few more liquids and vowels perchance in the language, to make us locate our ideals at once. I began to dream of Provence and the Troubadours, and of places and things which have no existence on the earth. They veiled the Indian and the primitive forest, and the woods toward Hudson's Bay, were only as the forests of France and Germany. I could not at once bring myself to believe that the inhabitants who pronounced daily those beautiful and, to me, significant names, lead as prosaic lives as we of New England. In short, the Canada which I saw was not merely a place for railroads to terminate in and for criminals to run to.

When I asked the man to whom I have referred, if there were any falls on the Rivière au Chien,—for I saw that it came over the same high bank with the Montmorenci and St. Anne,—he answered that there were. How far? I inquired. *Trois quatres lieue*. How high? *Je pense, quatre-vingt-dix pieds*;

that is, ninety feet. We turned aside to look at the falls of the
Rivière du Sault à la Puce, half a mile from the road, which
before we had passed in our haste and ignorance, and we pronounced them as beautiful as any that we saw; yet they
seemed to make no account of them there, and, when first we
inquired the way to the Falls, directed us to Montmorenci,
seven miles distant. It was evident that this was the country
for waterfalls; that every stream that empties into the St.
Lawrence, for some hundreds of miles, must have a great fall
or cascade on it, and in its passage through the mountains
was, for a short distance, a small Saguenay, with its upright
walls. This fall of La Puce, the least remarkable of the four
which we visited in this vicinity, we had never heard of till we
came to Canada, and yet, so far as I know, there is nothing of
the kind in New England to be compared with it. Most travellers in Canada would not hear of it, though they might go
so near as to hear it. Since my return I find that in the topographical description of the country mention is made of "two
or three romantic falls" on this stream, though we saw and
heard of but this one. Ask the inhabitants respecting any
stream, if there is a fall on it, and they will perchance tell you
of something as interesting as Bashpish or the Catskill, which
no traveller has ever seen, or if they have not found it, you
may possibly trace up the stream and discover it yourself. Falls
there are a drug; and we became quite dissipated in respect to
them. We had drank too much of them. Beside these which I
have referred to, there are a thousand other falls on the St.
Lawrence and its tributaries which I have not seen nor heard
of; and above all there is one which I have heard of, called
Niagara, so that I think that this river must be the most remarkable for its falls of any in the world.

At a house near the western boundary of Chateau Richer,
whose master was said to speak a very little English, having
recently lived at Quebec, we got lodging for the night. As
usual, we had to go down a lane to get round to the south
side of the house where the door was, away from the road.
For these Canadian houses have no front door, properly
speaking. Every part is for the use of the occupant exclusively,
and no part has reference to the traveller or to travel. Every
New England house, on the contrary, has a front and princi-

pal door opening to the great world, though it may be on the cold side, for it stands on the highway of nations, and the road which runs by it comes from the Old World and goes to the far West; but the Canadian's door opens into his back-yard and farm alone, and the road which runs behind his house leads only from the church of one saint to that of another. We found a large family, hired men, wife and children, just eating their supper. They prepared some for us afterwards. The hired men were a merry crew of short, black-eyed fellows, and the wife a thin-faced, sharp-featured French Canadian woman. Our host's English staggered us rather more than any French we had heard yet; indeed, we found that even we spoke better French than he did English, and we concluded that a less crime would be committed on the whole if we spoke French with him, and in no respect aided or abetted his attempts to speak English. We had a long and merry chat with the family this Sunday evening in their spacious kitchen. While my companion smoked a pipe and parlez-vous'd with one party, I parleyed and gesticulated to another. The whole family was enlisted, and I kept a little girl writing what was otherwise unintelligible. The geography getting obscure, we called for chalk, and the greasy oiled table-cloth having been wiped,—for it needed no French, but only a sentence from the universal language of looks on my part, to indicate that it needed it,—we drew the St. Lawrence, with its parishes, thereon, and thenceforward went on swimmingly, by turns handling the chalk and committing to the table-cloth what would otherwise have been left in a limbo of unintelligibility. This was greatly to the entertainment of all parties. I was amused to hear how much use they made of the word *oui* in conversation with one another. After repeated single insertions of it, one would suddenly throw back his head at the same time with his chair, and exclaim rapidly, "*oui! oui! oui! oui!*" like a Yankee driving pigs. Our host told us that the farms thereabouts were generally two acres, or three hundred and sixty French feet wide, by one and a half leagues, (?) or a little more than four and a half of our miles deep. This use of the word *acre* as long measure arises from the fact that the French acre or arpent, the arpent of Paris, makes a square of ten perches, of eighteen feet each on a side,

a Paris foot being equal to 1.06575 English feet. He said that
the wood was cut off about one mile from the river. The rest
was "bush," and beyond that the "Queen's bush." Old as the
country is, each landholder bounds on the primitive forest,
and fuel bears no price. As I had forgotten the French for
sickle, they went out in the evening to the barn and got one,
and so clenched the certainty of our understanding one another. Then, wishing to learn if they used the cradle, and not
knowing any French word for this instrument, I set up the
knives and forks on the blade of the sickle to represent one; at
which they all exclaimed that they knew and had used it.
When *snells* were mentioned they went out in the dark and
plucked some. They were pretty good. They said they had
three kinds of plums growing wild,—blue, white, and red, the
two former much alike and the best. Also they asked me if I
would have *des pommes*, some apples, and got me some. They
were exceedingly fair and glossy, and it was evident that there
was no worm in them; but they were as hard almost as a
stone, as if the season was too short to mellow them. We had
seen no soft and yellow apples by the roadside. I declined eating one, much as I admired it, observing that it would be
good *dans le printemps*, in the spring. In the morning when
the mistress had set the eggs a-frying she nodded to a thick-
set, jolly-looking fellow, who rolled up his sleeves, seized the
long-handled griddle, and commenced a series of revolutions
and evolutions with it, ever and anon tossing its contents into
the air, where they turned completely topsy-turvy and came
down t' other side up; and this he repeated till they were
done. That appeared to be his duty when eggs were concerned. I did not chance to witness this performance, but my
companion did, and he pronounced it a master-piece in its
way. This man's farm, with the buildings, cost seven hundred
pounds; some smaller ones, two hundred.

In 1827, Montmorenci County, to which the Isle of Orleans
has since been added, was nearly as large as Massachusetts,
being the eighth county out of forty (in Lower Canada) in extent; but by far the greater part still must continue to be
waste land, lying, as it were, under the walls of Quebec.

I quote these old statistics, not merely because of the difficulty of obtaining more recent ones, but also because I saw

there so little evidence of any recent growth. There were in this county, at the same date, five Roman Catholic churches, and no others, five curés and five presbyteries, two schools, two corn-mills, four saw-mills, one carding-mill,—no medical man, or notary or lawyer,—five shopkeepers, four taverns (we saw no sign of any, though, after a little hesitation, we were sometimes directed to some undistinguished hut as such), thirty artisans, and five river crafts, whose tonnage amounted to sixty-nine tons! This, notwithstanding that it has a frontage of more than thirty miles on the river, and the population is almost wholly confined to its banks. This describes nearly enough what we saw. But double some of these figures, which, however, its growth will not warrant, and you have described a poverty which not even its severity of climate and ruggedness of soil will suffice to account for. The principal productions were wheat, potatoes, oats, hay, peas, flax, maple-sugar, &c., &c.; linen, cloth, or *étoffe du pays*, flannel, and homespun, or *petite étoffe*.

In Lower Canada, according to Bouchette, there are two tenures,—the feudal and the socage. Tenanciers, censitaires, or holders of land *en roture*, pay a small annual rent to the seigneurs, to which "is added some article of provision, such as a couple of fowls, or a goose, or a bushel of wheat." "They are also bound to grind their corn at the *moulin banal*, or the lord's mill, where one fourteenth part of it is taken for his use" as toll. He says that the toll is one twelfth in the United States, where competition exists. It is not permitted to exceed one sixteenth in Massachusetts. But worse than this monopolizing of mill rents is what are called *lods et ventes*, or mutation fines. According to which the seigneur has "a right to a twelfth part of the purchase-money of every estate within his seigniory that changes its owner by sale." This is over and above the sum paid to the seller. In such cases, moreover, "the lord possesses the *droit de retrait*, which is the privilege of pre-emption at the highest bidden price within forty days after the sale has taken place,"—a right which, however, is said to be seldom exercised. "Lands held by Roman Catholics are further subject to the payment to their curates of one twenty-sixth part of all the grain produced upon them, and to occasional assessments for building and repairing churches,"

&c.,—a tax to which they are not subject if the proprietors change their faith; but they are not the less attached to their church in consequence. There are, however, various modifications of the feudal tenure. Under the socage tenure, which is that of the townships or more recent settlements, English, Irish, Scotch, and others, and generally of Canada West, the landholder is wholly unshackled by such conditions as I have quoted, and "is bound to no other obligations than those of allegiance to the king and obedience to the laws." Throughout Canada "a freehold of forty shillings yearly value, or the payment of ten pounds rent annually, is the qualification for voters." In 1846 more than one sixth of the whole population of Canada East were qualified to vote for members of Parliament,—a greater proportion than enjoy a similar privilege in the United States.

The population which we had seen the last two days,—I mean the habitans of Montmorenci County,—appeared very inferior, intellectually and even physically, to that of New England. In some respects they were incredibly filthy. It was evident that they had not advanced since the settlement of the country, that they were quite behind the age, and fairly represented their ancestors in Normandy a thousand years ago. Even in respect to the common arts of life, they are not so far advanced as a frontier town in the West three years old. They have no money invested in railroad stock, and probably never will have. If they have got a French phrase for a railroad, it is as much as you can expect of them. They are very far from a revolution; have no quarrel with Church or State, but their vice and their virtue is content. As for annexation, they have never dreamed of it; indeed, they have not a clear idea what or where the States are. The English government has been remarkably liberal to its Catholic subjects in Canada, permitting them to wear their own fetters, both political and religious, as far as was possible for subjects. Their government is even too good for them. Parliament passed "an act [in 1825] to provide for the extinction of feudal and seigniorial rights and burdens on lands in Lower Canada, and for the gradual conversion of those tenures into the tenure of free and common socage," &c. But as late as 1831, at least, the design of the act was likely to be frustrated, owing to the reluctance of the seigniors and peasants. It has been observed by another that the French Canadians do not extend nor perpetuate their influence. The British, Irish, and other immigrants, who have settled the townships, are found to have imitated the American settlers, and not the French. They reminded me in this of the Indians, whom they were slow to displace and to whose habits of life they themselves more readily conformed than the Indians to theirs. The Governor-General Denouville remarked, in 1685, that some had long thought that it was necessary to bring the Indians near them in order to Frenchify (*franciser*) them, but that they had every reason to think themselves in an error; for those who had come near them and were even collected in villages in the midst of the colony had not become French, but the French, who had haunted them, had become savages. Kalm said: "Though many nations imitate the French customs, yet I observed, on the contrary, that the French in Canada, in many respects, follow the customs of the Indians, with whom they converse every day. They make use of the tobacco-pipes, shoes, garters, and girdles of the Indians. They follow the Indian way of making war with exactness; they mix the same things with tobacco (he might have said that both French and English learned the use itself of this weed of the Indian); they make use of the Indian bark-boats, and row them in the Indian way; they wrap square pieces of cloth round their feet instead of stockings; and have adopted many other Indian fashions." Thus, while the descendants of the Pilgrims are teaching the English to make pegged boots, the descendants of the French in Canada are wearing the Indian moccasin still. The French, to their credit be it said, to a certain extent respected the Indians as a separate and independent people, and spoke of them and contrasted themselves with them as the English have never done. They not only went to war with them as allies, but they lived at home with them as neighbors. In 1627 the French king declared "that the descendants of the French, settled in" New France, "and the savages who should be brought to the knowledge of the faith, and should make profession of it, should be counted and reputed French born (*Naturels François*); and as such could emigrate to France, when it seemed good to them, and there acquire, will, inherit, &c., &c., without obtaining letters of naturalization." When the English had possession of Quebec, in 1630, the Indians, attempting to practise the same familiarity with them that they had with the French, were driven out of their houses with blows; which accident taught them a difference between the two races, and attached them yet more to the French. The impression made on me was, that the French Canadians were even sharing the fate of the Indians, or at least gradually disappearing in what is called the Saxon current.

The English did not come to America from a mere love of adventure, nor to truck with or convert the savages, nor to hold offices under the crown, as the French to a great extent did, but to live in earnest and with freedom. The latter overran a great extent of country, selling strong water, and collecting its furs, and converting its inhabitants,—or at least baptizing its dying infants (*enfans moribonds*),—without *improving* it. First, went the *coureur de bois* with the *eau de vie*; then followed, if he did not precede, the heroic missionary with the *eau d'immortalité*. It was freedom to hunt, and fish, and convert, not to work, that they sought. Hontan says that the *coureurs de bois* lived like sailors ashore. In no part of the seventeenth century could the French be said to have had a foothold in Canada; they held only by the fur of the wild animals which they were exterminating. To enable the poor seigneurs to get their living, it was permitted by a decree passed in the reign of Louis the Fourteenth, in 1685, "to all nobles and gentlemen settled in Canada, to engage in commerce, without being called to account or reputed to have done anything derogatory." The reader can infer to what extent they had engaged in agriculture, and how their farms must have shone by this time. The New England youth, on the other hand, were never *coureurs de bois* nor *voyageurs*, but backwoodsmen and sailors rather. Of all nations the English undoubtedly have proved hitherto that they had the most business here.

Yet I am not sure but I have most sympathy with that spirit of adventure which distinguished the French and Spaniards of those days, and made them especially the explorers of the American Continent,—which so early carried the former to the Great Lakes and the Mississippi on the north, and the latter to the same river on the south. It was long before our frontiers reached their settlements in the West. So far as inland discovery was concerned, the adventurous spirit of the English was that of sailors who land but for a day, and their enterprise the enterprise of traders.

There was apparently a greater equality of condition among the habitans of Montmorenci County than in New England. They are an almost exclusively agricultural, and so far independent, population, each family producing nearly all the necessaries of life for itself. If the Canadian wants energy, perchance he possesses those virtues, social and others, which the Yankee lacks, in which case he cannot be regarded as a poor man.

CHAPTER IV.
THE WALLS OF QUEBEC.

After spending the night at a farm-house in Chateau-Richer, about a dozen miles northeast of Quebec, we set out on our return to the city. We stopped at the next house, a picturesque old stone mill, over the *Chipré*,—for so the name sounded,—such as you will nowhere see in the States, and asked the millers the age of the mill. They went up stairs to call the master; but the crabbed old miser asked why we wanted to know, and would tell us only for some compensation. I wanted French to give him a piece of my mind. I had got enough to talk on a pinch, but not to quarrel; so I had to come away, looking all I would have said. This was the utmost incivility we met with in Canada. In Beauport, within a few miles of Quebec, we turned aside to look at a church which was just being completed,—a very large and handsome edifice of stone, with a green bough stuck in its gable, of some significance to Catholics. The comparative wealth of the Church in this country was apparent; for in this village we did not see one good house besides. They were all humble cottages; and yet this appeared to me a more imposing structure than any church in Boston. But I am no judge of these things.

Re-entering Quebec through St. John's Gate, we took a caleche in Market Square for the Falls of the Chaudière, about nine miles southwest of the city, for which we were to pay so much, beside forty sous for tolls. The driver, as usual, spoke French only. The number of these vehicles is very great for so small a town. They are like one of our chaises that has lost its top, only stouter and longer in the body, with a seat for the driver where the dasher is with us, and broad leather ears on each side to protect the riders from the wheel and keep children from falling out. They had an easy jaunting look, which, as our hours were numbered, persuaded us to be riders. We met with them on every road near Quebec these days, each with its complement of two inquisitive-looking foreigners and a Canadian driver, the former evidently enjoying their novel experience, for commonly it is only the horse whose language you do not understand; but they were one remove further from him by the intervention of an equally unintelligible driver. We crossed the St. Lawrence to Point Levi in a French-Canadian ferry-boat, which was inconvenient and dirty, and managed with great noise and bustle. The current was very strong and tumultuous, and the boat tossed enough to make some sick, though it was only a mile across; yet the wind was not to be compared with that of the day before, and we saw that the Canadians had a good excuse for not taking us over to the Isle of Orleans in a pirogue, however shiftless they may be for not having provided any other conveyance. The route which we took to the Chaudière did not afford us those views of Quebec which we had expected, and the country and inhabitants appeared less interesting to a traveller than those we had seen. The Falls of the Chaudière are three miles from its mouth on the south side of the St. Lawrence. Though they were the largest which I saw in Canada, I was not proportionately interested by them, probably from satiety. I did not see any *peculiar* propriety in the name *Chaudière*, or caldron. I saw here the most brilliant rainbow that I ever imagined. It was just across the stream below the precipice, formed on the mist which this tremendous fall produced; and I stood on a level with the key-stone of its arch. It was not a few faint prismatic colors merely, but a full semi-circle, only four or five rods in diameter, though as wide as usual, so intensely bright as to pain the eye, and apparently as substantial as an arch of stone. It changed its position and colors as we moved, and was the brighter because the sun shone so clearly and the mist was so thick. Evidently a picture painted on mist for the men and animals that came to the falls to look at; but for what special purpose beyond this, I know not. At the farthest point in this ride, and when most inland, unexpectedly at a turn in the road we descried the frowning citadel of Quebec in the horizon, like the beak of a bird of prey. We returned by the river-road under the bank, which is very high, abrupt, and rocky. When we were opposite to Quebec, I was surprised to see that in the Lower Town, under the shadow of the rock, the lamps were lit, twinkling not unlike crystals in a cavern, while the citadel high above, and we, too, on the south shore, were in broad daylight. As we were too late for the ferry-boat that night, we put up at a *maison de pension* at Point Levi. The usual two-story stove was here placed against an opening in the partition shaped like a fireplace, and so warmed several rooms. We could not understand their French here very well, but the *potage* was just like what we had had before. There were many small chambers with doorways but no doors. The walls of our chamber, all around and overhead, were neatly ceiled, and the timbers cased with wood unpainted. The pillows were checkered and tasselled, and the usual long-pointed red woollen or worsted night-cap was placed on each. I pulled mine out to see how it was made. It was in the form of a double cone, one end tucked into the other; just such, it appeared, as I saw men wearing all day in the streets. Probably I should have put it on if the cold had been then, as it is sometimes there, thirty or forty degrees below zero.

When we landed at Quebec the next morning, a man lay on his back on the wharf, apparently dying, in the midst of a crowd and directly in the path of the horses, groaning, *"O ma conscience!"* I thought that he pronounced his French more distinctly than any I heard, as if the dying had already acquired the accents of a universal language. Having secured the only unengaged berths in the Lord Sydenham steamer, which was to leave Quebec before sundown, and being resolved, now that I had seen somewhat of the country, to get an idea of the city, I proceeded to walk round the Upper Town, or fortified portion, which is two miles and three quarters in circuit, alone, as near as I could get to the cliff and the walls, like a rat looking for a hole; going round by the south-

west, where there is but a single street between the cliff and
the water, and up the long, wooden stairs, through the suburbs northward to the King's Woodyard, which I thought
must have been a long way from his fireplace, and under the
cliffs of the St. Charles, where the drains issue under the
walls, and the walls are loop-holed for musketry; so returning
by Mountain Street and Prescott Gate to the Upper Town.
Having found my way by an obscure passage near the St.
Louis Gate to the glacis on the north of the citadel proper,—
I believe that I was the only visitor then in the city who got
in there,—I enjoyed a prospect nearly as good as from within
the citadel itself, which I had explored some days before. As I
walked on the glacis I heard the sound of a bagpipe from the
soldiers' dwellings in the rock, and was further soothed and
affected by the sight of a soldier's cat walking up a cleeted
plank into a high loop-hole, designed for *mus-catry*, as serene
as Wisdom herself, and with a gracefully waving motion of
her tail, as if her ways were ways of pleasantness and all her
paths were peace. Scaling a slat fence, where a small force
might have checked me, I got out of the esplanade into the
Governor's Garden, and read the well-known inscription on
Wolfe and Montcalm's monument, which for saying much in
little, and that to the purpose, undoubtedly deserved the
prize medal which it received:

> MORTEM . VIRTUS . COMMUNEM .
> FAMAM . HISTORIA .
> MONUMENTUM . POSTERITAS .
> DEDIT.

Valor gave them one death, history one fame, posterity one
monument. The Government Garden has for nosegays, amid
kitchen vegetables, beside the common garden flowers, the
usual complement of cannon directed toward some future
and possible enemy. I then returned up St. Louis Street to the
esplanade and ramparts there, and went round the Upper
Town once more, though I was very tired, this time on the
inside of the wall; for I knew that the wall was the main thing
in Quebec, and had cost a great deal of money, and therefore
I must make the most of it. In fact, these are the only remarkable walls we have in North America, though we have a

good deal of Virginia fence, it is true. Moreover, I cannot say but I yielded in some measure to the soldier instinct, and, having but a short time to spare, thought it best to examine the wall thoroughly, that I might be the better prepared if I should ever be called that way again in the service of my country. I committed all the gates to memory in their order, which did not cost me so much trouble as it would have done at the hundred-gated city, there being only five; nor were they so hard to remember as those seven of Bœotian Thebes; and, moreover, I thought that, if seven champions were enough against the latter, one would be enough against Quebec, though he bore for all armor and device only an umbrella and a bundle. I took the nunneries as I went, for I had learned to distinguish them by the blinds; and I observed also the foundling hospitals and the convents, and whatever was attached to, or in the vicinity of the walls. All the rest I omitted, as naturally as one would the inside of an inedible shellfish. These were the only pearls, and the wall the only mother-of-pearl for me. Quebec is chiefly famous for the thickness of its parietal bones. The technical terms of its conchology may stagger a beginner a little at first, such as *banlieue, esplanade, glacis, ravelin, cavalier,* &c., &c., but with the aid of a comprehensive dictionary you soon learn the nature of your ground. I was surprised at the extent of the artillery barracks, built so long ago,—*Casernes Nouvelles,* they used to be called,—nearly six hundred feet in length by forty in depth, where the sentries, like peripatetic philosophers, were so absorbed in thought, as not to notice me when I passed in and out at the gates. Within, are "small arms of every description, sufficient for the equipment of twenty thousand men," so arranged as to give a startling *coup d'œil* to strangers. I did not enter, not wishing to get a black eye; for they are said to be "in a state of complete repair and readiness for immediate use." Here, for a short time, I lost sight of the wall, but I recovered it again on emerging from the barrack yard. There I met with a Scotchman who appeared to have business with the wall, like myself; and, being thus mutually drawn together by a similarity of tastes, we had a little conversation *sub mœnibus,* that is, by an angle of the wall which sheltered us. He lived about thirty miles northwest of

Quebec; had been nineteen years in the country; said he was disappointed that he was not brought to America after all, but found himself still under British rule and where his own language was not spoken; that many Scotch, Irish, and English were disappointed in like manner, and either went to the States, or pushed up the river to Canada West, nearer to the States, and where their language was spoken. He talked of visiting the States some time; and, as he seemed ignorant of geography, I warned him that it was one thing to visit the State of Massachusetts, and another to visit the State of California. He said it was colder there than usual at that season, and he was lucky to have brought his thick togue, or frock-coat, with him; thought it would snow, and then be pleasant and warm. That is the way we are always thinking. However, his words were music to me in my thin hat and sack.

At the ramparts on the cliff near the old Parliament House I counted twenty-four thirty-two-pounders in a row, pointed over the harbor, with their balls piled pyramid-wise between them,—there are said to be in all about one hundred and eighty guns mounted at Quebec,—all which were faithfully kept dusted by officials, in accordance with the motto, "In time of peace prepare for war"; but I saw no preparations for peace: she was plainly an uninvited guest.

Having thus completed the circuit of this fortress, both within and without, I went no farther by the wall for fear that I should become wall-eyed. However, I think that I deserve to be made a member of the Royal Sappers and Miners.

In short, I observed everywhere the most perfect arrangements for keeping a wall in order, not even permitting the lichens to grow on it, which some think an ornament; but then I saw no cultivation nor pasturing within it to pay for the outlay, and cattle were strictly forbidden to feed on the glacis under the severest penalties. Where the dogs get their milk I don't know, and I fear it is bloody at best.

The citadel of Quebec says, "I *will* live here, and you sha'n't prevent me." To which you return, that you have not the slightest objection; live and let live. The Martello towers looked, for all the world, exactly like abandoned wind-mills which had not had a grist to grind these hundred years. Indeed, the whole castle here was a "folly,"—England's folly,—and, in more senses than one, a castle in the air. The inhabitants and the government are gradually waking up to a sense of this truth; for I heard something said about their abandoning the wall around the Upper Town, and confining the fortifications to the citadel of forty acres. Of course they will finally reduce their intrenchments to the circumference of their own brave hearts.

The most modern fortifications have an air of antiquity about them; they have the aspect of ruins in better or worse repair from the day they are built, because they are not really the work of this age. The very place where the soldier resides has a peculiar tendency to become old and dilapidated, as the word *barrack* implies. I couple all fortifications in my mind with the dismantled Spanish forts to be found in so many parts of the world; and if in any place they are not actually dismantled, it is because that there the intellect of the inhabitants is dismantled. The commanding officer of an old fort near Valdivia in South America, when a traveller remarked to him that, with one discharge, his gun-carriages would certainly fall to pieces, gravely replied, "No, I am sure, sir, they would stand two." Perhaps the guns of Quebec would stand three. Such structures carry us back to the Middle Ages, the siege of Jerusalem, and St. Jean d'Acre, and the days of the Bucaniers. In the armory of the citadel they showed me a clumsy implement, long since useless, which they called a Lombard gun. I thought that their whole citadel was such a Lombard gun, fit object for the museums of the curious. Such works do not consist with the development of the intellect. Huge stone structures of all kinds, both in their erection and by their influence when erected, rather oppress than liberate the mind. They are tombs for the souls of men, as frequently for their bodies also. The sentinel with his musket beside a man with his umbrella is spectral. There is not sufficient reason for his existence. Does my friend there, with a bullet resting on half an ounce of powder, think that he needs that argument in conversing with me? The fort was the first institution that was founded here, and it is amusing to read in Champlain how assiduously they worked at it almost from the first day of the settlement. The founders of the colony thought this an excellent site for a wall,—and no doubt it was a better site, in some respects, for a wall than for a city,—but it chanced that a city got behind it. It chanced, too, that a Lower Town got before it, and clung like an oyster to the outside of the crags, as you may see at low tide. It is as if you were to come to a country village surrounded by palisades in the old Indian fashion,—interesting only as a relic of antiquity and barbarism. A fortified town is like a man cased in the heavy armor of antiquity, with a horse-load of broadswords and small arms slung to him, endeavoring to go about his business. Or is this an indispensable machinery for the good government of the country? The inhabitants of California succeed pretty well, and are doing better and better every day, without any such institution. What use has this fortress served, to look at it even from the soldiers' point of view? At first the French took care of it; yet Wolfe sailed by it with impunity, and took the town of Quebec without experiencing any hinderance at last from its fortifications. They were only the bone for which the parties fought. Then the English began to take care of it. So of any fort in the world,—that in Boston harbor, for instance. We shall at length hear that an enemy sailed by it in the night, for it cannot sail itself, and both it and its inhabitants are always benighted. How often we read that the enemy occupied a position which commanded the old, and so the fort was evacuated. Have not the school-house and the printing-press occupied a position which commands such a fort as this?

However, this is a ruin kept in remarkably good repair. There are some eight hundred or thousand men there to exhibit it. One regiment goes bare-legged to increase the attraction. If you wish to study the muscles of the leg about the knee, repair to Quebec. This universal exhibition in Canada of the tools and sinews of war reminded me of the keeper of a menagerie showing his animals' claws. It was the English leopard showing his claws. Always the *royal* something or other; as, at the menagerie, the Royal Bengal Tiger. Silliman states that "the cold is so intense in the winter nights, particularly on Cape Diamond, that the sentinels cannot stand it more than one hour, and are relieved at the expiration of that time"; "and even, as it is said, at much shorter intervals, in case of the most extreme cold." What a natural or unnatural

fool must that soldier be,—to say nothing of his government,—who, when quicksilver is freezing and blood is ceasing
to be quick, will stand to have his face frozen, watching the
walls of Quebec, though, so far as they are concerned, both
honest and dishonest men all the world over have been in
their beds nearly half a century,—or at least for that space
travellers have visited Quebec only as they would read history.
I shall never again wake up in a colder night than usual, but I
shall think how rapidly the sentinels are relieving one another
on the walls of Quebec, their quicksilver being all frozen, as
if apprehensive that some hostile Wolfe may even then be
scaling the Heights of Abraham, or some persevering Arnold
about to issue from the wilderness; some Malay or Japanese,
perchance, coming round by the northwest coast, have chosen that moment to assault the citadel! Why I should as
soon expect to find the sentinels still relieving one another
on the walls of Nineveh, which have so long been buried to
the world! What a troublesome thing a wall is! I thought it
was to defend me, and not I it. Of course, if they had no wall
they would not need to have any sentinels.

You might venture to advertise this farm as well fenced
with substantial stone walls (saying nothing about the eight
hundred Highlanders and Royal Irish who are required to
keep them from toppling down); stock and tools to go with
the land if desired. But it would not be wise for the seller to
exhibit his farm-book.

Why should Canada, wild and unsettled as it is, impress us
as an older country than the States, unless because her institutions are old? All things appeared to contend there, as I
have implied, with a certain rust of antiquity,—such as forms
on old armor and iron guns,—the rust of conventions and
formalities. It is said that the metallic roofs of Montreal and
Quebec keep sound and bright for forty years in some cases.
But if the rust was not on the tinned roofs and spires, it was
on the inhabitants and their institutions. Yet the work of bur-
nishing goes briskly forward. I imagined that the government
vessels at the wharves were laden with rotten-stone and oxalic
acid,—that is what the first ship from England in the spring
comes freighted with,—and the hands of the colonial legislature are cased in wash-leather. The principal exports must be

*gun*ny bags, verdigrease, and iron rust. Those who first built this fort, coming from Old France with the memory and tradition of feudal days and customs weighing on them, were unquestionably behind their age; and those who now inhabit and repair it are behind their ancestors or predecessors. Those old chevaliers thought that they could transplant the feudal system to America. It has been set out, but it has not thriven. Notwithstanding that Canada was settled first, and, unlike New England, for a long series of years enjoyed the fostering care of the mother country,—notwithstanding that, as Charlevoix tells us, it had more of the ancient *noblesse* among its early settlers than any other of the French colonies, and perhaps than all the others together,—there are in both the Canadas but 600,000 of French descent to-day,—about half so many as the population of Massachusetts. The whole population of both Canadas is but about 1,700,000 Canadians, English, Irish, Scotch, Indians, and all, put together! Samuel Laing, in his essay on the Northmen, to whom especially, rather than the Saxons, he refers the energy and indeed the excellence of the English character, observes that, when they occupied Scandinavia, "each man possessed his lot of land without reference to, or acknowledgment of, any other man,—without any local chief to whom his military service or other quit-rent for his land was due,—without tenure from, or duty or obligation to, any superior, real or fictitious, except the general sovereign. The individual settler held his land, as his descendants in Norway still express it, by the same right as the king held his crown,—by udal right, or adel,—that is, noble right." The French have occupied Canada, not *udally*, or by noble right, but *feudally*, or by ignoble right. They are a nation of peasants.

It was evident that, both on account of the feudal system and the aristocratic government, a private man was not worth so much in Canada as in the United States; and, if your wealth in any measure consists in manliness, in originality, and independence, you had better stay here. How could a peaceable, freethinking man live neighbor to the Forty-ninth Regiment? A New-Englander would naturally be a bad citizen, probably a rebel, there,—certainly if he were already a rebel at home. I suspect that a poor man who is not servile is a much rarer phenomenon there and in England than in the Northern United States. An Englishman, methinks,—not to speak of other European nations,—habitually regards himself merely as a constituent part of the English nation; he is a member of the royal regiment of Englishmen, and is proud of his company, as he has reason to be proud of it. But an American,—one who has made a tolerable use of his opportunities,—cares, comparatively, little about such things, and is advantageously nearer to the primitive and the ultimate condition of man in these respects. It is a government, that English one,—like most other European ones,—that cannot afford to be forgotten, as you would naturally forget it; under which one cannot be wholesomely neglected, and grow up a man and not an Englishman merely,—cannot be a poet even without danger of being made poet-laureate! Give me a country where it is the most natural thing in the world for a government that does not understand you to let you alone. One would say that a true Englishman could speculate only within bounds. (It is true the Americans have proved that they, in more than one sense, can *speculate* without bounds.) He has to pay his respects to so many things, that, before he knows it, he *may* have paid away all he is worth. What makes the United States government, on the whole, more tolerable,—I mean for us lucky white men,—is the fact that there is so much less of government with us. Here it is only once in a month or a year that a man *needs* remember that institution; and those who go to Congress can play the game of the Kilkenny cats there without fatal consequences to those who stay at home,—their term is so short: but in Canada you are reminded of the government every day. It parades itself before you. It is not content to be the servant, but will be the master; and every day it goes out to the Plains of Abraham or to the Champ de Mars and exhibits itself and its tools. Everywhere there appeared an attempt to make and to preserve trivial and otherwise transient distinctions. In the streets of Montreal and Quebec you met not only with soldiers in red, and shuffling priests in unmistakable black and white, with Sisters of Charity gone into mourning for their deceased relative,—not to mention the nuns of various orders depending on the fashion of a tear, of whom you heard,—but youths belonging to some seminary or other, wearing coats edged with white, who looked as if their expanding hearts were already repressed with a piece of tape. In short, the inhabitants of Canada appeared to be suffering between two fires,—the soldiery and the priesthood.

CHAPTER V.
THE SCENERY OF QUEBEC; AND THE RIVER ST. LAWRENCE.

About twelve o'clock this day, being in the Lower Town, I looked up at the signal-gun by the flag-staff on Cape Diamond, and saw a soldier up in the heavens there making preparations to fire it,—both he and the gun in bold relief against the sky. Soon after, being warned by the boom of the gun to look up again, there was only the cannon in the sky, the smoke just blowing away from it, as if the soldier, having touched it off, had concealed himself for effect, leaving the sound to echo grandly from shore to shore, and far up and down the river. This answered the purpose of a dinner-horn.

There are no such restaurateurs in Quebec or Montreal as there are in Boston. I hunted an hour or two in vain in this town to find one, till I lost my appetite. In one house, called a restaurateur, where lunches were advertised, I found only tables covered with bottles and glasses innumerable, containing apparently a sample of every liquid that has been known since the earth dried up after the flood, but no scent of solid food did I perceive gross enough to excite a hungry mouse. In short, I saw nothing to tempt me there, but a large map of Canada against the wall. In another place I once more got as far as the bottles, and then asked for a bill of fare; was told to walk up stairs; had no bill of fare, nothing but fare. "Have you any pies or puddings?" I inquired, for I am obliged to keep my savageness in check by a low diet. "No, sir; we've nice mutton-chop, roast beef, beef-steak, cutlets," and so on. A burly Englishman, who was in the midst of the siege of a piece of roast beef, and of whom I have never had a front view to this day, turned half round, with his mouth half full, and remarked, "You'll find no pies nor puddings in Quebec, sir; they don't make any here." I found that it was even so, and therefore bought some musty cake and some fruit in the open market-place. This market-place by the water-side, where the old women sat by their tables in the open air, amid a dense crowd jabbering all languages, was the best place in Quebec to observe the people; and the ferry-boats, continually coming and going with their motley crews and cargoes, added much to the entertainment. I also saw them getting water from the river, for Quebec is supplied with water by cart and barrel. This city impressed me as wholly foreign and French, for I scarcely heard the sound of the English language in the streets. More than three fifths of the inhabitants are of French origin; and if the traveller did not visit the fortifications particularly, he might not be reminded that the English have any foothold here; and, in any case, if he looked no farther than Quebec, they would appear to have planted themselves in Canada only as they have in Spain at Gibraltar; and he who plants upon a rock cannot expect much increase. The novel sights and sounds by the water-side made me think of such ports as Boulogne, Dieppe, Rouen, and Havre de Grace, which I have never seen; but I have no doubt that they present similar scenes. I was much amused from first to last with the sounds made by the charette and caleche drivers. It was that part of their foreign language that you heard the most of,—the French they talked to their horses,—and which they talked the loudest. It was a more novel sound to me than the French of conversation. The streets resounded with the cries, "*Qui donc!*" "*March tôt!*" I suspect that many of our horses which came from Canada would prick up their ears at these sounds. Of the shops, I was most attracted by those where furs and Indian works were sold, as containing articles of genuine Canadian manufacture. I have been told that two townsmen of mine, who were interested in horticulture, travelling once in Canada, and being in Quebec, thought it would be a good opportunity to obtain seeds of the real Canada crook-neck squash. So they went into a shop where such things were advertised, and inquired for the same. The shopkeeper had the very thing they wanted. "But are you sure," they asked, "that these are the genuine Canada crook-neck?" "O yes, gentlemen," answered he, "they are a lot which I have received directly from Boston." I resolved that my Canada crook-neck seeds should be such as had grown in Canada.

Too much has not been said about the scenery of Quebec. The fortifications of Cape Diamond are omnipresent. They preside, they frown over the river and surrounding country. You travel ten, twenty, thirty miles up or down the river's banks, you ramble fifteen miles amid the hills on either side, and then, when you have long since forgotten them, perchance slept on them by the way, at a turn of the road or of your body, there they are still, with their geometry against the sky. The child that is born and brought up thirty miles distant, and has never travelled to the city, reads his country's history, sees the level lines of the citadel amid the cloud-built citadels in the western horizon, and is told that that is Quebec. No wonder if Jacques Cartier's pilot exclaimed in Norman French, *Que bec!*—"What a beak!"—when he saw this cape, as some suppose. Every modern traveller involuntarily uses a similar expression. Particularly it is said that its sudden apparition on turning Point Levi makes a memorable impression on him who arrives by water. The view from Cape Diamond has been compared by European travellers with the most remarkable views of a similar kind in Europe, such as from Edinburgh Castle, Gibraltar, Cintra, and others, and preferred by many. A main peculiarity in this, compared with other views which I have beheld, is that it is from the ramparts of a fortified city, and not from a solitary and majestic river cape alone that this view is obtained. I associate the beauty of Quebec with the steel-like and flashing air, which may be peculiar to that season of the year, in which the blue flowers of the succory and some late golden-rods and buttercups on the summit of Cape Diamond were almost my only companions,—the former bluer than the heavens they faced. Yet even I yielded in some degree to the influence of historical associations, and found it hard to attend to the geology of Cape Diamond or the botany of the Plains of Abraham. I still remember the harbor far beneath me, sparkling like silver in the sun,—the answering highlands of Point Levi on the southeast,—the frowning Cap Tourmente abruptly bounding the seaward view far in the northeast,—the villages of Lorette and Charlesbourg on the north,—and further west the distant

Val Cartier, sparkling with white cottages, hardly removed by distance through the clear air,—not to mention a few blue mountains along the horizon in that direction. You look out from the ramparts of the citadel beyond the frontiers of civilization. Yonder small group of hills, according to the guide-book, forms "the portal of the wilds which are trodden only by the feet of the Indian hunters as far as Hudson's Bay." It is but a few years since Bouchette declared that the country ten leagues north of the British capital of North America was as little known as the middle of Africa. Thus the citadel under my feet, and all historical associations, were swept away again by an influence from the wilds and from nature, as if the beholder had read her history,—an influence which, like the Great River itself, flowed from the Arctic fastnesses and Western forests with irresistible tide over all.

The most interesting object in Canada to me was the River St. Lawrence, known far and wide, and for centuries, as the Great River. Cartier, its discoverer, sailed up it as far as Montreal in 1535,—nearly a century before the coming of the Pilgrims; and I have seen a pretty accurate map of it so far, containing the city of "Hochelaga" and the river "Saguenay," in Ortelius's *Theatrum Orbis Terrarum*, printed at Antwerp in 1575,—the first edition having appeared in 1570,—in which the famous cities of "Norumbega" and "Orsinora" stand on the rough-blocked continent where New England is to-day, and the fabulous but unfortunate Isle of Demons, and Frislant, and others, lie off and on in the unfrequented sea, some of them prowling near what is now the course of the Cunard steamers. In this ponderous folio of the "Ptolemy of his age," said to be the first general atlas published after the revival of the sciences in Europe, only one page of which is devoted to the topography of the *Novus Orbis*, the St. Lawrence is the only large river, whether drawn from fancy or from observation, on the east side of North America. It was famous in Europe before the other rivers of North America were heard of, notwithstanding that the mouth of the Mississippi is said to have been discovered first, and its stream was reached by Soto not long after; but the St. Lawrence had attracted settlers to its cold shores long before the Mississippi, or even the Hudson, was known to the world. Schoolcraft was misled by

Gallatin into saying that Narvaez discovered the Mississippi. De Vega does *not* say so. The first explorers declared that the summer in that country was as warm as France, and they named one of the bays in the Gulf of St. Lawrence the Bay of Chaleur, or of warmth; but they said nothing about the winter being as cold as Greenland. In the manuscript account of Cartier's second voyage, attributed by some to that navigator himself, it is called "the greatest river, without comparison, that is known to have ever been seen." The savages told him that it was the "*chemin du Canada,*"—the highway to Canada,—"which goes so far that no man had ever been to the end that they had heard." The Saguenay, one of its tributaries, which the panorama has made known to New England within three years, is described by Cartier, in 1535, and still more particularly by Jean Alphonse, in 1542, who adds, "I think that this river comes from the sea of Cathay, for in this place there issues a strong current, and there runs there a terrible tide." The early explorers saw many whales and other sea-monsters far up the St. Lawrence. Champlain, in his map, represents a whale spouting in the harbor of Quebec, three hundred and sixty miles from what is called the mouth of the river; and Charlevoix takes his reader to the summit of Cape Diamond to see the "porpoises, white as snow," sporting on the surface of the harbor of Quebec. And Boucher says in 1664, "from there (Tadoussac) to Montreal is found a great quantity of *Marsouins blancs.*" Several whales have been taken pretty high up the river since I was there. P. H. Gosse, in his "Canadian Naturalist," p. 171 (London, 1840), speaks of "the white dolphin of the St. Lawrence (*Delphinus Canadensis*)," as considered different from those of the sea. "The Natural History Society of Montreal offered a prize, a few years ago, for an essay on the *Cetacea* of the St. Lawrence, which was, I believe, handed in." In Champlain's day it was commonly called "the Great River of Canada." More than one nation has claimed it. In Ogilby's "America of 1670," in the map *Novi Belgii,* it is called "De Groote Rivier van Niew Nederlandt." It bears different names in different parts of its course, as it flows through what were formerly the territories of different nations. From the Gulf to Lake Ontario it is called at present the St. Lawrence; from Montreal to the same place it is frequently called the Cateraqui; and higher up it is known successively as the Niagara, Detroit, St. Clair, St. Mary's, and St. Louis rivers. Humboldt, speaking of the Orinoco, says that this name is unknown in the interior of the country; so likewise the tribes that dwell about the sources of the St. Lawrence have never heard the name which it bears in the lower part of its course. It rises near another father of waters,—the Mississippi,—issuing from a remarkable spring far up in the woods, called Lake Superior, fifteen hundred miles in circumference; and several other springs there are thereabouts which feed it. It makes such a noise in its tumbling down at one place as is heard all round the world. Bouchette, the Surveyor-General of the Canadas, calls it "the most splendid river on the globe"; says that it is two thousand statute miles long (more recent geographers make it four or five hundred miles longer); that at the Rivière du Sud it is eleven miles wide; at the Traverse, thirteen; at the Paps of Matane, twenty-five; at the Seven Islands, seventy-three; and at its mouth, from Cape Rosier to the Mingan Settlements in Labrador, near one hundred and five (?) miles wide. According to Captain Bayfield's recent chart it is about *ninety-six* geographical miles wide at the latter place, measuring at right angles with the stream. It has much the largest estuary, regarding both length and breadth, of any river on the globe. Humboldt says that the river Plate, which has the broadest estuary of the South American rivers, is ninety-two geographical miles wide at its mouth; also he found the Orinoco to be more than three miles wide at five hundred and sixty miles from its mouth; but he does not tell us that ships of six hundred tons can sail up it so far, as they can up the St. Lawrence to Montreal,—an equal distance. If he had described a fleet of such ships at anchor in a city's port so far inland, we should have got a very different idea of the Orinoco. Perhaps Charlevoix describes the St. Lawrence truly as the most *navigable* river in the world. Between Montreal and Quebec it averages about two miles wide. The tide is felt as far up as Three Rivers, four hundred and thirty-two miles, which is as far as from Boston to Washington. As far up as Cap aux Oyes, sixty or seventy miles below Quebec, Kalm found a great part of the plants near the shore to be marine, as glass-wort (*Salicornia*), seaside pease (*Pisum maritimum*), sea-milkwort (*Glaux*), beach-grass (*Psamma arenarium*), seaside plantain (*Plantago maritima*), the sea-rocket (*Bunias cakile*), &c.

The geographer Guyot observes that the Maranon is three thousand miles long, and gathers its waters from a surface of a million and a half square miles; that the Mississippi is also three thousand miles long, but its basin covers only from eight to nine hundred thousand square miles; that the St. Lawrence is eighteen hundred miles long, and its basin covers more than a million square miles (Darby says five hundred thousand); and speaking of the lakes, he adds, "These vast fresh-water seas, together with the St. Lawrence, cover a surface of nearly one hundred thousand square miles, and it has been calculated that they contain about one half of all the fresh water on the surface of our planet." But all these calculations are necessarily very rude and inaccurate. Its tributaries, the Ottawa, St. Maurice, and Saguenay, are great rivers themselves. The latter is said to be more than one thousand (?) feet deep at its mouth, while its cliffs rise perpendicularly an equal distance above its surface. Pilots say there are no soundings till one hundred and fifty miles up the St. Lawrence. The greatest sounding in the river, given on Bayfield's chart of the gulf and river, is two hundred and twenty-eight fathoms. McTaggart, an engineer, observes that "the Ottawa is larger than all the rivers in Great Britain, were they running in one." The traveller Grey writes: "A dozen Danubes, Rhines, Taguses, and Thameses would be nothing to twenty miles of fresh water in breadth (as where he happened to be), from ten to forty fathoms in depth." And again: "There is not perhaps in the whole extent of this immense continent so fine an approach to it as by the river St. Lawrence. In the Southern States you have, in general, a level country for many miles inland; here you are introduced at once into a majestic scenery, where everything is on a grand scale,—mountains, woods, lakes, rivers, precipices, waterfalls."

We have not yet the data for a minute comparison of the St. Lawrence with the South American rivers; but it is obvious that, taking it in connection with its lakes, its estuary, and its falls, it easily bears off the palm from all the rivers on the globe; for though, as Bouchette observes, it may not carry to the ocean a greater volume of water than the Amazon and Mississippi, its surface and cubic mass are far greater than theirs. But, unfortunately, this noble river is closed by ice from the beginning of December to the middle of April. The arrival of the first vessel from England when the ice breaks up is, therefore, a great event, as when the salmon, shad, and alewives come up a river in the spring to relieve the famishing inhabitants on its banks. Who can say what would have been the history of this continent if, as has been suggested, this river had emptied into the sea where New York stands!

After visiting the Museum and taking one more look at the wall, I made haste to the Lord Sydenham steamer, which at five o'clock was to leave for Montreal. I had already taken a seat on deck, but finding that I had still an hour and a half to spare, and remembering that large map of Canada which I had seen in the parlor of the restaurateur in my search after pudding, and realizing that I might never see the like out of the country, I returned thither, asked liberty to look at the map, rolled up the mahogany table, put my handkerchief on it, stood on it, and copied all I wanted before the maid came in and said to me standing on the table, "Some gentlemen want the room, sir"; and I retreated without having broken the neck of a single bottle, or my own, very thankful and willing to pay for all the solid food I had got. We were soon abreast of Cap Rouge, eight miles above Quebec, after we got underway. It was in this place, then called "*Fort du France Roy*," that the Sieur de Roberval with his company, having sent home two of his three ships, spent the winter of 1542–43. It appears that they fared in the following manner (I translate from the original): "Each mess had only two loaves, weighing each a pound, and half a pound of beef. They ate pork for dinner, with half a pound of butter, and beef for supper, with about two handfuls of beans, without butter. Wednesdays, Fridays, and Saturdays they ate salted cod, and sometimes green, for dinner, with butter; and porpoise and beans for supper. Monsieur Roberval administered good justice, and punished each according to his offence. One, named Michel Gaillon, was hung for theft; John of Nantes was put in irons and imprisoned for his fault; and others were likewise put in irons; and many were whipped, both men and women; by which means they lived in peace and tranquillity." In an account of a voyage up this river, printed in the Jesuit Relations in the year 1664, it is said: "It was an interesting navigation for us in ascending the river from Cap Tourment to Quebec, to see on this side and on that, for the space of eight leagues, the farms and the houses of the company, built by our French, all along these shores. On the right, the seigniories of Beauport, of Notre Dames des Anges; and on the left, this beautiful Isle of Orleans." The same traveller names among the fruits of the country observed at the Isles of Richelieu, at the head of Lake St. Peter, "kinds (*des espèces*) of little apples or haws (*semelles*), and of pears, which only ripen with the frost."

Night came on before we had passed the high banks. We had come from Montreal to Quebec in one night. The return voyage, against the stream, takes but an hour longer. Jacques Cartier, the first white man who is known to have ascended this river, thus speaks of his voyage from what is now Quebec to the foot of Lake St. Peter, or about half-way to Montreal: "From the said day, the 19th, even to the 28th of the said month, [September, 1535] we had been navigating up the said river without losing hour or day, during which time we had seen and found as much country and lands as level as we could desire, full of the most beautiful trees in the world," which he goes on to describe. But we merely slept and woke again to find that we had passed through all that country which he was eight days in sailing through. He must have had a troubled sleep. We were not long enough on the river to realize that it had length; we got only the impression of its breadth, as if we had passed over a lake a mile or two in breadth and several miles long, though we might thus have slept through a European kingdom. Being at the head of Lake St. Peter, on the above-mentioned 28th of September, dealing with the natives, Cartier says: "We inquired of them by signs if this was the route to Hochelaga [Montreal]; and they answered that it was, and that there were yet three days' journeys to go there." He finally arrived at Hochelaga on the 2d of October.

When I went on deck at dawn we had already passed through Lake St. Peter, and saw islands ahead of us. Our boat advancing with a strong and steady pulse over the calm surface, we felt as if we were permitted to be awake in the scenery of a dream. Many vivacious Lombardy poplars along the distant shores gave them a novel and lively, though artificial, look, and contrasted strangely with the slender and graceful elms on both shores and islands. The church of Varennes, fifteen miles from Montreal, was conspicuous at a great distance before us, appearing to belong to, and rise out of, the river; and now, and before, Mount Royal indicated where the city was. We arrived about seven o'clock, and set forth immediately to ascend the mountain, two miles distant, going across lots in spite of numerous signs threatening the severest penalties to trespassers, past an old building known as the Mac Tavish property,—Simon Mac Tavish, I suppose, whom Silliman refers to as "in a sense the founder of the Northwestern Company." His tomb was behind in the woods, with a remarkably high wall and higher monument. The family returned to Europe. He could not have imagined how dead he would be in a few years, and all the more dead and forgotten for being buried under such a mass of gloomy stone, where not even memory could get at him without a crowbar. Ah! poor man, with that last end of his! However, he may have been the worthiest of mortals for aught that I know. From the mountain-top we got a view of the whole city; the flat, fertile, extensive island; the noble sea of the St. Lawrence swelling into lakes; the mountains about St. Hyacinth, and in Vermont and New York; and the mouth of the Ottawa in the west, overlooking that St. Ann's where the voyageur sings his "parting hymn," and bids adieu to civilization,—a name, thanks to Moore's verses, the most suggestive of poetic associations of any in Canada. We, too, climbed the hill which Cartier, first of white men, ascended, and named Mont-real, (the 3d of October, O. S., 1535,) and, like him, "we saw the said river as far as we could see, *grand, large, et spacieux*, going to the southwest," toward that land whither Donnacona had told the discoverer that he had been a month's journey from Canada, where there grew "*force Canelle et Girofle*," much cinnamon and cloves, and where also, as the natives told him, were three great lakes and afterward *une mer douce*,—a sweet sea,—*de laquelle n'est mention avoir vu le bout*, of which there is no mention to have seen the end. But instead of an Indian town far in the interior of a new world, with guides to show us where the river came from, we found a splendid and bustling stone-built city of white men, and only a few squalid Indians offered to sell us baskets at the Lachine Railroad Depot, and Hochelaga is, perchance, but the fancy name of an engine company or an eating-house.

We left Montreal Wednesday, the 2d of October, late in the afternoon. In the La Prairie cars the Yankees made themselves merry, imitating the cries of the charette-drivers to perfection, greatly to the amusement of some French-Canadian travellers, and they kept it up all the way to Boston. I saw one person on board the boat at St. John's, and one or two more elsewhere in Canada, wearing homespun gray great-coats, or capotes, with conical and comical hoods, which fell back between their shoulders like small bags, ready to be turned up over the head when occasion required, though a hat usurped that place now. They looked as if they would be convenient and proper enough as long as the coats were new and tidy, but would soon come to have a beggarly and unsightly look, akin to rags and dust-holes. We reached Burlington early in the morning, where the Yankees tried to pass off their Canada coppers, but the news-boys knew better. Returning through the Green Mountains, I was reminded that I had not seen in Canada such brilliant autumnal tints as I had previously seen in Vermont. Perhaps there was not yet so great and sudden a contrast with the summer heats in the former country as in these mountain valleys. As we were passing through Ashburnham, by a new white house which stood at some distance in a field, one passenger exclaimed, so that all in the car could hear him, "There, there's not so good a house as that in all Canada!" I did not much wonder at his remark, for there is a neatness, as well as evident prosperity, a certain elastic easiness of circumstances, so to speak, when not rich, about a New England house, as if the proprietor could at least afford to make repairs in the spring, which the Canadian houses do not suggest. Though of stone, they are not better constructed than a stone barn would be with us; the only building, except the chateau, on which money and taste are expended, being the church. In Canada an ordinary New

England house would be mistaken for the chateau, and while every village here contains at least several gentlemen or "squires," *there* there is but one to a seigniory.

I got home this Thursday evening, having spent just one week in Canada and travelled eleven hundred miles. The whole expense of this journey, including two guide-books and a map, which cost one dollar twelve and a half cents, was twelve dollars seventy-five cents. I do not suppose that I have seen all British America; that could not be done by a cheap excursion, unless it were a cheap excursion to the Icy Sea, as seen by Hearne or McKenzie, and then, no doubt, some interesting features would be omitted. I wished to go a little way behind that word *Canadense*, of which naturalists make such frequent use; and I should like still right well to make a longer excursion on foot through the wilder parts of Canada, which perhaps might be called *Iter Canadense*.

Love

WHAT the essential difference between man and woman is that they should be thus attracted to one another, no one has satisfactorily answered. Perhaps we must acknowledge the justness of the distinction which assigns to man the sphere of wisdom, and to woman that of love, though neither belongs exclusively to either. Man is continually saying to woman, Why will you not be more wise? Woman is continually saying to man, Why will you not be more loving? It is not in their wills to be wise or to be loving; but, unless each is both wise and loving, there can be neither wisdom nor love.

All transcendent goodness is one, though appreciated in different ways, or by different senses. In beauty we see it, in music we hear it, in fragrance we scent it, in the palatable the pure palate tastes it, and in rare health the whole body feels it. The variety is in the surface or manifestation; but the radical identity we fail to express. The lover sees in the glance of his beloved the same beauty that in the sunset paints the western skies. It is the same daimon, here lurking under a human eyelid, and there under the closing eyelids of the day. Here, in small compass, is the ancient and natural beauty of evening and morning. What loving astronomer has ever fathomed the ethereal depths of the eye?

The maiden conceals a fairer flower and sweeter fruit than any calyx in the field; and, if she goes with averted face, confiding in her purity and high resolves, she will make the heavens retrospective, and all nature humbly confess its queen.

Under the influence of this sentiment, man is a string of an Æolian harp, which vibrates with the zephyrs of the eternal morning.

There is at first thought something trivial in the commonness of love. So many Indian youths and maidens along these banks have in ages past yielded to the influence of this great civilizer. Nevertheless, this generation is not disgusted nor discouraged, for love is no individual's experience; and though we are imperfect mediums, it does not partake of our imperfection; though we are finite, it is infinite and eternal;

and the same divine influence broods over these banks, whatever race may inhabit them, and perchance still would, even if the human race did not dwell here.

Perhaps an instinct survives through the intensest actual love, which prevents entire abandonment and devotion, and makes the most ardent lover a little reserved. It is the anticipation of change. For the most ardent lover is not the less practically wise, and seeks a love which will last forever.

Considering how few poetical friendships there are, it is remarkable that so many are married. It would seem as if men yielded too easy an obedience to nature without consulting their genius. One may be drunk with love without being any nearer to finding his mate. There is more of good nature than of good sense at the bottom of most marriages. But the good nature must have the counsel of the good spirit or Intelligence. If common sense had been consulted, how many marriages would never have taken place; if uncommon or divine sense, how few marriages such as we witness would ever have taken place!

Our love may be ascending or descending. What is its character, if it may be said of it,—

> "We must *respect* the souls above,
> But only *those below* we *love*."

Love is a severe critic. Hate can pardon more than love. They who aspire to love worthily, subject themselves to an ordeal more rigid than any other.

Is your friend such a one that an increase of worth on your part will surely make her more your friend? Is she retained,—is she attracted,—by more nobleness in you,—by more of that virtue which is peculiarly yours; or is she indifferent and blind to that? Is she to be flattered and won by your meeting her on any other than the ascending path? Then duty requires that you separate from her.

Love must be as much a light as a flame.

Where there is not discernment, the behavior even of the purest soul may in effect amount to coarseness.

A man of fine perceptions is more truly feminine than a merely sentimental woman. The heart is blind, but Love is not blind. None of the gods is so discriminating.

In Love & Friendship the imagination is as much exercised as the heart, and if either is outraged, the other will be estranged. It is commonly the imagination which is wounded first, rather than the heart, it is so much the more sensitive.

Comparatively, we can excuse any offence against the heart, but not against the imagination. The imagination knows— nothing escapes its glance from out its eyry—and it controls the breast. My heart may still yearn toward the valley, but my imagination will not permit me to jump off the precipice that debars me from it, for it is wounded, its wings are clipt, and it cannot fly, even descendingly. Our "blundering hearts"! some poet says. The imagination never forgets, it is a re-membering. It is not foundationless, but most reasonable, and it alone uses all the knowledge of the intellect.

Love is the profoundest of secrets. Divulged, even to the beloved, it is no longer Love. As if it were merely I that loved you. When love ceases, then it is divulged.

In our intercourse with one we love, we wish to have answered those questions at the end of which we do not raise our voice; against which we put no interrogation-mark,—answered with the same unfailing, universal aim toward every point of the compass.

I require that thou knowest everything without being told anything. I parted from my beloved because there was one thing which I had to tell her. She *questioned* me. She should have known all by sympathy. That I had to tell it her was the difference between us,—the misunderstanding.

A lover never hears anything that is *told*, for that is commonly either false or stale; but he hears things taking place, as the sentinels heard Trenck mining in the ground, and thought it was moles.

The relation may be profaned in many ways. The parties may not regard it with equal sacredness. What if the lover should learn that his beloved dealt in incantations and philters! What if he should hear that she consulted a clairvoyant! The spell would be instantly broken.

If to chaffer and higgle are bad in trade, they are much worse in Love. It demands directness as of an arrow.

There is danger that we lose sight of what our friend is absolutely, while considering what she is to us alone.

The lover wants no partiality. He says, Be so kind as to be just.

> Canst thou love with thy mind,
>   And reason with thy heart?
> Canst thou be kind,
>   And from thy darling part?
>
> Canst thou range earth, sea, and air,
>   And so meet me everywhere?
> Through all events I will pursue thee,
>   Through all persons I will woo thee.

I need thy hate as much as thy love. Thou wilt not repel me entirely when thou repellest what is evil in me.

> Indeed, indeed, I cannot tell,
> Though I ponder on it well,
> Which were easier to state,
> All my love or all my hate.
> Surely, surely, thou wilt trust me
> When I say thou dost disgust me.
> O I hate thee with a hate
> That would fain annihilate;
> Yet, sometimes, against my will,
> My dear Friend, I love thee still.
> It were treason to our love,
> And a sin to God above,
> One iota to abate
> Of a pure, impartial hate.

It is not enough that we are truthful; we must cherish and carry out high purposes to be truthful about.

It must be rare, indeed, that we meet with one to whom we are prepared to be quite ideally related, as she to us. We should have no reserve; we should give the whole of ourselves to that society; we should have no duty aside from that. One who could bear to be so wonderfully and beautifully exaggerated every day. I would take my friend out of her low self and set her higher, infinitely higher, and *there* know her. But, commonly, men are as much afraid of love as of hate. They have lower engagements. They have near ends to serve. They have not imagination enough to be thus employed about a human being, but must be coopering a barrel, forsooth.

What a difference, whether, in all your walks, you meet only strangers, or in one house is one who knows you, and whom you know. To have a brother or a sister! To have a gold mine on your farm! To find diamonds in the gravel heaps before your door! How rare these things are! To share the day with you,—to people the earth. Whether to have a god or a goddess for companion in your walks, or to walk alone with hinds and villains and carles. Would not a friend enhance the beauty of the landscape as much as a deer or hare? Everything would acknowledge and serve such a relation; the corn in the field, and the cranberries in the meadow. The flowers would bloom, and the birds sing, with a new impulse. There would be more fair days in the year.

The object of love expands and grows before us to eternity, until it includes all that is lovely, and we become all that can love.

Chastity & Sensuality

THE SUBJECT of Sex is a remarkable one, since, though its phenomena concern us so much both directly and indirectly, and, sooner or later it occupies the thoughts of all, yet, all mankind, as it were, agree to be silent about it, at least the sexes commonly one to another. One of the most interesting of all human facts is veiled more completely than any mystery. It is treated with such secrecy and awe, as surely do not go to any religion. I believe that it is unusual even for the most intimate friends to communicate the pleasures and anxieties connected with this fact,—much as the external affairs of love, its comings & goings, are bruited. The Shakers do not exaggerate it so much by their manner of speaking of it, as all mankind by their manner of keeping silence about it. Not that men should speak on this or any subject without having any thing worthy to say; but it is plain that the education of man has hardly commenced, there is so little genuine intercommunication.

In a pure society, the subject of copulation would not be so often avoided from shame and not from reverence, winked out of sight, and hinted at only, but treated naturally and simply,—perhaps simply avoided, like the kindred mysteries. If it cannot be spoken of for shame, how can it be acted of? But doubtless there is far more purity as well as more impurity, than is apparent.

Men commonly couple with their idea of marriage a slight degree at least of sensuality, but every lover, the world over, believes in its inconceivable purity.

If it is the result of a pure love, there can be nothing sensual in marriage. Chastity is something positive, not negative. It is the virtue of the married especially. All lusts or base pleasures must give place to loftier delights. They who meet as superior beings cannot perform the deeds of inferior ones. The deeds of love are less questionable than any action of an individual can be, for, it being founded on the rarest mutual respect, the parties incessantly stimulate each other to a loftier and purer life, and the act in which they are associated must be pure and noble indeed, for innocence and purity can have no equal. In this relation we deal with one whom we respect more religiously even than we respect our better selves, and we shall necessarily conduct as in the presence of God. What presence can be more awful to the lover than that of his beloved?

If you seek the warmth even of affection from a similar motive to that from which cats and dogs and slothful persons hug the fire, because your temperature is low through sloth, you are on the downward road, and it is but to plunge yet deeper into sloth. Better the cold affection of the sun reflected from fields of ice and snow, or his warmth in some still wintry dell. The warmth of celestial love does not relax, but nerves and braces its enjoyer. Warm your body by healthful exercise, not by cowering over a stove. Warm your spirit by performing independently noble deeds, not by ignobly seeking the sympathy of your fellows who are no better than yourself. A man's social and spiritual discipline must answer to his corporeal. He must lean on a friend who has a hard breast, as he would lie on a hard bed. He must drink cold water for his only beverage. So he must not hear sweetened and colored words, but pure and refreshing truths. He must daily bathe in truth cold as spring water, not warmed by the sympathy of friends.

Can love be in aught allied to dissipation? Let us love by refusing not accepting one another. Love and lust are far asunder. The one is good, the other bad. When the affectionate sympathize by their higher natures, there is love; but there is danger that they will sympathize by their lower natures, and then there is lust. It is not necessary that this be deliberate, hardly even conscious, but in the close contact of affection there is danger that we may stain and pollute one another, for we cannot embrace but with an entire embrace.

We must love our friend so much that she shall be associated with our purest and holiest thoughts alone. When there is impurity, we have "descended to meet," though we knew it not.

The *luxury* of affection,—there's the danger. There must be some nerve and heroism in our love, as of a winter morning. In the religion of all nations a purity is hinted at, which,

I fear, men never attain to. We may love and not elevate one another. The love that takes us as it finds us, degrades us. What watch we must keep over the fairest and purest of our affections, lest there be some taint about them. May we so love as never to have occasion to repent of our love.

There is to be attributed to sensuality the loss to language of how many pregnant symbols.

Flowers, which, by their infinite hues and fragrance celebrate the marriage of the plants are intended for a symbol of the open and unsuspected beauty of all true marriage, when man's flowering season arrives.

Virginity too is a budding flower, and by an impure marriage the virgin is deflowered. Whoever loves flowers, loves virgins and chastity. Love and lust are as far asunder as a flower garden is from a brothel.

J. Biberg, in the "Amoenitates Botanicae", edited by Linnaeus, observes, (I translate from the Latin) "the organs of generation which in the animal kingdom are for the most part concealed by nature as if they were to be ashamed of, in the vegetable kingdom are exposed to the eyes of all; and when the nuptials of plants are celebrated, it is wonderful what delight they afford to the beholder, refreshing the senses with the most agreeable color and the sweetest odor, and at the same time bees and other insects, not to mention the humming bird, extract honey from their nectaries, and gather wax from their effete pollen." Linnaeus himself calls the calyx the *thalamus*, or bridal chamber, and the corolla the *aulaeum* or tapestry of it, and proceeds to explain thus every part of the flower.

Who knows but evil spirits might corrupt the flowers themselves, rob them of their fragrance and their fair hues, and turn their marriage into a secret shame & defilement? Already they are of various qualities, and there is one whose nuptials fill the lowlands in June with the odor of carrion.

The intercourse of the sexes, I have dreamed, is incredibly beautiful, too fair to be remembered. I have had thoughts about it, but they are among the most fleeting and irrecoverable in my experience. It is strange that men will talk of miracles, revelation, inspiration, and the like, as things past, while love remains.

A true marriage will differ in no wise from illumination. In all perception of the truth there is a divine ecstasy, an inexpressible delirium of joy, as when a youth embraces his betrothed virgin. The ultimate delights of a true marriage are one with this.

No wonder that out of such a union, not as end, but as accompaniment, comes the undying race of man. The womb is a most fertile soil.

Some have asked if the stock of men could not be improved,—if they could not be bred as cattle. Let Love be purified and all the rest will follow. A pure love is thus indeed the panacea for all the ills of the world.

The only excuse for reproduction is improvement. Nature abhors repetition. Beasts merely propagate their kind, but the offspring of noble men & women will be superior to themselves, as their aspirations are. By their fruits ye shall know them.

Slavery in Massachusetts

I LATELY attended a meeting of the citizens of Concord, expecting, as one among many, to speak on the subject of slavery in Massachusetts; but I was surprised and disappointed to find that what had called my townsmen together was the destiny of Nebraska, and not of Massachusetts, and that what I had to say would be entirely out of order. I had thought that the house was on fire, and not the prairie; but though several of the citizens of Massachusetts are now in prison for attempting to rescue a slave from her own clutches, not one of the speakers at that meeting expressed regret for it, not one even referred to it. It was only the disposition of some wild lands a thousand miles off, which appeared to concern them. The inhabitants of Concord are not prepared to stand by one of their own bridges, but talk only of taking up a position on the highlands beyond the Yellowstone river. Our Buttricks, and Davises, and Hosmers are retreating thither, and I fear that they will have no Lexington Common between them and the enemy. There is not one slave in Nebraska; there are perhaps a million slaves in Massachusetts.

They who have been bred in the school of politics fail now and always to face the facts. Their measures are half measures and make-shifts, merely. They put off the day of settlement indefinitely, and meanwhile, the debt accumulates. Though the Fugitive Slave Law had not been the subject of discussion on that occasion, it was at length faintly resolved by my townsmen, at an adjourned meeting, as I learn, that the compromise compact of 1820 having been repudiated by one of the parties, 'Therefore, . . . the Fugitive Slave Law must be repealed.' But this is not the reason why an iniquitous law should be repealed. The fact which the politician faces is merely, that there is less honor among thieves than was supposed, and not the fact that they are thieves.

As I had no opportunity to express my thoughts at that meeting, will you allow me to do so here?

Again it happens that the Boston Court House is full of armed men, holding prisoner and trying a MAN, to find out if

he is not really a SLAVE. Does any one think that Justice or
God awaits Mr. Loring's decision? For him to sit there deciding still, when this question is already decided from eternity
to eternity, and the unlettered slave himself, and the multitude around, have long since heard and assented to the decision, is simply to make himself ridiculous. We may be tempted
to ask from whom he received his commission, and who he is
that received it; what novel statutes he obeys, and what precedents are to him of authority. Such an arbiter's very existence
is an impertinence. We do not ask him to make up his mind,
but to make up his pack.

I listen to hear the voice of a Governor, Commander-in-
Chief of the forces of Massachusetts. I hear only the creaking
of crickets and the hum of insects which now fill the summer
air. The Governor's exploit is to review the troops on muster
days. I have seen him on horseback, with his hat off, listening
to a chaplain's prayer. It chances that is all I have ever seen of
a Governor. I think that I could manage to get along without
one. If *he* is not of the least use to prevent my being kidnapped, pray of what important use is he likely to be to me?
When freedom is most endangered, he dwells in the deepest
obscurity. A distinguished clergyman told me that he chose
the profession of a clergyman, because it afforded the most
leisure for literary pursuits. I would recommend to him the
profession of a Governor.

Three years ago, also, when the Simm's tragedy was acted,
I said to myself, there is such an officer, if not such a man, as
the Governor of Massachusetts,—what has he been about the
last fortnight? Has he had as much as he could do to keep on
the fence during this moral earthquake? It seemed to me that
no keener satire could have been aimed at, no more cutting
insult have been offered to that man, than just what happened—the absence of all inquiry after him in that crisis. The
worst and the most I chance to know of him is, that he did
not improve that opportunity to make himself known, and
worthily known. He could at least have *resigned* himself into
fame. It appeared to be forgotten that there was such a man,
or such an office. Yet no doubt he was endeavoring to fill the
gubernatorial chair all the while. He was no Governor of
mine. He did not govern me.

But at last, in the present case, the Governor was heard from. After he and the United States Government had perfectly succeeded in robbing a poor innocent black man of his liberty for life, and, as far as they could, of his Creator's likeness in his breast, he made a speech to his accomplices, at a congratulatory supper!

I have read a recent law of this State, making it penal for 'any officer of the Commonwealth' to 'detain, or aid in the . . . detention,' any where within its limits, 'of any person, for the reason that he is claimed as a fugitive slave.' Also, it was a matter of notoriety that a writ of replevin to take the fugitive out of the custody of the United States Marshal could not be served, for want of sufficient force to aid the officer.

I had thought that the Governor was in some sense the executive officer of the State; that it was his business, as a Governor, to see that the laws of the State were executed; while, as a man, he took care that he did not, by so doing, break the laws of humanity; but when there is any special important use for him, he is useless, or worse than useless, and permits the laws of the State to go unexecuted. Perhaps I do not know what are the duties of a Governor; but if to be a Governor requires to subject one's self to so much ignominy without remedy, if it is to put a restraint upon my manhood, I shall take care never to be Governor of Massachusetts. I have not read far in the statutes of this Commonwealth. It is not profitable reading. They do not always say what is true; and they do not always mean what they say. What I am concerned to know is, that that man's influence and authority were on the side of the slaveholder, and not of the slave—of the guilty, and not of the innocent —of injustice, and not of justice. I never saw him of whom I speak; indeed, I did not know that he was Governor until this event occurred. I heard of him and Anthony Burns at the same time, and thus, undoubtedly, most will hear of him. So far am I from being governed by him. I do not mean that it was any thing to his discredit that I had not heard of him, only that I heard what I did. The worst I shall say of him is, that he proved no better than the majority of his constituents would be likely to prove. In my opinion, he was not equal to the occasion.

The whole military force of the State is at the service of a Mr. Suttle, a slaveholder from Virginia, to enable him to catch a man whom he calls his property; but not a soldier is offered to save a citizen of Massachusetts from being kidnapped! Is this what all these soldiers, all this *training* has been for these seventy-nine years past? Have they been trained merely to rob Mexico, and carry back fugitive slaves to their masters?

These very nights, I heard the sound of a drum in our streets. There were men *training* still; and for what? I could with an effort pardon the cockerels of Concord for crowing still, for they, perchance, had not been beaten that morning; but I could not excuse this rub-a-dub of the 'trainers.' The slave was carried back by exactly such as these, i.e., by the soldier, of whom the best you can say in this connection is, that he is a fool made conspicuous by a painted coat.

Three years ago, also, just a week after the authorities of Boston assembled to carry back a perfectly innocent man, and one whom they knew to be innocent, into slavery, the inhabitants of Concord caused the bells to be rung and the cannons to be fired, to celebrate their liberty—and the courage and love of liberty of their ancestors who fought at the bridge. As if *those* three millions had fought for the right to be free themselves, but to hold in slavery three million others. Now-a-days, men wear a fool's cap, and call it a liberty cap. I do not know but there are some, who, if they were tied to a whipping-post, and could but get one hand free, would use it to ring the bells and fire the cannons, to celebrate *their* liberty. So some of my townsmen took the liberty to ring and fire; that was the extent of their freedom; and when the sound of the bells died away, their liberty died away also; when the powder was all expended, their liberty went off with the smoke.

The joke could be no broader, if the inmates of the prisons were to subscribe for all the powder to be used in such salutes, and hire the jailers to do the firing and ringing for them, while they enjoyed it through the grating.

This is what I thought about my neighbors.

Every humane and intelligent inhabitant of Concord, when he or she heard those bells and those cannons, thought not with pride of the events of the 19th of April, 1775, but with

shame of the events of the 12th of April, 1851. But now we
have half buried that old shame under a new one.

Massachusetts sat waiting Mr. Loring's decision, as if it
could in any way affect her own criminality. Her crime, the
most conspicuous and fatal crime of all, was permitting him
to be the umpire in such a case. It was really the trial of
Massachusetts. Every moment that she hesitated to set this
man free—every moment that she now hesitates to atone for
her crime, she is convicted. The Commissioner on her case is
God; not Edward G. God, but simple God.

I wish my countrymen to consider, that whatever the human law may be, neither an individual nor a nation can ever
commit the least act of injustice against the obscurest individual, without having to pay the penalty for it. A government
which deliberately enacts injustice, and persists in it, will at
length ever become the laughing-stock of the world.

Much has been said about American slavery, but I think
that we do not even yet realize what slavery is. If I were seriously to propose to Congress to make mankind into sausages,
I have no doubt that most of the members would smile at my
proposition, and if any believed me to be in earnest, they
would think that I proposed something much worse than
Congress had ever done. But if any of them will tell me that
to make a man into a sausage would be much worse,—would
be any worse, than to make him into a slave,—than it was to
enact the Fugitive Slave Law, I will accuse him of foolishness,
of intellectual incapacity, of making a distinction without a
difference. The one is just as sensible a proposition as the
other.

I hear a good deal said about trampling this law under foot.
Why, one need not go out of his way to do that. This law rises
not to the level of the head or the reason; its natural habitat
is in the dirt. It was born and bred, and has its life only in the
dust and mire, on a level with the feet, and he who walks with
freedom, and does not with Hindoo mercy avoid treading on
every venomous reptile, will inevitably tread on it, and so
trample it under foot,—and Webster, its maker, with it, like
the dirt-bug and its ball.

Recent events will be valuable as a criticism on the administration of justice in our midst, or, rather, as showing what

are the true resources of justice in any community. It has come to this, that the friends of liberty, the friends of the slave, have shuddered when they have understood that his fate was left to the legal tribunals of the country to be decided. Free men have no faith that justice will be awarded in such a case; the judge may decide this way or that; it is a kind of accident, at best. It is evident that he is not a competent authority in so important a case. It is no time, then, to be judging according to his precedents, but to establish a precedent for the future. I would much rather trust to the sentiment of the people. In their vote, you would get something of some value, at least, however small; but, in the other case, only the trammelled judgment of an individual, of no significance, be it which way it might.

It is to some extent fatal to the courts, when the people are compelled to go behind them. I do not wish to believe that the courts were made for fair weather, and for very civil cases merely,—but think of leaving it to any court in the land to decide whether more than three millions of people, in this case, a sixth part of a nation, have a right to be freemen or not! But it has been left to the courts of *justice*, so-called—to the Supreme Court of the land—and, as you all know, recognizing no authority but the Constitution, it has decided that the three millions are, and shall continue to be, slaves. Such judges as these are merely the inspectors of a pick-lock and murderer's tools, to tell him whether they are in working order or not, and there they think that their responsibility ends. There was a prior case on the docket, which they, as judges appointed by God, had no right to skip; which having been justly settled, they would have been saved from this humiliation. It was the case of the murderer himself.

The law will never make men free; it is men who have got to make the law free. They are the lovers of law and order, who observe the law when the government breaks it.

Among human beings, the judge whose words seal the fate of a man furthest into eternity, is not he who merely pronounces the verdict of the law, but he, whoever he may be, who, from a love of truth, and unprejudiced by any custom or enactment of men, utters a true opinion or *sentence* concerning him. He it is that *sentences* him. Whoever has discerned truth, has received his commission from a higher source than the chiefest justice in the world, who can discern only law. He finds himself constituted judge of the judge.—Strange that it should be necessary to state such simple truths.

I am more and more convinced that, with reference to any public question, it is more important to know what the country thinks of it, than what the city thinks. The city does not *think* much. On any moral question, I would rather have the opinion of Boxboro than of Boston and New York put together. When the former speaks, I feel as if somebody *had* spoken, as if *humanity* was yet, and a reasonable being had asserted its rights,—as if some unprejudiced men among the country's hills had at length turned their attention to the subject, and by a few sensible words redeemed the reputation of the race. When, in some obscure country town, the farmers come together to a special town meeting, to express their opinion on some subject which is vexing the land, that, I think, is the true Congress, and the most respectable one that is ever assembled in the United States.

It is evident that there are, in this Commonwealth, at least, two parties, becoming more and more distinct—the party of the city, and the party of the country. I know that the country is mean enough, but I am glad to believe that there is a slight difference in her favor. But as yet, she has few, if any organs, through which to express herself. The editorials which she reads, like the news, come from the sea-board. Let us, the inhabitants of the country, cultivate self-respect. Let us not send to the city for aught more essential than our broadcloths and groceries, or, if we read the opinions of the city, let us entertain opinions of our own.

Among measures to be adopted, I would suggest to make as earnest and vigorous an assault on the Press as has already been made, and with effect, on the Church. The Church has much improved within a few years; but the Press is almost, without exception, corrupt. I believe that, in this country, the press exerts a greater and a more pernicious influence than the Church did in its worst period. We are not a religious people, but we are a nation of politicians. We do not care for the Bible, but we do care for the newspaper. At any meeting of politicians,—like that at Concord the other evening, for instance,—how impertinent it would be to quote from the Bible! how pertinent to quote from a newspaper or from the Constitution! The newspaper is a Bible which we read every morning and every afternoon, standing and sitting, riding and walking. It is a Bible which every man carries in his pocket, which lies on every table and counter, and which the mail, and thousands of missionaries, are continually dispensing. It is, in short, the only book which America has printed, and which America reads. So wide is its influence. The editor is a preacher whom you voluntarily support. Your tax is commonly one cent daily, and it costs nothing for pew hire. But how many of these preachers preach the truth? I repeat the testimony of many an intelligent foreigner, as well as my own convictions, when I say, that probably no country was ever ruled by so mean a class of tyrants as, with a few noble exceptions, are the editors of the periodical press in *this* country. And as they live and rule only by their servility, and appealing to the worst, and not the better nature of man, the people who read them are in the condition of the dog that returns to his vomit.

The *Liberator* and the *Commonwealth* were the only papers in Boston, as far as I know, which made themselves heard in condemnation of the cowardice and meanness of the authorities of that city, as exhibited in '51. The other journals, almost without exception, by their manner of referring to and speaking of the Fugitive Slave Law, and the carrying back of the slave Simms, insulted the common sense of the country, at least. And, for the most part, they did this, one would say, because they thought so to secure the approbation of their patrons, not being aware that a sounder sentiment prevailed to any extent in the heart of the Commonwealth. I am told that some of them have improved of late; but they are still eminently time-serving. Such is the character they have won.

But, thank fortune, this preacher can be even more easily reached by the weapons of the reformer than could the recreant priest. The free men of New England have only to refrain from purchasing and reading these sheets, have only to withhold their cents, to kill a score of them at once. One whom I respect told me that he purchased Mitchell's *Citizen* in the cars, and then threw it out the window. But would not his contempt have been more fatally expressed, if he had not bought it?

Are they Americans? are they New Englanders? are they inhabitants of Lexington, and Concord, and Framingham, who read and support the Boston *Post, Mail, Journal, Advertiser, Courier,* and *Times?* Are these the Flags of our Union? I am not a newspaper reader, and may omit to name the worst.

Could slavery suggest a more complete servility than some of these journals exhibit? Is there any dust which their conduct does not lick, and make fouler still with its slime? I do not know whether the Boston *Herald* is still in existence, but I remember to have seen it about the streets when Simms was carried off. Did it not act its part well—serve its master faithfully? How could it have gone lower on its belly? How can a man stoop lower than he is low? do more than put his extremities in the place of the head he has? than make his head his lower extremity? When I have taken up this paper with my cuffs turned up, I have heard the gurgling of the sewer through every column. I have felt that I was handling a paper picked out of the public gutters, a leaf from the gospel of the gambling-house, the groggery and the brothel, harmonizing with the gospel of the Merchants' Exchange.

The majority of the men of the North, and of the South, and East, and West, are not men of principle. If they vote, they do not send men to Congress on errands of humanity, but while their brothers and sisters are being scourged and hung for loving liberty, while——I might here insert all that slavery implies and is,——it is the mismanagement of wood and iron and stone and gold which concerns them. Do what you will, O Government! with my wife and children, my mother and brother, my father and sister, I will obey your commands to the letter. It will indeed grieve me if you hurt them, if you deliver them to overseers to be hunted by hounds or to be whipped to death; but nevertheless, I will peaceably pursue my chosen calling on this fair earth, until perchance, one day, when I have put on mourning for them dead, I shall have persuaded you to relent. Such is the attitude, such are the words of Massachusetts.

Rather than do thus, I need not say what match I would touch, what system endeavor to blow up,—but as I love my life, I would side with the light, and let the dark earth roll from under me, calling my mother and my brother to follow.

I would remind my countrymen, that they are to be men first, and Americans only at a late and convenient hour. No matter how valuable law may be to protect your property, even to keep soul and body together, if it do not keep you and humanity together.

I am sorry to say, that I doubt if there is a judge in Massachusetts who is prepared to resign his office, and get his living innocently, whenever it is required of him to pass sentence under a law which is merely contrary to the law of God. I am compelled to see that they put themselves, or rather, are by character, in this respect, exactly on a level with the marine who discharges his musket in any direction he is ordered to. They are just as much tools and as little men. Certainly, they are not the more to be respected, because their master enslaves their understandings and consciences, instead of their bodies.

The judges and lawyers,—simply as such, I mean,—and all men of expediency, try this case by a very low and incompetent standard. They consider, not whether the Fugitive Slave Law is right, but whether it is what they call *constitutional*. Is virtue constitutional, or vice? Is equity constitutional, or iniquity? In important moral and vital questions like this, it is just as impertinent to ask whether a law is constitutional or not, as to ask whether it is profitable or not. They persist in being the servants of the worst of men, and not the servants of humanity. The question is not whether you or your grandfather, seventy years ago, did not enter into an agreement to serve the devil, and that service is not accordingly now due; but whether you will not now, for once and at last, serve God,—in spite of your own past recreancy, or that of your ancestor,—by obeying that eternal and only just CONSTITUTION, which He, and not any Jefferson or Adams, has written in your being.

The amount of it is, if the majority vote the devil to be God, the minority will live and behave accordingly, and obey the successful candidate, trusting that some time or other, by some Speaker's casting vote, perhaps, they may reinstate God. This is the highest principle I can get out of or invent for my neighbors. These men act as if they believed that they could safely slide down hill a little way—or a good way—and would surely come to a place, by and by, where they could begin to slide up again. This is expediency, or choosing that course which offers the slightest obstacles to the feet, that is, a down-hill one. But there is no such thing as accomplishing a righteous reform by the use of 'expediency.' There is no such thing as sliding up hill. In morals, the only sliders are back-sliders.

Thus we steadily worship Mammon, both School, and State, and Church, and the Seventh Day curse God with a tin-tamar from one end of the Union to the other.

Will mankind never learn that policy is not morality—that it never secures any moral right, but considers merely what is expedient? chooses the available candidate, who is invariably the devil,—and what right have his constituents to be sur-prised, because the devil does not behave like an angel of light? What is wanted is men, not of policy, but of probity—who recognize a higher law than the Constitution, or the de-cision of the majority. The fate of the country does not depend on how you vote at the polls—the worst man is as strong as the best at that game; it does not depend on what kind of paper you drop into the ballot-box once a year, but on what kind of man you drop from your chamber into the street every morning.

What should concern Massachusetts is not the Nebraska Bill, nor the Fugitive Slave Bill, but her own slaveholding and servility. Let the State dissolve her union with the slaveholder. She may wriggle and hesitate, and ask leave to read the Constitution once more; but she can find no respectable law or precedent which sanctions the continuance of such a Union for an instant.

Let each inhabitant of the State dissolve his union with her, as long as she delays to do her duty.

The events of the past month teach me to distrust Fame. I see that she does not finely discriminate, but coarsely hurrahs. She considers not the simple heroism of an action, but only as it is connected with its apparent consequences. She praises till she is hoarse the easy exploit of the Boston tea party, but will be comparatively silent about the braver and more disinterestedly heroic attack on the Boston Court-House, simply because it was unsuccessful!

Covered with disgrace, the State has sat down coolly to try for their lives and liberties the men who attempted to do its duty for it. And this is called *justice*! They who have shown that they can behave particularly well may perchance be put under bonds for *their good behavior.* They whom truth requires at present to plead guilty, are of all the inhabitants of the State, pre-eminently innocent. While the Governor, and the Mayor, and countless officers of the Commonwealth, are at large, the champions of liberty are imprisoned.

Only they are guiltless, who commit the crime of contempt of such a Court. It behoves every man to see that his influence is on the side of justice, and let the courts make their own characters. My sympathies in this case are wholly with the accused, and wholly against the accusers and their judges. Justice is sweet and musical; but injustice is harsh and discordant. The judge still sits grinding at his organ, but it yields no music, and we hear only the sound of the handle. He believes that all the music resides in the handle, and the crowd toss him their coppers the same as before.

Do you suppose that that Massachusetts which is now doing these things,—which hesitates to crown these men, some of whose lawyers, and even judges, perchance, may be driven to take refuge in some poor quibble, that they may not wholly outrage their instinctive sense of justice,—do you suppose that she is any thing but base and servile? that she is the champion of liberty?

Show me a free State, and a court truly of justice, and I will fight for them, if need be; but show me Massachusetts, and I refuse her my allegiance, and express contempt for her courts.

The effect of a good government is to make life more valuable,—of a bad one, to make it less valuable. We can afford that railroad, and all merely material stock, should lose some of its value, for that only compels us to live more simply and economically; but suppose that the value of life itself should be diminished! How can we make a less demand on man and nature, how live more economically in respect to virtue and all noble qualities, than we do? I have lived for the last month,—and I think that every man in Massachusetts capable of the sentiment of patriotism must have had a similar experience,—with the sense of having suffered a vast and indefinite loss. I did not know at first what ailed me. At last it occurred to me that what I had lost was a country. I had never respected the Government near to which I had lived, but I had foolishly thought that I might manage to live here, minding my private affairs, and forget it. For my part, my old and worthiest pursuits have lost I cannot say how much of their attraction, and I feel that my investment in life here is worth many per cent. less since Massachusetts last deliberately sent back an innocent man, Anthony Burns, to slavery. I dwelt before, perhaps, in the illusion that my life passed somewhere only *between* heaven and hell, but now I cannot persuade myself that I do not dwell *wholly within* hell. The site of that political organization called Massachusetts is to me morally covered with volcanic scoriæ and cinders, such as Milton describes in the infernal regions. If there is any hell more unprincipled than our rulers, and we, the ruled, I feel curious to see it. Life itself being worth less, all things with it, which minister to it, are worth less. Suppose you have a small library, with pictures to adorn the walls—a garden laid out around— and contemplate scientific and literary pursuits, &c., and discover all at once that your villa, with all its contents, is located in hell, and that the justice of the peace has a cloven foot and forked tail—do not these things suddenly lose their value in your eyes?

I feel that, to some extent, the State has fatally interfered with my lawful business. It has not only interrupted me in my passage through Court street on errands of trade, but it has interrupted me and every man on his onward and upward path, on which he had trusted soon to leave Court street far behind. What right had it to remind me of Court street? I have found that hollow which even I had relied on for solid.

I am surprised to see men going about their business as if nothing had happened. I say to myself—Unfortunates! they have not heard the news. I am surprised that the man whom I just met on horseback should be so earnest to overtake his newly-bought cows running away—since all property is insecure—and if they do not run away again, they may be taken away from him when he gets them. Fool! does he not know that his seed-corn is worth less this year—that all beneficent harvests fail as you approach the empire of hell? No prudent man will build a stone house under these circumstances, or engage in any peaceful enterprise which it requires a long time to accomplish. Art is as long as ever, but life is more interrupted and less available for a man's proper pursuits. It is not an era of repose. We have used up all our inherited freedom. If we would save our lives, we must fight for them.

I walk toward one of our ponds, but what signifies the beauty of nature when men are base? We walk to lakes to see our serenity reflected in them; when we are not serene, we go not to them. Who can be serene in a country where both the rulers and the ruled are without principle? The remembrance of my country spoils my walk. My thoughts are murder to the State, and involuntarily go plotting against her.

But it chanced the other day that I scented a white water-lily, and a season I had waited for had arrived. It is the emblem of purity. It bursts up so pure and fair to the eye, and so sweet to the scent, as if to show us what purity and sweetness reside in, and can be extracted from, the slime and muck of earth. I think I have plucked the first one that has opened for a mile. What confirmation of our hopes is in the fragrance of this flower! I shall not so soon despair of the world for it, notwithstanding slavery, and the cowardice and want of principle of Northern men. It suggests what kind of laws have prevailed longest and widest, and still prevail, and that the time may come when man's deeds will smell as sweet. Such is the odor which the plant emits. If Nature can compound this fragrance still annually, I shall believe her still young and full of vigor, her integrity and genius unimpaired, and that there is virtue even in man, too, who is fitted to perceive and love it. It reminds me that Nature has been partner to no Missouri Compromise. I scent no compromise in the fragrance of the water-lily. It is not a *Nymphœa Douglassii*. In it, the sweet, and pure, and innocent, are wholly sundered from the obscene and baleful. I do not scent in this the time-serving irresolution of a Massachusetts Governor, nor of a Boston Mayor. So behave that the odor of your actions may enhance the general sweetness of the atmosphere, that when we behold or scent a flower, we may not be reminded how inconsistent your deeds are with it; for all odor is but one form of advertisement of a moral quality, and if fair actions had not been performed, the lily would not smell sweet. The foul slime stands for the sloth and vice of man, the decay of humanity; the fragrant flower that springs from it, for the purity and courage which are immortal.

Slavery and servility have produced no sweet-scented flower annually, to charm the senses of men, for they have no real life: they are merely a decaying and a death, offensive to all healthy nostrils. We do not complain that they *live*, but that they do not *get buried*. Let the living bury them; even they are good for manure.

Life Without Principle

A T a lyceum, not long since, I felt that the lecturer had chosen a theme too foreign to himself, and so failed to interest me as much as he might have done. He described things not in or near to his heart, but toward his extremities and superficies. There was, in this sense, no truly central or centralizing thought in the lecture. I would have had him deal with his privatest experience, as the poet does. The greatest compliment that was ever paid me was when one asked me what *I thought*, and attended to my answer. I am surprised, as well as delighted, when this happens, it is such a rare use he would make of me, as if he were acquainted with the tool. Commonly, if men want anything of me, it is only to know how many acres I make of their land,—since I am a surveyor,—or, at most, what trivial news I have burdened myself with. They never will go to law for my meat; they prefer the shell. A man once came a considerable distance to ask me to lecture on Slavery; but on conversing with him, I found that he and his clique expected seven-eighths of the lecture to be theirs, and only one-eighth mine; so I declined. I take it for granted, when I am invited to lecture anywhere,—for I have had a little experience in that business,—that there is a desire to hear what *I think* on some subject, though I may be the greatest fool in the country,—and not that I should say pleasant things merely, or such as the audience will assent to; and I resolve, accordingly, that I will give them a strong dose of myself. They have sent for me, and engaged to pay for me, and I am determined that they shall have me, though I bore them beyond all precedent.

So now I would say something similar to you, my readers. Since *you* are my readers, and I have not been much of a traveller, I will not talk about people a thousand miles off, but come as near home as I can. As the time is short, I will leave out all the flattery, and retain all the criticism.

Let us consider the way in which we spend our lives.

This world is a place of business. What an infinite bustle! I am awaked almost every night by the panting of the locomotive. It interrupts my dreams. There is no sabbath. It would be glorious to see mankind at leisure for once. It is nothing but work, work, work. I cannot easily buy a blank-book to write thoughts in; they are commonly ruled for dollars and cents. An Irishman, seeing me making a minute in the fields, took it for granted that I was calculating my wages. If a man was tossed out of a window when an infant, and so made a cripple for life, or scared out of his wits by the Indians, it is regretted chiefly because he was thus incapacitated for—business! I think that there is nothing, not even crime, more opposed to poetry, to philosophy, ay, to life itself, than this incessant business.

There is a coarse and boisterous money-making fellow in the outskirts of our town, who is going to build a bank-wall under the hill along the edge of his meadow. The powers have put this into his head to keep him out of mischief, and he wishes me to spend three weeks digging there with him. The result will be that he will perhaps get some more money to hoard, and leave for his heirs to spend foolishly. If I do this, most will commend me as an industrious and hard-working man; but if I choose to devote myself to certain labors which yield more real profit, though but little money, they may be inclined to look on me as an idler. Nevertheless, as I do not need the police of meaningless labor to regulate me, and do not see anything absolutely praiseworthy in this fellow's undertaking, any more than in many an enterprise of our own or foreign governments, however amusing it may be to him or them, I prefer to finish my education at a different school.

If a man walk in the woods for love of them half of each day, he is in danger of being regarded as a loafer; but if he spends his whole day as a speculator, shearing off those woods and making earth bald before her time, he is esteemed an industrious and enterprising citizen. As if a town had no interest in its forests but to cut them down!

Most men would feel insulted, if it were proposed to employ them in throwing stones over a wall, and then in throwing them back, merely that they might earn their wages. But many are no more worthily employed now. For instance: just after sunrise, one summer morning, I noticed one of my neighbors walking beside his team, which was slowly drawing a heavy hewn stone swung under the axle, surrounded by an atmosphere of industry,—his day's work begun,—his brow commenced to sweat,—a reproach to all sluggards and idlers,—pausing abreast the shoulders of his oxen, and half turning round with a flourish of his merciful whip, while they gained their length on him. And I thought, Such is the labor which the American Congress exists to protect, honest, manly toil,—honest as the day is long,—that makes his bread taste sweet, and keeps society sweet,—which all men respect and have consecrated: one of the sacred band, doing the needful, but irksome drudgery. Indeed, I felt a slight reproach, because I observed this from the window, and was not abroad and stirring about a similar business. The day went by, and at evening I passed the yard of another neighbor, who keeps many servants, and spends much money foolishly, while he adds nothing to the common stock, and there I saw the stone of the morning lying beside a whimsical structure intended to adorn this Lord Timothy Dexter's premises, and the dignity forthwith departed from the teamster's labor, in my eyes. In my opinion, the sun was made to light worthier toil than this. I may add, that his employer has since run off, in debt to a good part of the town, and, after passing through Chancery, has settled somewhere else, there to become once more a patron of the arts.

The ways by which you may get money almost without exception lead downward. To have done anything by which you earned money *merely* is to have been truly idle or worse. If the laborer gets no more than the wages which his employer pays him, he is cheated, he cheats himself. If you would get money as a writer or lecturer, you must be popular, which is to go down perpendicularly. Those services which the community will most readily pay for it is most disagreeable to render. You are paid for being something less than a man. The State does not commonly reward a genius any more wisely. Even the poet-laureate would rather not have to celebrate the accidents of royalty. He must be bribed with a pipe of wine; and perhaps another poet is called away from his muse to gauge that very pipe. As for my own business, even that kind of surveying which I could do with most satisfaction my employers do not want. They would prefer that I should do my work coarsely and not too well, ay, not well enough. When I observe that there are different ways of surveying, my employer commonly asks which will give him the most land, not which is most correct. I once invented a rule for measuring cord-wood, and tried to introduce it in Boston; but the measurer there told me that the sellers did not wish to have their wood measured correctly,—that he was already too accurate for them, and therefore they commonly got their wood measured in Charlestown before crossing the bridge.

The aim of the laborer should be, not to get his living, to get "a good job," but to perform well a certain work; and, even in a pecuniary sense, it would be economy for a town to pay its laborers so well that they would not feel that they were working for low ends, as for a livelihood merely, but for scientific, or even moral ends. Do not hire a man who does your work for money, but him who does it for love of it.

It is remarkable that there are few men so well employed, so much to their minds, but that a little money or fame would commonly buy them off from their present pursuit. I see advertisements for *active* young men, as if activity were the whole of a young man's capital. Yet I have been surprised when one has with confidence proposed to me, a grown man, to embark in some enterprise of his, as if I had absolutely nothing to do, my life having been a complete failure hitherto. What a doubtful compliment this is to pay me! As if he had met me half-way across the ocean beating up against the wind, but bound nowhere, and proposed to me to go along with him! If I did, what do you think the underwriters would say? No, no! I am not without employment at this stage of the voyage. To tell the truth, I saw an advertisement for able-bodied seamen, when I was a boy, sauntering in my native port, and as soon as I came of age I embarked.

The community has no bribe that will tempt a wise man. You may raise money enough to tunnel a mountain, but you cannot raise money enough to hire a man who is minding *his own* business. An efficient and valuable man does what he can, whether the community pay him for it or not. The inefficient offer their inefficiency to the highest bidder, and are forever expecting to be put into office. One would suppose that they were rarely disappointed.

Perhaps I am more than usually jealous with respect to my freedom. I feel that my connection with and obligation to society are still very slight and transient. Those slight labors which afford me a livelihood, and by which it is allowed that I am to some extent serviceable to my contemporaries, are as yet commonly a pleasure to me, and I am not often reminded that they are a necessity. So far I am successful. But I foresee, that, if my wants should be much increased, the labor required to supply them would become a drudgery. If I should sell both my forenoons and afternoons to society, as most appear to do, I am sure, that, for me, there would be nothing left worth living for. I trust that I shall never thus sell my birthright for a mess of pottage. I wish to suggest that a man may be very industrious, and yet not spend his time well. There is no more fatal blunderer than he who consumes the greater part of his life getting his living. All great enterprises are self-supporting. The poet, for instance, must sustain his body by his poetry, as a steam planing-mill feeds its boilers with the shavings it makes. You must get your living by loving. But as it is said of the merchants that ninety-seven in a hundred fail, so the life of men generally, tried by this standard, is a failure, and bankruptcy may be surely prophesied.

Merely to come into the world the heir of a fortune is not to be born, but to be still-born, rather. To be supported by the charity of friends, or a government-pension,—provided you continue to breathe,—by whatever fine synonymes you describe these relations, is to go into the almshouse. On Sundays the poor debtor goes to church to take an account of stock, and finds, of course, that his outgoes have been greater than his income. In the Catholic Church, especially, they go into Chancery, make a clean confession, give up all, and think to start again. Thus men will lie on their backs, talking about the fall of man, and never make an effort to get up.

As for the comparative demand which men make on life, it is an important difference between two, that the one is satisfied with a level success, that his marks can all be hit by point-blank shots, but the other, however low and unsuccessful his life may be, constantly elevates his aim, though at a very slight angle to the horizon. I should much rather be the last man,—though, as the Orientals say, "Greatness doth not approach him who is forever looking down; and all those who are looking high are growing poor."

It is remarkable that there is little or nothing to be remembered written on the subject of getting a living: how to make getting a living not merely honest and honorable, but altogether inviting and glorious; for if *getting* a living is not so, then living is not. One would think, from looking at literature, that this question had never disturbed a solitary individual's musings. Is it that men are too much disgusted with their experience to speak of it? The lesson of value which money teaches, which the Author of the Universe has taken so much pains to teach us, we are inclined to skip altogether. As for the means of living, it is wonderful how indifferent men of all classes are about it, even reformers, so called,—whether they inherit, or earn, or steal it. I think that society has done nothing for us in this respect, or at least has undone what she has done. Cold and hunger seem more friendly to my nature than those methods which men have adopted and advise to ward them off.

The title *wise* is, for the most part, falsely applied. How can one be a wise man, if he does not know any better how to live than other men?—if he is only more cunning and intellectually subtle? Does Wisdom work in a tread-mill? or does she teach how to succeed *by her example*? Is there any such thing as wisdom not applied to life? Is she merely the miller who grinds the finest logic? It is pertinent to ask if Plato got his *living* in a better way or more successfully than his contemporaries,—or did he succumb to the difficulties of life like other men? Did he seem to prevail over some of them merely by indifference, or by assuming grand airs? or find it easier to live, because his aunt remembered him in her will? The ways in which most men get their living, that is, live, are mere make-shifts, and a shirking of the real business of life,—chiefly because they do not know, but partly because they do not mean, any better.

The rush to California, for instance, and the attitude, not merely of merchants, but of philosophers and prophets, so called, in relation to it, reflect the greatest disgrace on mankind. That so many are ready to live by luck, and so get the means of commanding the labor of others less lucky, without contributing any value to society! And that is called enterprise! I know of no more startling development of the immorality of trade, and all the common modes of getting a living. The philosophy and poetry and religion of such a mankind are not worth the dust of a puff-ball. The hog that gets his living by rooting, stirring up the soil so, would be ashamed of such company. If I could command the wealth of all the worlds by lifting my finger, I would not pay *such* a price for it. Even Mahomet knew that God did not make this world in jest. It makes God to be a moneyed gentleman who scatters a handful of pennies in order to see mankind scramble for them. The world's raffle! A subsistence in the domains of Nature a thing to be raffled for! What a comment, what a satire on our institutions! The conclusion will be, that mankind will hang itself upon a tree. And have all the precepts in all the Bibles taught men only this? and is the last and most admirable invention of the human race only an improved muck-rake? Is this the ground on which Orientals and Occidentals meet? Did God direct us so to get our living, digging where we never planted,—and He would, perchance, reward us with lumps of gold?

God gave the righteous man a certificate entitling him to food and raiment, but the unrighteous man found a *facsimile* of the same in God's coffers, and appropriated it, and obtained food and raiment like the former. It is one of the most extensive systems of counterfeiting that the world has seen. I did not know that mankind were suffering for want of gold. I have seen a little of it. I know that it is very malleable, but not so malleable as wit. A grain of gold will gild a great surface, but not so much as a grain of wisdom.

The gold-digger in the ravines of the mountains is as much a gambler as his fellow in the saloons of San Francisco. What difference does it make, whether you shake dirt or shake dice? If you win, society is the loser. The gold-digger is the enemy of the honest laborer, whatever checks and compensations there may be. It is not enough to tell me that you worked hard to get your gold. So does the Devil work hard. The way of transgressors may be hard in many respects. The humblest observer who goes to the mines sees and says that gold-digging is of the character of a lottery; the gold thus obtained is not the same thing with the wages of honest toil. But, practically, he forgets what he has seen, for he has seen only the fact, not the principle, and goes into trade there, that is, buys a ticket in what commonly proves another lottery, where the fact is not so obvious.

After reading Howitt's account of the Australian gold-diggings one evening, I had in my mind's eye, all night, the numerous valleys, with their streams, all cut up with foul pits, from ten to one hundred feet deep, and half a dozen feet across, as close as they can be dug, and partly filled with water,—the locality to which men furiously rush to probe for their fortunes,—uncertain where they shall break ground,—not knowing but the gold is under their camp itself,—sometimes digging one hundred and sixty feet before they strike the vein, or then missing it by a foot,—turned into demons, and regardless of each other's rights, in their thirst for riches,—whole valleys, for thirty miles, suddenly honey-combed by the pits of the miners, so that even hundreds are drowned in them,—standing in water, and covered with mud and clay, they work night and day, dying of exposure and disease. Having read this, and partly forgotten it, I was thinking, accidentally, of my own unsatisfactory life, doing as others do; and with that vision of the diggings still before me, I asked myself, why *I* might not be washing some gold daily, though it were only the finest particles,—why *I* might not sink a shaft down to the gold within me, and work that mine. *There* is a Ballarat, a Bendigo for you,—what though it were a Sulky Gully? At any rate, I might pursue some path, however solitary and narrow and crooked, in which I could walk with love and reverence. Wherever a man separates from the multitude, and goes his own way in this mood, there indeed is a fork in the road, though ordinary travellers may see only a gap in the paling. His solitary path across-lots will turn out the *higher way* of the two.

Men rush to California and Australia as if the true gold were to be found in that direction; but that is to go to the very opposite extreme to where it lies. They go prospecting farther and farther away from the true lead, and are most unfortunate when they think themselves most successful. Is not our *native* soil auriferous? Does not a stream from the golden mountains flow through our native valley? and has not this for more than geologic ages been bringing down the shining particles and forming the nuggets for us? Yet, strange to tell, if a digger steal away, prospecting for this true gold, into the unexplored solitudes around us, there is no danger that any will dog his steps, and endeavor to supplant him. He may claim and undermine the whole valley even, both the cultivated and the uncultivated portions, his whole life long in peace, for no one will ever dispute his claim. They will not mind his cradles or his toms. He is not confined to a claim twelve feet square, as at Ballarat, but may mine anywhere, and wash the whole wide world in his tom.

Howitt says of the man who found the great nugget which weighed twenty-eight pounds, at the Bendigo diggings in Australia:—"He soon began to drink; got a horse and rode all about, generally at full gallop, and when he met people, called out to inquire if they knew who he was, and then kindly informed them that he was 'the bloody wretch that had found the nugget.' At last he rode full speed against a tree, and nearly knocked his brains out." I think, however, there was no danger of that, for he had already knocked his brains out against the nugget. Howitt adds, "He is a hopelessly ruined man." But he is a type of the class. They are all fast men. Hear some of the names of the places where they dig:—"Jackass Flat,"—"Sheep's-Head Gully,"—"Murderer's Bar," etc. Is there no satire in these names? Let them carry their ill-gotten wealth where they will, I am thinking it will still be "Jackass Flat," if not "Murderer's Bar," where they live.

The last resource of our energy has been the robbing of graveyards on the Isthmus of Darien, an enterprise which appears to be but in its infancy; for, according to late accounts, an act has passed its second reading in the legislature of New Granada, regulating this kind of mining; and a correspondent of the *Tribune* writes:—"In the dry season, when the weather will permit of the country being properly prospected, no doubt other rich '*guacas*' [that is, graveyards] will be found." To emigrants he says:—"Do not come before December; take the Isthmus route in preference to the Boca del Toro one; bring no useless baggage, and do not cumber yourself with a tent; but a good pair of blankets will be necessary; a pick, shovel, and axe of good material will be almost all that is required": advice which might have been taken from the "Burker's Guide." And he concludes with this line in Italics and small capitals: "*If you are doing well at home,* STAY THERE," which may fairly be interpreted to mean, "If you are getting a good living by robbing graveyards at home, stay there."

But why go to California for a text? She is the child of New England, bred at her own school and church.

It is remarkable that among all the preachers there are so few moral teachers. The prophets are employed in excusing the ways of men. Most reverend seniors, the *illuminati* of the age, tell me, with a gracious, reminiscent smile, betwixt an aspiration and a shudder, not to be too tender about these things,—to lump all that, that is, make a lump of gold of it. The highest advice I have heard on these subjects was grovelling. The burden of it was,—It is not worth your while to undertake to reform the world in this particular. Do not ask how your bread is buttered; it will make you sick, if you do,—and the like. A man had better starve at once than lose his innocence in the process of getting his bread. If within the sophisticated man there is not an unsophisticated one, then he is but one of the Devil's angels. As we grow old, we live more coarsely, we relax a little in our disciplines, and, to some extent, cease to obey our finest instincts. But we should be fastidious to the extreme of sanity, disregarding the gibes of those who are more unfortunate than ourselves.

In our science and philosophy, even, there is commonly no true and absolute account of things. The spirit of sect and bigotry has planted its hoof amid the stars. You have only to discuss the problem, whether the stars are inhabited or not, in order to discover it. Why must we daub the heavens as well as the earth? It was an unfortunate discovery that Dr. Kane was a Mason, and that Sir John Franklin was another. But it was a more cruel suggestion that possibly that was the reason why the former went in search of the latter. There is not a popular magazine in this country that would dare to print a child's thought on important subjects without comment. It must be submitted to the D. D.s. I would it were the chicka-dee-dees.

You come from attending the funeral of mankind to attend

to a natural phenomenon. A little thought is sexton to all the world.

I hardly know an *intellectual* man, even, who is so broad and truly liberal that you can think aloud in his society. Most with whom you endeavor to talk soon come to a stand against some institution in which they appear to hold stock,—that is, some particular, not universal, way of viewing things. They will continually thrust their own low roof, with its narrow skylight, between you and the sky, when it is the unobstructed heavens you would view. Get out of the way with your cobwebs, wash your windows, I say! In some lyceums they tell me that they have voted to exclude the subject of religion. But how do I know what their religion is, and when I am near to or far from it? I have walked into such an arena and done my best to make a clean breast of what religion I have experienced, and the audience never suspected what I was about. The lecture was as harmless as moonshine to them. Whereas, if I had read to them the biography of the greatest scamps in history, they might have thought that I had written the lives of the deacons of their church. Ordinarily, the inquiry is, Where did you come from? or, Where are you going? That was a more pertinent question which I overheard one of my auditors put to another once,—"What does he lecture for?" It made me quake in my shoes.

To speak impartially, the best men that I know are not serene, a world in themselves. For the most part, they dwell in forms, and flatter and study effect only more finely than the rest. We select granite for the underpinning of our houses and barns; we build fences of stone; but we do not ourselves rest on an underpinning of granitic truth, the lowest primitive rock. Our sills are rotten. What stuff is the man made of who is not coexistent in our thought with the purest and subtilest truth? I often accuse my finest acquaintances of an immense frivolity; for, while there are manners and compliments we do not meet, we do not teach one another the lessons of honesty and sincerity that the brutes do, or of steadiness and solidity that the rocks do. The fault is commonly mutual, however; for we do not habitually demand any more of each other.

That excitement about Kossuth, consider how characteristic, but superficial, it was!—only another kind of politics or dancing. Men were making speeches to him all over the country, but each expressed only the thought, or the want of thought, of the multitude. No man stood on truth. They were merely banded together, as usual, one leaning on another, and all together on nothing; as the Hindoos made the world rest on an elephant, the elephant on a tortoise, and the tortoise on a serpent, and had nothing to put under the serpent. For all fruit of that stir we have the Kossuth hat.

Just so hollow and ineffectual, for the most part, is our ordinary conversation. Surface meets surface. When our life ceases to be inward and private, conversation degenerates into mere gossip. We rarely meet a man who can tell us any news which he has not read in a newspaper, or been told by his neighbor; and, for the most part, the only difference between us and our fellow is, that he has seen the newspaper, or been out to tea, and we have not. In proportion as our inward life fails, we go more constantly and desperately to the post-office. You may depend on it, that the poor fellow who walks away with the greatest number of letters, proud of his extensive correspondence, has not heard from himself this long while.

I do not know but it is too much to read one newspaper a week. I have tried it recently, and for so long it seems to me that I have not dwelt in my native region. The sun, the clouds, the snow, the trees say not so much to me. You cannot serve two masters. It requires more than a day's devotion to know and to possess the wealth of a day.

We may well be ashamed to tell what things we have read or heard in our day. I do not know why my news should be so trivial,—considering what one's dreams and expectations are, why the developments should be so paltry. The news we hear, for the most part, is not news to our genius. It is the stalest repetition. You are often tempted to ask, why such stress is laid on a particular experience which you have had,—that, after twenty-five years, you should meet Hobbins, Registrar of Deeds, again on the sidewalk. Have you not budged an inch, then? Such is the daily news. Its facts appear to float in the atmosphere, insignificant as the sporules of fungi, and impinge on some neglected *thallus*, or surface of our minds, which affords a basis for them, and hence a parasitic growth. We should wash ourselves clean of such news. Of what consequence, though our planet explode, if there is no character involved in the explosion? In health we have not the least curiosity about such events. We do not live for idle amusement. I would not run round a corner to see the world blow up.

All summer, and far into the autumn, perchance, you unconsciously went by the newspapers and the news, and now you find it was because the morning and the evening were full of news to you. Your walks were full of incidents. You attended, not to the affairs of Europe, but to your own affairs in Massachusetts fields. If you chance to live and move and have your being in that thin stratum in which the events that make the news transpire,—thinner than the paper on which it is printed,—then these things will fill the world for you; but if you soar above or dive below that plane, you cannot remember nor be reminded of them. Really to see the sun rise or go down every day, so to relate ourselves to a universal fact, would preserve us sane forever. Nations! What are nations? Tartars, and Huns, and Chinamen! Like insects, they swarm. The historian strives in vain to make them memorable. It is for want of a man that there are so many men. It is individuals that populate the world. Any man thinking may say with the Spirit of Lodin,—

> "I look down from my height on nations,
>   And they become ashes before me;—
> Calm is my dwelling in the clouds;
>   Pleasant are the great fields of my rest."

Pray, let us live without being drawn by dogs, Esquimaux-fashion, tearing over hill and dale, and biting each other's ears.

Not without a slight shudder at the danger, I often perceive how near I had come to admitting into my mind the details of some trivial affair,—the news of the street; and I am astonished to observe how willing men are to lumber their minds with such rubbish,—to permit idle rumors and incidents of the most insignificant kind to intrude on ground which should be sacred to thought. Shall the mind be a

public arena, where the affairs of the street and the gossip of
the tea-table chiefly are discussed? Or shall it be a quarter of
heaven itself,—an hypæthral temple, consecrated to the service of the gods? I find it so difficult to dispose of the few
facts which to me are significant, that I hesitate to burden my
attention with those which are insignificant, which only a divine mind could illustrate. Such is, for the most part, the
news in newspapers and conversation. It is important to preserve the mind's chastity in this respect. Think of admitting
the details of a single case of the criminal court into our
thoughts, to stalk profanely through their very *sanctum sanctorum* for an hour, ay, for many hours! to make a very bar-
room of the mind's inmost apartment, as if for so long the
dust of the street had occupied us,—the very street itself, with
all its travel, its bustle, and filth had passed through our
thoughts' shrine! Would it not be an intellectual and moral
suicide? When I have been compelled to sit spectator and auditor in a court-room for some hours, and have seen my
neighbors, who were not compelled, stealing in from time to
time, and tiptoeing about with washed hands and faces, it has
appeared to my mind's eye, that, when they took off their
hats, their ears suddenly expanded into vast hoppers for
sound, between which even their narrow heads were
crowded. Like the vanes of windmills, they caught the broad,
but shallow stream of sound, which, after a few titillating gy-
rations in their coggy brains, passed out the other side. I
wondered if, when they got home, they were as careful to
wash their ears as before their hands and faces. It has seemed
to me, at such a time, that the auditors and the witnesses, the
jury and the counsel, the judge and the criminal at the bar,—
if I may presume him guilty before he is convicted,—were all
equally criminal, and a thunderbolt might be expected to descend and consume them all together.

By all kinds of traps and sign-boards, threatening the extreme penalty of the divine law, exclude such trespassers from
the only ground which can be sacred to you. It is so hard
to forget what it is worse than useless to remember! If I am to
be a thoroughfare, I prefer that it be of the mountain-brooks,
the Parnassian streams, and not the town-sewers. There is inspiration, that gossip which comes to the ear of the attentive

mind from the courts of heaven. There is the profane and stale revelation of the bar-room and the police court. The same ear is fitted to receive both communications. Only the character of the hearer determines to which it shall be open, and to which closed. I believe that the mind can be permanently profaned by the habit of attending to trivial things, so that all our thoughts shall be tinged with triviality. Our very intellect shall be macadamized, as it were,—its foundation broken into fragments for the wheels of travel to roll over; and if you would know what will make the most durable pavement, surpassing rolled stones, spruce blocks, and asphaltum, you have only to look into some of our minds which have been subjected to this treatment so long.

If we have thus desecrated ourselves,—as who has not?—the remedy will be by wariness and devotion to reconsecrate ourselves, and make once more a fane of the mind. We should treat our minds, that is, ourselves, as innocent and ingenuous children, whose guardians we are, and be careful what objects and what subjects we thrust on their attention. Read not the Times. Read the Eternities. Conventionalities are at length as bad as impurities. Even the facts of science may dust the mind by their dryness, unless they are in a sense effaced each morning, or rather rendered fertile by the dews of fresh and living truth. Knowledge does not come to us by details, but in flashes of light from heaven. Yes, every thought that passes through the mind helps to wear and tear it, and to deepen the ruts, which, as in the streets of Pompeii, evince how much it has been used. How many things there are concerning which we might well deliberate, whether we had better know them,—had better let their peddling-carts be driven, even at the slowest trot or walk, over that bridge of glorious span by which we trust to pass at last from the farthest brink of time to the nearest shore of eternity! Have we no culture, no refinement,—but skill only to live coarsely and serve the Devil?—to acquire a little worldly wealth, or fame, or liberty, and make a false show with it, as if we were all husk and shell, with no tender and living kernel to us? Shall our institutions be like those chestnut-burs which contain abortive nuts, perfect only to prick the fingers?

America is said to be the arena on which the battle of freedom is to be fought; but surely it cannot be freedom in a merely political sense that is meant. Even if we grant that the American has freed himself from a political tyrant, he is still the slave of an economical and moral tyrant. Now that the republic—the *res-publica*—has been settled, it is time to look after the *res-privata*,—the private state,—to see, as the Roman senate charged its consuls, *"ne quid res-*PRIVATA *detrimenti caperet,"* that the *private* state receive no detriment.

Do we call this the land of the free? What is it to be free from King George and continue the slaves of King Prejudice? What is it to be born free and not to live free? What is the value of any political freedom, but as a means to moral freedom? Is it a freedom to be slaves, or a freedom to be free, of which we boast? We are a nation of politicians, concerned about the outmost defences only of freedom. It is our children's children who may perchance be really free. We tax ourselves unjustly. There is a part of us which is not represented. It is taxation without representation. We quarter troops, we quarter fools and cattle of all sorts upon ourselves. We quarter our gross bodies on our poor souls, till the former eat up all the latter's substance.

With respect to a true culture and manhood, we are essentially provincial still, not metropolitan,—mere Jonathans. We are provincial, because we do not find at home our standards,—because we do not worship truth, but the reflection of truth,—because we are warped and narrowed by an exclusive devotion to trade and commerce and manufactures and agriculture and the like, which are but means, and not the end.

So is the English Parliament provincial. Mere country-bumpkins, they betray themselves, when any more important question arises for them to settle, the Irish question, for instance,—the English question why did I not say? Their natures are subdued to what they work in. Their "good breeding" respects only secondary objects. The finest manners in the world are awkwardness and fatuity, when contrasted with a finer intelligence. They appear but as the fashions of past days,—mere courtliness, knee-buckles and small-clothes, out of date. It is the vice, but not the excellence of manners, that they are continually being deserted by the character; they are cast-off clothes or shells, claiming the respect which belonged to the living creature. You are presented with the shells instead of the meat, and it is no excuse generally, that, in the case of some fishes, the shells are of more worth than the meat. The man who thrusts his manners upon me does as if he were to insist on introducing me to his cabinet of curiosities, when I wished to see himself. It was not in this sense that the poet Decker called Christ "the first true gentleman that ever breathed." I repeat that in this sense the most splendid court in Christendom is provincial, having authority to consult about Transalpine interests only, and not the affairs of Rome. A praetor or proconsul would suffice to settle the questions which absorb the attention of the English Parliament and the American Congress.

Government and legislation! these I thought were respectable professions. We have heard of heaven-born Numas, Lycurguses, and Solons, in the history of the world, whose *names* at least may stand for ideal legislators; but think of legislating to *regulate* the breeding of slaves, or the exportation of tobacco! What have divine legislators to do with the exportation or the importation of tobacco? What humane ones with the breeding of slaves? Suppose you were to submit the question to any son of God,—and has He no children in the nineteenth century? is it a family which is extinct?— in what condition would you get it again? What shall a State like Virginia say for itself at the last day, in which these have been the principal, the staple productions? What ground is there for patriotism in such a State? I derive my facts from statistical tables which the States themselves have published.

A commerce that whitens every sea in quest of nuts and raisins, and makes slaves of its sailors for this purpose! I saw, the other day, a vessel which had been wrecked, and many lives lost, and her cargo of rags, juniper-berries, and bitter almonds were strewn along the shore. It seemed hardly worth the while to tempt the dangers of the sea between Leghorn and New York for the sake of a cargo of juniper-berries and bitter almonds. America sending to the Old World for her bitters! Is not the sea-brine, is not shipwreck, bitter enough to make the cup of life go down here? Yet such, to a great extent, is our boasted commerce; and there are those who style themselves statesmen and philosophers who are so blind as to think that progress and civilization depend on precisely this kind of interchange and activity,—the activity of flies about a molasses-hogshead. Very well, observes one, if men were oysters. And very well, answer I, if men were mosquitoes.

Lieutenant Herndon, whom our Government sent to explore the Amazon, and, it is said, to extend the area of Slavery, observed that there was wanting there "an industrious and active population, who know what the comforts of life are, and who have artificial wants to draw out the great resources of the country." But what are the "artificial wants" to be encouraged? Not the love of luxuries, like the tobacco and slaves of, I believe, his native Virginia, nor the ice and granite and other material wealth of our native New England; nor are "the great resources of a country" that fertility or barrenness of soil which produces these. The chief want, in every State that I have been into, was a high and earnest purpose in its inhabitants. This alone draws out "the great resources" of Nature, and at last taxes her beyond her resources; for man naturally dies out of her. When we want culture more than potatoes, and illumination more than sugar-plums, then the great resources of a world are taxed and drawn out, and the result, or staple production, is, not slaves, nor operatives, but men,—those rare fruits called heroes, saints, poets, philosophers, and redeemers.

In short, as a snow-drift is formed where there is a lull in the wind, so, one would say, where there is a lull of truth, an institution springs up. But the truth blows right on over it, nevertheless, and at length blows it down.

What is called politics is comparatively something so superficial and inhuman, that, practically, I have never fairly recognized that it concerns me at all. The newspapers, I perceive, devote some of their columns specially to politics or government without charge; and this, one would say, is all that saves it; but, as I love literature, and, to some extent, the truth also, I never read those columns at any rate. I do not wish to blunt my sense of right so much. I have not got to answer for having read a single President's Message. A strange age of the world this, when empires, kingdoms, and republics come a-begging to a private man's door, and utter their complaints at his elbow! I cannot take up a newspaper but I find that some wretched government or other, hard pushed, and on its last legs, is interceding with me, the reader, to vote for it,—more importunate than an Italian beggar; and if I have a mind to look at its certificate, made, perchance, by some benevolent merchant's clerk, or the skipper that brought it over, for it cannot speak a word of English itself, I shall probably read of the eruption of some Vesuvius, or the overflowing of some Po, true or forged, which brought it into this condition. I do not hesitate, in such a case, to suggest work, or the almshouse; or why not keep its castle in silence, as I do commonly? The poor President, what with preserving his popularity and doing his duty, is completely bewildered. The newspapers are the ruling power. Any other government is reduced to a few marines at Fort Independence. If a man neglects to read the Daily Times, Government will go down on its knees to him, for this is the only treason in these days.

Those things which now most engage the attention of men, as politics and the daily routine, are, it is true, vital functions of human society, but should be unconsciously performed, like the corresponding functions of the physical body. They are *infra*-human, a kind of vegetation. I sometimes awake to a half-consciousness of them going on about me, as a man may become conscious of some of the processes of digestion in a morbid state, and so have the dyspepsia, as it is called. It is as if a thinker submitted himself to be rasped by the great gizzard of creation. Politics is, as it were, the gizzard of society, full of grit and gravel, and the two political parties are its two opposite halves,—sometimes split into quarters, it may be, which grind on each other. Not only individuals, but States, have thus a confirmed dyspepsia, which expresses itself, you can imagine by what sort of eloquence. Thus our life is not altogether a forgetting, but also, alas! to a great extent, a remembering of that which we should never have been conscious of, certainly not in our waking hours. Why should we not meet, not always as dyspeptics, to tell our bad dreams, but sometimes as *eu*peptics, to congratulate each other on the ever glorious morning? I do not make an exorbitant demand, surely.

Autumnal Tints

EUROPEANS coming to America are surprised by the brilliancy of our autumnal foliage. There is no account of such a phenomenon in English poetry, because the trees acquire but few bright colors there. The most that Thomson says on this subject in his "Autumn" is contained in the lines,—

"But see the fading many-colored woods,
    Shade deepening over shade, the country round
    Imbrown; a crowded umbrage, dusk and dun,
    Of every hue, from wan declining green to sooty dark":—

and in the line in which he speaks of

"Autumn beaming o'er the yellow woods."

The autumnal change of our woods has not made a deep impression on our own literature yet. October has hardly tinged our poetry.

A great many, who have spent their lives in cities, and have never chanced to come into the country at this season, have never seen this, the flower, or rather the ripe fruit, of the year. I remember riding with one such citizen, who, though a fortnight too late for the most brilliant tints, was taken by surprise, and would not believe that there had been any brighter. He had never heard of this phenomenon before. Not only many in our towns have never witnessed it, but it is scarcely remembered by the majority from year to year.

Most appear to confound changed leaves with withered ones, as if they were to confound ripe apples with rotten ones. I think that the change to some higher color in a leaf is an evidence that it has arrived at a late and perfect maturity, answering to the maturity of fruits. It is generally the lowest and oldest leaves which change first. But as the perfect winged and usually bright-colored insect is short-lived, so the leaves ripen but to fall.

Generally, every fruit, on ripening, and just before it falls, when it commences a more independent and individual existence, requiring less nourishment from any source, and that not so much from the earth through its stem as from the sun and air, acquires a bright tint. So do leaves. The physiologist says it is "due to an increased absorption of oxygen." That is the scientific account of the matter,—only a reassertion of the fact. But I am more interested in the rosy cheek than I am to know what particular diet the maiden fed on. The very forest and herbage, the pellicle of the earth, must acquire a bright color, an evidence of its ripeness,—as if the globe itself were a fruit on its stem, with ever a cheek toward the sun.

Flowers are but colored leaves, fruits but ripe ones. The edible part of most fruits is, as the physiologist says, "the parenchyma or fleshy tissue of the leaf" of which they are formed.

Our appetites have commonly confined our views of ripeness and its phenomena, color, mellowness, and perfectness, to the fruits which we eat, and we are wont to forget that an immense harvest which we do not eat, hardly use at all, is annually ripened by Nature. At our annual Cattle Shows and Horticultural Exhibitions, we make, as we think, a great show of fair fruits, destined, however, to a rather ignoble end, fruits not valued for their beauty chiefly. But round about and within our towns there is annually another show of fruits, on an infinitely grander scale, fruits which address our taste for beauty alone.

October is the month of painted leaves. Their rich glow now flashes round the world. As fruits and leaves and the day itself acquire a bright tint just before they fall, so the year near its setting. October is its sunset sky; November the later twilight.

I formerly thought that it would be worth the while to get a specimen leaf from each changing tree, shrub, and herbaceous plant, when it had acquired its brightest characteristic color, in its transition from the green to the brown state, outline it, and copy its color exactly, with paint, in a book, which should be entitled, *"October, or Autumnal Tints"*;—beginning with the earliest reddening,—Woodbine and the lake of radical leaves, and coming down through the Maples, Hickories, and Sumachs, and many beautifully freckled leaves less generally known, to the latest Oaks and Aspens. What a memento such a book would be! You would need only to turn over its leaves to take a ramble through the autumn woods whenever you pleased. Or if I could preserve the leaves themselves, un-faded, it would be better still. I have made but little progress toward such a book, but I have endeavored, instead, to de-scribe all these bright tints in the order in which they present themselves. The following are some extracts from my notes.

THE PURPLE GRASSES.

By the twentieth of August, everywhere in woods and swamps, we are reminded of the fall, both by the richly spot-ted Sarsaparilla-leaves and Brakes, and the withering and blackened Skunk-Cabbage and Hellebore, and, by the river-side, the already blackening Pontederia.

The Purple Grass (*Eragrostis pectinacea*) is now in the height of its beauty. I remember still when I first noticed this grass particularly. Standing on a hill-side near our river, I saw, thirty or forty rods off, a stripe of purple half a dozen rods long, under the edge of a wood, where the ground sloped to-ward a meadow. It was as high-colored and interesting, though not quite so bright, as the patches of Rhexia, being a darker purple, like a berry's stain laid on close and thick. On going to and examining it, I found it to be a kind of grass in bloom, hardly a foot high, with but few green blades, and a fine spreading panicle of purple flowers, a shallow, purplish mist trembling around me. Close at hand it appeared but a dull purple, and made little impression on the eye; it was even difficult to detect; and if you plucked a single plant, you were surprised to find how thin it was, and how little color it had. But viewed at a distance in a favorable light, it was of a fine lively purple, flower-like, enriching the earth. Such puny causes combine to produce these decided effects. I was the more surprised and charmed because grass is commonly of a sober and humble color.

With its beautiful purple blush it reminds me, and supplies the place, of the Rhexia, which is now leaving off, and it is one of the most interesting phenomena of August. The finest patches of it grow on waste strips or selvages of land at the base of dry hills, just above the edge of the meadows, where the greedy mower does not deign to swing his scythe; for this is a thin and poor grass, beneath his notice. Or, it may be, because it is so beautiful he does not know that it exists; for the same eye does not see this and Timothy. He carefully gets the meadow hay and the more nutritious grasses which grow next to that, but he leaves this fine purple mist for the walker's harvest,—fodder for his fancy stock. Higher up the hill, perchance, grow also Blackberries, John's-Wort, and neglected, withered, and wiry June-Grass. How fortunate that it grows in such places, and not in the midst of the rank grasses which are annually cut! Nature thus keeps use and beauty distinct. I know many such localities, where it does not fail to present itself annually, and paint the earth with its blush. It grows on the gentle slopes, either in a continuous patch or in scattered and rounded tufts a foot in diameter, and it lasts till it is killed by the first smart frosts.

In most plants the corolla or calyx is the part which attains the highest color, and is the most attractive; in many it is the seed-vessel or fruit; in others, as the Red Maple, the leaves; and in others still it is the very culm itself which is the principal flower or blooming part.

The last is especially the case with the Poke or Garget (*Phytolacca decandra*). Some which stand under our cliffs quite dazzle me with their purple stems now and early in September. They are as interesting to me as most flowers, and one of the most important fruits of our autumn. Every part is flower, (or fruit,) such is its superfluity of color,—stem, branch, peduncle, pedicel, petiole, and even the at length yellowish purple-veined leaves. Its cylindrical racemes of berries of various hues, from green to dark purple, six or seven inches long, are gracefully drooping on all sides, offering repasts to the birds; and even the sepals from which the birds have picked the berries are a brilliant lake-red, with crimson flame-like reflections, equal to anything of the kind,—all on fire with ripeness. Hence the *lacca*, from *lac*, lake. There are at the same time flower-buds, flowers, green berries, dark purple or ripe ones, and these flower-like sepals, all on the same plant.

We love to see any redness in the vegetation of the temperate zone. It is the color of colors. This plant speaks to our blood. It asks a bright sun on it to make it show to best advantage, and it must be seen at this season of the year. On warm hill-sides its stems are ripe by the twenty-third of August. At that date I walked through a beautiful grove of them, six or seven feet high, on the side of one of our cliffs, where they ripen early. Quite to the ground they were a deep brilliant purple with a bloom, contrasting with the still clear green leaves. It appears a rare triumph of Nature to have produced and perfected such a plant, as if this were enough for a summer. What a perfect maturity it arrives at! It is the emblem of a successful life concluded by a death not premature, which is an ornament to Nature. What if we were to mature as perfectly, root and branch, glowing in the midst of our decay, like the Poke! I confess that it excites me to behold them. I cut one for a cane, for I would fain handle and lean on it. I love to press the berries between my fingers, and see their juice staining my hand. To walk amid these upright, branching casks of purple wine, which retain and diffuse a sunset glow, tasting each one with your eye, instead of counting the pipes on a London dock, what a privilege! For Nature's vintage is not confined to the vine. Our poets have sung of wine, the product of a foreign plant which commonly they never saw, as if our own plants had no juice in them more than the singers. Indeed, this has been called by some the American Grape, and, though a native of America, its juices are used in some foreign countries to improve the color of the wine; so that the poetaster may be celebrating the virtues of the Poke without knowing it. Here are berries enough to paint afresh the western sky, and play the bacchanal with, if you will. And what flutes its ensanguined stems would make, to be used in such a dance! It is truly a royal plant. I could spend the evening of the year musing amid the Poke-stems. And perchance amid these groves might arise at last a new school of philosophy or poetry. It lasts all through September.

At the same time with this, or near the end of August, a to me very interesting genus of grasses, Andropogons, or Beard-Grasses, is in its prime. *Andropogon furcatus*, Forked Beard-Grass, or call it Purple-Fingered Grass; *Andropogon scoparius*, Purple Wood-Grass; and *Andropogon* (now called *Sorghum*) *nutans*, Indian-Grass. The first is a very tall and slender-culmed grass, three to seven feet high, with four or five purple finger-like spikes raying upward from the top. The second is also quite slender, growing in tufts two feet high by one wide, with culms often somewhat curving, which, as the spikes go out of bloom, have a whitish fuzzy look. These two are prevailing grasses at this season on dry and sandy fields and hill-sides. The culms of both, not to mention their pretty flowers, reflect a purple tinge, and help to declare the ripeness of the year. Perhaps I have the more sympathy with them because they are despised by the farmer, and occupy sterile and neglected soil. They are high-colored, like ripe grapes, and express a maturity which the spring did not suggest. Only the August sun could have thus burnished these culms and leaves. The farmer has long since done his upland haying, and he will not condescend to bring his scythe to where these slender wild grasses have at length flowered thinly; you often see spaces of bare sand amid them. But I walk encouraged between the tufts of Purple Wood-Grass, over the sandy fields, and along the edge of the Shrub-Oaks, glad to recognize these simple contemporaries. With thoughts cutting a broad swathe I "get" them, with horse-raking thoughts I gather them into windrows. The fine-eared poet may hear the whetting of my scythe. These two were almost the first grasses that I learned to distinguish, for I had not known by how many friends I was surrounded,—I had seen them simply as grasses standing. The purple of their culms also excites me like that of the Poke-Weed stems.

Think what refuge there is for one, before August is over, from college commencements and society that isolates! I can skulk amid the tufts of Purple Wood-Grass on the borders of the "Great Fields." Wherever I walk these afternoons, the Purple-Fingered Grass also stands like a guide-board, and points my thoughts to more poetic paths than they have lately travelled.

A man shall perhaps rush by and trample down plants as high as his head, and cannot be said to know that they exist, though he may have cut many tons of them, littered his stables with them, and fed them to his cattle for years. Yet, if he ever favorably attends to them, he may be overcome by their beauty. Each humblest plant, or weed, as we call it, stands there to express some thought or mood of ours; and yet how long it stands in vain! I had walked over those Great Fields so many Augusts, and never yet distinctly recognized these purple companions that I had there. I had brushed against them and trodden on them, forsooth; and now, at last, they, as it were, rose up and blessed me. Beauty and true wealth are always thus cheap and despised. Heaven might be defined as the place which men avoid. Who can doubt that these grasses, which the farmer says are of no account to him, find some compensation in your appreciation of them? I may say that I never saw them before,—though, when I came to look them face to face, there did come down to me a purple gleam from previous years; and now, wherever I go, I see hardly anything else. It is the reign and presidency of the Andropogons.

Almost the very sands confess the ripening influence of the August sun, and methinks, together with the slender grasses waving over them, reflect a purple tinge. The impurpled sands! Such is the consequence of all this sunshine absorbed into the pores of plants and of the earth. All sap or blood is now wine-colored. At last we have not only the purple sea, but the purple land.

The Chestnut Beard-Grass, Indian-Grass, or Wood-Grass, growing here and there in waste places, but more rare than the former, (from two to four or five feet high,) is still handsomer and of more vivid colors than its congeners, and might well have caught the Indian's eye. It has a long, narrow, one-sided, and slightly nodding panicle of bright purple and yellow flowers, like a banner raised above its reedy leaves. These bright standards are now advanced on the distant hill-sides, not in large armies, but in scattered troops or single file, like the red men. They stand thus fair and bright, representative of the race which they are named after, but for the most part unobserved as they. The expression of this grass haunted me for a week, after I first passed and noticed it, like the glance of an eye. It stands like an Indian chief taking a last look at his favorite hunting-grounds.

THE RED MAPLE.

By the twenty-fifth of September, the Red Maples generally are beginning to be ripe. Some large ones have been conspicuously changing for a week, and some single trees are now very brilliant. I notice a small one, half a mile off across a meadow, against the green wood-side there, a far brighter red than the blossoms of any tree in summer, and more conspicuous. I have observed this tree for several autumns invariably changing earlier than its fellows, just as one tree ripens its fruit earlier than another. It might serve to mark the season, perhaps. I should be sorry, if it were cut down. I know of two or three such trees in different parts of our town, which might, perhaps, be propagated from, as early ripeners or September trees, and their seed be advertised in the market, as well as that of radishes, if we cared as much about them.

At present, these burning bushes stand chiefly along the edge of the meadows, or I distinguish them afar on the hillsides here and there. Sometimes you will see many small ones in a swamp turned quite crimson when all other trees around are still perfectly green, and the former appear so much the brighter for it. They take you by surprise, as you are going by on one side, across the fields, thus early in the season, as if it were some gay encampment of the red men, or other foresters, of whose arrival you had not heard.

Some single trees, wholly bright scarlet, seen against others of their kind still freshly green, or against evergreens, are more memorable than whole groves will be by-and-by. How beautiful, when a whole tree is like one great scarlet fruit full of ripe juices, every leaf, from lowest limb to topmost spire, all aglow, especially if you look toward the sun! What more remarkable object can there be in the landscape? Visible for miles, too fair to be believed. If such a phenomenon occurred but once, it would be handed down by tradition to posterity, and get into the mythology at last.

The whole tree thus ripening in advance of its fellows attains a singular preëminence, and sometimes maintains it for a week or two. I am thrilled at the sight of it, bearing aloft its scarlet standard for the regiment of green-clad foresters around and I go half a mile out of my way to examine it. A single tree becomes thus the crowning beauty of some meadowy vale, and the expression of the whole surrounding forest is at once more spirited for it.

A small Red Maple has grown, perchance, far away at

the head of some retired valley, a mile from any road, un-observed. It has faithfully discharged the duties of a Maple there, all winter and summer, neglected none of its econo-mies, but added to its stature in the virtue which belongs to a Maple, by a steady growth for so many months, never having gone gadding abroad, and is nearer heaven than it was in the spring. It has faithfully husbanded its sap, and afforded a shelter to the wandering bird, has long since ripened its seeds and committed them to the winds, and has the satisfaction of knowing, perhaps, that a thousand little well-behaved Maples are already settled in life somewhere. It deserves well of Mapledom. Its leaves have been asking it from time to time, in a whisper, "When shall we redden?" And now, in this month of September, this month of travel-ling, when men are hastening to the sea-side, or the moun-tains, or the lakes, this modest Maple, still without budging an inch, travels in its reputation,—runs up its scarlet flag on that hill-side, which shows that it has finished its summer's work before all other trees, and withdraws from the contest. At the eleventh hour of the year, the tree which no scrutiny could have detected here when it was most industrious is thus, by the tint of its maturity, by its very blushes, revealed at last to the careless and distant traveller, and leads his thoughts away from the dusty road into those brave soli-tudes which it inhabits. It flashes out conspicuous with all the virtue and beauty of a Maple,—*Acer rubrum*. We may now read its title, or *rubric*, clear. Its *virtues*, not its sins, are as scarlet.

Notwithstanding the Red Maple is the most intense scarlet of any of our trees, the Sugar-Maple has been the most cele-brated, and Michaux in his "Sylva" does not speak of the au-tumnal color of the former. About the second of October, these trees, both large and small, are most brilliant, though many are still green. In "sprout-lands" they seem to vie with one another, and ever some particular one in the midst of the crowd will be of a peculiarly pure scarlet, and by its more in-tense color attract our eye even at a distance, and carry off the palm. A large Red-Maple swamp, when at the height of its change, is the most obviously brilliant of all tangible things, where I dwell, so abundant is this tree with us. It varies much both in form and color. A great many are merely yellow, more scarlet, others scarlet deepening into crimson, more red than common. Look at yonder swamp of Maples mixed with Pines, at the base of a Pine-clad hill, a quarter of a mile off, so that you get the full effect of the bright colors, without detecting the imperfections of the leaves, and see their yellow, scarlet, and crimson fires, of all tints, mingled and contrasted with the green. Some Maples are yet green, only yellow or crimson-tipped on the edges of their flakes, like the edges of a Hazel-Nut burr; some are wholly brilliant scarlet, raying out regularly and finely every way, bilaterally, like the veins of a leaf; others, of more irregular form, when I turn my head slightly, emptying out some of its earthiness and concealing the trunk of the tree, seem to rest heavily flake on flake, like yellow and scarlet clouds, wreath upon wreath, or like snow-drifts driving through the air, stratified by the wind. It adds greatly to the beauty of such a swamp at this season, that, even though there may be no other trees interspersed, it is not seen as a simple mass of color, but, different trees being of different colors and hues, the outline of each crescent tree-top is distinct, and where one laps on to another. Yet a painter would hardly venture to make them thus distinct a quarter of a mile off.

As I go across a meadow directly toward a low rising ground this bright afternoon, I see, some fifty rods off toward the sun, the top of a Maple swamp just appearing over the sheeny russet edge of the hill, a stripe apparently twenty rods long by ten feet deep, of the most intensely brilliant scarlet, orange, and yellow, equal to any flowers or fruits, or any tints ever painted. As I advance, lowering the edge of the hill which makes the firm foreground or lower frame of the picture, the depth of the brilliant grove revealed steadily increases, suggesting that the whole of the inclosed valley is filled with such color. One wonders that the tithing-men and fathers of the town are not out to see what the trees mean by their high colors and exuberance of spirits, fearing that some mischief is brewing. I do not see what the Puritans did at this season, when the Maples blaze out in scarlet. They certainly could not have worshipped in groves then. Perhaps that is what they built meeting-houses and fenced them round with horse-sheds for.

THE ELM.

Now, too, the first of October, or later, the Elms are at the height of their autumnal beauty, great brownish-yellow masses, warm from their September oven, hanging over the highway. Their leaves are perfectly ripe. I wonder if there is any answering ripeness in the lives of the men who live beneath them. As I look down our street, which is lined with them, they remind me both by their form and color of yellowing sheaves of grain, as if the harvest had indeed come to the village itself, and we might expect to find some maturity and *flavor* in the thoughts of the villagers at last. Under those bright rustling yellow piles just ready to fall on the heads of the walkers, how can any crudity or greenness of thought or act prevail? When I stand where half a dozen large Elms droop over a house, it is as if I stood within a ripe pumpkin-rind, and I feel as mellow as if I were the pulp, though I may be somewhat stringy and seedy withal. What is the late greenness of the English Elm, like a cucumber out of season, which does not know when to have done, compared with the early and golden maturity of the American tree? The street is the scene of a great harvest-home. It would be worth the while to set out these trees, if only for their autumnal value. Think of these great yellow canopies or parasols held over our heads and houses by the mile together, making the village all one and compact,—an *ulmarium*, which is at the same time a nursery of men! And then how gently and unobserved they drop their burden and let in the sun when it is wanted, their leaves not heard when they fall on our roofs and in our streets; and thus the village parasol is shut up and put away! I see the market-man driving into the village, and disappearing under its canopy of Elm-tops, with *his* crop, as into a great granary or barnyard. I am tempted to go thither as to a husking of thoughts, now dry and ripe, and ready to be separated from their integuments; but, alas! I foresee that it will be chiefly husks and little thought, blasted pig-corn, fit only for cob-meal,—for, as you sow, so shall you reap.

FALLEN LEAVES.

By the sixth of October the leaves generally begin to fall, in successive showers, after frost or rain; but the principal leaf-harvest, the acme of the *Fall*, is commonly about the sixteenth. Some morning at that date there is perhaps a harder frost than we have seen, and ice formed under the pump, and now, when the morning wind rises, the leaves come down in denser showers than ever. They suddenly form thick beds or carpets on the ground, in this gentle air, or even without wind, just the size and form of the tree above. Some trees, as small Hickories, appear to have dropped their leaves instantaneously, as a soldier grounds arms at a signal; and those of the Hickory, being bright yellow still, though withered, reflect a blaze of light from the ground where they lie. Down they have come on all sides, at the first earnest touch of autumn's wand, making a sound like rain.

Or else it is after moist and rainy weather that we notice how great a fall of leaves there has been in the night, though it may not yet be the touch that loosens the Rock-Maple leaf. The streets are thickly strewn with the trophies, and fallen Elm-leaves make a dark brown pavement under our feet. After some remarkably warm Indian-summer day or days, I perceive that it is the unusual heat which, more than anything, causes the leaves to fall, there having been, perhaps, no frost nor rain for some time. The intense heat suddenly ripens and wilts them, just as it softens and ripens peaches and other fruits, and causes them to drop.

The leaves of late Red Maples, still bright, strew the earth, often crimson-spotted on a yellow ground, like some wild apples,—though they preserve these bright colors on the ground but a day or two, especially if it rains. On causeways I go by trees here and there all bare and smoke-like, having lost their brilliant clothing; but there it lies, nearly as bright as ever, on the ground on one side, and making nearly as regular a figure as lately on the tree. I would rather say that I first observe the trees thus flat on the ground like a permanent colored shadow, and they suggest to look for the boughs that bore them. A queen might be proud to walk where these gallant trees have spread their bright cloaks in

the mud. I see wagons roll over them as a shadow or a reflection, and the drivers heed them just as little as they did
their shadows before.

Birds'-nests, in the Huckleberry and other shrubs, and in
trees, are already being filled with the withered leaves. So
many have fallen in the woods, that a squirrel cannot run after a falling nut without being heard. Boys are raking them in
the streets, if only for the pleasure of dealing with such clean
crisp substances. Some sweep the paths scrupulously neat, and
then stand to see the next breath strew them with new
trophies. The swamp-floor is thickly covered, and the
Lycopodium lucidulum looks suddenly greener amid them. In
dense woods they half-cover pools that are three or four rods
long. The other day I could hardly find a well-known spring,
and even suspected that it had dried up, for it was completely
concealed by freshly fallen leaves; and when I swept them
aside and revealed it, it was like striking the earth, with
Aaron's rod, for a new spring. Wet grounds about the edges
of swamps look dry with them. At one swamp, where I was
surveying, thinking to step on a leafy shore from a rail, I got
into the water more than a foot deep.

When I go to the river the day after the principal fall of
leaves, the sixteenth, I find my boat all covered, bottom and
seats, with the leaves of the Golden Willow under which it is
moored, and I set sail with a cargo of them rustling under my
feet. If I empty it, it will be full again to-morrow. I do not regard them as litter, to be swept out, but accept them as suitable straw or matting for the bottom of my carriage. When I
turn up into the mouth of the Assabet, which is wooded,
large fleets of leaves are floating on its surface, as it were getting out to sea, with room to tack; but next the shore, a little
farther up, they are thicker than foam, quite concealing the
water for a rod in width, under and amid the Alders, Button-
Bushes, and Maples, still perfectly light and dry, with fibre
unrelaxed; and at a rocky bend where they are met and
stopped by the morning wind, they sometimes form a broad
and dense crescent quite across the river. When I turn my
prow that way, and the wave which it makes strikes them, list
what a pleasant rustling from these dry substances grating on
one another! Often it is their undulation only which reveals

the water beneath them. Also every motion of the wood-turtle on the shore is betrayed by their rustling there. Or even in mid-channel, when the wind rises, I hear them blown with a rustling sound. Higher up they are slowly moving round and round in some great eddy which the river makes, as that at the "Leaning Hemlocks," where the water is deep, and the current is wearing into the bank.

Perchance, in the afternoon of such a day, when the water is perfectly calm and full of reflections, I paddle gently down the main stream, and, turning up the Assabet, reach a quiet cove, where I unexpectedly find myself surrounded by myriads of leaves, like fellow-voyagers, which seem to have the same purpose, or want of purpose with myself. See this great fleet of scattered leaf-boats which we paddle amid, in this smooth river-bay, each one curled up on every side by the sun's skill, each nerve a stiff spruce-knee,—like boats of hide, and of all patterns, Charon's boat probably among the rest, and some with lofty prows and poops, like the stately vessels of the ancients, scarcely moving in the sluggish current,—like the great fleets, the dense Chinese cities of boats, with which you mingle on entering some great mart, some New York or Canton, which we are all steadily approaching together. How gently each has been deposited on the water! No violence has been used towards them yet, though, perchance, palpitating hearts were present at the launching. And painted ducks, too, the splendid wood-duck among the rest, often come to sail and float amid the painted leaves,—barks of a nobler model still!

What wholesome herb-drinks are to be had in the swamps now! What strong medicinal, but rich, scents from the decaying leaves! The rain falling on the freshly dried herbs and leaves, and filling the pools and ditches into which they have dropped thus clean and rigid, will soon convert them into tea,—green, black, brown, and yellow teas, of all degrees of strength, enough to set all Nature a-gossiping. Whether we drink them or not, as yet, before their strength is drawn, these leaves, dried on great Nature's coppers, are of such various pure and delicate tints as might make the fame of Oriental teas.

How they are mixed up, of all species, Oak and Maple and Chestnut and Birch! But Nature is not cluttered with them; she is a perfect husbandman; she stores them all. Consider what a vast crop is thus annually shed on the earth! This, more than any mere grain or seed, is the great harvest of the year. The trees are now repaying the earth with interest what they have taken from it. They are discounting. They are about to add a leaf's thickness to the depth of the soil. This is the beautiful way in which Nature gets her muck, while I chaffer with this man and that, who talks to me about sulphur and the cost of carting. We are all the richer for their decay. I am more interested in this crop than in the English grass alone or in the corn. It prepares the virgin mould for future cornfields and forests, on which the earth fattens. It keeps our homestead in good heart.

For beautiful variety no crop can be compared with this. Here is not merely the plain yellow of the grains, but nearly all the colors that we know, the brightest blue not excepted: the early blushing Maple, the Poison-Sumach blazing its sins as scarlet, the mulberry Ash, the rich chrome-yellow of the Poplars, the brilliant red Huckleberry, with which the hills' backs are painted, like those of sheep. The frost touches them, and, with the slightest breath of returning day or jarring of earth's axle, see in what showers they come floating down! The ground is all party-colored with them. But they still live in the soil, whose fertility and bulk they increase, and in the forests that spring from it. They stoop to rise, to mount higher in coming years, by subtle chemistry, climbing by the sap in the trees, and the sapling's first fruits thus shed, transmuted at last, may adorn its crown, when, in after-years, it has become the monarch of the forest.

It is pleasant to walk over the beds of these fresh, crisp, and rustling leaves. How beautifully they go to their graves! how gently lay themselves down and turn to mould!—painted of a thousand hues, and fit to make the beds of us living. So they troop to their last resting-place, light and frisky. They put on no weeds, but merrily they go scampering over the earth, selecting the spot, choosing a lot, ordering no iron fence, whispering all through the woods about it,—some choosing the spot where the bodies of men are mouldering beneath, and meeting them half-way. How many flutterings before they rest quietly in their graves! They that soared so loftily, how contentedly they return to dust again, and are laid low, re-

signed to lie and decay at the foot of the tree, and afford
nourishment to new generations of their kind, as well as to
flutter on high! They teach us how to die. One wonders if the
time will ever come when men, with their boasted faith in immortality, will lie down as gracefully and as ripe,—with such
an Indian-summer serenity will shed their bodies, as they do
their hair and nails.

When the leaves fall, the whole earth is a cemetery pleasant
to walk in. I love to wander and muse over them in their
graves. Here are no lying nor vain epitaphs. What though you
own no lot at Mount Auburn? Your lot is surely cast somewhere in this vast cemetery, which has been consecrated from
of old. You need attend no auction to secure a place. There is
room enough here. The Loose-strife shall bloom and the
Huckleberry-bird sing over your bones. The woodman and
hunter shall be your sextons, and the children shall tread upon
the borders as much as they will. Let us walk in the cemetery
of the leaves,—this is your true Greenwood Cemetery.

THE SUGAR-MAPLE.

But think not that the splendor of the year is over; for as
one leaf does not make a summer, neither does one fallen
leaf make an autumn. The smallest Sugar-Maples in our
streets make a great show as early as the fifth of October,
more than any other trees there. As I look up the Main
Street, they appear like painted screens standing before the
houses; yet many are green. But now, or generally by the seventeenth of October, when almost all Red Maples, and some
White Maples, are bare, the large Sugar-Maples also are in
their glory, glowing with yellow and red, and show unexpectedly bright and delicate tints. They are remarkable for
the contrast they often afford of deep blushing red on one
half and green on the other. They become at length dense
masses of rich yellow with a deep scarlet blush, or more than
blush, on the exposed surfaces. They are the brightest trees
now in the street.

The large ones on our Common are particularly beautiful.
A delicate, but warmer than golden yellow is now the prevailing color, with scarlet cheeks. Yet, standing on the east side of

the Common just before sundown, when the western light is transmitted through them, I see that their yellow even, compared with the pale lemon yellow of an Elm close by, amounts to a scarlet, without noticing the bright scarlet portions. Generally, they are great regular oval masses of yellow and scarlet. All the sunny warmth of the season, the Indian summer, seems to be absorbed in their leaves. The lowest and inmost leaves next the bole are, as usual, of the most delicate yellow and green, like the complexion of young men brought up in the house. There is an auction on the Common to-day, but its red flag is hard to be discerned amid this blaze of color.

Little did the fathers of the town anticipate this brilliant success, when they caused to be imported from farther in the country some straight poles with their tops cut off, which they called Sugar-Maples; and, as I remember, after they were set out, a neighboring merchant's clerk, by way of jest, planted beans about them. Those which were then jestingly called bean-poles are to-day far the most beautiful objects noticeable in our streets. They are worth all and more than they have cost,—though one of the selectmen, while setting them out, took the cold which occasioned his death,—if only because they have filled the open eyes of children with their rich color unstintedly so many Octobers. We will not ask them to yield us sugar in the spring, while they afford us so fair a prospect in the autumn. Wealth in-doors may be the inheritance of few, but it is equally distributed on the Common. All children alike can revel in this golden harvest.

Surely trees should be set in our streets with a view to their October splendor; though I doubt whether this is ever considered by the "Tree Society." Do you not think it will make some odds to these children that they were brought up under the Maples? Hundreds of eyes are steadily drinking in this color, and by these teachers even the truants are caught and educated the moment they step abroad. Indeed, neither the truant nor the studious is at present taught color in the schools. These are instead of the bright colors in apothecaries' shops and city windows. It is a pity that we have no more *Red* Maples, and some Hickories, in our streets as well. Our paint-box is very imperfectly filled. Instead of, or beside, supplying such paint-boxes as we do, we might supply these natural colors to the young. Where else will they study color under greater advantages? What School of Design can vie with this? Think how much the eyes of painters of all kinds, and of manufacturers of cloth and paper, and paper-stainers, and countless others, are to be educated by these autumnal colors. The stationer's envelopes may be of very various tints, yet not so various as those of the leaves of a single tree. If you want a different shade or tint of a particular color, you have only to look farther within or without the tree or the wood. These leaves are not many dipped in one dye, as at the dye-house, but they are dyed in light of infinitely various degrees of strength, and left to set and dry there.

Shall the names of so many of our colors continue to be derived from those of obscure foreign localities, as Naples yellow, Prussian blue, raw Sienna, burnt Umber, Gamboge?— (surely the Tyrian purple must have faded by this time)—or from comparatively trivial articles of commerce,—chocolate, lemon, coffee, cinnamon, claret?—(shall we compare our Hickory to a lemon, or a lemon to a Hickory?)—or from ores and oxides which few ever see? Shall we so often, when describing to our neighbors the color of something we have seen, refer them, not to some natural object in our neighborhood, but perchance to a bit of earth fetched from the other side of the planet, which possibly they may find at the apothecary's, but which probably neither they nor we ever saw? Have we not an *earth* under our feet,—ay, and a sky over our heads? Or is the last *all* ultramarine? What do we know of sapphire, amethyst, emerald, ruby, amber, and the like,—most of us who take these names in vain? Leave these precious words to cabinet-keepers, virtuosos, and maids-of-honor,—to the Nabobs, Begums, and Chobdars of Hindostan, or wherever else. I do not see why, since America and her autumn woods have been discovered, our leaves should not compete with the precious stones in giving names to colors; and, indeed, I believe that in course of time the names of some of our trees and shrubs, as well as flowers, will get into our popular chromatic nomenclature.

But of much more importance than a knowledge of the names and distinctions of color is the joy and exhilaration which these colored leaves excite. Already these brilliant trees throughout the street, without any more variety, are at least equal to an annual festival and holiday, or a week of such. These are cheap and innocent gala-days, celebrated by one and all without the aid of committees or marshals, such a show as may safely be licensed, not attracting gamblers or rum-sellers, nor requiring any special police to keep the peace. And poor indeed must be that New-England village's October which has not the Maple in its streets. This October festival costs no powder, nor ringing of bells, but every tree is a living liberty-pole on which a thousand bright flags are waving.

No wonder that we must have our annual Cattle-Show, and Fall Training, and perhaps Cornwallis, our September Courts, and the like. Nature herself holds her annual fair in October, not only in the streets, but in every hollow and on every hill-side. When lately we looked into that Red-Maple swamp all a-blaze, where the trees were clothed in their vestures of most dazzling tints, did it not suggest a thousand gypsies beneath,—a race capable of wild delight,—or even the fabled fawns, satyrs, and wood-nymphs come back to earth? Or was it only a congregation of wearied wood-choppers, or of proprietors come to inspect their lots, that we thought of? Or, earlier still, when we paddled on the river through that fine-grained September air, did there not appear to be something new going on under the sparkling surface of the stream, a shaking of props, at least, so that we made haste in order to be up in time? Did not the rows of yellowing Willows and Button-Bushes on each side seem like rows of booths, under which, perhaps, some fluviatile egg-pop equally yellow was effervescing? Did not all these suggest that man's spirits should rise as high as Nature's,—should hang out their flag, and the routine of his life be interrupted by an analogous expression of joy and hilarity?

No annual training or muster of soldiery, no celebration with its scarfs and banners, could import into the town a hundredth part of the annual splendor of our October. We have only to set the trees, or let them stand, and Nature will find the colored drapery,—flags of all her nations, some of whose private signals hardly the botanist can read,—while we walk under the triumphal arches of the Elms. Leave it to Nature to appoint the days, whether the same as in neighboring States or not, and let the clergy read her proclamations, if they can understand them. Behold what a brilliant drapery is her Woodbine flag! What public-spirited merchant, think you, has contributed this part of the show? There is no handsomer shingling and paint than this vine, at present covering a whole side of some houses. I do not believe that the Ivy *never sear* is comparable to it. No wonder it has been extensively introduced into London. Let us have a good many Maples and Hickories and Scarlet Oaks, then, I say. Blaze away! Shall that dirty roll of bunting in the gun-house be all the colors a village can display? A village is not complete, unless it have these trees to mark the season in it. They are important, like the town-clock. A village that has them not will not be found to work well. It has a screw loose, an essential part is wanting. Let us have Willows for spring, Elms for summer, Maples and Walnuts and Tupeloes for autumn, Evergreens for winter, and Oaks for all seasons. What is a gallery in a house to a gallery in the streets, which every market-man rides through, whether he will or not? Of course, there is not a picture-gallery in the country which would be worth so much to us as is the western view at sunset under the Elms of our main street. They are the frame to a picture which is daily painted behind them. An avenue of Elms as large as our largest and three miles long would seem to lead to some admirable place, though only C—— were at the end of it.

A village needs these innocent stimulants of bright and cheering prospects to keep off melancholy and superstition. Show me two villages, one embowered in trees and blazing with all the glories of October, the other a merely trivial and treeless waste, or with only a single tree or two for suicides, and I shall be sure that in the latter will be found the most starved and bigoted religionists and the most desperate drinkers. Every wash-tub and milk-can and gravestone will be exposed. The inhabitants will disappear abruptly behind their barns and houses, like desert Arabs amid their rocks, and I shall look to see spears in their hands. They will be ready to accept the most barren and forlorn doctrine,—as that the world is speedily coming to an end, or has already got to it, or that they themselves are turned wrong side outward. They will perchance crack their dry joints at one another and call it a spiritual communication.

But to confine ourselves to the Maples. What if we were to take half as much pains in protecting them as we do in setting them out,—not stupidly tie our horses to our dahlia-stems?

What meant the fathers by establishing this *perfectly living* institution before the church,—this institution which needs no repairing nor repainting, which is continually enlarged and repaired by its growth? Surely they

> "Wrought in a sad sincerity;
> Themselves from God they could not free;
> They *planted* better than they knew;—
> The conscious *trees* to beauty grew."

Verily these Maples are cheap preachers, permanently settled, which preach their half-century, and century, ay, and century-and-a-half sermons, with constantly increasing unction and influence, ministering to many generations of men; and the least we can do is to supply them with suitable colleagues as they grow infirm.

THE SCARLET OAK.

Belonging to a genus which is remarkable for the beautiful form of its leaves, I suspect that some Scarlet-Oak leaves surpass those of all other Oaks in the rich and wild beauty of their outlines. I judge from an acquaintance with twelve species, and from drawings which I have seen of many others.

Stand under this tree and see how finely its leaves are cut against the sky,—as it were, only a few sharp points extending from a midrib. They look like double, treble, or quadruple crosses. They are far more ethereal than the less deeply scolloped Oak-leaves. They have so little leafy *terra firma* that they appear melting away in the light, and scarcely obstruct our view. The leaves of very young plants are, like those of full-grown Oaks of other species, more entire, simple, and lumpish in their outlines; but these, raised high on old trees, have solved the leafy problem. Lifted higher and higher, and sublimated more and more, putting off some earthiness and cultivating more intimacy with the light each year, they have at length the least possible amount of earthy matter, and the greatest spread and grasp of skyey influences. There they dance, arm in arm with the light,—tripping it on fantastic points, fit partners in those aërial halls. So intimately mingled are they with it, that, what with their slenderness and their glossy surfaces, you can hardly tell at last what in the dance is leaf and what is light. And when no zephyr stirs, they are at most but a rich tracery to the forest-windows.

I am again struck with their beauty, when, a month later, they thickly strew the ground in the woods, piled one upon another under my feet. They are then brown above, but purple beneath. With their narrow lobes and their bold deep scollops reaching almost to the middle, they suggest that the material must be cheap, or else there has been a lavish expense in their creation, as if so much had been cut out. Or else they seem to us the remnants of the stuff out of which leaves have been cut with a die. Indeed, when they lie thus one upon another, they remind me of a pile of scrap-tin.*

Or bring one home, and study it closely at your leisure, by the fireside. It is a type, not from any Oxford font, not in the Basque nor the arrow-headed character, not found on the Rosetta Stone, but destined to be copied in sculpture one day, if they ever get to whittling stone here. What a wild and pleasing outline, a combination of graceful curves and angles! The eye rests with equal delight on what is not leaf and on what is leaf,—on the broad, free, open sinuses, and on the long, sharp, bristle-pointed lobes. A simple oval outline would include it all, if you connected the points of the leaf; but how much richer is it than that, with its half-dozen deep scollops, in which the eye and thought of the beholder are embayed! If I were a drawing-master, I would set my pupils to copying these leaves, that they might learn to draw firmly and gracefully.

Regarded as water, it is like a pond with half a dozen broad rounded promontories extending nearly to its middle, half from each side, while its watery bays extend far inland, like

---

*The original of the leaf copied on the next page was picked from such a pile.

sharp friths, at each of whose heads several fine streams empty in,—almost a leafy archipelago.

But it oftener suggests land, and, as Dionysius and Pliny compared the form of the Morea to that of the leaf of the Oriental Plane-tree, so this leaf reminds me of some fair wild island in the ocean, whose extensive coast, alternate rounded bays with smooth strands, and sharp-pointed rocky capes, mark it as fitted for the habitation of man, and destined to be-

come a centre of civilization at last. To the sailor's eye, it is a much-indented shore. Is it not, in fact, a shore to the aërial ocean, on which the windy surf beats? At sight of this leaf we are all mariners,—if not vikings, buccaneers, and filibusters. Both our love of repose and our spirit of adventure are addressed. In our most casual glance, perchance, we think, that, if we succeed in doubling those sharp capes, we shall find deep, smooth, and secure havens in the ample bays. How different from the White-Oak leaf, with its rounded headlands, on which no light-house need be placed! That is an England, with its long civil history, that may be read. This is some still unsettled New-found Island or Celebes. Shall we go and be rajahs there?

By the twenty-sixth of October the large Scarlet Oaks are in their prime, when other Oaks are usually withered. They have been kindling their fires for a week past, and now generally burst into a blaze. This alone of *our* indigenous deciduous trees (excepting the Dogwood, of which I do not know half a dozen, and they are but large bushes) is now in its glory. The two Aspens and the Sugar-Maple come nearest to it in date, but they have lost the greater part of their leaves. Of evergreens, only the Pitch-Pine is still commonly bright.

But it requires a particular alertness, if not devotion to these phenomena, to appreciate the wide-spread, but late and unexpected glory of the Scarlet Oaks. I do not speak here of the small trees and shrubs, which are commonly observed, and which are now withered, but of the large trees. Most go in and shut their doors, thinking that bleak and colorless November has already come, when some of the most brilliant and memorable colors are not yet lit.

This very perfect and vigorous one, about forty feet high, standing in an open pasture, which was quite glossy green on the twelfth, is now, the twenty-sixth, completely changed to bright dark scarlet,—every leaf, between you and the sun, as if it had been dipped into a scarlet dye. The whole tree is much like a heart in form, as well as color. Was not this worth waiting for? Little did you think, ten days ago, that that cold green tree would assume such color as this. Its leaves are still firmly attached, while those of other trees are falling around it. It seems to say,—"I am the last to blush, but I blush deeper than any of ye. I bring up the rear in my red coat. We Scarlet ones, alone of Oaks, have not given up the fight."

The sap is now, and even far into November, frequently flowing fast in these trees, as in Maples in the spring; and apparently their bright tints, now that most other Oaks are withered, are connected with this phenomenon. They are full of life. It has a pleasantly astringent, acorn-like taste, this strong Oak-wine, as I find on tapping them with my knife.

Looking across this woodland valley, a quarter of a mile wide, how rich those Scarlet Oaks, embosomed in Pines, their bright red branches intimately intermingled with them! They have their full effect there. The Pine-boughs are the green calyx to their red petals. Or, as we go along a road in the woods, the sun striking endwise through it, and lighting up the red tents of the Oaks, which on each side are mingled with the liquid green of the Pines, makes a very gorgeous scene. Indeed, without the evergreens for contrast, the autumnal tints would lose much of their effect.

The Scarlet Oak asks a clear sky and the brightness of late October days. These bring out its colors. If the sun goes into a cloud, they become comparatively indistinct. As I sit on a cliff in the southwest part of our town, the sun is now getting low, and the woods in Lincoln, south and east of me, are lit up by its more level rays; and in the Scarlet Oaks, scattered so equally over the forest, there is brought out a more brilliant redness than I had believed was in them. Every tree of this species which is visible in those directions, even to the horizon, now stands out distinctly red. Some great ones lift their red backs high above the woods, in the next town, like huge roses with a myriad of fine petals; and some more slender ones, in a small grove of White Pines on Pine Hill in the east, on the very verge of the horizon, alternating with the Pines on the edge of the grove, and shouldering them with their red coats, look like soldiers in red amid hunters in green. This time it is Lincoln green, too. Till the sun got low, I did not believe that there were so many redcoats in the forest army. Theirs is an intense burning red, which would lose some of its strength, methinks, with every step you might take toward them; for the shade that lurks amid their foliage does not report itself at this distance, and they are unanimously red. The focus of their reflected color is in the atmosphere far on this side. Every such tree becomes a nucleus of red, as it were, where, with the declining sun, that color grows and glows. It is partly borrowed fire, gathering strength from the sun on its way to your eye. It has only some comparatively dull red leaves for a rallying-point, or kindling-stuff, to start it, and it becomes an intense scarlet or red mist, or fire, which finds fuel for itself in the very atmosphere. So vivacious is redness. The very rails reflect a rosy light at this hour and season. You see a redder tree than exists.

If you wish to count the Scarlet Oaks, do it now. In a clear day stand thus on a hill-top in the woods, when the sun is an hour high, and every one within range of your vision, excepting in the west, will be revealed. You might live to the age of Methuselah and never find a tithe of them, otherwise. Yet sometimes even in a dark day I have thought them as bright as I ever saw them. Looking westward, their colors are lost in a blaze of light; but in other directions the whole forest is a flower-garden, in which these late roses burn, alternating with green, while the so-called "gardeners," walking here and there, perchance, beneath, with spade and water-pot, see only a few little asters amid withered leaves.

These are *my* China-asters, *my* late garden-flowers. It costs me nothing for a gardener. The falling leaves, all over the forest, are protecting the roots of my plants. Only look at what is to be seen, and you will have garden enough, without deepening the soil in your yard. We have only to elevate our view a little, to see the whole forest as a garden. The blossoming of the Scarlet Oak,—the forest-flower, surpassing all in splendor (at least since the Maple)! I do not know but they interest me more than the Maples, they are so widely and equally dispersed throughout the forest; they are so hardy, a nobler tree on the whole;—our chief November flower, abiding the approach of winter with us, imparting warmth to early November prospects. It is remarkable that the latest bright color that is general should be this deep, dark scarlet and red, the intensest of colors. The ripest fruit of the year; like the cheek of a hard, glossy, red apple from the cold Isle of Orleans, which will not be mellow for eating till next spring! When I rise to a hill-top, a thousand of these great Oak roses, distributed on every side, as far as the horizon! I admire them four or five miles off! This my unfailing prospect for a fortnight past! This late forest-flower surpasses all that spring or summer could do. Their colors were but rare and dainty specks comparatively, (created for the near-sighted, who walk amid the humblest herbs and underwoods,) and made no impression on a distant eye. Now it is an extended forest or a mountain-side, through or along which we journey from day to day, that bursts into bloom. Comparatively, our gardening is on a petty scale,—the gardener still nursing a few asters amid dead weeds, ignorant of the gigantic asters and roses, which, as it were, overshadow him, and ask for none of his care. It is like a little red paint ground on a saucer, and held up against the sunset sky. Why not take more elevated and broader views, walk in the great garden, not skulk in a little "debauched" nook of it? consider the beauty of the forest, and not merely of a few impounded herbs?

Let your walks now be a little more adventurous; ascend the hills. If about the last of October, you ascend any hill in the outskirts of our town, and probably of yours, and look over the forest, you may see——well, what I have endeavored to describe. All this you surely *will* see, and much more, if you are prepared to see it,—if you *look* for it. Otherwise, regular and universal as this phenomenon is, whether you stand on the hill-top or in the hollow, you will think for threescore years and ten that all the wood is, at this season, sear and brown. Objects are concealed from our view, not so much because they are out of the course of our visual ray as because we do not bring our minds and eyes to bear on them; for there is no power to see in the eye itself, any more than in any other jelly. We do not realize how far and widely, or how near and narrowly, we are to look. The greater part of the phenomena of Nature are for this reason concealed from us all our lives. The gardener sees only the gardener's garden. Here, too, as in political economy, the supply answers to the demand. Nature does not cast pearls before swine. There is just as much beauty visible to us in the landscape as we are prepared to appreciate,—not a grain more. The actual objects which one man will see from a particular hill-top are just as different from those which another will see as the beholders are different. The Scarlet Oak must, in a sense, be in your eye when you go forth. We cannot see anything until we are possessed with the idea of it, take it into our heads,—and then we can hardly see anything else. In my botanical rambles, I find, that, first, the idea, or image, of a plant occupies my thoughts, though it may seem very foreign to this locality,— no nearer than Hudson's Bay,—and for some weeks or months I go thinking of it, and expecting it, unconsciously, and at length I surely see it. This is the history of my finding a score or more of rare plants, which I could name. A man sees only what concerns him. A botanist absorbed in the study of grasses does not distinguish the grandest Pasture Oaks. He, as it were, tramples down Oaks unwittingly in his walk, or at most sees only their shadows. I have found that it required a different intention of the eye, in the same locality, to see different plants, even when they were closely allied, as *Juncaceæ* and *Gramineæ*: when I was looking for the former, I did not see the latter in the midst of them. How much more, then, it requires different intentions of the eye and of the mind to attend to different departments of knowledge! How differently the poet and the naturalist look at objects!

Take a New-England selectman, and set him on the highest of our hills, and tell him to look,—sharpening his sight to the utmost, and putting on the glasses that suit him best, (ay, using a spy-glass, if he likes,)—and make a full report. What, probably, will he *spy?*—what will he *select* to look at? Of course, he will see a Brocken spectre of himself. He will see several meeting-houses, at least, and, perhaps, that somebody ought to be assessed higher than he is, since he has so handsome a wood-lot. Now take Julius Cæsar, or Immanuel Swedenborg, or a Fegee-Islander, and set him up there. Or suppose all together, and let them compare notes afterward. Will it appear that they have enjoyed the same prospect? What they will see will be as different as Rome was from Heaven or Hell, or the last from the Fegee Islands. For aught we know, as strange a man as any of these is always at our elbow.

Why, it takes a sharp-shooter to bring down even such trivial game as snipes and woodcocks; he must take very particular aim, and know what he is aiming at. He would stand a very small chance, if he fired at random into the sky, being told that snipes were flying there. And so is it with him that shoots at beauty; though he wait till the sky falls, he will not bag any if he does not already know its seasons and haunts, and the color of its wing,—if he has not dreamed of it, so that he can *anticipate* it; then, indeed, he flushes it at every step, shoots double and on the wing, with both barrels, even in cornfields. The sportsman trains himself, dresses and watches unweariedly, and loads and primes for his particular game. He prays for it, and offers sacrifices, and so he gets it. After due and long preparation, schooling his eye and hand, dreaming awake and asleep, with gun and paddle and boat he goes out after meadow-hens, which most of his townsmen never saw nor dreamed of, and paddles for miles against a head-wind, and wades in water up to his knees, being out all day without his dinner, and *therefore* he gets them. He had them half-way into his bag when he started, and has only to shove them down. The true sportsman can shoot you almost any of his game from his windows: what else has he windows or eyes for? It comes and perches at last on the barrel of his gun; but the rest of the world never see it *with the feathers on*. The geese fly exactly under his zenith, and honk when they get there, and he will keep himself supplied by firing up his chimney; twenty musquash have the refusal of each one of his traps before it is empty. If he lives, and his game-spirit increases, heaven and earth shall fail him sooner than game; and when he dies, he will go to more extensive, and, perchance, happier hunting-grounds. The fisherman, too, dreams of fish, sees a bobbing cork in his dreams, till he can almost catch them in his sink-spout. I knew a girl who, being sent to pick huckleberries, picked wild gooseberries by the quart, where no one else knew that there were any, because she was accustomed to pick them up country where she came from. The astronomer knows where to go star-gathering, and sees one clearly in his mind before any have seen it with a glass. The hen scratches and finds her food right under where she stands; but such is not the way with the hawk.

These bright leaves which I have mentioned are not the exception, but the rule; for I believe that all leaves, even grasses and mosses, acquire brighter colors just before their fall. When you come to observe faithfully the changes of each humblest plant, you find that each has, sooner or later, its peculiar autumnal tint; and if you undertake to make a complete list of the bright tints, it will be nearly as long as a catalogue of the plants in your vicinity.

A Plea for Captain John Brown

I TRUST that you will pardon me for being here. I do not
wish to force my thoughts upon you, but I feel forced myself. Little as I know of Captain Brown, I would fain do my
part to correct the tone and the statements of the newspapers,
and of my countrymen generally, respecting his character and
actions. It costs us nothing to be just. We can at least express
our sympathy with, and admiration of, him and his companions, and that is what I now propose to do.

First, as to his history.

I will endeavor to omit, as much as possible, what you have
already read. I need not describe his person to you, for probably most of you have seen and will not soon forget him. I am
told that his grandfather, John Brown, was an officer in the
Revolution; that he himself was born in Connecticut about
the beginning of this century, but early went with his father
to Ohio. I heard him say that his father was a contractor who
furnished beef to the army there, in the war of 1812; that he
accompanied him to the camp, and assisted him in that employment, seeing a good deal of military life, more, perhaps,
than if he had been a soldier, for he was often present at the
councils of the officers. Especially, he learned by experience
how armies are supplied and maintained in the field—a work
which, he observed, requires at least as much experience and
skill as to lead them in battle. He said that few persons had
any conception of the cost, even the pecuniary cost, of firing
a single bullet in war. He saw enough, at any rate, to disgust
him with a military life, indeed to excite in him a great ab-
horrence of it; so much so, that though he was tempted by
the offer of some petty office in the army, when he was about
eighteen, he not only declined that, but he also refused to
train when warned, and was fined for it. He then resolved that
he would never have anything to do with any war, unless it
were a war for liberty.

When the troubles in Kansas began, he sent several of his
sons thither to strengthen the party of the Free State men, fitting them out with such weapons as he had; telling them that

if the troubles should increase, and there should be need of him, he would follow to assist them with his hand and counsel. This, as you all know, he soon after did; and it was through his agency, far more than any other's, that Kansas was made free.

For a part of his life he was a surveyor, and at one time he was engaged in wool-growing, and he went to Europe as an agent about that business. There, as every where, he had his eyes about him, and made many original observations. He said, for instance, that he saw why the soil of England was so rich, and that of Germany (I think it was) so poor, and he thought of writing to some of the crowned heads about it. It was because in England the peasantry live on the soil which they cultivate, but in Germany they are gathered into villages, at night. It is a pity that he did not make a book of his observations.

I should say that he was an old-fashioned man in his respect for the Constitution, and his faith in the permanence of this Union. Slavery he deemed to be wholly opposed to these, and he was its determined foe.

He was by descent and birth a New England farmer, a man of great common sense, deliberate and practical as that class is, and tenfold more so. He was like the best of those who stood at Concord Bridge once, on Lexington Common, and on Bunker Hill, only he was firmer and higher principled than any that I have chanced to hear of as there. It was no abolition lecturer that converted him. Ethan Allen and Stark, with whom he may in some respects be compared, were rangers in a lower and less important field. They could bravely face their country's foes, but he had the courage to face his country herself, when she was in the wrong. A Western writer says, to account for his escape from so many perils, that he was concealed under a "rural exterior;" as if, in that prairie land, a hero should, by good rights, wear a citizen's dress only.

He did not go to the college called Harvard, good old Alma Mater as she is. He was not fed on the pap that is there furnished. As he phrased it, "I know no more of grammar than one of your calves." But he went to the great university of the West, where he sedulously pursued the study of Liberty, for which he had early betrayed a fondness, and having taken many degrees, he finally commenced the public practice of Humanity in Kansas, as you all know. Such were *his humanities*, and not any study of grammar. He would have left a Greek accent slanting the wrong way, and righted up a falling man.

He was one of that class of whom we hear a great deal, but, for the most part, see nothing at all—the Puritans. It would be in vain to kill him. He died lately in the time of Cromwell, but he reappeared here. Why should he not? Some of the Puritan stock are said to have come over and settled in New England. They were a class that did something else than celebrate their forefathers' day, and eat parched corn in remembrance of that time. They were neither Democrats nor Republicans, but men of simple habits, straightforward, prayerful; not thinking much of rulers who did not fear God, not making many compromises, nor seeking after available candidates.

"In his camp," as one has recently written, and as I have myself heard him state, "he permitted no profanity; no man of loose morals was suffered to remain there, unless, indeed, as a prisoner of war. 'I would rather,' said he, 'have the small-pox, yellow fever, and cholera, all together in my camp, than a man without principle. . . . It is a mistake, sir, that our people make, when they think that bullies are the best fighters, or that they are the fit men to oppose these Southerners. Give me men of good principles,—God-fearing men,—men who respect themselves, and with a dozen of them I will oppose any hundred such men as these Buford ruffians.' " He said that if one offered himself to be a soldier under him, who was forward to tell what he could or would do, if he could only get sight of the enemy, he had but little confidence in him.

He was never able to find more than a score or so of recruits whom he would accept, and only about a dozen, among them his sons, in whom he had perfect faith. When he was here, some years ago, he showed to a few a little manuscript book,—his "orderly book" I think he called it,—containing the names of his company in Kansas, and the rules by which they bound themselves; and he stated that several of them had already sealed the contract with their blood. When some one remarked that, with the addition of a chaplain, it would have been a perfect Cromwellian troop, he observed that he would have been glad to add a chaplain to the list, if he could have found one who could fill that office worthily. It is easy enough to find one for the United States army. I believe that he had prayers in his camp morning and evening, nevertheless.

He was a man of Spartan habits, and at sixty was scrupulous about his diet at your table, excusing himself by saying that he must eat sparingly and fare hard, as became a soldier or one who was fitting himself for difficult enterprises, a life of exposure.

A man of rare common sense and directness of speech, as of action; a transcendentalist above all, a man of ideas and principles,—that was what distinguished him. Not yielding to a whim or transient impulse, but carrying out the purpose of a life. I noticed that he did not overstate any thing, but spoke within bounds. I remember, particularly, how, in his speech here, he referred to what his family had suffered in Kansas, without ever giving the least vent to his pent-up fire. It was a volcano with an ordinary chimney-flue. Also referring to the deeds of certain Border Ruffians, he said, rapidly paring away his speech, like an experienced soldier, keeping a reserve of force and meaning, "They had a perfect right to be hung." He was not in the least a rhetorician, was not talking to Buncombe or his constituents any where, had no need to invent any thing, but to tell the simple truth, and communicate his own resolution; therefore he appeared incomparably strong, and eloquence in Congress and elsewhere seemed to me at a discount. It was like the speeches of Cromwell compared with those of an ordinary king.

As for his tact and prudence, I will merely say, that at a time when scarcely a man from the Free States was able to reach Kansas by any direct route, at least without having his arms taken from him, he, carrying what imperfect guns and other weapons he could collect, openly and slowly drove an ox-cart through Missouri, apparently in the capacity of a surveyor, with his surveying compass exposed in it, and so passed unsuspected, and had ample opportunity to learn the designs of the enemy. For some time after his arrival he still followed the same profession. When, for instance, he saw a knot of the ruffians on the prairie, discussing, of course, the single topic which then occupied their minds, he would, perhaps, take his compass and one of his sons, and proceed to run an imaginary line right through the very spot on which that conclave had assembled, and when he came up to them, he would naturally pause and have some talk with them, learning their news, and, at last, all their plans perfectly; and having thus completed his real survey, he would resume his imaginary one, and run on his line till he was out of sight.

When I expressed surprise that he could live in Kansas at all, with a price set upon his head, and so large a number, including the authorities, exasperated against him, he accounted for it by saying, "It is perfectly well understood that I will not be taken." Much of the time for some years he has had to skulk in swamps, suffering from poverty and from sickness, which was the consequence of exposure, befriended only by Indians and a few whites. But though it might be known that he was lurking in a particular swamp, his foes commonly did not care to go in after him. He could even come out into a town where there were more Border Ruffians than Free State men, and transact some business, without delaying long, and yet not be molested; for said he, "No little handful of men were willing to undertake it, and a large body could not be got together in season."

As for his recent failure, we do not know the facts about it. It was evidently far from being a wild and desperate attempt. His enemy, Mr. Vallandigham, is compelled to say, that "it was among the best planned and executed conspiracies that ever failed."

Not to mention his other successes, was it a failure, or did it show a want of good management, to deliver from bondage a dozen human beings, and walk off with them by broad daylight, for weeks if not months, at a leisurely pace, through one State after another, for half the length of the North, conspicuous to all parties, with a price set upon his head, going into a court room on his way and telling what he had done, thus convincing Missouri that it was not profitable to try to hold slaves in his neighborhood?—and this, not because the government menials were lenient, but because they were afraid of him.

Yet he did not attribute his success, foolishly, to "his star," or to any magic. He said, truly, that the reason why such greatly superior numbers quailed before him, was, as one of his prisoners confessed, because they *lacked a cause*—a kind of armor which he and his party never lacked. When the time came, few men were found willing to lay down their lives in defence of what they knew to be wrong; they did not like that this should be their last act in this world.

But to make haste to *his* last act, and its effects.

The newspapers seem to ignore, or perhaps are really ignorant of the fact, that there are at least as many as two or three individuals to a town throughout the North, who think much as the present speaker does about him and his enterprise. I do not hesitate to say that they are an important and growing party. We aspire to be something more than stupid and timid chattels, pretending to read history and our bibles, but desecrating every house and every day we breathe in. Perhaps anxious politicians may prove that only seventeen white men and five negroes were concerned in the late enterprise, but their very anxiety to prove this might suggest to themselves that all is not told. Why do they still dodge the truth? They are so anxious because of a dim consciousness of the fact, which they do not distinctly face, that at least a million of the free inhabitants of the United States would have rejoiced if it had succeeded. They at most only criticise the tactics. Though we wear no crape, the thought of that man's position and probable fate is spoiling many a man's day here at the North for other thinking. If any one who has seen him here can pursue successfully any other train of thought, I do not know what he is made of. If there is any such who gets his usual allowance of sleep, I will warrant him to fatten easily under any circumstances which do not touch his body or purse. I put a piece of paper and a pencil under my pillow, and when I could not sleep, I wrote in the dark.

On the whole, my respect for my fellow-men, except as one may outweigh a million, is not being increased these days. I have noticed the cold-blooded way in which newspaper writers and men generally speak of this event, as if an ordinary malefactor, though one of unusual "pluck,"—as the Governor of Virginia is reported to have said, using the language of the cock-pit, "the gamest man he ever saw,"—had been caught, and were about to be hung. He was not dreaming of his foes when the governor thought he looked so brave. It turns what sweetness I have to gall, to hear, or hear of, the remarks of some of my neighbors. When we heard at first that he was dead, one of my townsmen observed that "he died as the fool dieth;" which, pardon me, for an instant suggested a likeness in him dying to my neighbor living. Others, craven-hearted, said disparagingly, that "he threw his life away," because he resisted the government. Which way have they thrown *their* lives, pray?—Such as would praise a man for attacking singly an ordinary band of thieves or murderers. I hear another ask, Yankee-like, "What will he gain by it?" as if he expected to fill his pockets by this enterprise. Such a one has no idea of gain but in this worldly sense. If it does not lead to a "surprise" party, if he does not get a new pair of boots, or a vote of thanks, it must be a failure. "But he won't gain any thing by it." Well, no, I don't suppose he could get four-and-six-pence a day for being hung, take the year round; but then he stands a chance to save a considerable part of his soul—and *such* a soul!—when *you* do not. No doubt you can get more in your market for a quart of milk than for a quart of blood, but that is not the market that heroes carry their blood to.

Such do not know that like the seed is the fruit, and that, in the moral world, when good seed is planted, good fruit is inevitable, and does not depend on our watering and cultivating; that when you plant, or bury, a hero in his field, a crop of heroes is sure to spring up. This is a seed of such force and vitality, that it does not ask our leave to germinate.

The momentary charge at Balaclava, in obedience to a blundering command, proving what a perfect machine the soldier is, has, properly enough, been celebrated by a poet laureate; but the steady, and for the most part successful charge of this man, for some years, against the legions of Slavery, in obedience to an infinitely higher command, is as much more memorable than that, as an intelligent and con-scientious man is superior to a machine. Do you think that that will go unsung?

"Served him right"—"A dangerous man"—"He is un-doubtedly insane." So they proceed to live their sane, and wise, and altogether admirable lives, reading their Plutarch a little, but chiefly pausing at that feat of Putnam, who was let down into a wolf's den; and in this wise they nourish themselves for brave and patriotic deeds some time or other. The Tract Society could afford to print that story of Putnam. You might open the district schools with the reading of it, for there is nothing about Slavery or the Church in it; unless it occurs to the reader that some pastors are *wolves* in sheep's clothing. "The American Board of Commissioners for Foreign Missions" even, might dare to protest against *that* wolf. I have heard of boards, and of American boards, but it chances that I never heard of this particular lumber till lately. And yet I hear of Northern men, women, and children, by families, buying a "life membership" in such societies as these;—a life-membership in the grave! You can get buried cheaper than that.

Our foes are in our midst and all about us. There is hardly a house but is divided against itself, for our foe is the all but universal woodenness of both head and heart, the want of vitality in man, which is the effect of our vice; and hence are begotten fear, superstition, bigotry, persecution, and slavery of all kinds. We are mere figure-heads upon a hulk, with livers in the place of hearts. The curse is the worship of idols, which at length changes the worshipper into a stone image himself; and the New Englander is just as much an idolater as the Hindoo. This man was an exception, for he did not set up even a political graven image between him and his God.

A church that can never have done with excommunicating Christ while it exists! Away with your broad and flat churches, and your narrow and tall churches! Take a step forward, and invent a new style of out-houses. Invent a salt that will save you, and defend our nostrils.

The modern Christian is a man who has consented to say all the prayers in the liturgy, provided you will let him go straight to bed and sleep quietly afterward. All his prayers begin with "Now I lay me down to sleep," and he is forever looking forward to the time when he shall go to his "*long* rest." He has consented to perform certain old established charities, too, after a fashion, but he does not wish to hear of any new-fangled ones; he doesn't wish to have any supplementary articles added to the contract, to fit it to the present time. He shows the whites of his eyes on the Sabbath, and the blacks all the rest of the week. The evil is not merely a stagnation of blood, but a stagnation of spirit. Many, no doubt, are well disposed, but sluggish by constitution and by habit, and they cannot conceive of a man who is actuated by higher motives than they are. Accordingly they pronounce this man insane, for they know that *they* could never act as he does, as long as they are themselves.

We dream of foreign countries, of other times and races of men, placing them at a distance in history or space; but let some significant event like the present occur in our midst, and we discover, often, this distance and this strangeness between us and our nearest neighbors. *They* are our Austrias, and Chinas, and South Sea Islands. Our crowded society becomes well spaced all at once, clean and handsome to the eye, a city of magnificent distances. We discover why it was that we never got beyond compliments and surfaces with them before; we become aware of as many versts between us and them as there are between a wandering Tartar and a Chinese town. The thoughtful man becomes a hermit in the thoroughfares of the market-place. Impassable seas suddenly find their level between us, or dumb steppes stretch themselves out there. It is the difference of constitution, of intelligence, and faith, and not streams and mountains, that make the true and impassable boundaries between individuals and between states. None but the like-minded can come plenipotentiary to our court.

I read all the newspapers I could get within a week after this event, and I do not remember in them a single expression of sympathy for these men. I have since seen one noble statement, in a Boston paper, not editorial. Some voluminous sheets decided not to print the full report of Brown's words to the exclusion of other matter. It was as if a publisher should reject the manuscript of the New Testament, and print Wilson's last speech. The same journal which contained this pregnant news, was chiefly filled, in parallel columns, with the reports of the political conventions that were being held. But the descent to them was too steep. They should have been spared this contrast, been printed in an extra at least. To turn from the voices and deeds of earnest men to the *cackling* of political conventions! Office seekers and speech-makers, who do not so much as lay an honest egg, but wear their breasts bare upon an egg of chalk! Their great game is the game of straws, or rather that universal aboriginal game of the platter, at which the Indians cried *hub, hub!* Exclude the reports of religious and political conventions, and publish the words of a living man.

But I object not so much to what they have omitted as to what they have inserted. Even the *Liberator* called it "a misguided, wild, and apparently insane . . . effort." As for the herd of newspapers and magazines, I do not chance to know an editor in the country who will deliberately print anything which he knows will ultimately and permanently reduce the number of his subscribers. They do not believe that it would be expedient. How then can they print truth? If we do not say pleasant things, they argue, nobody will attend to us. And so they do like some travelling auctioneers, who sing an obscene song in order to draw a crowd around them. Republican editors, obliged to get their sentences ready for the morning edition, and accustomed to look at every thing by the twilight of politics, express no admiration, nor true sorrow even, but call these men "deluded fanatics"—"mistaken men"—"insane," or "crazed." It suggests what a *sane* set of editors we are blessed with, *not* "mistaken men"; who know very well on which side their bread is buttered, at least.

A man does a brave and humane deed, and at once, on all sides, we hear people and parties declaring, "I didn't do it, nor countenance *him* to do it, in any conceivable way. It can't be fairly inferred from my past career." I, for one, am not interested to hear you define your position. I don't know that I ever was, or ever shall be. I think it is mere egotism, or impertinent at this time. Ye needn't take so much pains to wash your skirts of him. No intelligent man will ever be convinced that he was any creature of yours. He went and came, as he himself informs us, "under the auspices of John Brown and nobody else." The Republican party does not perceive how many his *failure* will make to vote more correctly than they would have

them. They have counted the votes of Pennsylvania & Co.,
but they have not correctly counted Captain Brown's vote. He
has taken the wind out of their sails, the little wind they had,
and they may as well lie to and repair.

What though he did not belong to your clique! Though
you may not approve of his method or his principles, recognize his magnanimity. Would you not like to claim kindredship with him in that, though in no other thing he is like, or
likely, to you? Do you think that you would lose your reputation so? What you lost at the spile, you would gain at the
bung.

If they do not mean all this, then they do not speak the
truth, and say what they mean. They are simply at their old
tricks still.

"It was always conceded to him," *says one who calls him
crazy*, "that he was a conscientious man, very modest in his
demeanor, apparently inoffensive, until the subject of Slavery
was introduced, when he would exhibit a feeling of indignation unparalleled."

The slave-ship is on her way, crowded with its dying victims; new cargoes are being added in mid ocean; a small crew
of slaveholders, countenanced by a large body of passengers,
is smothering four millions under the hatches, and yet the
politician asserts that the only proper way by which deliverance is to be obtained, is by "the quiet diffusion of the sentiments of humanity," without any "outbreak." As if the
sentiments of humanity were ever found unaccompanied by
its deeds, and you could disperse them, all finished to order,
the pure article, as easily as water with a watering-pot, and
so lay the dust. What is that that I hear cast overboard? The
bodies of the dead that have found deliverance. That is the
way we are "diffusing" humanity, and its sentiments with it.

Prominent and influential editors, accustomed to deal with
politicians, men of an infinitely lower grade, say, in their ignorance, that he acted "on the principle of revenge." They do
not know the man. They must enlarge themselves to conceive
of him. I have no doubt that the time will come when they
will begin to see him as he was. They have got to conceive of
a man of faith and of religious principle, and not a politician
or an Indian; of a man who did not wait till he was personally

interfered with, or thwarted in some harmless business, before he gave his life to the cause of the oppressed.

If Walker may be considered the representative of the South, I wish I could say that Brown was the representative of the North. He was a superior man. He did not value his bodily life in comparison with ideal things. He did not recognize unjust human laws, but resisted them as he was bid. For once we are lifted out of the trivialness and dust of politics into the region of truth and manhood. No man in America has ever stood up so persistently and effectively for the dignity of human nature, knowing himself for a man, and the equal of any and all governments. In that sense he was the most American of us all. He needed no babbling lawyer, making false issues, to defend him. He was more than a match for all the judges that American voters, or office-holders of whatever grade, can create. He could not have been tried by a jury of his peers, because his peers did not exist. When a man stands up serenely against the condemnation and vengeance of mankind, rising above them literally *by a whole body*,—even though he were of late the vilest murderer, who has settled that matter with himself,—the spectacle is a sublime one,—didn't ye know it, ye Liberators, ye Tribunes, ye Republicans?—and we become criminal in comparison. Do yourselves the honor to recognize him. He needs none of your respect.

As for the Democratic journals, they are not human enough to affect me at all. I do not feel indignation at any thing they may say.

I am aware that I anticipate a little, that he was still, at the last accounts, alive in the hands of his foes; but that being the case, I have all along found myself thinking and speaking of him as physically dead.

I do not believe in erecting statues to those who still live in our hearts, whose bones have not yet crumbled in the earth around us, but I would rather see the statue of Captain Brown in the Massachusetts State-House yard, than that of any other man whom I know. I rejoice that I live in this age—that I am his contemporary.

What a contrast, when we turn to that political party which is so anxiously shuffling him and his plot out of its way, and

looking around for some available slaveholder, perhaps, to be
its candidate, at least for one who will execute the Fugitive
Slave Law, and all those other unjust laws which he took up
arms to annul!

Insane! A father and six sons, and one son-in-law, and several more men besides,—as many at least as twelve disciples,—
all struck with insanity at once; while the sane tyrant holds with
a firmer gripe than ever his four millions of slaves, and a thousand sane editors, his abettors, are saving their country and
their bacon! Just as insane were his efforts in Kansas. Ask the
tyrant who is his most dangerous foe, the sane man or the insane. Do the thousands who know him best, who have rejoiced
at his deeds in Kansas, and have afforded him material aid
there, think him insane? Such a use of this word is a mere trope
with most who persist in using it, and I have no doubt that
many of the rest have already in silence retracted their words.

Read his admirable answers to Mason and others. How
they are dwarfed and defeated by the contrast! On the one
side, half brutish, half timid questioning; on the other, truth,
clear as lightning, crashing into their obscene temples. They
are made to stand with Pilate, and Gessler, and the
Inquisition. How ineffectual their speech and action! and
what a void their silence! They are but helpless tools in this
great work. It was no human power that gathered them about
this preacher.

What have Massachusetts and the North sent a few *sane*
representatives to Congress for, of late years?—to declare with
effect what kind of sentiments? All their speeches put together
and boiled down,—and probably they themselves will confess
it,—do not match for manly directness and force, and for simple truth, the few casual remarks of crazy John Brown, on the
floor of the Harper's Ferry engine house;—that man whom
you are about to hang, to send to the other world, though
not to represent *you* there. No, he was not our representative
in any sense. He was too fair a specimen of a man to represent the like of us. Who, then, *were* his constituents? If you
read his words understandingly you will find out. In his case
there is no idle eloquence, no made, nor maiden speech, no
compliments to the oppressor. Truth is his inspirer, and
earnestness the polisher of his sentences. He could afford to

lose his Sharps' rifles, while he retained his faculty of speech, a Sharps' rifle of infinitely surer and longer range.

And the *New York Herald* reports the conversation "*verbatim*"! It does not know of what undying words it is made the vehicle.

I have no respect for the penetration of any man who can read the report of that conversation, and still call the principal in it insane. It has the ring of a saner sanity than an ordinary discipline and habits of life, than an ordinary organization, secure. Take any sentence of it—"Any questions that I can honorably answer, I will; not otherwise. So far as I am myself concerned, I have told every thing truthfully. I value my word, sir." The few who talk about his vindictive spirit, while they really admire his heroism, have no test by which to detect a noble man, no amalgam to combine with his pure gold. They mix their own dross with it.

It is a relief to turn from these slanders to the testimony of his more truthful, but frightened, jailers and hangmen. Governor Wise speaks far more justly and appreciatingly of him than any Northern editor, or politician, or public personage, that I chance to have heard from. I know that you can afford to hear him again on this subject. He says: "They are themselves mistaken who take him to be a madman. . . . He is cool, collected, and indomitable, and it is but just to him to say, that he was humane to his prisoners. . . . And he inspired me with great trust in his integrity as a man of truth. He is a fanatic, vain and garrulous," (I leave that part to Mr. Wise) "but firm, truthful, and intelligent. His men, too, who survive, are like him. . . . Colonel Washington says that he was the coolest and firmest man he ever saw in defying danger and death. With one son dead by his side, and another shot through, he felt the pulse of his dying son with one hand, and held his rifle with the other, and commanded his men with the utmost composure, encouraging them to be firm, and to sell their lives as dear as they could. Of the three white prisoners, Brown, Stevens, and Coppoc, it was hard to say which was most firm. . . ."

Almost the first Northern men whom the slaveholder has learned to respect!

The testimony of Mr. Vallandigham, though less valuable,

is of the same purport, that "it is vain to underrate either the man or his conspiracy. . . . He is the farthest possible remove from the ordinary ruffian, fanatic, or madman."

"All is quiet at Harper's Ferry," say the journals. What is the character of that calm which follows when the law and the slaveholder prevail? I regard this event as a touchstone designed to bring out, with glaring distinctness, the character of this government. We needed to be thus assisted to see it by the light of history. It needed to see itself. When a government puts forth its strength on the side of injustice, as ours to maintain Slavery and kill the liberators of the slave, it reveals itself a merely brute force, or worse, a demoniacal force. It is the head of the Plug Uglies. It is more manifest than ever that tyranny rules. I see this government to be effectually allied with France and Austria in oppressing mankind. There sits a tyrant holding fettered four millions of slaves; here comes their heroic liberator. This most hypocritical and diabolical government looks up from its seat on the gasping four millions, and inquires with an assumption of innocence, "What do you assault me for? Am I not an honest man? Cease agitation on this subject, or I will make a slave of you, too, or else hang you."

We talk about a *representative* government; but what a monster of a government is that where the noblest faculties of the mind, and the *whole* heart, are not *represented*. A semi-human tiger or ox, stalking over the earth, with its heart taken out and the top of its brain shot away. Heroes have fought well on their stumps when their legs were shot off, but I never heard of any good done by such a government as that.

The only government that I recognize,—and it matters not how few are at the head of it, or how small its army,—is that power that establishes justice in the land, never that which establishes injustice. What shall we think of a government to which all the truly brave and just men in the land are enemies, standing between it and those whom it oppresses? A government that pretends to be Christian and crucifies a million Christs every day!

Treason! Where does such treason take its rise? I cannot help thinking of you as you deserve, ye governments. Can you dry up the fountains of thought? High treason, when it is resistance to tyranny here below, has its origin in, and is first committed by the power that makes and forever recreates man. When you have caught and hung all these human rebels, you have accomplished nothing but your own guilt, for you have not struck at the fountain head. You presume to contend with a foe against whom West Point cadets and rifled cannon *point* not. Can all the art of the cannon-founder tempt matter to turn against its maker? Is the form in which the founder thinks he casts it more essential than the constitution of it and of himself?

The United States have a coffle of four millions of slaves. They are determined to keep them in this condition; and Massachusetts is one of the confederated overseers to prevent their escape. Such are not all the inhabitants of Massachusetts, but such are they who rule and are obeyed here. It was Massachusetts, as well as Virginia, that put down this insurrection at Harper's Ferry. She sent the marines there, and she will have to pay the penalty of her sin.

Suppose that there is a society in this State that out of its own purse and magnanimity saves all the fugitive slaves that run to us, and protects our colored fellow-citizens, and leaves the other work to the Government, so-called. Is not that government fast losing its occupation, and becoming contemptible to mankind? If private men are obliged to perform the offices of government, to protect the weak and dispense justice, then the government becomes only a hired man, or clerk, to perform menial or indifferent services. Of course, that is but the shadow of a government whose existence necessitates a Vigilant Committee. What should we think of the oriental Cadi even, behind whom worked in secret a Vigilant Committee? But such is the character of our Northern States generally; each has its Vigilant Committee. And, to a certain extent, these crazy governments recognize and accept this relation. They say, virtually, "We'll be glad to work for you on these terms, only don't make a noise about it." And thus the government, its salary being insured, withdraws into the back shop, taking the constitution with it, and bestows most of its labor on repairing that. When I hear it at work sometimes, as I go by, it reminds me, at best, of those farmers who in winter contrive to turn a penny by following the cooping business. And what kind of spirit is their barrel made to hold? They speculate in stocks, and bore holes in mountains, but they are not competent to lay out even a decent highway. The only *free* road, the Underground Railroad, is owned and managed by the Vigilant Committee. *They* have tunnelled under the whole breadth of the land. Such a government is losing its power and respectability as surely as water runs out of a leaky vessel, and is held by one that can contain it.

I hear many condemn these men because they were so few. When were the good and the brave ever in a majority? Would you have had him wait till that time came?—till you and I came over to him? The very fact that he had no rabble or troop of hirelings about him would alone distinguish him from ordinary heroes. His company was small indeed, because few could be found worthy to pass muster. Each one who there laid down his life for the poor and oppressed, was a picked man, called out of many thousands, if not millions; apparently a man of principle, of rare courage and devoted humanity, ready to sacrifice his life at any moment for the benefit of his fellow man. It may be doubted if there were as many more their equals in these respects in all the country—I speak of his followers only—for their leader, no doubt, scoured the land far and wide, seeking to swell his troop. These alone were ready to step between the oppressor and the oppressed. Surely, they were the very best men you could select to be hung. That was the greatest compliment which this country could pay them. They were ripe for her gallows. She has tried a long time, she has hung a good many, but never found the right one before.

When I think of him, and his six sons, and his son in law,—not to enumerate the others,—enlisted for this fight; proceeding coolly, reverently, humanely to work, for months if not years, sleeping and waking upon it, summering and wintering the thought, without expecting any reward but a good conscience, while almost all America stood ranked on the other side, I say again that it affects me as a sublime spectacle. If he had had any journal advocating *"his cause,"* any organ as the phrase is, monotonously and wearisomely playing the same old tune, and then passing round the hat, it would have been fatal to his efficiency. If he had acted in any way so as to be let alone by the government, he might have been suspected. It was the fact that the tyrant must give place to him, or he to the tyrant, that distinguished him from all the reformers of the day that I know.

It was his peculiar doctrine that a man has a perfect right to interfere by force with the slaveholder, in order to rescue the slave. I agree with him. They who are continually shocked by slavery have some right to be shocked by the violent death of the slaveholder, but no others. Such will be more shocked by his life than by his death. I shall not be forward to think him mistaken in his method who quickest succeeds to liberate the slave. I speak for the slave when I say, that I prefer the philanthropy of Captain Brown to that philanthropy which neither shoots me nor liberates me. At any rate, I do not think it is quite sane for one to spend his whole life in talking or writing about this matter, unless he is continuously inspired, and I have not done so. A man may have other affairs to attend to. I do not wish to kill nor to be killed, but I can foresee circumstances in which both these things would be by me unavoidable. We preserve the so-called "peace" of our community by deeds of petty violence every day. Look at the policeman's billy and hand cuffs! Look at the jail! Look at the gallows! Look at the chaplain of the regiment! We are hoping only to live safely on the outskirts of *this* provisional army. So we defend ourselves and our hen roosts, and maintain slavery. I know that the mass of my countrymen think that the only righteous use that can be made of Sharps' rifles and revolvers is to fight duels with them, when we are insulted by other nations, or to hunt Indians, or shoot fugitive slaves with them, or the like. I think that for once the Sharps' rifles and the revolvers were employed in a righteous cause. The tools were in the hands of one who could use them.

The same indignation that is said to have cleared the temple once will clear it again. The question is not about the weapon, but the spirit in which you use it. No man has appeared in America as yet who loved his fellow man so well, and treated him so tenderly. He lived for him. He took up his life and he laid it down for him. What sort of violence is that which is encouraged, not by soldiers but by peaceable citizens, not so much by lay-men as by ministers of the gospel, not so much by the fighting sects as by the Quakers, and not so much by Quaker men as by Quaker women?

This event advertises me that there is such a fact as death—the possibility of a man's dying. It seems as if no man had ever died in America before, for in order to die you must first have lived. I don't believe in the hearses and palls and funerals that they have had. There was no death in the case, because there had been no life; they merely rotted or sloughed off, pretty much as they had rotted or sloughed along. No temple's vail was rent, only a hole dug somewhere. Let the dead bury their dead. The best of them fairly ran down like a clock. Franklin—Washington—they were let off without dying; they were merely missing one day. I hear a good many pretend that they are going to die;—or that they have died for aught that I know. Nonsense! I'll defy them to do it. They haven't got life enough in them. They'll deliquesce like fungi, and keep a hundred eulogists mopping the spot where they left off. Only half a dozen or so have died since the world began. Do you think that you are going to die, sir? No! there's no hope of you. You haven't got your lesson yet. You've got to stay after school. We make a needless ado about capital punishment—taking lives, when there is no life to take. *Memento mori!* We don't understand that sublime sentence which some worthy got sculptured on his gravestone once. We've interpreted it in a grovelling and snivelling sense; we've wholly forgotten how to die.

But be sure you do die, neverthless. Do your work, and finish it. If you know how to begin, you will know when to end.

These men, in teaching us how to die, have at the same time taught us how to live. If this man's acts and words do not create a revival, it will be the severest possible satire on the acts and words that do. It is the best news that America has ever heard. It has already quickened the feeble pulse of the North, and infused more and more generous blood into her veins and heart, than any number of years of what is called commercial and political prosperity could. How many a man who was lately contemplating suicide has now something to live for!

One writer says that Brown's peculiar monomania made him to be "dreaded by the Missourians as a supernatural being." Sure enough, a hero in the midst of us cowards is always so dreaded. He is just that thing. He shows himself superior to nature. He has a spark of divinity in him.

> "Unless above himself he can
> Erect himself, how poor a thing is man!"

Newspaper editors argue also that it is a proof of his *insanity* that he thought he was appointed to do this work which he did—that he did not suspect himself for a moment! They talk as if it were impossible that a man could be "divinely appointed" in these days to do any work whatever; as if vows and religion were out of date as connected with any man's daily work,—as if the agent to abolish Slavery could only be somebody appointed by the President, or by some political party. They talk as if a man's death were a failure, and his continued life, be it of whatever character, were a success.

When I reflect to what a cause this man devoted himself, and how religiously, and then reflect to what cause his judges and all who condemn him so angrily and fluently devote themselves, I see that they are as far apart as the heavens and earth are asunder.

The amount of it is, our *"leading men"* are a harmless kind of folk, and they know *well enough* that *they* were not divinely appointed, but elected by the votes of their party.

Who is it whose safety requires that Captain Brown be hung? Is it indispensable to any Northern man? Is there no resource but to cast these men also to the Minotaur? If you do not wish it say so distinctly. While these things are being done, beauty stands veiled and music is a screeching lie. Think of him—of his rare qualities! such a man as it takes ages to make, and ages to understand; no mock hero, nor the representative of any party. A man such as the sun may not rise upon again in this benighted land. To whose making went the costliest material, the finest adamant; sent to be the redeemer of those in captivity. And the only use to which you can put him is to hang him at the end of a rope! You who pretend to care for Christ crucified, consider what you are about to do to him who offered himself to be the savior of four millions of men.

Any man knows when he is justified, and all the wits in the world cannot enlighten him on that point. The murderer always knows that he is justly punished; but when a government takes the life of a man without the consent of his conscience, it is an audacious government, and is taking a step towards its own dissolution. Is it not possible that an individual may be right and a government wrong? Are laws to be enforced simply because they were made? or declared by any number of men to be good, if they are *not* good? Is there any necessity for a man's being a tool to perform a deed of which his better nature disapproves? Is it the intention of lawmakers that *good* men shall be hung ever? Are judges to interpret the law according to the letter, and not the spirit? What right have *you* to enter into a compact with yourself that you *will* do thus or so, against the light within you? Is it for *you* to *make up* your mind—to form any resolution whatever—and not accept the convictions that are forced upon you, and which ever pass your understanding? I do not believe in lawyers, in that mode of attacking or defending a man, because you descend to meet the judge on his own ground, and, in cases of the highest importance, it is of no consequence whether a man breaks a human law or not. Let lawyers decide trivial cases. Business men may arrange that among themselves. If they were the interpreters of the everlasting laws which rightfully bind man, that would be another thing. A counterfeiting law-factory, standing half in a slave land and half in a free! What kind of laws for free men can you expect from that?

I am here to plead his cause with you. I plead not for his life, but for his character—his immortal life; and so it becomes your cause wholly, and is not his in the least. Some eighteen hundred years ago Christ was crucified; this morning, perchance, Captain Brown was hung. These are the two ends of a chain which is not without its links. He is not Old Brown any longer; he is an Angel of Light.

I see now that it was necessary that the bravest and humanest man in all the country should be hung. Perhaps he saw it himself. I *almost fear* that I may yet hear of his deliverance, doubting if a prolonged life, if *any* life, can do as much good as his death.

"Misguided"! "Garrulous"! "Insane"! "Vindictive"! So ye write in your easy chairs, and thus he wounded responds from the floor of the Armory, clear as a cloudless sky, true as the voice of nature is: "No man sent me here; it was my own prompting and that of my Maker. I acknowledge no master in human form."

And in what a sweet and noble strain he proceeds, addressing his captors, who stand over him: "I think, my friends, you are guilty of a great wrong against God and humanity, and it would be perfectly right for any one to interfere with you so far as to free those you wilfully and wickedly hold in bondage."

And referring to his movement: "It is, in my opinion, the greatest service a man can render to God."

"I pity the poor in bondage that have none to help them; that is why I am here; not to gratify any personal animosity, revenge, or vindictive spirit. It is my sympathy with the oppressed and the wronged, that are as good as you, and as precious in the sight of God."

You don't know your testament when you see it.

"I want you to understand that I respect the rights of the poorest and weakest of colored people, oppressed by the slave power, just as much as I do those of the most wealthy and powerful."

"I wish to say, furthermore, that you had better, all you people at the South, prepare yourselves for a settlement of that question, that must come up for settlement sooner than you are prepared for it. The sooner you are prepared the better. You may dispose of me very easily. I am nearly disposed of now; but this question is still to be settled—this negro question, I mean; the end of that is not yet."

I foresee the time when the painter will paint that scene, no longer going to Rome for a subject; the poet will sing it; the historian record it; and, with the Landing of the Pilgrims and the Declaration of Independence, it will be the ornament of some future national gallery, when at least the present form of Slavery shall be no more here. We shall then be at liberty to weep for Captain Brown. Then, and not till then, we will take our revenge.

Martyrdom of John Brown

So universal and widely related is any transcendent moral greatness—so nearly identical with greatness every where and in every age, as a pyramid contracts the nearer you approach its apex—that, when I now look over my commonplace book of poetry, I find that the best of it is oftenest applicable, in part or wholly, to the case of Captain Brown. Only what is true, and strong, and solemnly earnest will recommend itself to our mood at this time. Almost any noble verse may be read, either as his elegy, or eulogy, or be made the text of an oration on him. Indeed, such are now discerned to be the parts of a universal liturgy, applicable to those rare cases of heroes and martyrs, for which the ritual of no church has provided. This is the formula established on high,—their burial service—to which every great genius has contributed its stanza or line. As Marvell wrote,

> "When the sword glitters o'er the judge's head,
> And fear has coward churchmen silenced,
> Then is the poet's time; 'tis then he draws,
> And single fights forsaken virtue's cause.
> He when the wheel of empire whirleth back,
> And though the world's disjointed axel crack,
> Sings still of ancient rights and better times,
> Seeks suff'ring good, arraigns successful crimes."

The sense of grand poetry, read by the light of this event, is brought out distinctly, like an invisible writing held to the fire.

> "All heads must come
> To the cold tomb,
> Only the actions of the just
> Smell sweet and blossom in the dust."

We have heard that the Boston lady who recently visited our hero in prison found him wearing still the clothes all cut and torn by sabres and by bayonet thrusts, in which he had been taken prisoner; and thus he had gone to his trial, and without a hat. She spent her time in the prison mending those clothes, and, for a memento, brought home a pin covered with blood.—What are the clothes that endure?

> "The garments lasting evermore
>   Are works of mercy to the poor;
> And neither tetter, time, nor moth
>   Shall fray that silk, or fret this cloth."

The well known verses called "The Soul's Errand," supposed, by some, to have been written by Sir Walter Raleigh, when he was expecting to be executed the following day, are at least worthy of such an origin, and are equally applicable to the present case. Hear them.

> Go, Soul, the body's guest,
>   Upon a thankless arrant;
> Fear not to touch the best,
>   The truth shall be thy warrant:
>   Go, since I needs must die,
>   And give the world the lie.
>
> Go, tell the court it glows
>   And shines like rotten wood;
> Go, tell the church it shows
>   What's good, and doth no good;
>   If church and court reply,
>   Then give them both the lie.
>
> Tell potentates they live
>   Acting by others' actions;
> Not loved unless they give,
>   Not strong but by their factions:
>   If potentates reply,
>   Give potentates the lie.
>
> Tell men of high condition,
>   That rule affairs of state,
> Their purpose is ambition,
>   Their practice only hate;
>   And if they once reply,
>   Then give them all the lie.

Tell zeal, it lacks devotion;
　Tell love, it is but lust;
Tell time, it is but motion;
　Tell flesh, it is but dust;
　　And wish them not reply,
　　For thou must give the lie.

Tell age, it daily wasteth;
　Tell honor, how it alters;
Tell beauty, how she blasteth;
　Tell favor, how she falters;
　　And as they shall reply,
　　Give each of them the lie.

Tell fortune of her blindness;
　Tell nature of decay;
Tell friendship of unkindness;
　Tell justice of delay;
　　And if they dare reply,
　　Then give them all the lie.

And when thou hast, as I
　Commanded thee, done blabbing,
Although to give the lie
　Deserves no less than stabbing,
　　Yet stab at thee who will,
　　No stab the soul can kill.

"When I am dead,
　Let not the day be writ—"
Nor bell be tolled—*
　　"Love will remember it"
When hate is cold.

You, Agricola, are fortunate, not only because your life was
glorious, but because your death was timely. As they tell
us who heard your last words, unchanged and willing you

---

*The selectmen of the town refused to allow the bell to be tolled on this
occasion.

accepted your fate; as if, as far as in your power, you would make the emperor appear innocent. But, besides the bitterness of having lost a parent, it adds to our grief, that it was not permitted us to minister to your health, . . . to gaze on your countenance, and receive your last embrace; surely, we might have caught some words and commands which we could have treasured in the inmost part of our souls. This is our pain, this our wound. . . . You were buried with the fewer tears, and in your last earthly light, your eyes looked around for something which they did not see.

If there is any abode for the spirits of the pious; if, as wise men suppose, great souls are not extinguished with the body, may you rest placidly, and call your family from weak regrets, and womanly laments, to the contemplation of your virtues, which must not be lamented, either silently or aloud. Let us honor you by our admiration, rather than by short-lived praises, and, if nature aid us, by our emulation of you. That is true honor, that the piety of whoever is most akin to you. This also I would teach your family, so to venerate your memory, as to call to mind all your actions and words, and embrace your character and the form of your soul, rather than of your body; not because I think that statues which are made of marble or brass are to be condemned, but as the features of men, so images of the features, are frail and perishable. The form of the soul is eternal; and this we can retain and express, not by a foreign material and art, but by our own lives. Whatever of Agricola we have loved, whatever we have admired, remains, and will remain, in the minds of men, and the records of history, through the eternity of ages. For oblivion will overtake many of the ancients, as if they were inglorious and ignoble: Agricola, described and transmitted to posterity, will survive.

The Last Days of John Brown

JOHN BROWN'S career for the last six weeks of his life was meteor-like, flashing through the darkness in which we live. I know of nothing so miraculous in our history.

If any person, in a lecture or conversation at that time, cited any ancient example of heroism, such as Cato or Tell or Winkelried, passing over the recent deeds and words of Brown, it was felt by any intelligent audience of Northern men to be tame and inexcusably far-fetched.

For my own part, I commonly attend more to nature than to man, but any affecting human event may blind our eyes to natural objects. I was so absorbed in him as to be surprised whenever I detected the routine of the natural world surviving still, or met persons going about their affairs indifferent. It appeared strange to me that the 'little dipper' should be still diving quietly in the river, as of yore; and it suggested that this bird might continue to dive here when Concord should be no more.

I felt that he, a prisoner in the midst of his enemies, and under sentence of death, if consulted as to his next step or resource, could answer more wisely than all his countrymen beside. He best understood his position; he contemplated it most calmly. Comparatively, all other men, North and South, were beside themselves. Our thoughts could not revert to any greater or wiser or better man with whom to contrast him, for he, then and there, was above them all. The man this country was about to hang appeared the greatest and best in it.

Years were not required for a revolution of public opinion; days, nay, hours, produced marked changes in this case. Fifty who were ready to say on going into our meeting in honor of him in Concord, that he ought to be hung, would not say it when they came out. They heard his words read, they saw the earnest faces of the congregation; and perhaps they joined at last in singing the hymn in his praise.

The order of instructors was reversed. I heard that one preacher, who at first was shocked and stood aloof, felt obliged at last, after he was hung, to make him the subject of a sermon, in which, to some extent, he eulogized the man, but said that his act was a failure. An influential class-teacher thought it necessary, after the services, to tell his grown-up pupils, that at first he thought as the preacher did then, but now he thought that John Brown was right. But it was understood that his pupils were as much ahead of the teacher, as he was ahead of the priest; and I know for a certainty, that very little boys at home had already asked their parents, in a tone of surprise, why God did not interfere to save him. In each case, the constituted teachers were only half conscious that they were not *leading*, but being *dragged*, with some loss of time and power.

The more conscientious preachers, the Bible men, they who talk about principle, and doing to others as you would that they should do unto you,—how could they fail to recognize him, by far the greatest preacher of them all, with the Bible in his life and in his acts, the embodiment of principle, who actually carried out the golden rule? All whose moral sense had been aroused, who had a calling from on high to preach, sided with him. What confessions he extracted from the cold and conservative! It is remarkable, but on the whole it is well, that it did not prove the occasion for a new sect of *Brownites* being formed in our midst.

They, whether within the Church or out of it, who adhere to the spirit and let go the letter, and are accordingly called infidel, were as usual foremost to recognize him. Men have been hung in the South before for attempting to rescue slaves, and the North was not much stirred by it. Whence, then, this wonderful difference? We were not so sure of *their* devotion to principle. We made a subtle distinction, forgot human laws, and did homage to an idea. The North, I mean the *living* North, was suddenly all transcendental. It went behind the human law, it went behind the apparent failure, and recognized eternal justice and glory. Commonly, men live according to a formula, and are satisfied if the order of law is observed, but in this instance they, to some extent, returned to original perceptions, and there was a slight revival of old religion. They saw that what was called order was confusion, what was called justice, injustice, and that the best was deemed the worst. This attitude suggested a more intelligent

and generous spirit than that which actuated our forefathers, and the possibility, in the course of ages, of a revolution in behalf of another and an oppressed people.

Most Northern men, and a few Southern ones, were wonderfully stirred by Brown's behavior and words. They saw and
felt that they were heroic and noble, and that there had been
nothing quite equal to them in their kind in this country, or
in the recent history of the world. But the minority were unmoved by them. They were only surprised and provoked by
the attitude of their neighbors. They saw that Brown was
Brave, and that he believed that he had done right, but they
did not detect any further peculiarity in him. Not being accustomed to make fine distinctions, or to appreciate magnanimity, they read his letters and speeches as if they read them
not. They were not aware when they approached a heroic
statement—they did not know when they *burned*. They did
not feel that he spoke with authority, and hence they only remembered that the *law* must be executed. They remembered
the old formula, but did not hear the new revelation. The
man who does not recognize in Brown's words a wisdom and
nobleness, and therefore an authority, superior to our laws, is
a modern Democrat. This is the test by which to discover
him. He is not wilfully but constitutionally blind on this side,
and he is consistent with himself. Such has been his past life;
no doubt of it. In like manner he has read history and his
Bible, and he accepts, or seems to accept, the last only as an
established formula, and not because he has been convicted
by it. You will not find kindred sentiments in his commonplace book, if he has one.

When a noble deed is done, who is likely to appreciate it?
They who are noble themselves. I was not surprised that certain of my neighbors spoke of John Brown as an ordinary
felon, for who are they? They have either much flesh, or much
office, or much coarseness of some kind. They are not etherial natures in any sense. The dark qualities predominate in
them. Several of them are decidedly pachydermatous. I say it
in sorrow, not in anger. How can a man behold the light, who
has no answering inward light? They are true to their *right*,
but when they look this way they *see* nothing, they are blind.
For the children of the light to contend with them is as if

there should be a contest between eagles and owls. Show me a man who feels bitterly toward John Brown, and let me hear what noble verse he can repeat. He'll be as dumb as if his lips were stone.

It is not every man who can be a Christian, even in a very moderate sense, whatever education you give him. It is a matter of constitution and temperament, after all. He may have to be born again many times. I have known many a man who pretended to be a Christian, in whom it was ridiculous, for he had no genius for it. It is not every man who can be a freeman, even.

Editors persevered for a good while in saying that Brown was crazy: but at last they said only that it was 'a crazy scheme,' and the only evidence brought to prove it was that it cost him his life. I have no doubt that if he had gone with five thousand men, liberated a thousand slaves, killed a hundred or two slaveholders, and had as many more killed on his own side, but not lost his own life, these same editors would have called it by a more respectable name. Yet he has been far more successful than that. He has liberated many thousands of slaves, both North and South. They seem to have known nothing about living or dying for a principle. They all called him crazy then; who calls him crazy now?

All through the excitement occasioned by his remarkable attempt and subsequent behavior, the Massachusetts Legislature, not taking any steps for the defence of her citizens who were likely to be carried to Virginia as witnesses and exposed to the violence of a slaveholding mob, was wholly absorbed in a liquor-agency question, and indulging in poor jokes on the word 'extension.' Bad spirits occupied their thoughts. I am sure that no statesman up to the occasion could have attended to that question at all at that time,—a very vulgar question to attend to at any time.

When I looked into a liturgy of the Church of England, printed near the end of the last century, in order to find a service applicable to the case of Brown, I found that the only martyr recognized and provided for by it was King Charles the First, an eminent scamp. Of all the inhabitants of England and of the world, he was the only one according to this authority, whom that church had made a martyr and saint of;

and for more than a century it had celebrated his martyrdom, so called, by an annual service. What a satire on the Church is that!

Look not to legislatures and churches for your guidance, nor to any soulless, *incorporated* bodies, but to *inspirited* or inspired ones.

What avail all your scholarly accomplishments and learning, compared with wisdom and manhood? To omit his other behavior, see what a work this comparatively unread and unlettered man wrote within six weeks. Where is our professor of *belles lettres* or of logic and rhetoric, who can write so well? He wrote in prison, not a history of the world, like Raleigh, but an American book which I think will live longer than that. I do not know of such words, uttered under such circumstances, and so copiously withal, in Roman or English or any history. What a variety of themes he touched on in that short space! There are words in that letter to his wife, respecting the education of his daughters, which deserve to be framed and hung over every mantlepiece in the land. Compare this earnest wisdom with that of Poor Richard.

The death of Irving, which at any other time would have attracted universal attention, having occurred while these things were transpiring, went almost unobserved. I shall have to read of it in the biography of authors.

Literary gentlemen, editors and critics, think that they know how to write, because they have studied grammar and rhetoric; but they are egregiously mistaken. The *art* of composition is as simple as the discharge of a bullet from a rifle, and its master-pieces imply an infinitely greater force behind them. This unlettered man's speaking and writing are standard English. Some words and phrases deemed vulgarisms and Americanisms before, he has made standard American; such as *'It will pay.'* It suggests that the one great rule of composition—and if I were a professor of rhetoric, I should insist on this—is to *speak the truth*. This first, this second, this third; pebbles in your mouth or not. This demands earnestness and manhood chiefly.

We seem to have forgotten that the expression, a *liberal* education, originally meant among the Romans one worthy of *free* men; while the learning of trades and professions by which to get your livelihood merely, was considered worthy of *slaves* only. But taking a hint from the word, I would go a step further and say, that it is not the man of wealth and leisure simply, though devoted to art, or science, or literature, who, in a true sense, is *liberally* educated, but only the earnest and *free* man. In a slaveholding country like this, there can be no such thing as a *liberal* education tolerated by the State; and those scholars of Austria and France who, however learned they may be, are contented under their tyrannies, have received only a *servile* education.

Nothing could his enemies do, but it redounded to his infinite advantage—that is, to the advantage of his cause. They did not hang him at once, but reserved him to preach to them. And then there was another great blunder. They did not hang his four followers with him; that scene was still postponed; and so his victory was prolonged and completed. No theatrical manager could have arranged things so wisely to give effect to his behavior and words. And who, think you, *was* the manager? Who placed the slave woman and her child, whom he stooped to kiss for a symbol, between his prison and the gallows?

We soon saw, as he saw, that he was not to be pardoned or rescued by men. That would have been to disarm him, to restore to him a material weapon, a Sharps' rifle, when he had taken up the sword of the spirit—the sword with which he has really won his greatest and most memorable victories. Now he has not laid aside the sword of the spirit, for he is pure spirit himself, and his sword is pure spirit also.

> 'He nothing common did or mean
> Upon that memorable scene,
> Nor called the gods with vulgar spite,
> To vindicate his helpless right;
> But bowed his comely head
> Down as upon a bed.'

What a transit was that of his horizontal body alone, but just cut down from the gallows-tree! We read, that at such a time it passed through Philadelphia, and by Saturday night had reached New York. Thus, like a meteor it shot through the Union from the southern regions toward the north! No

such freight had the cars borne since they carried him southward alive.

On the day of his translation, I heard, to be sure, that he
was *hung*, but I did not know what that meant; I felt no sorrow on that account; but not for a day or two did I even *hear*
that he was *dead*, and not after any number of days shall I believe it. Of all the men who were said to be my contemporaries, it seemed to me that John Brown was the only one
who *had not died*. I never hear of a man named Brown
now,—and I hear of them pretty often,—I never hear of any
particularly brave and earnest man, but my first thought is of
John Brown, and what relation he may be to him. I meet him
at every turn. He is more alive than ever he was. He has
earned immortality. He is not confined to North Elba nor to
Kansas. He is no longer working in secret. He works in public, and in the clearest light that shines on this land.

The Succession of Forest Trees

AN ADDRESS BEFORE THE MIDDLESEX (MASS.)
AGRICULTURAL SOCIETY.

EVERY man is entitled to come to Cattle-shows, even a transcendentalist; and for my part I am more interested in the men than in the cattle. I wish to see once more those old familiar faces, whose names I do not know, which for me represent the Middlesex country, and come as near being indigenous to the soil as a white man can; the men who are not above their business, whose coats are not too black, whose shoes do not shine very much, who never wear gloves to conceal their hands. It is true there are some queer specimens of humanity attracted to our festival, but all are welcome. I am pretty sure to meet once more that weak-minded and whimsical fellow, generally weak-bodied too, who prefers a crooked stick for a cane; perfectly useless, you would say, only bizarre, fit for a cabinet, like a petrified snake. A ram's horn would be as convenient, and is yet more curiously twisted. He brings that much indulged bit of the country with him, from some town's end or other, and introduces it to Concord groves as if he had promised it so much sometime.

So some, it seems to me, elect their rulers for their crookedness. But I think that a straight stick makes the best cane, and an upright man the best ruler. Or why choose a man to do plain work who is distinguished for his "oddity?" However, I do not know but you will think that they have committed this mistake who invited me to speak to you to-day.

In my capacity of surveyor, I have often talked with some of you, my employers, at your dinner-tables, after having gone round and round and behind your farming, and ascertained exactly what its limits were. Moreover, taking a surveyor's and a naturalist's liberty, I have been in the habit of going across your lots much oftener than is usual as many of you, perhaps to your sorrow, are aware. Yet many of you, to my relief, have seemed not to be aware of it; and when I came across you in some out-of-the-way nook of your farms, have inquired, with an air of surprise, if I were not lost, since you had never seen me in that part of the town or county before; when, if the truth were known, and it had not been for betraying my secret, I might with more propriety have inquired if *you* were not lost, since I had never seen *you* there before. I have several times shown the proprietor the shortest way out of his wood-lot.

Therefore, it would seem that I have some title to speak to you to-day; and, considering what that title is, and the occasion that has called us together, I need offer no apology if I invite your attention for the few moments that are allotted me, to a purely scientific subject.

At those dinner tables referred to, I have often been asked as many of you have been, if I could tell how it happened that when a pine wood was cut down an oak one sprang up, and *vice versa*. To which I have answered, and now answer, that I can tell—that it is no mystery to me. As I am not aware that this has been clearly shown by any one, I shall lay the more stress on this point. Let me lead you back into your wood-lots again.

When a single tree or a forest springs up naturally where none of its kind grew before, I do not hesitate to say, though in some quarters still it may sound paradoxical, that it came from a seed. Of the various ways by which trees are *known* to be propagated—by transplanting, cuttings, and the like—this is the only supposable one under these circumstances. No such tree has ever been known to spring from any thing else. If any one asserts that it sprang from something else, or from nothing the burden of proof lies with him.

It remains then only to show how the seed is transported from where it grows, to where it is planted. This is done chiefly by the agency of the wind, water and animals. The lighter seeds, as those of pines and maples, are transported chiefly by wind and water; the heavier, as acorns and nuts, by animals.

In all the pines, a very thin membrane, in appearance much like an insect's wing, grows over and around the seed, and independent of it, while the latter is being developed within its base. Indeed, this is often perfectly developed though the seed is abortive, nature being, you would say, more sure to provide the means of transporting the seed, than to provide the seed to be transported. In other words, a beautiful thin sack is woven around the seed, with a handle to it such as the wind can take hold of, and it is then committed to the wind, expressly that it may transport the seed and extend the range of the species; and this it does as effectually as when seeds are sent by mail in a different kind of sack from the patent office. There is a patent office at the seat of government of the universe, whose managers are as much interested in the dispersion of seeds as any body at Washington can be, and their operations are infinitely more extensive and regular.

There is then no necessity for supposing that the pines have sprung up from nothing, and I am aware that I am not at all peculiar in asserting that they come from seeds, though the mode of their propagation *by nature* has been but little attended to. They are very extensively raised from the seed in Europe, and are beginning to be here.

When you cut down an oak wood, a pine wood will not *at once* spring up there unless there are, or have been, quite recently, seed-bearing pines near enough for the seeds to be blown from them. But, adjacent to a forest of pines, if you prevent other crops from growing there, you will surely have an extension of your pine forest, provided the soil is suitable.

As for the heavy seeds and nuts which are not furnished with wings, the notion is still a very common one that, when the trees which bear these spring up where none of their kind were noticed before, they have come from seeds or other principles spontaneously generated there in an unusual manner, or which have lain dormant in the soil for centuries, or perhaps been called into activity by the heat of a burning. I do not believe these assertions and I will state some of the ways in which, according to my observation, such forests are planted and raised.

Every one of these seeds, too, will be found to be winged or legged in another fashion. Surely it is not wonderful that cherry trees of all kinds are widely dispersed, since their fruit is well known to be the favorite feed of various birds. Many kinds are called bird-cherries and they appropriate many more kinds, which are not so called. Eating cherries is a bird-like employment, and unless we disperse the seeds occasionally as they do I shall think that the birds have the best right to them. See how artfully the seed of a cherry is placed in order that a bird may be compelled to transport it—in the very midst of a tempting pericarp, so that the creature that would devour this must commonly take the stone also into its mouth or bill. If you ever ate a cherry, and did not make two bites of it, you must have perceived it—right in the center of the luscious morsel, a large earthly residuum left on the tongue. We thus take into our mouths cherry stones as big as peas, a dozen at once, for Nature can persuade us to do almost anything when she would compass her ends. Some wild men and children instinctively swallow these, like the birds when in a hurry, as the shortest way to get rid of them. Thus, though these seeds are not provided with vegetable wings, Nature has impelled the thrush tribe to take them into their bills and fly away with them, and they are winged in another sense, and more effectually than the seeds of pines, for these are carried even against the wind. The consequence is, that cherry trees grow not only here but there. The same is true of a great many other seeds.

But to come to the observation which suggested these remarks. As I have said, I suspect that I can throw some light on the fact, that when hereabouts a dense pine wood is cut down, oaks and other hard woods may at once take its place. I have got only to show that the acorns and nuts, provided they are grown in the neighborhood, are regularly planted in such woods; for I assert that if an oak tree has not grown within ten miles, and man has not carried acorns thither, then the oak wood will not spring up at once when a pine wood is cut down.

Apparently, there were only pines there before. They are cut off, and after a year or two you see oaks and other hard woods springing up there, with scarcely a pine amid them, and the wonder commonly is how the seed could have been lying in the ground so long without decaying. But the truth is, that it has not been lying in the ground so long, but is regularly planted each year by various quadrupeds and birds.

In this neighborhood, where oaks and pines are about equally dispersed, if you look through the thickest pine wood, even the seemingly exclusive pitch-pine ones, you will commonly detect many little oaks, birches, and other hard woods sprung from seeds carried into the thicket by squirrels and other animals, and also blown thither, but which are over-shadowed and choaked by the pines. The denser the ever-green wood, the more likely it is to be well planted with these seeds, because the planters incline to resort with their forage to the closest covert. They also carry it into birch and other woods. This planting is carried on annually, and the plants annually die; but when the pines are cleared off, the oaks having got just the start they want, and now secured favorable conditions, immediately spring up to trees.

Apparently, the shade of a dense pine wood is more unfavorable to the springing up of pines than of oaks within it, though the former may come up abundantly when the pines are cut, if there chance to be sound seed in the ground.

But when you cut off a lot of hard wood, very often the little pines mixed with it, have a similar start, for the squirrels have carried off the nuts to the pines and not to the more open wood, and they commonly make pretty clean work of it—to say nothing about the soil being, in a measure, exhausted for the same kind of crop.

If a pine wood is surrounded by a white oak one chiefly, white oak may be expected to succeed when the pines are cut. If it is surrounded instead by an edging of shrub oaks, then you will probably have a dense shrub-oak thicket.

I have no time to go into details, but will say, in a word, that while the wind is conveying the seeds of pines into hard woods and open lands, the squirrels and other animals are conveying the seeds of oaks and walnuts into the pine woods, and thus a rotation of crops is kept up.

I affirmed this confidently many years ago, and an occasional examination of dense pine woods confirmed me in my opinion. It has long been known to observers that squirrels bury nuts in the ground, but I am not aware that any one has thus accounted for the regular succession of forests.

On the 24th of September, in '57, as I was paddling down the Assabet, in this town, I saw a red squirrel run along the bank under some herbage, with something large in its mouth. It stopped near the foot of a hemlock, within a couple of rods of me, and, hastily pawing a hole with its fore feet, dropped its booty into it and covered it up and retreated part way up the trunk of the tree. As I approached the shore to examine

the deposit, the squirrel, descending part way, betrayed no little anxiety about its treasure, and made two or three motions
to recover it before it finally retreated. Digging there, I found
two green pig nuts joined together, with the thick husks on,
buried about an inch and a half under the reddish soil of decayed hemlock leaves, just the right depth to plant it. In
short, this squirrel was then engaged in accomplishing two
objects, to wit, laying up a store of Winter food for itself, and
planting a hickory wood for all creation. If the squirrel was
killed, or neglected its deposit, a hickory would spring up.
The nearest hickory tree was twenty rods distant. These nuts
were there still just fourteen days later, but were gone when I
looked again, Nov. 21, or six weeks later still.

I have since examined more carefully several dense woods,
which are said to be, and are apparently exclusively pine, and
always with the same result. For instance, I walked the same
day to a small, but very dense and handsome white-pine
grove, about fifteen rods square, in the east part of this town.
The trees are large for Concord, being from ten to twenty
inches in diameter, and as exclusively pine as any wood that I
know. Indeed, I selected this wood because I thought it the
least likely to contain anything else. It stands on an open plain
or pasture, except that it adjoins another small pine wood,
which has a few little oaks in it, on the south-east side. On
every other side, it was at least thirty rods from the nearest
woods. Standing on the edge of this grove and looking
through it, for it is quite level and free from underwood, for
the most part bare, red carpeted ground, you would have said
that there was not a hard wood tree on it, young or old. But
on looking carefully along over its floor I discovered, though
it was not till my eye had got used to the search, that, alternating with their ferns, and small blueberry bushes, there was
not merely here and there, but as often as every five feet, and
with a degree of regularity, a little oak, from three to twelve
inches high, and in one place I found a green acorn dropped
by the base of a pine.

I confess I was surprised to find my theory so perfectly
proved in this case. One of the principal agents in this planting, the red squirrels, were all the while curiously inspecting
me, while I was inspecting their plantation. Some of the little

oaks had been browsed by cows, which resorted to this wood for shade.

After some years the hard woods, as I have said, evidently find such a locality unfavorable to their growth, the pines being allowed to stand. As an evidence of this, I observed a red maple, twenty-five feet long, which had been recently prostrated, as if by the wind, though it was still covered with green leaves, the only maple in any position in the wood.

But although these oaks almost invariably die if the pines are not cut down, it is probable that they do better for a few years under their shelter than they would anywhere else.

The very extensive and thorough experiments of the English have at length led them to adopt a method of raising oaks almost precisely like this, which somewhat earlier had been adopted by nature and her squirrels here; they have simply rediscovered the value of pines as nurses for oaks. The English experimenters seem early and generally to have found out the importance of using trees of some kind as nurse plants for the young oaks. I quote from Loudon what he describes as "the ultimatum on the subject of planting and sheltering oaks"—an "abstract of the practice adopted by the Government officers in the national forests" of England, prepared by Alexander Milne.

At first some oaks had been planted by themselves, and others mixed with Scotch pines; "but in all cases," says Mr. Milne, "where oaks were planted actually among the pines, and surrounded by them [though the soil be inferior], the oaks were bound to be much the best." . . . "For several years past, the plan pursued has been to plant the inclosures with Scotch pines only [a tree very similar to our pitch pine]. . . And when the pines have got to the hight of five or six feet, then to put in good strong oak plants of about four or five years' growth among the pines—not cutting away any pines at first, unless they happen to be so strong and thick as to overshadow the oaks. In about two years, it becomes necessary to shred the branches of the pines, to give light and air to the oaks, and in about two or three more years to begin gradually to remove the pines altogether, taking out a certain number each year, so that, at the end of twenty or twenty-five years, not a single Scotch pine shall be left; although, for the first ten or twelve years, the plantation may have appeared to contain nothing else but pine. The advantage of this mode of planting has been found to be that the pines dry and ameliorate the soil, destroying the coarse grass and brambles which frequently choke and injure oaks; and that no mending over is necessary, as scarcely an oak so planted is found to fail."

Thus much the English planters have discovered by patient experiment, and, for aught I know, they have taken out a patent for it; but they appear not to have discovered that it was discovered before, and that they are merely adopting the method of Nature, which she long ago made patent to all. She is all the while planting the oaks amid the pines without our knowledge, and at last, instead of Government officers, we send a party of wood-choppers to cut down the pines, and so rescue an oak forest, at which we wonder as if it had dropped from the skies.

As I walk amid hickories even in August, I hear the sound of green pig-nuts falling from time to time, cut off by the chickaree over my head. In the Fall, I notice on the ground, either within or in the neighborhood of oak woods, on all sides of the town, stout oak twigs three or four inches long, bearing half-a-dozen empty acorn-cups, which have been gnawed off by squirrels, on both sides of the nuts, in order to make them more portable.

The jays scream and the red squirrels scold while you are clubbing and shaking the chestnut trees, for they are there on the same errand, and two of a trade never agree. I frequently see a red or gray squirrel cast down a green chestnut bur, as I am going through the woods, and I used to think, sometimes, that they were cast at me. In fact, they are so busy about it in the midst of the chestnut season, that you cannot stand long in the woods without hearing one fall.

A sportsman told me that he had, the day before—that was in the middle of October—seen a green chestnut bur dropt on our great river meadow, fifty rods from the nearest wood, and much further from the nearest chestnut tree, and he could not tell how it came there.

Occasionally, when chestnuting in midwinter, I find thirty or forty nuts in a pile, left in its gallery, just under the leaves, by the common wood-mouse (*mus leucopus*).

But especially in the Winter the extent to which this trans-portation and planting of nuts is carried on is made apparent by the snow. In almost every wood, you will see where the red or gray squirrels have pawed down through the snow in a hundred places, sometimes two feet deep, and almost always directly to a nut or a pine-cone, as directly as if they had started from it and bored upward—which you and I could not have done. It would be difficult for us to find one before the snow falls. Commonly, no doubt, they had deposited them there in the Fall. You wonder if they remember the lo-calities, or discover them by the scent. The red squirrel com-monly has its Winter abode in the earth under a thicket of evergreens, frequently under a small clump of evergreens in the midst of a deciduous wood. If there are any nut-trees, which still retain their nuts, standing at a distance without the wood, their paths often lead directly to and from them. We, therefore, need not suppose an oak standing here and there *in* the wood in order to seed it, but if a few stand within twenty or thirty rods of it, it is sufficient.

I think that I may venture to say that every white-pine cone that falls to the earth naturally in this town, before opening and losing its seeds and almost every pitch-pine one that falls at all, is cut off by a squirrel, and they begin to pluck them long before they are ripe, so that when the crop of white-pine cones is a small one, as it commonly is, they cut off thus almost every one of those before it fairly ripens. I think, moreover, that their design, if I may so speak, in cut-ting them off green, is partly to prevent their opening and losing their seeds, and these are the ones for which they dig through the snow, and the only white-pine cones which con-tain anything then. I have counted in one heap, within a di-ameter of four feet, the cores of 239 pitch-pine cones which had been cut off and stripped by the red squirrel the previ-ous Winter.

The nuts thus left on the surface, or buried just beneath it, are placed in the most favorable circumstances for germinat-ing. I have sometimes wondered how those which merely fell on the surface of the earth got planted; but, by the end of December, I find the chestnuts of the same year partially mixed with the mold, as it were, under the decaying and moldy leaves, where there is all the moisture and manure they want, for the nuts fall first. In a plentiful year, a large proportion of the nuts are thus covered loosely an inch deep, and are, of course, somewhat concealed from squirrels. One Winter, when the crop had been abundant, I got, with the aid of a rake, many quarts of these nuts as late as the 10th of January, and though some bought at the store the same day were more than half of them moldy, I did not find a single moldy one among these which I picked from under the wet and moldy leaves, where they had been snowed on once or twice. Nature knows how to pick them best. They were still plump and tender. Apparently, they do not heat there, though wet. In the Spring, they were all sprouting.

Loudon says that "when the nut [of the common walnut of Europe] is to be preserved through the Winter for the purpose of planting in the following Spring, it should be laid in a rot heap, as soon as gathered, with the husk on; and the heap should be turned over frequently in the course of the Winter."

Here, again, he is stealing Nature's "thunder." How can a poor mortal do otherwise? for it is she that finds fingers to steal with, and the treasure to be stolen. In the planting of the seeds of most trees, the best gardeners do no more than follow nature, though they may not know it. Generally, both large and small ones are most sure to germinate, and succeed best, when only beaten into the earth with the back of a spade and then covered with leaves or straw. These results to which planters have arrived, remind us of the experience of Kane and his companions at the North, who, when learning to live in that climate, were surprised to find themselves steadily adopting the customs of the natives, simply becoming Esquimaux. So, when we experiment in planting forests, we find ourselves at last doing as Nature does. Would it not be well to consult with Nature in the outset? for she is the most extensive and experienced planter of us all, not excepting the Dukes of Athol.

In short, they who have not attended particularly to this subject, are but little aware to what an extent quadrupeds and birds are employed, especially in the Fall, in collecting, and so disseminating and planting the seeds of trees. It is the most constant employment of the squirrels at that season, and you rarely meet with one that has not a nut in its mouth, or is not just going to get one. One squirrel-hunter of this town told me that he knew of a walnut tree which bore particularly good nuts, but that on going to gather them one Fall, he found that he had been anticipated by a family of a dozen red squirrels. He took out of the tree, which was hollow, one bushel and three pecks by measurement without the husks, and they supplied him and his family for the Winter. It would be easy to multiply instances of this kind. How commonly in the Fall you see the cheek-pouches of the striped squirrel distended by a quantity of nuts! This species gets its scientific name *Tamias*, or the steward, from its habit of storing up nuts and other seeds. Look under a nut-tree a month after the nuts have fallen and see what proportion of sound nuts to the abortive ones and shells, you will find ordinarily. They have been already eaten, or dispersed far and wide. The ground looks like a platform before a grocery, where the gossips of the village sit and crack nuts and less savory jokes. You have come, you would say, after the feast was over, and are presented with the shells only.

Occasionally, when threading the woods in the Fall, you will hear a sound as if some one had broken a twig, and, looking up, see a jay pecking at an acorn, or you will see a flock of them at once about it, in the top of an oak, and hear them break them off. They then fly to a suitable limb, and, placing the acorn under one foot, hammer away at it busily, making a sound like a wood pecker's tapping, looking round from time to time to see if any foe is approaching, and soon reach the meat, and nibble at it, holding up their heads to swallow, while they hold the remainder very firmly with their claws. Nevertheless, it often drops to the ground before the bird has done with it. I can confirm what Wm. Bartram wrote to Wilson, the Ornithologist, that "The jay is one of the most useful agents in the economy of nature, for disseminating forest trees and other nuciferous and hard-seeded vegetables on which they feed. Their chief employment during the Autumnal season is foraging to supply their Winter stores. In performing this necessary duty they drop abundance of seed in their flight over fields, hedges, and by fences where they alight to deposit them in the post-holes, &c. It is remarkable what numbers of young trees rise up in fields and pastures after a wet Winter and Spring. These birds alone are capable, in a few years time, to replant all the cleared lands."

I have noticed that squirrels also frequently drop their nuts in open land, which will still further account for the oaks and walnuts which spring up in pastures, for, depend on it, every new tree comes from a seed. When I examine the little oaks, one or two years old, in such places, I invariably find the empty acorn from which they sprung.

So far from the seed having lain dormant in the soil since oaks grew there before, as many believe, it is well known that it is difficult to preserve the vitality of acorns long enough to transport them to Europe; and it is recommended in Loudon's Arboretum, as the safest course, to sprout them in pots on the voyage. The same authority states that "very few acorns of any species will germinate after having been kept a year," that beach mast "only retains its vital properties one year," and the black walnut "seldom more than six months after it has ripened." I have frequently found that in November almost every acorn left on the ground had sprouted. What with frost, drouth, moisture, and worms, the greater part are soon destroyed. Yet it is stated by one botanical writer that "Acorns that have lain for centuries, on being plowed up, have soon vegetated."

Mr. George B. Emerson, in his valuable Report on the Trees and Shrubs of this State, says of the pines: "The tenacity of life of the seeds is remarkable. They will remain for many years unchanged in the ground, protected by the coolness and deep shade of the forest above them. But when the forest is removed, and the warmth of the sun admitted, they immediately vegetate." Since he does not tell us on what observations his remark is founded, I must doubt its truth. Besides, the experience of nursery men makes it the more questionable.

The stories of wheat raised from seed buried with an ancient Egyptian, and of raspberries raised from seed found in the stomach of a man in England, who is supposed to have died sixteen or seventeen hundred years ago, are generally discredited, simply because the evidence is not conclusive.

Several men of science, Dr. Carpenter among them, have used the statement that beach-plums sprang up in sand which was dug up forty miles inland in Maine, to prove that the seed had lain there a very long time, and some have inferred that the coast has receded so far. But it seems to me necessary to their argument to show, first, that beach-plums grow only on a beach. They are not uncommon here, which is about half that distance from the shore, and I remember a dense patch a few miles north of us twenty five miles inland, from which the fruit was annually carried to market. How much further inland they grow, I know not. Dr. Chas. T. Jackson speaks of finding beach-plums (perhaps they were this kind), more than 100 miles inland in Maine.

It chances that similar objections lie against all the more notorious instances of the kind on record.

Yet I am prepared to believe that some seeds, especially small ones, may retain their vitality for centuries under favorable circumstances. In the Spring of 1859, the old Hunt House, so called, in this town, whose chimney bore the date 1703, was taken down. This stood on land which belonged to John Winthrop the first Governor of Massachusetts, and a part of the house was evidently much older than the above date, and belonged to the Winthrop family. For many years, I have ransacked this neighborhood for plants, and consider myself familiar with its productions. Thinking of the seed which are said to be sometimes dug up at an unusual depth in the earth, and thus to reproduce long extinct plants, it occurred to me last Fall that some new or rare plants might have sprung up in the cellar of this house, which had been covered from the light so long. Searching there on the 22d of September I found, among other rank weeds, a species of nettle (Urtica urens) which I had not found before; dill, which I had not seen growing spontaneously; the Jerusalem oak (Chenopodium botrys) which I had seen wild in but one place; black nightshade (Solanium nigrum), which is quite rare hereabouts, and common tobacco, which, though it was often cultivated here in the last century, has for fifty years been an unknown plant in this town, and a few months before this not even I had heard that one man in the north part of the town was cultivating a few plants for his own use. I have no doubt that some or all of these plants sprang from seeds which had long been buried under or about that house, and that that tobacco is an additional evidence that the plant was formerly cultivated here. The cellar has been filled up this year, and four of those plants, including the tobacco, are now again extinct in that locality.

It is true, I have shown that the animals consume a great part of the seeds of trees, and so, at least, effectually prevent their becoming trees; but in all these cases, as I have said, the consumer is compelled to be at the same time the disperser and planter, and this is the tax which he pays to nature. I think it is Linnæus, who says that while the swine is rooting for acorns he is planting acorns.

Though I do not believe that a plant will spring up where no seed has been, I have great faith in a seed—a, to me, equally mysterious origin for it. Convince me that you have a seed there, and I am prepared to expect wonders. I shall even believe that the millennium is at hand, and that the reign of justice is about to commence, when the Patent Office, or Government, begins to distribute, and the people to plant the seeds of these things.

In the Spring of '57, I planted six seeds sent to me from the Patent Office and labeled, I think, *"Poitrine jaune grosse,"* large yellow squash, two came up, and one bore a squash which weighed 123½ pounds, the other bore four, weighing together 186¼ pounds. Who would have believed that there were 310 pounds of *Poitrine jaune grosse* in that corner of my garden? These seeds were the bait I used to catch it, my ferrets which I sent into its burrow, my brace of terriers which unearthed it. A little mysterious hoeing and manuring was all the *abra cadabra presto-change,* that I used, and lo! true to the label, they found for me 310 pounds of *poitrine jaune grosse* there, where it was never known to be, nor was before. These talismen had perchance sprung from America at first, and returned to it with unabated force. The big squash took a premium at your fair that Fall, and I understood that the man who bought it intended to sell the seeds for 10 cents a piece—(were they not cheap at that)? But I have more hounds of the same breed. I learn that one which I dispatched to a distant town, true to its instinct, points the large yellow squash there too, where no hound ever found it before, as its ancestors did here and in France.

Other seeds I have which will find other things in that corner of my garden, in like fashion, almost any fruit you wish, every year for ages, until the crop more than fills the whole garden. You have but little more to do than throw up your cap for entertainment these American days. Perfect alchemists I keep, who can transmute substances without end; and thus the corner of my garden is an inexhaustible treasure chest. Here you can dig, not gold, but the value which gold merely represents; and there is no Signor Blitz about it. Yet farmers' sons will stare by the hour to see a juggler draw ribbons from his throat, though he tells them it is all deception. Surely, men love darkness rather than light.

Wild Apples

THE HISTORY OF THE APPLE-TREE.

IT IS remarkable how closely the history of the Apple-tree is connected with that of man. The geologist tells us that the order of the *Rosaceæ*, which includes the Apple, also the true Grasses, and the *Labiatæ*, or Mints, were introduced only a short time previous to the appearance of man on the globe.

It appears that apples made a part of the food of that unknown primitive people whose traces have lately been found at the bottom of the Swiss lakes, supposed to be older than the foundation of Rome, so old that they had no metallic implements. An entire black and shrivelled Crab-Apple has been recovered from their stores.

Tacitus says of the ancient Germans, that they satisfied their hunger with wild apples (*agrestia poma*) among other things.

Niebuhr observes that "the words for a house, a field, a plough, ploughing, wine, oil, milk, sheep, apples, and others relating to agriculture and the gentler way of life, agree in Latin and Greek, while the Latin words for all objects pertaining to war or the chase are utterly alien from the Greek." Thus the apple-tree may be considered a symbol of peace no less than the olive.

The apple was early so important, and generally distributed, that its name traced to its root in many languages signifies fruit in general. Μῆλον, in Greek, means an apple, also the fruit of other trees, also a sheep and any cattle, and finally riches in general.

The apple-tree has been celebrated by the Hebrews, Greeks, Romans, and Scandinavians. Some have thought that the first human pair were tempted by its fruit. Goddesses are fabled to have contended for it, dragons were set to watch it, and heroes were employed to pluck it.

The tree is mentioned in at least three places in the Old Testament, and its fruit in two or three more. Solomon sings,—"As the apple-tree among the trees of the wood, so is my beloved among the sons." And again,—"Stay me with flagons, comfort me with apples." The noblest part of man's noblest feature is named from this fruit, "the apple of the eye."

The apple-tree is also mentioned by Homer and Herodotus. Ulysses saw in the glorious garden of Alcinoüs "pears and pomegranates, and apple-trees bearing beautiful fruit" (καὶ μηλέαι ἀγλαόκαρποι). And according to Homer, apples were among the fruits which Tantalus could not pluck, the wind ever blowing their boughs away from him. Theophrastus knew and described the apple-tree as a botanist.

According to the Prose Edda, "Iduna keeps in a box the apples which the gods, when they feel old age approaching, have only to taste of to become young again. It is in this manner that they will be kept in renovated youth until Ragnarök" (or the destruction of the gods).

I learn from Loudon that "the ancient Welsh bards were rewarded for excelling in song by the token of the apple-spray"; and "in the Highlands of Scotland the apple-tree is the badge of the clan Lamont."

The apple-tree (*Pyrus malus*) belongs chiefly to the northern temperate zone. Loudon says, that "it grows spontaneously in every part of Europe except the frigid zone, and throughout Western Asia, China, and Japan." We have also two or three varieties of the apple indigenous in North America. The cultivated apple-tree was first introduced into this country by the earliest settlers, and it is thought to do as well or better here than anywhere else. Probably some of the varieties which are now cultivated were first introduced into Britain by the Romans.

Pliny, adopting the distinction of Theophrastus, says,—"Of trees there are some which are altogether wild (*sylvestres*), some more civilized (*urbaniores*)." Theophrastus includes the apple among the last; and, indeed, it is in this sense the most civilized of all trees. It is as harmless as a dove, as beautiful as a rose, and as valuable as flocks and herds. It has been longer cultivated than any other, and so is more humanized; and who knows but, like the dog, it will at length be no longer traceable to its wild original? It migrates with man, like the dog and horse and cow: first, perchance, from Greece to Italy, thence to England, thence to America; and our Western emigrant is still marching steadily toward the setting sun with the seeds of the apple in his pocket, or perhaps a few young trees strapped to his load. At least a million apple-trees are thus set farther westward this year than any cultivated ones grew last year. Consider how the Blossom-Week, like the Sabbath, is thus annually spreading over the prairies; for when man migrates, he carries with him not only his birds, quadrupeds, insects, vegetables, and his very sward, but his orchard also.

The leaves and tender twigs are an agreeable food to many domestic animals, as the cow, horse, sheep, and goat; and the fruit is sought after by the first, as well as by the hog. Thus there appears to have existed a natural alliance between these animals and this tree from the first. "The fruit of the Crab in the forests of France" is said to be "a great resource for the wild-boar."

Not only the Indian, but many indigenous insects, birds, and quadrupeds, welcomed the apple-tree to these shores. The tent-caterpillar saddled her eggs on the very first twig that was formed, and it has since shared her affections with the wild cherry; and the canker-worm also in a measure abandoned the elm to feed on it. As it grew apace, the blue-bird, robin, cherry-bird, king-bird, and many more, came with haste and built their nests and warbled in its boughs, and so became orchard-birds, and multiplied more than ever. It was an era in the history of their race. The downy woodpecker found such a savory morsel under its bark, that he perforated it in a ring quite round the tree, before he left it,—a thing which he had never done before, to my knowledge. It did not take the partridge long to find out how sweet its buds were, and every winter eve she flew, and still flies, from the wood, to pluck them, much to the farmer's sorrow. The rabbit, too, was not slow to learn the taste of its twigs and bark; and when the fruit was ripe, the squirrel half-rolled, half-carried it to his hole; and even the musquash crept up the bank from the brook at evening, and greedily devoured it, until he had worn a path in the grass there; and when it was frozen and thawed, the crow and the jay were glad to taste it occasionally. The owl crept into the first apple-tree that became hollow, and fairly hooted with delight, finding it just the place for him; so, settling down into it, he has remained there ever since.

My theme being the Wild Apple, I will merely glance at some of the seasons in the annual growth of the cultivated apple, and pass on to my special province.

The flowers of the apple are perhaps the most beautiful of any tree's, so copious and so delicious to both sight and scent. The walker is frequently tempted to turn and linger near some more than usually handsome one, whose blossoms are two-thirds expanded. How superior it is in these respects to the pear, whose blossoms are neither colored nor fragrant!

By the middle of July, green apples are so large as to remind us of coddling, and of the autumn. The sward is commonly strewed with little ones which fall still-born, as it were,—Nature thus thinning them for us. The Roman writer Palladius said,—"If apples are inclined to fall before their time, a stone placed in a split root will retain them." Some such notion, still surviving, may account for some of the stones which we see placed to be overgrown in the forks of trees. They have a saying in Suffolk, England,—

> "At Michaelmas time, or a little before,
> Half an apple goes to the core."

Early apples begin to be ripe about the first of August; but I think that none of them are so good to eat as some to smell. One is worth more to scent your handkerchief with than any perfume which they sell in the shops. The fragrance of some fruits is not to be forgotten, along with that of flowers. Some gnarly apple which I pick up in the road reminds me by its fragrance of all the wealth of Pomona,—carrying me forward to those days when they will be collected in golden and ruddy heaps in the orchards and about the cider-mills.

A week or two later, as you are going by orchards or gardens, especially in the evenings, you pass through a little region possessed by the fragrance of ripe apples, and thus enjoy them without price, and without robbing anybody.

There is thus about all natural products a certain volatile and ethereal quality which represents their highest value, and which cannot be vulgarized, or bought and sold. No mortal has ever enjoyed the perfect flavor of any fruit, and only the godlike among men begin to taste its ambrosial qualities. For nectar and ambrosia are only those fine flavors of every earthly fruit which our coarse palates fail to perceive,—just as we occupy the heaven of the gods without knowing it. When I see a particularly mean man carrying a load of fair and fragrant early apples to market, I seem to see a contest going on between him and his horse, on the one side, and the apples on the other, and, to my mind, the apples always gain it. Pliny says that apples are the heaviest of all things, and that the oxen begin to sweat at the mere sight of a load of them. Our driver begins to lose his load the moment he tries to transport them to where they do not belong, that is, to any but the most beautiful. Though he gets out from time to time, and feels of them, and thinks they are all there, I see the stream of their evanescent and celestial qualities going to heaven from his cart, while the pulp and skin and core only are going to market. They are not apples, but pomace. Are not these still Iduna's apples, the taste of which keeps the gods forever young? and think you that they will let Loki or Thjassi carry them off to Jötunheim, while they grow wrinkled and gray? No, for Ragnarök, or the destruction of the gods, is not yet.

There is another thinning of the fruit, commonly near the end of August or in September, when the ground is strewn with windfalls; and this happens especially when high winds occur after rain. In some orchards you may see fully three-quarters of the whole crop on the ground, lying in a circular form beneath the trees, yet hard and green,—or, if it is a hillside, rolled far down the hill. However, it is an ill wind that blows nobody any good. All the country over, people are busy picking up the windfalls, and this will make them cheap for early apple-pies.

In October, the leaves falling, the apples are more distinct on the trees. I saw one year in a neighboring town some trees fuller of fruit than I remembered to have ever seen before, small yellow apples hanging over the road. The branches were gracefully drooping with their weight, like a barberry-bush, so that the whole tree acquired a new character. Even the topmost branches, instead of standing erect, spread and drooped in all directions; and there were so many poles supporting the lower ones, that they looked like pictures of banian-trees. As an old English manuscript says, "The mo appelen the tree bereth, the more sche boweth to the folk."

Surely the apple is the noblest of fruits. Let the most beautiful or the swiftest have it. That should be the "going" price of apples.

Between the fifth and twentieth of October I see the barrels lie under the trees. And perhaps I talk with one who is selecting some choice barrels to fulfil an order. He turns a specked one over many times before he leaves it out. If I were to tell what is passing in my mind, I should say that every one was specked which he had handled; for he rubs off all the bloom, and those fugacious ethereal qualities leave it. Cool evenings prompt the farmers to make haste, and at length I see only the ladders here and there left leaning against the trees.

It would be well, if we accepted these gifts with more joy and gratitude, and did not think it enough simply to put a fresh load of compost about the tree. Some old English customs are suggestive at least. I find them described chiefly in Brand's "Popular Antiquities." It appears that "on Christmas eve the farmer and their men in Devonshire take a large bowl of cider, with a toast in it, and carrying it in state to the orchard, they salute the apple-trees with much ceremony, in order to make them bear well the next season." This salutation consists in "throwing some of the cider about the roots of the tree, placing bits of the toast on the branches," and then, "encircling one of the best bearing trees in the orchard, they drink the following toast three several times:—

'Here 's to thee, old apple-tree,
Whence thou mayst bud, and whence thou mayst blow,
And whence thou mayst bear apples enow!
Hats-full! caps-full!
Bushel, bushel, sacks-full!
And my pockets full, too! Hurra!' "

Also what was called "apple-howling" used to be practised in various counties of England on New-Year's eve. A troop of boys visited the different orchards, and, encircling the apple-trees, repeated the following words:—

> "Stand fast, root! bear well, top!
> Pray God send us a good howling crop:
> Every twig, apples big;
> Every bough, apples enow!"

"They then shout in chorus, one of the boys accompanying them on a cow's horn. During this ceremony they rap the trees with their sticks." This is called "wassailing" the trees, and is thought by some to be "a relic of the heathen sacrifice to Pomona."

Herrick sings,—

> "Wassaile the trees that they may beare
> You many a plum and many a peare;
> For more or less fruits they will bring
> As you so give them wassailing."

Our poets have as yet a better right to sing of cider than of wine; but it behooves them to sing better than English Phillips did, else they will do no credit to their Muse.

THE WILD APPLE.

So much for the more civilized apple-trees (*ubaniores*, as Pliny calls them). I love better to go through the old orchards of ungrafted apple-trees, at whatever season of the year,—so irregularly planted: sometimes two trees standing close together; and the rows so devious that you would think that they not only had grown while the owner was sleeping, but had been set out by him in a somnambulic state. The rows of grafted fruit will never tempt me to wander amid them like these. But I now, alas, speak rather from memory than from any recent experience, such ravages have been made!

Some soils, like a rocky tract called the Easterbrooks Country in my neighborhood, are so suited to the apple, that it will grow faster in them without any care, or if only the ground is broken up once a year, than it will in many places with any amount of care. The owners of this tract allow that the soil is excellent for fruit, but they say that it is so rocky that they have not patience to plough it, and that, together with the distance, is the reason why it is not cultivated. There are, or were recently, extensive orchards there standing without order. Nay, they spring up wild and bear well there in the midst of pines, birches, maples, and oaks. I am often surprised to see rising amid these trees the rounded tops of apple-trees glowing with red or yellow fruit, in harmony with the autumnal tints of the forest.

Going up the side of a cliff about the first of November, I saw a vigorous young apple-tree, which, planted by birds or cows, had shot up amid the rocks and open woods there, and had now much fruit on it, uninjured by the frosts, when all cultivated apples were gathered. It was a rank wild growth, with many green leaves on it still, and made an impression of thorniness. The fruit was hard and green, but looked as if it would be palatable in the winter. Some was dangling on the twigs, but more half-buried in the wet leaves under the tree, or rolled far down the hill amid the rocks. The owner knows nothing of it. The day was not observed when it first blossomed, nor when it first bore fruit, unless by the chickadee. There was no dancing on the green beneath it in its honor, and now there is no hand to pluck its fruit,—which is only gnawed by squirrels, as I perceive. It has done double duty,— not only borne this crop, but each twig has grown a foot into the air. And this is *such* fruit! bigger than many berries, we must admit, and carried home will be sound and palatable next spring. What care I for Iduna's apples so long as I can get these?

When I go by this shrub thus late and hardy, and see its dangling fruit, I respect the tree, and I am grateful for Nature's bounty, even though I cannot eat it. Here on this rugged and woody hill-side has grown an apple-tree, not planted by man, no relic of a former orchard, but a natural growth, like the pines and oaks. Most fruits which we prize and use depend entirely on our care. Corn and grain, potatoes, peaches, melons, etc., depend altogether on our planting; but the apple emulates man's independence and enterprise. It is not simply carried, as I have said, but, like him, to some extent, it has migrated to this New World, and is even, here and there, making its way amid the aboriginal trees; just as the ox and dog and horse sometimes run wild and maintain themselves.

Even the sourest and crabbedest apple, growing in the most unfavorable position, suggests such thoughts as these, it is so noble a fruit.

THE CRAB.

Nevertheless, *our* wild apple is wild only like myself, perchance, who belong not to the aboriginal race here, but have strayed into the woods from the cultivated stock. Wilder still, as I have said, there grows elsewhere in this country a native and aboriginal Crab-Apple, *Malus coronaria*, "whose nature has not yet been modified by cultivation." It is found from Western New-York to Minnesota, and southward. Michaux says that its ordinary height "is fifteen or eighteen feet, but it is sometimes found twenty-five or thirty feet high," and that the large ones "exactly resemble the common apple-tree." "The flowers are white mingled with rose-color, and are collected in corymbs." They are remarkable for their delicious odor. The fruit, according to him, is about an inch and a half in diameter, and is intensely acid. Yet they make fine sweetmeats, and also cider of them. He concludes, that, "if, on being cultivated, it does not yield new and palatable varieties, it will at least be celebrated for the beauty of its flowers, and for the sweetness of its perfume."

I never saw the Crab-Apple till May, 1861. I had heard of it through Michaux, but more modern botanists, so far as I know, have not treated it as of any peculiar importance. Thus it was a half-fabulous tree to me. I contemplated a pilgrimage to the "Glades," a portion of Pennsylvania where it was said to grow to perfection. I thought of sending to a nursery for it, but doubted if they had it, or would distinguish it from European varieties. At last I had occasion to go to Minnesota, and on entering Michigan I began to notice from the cars a tree with handsome rose-colored flowers. At first I thought it some variety of thorn; but it was not long before the truth flashed on me, that this was my long-sought Crab-Apple. It was the prevailing flowering shrub or tree to be seen from the cars at that season of the year—about the middle of May. But the cars never stopped before one, and so I was launched on the bosom of the Mississippi without having touched one, experiencing the fate of Tantalus. On arriving at St. Anthony's Falls, I was sorry to be told that I was too far north for the Crab-Apple. Nevertheless I succeeded in finding it about eight miles west of the Falls; touched it and smelled it, and secured a lingering corymb of flowers for my herbarium. This must have been near its northern limit.

HOW THE WILD APPLE GROWS.

But though these are indigenous, like the Indians, I doubt whether they are any hardier than those backwoodsmen among the apple-trees, which, though descended from culti-vated stocks, plant themselves in distant fields and forests, where the soil is favorable to them. I know of no trees which have more difficulties to contend with, and which more stur-dily resist their foes. These are the ones whose story we have to tell. It oftentimes reads thus:—

Near the beginning of May, we notice little thickets of apple-trees just springing up in the pastures where cattle have been,—as the rocky ones of our Easterbrooks Country, or the top of Nobscot Hill, in Sudbury. One or two of these perhaps survive the drought and other accidents,—their very birth-place defending them against the encroaching grass and some other dangers, at first.

> In two years' time 't had thus
>   Reached the level of the rocks,
> Admired the stretching world,
>   Nor feared the wandering flocks.
>
> But at this tender age
>   Its sufferings began:
> There came a browsing ox
>   And cut it down a span.

This time, perhaps, the ox does not notice it amid the grass; but the next year, when it has grown more stout, he recog-nizes it for a fellow-emigrant from the old country, the flavor of whose leaves and twigs he well knows; and though at first he pauses to welcome it, and express his surprise, and gets for answer, "The same cause that brought you here brought me," he nevertheless browses it again, reflecting, it may be, that he has some title to it.

Thus cut down annually, it does not despair; but, putting forth two short twigs for every one cut off, it spreads out low along the ground in the hollows or between the rocks, growing more stout and scrubby, until it forms, not a tree as yet, but a little pyramidal, stiff, twiggy mass, almost as solid and impenetrable as a rock. Some of the densest and most impenetrable clumps of bushes that I have ever seen, as well on account of the closeness and stubbornness of their branches as of their thorns, have been these wild-apple scrubs. They are more like the scrubby fir and black spruce on which you stand, and sometimes walk, on the tops of mountains, where cold is the demon they contend with, than anything else. No wonder they are prompted to grow thorns at last, to defend themselves against such foes. In their thorniness, however, there is no malice, only some malic acid.

The rocky pastures of the tract I have referred to—for they maintain their ground best in a rocky field—are thickly sprinkled with these little tufts, reminding you often of some rigid gray mosses or lichens, and you see thousands of little trees just springing up between them, with the seed still attached to them.

Being regularly clipped all around each year by the cows, as a hedge with shears, they are often of a perfect conical or pyramidal form, from one to four feet high, and more or less sharp, as if trimmed by the gardener's art. In the pastures on Nobscot Hill and its spurs, they make fine dark shadows when the sun is low. They are also an excellent covert from hawks for many small birds that roost and build in them. Whole flocks perch in them at night, and I have seen three robins' nests in one which was six feet in diameter.

No doubt many of these are already old trees, if you reckon from the day they were planted, but infants still when you consider their development and the long life before them. I counted the annual rings of some which were just one foot high, and as wide as high, and found that they were about twelve years old, but quite sound and thrifty! They were so low that they were unnoticed by the walker, while many of their contemporaries from the nurseries were already bearing considerable crops. But what you gain in time is perhaps in this case, too, lost in power,—that is, in the vigor of the tree. This is their pyramidal state.

The cows continue to browse them thus for twenty years or more, keeping them down and compelling them to spread, until at last they are so broad that they become their own fence, when some interior shoot, which their foes cannot reach, darts upward with joy: for it has not forgotten its high calling, and bears its own peculiar fruit in triumph.

Such are the tactics by which it finally defeats its bovine foes. Now, if you have watched the progress of a particular shrub, you will see that it is no longer a simple pyramid or cone, but that out of its apex there rises a sprig or two, growing more lustily perchance than an orchard-tree, since the plant now devotes the whole of its repressed energy to these upright parts. In a short time these become a small tree, an inverted pyramid resting on the apex of the other, so that the whole has now the form of a vast hour-glass. The spreading bottom, having served its purpose, finally disappears, and the generous tree permits the now harmless cows to come in and stand in its shade, and rub against and redden its trunk,which has grown in spite of them, and even to taste a part of its fruit, and so disperse the seed.

Thus the cows create their own shade and food; and the tree, its hour-glass being inverted, lives a second life, as it were.

It is an important question with some nowadays, whether you should trim young apple-trees as high as your nose or as high as your eyes. The ox trims them up as high as he can reach, and that is about the right height, I think.

In spite of wandering kine, and other adverse circumstances, that despised shrub, valued only by small birds as a covert and shelter from hawks, has its blossom-week at last, and in course of time its harvest, sincere, though small.

By the end of some October, when its leaves have fallen, I frequently see such a central sprig, whose progress I have watched, when I thought it had forgotten its destiny, as I had, bearing its first crop of small green or yellow or rosy fruit, which the cows cannot get at over the bushy and thorny hedge which surrounds it, and I make haste to taste the new and undescribed variety. We have all heard of the numerous varieties of fruit invented by Van Mons and Knight. This is the system of Van Cow, and she has invented far more and more memorable varieties than both of them.

Through what hardships it may attain to bear a sweet fruit! Though somewhat small, it may prove equal, if not superior, in flavor to that which has grown in a garden,—will perchance be all the sweeter and more palatable for the very difficulties it has had to contend with. Who knows but this chance wild fruit, planted by a cow or a bird on some remote and rocky hill-side, where it is as yet unobserved by man, may be the choicest of all its kind, and foreign potentates shall hear of it, and royal societies seek to propagate it, though the virtues of the perhaps truly crabbed owner of the soil may never be heard of,—at least, beyond the limits of his village? It was thus the Porter and the Baldwin grew.

Every wild-apple shrub excites our expectation thus, somewhat as every wild child. It is, perhaps, a prince in disguise. What a lesson to man! So are human beings, referred to the highest standard, the celestial fruit which they suggest and aspire to bear, browsed on by fate; and only the most persistent and strongest genius defends itself and prevails, sends a tender scion upward at last, and drops its perfect fruit on the ungrateful earth. Poets and philosophers and statesmen thus spring up in the country pastures, and outlast the hosts of unoriginal men.

Such is always the pursuit of knowledge. The celestial fruits, the golden apples of the Hesperides, are ever guarded by a hundred-headed dragon which never sleeps, so that it is an Herculean labor to pluck them.

This is one, and the most remarkable way, in which the wild apple is propagated; but commonly it springs up at wide intervals in woods and swamps, and by the sides of roads, as the soil may suit it, and grows with comparative rapidity. Those which grow in dense woods are very tall and slender. I frequently pluck from these trees a perfectly mild and tamed fruit. As Palladius says, *"Et injussu consternitur ubere mali"*: And the ground is strewn with the fruit of an unbidden apple-tree.

It is an old notion, that, if these wild trees do not bear a valuable fruit of their own, they are the best stocks by which to transmit to posterity the most highly prized qualities of others. However, I am not in search of stocks, but the wild fruit itself, whose fierce gust has suffered no "inteneration." It is not my

> "highest plot
> To plant the Bergamot."

THE FRUIT, AND ITS FLAVOR.

The time for wild apples is the last of October and the first of November. They then get to be palatable, for they ripen late, and they are still perhaps as beautiful as ever. I make a great account of these fruits, which the farmers do not think it worth the while to gather,—wild flavors of the Muse, vivacious and inspiriting. The farmer thinks that he has better in his barrels, but he is mistaken, unless he has a walker's appetite and imagination, neither of which can he have.

Such as grow quite wild, and are left out till the first of November, I presume that the owner does not mean to gather. They belong to children as wild as themselves,—to certain active boys that I know,—to the wild-eyed woman of the fields, to whom nothing comes amiss, who gleans after all the world,—and, moreover, to us walkers. We have met with them, and they are ours. These rights, long enough insisted upon, have come to be an institution in some old countries, where they have learned how to live. I hear that "the custom of grippling, which may be called apple-gleaning, is, or was formerly, practised in Herefordshire. It consists in leaving a few apples, which are called the gripples, on every tree, after the general gathering, for the boys, who go with climbing-poles and bags to collect them."

As for those I speak of, I pluck them as a wild fruit, native to this quarter of the earth,—fruit of old trees that have been dying ever since I was a boy and are not yet dead, frequented only by the woodpecker and the squirrel, deserted now by the owner, who has not faith enough to look under their boughs.

From the appearance of the tree-top, at a little distance, you would expect nothing but lichens to drop from it, but your faith is rewarded by finding the ground strewn with spirited fruit,—some of it, perhaps, collected at squirrel-holes, with the marks of their teeth by which they carried them,—some containing a cricket or two silently feeding within, and some, especially in damp days, a shelless snail. The very sticks and stones lodged in the tree-top might have convinced you of the savoriness of the fruit which has been so eagerly sought after in past years.

I have seen no account of these among the "Fruits and Fruit-Trees of America," though they are more memorable to my taste than the grafted kinds; more racy and wild American flavors do they possess, when October and November, when December and January, and perhaps February and March even, have assuaged them somewhat. An old farmer in my neighborhood, who always selects the right word, says that "they have a kind of bow-arrow tang."

Apples for grafting appear to have been selected commonly, not so much for their spirited flavor, as for their mildness, their size, and bearing qualities,—not so much for their beauty, as for their fairness and soundness. Indeed, I have no faith in the selected lists of pomological gentlemen. Their "Favorites" and "None-suches" and "Seek-no-farthers," when I have fruited them, commonly turn out very tame and forgetable. They are eaten with comparatively little zest and have no real *tang* nor *smack* to them.

What if some of these wildings are acrid and puckery, genuine *verjuice*, do they not still belong to the *Pomaceæ*, which are uniformly innocent and kind to our race? I still begrudge them to the cider-mill. Perhaps they are not fairly ripe yet.

No wonder that these small and high-colored apples are thought to make the best cider. Loudon quotes from the "Herefordshire Report," that "apples of a small size are always, if equal in quality, to be preferred to those of a larger size, in order that the rind and kernel may bear the greatest proportion to the pulp, which affords the weakest and most watery juice." And he says, that, "to prove this, Dr. Symonds, of Hereford, about the year 1800, made one hogshead of cider entirely from the rinds and cores of apples, and another from the pulp only, when the first was found of extraordinary strength and flavor, while the latter was sweet and insipid."

Evelyn says that the "Red-strake" was the favorite cider-apple in his day; and he quotes one Dr. Newburg as saying, "In Jersey 't is a general observation, as I hear, that the more of red any apple has in its rind, the more proper it is for this use. Pale-faced apples they exclude as much as may be from their cider-vat." This opinion still prevails.

All apples are good in November. Those which the farmer leaves out as unsalable, and unpalatable to those who frequent the markets, are choicest fruit to the walker. But it is remarkable that the wild apple, which I praise as so spirited and racy when eaten in the fields or woods, being brought into the house, has frequently a harsh and crabbed taste. The Saunterer's Apple not even the saunterer can eat in the house. The palate rejects it there, as it does haws and acorns, and demands a tamed one; for there you miss the November air, which is the sauce it is to be eaten with. Accordingly, when Tityrus, seeing the lengthening shadows, invites Melibœus to go home and pass the night with him, he promises him *mild* apples and soft chestnuts,—*mitia poma, astaneæ molles.* I frequently pluck wild apples of so rich and spicy a flavor that I wonder all orchardists do not get a scion from that tree, and I fail not to bring home my pockets full. But perchance, when I take one out of my desk and taste it in my chamber, I find it unexpectedly crude,—sour enough to set a squirrel's teeth on edge and make a jay scream.

These apples have hung in the wind and frost and rain till they have absorbed the qualities of the weather or season, and thus are highly *seasoned*, and they *pierce* and *sting* and *permeate* us with their spirit. They must be eaten in *season*, accordingly,—that is, out-of-doors.

To appreciate the wild and sharp flavors of these October fruits, it is necessary that you be breathing the sharp October or November air. The out-door air and exercise which the walker gets give a different tone to his palate, and he craves a fruit which the sedentary would call harsh and crabbed. They must be eaten in the fields, when your system is all aglow with exercise, when the frosty weather nips your fingers, the wind rattles the bare boughs or rustles the few remaining leaves, and the jay is heard screaming around. What is sour in the house a bracing walk makes sweet. Some of these apples might be labelled, "To be eaten in the wind."

Of course no flavors are thrown away; they are intended for the taste that is up to them. Some apples have two distinct flavors, and perhaps one-half of them must be eaten in the house, the other out-doors. One Peter Whitney wrote from Northborough in 1782, for the Proceedings of the Boston Academy, describing an apple-tree in that town "producing fruit of opposite qualities, part of the same apple being frequently sour and the other sweet"; also some all sour, and others all sweet, and this diversity on all parts of the tree.

There is a wild apple on Nawshawtuct Hill in my town which has to me a peculiarly pleasant bitter tang, not perceived till it is three-quarters tasted. It remains on the tongue. As you eat it, it smells exactly like a squash-bug. It is a sort of triumph to eat and relish it.

I hear that the fruit of a kind of plum-tree in Provence is "called *Prunes sibarelles*, because it is impossible to whistle after having eaten them, from their sourness." But perhaps they were only eaten in the house and in summer, and if tried out-of-doors in a stinging atmosphere, who knows but you could whistle an octave higher and clearer?

In the fields only are the sours and bitters of Nature appreciated; just as the wood-chopper eats his meal in a sunny glade, in the middle of a winter day, with content, basks in a sunny ray there and dreams of summer in a degree of cold which, experienced in a chamber, would make a student miserable. They who are at work abroad are not cold, but rather it is they who sit shivering in houses. As with temperatures, so with flavors; as with cold and heat, so with sour and sweet. This natural raciness, the sours and bitters which the diseased palate refuses, are the true condiments.

Let your condiments be in the condition of your senses. To appreciate the flavor of these wild apples requires vigorous and healthy senses, *papillæ* firm and erect on the tongue and palate, not easily flattened and tamed.

From my experience with wild apples, I can understand that there may be reason for a savage's preferring many kinds of food which the civilized man rejects. The former has the palate of an out-door man. It takes a savage or wild taste to appreciate a wild fruit.

What a healthy out-of-door appetite it takes to relish the apple of life, the apple of the world, then!

"Nor is it every apple I desire,
    Nor that which pleases every palate best;
'T is not the lasting Deuxan I require,
    Nor yet the red-cheeked Greening I request,
Nor that which first beshrewed the name of wife,
Nor that whose beauty caused the golden strife:
No, no! bring me an apple from the tree of life!"

So there is one *thought* for the field, another for the house. I would have my thoughts, like wild apples, to be food for walkers, and will not warrant them to be palatable, if tasted in the house.

THEIR BEAUTY.

Almost all wild apples are handsome. They cannot be too gnarly and crabbed and rusty to look at. The gnarliest will have some redeeming traits even to the eye. You will discover some evening redness dashed or sprinkled on some protuberance or in some cavity. It is rare that the summer lets an apple go without streaking or spotting it on some part of its sphere. It will have some red stains, commemorating the mornings and evenings it has witnessed; some dark and rusty blotches, in memory of the clouds and foggy, mildewy days that have passed over it; and a spacious field of green reflecting the general face of Nature,—green even as the fields; or a yellow ground, which implies a milder flavor,—yellow as the harvest, or russet as the hills.

Apples, these I mean, unspeakably fair,—apples not of Discord, but of Concord! Yet not so rare but that the homeliest may have a share. Painted by the frosts, some a uniform clear bright yellow, or red, or crimson, as if their spheres had regularly revolved, and enjoyed the influence of the sun on all sides alike,—some with the faintest pink blush imaginable,—some brindled with deep red streaks like a cow, or with hundreds of fine blood-red rays running regularly from the

stem-dimple to the blossom-end, like meridional lines, on a
straw-colored ground,—some touched with a greenish rust,
like a fine lichen, here and there, with crimson blotches or
eyes more or less confluent and fiery when wet,—and others
gnarly, and freckled or peppered all over on the stem side with
fine crimson spots on a white ground, as if accidentally sprinkled from the brush of Him who paints the autumn leaves.
Others, again, are sometimes red inside, perfused with a beautiful blush, fairy food, too beautiful to eat,—apple of the
Hesperides, apple of the evening sky! But like shells and pebbles on the sea-shore, they must be seen as they sparkle amid
the withering leaves in some dell in the woods, in the autumnal air, or as they lie in the wet grass, and not when they have
wilted and faded in the house.

THE NAMING OF THEM.

It would be a pleasant pastime to find suitable names for
the hundred varieties which go to a single heap at the cider-
mill. Would it not tax a man's invention,—no one to be
named after a man, and all in the *lingua vernacula*? Who shall
stand godfather at the christening of the wild apples? It would
exhaust the Latin and Greek languages, if they were used, and
make the *lingua vernacula* flag. We should have to call in the
sunrise and the sunset, the rainbow and the autumn woods
and the wild flowers, and the woodpecker and the purple
finch and the squirrel and the jay and the butterfly, the
November traveller and the truant boy, to our aid.

In 1836 there were in the garden of the London
Horticultural Society more than fourteen hundred distinct
sorts. But here are species which they have not in their catalogue, not to mention the varieties which our Crab might
yield to cultivation.

Let us enumerate a few of these. I find myself compelled,
after all, to give the Latin names of some for the benefit of
those who live where English is not spoken,—for they are
likely to have a world-wide reputation.

There is, first of all, the Wood-Apple (*Malus sylvatica*);
the Blue-Jay Apple; the Apple which grows in Dells in the
Woods, (*sylvestrivallis*,) also in Hollows in Pastures (*campe-*

strivallis); the Apple that grows in an old Cellar-Hole (*Malus cellaris*); the Meadow-Apple; the Partridge-Apple; the Truant's Apple, (*Cessatoris,*) which no boy will ever go by without knocking off some, however *late* it may be; the Saunterer's Apple,—you must lose yourself before you can find the way to that; the Beauty of the Air (*Decus Aëris*); December-Eating; the Frozen-Thawed, (*gelato-soluta,*) good only in that state; the Concord Apple, possibly the same with the *Musketaquidensis*; the Assabet Apple; the Brindled Apple; Wine of New England; the Chickaree Apple; the Green Apple (*Malus viridis*);—this has many synonymes; in an imperfect state, it is the *Cholera morbifera aut dysenterifera, puerulis dilectissima*;—the Apple which Atalanta stopped to pick up; the Hedge-Apple (*Malus Sepium*); the Slug-Apple (*limacea*); the Railroad-Apple, which perhaps came from a core thrown out of the cars; the Apple whose Fruit we tasted in our Youth; our Particular Apple, not to be found in any catalogue,— *Pedestrium Solatium*; also the Apple where hangs the Forgotten Scythe; Iduna's Apples, and the Apples which Loki found in the Wood; and a great many more I have on my list, too numerous to mention,—all of them good. As Bodæus exclaims, referring to the cultivated kinds, and adapting Virgil to his case, so I, adapting Bodæus,—

> "Not if I had a hundred tongues, a hundred mouths,
> An iron voice, could I describe all the forms
> And reckon up all the names of these *wild apples.*"

THE LAST GLEANING.

By the middle of November the wild apples have lost some of their brilliancy, and have chiefly fallen. A great part are decayed on the ground, and the sound ones are more palatable than before. The note of the chickadee sounds now more distinct, as you wander amid the old trees, and the autumnal dandelion is half-closed and tearful. But still, if you are a skilful gleaner, you may get many a pocket-full even of grafted fruit, long after apples are supposed to be gone out-of-doors. I know a Blue-Pearmain tree, growing within the edge of a swamp, almost as good as wild. You would not suppose that there was any fruit left there, on the first survey, but you must look according to system. Those which lie exposed are quite brown and rotten now, or perchance a few still show one blooming cheek here and there amid the wet leaves. Nevertheless, with experienced eyes, I explore amid the bare alders and the huckleberry-bushes and the withered sedge, and in the crevices of the rocks, which are full of leaves, and pry under the fallen and decaying ferns, which, with apple and alder leaves, thickly strew the ground. For I know that they lie concealed, fallen into hollows long since and covered up by the leaves of the tree itself,—a proper kind of packing. From these lurking-places, anywhere within the circumference of the tree, I draw forth the fruit, all wet and glossy, maybe nibbled by rabbits and hollowed out by crickets and perhaps with a leaf or two cemented to it, (as Curzon an old manuscript from a monastery's mouldy cellar,) but still with a rich bloom on it, and at least as ripe and well kept, if not better than those in barrels, more crisp and lively than they. If these resources fail to yield anything, I have learned to look between the bases of the suckers which spring thickly from some horizontal limb, for now and then one lodges there, or in the very midst of an alder-clump, where they are covered by leaves, safe from cows which may have smelled them out. If I am sharp-set, for I do not refuse the Blue-Pearmain, I fill my pockets on each side; and as I retrace my steps in the frosty eve, being perhaps four or five miles from home, I eat one first from this side, and then from that, to keep my balance.

I learn from Topsell's Gesner, whose authority appears to be Albertus, that the following is the way in which the hedge-hog collects and carries home his apples. He says,—"His meat is apples, worms, or grapes: when he findeth apples or grapes on the earth, he rolleth himself upon them, until he have filled all his prickles, and then carrieth them home to his den, never bearing above one in his mouth; and if it fortune that one of them fall off by the way, he likewise shaketh off all the residue, and walloweth upon them afresh, until they be all settled upon his back again. So, forth he goeth, making a noise like a cart-wheel; and if he have any young ones in his nest, they pull off his load wherewithal he is loaded, eating thereof what they please, and laying up the residue for the time to come."

THE "FROZEN-THAWED" APPLE.

Toward the end of November, though some of the sound ones are yet more mellow and perhaps more edible, they have generally, like the leaves, lost their beauty, and are beginning to freeze. It is finger-cold, and prudent farmers get in their barrelled apples, and bring you the apples and cider which they have engaged; for it is time to put them into the cellar. Perhaps a few on the ground show their red cheeks above the early snow, and occasionally some even preserve their color and soundness under the snow throughout the winter. But generally at the beginning of the winter they freeze hard, and soon, though undecayed, acquire the color of a baked apple.

Before the end of December, generally, they experience their first thawing. Those which a month ago were sour, crabbed, and quite unpalatable to the civilized taste, such at least as were frozen while sound, let a warmer sun come to thaw them, for they are extremely sensitive to its rays, are found to be filled with a rich sweet cider, better than any bottled cider that I know of, and with which I am better acquainted than with wine. All apples are good in this state, and your jaws are the cider-press. Others, which have more substance, are a sweet and luscious food,—in my opinion of more worth than the pine-apples which are imported from the West Indies. Those which lately even I tasted only to repent of it,— for I am semi-civilized,—which the farmer willingly left on the tree, I am now glad to find have the property of hanging on like the leaves of the young oaks. It is a way to keep cider sweet without boiling. Let the frost come to freeze them first, solid as stones, and then the rain or a warm winter day to thaw them, and they will seem to have borrowed a flavor from heaven through the medium of the air in which they hang. Or perchance you find, when you get home, that those which rattled in your pocket have thawed, and the ice is turned to cider. But after the third or fourth freezing and thawing they will not be found so good.

What are the imported half-ripe fruits of the torrid South, to this fruit matured by the cold of the frigid North? These are those crabbed apples with which I cheated my companion, and kept a smooth face that I might tempt him to eat. Now we both greedily fill our pockets with them,—bending to drink the cup and save our lappets from the overflowing juice,—and grow more social with their wine. Was there one that hung so high and sheltered by the tangled branches that our sticks could not dislodge it?

It is a fruit never carried to market, that I am aware of,—quite distinct from the apple of the markets, as from dried apple and cider,—and it is not every winter that produces it in perfection.

The era of the Wild Apple will soon be past. It is a fruit which will probably become extinct in New England. You may still wander through old orchards of native fruit of great extent, which for the most part went to the cider-mill, now all gone to decay. I have heard of an orchard in a distant town, on the side of a hill, where the apples rolled down and lay four feet deep against a wall on the lower side, and this the owner cut down for fear they should be made into cider. Since the temperance reform and the general introduction of grafted fruit, no native apple-trees, such as I see everywhere in deserted pastures, and where the woods have grown up around them, are set out. I fear that he who walks over these fields a century hence will not know the pleasure of knocking off wild apples. Ah, poor man, there are many pleasures which he will not know! Notwithstanding the prevalence of the Baldwin and the Porter, I doubt if so extensive orchards are set out to-day in my town as there were a century ago, when those vast straggling cider-orchards were planted, when men both ate and drank apples, when the pomace-heap was the only nursery, and trees cost nothing but the trouble of setting them out. Men could afford then to stick a tree by every wall-side and let it take its chance. I see nobody planting trees to-day in such out-of-the-way places, along the lonely roads and lanes, and at the bottom of dells in the wood. Now that they have grafted trees, and pay a price for them, they collect them into a plat by their houses, and fence them in,—and the end of it all will be that we shall be compelled to look for our apples in a barrel.

This is "The word of the Lord that came to Joel the son of Pethuel.

"Hear this, ye old men, and give ear, all ye inhabitants of the land! Hath this been in your days, or even in the days of your fathers? . . . .

"That which the palmer-worm hath left hath the locust eaten; and that which the locust hath left hath the canker-worm eaten; and that which the canker-worm hath left hath the caterpillar eaten.

"Awake, ye drunkards, and weep! and howl, all ye drinkers of wine, because of the new wine! for it is cut off from your mouth.

"For a nation is come up upon my land, strong, and without number, whose teeth are the teeth of a lion, and he hath the cheek-teeth of a great lion.

"He hath laid my vine waste, and barked my fig-tree; he hath made it clean bare, and cast it away; the branches thereof are made white. . . . .

"Be ye ashamed, O ye husbandmen! howl, O ye vine-dressers! . . . .

"The vine is dried up, and the fig-tree languisheth; the pomegranate-tree, the palm-tree also, and the apple-tree, even all the trees of the field, are withered: because joy is withered away from the sons of men."

Huckleberries

Agrestem tenui meditabor arundine musam
I am going to play a rustic strain on my slender reed—
non injussa cano—
but I trust that I do not sing unbidden things.

MANY public speakers are accustomed, as I think foolishly, to talk about what they call *little things* in a patronising way sometimes, advising, perhaps, that they be not wholly neglected; but in making this distinction they really use no juster measure than a ten-foot pole, and their own ignorance. According to this rule a small potatoe is a little thing, a big one a great thing. A hogshead-full of anything—the big cheese which it took so many oxen to draw—a national salute—a state-muster—a fat ox—the horse Columbus—or Mr. Blank—the Ossian Boy—there is no danger that any body will call these *little things*. A cartwheel is a great thing—a snow flake a little thing. The *Wellingtonia gigantea*—the famous California tree, is a great thing—the seed from which it sprang a little thing—scarcely one traveller has noticed the seed at all—and so with all the seeds or origins of things. But Pliny said—*In minimis Natura praestat*—Nature excels in the least things.

In this country a political speech, whether by Mr. Seward or Caleb Cushing, is a great thing, a ray of light a little thing. It would be felt to be a greater national calamity if you should take six inches from the corporeal bulk of one or two gentlemen in Congress, than if you should take a yard from their wisdom and manhood.

I have noticed that whatever is thought to be covered by the word *education*—whether reading, writing or 'rithmetick—is a great thing, but almost all that constitutes education is a little thing in the estimation of such speakers as I refer to. In short, whatever they know and care but *little* about is a little thing, and accordingly almost everything good or great is little in their sense, and is very slow to grow any bigger.

When the husk gets separated from the kernel, almost all men run after the husk and pay their respects to that. It is only the husk of Christianity that is so bruited and wide spread in this world, the kernel is still the very least and rarest of all things. There is not a single church founded on it. To obey the higher law is generally considered the last manifestation of littleness.

I have observed that many English naturalists have a pitiful habit of speaking of their proper pursuit as a sort of trifling or waste of time—a mere interruption to more important employments and 'severer studies'—for which they must ask pardon of the reader. As if they would have you believe that all the rest of their lives was consecrated to some truly great and serious enterprise. But it happens that we never hear more of this, as we certainly should, if it were only some great public or philanthropic service, and therefore conclude that they have been engaged in the heroic and magnanimous enterprise of feeding, clothing, housing and warming themselves and their dependents, the chief value of all which was that it enabled them to pursue just these studies of which they speak so slightingly. The 'severer study' they refer to was keeping their accounts. Comparatively speaking—what they call their graver pursuits and severer studies was the real trifling and misspense of life—and were they such fools as not to know it? It is, in effect at least, mere cant. All mankind have depended on them for this intellectual food.

I presume that every one of my audience knows what a huckleberry is—has seen a huckleberry—gathered a huckleberry—nay tasted a huckleberry—and that being the case, that you will not be averse to revisiting the huckleberry field in imagination this evening, though the pleasure of this excursion may fall as far short of the reality, as the flavor of a dried huckleberry is inferior to that of a fresh one.

Huckleberries begin to be ripe July third (or generally the thirteenth), are thick enough to pick about the twenty-second, at their height about the fifth of August, and last fresh till after the middle of that month.

This, as you know, is an upright shrub more or less stout depending on the exposure, with a spreading bushy top—a dark brown bark—red recent shoots and thick leaves. The flowers are smaller and much more red than those of the other species.

It is said to range from the Saskatchewan to the mountains of Georgia, and from the Atlantic to the Mississippi in this latitude—but it abounds over but a small part of this area, and there are large tracts where it is not found at all.

By botanists it is called of late, but I think without good reason, *Gaylussacia resinosa*, after the celebrated French chemist. If he had been the first to distil its juices and put them in this globular bag, he would deserve this honor, or if he had been a celebrated picker of huckleberries, perchance paid for his schooling so, or only notoriously a lover of them, we should not so much object. But it does not appear that he ever saw one. What if a committee of Parisian naturalists had been appointed to break this important news to an Indian maiden who had just filled her basket on the shore of Lake Huron! It is as if we should hear that the Daguerreotype had been *finally* named after the distinguished Chippeway conjurer, The-Wind-that-Blows. By another it has been called *Andromeda baccata*, the berry bearing andromeda—but he evidently lived far away from huckleberries and milk.

I observe green huckleberries by the nineteenth of June, and perhaps three weeks later, when I have forgotten them, I first notice on some hill side exposed to the light, some black or blue ones amid the green ones and the leaves, always sooner than I had expected, and though they may be manifestly premature, I make it a point to taste them, and so inaugurate the huckleberry season.

In a day or two the black are so thick among the green ones that they no longer incur the suspicion of being worm-eaten, and perhaps a day later I pluck a handful from one bush, and I do not fail to make report of it when I get home, though it is rarely believed, most people are so behind hand in their year's accounts.

Early in August, in a favorable year, the hills are black with them. At Nagog Pond I have seen a hundred bushels in one field—the bushes drooping over the rocks with the weight of them—and a very handsome sight they are, though you should not pluck one of them. They are of various forms, colors and flavors—some round—some pear-shaped—some glossy black—some dull black, some blue with a tough and thick skin (though they are never of the peculiar light blue of blueberries with a bloom)—some sweeter, some more insipid—etc., etc., more varieties than botanists take notice of.

To-day perhaps you gather some of those large, often pear-shaped, sweet blue ones which grow tall and thinly amid the rubbish where woods have been cut. They have not borne there before for a century—being over-shadowed and stinted by the forest—but they have the more concentrated their juices—and profited by the new recipes which nature has given them—and now they offer to you fruit of the very finest flavor, like wine of the oldest vintage.

And tomorrow you come to a strong moist soil where the black ones shine with such a gloss—every one its eye on you, and the blue are so large and firm, that you can hardly believe them to be huckleberries at all, or edible; but you seem to have travelled into a foreign country, or else are dreaming.

They are a firmer berry than most of the whortleberry family—and hence are the most marketable.

If you look closely at a huckleberry you will see that it is dotted, as if sprinkled over with a yellow dust or meal, which looks as if it could be rubbed off. Through a microscope, it looks like a resin which has exuded, and on the small green fruit is of a conspicuous light orange or lemon color, like small specks of yellow lichens. It is apparently the same with that shining resinous matter which so conspicously covers the leaves when they are unfolding, making them sticky to the touch—whence this species is called *resinosa* or resinous.

There is a variety growing in swamps—a very tall and slender bush drooping or bent like grass to one side—commonly three or four feet high, but often seven feet—the berries, which are later than the former, are round and glossy black—with resinous dots as usual—and grow in flattish topped racemes—sometimes ten or twelve together, though generally more scattered. I call it the swamp-huckleberry.

But the most marked variety is the *red*-huckleberry—the *white* of some, (for the less ripe are whitish)—which ripens at the same time with the black. It is red with a white cheek, often slightly pear-shaped, semitransparent with a luster, very finely and indistinctly white dotted. It is as easily distinguished from the common in the green state as when ripe. I know of but three or four places in the town where they grow. It might be called *Gaylussacia resinosa var. erythrocarpa*.

I once did some surveying for a man, who remarked, but not till the job was nearly done, that he did not know when he should pay me. I did not at first pay much heed to this observation, though it was unusual, supposing that he meant to pay me within a reasonable time. Nevertheless it occurred to me that if he did not know when he should pay me still less did I know when I should be paid. He added, however, that I was perfectly secure, for there were the pigs in the stye (and as nice pigs as ever were seen) and there was his farm itself which I had surveyed, and knew was there as much as he. All this had its due influence in increasing my sense of security, as you may suppose. After many months he sent me a quart of red huckleberries, for they grew on his farm, and this I thought was ominous; he distinguished me altogether too much by this gift, since I was not his particular friend. I saw that it was the first installment of my dues—and that it would go a great way toward being the last. In the course of years he paid a part of the debt in money, and that is the last that I have heard of it. I shall beware of red huckleberry gifts in the future.

Then there is the Late Whortleberry—Dangleberry or Blue Tangles—whose fruit does not begin to be ripe until about a month after huckleberries begin, when these and blueberries are commonly shrivelled and spoiling—on about August seventh, and is in its prime near the end of August.

This is a tall and handsome bush about twice as high as a huckleberry bush, with altogether a glaucous aspect, growing in shady copses where it is rather moist, and to produce much fruit it seems to require wet weather.

The fruit is one of the handsomest of berries, smooth, round and blue, larger than most huckleberries and more transparent, on long stems dangling two or three inches, and more or less tangled. By the inexperienced it is suspected to be poisonous, and so avoided, and perhaps is the more fair and memorable to them on that account. Though quite good to eat, it has a peculiar, slightly astringent, and compared with most huckleberries, not altogether pleasant flavor, and a tough skin.

At the end of the first week of September, they are commonly the only edible Whortleberries which are quite fresh. They are rare hereabouts however, and it is only in certain years that you can find enough for a pudding.

There is still another kind of Huckleberry growing in this town, called the *Hairy Huckleberry*, which ripens about the same time with the last. It is quite rare, growing only in the wildest and most neglected places, such as cold sphagnous swamps where the *Andromeda polifolia* and *Kalmia glauca* are found, and in some almost equally neglected but firmer low ground. The berries are oblong and black, and, with us, roughened with short hairs. It is the only species of *Vaccinieae* that I know of in this town whose fruit is inedible; though I have seen another kind of Whortleberry, the *Deerberry* or Squaw Huckleberry, growing in another part of the state, whose fruit is said to be equally inedible. The former is merely insipid however. Some which grow on firmer ground have a little more flavor, but the thick and shaggy-feeling coats of the berries left in the mouth are far from agreeable to the palate.

Both these and Dangleberries are placed in the same genus (or section) with the common huckleberry.

Huckleberries are very apt to dry up and not attain their proper size—unless rain comes to save them before the end of July. They will be dried quite hard and black by drought even before they have ripened. On the other hand they frequently burst open and are so spoiled in consequence of copious rains when they are fully ripe.

They *begin* to be soft and wormy as early as the middle of August, and generally about the twentieth the children cease to carry them round to sell, as they are suspected by the purchasers.

How late when the huckleberries begin to be wormy and the pickers are deserting the fields! The walker feels very solitary now.

But in woods and other cool places they commonly last quite fresh a week or more longer, depending on the season. In some years when there are far more berries than pickers or even worms, and the birds appear to pass them by, I have found them plump, fresh, and quite thick, though with a somewhat dried taste, the fourteenth of October, when the bushes were mostly leafless, and the leaves that were left, were all red, and they continued to hold on after the leaves had all fallen, till they were softened and spoiled by rain.

Sometimes they begin to dry up generally by the middle of August—after they are ripe, but before spoiling, and by the end of that month I have seen the bushes so withered and brown owing to the drought, that they appeared dead like those which you see broken off by the pickers, or as if burnt.

I have seen the hills still black with them, though hard and shrivelled as if dried in a pan, late in September. And one year I saw an abundance of them still holding on the eleventh of December, they having dried ripe prematurely, but these had no sweetness left. The sight of them thus dried by nature may have originally suggested to the Indians to dry them artificially.

High-blueberries, the second kind of low-blueberries, huckleberries and low-blackberries are all at their height generally during the first week of August. In the dog-days (or the first ten of them) they abound and attain their full size.

Huckleberries are classed by botanists with the cranberries (both bog and mountain)—snowberry, bearberry—mayflower, checkerberry—the andromedas, clethra, laurels, azaleas, rhodora, ledum, pyrolas, prince's pine, Indian pipes, and many other plants, and they are called all together the Heath Family, they being in many respects similar to and occupying similar ground with the heaths of the Old World, which we have not. If the first botanists had been American this might have been called the Huckleberry Family including the heaths. Plants of this order (*Ericaceae*) are said to be among the earliest ones found in a fossil state, and one would say that they promised to last as long as any on this globe. George B. Emerson says that the whortleberry differs from the heath proper, 'essentially only in its juicy fruit surrounded by the calyx segments.'

The genus to which the whortleberries belong, is called by most botanists *Vaccinium*, which I am inclined to think is properly derived from *bacca*, a berry, as if these were the chief of all berries, though the etymology of this word is in dispute.

Whortle- or Hurtleberry, Bilberry, and Blae or Blea, that is *blue* berry are the names given in England originally to the fruit of the *Vaccinium myrtillus* which we have not in New England and also to the more scarce and local *Vaccinium uliginosum* which we have.

The word whortleberry is said to be derived from the Saxon *heort-berg* (or *heorot-berg*), the hart's berry.

Hurts is an old English word used in heraldry, where, according to Bailey, it is 'certain balls resembling hurtleberries.'

The Germans say *Heidel-beere*, that is *heath berry*.

Huckleberry—this word is used by Lawson in 1709—appears to be an American word derived from Whortleberry—and applied to fruits of the same family, but for the most part of different species from the English whortleberries. According to the Dictionary the word berry is from the Saxon *beria*—a grape or cluster of grapes. A French name of whortleberry is 'raisin des bois'—grape of the woods. It is evident that the word berry has a new significance in America.

We do not realize how rich our country is in berries. The ancient Greeks and Romans appear not to have made much account of strawberries, huckleberries, melons etc. because they had not got them.

The Englishman Lindley, in his *Natural System of Botany*, says that the *Vaccinieae* are 'Natives of North America, where they are found in great abundance as far as high northern latitudes; sparingly in Europe; and not uncommonly on high land in the Sandwich Islands.'

Or as George B. Emerson states it, they 'are found chiefly in the temperate, or on mountains in the warmer regions of America. Some are found in Europe; some on the continent and islands of Asia, and on islands in the Atlantic, Pacific and Indian Oceans.' 'The whortleberries and cranberries,' says he, 'take the place, throughout the northern part of this continent, of the heaths of the corresponding climates of Europe; and fill it with no less of beauty, and incomparably more of use.'

According to the last arrangement of our plants, we have fourteen species of the Whortleberry Family (*Vaccinieae*) in New England, eleven of which bear edible berries, eight, berries which are eaten raw, and five of the last kind are abundant—to wit—the huckleberry—the bluet or Pennsylvania blueberry—the Canada blueberry (in the northern part of New England)—the second or common low blueberry—and the high or swamp-blueberry (not to mention the Dangle-berry, which is common in some seasons and localities).

On the other hand I gather from Loudon and others that there are only two species growing in England, which are eaten raw, answering to our eight—to wit, the Bilberry (*V. myrtillus*) and the Blea-berry or Bog Whortleberry (*V. uliginosum*), both of which are found in North America, and the last is the common one on the summit of the White Mountains, but in Great Britain it is found only in the northern part of England and in Scotland. This leaves only one in England to our five which are abundant.

In short, it chances that of the thirty-two species of *Vaccinium* which Loudon describes, all except the above two and four more are referred to North America alone, and only three or possibly four are found in Europe.

Yet the few Englishmen with whom I have spoken on this subject love to think and to say that they have as many huckleberries as we. I will therefore quote the most which their own authorities say not already quoted, about the abundance and value of their only two kinds which are eaten raw.

Loudon says of the bog whortleberry (*V. uliginosum*), 'The berries are agreeable but inferior in flavor to those of *Vaccinium myrtillus* [the bilberry]; eaten in large quantities, they occasion giddiness, and a slight headache.'

And of their only common whortleberry (*V. myrtillus*), he says, 'It is found in every country in Britain, from Cornwall to Caithness, least frequently in the south-eastern countries, and increases in quantity as we advance northward.' It 'is an elegant and also a fruit-bearing plant.' The berries 'are eaten in tarts or with cream, or made into a jelly, in the northern and western counties of England; and, in other parts of the country they are made into pies and puddings.' They 'are very acceptable to children either eaten by themselves, or with milk' or otherwise. They 'have an astringent quality.'

Coleman in his "Woodlands, Heaths, and Hedges," says 'The traveller in our upland and mountain districts can hardly have failed to notice, as his almost constant companion, this cheerful little shrub, . . . it flourishes best in a high airy situation, only the summits of the very loftiest mountains of which this country can boast being too elevated for this hardy little mountaineer.' 'In Yorkshire, and many parts of the north, large quantities of bilberries are brought into the market, being extensively used as an ingredient in pies and puddings, or preserved in the form of jam. . . . Much, however, of the relish of these wilding fruits must be set down to the exhilarating air, and those charms of scenery that form the accessories of a mountain feast; . . . One of the prettiest sights that greet one's eye in the districts where it abounds, is that of a party of rustic children "a-bilberrying" (for the greater portion of those that come to market are collected by children); there they may be seen, knee deep in the "wires," or clambering over the broken gray rocks to some rich nest of berries, their tanned faces glowing with health, and their picturesque dress (or undress)—with here and there bits of bright red, blue, or white—to the painter's eye contrasting beautifully with the purple, gray and brown of the moorland, and forming altogether rich pictorial subjects.'

These authorities tell us that children and others eat the fruit, just as they tell us that the birds do. It is evident from all this that whortleberries do not make an important part of the regular food of the Old English people in their season, as they do of the New Englanders. What should we think of a summer in which we did not taste a huckleberry pudding? That is to Jonathan what his plum pudding is to John Bull.

Yet Dr. Manassah Cutler, one of the earliest New England botanists, speaks of the huckleberry lightly as being merely a fruit which children love to eat with their milk. What ingratitude thus to shield himself behind the children! I should not wonder if it turned out that Dr. Manassah Cutler ate his huckleberry pudding or pie regularly through the season, as many his equals do. I should have pardoned him had he frankly put in his thumb and pulled out a plum, and cried 'What a Great Doctor am I?' But probably he was lead astray by reading English books or it may be that the Whites did not make so much use of them in his time.

Widely dispersed as their bilberry may still be in England, it was undoubtedly far more abundant there once. One botanist says that 'This is one of the species, that if allowed, would overrun Britain, and form, with *Culluna vulgaris* (heather) and *Empetrum nigrum* (crowberry, which grows on our

White Mountains), much of the natural physiognomical character of its vegetation.'

The genus *Gaylussacia*, to which our huckleberry belongs, has no representative in Great Britain, nor does our species extend very far northward in this country.

So I might say of edible berries generally, that there are far fewer kinds in Old than in New England.

Take the *rubuses* or what you might call bramble berries, for instance, to which genus our raspberries, blackberries and thimbleberries belong. According to Loudon there are five kinds indigenous in Britain to our eight. But of these five only two appear to be at all common, while we have four kinds both very common and very good. The Englishman Coleman says of their best, the English raspberry, which species we also cultivate, that 'the wilding is not sufficiently abundant to have much importance.'

And the same is true of wild fruits generally. Hips and haws are much more important comparatively there than here, where they have hardly got any popular name.

I state this to show how contented and thankful we ought to be.

It is to be remembered that the vegetation of Great Britain is that of a much more northern latitude than where we live, that some of our alpine shrubs are found on the plain there and their two whortleberries are alpine or extreme northern plants with us.

If you look closely you will find blueberry and huckleberry bushes under your feet, though they may be feeble and barren, throughout all our woods, the most persevering Native Americans, ready to shoot up into place and power at the next election among the plants, ready to reclothe the hills when man has laid them bare and feed all kinds of pensioners. What though the woods be cut down; it appears that this emergency was long ago anticipated and provided for by Nature, and the interregnum is not allowed to be a barren one. She not only begins instantly to heal that scar, but she compensates us for the loss and refreshes us with fruits such as the forest did not produce. As the sandal wood is said to diffuse a perfume around the woodman who cuts it—so in this case Nature rewards with unexpected fruits the hand that lays her waste.

I have only to remember each year where the woods have been cut just long enough to know where to look for them. It is to refresh us thus once in a century that they bide their time on the forest floor. If the farmer mows and burns over his overgrown pasture for the benefit of the grass, or to keep the children out, the huckleberries spring up there more vigorous than ever, and the fresh blueberry shoots tinge the earth crimson. All our hills are, or have been, huckleberry hills, the three hills of Boston and no doubt Bunker Hill among the rest. My mother remembers a woman who went a-whortleberrying where Dr. Lowell's church now stands.

In short the whortleberry bushes in the Northern States and British America are a sort of miniature forest surviving under the great forest, and reappearing when the latter is cut, and also extending northward beyond it. The small berry-bearing shrubs of this family, as the crowberry, bilberry, and cranberry, are called by the Esquimaux in Greenland, 'berry grass,' and Crantz says that the Greenlanders cover their winter houses with 'bilberry bushes,' together with turf and earth. They also burn them; and I hear that some body in this neighborhood has invented a machine for cutting up huckleberry bushes for fuel.

It is remarkable how universally, as it respects soil and exposure, the whortleberry family is distributed with us, almost we may say a new species for every thousand feet of elevation. One kind or another, of those of which I am speaking, flourishing in every soil and locality.

There is the high blueberry in swamps—the second low blueberry, with the huckleberry, on almost all fields and hills—the Pennsylvanian and Canada blueberries especially in cool and airy places in openings in the woods and on hills and mountains, while we have two kinds confined to the alpine tops of our highest mountains—the family thus ranging from the lowest valleys to the highest mountain tops, and forming the prevailing small shrubbery of a great part of New England.

The same is true *hereabouts* of a single species of this family, the huckleberry proper. I do not know of a spot where any shrub grows in this neighborhood, but one or another variety of the huckleberry may also grow there. It is stated in

Loudon that all the plants of this order 'require a peat soil, or a soil of a close cohesive nature,' but this is not the case with the huckleberry. It grows on the tops of our highest hills—no pasture is too rocky or barren for it—it grows in such deserts as we have, standing in pure sand—and at the same time it flourishes in the strongest and most fertile soil. One variety is peculiar to quaking bogs where there can hardly be said to be any soil beneath, to say nothing of another but unpalatable species, the hairy huckleberry, which is found there. It also extends through all our woods more or less thinly, and a distinct species, the dangleberry, belongs especially to moist woods and thickets.

Such care has Nature taken to furnish to birds and quadrupeds, and to men, a palatable berry of this kind, slightly modified by soil and climate, wherever the consumer may chance to be. Corn and potatoes, apples and pears, have comparatively a narrow range, but we can fill our basket with whortleberries on the summit of Mount Washington, above almost all other shrubs with which we are familiar, the same kind which they have in Greenland, and again when we get home, with another species in our lowest swamps, such as the Greenlanders never dreamed of.

The berries *which I celebrate*, appear to have a range, most of them, very nearly coterminous with what has been called the Algonquin Family of Indians, whose territories embraced what are now the Eastern, Middle and Northwestern States—and the Canadas—and surrounded those of the Iroquois in what is now New York. These were the small fruits of the Algonquin and Iroquois Families.

Of course the Indians naturally made a much greater account of wild fruits than we do, and among the most important of these were huckleberries.

They taught us not only the use of corn and how to plant it, but also of whortleberries and how to dry them for winter. We should have hesitated long before we tasted some kinds if they had not set us the example, knowing by old experience that they were not only harmless but salutary. I have added a few to my number of edible berries, by walking behind an Indian in Maine, and observing that he ate some which I never thought of tasting before.

To convince you of the extensive use which the Indians made of huckleberries, I will quote at length the testimony of the most observing travellers, on this subject, as nearly as possible in the order in which it was given us; for it is only after listening patiently to such reiterated and concurring testimony, of various dates—and respecting widely distant localities—that we come to realize the truth.

But little is said by the discoverers of the use which the Indians made of the fresh berries in their season—the hand to mouth use of them—because there was little to be said—though in this form they may have been much the most important to them. We have volumes of recipes, called cookbooks—but when a fruit or a tart is ready for the table, nothing remains but to eat it without any more words. We therefore have few or no accounts of Indians going a-huckleberrying—though they had more than a six weeks' vacation for that purpose, and probably camped on the huckleberry field.

I will go far enough back for my authorities to show that they did not learn the use of these berries from us whites.

In the year 1615, Champlain, the founder of Quebec, being far up the Ottawa spying out the land and taking notes among the Algonquins, on his way to the Fresh Water Sea since called Lake Huron—observed that the natives made a business of collecting and drying for winter use, a small berry which he calls blues, and also raspberries—the former is the common blueberry of those regions, by some considered a variety of our early low blueberry (*Vaccinium Pennsylvanicum*); and again when near the lake he observes that the natives make a kind of bread of pounded corn sifted and mixed with mashed beans which have been boiled—and sometimes they put dried blueberries and raspberries into it.

This was five years before the Pilgrims crossed the Atlantic, and is the first account of huckleberry cake that I know of.

Gabriel Sagard, a Franciscan Friar, in the account of his visit to the Huron Country in 1624, says, 'There is so great a quantity of blues, which the Hurons call *Ohentaque*, and other little fruits which they call by a general name *Hahique*, that the savages regularly dry them for the winter, as we do prunes in the sun, and that serves them for comfits for the sick, and to give taste to their *sagamite* [or gruel, making a kind of plum porridge], and also to put into the little loaves (or cakes, *pains*) which they cook under the ashes.'

According to him they put not only blueberries and raspberries into their bread but strawberries, 'wild mulberries (*meures champestres*) and other little fruits dry and green.'

Indeed the gathering of blueberries by the savages is spoken of by the early French explorers as a regular and important harvest with them.

Le Jeune, the Superior of the Jesuits in Canada—residing at Quebec—in his Relation for 1639—says of the savages that 'Some figure to themselves a paradise full of *bluets*.'

Roger Williams, who knew the Indians well, in his account of those in his neighborhood—published in 1643—tells us that '*Sautaash* are those currants (grapes and whortleberries) dried by the natives, and so preserved all the year, which they beat to powder and mingle it with their parched meal, and make a delicate dish which they call *Sautauthig*, which is as sweet to them as plum or spice cake to the English.'

But Nathaniel Morton, in his *New England's Memorial*, printed in 1669—speaking of white men going to treat with Canonicus, a Narraghanset Indian, about Mr. Oldham's death in 1636—says 'Boiled chestnuts is their white bread, and because they would be extraordinary in their feasting, they strove for variety after the English manner, boiling puddings made of beaten corn, putting therein great store of black berries, somewhat like currants'—no doubt whortleberries. This *seems* to *imply* that the Indians imitated the English—or set before their guests dishes to which they themselves were not accustomed—or which were extra-ordinary. But we have seen that these dishes were not new or unusual to them and it was the whites who imitated the Indians rather.

John Josselyn—in his *New England's Rarities*, published in 1672—says under the fruits of New England, 'Bill-berries, two kinds, black and sky colored, which is more frequent. . . . The Indians dry them in the sun and sell them to the English by the bushel, who make use of them instead of currence, putting of them into puddens, both boyled and baked, and into water gruel.'

The largest Indian huckleberry party that I have heard of is mentioned in the life of Captain Church who, it is said, when in pursuit of King Phillip in the summer of 1676, came across a large body of Indians, chiefly squaws, gathering whortleberries on a plain near where New Bedford now is, and killed and took prisoner sixty-six of them—some throwing away their baskets and their berries in their flight. They told him that their husbands and brothers, a hundred of them, who with others had their rendezvous in a great cedar swamp nearby, had recently left them to gather whortleberries there, while they went to Sconticut Neck to kill cattle and horses for further and more substantial provisions.

La Hontan in 1689, writing from the Great Lakes, repeats what so many French travellers had said about the Indians drying and preserving blueberries—saying, 'The savages of the north make a great harvest of them in summer, which is a great resource especially when the chase fails them.' They were herein more provident than we commonly suppose.

Father Rasles—who was making a Dictionary of the Abenaki Language in 1691 (at Norridgewock?)—says that their word for blueberries was fresh *Satar*, dry *Sakisatar*—and the words in their name for July meant when the blueberries are ripe. This shows how important they were to them.

Father Hennepin—who writes in 1697—says that his captors, Naudowessi (the Sioux!), near the falls of St. Anthony, feasted on wild-rice seasoned with blueberries, 'which they dry in the sun during the summer, and which are as good as raisins of Corinth'—[that is, the imported currants].

The Englishman John Lawson, who published an account of the Carolinas in 1709, says of North Carolina, 'The hurts, huckleberries or blues of this country are four sorts. . . . The first sort is the same blue or bilberry that grows plentifully in the North of England.' 'The second sort grows on a small bush,' the fruit being larger than the last. The third grows three or four feet high in low land. 'The fourth sort grows upon trees, some ten and twelve foot high, and the thickness of a man's arm; these are found in the runs and low grounds. . . . The Indians get many bushels, and dry them on mats, whereof they make plum bread, and many other eatables.' He is the first author that I remember who uses the word 'huckleberry.'

The well known natural botanist John Bartram, when returning to Philadelphia in 1743 from a Journey through what was then the wilderness of Pennsylvania and New York, to the Iroquois and Lake Ontario, says that he 'found [when in Pennsylvania] an Indian squaw drying huckleberries. This is done by setting four forked sticks in the ground, about three or four feet high, then others across, over them the stalks of our common *Jacea* or *Saratula*, on these lie the berries, as malt is spread on the hair cloth over the kiln. Underneath she had kindled a smoke fire, which one of her children was tending.'

Kalm, in his travels in this country in 1748–9, writes, 'On my travels through the country of the Iroquois, they offered me, whenever they designed to treat me well, fresh maize bread, baked in an oblong shape, mixed with dried huckleberries, which lay as close in it as the raisins in a plumb pudding.'

The Moravian missionary Heckewelder, who spent a great part of his life among the Delawares toward the end of the last century, states that they mixed with their bread, which was six inches in diameter by one inch thick—'whortleberries green or dry, but not boiled.'

Lewis and Clarke in 1805 found the Indians west of the Rocky Mountains using dried berries extensively.

And finally in Owen's Geological Survey of *Wisconsin, Iowa and Minnesota*—published in 1852—occurs the following. '*Vaccinium Pennsylvanicum (Lam.)* [that is, our early low blueberry]—Barrens on the upper St. Croix. This is the common Huckleberry, associated with the characteristic growth of the *Pinus Banksiana*, covering its sandy ridges with a verdant undergrowth, and an unsurpassed luxuriance of fruit. By the Indians these are collected and smoke dried in great quantities, and in this form constitute an agreeable article of food.'

Hence you see that the Indians from time immemorial, down to the present day, all over the northern part of America—have made far more extensive use of the whortleberry—at all seasons and in various ways—than we—and that they were far more important to them than to us.

It appears from the above evidence that the Indians used their dried berries commonly in the form of a cake, and also of huckleberry porridge or pudding.

What we call huckleberry cake made of Indian meal and huckleberries was evidently the principal cake of the aborigines—though they also used other berries and fruits in a similar manner and often put things into their cake which would not have been agreeable to our palates—though I do not hear that they ever put any soda or pearl ash or alum into it. We have no national cake so universal and well known as this was in all parts of the country where corn and huckleberries grew.

They enjoyed it all alone ages before our ancestors heard of their Indian corn—or their huckleberries—and probably if you had travelled here a thousand years ago it would have been offered you alike on the Connecticut, the Potomac, the Niagara, the Ottawa and the Mississippi.

The last Indian of Nantucket, who died a few years ago, was very properly represented in a painting which I saw there, with a basket full of huckleberries in his hand, as if to hint at the employment of his last days. I trust that I may not outlive the last of the huckleberries.

Tanner, who was taken captive by the Indians in 1789, and spent a good part of his life as an Indian, gives the Chippeway names of at least five kinds of whortleberries. He gives '*meen*—blue berry, *meen-un*—blue berries,' and says that 'this is a word that enters into the composition of almost all words which are used as the names of fruits,' that is as a terminal syllable. Hence this would appear to have been the typical berry—or berry of berries—among the Chippeway as it is among us.

I think that it would be well if the Indian names, were as far as possible restored and applied to the numerous species of huckleberries, by our botanists—instead of the very inadequate—Greek and Latin or English ones at present used. They might serve both a scientific and popular use. Certainly it is not the best point of view to look at this peculiarly American family as it were from the other side of the Atlantic. It is still in doubt whether the Latin word for the genus *Vaccinium* means a berry or a flower.

Botanists, on the look out for what they thought a respectable descent, have long been inclined to trace this family backward to Mount Ida. Tourneforte does not hesitate to give it the ancient name of *Vine of Mount Ida*. The common English Raspberry also is called *Rubus Idaea* or the Mount

Ida bramble—from the old Greek name. The truth of it seems to be that blueberries and raspberries flourish best in cool and airy situations, on hills and mountains, and I can easily believe that something *like* these at least grows on Mount Ida. But Mount Monadnoc is as good as Mount Ida, and probably better for blueberries, though its name is said to mean *Bad Rock*. But the worst rocks are the best for poets' uses. Let us then exchange that oriental uncertainty for this western certainty.

We have in the northern states a few wild plums and inedible crab apples—a few palatable grapes—and many tolerable nuts—but I think that the various species of berries are our *wild fruits* which are to be compared with the more celebrated ones of the tropics, and for my part I would not exchange fruits with them—for the object is not merely to get a ship-load of something which you can eat or sell, but the pleasure of gathering it is to be taken into the account.

What is the pear crop as yet to the huckleberry crop? Horticulturists make a great ado about their pears, but how many families raise or buy a barrel of pears in a year all told? They are comparatively insignificant. I do not taste more than half a dozen pears annually, and I suspect that the majority fare worse even than I. (This was written before my neighbor's pear-orchard began to bear. Now he frequently fills my own and others' pockets with the fruit.) But Nature heaps the table with berries for six weeks or more. Indeed the apple crop is not so important as the huckleberry crop. Probably the apples consumed in this town annually do not amount to more than one barrel per family. But what is this to a month or more of huckleberrying to every man, woman and child, and the birds into the bargain. Even the crop of oranges, lemons, nuts, raisins, figs, quinces, etc. is of little importance to us compared with these.

They are not unprofitable in a pecuniary sense; I hear that some of the inhabitants of Ashby sold $2000 worth of huckleberries in '56.

In May and June all our hills and fields are adorned with a profusion of the pretty little more or less bell-shaped flowers of this family, commonly turned toward the earth and more or less tinged with red or pink, and resounding with the hum

of insects, each one the forerunner of a berry the most natural, wholesome and palatable that the soil can produce. I
think to myself, these are the blossoms of the *Vaccinieae* or
Whortleberry family, which affords so large a portion of our
berries; the berry-promising flower of the *Vaccinieae*! This
crop grows wild all over the country—wholesome, bountiful
and free, a real ambrosia. And yet men, the foolish demons
that they are, devote themselves to the culture of tobacco, in-
venting slavery and a thousand other curses for that purpose—with infinite pains and inhumanity go raise tobacco all
their lives, and that is the staple instead of huckleberries.
Wreathes of tobacco smoke go up from this land, the only incense which its inhabitants burn in honor of their gods. With
what authority can such as we distinguish between Christians
and Mahometans? Almost every interest, as the codfish and
mackerel interest, gets represented at the General Court—but
not the huckleberry interest. The first discoverers and explorers of the land make report of this fruit—but the last make
comparatively little account of them.

Blueberries and huckleberries are such simple, wholesome
and universal fruits that they concern our race much. It is
hard to imagine any country without this kind of berry, on
which men live like birds. Still covering our hills as when the
red men lived here. Are they not the the principal wild fruit?

What means this profusion of berries at this season only?
Nature does her best to feed her children, and the broods of
birds just matured find plenty to eat now. Every bush and
vine does its part and offers a wholesome and palatable diet to
the way-farer. He need not go out of the road to get as many
berries as he wants—of various kinds and qualities according
as his road leads him over high or low, wooded or open
ground—huckleberries of different colors and flavors almost
everywhere—the second kind of low blueberry largest in the
moist ground—high blueberries with their agreeable acid
when his way lies through a swamp, and low blackberries of
two or more varieties on almost every sandy plain and bank
and stone heap.

Man at length stands in such a relation to Nature as the animals which pluck and eat as they go. The fields and hills are a
table constantly spread. Diet-drinks, cordials, wines of all kinds

and qualities, are bottled up in the skins of countless berries for their refreshment, and they quaff them at every turn. They seem offered to us not so much for food as for sociality, inviting us to a pic-nic with Nature. We pluck and eat in remembrance of her. It is a sort of sacrament—a communion—the *not* forbidden fruits, which no serpent tempts us to eat. Slight and innocent savors which relate us to Nature, make us her guests, and entitle us to her regard and protection.

When I see, as now, in climbing one of our hills, huckleberry and blueberry bushes bent to the ground with fruit, I think of them as fruits fit to grow on the most Olympian or heaven-pointing hills.

It does not occur to you at first that where such thoughts are suggested is Mount Olympus, and that you who taste these berries are a god. Why in his only royal moments should man abdicate his throne?

You eat these berries in the dry pastures where they grow not to gratify an appetite, but as simply and naturally as thoughts come into your mind, as if they were the food of thought, dry as itself, and surely they nourish the brain there.

Occasionally there is an unusual profusion of these fruits to compensate for the scarcity of a previous year. I remember some seasons when favorable moist weather had expanded the berries to their full size, so that the hill-sides were literally black with them. There were infinitely more of all kinds than any and all creatures could use.

One such year, on the side of Conantum Hill, they were literally five or six species deep. First, if you searched low down in the shade under all, you found still fresh the great light blue earliest blueberries, bluets, in heavy clusters—that most Olympian fruit of all—delicate flavored, thin-skinned and cool—then, next above, the still denser masses or clusters of the second low blueberry of various varieties, firm and sweet food—and rising above these large blue and black huckleberries of various qualities—and over these ran rampant the low blackberry weighing down the thicket with its wreathes of black fruit, and binding it together in a trembling mass— while here and there the high blackberry, just beginning to be ripe, towered over all the rest. Thus, as it were, the berries hung up lightly in masses or heaps, separated by their leaves and twigs so that the air could circulate through and preserve them; and you went daintily wading through this thicket, picking perhaps only the finest of the high blackberries, as big as the end of your thumb, however big that may be, or clutching here and there a handful of huckleberries for variety, but never suspecting the delicious, cool blue-bloomed ones, which you were crushing with your feet under all. I have in such a case spread aside the bushes and revealed the last kind to those who had never in all their lives seen or heard of it before.

Each such patch, each bush—seems fuller and blacker than the last, as you proceed, and the huckleberries at length swell so big, as if aping the blackberries, that you mark the spot for future years.

There is all this profusion and yet you see neither birds nor beasts eating them—only ants and the huckleberry-bug. It seems fortunate for us that those cows in their pasture do not love them, but pass them by. We do not perceive that birds and quadrupeds make any use of them because they are so abundant we do not miss them, and they are not compelled to come when we are for them. Yet they are far more important to them than to us. We do not notice the robin when it plucks a huckleberry as we do when it visits our favorite cherry tree—and the fox pays his visits to the fields when we are not there.

I once carried my arms full of these bushes to my boat, and while I was rowing homeward two ladies, who were my companions, picked three pints from these alone, casting the bare bushes into the stream from time to time.

Even in ordinary years, when berries are comparatively scarce, I sometimes unexpectedly find so many in some distant and unfrequented part of the town, between and about the careless farmers' houses and walls, that the soil seems more fertile than where I live. Every bush and bramble bears its fruit. The very sides of the road are a fruit garden. The earth there teems with blackberries, huckleberries, thimbleberries, fresh and abundant—no signs of drought nor of pickers. Great shining black berries peep out at me from under the leaves upon the rocks. Do the rocks hold moisture? or are there no fingers to pluck these fruits? I seem to have wandered into a land of greater fertility—some up country Eden. These are the Delectable Hills. It is a land flowing with milk and huckleberries, only they have not yet put the berries into the milk. *There* the herbage never withers, *there* are abundant dews. I ask myself, What are the virtues of the inhabitants that they are thus blessed?

O fortunatos nimium, sua si bona norint Agricolas—
O too fortunate husbandmen if they knew their own
   happiness.

These berries are further important as introducing children to the fields and woods. The season of berrying is so far respected that the school children have a vacation then—and many little fingers are busy picking these small fruits. It is even a pastime, not a drudgery—though it often pays well beside. The First of August is to them the anniversary of Emancipation in New England.

Women and children who never visit distant hills, fields and swamps on any other errand are seen making haste thither now with half their domestic utensils in their hands. The wood-chopper goes into the swamp for fuel in the winter; his wife and children for berries in the summer.

Now you will see who is the thorough countrywoman who does not go to the beach—conversant with berries and nuts— a masculine wild-eyed woman of the fields.

Now for a ride in the hay-rigging to that far off Elysium that Zachariah See-all alighted on—but has not mentioned to every person—in the hay-rigging without springs—trying to sensitive nerves and to full pails, for all alike sit on the bottom—such a ride is favorable to conversation for the incessant rumble hides all defects and fills the otherwise aweful pauses—to be introduced to new scenes more memorable than the berries—but to the old walker the straggling party itself half concealed amid the bushes is the most novel and interesting feature. If hot the boys break up the bushes and carry them to some shady place where the girls can pick them at their ease. But this is a lazy and improvident way— and gives an unsightly look to the hill. There are many events not in the program. If you have an ear for music— perhaps one is the sound of a cow bell—never heard before—

or a sudden thunder shower putting you to flight—or a breakdown.

I served my apprenticeship and have since done considerable journeywork in the huckleberry field. Though I never paid for my schooling and clothing in that way, it was some of the best schooling that I got and paid for itself. Theodore Parker is not the only New England boy who has got his education by picking huckleberries, though he may not have gone to Harvard thereafter, nor to any school more distant than the huckleberry field. *There* was the university itself where you could learn the everlasting Laws, and Medicine and Theology, not under Story, and Warren, and Ware, but far wiser professors than they. Why such haste to go from the huckleberry field to the College yard?

As in old times they who dwelt on the heath, remote from towns, being backward to adopt the doctrines which prevailed in towns, were called heathen in a bad sense, so I trust that we dwellers in the huckleberry pastures, which are our heathlands, shall be slow to adopt the notions of large towns and cities, though perchance we may be nicknamed huckleberry people. But the worst of it is that the emissaries of the towns come more for our berries than they do for our salvation.

Occasionally, in still summer forenoons, when perhaps a mantua-maker was to be dined, and a huckleberry pudding had been decided on (by the authorities), I a lad of ten was despatched to a neighboring hill alone. My scholastic education could be thus far tampered with, and an excuse might be found. No matter how scarce the berries on the near hills, the exact number necessary for a pudding could surely be collected by eleven o'clock—and all ripe ones too though I turned some round three times to be sure they were not premature. My rule in such cases was never to eat one till my dish was full; for going a-berrying implies more things than eating the berries. They at home got nothing but the pudding, a comparatively heavy affair—but I got the forenoon out of doors—to say nothing about the appetite for the pudding. They got only the plums that were in the pudding, but I got the far sweeter plums that never go into it.

At other times, when I had companions, some of them used to bring such remarkably shaped dishes, that I was often curious to see how the berries disposed of themselves in them. Some brought a coffee-pot to the huckleberry field, and such a vessel possessed this advantage at least, that if a greedy boy had skimmed off a handful or two on his way home, he had only to close the lid and give his vessel a shake to have it full again. I have seen this done all round when the party got as far homeward as the Dutch House. It can prob ably be done with any vessel that has much side to it.

There was a Young America then, which has become Old America, but its principles and motives are still the same, only applied to other things. Sometimes, just before reaching the spot—every boy rushed to the hill side and hastily selecting a spot—shouted 'I speak for this place,' indicating its bounds, and another 'I speak for that,' and so on—and this was some-times considered good law for the huckleberry field. At any rate it is a law similar to this by which we have taken posses-sion of the territory of Indians and Mexicans.

I once met with a whole family, father, mother, and chil-dren, ravaging a huckleberry field in this wise. They cut up the bushes as they went and beat them over the edge of a bushel basket, till they had it full of berries, ripe and green, leaves, sticks etc., and so they passed along out of my sight like wild men.

I well remember with what a sense of freedom and spirit of adventure I used to take my way across the fields with my pail, some years later, toward some distant hill or swamp, when dismissed for all day, and I would not now exchange such an expansion of all my being for all the learning in the world. Liberation and enlargement—such is the fruit which all culture aims to secure. I suddenly knew more about my books than if I had never ceased studying them. I found my-self in a schoolroom where I could not fail to see and hear things worth seeing and hearing—where I could not help get-ting my lesson—for my lesson came to me. Such experience often repeated, was the chief encouragement to go to the Academy and study a book at last.

But ah we have fallen on evil days! I hear of pickers or-dered out of the huckleberry fields, and I see stakes set up with written notices forbidding any to pick them. Some let their fields or allow so much for the picking. *Sic transit gloria ruris.* I do not mean to blame any, but all—to bewail our fates generally. We are not grateful enough that we have lived a part of our lives before these things occurred. What becomes of the true value of country life—what, if you must go to market for it? It has come to this, that the butcher now brings round our huckleberries in his cart. Why, it is as if the hangman were to perform the marriage ceremony. Such is the inevitable tendency of our civilization, to reduce huckleberries to a level with beef-steaks—that is to blot out four fifths of it, or the going a-huckleberrying, and leave only a pudding, that part which is the fittest accompaniment to a beef-steak. You all know what it is to go a-beef-steaking. It is to knock your old fellow laborer Bright on the head to begin with—or possibly to cut a steak from him running in the Abyssinian fashion and wait for another to grow there. The butcher's item in chalk on the door is now 'Calf's head and huckleberries.'

I suspect that the inhabitants of England and the continent of Europe have thus lost in a measure their natural rights, with the increase of population and monopolies. The wild fruits of the earth disappear before civilization, or only the husks of them are to be found in large markets. The whole country becomes, as it were, a town or beaten common, and almost the only fruits left are a few hips and haws.

What sort of a country is that where the huckleberry fields are private property? When I pass such fields on the highway, my heart sinks within me. I see a blight on the land. Nature is under a veil there. I make haste away from the accursed spot. Nothing could deform her fair face more. I cannot think of it ever after but as the place where fair and palatable berries, are converted into money, where the huckleberry is desecrated.

It is true, we have as good a right to make berries private property, as to make wild grass and trees such—it is not worse than a thousand other practices which custom has sanctioned—but that is the worst of it, for it suggests how bad the rest are, and to what result our civilization and division of labor naturally tend, to make all things venal.

A., a professional huckleberry picker, has hired B.'s field, and, we will suppose, is now gathering the crop, with a patent huckleberry horse rake.

C., a professed cook, is superintending the boiling of a pudding made of some of the berries.

While Professor D.—for whom the pudding is intended, sits in his library writing a book—a work on the *Vaccinieae* of course.

And now the result of this downward course will be seen in that work—which should be the ultimate fruit of the huckleberry field. It will be worthless. It will have none of the spirit of the huckleberry in it, and the reading of it will be a weariness of the flesh.

I believe in a different kind of division of labor—that Professor D. should be encouraged to divide himself freely between his library and the huckleberry field.

What I chiefly regret in this case, is the in effect dog-in-the-manger result; for at the same time that we exclude mankind from gathering berries in our field, we exclude them from gathering health and happiness and inspiration, and a hundred other far finer and nobler fruits than berries, which are found there, but which we have no notion of gathering and shall not gather ourselves, nor ever carry to market, for there is no market for them, but let them rot on the bushes.

We thus strike only one more blow at a simple and wholesome relation to nature. I do not know but this is the excuse of those who have lately taken to swinging bags of beans and ringing dumb bells. As long as the berries are free to all comers they are beautiful, though they may be few and small, but tell me that this is a blueberry swamp which somebody has hired, and I shall not want even to look at it. We so commit the berries to the wrong hands, that is to the hands of those who cannot appreciate them. This is proved by the fact that if we do not pay them some money, these parties will at once cease to pick them. They have no other interest in berries but a pecuniary one. Such is the constitution of our society that we make a compromise and permit the berries to be degraded, to be enslaved, as it were.

Accordingly in laying claim for the first time to the spontaneous fruit of our pastures, we are inevitably aware of a little meanness, and the merry berry party which we turn away naturally looks down on and despises us. If it were left to the berries to say who should have them, is it not likely that they would prefer to be gathered by the party of children in the hay-rigging, who have come to have a good time merely?

This is one of the taxes which we pay for having a rail-road. All our improvements, so called, tend to convert the country into the town. But I do not see clearly that these successive losses are ever quite made up to us. This suggests, as I have said, what origin and foundation many of our institutions have. I do not say this by way of complaining of this custom in particular, which is beginning to prevail—not that I love Caesar less but Rome more. It is my own way of living that I complain of as well as yours—and therefore I trust that my remarks will come home to you. I hope that I am not so poor a shot, like most clergymen, as to fire into a crowd of a thousand men without hitting somebody—though I do not aim at any one.

Thus we behave like oxen in a flower garden. The true fruit of Nature can only be plucked with a fluttering heart and a delicate hand, not bribed by any earthly reward. No hired man can help us to gather that crop.

Among the Indians, the earth and its productions generally were common and free to all the tribe, like the air and water—but among us who have supplanted the Indians, the public retain only a small yard or common in the middle of the village, with perhaps a grave-yard beside it, and the right of way, by sufferance, by a particular narrow route, which is annually becoming narrower, from one such yard to another. I doubt if you can ride out five miles in any direction without coming to where some individual is tolling in the road—and he expects the time when it will all revert to him or his heirs. This is the way we civilized men have arranged it.

I am not overflowing with respect and gratitude to the fathers who thus laid out our New England villages, whatever precedent they were influenced by, for I think that a 'prentice hand liberated from Old English prejudices could have done much better in this new world. If they were in earnest seeking thus far away 'freedom to worship God,' as some assure us—why did they not secure a little more of it, when it was so cheap and they were about it? At the same time that they built meeting-houses why did they not preserve from desecration and destruction far grander temples not made with hands?

What are the natural features which make a township handsome—and worth going far to dwell in? A river with its waterfalls—meadows, lakes—hills, cliffs or individual rocks, a forest and single ancient trees—such things are beautiful. They have a high use which dollars and cents never represent. If the inhabitants of a town were wise they would seek to preserve these things though at a considerable expense. For such things educate far more than any hired teachers or preachers, or any at present recognized system of school education.

I do not think him fit to be the founder of a state or even of a town who does not foresee the use of these things, but legislates as it were, for oxen chiefly.

It would be worth the while if in each town there were a committee appointed, to see that the beauty of the town received no detriment. If here is the largest boulder in the country, then it should not belong to an individual nor be made into door-steps. In some countries precious metals belong to the crown—so here more precious objects of great natural beauty should belong to the public.

Let us try to keep the new world new, and while we make a wary use of the city, preserve as far as possible the advantages of living in the country.

I think of no natural feature which is a greater ornament and treasure to this town than the river. It is one of the things which determine whether a man will live here or in another place, and it is one of the first objects which we show to a stranger. In this respect we enjoy a great advantage over those neighboring towns which have no river. Yet the town, as a corporation, has never turned any but the most purely utilitarian eyes upon it—and has done nothing to preserve its natural beauty.

They who laid out the town should have made the river available as a common possession forever. The town collectively should at least have done as much as an individual of taste who owns an equal area commonly does in England. Indeed I think that not only the channel but one or both banks of every river should be a public highway—for a river is not useful merely to float on. In this case, one bank might have been reserved as a public walk and the trees that adorned it have been protected, and frequent avenues have been provided leading to it from the main street. This would have cost but few acres of land and but little wood, and we should all have been gainers by it. Now it is accessible only at the bridges at points comparatively distant from the town, and there there is not a foot of shore to stand on unless you trespass on somebody's lot—and if you attempt a quiet stroll down the bank—you soon meet with fences built at right angles with the stream and projecting far over the water—where individuals, naturally enough, under the present arrangement—seek to monopolize the shore. At last we shall get our only view of the stream from the meeting house belfry.

As for the trees which fringed the shore within my remembrance—where are they? and where will the remnant of them be after ten years more?

So if there is any central and commanding hill-top, it should be reserved for the public use. Think of a mountain top in the township—even to the Indians a sacred place—only accessible through private grounds. A temple as it were which you cannot enter without trespassing—nay the temple itself private property and standing in a man's cow yard—for such is commonly the case. New Hampshire courts have lately been deciding, as if it was for them to decide, whether the top of Mount Washington belonged to A or B—and it being decided in favor of B, I hear that he went up one winter with the proper officers and took formal possession. That area should be left unappropriated for modesty and reverence's sake—if only to suggest that the traveller who climbs thither in a degree rises above himself, as well as his native valley, and leaves some of his grovelling habits behind.

I know it is a mere figure of speech to talk about temples nowadays, when men recognize none, and associate the word with heathenism. Most men, it appears to me, do not care for Nature, and would sell their share in all her beauty, for as long as they may live, for a stated and not very large sum. Thank God they cannot yet fly and lay waste the sky as well as the earth. We are safe on that side for the present. It is for the very reason that some do not care for these things that we need to combine to protect all from the vandalism of a few.

It is true, we as yet take liberties and go across lots in most directions but we naturally take fewer and fewer liberties every year, as we meet with more resistance, and we shall soon be reduced to the same straights they are in England, where going across lots is out of the question—and we must ask leave to walk in some lady's park.

There are a few hopeful signs. There is the growing *library*—and then the town does set trees along the highways. But does not the broad landscape itself deserve attention?

We cut down the few old oaks which witnessed the transfer of the township from the Indian to the white man, and perchance commence our museum with a cartridge box taken from a British soldier in 1775. How little we insist on truly grand and beautiful natural features. There may be the most beautiful landscapes in the world within a dozen miles of us, for aught we know—for their inhabitants do not value nor perceive them—and so have not made them known to others—but if a grain of gold were picked up there, or a pearl found in a fresh-water clam, the whole state would resound with the news.

Thousands annually seek the White Mountains to be refreshed by their wild and primitive beauty—but when the country was discovered a similar kind of beauty prevailed all over it—and much of this might have been preserved for our present refreshment if a little foresight and taste had been used.

I do not believe that there is a town in this country which realizes in what its true wealth consists.

I visited the town of Boxboro only eight miles west of us last fall—and far the handsomest and most memorable thing which I saw there, was its noble oak wood. I doubt if there is a finer one in Massachusetts. Let it stand fifty years longer and men will make pilgrimages to it from all parts of the country, and for a worthier object than to shoot squirrels in it—and yet I said to myself, Boxboro would be very like the rest of New England, if she were ashamed of that wood-land. Probably, if the history of this town is written, the historian will have omitted to say a word about this forest—the most interesting thing in it—and lay all the stress on the history of the parish.

It turned out that I was not far from right—for not long after I came across a very brief historical notice of Stow—which then included Boxboro—written by the Reverend John Gardiner in the *Massachusetts Historical Collections*, nearly a hundred years ago. In which Mr. Gardiner, after telling us who was his predecessor in the ministry, and when he himself was settled, goes on to say, 'As for any remarkables, I am of mind there have been the fewest of any town of our standing in the Province. . . . I can't call to mind above one thing worthy of public notice, and that is the grave of Mr. John Green' who, it appears, when in England, 'was made clerk of the exchequer' by Cromwell. 'Whether he was excluded the act of oblivion or not I cannot tell,' says Mr. Gardiner. At any rate he returned to New England and as Gardiner tells us 'lived and died, and lies buried in this place.'

I can assure Mr. Gardiner that he was not excluded from the act of oblivion.

It is true Boxboro was less peculiar for its woods at that date—but they were not less interesting absolutely.

I remember talking a few years ago with a young man who had undertaken to write the history of his native town—a wild and mountainous town far up country, whose very name suggested a hundred things to me, and I almost wished I had the task to do myself—so few of the original settlers had been driven out—and not a single clerk of the exchequer buried in it. But to my chagrin I found that the author was complaining of want of materials, and that the crowning fact of his story was that the town had been the residence of General C— and the family mansion was still standing.

I have since heard, however, that Boxboro is content to have that forest stand, instead of the houses and farms that might supplant it—not because of its beauty—but because the land pays a much larger tax now than it would then.

Nevertheless it is likely to be cut off within a few years for ship-timber and the like. It is too precious to be thus disposed of. I think that it would be wise for the state to purchase and preserve a few such forests.

If the people of Massachusetts are ready to found a professorship of Natural History—so they must see the importance of preserving some portions of nature herself unimpaired.

I find that the rising generation in this town do not know what an oak or a pine is, having seen only inferior specimens. Shall we hire a man to lecture on botany, on oaks for instance, our noblest plants—while we permit others to cut down the few best specimens of these trees that are left? It is like teaching children Latin and Greek while we burn the books printed in those languages.

I think that each town should have a park, or rather a primitive forest, of five hundred or a thousand acres, either in one body or several—where a stick should never be cut for fuel—nor for the navy, nor to make wagons, but stand and decay for higher uses—a common possession forever, for instruction and recreation.

All Walden wood might have been reserved, with Walden in the midst of it, and the Easterbrooks country, an uncultivated area of some four square miles in the north of the town, might have been our huckleberry field. If any owners of these tracts are about to leave the world without natural heirs who need or deserve to be specially remembered, they will do wisely to abandon the possession to all mankind, and not will them to some individual who perhaps has enough already—and so correct the error that was made when the town was laid out. As some give to Harvard College or another Institution, so one might give a forest or a huckleberry field to Concord. This town surely is an institution which deserves to be remembered. Forget the heathen in foreign parts, and remember the pagans and savages here.

We hear of cow commons and ministerial lots, but we want *men* commons and *lay* lots as well. There is meadow and pasture and woodlot for the town's poor, why not a forest and huckleberry field for the town's rich?

We boast of our system of education, but why stop at schoolmasters and schoolhouses? We are all schoolmasters and our schoolhouse is the universe. To attend chiefly to the desk or schoolhouse, while we neglect the scenery in which it is placed, is absurd. If we do not look out we shall find our fine schoolhouse standing in a cow yard at last.

It frequently happens that what the city prides itself on most is its park—those acres which require to be the least altered from their original condition.

Live in each season as it passes; breathe the air, drink the drink, taste the fruit, and resign yourself to the influences of each. Let these be your only diet-drink and botanical medicines.

In August live on berries, not dried meats and pemmican as if you were on shipboard making your way through a waste ocean, or in the Darien Grounds, and so die of ship-fever and scurvy. Some will die of ship-fever and scurvy in an Illinois prairie, they lead such stifled and scurvy lives.

Be blown on by all the winds. Open all your pores and bathe in all the tides of nature, in all her streams and oceans, at all seasons. Miasma and infection are from within, not without. The invalid brought to the brink of the grave by an unnatural life, instead of imbibing the great influence that nature is—drinks only of the tea made of a particular herb— while he still continues his unnatural life—saves at the spile and wastes at the bung. He does not love nature or his life and so sickens and dies and no doctor can save him.

Grow green with spring—yellow and ripe with autumn. Drink of each season's influence as a vial, a true panacea of all remedies mixed for your especial use. The vials of summer never made a man sick, only those which he had stored in his cellar. Drink the wines not of your own but of nature's bottling—not kept in a goat- or pig-skin, but in the skins of a myriad fair berries.

Let Nature do your bottling, as also your pickling and preserving.

For all nature is doing her best each moment to make us well. She exists for no other end. Do not resist her. With the least inclination to be well we should not be sick. Men have discovered, or think that they have discovered the salutariness of a few wild things only, and not of all nature. Why nature is but another name for health. Some men think that they are not well in Spring or Summer or Autumn or Winter, (if you will excuse the pun) it is only because they are not indeed *well*, that is fairly *in* those seasons.

POEMS

POEMS

In days of yore, tis said, the swimming alder
Fashioned rude, with branches lopt, and stripped of its
    smooth coat,
Where fallen tree was none, and rippling streams vast breadth
Forbade adventurous leap, the brawny swain did bear
Secure to farthest shore.
The book has passed away, and with the book the lay
Which in my youthful days I loved to ponder.
Of curious things it told, how wise men 3 of Gotham
In a bowl did venture out to sea,
And darkly hints their awful fate
If men have dared the main to tempt in such frail barks,
Why may not wash tub round, or bread-troughs square
    oblong
Suffice to cross the purling wave and gain the destin'd port.

Fair Haven

When little hills like lambs did skip,
  And Joshua ruled in heaven,
Unmindful rolled Musketuquid,
    Nor budged an inch Fair Haven.

When principle is like to yield,
  To selfish fear, or craven,
And fickle mortals round me fall,
    I'll not forget Fair Haven.

If there's a cliff in this wide world,
  'S, a stepping stone to heaven,
A pleasant, craggy, short hand cut,
    It sure must be Fair Haven.

Oft have I climbed thy craggy steep,
Where ceaseless wheels the raven,
And whiled away an hour at e'en,
   For love of thee, Fair Haven.

If e'er my bark be tempest-tossed,
And every hope the wave in,
And this frail hulk shall spring a leak,
   I'll steer for thee, Fair Haven.

When cares press heavy on my soul,
And devils blue are craven,
Or e'er I lay me down to rest,
   I'll think of thee, Fair Haven.

And when I take my last long rest,
And quiet sleep my grave in,
What kindlier covering for my breast,
   Than thy warm turf Fair Haven.

Voyagers Song

Gentle river, gentle river
Swift as glides thy stream along,
Many a bold Canadian voyageur,
Bravely swelled the gay chanson

Thus of old our valiant fathers,
Many a lagging year agone
Gliding oer the rippling waters,
Taught to banish care in song.

Now the sun's behind the willows,
Now he gleams along the lake,
Hark across the bounding billows
Liquid songs the echoes wake.

Rise Apollo up before us,
E'ne the lark's begun her lay
Let us all in deafning chorus
Praise the glorious king of day.

Thus we lead a life of pleasure,
Thus we while the hours away,
Thus we revel beyond measure,
Gaily live we while we may.

———

Life is a summer's day
When as it were for aye
    We sport and play.

Anon the night comes on,
The ploughman's work is done,
    And day is gone.

We read in this one page
Both Youth, Manhood, and Age
    That hoary Sage.

The morning is our prime,
That laughs to scorn old Time,
    And knows no crime.

The noon comes on apace,
And then with swel'tring face
    We run our race.

When eve comes stealing o'er
We ponder at our door
    On days of yore.

The patient kine, they say,
At dawn do frisk and play,
    And well they may.

By noon their sports abate,
For then, as bards relate,
    They vegetate.

When eventide hath come,
And grey flies cease their hum,
    And now are dumb,

They leave the tender bud,
That's cooling to the blood,
    And chew the cud.

———

Let's make the most of morn,
Ere grey flies wind their horn,
    And it is gone.

———

"Long life and success to you."
                    UBIQUE.

I love a careless streamlet,
That takes a mad-cap leap,
And like a sparkling beamlet
Goes dashing down the steep.

———

Like torrents of the mountain
We've coursed along the lea,
From many a crystal fountain
Toward the far-distant sea.

And now we've gained life's valley,
And through the lowlands roam,
No longer may'st thou dally,
No longer spout and foam.

May pleasant meads await thee,
Where thou may'st freely roll
Towards that bright heavenly sea,
Thy resting place and goal.

And when thou reach'st life's down-hill,
So gentle be thy stream,
As would not turn a grist-mill
Without the aid of steam.

———

Pens to mend, and hands to guide.
Oh who would a schoolmaster be?

———

Each summer sound
Is a summer round.

Friendship

I think awhile of Love, and while I think,
  Love is to me a world,
  Sole meat and sweetest drink,
  And close connecting link
   Tween heaven and earth.

I only know it is, not how or why,
  My greatest happiness;
  However hard I try,
  Not if I were to die,
   Can I explain.

I fain would ask my friend how it can be,
  But when the time arrives,
  Then Love is more lovely
  Than anything to me,
   And so I'm dumb.

For if the truth were known, Love cannot speak,
  But only thinks and does;
  Though surely out 'twill leak
  Without the help of Greek,
   Or any tongue.

A man may love the truth and practise it,
  Beauty he may admire,
  And goodness not omit,
  As much as may befit
   To reverence.

But only when these three together meet,
  As they always incline,
  And make one soul the seat,
  And favorite retreat
   Of loveliness;

When under kindred shape, like loves and hates
  And a kindred nature,
  Proclaim us to be mates,
  Exposed to equal fates
   Eternally;

And each may other help, and service do,
  Drawing Love's bands more tight,
  Service he ne'er shall rue
  While one and one make two,
   And two are one;

In such case only doth man fully prove
  Fully as man can do,
  What power there is in Love
  His inmost soul to move
   Resistlessly.

—

Two sturdy oaks I mean, which side by side,
  Withstand the winter's storm,
  And spite of wind and tide,
  Grow up the meadow's pride,
   For both are strong

Above they barely touch, but undermined
  Down to their deepest source,
  Admiring you shall find
  Their roots are intertwined
   Insep'rably.

When breathless noon hath paused on hill and vale,
And now no more the woodman plies his axe,
Nor mower whets his scythe,
Somewhat it is, sole sojourner on earth,
To hear the veery on her oaken perch
Ringing her modest trill—
Sole sound of all the din that makes a world,
And I sole ear.
Fondly to nestle me in that sweet melody,
And own a kindred soul, speaking to me
From out the depths of universal being.
O'er birch and hazle, through the sultry air,
Comes that faint sound this way,
On Zephyr borne, straight to my ear.
No longer time or place, nor faintest trace
Of earth, the landscape's shimmer is my only space,
Sole remnant of a world.
Anon that throat has done, and familiar sounds
Swell strangely on the breeze, the low of cattle,
And the novel cries of sturdy swains
That plod the neighboring vale—
And I walk once more confounded a denizen of earth.

The Bluebirds

In the midst of the poplar that stands by our door,
We planted a bluebird box,
And we hoped before the summer was o'er
A transient pair to coax.

One warm summer's day the bluebirds came
And lighted on our tree,
But at first the wand'rers were not so tame
But they were afraid of me.

They seemed to come from the distant south,
Just over the Walden wood,
And they skimmed it along with open mouth
Close by where the bellows stood.

Warbling they swept round the distant cliff,
And they warbled it over the lea,
And over the blacksmith's shop in a jiff
Did they come warbling to me.

They came and sat on the box's top
Without looking into the hole,
And only from this side to that did they hop,
As 'twere a common well-pole.

Methinks I had never seen them before,
Nor indeed had they seen me,
Till I chanced to stand by our back door,
And they came to the poplar tree.

In course of time they built their nest
And reared a happy brood,
And every morn they piped their best
As they flew away to the wood.

Thus wore the summer hours away
To the bluebirds and to me,
And every hour was a summer's day,
So pleasantly lived we.

They were a world within themselves,
And I a world in me,
Up in the tree—the little elves—
With their callow family.

One morn the wind blowed cold and strong,
And the leaves when whirling away;
The birds prepared for their journey long
That raw and gusty day.

Boreas came blust'ring down from the north,
And ruffled their azure smocks,
So they launched them forth, though somewhat loth,
By way of the old Cliff rocks.

Meanwhile the earth jogged steadily on
In her mantle of purest white,
And anon another spring was born
When winter was vanished quite.

And I wandered forth o'er the steamy earth,
And gazed at the mellow sky,
But never before from the hour of my birth
Had I wandered so thoughtfully.

For never before was the earth so still,
And never so mild was the sky,
The river, the fields, the woods, and the hill,
Seemed to heave an audible sigh.

I felt that the heavens were all around,
And the earth was all below,
As when in the ears there rushes a sound
Which thrills you from top to toe.

I dreamed that I was an waking thought—
A something I hardly knew—
Not a solid piece, nor an empty nought,
But a drop of morning dew.

'Twas the world and I at a game of bo-peep,
As a man would dodge his shadow,
An idea becalmed in eternity's deep—
'Tween Lima and Segraddo.

Anon a faintly warbled note
From out the azure deep,
Into my ears did gently float
As is the approach of sleep.

It thrilled but startled not my soul;
Across my mind strange mem'ries gleamed,
As often distant scenes unroll
When we have lately dreamed

The bluebird had come from the distant South
To his box in the poplar tree,
And he opened wide his slender mouth,
On purpose to sing to me.

May Morning

The school boy loitered on his way to school,
Scorning to live so rare a day by rule.
So mild the air a pleasure 'twas to breathe,
For what seems heaven above was earth beneath.

Soured neighbors chatted by the garden pale,
Nor quarrelled who should drive the needed nail—
The most unsocial made new friends that day,
As when the sun shines husbandmen make hay

How long I slept I know not, but at last
I felt my consciousness returning fast,
For Zephyr rustled past with leafy tread,
And heedlessly with one heel grazed my head.

My eyelids opened on a field of blue,
For close above a nodding violet grew,
A part of heaven it seemed, which one could scent,
Its blue commingling with the firmament.

Walden

—True, our converse a stranger is to speech,
Only the practised ear can catch the surging words,
That break and die upon thy pebbled lips.
Thy flow of thought is noiseless as the lapse of thy own
            waters,
Wafted as is the morning mist up from thy surface,
So that the passive Soul doth breathe it in,
And is infected with the truth thou wouldst express.

E'en the remotest stars have come in troops
And stooped low to catch the benediction
Of thy countenance. Oft as the day came round,
Impartial has the sun exhibited himself
Before thy narrow skylight—nor has the moon
For cycles failed to roll this way
As oft as elsewhither, and tell thee of the night.
No cloud so rare but hitherward it stalked,
And in thy face looked doubly beautiful.
O! tell me what the winds have writ within these thousand
            years,
On the blue vault that spans thy flood—
Or sun transferred and delicately reprinted
For thy own private reading. Somewhat
Within these latter days I've read,
But surely there was much that would have thrilled the Soul,
Which human eye saw not
I would give much to read that first bright page,
Wet from a virgin press, when Eurus—Boreas—
And the host of airy quill-drivers
First dipped their pens in mist.

———

Truth—Goodness—Beauty—those celestial thrins,
Continually are born; e'en now the Universe,
With thousand throats—and eke with greener smiles,
Its joy confesses at their recent birth.

Strange that so many fickle gods, as fickle as the weather,
Throughout Dame Natures provinces should always pull
    together.

In the busy streets, domains of trade,
Man is a surly porter, or a vain and hectoring bully,
Who can claim no nearer kindredship with me
Than brotherhood by law.

I knew a man by sight,
    A blameless wight,
Who, for a year or more,
Had daily passed my door,
Yet converse none had had with him.

I met him in a lane,
    Him and his cane,
About three miles from home,
Where I had chanced to roam,
And volumes stared at him, and he at me.

In a more distant place
    I glimpsed his face,
And bowed instinctively;
    Starting he bowed to me,
Bowed simultaneously, and passed along.

Next, in a foreign land
  I grasped his hand,
And had a social chat,
  About this thing and that,
As I had known him well a thousand years.

Late in a wilderness
  I shared his mess,
For he had hardships seen,
  And I a wanderer been;
He was my bosom friend, and I was his.

And as, methinks, shall all,
  Both great and small,
That ever lived on earth,
  Early or late their birth,
Stranger and foe, one day each other know.

Cliffs

The loudest sound that burdens here the breeze
Is the wood's whisper; 'tis when we choose to list
Audible sound, and when we list not,
It is calm profound. Tongues were provided
But to vex the ear with superficial thoughts.
When deeper thoughts upswell, the jarring discord
Of harsh speech is hushed, and senses seem
As little as may be to share the extacy.

My Boots

Anon with gaping fearlessness they quaff
The dewy nectar with a natural thirst,
Or wet their leathern lungs where cranberries lurk,
With sweeter wine than Chian, Lesbian, or Falernian far.
Theirs was the inward lustre that bespeaks

An open sole—unknowing to exclude
The cheerful day—a worthier glory far
Than that which gilds the outmost rind with darkness
    visible—
Virtues that fast abide through lapse of years,
Rather rubbed in than off.

Noon

What time the bittern, solitary bird,
Hides now her head amid the whispering fern,
And not a paddock vexes all the shore—
Nor feather ruffles the incumbent air,
Save where the wagtail interrupts the noon.

Fair Haven

When Winter fringes every bough
    With his fantastic wreath,
And puts the seal of silence now
    Upon the leaves beneath;

When every stream in its pent-house
    Goes gurgling on its way,
And in his gallery the mouse
    Nibbleth the meadow hay;

Methinks the summer still is nigh,
    And lurketh underneath,
As that same meadow mouse doth lie
    Snug in the last year's heath.

And if perchance the chicadee
    Lisp a faint note anon,
The snow in summer's canopy,
    Which she herself put on.

Fair blossoms deck the cheerful trees,
  And dazzling fruits depend,
The north wind sighs a summer breeze,
  The nipping frosts to fend,

Bringing glad tidings unto me,
  The while I stand all ear,
Of a serene eternity,
  Which need not winter fear.

Out on the silent pond straightway
  The restless ice doth crack,
And pond sprites merry gambols play
  Amid the deafening rack.

Eager I hasten to the vale,
  As if I heard brave news,
How nature held high festival,
  Which it were hard to lose.

I gambol with my neighbor ice,
  And sympathizing quake,
As each new crack darts in a trice
  Across the gladsome lake.

One with the cricket in the ground,
  And faggot on the hearth,
Resounds the rare domestic sound
  Along the forest path.

The Thaw

—

I saw the civil sun drying earth's tears—
Her tears of joy that only faster flowed,

—

Fain would I stretch me by the highway side,
To thaw and trickle with the melting snow,
That mingled soul and body with the tide,
I too may through the pores of nature flow.

—

But I alas nor tinkle can nor fume,
One jot to forward the great work of Time,
'Tis mine to hearken while these ply the loom,
So shall my silence with their music chime.

—

Last night as I lay gazing with shut eyes
     Into the golden land of dreams,
  I thought I gazed adown a quiet reach
    Of land and water prospect,
      Whose low beach
Was peopled with the now subsiding hum
Of happy industry—whose work is done.

And as I turned me on my pillow o'er,
I heard the lapse of waves upon the shore,
Distinct as it had been at broad noonday,
An I were wandering at Rockaway.

Love

We two that planets erst had been
Are now a double star,
And in the heavens may be seen,
Where that we fixed are.

Yet whirled with subtle power along,
Into new space we enter,
And evermore with spheral song
Revolve about one centre.

———

The deeds of king and meanest hedger,
Stand side by side in heaven's ledger.

———

'T will soon appear if we but look
At evening into earth's day book,
Which way the great account doth stand
Between the heavens and the land.

The Evening Wind

The eastern mail comes lumbering in
With outmost waves of Europe's din;
The western sighs adown the slope,
Or mid the rustling leaves doth grope,
Laden with news from Californ',
Whateer transpired hath since morn,
How wags The world by brier and brake,
From hence to Athabasca lake.

The Peal of the Bells

When the world grows old by the chimney side,
Then forth to the youngling rocks I glide—
Where over the water, and over the land,
The bells are booming on either hand.

Now up they go ding, then down again dong,
And awhile they swing to the same old song,
And the metal goes round 't a single bound,
A-lulling the fields with its measured sound—
Till the tired tongue falls with a lengthened boom,
As solemn and loud as the crack of doom.
Then changed is their measure to tone upon tone,
And seldom it is that one sound comes alone,
For they ring out their peals in a mingled throng,
And the breezes waft the loud ding-dong along.

When the echo has reached me in this lone vale,
I am straightway a hero in coat of mail,
I tug at my belt and I march on my post,
And feel myself more than a match for a host.

I am on the alert for some wonderful Thing,
Which somewhere's a taking place,
'Tis perchance the salute which our planet doth ring
When it meeteth another in space.

The Shrike

Hark—hark—from out the thickest fog
Warbles with might and main
The fearless shrike, as all agog
To find in fog his gain.

His steady sail he never furls
At any time o' year,
And perched now on winter's curls,
He whistles in his ear.

Sympathy

Lately alas I knew a gentle boy,
Whose features all were cast in Virtue's mould,
As one she had designed for Beauty's toy,
But after manned him for her own stronghold.

On every side he open was as day,
That you might see no lack of strength within,
For walls and ports do only serve alway
For a pretence to feebleness and sin.

Say not that Caesar was victorious,
With toil and strife who stormed the House of Fame
In other sense this youth was glorious,
Himself a kingdom wheresoe'er he came.

No strength went out to get him victory,
When all was income of its own accord;
For where he went none other was to see,
But all were parcel of their noble lord.

He forayed like the subtle haze of summer,
That stilly shows fresh landscapes to our eyes,
And revolutions works without a murmur,
Or rustling of a leaf beneath the skies.

So was I taken unawares by this,
I quite forgot my homage to confess;
Yet now am forced to know, though hard it is,
I might have loved him, had I loved him less.

Each moment, as we nearer drew to each,
A stern respect withheld us farther yet,
So that we seemed beyond each other's reach,
And less acquainted than when first we met.

We two were one while we did sympathize
So could we not the simplest bargain drive;
And what avails it now that we are wise,
If absence doth this doubleness contrive?

Eternity may not the chance repeat,
But I must tread my single way alone,
In sad remembrance that we once did meet,
And know that bliss irrevocably gone.

The spheres henceforth my elegy shall sing,
For elegy has other subject none;
Each strain of music in my ears shall ring
Knell of departure from that other one.

Make haste and celebrate my tragedy;
With fitting strain resound ye woods and fields;
Sorrow is dearer in such case to me
Than all the joys other occasion yields.

Is't then too late the damage to repair?
Distance, forsooth, from my weak grasp hath reft
The empty husk, and clutched the useless tare,
But in my hands the wheat and kernel left.

If I but love that virtue which he is,
Though it be scented in the morning air,
Still shall we be truest acquaintances,
Nor mortals know a sympathy more rare.

The "Book of Gems"

—With cunning plates the polished leaves were decked,
Each one a window to the poet's world,
So rich a prospect that you might suspect
In that small space all paradise unfurled.
It was a right delightful road to go,
   marching through pastures of such fair herbage,
O'er hill and dale it lead, and to and fro,
From bard to bard, making an easy stage.

Where ever and anon I slaked my thirst
Like a tired traveller at some poet's well,
Which from the teeming ground did bubbling burst,
And tinkling thence adown the page it fell.
Still through the leaves its music you might hear,
Till other springs fell faintly on the ear.

The Assabet

Up this pleasant stream let's row
For the livelong summer's day,
Sprinkling foam where'er we go
In wreaths as white as driven snow—
Ply the oars, away! away!

Now we glide along the shore,
Chucking lilies as we go,
While the yellow-sanded floor
Doggedly resists the oar,
Like some turtle dull and slow.

Now we stem the middle tide
Ploughing through the deepest soil,
Ridges pile on either side,
While we through the furrow glide,
Reaping bubbles for our toil.

Dew before and drought behind,
Onward all doth seem to fly;
Nought contents the eager mind,
Only rapids now are kind,
Forward are the earth and sky.

Sudden music strikes the ear,
Leaking out from yonder bank,
Fit such voyagers to cheer—
Sure there must be naiads here,
Who have kindly played this prank.

There I know the cunning pack
Where yon self-sufficient rill
All its telltale hath kept back,
Through the meadows held its clack,
And now babbleth its fill.

Silent flows the parent stream,
And if rocks do lie below
Smothers with her waves the din,
As it were a youthful sin,
Just as still and just as slow.

But this gleeful little rill,
Purling round its storied pebble,
Tinkles to the self same tune
From December until June,
Nor doth any drought enfeeble.

See the sun behind the willows,
Rising through the golden haze,
How he gleams along the billows—
Their white crests the easy pillows
Of his dew besprinkled rays.

Forward press we to the dawning,
For Aurora leads the way,
Sultry noon and twilight scorning,
In each dew drop of the morning
Lies the promise of a day.

Rivers from the sun do flow,
Springing with the dewy morn,
Voyageurs 'gainst time do row,
Idle noon nor sunset know,
Even even with the dawn.

Since that first away! away!
Many a lengthy league we've rowed,
Still the sparrow on the spray,
Hastes to usher in the day
With her simple stanza'd ode.

The Breeze's Invitation

Come let's roam the breezy pastures,
Where the freest zephyrs blow,
Batten on the oak tree's rustle,
And the pleasant insect bustle,
Dripping with the streamlet's flow.

What if I no wings do wear,
Thro' this solid seeming air
I can skim like any swallow
Who so dareth let her follow,
And we'll be a jovial pair.

Like two careless swifts let's sail,
Zephyrus shall think for me—
Over hill and over dale,
Riding on the easy gale,
We will scan the earth and sea.

Yonder see that willow tree
Winnowing the buxom air,
You a gnat and I a bee,
With our merry minstrelsy
We will make a concert there.

One green leaf shall be our screen,
Till the sun doth go to bed,
I the king and you the queen
Of that peaceful little green,
Without any subject's aid.

To our music Time will linger,
And earth open wide her ear,
Nor shall any need to tarry
To immortal verse to marry
Such sweet music as he'll hear.

Stanzas

Nature doth have her dawn each day,
But mine are far between;
Content, I cry, for sooth to say,
Mine brightest are, I ween.

For when my sun doth deign to rise,
Though it be her noontide,
Her fairest field in shadow lies,
Nor can my light abide.

Sometimes I bask me in her day,
Conversing with my mate;
But if we interchange one ray,
Forthwith her heats abate.

Through his discourse I climb and see,
As from some eastern hill,
A brighter morrow rise to me
Than lieth in her skill.

As 't were two summer days in one,
Two Sundays come together,
Our rays united make one Sun,
With fairest summer weather.

Loves Farewell

Light hearted, careless, shall I take my way,
When I to thee this being have resigned,
Well knowing where upon a future day,
With usurer's craft, more than myself to find.

Each more melodious note I hear
Brings this reproach to me,
That I alone afford the ear,
Who would the music be.

The Fisher's Son

I know the world where land and water meet,
By yonder hill abutting on the main,
One while I hear the waves incessant beat,
Then turning round survey the land again.

Within a humble cot that looks to sea
Daily I breathe this curious warm life,
Beneath a friendly haven's sheltering lea
My noiseless day with myst'ry still is rife.

'Tis here, they say, my simple life began,
And easy credit to the tale I lend,
For well I know 'tis here I am a man,
But who will simply tell me of the end?

These eyes fresh opened spied the far off Sea,
Which like a silent godfather did stand,
Nor uttered one explaining word to me,
But introduced straight godmother Land.

And yonder still stretches that silent main,
With many glancing ships besprinkled o'er,
And earnest still I gaze and gaze again
Upon the self same waves and friendly shore.

Till like a watery humor on the eye
It still appears whichever way I turn,
Its silent waste and mute oerarching sky
With close shut eyes I clearly still discern.

And yet with lingering doubt I haste each morn
To see if Ocean still my gaze will greet,
And with each day once more to life am born,
And tread the earth once more with tott'ring feet.

———

My years are like a stroll upon the beach,
As near the ocean's edge as I can go;
My tardy steps its waves sometimes o'erreach,
Sometimes I stay to let them overflow.

Infinite work my hands find there to do,
Gathering the relics which the waves up cast;
Each tempest scours the deep for something new,
And every time the strangest is the last.

My sole employment 'tis and scrupulous care,
To place my gains beyond the reach of tides,
Each smoother pebble and each shell more rare
Which Ocean kindly to my hand confides.

I have but few companions on the shore,
They scorn the strand who sail upon the sea,
Yet oft I think the ocean they've sailed oer
Is deeper known upon the strand to me.

My neighbors sometimes come with lumb'ring carts,
As if they wished my pleasant toil to share,
But straight they go again to distant marts
For only weeds and ballast are their care.

———

'Tis by some strange coincidence if I
Make common cause with Ocean when he storms
Who can so well support a separate sky,
And people it with multitude of forms.

Oft in the stillness of the night I hear
Some restless bird presage the coming din,
And distant murmurs faintly strike my ear
From some bold bluff projecting far within.

My stillest depths straightway do inly heave
More genially than rests the summer's calm,
The howling winds through my soul's cordage grieve,
Till every shelf and ledge gives the alarm.

Oft at some ruling star my tide has swelled,
The sea can scarcely brag more wrecks than I,
Ere other influence my waves has quelled
The staunchest bark that floats is high and dry.

Friendship

"Friends, Romans, Countrymen, and Lovers."

Let such pure hate still underprop
Our love, that we may be
Each other's conscience,
And have our sympathy
Mainly from thence.

We'll one another treat like gods,
And all the faith we have
In virtue and in truth, bestow
On either, and suspicion leave
To gods below.

Two solitary stars—
Unmeasured systems far
Between us roll,
But by our conscious light we are
Determined to one pole.

What need confound the sphere—
God can afford to wait,
For him no hour's too late
That witnesseth one duty's end,
Or to another doth beginning lend.

Love will subserve no use,
More than the tints of flowers,
Only the independent guest
Frequents its bowers,
Inherits its bequest.

No speech though kind has it,
But kinder silence doles
Unto its mates,
By night consoles,
By day congratulates.

What saith the tongue to tongue?
What heareth ear of ear?
By the decrees of fate
From year to year,
Does it communicate.

Pathless the gulf of feeling yawns—
No trivial bridge of words,
Or arch of boldest span,
Can leap the moat that girds
The sincere man.

No show of bolts and bars
Can keep the foeman out,
Or 'scape his secret mine
Who entered with the doubt
That drew the line.

No warder at the gate
Can let the friendly in,
But like the sun o'er all
He will the castle win,
And shine along the wall.

There's nothing in the world I know
That can escape from love,
For every depth it goes below,
And every height above.

It waits as waits the sky,
Until the clouds go by,
Yet shines serenely on
With an eternal day,
Alike when they are gone,
And when they stay.

Implacable is Love,—
Foes may be bought or teased
From their hostile intent,
But he goes unappeased
Who is on kindness bent.

The Freshet

——A stir is on the Worc'ter hills,
And Nobscott too the valley fills—
Where scarce you'd fill an acorn cup
In summer when the sun was up,
No more you'll find a cup at all,
But in its place a waterfall.

Oh that the moon were in conjunction
To the dry land's extremest unction,
Till every dyke and pier were flooded,
And all the land with islands studded,
For once to teach all human kind,
Both those that plough and those that grind,
There is no fixture in the land,
But all unstable is as sand.

—
—

The river swelleth more and more,
Like some sweet influence stealing o'er
The passive town; and for awhile
Each tussock makes a tiny isle,
Where, on some friendly Ararat,
Resteth the weary water rat.

No ripple shows Musketaquid,
Her very current e'en is hid,
As deepest souls do calmest rest
When thoughts are swelling in the breast;
And she that in the summer's drought
Doth make a rippling and a rout,
Sleeps from Nawshawtuct to the cliff,
Unruffled by a single skiff;
So like a deep and placid mind
Whose currents underneath it wind—
For by a thousand distant hills
The louder roar a thousand rills,
And many a spring which now is dumb,
And many a stream with smothered hum,
Doth faster well and swifter glide
Though buried deep beneath the tide.

Our village shows a rural Venice,
Its broad lagunes where yonder fen is,
Far lovelier than the Bay of Naples
Yon placid cove amid the maples,
And in my neighbor's field of corn
I recognise the Golden Horn.

Here Nature taught from year to year,
When only red men came to hear,
Methinks 'twas in this school of art
Venice and Naples learned their part,
But still their mistress, to my mind,
Her young disciples leaves behind.

The Poet's Delay

In vain I see the morning rise,
In vain observe the western blaze,
Who idly look to other skies,
Expecting life by other ways.

Amidst such boundless wealth without,
I only still am poor within,
The birds have sung their summer out,
But still my spring does not begin.

Shall I then wait the autumn wind,
Compelled to seek a milder day,
And leave no curious nest behind,
No woods still echoing to my lay?

The Summer Rain

My books I'd fain cast off, I cannot read,
'Twixt every page my thoughts go stray at large
Down in the meadow, where is richer feed,
And will not mind to hit their proper targe.

Plutarch was good, and so was Homer too,
Our Shakspeare's life was rich to live again,
What Plutarch read that was not good nor true,
Nor Shakspeare's books, unless his books were men.

Here while I lie beneath this walnut bough,
What care I for the Greeks, or for Troy town,
If juster battles are enacted now
Between the ants upon this hummock's crown.

Bid Homer wait till I the issue learn,
If red or black the gods will favor most,
Or yonder Ajax will the phalanx turn,
Struggling to heave some rock against the host.

Tell Shakspeare to attend some leisure hour,
For now I've business with this drop of dew,
And see you not, the clouds prepare a shower,—
I'll meet him shortly when the sky is blue.

This bed of herdsgrass and wild oats was spread
Last year with nicer skill than monarchs use,
A clover tuft is pillow for my head,
And violets quite overtop my shoes.

And now the cordial clouds have shut all in,
And gently swells the wind to say all's well,
The scattered drops are falling fast and thin,
Some in the pond, some in the lily bell.

Drip, drip the trees for all the country round,
And richness rare distils from every bough,
The wind alone it is makes every sound,
Shaking down crystals on the leaves below.

For shame the sun will never show himself,
Who could not with his beams e'er melt me so,
My dripping locks—they would become an elf
Who in a beaded coat does gaily go.

Guido's Aurora

The God of day rolls his car up the slopes,
Reining his prancing steeds with steady hand,
The moon's pale orb through western shadows gropes,
While morning sheds its light o'er sea and land.

Castles and cities by the sounding main
Resound with all the busy din of life,
The fisherman unfurls his sails again
And the recruited warrior bides the strife.

The early breeze ruffles the poplar leaves,
The curling waves reflect the washed light,
The slumbering sea with the day's impulse heaves,
While o'er the western hills retires the drowsy night.

The sea birds dip their bills in ocean's foam,
Far circling out over the frothy waves—

I've heard my neighbor's pump at night,
Long after Lyra sunk her light,
As if it were a natural sound,
And proper utterance of the ground—
Perchance some bittern in a fen—
Or else the squeak of a meadow hen.

Who sleeps by day and walks by night,
Will meet no spirit but some sprite.

When with pale cheek and sunken eye I sang
Unto the slumbering world at midnights hour,
How it no more resounded with war's clang,
And virtue was decayed in Peace's bower;

How in these days no hero was abroad,
But puny men, afraid of war's alarms,
Stood forth to fight the battles of their Lord,
Who scarce could stand beneath a hero's arms;

A faint, reproachful, reassuring strain,
From some harp's strings touched by unskilful hands
Brought back the days of chivalry again,
And the surrounding fields made holy lands.

A bustling camp and an embattled host
Extending far on either hand I saw,
For I alone had slumbered at my post,
Dreaming of peace when all around was war.

I arose before light
To work with all my might,
With my arms braced for toil
Which no obstacle could foil,
For it robbed me of my rest
Like an anvil on my breast.

But as a brittle cup
I've held the hammer up,
And no sound from my forge
Has been heard in the gorge.
I look forward into night,
And seem to get some light;
E're long the forge will ring
With its ding-dong-ding,
For the iron will be hot
And my wages will be got.

I'm guided in the darkest night
By flashes of auroral light,
Which over dart thy eastern home
And teach me not in vain to roam.
Thy steady light on t'other side
Pales the sunset, makes day abide,
And after sunrise stays the dawn,
Forerunner of a brighter morn.

There is no being here to me
But staying here to be
When others laugh I am not glad,
When others cry I am not sad,
But be they grieved or be they merry
I'm supernumerary.
I am a miser without blame

Am conscience stricken without shame.
An idler am I without leisure,
A busy body without pleasure.
I did not think so bright a day
Would issue in so dark a night.
I did not think such sober play
Would leave me in so sad a plight,
And I should be most sorely spent
Where first I was most innocent.
I thought by loving all beside
To prove to you my love was wide,
And by the rites I soared above
To show you my peculiar love.

———

　　Friends—
They cannot help,
They cannot hurt,
Nor in indifference rest,
But when for a host's service girt,
They are a mutual guest.

They are a single power
Plenipotentiary,
No minister of state,
Anxious and wary
Decides their fate.

Where interest's self is
There is no go-between,
But where another reaps,
They do but glean
In scanty heaps.

They have learned well to hate,
And never grant reprieve,
Nor e'er succumb to love,
But sternly grieve,
And look above.

If faults arise, my friend will send for me
As some great god,
Who will the matter try,
Holding the scales, even or odd,
Under the sky—

Who will award strict justice
All the while,
Confounding mine and thine,
And share his smile,
When they 'gainst me incline.

When in some cove I lie,
A placid lake at rest,
Scanning the distant hills,
A murmur from the west,
And gleam of thousand rills
Which gently swell my breast,
Announce the friendly thought,
And in one wave sun-lit
I'm softly brought
Seaward with it.

Who hears the parson
Will not hear the bell,
But if he deafly pass on
He will hear of hell.

I' faith the people go to church
To leave the devil in the lurch,
But since they've carpeted the pews
To squat with hymn book he doth use.

Sic Vita

I am a parcel of vain strivings tied
    By a chance bond together,
Dangling this way and that, their links
        Were made so loose and wide,
                Methinks,
            For milder weather.

A bunch of violets without their roots,
        And sorrel intermixed,
Encircled by a wisp of straw
            Once coiled about their shoots,
                The law
            By which I'm fixed.

A nosegay which Time clutched from out
        Those fair Elysian fields,
With weeds and broken stems, in haste,
            Doth make the rabble rout
                That waste
            The day he yields.

And here I bloom for a short hour unseen,
        Drinking my juices up,
Which have no root in the land
            To keep my branches green,

But stand
In a bare cup.

Some tender buds were left upon my stem
In mimicry of life,
But ah! the children will not know
Till time has withered them,
The woe
With which they're rife.

But now I see I was not plucked for nought,
And after in life's vase
Of glass set while I might survive,
But by a kind hand brought
Alive
To a strange place.

That stock thus thinned will soon redeem its hours,
And by another year
Such as God knows, with freer air,
More fruits and fairer flowers
Will bear,
While I droop here.

———

Wait not till I invite thee, but observe
I'm glad to see thee when thou com'st.

Friendship

Now we are partners in such legal trade,
We'll look to the beginnings, not the ends,
Nor to pay day—knowing true wealth is made
For current stock and not for dividends.

On the Sun Coming Out in the Afternoon

Methinks all things have travelled since you shined,
But only Time, and clouds, Time's team, have moved;
Again foul weather shall not change my mind,
But In the shade I will believe what in the sun I loved.

———

They who prepare my evening meal below
Carelessly hit the kettle as they go
With tongs or shovel,
And ringing round and round,
Out of this hovel
It makes an eastern temple by the sound.

At first I thought a cow-bell right at hand
Mid birches sounded o'er the open land,
Where I plucked flowers
Many years ago,
Spending midsummer hours
With such secure delight they hardly seemed to flow.

———

My ground is high,
But 'tis not dry,
What you call dew
Comes filtering through;
Though in the sky,
It still is nigh;
Its soil is blue
And virgin too.

———

If from your price ye will not swerve,
Why then Ill think the gods reserve
A greater bargain there above,
Out of their sup'rabundant love,
Have meantime better for me cared,
And so will get my stock prepared,
Plows of new pattern, hoes the same,
Designed a different soil to tame,
And sow my seed broadcast in air,
Certain to reap my harvest there.

⸻

Death cannot come too soon
Where it can come at all,
But always is too late
Unless the fates it call.

The Mountains in the Horizon

With frontier strength ye stand your ground—
With grand content ye circle round—
Tumultuous silence for all sound,
Ye springing nursery of rills,
Monadnock and the Peterborough hills—
Staid argument that never stirs,
Outcircling the philosophers.
While we enjoy a lingering ray,
Ye still oertop the western day,
Reposing yonder on God's croft
Like solid stacks of hay.
The iris of the sky,
Ye run
Round the horizon of its eye
Whose pupil is the sun.

Upon a fresh and airy day,
When our globe ploughs its way
In salter seas of light,
Right opposite the bight
Of some elysian bay,
Ye are its dorsal fin,
Tossing th'etherial spray
With breezy din.
From on Fair Haven's pier,
For many a year.
I've seen ye westward bound,
Without a sound,
Like some vast fleet
Sailing through rain and sleet,
Through winters cold and summer's heat.
Ships of the line each one
That westward run,
Always before the gale,
Under a press of sail,
Convoying clouds
Which cluster in your shrouds—
With your slant masts 'tis sixes and sevens
But that ye rake the heavens,
So near the edge ye go,
Under the roof so low;
With weight of metal all untold,
I seem to feel ye in my firm seat here,
Immeasurable depth of hold,
And breadth of beam, and length of running gear.
The vessels on the sea
Are relative to ye,
Sailing by sympathy.
Late enterprises of mankind
Some near income to find.
Flitting from shore to shore,
Their voyages soon are oer,
But ye hold on upon your high emprise,
Until ye find a shore
Amid the skies.

Crossing the pliant flood
By swifter period,
They with the noontide weigh,
And glide before its ray
To some retired bay,
Their haunt—
Whence under tropic sun,
They ceaseless run,
Bearing gum Senegal and Tragicant.
For such small ends
Time gladly spends
Itself into eternity,
For this was ocean meant,
For this the sun was sent,
And moon was lent,
And 'tis the winds' employment.
Time waits but till the field is tilled,
With such small deeds
His lap is filled
As that with seeds.

Man's little acts are grand
Beheld from land to land,
There as they lie in time
Within their native clime
For which the world did wait,
They are so great.
        No doubt that in the port from whence ye hail
        Your masters did not fail
        To register your wealth,
        For ye sail not by stealth,
        Skulking close in to land,
        With cargo contraband,
        But they who sent a venture out by ye
        Have set the sun to see
        Their honesty.

Especial I remember thee,
Wachusett, who like me
Standest alone without society.

My life is like a western sky
Unto an eastern eye
Of calm repose,
Each moment tinted variously
As the wind blows.
Now streaming like the northern light,
Each yet more north, more high, more bright,
Subsiding on the shores of night,
Like yonder field of grain
It alway doth remain
Firm at its root,
Bending through all its length
With graceful strength,
Only the shadows glide
From side to side,
But still the deep grain doth abide.
 Anon it sighs along
 Like the breath of a song,
 Or the wind on the sedge,
 Or a tempest on the ledge,
 First swells then dies away
 Like a harp strain,
 Only a string doth stay
 To invite the wind again,—
 But thou art far and blue and still,
 Mocking my infirm will,
 Thou steadfast hill.
 Upholding heaven, holding down earth,
 Thy pastime from thy birth,
 Not steadied by the one nor leaning on the other,
 May I approve myself thy worthy brother.

 Thy far blue eye,
 A remnant of the sky,
 See through the clearing or the gorge,
 Or from the windows of the forge
 Doth leaven all it passes by.
 Thou art our rostrum in the west,
 Some ancient victory's bequest,

With nature's trophies fringed,
And natural colors tinged,
Not with the Tyrian dye,
But with the azure of the sky
Fronting an amphitheater of glory
Greater than Greek or Roman story—
Their old nobility westering with the sun,
Here to be done, perchance, or else begun.

Nothing is true
But stands 'tween me and you,
Thou western pioneer
Who know'st not shame nor fear,
By venturous spirit driven
Under the eaves of heaven,
And canst expand thee there?
And breath enough of air?
The sun doth go behind thee not before,
Briefly to mend his store,
Even beyond the west
With thy small stock thou migratest
Into unclouded tracts,
Without a pilgrims axe,
Upon a loftier way
Than our low western rout,
Cleaving thy road on high
With thy well tempered brow,
And mak'st thyself a clearing in the sky.

The needles of the pine,
All to the west incline.

The Echo of the Sabbath Bell—

heard in the Woods

Dong—sounds the brass in the east—
As if for a civic feast,
But I like that sound the best
Out of the fluttering west.

The steeple rings a knell,
But the fairies' silvery bell
Is the voice of that gentle folk—
Or else the horizon that spoke.

Its metal is not of brass,
But air and water and glass,
And under a cloud it is swung,
And by the wind is rung,
With a slim silver tongue

When the steeple tolls the noon
It soundeth not so soon,
Yet it rings an earlier hour,
And the sun has not reached its tower.

———

Low in the eastern sky
Is set thy glancing eye;
And though its gracious light
Ne'er riseth to my sight,
Yet every star that climbs
Above the gnarled limbs
  Of yonder hill,
Conveys thy gentle will.

Believe I knew thy thought,
And that the zephyrs brought
Thy kindest wishes through,
As mine they bear to you,

That some attentive cloud
Did pause amid the crowd
    Over my head,
While gentle things were said.

Believe the thrushes sung,
And that the flower-bells rung,
That herbs exhaled their scent,
And beasts knew what was meant,
The trees a welcome waved,
And lakes their margins laved,
    When thy free mind
To my retreat did wind.

It was a summer eve,
The air did gently heave
While yet a low-hung cloud
Thy eastern skies did shroud;
The lightning's silent gleam,
Startling my drowsy dream,
    Seemed like the flash
Under thy dark eyelash.

Still will I strive to be
As if thou wert with me;
Whatever path I take,
It shall be for thy sake,
Of gentle slope and wide,
As thou wert by my side,
    Without a root
To trip thy gentle foot.

I'll walk with gentle pace,
And choose the smoothest place,
And careful dip the oar,
And shun the winding shore,
And gently steer my boat
Where water-lilies float,
    And cardinal flowers
Stand in their sylvan bowers.

My life has been the poem I would have writ,
But I could not both live and utter it.

To the Mountains

And when the sun puts out his lamp
We'll sleep serene within the camp,
Trusting to his invet'rate skill
Who leads the stars oer yonder hill,
Whose discipline doth never cease
To watch the slumberings of peace,
And from the virtuous hold afar
The melancholy din of war.—
For ye our sentries still outlie,
The earth your pallet and your screen the sky.

From steadfastness I will not swerve
Remembering my sweet reserve.

With all your kindness shown from year to year
Ye do but civil demons still appear,
Still to my mind
Ye are inhuman and unkind,
And bear an untamed aspect to my sight
After the "civil-suited" night
As if ye had lain out
Like to the Indian scout
Who lingers in the purlieus of the towns
With unexplored grace and savage frowns.

Greater is the depth of sadness
Than is any height of gladness.

———

Where I have been
There was none seen.

———

Better wait
Than be too late.

Independence

My life more civil is and free
Than any civil polity.

Ye princes keep your realms
And circumscribed power,
Not wide as are my dreams,
Nor rich as is this hour.

What can ye give which I have not?
What can ye take which I have got?
Can ye defend the dangerless?
Can ye inherit nakedness?

To all true wants times ear is deaf,
Penurious states lend no relief
Out of their pelf—
But a free soul—thank God—
Can help itself.

Be sure your fate
Doth keep apart its state—
Not linked with any band—
Even the nobles of the land

In tented fields with cloth of gold—
No place doth hold
But is more chivalrous than they are.
And sigheth for a nobler war.
A finer strain its trumpet sings—
A brighter gleam its armor flings.

The life that I aspire to live
No man proposeth me—
No trade upon the street
Wears its emblazonry.

Cock-crowing

Upon my bed at early dawn
I hear the cocks proclaim the day,
Though the moon shines serenely on,
As if her queenly course they could not stay—

———

Nor pull her down with their faint din
From riding at that lofty height,
Who in her shining knows no sin,
As if unconscious of a nobler light.

———

Far in the east their larum rings,
As if a watchful host there thronged,
Where now its early clarion sings,
So bravely is their martial note prolonged.

———

One on more distant perch, more clear,
But fainter brags him still,
But ah! he promises, I fear,
More than his master's household will fulfill.

———

The stars withhold their shining not
Or singly or in scattered crowds,
But seem like Parthian arrows shot
By yielding night 'mid the advancing clouds.

———

Some wakeful steer exalts his trump
Afar oer the sonorous ground,
And with a sounding eastern pomp
It grandly marcheth the horizon round.

———

Invades each recess of the wood,
Awakes each slumbering bird,
Till every fowl leads forth her brood,
Which on her nest the tuneful summons heard.

———

Methinks that Time has reached his prime,
Eternity is in the flower,
I hear their faint confused chime
Now ushering in the sacred hour.

———

Over the hill top I have run
For fear to be too late,
I've left behind the luggard sun,
Travelling at such a rate,
To be in at creation,
To be up with fate.

———

And has time got so forward then?
From what perennial fount of joy,
Do ye inspire the hearts of men,
And teach them how the day-light to employ?

———

From your abundance pray impart
Who dost so freely spill,
Some bravery unto my heart,
Or let me taste of thy perennial rill.

——

There is such health and length of years
In the elixir of that note,
That God himself more young appears,
And a more youthful world through space doth float.

——

The tidy night with woolen feet,
I'm sure has lately passed this way,
And with her trim despatch so neat,
She has arranged the furniture of the day.

——

In yon thin sheet of mist spread oer
The lowland trees of leaves bereft,
Which round her head at eve she wore,
Methinks I see the housewife's duster left.

——

The fragrant mist exhales the scent
Of aromatic herbs, so you
Would say she blest whereer she went,
And through the fields had sprinkled perfumed dew.

Inspiration

Whate'er we leave to God, God does,
    And blesses us;
The work we choose should be our own,
    God lets alone.

——

If with light head erect I sing,
Though all the muses lend their force,
From my poor love of anything,
The verse is weak and shallow as its source.

———

But if with bended neck I grope,
Listening behind me for my wit,
With faith superior to hope,
More anxious to keep back than forward it,

———

Making my soul accomplice there
Unto the flame my heart hath lit,
Then will the verse forever wear,
Time cannot bend the line which God hath writ.

———

Always the general show of things
Floats in review before my mind,
And such true love and reverence brings,
That sometimes I forget that I am blind.

———

But soon there comes unsought, unseen,
Some clear divine electuary,
And I, who had but sensual been,
Grow sensible, and as God is am wary.

———

I hearing get who had but ears,
And sight who had but eyes before,
I moments live who lived but years,
And truth discern who knew but learning's lore.

———

I hear beyond the range of sound,
I see beyond the verge of sight,
New earths—new skies—new seas—around,
And in my noon the sun doth pale his light.

—

A clear and ancient harmony
Peirces my soul through all its din,
As through its utmost melody,
Further behind than they, further within.

—

More swift its bolt than lightning is,
Its voice than thunder is more loud,
It doth expand my privacies
To all, and leave me single in the crowd.

—

It speaks with such authority,
With so serene and lofty tone,
That idle Time runs gadding by,
And leaves me with Eternity alone.

—

Then chiefly is my natal hour,
And only then my prime of life,
Of manhood's strength it is the flower,
'T is peace's end and wars beginning strife.

—

'T hath come in summer's broadest noon,
By a grey wall or some chance place,
Unseasoned time, insulted June,
And vexed the day with its presuming face.

—

Such fragrance round my sleep it makes,
More rich than are Arabian drugs,
That my soul scents its life, and wakes
The body up—from 'neath its perfumed rugs.

—

—

Such is the Muse—the heavenly maid,
The star that guides our mortal course,
Which shows where life's true kernel's laid,
Its wheat's fine flower, and its undying force.

—

Who with one breath attunes the spheres,
And also my poor human heart,
With one impulse propels the years
Around, and gives my throbbing pulse its start.

—

I will not doubt forever more,
Nor falter from an iron faith,
For if the system be turned oer,
God takes not back the word which once he saith.

—

I will believe the love untold,
Which not my worth nor want hath bought,
Which wood me young and woos me old,
And call the stars to witness now my thought.

—

My memory I'll educate
To know the one historic truth,
Remembering to the latest date
The only true, and sole immortal youth.

—

Be but thy inspiration given,
No matter through what dangers sought,
I'll fathom hell or climb to heaven,
And yet esteem that cheap which love has bought.

Fame cannot tempt the bard
    Who's famous with his God,
    Nor laurel him reward,
    Who hath his maker's nod.

The Soul's Season

Thank God who seasons thus the year,
And sometimes kindly slants his rays,
For in his winter he's most near,
And plainest seen upon the shortest days.

———

Who gently tempers now his heats,
And then his harsher cold, lest we
Should surfeit on the Summer's sweets,
Or pine upon the Winter's crudity.

———

Grown tired of this rank summer's wealth,
Its raw and superficial show,
I fain would hie away by stealth
Where no roads meet, but still 't doth trivial grow.

———

Methinks by dalliance it hath caught
The shallow habits of the town,
Itself infected most, which ought
With sterner face upon our tameness frown.

———

A sober mind will walk alone
Apart from nature if need be,
And only its own seasons own,
For nature having its humanity.

———

Sometimes a late Autumnal thought
Has crossed my mind in green July,
And to its early freshness brought
Late ripened fruits and an autumnal sky.

A dry but golden thought which gleamed
Across the greenness of my mind,
And prematurely wise it seemed,
Too ripe 'mid summer's youthful bowers to find.

—

So have I seen one yellow leaf
Amid the glossy leaves of June,
Which pensive hung, though not with grief,
Like some fair flower, it had changed so soon.

—

I scent my med'cine from afar,
Where the rude simpler of the year,
October leads the rustling war,
And strews his honors on the summer's bier.

The Fall of the Leaf

Grown tired of this rank summer's wealth,
  Its raw and superficial show,
I fain would hie away by stealth
  Where no roads meet, but still 't doth trivial grow.

A sober mind will walk alone,
  Apart from nature if need be,
And only its own seasons own,
  For nature having its humanity.

Sometimes a late autumnal thought
  Has crossed my mind in green July,
And to its early freshness brought
  Late ripend fruits and an autumnal sky.

A dry but golden thought which gleamed
  Athwart the greenness of my mind,
And prematurely wise it seemed,
  Too ripe mid summer's youthful bowers to find.

So have I seen one yellow leaf
  Amid the glossy leaves of June,
Which pensive hung, though not with grief,
  Like some fair flower, it had changed so soon.

I scent my med'cine from afar,
   Where the rude simpler of the year
October leads the rustling war,
   And strews his honors on the summer's bier.

The evening of the year draws on,
   The fields a later aspect wear,
Since summer's garishness is gone
   Some grains of night tincture the noontide air.

Behold the shadows of the trees
   Now circle wider 'bout their stem,
Like sentries which by slow degrees
   Perform their rounds, gently protecting them.

And as the season doth decline
   The sun affords a scantier light,
Behind each needle of the pine
   There lurks a small auxiliar of the night.

After each shrub and straggling fence
   That marks the meadow's pensive green,
And shows the meadow's opulence,
   Evening's insidious foot at noon is seen.

Wave upon wave a mellower air
   Flows over all the region,
As if there were some tincture there
   Of ripeness caught from the long summer's sun.

I hear the cricket's slumbrous lay
   Around, beneath me, and on high,
It rocks the night, it lulls the day,
   And everywhere 'tis nature's lullaby.

But most he chirps beneath the sod,
   Where he hath made his winter's bed,
His creak grown fainter, but more broad,
   A film of autumn o'er the summer spread.

Upon my bed at early dawn
   I hear the cocks proclaim the day,
Though the moon shines serenely on
   As if her queenly course they could not stay;

Nor pull her down with their faint din
   From riding at that lofty height,
Who in her shining knows no sin,
   But is unconscious of a nobler light.

The stars withhold their shining not
   Or singly or in scattered crowds,
But seem like Parthian arrows shot
   By yielding night 'mid the advancing clouds.

And has time got so forward then?
   From what perennial fount of joy
Do ye inspire the hearts of men,
   And teach them how the daylight to employ?

From your abundance pray impart,
   Who dost so freely spill,
Some bravery unto my heart,
   Or let me taste of thy perennial rill.

Small birds in fleets migrating by
   Now beat across some meadow's bay,
And as they tack and veer on high,
   With faint and hurried click beguile the way.

The moon is ripe fruit in the sky
   Which overhangs her harvest now,
The sun doth break his stem well nigh
   From summer's height he has declined so low.

The greedy earth doth pluck his fruit,
   And cast it in night's lap,
The stars more brightly glisten, mute
   Though their tears be, to see their lords mishap.

The harvest rattles in the wind,
   Ripe apples overhang the hay,
The cereal flavor of my mind
   Natheless, tells me I am as ripe as they.

I hearing get who had but ears,
   And sight who had but eyes before,
I moments live who lived but years,
   And truth discern who knew but learning's lore.

Far in the woods these golden days
   Some leaf obeys its maker's call,
And through their hollow aisles it plays
   With delicate touch the prelude of the fall.

Gently withdrawing from its stem
   It lightly lays itself along,
Where the same hand hath pillowed them
   Resigned to sleep upon the old year's throng.

The loneliest birch is brown and sere,
   The farthest pool is strewn with leaves,
Which float upon their watery bier,
   Where is no eye that sees, no heart that grieves.

I marked when first the wind grew rude
   Each leaf curled like a living thing,
As if with the ripe air it would
   Secure some faint memorial of the spring.

Then for its sake it turned a boat
   And dared new elements to brave,
A painted palace which did float
   A summer's hoarded wealth to save.

Oh could I catch these sounds remote,
   Could I preserve to human ear,
The strains which on the breezes float,
   And sing the requiem of the dying year.

I stood beside an oaken copse
   When the first gale of autumn sighed,
It gently waved the birch tree tops
   Then rustled the oak leaves and died

But not the strains which it awoke,
   For in my inmost sense I hear
The melody of which it spoke
   Still faintly rising on my inward ear.

A ripple on the river fell,
   A shadow o'er the landscape passed,
And still the whispering ferns could tell
   Whither the stranger travelled so fast.

How stand the cottages of men
   In these so fair October days,
Along the wood along the fen
   I see them looming through the mellow haze.

Immersed in Nature there they lie
   Against some cliff or chestnuts shade
Scarce obvious to the travellers eye
   Who thoughtful traverses the forest glade.

The harvest lies about the door
   The chestnut drops its burs around
As if they were the stock that bore
   The yellow crops that strew the ground.

The lily loves the river's tide
   The meadow's are the daisy's haunt
The aspens on the mountain side
   Here child of nature grows the human plant.

The jay screams through the chestnut wood
   The crisped and yellow leaves around
Are hue and texture of my mood,
   And these rough burs my heirlooms on the ground.

The thread bare trees so poor and thin
    They are no wealthier than I,
But with as brave a core within
    They rear their boughs to the October sky.

Poor knights they are which bravely wait
    The charge of winter's cavalry,
Keeping a simple Roman state
    Discumbered of their Persian luxury.

Thank God who seasons thus the year
    And sometimes kindly slants his rays,
For in his winter he's most near
    And plainest seen upon the shortest days.

Who gently tempers now his heats
    And then his harsher cold, lest we
Should surfeit on the summer's sweets,
    Or pine upon the winter's crudity.

Delay

No generous action can delay
Or thwart our higher, steadier aims,
But if sincere and true are they,
It will arouse our sight and nerve our frames.

Inspiration

If thou wilt but stand by my ear,
When through the field thy anthem's rung,
When that is done I will not fear
But the same power will abet my tongue.

Ive searched my faculties around
To learn why life to me was lent
I will attend his faintest sound
And then declare to man what God hath meant

Who equallest the coward's haste
And still inspires the faintest heart
Whose lofty fame is not disgraced
Though it assume the lowest part

The Vireo

Upon the lofty elm tree sprays
The vireo rings the changes sweet,
During the trivial summer days,
Striving to lift our thoughts above the street.

The coward ever sings no song,
He listens to no chime,
He has no heart, he has no tongue,
To build the lofty rhyme.

Only the slave knows of the slave,
Only the free the free,
For what ye principally have,
That only can ye see.

———

Great God, I ask thee for no meaner pelf
Than that I may not disappoint myself,
That in my action I may soar as high,
As I can now discern with this clear eye.

And next in value, which thy kindness lends,
That I may greatly disappoint my friends,
Howe'er they think or hope that it may be,
They may not dream how thou'st distinguished me.

That my weak hand may equal my firm faith,
And my life practice more than my tongue saith;
That my low conduct may not show,
Nor my relenting lines,
That I thy purpose did not know,
Or overrated thy designs.

The Inward Morning

Packed in my mind lie all the clothes
    Which outward nature wears,
And in its fashion's hourly change
    It all things else repairs.

In vain I look for change abroad,
    And can no difference find,
Till some new ray of peace uncalled
    Illumes my inmost mind.

What is it gilds the trees and clouds,
　　And paints the heavens so gay,
But yonder fast abiding light
　　With its unchanging ray?

Lo, when the sun streams through the wood
　　Upon a winter's morn,
Wher'er his silent beams intrude
　　The murky night is gone.

How could the patient pine have known
　　The morning breeze would come,
Or humble flowers anticipate
　　The insect's noonday hum?

Till the new light with morning cheer
　　From far streamed through the aisles,
And nimbly told the forest trees
　　For many stretching miles.

I've heard within my inmost soul
　　Such cheerful morning news,
In the horizon of my mind
　　Have seen such orient hues,

As in the twilight of the dawn,
　　When the first birds awake,
Are heard within some silent wood,
　　Where they the small twigs break,

Or in the eastern skies are seen,
　　Before the sun appears,
The harbingers of summer heats
　　Which from afar he bears.

Within the circuit of this plodding life
There enter moments of an azure hue,
Untarnished fair as is the violet
Or anemone, when the spring strews them
By some meandering rivulet, which make
The best philosophy untrue that aims
But to console man for his grievances.
I have remembered when the winter came,
High in my chamber in the frosty nights,
When in the still light of the cheerful moon,
On every twig and rail and jutting spout,
The icy spears were adding to their length
Against the arrows of the coming sun,
How in the shimmering noon of summer past
Some unrecorded beam slanted across
The upland pastures where the Johnswort grew;
Or heard, amid the verdure of my mind,
The bee's long smothered hum, on the blue flag
Loitering amidst the mead; or busy rill,
Which now through all its course stands still and dumb
Its own memorial,—purling at its play
Along the slopes, and through the meadows next,
Until its youthful sound was hushed at last
In the staid current of the lowland stream;
Or seen the furrows shine but late upturned,
And where the fieldfare followed in the rear,
When all the fields around lay bound and hoar
Beneath a thick integument of snow.
So by God's cheap economy made rich
To go upon my winter's task again.

To Edith

Thou little bud of being, Edith named,
With whom I've made acquaintance on this earth,
Who knowest me without impediment,
As flowers know the winds that stir their leaves,

And rid'st upon my shoulders as the sphere,
Turning on me thy sage reserved eye,
Behind whose broad & charitable gaze
Floats the still true & universal soul
With the pure azure of the general day,
Not yet a peopled & a vulgar town,
Rather a pure untarnished country ground;
For thou art whole, not yet begun to die,
While men look on me with their shrivelled rays
Streaming through some small chink of the broad sky;
Pure youthful soul, thou hast begun to be,
To cumulate thy sin & piety.

Delay in Friendship

The blossoms on the tree
Swell not too fast for me.
God does not want quick work but sure
Not to be tempted by so cheap a lure.

Owing to slow steps I shall be never
By my friend out run,
More than the tide can land from ocean sever,
Or earth distance the sun.

The friend is patient, he can stay
Some centuries yet,
Though then I may not get
So on my way
As fit to be his mate.

Wilt thou not wait for me my friend,
Or give a longer lease?
Why think I can wait for myself,
If so I please.

Now as ye take one step away
Thinking to leave me here—
The heavens will still beyond ye lay,
And though ye are far they will be near.

Ye will be pilgrims on the road
Whither my heart has single gone,
And never looks back from its abode
On ye thus left forlorn.

Love equals swift and slow
And high & low—
Racer and lame—
The hunter and his game.

———

Ah, 'tis in vain the peaceful din
    That wakes the ignoble town,
Not thus did braver spirits win
    A patriot's renown.

There is one field beside this stream,
    Wherein no foot does fall,
But yet it beareth in my dream
    A richer crop than all.

Let me believe a dream so dear,
    Some heart beat high that day,
Above the petty Province here,
    And Britain far away;

Some hero of the ancient mould,
    Some arm of knightly worth,
Of strength unbought, and faith unsold,
    Honored this spot of earth;

Who sought the prize his heart described,
  And did not ask release,
Whose free-born valor was not bribed
  By prospect of a peace.

The men who stood on yonder height
  That day are long since gone;
Not the same hand directs the fight
  And monumental stone.

Ye were the Grecian cities then,
  The Romes of modern birth,
Where the New England husbandmen
  Have shown a Roman worth.

In vain I search a foreign land
  To find our Bunker Hill,
And Lexington and Concord stand
  By no Laconian rill.

———

Between the traveller and the setting sun,
Upon some drifting sand heap of the shore,
A hound stands o'er the carcass of a man.

———

Have ye no work for a man to do—
No earnest work that will expand the frame,
And give a soundness to the muscles too?
How ye do waste your time!
Pray make it worth the while to live,
Or worth the while to die.
Show us great actions piled on high,
Tasking our utmost strength touching the sky,

As if we lived in a mountainous country.
　　Hell were not quite so hard to bear
　If one were honored with its hottest place.
And did ye fear ye should spoil Hell
By making it sublime?

———

I sailed up a river with a pleasant wind,
New lands, new people, and new thoughts to find;
Many fair reaches and headlands appeared,
And many dangers were there to be feared;
But when I remember where I have been,
And the fair landscapes that I have seen,
THOU seemest the only permanent shore,
The cape never rounded, nor wandered o'er.

———

I was made erect and lone
And within me is the bone
Still my vision will be clear
Still my life will not be drear
To the center all is near
Where I sit there is my throne
If age choose to sit apart
If age choose give me the start
Take the sap and leave the heart

———

I'm not alone
If I stand by myself,
But more than one,
And not in my own pelf.

I'm understood
If my intent is good,
For who obeys
The truth finds his own praise.

Our Country

It is a noble country where we dwell,
Fit for a stalwart race to summer in;
From Madawaska to Red River raft,
From Florid keys to the Missouri forks,
See what unwearied (and) copious streams
Come tumbling to the east and southern shore,
To find a man stand on their lowland banks:
Behold the innumerous rivers and the licks
Where he may drink to quench his summer's thirst,
And the broad corn and rice fields yonder, where
His hands may gather for his winter's store.

See the fair reaches of the northern lakes
To cool his summer with their inland breeze,
And the long slumbering Appalachian range
Offering its slopes to his unwearied knees!
See what a long-lipped sea doth clip the shores,
And noble strands where navies may find port;
See Boston, Baltimore, and New York stand
Fair in the sunshine on the eastern sea,
And yonder too the fair green prairie.

See the red race with sullen step retreat,
Emptying its graves, striking the wigwam tent,
And where the rude camps of its brethren stand,
Dotting the distant green, their herds around;

In serried ranks, and with a distant clang,
Their fowl fly o'er, bound to the northern lakes,
Whose plashing waves invite their webbéd feet.
Such the fair reach and prospect of the land,
The journeying summer creeps from south to north
With wearied feet, resting in many a vale;
Its length doth tire the seasons to o'ercome,
Its widening breadth doth make the sea-breeze pause
And spend its breath against the mountain's side:
Still serene Summer paints the southern fields,
While the stern Winter reigns on northern hills.

Look nearer,—know the lineaments of each face,—
Learn the far-travelled race, and find here met
The so long gathering congress of the world!
The Afric race brought here to curse its fate,
Erin to bless,—the patient German too,
Th' industrious Swiss, the fickle, sanguine Gaul,
And manly Saxon, leading all the rest.
All things invite this earth's inhabitants
To rear their lives to an unheard-of height,
And meet the expectation of the land;
To give at length the restless race of man
A pause in the long westering caravan.

———

Pray to what earth does this sweet cold belong,
Which asks no duties and no conscience?
The moon goes up by leaps her cheerful path
In some far summer stratum of the sky,
While stars with their cold shine bedot her way.
The fields gleam mildly back upon the sky,
And far and near upon the leafless shrubs
The snow dust still emits a silvery light.
Under the hedge, where drift banks are their screen,
The titmice now pursue their downy dreams,
As often in the sweltering summer nights

The bee doth drop asleep in the flower cup,
When evening overtakes him with his load.
By the brooksides, in the still genial night,
The more adventurous wanderer may hear
The crystals shoot and form, and winter slow
Increase his rule by gentlest summer means.

True kindness is a pure divine affinity,
Not founded upon human consanguinity.
It is a spirit, not a blood relation,
Superior to family and station.

Until at length the north winds blow,
And beating high mid ice and snow,
The sturdy goose brings up the rear,
Leaving behind the cold cold year.

Spes sibi quisque
Each one his own hope

Wait not till slaves pronounce the word
To set the captive free,
Be free yourselves, be not deferred,
And farewell slavery.

Ye are all slaves, ye have your price,
And gang but cries to gang.
Then rise, the highest of ye rise,
I hear your fetters clang.

Think not the tyrant sits afar
   In your own breasts ye have
The District of Columbia
   And power to free the Slave.

The warmest heart the north doth breed,
   Is still too cold and far,
The colored man's release must come
   From outcast Africa.

Make haste & set the captive free!—
   Are ye so free that cry?
The lowest depths of slavery
   Leave freedom for a sigh.

The Funeral Bell

One more is gone
Out of the busy throng
That tread these paths;
The church bell tolls,
Its sad knell rolls
To many hearths.

   Flower bells toll not,
   Their echoes roll not
   Unto my ear;—
   There still perchance,
   That gentle spirit haunts
   A fragrant bier.

Low lies the pall,
Lowly the mourners all
Their passage grope;—
No sable hue
Mars the serene blue
Of heaven's cope.

In distant dell
Faint sounds the funeral bell,
A heavenly chime;
Some poet there
Weaves the light burthened air
Into sweet rhyme.

———

Sometimes I hear the veery's clarion,
Or brazen trump of the impatient jay,
And in secluded woods the chicadee
Doles out her scanty notes, which sing the praise
Of heroes, and set forth the loveliness
Of virtue evermore.

———

Thou dusky spirit of the wood,
Bird of an ancient brood,
Flitting thy lonely way,
A meteor in the summer's day,
From wood to wood, from hill to hill,
Low over forest, field and rill,
What wouldst thou say?
Why shouldst thou haunt the day?
What makes thy melancholy float?
What bravery inspires thy throat,
And bears thee up above the clouds,
Over desponding human crowds,
Which far below
Lay thy haunts low?

Not unconcerned Wachusett rears his head
Above the fields so late from nature won
With patient brow unmoved as one who read
New annals in the history of man.

Nature

O nature I do not aspire
To be the highest in thy quire,
To be a meteor in the sky
Or comet that may range on high,
Only a zephyr that may blow
Among the reeds by the river low.
Give me thy most privy place
Where to run my airy race.
In some withdrawn unpublic mead
Let me sigh upon a reed,
Or in the woods with leafy din
Whisper the still evening in,
For I had rather be thy child
And pupil in the forest wild
Than be the king of men elsewhere
And most sovereign slave of care
To have one moment of thy dawn
Than share the city's year forlorn.
Some still work give me to do
Only be it near to you.

Godfrey of Boulogne

The moon hung low o'er Provence vales,
   'Twas night upon the sea,
Fair France was woo'd by Afric gales
   And paid in minstrelsy.
Along the Rhone then moves a band,
   Their banner in the breeze,
Of mail-clad men with iron hand,
   And steel on breast and knees.
The herdsman following his droves
   Far in the night alone,
Read faintly through the olive groves,—
   'Twas Godfrey of Boulogne

The mist still slumbered on the heights
   The glaciers lay in shade,
The stars withdrew with faded lights,
   The moon went down the glade.
Proud Jura saw the day from far,
   And showed it to the plain;
She heard the din of coming war,
   But told it not again.
The goatherd seated on the rocks,
   Dreaming of battles none
Was wakened by his startled flocks,—
   'Twas Godfrey of Boulogne.

Night hung upon the Danube's stream,
   Deep midnight on the vales,
Along the shore no beacons gleam,
   No sound is on the gales.
The Turkish lord has banished care
   The harem sleeps profound,
Save one fair Georgian sitting there
   Upon the Moslem ground.
The lightning flashed a transient gleam,
   A glancing banner shone,
A host swept swiftly down the stream,—
   'Twas Godfrey of Boulogne.

'Twas noon upon Byzantium,
    On street and tower and sea,
On Europe's edge a warlike hum
    Of gathered chivalry.
A troop went boldly through the throng,
    Of Ethiops, Arabs, Huns,
Jews Greeks and Turk, to right their wrong
    Their swords flashed thousand suns.
Their banner cleaved Byzantium's dust,
    And like the sun it shone,
their armor had acquired no rust,—
    'Twas Godfrey of Boulogne.

———

The Rabbit leaps
The mouse outcreeps
The flag out-peeps
    Beside the brook.

The ferret weeps
The marmot sleeps
The owlet keeps
    In his snug nook.

The apples thaw
The ravens caw
The squirrels gnaw
    The frozen fruit;

To their retreat
We track the feet
Of mice that eat
    The apples root.

The willows droop
The alders stoop
The pheasants group
    Beneath the snow.

The catkins green
Cast o'er the scene
A summer sheen
    A genial glow.

The snow dust falls
The otter crawls
The partridge calls
    Far in the wood

The traveller dreams
The tree-ice gleams
The blue jay screams
    In angry mood.

———

I am the Autumnal sun,
With Autumn gales my race is run.
When will the hazle put forth its flowers,
And the grape ripen under my bowers?
When will the harvest and the hunter's moon
Turn my midnight into midnoon?
    I am all sere & yellow,
    And to my core mellow.
The mast is dropping within my woods
The winter is lurking within my moods
And the rustling of the withered leaf
Is the constant music of my grief,
    My gay colored grief,
    My autumnal relief.

———

Where'er thou sail'st who sailed with me,
Though now thou climbest loftier mounts
And fairer rivers dost ascend
Be thou my muse, my Brother.

I was born upon thy bank river
My blood flows in thy stream
And thou meanderest forever
  At the bottom of my dream

Salmon Brook
Pennichook
Ye sweet waters of my brain
  When shall I look
  Or cast the hook
  In thy waves again?

Silver eels
Wooden creels
These the baits that still allure
  And dragon fly
  That floated by
  May they still endure?

The moon now rises to her absolute rule,
And the husbandman and hunter
Acknowledge her for their mistress.
Asters and golden reign in the fields
And the life everlasting withers not.
The fields are reaped and shorn of their pride
But an inward verdure still crowns them
The thistle scatters its down on the pool
And yellow leaves clothe the river—
And nought disturbs the serious life of men.

But behind the sheaves and under the sod
There lurks a ripe fruit which the reapers have not gathered
The true harvest of the year—the boreal fruit
Which it bears forever.
With fondness annually watering and maturing it.
But man never severs the stalk
Which bears this palatable fruit.

My friends, why should we live?
Life is an idle war a toilsome peace;
    To-day I would not give
One small consent for its securest ease.

    Shall we out-wear the year
In our pavilions on its dusty plain
    And yet no signal hear
To strike our tents and take the road again?

    Or else drag up the slope
The heavy ordnance of nature's train?
    Useless but in the hope,
Some far remote and heavenward hill to gain.

I mark the summer's swift decline
The springing sward its grave clothes weaves
Whose rustling woods the gales confine
The aged year turns on its couch of leaves.

Oh could I catch the sounds remote
Could I but tell to human ear—
The strains which on the breezes float
And sing the requiem of the dying year.

My love must be as free
    As is the eagle's wing,
Hovering o'er land and sea
    And everything.

I must not dim my eye
    In thy saloon,
I must not leave my sky
    And nightly moon.

Be not the fowler's net
    Which stays my flight,
And craftily is set
    T' allure the sight.

But be the favoring gale
    That bears me on,
And still doth fill my sail
    When thou art gone.

I cannot leave my sky
    For thy caprice,
True love would soar as high
    As heaven is.

The eagle would not brook
    Her mate thus won,
Who trained his eye to look
    Beneath the sun.

The Moon

Time wears her not; she doth his chariot guide;
Mortality below her orb is placed.
—RALEIGH.

The full-orbed moon with unchanged ray
Mounts up the eastern sky,
Not doomed to these short nights for aye,
But shining steadily.

She does not wane, but my fortune,
Which her rays do not bless,
My wayward path declineth soon,
But she shines not the less.

And if she faintly glimmers here,
And paled is her light,
Yet always in her proper sphere
She's mistress of the night.

Rumors From an Aeolian Harp

There is a vale which none hath seen,
Where foot of man has never been,
Such as here lives with toil and strife,
An anxious and a sinful life.

There every virtue has its birth,
Ere it descends upon the earth,
And thither every deed returns,
Which in the generous bosom burns.

There love is warm, and youth is young,
And poetry is yet unsung,
For Virtue still adventures there,
And freely breathes her native air.

And ever, if you hearken well,
You still may hear its vesper bell,
And tread of high-souled men go by,
Their thoughts conversing with the sky.

———

On shoulders whirled in some eccentric orbit
Just by old Paestum's temples and the perch
Where Time doth plume his wings.

———

    Far oer The bow
Amid the drowsy noon
Souhegan creeping slow
    Appeareth soon.

Where gleaming fields of haze
Meet the voyageurs gaze,
And above the heated air
Seems to make a river there.

The pines stand up with pride
By the Souhegan's side,
And the hemlock and the larch
With their triumphal arch
Have accompanied its march
    To the sea.

No wind stirs its waves
But the spirits of the braves
    Hov'ring o'er
Whose antiquated graves
Its still water laves
    On the shore.

But with an Indian's stealthy tread
It goes sleeping in its bed
Without joy or grief
Or the rustle of a leaf
From the Lyndeboro' hills
To the merrimack mills

Without a ripple or a billow
Or the sigh of a willow
Which trails in its stream
The mid current of its dream.

Not a sound is floated o'er
save the mallet on shore
Which echoing on high
Seems a caulking the sky.

experienced river
Hast thou flown for ever?
Souhegan soundeth old
But the half is not told.

What names hast thou borne
In the ages far gone?
When the Xanthus and Meander
Commenced to wander—
Eer the brown bear hunted
On thy forest floor
Or nature had planted
The pines by thy shore.

With a louder din
Did thy current begin
When melted the snow
On the far mountain's brow
And the drops came together
In that rainy weather.

Methinks that by a strict behavior
I could elicit back the brightest star
That lurks behind a cloud.

I have rolled near some other spirits path
And with a pleased anxiety have felt
Its purer influence on my opaque mass
But always was I doomed to learn, alas!
I had scarce changed its sidireal time.

Fog

Thou drifting meadow of the air
Where bloom The dasied banks & violets
And in whose fenny labyrinths
The bittern booms, and curlew peeps
The heron wades and boding rain crow clucks;
  Low anchored cloud,
  Newfoundland air,
Fountain head and source of rivers,
Ocean branch that flowest to the sun,
Diluvian spirit, or Deucaleon shroud,
Dew cloth dream drapery
And napkin spread by fays—
Spirit of lakes and seas and rivers—
   Sea fowl that with the east wind
 Seeks't the shore— Groping thy way inland
By which ever name I please to call thee
 Bear only perfumes and the scent
 Of healing herbs to just men's fields.

How little curious is man
Who hath not searched his mystery a span
But dreams of mines of treasure
Which he neglects to measure
For three score years and ten
Walks to and fro amid his fellow men
Oer this firm tract of continental land
His fancy bearing no divining wand.
Our uninquiring corpses lie more low
Than our lifes curiosity doth go
Our most ambitious steps climb not so high
As in their hourly sport the sparrows fly.
And yonder cloud's blown farther in a day
Than our most vagrant feet may ever stray.
Surely, O Lord, he hath not greatly erred
Who hath so little from his birth place stirred.
He wanders through this low and shallow world
Scarcely his bolder thoughts and hopes unfurled
Through this low walled world which his huge sin
Hath hardly room to rest and harbor in.
Bearing his head just oer some fallow ground
Some cowslip'd meadows where the bitterns sound.
He wanders round until his end draws nigh
And then lays down his aged head to die.
And this is life—this is that famous strife.

    His head doth coast a fathom from the land
    Six feet from where his grovelling feet do stand.

To the Comet

My sincerity doth surpass
   The pretence of optic glass.

Say what are the highlands yonder
Which do keep the spheres asunder
The streams of light which centre in our sun
And those which from some other system run?

Distinguished stranger, system ranger,
Plenipotentiary to our sphere,
Dost thou know of any danger,
War or famine near?

Special envoy, foreign minister,
From the empire of the sky,
Dost thou threaten aught that's sinister
By thy course on high?

Runner of the firmament
On what errand wast thou sent,
Art thou some great general's scout
Come to spy our weakness out?
Sculling thy way without a sail,
Mid the stars and constellations,
The pioneer*er* of a tail
Through the stary nations.
    Thou celestial privateer
We entreat thee come not near.

Haze

Woof of the sun, ethereal gauze,
Woven of Nature's richest stuffs,
Visible heat, air-water, and dry sea,
Last conquest of the eye;
Toil of the day displayed, sun-dust,
Aerial surf upon the shores of earth,
Ethereal estuary, frith of light,
Breakers of air, billows of heat,
Fine summer spray on inland seas;
Bird of the sun, transparent-winged
Owlet of noon, soft-pinioned,
From heath or stubble rising without song;
Establish thy serenity o'er the fields.

Smoke

Light-winged smoke, Icarian bird,
Melting thy pinions in thy upward flight,
Lark without song, and messenger of dawn,
Circling above the hamlets as thy nest;
Or else, departing dream, and shadowy form
Of midnight vision, gathering up thy skirts;
By night star-veiling, and by day
Darkening the light and blotting out the sun;
Go thou my incense upward from this hearth,
And ask the Gods to pardon this clear flame.

To a Stray Fowl

Poor bird! destined to lead thy life
    Far in the adventurous west,
And here to be debarred to-night
    From thy accustomed nest;
Must thou fall back upon old instinct now—
Well nigh extinct under man's fickle care?
Did heaven bestow its quenchless inner light
So long ago, for thy small want to-night?
Why stand'st upon thy toes to crow so late?
The moon is deaf to thy low feathered fate;
Or dost thou think so to possess the night,
And people the drear dark with thy brave sprite?
And now with anxious eye thou look'st about,
While the relentless shade draws on its veil,
For some sure shelter from approaching dews,
And the insidious steps of nightly foes.
I fear imprisonment has dulled thy wit,
Or ingrained servitude extinguished it.
But no,—dim memory of the days of yore,
By Brahmapootra and the Jumna's shore,
Where thy proud race flew swiftly o'er the heath,
And sought its food the jungle's shade beneath,
Has taught thy wings to seek yon friendly trees,
As erst by Indus' bank and far Ganges.

The Departure

In this roadstead I have ridden
In this covert I have hidden
Friendly thoughts were cliffs to me
And I hid beneath their lea.

This true people took the stranger
And warm hearted housed the ranger
They received their roving guest,
And have fed him with the best

Whatsoe'er the land afforded
To the stranger's wish accorded,
Shook the olive, stripped the vine,
And expressed the strengthening wine.

And at night they did spread o'er him
What by day they spread before him,
That good-will which was repast
Was his covering at last.

The stranger moored him to their pier
Without anxiety or fear;
By day he walked the sloping land,
    By night the gentle heavens he scanned.

When first his bark stood inland
To the coast of this far Finland,
Sweet-watered brooks came tumbling to the shore
The weary mariner to restore.

And still he stayed from day to day
If he their kindness might repay
But more and more
The sullen waves came rolling to the shore.

And still the more the stranger waited
The less his argosy was freighted,
And still the more he stayed
The less his debt was paid.

So He unfurled his mast
To receive the fragrant blast,
And that same refreshing gale
Which had woo'd him to remain
    Again and again—
It was that filled his sail
    And drove him to the main.

All day the low hung clouds
    Dropt tears into the sea
And the wind amid the shrouds
    Sighed plaintively.

———

Brother where dost thou dwell?
    What sun shines for thee now?
Dost thou indeed farewell?
    As we wished here below.

What season didst thou find?
    'Twas winter here.
Are not the fates more kind
    Than they appear?

Is thy brow clear again
    As in thy youthful years?
And was that ugly pain
    The summit of thy fears?

Yet thou wast cheery still,
    They could not quench thy fire,
Thou dids't abide their will,
    And then retire.

Where chiefly shall I look
    To feel thy presence near?
Along the neighboring brook
    May I thy voice still hear?

Dost thou still haunt the brink
    Of yonder river's tide?
And may I ever think
    That thou art at my side?

What bird wilt thou employ
    To bring me word of thee?
For it would give them joy,
    'Twould give them liberty,
    To serve their former lord
    With wing and minstrelsy.

A sadder strain has mixed with their song,
    They've slowlier built their nests,
Since thou art gone
    Their lively labor rests.

Where is the finch—the thrush,
    I used to hear?
Ah! they could well abide
    The dying year.

Now they no more return,
    I hear them not;
They have remained to mourn,
    Or else forgot.

———

All things are current found
Oer the uneven ground.
    Spirits and elements
    Have their descents.

Night and day—year on year,
    High and low far and near,
    These are our own aspects
    These are our own regrets.

Ye gods of the shore
Who abide evermore,
I see your far headland
Stretching on either hand.

I hear the sweet evening sounds
From your undecaying grounds
Cheat me no more with time
Take me to your clime.

On fields oer which the reaper's hand has passed,
Lit by the harvest moon and autumn sun,
My thoughts like stubble floating in the wind
And of such fineness as October airs,
There after harvest could I glean my life
A richer harvest reaping without toil,
And weaving gorgeous fancies at my will
In subtler webs than finest summer haze.

Epitaph on an Engraver

By death's favor
Here lies the engraver
And now I think o't
Where lies he not?
If the archangel look but where he lies
He ne'er will get translated to the skies.

Epitaph on Pursy

Traveller, this is no prison,
He is not dead, but risen.
    Then is there need,
    To fill his grave,
    And truth to save,
    That we should read,—
    In Pursy's favor
    Here lies the engraver.

Ep on a Good Man

Here lies—the world
There rises one.

Epitaph

Here lies an honest man
    Rear Admiral Van.
Faith, then ye have
Two in one grave,
For by your favor
Here too lies the engraver.

Ep on the World

Here lies the body of this world,
Whose soul alas to hell is hurled.
This golden youth long since was past,
Its silver manhood went as fast,
And iron age drew on at last;
'Tis vain its character to tell,
The several fates which it befell,
What year it died, when 'twill arise,
We only know that here it lies.

The sluggish smoke curls up from some deep dell,
The stiffened air exploring in the dawn,
And making slow acquaintance with the day;
Delaying now upon its heavenward course,
In wreathed loiterings dallying with itself,
With as uncertain purpose and slow deed,
As its half-wakened master by the hearth,
Whose mind still slumbering and sluggish thoughts
Have not yet swept into the onward current
Of the new day;—and now it streams afar,
The while the chopper goes with step direct,
And mind intent to swing the early axe.

First in the dusky dawn he sends abroad
His early scout, his emissary, smoke,
The earliest, latest pilgrim from the roof,
To feel the frosty air, inform the day;
And while he crouches still beside the hearth,
Nor musters courage to unbar the door,
It has gone down the glen with the light wind,
And o'er the plain unfurled its venturous wreath,
Draped the tree tops, loitered upon the hill,
And warmed the pinions of the early bird;
And now, perchance, high in the crispy air,
Has caught sight of the day o'er the earth's edge,
And greets its master's eye at his low door,
As some refulgent cloud in the upper sky.

———

On Ponkawtasset, since, we took our way,
Down this still stream to far Billericay,
A poet wise has settled, whose fine ray
Doth often shine on Concord's twilight day.

Like those first stars, whose silver beams on high,
Shining more brightly as the day goes by,
Most travellers cannot at first descry,
But eyes that wont to range the evening sky,

And know celestial lights, do plainly see,
And gladly hail them, numbering two or three;
For lore that's deep must deeply studied be,
As from deep wells men read star-poetry.

These stars are never paled, though out of sight,
But like the sun they shine forever bright;
Ay, *they* are suns, though earth must in its flight
Put out its eyes that it may see their light.

Who would neglect the least celestial sound,
Or faintest light that falls on earthly ground,
If he could know it one day would be found
That star in Cygnus whither we are bound,
And pale our sun with heavenly radiance round?

To a Marsh Hawk in Spring

There is health in thy gray wing
Health of nature's furnishing.
Say thou modern-winged antique,
Was thy mistress ever sick?
In each heaving of thy wing
Thou dost health and leisure bring,
Thou dost waive disease & pain
And resume new life again.

Great Friend

I walk in nature still alone
　And know no one
Discern no lineament nor feature
　Of any creature.

Though all the firmament
  Is oer me bent,
Yet still I miss the grace
  Of an intelligent and kindred face.

I still must seek the friend
Who does with nature blend,
Who is the person in her mask,
He is the man I ask.

Who is the expression of her meaning,
Who is the uprightness of her leaning,
Who is the grown child of her weaning

The center of this world,
The face of nature,
The site of human life,
Some sure foundation
And nucleus of a nation—
At least a private station.

We twain would walk together
Through every weather,
And see this aged nature,
Go with a bending stature.

The offer

I make ye an offer,
Ye gods hear the scoffer,
The scheme will not hurt you,
If ye will find goodness I will find virtue.
Though I am your creature,
And child of your nature,
I have pride still unbended,
And blood undescended,
Some free independence,
And my own descendents.

If ye will deal plainly,
I will strive mainly,
If ye will discover
Great plans to your lover,
And give him a sphere
Somewhat larger than here.

Morning

Thou unconverted saint
Early Christian without taint—
Heathen without reproach
Who dost upon the evil day encroach,
Who ever since thy birth
Hast trod the outskirts of the earth.
Strict anchorite who dost simply feast
On freshest dews—I'll be thy guest,
And daily bend my steps to east
While the late risen world goes west.

The Friend

The great friend
Dwells at the land's end,
There lives he
Next to the sea.
Fleets come and go,
Carrying commerce to and fro,
But still sits he on the sand
And maketh firm that headland.
Mariners steer them by his light
Safely in the darkest night,
He holds no visible communion
For his friendship is a union.
Many men dwell far inland,
But he alone sits on the strand,
Whether he ponders men or books
Ever still he seaward looks,

Feels the sea-breeze on his cheek,
At each word the landsmen speak;
From some distant port he hears
Of the ventures of past years
In the sullen ocean's roar
Of wrecks upon a distant shore;
In every companion's eye
A sailing vessel doth descry;
Marine news he ever reads
And the slightest glances heeds.
Near is India to him
Though his native shore is dim,
But the bark which long was due,
Never—never—heaves in view,
Which shall put an end to commerce
And bring back what it took from us,
(Which shall make Siberia free
Of the climes beyond the sea)
Fetch the Indies in its hold,
All their spices and their gold,
    And men sail the sea no more
    The sea itself become a shore,
    To a broader deeper sea,
    A profounder mystery.

———

Yet let us Thank the purblind race,
    Who still have thought it good
With lasting stone to mark the place
    Where braver men have stood.

In concord, town of quiet name
    And quiet fame as well,

———

Ye do command me to all virtue ever
And simple truth the law by which we live
Methinks that I can trust your clearer sense
And your immediate knowledge of the truth.
I would obey your influence—one with fate

———

Ive seen ye, sisters, on the mountain-side
When your green mantles fluttered in the wind
Ive seen your foot-prints on the lakes smooth shore
Lesser than man's, a more ethereal trace,
I have heard of ye as some far-famed race—
Daughters of gods whom I should one day meet—
Or mothers I might say of all our race.
I reverence your natures so like mine
Yet strangely different, like but still unlike
Thou only stranger that hast crossed my path
Accept my hospitality—let me hear
The message which thou bring'st
　　　Made different from me
　　Perchance thou't made to be
　　The creature of a different destiny.
I know not who ye are that meekly stand
Thus side by side with man in every land.
When did ye form alliance with our race
Ye children of the moon who in placid nights
Vaulted upon the hills and sought this earth.
Reveal that which I fear ye can not tell
Wherein ye are not I, wherein ye dwell
Where I can never come.
What boots it that I do regard ye so
Does it make suns to shine or crops to grow?
What boots that I never should forget
Thee, I have sisters sitting for me yet
And what are sisters
The robust man who can so stoutly strive
In this bleak world is hardly kept alive.
And who is it protects *ye* smooths *your* way

I am bound, I am bound, for a distant shore,
By a lonely isle, by a far Azore,
There it is, there it is, the treasure I seek,
On the barren sands of a desolate creek.

The Hero

What doth he ask?
Some worthy task.
Never to run
Till that be done,
that never done
Under the sun.
Here to begin
All things to win
By his endeavor
Forever and ever—
Happy and well
On this ground to dwell
This soil subdue
Plant and renew.
By might & main
Health & strength gain
So to give nerve
To his slenderness
Yet Some mighty pain
He would sustain.
So to preserve
His tenderness.
Not be deceived
Of suffring bereaved
Not lose his life
By living too well
Nor escape strife

In his lonely cell
And so find out Heaven
By not knowing Hell.
Strength like the rock
To withstand any shock—
Yet some Aaron's rod
Some smiting by god
Occasion to gain
To shed human tears
And to entertain
Still divine fears.
Not once for all, forever, blest,
Still to be cheered out of the west
Not from his heart to banish all sighs
Still be encouraged by the sun rise
Forever to love and to love and to love
Within him, around him—beneath him above
To love is to know, is to feel, is to be
At once 'tis his birth & his destiny
For earthly pleasures
Celestial pains
Heavenly losses
For earthly gains.
Must we still eat
The bread we have spurned
Must we rekindle
The faggots we've burned—
Must we go out
By the poor man's gate
Die by degrees
Not by new fate.
Is then no road
This way my friend
Is there no road
Without any end—
When I have slumbered
I have heard sounds

As travellers passing
Over my grounds—
'Twas a sweet music
Wafted them by
I could not tell
If far off or nigh.
Unless I dreamed it
This was of yore—
But I never told it
To mortal before—
Never remembered
But in my dreams
What to me waking
A miracle seems
If you will give of your pulse or your grain
We will rekindle those flames again
Here will we tarry it is without doubt
Till a miracle putteth that fire out.

At midnight's hour I raised my head
The owls were seeking for their bread
The foxes barked impatient still
At their wan fate they bear so ill—
I thought me of eternities delayed
And of commands but half obeyed—
The night wind rustled through the glade
As if a force of men there staid
The word was whispered through the ranks
And every hero seized his lance
The word was whispered through the ranks
        Advance.

I seek the Present Time,
No other clime,
Life in to-day,
Not to sail another way,
To Paris or to Rome,
Or farther still from home.
That man, whoe'er he is,
Lives but a moral death,
Whose life is not coeval
With his breath.
What are deeds done
Away from home?
What the best essay
On the Ruins of Rome?
The dusty highways,
What Scripture says,
This pleasant weather
And all signs together—
The river's meander,
All things, in short,
Forbid me to wander
In deed or in thought.
In cold or in drouth,
seek Not the sunny South,
But make the whole tour
Of the sunny Present Hour.
For here if thou fail,
Where canst thou prevail?
If you love not
Your own land most,
You'll find nothing lovely
Upon a distant coast.
If you love not
The latest sunset,
What is there in pictures
Or old gems set?

If no man should travel
Till he had the means,
There'd be little travelling

For kings or for Queens.
The means, what are they!
They are the wherewithal
Great expenses to pay;—
Life got, and some to spare,
Great works on hand,
And freedom from care.
Plenty of time well spent,
To use,—
Clothes paid for, and no rent
In your shoes;—
Something to eat,
And something to burn,
And, above all, no need to return;—
For they who come back,
,have they not failed,
Wherever they've ridden
Or steamed it, or sailed?
All your grass hayed,—
All your debts paid,—
All your wills made?
Then you might as well have stayed,
For are you not dead,
Only not buried?

The way unto "Today",
The rail road to "Here,"
They never'll grade that way,
Nor shorten it, I fear.
There are plenty of depots
All the world o'er,
But not a single station
At a man's door;
If we would get near
To the secret of things,
We shall not have to hear
When the engine bell rings.

Tell me ye wise ones if ye can
Whither and whence the race of man.
For I have seen his slender clan
Clinging to hoar hills with their feet
Threading the forest for their meat
Moss and lichens bark & grain
They racke together with might & main
And they digest them with anxiety & pain.
I meet them in their rags and unwashed hair
Instructed to eke out their scanty fare
Brave race—with a yet humbler prayer
Beggars they are aye on the largest scale
They beg their daily bread at heavens door
   And if their this years crop alone shoud fail
They neither bread nor begging would know more.
   They are the Titmans of their race
   And hug the vales with mincing pace
   Like Troglodites, and fight with cranes
   We walk 'mid great relations feet
   What they let fall alone we eat
   We are only able
   to catch the fragments from their table
     These elder brothers of our race
     By us unseen with larger pace
     Walk oer our heads, and live our lives
     embody our desires and dreams
     Anticipate our hoped for gleams
       We grub the earth for our food
       We know not what is good.
     Where does the fragrance of our orchards go
     Our vineyards whiie we toil below—
     A finer race and finer fed
     Feast and revel above our head.
     The tints and fragrance of the flowers & fruits
     Are but the crumbs from off their table
     While we consume the pulp and roots
     Some times we do assert our kin
     And stand a moment where once they have been
     We hear their sounds and see their sights

And we experience their delights—
But for the moment that we stand
Astonished on the Olympian land.
We do discern no traveller's face
No elder brother of our race.
To lead us to the monarch's court
And represent our case.
But straightway we must journey back
retracing slow the arduous track
Without the privelege to tell
Even, the sight we know so well

———

Behold these flowers—
let us be up with Time
not dreaming of 3000 years
ago. Erect ourselves and let
those columns lie—not stoop
to raise a foil against the
sky— Where is the *spirit*
of that time but in this
present day this present line
3000 years ago are not
agone—they are still lingering
here aye every one, Where
there is memory which com-
pelleth time the muse's mother
and the muses nine— There are
all ages—past and future
time unwearied memory that
does not forget the actions
of the past—that does
not forego—to stamp them
freshly—. That old mortality
industrious to retouch the monuments of time, in the world's

cemetery through-out every clime/
And Memnon's mother sprightly greets us now
Wears still her youthful blushes on her brow
And Carnac's columns why stand they on the plain?
T'enjoy our opportunities they would fain remain

This is my Carnac whose unmeasured dome
Shelters the measuring art & measurer's home
Whose propylaeum is the system nigh
And sculptured facade the visible sky

My friends, my noble friends, know ye—
That in my waking hours I think of ye
—Ever in godlike band uncompromised & free

The Earth

Which seems so barren once gave birth
To heroes—who oerran her plains,
Who plowed her seas and reaped her grains

But now "no war nor battle's sound"
Invades this peaceful battleground
But waves of Concord murmuring by
flowing with gentle harmony.
Yet since we sailed, some things have failed
And many a dream gone down the stream
Here then an aged shepherd dwellt

Who to his flock his substance dealt
And ruled them with a vigorous crook
According to the sacred Book.
But he the pierless bridge passed o'er
And solitary left the shore
Anon a youthful pastor came
Whose crook was not unknown to fame
His lambs he viewed with gentle glance
Spread oer the country's wide expanse
And fed with "mosses from the manse"—
Yonder the rocky seat where late
With soothed and patient ear we sat
Beside our Hawthorne in the dale
And listened to his Twice told Tale.—

Such water do the gods distill
And pour down every hill
For their new England men.
A draught of this wild water bring
And I will never taste the spring
Of Helicon again.
But yesterday in dew it fell
This morn its streams began to swell
And with the sun it downward flowd
So fresh it hardly knew its road.

Die and be buried who will,
I mean to live my fill.
My nature grows ever more young
The primitive pines among.

I have seen some frozenfaced connecticut
Or Down east man in his crack coaster
With tort sail, with folded arms standing
Beside his galley with his dog & man
While his cock crowed aboard, scud thro the surf
By some fast anchored Staten island farm,
But just outside the vast and stirring line
Where the astonished Dutchman digs his clams
Or but half ploughs his cabbage garden plot
With unbroken steeds & ropy harness—
And some squat bantam whom the shore wind drownd
Feebly responded there for all reply,
While the triumphant Yankee's farm swept by.

———

Such near aspects had we
Of our life's scenery.

Travelling

If e'er our minds be ill at ease
It is in vain to cross the seas
Or when the fates do prove unkind
To leave our native land behind.
The ship becalmed at length stands still
The steed will rest beneath the hill.
But swiftly still our fortunes pace
To find us out in every place.

The Atlantides

The smothered streams of love, which flow
More bright than Phlegethon, more low,
Island us ever, like the sea,
In an Atlantic mystery.
Our fabled shores none ever reach,
No mariner has found our beach,
Scarcely our mirage now is seen,
And neighboring waves with floating green,
Yet still the oldest charts contain
Some dotted outline of our main;
In ancient times midsummer days
Unto the western islands' gaze,
To Teneriffe and the Azores,
Have shown our faint and cloud-like shores.

But sink not yet, ye desolate isles,
Anon your coast with commerce smiles,
And richer freights ye'll furnish far
Than Africa or Malabar.
Be fair, be fertile evermore,
Ye rumored but untrodden shore,
Princes and monarchs will contend
Who first unto your land shall send,
And pawn the jewels of the crown
To call your distant soil their own.

—

Conscience is instinct bred in the house,
Feeling and Thinking propagate the sin
By an unnatural breeding in and in.
I say, Turn it out doors,
Into the moors.
I love a life whose plot is simple,
And does not thicken with every pimple,
A soul so sound no sickly conscience binds it,

That makes the universe no worse than 't finds it.
I love an earnest soul,
Whose mighty joy and sorrow
Are not drowned in a bowl,
And brought to life to-morrow;
That lives one tragedy,
And not seventy;
A conscience worth keeping,
Laughing not weeping;
A conscience wise and steady,
And forever ready;
Not changing with events,
Dealing in compliments;
A conscience exercised about
Large things, where one *may* doubt.
I love a soul not all of wood,
Predestinated to be good,
But true to the backbone
Unto itself alone,
And false to none;
Born to its own affairs,
Its own joys and own cares;
By whom the work which God begun
Is finished, and not undone;
Taken up where he left off,
Whether to worship or to scoff;
If not good, why then evil,
If not good god, good devil.
Goodness! you hypocrite, come out of that,
Live your life, do your work, then take your hat.
I have no patience towards
Such conscientious cowards.
Give me simple laboring folk,
Who love their work,
Whose virtue is a song
To cheer God along.

That Phaeton of our day,
Who'd make another milky way,
And burn the world up with his ray;

By us an undisputed seer,—
Who'd drive his flaming car so near
Unto our shuddering mortal sphere,

Disgracing all our slender worth,
And scorching up the living earth,
To prove his heavenly birth.

The silver spokes, the golden tire,
Are glowing with unwonted fire,
And ever nigher roll and nigher;

The pins and axle melted are,
The silver radii fly afar,
Ah, he will spoil his Father's car!

Who let him have the steeds he cannot steer?
Henceforth the sun will not shine for a year;
And we shall Ethiops all appear.

———

Then spend an age in whetting thy desire,
Thou needs't not *hasten* if thou dost *stand fast*.

———

We see the *planet* fall,
And that is all.

———

We should not mind if on our ear there fell
Some less of cunning, more of oracle.

———

Men say they know many things
But lo! they have taken wings,
The arts & sciences.
And a thousand appliances—
The wind that blows
Is all that anybody knows.

———

Away! away! away! away!
   Ye have not kept your secret well,
I will abide that other day,
   Those other lands ye tell.

Has time no leisure left for these,
   The acts that ye rehearse?
Is not eternity a lease
   For better deeds than verse?

'T is sweet to hear of heroes dead,
   To know them still alive,
But sweeter if we earn their bread,
   And in us they survive.

Our life should feed the springs of fame
   With a perennial wave,
As ocean feeds the babbling founts
   Which find in it their grave.

Ye skies drop gently round my breast,
   And be my corselet blue,
Ye earth receive my lance in rest,
   My faithful charger you;

Ye stars my spear-heads in the sky,
   My arrow-tips ye are,—
I see the routed foemen fly,
   My bright spears fixed are.

Give me an angel for a foe,
   Fix now the place and time,
And straight to meet him I will go
   Above the starry chime.

And with our clashing bucklers' clang
   The heavenly spheres shall ring,
While bright the northern lights shall hang
   Beside our tourneying.

And if she lose her champion true,
   Tell Heaven not despair,
For I will be her champion new,
   Her fame I will repair.

———

In the East fames are won,
In the West deeds are done.

———

The good how can we trust?
Only the wise are just.
The good we use,
The wise we cannot choose.
These there are none above;
The good they know & love,
But are not known again
By those of lesser ken.—
They do not charm us with their eyes,
But they transfix with their advice.
No partial sympathy they feel,
With private woe or private weal,
But with the Universe joy & sigh,
Whose knowledge is their sympathy.

Greece

When life contracts into a vulgar span
And human nature tires to be a man,
I thank the gods for Greece
That permanent realm of peace,
For as the rising moon far in the night
Checquers the shade with her forerunning light,
So in my darkest hour my senses seem
To catch from her Acropolis a gleam,
Greece who am I that should remember thee?
Thy Marathon and thy Thermopylae
Is my life vulgar my fate mean
Which on such golden memories can lean?

Poverty

If I am poor it is that I am proud,
If God has made me naked and a boor
He did not think it fit his work to shroud.

The poor man comes from heaven direct to earth
As stars drop down the sky and tropic beams.
The rich receives in our gross air his birth,
As from low suns are slanted golden gleams.

Men are by birth equal in this that given
Themselves and their condition they are even.
The less of inward essence is to leaven
The more of outward circumstance is given.

Yon sun is naked bare of satellite
Unless our earths and moons that office hold,
Though his perpetual day feareth no night
And his perennial summer dreads no cold.

Where are his gilded rays but in our sky?
His solid disk doth float far from us still,
The orb which through the central way doth fly
Shall naked seem though proudly circumstanced.

Ill leave my mineral wealth hoarded in earth?
Buried in seas in mines and ocean caves
More safely kept than is the merchant's worth,
Which every storm committeth to the waves.

Man kind may delve but cannot my wealth spend,
If I no partial store appropriate
no armed ships into the Indies send
To rob me of my orient estate

The rich man's clothes keep out the genial sun
But scarce defend him from the piercing cold
If he did not his heavenly garment shun
He would not need to hide beneath a fold.

The respectable folks,
Where dwell they?
They whisper in the oaks,
And they sigh in the hay,
Summer and winter, night and day,
Out on the meadow, there dwell they.
They drink at the brooks and the pilgrim's cup,
And with the owl and the nighthawk sup;
They suck the breath of the morning wind,
And they make their own all the good they find.
They never die,
Nor snivel nor cry,
For they have a lease of immortality.
A sound estate forever they mend,
To every asker readily lend,
To the ocean wealth,
To the meadow health,
To Time his length,
To the rocks strength,
To the stars light
To the weary night,
To the busy day,
To the idle play,
And so their good cheer never ends,
For all are their debtors and all their friends.

Farewell

Whether we've far withdrawn
   Or come more near
Equally the outward form
   Doth no more appear.
Not thou by distance lost
No—for regret doth bind
Me faster to thee now
   Than neighborhood confined.

Where thy love followeth me
Is enough society.
Thy indelible mild eye
   Is my sky.
Whether by land or sea
   I wander to and fro,
Oft as I think of thee
   The heavens hang more low
The pure glance of thy eye
Doth purge the summer's sky,
And thy breath so rare
Doth refine the winter's air.
my feet would weary be
Ere they travelled from thee.
I discover by thy face
That we are of one race
Flowed in one vein our blood
Ere the sea found its flood
The worm may be divided
And each part become a whole,
But the nobler creature man
May not separate a span.

—

For though the eaves were rabitted,
   And the well sweeps were slanted,
Each house seemed not inhabited
   But haunted.

The pensive traveller held his way,
   Silent & melancholy,
For every man an ideot was,
   And every house a folly.

—

You Boston folks & Roxbury people
Will want Tom Hyde to mend your kettle

———

I will obey the strictest law of love
As if I dealt with cherubim above.
 I will accept no half gift from my friend
 By which he thinks for hate to make amend.
But every friendly thought
Will come to me unbought
 My friend may do whate'er he will
  And I shall love him
   If he doth it from love.
 But let him do whateer he will
 I think that I must hate him still
  If lower motives move.

 I love not all
  I love not one alway
 But that I love is one & all
  And lasteth ever and aye.

 I will leave him I hate
  And cleave to him I love
 I will forsake my earthly mate
  And seek my mate above.

Though my friends are dull and cold
I will be quick and warm.
Though their love groweth old
Mine shall be new born

Though they understand me not
 I shall be understood
Though by them I am forgot
 Not therefore by the good.

My friend can wound me
For to him I bare my breast—
But his wounds save me
From a foe's embrace
  But these are honorable scars
  And fit the wounded heart for Love's more glorious
     wars.

These wounds are not fatal though inflicted on the heart
For the heart's not less a vital than a mortal part.
    Unlike the inferior part
     The wounded heart
     Is not repaired with wood
     But by fresh currents from above
     Which fit it for a purer love
For all that's true & beautiful & good.

Why toll the bell today—
Its knell has died away—

  And once again
When I went a-maying—
& once or twice more I had seen thee before.
For there grow the May flower
  (*Epigaea repens*)
& the mt cranberry
  & the screech owl *strepens*

The Old Marlborough Road

Where they once dug for money,
But never found any;
Where sometimes Martial Miles
Singly files,
And Elijah Wood,
I fear for no good:
No other man,
Save Elisha Dugan,—
O man of wild habits,
Partridges and rabbits,
Who hast no cares
Only to set snares,
Who liv'st all alone,
Close to the bone,
And where life is sweetest
Constantly eatest.
When the spring stirs my blood
With the instinct to travel,
I can get enough gravel
On the Old Marlborough Road.
Nobody repairs it,
For nobody wears it;
It is a living way,
As the Christians say.
Not many there be
Who enter therein,
Only the guests of the
Irishman Quin.
What is it, what is it,
But a direction out there,
And the bare possibility
Of going somewhere?
Great guide-boards of stone,
But travellers none;
Cenotaphs of the towns
Named on their crowns.
It is worth going to see
Where you *might* be.

What king
Did the thing,
I am still wondering;
Set up how or when,
By what selectmen,
Gourgas or Lee,
Clark or Darby?
They're a great endeavor
To be something forever;
Blank tablets of stone,
Where a traveller might groan,
And in one sentence
Grave all that it known;
Which another might read,
In his extreme need.
I know one or two
Lines that would do,
Literature that might stand
All over the land,
Which a man could remember
Till next December,
And read again in the spring,
After the thawing.
If with fancy unfurled
　You leave your abode,
You may go round the world
　By the Old Marlborough Road.

———

Old meeting-house bell
I love thy music well
It peals through the air
Sweetly full & fair
As in the early times
When I listened to its chimes.

It is a real place,
Boston, I tell it to your face.
And no dream of mine
To ornament a line
I can not come nearer to God & Heaven
Than I live to Walden even.
It is a part of me which I have not prophaned
I live by the shore of me detained.
Laden with my dregs
I stand on my legs,
While all my pure wine
I to nature consign.
I am its stoney shore
And the breeze that passes o'er
In the hollow of my hand
Are its water and its sand;
Its deepest resort
Lies high in my thought,

Among the worst of men that ever lived
However we did seriously attend
A little space we let our thoughts ascend
Experienced our religion & confessed
'Twas good for us to be there—be anywhere
Then to a heap of apples we addressed
& cleared the topmost rider *sine* care
But our Icarian thoughts returned to ground
And we went on to heaven the long way round.

What's the rail-road to me?
I never go to see
Where it ends
It fills a few hollows
And makes banks for the swallows
It sets the sand a flowing
And blackberries a growing

Tall Ambrosia

Among the signs of autumn I perceive
The Roman wormwood (called by learned men
Ambrosia elatior, food for gods,—
For to impartial science the humblest weed
Is as immortal once as the proudest flower—)
Sprinkles its yellow dust over my shoes
As I cross the now neglected garden
—We trample under foot the food of gods
& spill their nectar in each drop of dew—
My honest shoes Fast friends that never stray
far from my couch thus powdered countryfied
Bearing many a mile the marks of their adventure
At the post-house disgrace the Gallic gloss
Of those well dressed ones who no morning dew
Nor Roman wormwood ever have been through
Who never walk but are *transported* rather—
For what old crime of theirs I do not gather

'Tis very fit the ambrosia of the gods
Should be a weed on earth. As nectar is
The morning dew with which we wet our shoes
For the gods are simple folks and we should pine
                    upon their humble fare

I saw a delicate flower had grown up 2 feet high
Between the horse's paths & the wheel track
Which Dakin's & Maynards wagons had
Passed over many a time
An inch more to right or left had sealed its fate
Or an inch higher. And yet it lived & flourished
As much as if it had a thousand acres
Of untrodden space around it—and never
Knew the danger it incurred.
It did not borrow trouble nor invite an
Evil fate by apprehending it.
For though the distant market-wagon
Every other day—inevitably rolled
This way—it just as inevitably rolled
In those ruts—And the same
Charioteer who steered the flower
Upward—guided the horse & cart aside from it.
There were other flowers which you would say
Incurred less danger grew more out of the way
Which no cart rattled near, no walker daily passed.
But at length one rambling deviously
For no rut restrained plucked them
And then it appeared that they stood
Directly in his way though he had come
From farther than the market wagon—

To day I climbed a handsome rounded hill
Covered with hickory trees wishing to see
The country from its top—for low hills
show unexpected prospects—I looked
many miles over a woody low-land
Toward Marlborough Framingham & Sudbury
And as I sat amid the hickory trees

I am the little Irish boy
   That lives in the shanty
I am four years old today
   And shall soon be one and twenty
   I shall grow up
   And be a great man
   And shovel all day
   As hard as I can.

   Down in the deep cut
   Where the men lived
   Who made the Rail road.

for supper
   I have some potatoe
   And sometimes some bread
   And then if it's cold
     I go right to bed.

   I lie on some straw
   Under my fathers coat

   My mother does not cry
   And my father does not scold
   For I am a little Irish Boy
   And I'm four years old.

   Every day I go to school
   Along the Railroad
   It was so cold it made me cry
   The day that it snowed.

   And if my feet ache
   I do not mind the cold
   For I am a little Irish boy
   & I'm four years old.

In Adams fall
We sinned all.
In the new Adam's rise
We shall all reach the skies.

Life

My life is like a stately warrior horse,
That walks with fluent pace along the way,
And I the upright horseman that bestrides
His flexuous back, feeding my private thoughts.—
Alas, when will this rambling head and neck
Be welded to that firm and brawny breast?—
But still my steady steed goes proudly forth,
Mincing his stately steps along the road;
The sun may set, the silver moon may rise,
But my unresting steed holds on his way.
He is far gone ere this, you fain would say,
He is far going. Plants grow and rivers run;
You ne'er may look upon the ocean waves,
At morn or eventide, but you will see
Far in th' horizon with expanded sail,
Some solitary bark stand out to sea,
Far bound—well so my life sails far,
To double some far cape not yet explored.
A cloud ne'er standeth in the summer's sky,
The eagle sailing high, with outspread wings
Cleaving the silent air, resteth him not
A moment in his flight, the air is not his perch.
Nor doth my life fold its unwearied wings,
And hide its head within its downy breast,
But still it plows the shoreless seas of time,
Breasting the waves with an unsanded bow.

The moon moves up her smooth and sheeny path
Without impediment; and happily
The brook Glides by lulled by its tinkling;
Meteeors drop down the sky without chagrin
And rise again; but my cares never rest.
No charitable laws alas cut me
An easy orbit round the sun, but I
Must make my way through rocks and seas and earth
my steep and devious way Uncertain still.
My current never rounds into a lake
In whose fair heart the heavens come to bathe
Nor does my life drop freely but a rod
By its resistless course
As Meteors do.

I'm thankful that my life doth not deceive
Itself with a low loftiness, half height,
And think it soars when still it dip its way
Beneath the clouds on noiseless pinion
Like the crow or owl, but it doth know
The full extent of all its trivialness,
Compared with the splendid heights above.
    See how it waits to watch the mail come in
While 'hind its back *the sun goes out perchance.*
And yet their lumbering cart brings me no word
Not one scrawled leaf such as my neighbors get
To cheer them with the slight events forsooth
Faint ups and downs of their far distant friends—
And now tis passed. What next? See the long train
Of teams wreathed in dust, their atmosphere;
Shall I attend until the last is passed?
Else why these ears that hear the leader's bells
Or eyes that link me in procession.

But hark! the drowsy day has done its task,
Far in yon hazy field where stands a barn
Unanxious hens improve the sultry hour
And with contented voice now brag their deed—
A new laid egg—Now let the day decline—
They'll lay another by tomorrow's sun.

Manhood

I love to see the man, a long-lived child,
As yet uninjured by all worldly taint
As the fresh infant whose whole life is play.
'Tis a serene spectacle for a serene day;
But better still I love to contemplate
The mature soul of lesser innocence,
Who hath travelled far on life's dusty road
Far from the starting point of infancy
And proudly bears his small degen'racy
Blazon'd on his memorial standard high
Who from the sad experience of his fate
Since his bark struck on that unlucky rock
Has proudly steered his life with his own hands.
Though his face harbors less of innocence
Yet there do chiefly lurk within its depths
Furrowed by care, but yet all over spread
With the ripe bloom of a self-wrought content
Noble resolves which do reprove the gods
And it doth more assert man's eminence
Above the happy level of the brute
And more doth advertise me of the heights
To which no natural path doth ever lead
No natural light can ever light our steps,
—But the far-piercing ray that shines
From the recesses of a brave man's eye.

Music

Far from this atmosphere that music sounds
Bursting some azure chink in the dull clouds
Of sense that overarch my recent years
And steal his freshness from the noonday sun.
Ah, I have wandered many ways and lost
The boyant step, the whole responsive life
That stood with joy to hear what seemed then
Its echo, its own harmony borne back
Upon its ear. This tells of better space,
Far far beyond the hills the woods the clouds
That bound my low and plodding valley life,
Far from my sin, remote from my distrust,
When first my healthy morning life perchance
Trod lightly as on clouds, and not as yet
My weary and faint hearted noon had sunk
Upon the clod while the bright day went by.

Lately, I feared my life was empty, now
I know though a frail tenement that it still
Is worth repair, if yet its hollowness
Doth entertain so fine a guest within, and through
Its empty aisles there still doth ring
Though but the echo of so high a strain;
It shall be swept again and cleansed from sin
To be a thoroughfare for celestial airs;
Perchance the God who is proprietor
Will pity take on his poor tenant here
And countenance his efforts to improve
His property and make it worthy to revert,
At some late day Unto himself again.

The Just Made Perfect

A stately music rises on my ear,
Borne on the breeze from some adjacent vale;
A host of knights, my own true ancestors,
Tread to the lofty strains and pass away
In long procession; to this music's sound
The Just move onward in deep serried ranks,
With looks serene of hope, and gleaming brows,
As if they were the temples of the Day.

Gilt by an unseen sun's resplendent ray
They firmly move, sure as the lapse of Time;
Departed worth, leaving these trivial fields
Where sedate valor finds no worthy aim,
And still is Fame the noblest cause of all.

Forward they press and with exalted eye,
As if their road, which seems a level plain,
Did still ascend, and were again subdued
'Neath their proud feet. Forward they move, and leave
The sun and moon and stars alone behind:
And now, by the still fainter strains, I know
They surely pass; and soon their quivering harp,
And faintly clashing cymbal, will have ceased
To feed my ear.

It is the steadiest motion eye hath seen,
A Godlike progress; e'en the hills and rocks
Do forward come, so to congratulate
Their feet; the rivers eddy backward, and
The waves recurl to accompany their march.

Onward they move, like to the life of man,
Which cannot rest, but goes without delay
Right to the gates of Death, not losing time
In its majestic tread to Eternity,
As if Man's blood, a river, flowed right on
Far as the eye could reach, to the Heart of hearts,
Nor eddied round about these complex limbs.

'Tis the slow march of life,—I feel the feet
Of tiny drops go pattering through *my* veins;
Their arteries flow with an Assyrian pace,
And empires rise and fall beneath their stride.

Still, as they move, flees the horizon wall;
The low-roofed sky o'erarches their true path;
For they have caught at last the pace of Heaven,
Their great Commander's true and timely tread.

Lo! how the sky before them is cast up
Into an archèd road, like to the gallery
Of the small mouse that bores the meadow's turf:
Chapels of ease swift open o'er the path,
And domes continuous span the lengthening way.

I do not fear my thoughts will die
For never yet it was so dry
as to scorch the azure of the sky.
It knows no withering & no drought
Though all eyes crop it ne'er gives out
My eyes my flocks are
Mountains my crops are
I do not fear my flocks will stray
For they were made to roam the day
For they can wander with the latest light
Yet be at home at night.

I'm contented you should stay
For ever and aye
If you can take yourself away
Any day.

Man Man is the Devil
The source of all evil.

You must not only aim aright,
But draw the bow with all your might.

He knows no change who knows the true,
    And on it keeps his eye,
Who always still the unseen doth view;
    Only the false & the apparent die.

Things change, but change not far
    From what they are not but to what they are,
Or rather 'tis our ignorance that dies;
    Forever lives the knowledge of the wise.

When the toads begin to ring,
Then thinner clothing bring
or Off your greatcoat fling

The chicadee
Hops near to me.

—————

'Twas 30 years ago
In a rocky pasture field
Sprang an infant apple grove
low planted & concealed—
I sing the wild apple theme enough for me.
I love the racy fruit & I reverence the tree—
In that small family there was one that
loved the sun—which sent its root down deep/—
& took fast hold on life/—while the others
went to sleep
In 2 years time 't had thus
Reached the level of the rocks—
Admired the stretching world
Nor feared the wandering flocks—

But at this tender age
Its sufferings began—
There came a browsing ox
And cut it down a span.

Its heart did bleed all day
& When the birds were hushed—

—————

Forever in my dream & in my morning thought
Eastward a mount ascends—
But when in the sunbeam its hard outline is sought—
It all dissolves & ends.
The woods that way are gates—the pastures too slope up
To an unearthly ground—
But when I ask my mates, to take the staff & cup,
It can no more be found—
Perchance I have no shoes fit for the lofty soil
Where my thoughts graze—

No properly spun clues—nor well strained mid day oil
    Or—must I mend my ways?
It is a promised land which I have not yet earned,
    I have not made beginning
With consecrated hand—I have not even learned
    To lay the underpinning.
The mountain sinks by day—as do my lofty thoughts,
    Because I'm not highminded.
If I could think alway above these hills & warts
    I should see it, though blinded.
It is a spiral path within the pilgrim's soul
    Leads to this mountain's brow
Commencing at his hearth he reaches to this goal
    He knows not when nor how.

———

Except, returning, by the Marlboro,
A way, methinks, might safely be allowed
To pilgrims of the holiest character
We marked, I say, the barberry's brilliant fruit,
Which on our hill & pasture grows to waste
Not the less sweet to see though sour to taste—
And in a rocky lane through which we passed
Not so much lengthwise as diagonally
In our saint-terrering over hill & valley
We plucked wild apples of the fairest hew
Filling our pockets out with eagerness,
Excellent whether to eat or look at,
Or to throw at one another & the
Squirrels in sport; & afterward tame ones
In orchards heaped by a penurious hind,
Who saw but heaps of dollars in his mind;
Some what less tame to us for being stolen,
Although our pockets were already swolen;
And, one more proof, I saw at Willis Lake
Where we had come our nature's thirst to slake
The willow bed which ornaments its edge

Mixed with the cranberry—button bush & sedge
Touched by the frost send forth its scarlet flames,
Which far surpassed all oriental dyes
Reminding me of the wild wealth of the skies
And of the red man who once on this shore
Beheld it, ere *his* last summer was oer.
So we returned from Willis Pond & Hill,
I climb the last & drink the former still.

The Rosa Sanguinea

As often as a martyr dies,
This opes its petals to the skies;
And Nature by this trace alone
Informs us which way he is gone.

———

Any fool can make a rule
And every fool will mind it.

———

All things decay
& so must our sleigh

CHRONOLOGY

NOTE ON THE TEXTS

NOTES

INDEX OF TITLES AND FIRST LINES

Chronology

1817   Born July 12, in Concord, Massachusetts, third of four
              children (Helen, b. 1812, John, b. 1815, and Sophia, b. 1819)
              of John and Cynthia (Dunbar) Thoreau, and christened
              October 12 as David Henry Thoreau. (Grandfather Jean
              Thoreau, a descendant of French Protestant refugees,
              came to Boston from the Isle of Jersey in 1773, served on
              Revolutionary War privateers, and became a prosperous
              merchant; after his death his estate was plundered by its
              executor. Maternal grandfather, the Rev. Asa Dunbar, re-
              signed from the ministry in 1779 because of poor health
              and practiced law in Keene, New Hampshire. Maternal
              grandmother, Mary Jones, of a wealthy Loyalist family,
              helped her brothers escape to Canada during the Revolu-
              tion.) Father farms, and manages store in Concord.

1818–21   Family moves to Chelmsford, a village ten miles north of
              Concord, where father opens grocery store. Thoreau en-
              joys sledding and suffers a series of accidents, including
              the loss of part of a toe while playing with an axe. In 1821,
              father closes failing grocery store and moves family to
              Boston, where he teaches school.

1822   Sees Walden Pond for the first time while visiting grand-
              mother Mary Jones. (Later writes: "That woodland vision
              for a long time made the drapery of my dreams.")

1823–27   Family returns to Concord, where father takes over pen-
              cil-making business started by brother-in-law Charles
              Dunbar. Attends Phoebe Wheeler's private "infant school"
              and then the town-run Center School. Memorizes pas-
              sages from the Bible, Shakespeare, Bunyan, and Samuel
              Johnson. Classmates call him "the Judge" because of
              his stern demeanor. Financial uncertainty causes mother
              to take in boarders and family to move twice within
              Concord. Begins lifelong exploration of surrounding
              countryside. Mother becomes active in town charity
              work.

1828   Thoreau and brother, John, enroll in Concord Academy,
              a private school founded in 1822 by prominent town

citizens. Studies French, Latin, Greek, geography, history, and science.

1829   Attends lectures in natural history at newly founded Concord Lyceum.

1833   Family is able to send only one son to college, and Henry is considered the more scholarly; he enrolls in Harvard College after barely passing entrance examinations. John and Helen, now schoolteachers, and Thoreau's aunts help parents pay his expenses. Goes beyond the required curriculum by taking Italian, French, German, and Spanish and attending lectures on mineralogy, anatomy, and natural history. Remembered by a classmate as being "cold and unimpressionable," his academic performance is above average but not exceptional. Spends much time alone, reading and walking.

1835–36   Ralph Waldo Emerson moves to Concord. Thoreau takes a leave of absence for winter term to earn money by teaching in Canton, Massachusetts. Boards for six weeks with Orestes Brownson, Unitarian minister and New England intellectual, and studies German with him. (Later writes of these weeks: "They were an era in my life—the morning of a new Lebenstag. They are to me as a dream that is dreamt, but which returns from time to time in all its original freshness.") In May 1836, briefly leaves Harvard because of illness, possibly first attack of tuberculosis. Attends dedication of Concord Bridge Memorial in July and joins with choir in singing Emerson's "Concord Hymn." Lives for six weeks in hut on shore of Flint's Pond in Lincoln with Harvard friend Charles Stearns Wheeler. Visits New York City with father to sell pencils.

1837   Receives grant of $25 from Harvard Corporation after Emerson writes recommendation to President Quincy. Graduates nineteenth in his class of approximately fifty, taking part in commencement honors conference on "The Commercial Spirit of Modern Times." ("This curious world which we inhabit is more wonderful than convenient; more beautiful than it is useful; it is more to be admired and enjoyed than used.") Begins teaching at Center School, but resigns after flogging six students (including a family servant) against his own wishes at the direction of a superior. Becomes member of informal group of New England Transcendentalists, the "Hedge Club," including Brownson, Margaret Fuller, Frederic Henry Hedge, George Ripley, Jones Very, Elizabeth Peabody, Bronson Alcott, and Theodore Parker, who meet irregularly in Emerson's study. Begins his journal, ultimately to comprise nearly two million words, on October 22. Works on improving lead quality in pencils; learns from Scottish encyclopedia in Harvard Library to mix graphite with Bavarian clay, designs grinding mill to produce more finely powdered graphite. Changes name from David Henry to Henry David.

1838   Plans to go with brother to Kentucky in search of work; trip is postponed and then abandoned when John finds job in Roxbury. Goes to Maine in futile search for teaching job. June, opens small private school in parents' house, then takes over Concord Academy in September. Delivers first lecture to Concord Lyceum, "Society," on April 11, and is elected Lyceum secretary and curator in fall, serving two years.

1839   Increased enrollment (approximately 25 students) allows John to join Thoreau at the Concord Academy. John teaches "English branches"; Henry teaches Latin, Greek, French, and sciences. (One pupil reports later that John "was more human, loving" and Henry "rigid," but most remember both brothers with great affection: "It was a peculiar school, there was never a boy flogged or threatened, yet I never saw so absolutely military discipline. . . . Even the incorrigible were brought into line.") Innovative curriculum stresses reasoning over rote memorization and features field trips to workshops and countryside. In July Thoreau meets Ellen Sewall of Scituate, Massachusetts, 17-year-old sister of one of his students, and both he and John fall in love with her. August 31, Henry and John leave for two-week trip on the Concord and Merrimack rivers in their homemade boat, *Musketaquid*. Emerson helps found Transcendentalist quarterly *The Dial* and writes, "My Henry Thoreau will be a great poet for such a company & one of these days for all companies."

1840   Louisa May Alcott enrolls in Concord Academy, beginning her lifelong admiration for Thoreau. First issue of
The Dial, edited by Margaret Fuller, appears in July, with
Thoreau's poem "Sympathy" and essay "Aulus Persius
Flaccus"; Thoreau eventually publishes 31 poems, essays,
and translations in *The Dial*'s 16 issues. Ellen Sewall rejects as suitors first John and then Henry. Thoreau
teaches himself surveying, later an important source of income. Meets Ellery Channing, poet and nephew of Unitarian minister William Ellery Channing, who becomes
intimate friend and (in 1873) first biographer.

1841   Declines invitation to join Brook Farm community ("I
had rather keep bachelor's hall in hell than go board in
heaven"). Closes Concord Academy on April 1 because of
John's poor health and moves into Emerson household
for two years as handyman and gardener. Borrows from
Emerson's library to read further in Greek classics and
English poetry, and begins reading Oriental literature.
Transcribes edited version of first two volumes of journal
into new notebooks. Composes longest poem of his career. Still seeking a way to support himself, nearly buys
rundown farm, and dreams of going to live by Flint's
Pond in Lincoln. ("My friends ask what I will do when I
get there. Will it not be employment enough to watch
the progress of the seasons?") The Flints, owners of the
land, refuse permission to build cabin.

1842   January 1, John suffers razor cut, develops lockjaw, and
dies on January 11 in Thoreau's arms. Soon afterward
Thoreau is stricken for weeks with psychosomatic attack
of the same paralytic symptoms, followed by months of
depression. In summer meets Nathaniel Hawthorne, who
becomes an intermittent literary sponsor after reading "A
Natural History of Massachusetts" in the July 1842 *Dial*.
Hawthorne describes him as "a young man with much of
wild original nature still remaining in him. . . . He is as
ugly as sin, long-nosed, queer-mouthed, and with un-
couth and somewhat rustic, although courteous manners,
corresponding very well with such an exterior. He was educated, I believe, at Cambridge, . . . but for two or
three years back, he has repudiated all regular modes of
getting a living, and seems inclined to lead a sort of Indian life among civilized men—an Indian life, I mean, as

respects the absence of any systematic effort for a livelihood." Sells Hawthorne *Musketaquid* for seven dollars
and teaches him to paddle. In the winter goes skating
with Emerson and Hawthorne; Hawthorne's wife,
Sophia, describes him "figuring dithyrambic dances and
Bacchic leaps on the ice—very remarkable, but very ugly,
methought."

1843   Lectures on "Sir Walter Raleigh" in February. Edits April
issue of *The Dial*, substituting for Emerson, and includes
in it "Dark Ages," a short essay on ancient history. In May
goes to Staten Island, New York, as tutor to children of
Emerson's brother William. Meets Horace Greeley, Henry
James, Sr., and the abolitionist William Tappan; hears social reformer Lucretia Mott at Quaker meeting and is favorably impressed. Enjoys walks along Staten Island shore
and frequents various New York libraries, reading Ossian
and Francis Quarles with particular interest, but writes of
New York City: "It is a thousand times meaner than I
could have imagined." Homesick, he returns to Concord
in December and moves back into family home. "Paradise
(To Be) Regained," criticizing technological utopianism,
published in *United States Magazine and Democratic Review*, November.

1844   In series of lectures and discussions on reform at Boston's
Amory Hall, delivers "The Conservative and the Re-
former." Writes essay for *The Dial* praising Nathaniel P.
Rogers, abolitionist publisher who advocates the dissolution of antislavery societies on the grounds that they re-
strict the exercise of individual freedom. Devises a drilling
machine that allows lead to be inserted into pencils without splitting the wood; develops different grades of lead
hardness. April 30, on camping trip with Edward Hoar,
accidentally sets fire to three hundred acres of Concord
woods, causing over $2,000 damage. Meets Isaac Thomas
Hecker, future founder of the Paulist Fathers, who proposes that they make a pilgrimage to Rome "in the old
middleage fashion." Thoreau declines, and resists
Hecker's attempts to convert him to Roman Catholicism.
July, takes walking trip through Berkshires and Catskills
with Ellery Channing. August 1, rings First Parish Church
bell to summon town to annual fair of Concord Women's
Anti-Slavery Society (which his mother had helped

found); there Emerson delivers address on West Indian Emancipation, which Thoreau arranges to be published as a pamphlet. In fall, helps build new family house in the open southwestern "prairie" of Concord (the "Texas house").

1845 Spring, starts building cabin in Emerson's woodlot at Walden Pond, and moves in July 4. Works on manuscript about 1839 boat trip with John on Concord and Merrimack rivers, and on a lecture about Thomas Carlyle. Throughout his 26-month stay, remains in close contact with family and friends.

1846 Begins writing *Walden*. Delivers Carlyle lecture at Concord Lyceum in February. July, arrested and jailed for one night by Concord constable Sam Staples for not paying several years' poll tax in protest against role of the state in perpetuating slavery. (Emerson writes disapprovingly in his journal: "Don't run amuck against the world. As long as the state means you well, do not refuse your pistareen." Alcott, arrested in 1843 for failure to pay his town tax, praises Thoreau's "dignified non-compliance with the injunction of civil power.") Tax is paid that evening by anonymous person (probably aunt Maria Thoreau). The next morning Thoreau is thrown out of jail when he refuses to leave. For the remainder of his life, his aunt and others pay tax to avoid further confrontation. August 1, Anti-Slavery Society fair held at Walden. August 31 through early September, trip to Maine to climb Mount Katahdin with cousin George Thatcher of Bangor.

1847 Reads "A History of Myself," part of first draft of *Walden*, at Concord Lyceum in February. Collects zoological specimens for Louis Agassiz of Harvard. Leaves Walden on September 6, having finished his manuscript of *A Week on the Concord and Merrimack Rivers* and most or all of the first version of *Walden*. In October moves into Emerson house for ten months to help care for Lydia Emerson and the children while Waldo is in Europe. Responds to tenth anniversary questionnaire from his Harvard class: "I am a Schoolmaster—a private Tutor, a Surveyor—a Gardener, a Farmer—a Painter, I mean a House Painter, a Carpenter, a Mason, a Day-Laborer, a

Pencil-Maker, a Glass-paper Maker, a Writer, and some-times a Poetaster."

1848 January 26, delivers lecture to Concord Lyceum on "the relation of the individual to the State," published in 1849 as "Resistance to Civil Government" (posthumously re-titled "Civil Disobedience") in Elizabeth Peabody's *Aes-thetic Papers*. Responding to appreciative letter, begins extensive correspondence with Worcester, Massachusetts, schoolteacher Harrison Blake. July–November, "Ktaadn, and the Maine Woods" serialized in John Sartain's *Union Magazine* and strongly promoted in the New York *Tri-bune* by Horace Greeley, now Thoreau's enthusiastic backer and literary agent. Begins more extensive lecturing in New England. Satirized by James Russell Lowell in "A Fable for Critics" (published October 31) as a mere shadow of Emerson. Extensively revises *A Week* and be-gins second version of *Walden*.

1849 *A Week on the Concord and Merrimack Rivers* published May 30 by James Munroe and Company of Boston after Thoreau agrees to pay the cost from his royalties. It re-ceives mixed reviews and sells poorly. Continues to correct and revise text. (In 1853 Thoreau takes back 706 of the original 1,000 copies and stores them in the family attic, remarking, "I have now a library of nearly nine hundred volumes, over seven hundred of which I wrote myself.") June 14, sister Helen dies of tuberculosis. Autumn, family buys larger house nearer to center of Concord (the "Yel-low House") out of growing profits from pencil business, which has begun to concentrate on supplying ground lead for electrotyping. Finds surveying a preferable way to sup-port himself and establishes a reputation for extreme accu-racy. Friendship with Emerson cools. Emerson writes in his journal: "Thoreau wants a little ambition in his mix-ture. . . . Instead of being the head of American engi-neers, he is captain of a huckleberry party." Thoreau is suspicious of the effect on Emerson of growing fame and acceptance, annoyed by charge that he is merely Emer-son's follower, and offended that Emerson does not do more to promote *A Week*. October, first trip to Cape Cod, with Ellery Channing, going via Cohasset and Sand-wich, returning by steamer from Provincetown.

1850   Increases reading on natural history and American Indi-
            ans, recording nearly 3,000 pages of notes and quotations
            in "Indian Books" between 1847 and 1861. Collects in his
            attic room in the Yellow House hundreds of arrowheads
            and other Indian artifacts, as well as hundreds of dried
            plant specimens. June, second trip to Cape Cod, alone, by
            steamer to Provincetown and back to Boston. July, sent
            by Emerson to Fire Island, New York, to search for body
            and manuscripts of Margaret Fuller Ossoli, who had died
            in a shipwreck with her husband and child and Horace
            Sumner, brother of Massachusetts senator Charles Sum-
            ner. The wreck is plundered before he arrives and he finds
            only a few insignificant items. Writes of an unidentifiable
            skeleton he saw: "It reigned over the shore. That dead
            body possessed the shore as no living one could. It
            showed a title to the sands which no living ruler could."
            September, trip to Montreal, Quebec City, and the north-
            ern bank of the St. Lawrence with Ellery Channing.

1851   Stops removing leaves from journal volumes for use in
            drafts of lectures and essays and begins to record detailed
            observations of natural phenomena that he uses later in
            essays and phrenological charts. Passage of Fugitive Slave
            Act enrages him; writes in journal: "I do not believe that
            the North will soon come to blows with the South on this
            question. It would be too bright a page to be written . . .
            at present." Becomes increasingly involved in Under-
            ground Railroad, which he has been assisting for several
            years, sheltering escaped slaves in the family house and
            aiding their flight to Canada.

1852   Excerpts from fourth version of *Walden* published in
            Union Magazine attract little attention, and Thoreau re-
            ceives no money when the magazine ceases publication.

1853   January–March, first three installments of "A Yankee in
            Canada," based on 1850 trip, appear in *Putnam's Monthly
            Magazine*. Publication stops when Thoreau objects to ed-
            itor George William Curtis removing passages Curtis con-
            siders "heresies." Declines invitation to join American
            Association for the Advancement of Science. September,
            second trip to Maine, with George Thatcher and Indian
            guide Joe Aitteon.

1854   Arrest in Boston of fugitive slave Anthony Burns incites
        Thoreau to write "Slavery in Massachusetts" and read it
        at Framingham, Massachusetts, rally organized by
        William Lloyd Garrison, July 4. It is printed in the *Anti-
        Slavery Standard*, *The Liberator*, and the New York *Tri-
        bune*. *Walden* published August 9 by Boston firm of
        Ticknor and Fields in an edition of 2,000, the result of
        over seven years of work and seven major revisions of the
        text. Although a few reviews are harsh (*Boston Atlas*:
        "There is not a page . . . giving one sign of liberality,
        charitableness, kind feeling, generosity, in a word—
        heart"; *Knickerbocker* reviews it with P. T. Barnum's auto-
        biography under the title "Town and Rural Humbugs"),
        most are very enthusiastic. (The popular *Graham's Maga-
        zine* concludes: "Through all the audacities of his eccen-
        tric protests, a careful eye can easily discern the movement
        of a powerful and accomplished mind.") By the end of the
        year, 1,744 copies are sold, plus several hundred more be-
        fore it goes out of print in 1859. (Some are shipped to
        England, where George Eliot favorably reviews it in 1856:
        ". . . we have a bit of pure American life . . . animated
        by that energetic, yet calm spirit of innovation, that prac-
        tical as well as theoretic independence of formulae, which
        is peculiar to some of the finer American minds.") En-
        couraged by *Walden's* success, Thoreau urges Ticknor and
        Fields to reissue *A Week*, but they decline. Enjoys wider
        popularity as lecturer throughout the Northeast; intro-
        duces "Getting a Living," critique of American acquisi-
        tiveness (later published as "Life without Principle").
        Begins to attract a circle of admirers, including English
        traveler and author Thomas Cholmondeley; Quaker
        Daniel Ricketson, later historian of New Bedford; and
        abolitionist, educator, and writer F. B. Sanborn.

1855   Develops weakness in legs that afflicts him intermittently
        for the next two years. "Cape Cod," drawn from visits
        to region, published in *Putnam's Monthly Magazine*
        June–August. Curtis cancels publication of further install-
        ments, probably fearing that Cape Cod residents will be
        offended by Thoreau's depictions. July, third trip to Cape
        Cod, accompanied by Ellery Channing, taking a schooner
        to Provincetown, spending two weeks at Highland Light,
        and returning by sailboat *Olata* from Provincetown to

Boston. In return for Thoreau's hospitality in Concord, Thomas Cholmondeley sends 44 volumes of Oriental philosophy, religion, and history, for which Thoreau makes a special bookcase from Concord River driftwood. Sends Cholmondeley *Walden*, Emerson's poems, and Whitman's *Leaves of Grass*.

1856   October, goes to Perth Amboy, New Jersey, to survey at Eagleswood, a former utopian community being converted into suburban estates. In early November visits with Bronson Alcott in New York. They hear Henry Ward Beecher preach at Plymouth Church in Brooklyn; Thoreau is unimpressed. The next day Thoreau and Alcott meet Walt Whitman. ("He is apparently the greatest democrat the world has seen," Thoreau later writes to Harrison Blake. "Kings and aristocracy go by the board at once, as they have long deserved to. A remarkably strong though coarse nature, of a sweet disposition, and much prized by his friends.") Whitman presents him with an inscribed copy of the 1856 *Leaves of Grass*. Thoreau is dismayed by its sensuality but calls it "a great primitive poem,—an alarum or trumpet note ringing through the American camp."

1857   Meets John Brown in early March when Brown visits F. B. Sanborn in Concord and takes noon meal at Thoreau's house. Hears Brown speak and makes small monetary contribution; writes that Brown "had the courage to face his country herself when she was in the wrong." June 12–22, makes his last visit to Cape Cod, alone. (Only trip not described in *Cape Cod*, published by Ticknor and Fields in 1865.) July 20–August 7, travels through Maine with Edward Hoar and Indian guide Joe Polis. Grows full beard.

1858   James Russell Lowell solicits account of 1857 Maine travels for *Atlantic Monthly*. Fearing that his portrayal of Polis is too candid, Thoreau submits instead "Chesuncook," drawn from 1853 trip, published June–August. When sentence praising a pine tree—"It is as immortal as I am, and perchance will go to as high a heaven"—is omitted from July installment against Thoreau's explicit instructions, writes to Lowell, "I do not ask anybody to adopt my opinions, but I do expect that when they ask for them in print, they will print them, or obtain my consent to their alteration or omission." Demands that Lowell print the omitted sentence in the August issue. Lowell does not, and delays paying Thoreau $198 owed to him. (Revised versions of "Ktaadn," "Chesuncook," and 1857 trip account, together with appendix, published as *The Maine Woods* by Ticknor and Fields in 1864.) Travels through the White Mountains and climbs Mount Washington, July 2–19.

1859   February 3, father dies, leaving Thoreau financially responsible for mother and sister. Begins writing "Wild Fruits" (unpublished until 2000). May 8, hears John Brown speak at Concord Town Hall. October, news of Brown's raid on Harpers Ferry reaches Concord. Thoreau delivers a defiant tribute, "A Plea for Captain John Brown," to large audiences in Concord, Boston, and Worcester, October 30 to November 3. Helps organize and speaks at memorial meeting in Concord on Brown's execution day, December 2. Aids fugitive member of Brown's band in escape to Canada.

1860   Reads Darwin's *Origin of Species* and defends it to Emerson against Louis Agassiz's attacks. Visited by William Dean Howells, who finds Thoreau "dreamy" and "orphic," and later describes the encounter as "a rout" of his hopes. Joins townspeople in protecting F. B. Sanborn against arrest by federal marshals trying to subpoena him to appear before Senate investigation of Harpers Ferry raid. Writes "The Last Days of John Brown." Begins expanding "The Succession of Forest Trees" into "The Dispersion of Seeds." December, catches a bad cold that quickly turns to bronchitis.

1861   Comments on Civil War in a letter to cousin George Thatcher: "If the people of the north thus come to see clearly that there can be no *Union* between freemen & slaveholders, & vote & act accordingly, I shall think that we have purchased that progress cheaply by this revolution. A nation of 20 millions of freemen will be far more respectable & powerful, than if 10 millions of slaves & slave holders were added to them." Seeking to improve his health, to observe Indians, and to compare flora and fauna of Concord with that of the Middle West, he goes to Minnesota in May with young friend Horace Mann, Jr.

They collect botanical specimens and take an excursion steamer to Lower Sioux Agency at Redwood, where Thoreau witnesses annual government payment to Indians and sees Chief Little Crow, who will lead the 1862 Sioux uprising. Observes and sympathizes with the Indians' discontent. Returns to Concord in early July, tired and no better. Resigned to an early death, makes last revisions in *A Week* (posthumous new edition is published by Ticknor and Fields in 1868). Arranges with sister for posthumous publication of *The Maine Woods*, *Cape Cod*, and other writings. "You know it's respectable to leave an estate to one's friends," he tells one of his many bedside visitors. Makes last visit to Walden Pond in September and final journal entry on November 3.

1862   Confined to his house, refuses opiates and continues to receive visitors. February–April, works to complete "Life without Principle," "Autumnal Tints," "Walking," and "Wild Apples" for publication in James T. Fields's *Atlantic Monthly*. April 12, sells attic stock of *A Week* to publisher James T. Fields, who reissues it two months later with new title page. Dies May 6 of tuberculosis, his last intelligible words "moose" and "Indian." Buried May 9, in New Burying Ground, Concord, later moved to nearby Sleepy Hollow Cemetery.

Note on the Texts

When Henry David Thoreau died of tuberculosis in 1862, he left behind few published works. His first book, *A Week on the Concord and Merrimack Rivers*, was based on a trip he had made with his brother John in 1839, two years after he had graduated from Harvard College. It was drafted at Walden Pond, where he lived from 1845 to 1847, and was published in 1849 by James Munroe and Company. Meanwhile Thoreau had begun work on *Walden*, which was advertised in *A Week* as soon to be published. But the commercial failure of his first book discouraged the publisher from undertaking a second, and throughout the early 1850s Thoreau reworked *Walden* into the form we know. It was published by the newly established firm of Ticknor and Fields in 1854. Apart from these two books, Thoreau's published work consisted of a number of essays and poems that had appeared in *The Dial*, *The Atlantic Monthly*, and other journals.

This printed material, however, represented a mere fraction of Thoreau's literary output, left in manuscript at his death. There were the speeches and lectures he had delivered almost annually since the late 1830s, new essays and chapters and revised versions of the printed ones, numerous poems, notes and extracts from his voluminous reading about the Indians, and the nearly two million words of his journal, from which the finished pieces had been quarried.

Some of this large mass of material was pulled into shape by Thoreau's sister Sophia with the assistance of his good friend Ellery Channing. Ticknor and Fields, which had done a small reprinting of *A Week* and *Walden* immediately following Thoreau's death, issued five new volumes in the next few years: *Excursions* (1863), *The Maine Woods* (1864), *Cape Cod* (1865), *Letters to Various Persons* (1865, edited by Emerson), and *A Yankee in Canada with Anti-Slavery and Reform Papers* (1866), in addition to a new and revised edition of *A Week* in 1868.

The present volume contains two of the four works that Thoreau planned as unified, full-length books—one published during his lifetime, *Walden; or, Life in the Woods*, and one posthumously published, *The Maine Woods*. The texts of these two works suffered, to a greater or lesser extent, from misreading Thoreau's difficult handwriting and occasionally from a compositor missing or ignoring the author's instructions. Because Thoreau did not live to see *The Maine Woods* through the press in book form or to supervise a corrected second edition of *Walden*, errors introduced during initial publication frequently went undetected and were carried over into subsequent printings and editions. This volume also contains 27 essays and 203 poems by Thoreau, arranged in the approximate order of their composition between 1836 and 1862. Most of the essays were published during the author's lifetime, but most of the poems were not and existed only in manuscript at the time of his death. Detection of errors in these two books as well as in the essays and poems has benefited greatly from the work of the editors and scholars of the Princeton University Press edition of *The Writings of Henry D. Thoreau*. The texts of this edition have been prepared according to the standards established by the Center for Editions of American Authors. (See its Statement of Editorial Principles and Procedures, revised edition, 1972.)

Walden and the earlier *A Week on the Concord and Merrimack Rivers* were the only two books that Thoreau lived to see published. Like *A Week*, *Walden* was first drafted during his 1845–47 stay at Walden Pond and, again like his first book, considerably revised and expanded prior to its 1854 publication by Ticknor and Fields. In fact the manuscript he submitted as the printer's copy, apparently no longer extant, represented the eighth version of the work. The page proofs for the first edition, with Thoreau's more than 1,000 corrections, demonstrate that he read proof carefully. Some of his changes on proof correct the printer's misreading of his handwriting. The great majority involve punctuation, and it is often unclear whether these changes represent corrections or revisions. In any event, all but a small percentage of Thoreau's requested alterations were made in the first edition. Of the differences between the first edition and the page proofs, some are corrections of typographical errors that Thoreau missed in proofreading, while others are a matter of house style or spelling conventions. The rest are printer's errors, a few of which Thoreau later corrected in a copy of the book.

The 1854 first edition thus has the authority of Thoreau's supervision and, unlike *A Week*, was not superseded by a "revised" edition: omissions in the first edition and the few post-1854 changes were not incorporated in a posthumous volume by Thoreau's literary executors. The first edition text is reprinted here. Printer's errors are corrected by reference to Thoreau's own copy of *Walden*, and, more important, by comparison with the page proofs containing Thoreau's markings. Systematic changes by the printer in spelling, punctuation, or typography are considered features of the edition reprinted here; other oversights and omissions are corrected.

For *The Maine Woods*, the present volume reprints the text of the 1864 first edition. Prepared by Ellery Channing and Sophia Thoreau,

the first edition consisted of three essays and an appendix of technical terms. Although it was a composite volume, Thoreau unquestionably intended to issue the four parts as a single book in the order
of the 1864 edition. He left a rough plan for the organization of the
essays and a statement of the volume's collective title, and he drew
on all three chapters in compiling the appendix.

Two of the essays, "Ktaadn" and "Chesuncook," had already been
printed in periodicals, but Thoreau afterwards revised them for future book publication. "Ktaadn" was heavily revised from its 1848
printing in John Sartain's *Union Magazine*: Thoreau corrected obvious misreadings of his handwriting, revised the style, and inserted
several substantial passages and footnotes. "Chesuncook" was more
lightly revised following its 1858 publication in James Russell Lowell's
Atlantic Monthly. The most significant change was the restoration, in
revised form, of the sentence about a pine tree at 365.33–34 that
Lowell had struck out despite Thoreau's objections.

For the rest of the first edition of *The Maine Woods*, the third piece,
"The Allegash and East Branch," and the appendix were printed for
the first time. Thoreau apparently did not have time before he died
to prepare a fair copy of his manuscript for the printer, and these last
two sections, for which no previous printed text existed, suffered
most from the lack of authorial proofreading and supervision. Apart
from routine compositor's errors (here more common than usual
because of the large number of unfamiliar botanical terms and Indian
place names), there are corruptions probably introduced by Sophia
while transcribing especially messy pages of her brother's last draft
for the printer. In several instances she (or conceivably the compositor) misread Thoreau's handwriting, introducing errors into the first
edition that were reproduced in subsequent editions. The compositor who set the appendix consistently substituted the more familiar
"ü" for the unusual "ñ" used by Thoreau's sources to transcribe an
American Indian sound. It was probably Sophia, however, who at
502.10 misread "as fast as the stage on the bank," the reading of one
of the fragments of last-draft "Allegash" manuscript now at the
Huntington and Houghton libraries, as "as fast as the stage or the
boat." Where last-draft manuscript does not exist, Thoreau's journal
(at the Pierpont Morgan Library and elsewhere) helps detect the
more obvious errors, as when "memorable parts" of a stream
(481.16) appears absurdly in the 1864 text as "more arable parts."

Of the 27 essays included in this volume, the texts of 16 are taken
from *Reform Papers* and *Early Essays and Miscellanies*, two volumes
of the Princeton University Press edition of *The Writings of Henry D.
Thoreau*. The texts printed in this volume of "The Service," "Paradise
(To Be) Regained," "Herald of Freedom," "Wendell Phillips Before

Concord Lyceum," "Slavery in Massachusetts," "Life Without Principle," "A Plea for Captain John Brown," "Martyrdom of John Brown," and "The Last Days of John Brown" are taken from *Reform Papers*, edited by Wendell Glick (Princeton: Princeton University Press, 1973), while the texts of "Aulus Persius Flaccus," "Sir Walter Raleigh," "Dark Ages," "Homer. Ossian. Chaucer.," "Thomas Carlyle and His Works," "Love," and "Chastity & Sensuality" are taken from *Early Essays and Miscellanies*, edited by Joseph J. Moldenhauer, Edwin Moser, and Alexander Kern (Princeton: Princeton University Press, 1975). The essays from *Reform Papers* and *Early Essays and Miscellanies* from *The Writings of Henry D. Thoreau*, edited by Elizabeth Witherell, © 1972 Princeton University Press, are printed by permission of Princeton University Press. "Huckleberries," a section of a long manuscript on fruits that Thoreau worked on toward the end of his life, is taken from an edition prepared by Leo Stoller and published in 1970 by the Windhover Press of the University of Iowa and the New York Public Library. *Huckleberries*, © 1970 the New York Public Library, Astor, Lenox, and Tilden Foundations, is reprinted with permission. The texts of the ten remaining essays are taken from periodical or book publications published during Thoreau's lifetime or shortly after his death.

Thoreau wrote "Aulus Persius Flaccus" and "The Service" in 1840 and submitted both essays to *The Dial* for publication. "Aulus Persius Flaccus" was edited by Ralph Waldo Emerson and printed in *The Dial* in July 1840. Thoreau incorporated the essay in the "Thursday" chapter of *A Week on the Concord and Merrimack Rivers* (1849), making a few changes of wording and cutting three sentences. The text in *Reform Papers* (1973), based on Thoreau's copy of the July 1840 *Dial* with his corrections, is printed here. "The Service" was rejected by Margaret Fuller, editor of *The Dial*, and was not printed during Thoreau's lifetime. The text in *Reform Papers*, based on manuscripts at the Pierpont Morgan Library, is the text printed here.

Thoreau composed "Natural History of Massachusetts" in spring 1842, after Emerson asked him to write an essay for *The Dial* about several scientific surveys of the state. It was published in *The Dial* in July 1842, and *The Dial* text is printed here. In the autumn of 1842 Thoreau wrote "A Walk to Wachusett," which was published in *The Boston Miscellany* in January 1843. *The Boston Miscellany* text is printed here.

"Sir Walter Raleigh," "Dark Ages," "A Winter Walk," "The Landlord," "Paradise (To Be) Regained," and "Homer. Ossian. Chaucer." were written in 1843. Thoreau gave a lecture on Raleigh at the Concord Lyceum on February 8, 1843, and he may have submitted "Sir Walter Raleigh" to *The Dial* later that year. Part of the essay was included in *A Week on the Concord and Merrimack Rivers*. The text in *Early Essays and Miscellanies* is based on a manuscript at the Huntington Library and is the text printed here. "Dark Ages" was published in *The Dial* in April 1843 and was later incorporated in the "Monday" chapter of *A Week on the Concord and Merrimack Rivers*; this volume prints the text from *Early Essays and Miscellanies*, which is based on Thoreau's copy of the magazine printing. "A Winter Walk" appeared in *The Dial* in October 1843, and *The Dial* text is printed here. "The Landlord" and "Paradise (To Be) Regained" were published in *The United States Magazine, and Democratic Review* in October 1843 and November 1843, respectively. The text printed here of "The Landlord" is taken from *The United States Magazine, and Democratic Review*. The text of "Paradise (To Be) Regained" in *Reform Papers* (1973) is based on the version published in *The United States Magazine, and Democratic Review*, and is the text printed here. "Homer. Ossian. Chaucer." was published in *The Dial* in January 1844 after a version of the essay was presented as a lecture entitled "Ancient Poets" at the Concord Lyceum on November 23, 1843. *Early Essays and Miscellanies* bases its text on the version published in *The Dial* and incorporates some of the corrections Thoreau made in his copy of the magazine printing. The *Early Essays and Miscellanies* text is printed here.

Thoreau wrote "Herald of Freedom" in the spring of 1844. It was first published in the April 1844 issue of *The Dial*, and then appeared in a slightly different version the following month in *Herald of Freedom*, the antislavery periodical edited by Nathaniel Rogers. After Rogers' death on October 16, 1846, Thoreau wrote several additional paragraphs about Rogers and his periodical. A revised version of the essay appeared in the posthumous collection *A Yankee in Canada, with Anti-Slavery and Reform Papers* (Boston: Ticknor and Fields, 1866). The text in *Reform Papers* (1973) is based on the version printed in *The Dial* and incorporates the four manuscript pages Thoreau wrote after Rogers' death, citing evidence that Thoreau planned to publish this expanded version of "Herald of Freedom." The *Reform Papers* text is printed here.

When Wendell Phillips was invited to speak against slavery at the Concord Lyceum in March 1845, three of the Lyceum's curators resigned in protest. Thoreau, Emerson, and Samuel Barrett replaced them, and Phillips delivered his speech on March 11. Thoreau sent a letter defending Phillips to *The Liberator*, where it was published on March 28, 1845. The letter was reprinted under the title "Wendell Phillips Before the Concord Lyceum" in *A Yankee in Canada, with Anti-Slavery and Reform Papers* (1866). The text in *Reform Papers* (1973), based on Thoreau's letter in *The Liberator*, is printed here.

"Thomas Carlyle and His Works," originally presented as a lecture at the Concord Lyceum on February 4, 1846, was first published in two installments of *Graham's American Monthly Magazine* (March and April 1847). A shorter version was published in *A Yankee in Canada, with Anti-Slavery and Reform Papers* (1866). This volume prints the text from *Early Essays and Miscellanies*, which is based on the version in *Graham's American Monthly Magazine*.

"Civil Disobedience" is derived from two lectures Thoreau delivered at the Concord Lyceum early in 1848. The lectures were given —at least in part—in response to his neighbors' curiosity about why he had chosen in July 1846 to spend a night in prison rather than pay his poll tax. In the spring of 1849 Thoreau was invited by Elizabeth Peabody to submit a written version to her periodical *Aesthetic Papers*, where the essay appeared under the title of "Resistance to Civil Government" on May 14, 1849. It was published posthumously under the title "Civil Disobedience" in *A Yankee in Canada, with Anti-Slavery and Reform Papers* (1866), in a version that differs from the *Aesthetic Papers* version in four significant readings, including the title. Because of a lack of holographic evidence, it cannot be known definitively if Thoreau was responsible for these revisions. However, two passages that appear in the version published in *A Yankee in Canada, with Anti-Slavery and Reform Papers* have sources in commonplace books Thoreau kept and consulted for quotations as he worked on pieces from the 1840s until just before his death in 1862: lines from George Peele's "The Battle of Alcazar" and a sentence about Mencius's belief that the individual is the basis for the empire. It is unlikely that anyone but Thoreau would have made these changes; accepting them as authoritative acknowledges Thoreau's involvement in revising the essay and raises the strong possibility that he made the other two changes as well. The version of the essay that appears in *Reform Papers* (1973) as "Resistance to Civil Government" is based on the 1849 *Aesthetic Papers* text and does not include these changes. The present volume prints the text of "Civil Disobedience" that appeared in *A Yankee in Canada, with Anti-Slavery and Reform Papers* (1866).

Thoreau delivered a lecture entitled "The Wild" at the Concord Lyceum on April 23, 1851. This lecture was revised and expanded into two lectures, "Walking" and "The Wild," that Thoreau delivered frequently during the 1850s, sometimes combined as a single lecture. Shortly before his death, he sold an essay titled "Walking" to *The Atlantic Monthly*, which published it in July 1862. *The Atlantic Monthly* text is printed here.

In September 1850 Thoreau and Ellery Channing traveled to Montreal, Quebec City, and the northern bank of the St. Lawrence. Soon after his return in October, Thoreau began writing about the trip. He worked on the essay during the winter of 1850 and throughout 1851, reading accounts of Canadian history and filling a notebook with quotations about Canada. He delivered two lectures adapted from his essay at the Concord Lyceum in 1852, the first on January 7, the second on March 17. Horace Greeley then suggested revisions that might be made in the manuscript, now titled "A Yankee in Canada." After two magazines rejected it, the essay was accepted by *Putnam's Monthly Magazine*. George William Curtis, Thoreau's friend and an editor at *Putnam's*, removed passages that he called "heresies," such as Thoreau's statement that "I am not sure but this Catholic religion would be an admirable one if the priests were quite omitted," from the three serial installments published in the magazine's January, February, and March numbers in 1853. The remaining installments in *Putnam's* were canceled after Thoreau objected to the editing and asked for the return of his manuscript. "A Yankee in Canada" was not published in full until the posthumous *A Yankee in Canada, with Anti-Slavery and Reform Papers* (1866), which is the text printed here.

"Love" and "Chastity & Sensuality" were enclosed in a letter to Thoreau's friend Harrison G. O. Blake in September 1852. Both essays were first published in the posthumous *Letters to Various Persons* (Boston: Ticknor and Fields, 1865), edited by Emerson. An incomplete draft of "Love" is in a manuscript now at the Huntington Library. *Early Essays and Miscellanies* bases its text of "Love" on this manuscript and on the version printed in *Letters to Various Persons*, and it is the source of the text printed here. A complete manuscript of "Chastity & Sensuality" is in the Huntington Library. The text in *Early Essays and Miscellanies* is based on this manuscript and is the text printed here.

"Slavery in Massachusetts" originated in a lecture given by Thoreau at Framingham, Massachusetts, on July 4, 1854. A longer version of the speech was published in the July 21, 1854 number of *The Liberator*, and versions also appeared in *The New-York Daily Tribune*, August 2, 1854, and in *The National Anti-Slavery Standard*, August 12, 1854. It was included in *A Yankee in Canada, with Anti-Slavery and Reform Papers* (1866). The text in *Reform Papers* (1973) is based on the version that was published in *The Liberator* and is the text printed here.

Thoreau gave a lecture entitled "Getting a Living" in New Bedford, Massachusetts, on December 26, 1854. He revised and delivered this lecture often between 1854 and 1860, using the titles "The Connection Between Man's Employment and His Higher Life," "What Shall It Profit?," and "Life Misspent." Shortly before his death,

Thoreau sent a manuscript of the essay, prepared with the help of his sister Sophia and using the working title "The Higher Law," to *The Atlantic Monthly*. He gave the essay the title "Life without Principle," in a letter dated March 4, 1862, to James T. Field of *The Atlantic Monthly*. The essay appeared in the October 1863 number of *The Atlantic Monthly* and was reprinted in *A Yankee in Canada, with Anti-Slavery and Reform Papers* (1866). The text in *Reform Papers* (1973), based on *The Atlantic Monthly* version, is the text printed here.

"Autumnal Tints" was first delivered as a lecture in Worcester on February 22, 1859; Thoreau repeated the lecture on several occasions in 1859. It appeared posthumously in *The Atlantic Monthly* in November 1862, which is the source of the text printed here.

"A Plea for John Brown," "Martyrdom of John Brown," and "The Last Days of John Brown" were written in the aftermath of Brown's raid on Harpers Ferry in October 1859. "A Plea for John Brown" was given as a speech on October 18, 1859, and delivered several times in the weeks that followed. It was first published in *Echoes of Harper's Ferry* (Boston: Thayer and Eldridge, 1860), a collection of essays edited by James Redpath. The text in *Reform Papers* (1973) is based on the version that appears in *Echoes of Harper's Ferry* and is the text printed here. "Martyrdom of John Brown" was delivered as a speech at the Concord Town Hall on December 2, 1859, the day of Brown's execution, and then published as a broadside. It also appeared in *Echoes of Harper's Ferry*, under the title "Remarks at Concord on the Day of the Execution of John Brown." The *Reform Papers* text, based on the printer's copy of the December 1859 broadside, is printed here. "The Last Days of John Brown" was derived from entries in Thoreau's journal, dating from November and December 1859, that he did not incorporate into his two speeches about Brown. It was first published as an untitled piece in *The Liberator* on July 27, 1860, and was printed under the title "The Last Days of John Brown" in *A Yankee in Canada, with Anti-Slavery and Reform Papers* (1866). The text in *Reform Papers* (1973) is based on *The Liberator* version but uses the title from *A Yankee in Canada, with Anti-Slavery and Reform Papers*, and it is the text printed here.

Thoreau delivered "The Succession of Forest Trees" as a lecture to the Middlesex Agricultural Society at the Concord Town Hall on September 20, 1860. The text of the lecture appeared in the *New York Weekly Tribune* on October 6, 1860. It was also reprinted in the *Transactions of the Middlesex Agricultural Society* and, in shortened form, in a report of the Massachusetts Board of Agriculture published in 1860. It was incorporated into a longer work on seed dispersion that Thoreau did not live to complete. This volume prints the *New York Weekly Tribune* text.

"Wild Apples" was first given as a lecture at the Concord Lyceum on February 8, 1860, although much of it is derived from journal entries composed in the early 1850s. Thoreau revised the essay after delivering it as a lecture, and it was published for the first time in *The Atlantic Monthly* in November 1862. It was also incorporated into "Wild Fruits," a manuscript that Thoreau worked on during the last years of his life and did not live to finish. This volume prints *The Atlantic Monthly* text.

"Huckleberries" is also part of "Wild Fruits." The writings on huckleberries exist in a more advanced form than the other essays in "Wild Fruits," with the exception of "Wild Apples." The text of "Huckleberries" printed here is taken from the edition prepared by Leo Stoller in *Huckleberries*, published in 1970 by the Windhover Press of the University of Iowa and the New York Public Library, © 1970 the New York Public Library, Astor, Lenox, and Tilden Foundations; reprinted with permission.

Thoreau wrote more than 200 poems, 85 of which were published in some form in his lifetime. Most of his poems were written between 1837 and 1845. Fifteen were published in *The Dial*, excluding translations and poems that appear in essays; one additional poem, "Great God, I ask thee for no meaner pelf," was included in Emerson's essay "Prayers," which appeared in *The Dial* in July 1842. The majority of Thoreau's published poems are interspersed throughout *A Week on the Concord and Merrimack Rivers,* and other poems appear in *Walden, The Maine Woods,* and in several of his essays. The poems Thoreau included in his essays and books were usually written before the prose works, and they are often longer in their manuscript versions, since he would excerpt lines from these manuscripts when incorporating his poetry into his essays and books. For example, "The Assabet," composed in 1839, contains lines that appear in revised form in three separate passages in *A Week on the Concord and Merrimack Rivers* as "Some tumultuous little rill," "Ply the oars! away! away!," and "Since that first 'away! away!'"

Drafts of many poems appear in the journal that Thoreau kept from 1837 until the end of his life, although he wrote few poems after 1847. In some instances Thoreau revised these drafts for separate publication in *The Dial*, or in his prose works, or for subsequent manuscript versions of the poem. In other cases the journal version of the poem is the only surviving version. Journal entries that are dated between October 1837 and September 1841 are usually taken from the five manuscript volumes that Thoreau used to copy entries from two volumes of an earlier journal, of which only a few leaves survive. When Thoreau copied these entries in the fall of 1841, he gave the transcribed entries their original dates. Drafts of poems also appear in the "Long Book," a manuscript volume that contains transcribed journal entries and original material, including a version of "Wendell Phillips at the Concord Lyceum" and a draft of a lecture on the Concord River delivered in March 1845. Thoreau began copying passages from earlier journals into the Long Book in fall 1844, gathering material for what would eventually become A *Week on the Concord and Merrimack Rivers*. Most of the entries in the Long Book are not dated; the latest entries were composed in 1846.

During the last ten years of his life, Thoreau virtually stopped writing poetry, and he never collected his poems. The first posthumous edition of his poetry, *Poems of Nature* (1895), edited by Henry S. Salt and Franklin B. Sanborn, contained unauthorized changes. The first critical edition, *Collected Poems of Henry Thoreau*, edited by Carl Bode, was published in 1943; a revised and expanded version, containing 16 additional poems and omitting two poems incorrectly attributed to Thoreau in the first edition, was published in 1964 by Johns Hopkins University Press.

Since *Collected Poems of Henry Thoreau* was published, a new edition of some of Thoreau's poems has appeared as a doctoral dissertation by Elizabeth Hall Witherell, "The Poetry of Henry David Thoreau: A Selected Critical Edition" (1979). The present volume uses the Witherell edition as the source for the 49 poems it contains, since Witherell had access to more manuscripts than Bode and was able to clarify the relationship among versions of what might be considered the same poem. Five additional poems are printed from Witherell's article "Thoreau's Watershed Season as a Poet: The Hidden Fruits of the Summer and Fall of 1841," published in the 1990 volume of *Studies in the American Renaissance*, edited by Joel Myerson; this article is an expanded version of an appendix to the Witherell edition. The texts of 141 poems are printed from the 1964 revised edition of Carl Bode's *Collected Poems of Henry Thoreau*. (*Collected Poems* is the source of "Delay in Friendship," one of the poems in the Witherell edition.) In printing poems from *Collected Poems of Henry Thoreau*, this volume sometimes adopts the alternate titles listed in its table of contents but does not follow its practice of printing the first line of an untitled poem as its title; instead, the present volume prints the poem without a title. Nine poems are printed from manuscript sources.

Witherell's "The Poetry of Henry David Thoreau: A Selected Critical Edition" presents texts grouped together on the basis of shared content, such as a line or lines in common. For example, "The Inward Morning," published in the October 1842 *Dial* and included in A *Week on the Concord and Merrimack Rivers*, contains lines that appear in two manuscript poems in Thoreau's journal, "Packed in my mind lie all the clothes" and "What is it gilds the trees and clouds." The Witherell edition regards these four texts together as versions of a single poem. The present volume follows the Witherell edition's groupings of manuscript and printed sources, but it prints only one version of each poem. For poems included in the Witherell edition that were published during Thoreau's lifetime, this volume prints the published version with Thoreau's latest revisions, unless the published version was part of a larger prose work such as *A Week on the Concord and Merrimack Rivers*, *Walden*, or one of Thoreau's essays. For poems included in the Witherell edition that appear in Thoreau's prose works, this volume prints the version with Thoreau's latest revisions before the poem was made part of a prose work. In the case of poems included *A Week on the Concord and Merrimack Rivers* for which no earlier manuscript version is known to survive, this volume prints texts from the Witherell edition that are based on the proofsheets of *A Week* (now at the Huntington Library), which Thoreau continued to correct and revise after the book was published in 1849. When the only existing version of a poem appeared in a prose work other than *A Week*, this volume prints the text from the Witherell edition in which the text is based on the published prose work.

"Independence," "Cock-crowing," "Inspiration" ("Whate'er we leave to God, God does"), "The Soul's Season," and "The Fall of the Leaf" are part of a group of interrelated poems that Thoreau worked on during the summer and fall of 1841, of which nearly 20 versions survive, ranging in length from four to about 300 lines. Versions of these five poems survive as titled fair copies, written out in ink by Thoreau. The texts of "Independence," "Cock-crowing," "Inspiration," "The Soul's Season," and "The Fall of the Leaf" printed here are taken from Elizabeth Hall Witherell, "Thoreau's Watershed Season as a Poet: The Hidden Fruits of the Summer and Fall of 1841," published in *Studies in the American Renaissance 1990*, edited by Joel Myerson (Charlottesville: University Press of Virginia, 1991).

The texts printed here of two poems that were included in *Collected Poems of Henry Thoreau* are transcribed from manuscripts not available to Bode when he was preparing his edition. "In days of yore, 'tis said, the swimming alder," appeared in *Collected Poems* as "In times of yore, 'tis said, the swimming alder," based on a version that appeared in *The Life of Henry Thoreau* by Franklin B. Sanborn (Boston: Houghton Mifflin, 1917). The text printed here is taken from a manuscript at the University of Illinois. "The Rabbit leaps" appeared in *Collected Poems* as "A Winter and a Spring Scene," also based on a version published in *The Life of Henry Thoreau*. The text printed here is based on a manuscript at Southern Illinois University.

Seven poems included in this volume—"Pens to mend and hands to glide," "The coward ever sings no song," "Only the slave knows of the slave," "I have seen some frozenfaced connecticut," "You Boston folk & Roxbury people," "Why toll the bell today—," and "Except, returning, by the Marlboro"—are taken from manuscript sources listed below.

The following is a list, in the approximate order of composition, of the poems contained in this volume, indicating the source text and other relevant information. Abbreviations refer to the following:

CP   *Collected Poems of Henry Thoreau*, revised and expanded edition, edited by Carl Bode (Baltimore: Johns Hopkins University Press, 1964).

EHW   Elizabeth Hall Witherell, "The Poetry of Henry David Thoreau: A Selected Critical Edition." Doctoral dissertation, University of Wisconsin, 1979.

SAR   Elizabeth Hall Witherell, "Thoreau's Watershed Season as a Poet: The Hidden Fruits of the Summer and Fall of 1841," in Joel Myerson (ed.), *Studies in the American Renaissance 1990* (Charlottesville: University Press of Virginia, 1991), pp. 49–106.

A Week *A Week on the Concord and Merrimack Rivers* (Boston: James Munroe and Company, 1849).

In days of yore, tis said, the swimming alder. Manuscript, University of Illinois Rare Book Room, in holograph copy of August 5, 1836, letter from Thoreau to Charles Wyatt Rice. Reprinted with permission.

Fair Haven ("When little hills like lambs did skip"). *CP.*

Voyagers Song. *CP.* A revised version of the second and the third stanzas appear in *A Week.*

Life is a summer's day. *CP.*

I love a careless streamlet. *CP.*

Pens to mend and hands to guide. Manuscript, New York Public Library, Berg Collection, in a letter from Thoreau to Henry Vose, October 13, 1837. Reprinted with permission of the New York Public Library, Berg Collection, Astor, Lenox, and Tilden Foundations.

Each summer sound. *CP.* Appears in journal, February 19, 1838, and is included in "Natural History of Massachusetts."

Friendship ("I think awhile of Love, and while I think"). *CP.* Appears in journal, April 8, 1838.

When breathless noon hath paused on hill and vale. *CP*, under the title "The Cliffs & Springs."

The Bluebirds. *CP.* Appears in journal, April 26, 1838.

May Morning. *CP*. Appears in journal, May 21, 1838.

Walden. *CP*. Appears in journal, June 3, 1838.

Truth—Goodness—Beauty—those celestial thrins. *CP*. Appears in journal, June 14, 1838.

Strange that so many fickle gods, as fickle as the weather. *CP*. Appears in journal, June 14, 1838.

In the busy streets, domains of trade. *CP*. Appears in journal, June 16, 1838.

I knew a man by sight. *CP*.

Cliffs. *CP*. Appears in journal, July 8, 1838.

My Boots. *CP*. Appears in journal, October 16, 1838.

Noon. *CP*. Appears in journal, October 16, 1838.

Fair Haven ("When Winter fringes every bough"). *CP*. Appears in journal, December 15, 1838. An untitled version of the poem was included in "A Winter Walk."

The Thaw. *EHW*, from journal, January 11, 1839, MA 1302:1. Reprinted with permission of the Pierpont Morgan Library, New York. Published in *The Dial*, July 1842. A slightly revised version of the opening couplet appears in "The Natural History of Massachusetts." A version of lines 3–6 appears in Long Book.

Last night as I lay gazing with shut eyes. *EHW*, from journal, January 20, 1839, MA 1302:1, with pencil revisions made after December 1843. Reprinted with permission of the Pierpont Morgan Library, New York. A version of the last stanza appears in *A Week*.

Love. *CP*. Appears in journal, January 20, 1839.

The deeds of king and meanest hedger. *CP*. Appears in journal, February 3, 1839.

'Twill soon appear if we but look. *CP*. Appears in journal, February 3, 1839.

The Evening Wind. *EHW*, from journal, February 13, 1839, MA 1302:1. Reprinted with permission of the Pierpont Morgan Library, New York. A revised version of the poem is included in *A Week*.

The Peal of the Bells. *CP*. Appears in journal, February 10, 1839.

The Shrike. *EHW*, from journal, February 25, 1839, MA 1302:1. Reprinted with permission of the Pierpont Morgan Library, New York. The second stanza is included in "The Natural History of Massachusetts."

Sympathy. *EHW*, from journal, June 24, 1839, MA 1302:1. Reprinted with permission of the Pierpont Morgan Library, New York. The poem was published in the July 1840 *Dial*, set from a copy by Emerson that contained misreadings and unauthorized revisions. The poem was revised for inclusion in *A Week*.

The "Book of Gems." *CP*. Appears in journal, July 4, 1839.

The Assabet. *EHW*, from journal, July 18, 1839, MA 1302:1. Reprinted with permission of the Pierpont Morgan Library, New York. A later manuscript version contains two stanzas, the eleventh and the tenth, of "The Assabet." Lines originating in "The Assabet" appear in *A Week* in three places: a version of stanzas six and seven appear in "Sunday"; two stanzas beginning "Ply the oars! away! away!" and a version of the last stanza appears in "Tuesday."

The Breeze's Invitation, *CP*. Appears in journal, July 20, 1839.

Stanzas. *EHW*, from *The Dial*, January 1841. A version of the poem appears in journal, July 24, 1839. It is included without a title in *A Week*.

Loves Farewell. *CP*. Appears under the title "Farewell" in journal, November 19, 1839.

Each more melodious note I hear. *CP*. Appears in journal, December 1839, and is included in "The Service."

The Fisher's Son. *EHW*, from manuscript, Abernathy Library, Middlebury College, on two single leaves of an early journal that Thoreau apparently saved because they were blank, though the poem is not part of that journal. The manuscript contains Thoreau's pencil revisions. Reprinted with permission. A version of the poem appears in Thoreau's journal, January 10, 1840; stanzas eight, ten, eleven, and twelve were revised and included in *A Week*.

Friendship ("Let such pure hate still underprop"). *EHW*, from Thoreau's corrected copy of the October 1841 *Dial*, where the poem was first published. Thoreau corrected two errors in his copy. The poem appeared without a title in *A Week*. A quatrain that was the final stanza of an early draft of the poem appears in Thoreau's journal, January 19, 1840.

The Freshet. *EHW*, from journal, February 24, 1840, MA 1302:2. Reprinted with permission of the Pierpont Morgan Library, New York. A revised version was included in "Natural History of Massachusetts." A version of the first stanza appears in Long Book.

The Poet's Delay. *EHW*, from *The Dial*, October 1842. An untitled version, with two additional stanzas and the order of the first and second stanzas reversed, appears in Thoreau's journal between entries dated March 8, 1840, and March 16, 1840. The poem was reprinted in *A Week*.

The Summer Rain. *EHW*, from Thoreau's copy of the October 1842 *Dial*, where Thoreau changed "greater" to "juster" in the third stanza. A revised version of the poem was included in *A Week*.

Guido's Aurora. *CP*.

I've heard my neighbor's pump at night. *CP*, which erroneously prints "Who sleeps by day and walks by night" as its final couplet. This volume follows *CP*'s transcription of Thoreau's manuscript but prints "I've heard my neighbor's pump at night" and "Who sleeps by day and walks by night" as separate poems. Both poems appear on the flyleaf of the third volume of Thoreau's journal.

Who sleeps by day and walks by night. *CP*. It was included in *A Week*.

When with pale cheek and sunken eye I sang. *CP*. Appears in journal, August 12, 1840.

I arose before light. *CP*. Appears in journal, October 14, 1840.

I'm guided in the darkest night. *CP*. Appears in journal, November 7, 1840.

Friends—. *CP*. Published in *The Dial*, December 28, 1841, and copied into journal, January 1841.

When in some cove I lie. *CP*. Appears in journal, January 1841.

Who hears the parson. *CP*. Appears in journal, January 10, 1841.

Sic Vita. *EHW*, from *The Dial*, July 1841. The poem appears without a title in *A Week*, and in journal.

Wait not till I invite thee, but observe. *CP*. Appears in journal, April 7, 1841.

Friendship ("Now we are partners in such legal trade"). *CP*. Appears in journal, March 30, 1841.

On the Sun Coming Out in the Afternoon. *CP*. Appears in journal, April 1, 1841.

They who prepare my evening meal below. *CP*. Appears in journal, April 4, 1841.

My ground is high. *CP*. Appears in journal, April 7, 1841.

If from your price ye will not swerve. *CP*. Appears in journal, April 7, 1841.

Death cannot come too soon. *CP*. Appears in journal, April 18, 1841.

The Mountains in the Horizon. *EHW*, from manuscript, Am 1280.214.1 (2), Houghton Library, Harvard University. Reprinted with permission. Revised versions of the poem were included in "A Walk to Wachusett" and *A Week*.

The needles of the pine. *CP*. Appears in journal, May 9, 1841, and in "A Walk to Wachusett."

The Echo of the Sabbath Bell—. *EHW*, from journal, May 9, 1841, MA 1302:5. Reprinted with permission of the Pierpont Morgan Library, New York. A revised version, untitled, was included in *A Week*.

Low in the eastern sky. *CP*. First published under the title, "To the Maiden in the East," in *The Dial*, October 1842. Thoreau omitted three stanzas when including the poem in *A Week*. The version in *CP* reflects these revisions.

My life has been the poem I would have writ. *CP*. Appears in journal, August 28, 1841, and in *A Week*.

To the Mountains. *CP*.

Greater is the depth of sadness. *CP*. Appears in journal, September 5, 1841.

Where I have been. *CP*. Appears in journal, September 7, 1841.

Better wait. *CP*. Appears in journal, September 30, 1841.

Independence. *SAR*. Manuscript dated July 30, 1841, now in the Yale University Collection of American Literature, Beinecke Rare Book and Manuscript Library. A version titled "The Black Knight" was published in *The Dial*, October 1842.

Cock-crowing. *SAR*. Manuscript, Berg Collection, New York Public Library. Reprinted with permission of the New York Public Library, Berg Collection, Astor, Lenox, and Tilden Foundations.

Inspiration ("Whate'er we leave to God, God does"). *SAR*. Based on a photograph of an unlocated manuscript made from a negative by Herbert Cahoon, formerly Robert H. Taylor Curator of Autograph Manuscripts at the Pierpont Morgan Library, New York.

The Soul's Season. *SAR*. Manuscript, Robert H. Taylor Collection, Department of Rare Books and Special Collections, Princeton University Library. Reprinted with permission.

The Fall of the Leaf. *SAR*. Manuscript, Berg Collection, New York Public Library. Reprinted with permission of the New York Public Library, Berg Collection, Astor, Lenox, and Tilden Foundations.

Delay. *CP*.

Inspiration ("If thou wilt but stand by my ear"). *CP*.

Ive searched my faculties around. *CP*.

Who equallest the coward's haste. *CP*.

The Vireo. *CP*. The lines appear without a title in "Natural History of Massachusetts."

The coward ever sings no song. Manuscript, MS Am 1280 (137), Houghton Library, Harvard University. Reprinted with permission.

Only the slave knows of the slave. Manuscript, MS Am 1280 (137), Houghton Library, Harvard University. Reprinted with permission.

Great God, I ask thee for no meaner pelf. *CP*. The poem appeared under the heading "Metrical Prayer" in Emerson's essay "Prayers," which was published in *The Dial*, July 1842.

The Inward Morning. *EHW*, from *The Dial*, October 1842. The poem was included in *A Week*. Early drafts appear in journal, November–December 1841.

Within the circuit of this plodding life. *EHW*, from manuscript, dated December 30, 1841, MA 1302:6. Reprinted with permission of the Pierpont Morgan Library, New York. A revised version appears in "Natural History of Massachusetts."

To Edith. *CP.*

Delay in Friendship. *CP.* Appears in *EHW*, which uses *CP* as its text. A version of the final stanza appears in *A Week.*

Ah, 'tis in vain the peaceful din. *CP.* Included in *A Week.*

Between the traveller and the setting sun. *CP.*

Have ye no work for a man to do—. *CP.*

I sailed up a river with a pleasant wind. *CP.* Included in *A Week.*

I was made erect and lone. *CP.*

I'm not alone. *CP.*

Our Country. *CP.*

Pray to what earth does this sweet cold belong. *CP.*

True kindness is a pure divine affinity. *CP.* Included in *A Week.*

Until at length the north winds blow. *CP.*

Wait not till slaves pronounce the word. *CP.*

The Funeral Bell. *CP.* The first eight lines appear in journal, July 18, 1842.

Sometimes I hear the veery's clarion. *CP.* The lines are included in "Natural History of Massachusetts." A prose version dated 1838 appears in Thoreau's journal.

Thou dusky spirit of the wood. *CP.* The lines are included in "Natural History of Massachusetts."

Not unconcerned Wachusett rears his head. *EHW,* from "A Walk to Wachusett," *Boston Miscellany,* January 1843.

Nature. *CP.*

Godfrey of Boulogne. *CP.* A draft appears in journal, 1842 (after August 23).

The Rabbit leaps. Manuscript, VFM 1091, Special Collections, Morris Library, Southern Illinois University, Carbondale. Drafts of the poem appear in journal, 1842 (after August 23).

I am the Autumnal sun. *EHW,* from Long Book, MA 1303. Reprinted with permission of the Pierpont Morgan Library, New York. Appears in *A Week.*

Where'er thou sail'st who sailed with me. *EHW,* from manuscript, from Long Book, 1842, MA 1303. Reprinted with permission of the Pierpont Morgan Library, New York. It was included in *A Week.*

I was born upon thy bank river. *CP.* Appears in Long Book, 1842.

Salmon Brook. *EHW,* from Long Book, September 1, 1842, MA 1303. Reprinted with permission of the Pierpont Morgan Library, New York. Appears in *A Week.*

The moon now rises to her absolute rule. *CP.* Appears in Long Book, September 1842.

My friends, why should we live? *CP.* Appears in Long Book, September 1842.

I mark the summer's swift decline. *CP*. Appears in Long Book, September 1842.

My love must be as free. *CP*. Published as "Free Love" in *The Dial*, October 1842; included without a title in *A Week*.

The Moon. CP. Published in *The Dial*, October 1842.

Rumors From an Aeolian Harp. *CP*. Published in *The Dial*, October 1842, and revised for inclusion in *A Week*.

On shoulders whirled in some eccentric orbit. *CP*.

Far oer The bow. *EHW*, from Long Book, MA 1303. Reprinted with permission of the Pierpont Morgan Library, New York. Lines that appear in two places in *A Week*, "The waves slowly beat" and "Where gleaming fields of haze," have their origin in this poem.

Methinks that by a strict behavior. *CP*. Appears in Long Book.

I have rolled near some other spirits path. *CP*. Appears in Long Book.

Fog. *EHW*, from Long Book, MA 1303. Reprinted with permission of the Pierpont Morgan Library, New York. A draft appears in journal, 1843 (after January 16). A revised version of the poem beginning with the line "Low-anchored cloud" is included in *A Week*.

How little curious is man. *EHW*, from Long Book, with Thoreau's pencil revisions. Lines 9–10 were incorporated into *A Week*.

To the Comet. *CP*.

Haze. *CP*. Published in *The Dial*, April 1843, then included, without a title, in *A Week*.

Smoke. *EHW*, from *The Dial*, April 1843. Appeared without a title in *Walden*.

To a Stray Fowl. *EHW*, from *The Dial*, April 1843. A slightly revised version of the poem was incorporated into an early draft of *Walden*.

The Departure. *CP*.

Brother where dost thou dwell? *CP*.

All things are current found. *EHW*, from Long Book, MA 1303, with Thoreau's ink revisions. Reprinted with permission of the Pierpont Morgan Library, New York. The poem was included in *A Week*.

On fields oer which the reaper's hand has passed. *CP*. Appears in Long Book.

Epitaph on an Engraver. *CP*. Versions appear in journal, October 22, 1843, in Long Book, and in *A Week*.

Epitaph on Pursy. *CP*. Appears in journal, October 22, 1843.

Ep on a Good Man. *CP*. Appears in journal, October 22, 1843, and in Long Book.

Epitaph. *EHW*, from Long Book, Collection of W. Stephen Thomas, Rochester, New York. A slightly revised version was included in *A Week*.

Ep on the World. *CP*. Appears in journal, October 22, 1843.

The sluggish smoke curls up from some deep dell. *CP.* Included in "A Winter Walk."

On Ponkawtasset, since, we took our way. *CP.* Included in *A Week.*

To a Marsh Hawk in Spring. *CP.* Appears in Long Book.

Great Friend. *CP.* Version appears in Long Book.

The offer. *EHW,* from manuscript, from Long Book, MA 1303. A slightly revised version of the poem appears in *A Week.* Reprinted with permission of the Pierpont Morgan Library, New York.

Morning. *EHW,* from manuscript, from Long Book. Reprinted by permission of the Huntington Library, San Marino, California, HM 13188. The six lines in *A Week* beginning "An early unconverted saint" were revised from this version of the poem.

The Friend. *EHW,* from Long Book. Reprinted by permission of the Huntington Library, San Marino, California, HM 13188. A revised version of the poem appears in *A Week.*

Yet let us Thank the purblind race. *CP.* Appears in Long Book.

Ye do command me to all virtue ever. *CP.* Appears in Long Book.

Ive seen ye, sisters, on the mountain-side. *CP.* Appears in Long Book.

I am bound, I am bound, for a distant shore. *EHW,* from proofsheets of *A Week.* A version appears in Long Book, 1845 (after March 11).

The Hero. *CP.* A version of this poem appears in a draft of *Walden.*

At midnight's hour I raised my head. *CP.*

I seek the Present Time. *CP.* A version of this poem appears in a draft of *Walden* but was not included in the published work.

Tell me ye wise ones if ye can. *EHW,* from journal. Lines 33 to 42 were revised and appear as an 8-line poem in *A Week.*

Behold these flowers—. *EHW,* from journal, August 6, 1845, MA 1302:8, with Thoreau's ink revisions. Reprinted with permission of the Pierpont Morgan Library, New York. The final stanza was revised and included in *A Week.*

My friends, my noble friends, know ye—. *CP.*

The Earth. *CP.*

But now "no war nor battle's sound". *EHW,* from journal (after July 24, 1846), Berg Collection, New York Public Library, with Thoreau's revisions made in pencil and ink. Reprinted with permission of the New York Public Library, Berg Collection, Astor, Lenox, and Tilden Foundations. It was revised for inclusion in *A Week.*

Such water do the gods distill. *EHW,* from journal (after July 24, 1846), Berg Collection, New York Public Library, with Thoreau's revisions, Reprinted with permission of the New York Public Library, Berg Collection, Astor, Lenox, and Tilden Foundations. It was revised for inclusion in *A Week.*

Die and be buried who will. *EHW,* from manuscript draft of

"Ktaadn" that Thoreau wrote in late 1846 or 1847, now at the Brown University Library. Reprinted with permission. The quatrain appears in slightly altered form in *The Maine Woods*.

I have seen some frozenfaced connecticut. Manuscript, Robert H. Taylor Collection, Department of Rare Books and Special Collections, Princeton University Library. Reprinted with permission.

Such near aspects had we. *EHW*, from proofsheets of *A Week*. Reprinted by permission of the Huntington Library, San Marino, California, HM 13195.

Travelling ("If e'er our minds be ill at ease"). *EHW*, from manuscript, MA 920. Reprinted with permission of the Pierpont Morgan Library, New York. A longer version, beginning with the line "Though all the fates should prove unkind," was published in *A Week*.

The Atlantides. *CP*. Included in *A Week*.

Conscience is instinct bred in the house. *CP*. Included in *A Week*.

That Phaeton of our day. *CP*. Included in *A Week*.

Then spend an age in whetting thy desire. *CP*. Included in *A Week*.

We see the *planet* fall. *CP*. Included in *A Week*.

We should not mind if on our ear there fell. *CP*. Included in *A Week*.

Men say they know many things. *EHW*, from proofsheets of *Walden*. Reprinted by permission of The Huntington Library, San Marino, California, HM 924.

Away! away! away! away! *EHW*, from proofsheets of *A Week*.

In the East fames are won. *CP*. Appears in "Thomas Carlyle and His Works."

The good how can we trust? *EHW*, from manuscript, New York Public Library, included in a letter to Emerson dated December 29, 1847. Reprinted with permission of the New York Public Library, Berg Collection, Astor, Lenox, and Tilden Foundations. The poem appears in *A Week*.

Greece. *EHW*, from manuscript, MA 920. Reprinted with permission of the Pierpont Morgan Library, New York. A version of the last 4 lines were included in *A Week*.

Poverty. *EHW*, from manuscript, MA 920. Reprinted with permission of the Pierpont Morgan Library, New York. Versions of lines 8–9 and 24–27 appear in *A Week*.

The respectable folks. *EHW*, from proofsheets of *A Week*. Reprinted by permission of the Huntington Library, San Marino, California, HM 13182.

Farewell. *CP*.

For though the eaves were rabitted. *CP*. *CP*'s transcription of "caves" in the poem's first line is here emended to "eaves," based on a review of the manuscript. Appears in journal (after September 11, 1849).

You Boston folks & Roxbury people. Manuscript, the Huntington Library, San Marino, California, HM 13182. Reprinted with permission.

I will obey the strictest law of love. *CP.* A version appears in journal (after October 28, 1849).

Why toll the bell today—. Manuscript, the Huntington Library, San Marino, California, HM 13182. Reprinted with permission.

And once again. *CP.* Appears in journal, 1850 (after July 29).

The Old Marlborough Road. *CP.* Versions appear in journal, 1850 (after July 29), and in "Walking."

Old meeting-house bell. *CP.* Appears in journal, 1850.

It is a real place. *EHW,* from a draft of *Walden.* Reprinted by permission of the Huntington Library, San Marino, California, HM 924. The manuscript is incomplete. An incomplete draft of the poem appears in the journal, 1850 (between July 29, 1850, and August 31, 1850). A version of the poem, beginning with the line "It is no dream of mine," appears in *Walden.*

Among the worst of men that ever lived. *CP.* Appears in journal, August 1850.

What's the rail-road to me? *EHW,* from journal (between July 29, 1850, and August 31, 1850), MA 1302:9. Reprinted with permission of the Pierpont Morgan Library, New York. The poem was included in *Walden.*

Tall Ambrosia. *CP.* Appears in journal, August 31, 1850.

'Tis very fit the ambrosia of the gods. *CP. CP* prints two versions as a single poem, "Th'ambrosia of the Gods 's a weed on earth." The present volume prints the final five lines of *CP*'s "Th'ambrosia of the Gods 's a weed on earth," since this is the final version of the poem. The first version reads: "Th'ambrosia of the Gods 's a weed on earth / Their nectar is the morning dew which on / 'ly our shoes taste—For they are simple folks". Appears in journal, August 31, 1850.

I saw a delicate flower had grown up 2 feet high. *CP.* Appears in journal, September 9, 1850.

To day I climbed a handsome rounded hill. *CP.* Appears in journal, September 6, 1850.

I am the little Irish boy. *CP.* Appears in journal, November 28, 1850.

In Adams fall. *CP.* Appears in journal, February 12, 1851.

Life. *CP.*

The moon moves up her smooth and sheeny path. *CP.*

I'm thankful that my life does not deceive. *CP.*

Manhood. *CP*.

Music. *CP*.

The Just Made Perfect. *CP*.

I do not fear my thoughts will die. *CP*. Appears in journal, November 13, 1851.

I'm contented you should stay. *CP*.

Man man is the Devil. *CP*. Appears in journal, January 3, 1853.

You must not only aim aright. *CP*.

He knows no change who knows the true. *CP*.

When the toads begin to ring. *CP*. Appears in journal, April 26, 1854.

The chicadee. *CP*. Appears in journal, November 8, 1857.

'Twas 30 years ago. *EHW*, from journal, October 28, 1857, MA 1302:30. Reprinted with permission of the Pierpont Morgan Library, New York. A version of lines 11–18 was included in "Wild Apples."

Forever in my dream & in my morning thought. Appears in journal October 29, 1857. *CP*.

Except, returning, by the Marlboro. Manuscript, New York Public Library, with papers related to manuscript "The Dispersion of Seeds." Reprinted with permission of the New York Public Library, Berg Collection, Astor, Lenox, and Tilden Foundations.

The Rosa Sanguinea. *CP*.

Any fool can make a rule. *CP*. Appears in journal, February 3, 1860.

All things decay. *CP*. Appears in journal, March 25, 1860.

The standards for American English continue to fluctuate and in some ways are now conspicuously different from what they were in earlier periods. In nineteenth-century writing a word might be spelled in more than one way even in the same work. Commas (and other punctuation) were sometimes used expressively to suggest the movement of voice; capitals were sometimes meant to give added significance to a word or phrase. Because modernization would remove such effects, this volume preserves the texts as they were originally printed. In addition this volume is concerned with only the texts of the works chosen for inclusion; it does not attempt to reproduce features of typographic design or layout, such as display capitalization of chapter openings. The text is presented without change, even when it appears to be inconsistent or irregular; typographical errors, however, have been corrected. Footnotes within the text are those supplied by Thoreau. Open contractions are retained if they appear in the original version.

The following is a list of pages where a stanza break coincides with the foot of the page (except where such breaks are apparent from the regular stanzaic structure of the poem): 568, 752, 1051, 1059, 1060,

1071, 1072, 1079, 1097, 1114, 1117, 1120, 1121, 1126, 1128, 1146, 1150, 1162.

In addition to a customary reference to other printed versions of the text, the list of typographical errors corrected in this volume was determined by reference to certain extant documents: for *Walden*, Thoreau's marked proof for the first edition; for *The Maine Woods*, Thoreau's journal (Pierpont Morgan and New York Public libraries), his marked set of the *Union Magazine* printing of "Ktaadn, and the Maine Woods" (New York Public Library), a fragmentary fair-copy manuscript for *The Atlantic Monthly* printing of "Chesuncook" (Harvard University's Houghton Library), and the fragments of the last draft of "Allegash" at the Huntington and Houghton libraries.

These materials were used to detect both simple typographical errors and the unintentional alterations of Thoreau's texts that were to a certain extent inevitable, given his handwriting, his tendency to continue to revise his work on page proofs, and the fact that most of his books were prepared for publication after he could no longer supervise or proofread them. Intentional, systematic changes such as house styling were considered features of the editions reprinted here —so, for example, an editor's or compositor's preference for "farther" over Thoreau's "further" or Sophia's expansion of Thoreau's characteristic abbreviations are allowed to stand.

Of the manuscripts, the *Walden* page proofs are very significant insofar as no document intervened between these proofs and the text of the first edition presented here. In this case, as with the extant fragments of the "Allegash" draft, the author's last word exists, and it is thus possible to distinguish the copyist's or compositor's errors and omissions from authorial revisions.

The following is a list of typographical errors corrected, cited by page and line number: 19.20, post; 33.7, fail, or the; 39.40, cornice,; 41.29, timber,; 43.26, fingers? . . . ; 45.30, manure whatever; 46.10, There; 47.33–34, oxen, cows,; 53.17, named.; 55.24, all—; 55.26, neck—; 59.7–8, not proportionally more expensive than; 67.26, orchard, woodlot,; 67.36, place; 68.16, [line not indented]; 69.36, day; 78.7, Kieou-he-yu; 79.28, reality that; 86.33, on to; 93.13, *cerasus*; 93.18, *rhus*; 95.21, beneficent as; 95.36, plough plough; 100.11, by; 101.33, wood-side;; 104.31, gate—; 108.26, issue,; 110.32, tolerable; 111.24, north star; 124.16–17, occcasionally; 132.8, particular,; 132.10, farmers,; 132.25, small,; 133.20, orchards,; 134.2, ground:; 139.6, road; 145.13, neighborhood; 150.20, over it, and the peetweets; 163.32, *celtis*; 166.12, tight, light,; 174.31, carniverous; 185.7, nearer; 185.8, attention,; 194.9, masonry; 212.6, them,; 220.16, gratui/tous; 220.27, brisk; 221.26, which,; 221.28, and,; 232.8, have; 237.15, was,—; 247.38–39, —*labium*, from *labor* (?)—; 251.8, as in; 252.20, Nabathacaque;

257.27, eye right; 266.28, might, perhaps,; 281.18, canalès; 288.16, villagers; 290.39, ceilings; 308.22, our question; 314.25, land, still; 337.6, Manhegan; 339.21, Moose-horns; 346.19, name, one or; 351.40, thus; 352.23, chickadee; 366.20, *Katahdinauquoh*; 371.36, be there,—the; 386.4, character; 391.40, poet's; 393.14, on the; 393.15, told me; 395.4, provisions; 396.16, Pistigouche; 398.6, singing; 398.7, season; 402.19, *ne*; 403.23, lake, she; 408.22, (the *V. Pennsylvanicum*); 415.14, exactly; 418.3, he, 423.11, white-beaked; 426.1, [The figure of a bear in a boat.]; 426.3, *Niasoseb.*; 426.4, Joseph.; 426.5, *clioi*; 426.9, *ouke*; 426.11, quambi; 428.3, *Caucomgomoc-took!* there; 435.2, narrowest point; 435.15, nearest bend; 443.32, Tebos; 447.16, main hardly; 447.16–17, washing and; 447.23, northeasterly; 447.35, not intend; 449.25, life.; 453.33, abundant.; 453.33–34, *minatus*; 453.34–35, *margaraticea*; 463.33–34, *Madunkchunk*; 463.34–35, *Madunkchunk-gamooc*; 466.29, paths; 472.14, without rocks; 476.29, ripple; 476.37, loon; 477.9, crushing; 478.24, scarred; 480.18–21, high. Richardson; 481.5–6, Madunkchunk; 481.14, water and forks; 481.16, more arable parts; 481.29, ridge; 486.1, [72 lines transposed to 494.4–495.36]; 486.28, tnat; 487.30, lodges; 492.6, told me; 493.37, Rocks (locks); 498.19, Matanancook; 501.27–28, accord/ing; 502.10, stage or the boat; 505.16, 1858; 510.27, Cham/berlain; 515.14, *monocea*; 517.35, Schoonis; 519.5, *albicola*; 520.33, *Mt.*; 520.34, *Kitadaügan*; 521.14, *Ibibimin*; 521.17, ceinture."; 521.19, *Ouaürinaügamek*; 522.9, *Bematruichtik*; 522.9, *Mt.*; 522.32, *Pagadaükoueouérré*; 522.34, *Bororquasis*; 522.37, *Apmoojeuegamook*; 523.17, *Paüsidaükioui*; 523.20, *Ouramaü*; 523.21, ho,; 523.22–23, *Saüghedétegoue*; 523.24, *saüktaüoui*; 524.36, *Telasiuis*; 525.3, *Schunk*; 525.5, Schunk; 525.10, *Schunk-auke*; 550.25, skiful; 573.14, side, is by; 577.14, attis; 579.22, Massachussets; 624.36, phæbes; 634.37, fair-weather-and foul; 635.40, essentiais; 636.28, ascends; 656.18, even crystal; 687.4, "*he*; 748.40, slavery, but; 881.30, Where-/ever; 891.37, Message,; 940.6, dont; 955.30–31, as certained; 958.5, the of; 962.40, *leuco pus*; 964.40, dissemminating; 965.11, cheeck-pouches; 969.11, farmers; 994.15, Oinan; 999.8–9, sphagneous; 1003.6, exhilirating; 1007.2, testimomony; 1009.19, Raslles; 1026.27, salvages; 1050.13, whereso'eer.

Notes

In the notes below, the reference numbers denote page and line of this volume (the line count includes chapter headings). No note is made for material included in standard desk-reference books such as Webster's *Collegiate*, *Biographical*, and *Geographical* dictionaries. Biblical quotations are keyed to the King James Version. Quotations from Shakespeare are keyed to *The Riverside Shakespeare*, ed. G. Blakemore Evans (Boston: Houghton Mifflin, 1974). For further biographical information than is contained in the Chronology, see William Ellery Channing II, *Thoreau, the Poet-Naturalist*, enlarged edition, edited by Franklin B. Sanborn (Boston: Charles E. Goodspeed, 1902); Edward Waldo Emerson, *Henry Thoreau as Remembered by a Young Friend* (Boston: Houghton Mifflin, 1917); Steven Fink, *Prophet in the Marketplace: Thoreau's Development as a Professional Writer* (Princeton: Princeton University Press, 1992); Walter Harding, *The Days of Henry Thoreau*, revised edition (Princeton: Princeton University Press, 1982); Richard Lebeaux, *Young Man Thoreau* (Amherst: University of Massachusetts Press, 1977); Richard Lebeaux, *Thoreau's Seasons* (Amherst: University of Massachusetts Press, 1984); Robert D. Richardson, Jr., *Henry Thoreau: A Life of the Mind* (Berkeley: University of California Press, 1986). For textual background see the Princeton University Press edition of *The Writings of Henry D. Thoreau: Walden*, edited by J. Lyndon Shanley (1971); *The Maine Woods*, edited by Joseph J. Moldenhauer (1972); *Reform Papers*, edited by Wendell Glick (1973); *Early Essays and Miscellanies*, edited by Joseph J. Moldenhauer, Edwin Moser, and Alexander Kern (1975). Notes at the foot of the page in the text are Thoreau's own.

WALDEN
7.13–14   Inde . . . nati]   Ovid, *Metamorphoses*, I, 414–15. The translation (7.16–18) is from Sir Walter Raleigh, *History of the World.*

10.23–27   Evelyn . . . neighbor."]   John Evelyn, *Silva, or a Discourse of Forest-Trees* (1664).

10.34–36   "be not . . . undone?"]   *The Vishñu Puráña*, tr. H. H. Wilson (London, 1840).

11.35–37   "To . . . knowledge."]   *Confucian Analects*, Bk. II, ch. 17.

12.40–13.1   "to . . . roasting."]   Charles Darwin, *Journal of Researches . . . during the Voyage of H.M.S. Beagle* (New York, 1846).

19.15   tare and tret]   Tare is a deduction from gross weight made for the weight of the container; tret is a further deduction of four pounds from every 104 pounds.

20.34–36   "was now . . . clothes."] Madam Ida Pfeiffer, *A Lady's Voyage Round the World* (New York, 1852).

24.8–13   "The Laplander . . . people."] Samuel Laing, *Journal of a Residence in Norway* (London, 1837).

26.9–18   "The best . . . houses."] Daniel Gookin (1612–87), *Historical Collections of the Indians of New England.*

27.8–9   Rumford fireplace] A non-smoking stove named for its inventor, Benjamin Thompson, Count Rumford (1753–1814).

27.9   back plastering] Plaster between the exterior and interior walls.

28.3   the poor . . . with you] Matthew 26:11.

28.4–5   the fathers . . . edge?] Ezekiel 18:2.

28.6–7   "As I . . . Israel."] Ezekiel 18:3.

28.8–10   "Behold . . . die."] Ezekiel 18:4.

29.3   suent] Running smoothly.

29.7   springe] In several earlier drafts, "spring."

29.12–15   Chapman . . . air."] George Chapman (1559?–1634), *The Tragedy of Caesar and Pompey*, V, ii.

29.19–21   "had . . . avoided;"] John Lempriere, *Bibliotheca Classica* (New York, 1842), "Momus."

30.4   "silent poor."] People who were silent about their poverty in order to avoid the poorhouse. A fund was established in Concord in the eighteenth century to help them.

31.11   glow-shoes] Variant spelling of galoshes.

33.16   Johnson . . . Providence,"] Edward Johnson, *A History of New-England.*

33.28–34.8   "those . . . thousands."] In E. B. O'Callaghan, *The Documentary History of New York* (Albany, 1851).

44.17–18   Flying Childers] A famous eighteenth-century English racehorse.

52.29–32   "Panem . . . testu."] *De Agri Cultura*, ch. 74.

53.17–20   "For . . . chips."] Anonymous poem in John Warner Barber, *Historical Collections . . . of . . . Massachusetts* (Worcester, 1839).

56.5   "The evil . . . them."] Shakespeare, *Julius Caesar*, III, ii, 76.

56.20–57.3   "busk . . . themselves."] William Bartram, *Travels through North and South Carolina* . . . (*Philadelphia*, 1791).

57.4–6   The Mexicans . . . end.] See William H. Prescott, *History of the Conquest of Mexico* (New York, 1843), Bk. I, ch. 4.

57.37   flocks of Admetus.] When Apollo was banished from heaven, he was forced to tend the flocks of Admetus, King of Pherae, for nine years.

61.27   Howard] John Howard (1726–90), English prison reformer.

66.3–29   "Thou . . . Carew.] Thomas Carew (?1595–?1645), *Coelum Britannicum*, ll. 642–68.

68.15–16   "I . . . dispute."] William Cowper (1731–1800), "Verses Supposed to be Written by Alexander Selkirk."

70.28–29   "An abode . . . seasoning."] M. A. Langlois (tr.), *Harivansa, ou Histoire de la Famille de Hari* (Paris, 1834); Thoreau's translation from French. "Harivamsa," or "genealogy of the god Hari (Krishna)" is a supplement to the Sanskrit epic *Mahabharata*.

72.14–15   "There . . . Damodara,] See note 70.28–29. Damodara is one of the names for Krishna.

72.32–35   "There . . . by."] Fragment of an anonymous Jacobean poem set to music by Robert Jones (fl. 1616) in *The Muses Garden for Delights*. Also in Thomas Evans, *Old Ballads* (London, 1810).

73.5–6   "Renew . . . again."] Confucius, *The Great Learning*, "Commentary of the Philosopher Tsang."

75.4   "glorify . . . forever."] From the opening lines of "The Shorter Catechism," in *The New England Primer*, the seventeenth-century Calvinist schoolbook.

78.7–15   "Kieou-pe-yu . . . messenger!"] *Confucian Analects*, Bk. XIV, ch. 26.

80.18   Nilometer] An ancient Egyptian instrument for measuring the rise of the Nile, or, generally, a graduated scale cut in rock to measure a river's height.

82.23–27   Mîr . . . doctrines."] M. Garcin de Tassy, *Histoire de la Littérature Hindoui* (Paris, 1839). Mîr Camar Uddîn Mast was an eighteenth-century Hindu poet.

88.32   tit-men] Dwarfs. "Titman" is a regionalism for the smallest pig in a litter.

90.18   "Olive-Branches"] The *Olive Branch* was a Methodist weekly published in Boston.

92.5–8   "for . . . day."] Pfeiffer, *A Lady's Voyage*. The Puri Indians were natives of eastern Brazil.

94.13–15   "In truth . . . Concord."] Channing, "Walden Spring," ll. 30–32, in *The Woodman and Other Poems* (Boston, 1849).

97.7   Buena Vista] Battlefield during the Mexican War, 1847.

99.16–17   "to be . . . ammiral."] Milton, *Paradise Lost*, I, 293–94.

102.29   single spruce] Thoreau changed "single" (white) spruce to "double" (black) spruce in a copy of the book.

106.20–21   "the world . . . me,"] Thomas Gray, "Elegy Written in a Country Churchyard" (1751), l. 4.

107.28–30   "Mourning . . . Toscar."] *Croma*, ll. 52–54, in Patrick Mac-Gregor, *The Genuine Remains of Ossian* (London, 1841).

109.9–18   "How vast . . . sides."] Confucius, *The Doctrine of the Mean*, XVI, 1–3.

109.22–24   "Virtue . . . neighbors."] *Confucian Analects*, Bk. IV, ch. 25.

109.29   Indra] Hindu god of air, rain, thunder, and earth.

112.21   old Parrs] Thomas Parr was an Englishman who reportedly lived from 1483 to 1635, 152 years.

116.11–14   "Arrivéd . . . has."] Spenser, *The Faerie Queene*, I, canto I, stanza 35.

116.20–117.5   "He laid . . . respect.] Edward Winslow, *A Relation or Journall of the Beginning and Proceedings of the English Plantation Setled at Plimouth in New England* (London, 1622), better known as *Mourt's Relation*.

117.30–35   "Why . . . grieve."] *Iliad*, XVI, 8, 16–19.

123.34   the fox in the fable] Aesop's "The Cock and the Fox."

125.15–16   "Welcome . . . Englishmen!"] The Indian Samoset's legendary greeting to the Pilgrims at Plymouth.

127.34   *agricola laboriosus*] Hard-working farmer.

128.16–17   Mr. Coleman's report] Rev. Henry Colman (1785–1849) was commissioned in 1837 to make an agricultural survey of Massachusetts. His four extensive reports were published by the state from 1838 to 1841. Colman went on to publish studies of British and European agriculture.

128.28   *Rans des Vaches*] A Swiss cowherd's song.

130.7   canker-rash] Sore throat.

131.35–132.3   "there . . . improvement."] John Evelyn, *Terra: a Philosophical Discourse of Earth* (London, 1729).

132.8–9   Mr. Coleman]   See note 128.16–17.

132.21–22   patrem . . . oportet]   The master should have the selling habit, not the buying habit. Cato, *De Agri Cultura*, ch. 2.

134.3–4   "And as . . . again,"]   Frances Quarles, "The Shepherd's Oracles," Eclogue V.

134.26   (*maximeque pius questus,*)]   Cato, *De Agri Cultura*, Introduction.

134.27–30   "called . . . Saturn."]   Varro, *Rerum Rusticarum*, III, i.

136.22   Redding & Company's]   Boston bookseller.

137.27–29   "loudly . . . danger."]   Apollonius Rhodius (late third or early second century B.C.), *Argonautica*, 4, 903.

138.6   "as I sailed."]   From "Ballad of Captain Robert Kidd."

140.19–22   "Nec . . . request."]   *Elegies of Tibullus*, 3, 7–8; quoted in John Evelyn, *Silva*.

140.23–27   "You who . . . bends."]   *Confucian Analects*, Bk. XII, ch. 19.

149.11   Boiling Spring]   A bubbling spring west of Walden.

149.29   breams]   Thoreau inserted "*Pomotis obesus*" in a copy of the book.

150.5   *reticulatus*]   Net-like.

150.6   *guttatus*]   Speckled.

150.20   kingfishers . . . it]   In a copy of the book, Thoreau revised this phrase, which was omitted from the first edition, to "kingfishers dart away from its coves."

156.18   Moore . . . Deep Cut]   "But More of More-Hall, with nothing at all,/He slew the dragon of Wantley." From "The Dragon of Wantley," in Percy's *Reliques*. The Deep Cut had been dug in a hillside between Walden and Concord for the railroad.

159.38   "still . . . resounds."]   William Drummond, "Icarus," l. 10, in *Madrigals and Epigrams* (1616).

163.10   white-spruce]   Thoreau changed this to "black spruce" in a copy of the book.

164.30–35   "Thy . . . about."]   Channing, "Baker Farm," ll. 1–6. Channing included this poem, written in 1848, in his *Thoreau: The Poet Naturalist*.

164.37   musquash]   Indian name for muskrat.

165.15–18   "And here . . . steers."]   Channing, "Baker Farm," ll. 36–38.

168.22–35   "Landscape . . . trees!"]   Channing, "Baker Farm," ll. 11–12, 21–22, and 78–87.

172.1–2   "yave . . . men."]   Chaucer, in the Prologue to *Canterbury Tales*, ll. 177–78, describing the Monk, not the Nun.

174.3–9   "some . . . fly,"]   William Kirby and William Spence, *An Introduction to Entomology* (Philadelphia, 1846).

176.10–14   "he who . . . distress."]   Rajah Rammohun Roy, *Translation of Several . . . of the Veds* (London, 1832).

1/0.20–23   "The soul . . . food."]   Confucius, *The Great Learning*, "Commentary of the Philosopher Tsang," ch. 7.

177.22–25   "That . . . carefully."]   *Works of Mencius*, Bk. IV ("Le Low"), pt. II, ch. 19.

177.27–30   "A command . . . God."]   Roy, *Translation*.

178.7–13   "How . . . worse."]   Donne, "To Sire Edward Herbert at Iulyers."

182.38   Pilpay]   Also known as Bidpai; reputed author of East Indian animal fables. See *The Dial*, III (1842), 82–85.

183.5   wild native kind]   Thoreau inserted "(*Mus leucopus*)" in a copy of the book.

187.32   Kirby and Spence]   See note 174.3–9.

195.31   keeping-room]   New England term for sitting room.

195.34–36   "cellam. . . erit,"]   Cato, *De Agri Cultura*, ch. 3.

198.27–28   cadis worms]   Larva of the mayfly and others that live in water and form cylindrical cases.

201.16–20   "the encroachments . . . *forestæ*, &c.,"]   William Gilpin, *Remarks on Forest Scenery* (Edinburgh, 1834).

201.31–35   consecrated . . . children, &c.]   Cato, *De Agri Cultura*, ch. 139.

202.3–7   "nearly . . . plains."]   F. Andrew Michaux, *North American Sylva*, edition of 1819.

202.30   "jump"]   To flatten the head by heating and pounding, thus pinching the handle.

205.1–19   "Never . . . talked."]   Ellen Sturgis Hooper (1816–48), "The Wood-Fire." See *The Dial*, I (1840), 193. Thoreau wrote "Mrs. Hooper" after this poem in a copy of the book.

209.13   "tub,"]   Hand-drawn fire truck.

209.16–19   Gondibert . . . powder."]   Sir William Davenant (1606–68), "Author's Preface" to *Gondibert: An Heroic Poem*.

210.2   "rider."]   Top rail of the fence.

211.32–33   "fate . . . absolute,"]   Milton, *Paradise Lost*, II, 560.

214.28   meadow mouse]   Thoreau changed this to "deer mouse" in a copy of the book.

216.1   "How. . . serenity!"]   Thomas Storer (1571–1604), *The Life and Death of Thomas Wolsey*, Sec. 2, stanza 77, l. 5.

217.9–12   "The house-holder . . . guest."]   See note 10.34–36.

228.7   fear-naughts]   Thick wool coats.

231.27–32   "a bay . . . appeared!]   William Gilpin, *Observations on . . . the High-lands of Scotland* (London, 1808).

231.33–35   So high . . . waters—."]   Milton, *Paradise Lost*, VII, 288–90.

240.1   periplus of Hanno]   The report of the Carthaginian Hanno on his exploration of the west coast of Africa in 480 B.C.

240.1   Ternate and Tidore]   Spice Islands in the Dutch East Indies.

248.16   lights]   Lungs of a slaughtered animal.

250.7–8   "et primitus . . . evocate,"]   Varro, *Rerum Rusticarum*, II, ii: "and the grass which is called forth by the early rains is just growing."

252.20–31   "Eurus . . . heaven."]   Ovid, *Metamorphoses*, I, 61–2, 78–81.

253.5–6   While . . . return.]   Cf. Isaac Watts, *Hymns and Spiritual Songs*, Bk. I, Hymn 88: "And while the lamp . . . return."

253.27–254.2   "A return . . . man?"]   *Words of Mencius*, Bk. VI, "Kaou Tsze," pt. I, ch. 8.

254.3–15   "The Golden . . . seed."]   Ovid, *Metamorphoses*, I, 89–96, 107–8.

256.30   "rills . . . lotus."]   Calidas, *Sacontalá; or The Fatal Ring*, tr. Sir William Jones. Speech of Dushmanta, Act V.

257.27–30   "Direct . . . home-cosmography."]   William Habington, "To My Honoured Friend Sir Ed. P. Knight," in *Castara* (1634).

258.24–25   "Erret . . . viæ."]   Adapted from Claudian, "De Sene Veronensi," ll. 21–22. Thoreau changed "Iberos" (Iberians) to "Australians."

259.8–14   "to ascertain . . . resolve."]   Thoreau copied this anecdote from *Harper's New Monthly*, I (October 1850) into his journal for July 21, 1851.

261.11–14   "They . . . Vedas;"]   M. Garcin de Tassy, *Histoire de la Littérature Hindoui* (Paris, 1839). Thoreau's translation.

262.7–263.3   There was . . . wonderful?]   In the *Bhagavad-Gita*, Kooroo is a nation, and Kalpa is the period between the creation and destruction of the world, reportedly over four billion years. A day and night, to Brahma, is one Kalpa. See *The Dial*, III (1843), 332.

263.38–264.1   "From . . . thought."]   *Confucian Analects*, Bk. 9, ch. 25.

264.4–5   "and lo! . . . view."]   Joseph Blanco White (1775–1841), Sonnet: "To Night."

264.29–30   Mameluke bey.]   In 1811 the Turkish viceroy of Egypt ordered the massacre of all the Mamelukes, a military caste. One leaped from the citadel to his horse and fled to Syria.

265.4   kittlybenders.]   children's game of running across thin ice.

265.16   furrowing]   Furring.

THE MAINE WOODS

274.13   clothing and articles]   Thoreau's annotated copy of the *Union Magazine* printing of "Ktaadn" has "clothing and other articles."

276.37–38   Passadumkeag . . . implies]   See Appendix, 524.24.

282.18–19   Province man]   A man from the Canadian province of New Brunswick.

284.28–30   "Village . . . blood,"]   Phrases from lines 57–60 of Gray's "Elegy Written in a Country Churchyard."

284.31–34   "Perchance . . . lyre."]   Gray, "Elegy," ll. 45–48.

289.14   idle]   In the *Union Magazine* version, "idler."

300.21–22   "Row . . . past!"]   Thomas Moore (1779–1852), "The Canadian Boat Song," ll. 5–6.

300.28–33   "Why . . . sson."]   Moore, "Boat Song," ll. 7–10 and 13–14.

301.1–2   "Saint . . . airs!"]   Moore, "Boat Song," ll. 15–16.

304.23   feruled]   Ferruled; wrapped with a metal ring or cap.

304.33   Michaux]   François André Michaux (1770–1855), whose *Histoire des Arbres Forestiers de l'Amérique Septentrionale* (translated as *The North American Sylva*) is quoted here and below.

304.40   Springer]   John S. Springer, whose *Forest Life and Forest Trees* (New York, 1851) Thoreau quotes here and below.

305.21   drawn]   In one English edition of Michaux's *The North American Sylva* (Philadelphia, 1855), the sentence reads: "The logs are not sawn the first year."

307.4   outlet]   Possibly Thoreau meant "inlet."

308.39–40   there . . . least] Thoreau probably intended "of the whole Penobscot River" to modify "a perpendicular fall" rather than "the worst place." His 1846 journal has: "As near as I can remember there was a perpendicular fall here of the whole Penobscot River 2 or 3 feet at least."

313.10–11   "qu'en . . . chaude."] Marc Lescarbot, *Histoire de la Nouvelle France* (Paris, 1612): "that they would put the kettle on the fire and catch enough fish for dinner before the water was hot."

318.24–26   "Nigh . . . flying."] Milton, *Paradise Lost*, II, 940–42.

321.6–10   "Chaos . . . light."] *Paradise Lost*, II, 970–74.

327.14   Hodge] The quotations from James Hodge, here and below, are from Charles T. Jackson, *Maine Geological Survey* (Augusta, 1838), also the source for quotations from Jackson.

359.15–18   [Indeed, . . . woods.]] This sentence, which did not appear in earlier versions, appears with brackets in the first edition.

370.15–16   Aroostook or Penobscot war] The Aroostook War was the name given to a boundary dispute over timberlands between Maine and New Brunswick in 1839. The Penobscot War could refer to the long conflict, 1631–1759, between England and France over a trading post on the Penobscot Peninsula, or to the attempt by Massachusetts to take it from the British in 1779.

372.14   Arnold's expedition] Benedict Arnold's attempt to capture Quebec in 1775 was one of the boldest expeditions of the American Revolution.

375.11–12   With, . . . 1588] John White (or Wyth, or With) was a member of the Roanoke Island colony. His watercolors, the first European paintings of life in America, were the basis of engravings in Théodore de Bry's *Collectio Peregrinationum* (Collection of Voyages), published in Frankfurt-on-Main, 1590–1629, which also had illustrations of the Brazilian *boucan*. Thoreau's "1588" is probably an error for "1590."

376.8   hylodes] A "genus of American toads" (*Oxford English Dictionary*), or a "large genus of New World frogs" (Mitford M. Matthews, *Dictionary of Americanisms*, 1951). Both cite this passage.

376.40   Paugus] A war-chief of the Pequawkets killed at Lovewell's Fight.

378.33   Father Rasles] Father Sébastien Rasles (also spelled Rale, Rasle, and Ralle), 1652–1724, was a missionary to the Abnaki people at Norridgewock from 1694 until his death in an English raid on the village. His *Dictionary of the Abnaki Language*, stolen in the raid, was published in 1833 as the first volume of the *Memoirs of the American Academy of Arts and Sciences*. Thoreau used it extensively in preparing the Appendix to *The Maine Woods*.

380.12   Josselyn]   John Josselyn, *An Account of Two Voyages to New-England* (1674).

380.26   Cusabesex]   "Cusabexsex" in Thoreau's journal for 1853.

382.23   at once.]   The 1858 *Atlantic Monthly* version adds the following passage:
At the carry-man's camp I saw many little birds, brownish and yellowish, with some white tail-feathers, hopping on the wood-pile, in company with the slate-colored snow-bird, (*Fringilla hiemalis*,) but more familiar than they. The lumberers said that they came round their camps, and they gave them a vulgar name. Their simple and lively note, which was heard in all the woods, was very familiar to me, though I had never before chanced to see the bird while uttering it, and it interested me not a little, because I had had many a vain chase in a spring-morning in the direction of that sound, in order to identify the bird. On the 28th of the next month. (October,) I saw in my yard, in a drizzling day, many of the same kind of birds flitting about amid the weeds, and uttering a faint *chip* merely. There was one full-plumaged Yellow-crowned Warbler (*Sylva coronata*) among them, and I saw that the others were the young birds of that season. They had followed me from Moosehead and the North. I have since frequently seen the full-plumaged ones while uttering that note in the spring.

389.23   top]   In Thoreau's source, William Gilpin's *Observations on the Western Parts of England* (London, 1808), "tops."

398.5   hylodes]   See note 376.8.

400.17   cunningly.]   In his journal, Thoreau notes here: "The Indian thought that the mother had perhaps been killed."

411.33–34   "a pagan . . . creed"]   Wordsworth, "The World is Too Much with Us," l. 10.

419.22   Wrangel]   Ferdinand Petrovitch Wrangel, *Narrative of an Expedition to the Polar Sea* (London, 1840).

422.12   Eastham]   Eastham, Massachusetts, was famous as a site for revival meetings.

426.2   July 26,]   The first edition has the words "[The figure of a bear in a boat.]" instead of the sketch above, which is reproduced from Thoreau's journal draft.

428.32   kingfisher (tweezer bird)]   Since "tweezer bird" is not another name for kingfisher, the parentheses, also in Thoreau's journal, may indicate that Thoreau considered deleting the name.

430.29–30   "the turpentine . . . pork-bag."]   "Arnold's Letters on his Expedition to Canada in 1775," *Maine Historical Society Collections*, 3rd ser., I (1831).

444.5   Paugus] See note 376.40.

447.38   by good rights] These words appear within quotation marks in Thoreau's last draft of the passage.

448.38–40   When . . . university.] In Thoreau's last draft of the passage, this sentence, inserted in the margin, is in his sister Sophia's handwriting.

454.33–34   forks of the Nickatou] Since Nickatou is an island, not a river, the journal reading "forks at Nickatou" is more appropriate.

460.23–24   on a deserted log] In Thoreau's journal, the bread is found in a "deserted log hut."

463.11   Montresor] Col. John Montresor (1736–99). See *Maine Historical Society Collections*, 3rd ser., I.

472.14   not of rocks] Thoreau's journal draft of the passage has "trees (not of rocks)."

480.18–21   high, . . . Richardson] The first edition omits the words between "thirty-five feet high" and "Richardson." In the last-draft manuscript, the word "high" occurs in the same position in the line several lines apart; probably the copyist or compositor accidentally skipped down.

491.7–13   "and so . . . it."] Jérôme Lalemant, in *Relation de ce qui s'est passé en la Nouvelle France en les années 1661 et 1662* (Paris, 1663).

508.3–4   (Those . . . woods.)] In the list in Thoreau's journal, five more plants than those asterisked here are marked for special treatment: *Betula alba* (508.23), *Vaccinium corymbosum* (509.18), *A lemna* (513.17), *Galeopsis tetrahit* (514.13), and *Lobelia Dartmanna* (514.36).

520.33   Rale] See note 378.33.

522.12–13   (Williamson . . . (Hodge.)] This punctuation does not make clear that William D. Williamson is the authority for the definition "flint," while James Hodge is Thoreau's source for deriving the name *Kineo* from that of an old Indian hunter.

ESSAYS

529.6–7   "Ipse . . . nostrum."] "I half pagan / Bring my verses to the shrine of the poets." (Thoreau's translation.)

529.32–33   *particeps criminis*] Party to the crime; an accomplice.

531.1–3   "Haud . . . voto."] "It is not easy for every one to take murmurs and low / Whispers out of the temples, and live with open vow." (Thoreau's translation.)

531.23–25   "Est aliquid . . . vivis?"] "Is there anything to which thou tendest, and against which thou directest thy bow? / Or dost thou pursue crows, at random, with pottery or clay, / Careless whither thy feet bear thee, and live *ex tempore?*" (Thoreau's translation.)

532.26–27   "Stat . . . agendo."] "Reason opposes, and whispers in the secret ear, / That it is not lawful to do that which one will spoil by doing." (Thoreau's translation.)

534.3–4   Spes . . . hope.] *Aeneid*, Book XI.

534.18–21   "bearing . . . wish."] Aeschylus, *The Seven Against Thebes*.

535.16   "Discretion . . . soul,"] John Donne, "To the Countesse of Bedford (Honour Is So Sublime Perfection)" (c. 1600), line 40.

535.24   colures] Two large circles that intersect at right angles at the poles.

537.8   "made Fortune sirname to Fortitude,"] Plutarch, *Morals*, IV.

537.11–12   *vir summae fortis*] Man of highest courage.

537.12–13   "carry Caesar and Caesar's fortune."] According to Plutarch, Caesar was a hidden passenger on a boat when a storm caused the captain to order the vessel turned around. Caesar revealed himself to the captain and convinced him to proceed through the storm, saying, "Go on, my friend, and fear nothing; you carry Caesar and his fortune in your boat."

537.17–18   "Tumble . . . yet."] Robert Herrick, "To Fortune," lines 1–2.

538.2–5   "things terrestrial . . . right hand."] Plutarch, *Morals*, II.

539.33–40   "Plato . . . agreement."] Plutarch, *Morals*, I.

541.4–5   "What's brave . . . Roman fashion."] *Antony and Cleopatra*, IV.xv.87.

541.9   cope] The firmament.

541.18   Idomeneus] Cretan king, son of Minos, who fights against the Trojans in the *Iliad*.

541.21   bay of Aulis] Harbor where the ships of the Greek fleet assembled before sailing to Troy.

542.15–20   —returns . . . Surrounds—] Milton, *Paradise Lost*, Book III, lines 41–46.

542.34–36   "Sit not down . . . unto God."] From Sir Thomas Browne, *A Letter to a Friend*, published posthumously in 1690.

543.10–12   before . . . close] Milton, *Paradise Lost*, Book II, lines 535–37.

544.30–31   Guido's Aurora] "Phoebus and the Hours, Preceded by Aurora," fresco (1613) by the Bolognese artist Guido Reni (1575–1642).

545.9   Godfrey and Gonzalo] Godfrey of Bouillon (c. 1060–1100), Duke of Lower Lorraine who participated in the First Crusade in 1096; Godfrey is the hero of Torquato Tasso's *Jerusalem Delivered* (1581). Hernandez Gonzalo de Cordoba (1453?–1515), Spanish general and subject of novel *Gonsalve de Cardoue* (1791) by Jean Pierre Claris de Florian.

546.18–19   Isaak Walton and White of Selborne] Isaak Walton (1593–1683), English author of *The Compleat Angler* (1653); Gilbert White (1720–93), English naturalist and curate, author of *The Natural History of Selborne* (1851).

548.11   life-everlasting] American cudweed.

550.9–27   Anacreon's ode . . . like the gods."] This poem and the poem at 551.20–552.3 are from the "Anacreontea," poems incorrectly attributed to Anacreon.

552.9   harrows] Diagonal arrangements of migratory fowl in the air.

552.26   Nuttall] Thomas Nuttall (1786–1859), American botanist and ornithologist, author of *A Manual of the Ornithology of the United States and Canada* (1832–34).

552.37–38   the Argonautic expedition] In Greek legend, the ship *Argo* carried Jason and his companions on a mission to retrieve the Golden Fleece.

553.1   described by Goldsmith] See "The Deserted Village" (1770), line 44: "The hollow-sounding bittern guards its nest."

557.15   Pilpay] Also known as Bidpai, supposed author of a version of the Sanskrit collection of tales the *Panchatantra*.

558.26   Angler's Souvenir] Popular English fisherman's guide (1835) by "P. Fisher Esq.," pseudonym of William Andrew Chatto (1799–1864).

558.28–29   "Can these . . . cloud?"] Shakespeare, *Macbeth*, III.iv.109–10.

561.1   cucullo] Also "cucuyo," the West Indian firefly.

563.18   "winter of *their* discontent"] Cf. Shakespeare, *Richard III*, I.i.1.

566.33   Bigelow] Jacob Bigelow (1786–1879), an American physician, botanist, and author of *Florula Bostoniensis* (1814) and *American Medical Botany* (1817–20).

570.16   Rasselas] Hero of Samuel Johnson's *The History of Rasselas, Prince of Abissinia* (1759), whose home is the Happy Valley.

571.1   rifle] A piece of wood used by mowers to sharpen their scythes.

572.16–17   We could get no further . . . Romæ] The seventh line of Virgil's *Aeneid*.

572.28–32   "He shook . . . the flint."] *Georgics*, Book 1.

572.38   the wars of . . . Lancaster] King Philip's War (1675–76).

573.17   *gelidæ valles*]   Cold valleys.

573.20–21   "The sultry . . . was nigh,"]   William Collins, "Hassan; or the Camel-Driver," from *Persian Eclogues* (1742), lines 7–8.

573.23–25   our fellow-traveller . . . my way."]   Collins, "Hassan; or the Camel-Driver," lines 13–14.

576.24–30   "And he . . . stars."]   Wordsworth, *Peter Bell* (1798), Part First, lines 34–40.

576.31   Helvellyn]   Mountain in the Lake District in England.

577.13–16   Et jam summa . . . high mountains.]   The final lines of Virgil's first eclogue.

580.32–33   the scene of Mrs. Rowlandson's capture]   On February 10, 1676, during King Philip's War, Mary Rowlandson (c. 1635–c. 1678) was captured during a Narrangansett raid on Lancaster and held prisoner for 82 days. She wrote of her captivity in *The Sovereignty & Goodness of God, Together with the Faithfulness of His Promises Displayed; Being a Narrative of the Captivity and Restauration of Mrs. Mary Rowlandson* (1682).

581.2–3   Paugus . . . Church, or Lovell]   Paugus was a war-chief of the Pequawkets killed in King Philip's War; Captain Benjamin Church (1639–1718) and John Lovewell (1691–1725) were prominent soldiers fighting for the Puritans in King Philip's War.

581.11–12   Robin Hood ballads]   Thoreau's source is *Robin Hood: A Collection of All the Ancient Poems, Songs, and Ballads*, compiled by Joseph Ritson (1795).

583.1   *Sir Walter Raleigh*]   Thoreau's source for most of his quotations by Raleigh is *The Works of Sir Walter Raleigh, Kt. now first collected: to which are prefixed the lives of the author by Oldys and Birch*. (8 vols., Oxford: The University Press, 1829).

583.9   the Bayard]   Pierre Terrail, Seigneur de Bayard (c. 1473–1524), French knight and soldier.

587.35–36   the incident of the cloak]   According to tradition, Raleigh spread his cloak in the mud for Queen Elizabeth I to walk over.

589.31   Roger Ashton]   Catholic martyr, executed in 1592.

590.18–19   his connexion . . . prince Henry]   At the request of Prince Henry, the eldest son of James I, Raleigh argued against a proposal to marry Henry and his sister Elizabeth to Spanish royalty. Raleigh wrote in the preface to his *History of the World* that the work was written "for the service of that inestimable Prince Henry."

592.21   watched]   Also "watchet," a shade of light blue.

595.26   Lord Mayor's day]   November 9, when the Lord Mayor and other city dignitaries march in procession to Westminster to receive the Crown's assent to the election.

596.19   Hic Iacet]   "Here lies," a phrase used in epitaphs.

596.24   Fuller]   Thomas Fuller (1608–61), English clergyman and author.

602.22   Syracides]   Joshua ben Sira, author of the Apocryphal Book of Ecclesiasticus. Thoreau quotes Ecclesiasticus 43:16.

603.17   Dubartas']   French Protestant poet (1544–90).

604.1–5   *Inde genus* . . . stony nature are.]   Ovid, *Metamorphoses*, Book I.

611.33   Aubrey]   John Aubrey (1626–97), English author.

614.34–38   *"Largior* . . . stars.]   *Aeneid*, Book VI.

615.30   Alwákidi's Arabian Chronicle]   Chronicle of Moslem conquest of Syria; Thoreau's source for the quotation that follows is the first volume of Simon Ockley's *History of the Saracens* (1708–18).

623.10–11   "The foodless . . . inhabitants."]   James Thomson, "Winter: A Poem" (1726), lines 233–34.

623.22   Plicipennes]   Name given to the caddis fly by French entomologist Pierre Latreille (1762–1833).

626.18   Abu Musa]   Arab alchemist and mystic (c. 721–c. 815).

629.33   "the mower whet his scythe,"]   Milton, "L'Allegro" (1631), line 66.

630.5   *hortus siccus*]   A dry garden; herbarium.

631.31–36   "The snow flakes . . . the waves."]   Homer, *Iliad*, Book XII.

632.4–6   "Drooping . . . toil."]   Thomson, "Winter," lines 228–30.

633.9–12   "The full . . . pole."]   Thomson, "Winter," lines 738–41.

642.26   Hygeian]   Hygeia, Greek goddess of health.

644.3   Hymettus and Hybla]   Sites renowned in antiquity for their honey. Hymettus was a mountain in Attica, Hybla a Sicilian town.

644.8   Columella]   Roman author (1st century A.D.) of treatise on agriculture, *De re rustica*.

655.7–8   "tie up . . . the wind,"]   Sir Thomas Browne, *Christian Morals*, published posthumously in 1716.

655.13–14   George Fox's suit of leather]   George Fox, the founder of the Society of Friends, was known for wearing a leather suit that he was supposed to have made himself.

660.32 The Divine . . . nature] From Euripides' *Orestes*, a translation of the Greek line at 134.31.

662.36 Veeshnoo Sarma] In the July 1842 issue of *The Dial*, Thoreau wrote an introduction to "Extracts from *The Heetopades of Veeshnoo-Sarma*," also known as *The Amicable Instructions of Veeshno Sarma*, translated by Charles Wilkins (1787). The *Heetopades* are instructive fables told by an aged Hindu priest to educate the sons of the king.

665.5–10 "As from the clouds . . . Zeus."] *Iliad*, Book XI.

665.14–24 "While it was dawn . . . rank to rank."] *Iliad*, Book XI.

665.28–666.2 "They, thinking . . . before Ilium."] *Iliad*, Book VIII.

666.5–10 "Went down . . . Olympus."] *Iliad*, Book XV.

666.20–21 The statue of Memnon is cast down] A colossal statue near Thebes was believed to represent Memnon, a son of the goddess of dawn. According to legend, it made a musical sound when struck by rays of the morning sun, said to be Memnon's greeting to his mother. The statue was later destroyed in an earthquake.

668.1–4 "The wrathful . . . move."] *Ca-Lodin*, III, 138–41.

668.13–14 "Mounds . . . years."] *Timora*, VI, 391–92.

668.21–23 "His soul . . . bleak."] *Ca-Lodin*, II, 134–36.

668.26–27 "The weak . . . bend it."] *Fingal*, V, 280–81.

669.5–6 "I straightway . . . verse."] *Oinamoru*, I, 182–83.

669.9–21 "Whence . . . times."] *Ca-Lodin*, II, 137–49.

669.23–28 "Strangers . . . in song.'"] *Carric*, 167–72.

670.1 "Thou . . . ships."] *Ca-Lodin*, I, 125.

670.3–4 "With murmurs . . . moved."] *Ca-Lodin*, II, 132–33.

670.6–8 "dragging . . . it dies."] *Fingal*, III, 252–54.

670.10–11 "A thousand . . . Fingal."] *Garon*, 176–77.

670.15–17 "Thy mother . . . her son."] *Fingal*, VI, 292–94.

670.26–30 "He strode . . . lance."] *Timora*, III, 343–47.

671.1–13 "'My eyes . . . Croma.'"] *Croma*, 195–207.

671.16–17 "How beauteous . . . strength?"] *Garon*, 176–77.

673.38–39 "right as divers . . . to Rome."] From the opening of Chaucer's *A Treatise on the Astrolabe* (c. 1391).

673.39 Testament of Love] Now attributed to Thomas Usk (d. 1388), a contemporary of Chaucer.

675.3   the Black Prince] Edward, Prince of Wales (1453–71).

675.27–28   "For first . . . mouth astart."] From stanza 187 of "The Court of Life," a poem once attributed to Chaucer.

677.20–22   "if that God . . . semeliness."] Chaucer, *The Legend of Good Women* (c. 1385), lines 1039–41.

683.22   *Moses Norris's*] Democratic congressman (1799–1855) from New Hampshire.

683.36   'hinds' feet'] Cf. Habakkuk 3:19, Psalm 18:32–33, and II Samuel 22:34.

683.42   'on Fabyan's White Mountain horn.'] Fabyan is a town in the White Mountains of New Hampshire.

685.26   Webster's plea] Daniel Webster represented relatives of Philadelphia merchant Stephen Girard (1750–1831) who challenged provisions of Girard's will which established a boarding school for white orphan boys. Unsuccessfully arguing the case before the U.S. Supreme Court in 1844, Webster criticized the will's provision excluding clergymen from the school.

685.29   the Comeouters] Abolitionist group that advocated "coming out" of the church because of its toleration of slavery.

685.36   the conflict with Carolina Hayne] In January 1830, Webster opposed Senator Robert Young Hayne (1791–1831) in a series of debates where the topics included slavery, tariffs, and federalism.

686.2   the President's] John Tyler's.

688.1   *Wendell . . . Lyceum*] When the abolitionist Wendell Phillips was invited to speak on the subject of slavery at the Concord Lyceum in 1845, three of the Lyceum's curators resigned in protest. Thoreau, Emerson, and Samuel Barrett replaced them and Phillips delivered his speech on March 11. Thoreau's letter defending Phillips was published in *The Liberator* on March 28.

690.26   Paynim] Pagan or non-Christian, especially Islamic.

690.30   the Red-cross knight] Hero of the first book (1590) of Edmund Spenser's *The Faerie Queene*.

691.13   Edward Irving] Scottish clergyman (1792–1834), whose followers founded the Catholic Apostolic Church.

693.32   moss-troopers] Bandits who made raids along the Scottish border in the 17th century.

695.38   Arethuse] Fountain of the Muses.

696.1   Hercynian forest] Wooded mountains of Thuringia and Bohemia.

698.30   "Lieferung."] Installment.

699.8–9 "sire, . . . revolution."] Reply of Duc de La Rochefoucauld-Laincourt to Louis XVI's statement, "Why, it's only a revolt," upon hearing of the storming of the Bastille.

700.30 "Sauerteig,"] One of Carlyle's ironic personae; others include Dryasdust, Smelfungus, Plugson of Undershot, and Sir Jabesh Windbag.

702.1 Richter's] Jean Paul Friedrich Richter (1763–1825), German writer.

703.13 "Past and Present,"] 1843 book by Carlyle.

703.22 *Opera Omnia*] Complete works.

704.14 dandy pumps] Shoes worn by Victorian men for ballroom dancing.

711.34–35 The condition of England question] Phrase appearing in Carlyle's 1839 pamphlet *Chartism*, which discusses the conflict between the extremes of wealth and poverty resulting from the Industrial Revolution.

713.9–10 reminded of the "Brest Shipping,"] See *The French Revolution*, II.5.iv.

714.2 Jötuns] In the Norse Eddas, the oldest of all living creatures and the main foes of the gods.

714.27 *Oratoris est celare artem*] "The speaker conceals his art," a variation of *Ars est celare artem*, "Art lies in concealing art" (Ovid, *Art of Love*).

715.30–31 "sacred . . . matter"] From Carlyle's *Heroes, Hero-Worship, and the Heroic in History* (1840).

718.24 Serbonian bog] Lake Serbonis in Lower Egypt. See Milton, *Paradise Lost*, Book II, line 592.

719.3 Lubberland] An imaginary land of abundance for those who are lazy.

719.16 Baphometic Baptism] The Templars were accused of worshipping Baphomet, an idol. See Carlyle, *Sartor Resartus* (1833–34), II.vii, "My Spiritual New-birth, or Baphometic Fire-baptism."

723.13 blown his ram's horn about Jericho] Cf. Joshua 6:4–5.

723.16–17 those dibblers of beans on St. George's Hill] On April 16, 1649, a group of twenty to thirty peasants, part of a movement known as "the Diggers," overtook St. George's Hill in Weybridge, Surrey. They established a squatter's colony there, planting parsnips, carrots, and beans to "lay the Foundation of making the Earth a Common Treasury for All, both Rich and Poor."

723.30–31 "Our chief . . . fortitude."] Milton, "To the Lord General Cromwell" (1652), lines 1, 3.

730.39–40   powder-monkeys] Boys employed on ships to carry gunpowder from the powder room to the guns.

731.14–17   "Not a drum . . . we buried."] Charles Wolfe, "The Burial of Sir John Moore at Corunna" (1817).

731.36–37   "stop a hole to keep the wind away"] Shakespeare, *Hamlet*, V.i.214.

732.1–4   "I am . . . the world."] Shakespeare, *King John*, V.ii.79–82.

732.33–733.5   Paley . . . the other."] William Paley, *The Principles of Moral and Political Philosophy*, 2 vols. (1806).

733.19–21   "A drab of state . . . the dirt."] Cyril Tourneur, *The Revenger's Tragedie* (1607), Act V.

740.30–40   Christ . . . to know] See Matthew 22:19–22.

741.19–23   Confucius said . . . of shame."] Thoreau's translation from Jean-Pierre-Guillaume Pauthier, *Confucius et Mencius ou les quatres livres de philosophie moral et politique de la Chine* (Paris: Charpentier, 1841).

745.30   "My Prisons."] Autobiography of Sylvio Pellico (1789–1854), translated into English in 1836.

748.15–20   "We must affect . . . or benefit."] George Peele, *The Battle of Alcazar* (1594), II.ii.425–30.

751.30   Peter the Hermit] Also called Peter of Amiens (c. 1050–1115), French monk and leader of the First Crusade, who made pilgrimages to reclaim Christ's tomb. He is the basis for a character in Tasso's *Jerusalem Delivered* (1581).

752.27   *Ambulator nascitur, non fit*] "The walker is born, not made," adaptation of Latin motto *Poeta nascitur, non fit* ("The poet is born, not made").

752.36–753.4   "When he came . . . donne dere."] Two stanzas from the final eight of Chaucer's "A Gest of Robyn Hode."

753.28–29   Bonaparte may talk . . . courage] As recorded in his memoirs, *Mémorial de Ste-Hélène* (1823), dictated to Emmanuel de Las Cases, Napoleon said, " I have very rarely met with the two o'clock in the morning courage: I mean unprepared courage."

759.6   Varro] Marcus Terentius Varro (116–27 B.C.), Roman author.

757.22   Menu] Menu, or Manu, son of Brahma, the Hindu progenitor of and lawgiver to the human race, to whom is ascribed *Institutes of Hindu Law*, rules governing ritual and daily life, compiled 200 B.C.–A.D. 200.

758.39–40   Gourgas . . . Darby?] F. R. Gourgas, William Lee, Daniel Clark, and Joseph Darby, Concord town officials during the 1840s.

761.31–32 "Than longen folk . . . strondes."] Chaucer, the General Prologue to *The Canterbury Tales*, lines 9–10.

762.10–13 "And now the sun . . . pastures new."] Milton, *Lycidas* (1637), lines 190–93.

762.17 Michaux] François-André Michaux (1770–1855), French botanist and traveler; author of *The North American Sylva* (1819).

764.21 "Westward the star . . . its way."] Cf. George Berkeley, "Verses on the Prospect of Planting Arts and Learning in America" (1752).

765.24 Romulus and Remus] According to Roman legend, twin sons of Mars and Rhea Silvia who were cast into the Tiber to drown, but, protected by the gods, washed ashore and were suckled by a she-wolf. Romulus became the founder of Rome.

766.32 "How near to good is what is fair!"] From the "Song of the Second Priest" in Jonson's masque *Love Freed from Ignorance and Folly* (1616).

773.15–16 stop . . . away] See note 731.36–37.

773.17–19 Confucius . . . tanned."] Cf. *Analects* 12.8.

775.20–21 letters . . . Cadmus invented] In Greek mythology, Cadmus, founder of Thebes, invented the alphabet.

775.25–26 Society . . . Knowledge] Organization founded in Boston in 1829.

776.27 Chaldean Oracles] A prophetic poem written during Marcus Aurelius' rule (A.D. 196–217), attributed to Julianus of Chaldea.

776.36 Vishnu Purana] Hindu sacred texts; Thoreau read H. H. Wilson's 1840 translation *The Vishnu Parána, a System of Hindu Mythology and Tradition*.

777.35 moss-trooper] See note 693.32.

782.4 JOSSELYN'S RARITIES] *New Englands Rarities Discovered* (1672) by the English scientific writer John Josselyn (fl. 1638–75).

784.4–5 "my cousin Westmoreland"] Shakespeare, *Henry V*, IV.iii.18–19.

787.4–5 the Acton Blues] Militia of Acton, Massachusetts.

791.9–10 "Truth never . . . upon him."] Thomas Middleton and William Rowley, *A Fair Quarrel* (1617), III.i.196–97.

794.28 Kalm] Pehr Kalm (1716–1779), Swedish scientist, came to America in 1748 and stayed three years; an account of his journey was translated into English and published as *Travels into North America* (1770–71).

794.34 Hontan] French officer and traveler Louis Armand De Lom D'Arce, Baron de La Hontan (1666–1715) was in Canada intermittently from

1683 to 1693, and published an account of his travels in *Voyages du Baron de La Hontan dans l'Amérique Septentrionale* (1705).

795.9   the spot where . . . 1775]   Major General Richard Montgomery (b. 1736) was killed at the Siege of Quebec, December 31, 1775.

795.35   in his relation]   Accounts of the missionaries in New France to their Superior General in Quebec were published annually in Paris as *Relations de ce qui s'est passé en la Nouvelle France* (1632–73).

796.4–5   Froissart's Chronicles]   The history of Europe from 1325 to 1400 by Jean Froissart (1333?–c. 1405).

796.8   Castle William]   A large round fort on Governor's Island in New York Harbor, completed in 1811.

796.30   bungtown coppers]   Valueless coins.

797.31–32   those lines . . . Verona]   Cf. Roman poet Claudian (A.D. 370–405), *Carmina minores*, 20: "Of an old man of Verona who never left his home."

798.37   bladder-campion]   Common name of *Silene inflata*, named for its inflated calyx.

799.23–25   Olaf Trygesson the Northman . . . his bride]   Olaf Tryggvesson (c. 964–1000), king of Norway, married Gyda, princess of Dublin, and lived in England and Ireland for several years.

800.14   sawing logs pit-fashion]   Using a long two-handed saw, two men, one at the bottom of a pit and the other on a raised platform, saw logs placed over the pit.

800.21–23   Warburton, remarked . . . men]   In *Hochelaga; or, England in the New World* (1846), by George Draught Warburton.

800.39   Charlevoix]   Pierre François Xavier de Charlevoix (1682–1761), French Jesuit missionary and author of *Histoire et Description Générale de la Nouvelle France* (1744).

801.25   Oak Hall]   A large Boston clothing store.

804.28   *Pouvez-vous . . . nuit?*]   Can you give us a bed for the night?

804.34–35   *Y a-t-il . . . ici?*]   Is there an inn here?

804.35   *auberge*]   Inn, hostel.

805.16   literal signification]   "To God."

806.30–31   Roberval's pilot . . . 1542]   The account of Jean Alphonse de Xanctoigne (né Jean de Fonteneau), who guided Jean François de Roberval's fleet up the St. Lawrence River, was published in *Voyages de découverte au Canada, entre les années 1534 et 1542*.

808.2   Bouchette's]   Joseph Bouchette (1774–1841), Canadian geographer.

809.18   *censitaires*]   According to feudal custom, freemen who have obtained legal immunity from servitude by paying "quit-rent."

811.15   *pour la vierge*]   For the virgin.

811.15   *Iniri*]   (*Iesus Nazarenus Rex Iudaeorum*) Jesus of Nazareth, King of the Jews.

812.4   *"Ici git"*]   "Here lies."

812.5   *"Priez pour lui."*]   "Pray for him."

812.6   Père la Chaise]   Père Lachaise, a cemetery in Paris.

812.18–19   *appris . . . dans les États-Unis*]   Learned to speak French in the United States.

812.28   Sir Francis Head]   English traveler and author (1793–1845) who served as lieutenant of Upper Canada from 1835 to 1837.

813.4   according to Richardson]   Sir John Richardson, *Fauna borealiamericana; or The Zoology of the Northern Parts of British America* (1829–37).

813.5   Rupert's Land]   The Hudson Bay Territory, incorporated into Canada in 1870.

816.11   Potherie]   Claude-Charles le Roy Bacqueville de la Potherie (1663–1736), *Histoire de l'Amérique septentrionale* (1722).

819.4   *Friponne*]   A female swindler.

819.40   *Trois quatres lieue*]   Three-quarter league, or about 7½ miles.

823.21   *en roture*]   Obliged to a lord for land.

828.4   dasher]   Dashboard.

831.9–11   those seven . . . the latter]   In Greek mythology, seven princes attempted to install Oedipus' son Polynices as King of Thebes, which was ruled by Polynices' brother Eteocles. Each prince attacked a different gate of the city.

833.22–23   the siege of Jerusalem, and St. Jean d'Acre]   Jerusalem was sacked in A.D. 70. St. Jean d'Acre, now known as Akko, Israel, was battled over during the First and Third Crusades.

834.35–40   Silliman states . . . cold."]   In *Remarks Made on a Short Tour between Hartford and Quebec, in the Autumn of 1819* (1824), by the American chemist, geologist, and physicist Benjamin Silliman (1779–1864).

835.40   wash-leather]   A soft kind of sheepskin leather dressed to imitate chamois leather.

836.18   his essay on the Northmen] *Journal of a Residence in Norway during the years 1834, 1835, & 1836* (1837).

837.27–28   play the game of the Kilkenny cats] Destroy each other. The phrase is derived from a popular limerick; Kilkenny is a city in Ireland.

841.26   fabulous . . . Frislant] Legendary islands that appeared on early maps of the North Atlantic. On his 1542 voyage to the New World, Roberval, enraged at his niece's affair with one of his officers, banished the couple and a nurse to an island off the coast of Newfoundland. The officer, the nurse, and the child of the couple died there; Marguerite was rescued two years and five months after her banishment. She told her story, in which she claimed to be attacked by demons, to André Trevet, whose *The Peculiarities of Antarctic France, Also Called America* (1558) reported accounts of fantastic beasts on the Isle of Demons. Frisland, an imaginary island bearing characteristics of Iceland and the Faroe Islands, was first described by the Venetian traveler Niccolò Zeno after his 1380 voyage to the North Sea.

842.24–25   Boucher says in 1664] In *Histoire véritable et naturelle des moeurs et productions du pays de la Nouvelle France, vulgairement dite la Canada*.

844.27   Grey writes] In Hugh Gray, *Letters from Canada, Written During a Residence There in the Years 1806, 1807, 1808* (1809).

846.3   Jesuit Relations] See note 795.35.

847.30   Moore's verses] "Canadian Boat Song," ballad by the Irish poet Thomas Moore (1779–1852), who traveled to North America in 1804.

847.36   Donnacona] Iroquois chief who met Cartier during the explorer's second New World expedition in 1535; Cartier kidnapped him and brought him to France, where he died.

849.11   Hearne or McKenzie] Samuel Hearne (1745–92), English explorer; Sir Alexander Mackenzie (1764–1820), Scottish explorer.

852.30   Trenck mining in the ground] Baron Friedrick von der Trenck (1726–94) was imprisoned in 1754 for ten years by Frederick the Great, and made several attempts to escape by digging his way out.

859.6   destiny of Nebraska] In January 1854 Senator Stephen A. Douglas of Illinois introduced legislation for organizing Kansas and Nebraska as federal territories that repealed the prohibition against slavery in federal territory north of 36°30′ and allowed the question of whether slavery would be permitted in the new territories to be decided by their elected legislatures. The Kansas-Nebraska Act was passed by the Senate, 37–14, on March 4 and by the House of Representatives, 113–100, on May 22, then signed into law by President Franklin Pierce on May 30, 1854.

859.16–17   Our Buttricks . . . Hosmers] In the fighting at the North

Bridge in Concord on April 19, 1775, John Buttrick gave the initial order to the Massachusetts militia to open fire after British shots killed Isaac Davis and Abner Hosmer.

859.25 Fugitive Slave Law] In 1793 Congress adopted a fugitive slave law allowing slaveholders to use the federal courts to regain possession of runaway slaves. As part of the Compromise of 1850 Congress passed a new fugitive slave law that gave jurisdiction over fugitive slave cases to federal commissioners appointed by the courts, authorized federal marshals to summon all citizens to assist in enforcing the law, and established criminal penalties for harboring fugitives. Both the 1793 and 1850 laws denied persons accused of being runaway slaves the right to seek a writ of habeas corpus, to be tried by a jury, or to testify on their own behalf.

859.27–28 compromise compact of 1820] In March 1820 Congress voted to admit Missouri as a slave state while prohibiting slavery in the remainder of the Louisiana Purchase north of latitude 36°30′ N. The prohibition was repealed by the Kansas-Nebraska Act in 1854.

859.36–860.1 Again it happens . . . slave.] Anthony Burns (1834–62), a fugitive from Virginia, was arrested in Boston on May 24, 1854. On May 26 a federal deputy marshal was fatally shot when a crowd led by the Rev. Thomas Wentworth Higginson stormed the courthouse in an unsuccessful attempt to rescue Burns. With the approval of President Franklin Pierce, several companies of soldiers and marines were sent to guard the courthouse against further assault. On June 2 Burns was taken on board a federal revenue cutter as 1,500 militiamen stood guard. Higginson, Theodore Parker, Wendell Phillips, and five other men were charged for their role in the May 26 riot, but the indictments were dismissed in 1855 on a technicality.

860.2 Mr. Loring's decision] U.S. Commissioner Edward G. Loring presided over Burns's case and ruled that he be sent back to slavery.

860.12 Governor] Emory Washburn (1800–77), governor in 1854, a Whig.

860.26 Simm's tragedy] Thomas Sims, a fugitive slave from Georgia, was arrested in Boston on April 3, 1851, and kept in the courthouse under heavy guard until April 12, when he was escorted to the harbor by 300 armed deputies and militiamen and placed on a ship bound for Savannah, Georgia. Efforts to buy his freedom were unsuccessful, and Sims was sold at auction.

860.28 Governor of Massachusetts] George Sewall Boutwell (1818–1905), governor in 1851.

862.16–18 Three years ago . . . into slavery] See note 860.26.

863.1 the events of the 12th of April, 1851] See note 860.26.

866.19–20 the dog that returns to his vomit] See Proverbs 26:11, II Peter 2:22.

866.39   Mitchell's *Citizen*]   John Mitchell (1815–75), an Irish nationalist, was convicted of treason in 1848 and sentenced to 14 years transportation. In 1853 he escaped from Van Diemen's Land (Tasmania) and went to New York, where he began publishing *The Citizen*, a proslavery newspaper, in January 1854.

869.11–12   tintamar]   Uproar, clamor.

872.32–33   Missouri Compromise]   See note 859.27–28.

872.33–34   *Nymphæa Douglassii*]   Senator Stephen A. Douglas, a Democrat from Illinois, was the author of the Kansas-Nebraska Act and had played a major role in winning passage through Congress of the measures regarding slavery known as the Compromise of 1850.

872.37–38   Boston Mayor]   Jerome V. C. Smith (1800–79), mayor of Boston from 1854 to 1855.

878.12–13   I shall never . . . pottage.]   See Genesis 27:1–41.

881.6–7   Howitt's account . . . gold-diggings]   William Howitt, *Land, Labour, and Gold; or, Two Years in Victoria* (1855).

881.27–28   Ballarat . . . Sulky Gully]   Gold-diggings mentioned in *Land, Labour, and Gold*.

882.9–10   cradles . . . toms]   Equipment for digging gold.

883.3   "Burker's Guide."]   Refers to the murderer William Burke (1792–29), who (with William Hare) sold corpses of his victims to Edinburgh medical schools. Burke and Hare also robbed graves for the same purpose.

883.32–33   Dr. Kane . . . Sir John Franklin]   Elisha Kent Kane (1820–57), American explorer who traveled to the Arctic to search for Sir John Franklin (1786–1847), an English explorer who perished in an earlier expedition.

883.38   D.D.s]   Doctors of Divinity.

885.1   Kossuth]   Lajos Kossuth (1802–94), Hungarian patriot and revolutionary who in 1851–52 toured the United States seeking support for the Hungarian revolt against Austria. His visit was widely publicized in American newspapers.

890.7–8   "the first true gentleman that ever breathed."]   Thomas Dekker and Thomas Middleton, *The Honest Whore* (1604), Part One, act I, scene 12.

891.5–10   Lieutenant Herndon . . . country]   In William L. Herndon and Lardner Gibbon, *Exploration of the Valley of the Amazon, Made Under the Direction of the Navy Department* (1853–54).

905.12   *Lycopodium lucidulum*]   Shining clubmoss.

905.17–18   it was like . . . new spring]   See Numbers 20:10–11.

906.17   Charon's boat]   A boat-shaped leaf (*cymbifolius*), named for the ferry that crossed the river Styx.

908.11   Mount Auburn]   Cemetery in Cambridge and Watertown, Massachusetts.

908.18   Greenwood Cemetery]   In Brooklyn, New York.

910.32   Chobdars]   Attendants.

911.30   egg-pop]   Eggnog.

912.8   Ivy *never sear*]   Cf. Milton, "Lycidas," line 2.

913.11–14   "Wrought . . . beauty grew."]   Ralph Waldo Emerson, "The Problem," lines 21–24.

915.3–5   as Dionysius . . . Oriental Plane-tree]   According to John Claudius Loudon, *Arboretum et Fruticetum Brittanicum* (1844).

920.8–9   *Juncaceæ* and *Gramineæ*]   Rushes and grasses.

920.19   Brocken spectre]   An optical phenomenon seen at high altitudes in which a shadow, ringed with a halo, appears on a cloud.

922.1   *Captain John Brown*]   On October 16, 1859, John Brown (1800–59) led a raid on a federal arsenal at Harpers Ferry, Virginia (now West Virginia), with intent to use its weapons in a slave insurrection. Brown and 21 of his followers occupied the arsenal until forced out by troops commanded by Colonel Robert E. Lee. Ten of Brown's followers were killed in the fighting, and Brown was wounded and captured. Tried and convicted of treason, Brown was hanged on December 2, 1859. (Brown had previously held the rank of captain with the Pottawatomie Rifles, an antislavery militia in Kansas.)

922.35   the troubles in Kansas]   Armed conflict broke out in Kansas in 1856 between proslavery and antislavery settlers. About 200 people were killed before federal troops suppressed the fighting in the fall of 1856.

923.27   Stark]   John Stark (1728–1822), Revolutionary War officer who fought at Bunker Hill in June 1775 and commanded the forces that defeated the British at Bennington, Vermont, in August 1777.

924.28   Buford ruffians]   Jefferson Buford of Alabama organized the emigration of about 300 men from the South to Kansas in 1856.

925.24–25   talking to Buncombe]   Giving a long-winded and politically expedient speech, a phrase allegedly derived from an address by North Carolina congressman Felix Walker (1753–1828), whose district included Buncombe County.

926.27   Mr. Vallandigham]   Clement Larid Vallandigham (1820–71), Democratic Ohio congressman who met with Brown after his capture and claimed that Brown had acted as part of a national abolitionist conspiracy.

927.39–40   Governor of Virginia] Henry A. Wise (1807–76), governor of Virginia from 1856 to 1860, who signed Brown's death warrant.

928.30–33   The momentary charge . . . poet laureate] Tennyson, in "The Charge of the Light Brigade" (1854).

929.2   that feat of Putnam] A legend about Revolutionary War soldier Israel Putnam claimed that he killed a she-wolf that had been terrorizing flocks of sheep in Pomfret, Connecticut.

929.5   Tract Society] The American Tract Society, benevolent society and publisher whose evangelical pamphlets were often aimed at eradicating social ills such as gambling and alcoholism.

930.36   Wilson's last speech] Henry Wilson (1812–75) was an antislavery U.S. senator from Massachusetts.

933.3–4   Walker . . . South] Robert J. Walker (1801–69), senator from Mississippi, 1835–45, secretary of the treasury, 1845–49, was governor of Kansas Territory from April 1857 to December 1857. Walker resigned in protest when the Buchanan administration refused to submit the proslavery constitution drafted at Lecompton to a fair referendum.

934.2–3   Fugitive Slave Law] See note 859.25.

934.17   Read . . . Mason and others] Shortly after his capture, Brown was visited by Virginia senator James Murray Mason, Virginia governor Henry Wise, Ohio congressman Clement Vallandigham, and a correspondent for the New York World, among others. Brown's remarks during this interview were widely circulated in Northern newspapers.

934.21   Gessler] Austrian bailiff who, according to legend, ordered William Tell to shoot an apple off his own son's head as punishment for defying Gessler's authority.

935.29   Colonel Washington] Lewis W. Washington, a colonel on the staff of Virginia governor Henry Wise, who was among the hostages taken during Brown's raid.

935.38–39   Almost . . . respect!] Cf. Chief Justice Roger B. Taney's opinion in Dred Scott v. Sanford (1857), which stated that blacks "had no rights which . . . white man was bound to respect."

936.13   the Plug Uglies] Ardent proslavery advocates in the struggle for Kansas (see note 922.35).

937.11   coffle] A train of slaves fastened together.

937.29   Vigilant Committee] An organization dedicated to aiding fugitive slaves.

937.30   Cadi] In the Middle East and Asia Minor, a civil judge, usually of a town or village.

939.33–34   cleared the temple]   Cf. Matthew 21:12–13, Jesus and the moneychangers.

941.4–5   "Unless above . . . is man!"]   Samuel Daniel, "To the Lady Margaret, Countess of Cumberland" (c. 1600), lines 95–96.

944.17–24   "When the sword . . . successful crimes."]   Marvell, "Tom May's Death" (ca. 1650).

944.24   suff'ring]   Marvell's poem reads "wretched".

944.27–30   "All heads . . . in the dust."]   Adapted from James Shirley, "Contention of Ajax and Ulysses" (1659).

946.30   Agricola]   Roman general who was the subject of a biography by his son-in-law, Tacitus (in A.D. 98).

948.7   Winkelried]   Legendary Swiss patriot said to have won the battle of Sempach for his countrymen in 1386.

952.21   death of Irving]   Washington Irving died on November 28, 1859.

952.36   pebbles in your mouth or not]   According to Plutarch, Demosthenes overcame a stammer and his difficulty in articulating words by speaking with pebbles in his mouth.

953.29–34   'He nothing common . . . upon a bed.']   Marvell, "An Horatian Ode upon Cromwell's Return from Ireland" (1650), lines 57–64.

961.19   Loudon]   John Claudius Loudon (1783–1843), Scottish horticultural writer, author of *Arboretum et Fruticetum Britannicum* (1844), *An Encyclopedia of Agriculture* (1844), and *Encyclopedia of plants* (1855).

964.28–32   the experience of Kane . . . becoming Esquimaux]   See note 883.32–33.

964.36   Dukes of Athol]   James, Duke of Athol, and his son John were Scottish planters, with estates at Dunkeld and Athol; Duke John added 14 million larch trees to the Athol estate.

965.36   nuciferous]   Bearing nuts.

967.1   Dr. Carpenter]   William Carpenter, author of *Vegetable Physiology, and Systematic Botany* (1858).

967.11   Dr. Chas. T. Jackson]   State geologist of Maine and brother-in-law of Ralph Waldo Emerson; he published yearly reports (1838, 1839) on the geology of Maine and Massachusetts.

969.11   Signor Blitz]   Antonio Blitz (1810–77), German-born magician and ventriloquist.

970.8–10   that unknown primitive people . . . Swiss lakes]   The first systematic excavation of prehistoric settlements on Lake Zurich was initiated by Swiss archaeologist Ferdinand Keller in 1854, followed by excavations at other Swiss lakes.

970.16   Niebuhr] German philologist and historian Barthold Georg Niebuhr (1776–1831), author of a 3-volume history of early Rome (1835).

970.35–36   "As the apple-tree . . . sons."] Song of Solomon 2:3.

970.36–971.1   "Stay me . . . apples."] Song of Solomon 2:5.

971.5–6   Ulysses saw . . . fruit"] *Odyssey,* Book VII.

971.11   Prose Edda] Collection of Old Norse myths compiled and written by Snorri Sturluson.

973.28   Pomona] Roman goddess of fruits.

974.17–20   Iduna's apples . . . wrinkled and gray] In Norse mythology, Loki, the god of destruction, and the giant Thjazi kidnap Iduna, the goddess who watches over the apples that preserve eternal youth. The gods age rapidly and the state of the world declines until Thjazi is destroyed by fire. The gods summon up the last of their strength and force Loki to bring back Iduna's tree, whose apples restore their youth.

976.10–14   "Wassaile . . . wassailing."] Robert   Herrick,   "Another (Ceremonie for Christmas)."

976.15–17   to sing of cider . . . better than English Phillips] The English poet John Phillips (1676–1709) was the author of "Cyder, in Two Books" (1708).

978.24   Michaux] See note 762.17.

982.3   Van Mons and Knight] The horticulturists and botanists Jean-Baptiste Van Mons (1765–1842) and Thomas Andrew Knight (1759–1824).

983.7–8   "highest plot . . . Bergamot."] Andrew Marvell, "An Horatian Ode upon Cromwell's Return from Ireland" (1650), lines 31–32.

984.11–12   "Fruits and Fruit-Trees of America,"] 1845 book by Andrew J. Downing.

985.3   Evelyn says] In *Sylva, or a Discourse on Forest-Trees* (1679), by John Evelyn.

985.19–21   Tityrus . . . chestnuts] See Virgil's *Eclogues,* I, lines 80–81.

986.19   *Prunes sibarelles*] Whistling plums.

989.12–13   *Cholera morbifera . . . dilectissima*] "Cholera Moribus and dysentery, esteemed by young boys."

989.13   the Apple which Atalanta stopped to pick up] In Greek mythology, Atalanta agreed to marry the suitor who could defeat her in a race.

During a race with Milanion, she stopped to pick up three golden apples that he had dropped, causing her to lose the race and become his wife.

989.18   *Pedestrium Solatium*]   Solitary walker.

989.21–26   As Bodæus exclaims . . . *wild apples.*"]   From the commentary on Theophrastus by Johannes Bodaeus, published in 1644.

990.15–16   (as Curzon . . . mouldy cellar)]   Robert Curzon, 14th Baron Zouche (1810–72) conducted a tour from 1834 to 1837 collecting ecclesiastical manuscripts. In an Egyptian monastery, he found a cellar filled with rotting manuscripts being used as lids for storage containers. He published an account of the trip in *The Monasteries of the Levant* (1849).

990.29   Topsell's Gesner]   *The Historie of Four-Footed Beasts and Serpents and Insects*, Edward Topsell's 1607 translation of zoological writings by the Swiss naturalist Konrad von Gesner (1516–65).

993.3–26   "The word of the Lord . . . sons of men."]   Joel 1:1–12.

994.2–5   *Agrestem . . . things.*]   Virgil, *Eclogues*, Book VI, lines 8–9.

994.14–15   the horse Columbus—or Mr. Blank]   In 1860 Columbus was considered to be the fastest horse alive. "Mr. Blank" was John C. Heenan (1833–73), a professional boxer known as "the Benecia boy."

994.23–24   Mr. Seward or Caleb Cushing]   Senators from, respectively, New York and Massachusetts.

996.8–9   French chemist]   Joseph Louis Gay-Lussac (1778–1850).

998.3   *Gaylussacia resinosa var. erythrocarpa*]   Red huckleberry.

999.9–10   *Andromeda polifolia* and *Kalmia glauca*]   Bog rosemary and pale laurel.

1000.32   George B. Emerson]   Naturalist and educator (1797–1881), author of *A Report on the Trees and Shrubs Growing Naturally in the Forests of Massachusetts* (1846).

1001.9   Lawson in 1709]   In *A New Voyage to Carolina* by John Lawson (d. 1711), surveyor-general of North Carolina.

1002.3   Loudon]   See note 961.19.

1002.35   Coleman in his "Woodland, Heaths, and Hedges,"]   *Our Woodlands, Heaths, and Hedges: A Popular Description of Trees, Shrubs, Wild Fruits, etc.* (1859) by the English naturalist William Stephen Coleman (1829–1904).

1003.25   Dr. Manassah Cutler]   Clergyman and botanist (1743–1823) who published an account of American plants in the first volume of *Memoirs of the American Academy of Arts and Sciences* (1785).

1005.18   Crantz says]   In David Crantz, *The History of Greenland* (1767).

1007.36–37   Gabriel Sagard . . . 1624]   In *Le grand voyage du pays des Hurons* (1632).

1008.23–24   Mr. Oldham's death in 1636]   John Oldham (c. 1600–36) was killed by Pequot Indians while on a trading expedition to Block Island.

1009.2   in the life of Captain Church]   Thomas Church's *Entertaining Passages Relating to Philip's War* (1716), based on the notes of his father, Captain Benjamin Church.

1009.13   La Hontan in 1689]   See note 794.34.

1009.19   Father Rasles]   Father Sébastien Rasles (also spelled Rale, Rasle, and Ralle), 1652–1724, was a missionary to the Abnaki people from 1694 until his death in an English raid on the village. His *Dictionary of the Abnaki Language in North America*, stolen in the raid, was published in 1833.

1010.8   *Jacea* or *Saratula*]   *Centauria Jacea* is also known as brown knapweed. *Serratula* is sawwort.

1010.11   Kalm]   See note 794.28.

1010.29   *Pinus Banksiana*]   Jack pine, also called scrub pine or Hudson Bay pine.

1011.38–39   Tourneforte . . . *Mount Ida*]   Joseph Tournefort (1656–1708), French botanist, a founder of modern systematic botany, and author of *Éléments de botanique* (1694). Mount Ida was a sacred place for Cybele, the mother of gods.

1017.24   mantua-maker]   The maker of a loose gown.

1019.1–2   *Sic transit gloria ruris*]   "So the glory of the countryside passes away," adaptation of Latin motto *Sic transit gloria mundis* ("So the glory of the world passes away").

1021.12–13   not that . . . Rome more]   Cf. Shakespeare, *Julius Caesar*, III.ii.21–22.

1027.6   Darien Grounds]   The eastern coast of Panama.

POEMS

1031.10   wise men 3 of Gotham]   The magi. See Matthew 2:1–12.

1042.32   thrins]   Triplets.

1047.26   wandering at Rockaway]   Thoreau visited Rockaway Beach, in present-day New York City, while living on Staten Island, May–December 1843.

1058.10   "Friends, Romans, Countrymen, and Lovers."]   Cf. Shakespeare, *Julius Caesar*, III.ii.73.

1063.17   *Guido's Aurora*]   See note 544.30–31.

1081.3   Parthian arrows]   Parthian cavalry would shoot volleys of arrows at their enemies while retreating.

1103.18–19   Spes . . . hope]   See note 534.3–4.

1107.1   *Godfrey of Boulogne*]   See note 545.9.

1119.23   golden]   Goldenrod.

1113.2–4   Time . . . RALEIGH.]   From "Prais'd be Diana's fair and harmless light" (1593).

1113.17   *Aeolian Harp*]   A stringed instrument which produces musical sounds when struck by the wind.

1114.7   Paestum's temples]   Paestum, a coastal town in southern Italy, had Roman temples dedicated to Neptune and Ceres dating from the sixth and fifth centuries B.C.

1115.12–14   the mallet . . . caulking the sky]   A caulking mallet is used to strike an iron that drives loose rope fiber into the seams of a ship to prevent leaks.

1116.20   Deucaleon shroud]   In Greek myth, Deucalion, son of Prometheus and Clymene, survived a flood sent by Zeus. In order to renew the human race, Deucalion and his wife Pyrrha were told to shroud their faces and cast the bones of Clymene behind them. They threw stones instead, which were transformed into men and women.

1119.32   Brahmapootra and the Jumna's shore]   The Brahmaputra and the Jumna are tributaries of the Ganges.

1132.6   Aaron's rod]   See Numbers 20:10–11.

1136.16   Titmans]   See note 88.32.

1138.2   Memnon's mother]   See note 666.20–21.

1138.4   Carnac's columns]   A complex of menhirs, single stones stood on end, in Carnac, Brittany, France.

1139.13–14   Hawthorne . . . Twice told Tale.]   Nathaniel Hawthorne's collection of stories *Twice-told Tales* was first published in 1837.

1139.20–21   the spring of Helicon]   Hippocrene, a spring on Mount Helicon in Boeotia, legendary for giving inspiration to those who drink from it.

1140.3   tort]   Twisted.

1141.1   *The Atlantides*]   Daughters of Atlas and Hesperis, also called Hesperides.

1141.3   Phlegethon]   In   Greek   mythology,   a   river   of   fire   in   the
underworld.

1146.1–14   The   good   .   .   .   sympathy]   A   draft   of   this   poem   written   in
late 1847 reads:

> If Love fails in strife with love
> Then it boldly looks above
> And appeals to higher Love.
>
> My Friend, my Friend,
> I ask not Love but Hate without end.
> Erect me, restore me, hearten me then
> With some dear severity fatal to men.
> Sear my humanity,
> Cure my insanity,
> O wrack me, grind me, crush without end,
> And I will pronounce thee my dearest friend.
>
> With a tough tenderness
> Strengthen my slenderness,
> Waste me with care,
> Send me despair,
> Give me my deserts,
> Confound me with hurts.
> Be so kind as be just,
> Let me taste of the worst.
>
> Sweet Friend—sweet Friend,
> Let pity have end,
> I pray Thee let mercy cease,
> Let me have my release;
> Smile not again;
> Give me a glance that will wither my frame;
> With poisoned darts pierce me through & through,
> Only be true.
>
> O my Friend—my Friend,
> Let me feel once condemned.
> Then I will not doubt,
> Then I'll find the out,
> Then our love will be sure,
> Then our love will endure,
> Then I shall believe that thou knowest me well,
> And I shall not have a confession to tell.
>
> Give me some token
> That our first love is broken—

Then Love born of Love,
Love pure from above,
Will forge a true chain
To bind us again.

Love not me at all
But love all.
Know that I love not thee,
But thy destiny.
Canst thou range earth sea & air,
And so meet me everywhere?
Through all events I will pursue thee
Through all persons I will woo thee.
    Who loves me alone
    Is not flesh of my flesh, bone of my bone.
    Canst thou be kind
    To the north wind?
Dost thou affect sun, moon, & star,
And all creatures near & far?
Dost thou love the morning air,
And the creator every where?
Dost thou *love* God?
Is he thy mate—?
Hast thou feeling for the sod—
And sympathy with Death & Fate?
    Treat tenderly these powers,—
    Lend them some flowers,
    Give them some loving tears
    To soothe their sorrow,
    And all thy worthless years
    To gild their morrow.

Cant thou love with thy mind
And reason with thy heart?
Cant thou be kind,
And from thy darling part?

The good—how can we trust?
Only the wise are just.
Conform, Conform, with awe,
Think not thou mak'st the law
We're indiscriminately kind like clods,
But justice is the kindness of the Gods.
    The good we use,
    The wise we cannot choose.
    These there are none above.
    The good they know & love,

But are not known again
By those of lesser ken.—

They do not charm us with their eyes,
But they transfix with their advice.
No partial sympathy they feel
With private woe or private weal,
But with the universe joy & sigh
Whose knowledge is their sympathy.

1150.2   Tom Hyde] See *Walden*, "Conclusion": "Say what you have to say, not what you ought. Any truth is better than make-believe. Tom Hyde, the tinker, standing on the gallows, was asked if he had any thing to say. 'Tell the tailors,' said he, 'to remember to make a knot in their thread before they take the first stitch.' His companion's prayer is forgotten."

1153.6–7   Gourgas . . . Darby?] See note 758.39–40.

1154.27   *sine*] Latin, "without."

1156.4   Dakin's & Maynards] Neighbors of Thoreau.

1166.9   warts] From "warth," a flat meadow, especially one close to a stream.

1166.24   saint-terrering] See "Walking," 751.12–29.

Index of Titles and First Lines

Library of Congress Cataloging-in-Publication Data

Thoreau, Henry David, 1817–1862.
  [Selections. 2007]
  Walden, the Maine woods, and collected essays & poems /
    Henry David Thoreau. — 1st
  Library of America college ed.
      p. cm.
   ISBN 978-1-59853-010-0
      I. Thoreau, Henry David, 1817–1862. Walden. II. Thoreau,
Henry David, 1817–1862. Maine woods. III. Title.

PS3042 2007
818'.303—dc22   2006053007

ABOUT THE LIBRARY OF AMERICA

THE LIBRARY OF AMERICA is an award-winning, nonprofit publisher dedicated to preserving America's best and most significant writing in handsome, enduring volumes, featuring authoritative texts. Founded in 1979 with initial funding from the National Endowment for the Humanities and the Ford Foundation, the series, which now numbers over a hundred volumes, has been called "the most important book-publishing project in the nation's history."

For the first time, the full range of outstanding American writing will be permanently available in uniform, hardcover volumes, priced to reach a wide audience. Each volume contains up to 1600 pages and includes a number of works by our country's foremost novelists, historians, poets, essayists, journalists, philosophers, and statesmen. Authoritative, unabridged, scrupulously accurate texts are a hallmark of the volumes, which also feature a handsomely designed page, high-quality, acid-free paper bound in a cloth cover and sewn to lie flat when opened, a ribbon marker, and printed endpapers. The series includes acknowledged classics and neglected masterpieces, and new volumes are added each year.

Library of America hardcover volumes are available singly or by subscription. A jacketed edition, available in bookstores, is priced between $30.00 and $45.00. A slipcased edition is available by subscription at $26.95.

Library of America College Editions bring these authoritative and comprehensive editions to teachers and students for the first time in an affordable paperback format.

For more information, a complete list of titles, or to place an order, contact:

The Library of America
14 East 60th Street
New York, New York 10022
Telephone: (212) 308-3360
Fax: (212) 750-8352
E-Mail: info@loa.org
Websites: www.loa.org
　　　　www.LOAacademic.org

LIBRARY OF AMERICA COLLEGE EDITIONS

American Poetry: The Nineteenth Century
John Hollander, editor
ISBN 1-883011-36-1 $14.95 1040 pages

Willa Cather • NOVELS AND STORIES 1905–1918
Sharon O'Brien, editor
The Troll Garden, O Pioneers!, The Song of the Lark, My Ántonia
ISBN 1-883011-74-4 $13.95 975 pages

Stephen Crane • PROSE AND POETRY
J. C. Levenson, editor
*Maggie: A Girl of the Streets; The Red Badge of Courage; Stories;
Journalism; Poetry*
ISBN 1-883011-39-6 $15.95 1379 pages

Frederick Douglass • AUTOBIOGRAPHIES
Henry Louis Gates, Jr., editor
Narrative of the Life; My Bondage and My Freedom; Life and Times
ISBN 1-883011-30-2 $13.95 1126 pages

W.E.B. Du Bois • WRITINGS
Nathan I. Huggins, editor
*The Suppression of the African Slave-Trade; The Souls of Black Folk;
Dusk of Dawn; Essays & Articles from The Crisis*
ISBN 1-883011-31-0 $15.95 1334 pages

Ralph Waldo Emerson • ESSAYS AND POEMS
Joel Porte, Harold Bloom, and Paul Kane, editors
*Nature; Addresses, and Lectures; Essays: First and Second Series;
Representative Men; The Conduct of Life; Poems 1847;
May-Day and Other Poems; Uncollected Poems*
ISBN 1-883011-32-9 $15.95 1360 pages

Nathaniel Hawthorne • TALES AND SKETCHES
Roy Harvey Pearce, editor
Twice-told Tales; Masses from an Old Manse; The Snow Image
ISBN 1-883011-33-7 $15.95 1181 pages

Henry James • MAJOR STORIES AND ESSAYS
ISBN 1-883011-75-2 $11.95 705 pages

Sarah Orne Jewett • NOVELS AND STORIES
Michael Davitt Bell, editor
*Deephaven; A Country Doctor; The Country of the Pointed Firs;
Stories and Sketches*
ISBN 1-883011-34-5 $11.95 937 pages

Herman Melville • MOBY-DICK, BILLY BUDD, AND OTHER WRITINGS
G. Thomas Tanselle, Harrison Hayford, John Hollander, editors
Moby-Dick, Bartleby, The Scrivener, Benito Cereno, The Encantadas,
Billy Budd, Hawthorne and His Mosses, Selected Poems
ISBN 1-883011-89-2 $13.95   996 pages

Edgar Allan Poe • POETRY, TALES, AND SELECTED ESSAYS
Patrick F. Quinn and G. R. Thompson, editors
ISBN 1-883011-38-8 $16.95   1506 pages

Slave Narratives
William L. Andrews and Henry Louis Gates Jr., editors
ISBN 1-931082-11-1 $14.95   1035 pages

Henry David Thoreau • WALDEN, THE MAINE WOODS, AND COLLECTED
ESSAYS & POEMS
Robert F. Sayre and Elizabeth Hall Witherell, editors
ISBN 978-1-59853-010-0 $17.95   1247 pages

Mark Twain • HUCK FINN; PUDD'NHEAD WILSON; No. 44, THE
MYSTERIOUS STRANGER; AND OTHER WRITINGS
Guy Cardwell and Louis J. Budd, editors
ISBN 1-883011-88-4 $12.95   808 pages

Edith Wharton • FOUR NOVELS
R.W.B. Lewis and Cynthia Griffin Wolff, editors
The House of Mirth; Ethan Frome; The Custom of the Country;
The Age of Innocence
ISBN 1-883011-37-X $13.95   1156 pages

Walt Whitman • POETRY AND PROSE
Justin Kaplan, editor
Leaves of Grass 1855; Leaves of Grass 1891–92; Supplementary Poems;
Complete Prose
ISBN 1-883011-35-3 $17.95   1407 pages

Bookstore orders: Penguin Putnam Inc., Attn: Order Processing,
405 Murray Hill Parkway, East Rutherford, NJ 07073-2136;
tel: (800) 526-0275; fax: (800) 227-9604

Exam and Desk Copy Information: www.LOAacademic.org